Dictionary of Philosophy

DICTIONARY OF
PHILOSOPHY

edited by

Dagobert D. Runes

A HELIX BOOK

ROWMAN & ALLANHELD
Totowa, New Jersey

Library of Congress Cataloging in Publication Data
Main entry under title:

Dictionary of philosophy.

   1. Philosophy — Dictionaries. I. Runes, Dagobert
David, 1902- 1982
B41.D53   1982   103'.21   81-80240
ISBN 0-8022-2388-5   AACR2

Reprinted in 1984 as A HELIX BOOK, published by
Rowman & Allanheld, Publishers (a division of
Littlefield, Adams & Company) 81 Adams Drive,
Totowa, New Jersey, 07512

Φιλοσοφία Βίου Κυβερνήτης

CONTRIBUTORS

Initials	Names	Initials	Names
A.C.	Alonzo Church	*K.G.*	Katharine Gilbert
A.C.B.	A. Cornelius Benjamin	*L.E.D.*	Lester E. Denonn
A.C.E.	A. C. Ewing	*L.L.*	Leo Lieberman
A.C.P.	A. C. Pegis	*L.M.H.*	Lewis M. Hammond
A.G.A.B.	Albert G. A. Balz	*L.V.*	Lionello Venturi
A.J.B.	Archie J. Bahm	*L.W.*	Ledger Wood
B.A.G.F.	B. A. G. Fuller	*M.B.*	Max Black
C.A.B.	Charles A. Baylis	*M.T.K.*	Morris T. Keeton
C.A.H.	Charles A. Hart	*M.B.M.*	Marcus B. Mallett
C.G.H.	Carl G. Hempel	*M.F.*	Max Fishler
C.J.D.	C. J. Ducasse	*M.W.*	Meyer Waxmann
C.K.D.	C. K. Davenport	*O.F.K.*	Otto F. Kraushaar
C.L.	Corliss Lamont	*P.A.S.*	Paul A. Schilpp
D.C.	Dorion Cairns	*P.O.K.*	Paul O. Kristeller
E.A.M.	Ernest A. Moody	*P.P.W.*	Philip Paul Wiener
E.C.	Emmanuel Chapman	*P.W.*	Paul Weiss
E.F.	Erich Frank	*R.A.*	Rudolf Allers
E.H.	Eugene Holmes	*R.B.W.*	Ralph B. Winn
E.S.B.	Edgar Sheffield Brightman	*R.C.*	Rudolf Carnap
F.L.W.	Frederick L. Will	*R.M.J.*	Rufus M. Jones
F.K.	Fritz Kunz	*R.T.F.*	Ralph Tyler Flewelling
F.S.C.N.	F. S. C. Northrop	*S.E.N.*	St. Elmo Nauman, Jr.
G.B.	George Boas	*S.v.F.*	Sigmar von Fersen
G.R.M.	Glenn R. Morrow	*S.S.S.*	S. S. Stevens
G.W.C.	G. Watts Cunningham	*T.G.*	Thomas Greenwood
H.G.	Hunter Guthrie	*T.M.*	Thomas Munro
H.Go.	Heinrich Gomperz	*T.P.S.*	Thomas P. Steindler
H.H.	Herman Hausheer	*V.F.*	Vergilius Ferm
H.L.G.	H. L. Gordon	*V.J.B.*	Vernon J. Bourke
I.J.	Iredell Jenkins	*V.J.M.*	V. J. McGill
J.E.B.	John Edward Bentley	*W.E.*	Walter Eckstein
J.J.R.	J. J. Rolbiecki	*W.F.*	William Frankena
J.K.F.	James K. Feibleman	*W.L.*	Wilbur Long
J.M.	Joseph Maier	*W.M.M.*	William Marias Malisoff
J.A.F.	Jose A. Franquiz	*W.N.P.*	W. Norman Pittenger
J.M.S.	J. MacPherson Somerville	*W.S.W.*	William S. Weedon
J.R.W.	Julius R. Weinberg	*W.T.C.*	W. T. Chan
K.F.L.	Kurt F. Leidecker		

Preface To The Revised Edition

Much has changed in philosophy since the initial publication of this volume in 1942. New ideas, methods and conceptions of the very nature of the philosophical enterprise have come upon the scene. Some have risen to positions of prominence and influence, while most have eventually been eclipsed by newer ideas. A select few, as happens in every generation, are destined to become classics, which, by dint of repetition and reformulation by succeeding generations of scholars, shine, like polished stone, even more brilliantly with age.

In preparing the revised edition every attempt has been made to include the major figures and trends of the last forty years. Because philosophy is notably less capricious than many other human endeavors, this is slight in proportion to the original text of *Dictionary of Philosophy,* which, with minor corrections and updating, is presented in its entirety.

THE PUBLISHERS

Preface

The aim of this dictionary is to provide teachers, students and laymen interested in philosophy with clear, concise, and correct definitions and descriptions of the philosophical terms, throughout the range of philosophic thought. In the volume are represented all the branches as well as schools of ancient, medieval, and modern philosophy. In any such conspectus, it is increasingly recognized that the Oriental philosophies must be accorded ample space beside those of the western world.

The great field that must be compressed within the limits of a small volume makes omissions inevitable. If any topics, or phases of a subject, deserve space not here accorded them, it may be possible in future editions to allow them room; I take this occasion to invite suggestions and criticism, to that end.

Clarity and correctness would be more easily secured if there were concord among philosophers. Scarcely any two thinkers would define philosophy alike; nor are they likely to agree as to the significance of its basic concepts. The value of a one-volume dictionary, nonetheless, makes the effort worthwhile.

"Dictionaries are like watches," Samuel Johnson said; "the best cannot be expected to go quite true, but the worst is better than none."

I trust that the present volume will serve as reliably as the chronometer of today, in the time-pattern of the philosophic world.

I owe a debt of profound appreciation to every one of the many collaborators that have so generously contributed to the Dictionary. Especially do I wish to acknowledge my gratitude to Professors William Marias Malisoff and Ledger Wood. Needless to say, the final responsibility, as to the general plan of the volume, together with the burden of any short-comings, rests solely upon the editor.

THE EDITOR

ABBREVIATIONS

AS.—Anglo Saxon   *Gr.*—Greek
C.—Chinese   *Lat.*—Latin
Fr.—French   *Heb.*—Hebrew
Ger.—German   *Skr.*—Sanskrit

q.v.—quod vide
("see also")

A

Abbagnano, Nicola: (1901–   ) Italian existentialist. Born at Salerno, he studied at Naples and taught at Turin, editing the *Rivista de filosofia.* He opposed Croce's neo-Hegelianism. He worked at relating Kant and Kierkegaard. His books include *La Struttura dell' esistenza* (1939), *Possibilità e libertà* (1956), *Esistenzialismo positivo* (1948), and *Problemi di sociologia* (1959).—*S.E.N.*

Abbot, Francis Ellingwood: (1836–1903) American liberal theologian. Attacked intemperately by Josiah Royce for holding scientific realist views. Wrote *Scientific Theism* (1885), *The Way Out of Agnosticism* (1890) and *The Syllogistic Philosophy* (1906).—*S.E.N.*

Abbt, Thomas A.: (1738–1766) Popular philosophical writer, born at Ulm, Germany, author of *On Death for the Fatherland* (*Vom Tode fur's Vaterland,* 1761) supporting the "philosopher king" Frederick II of Prussia in The Seven Years War. *On Merit* (*Vom Verdienst,* 1765) was his second work, on educational ideals. He died before he was thirty.—*S.E.N.*

Abdera, School of: Founded by the Atomist Democritus. Important members, Metrodorus of Chios and Anaxarchus of Abdera (teacher of Pyrrho, into whose hands the school leadership fell), thus inspiring Pyrrhonism. See *Democritus, Pyrrhonism.*—*E.H.*

Abduction: (Gr. *apagoge*) In Aristotle's logic a syllogism whose major premiss is certain but whose minor premiss is only probable.—*G.R.M.*

In Peirce: type of inference yielding an explanatory hypothesis (*q.v.*), rather than a result of deductive application of a "rule" to a "case" or establishment of a rule by induction.

Ab esse ad posse valet, a posse ad esse non valet consequentia: Adage expressing the permissibility of arguing from facts to possibility and denying the validity of arguments proceeding from possibility to reality. —*J.J.R.*

Abelard, Peter: (1079–1142) Was born at Pallet in France; distinguished himself as a brilliant student of the trivium and quadrivium; studied logic with Roscelin and Wm. of Champeaux. He taught philosophy, with much emphasis on dialectic, at Melun, Corbeil, and the schools of St. Geneviève and Notre Dame in Paris. He was lecturing on theology in Paris c. 1113 when he was involved in the romantic and unfortunate interlude with Héloise. First condemned for heresy in 1121, he became Abbot of St. Gildas in 1125, and after returning to teach theology in Paris, his religious views were censured by the Council of Sens (1141). He died at Cluny after making his peace with God and his Church. Tactless, but very intelligent, Abelard set the course of mediaeval philosophy for two centuries with his interest in the problem of universals. He appears to have adopted a nominalistic solution, rather than the semi-realistic position attributed to him by the older historians. Chief works: *Sic et Non* (c. 1122), *Theologia Christiana* (c. 1124), *Scito Teipsum* (1125–1138) and several *Logical Glosses* (ed. B. Geyer, *Abaelard's Philos. Schrift.* BGPM, XXI, 1-3).

J. G. Sikes, *Peter Abailard* (Cambridge, Eng., 1932).—*V.J.B.*

Ābhāsa, ābhāsana: (Skr.) "Shining forth," the cosmopsychological process of the One becoming the Many as described by the Trika (*q.v.*) which regards the Many as a real aspect of the ultimate reality or Parama Siva (cf. Indian Philosophy). Reflection, objectivity. —*K.F.L.*

Abheda: (Skr. "not distinct") Identity, particularly in reference to any philosophy of monism which does not recognize the distinctness of spiritual and material, or divine and essentially human principles.—*K.F.L.*

Abravanel, Don Isaac: Exegete and philosopher (1437–1508), was born in Lisbon, Portugal, emigrated to Toledo, Spain, and after the expulsion settled in Italy. He wrote a number of philosophical works, among them a commentary on parts of the *Guide.* He follows in most of his views Maimonides but was also influenced by Crescas.—*M.W.*

Abravanel, Judah: or Judah Leon Medigo (1470–1530), son of Don Isaac, settled in Italy after the expulsion from Spain. In his *Dialoghi d'Amore,* i.e., Dialogues about Love, he conceives, in Platonic fashion, love as the principle permeating the universe. It emanates from God to the beings, and from the beings reverts back to God. It is possible that his conception of universal love exerted some influence upon the concept of Amor Dei of Spinoza.—*M.W.*

Absolute: (Lat. *absolvere* to release or set free) Of this term Stephanus Chauvin in the *Lexicon Philosophicum*, 1713, p.2 observes: "Because one thing is said to be free from another in many ways, so also the word absolute is taken by the philosophers in many senses." In Medieval Scholasticism this term was variously used, for example: freed or abstracted from material conditions, hence from contingency; hence applicable to all being; without limitations or restrictions; simply; totally; independent; unconditionally; uncaused; free from mental reservation.

Much of this Medieval usage is carried over and expanded in modern philosophy. Absolute and Absolutely signify perfection, completeness, universality, non-relativity, exemption from limitation or qualification, unconditionality; hence also the ineffable, unthinkable, indeterminable; strictly, literally, without reservation, not symbolically or metaphorically. *E.g.* "Absolute truth," "absolute space," "absolute Ego," "absolutely unconditioned," "absolutely true." —*W.L.*

Absolute Ego: In Fichte's philosophy, the Ego or Subject prior to its differentiation into an empirical (or historical) self and not-self.—*W.L.*

Absolute Idealism: See *Idealism, Hegel.*—*W.L.*

Absolute, The: (in Metaphysics) Most broadly, the terminus or ultimate referent of thought. The Unconditioned. The opposite of the Relative (Absolute). A distinction is to be made between the singular and generic use of the term.

A. While Nicholas of Cusa referred to God as "the absolute," the noun form of this term came into common use through the writings of Schelling and Hegel. Its adoption spread in France through Cousin and in Britain through Hamilton. According to Kant the Ideas of Reason seek both the absolute totality of conditions and their absolutely unconditioned Ground. This Ground of the Real Fichte identified with the Absolute Ego (*q.v.*). For Schelling the Absolute is a primordial World Ground, a spiritual unity behind all logical and ontological oppositions, the self-differentiating source of both Mind and Nature. For Hegel, however, the Absolute is the All conceived as a timeless, perfect, organic whole of self-thinking Thought. In England the Absolute has occasionally been identified with the Real considered as unrelated or "unconditioned" and hence as the "Unknowable" (Mansel, H. Spencer). Until recently, however, it was commonly appropriated by the Absolute Idealists to connote with Hegel the complete, the whole, the perfect, *i.e.* the Real conceived as an all-embracing unity that complements, fulfills, or transmutes into a higher synthesis the partial, fragmentary, and "self-contradictory" experiences, thoughts, purposes, values, and achievements of finite existence. The specific emphasis given to this all-inclusive perfection

varies considerably, *i.e.* logical wholeness or concreteness (Hegel), metaphysical completeness (Hamilton), mystical feeling (Bradley), aesthetic completeness (Bosanquet), moral perfection (Royce). The Absolute is also variously conceived by this school as an all-inclusive Person, a Society of persons, and as an impersonal whole of Experience.

More recently the term has been extended to mean also (a) the All or totality of the real, however understood, and (b) the World Ground, whether conceived idealistically or materialistically, whether pantheistically, theistically, or dualistically. It thus stands for a variety of metaphysical conceptions that have appeared widely and under various names in the history of philosophy. In China: the *Wu Chi* (Non-Being), *T'ai Chi* (Being), and, on occasion, *Tao*. In India: the Vedantic *Ātman* (Self) and *Brahman* (the Real), the Buddhist *Bhūtatathatā* (indeterminate Thatness), *Vignaptimatra* (the One, pure, changeless, eternal consciousness grounding all appearances), and the Void of Nāgārjuna. In Greece: the cosmic matrix of the Ionians, the One of the Eleatics, the Being or Good of Plato, the World Reason of Stoicism, the One of Neo-Platonism. In patristic and scholastic Christianity: the creator God, the Ens Realissimum, Ens Perfectissimum, Sui Causa, and the God of mysticism generally (Erigena, Hugo of St. Victor, Cusa, Boehme, Bruno). In modern thought: the Substance of Descartes and Spinoza, the God of Malebranche and Berkeley, the Energy of materialism, the Space-Time of realism, the Pure Experience of phenomenalism, the *ding-an-sich* (*q.v.*) of Kant.

B. Generically "an absolute" or "the absolute" (pl. "absolutes") means (a) the real (thing-in-itself) as opposed to appearance; (b) substance, the substantival, reals (possessing aseity or self-existence) as opposed to relations; (c) the perfect, non-comparative, complete of its kind; (d) the primordial or uncaused; (e) the independent or autonomous.

Logic. (a) Aristotelian logic involves such absolutes as the three laws of thought and changeless, objectively real classes or species. (b) In Kantian logic the categories and principles of judgment are absolutes, *i.e.* a priori, while the Ideas of reason seek absolute totality and unity. (c) In the organic or metaphysical logic of the Hegelian school, the Absolute is considered the ultimate terminus, referent, or subject of every judgment.

Ethics and Axiology. Moral and axiological values, norms, principles, maxims, laws are considered absolutes when universally valid objects of acknowledgment, whether conditionally or unconditionally (*e.g.* the law of the best possible, the utilitarian greatest happiness principle, the Kantian categorical imperative).

Aesthetics. Aesthetic absolutes are standards, norms, principles of aesthetic taste considered as objective, *i.e.* universally valid.—*W.L.*

Absolutism: The opposite of Relativism.

1. Metaphysics: the theory of the Absolute (*q.v.*).

2. Epistemology: the doctrine that objective or abso-

lute, and not merely relative and human, truth is possible.

3. Axiology: the view that standards of value (moral or aesthetic) are absolute, objective, superhuman, eternal.

4. Politics: Cult of unrestricted sovereignty located in the ruler.—*W.L.*

Absolutistic Personalism: The ascription of personality to the Absolute.—*R.T.F.*

Absorption: The name *law of absorption* is given to either of the two dually related theorems of the propositional calculus,

$$[p \vee pq] \equiv p, \qquad p[p \vee q] \equiv p,$$

or either of the two corresponding dually related theorems of the algebra of classes,

$$a \cup (a \cap b) = a, \quad a \cap (a \cup b) = a.$$

Any valid inference of the propositional calculus which amounts to replacing A v AB by A, or A[A v B] by A, or any valid inference of the algebra of classes which amounts to replacing A $\cup$ (A $\cap$ B) by A, or A $\cap$ (A $\cup$ B) by A, is called *absorption*.

Whitehead and Russell (*Principia Mathematica*) give the name *law of absorption* to the theorem of the propositional calculus,

$$[p \supset q] \equiv [p \equiv pq].—A.C.$$

Abstract: (Lat. *ab*, from + *trahere*, to draw) A designation applied to a partial aspect or quality considered in isolation from a total object, which is, in contrast, designated concrete.—*L.W.*

Abstracta: Such neutral, purely denotative entities as qualities, numbers, relations, logical concepts, appearing neither directly nor literally in time. (Broad)—*H.H.*

Abstractio imaginationis: According to the Scholastics a degree of abstraction below that of reason and above that of the senses, which do abstract from matter, but not from the presence of matter, whereas the imagination abstracts even from the presence of matter, but not from its *appendices*, or sensible qualities.—*J.J.R.*

Abstractio intellectus seu rationis: According to the Scholastics the highest degree of abstraction is that of reason which abstracts not only matter and its presence, but also from its *appendices*, that is, its sensible conditions and properties, considering essence or quiddity alone.—*J.J.R.*

Abstraction: (Lat. *ab*, from + *trahere*, to draw) The process of ideally separating a partial aspect or quality from a total object. Also the result or product of mental abstraction. Abstraction, which concentrates its attention on a single aspect, differs from *analysis* which considers all aspects on a par.—*L.W.*

In logic: Given a relation *R* which is transitive, symmetric, and reflexive, we may introduce or postulate new elements corresponding to the members of the field of *R*, in such a way that the same new element corresponds to two members *x* and *y* of the field of *R* if and only if *xRy* (see the article *relation*). These new elements are then said to be obtained by *abstraction* with respect to *R*. Peano calls this a method or kind of definition, and speaks, *e.g.*, of *cardinal numbers* (*q.v.*) as obtained from classes by abstraction with respect to

the relation of equivalence—two classes having the same cardinal number if and only if they are equivalent.

Given a formula A containing a free variable, say *x*, the process of forming a corresponding monadic *function* (*q.v.*)—defined by the rule that the value of the function for an argument *b* is that which A denotes if the variable *x* is taken as denoting *b*—is also called *abstraction*, or *functional abstraction*. In this sense, abstraction is an operation upon a *formula* A yielding a function, and is relative to a particular *system of interpretation* for the notations appearing in the formula, and to a particular *variable*, as *x*. The requirement that A shall contain *x* as a free variable is not essential: when A does not contain *x* as a free variable, the function obtained by abstraction relative to *x* may be taken to be the function whose value, the same for all arguments, is denoted by A.

In articles herein by the present writer, the notation $\lambda x[A]$ will be employed for the function obtained from A by abstraction relative to (or, as we may also say, with respect to) *x*. Russell, and Whitehead and Russell in *Principia Mathematica*, employ for this purpose the *formula* A with a circumflex ˆ placed over each (free) occurrence of *x*—but only for *propositional* functions. Frege (1893) uses a Greek vowel, say ϵ, as the variable relative to which abstraction is made, and employs the notation $\acute{\epsilon}$ (A) to denote what is essentially the *function in extension* (the "Werthverlauf" in his terminology) obtained from A by abstraction relative to ϵ.

There is also an analogous process of *functional abstraction* relative to two or more variables (taken in a given order), which yields a polyadic function when applied to a formula A.

Closely related to the process of functional abstraction is the process of forming a class by *abstraction* from a suitable formula A relative to a particular variable, say *x*. The formula A must be such that (under the given system of interpretation for the notations appearing in A) $\lambda x[A]$ denotes a propositional function. Then $x \ni$(A) (Peano), or $\hat{x}$ (A) (Russell), denotes the class determined by this propositional function. Frege's $\acute{\epsilon}$ (A) also belongs here, when the function corresponding to A (relatively to the variable ϵ) is a propositional function.

Similarly, a relation in extension may be formed by *abstraction* from a suitable formula A relative to two particular variables taken in a given order.—*A.C.*

Scholz and Schweitzer, *Die sogenannten Definitionen durch Abstraktion*, Leipzig, 1935.—W.V. Quine, *A System of Logistic*, Cambridge, Mass., 1934. A. Church, review of the preceding, Bulletin of the American Mathematical Society, vol. 41 (1935), pp. 498–603. W. V. Quine, *Mathematical Logic*, New York, 1940.

In psychology: the mental operation by which we proceed from individuals to concepts of classes, from individual dogs to the notion of "the dog." We abstract features common to several individuals, grouping them thus together under one name.

In Scholasticism: the operation by which the mind becomes cognizant of the universal (*q.v.*) as represented by the individuals. Aristotle and Thomas ascribe this operation to the active intellect (*q.v.*) which "illuminates" the image (phantasm) and disengages from it the universal nature to be received and made intelligible by the possible intellect.—*R.A.*

Abstractionism: (Lat. *ab,* from + *trahere,* to draw) The illegitimate use of abstraction, and especially the tendency to mistake abstractions for concrete realities. Cf. W. James, *The Meaning of Truth,* ch XIII. Equivalent to A. N. Whitehead's "Fallacy of misplaced concreteness."—*L.W.*

Abstractum (pl. *abstracta*): (Lat *ab* + *trahere,* to draw) An abstractum, in contrast to a concretum or existent is a quality or a relation envisaged by an abstract concept (*e.g.* redness, equality, truth etc.). The abstractum may be conceived either as an ideal object or as a real, subsistent universal.—*L.W.*

Ab universali ad particulare valet, a particulari ad universale non valet consequentia: Adage stating the validity of arguments making the transition from the general to the particular and denying the permissibility of the converse process.—*J.J.R.*

Academy: (Gr. *akademia*) A gymnasium in the suburbs of Athens, named after the hero Academus, where Plato first taught; hence, the Platonic school of philosophy. Plato and his immediate successors are called the Old Academy; the New Academy begins with Arcesilaus (*c.* 315—*c.* 241 B.C.), and is identified with its characteristic doctrine, probabilism (*q.v.*).—*G.R.M.*

Accident: (Lat. *accidens*) (in Scholasticism) Has no independent and self sufficient existence, but exists only in another being, a substance or another accident. As opposed to substance the accident is called *praedicamentale;* as naming features of the essence or quiddity of a being *accidens praedicabile.* Accidents may change, disappear or be added, while substance remains the same. Accidents are either proper, that is necessarily given with a definite essence (thus, the "faculties of the soul" are proper accidents, because to sense, strive, reason etc., is proper to the soul) or non-proper, contingent like color or size.—*R.A.*

In Aristotelian logic, whatever term can be predicated of, without being essential or peculiar to the subject (*q.v.*). Logical or predicable (*q.v.*) —opposed to property (*q.v.*)—is that quality which adheres to a subject in such a manner that it neither constitutes its essence nor necessarily flows from its essence; as, a man is *white* or *learned.*

Physical or predicamental (*q.v.*)—opposed to substance (*q.v.*)—that whose nature it is to exist not in itself but in some subject; as *figure, quantity, manner.*—*H.G.*

Accidentalism: The theory that some events are undetermined, or that the incidence of series of determined events is unpredictable (Aristotle, Cournot). In Epicureanism (*q.v.*) such indeterminism was applied to mental events and specifically to acts of will. The doctrine then assumes the special form: Some acts of will are unmotivated. See *Indeterminism.* A striking example of a more general accidentalism is Charles Peirce's

Tychism (*q.v.*). See *Chance, Contingency.*—*C.A.B.*

Acervus argument: A Sophistical argument to the effect that, given any number of stones which are not sufficient to constitute a heap, one does not obtain a heap by adding one more yet eventually, if this process is repeated, one has a heap.—*C.A.B.*

Achilles argument: Zeno of Elea used a reductio ad absurdum argument against the possibility of motion. He urged that if we assume it possible we are led to the absurdity that Achilles, the fastest runner in Greece, could not catch a proverbially slow tortoise. The alleged grounds for this are that during the time, $t_1 — t_2$, which it takes Achilles to traverse the distance between his position and that of the tortoise at time t_1, the latter even at his slow rate of speed would have moved on a finite distance farther.—*C.A.B.*

Cf. B. Russell, *Scientific Method in Philosophy*; Lewis Carroll, "Achilles and the Tortoise," *Mind.*

Acosmism: (Gr. *kosmos,* world) Theory of the non-existence of an external, physical world. See *Subjective Idealism.*—*W.L.*

Acquaintance, Knowledge by: (Lat. *adcognitare,* to make known) The apprehension of a quality, thing or person which is in the direct presence of the knowing subject. Acquaintance, in the strict sense, is restricted to the immediate data of experience but is commonly extended to include the things or persons perceived by means of such data. See *Description, Knowledge by.*—*L.W.*

Acroamatic: Communicated orally. Applied especially to Aristotle's more private teachings to his select advanced students. Hence, esoteric, abstruse.—*C.A.B.*

Act: (in Scholasticism) (1) Operation; as the intellect's *act.* In this sense, it is generally referred to as *second act* (see below).

(2) That which determines or perfects a thing; as *rationality perfects animality.*

Commanded: An act, originating in the will but executed by some other power; as *walking.*

Elicited: The proper and immediate act of the will, as *love* or *hate.*

First: (1) The prime form of a thing, in the sense of its essence or integrity. The *second act* is its operation. Thus the physical evil of blindness is the absence of the *first act,* i.e., a perfection due to man's integrity; while the moral evil of sin is an absence of the second act, i.e., a perfection demanded by righteous operation. (2) *First act* may also designate the faculty or principle of operation, as the *will,* while *second act* stands for its operations.

Human: (humanus) Deliberate act; e.g. painting.

Of Man: (hominis) Indeliberate act; e.g. digestion. Opposed to *passive* or *subjective* potency (*q.v.*).

Formal: A substantial or accidental form thought of as determining a thing to be what it is rather than to be something else. E.g. the substantial form of fire determines the composite in which it exists, to be fire and nothing else. Likewise the accidental form of heat determines a body to be warm rather than cold.

Informative: Form, or that which is like a form in

some composite, *e.g.* the soul in man or knowledge in the intelligent soul.—*H.G.*

Act-character: (Ger. *Aktcharakter*) In Husserl: Intentionality.—*D.C.*

Action: (in Scholasticism) *Immanent:* The terminus is received in the agent, as in a subject; as *contemplation.*

Transient: The terminus is received in a subject distinct from the agent; as *ball-throwing.*—*H.G.*

Activism: (Lat. *activus,* from *agere,* to act) The philosophical theory which considers activity, particularly spiritual activity, to be the essence of reality. The concept of pure act (*actus purus*), traceable to Aristotle's conception of divinity, was influential in Scholastic thought, and persists in Leibniz, Fichte and modern idealism.—*L.W.*

Negatively, a repudiation of the intellectualistic persuasion that an adequate solution of the truth problem can be found through an abstract intellectual inquiry. Positively, a view of action as the key to truth, similar to Fichte's view. The true and sound standard of action is an independent spiritual life, independent in bringing the world and life in accord with its values. Spiritual life grows by the active aid of human cooperation to ever higher dimensions. Spiritual being is achieved by the vital deeds of individuals. (Eucken)—*H.H.*

In the Personalistic sense activism applies not only to the continuous creative willing which underlies all reality but also to knowledge which calls for an unceasing divine activity which is a sort of occasionalism. (Malebranche: *Recherche de la vérité, Book* I, Chap. XIV.) Charles Sécrétan: "To be is to act."—*R.T.F.*

Act Psychology: (Lat. *actum,* a thing done) A type of psychology traceable to F. Brentano, *Psychologie vom empirischen Standpunkte* (1874) which considers the mental act (*e.g.* the act of sensing a red color patch) rather than the content (*e.g.* the red color) the proper subject matter of psychology. (See *Intentionalism.*)—*L.W.*

Acts: In ethics the main concern is usually said to be with acts or actions, particularly voluntary ones, in their moral relations, or with the moral qualities of acts and actions. By an act or action here is meant a bit of behavior or conduct, the origination or attempted origination of a change by some agent, the execution of some agent's choice or decision (so that not acting may be an act). As such, an act is often distinguished from its motive, its intention, and its maxim on the one hand, and from its consequences on the other, though it is not always held that its moral qualities are independent of these. Rather, it is frequently held that the rightness of an act, or its moral goodness, or both, depend at least in part on the character or value of its motive, intention, maxim, or consequences, or of the life or system of which it is a part. Another question concerning acts in ethics is whether they must be free (in the sense of being partially or wholly undetermined by previous causes), as well as voluntary, in order to be moral, and, if so, whether any acts are free in this sense. See *Agent.*—*W.K.F.*

Actual: In Husserl: see *Actuality*

Actual: (Lat. *actus,* act) 1. real or factual (opposed to *unreal* and *apparent*) 2. quality which anything possesses of having realized its potentialities or possibilities (opposed to *possible* and *potential*). In Aristotle: see *Energeia.*

Actuality: In Husserl: 1. (Ger. *Wirklichkeit*) Effective individual existence in space and time, as contrasted with mere possibility. 2. (Ger. *Aktualität*) The character of a conscious process as lived in by the ego, as contrasted with the "inactuality" of conscious processes more or less far from the ego. To say the ego lives in a particular conscious process is to say the ego is busied with the object intended in that process. Attending is a special form of being busied.—*D.C.*

Actuality: The mode of being in which things affect or are affected. The realm of fact; the field of happenings. Syn. with existence, sometimes with reality. Opposite of: possibility or potentiality. See *Energeia.*—*J.K.F.*

Actus Purus: See *Activism.*—*L.W.*

Ad hoc: A dubious assumption or argument arbitrarily introduced as explanation after the fact.

Adeism: Max Müller coined the term which means the rejection of the *devas,* or gods, of ancient India; similar to atheism which denies the one God.—*J.J.R.*

Adequation: (Ger. *Adäquation*) In Husserl: verification; fulfilment.—*D.C.*

(Lat. *adequatio*) In Aquinas: relation of truth to being.

Adhyātman: (Skr. *adhi,* over and *atman, q.v.*) A term for the Absolute which gained popularity with the reading of the Bhagavad Gitā (cf. 8.3) and which Ralph Waldo Emerson rendered appropriately "Oversoul" (cf. his essay *The Oversoul*).—*K.F.L.*

Adiaphora: (Gr. indifferent) A Stoic term designating entities which are morally indifferent.—*C.A.B.*

Adler, Alfred: (1870–1937) Originally a follower of Freud (see *Psychoanalysis; Freud*), he founded his own school in Vienna about 1912. In contrast to Freud, he tended to minimize the rôle of sexuality and to place greater emphasis on the ego. He investigated the feelings of inferiority resulting from organic abnormality and deficiency and described the unconscious attempt of the ego to compensate for such defects. (*Study of Organic Inferiority and its Psychical Compensations,* 1907). He extended the concept of the "inferiority complex" to include psychical as well as physical deficiencies and stressed the tendency of "compensation" to lead to *over*-correction. (*The Neurotic Constitution,* 1912; *Problems of Neurosis,* 1930.)—*L.W.*

Adler, Mortimer J.: (1902–) Speaking with a trace of scholasticism, Adler's breadth of mind communicated the ability to perform conceptual analysis with an existential enthusiasm unique in its time.

Born in New York, Adler graduated from Columbia (Ph. D. 1928) and taught there until 1929. He then taught philosophy of law at the University of Chicago from 1930 to 1952, and has been director of the Institute for Philosophical Research since that time. He has written over fourteen books, including *Dialectic* (1927), *The Idea of Freedom* (1958), *The Revolution in Educa-*

tion (1958), and *The Conditions of Philosophy: Its Checkered Past, Its Present Disorder, and Its Future Promise* (1965), *How to Think About God* (1980).—*S.E.N.*

Adoptionism: A christological doctrine prominent in Spain in the eighth century according to which Christ, inasmuch as He was man, was the Son of God by adoption only, acknowledging, however, that inasmuch as He was God, He was also the Son of God by nature and generation. The Church condemned the teaching. —*J.J.R.*

Adorno, Theodor W.: (1903-1969) Author of *The Authoritarian Personality* (1950), *Aesthetic Theory* (*Asthetische Theorie,* 1970), and other well-received and highly regarded works on social philosophy, music and literature.—*S.E.N.*

Advaita: (Skr. "non-duality") The Vedāntic (*q.v.*) doctrine of monism advocated by Sankara (*q.v.*) which holds the Absolute to be personal in relation to the world, especially the philosophically untutored, but supra-personal in itself (cf. *nirguna, saguna*); the world and the individual to be only relatively, or phenomenally, real; and salvation to consist in insight or *jñāna* (*q.v.*) after dispelling the *māyā* (*q.v.*) of separateness from the divine.—*K.F.L.*

Adventitious Ideas: Those ideas which appear to come from without, from objects outside the mind. Opposite of innate ideas. Descartes' form of the ontological argument for God was built upon the notion of adventitious ideas.—*V.F.*

Aenesidemus of Cnossos: (b. 1st century BC) Greek skeptic dialectician, revived Pyrrhonian principle of suspended judgment, a form of agnosticism in epistemology. Known through Sextus Empiricus (*q.v.*).—*S.E.N.*

Aeon: According to the Gnostics a being regarded as a subordinate heavenly power derived from the Supreme Being by a process of emanation. The totality of aeons formed the spiritual world which was intermediary between the Deity and the material world of sensible phenomena, which was held to be evil.—*J.J.R.*

Aequilibrium indifferentiae: The state or condition of exact balance between two actions, the motives being of equal strength. Thomas Aquinas held that in such a condition *"actus haberi non potest, nisi removeatur indifferentia."* This is effected by a determination *ab intrinseco,* or *ab extrinseco,* which disturbs the equipoise and makes it possible for the agent to act.—*J.J.R.*

Aesthetic Judgment: (German: *aesthetische Urteilskraft*) The power of judgment exercised upon data supplied by the feeling or sense of beauty. Kant devotes the first half of the *Critique of Judgment* to a "Critique of Aesthetic Judgment." (See *Kantianism* and *Feeling.*)—*O.F.K.*

On the origin of the term, see *Aesthetics.*

Aesthetics: (Gr. *aesthetikos,* perceptive) Traditionally, the branch of philosophy dealing with beauty or the beautiful, especially in art, and with taste and standards of value in judging art. Also, a theory or consistent attitude on such matters. The word *aesthetics* was first used by Baumgarten about 1750, to imply the science of sensuous knowledge, whose aim is beauty, as contrasted with logic, whose aim is truth. Kant used the term *transcendental aesthetic* in another sense, to imply the *a priori* principles of sensible experience. Hegel, in the 1820's, established the word in its present sense by his writings on art under the title of *Aesthetik.*

Aesthetics is now achieving a more independent status as the subject (whether it is or can be a "science" is a disputed issue) which studies (a) works of art, (b) the processes of producing and experiencing art, and (c) certain aspects of nature and human production outside the field of art—especially those which can be considered as beautiful or ugly in regard to form and sensory qualities. (E.g., sunsets, flowers, human beings, machines.)

While not abandoning its interest in beauty, artistic value, and other normative concepts, recent aesthetics has tended to lay increasing emphasis on a descriptive, factual approach to the phenomena of art and aesthetic experience. It differs from art history, archeology, and cultural history in stressing a theoretical organization of materials in terms of recurrent types and tendencies, rather than a chronological or genetic one. It differs from general psychology in focusing upon certain selected phases in psycho-physical activity, and on their application to certain types of objects and situations, especially those of art. It investigates the forms and characteristics of art, which psychology does not do. It differs from art criticism in seeking a more general, theoretical understanding of the arts than is usual in that subject, and in attempting a more consistently objective, impersonal attitude. It maintains a philosophic breadth, in comparing examples of all the arts, and in assembling data and hypotheses from many sources, including philosophy, psychology, cultural history, and the social sciences. But it is departing from traditional conceptions of philosophy in that writing labelled "aesthetics" now often includes much detailed, empirical study of particular phenomena, instead of restricting itself as formerly to abstract discussion of the meaning of beauty, the sublime, and other categories, their objective or subjective nature, their relation to pleasure and moral goodness, the purpose of art, the nature of aesthetic value, etc. There has been controversy over whether such empirical studies deserve to be called "aesthetics," or whether that name should be reserved for the traditional, dialectic or speculative approach; but usage favors the extension in cases where the inquiry aims at fairly broad generalizations.

Overlapping among all the above-mentioned fields is inevitable, as well as great differences in approach among individual writers. Some of these stress the nature and varieties of form in art, with attention to historic types and styles such as romanticism, the Baroque, etc., and in studying their evolution adopt the historian's viewpoint to some extent. Some stress the psychology of creation, appreciation, imagination, aesthetic experience, emotion, evaluation, and preference. Their work may be classed as "aesthetics," "aesthetic psychology," or "psychology of art." Within this psychological group, some can be further distinguished as laboratory or statistical psychologists, attempting more or less exact calculation and measurement. This approach (sometimes called "experimental aesthetics") follows the lead of Fechner, whose studies of aesthetic preference in 1876 helped to inaugurate modern experimental psychology as well as the empirical approach to aesthetics. It has dealt less with works of art than with preference for various arbitrary, simplified linear shapes, color-combinations and tone-combinations.

If the term "experimental" is broadly understood as implying a general mode of inquiry based on observation and the tentative application of hypotheses to particular cases, it includes many studies in aesthetics which avoid quantitative measurement and laboratory procedure. The full application of scientific method is still commonly regarded as impossible or unfruitful in dealing with the more subtle and complex phenomena of art. But the progress of aesthetics toward scientific status is being slowly made, through increasing use of an objective and logical approach instead of a dogmatic or personal one, and through bringing the results of other sciences to bear on aesthetic problems. Recent years have seen a vast increase in the amount and variety of artistic data available for the aesthetician, as a result of anthropological and archeological research and excavation, diversified museum collections, improved reproductions, translations, and phonograph records.—*T.M.*

Aetiology: (Gr. *aitiologeo*, to inquire into) An inquiry into causes. See *Etiology*.—*V.F.*

Aeviternity: (Lat. *aevum*, never-ending time) Eternity conceived as a whole, apart from the flux of time; an endless temporal medium in which objects and events are relatively fixed.—*R.B.W.*

Affect: (Lat. *ad + facere*, to do) The inner motive as distinguished from the intention or end of action. Cf. Spinoza, *Ethics*, bk. III.—*L.W.*

Affective: (Lat. *affectio*, from *afficere*, to affect) The generic character supposedly shared by pleasure, pain and the emotions as distinguished from the ideational and volitional aspects of consciousness. See *Affect*.—*L.W.*

Affinity (chemical): A potential of chemical energy; driving force; attraction. The term should be defined rigorously to mean the rate of change of chemical energy with changes in chemical mass.—*W.M.M.*

Affirmation of the consequent: The *fallacy of affirmation of the consequent* is the fallacious inference from B and A ⊃ B to A. The *law of affirmation of the consequent* is the theorem of the propositional calculus,

$$q \supset [p \supset q].—A.C.$$

Affirmative proposition: In traditional logic, propositions *A*, *I* were called *affirmative*, and *E*, *O*, *negative* (see *logic, formal*, § 4). It is doubtful whether this distinction can be satisfactorily extended to propositions (or even to sentences) generally.—*A.C.*

A fortiori: A phrase signifying all the more; applied to something which must be admitted for a still stronger reason.—*J.J.R.*

Āgama: (Skr.) One of a number of Indian treatises composed since the 1st cent. A.D. which are outside the Vedic (*q.v.*) tradition, but are regarded authoritative by the followers of Vishnuism, Shivaism, and Shaktism. Amid mythology, epic and ritualistic matter they contain much that is philosophical.—*K.F.L.*

Agathobiotik: A good life or the good life.—*C.A.B.*

Agathology: (Gr.) The science of the good.—*C.A.B.*

Agent: In ethics an agent is always a person who is acting, or has acted, or is contemplating action. Here it is usually held that to be a moral agent, i.e., an agent to whom moral qualities may be ascribed and who may be treated accordingly, one must be free and responsible, with a certain maturity, rationality, and sensitivity — which normal adult human beings are taken to have. Ethics is then concerned to determine when such an agent is morally good or virtuous, when morally bad or vicious, or, alternatively, when he is acting rightly and when wrongly, when virtuously and when viciously. See *Act*.—*W.K.F.*

Agglutination: (Lat. *ad + glutinare*, to paste) Philologically, a method of formation in language whereby a modification of meaning or of relation is given to a word by adherence or incorporation of distinct parts or elements.—*H.H.*

Aggregate: 1. In a general sense, a collection, a totality, a whole, a class, a group, a sum, an agglomerate, a cluster, a mass, an amount or a quantity of something, with certain definite characteristics in each case.

2. *In Logic and Mathematics,* a collection, a manifold, a multiplicity, a set, an ensemble, an assemblage, a totality of elements (usually numbers or points) satisfying a given condition or subjected to definite operational laws. According to Cantor, an aggregate is any collection of separate objects of thought gathered into a whole; or again, any multiplicity which can be thought as one; or better, any totality of definite elements bound up into a whole by means of a law. Aggregates have several properties: for example, they have the "same power" when their respective elements can be brought into one-to-one correspondence; and they are "enumerable" when they have the same power as the aggregate of natural numbers. Aggregates may be finite or infinite; and the laws applying to each type are different and often incompatible, thus raising difficult philosophical problems. See *One-One; Cardinal Number; Enumerable*. Hence the practice to isolate the mathematical notion of the aggregate from its metaphysical implications and to consider such collections as symbols of a certain kind which are to facilitate mathematical calculations in much the same way as numbers do. In spite of the controversial nature of infinite sets great progress has been made in mathematics by the introduction of the Theory of Aggregates in arithmetic, geometry and the theory of functions. (German, *Mannigfaltigkeit, Menge;* French, *Ensemble*).

3. *In logic,* an "aggregate meaning" is a form of

common or universal opinion or thought held by more than one person.

4. *In the philosophy of nature*, aggregate has various meanings: it is a mass formed into clusters (anat.); a compound or an organized mass of individuals (zool.); an agglomerate (bot.); an agglomeration of distinct minerals separable by mechanical means (geol.); or, in general, a compound mass in which the elements retain their essential individuality.—*T.G.*

(in mathematics): The concept of an *aggregate* is now usually identified with that of a *class* (*q.v.*)—although as a historical matter this does not, perhaps, exactly represent Cantor's notion.—*A.C.*

Agnoiology: (Gr. *agnoio* + *logos*, discourse on ignorance) J. F. Ferrier (1854) coined both this term and the term epistemology as connoting distinctive areas of philosophic inquiry in support of ontology. Agnoiology is the doctrine of ignorance which seeks to determine what we are necessarily ignorant of. It is a critique of agnosticism prior to the latter's appearance. Ignorance is defined in relation to knowledge since one cannot be ignorant of anything which cannot possibly be known.—*H.H.*

Agnosticism: (Gr. *agnostos,* unknowing) 1. (epist.) that theory of knowledge which asserts that it is impossible for man to attain knowledge of a certain subject-matter.
2. (theol.) that theory of religious knowledge which asserts that it is impossible for man to attain knowledge of God.

Agnosy: Ignorance, especially universal ignorance. —*C.A.B.*

Agrippa: (*fl. c.* AD 200) Greek skeptic known through Empiricus (*q.v.*), contributing five *tropoi,* ways of achieving doubt: everyone disagrees, nothing is self-evident, everything is relative, everything depends upon assumptions, and all arguments are circular.—*S.E.N.*

Agrippa von Nettesheim, Henricus Cornelius: (1487-1535) Stormy diplomat and adventurer, author of *De Occulta Philosophia* (1509/10, published 1531-3) and *De Incertitudine et Vanitate de Scientiarum et Artium* (*Of the Vanitie and Uncertaintie of Artes and Sciences,* 1530; London, 1569). Dismissed from Metz for defending a peasant woman accused of witchcraft.—*S.E.N.*

Aham brahma asmi: (Skr.) "I am brahman," the formula of the Brhadāraṇyaka Upanishad 1.4.10, denoting the full coincidence of the human and divine, arrived at not so much by a spontaneous mystic insight as by logical deduction from the nature of world and self.—*K.F.L.*

Ahamkāra: (Skr.) Literally "I-maker," the principle generating the consciousness of one's ego or personal identity; the ground of apperception.—*K.F.L.*

Ahantā: (Skr. "I-ness") Selfhood, state of being an ego; the subject in knowledge.—*K.F.L.*

Ahimsā: (Skr.) Non-injury, an ethical principle applicable to all living beings and subscribed to by most Hindus. In practice it would mean, e.g., abstaining from animal food, relinquishing war, rejecting all thought of taking life, regarding all living beings akin. It has led to such varied phenomena as the Buddhist's sweeping the path before him or straining the water, the almost reverential attitude toward the cow, and Gandhi's non-violent resistence campaign.—*K.F.L.*

Ahriman: (Middle Persian) Zoroaster, in building upon an ancient Indo-Iranian antecedent, expounded a thoroughgoing dualism in which Ormazd (*q.v.*) is the good, Ahriman the evil principle, corresponding to the Christian God and Devil, locked in combat on all levels of thought and existence. In that they are reciprocal and of a dialectic necessity, this dualism has, philosophically, the implication of a monism which was, indeed, ethically and eschatologically elaborated in the Zoroastrian optimism that postulates the ultimate victory of Ahura Mazdāh (*q.v.*) or Ormazd.—*K.F.L.*

Ai: (C.) Love; love for all people as a practical way to social welfare (chien ai) (Mo Tzú, between 500 and 396 B.C.); love for all, which is identical with true manhood (jên) (Han Yü, 767-824 A.D.).—*W.T.C.*

Ailly, Pierre d': (1350-1420) French Ockhamist, theologian, and cardinal, he supported the idea that church councils should be above the pope. A leader of the Council of Constance, which condemned John Hus, the Bohemian Reformer, Ailly wrote *De Anima* (*On the Soul,* 1492), *Concordentia astronomise cum Theologia* (*The Agreement of Astronomy with Theology,* 1490), and *De vita Christi* (*On the Life of Christ,* 1483).—*S.E.N.*

Ajdukiewicz, Kazimierz: (1890-1963) Polish logician and semanticist, student of Łukasiewicz at Lwów. Taught at Lwów, Poznań, and Warsaw. On Nagel's interpretation, interested in establishing a logic without metaphysics. Author of *Language and Meaning* (Chicago, 1951) and *Syntactic Connection* (Chicago, 1951).—*S.E.N.*

Akâsa: (Skr.) "Ether;" space; in Indian philosophy the continuum that is to be postulated in connection with the *paramānus* (*q.v.*)—*K.F.L.*

Aksara: (Skr.) "Imperishable," a descriptive synonym for *brahman* (*q.v.*), the Absolute, in the Upanishads (*q.v.*); has also the meaning of "syllable."—*K.F.L.*

Albert of Saxony: (*c.* 1316-1390) Medieval scientific writer, rector of the University of Paris (1357), bishop of Halberstadt, first rector of the University of Vienna (1365). He wrote: *Questions on Ockham's Logic* (1496), *Logica* (1522), *Sophismata* (1495), *About Aristotle's Heaven and Earth* (1492), *Super octo libros physicorum* (1516), *Super libros de generatione et corruptione* (1516), *De libris ethicorum,* and others.—*S.E.N.*

Albertists: The appellation is conferred on any disciple of Albertus Magnus. In particular it was applied to a group of Scholastics at the University of Cologne during the fifteenth and sixteenth centuries. It was the age of the struggles between the nominalists and the realists, who controlled the University of Cologne, but were themselves split into factions, the Thomists and the Albertists. The latter taught that the *universalia in re* and *post rem* were identical, and that logic was a speculative rather than a practical science. The principal Albertists were Heinrich von Kampen, Gerhard von Harderwyk, and Arnold von Lugde.—*J.J.R.*

Albertus, Magnus: St., O.P. (1193–1280) Count of Bollstädt, Bishop of Ratisbon, Doctor Universalis, was born at Lauingen, Bavaria, studied at Padua and Bologna, entered the Dominican Order in 1223. He taught theology at the Univ. of Paris from 1245-48, when he was sent to Cologne to organize a new course of studies for his Order; St. Thomas Aquinas was his student and assistant at this time. Later his time was given over to administrative duties and he was made Bishop of Ratisbon in 1260. In 1262 he gave up his bishopric and returned to a life of writing, teaching and controversy. Of very broad interests in science, philosophy and theology, Albert popularized a great part of the corpus of Aristotelian and Arabic philosophic writings in the 13th century. His thought incorporates elements of Augustinism, Aristotelianism, Neoplatonism, Avicennism, Boethianism into a vast synthesis which is not without internal inconsistencies. Due to the lack of critical editions of his works, a true estimate of the value of his philosophy is impossible at present. However, he must have had some influence on St. Thomas, and there was a lively Albertinian school lasting into the Renaissance. Chief works: *Summa de Creaturis, Comment, in IV Lib. Sent., Philos. Commentaries* on nearly all works of Aristotle, *De Causis, De intellectu et intellig., Summa Theologiae (Opera Omnia,* ed. Borgnet, 38 vol., Paris, 1890-99).—*V.J.B.*

Albo, Joseph: (1380-1444) Jewish philosopher in Spain, author of *The Book of Roots (Sefer ha-'Ikkarim,* 1485; English translation 1929-30).

Alcmaeon of Croton: Pre-socratic physician and philosopher, noted for combining theory ("What is health? Balance") with observation prior to the time of Hippocrates.—*S.E.N.*

Alcuin: (c.730-804) Was born in Northumbria and studied at the School of York under Egbert. In 781 he was called to head the Palatine School of Charlemagne. He died at St. Martin of Tours. It is his general influence on the revival of Christian learning that is significant in the history of philosophy. His psychology is a form of simplified Augustinianism. His treatise, *De animae ratione ad Eulaliam Virginem,* is extant (PL 101). —*V.J.B.*

Alembert, Jean Le Rond d': (1717-1783) Leading figure in the French Enlightenment, author of articles on science and mathematics. A skeptic on metaphysics, he wrote a brochure entitled *Histoire de la destruction des Jésuites (History of the Destruction of the Jesuits,* 1765).—*S.E.N.*

Alexander of Aphrodisias: (*c.* A.D. 160-220) Influential interpreter of Aristotle, teacher at Athens, author of commentaries on the *Metaphysics, De Anima, On Fate,* and *On Mixture.—S.E.N.*

Alexander of Hales: (*c.* 1185-1245) Medieval English Franciscan at the University of Paris, author of *Glossa, Disputed Questions,* and *Summa.* He defended Augus-

tinian positions.—*S.E.N.*

Alexander, Samuel: (1859-1938) English thinker who developed a non-psychic, neo-realistic metaphysics and synthesis. He makes the process of emergence a metaphysical principle. Although his inquiry is essentially *a priori, his* method is empirical. Realism at his hands becomes a quasi-materialism, an alternative to absolute idealism and ordinary materialism. It aims to combine the absoluteness of law in physics with the absolute unpredictability of emergent qualities. Whereas to the ancients and in the modern classical conception of physical science, the original stuff was matter and motion, after Minkowski, Einstein, Lorenz and others, it became indivisible space-time, instead of space *and* time.

Thus nature begins as a four-dimensional matrix in which it is the moving principle. Materiality, secondary qualities, life, mentality are all emergent modifications of proto-space-time. Mind is the nervous system blossoming out into the capacity of awareness. Contemplative knowledge, where the object is set over against the mind, and the actual being, or experiencing, or enjoying of reality, where there is no inner duplicity of subject and object, constitute the two forms of knowledge. Alexander conceives the deity as the next highest level to be emerged out of any given level. Thus for beings on the level of life mind is deity, but for beings possessing minds there is a *nisus* or urge toward a still higher quality. To such beings that dimly felt quality is deity. The quality next above any given level is deity to the beings on that level. For men deity has not yet emerged, but there is a *nisus* towards its emergence. S. Alexander, *Space, Time and Deity* (1920).—*H.H.*

Alexandrian School: A convenient designation for the various religious philosophies that flourished at Alexandria from the first to the fourth centuries of the Christian era, such as Neo-Pythagoreanism, the Jewish Platonism of Philo, Christian Platonism, and Neo-Platonism. Common to all these schools is the attempt to state Oriental religious beliefs in terms of Greek philosophy.—*G.R.M.*

Alexandrists: A term applied to a group of Aristotelians in Italy during the fifteenth and sixteenth centuries. Besides the Scholastic followers of Aristotle there were some Greeks, whose teaching was tinged with Platonism. Another group, the Averroists, followed Aristotle as interpreted by Ibn Rushd, while a third school interpreted Aristotle in the light of the commentaries of Alexander of Aphrodisias, hence were called Alexandrists. Against the Averroists who attributed a vague sort of immortality to the active intellect, common to all men, the Alexandrists, led by Pomponazzi, asserted the mortality of the individual human soul after its separation from universal reason.—*J.J.R.*

Al Farabi: Died 950, introduced Aristotelian logic into the world of Islam. He was known to posterity as the "second Aristotle." He continued the encyclopedic tradition inaugurated by Al Kindi. His metaphysical speculation influenced Avicenna who found in the works of his predecessor the fundamental notion of a distinction between existence and essence, the latter not implying necessarily in a contingent being the former which therefore has to be given by God. He also emphasizes the Aristotelian notion of the "first mover." The concretization of the universal nature in particular things points to a creative power which has endowed being with such a nature. Al Farabi's philosophy is dependent in certain parts on Neo-Platonism. Creation is emanation. There is an *anima mundi* the images of which become corporeal beings. Logic is considered as the preamble to all science. Physics comprises all factual knowledge, including psychology; metaphysics and ethics are the other parts of philosophy. Cl. Baeumker, *Alfarabi, Ueber den Ursprung der Wissenschaften*, Beitr. z. Gesch. d. Philos. d. MA. 1916. Vol. XIX. M. Horten, *Das Buch der Ringsteine Farabis. ibid.* 1906. Vol. V.—*R.A.*

Al Gazali: Born 1059 in Tus, in the country of Chorasan, taught at Bagdad, lived for a time in Syria, died in his home town 1111. He started as a sceptic in philosophy and became a mystic and orthodox afterwards. Philosophy is meaningful only as introduction to theology. His attitude resembles Neo-Platonic mysticism and is anti-Aristotelian. He wrote a detailed report on the doctrines of Farabi and Avicenna only to subject them to a scathing criticism in *Destructio philosophorum* where he points out the self-contradictions of philosophers. His main works are theological. In his writings on logic he wants to ensure to theology a reliable method of procedure. His metaphysics also is mainly based on theology: creation of the world out of nothing, resurrection, and so forth. Cf. H. Bauer, *Die Dogmatik Al-Ghazalis*, 1912.—*R.A.*

Algebraization: (Ger. *Algebraisierung*) In Husserl: Substitution of algebraic symbols (indeterminate terms) for the words (determinate terms) in which the material content of an objective sense is expressed. See *Formalization.*—*D.C.*

Algebra of logic is the name given to the Nineteenth Century form of the calculi of classes and propositions. It is distinguished from the contemporary forms of these calculi primarily by the absence of formalization as a *logistic system* (*q.v.*). The propositional calculus was also at first either absent or not clearly distinguished from the class calculus, the distinction between the two was made by Peirce and afterwards more sharply by Schröder (1891) but the identity of notation was retained.

Important names in the history of the subject are those of *Boole* (*q.v.*), *De Morgan* (*q.v.*), W.S. Jevons, *Peirce* (*q.v.*), Robert Grassmann, John Venn, Hugh MacColl, *Schröder* (*q.v.*), P.S. Poretsky.—*A.C.*

Algedonic: (Gr. *algos*, pain + *hēdonē*, pleasure) Term applied to feelings of pleasure or pain.—*L.W.*

Algorithm (or, less commonly, but etymologically more correctly, *algorism*) In its original usage, this word referred to the Arabic system of notation for numbers and to the elementary operations of arithmetic as performed in this notation. In mathematics, the word is used for a method or process of calculation with symbols (often, but not necessarily, numerical symbols) according to fixed rules which yields effectively the solution of any given problem of some class of problems.—*A.C.*

Aliotta, Antonio: (1881-1964) Italian philosopher, teacher at Padua and Naples, who combined methodological pragmatism (of the James and Mead variety) with an emphasis on the perennial character of human values. Author of *La reazione idealistica contro la scienza* (1914), *Relativismo e idealismo* (*Relativism and Idealism*, 1922), *Il sacrificio come significato del mondo* (1943), and *Le origini dell'irrazionalismo contemporaneo* (*The Origin of Contemporary Irrationalism*, 1950).—*S.E.N.*

Al Kindi: Of the tribe of Kindah, lived in Basra and Bagdad where he died 873. He is the first of the great Arabian followers of Aristotle whose influence is noticeable in Al Kindi's scientific and pyschological doctrines. He wrote on geometry, astronomy, astrology, arithmetic, music (which he developed on arithmetical principles), physics, medicine, psychology, meteorology, politics. He distinguishes the active intellect from the passive which is actualized by the former. Discursive reasoning and demonstration he considers as achievements of a third and a fourth intellect. In ontology he seems to hypostasize the categories, of which he knows five: matter, form, motion, place, time, and which he calls primary substances. Al Kindi inaugurated the encyclopedic form of philosophical treatises, worked out more than a century later by Avicenna (*q.v.*). He also was the first to meet the violent hostility of the orthodox theologians but escaped persecution. A. Nagy, *Die philos. Abhandlungen des Jacqub ben Ishaq al-Kindi*, Beitr, z. Gesch. d. Phil. d. MA. 1897, Vol. II.—*R.A.*

All: *All* and *every* are usual verbal equivalents of the universal quantifier. See *Quantifier.*—*A.C.*

Allen, Ethan: (1737-1789) Leader of the Green Mountain Boys and of their famous exploits during the American Revolution. He is less known but nonetheless significant as the earliest American deist. His *Reason, the Only Oracle of Man* (1784), expressed his opposition to the traditional Calvinism and its doctrine of original sin. He rejected prophecy and revelation but believed in immortality on moral grounds. He likewise believed in free will.—*L.E.D.*

Allgemeingültig: (Ger. *allgemein* + *gelten,* universally valid) A proposition or judgment which is universally valid, or necessary. Such propositions may be either empirical, i.e., dependent upon experience, or *a priori*, i.e., independent of all experience. In Kant's theoretical philosophy the necessary forms of the sensibility and understanding are declared to have universal validity *a priori*, because they are the *sine qua non* of any and all experience.—*O.F.K.*

Al-Mukamis, David Ibn Merwan: Early Jewish philosopher (died c. 937). His philosophic work, *Book of Twenty Tractates* shows influence of the teachings of the Kalam (*q.v.*); reasoning follows along lines similar to that of Saadia.—*M.W.*

Als Ob: (Ger. as if) Fictional; hypothetical; postulated;

pragmatic. The term was given currency by Hans Vaihinger's *Die Philosophie des Als Ob* (1911), which developed the thesis that our knowledge rests on a network of artfully contrived fictions which are not verifiable but pragmatically justifiable. While such fictions, employed in all fields of human knowledge and endeavor, deliberately falsify or circumvent the stream of immediate impressions, they greatly enhance reality.—*O.F.K.*

Alteration: (Lat. *alter*, other) In Aristotle's philosophy change of quality, as distinguished from change of quantity (growth and diminution) and from change of place (locomotion).—*G.R.M.*

Althusius, Johannes: (1557-1638) German social and political philosopher who lectured on Roman law at Herborn. Author of *Iurisprudentia Romana, vel Potius Iuris Romani Ars, 2 Libri, Comprehensa, et ad Leges Methodi Ramene Conformata* (1586), *Politica Methodice Digesta et Exemplis Sacris et Profanis Illustrata* (*Politics Methodologically Arranged and Illustrated by Holy and Profane Examples*, 1603), and *Dicaiologicae Libri Tres Totum et Universum Ius, Quo Utimur, Methodice Complectentes* (*Digest of Jurisprudence*, 1617).—*S.E.N.*

Altruism: (*Alter:* other) In general, the cult of benevolence; the opposite of Egoism (*q.v.*). Term coined by Comte and adopted in Britain by H. Spencer.

1. For Comte Altruism meant the discipline and eradication of self-centered desire, and a life devoted to the good of others; more particularly, selfless love and devotion to Society. In brief, it involved the self-abnegating love of Catholic Christianity redirected towards Humanity conceived as an ideal unity. As thus understood, altruism involves a conscious opposition not only to egoism (whether understood as excessive or moderate self-love), but also to the formal or theological pursuit of charity and to the atomic or individualistic social philosophy of 17th-18th century liberalism, of utilitarianism, and of French Ideology.

2. By extension the term has come to mean the pursuit of the good of others, whether motivated by either self-centered or other-centered interest, or whether by disinterested duty. By some it is identified with the protective and other-regarding feelings, attitudes, and behavior of animal life in general; while by others its use is restricted to mean such on the level of reflective intelligence.—*W.L.*

Ambiguity: In language, ambiguity is not necessarily the same as vagueness but rather refers to properties which have two or more meanings. For example, the word *base* may be connected with a favorite American sport or with the evil quality of an individual or it may even be the foundation of a structure. As a result base may be treated as three words with the same sound or one word with three different meanings. There are times when faulty antecedent may result in ambiguity such as when the antecedent of "her" is called into question in the sentence "Evelyn saw Lillian, but I didn't see *her.*" We often cite this example as an ambiguity of reference. Ambiguity has taken on importance to those who are philosophical linguists as well as to logicians.—*L.L.*

Ambiguous middle, fallacy of: See *quaternio terminorum*.

Amechanical: Term applied to psychologically conditioned movements. (Avenarius).—*H.H.*

Ammonius, Saccus: Teacher of Plotinus and Origen and reputed founder of Neo-Platonism.—*M.F.*

Amnestic: Characterized by amnesia, loss of memory.—*C.A.B.*

Amoral: Action, attitudes, state or character which is neither moral nor immoral, i.e., which is outside the moral realm. Neither right nor wrong. Ethically indifferent. Non-moral. Non-ethical. See Moral, Immoral, Ethics.—*A.J.B.*

Amphiboly: Any fallacy arising from ambiguity of grammatical construction (as distinguished from ambiguity of single words), a premiss being accepted, or proved, on the basis of one interpretation of the grammatical construction, and then used in a way which is correct only on the basis of another interpretation of the grammatical construction.—*A.C.*

Ampliative: (Lat. *ampliare*, to make wider; Ger. *Erweiterungsurteil*) Synthetic; serving to expand. In an *ampliative* judgment the predicate adds something not already contained in the meaning of the subject-term. Contrasted with *analytic* or *explicative*.—*O.F.K.*

Anādi: (Skr.) Beginningless, said of the Absolute and the world.—*K.F.L.*

Anagogic: (Gr. mystical) Usually employed as a noun in the plural, signifying an interpretation of Scripture pointing to a destiny to be hoped for and a goal to be attained; as an adjective it means, pertaining to the kind of interpretation described above.—*J.J.R.*

Analogies of Experience: (Ger. *Analogien der Erfahrung*) Kant's three dynamic principles (substantiality, reciprocity, and causality) of the understanding comprising the general category of *relation*, through which sense data are brought into the unity of experience. (See *Kantianism*.)—*O.F.K.*

Analogy: (in *Scholasticism*) Predication common to several inferiors of a name, which is accepted in different senses, in such a manner, nevertheless, that some principle warrants its common applicability. Accordingly as this principle is sought in the relations of cause and effect, proportion or proportionality there are distinguished various types of *analogy*.

Analogy of attribution: Is had when the principle of unity is found in a common concept to which the inferiors are related either by cause or effect. Moreover this common concept must refer principally and *per se* to a prime reality to which the inferiors are analogous. Thus food, medicine and pulse are said to be *healthy*. In this case the common concept is *health* which applies principally and *per se* to the animal; however, food, medicine and pulse are related to it through the various forms of cause and effect.

Analogy of proportion: Is had when the principle of unity is found, not in the relations of two or more to a common concept but in the interrelation of two concepts to themselves. This relation may be one of similitude or order. Thus *being* is predicated of substance and quantity, not because of their relations to a third reality which primordially contains this notion, but because of a relation both of similitude and order which they have to each other.

Analogy of proportionality: Is had when the principle of unity is found in an equality of proportions. This analogy is primarily used between material and spiritual realities. Thus *sight* is predicated of ocular vision and intellectual understanding *"eo quod sicut visus est in oculo, ita intellectus est in mente."—H.G.*

Analogy: Originally a mathematical term, Analogia, meaning equality of ratios (Euclid VII Df. 20, V. Dfs. 5, 6), which entered Plato's philosophy (*Republic* 534a6), where it also expressed the epistemological doctrine that sensed things are related as their mathematical and ideal correlates. In modern usage analogy was identified with a weak form of reasoning in which "from the similarity of two things in certain particulars, their similarity in other particulars is inferred." (*Century Dic.*) Recently, the analysis of scientific method has given the term new significance. The observable data of science are denoted by concepts by inspection, whose complete meaning is given by something immediately apprehendable; its verified theory designating unobservable scientific objects is expressed by concepts by postulation, whose complete meaning is prescribed for them by the postulates of the deductive theory in which they occur. To verify such theory relations, termed epistemic correlations (*J. Un. Sc.* IX: 125-128), are required. When these are one-one, analogy exists in a very precise sense, since the concepts by inspection denoting observable data are then related as are the correlated concepts by postulation designating unobservable scientific objects.—*F.S.C.N.*

Analogy of Pythagoras: (Gr. *analogia*) The equality of ratios, or proportion, between the lengths of the strings producing the consonant notes of the musical scale. The discovery of these ratios is credited to Pythagoras, who is also said to have applied the principle of mathematical proportion to the other arts, and hence to have discovered, in his analogy, the secret of beauty in all its forms.—*G.R.M.*

Analysis: (Chemical) The identification and estimation of chemical individuals in a mixture; the identification and estimation of elements in a compound; the identification and estimation of types of substances in complex mixtures; the identification and estimation of isotopes in an "element."—*W.M.M.*

Analysis, intentional: (Ger. *intentionale Analyse*) In Husserl: Explication and clarification of the essential structure of actual and potential (horizonal) synthesis by virtue of which objects are intentionally constituted. As *noematic,* intentional analysis discovers, explicates, and clarifies, the focally and horizontally intended objective sense (and the latter's quasi-objective substrates) in its manners of givenness, positedness, etc., and yields clues to the corresponding noetic synthesis. As *noetic* or *constitutional,* intentional analysis discovers, isolates, and clarifies these synthetically consti-

tuted structures of consciousness. See *Phenomenology.* —*D.C.*

Analysis (mathematical): The theory of real numbers, of complex numbers, and of functions of real and complex numbers. See *number; continuity; limit.*—*A.C.*

Analytic: (Gr. *analytike*) Aristotle's name for the technique of logical analysis. The *Prior Analytics* contains his analysis of the syllogism, the *Posterior Analytics* his analysis of the conditions of scientific or demonstrable knowledge.—*G.R.M.*

In Kant. One of two divisions of general logic (the other being *Dialectic*) which discovers by analysis all the functions of reason as exercised in thought, thus disclosing the formal criteria of experience and truth. (See *Kantianism.*)—*O.F.K.*

See also *Meaning, Kinds of.*

Analyticity: See *Meaning, Kinds of; Truth, semantical; Valid.*

Analytic Judgment: (Ger. *analytisches Urteil*) In Kant: A judgment in which the predicate concept is included within the subject concept, as analysis should or does disclose. Such a judgment does not require verification by experience; its sole criterion is the law of contradiction. (See *Kantianism.*)—*O.F.K.*

Analytic Philosophy: The dominant school in Great Britain, Australia, Scandinavia, and the United States, it emphasizes analysis as the proper method for philosophical investigation. Ideas must first be clarified before we attempt to do anything further with them, such as to investigate the nature of reality.

This clarification solves many philosophical puzzles because they literally *dis*solve upon analysis. The way we use language has caused many false problems for philosophy. The more careful use of language will lead to fewer problems.

The word "analysis" has two technical meanings: (1) philosophical (or reductive or "new-level") analysis, and (2) logical (or "same-level") analysis. The first reduces material objects to statements about the possibilities of sensation. The second concentrates on showing, as in the theory of descriptions, the correct logical form of ordinary sentences. It claims neutrality from making metaphysical assumptions about material objects. However, this second method was shown to be reductive as well, despite its claim of complete objectivity, as when it condemned certain ways of speaking and recommended others.

Three principles of analytic philosophy most generally held are (1) that philosophy as such is empirically uninformative, (2) that the primary function of philosophy is to engage in an analysis of the meaning of language, and (3) that the proper locus of meaning is in the proposition or statement.

Some well-known analytic philosophers are A. J. Ayer, G. E. Moore, G. Ryle, Urmson, and Passmore.—*S.E.N.*

Analytic, Transcendental: In Kant: The section of the *Critique of Pure Reason* which deals with the concepts and principles of the understanding. Its main purpose is the proof of the categories within the realm of phenomena.—*A.C.E.*

Analytical Jurisprudence: Theory of Austin, Markby, Holland, Salmond, etc., considering jurisprudence the formal science of positive law. Its main task is to analyze the necessary notions of law. Term coined by Henry Summer Maine.—*W.E.*

Anamnesis: (Gr. *anamnesis*) Calling to mind; recollection; in Plato, the process whereby the mind gains true knowledge, by recalling the vision of the Ideas which the soul experienced in a previous existence apart from the body.—*G.R.M.*

Ānanda: (Skr.) Joy, happiness, bliss, beatitude, associated in the thinking of many Indian philosophers with *moksa* (*q.v.*); a concomitant of perfection and divine consciousness (cf. *sat-cit-ānanda*).—*K.F.L.*

Ananya: (Skr. "not other") Designating the non-otherness of the cosmic principle from the individual. —*K.F.L.*

Anarchism: This doctrine advocates the abolition of political control within society: the State, it contends, is man's greatest enemy—eliminate it and the evils of human life will disappear. Positively, anarchism envisages a homely life devoted to unsophisticated activity and filled with simple pleasures. Thus it belongs in the "primitive tradition" of Western culture and springs from the philosophical concept of the inherent and radical goodness of human nature. Modern anarchism probably owes not a little, in an indirect way, to the influence of the primitivistic strain in the thought of Jean Jacques Rousseau. In a popular sense the word "anarchy" is often used to denote a state of social chaos, but it is obvious that the word can be used in this sense only by one who denies the validity of anarchism.—*M.B.M.*

Anattā-vāda: (Pali) Theory (*vāda*) of the non-existence of soul (*anattā*), one of the fundamental teachings of Gautama Buddha (*q.v.*) who regarded all ideas about the soul or self wrong, inadequate or illusory.—*K.F.L.*

Anaxagoras, of Klazomene: (about 430 B.C.) As a middle-aged man he settled in Athens; later he was accused of impiety and forced to leave the city. Anaxagoras taught that there is an infinity of simple substances, that is, such as are only divisible into parts of the same nature as the whole. These "seeds" are distributed throughout the universe. Their coming together gives rise to individual things, their separation entails the passing away of individual things. To account for the *cause of motion* of these "seeds" or elemental substances Anaxagoras conceived of a special kind of matter or "soul-substance" which alone is in motion itself and can communicate this motion to the rest. Now, since the universe displays harmony, order and purposiveness in its movements, Anaxagoras conceived this special substance as a mindstuff or an eternal, imperishable Reason diffused throughout the universe. Anaxagoras was thus the first to introduce the teleological principle into the explanation of the natural world. Cf. Burnet, *Early Greek Philosophy;* Diels, *Frag. d. Vorsokr.*—*M.F.*

Anaximander: (6th Cent. B.C.) With Thales and Anaximenes he formed the Milesian School of Greek Philosophy; with these and the other thinkers of the cosmological period he sought the ground of the manifold processes of nature in a single world-principle or cosmic stuff which he identified with "the Infinite." He was the first to step out of the realm of experience and ascribed to his "Infinite" the attributes of eternity, imperishability and inexhaustability. Cf. Burnet, *Early Greek Philosophy;* Diels, *Frag. d. Vorsokr.*—*M.F.*

Anaximenes: (6th Cent. B.C.) With Thales and Anaximander he belongs to the Milesian School of Greek Philosophy; as an Ionian he sought a cosmic material element which would explain the manifold processes of the natural world and declared this to be *air*. Air, he felt, had the attribute of infinity which would account for the varieties of nature more readily than water, which his predecessor Thales had postulated. Cf. Burnet, *Early Greek Philosophy*; Diels, *Frag. d. Vorsokr.*—*M.F.*

Anergy: The hypothesis interpreting sensations in terms of the infinite phases of negative energy, which is motion less than zero. (Montague.)—*H.H.*

Anglo-Catholic Philosophy: Anglo-Catholicism is the name frequently used to describe the Church of England and her sister communions, including the Episcopal Church in America. As a religious system, it may be described as the maintenance of the traditional credal, ethical and sacramental position of Catholic Christianity, with insistence on the incorporation into that general position of the new truth of philosophy, science and other fields of study and experience. Historically, the Anglo-Catholic divines (as in Hooker and the Caroline writers) took over the general Platonic-Aristotelian philosophy of the schools; their stress, however, was more on the Platonic than the Aristotelian side: "Platonism," Dr. Inge has said, "is the loving mother-nurse of Anglicanism." Statements of this position, modified by a significant agnosticism concerning areas into which reason (it is said) cannot penetrate, may be found collected in *Anglicanism* (edited by More and Cross). A certain empiricism has always marked Anglo-Catholic theological and philosophical speculation; this is brought out in recent writing by Taylor (*Faith of a Moralist*), the writers in *Lux Mundi* (edited by Gore) and its modern successor *Essays Catholic and Critical*.

In general, Anglo-Catholic philosophy has been an incarnational or sacramental one, finding God in the Biblical revelation culminating in Christ, but unwilling to limit his self-disclosure to that series of events. Incarnationalism provides, it is said, the setting for the historic Incarnation; general revelation is on sacramental lines, giving meaning to the particular sacraments. For Anglo-Catholic philosophical theology, in its central stream, the key to dogma is the cumulative experience of Christian people, tested by the Biblical revelation as source and standard of that experience and hence "classical" in its value. Revelation is the ultimate authority; the Church possesses a trustworthiness about her central beliefs, but *statement* of these may change from age to age. Sometimes this main tendency of Anglo-Catholic thought has been sharply criticized by thinkers, themselves Anglicans (cf. Tennant's *Philosophical Theology*); but these have, in general, served as useful warnings rather than as normal expressions of the Anglican mind.

In very recent years, a new stress has been laid upon the dogmatic side of Christianity as expressed in liturgy. This has been coupled with a revived interest in Thomism, found both in older philosophers such as A. E. Taylor and in younger men like A. G. Hebert (cf. his *Grace and Nature*, etc.).—*W.N.P.*

Angst: (Ger. dread) Concern or care, which are the essence of dread. (Heidegger.)—*H.H.*

Anima Mundi: See: *The World Soul, Bruno.*

Animalitarianism: A term used by Lovejoy in *Primitivism and Related Ideas in Antiquity* for the belief that animals are happier, more admirable, more "normal," or "natural," than human beings.—*G.B.*

Animism: (Lat. *anima*, soul) The doctrine of the reality of souls.
1. Anthropology: (a) the view that souls are attached to all things either as their inner principle of spontaneity or activity, or as their dwellers. (b) the doctrine that Nature is inhabited by various grades of spirits. (s. Spiritism).
2. Biology, Psychology: the view that the ground of life is immaterial soul rather than the material body.
3. Metaphysics: the theory that Being is animate, living, ensouled (s. Hylozoism, Personalism, Monadism).
4. Cosmology: the view that the World and the astronomical bodies possess souls (s. World Soul). —*W.L.*

Annihilationism: The doctrine of the complete extinction of the wicked or impenitent at death. Edward White in England in the last century taught the doctrine in opposition to the belief in the eternal punishment of those not to be saved.—*V.F.*

Anoetic: (Gr. *a* + *noetikos*, from *nous*, the mind) Applied to pure sensations, affective states and other pre-cognitive or non-cognitive states of mind.—*L.W.*

Anschauung: A German term used in epistemology to mean intuition or perception with a quality of directness or immediacy. It is a basic term in Kant's philosophy, denoting that which presents materials to the intellect through the forms of space and time. These forms predetermine what types of objects (schemata) can be set up when the understanding applies its own forms to the facts of sense. Kant distinguished "empirical" intuitions (*a posteriori*) of objects through sensation, and "pure" intuitions (*a priori*) with space and time as the forms of sensibility. The characteristics and functions of *Anschauung* are discussed in the first division (*Aesthetic*) of the *Critique of Pure Reason*. Caird disputes the equivalence of the Kantian *Anschauung* with intuition; but it is difficult to find an English word more closely related to the German term.—*T.G.*

Anselmian argument: Anselm (1033-1109) reasoned thus: I have an idea of a Being than which nothing greater can be conceived; this idea is that of the most perfect, complete, infinite Being, the greatest conceivable; now an idea which exists in reality (*in re*) is greater than one which exists in conception (*in intellectu*); hence, if my idea is the greatest it must exist in reality. Accordingly, God, the Perfect Idea, Being, exists. (Anselm's argument rests upon the basis of the realistic metaphysics of Plato.)—*V.F.*

Anselm of Canterbury, St.: (1033-1109) Was born at Aosta in Italy, educated by the Benedictines, entered the Order c. 1060. Most of his writings were done at the Abbey of Le Bec in Normandy, where he served as Abbot. In 1093 he became Archbishop of Canterbury, which post he occupied with distinction till his death. Anselm is most noted for his much discussed "ontological" argument to prove the existence of God. His theory of truth and his general philosophy are thoroughly Augustinian. Chief works: *Monologium, Proslogium, De Veritate, Cur Deus Homo* (in PL 158-9).—*V.J.B.*

An Sich: (Ger. literally in or by self. Lat. *in se*) Anything taken in itself without relation to anything else, especially without relation to a knowing consciousness. In Hegel's philosophy whatever has disowned its relations is *an sich*. In this status it reveals its inner potentialities. Thus in Hegel's system *an sich* frequently refers to that which is latent, undeveloped, or in certain connections, that which is unconscious. Kant used *an sich* more loosely to describe anything independent of consciousness or experience. Thus he contrasted the *"Ding-an-sich"* (thing-in-itself) with appearance (phenomenon), the latter being a function of consciousness, the former outside all consciousness.—*O.F.K.*

Ansichtslosigkeit: (Ger. point-of-viewlessness) Objectivity, or the unmediated approach to bare fact. (Heidegger.)—*H.H.*

Antar-ātman: (Skr.) "Inner self," a term for the self found in the Upanishads (*q.v.*). A similar concept is *antar-yāmin*, meaning "inner controller."—*K.F.L.*

Antecedent: In a sentence of the form A ⊃ B ("if A then B"), the constituent sentences A and B are called *antecedent* and *consequent* respectively. Or the same terminology may be applied to propositions expressed by these sentences.—*A.C.*

Anthropocentric: Literally, centering in man. A term which may be used in connection with extreme humanism, viewing the world in terms only of human experience.—*V.F.*

Anthropolatry: (Gr.) The worshipping or cult of a human being conceived as a god, and conversely of a god conceived as a human being. The deification of individual human beings was practiced by most early civilizations, and added much colour to the folklore and religion of such countries as Egypt, Greece, India and Japan. The human origin of *anthropolatry* is illustrated by the failure of Alexander the Great to obtain divine honours from his soldiers. In contrast, the Shinto religion in Japan still considers the emperor as a "visible deity," and maintains shrines devoted to brave warriors or heroes. Monotheistic religions consider *anthropolatry* as a superstition.—*T.G.*

Anthropology, Philosophical: (in Max Scheler) The philosophical science concerned with the questions about the essence of man.—*P.A.S.*

Anthropopathism: (Gr. *anthropos*, man; *pathein*, suffer) Sometimes referred to as the pathetic fallacy, i.e., attributing human feelings illegitimately to situations or things lacking such capacities.—*V.F.*

Anticipations: (Lat. *ante*, before + *capere*, to take) The foreknowledge of future events and experiences. Anticipation, in contrast to expectation, is allegedly immediate and non-inferential cognition of the future. See *Expectation; Foreknowledge*.—*L.W.*

In Lucretius, the Scholastics, Fr. Bacon, and Leibniz, it means a hypothesis without confirmation.

Anticipations of experience: In Kant's *Crit. of Pure Reason (Antizipationen der Wahrnehmung)* the second of two synthetic principles of the understanding (the other being "Axioms of Intuition") by which the mind is able to determine something *a priori* in regard to what is in itself empirical. While the mind cannot anticipate the specific qualities which are to be experienced, we can, nevertheless, Kant holds, predetermine or anticipate any sense experience that "in all appearances the real, which is an object of sensation, has intensive magnitude or degree."—*O.F.K.*

Antilogism: If in the syllogism in Barbara the conclusion is replaced by its contradictory there is obtained the following set of three (formulas representing) propositions,

$$M(x) \supset_x P(x), |S|(x) \supset_x M(x),$$
$$S(x) \wedge_x \sim P(x),$$

from any two of which the negation of the third may be inferred. Such an inconsistent triad of propositions is called an *antilogism*.

From the principle of the antilogism, together with obversion, simple conversion of *E* and *I*, and the fact that in the pairs, *A* and *O*, *E* and *I*, each proposition of the pair is equivalent to the negation of the other, all of the traditional valid moods of the syllogism may be derived except those which require a third (existential) premiss (see *logic, formal* §§ 4, 5). With the further aid of subalternation the remaining valid moods may be derived.

This extension of the traditional reductions of the syllogistic moods is due to Christine Ladd Franklin. She, however, stated the matter within the algebra of classes (see *logic, formal*, § 7), taking the three terms of the syllogism as classes. From this point of view the three propositions of an antilogism appear as follows:

$$m \cap -p = \Lambda, s \cap -m = \Lambda, s \cap -p \neq \Lambda.$$
—*A.C.*

A contradiction in terms, concepts, or propositions forming an inconsistent triad (Mrs. Ladd-Franklin), a set of three propositions such that if any two are true the third must be false; thus any two will strictly imply the contradictory of the third. An antilogism may be obtained from any strictly valid Aristotelian syllogism by contradicting the conclusion. q.v. Antilogism. —*C.A.B.*

Anti-metaphysics: 1. *Agnosticism* (*q.v.*). 2. *Logical Positivism* (see *Scientific Empiricism* (1)) holds that those metaphysical statements which are not confirmable by experiences (see *Verification* 4, 5) have no cognitive meaning and hence are pseudo-statements (see *Meaning, Kinds of*, 1, 5).—*R.C.*

Antinomies, logical: See *paradoxes, logical*.

Antinomianism: (Gr. *anti*, against, *nomos*, law) A term introduced by Martin Luther. Johann Agricola, contemporary of Luther, held that the gospel rather than the law is determinative in man's repentance. The term is used, more generally, to designate freedom from law or compulsion or external regulation to human living.—*V.F.*

Antinomy: (Ger. *Antinomie*) The mutual contradiction of two principles or inferences resting on premises of equal validity. Kant shows, in the Antinomies of pure Reason, that contradictory conclusions about the cosmos can be established with equal credit; from this he concluded that the Idea of the world, like other transcendent ideas of metaphysics, is a purely speculative, indeterminate notion. (See *Kantianism*.)—*O.F.K.*

Antisthenes: Of Athens (c. 444-368 B.C.) founder of the Cynic School of Greek Philosophy. See *Cynics*. —*M.F.*

Antistrophon argument: (Gr. *antistrophos*, turned in an opposite way) In rhetoric, any argument by an opponent which can be turned against him.—*J.K.F.*

Antithesis: (Gr. *anti*-against, *tithenai*- to set) In a general sense, the opposition or contrast of ideas or statements.

In philosophy, a proposition opposed to a given thesis expressing a fact or a positive statement. With Kant, it is the negative member of the antinomies of reason. With Hegel, it is the second phase of the dialectical process, which denies the first moment or *thesis*, and which contributes to the emergence of the *synthesis* blending the partial truths of the thesis and the antithesis, and transcending them both.

In rhetoric, the contrast involved by an antithesis is technically expressed by the position of opposite words in one or more sentences or clauses.—*T.G.*

Antitypy: The property of concepts or objects of thought to resist attribution of qualities or postulates incompatible with their semantic value and ontological nature. —*T.G.*

Anu: (Skr.) Atom; point.—*K.F.L.*

Anumăna: (Skr.) Inference.—*K.F.L.*

Aorist: (Gr.) Referring to unspecified past time without implication of continuance or repetition; indefinite; undefined.—*C.A.B.*

Apagoge: (Gr. *apagoge*) In Aristotle's logic (1) a syllogism whose major premiss is certain but whose minor premiss is only probable; abduction; (2) a method of indirect demonstration whereby the validity of a conclusion is established by assuming its contradiction and showing that impossible or unacceptable consequences follow; the *reductio ad impossibile*.—*G.R.M.*

A parte ante: A phrase the literal meaning of which is, from the part before, referring to duration previous to a given event.—*J.J.R.*

A parte post: A phrase the literal meaning of which is, from the part after, referring to duration subsequent to a given event.—*J.J.R.*

Apathia: (Gr. *apathia,* no feeling) In Epicurean (*q.v.*) and Stoic *(q.v.)* ethics: the inner equilibrium and peace of mind, freedom from emotion, that result from contemplation, for its own sake, on the ends of life.

Apeiron: (Gr. *apeiron*) The boundless; the indeterminate; the infinite. In the philosophy of Anaximander the apeiron is the primal indeterminate matter out of which all things come to be. The apeiron appears frequently elsewhere in early Greek philosophy, notably in the dualism of the Pythagoreans, where it is opposed to the principle of the Limit (peras), or number.—*G.R.M.*

Apercu: An immediate insight, not in itself analytical.—*C.A.B.*

Apocatastasis: (Gr. *apokatastasis,* complete restitution) In theology this term refers to a final restitution or universal salvation.—*V.F.*

Apodeictic: See *Modality.*

Apodictic Knowledge: (Gr. *apodeiktikos*) Knowledge of what must occur, as opposed to knowledge of what might occur or is capable of occurring, or of what is actual or occurring; opposed to *assertoric knowledge* and *problematic knowledge.*—*A.C.B.*

Apollinarianism: The view held by Apollinaris (310-390), a Christian bishop. He defended the deity of Jesus Christ in a manner regarded by the orthodox church as too extreme. Jesus, according to him, lacked a human soul, a human will, the Logos of God taking full possession.—*V.F.*

Apollonian: The art impulse in which one sees things as in a dream, detached from real experience. The theoretical, intellectual impulses striving after measure, order, and harmony. (Nietzsche, *Birth of Tragedy.*) In Spengler, *Decline of the West,* the classical spirit as contrasted with the Modern Faustian age.—*H.H.*

Apologetics: (Gr. *apologetikos,* fit for a defence) The discipline which deals with a defence of a position or body of doctrines. Traditional Christian theology gave over to Christian Apologetics (or, simply Apologetics) the task of defending the faith. As such the discipline was also called "Evidences of the Christian Religion." Each particular faith, however, developed its own particular type of apologetics.—*V.F.*

Apology: (Gr. *apologia*) A speech or writing in defense. Plato's *Apology of Socrates* purports to be the speech delivered by Socrates in his own defense at the trial in which he was condemned to death.—*G.R.M.*

Apophansis: A Greek word for *proposition* involving etymologically a reference to its realist ontological background (Greek root of phaos, light). In this sense, a proposition expresses the illumination of its subject by its predicate or predicates; or again, it makes explicit the internal luminosity of its subject by positing against it as predicates its essential or accidental constituents.

The Aristotelian *apophansis* or *logos apophantikos* denotes the fundamental subject-predicate form, either as an independent propositional form or as a syllogistic conclusion, to which all other types of propositions may be reduced by analysis and deduction. It cannot be said that the controversies initiated by modern symbolic logic have destroyed the ontological or operational value of the Aristotelian apophantic form.—*T.G.*

Apophantic: (Ger. *apophantisch*) In Husserl: Of, or pertaining to, predicative judgments or the theory of predicative judgments.—*D.C.*

Aporetics: (Gr. *aporetikos,* one who is inclined to doubt, who is at a loss about a matter) Obsolete term for sceptics.—*H.H.*

Aporia: (Gr. *aporia*) A theoretical difficulty or puzzle.—*G.R.M.*

A posteriori: (Lat. following after) (a) In psychology and epistemology: refers to the data of the mind which owe their origin to the outside world of human experience. Such data are acquired by the mind and do not belong to the mind's native equipment (*a priori*).

(b) In logic: a *posteriori* reasoning (as opposed to *a priori* reasoning) is inductive, i.e., the type which begins with observed facts and from these infers general conclusions.—*V.F.*

Apparent: (Lat. *ad* + *parere,* to come forth) 1. Property of seeming to be real or factual. 2. Obvious or clearly given to the mind or senses.

Appearance: 1. Neutrally, a presentation to an observer.

2. Epistemology: (a) A sensuously observable state of affairs.

(b) The mental or subjective correlate of a thing-in-itself.

(c) A sensuous object existent or possible, in space and time, related by the categories (Kant). It differs from illusion by its objectivity or logical validity.

3. Metaphysics: A degree of truth or reality; a fragmentary and self-contradictory judgment about reality.—*W.L.*

Appearances: (Ger. *Erscheinungen*) In Kant, applied to things as they are for human experience as opposed to things as they are for themselves.—*A.C.E.*

Apperception: (Lat. *ad* + *percipere,* to perceive) (a) *In epistemology:* The introspective or reflective apprehension by the mind of its own inner states. Leibniz, who introduced the term, distinguished between *perception,* (the inner state as representing outer things) and *apperception* (the inner state as reflectively aware of itself). *Principles of Nature and of Grace,* § 4. In Kant, apperception denotes the unity of self-consciousness pertaining to either the empirical ego ("empirical apperception") or to the pure ego ("transcendental apperception"), *Critique of Pure Reason,* A 106-8.

(b) *In psychology:* The process by which new experience is assimilated to and transformed by the residuum of past experiences of an individual to form a new whole. The residuum of past experience is called the apperceptive mass. Cf. Herbart, *Psychologie als Wissenschaft, Part* III, Sect. I, ch. 5.—*L.W.*

In Kant: (1) *Empirical apperception* (Ger. *empirische Apperzeption*). The consciousness of the concrete actual self with its changing states; sometimes, simply, the "inner sense." (2) *Transcendental apperception* (Ger. *transzendentale Apperzeption*). The pure, original, unchangeable consciousness which is the necessary condition of experience as such and the ultimate foundation of the synthetic unity of experience. (See *Kantianism*).—*O.F.K.*

Appetite: Name given in Scholastic psychology to all strivings. Sensitive appetites tend toward individual goods. They are concupiscible insofar as they are directed toward a sensible good or strive to avoid a sensible evil; irascible if the striving encounters obstacles. Their movements are the cause of emotions. Rational or intellectual appetite = will, tending towards the good as such and necessarily therefore towards God as the *summum bonum*.—*R.A.*

Appetition: (Lat. *ad + petere,* to seek) The internal drive which in the Leibnizian psychology effects the passage from one perception to another. Leibniz, *The Monadology,* § 15.—*L.W.*

To Spinoza, appetition is conscious desire. It is the essence of man insofar as he is conceived as determined to act by any of his affections.—*J.M.*

Appetitive: (Lat. *ad + petere,* to seek) Adjective of appetite. Applied to desire based on animal wants *e.g.* hunger, sex, etc. The appetitive, along with the ideational and the affective, are the three principal phases of the conscious life.—*L.W.*

Appreciation: (Royce) The faculty by which an individual feels, likes or hates, or, in general, evaluates certain experiences, as opposed to the faculty by which he describes them, communicates them, and renders them permanent through the use of forms or categories. (Royce: *Spirit of Modern Philosophy,* pp. 390-4.) —*A.C.B.*

Apprehension: (*ad + prehendere:* to seize) 1. Act involving the bare awareness of the presence of an object to consciousness; the general relation of subject to object as inclusive of the more special forms, such as perceiving or remembering, which the relation may take.

2. Act involving the awareness of the bare presence of an object to consciousness, as opposed to any act which involves judgment about such an object.—*A.C.B.*

Apprehension span: The extent or complexity of material which an individual is able to apprehend through a single, very brief act of attention. Also called *attention span*.—*A.C.B.*

Appresentation: (Ger. *Appräsentation*) In Husserl: The function of a presentation proper as motivating the experiential positing of something else as present along with the strictly presented object.—*D.C.*

A priori: (Kant) A term applied to all judgments and principles whose validity is independent of all impressions of sense. Whatever is pure *a priori* is unmixed with anything empirical. In Kant's doctrine, all the necessary conditions of experience (*i.e.,* forms and categories) are *a priori*. Whatever is *a priori* must possess universal and necessary validity. Sometimes used loosely to designate anything non-empirical, or something which can be known by reason alone. (See *Kantianism*).—*O.F.K.*

Aquinas, Thomas: (Born at Roccasocca, near Naples, in 1225; oblate at the Benedictine monastery, Monte Cassino, 1230-1239; student at the University of Naples, 1239-1244; having decided to become a Dominican, he studied at the University of Paris under St. Albert the Great, 1245-1248; until 1252 he was in Cologne with St. Albert at the newly opened *studium generale* of the Dominican Order; in 1252 he returned to study at the faculty of theology in the University of Paris where in 1256 he was given the *licentia docendi* in theology and where he taught until 1259; from 1259 until 1268 he taught at the papal curia in Rome; returned to the University of Paris to stem the tide against Averroism, 1269-1272; from 1272 he began teaching at the University of Naples. He died March 7, 1274 on the way to the Council of Lyons.)

St. Thomas was a teacher and a writer for some twenty years (1254-1273). Among his works are: (a) *Scriptum in IV Libros Sententiarum* (1254-1256), *Summa Contra Gentiles* (c. 1260), *Summa Theologica* (1265-1272); (b) commentaries on Boethius. *(De Trinitate,* c. 1257-1258), on Dionysius the Pseudo-Areopagite (*De Divinis Nominibus,* c. 1261), on the anonymous and important *Liber de Causis* (1268), and especially on Aristotle's works (1261-1272), *Physics, Metaphysics, Nicomachean Ethics, Politics, On the Soul, Posterior Analytics, On Interpretation, On the Heavens, On Generation and Corruption;* (c) *Quaestiones Disputatae,* which includes questions on such large subjects as *De Veritate* (1256-1259); *De Potentia* (1259-1263); *De Malo* (1263-1268); *De Spiritualibus Creaturis, De Anima* (1269-1270); (d) small treatises or *Opuscula,* among which especially noteworthy are the *De Ente et Essentia* (1256); *De Aeternitate Mundi* (1270), *De Unitate Intellectus* (1270), *De Substantiis Separatis* (1272).

While it is extremely difficult to grasp in its entirety the personality behind this complex theological and philosophical acitivity, some points are quite clear and beyond dispute. During the first five years of his activity as a thinker and a teacher, St. Thomas seems to have formulated his most fundamental ideas in their definite form, to have clarified his historical conceptions of Greek and Arabian philosophers, and to have made more precise and even corrected his doctrinal positions. (cf., e.g., the change on the question of creation between *In II Sent.,* d.1, q.1, a.3, and the later *De Potentia,* q. III, a.4). This is natural enough, though we cannot pretend to explain why he should have come to think as he did. The more he grew, and that very rapidly, towards maturity, the more his thought became inextricably involved in the defense of Aristotle (beginning with c. 1260), his texts and his ideas, against the Averroists, who were then beginning to become prominent in the faculty of arts at the University of Paris; against the traditional Augustinianism of a man like St. Bonaventure; as well as against that more subtle Augustinianism which could breathe some of the spirit of Augustine, speak the language of Aristotle, but expound, with increasing faithfulness and therefore more imminent disaster, Christian ideas through the Neoplatonic techniques of Avicenna. This last group includes such different thinkers as St. Albert the Great, Henry of Ghent, the many disciples of St. Bonaventure, including, some think, Duns Scotus himself, and Meister Eckhart of Hochheim.

To be an Aristotelian under such extremely complicated circumstances was the problem that St. Thomas set himself. What he did reduced itself fundamentally to three points: (a) He showed the Platonic orientation of St. Augustine's thought, the limitations that St. Augustine himself placed on his Platonism, and he inferred from this that St. Augustine could not be made the patron of the highly elaborated and sophisticated Platonism that an Ibn Gebirol expounded in his *Fons Vitae* or an Avicenna in his commentaries on the metaphysics and psychology of Aristotle. (b) Having singled out Plato as the thinker to search out behind St. Augustine, and having really eliminated St. Augustine from the Platonic controversies of the thirteenth century, St. Thomas is then concerned to diagnose the Platonic inspiration of the various commentators of Aristotle, and to separate what is to him the authentic Aristotle from those Platonic aberrations. In this sense, the philosophical activity of St. Thomas in the thirteenth century can be understood as a systematic critique and elimination of Platonism in metaphysics, psychology and epistemology. The Platonic World of Ideas is translated into a theory of substantial principles in a world of stable and intelligible individuals; the Platonic man, who was scarcely more than an incarcerated spirit, became a rational animal, containing within his being an interior economy which presented in a rational system his mysterious nature as a reality existing on the confines of two worlds, spirit and matter; the Platonic theory of knowledge (at least in the version of the *Meno* rather than that of the later dialogues where the doctrine of division is more prominent), which was regularly beset with the difficulty of accounting for the *origin* and the *truth* of knowledge, was translated into a theory of abstraction in which sensible experience enters as a necessary moment into the explanation of the origin, the growth and the use of knowledge, and in which the intelligible structure of sensible being becomes the measure of the truth of knowledge and of knowing. (c) The result of this elaborate critique of Platonism is sometimes called the Aristotelian-Thomistic synthesis. It is better, however, to call it simply a Thomistic synthesis, not only because St. Thomas criticized Aristotle on several occasions, but also because the real and historical meaning of Aristotle as a philosopher in the fourth century B.C. is still very much in dispute. In any case it ought to be pretty much beyond dispute that St. Thomas was quite aware that Aristotle was not the author of all the doctrines which he attributed to him.

What St. Thomas appears to have insisted on most in thus using Aristotle as a pillar of his own thought was the rehabilitation of man and the universe as stable realities and genuine causes. This insistence has been by some called his *naturalism*. Against the tendency of thirteenth century Augustinians to disparage the native ability of the human reason to know truth, St. Thomas insisted on the capacity of the reason to act as a genuine and sufficient cause of true knowledge within the natural order. Against the occasionalistic tendencies of Avicennian thought, which reduced both man and the world of change around him to the role of passive spectators of the sole activity of God (i.e., the *intellectus agens*), St. Thomas asserted the subordinate but autonomous causality of man in the production of knowledge and the genuine causality of sensible realities in the production of change. Ultimately, St. Thomas rests his defense of man and other beings as efficacious causes in their own order on the doctrine of creation; just as he shows that the occasionalism of Avicenna is ultimately based on the Neoplatonic doctrine of emanation.

This rebuilding of the notion of *creature* permits St. Thomas also to analyze the problems that Averroism was making more and more prominent. Philosophical truth was discovered by the Greeks and the Arabians neither completely nor adequately nor without error. What the Christian thinker must do in their presence is not to divide his allegiance between them and Christianity, but to discover the meaning of reason and the conditions of true thinking. That discovery will enable him to learn from the Greeks without also learning their errors; and it would thus show him the possibility of the harmony between reason and revelation. He must learn to be a philosopher, to discover the philosopher within the Christian man, in order to meet philosophers. In exploring the meaning of a *creature,* St. Thomas was building a philosophy which permitted his contemporaries (at least, if they listened to him) to free themselves from the old eternalistic and rigid world of the Greeks and to free their thinking, therefore, from the antinomies which this world could raise up for them. In the harmony of faith and reason which St. Thomas defended against Averroism, we must see the culminating point of his activity. For such a harmony meant ultimately not only a judicious and synthetic diagnosis of Greek philosophy, as well as a synthetic incorporation of Greek ideas in Christian thought, it meant also the final vindication of the humanism and the naturalism of Thomistic philosophy. The expression and the defense of this Christian humanism constitute one of St. Thomas' most enduring contributions to European thought.—*A.C.P.*

A quo: (Schol.) from which—indicates the principle, starting point, from which something proceeds. To whom (ad quem) or to which (ad quod) indicates the terminus, the end point to which something tends. For whom (cui) indicates for whom something is done. Thus alms giving is done from charity, *a que;* it tends to the relief of the poor, as *ad quod;* and it is a service done for God, as *cui.*—*H.G.*

Arabesque: Originally a method of ornament consisting of fantastic lines. Recently, inner design of a form.—*L.V.*

Arabic Philosophy: The contact of the Arabs with Greek civilization and philosophy took place partly in Syria, where Christian Arabic philosophy developed, partly in other countries, Asia Minor, Persia, Egypt and

Spain. The effect of this contact was not a simple reception of Greek philosophy, but the gradual growth of an original mode of thought, determined chiefly by the religious and philosophical tendencies alive in the Arab world. Eastern influences had produced a mystical trend, not unlike Neo-Platonism; the already existing "metaphysics of light," noticeable in the religious conception of the Quran, also helped to assimilate Plotinian ideas. On the other hand, Aristotelian philosophy became important, although more, at least in the beginning, as logic and methodology. The interest in science and medicine contributed to the spread of Aristotelian philosophy. The history of philosophy in the Arab world is determined by the increasing opposition of Orthodoxy against a more liberal theology and philosophy. Arab thought became influential in the Western world partly through European scholars who went to Spain and elsewhere for study, mostly however through the Latin translations which became more and more numerous at the end of the 12th and during the 13th centuries. Among the Christian Arabs Costa ben Luca (864-923) has to be mentioned whose *De Differentia spiritus et animae* was translated by Johannes Hispanus (12th century). The first period of Islamic philosophy is occupied mainly with translation of Greek texts, some of which were translated later into Latin. The *Liber de causis* (mentioned first by Alanus ab Insulis) is such a translation of an Arab text; it was believed to be by Aristotle, but is in truth, as Aquinas recognized, a version of the *Stoicheiosis theologike* by Proclus. The so-called *Theologia Aristotelis* is an excerpt of Plotinus Enn. IV-VI, written 840 by a Syrian. The fundamental trends of Arab philosophy are indeed Neo-Platonic, and the Aristotelian texts were mostly interpreted in this spirit. Furthermore, there is also a tendency to reconcile the Greek philosophers with theological notions, at least so long as the orthodox theologians could find no reason for opposition. In spite of this, some of the philosophers did not escape persecution. The Peripatetic element is more pronounced in the writings of later times when the technique of paraphrasis and commentary on Aristotelian texts had developed. Beside the philosophy dependent more or less on Greek, and partially even Christian influences, there is a mystical theology and philosophy whose sources are the Quran, Indian and, most of all, Persian systems. The knowledge of the "Hermetic" writings too was of some importance.

Al Kindi, Al Farabi, and Ibn Sinā (Avicenna) were the first great philosophers who made large use of Aristotelian books. Their writings are of truly encyclopedic character and comprise the whole edifice of knowledge in their time. Their Aristotelianism is, however, mainly Neo-Platonism with addition of certain peripatetic notions. Avicenna is more of an Aristotelian than his predecessors. Al Farabi, e.g., held that cognition is ultimately due to an illumination, whereas Avicenna adopted a more Aristotelian theory. While these thinkers had an original philosophy, Averroës (Ibn Roshd) endeavored to clarify the meaning of the Aristotelian

texts by extensive and minute commentaries. Translations from these writings first made known to medieval philosophy the non-logical works of the "Philosopher," although there existed, at the same time, some translations made directly from Greek texts.

The mystical trend is represented mostly by Al Gazali who also wrote a report on the philosophies of Farabi and Avicenna followed by a devastating criticism, known as *Destructio philosophorum*, translated by Dominicus Gundissalinus. Gazali's criticisms were answered by Averroës in his *Destructio destructionis*.

The importance of Arab philosophy has to be evaluated both in regard to the Oriental and the Western world. The latter was influenced, naturally, not by the originals but by the translations which do not always render exactly the spirit of the authors. In the East, theology remained victorious, but incorporated in its own teachings much of the philosophies it condemned. M. Horten, in Ueberweg-Heinze, *Geschichte der Philosophie*, 3d ed., Berlin, 1928, pp. 287-342. *Geschichte der Arabischen Litteratur*, Vol. I, II, Weimar, 1898-1902, Vol. III-VI, Leiden, 1936-1941. *The Encyclopedia of Islam*, Leiden, 1913-1918.—*R.A.*

Ārambha-vāda: (Skr.) The theory of evolution expounded by the Nyāya and Vaiśesika (*q.v.*), according to which atoms having been created combine to form the complex world, a sort of emergent evolution.—*K.F.L.*

Āranyaka: (Skr.) One of early Indian treatises composed in the forest (*aranya*) by Brahmans retired from life and devoting their time to an interpretation of the meaning of Vedic (*q.v.*) ritual and usage.—*K.F.L.*

Arbitrium, liberum: Livy used the expression, *libera arbitria*, signifying free decisions. Tertullian used either *liberum arbitrium* or *libertas arbitrii*, meaning freedom of choice. Augustine spoke of the *liberum voluntatis arbitrium*, free choice of the will. He held that *voluntas* and *liberum* are the same. Since *liberum arbitrium* implies the power to do evil, it is distinct from *libertas*, which is the good use of the *liberum arbitrium*. God is free, but He can do no wrong. Anselm preferred the term, *libertas arbitrii*. Thomas Aquinas taught that *voluntas* and *liberum arbitrium* are one potency. The expression has come to mean free will or choice. —*J.J.R.*

Arbor Porphyrii: (Tree of Porphyry) A representation of the series leading from the individual by means of the numerical and specific differences (corporeal, animate, sentient, rational) to the *genus subalternum et supremum*.—*R.A.*

Arcadic: Artificial art with the pretence of expressing pastoral simplicity.—*L.V.*

Arcanum: An old term almost identical with occultism, its recent equivalent. Arcana were originally used to cover the sacred objects, such as the Playthings of Dionysus in the Eleusinian rites, and a cognate is *ark*, as in the Ark of the Covenant.

Arcesilaus: (315-241 B.C.) Greek philosopher from Pitane in Aeolis. He succeeded Crates in the chair of the Platonic Academy and became the founder of the second or so-called middle academy. In opposition to both Stoicism and Epicureanism, he advocated a scepticism that was not so extreme as that of Pyrrho although he despaired of man's attaining truth. Suspended judgment was to him the best approach.—*L.E.D.*

Archaic: A style which is primitive and incomplete in comparison with a posterior style which is considered perfect and complete.—*L.V.*

Archaism: A revival of archaic style as a result of dissatisfaction with a manner previously considered perfect.—*L.V.*

Arche: (Gr. *arche*) The first in a series; that from which a thing either is or comes to be; origin; principle; first cause (Aristotle).—*G.R.M.*

Archelaus: A disciple of Anaxagoras; belonged to the Sophistic period; proclaimed the conventionality of all ethical judgments. He distinguished between man's natural impulses and dispositions and the dictates of human moral laws. The former he held to be superior guides to conduct.—*M.F.*

Archelogy: The science of first principles.—*C.A.B.*

Archetype: (Gr. *arche*, first; and *typos*, form) The original pattern of forms of which actual things are copies. (Platonic).—*J.K.F.*

Archeus: See *Paracelsus*.—*R.B.W.*

Architectonic: (Kant) (Gr. *architektonikos*; Ger. *Architektonik*) The formal scheme, structural design, or method of elucidation of a system. The architectonic of Kant's system rests throughout on the basic distinctions of the traditional logic.—*O.F.K.*

Ardigo, Roberto: (1828-1920) Was the leader in the Italian positivistic movement in philosophy. He was born in Padua and educated as a Catholic priest, but he became interested in the views of Comte, abandoned the ministry and became a professor at the Univ. of Padua. His emphasis on psychology differentiates his thought from Comtism. Chief works: *La psicologia come scienze positive* (1870), *La morale dei positivisti* (1885).—*V.J.B.*

Arete: See *Virtue*.

Aretology: That branch of ethics concerned with the nature of virtue.—*C.A.B.*

Argument: See *Function*.

Argumentum a fortiori: An argument from analogy which shows that the proposition advanced is more admissible than one previously conceded by an opponent.—*J.J.R.*

Argumentum ad baculum: An argument deriving its strength from appeal to human timidity or fears; it may contain, implicitly or explicitly, a threat.—*R.B.W.*

Argumentum ad hominem: An irrelevant or malicious appeal to personal circumstances; it consists in diverting an argument from sound facts and reasons to the personality of one's opponent, competitor or critic.—*R.B.W.*

Argumentum ad ignorantiam: An argument purporting to demonstrate a point or to persuade people, which avails itself of facts and reasons the falsity or inadequacy of which is not readily discerned; a misleading argument used in reliance on people's ignorance.—*R.B.W.*

Argumentum ad judicium: A reasoning grounded on the common sense of mankind and the judgment of the people.—*J.J.R.*

Argumentum ad misericordiam: An argument attempting to prove a point or to win a decision by appeal to pity and related emotions.—*R.B.W.*

Argumentum ad populum: An argument attempting to sway popular feeling or to win people's support by appealing to their sentimental weaknesses; it may avail itself of patriotism, group interests and loyalties, and customary preferences, rather than of facts and reasons.—*R.B.W.*

Argumentum ad rem: An argument to the point — distinguished from such evasions as *argumentum ad hominem* (*q.v.*), etc.—*A.C.*

Argumentum ad verecundiam: An argument availing itself of human respect for great men, ancient customs, recognized institutions, and authority in general, in order to strengthen one's point or to produce an illusion of proof.—*R.B.W.*

Argumentum ex concesso: An inference founded on a proposition which an opponent has already admitted.—*J.J.R.*

Arianism: A view named after Arius (256-336), energetic presbyter of Alexandria, condemned as a heretic by the ancient Catholic Church. Arius held that Jesus and God were not of the same substance (the orthodox position). He maintained that although the Son was subordinate to the Father he was of a similar nature. The controversy on the relation of Jesus to God involved the question of the divine status of Jesus. If he were not divine how could the church justify him as an object of worship, of trust, and adoration? If he is divine, how could such a belief square with the doctrine of one God (monotheism)? Arianism tended toward the doctrine of the subordination of Jesus to God, involving the extreme Arians who held Jesus to be unlike God and the moderate Arians who held that Jesus was of similar essence with God although not of the same substance. Some eighteen councils were convened to consider this burning question, parties in power condemning and placing each other under the ban. The Council of Nicea in 325 repudiated Arian tendencies but the issue was fought with uncertain outcome until the Council of Constantinople in 381 reaffirmed the orthodox view.—*V.F.*

Aristippus of Cyrene: (c. 435-366 B.C.) Originally a Sophist, then Socrates' disciple, and finally the founder of the Cyrenaic School. He taught that pleasure, understood as the sensation of gentle character, is the true end of life. All pleasures are equal in value, but differ in degree and duration; they should be controlled and moderated by reason.—*R.B.W.*

Aristippus the younger: A grandson of Aristippus of Cyrene, the founder of the Cyrenaic School; author of a physiological psychology which sought to trace the origin of human feelings. See *Cyrenaics*.—*M.F.*

Aristobulus: A philosopher of the second century B.C. who combined Greek philosophy with Jewish theology. —*M.F.*

Aristocracy: 1. In its original and etymological meaning (Greek: *aristos*-best, *kratos*-power), the government by the best; and by extension, the class of the chief persons in a country. As the standards by which the best can be determined and selected may vary, it is difficult to give a general definition of this term (Cf. C. Lewis, *Political Terms*, X. 73). But in particular, the implications of *aristocracy* may be rational, historical, political, pragmatic or analogical.

2. In its rational aspect, as developed especially by Plato and Aristotle, *aristocracy* is the rule of the best few, in a true, purposeful, law-abiding and constitutional sense. As a political ideal, it is a form of government by morally and intellectually superior men for the common good or in the general interests of the governed, but without participation of the latter. Owing to the difficulty of distinguishing the best men for directing the life of the community, and of setting in motion the process of training and selecting such models of human perfection, *aristocracy* becomes practically the rule of those who are thought to be the best. [Plato himself proposed his ideal State as "a model fixed in the heavens" for human imitation but not attainment; and in the *Laws* he offered a combination of monarchy and democracy as the best working form of government.] Though *aristocracy* is a type of government external to the governed, it is opposed to oligarchy (despotic) and to timocracy (militaristic). With monarchy and democracy, it exhausts the classification of the main forms of rational government.

3. In its historical aspect, *aristocracy* is a definite class or order known as hereditary nobility, which possesses prescriptive rank and privileges. This group developed from primitive monarchy, by the gradual limitation of the regal authority by those who formed the council of the king. The defense of their prerogatives led them naturally to consider themselves as a separate class fitted by birthright to monopolize government. But at the same time, they assumed a number of corresponding obligations (hence the aphorism *noblesse oblige*) particularly for maintaining justice, peace and security. [The characteristics of hereditary *aristocracy* are: (1) descent and birthright, (2) breeding and education, (3) power to command, (4) administrative and military capacities, (5) readiness to fulfill personal and national obligations, (6) interest in field sports, (7) social equality of its members, (8) aloofness and exclusiveness, (9) moral security in the possession of real values regardless of criticism, competition or advancement.] In certain societies as in Great Britain, birthright is not an exclusive factor: exceptional men are admitted by recognition into the aristocratic circle *(circulation of the élite)*, after a tincture of breeding satisfying its external standards. The decline of hereditary nobility was due to economic rather than to social or political changes. Now *aristocracy* can claim only a social influence.

4. In its political aspect, *aristocracy* is a form of government in which the sovereign power resides actually in a council composed of select persons (usually patricians), without a monarch, and exclusive of the common people (e.g. the Italian republics). It rules by decisions of the group arrived at by discussion; and tends to be absolute and oppressive.

5. In its pragmatic aspect, *aristocracy* is synonymous with the élite or the ruling class, and denotes those who hold active power in a totalitarian State. Their selection is by reference to some narrow and pragmatic principles of effective service to the State, of hierarchized leadership, or of training in accordance with the doctrines of the State.

6. In its analogical aspect, the term *aristocracy* is applied to the leading persons in a profession (intellectual or manual), who assume an attitude of exclusiveness or superiority on the strength of simply professional, religious or social motives.—*T.G.*

Aristotelianism: The philosophy of Aristotle (384-322 B.C.). Aristotle was born in the Greek colony of Stagira, in Macedon, the son of Nicomachus, the physician of King Amyntas of Macedon. In his eighteenth year Aristotle became a pupil of Plato at Athens and remained for nearly twenty years a member of the Academy. After the death of Plato he resided for some time at Atarneus, in the Troad, and at Mitylene, on the island of Lesbos, with friends of the Academy; then for several years he acted as tutor to the young Alexander of Macedon. In 335 he returned to Athens, where he spent the following twelve years as head of a school which he set up in the Lyceum. The school also came to be known as the Peripatetic, and its members Peripatetics, probably because of the peripatos, or covered walk, in which Aristotle lectured. As a result of the outburst of anti-Macedonian feeling at Athens in 323 after the death of Alexander, Aristotle retired to Chalcis, in Euboea, where he died a year later.

The extant works of Aristotle cover almost all the sciences known in his time. They are characterized by subtlety of analysis, sober and dispassionate judgment, and a wide mastery of empirical facts; collectively they constitute one of the most amazing achievements ever credited to a single mind. They may conveniently be arranged in seven groups: (1) *the Organon*, or logical treatises, viz. *Categories, De Interpretatione, Prior Analytics, Posterior Analytics, Topics* and *Sophistici Elenchi;* (2) the writings on physical science, viz. *Physics, De Coelo, De Generatione et Corruptione,* and *Meteorologica;* (3) the biological works, viz. *Historia Animalium, De Partibus Animalium, De Motu* and *De Incessu Animalium,* and *De Generatione Animalium;* (4) the treatises on psychology, viz. *De Anima* and a collection of shorter works known as the *Parva Naturalia;* (5) the *Metaphysics;* (6) the treatises on ethics and politics, viz. *Nicomachean Ethics, Eudemian Ethics, Politics, Constitution of Athens;* and (7) two works dealing with the literary arts, *Rhetoric* and *Poetics.* A large number of other works in these several fields are usually included in the Aristotelian corpus, though they are now generally believed not to have been written by Aristotle. It is probable also that portions of the works above listed are the work, not of Aristotle, but of his contemporaries or successors in the Lyceum.

Besides these treatises there are extant a large number of fragments of works now lost, some of them popular in character, others memoranda or collections of materials made in preparation for the systematic treatises. The most noteworthy member of the second class is the work dealing with the constitutions of one hundred fifty-eight Greek states, of which one part alone, the *Constitution of Athens,* has been preserved.

The standard edition of the Greek text is that of Bekker (5 vols. Berlin, 1831-1870). A complete English translation of the works included in the Berlin edition has recently been published (Oxford, 1908-1931) under the editorship of W. D. Ross.

Aristotle divides the sciences into the theoretical, the practical and the productive, the aim of the first being disinterested knowledge, of the second the guidance of conduct, and of the third the guidance of the arts. The science now called logic, by him known as "analytic," is a discipline preliminary to all the others, since its purpose is to set forth the conditions that must be observed by all thinking which has truth as its aim. Science, in the strict sense of the word, is demonstrated knowledge of the causes of things. Such demonstrated knowledge is obtained by syllogistic deduction from premises in themselves certain. Thus the procedure of science differs from dialectic, which employs probable premises, and from eristic, which aims not at truth but at victory in disputation. The center, therefore, of Aristotle's logic is the syllogism, or that form of reasoning whereby, given two propositions, a third follows necessarily from them. The basis of syllogistic inference is the presence of a term common to both premises (the middle term) so related as subject or predicate to each of the other two terms that a conclusion may be drawn regarding the relation of these two terms to one another. Aristotle was the first to formulate the theory of the syllogism, and his minute analysis of its various forms was definitive, so far as the subject-predicate relation is concerned; so that to this part of deductive logic but little has been added since his day. Alongside of deductive reasoning Aristotle recognizes the necessity of induction, or the process whereby premises, particularly first premises, are established. This involves passing from the particulars of sense experience (the things more knowable to us) to the universal and necessary principles involved in sense experience (the things more knowable in themselves). Aristotle attaches most importance, in this search for premises, to the consideration of prevailing beliefs (*endoxa*) and the examination of the difficulties (*aporiai*) that have been encountered in the solution of the problem in hand. At some stage in the survey of the field and the theories previously advanced the universal connection sought for is apprehended; and apprehended, Aristotle eventually says, by the intuitive reason, or *nous.* Thus knowledge ultimately rests upon an indubitable intellectual apprehension; yet for the proper employment of the intuitive reason a wide empirical acquaintance with the subject-matter is indispensable.

The causes which it is the aim of scientific inquiry to discover are of four sorts: the material cause (that of which a thing is made), the efficient cause (that by which it comes into being), the formal cause (its essence or nature, i.e. what it is), and the final cause (its end, or that for which it exists). In natural objects, as distinct from the products of art, the last three causes coincide; for the end of a natural object is the realization of its essence, and likewise it is this identical essence embodied in another individual that is the efficient cause in its production. Thus for Aristotle every object in the sense world is a union of two ultimate principles: the material constituents, or matter (*hyle*), and the form, structure, or essence which makes of these constituents the determinate kind of being it is. Nor is this union an external or arbitrary one; for the matter is in every case to be regarded as possessing the capacity for the form, as being potentially the formed matter. Likewise the form has being only in the succession of its material embodiments. Thus Aristotle opposes what he considers to be the Platonic doctrine that real being belongs only to the forms or universals, whose existence is independent of the objects that imperfectly manifest them. On the other hand, against the earlier nature-philosophies that found their explanatory principles in matter, to the neglect of form, Aristotle affirms that matter must be conceived as a locus of determinate potentialities that become actualized only through the activity of forms.

With these principles of matter and form, and the parallel distinction between potential and actual existence, Aristotle claims to have solved the difficulties that earlier thinkers had found in the fact of change. The changes in nature are to be interpreted not as the passage from non-being to being, which would make them unintelligible, but as the process by which what is merely potential being passes over, through form, into actual being, or entelechy. The philosophy of nature which results from these basic concepts views nature as a dynamic realm in which change is real, spontaneous, continuous, and in the main directed. Matter, though indeed capable of form, possesses a residual inertia which on occasion produces accidental effects; so that alongside the teleological causation of the forms Aristotle recognizes what he calls "necessity" in nature; but the products of the latter, since they are aberrations from form, cannot be made the object of scientific knowledge. Furthermore, the system of nature as developed by Aristotle is a graded series of existences, in which the simpler beings, though in themselves formed matter, function also as matter for higher forms. At the base of the series is prime matter, which as wholly unformed is mere potentiality, not actual being. The simplest formed matter is the so-called primary bodies—earth, water, air and fire. From these as matter arise by the intervention of successively more complex forms the composite inorganic bodies, organic tissues, and the world of organisms, characterized by varying degrees of complexity in structure and function. In this realization of form in matter Aristotle distinguishes three sorts of change: qualitative change, or alteration, quantitative change, or growth and diminution; and change of place, or locomotion, the last being primary, since it is presupposed in all the others. But Aristotle is far from suggesting a mechanical explanation of change, for not even locomotion can be explained by impact alone. The motion of the primary bodies is due to the fact that each has its natural place to which it moves when not opposed; earth to the center, then water, air, and fire to successive spheres about the center. The ceaseless motion of these primary bodies results from their ceaseless transformation into one another through the interaction of the forms of hot and cold, wet and dry. Thus qualitative differences of form underlie even the most elemental changes in the world of nature.

It is in his biology that the distinctive concepts of Aristotle show to best advantage. The conception of process as the actualization of determinate potentiality is well adapted to the comprehension of biological phenomena, where the immanent teleology of structure and function is almost a part of the observed facts. It is here also that the persistence of the form, or species, through a succession of individuals is most strikingly evident. His psychology is scarcely separable from his biology, since for Aristotle (as for Greek thought generally) the soul is the principle of life; it is "the primary actualization of a natural organic body." But souls differ from one another in the variety and complexity of the functions they exercise, and this difference in turn corresponds to differences in the organic structures involved. Fundamental to all other physical activities are the functions of nutrition, growth and reproduction, which are possessed by all living beings, plants as well as animals. Next come sensation, desire, and locomotion, exhibited in animals in varying degrees. Above all are deliberative choice and theoretical inquiry, the exercise of which makes the rational soul, peculiar to man among the animals. Aristotle devotes special attention to the various activities of the rational soul. Sense perception is the faculty of receiving the sensible form of outward objects without their matter. Besides the five senses Aristotle posits a "common sense," which enables the rational soul to unite the data of the separate senses into a single object, and which also accounts for the soul's awareness of these very activities of perception and of its other states. Reason is the faculty of apprehending the universals and first principles involved in all knowledge, and while helpless without sense perception it is not limited to the concrete and sensuous, but can grasp the universal and the ideal. The reason thus described as apprehending the intelligible world is in one difficult passage characterized as passive reason, requiring for its actualization a higher informing reason as the source of all intelligibility in things and of realized intelligence in man.

The necessity of assuming such a supreme form appears also from the side of physics. Since every movement or change implies a mover, and since the chain of causes cannot be infinite if the world is to be intelligible, there must be an unmoved first mover.

Furthermore, since motion is eternal (for time is eternal, and time is but the measure of motion), the first mover must be eternal. This eternal unmoved first mover, whose existence is demanded by physical theory, is described in the *Metaphysics* as the philosophical equivalent of the god or gods of popular religion. Being one, he is the source of the unity of the world process. In himself he is pure actuality, the only form without matter, the only being without extension. His activity consists in pure thought, that is, thought which has thought for its object; and he influences the world not by mechanical impulse, but by virtue of the perfection of his being, which makes him not only the supreme object of all knowledge, but also the ultimate object of all desire.

In the *Ethics* these basic principles are applied to the solution of the question of human good. The good for man is an actualization, or active exercise, of those faculties distinctive of man, that is the faculties of the rational, as distinct from the vegetative and sensitive souls. But human excellence thus defined shows itself in two forms, in the habitual subordination of sensitive and appetitive tendencies to rational rule and principle, and in the exercise of reason in the search for and contemplation of truth. The former type of excellence is expressed in the moral virtues, the latter in the dianoetic or intellectual virtues. A memorable feature of Aristotle's treatment of the moral virtues is his theory that each of them may be regarded as a mean between excess and defect; courage, for example, is a mean between cowardice and rashness, liberality a mean between stinginess and prodigality. In the *Politics* Aristotle sets forth the importance of the political community as the source and sustainer of the typically human life. But for Aristotle the highest good for man is found not in the political life, nor in any other form of practical activity, but in theoretical inquiry and contemplation of truth. This alone brings complete and continuous happiness, because it is the activity of the highest part of man's complex nature, and of that part which is least dependent upon externals, viz. the intuitive reason, or *nous*. In the contemplation of the first principles of knowledge and being man participates in that activity of pure thought which constitutes the eternal perfection of the divine nature.

The philosophy of Aristotle was continued after his death by other members of the Peripatetic school, the most important of whom were Theophrastus, Eudemus of Rhodes, and Strato of Lampsacus. In the Alexandrian Age, particularly after the editing of Aristotle's works by Andronicus of Rhodes (about 50 B.C.), Aristotelianism was the subject of numerous expositions and commentaries, such as those of Alexander of Aphrodisias, Themistius, John Philoponus, and Simplicius. With the closing of the philosophical schools in the sixth century the knowledge of Aristotle, except for fragments of the logical doctrine, almost disappeared in the west. It was preserved, however, by Arabian and Syrian scholars, from whom, with the revival of learning in the twelfth and thirteenth centuries, it passed again to western Europe and became in Thomas Aquinas the philosophical basis of Christian theology. For the next few centuries the prestige of Aristotle was immense; he was "the philosopher," "the master of those who know." With the rise of modern science his authority has greatly declined. Yet Aristotelianism is still a force in modern thought: in Neo-Scholasticism; in recent psychology, whose behavioristic tendencies are in part a revival of Aristotelian modes of thought; in the various forms of vitalism in contemporary biology; in the dynamism of such thinkers as Bergson; and in the more catholic naturalism which has succeeded the mechanistic materialism of the last century, and which, whether by appeal to a doctrine of levels or by emphasis on immanent teleology, seems to be striving along Aristotelian lines for a conception of nature broad enough to include the religious, moral and artistic consciousness. Finally, a very large part of our technical vocabulary, both in science and in philosophy, is but the translation into modern tongues of the terms used by Aristotle, and carries with it, for better or worse, the distinctions worked out in his subtle mind.—*G.R.M.*

Aristotle, medieval: Contrary to the esteem in which the Fathers held Platonic and especially Neo-Platonic philosophy, Aristotle plays hardly any rôle in early Patristic and Scholastic writings. Augustine seems not to have known much about him and admired him more as logician whereas he held Plato to be the much greater philosopher. The Middle Ages knew, until the end of the 12th and the beginning of the 13th century, only the logical texts, mostly in the translations made by Boethius of the texts and of the introduction by Porphyrius (*Isagoge*). During the latter third of the 12th, mostly however at the beginning of the 13th century appeared translations partly from Arabian texts and commentaries, partly from the Greek originals. Finally, Aquinas had William of Moerbeke translate the whole work of Aristotle, who soon came to be known as the Philosopher. Scholastic Aristotelianism is, however, not a simple revival of the Peripatetic views; Thomas is said to have "Christianized" the Philosopher as Augustine had done with Plato. Aristotle was differently interpreted by Aquinas and by the Latin Averroists (*q.v.* *Averroism*), especially in regard to the "unity of intellect" and the eternity of the created world.—*R.A.*

Aristotle's Dictum (or the *Dictum de Omni et Nullo*): The maxim that whatever may be predicated (i.e. affirmed or denied) of a whole may be predicated of any part of that whole; traditionally attributed to Aristotle, though perhaps on insufficient grounds. See Joseph, *Introduction to Logic*, p. 296, note. See also *Dictum de Omni et Nullo*.—*G.R.M.*

Aristotle's Experiment: An experiment frequently referred to by Aristotle in which an object held between two crossed fingers of the same hand is felt as two objects. *De Somniis* 460b 20; *Metaphysics* 1011a 33; *Problems* 958b 14, 959a, 15, 965a 36.—*G.R.M.*

Aristotle's Illusion: See *Aristotle's Experiment*.

Arithmetic, foundations of: Arithmetic (i.e., the mathematical theory of the non-negative integers, 0, 1,

2, . . .) may be based on the five following postulates, which are due to Peano (and Dedekind, from whom Peano's ideas were partly derived):

$N(0)$.

$N(x) \supset_x N(S(x))$.

$N(x) \supset_x [N(y) \supset_y [[S(x) = S(y)] \supset [x = y]]]$.

$N(x) \supset_x \sim [S(x) = 0]$.

$F(0) [N(x)F(x) \supset_x F(S(x))] \supset_F [N(x) \supset_x F(x)]$

The undefined terms are here 0, N, S, which may be interpreted as denoting, respectively, the non-negative integer 0, the propositional function to be a non-negative integer, and the function $+1$ (so that $S(x)$ is $x + 1$). The underlying logic may be taken to be the functional calculus of second order (*Logic, formal*, § 6), with the addition of notations for descriptions and for functions from individuals to individuals, and the individual constant 0, together with appropriate modifications and additions to the primitive formulas and primitive rules of inference (the axiom of infinity is not needed because the Peano postulates take its place). By adding the five postulates of Peano as primitive formulas to this underlying logic, a logistic system is obtained which is adequate to extant elementary number theory (arithmetic) and to all methods of proof which have found actual employment in elementary number theory (and are normally considered to belong to elementary number theory). But of course, the system, if consistent, is incomplete in the sense of Gödel's theorem (*Logic, formal*, § 6).

If the Peano postulates are formulated on the basis of an interpretation according to which the domain of individuals coincides with that of the non-negative integers, the undefined term N may be dropped and the postulates reduced to the three following:

$(x)(y) [[S(x) = S(y)] \supset [x = y]]$.

$(x) \sim [S(x) = 0]$.

$F(0) [F(x) \supset_x F(S(x))] \supset_F (x)F(x)$.

It is possible further to drop the undefined term 0 and to replace the successor function S by a dyadic propositional function S (the contemplated interpretation being that $S(x, y)$ is the proposition $y = x + 1$). The Peano postulates may then be given the following form:

$(x)(Ey) S(x,y)$.

$(x) [S(x,y) \supset_y [S(x,z) \supset_z [y = z]]]$.

$(x) [S(y,x) \supset_y [S(z,x) \supset_z [y = z]]]$.

$(Ez) [[(x) \sim S(x,y)] \equiv_y [y = z]]$.

$[(x) \sim S(x,z)] \supset_z [F(z)[F(x) \supset_x [S(x,y) \supset_y F(y)]] \supset_F (x)F(x)]$.

For this form of the Peano postulates the underlying logic may be taken to be simply the functional calculus of second order without additions. In this formulation, numerical functions can be introduced only by contextual definition as incomplete symbols.

In the Frege-Russell derivation of arithmetic from logic (see the article *Mathematics*) necessity for the postulates of Peano is avoided. If based on the theory of types, however, this derivation requires some form of the axiom of infinity—which may be regarded as a residuum of the Peano postulates.

See further the articles *Recursion, definition by,* and *Recursion, proof by.—A.C.*

B. Russell, *Introduction to Mathematical Philosophy,* London, 1919.

Arithmetic mean: The simple average. Thus the arithmetic mean of *n* quantities is the sum of these quantities divided by *n*. Contrast with geometric mean.—*C.A.B.*

Ars Combinatoria: (Leibniz) An art or technique of deriving or inventing complex concepts by a combination of a relatively few simple ones taken as primitive. This technique was proposed as a valuable subject for study by Leibniz in *De Arte Combinatoria* (1666) but was never greatly developed by him. Leibniz's program for logic consisted of two main projects: (1) the development of a universal characteristic *(characteristica universalis)*, and (2) the development of a universal mathematics *(mathesis universalis q.v.)*. The universal characteristic was to be a universal language for scientists and philosophers. With a relatively few basic symbols for the ultimately simple ideas, and a suitable technique for constructing compound ideas out of the simple ones, Leibniz thought that a language could be constructed which would be much more efficient for reasoning and for communication than the vague, complicated, and more or less parochial languages then available. This language would be completely universal in the sense that all scientific and philosophical concepts could be expressed in it, and also in that it would enable scholars in all countries to communicate over the barriers of their vernacular tongues. Leibniz's proposals in this matter, and what work he did on it, are the grand predecessors of a vast amount of research which has been done in the last hundred years on the techniques of language construction, and specifically on the invention of formal rules and procedures for introducing new terms into a language on the basis of terms already present, the general project of constructing a unified language for science and philosophy. L. Couturat, *La Logique de Leibniz,* Paris, 1901; C.I. Lewis, *A Survey of Symbolic Logic,* Berkeley, 1918.—*F.L.W.*

Ars magna Raymundi: A device by which Raymundus Lullus, Ramon Lul, thought to arrive at all possible conclusions from certain given principles or notions. A very imperfect precursor of Leibniz's mathesis universalis. See *Lullic art.—R.A.*

Art: (Gr. *techne*) (See *Aesthetics*) In Aristotle the science or knowledge of the principles involved in the production of beautiful or useful objects. As a branch of knowledge art is distinguished both from theoretical science and from practical wisdom; as a process of production it is contrasted with nature.—*G.R.M.*

In its narrower meaning, the fine arts and literature. The problem of the distinction and classification of the arts originated with Lessing in reaction to the interference of poetical values in painting and vice versa. He distinguished poetry dealing with consecutive actions from painting concerned with figures coexisting in space. Later, aestheticians divided the arts into many classifications. Zimmermann, a pupil of Herbart, distinguished three groups:

(1) arts of material representation (architecture, sculpture, etc.)

(2) arts of perceptive representation (painting, music).

(3) arts of the representation of thought (poetry).

This partition suggested to Fiedler the aesthetics of *pure visibility,* to Hanslick the aesthetics of *pure musicality.* And from Fiedler's idea was derived the so-called *Science of Art* independent of aesthetics.—*L.V.*

Art impulse: A term to account for the origin of all matter falling under the consideration of aesthetics by describing it as due to non-intellectualistic, psychical urges, thoroughly dynamic in nature, such as desire to imitate, proneness to please, exhibitionism, play, utilization of surplus vital energy, emotional expression, or compensation.—*K.F.L.*

Āsana: (Skr.) "Sitting;" posture, an accessory to the proper discipline of mind and thinking deemed important by the Yoga and other systems of Indian philosophy, according to psycho-physical presuppositions.—*K.F.L.*

Asat: (Skr.) "Non-being," a school concept dating back to Vedic *(q.v.)* times. It offers a theory of origination according to which being *(sat; q.v.)* was produced from non-being in the beginning; it was rejected by those who believe in being as the logical starting point in metaphysics.—*K.F.L.*

Asceticism: (Gr. *askesis,* exercise) The view—now and then appearing in conjunction with religion, particularly the Christian and Buddhistic one, or the striving for personal perfection or salvation for self and others—that the body is an evil and a detriment to a moral, spiritual, and god-pleasing life. Hence the negative adjustments to natural functions, desires, and even needs, manifesting themselves in abnegation of pleasures, denial of enjoyments, non-gratification of the senses, stifling of physical cravings, as well as self-torture which is meant to allay or kill off physical and worldly longings by destroying their root, in preparation for a happier, perhaps desireless future, in a *post mortem* existence.—*K.F.L.*

Aseitas: (Lat.) Being by and of itself, asserted only of God. All other beings are dependent in their existence on God as creator, they are *ab alio.—R.A.*

Asmitā: (Skr. "I am-ness") A kind of egoism repudiated by the Yogasutras *(q.v.)* in which lower states of mind are presumed to be the self or *purusa.* —*K.F.L.*

Asomatic: (Gr. *a + soma,* body, Disembodied) The condition of a mind after separation from its body.—*L.W.*

Assent: The act of the intellect adhering to a truth because of the evidence of the terms; a proof of the reason *(medium rationale),* or the command of the will.—*H.G*

Assertion: Frege introduced the assertion sign, in 1879, as a means of indicating the difference between asserting a proposition as true and merely naming a proposition (e.g., in order to make an assertion about it, that it has such and such consequences, or the like). Thus, with an appropriate expression A, the notation ⊢ A would be used to make the *assertion,* "The unlike magnetic poles attract one another," while the notation —A would correspond rather to the *noun clause,* "that the unlike magnetic poles attract one another." Later Frege adopted the usage that propositional expressions (as noun clauses) are proper names of truth values and modified his use of the assertion sign accordingly, employing say A (or — A) to denote the *truth value thereof that the unlike magnetic poles attract one another* and ⊢ A to express the assertion that this truth value is truth.

The assertion sign was adopted by Russell, and by Whitehead and Russell in *Principia Mathematica,* in approximately Frege's sense of 1879, and it is from this source that it has come into general use. Some recent writers omit the assertion sign, either as understood, or on the ground that the Frege-Russell distinction between asserted and unasserted propositions is illusory. Others use the assertion sign in a syntactical sense, to express that a formula is a theorem of a *logistic system* (*q.v.*); this usage differs from that of Frege and Russell in that the latter requires the assertion sign to be followed by a formula denoting a proposition, or a truth value, while the former requires it to be followed by the syntactical name of such a formula.

In the propositional calculus, the name *law of assertion* is given to the theorem:

$$p \supset [[p \supset q] \supset q].$$

(The associated form of inference from A and A ⊃ B to B is, however, known rather as *modus ponens*.)—*A.C.*

The act of declaring a proposition or propositional form to be true (or to be necessarily true, or to be a part of a system).

Assertoric: See *Modality.*

Assertoric knowledge: Knowledge of what is actual or occurring, as opposed to knowledge of what might occur or is capable of occurring, or of what must occur; opposed to *problematic knowledge* and *apodictic knowledge.*—*A.C.B.*

Association: (Lat. *ad* + *socius,* companion) The psychological phenomenon of connection or union between different items in consciousness. The term has been applied to two distinct types of connection: (a) the *natural* or original connection between sensations which together constitute a single perception and (b) the *acquired* connection whereby one sensation or idea tends to reinstate another idea. The first type of connection has sometimes been called *simultaneous* association and the second type *successive* association, but this terminology is misleading since successively apprehended sensations are often conjoined into the unity of a perception, *e.g.* the bell which I saw a moment ago and the sound which I now hear, while, on the other hand, an idea may in certain cases be contemporaneous with the sensation or idea by which it is revived. The dual application of the term association to both natural and acquired association was made by J. Locke: "Some of our ideas," says Locke "have a

natural correspondence or connection with one another . . . Besides this there is another connection of ideas wholly owing to chance or custom." *Essay Concerning Human Understanding* (1690) Bk. II, ch. 33. The usage of later authors, however, tends to restrict the term association to acquired connection ((b) above) and to adopt some other expression such as cohesion, correlation (see *Correlation, Sensory*) or combination (see *Combination*) to designate natural connections ((a) above).

A further distinction is drawn between two subvarieties of acquired associations viz. *spontaneous* or *free* association, in which the revival of associated ideas proceeds by chance and *voluntary* or *controlled* association in which it is guided by a dominant purpose. The distinction between chance and voluntary association was also recognized by Locke: "The strong combination of ideas not allied by nature makes itself either voluntarily or by chance." (*Ibid.*)

The phenomenon of acquired association has long been recognized by philosophers. Plato cites examples of association by contiguity and similarity (*Phaedo,* 73-6) and Aristotle in his treatment of memory enumerated similarity, contrast and contiguity as relations which mediate recollection. (*De Mem.* II 6-11 (451 b)). Hobbes also was aware of the psychological importance of the phenomenon of association and anticipated Locke's distinction between chance and controlled association (*Leviathan* (1651), ch. 3; *Human Nature* (1650), ch. 4). But it was Locke who introduced the phrase "association of ideas" and gave impetus to modern association psychology.

Following Locke, the phenomenon of association was investigated by G. Berkeley and D. Hume, both of whom were especially concerned with the relations mediating association. Berkeley enumerates similarity, causality and co-ëxistence or contiguity (*Theory of Vision Vindicated* (1733), § 39); Hume resemblance, contiguity in time or place and cause or effect (*Enquiry Concerning Human Understanding* (1748), § 3; *Treatise on Human Nature* (1739), Bk. I, Pt. I, § 4). English associationism is further developed by D. Hartley, *Observations on Man* (1749), esp. Prop. XII, J. Mill, *Analysis of the Phenomena of the Human Mind* (1829), esp. Ch. 3; A. Bain, *The Senses and the Intellect* (1855); J. S. Mill, *Examination of Sir William Hamilton's Philosophy* (1865). Continental exponents of association psychology are E. B. de Condillac (*Essai sur l'origines de connaissances humaines*) (1746); *Traité de sensations* (1754), J.F. Herbart *Lehrbuch der Psychologie* (1816).—*L.W.*

Association, Laws of: The psychological laws in accordance with which association takes place. The classical enumeration of the laws of association is contained in Aristotle's *De Memoria et Reminiscentia,* II, 451, b 18-20 which list similarity, contrast and contiguity as the methods of reviving memories. Hume (*A Treatise on Human Nature,* Part I, § 4 and *An Enquiry Concerning Human Understanding,* § 3) slightly revised the Aristotelian list by enumerating as the sole principles of association, resemblance, contiguity in time or place and causality; contrast was considered by Hume, "a mixture of causation and resemblance."—*L.W.*

Associationism: A theory of the structure and organization of mind which asserts that: (*a*) every mental state is resolvable into simple, discrete components (See *Mind-Stuff Theory, Psychological Atomism*) and (*b*) the whole of the mental life is explicable by the combination and recombination of these elemental states in conformity with the laws of association of ideas. (See *Association, Laws of*). Hume (*Treatise on Human Nature*, 1739) and Hartley (*Observations on Man*, 1749) may be considered the founders of associationism of which James Mill, J. S. Mill and A. Bain are later exponents.—*L.W.*

Associationist Psychology: See *Associationism.*—*L.W.*

Associative law: Any law of the form,

$$x \circ (y \circ z) = (x \circ y) \circ z,$$

where o is a dyadic operation (function) and $x \circ y$ is the result of applying the operation to x and y (the value of the function for the arguments x and y). Instead of the sign of equality, there may also appear the sign of the biconditional (in the propositional calculus), or of other relations having properties similar to equality in the discipline in question.

In arithmetic there are two associative laws, of addition and of multiplication:

$$x + (y + z) = (x + y) + z.$$
$$x \times (y \times z) = (x \times y) \times z.$$

Associative laws of addition and of multiplication hold also in the theory of real numbers, the theory of complex numbers, and various other mathematical disciplines.

In the propositional calculus there are the four following associative laws (two dually related pairs):

$$[p \vee [q \vee r]] \equiv [[p \vee q] \vee r].$$
$$[p \, [qr]] \equiv [[pq]r].$$
$$[p + [q + r]] \equiv [[p + q] + r].$$
$$[p \equiv [q \equiv r]] \equiv [[p \equiv q] \equiv r].$$

Also four corresponding laws in the algebra of classes.

As regards exclusive disjunction in the propositional calculus, the caution should be noted that, although $p + q$ is the exclusive disjunction of p and q, and although $+$ obeys an associative law, nevertheless $[p + q] + r$ is not the exclusive disjunction of the three propositions p, q, r — but is rather, "Either all three or one and one only of p, q, r."—*A.C.*

Assumption: A proposition which is taken or posed in order to draw inferences from it; or the act of so taking, posing, or *assuming* a proposition. The motive for an assumption may be (but need not necessarily be) a belief in the truth, or possible truth, of the proposition assumed; or the motive may be an attempt to refute the proposition by reductio ad absurdum (*q.v.*). The word *assumption* has also sometimes been used as a synonym of *axiom* or postulate (see the article *Mathematics.*).—*A.C.*

Āstika: (Skr.) "Orthodox;" one acknowledging the authority of the Veda (*q.v.*).—*K.F.L.*

Astikāya: (Skr.) Bodily or extended substance. In Jaina philosophy only time is not (*anasti*, the negation of *asti*)

like a body (*kāya*), hence non-extended.—*K.F.L.*

Ataraxia: The Epicurean doctrine that the complete peace of mind was a pleasurable state of equilibrium. See *Epicureanism.*—*E.H.*

Atheism: (Gr. *a*, no; *theos*, god) Two uses of the term: (a) The belief that there is no God (b) Some philosophers have been called "atheistic" because they have not held to a belief in a personal God. Atheism in this sense means "not theistic."

The former meaning of the term is a literal rendering. The latter meaning is a less rigorous use of the term although widely current in the history of thought.—*V.F.*

Ātman: (Skr.) Self, soul, ego, or I. Variously conceived in Indian philosophy, atomistically (cf. *anu*), monadically, etherially, as the hypothetical carrier of *karma* (*q.v.*), identical with the divine (cf. *ayam ātmā brahma; tat tvam asi*) or different from yet dependent on it, or as a metaphysical entity to be dissolved at death and reunited with the world ground. As the latter it is defined as "smaller than the small" (*anor aniyān*) or "greater than the great" (*mahato mahiyān*), i.e., magnitudeless as well as infinitely great.—*K.F.L.*

Atomism: (a) As contrasted with synechism, the view that there are discrete irreducible elements of finite spatial or temporal span. E.g., the atomic doctrine of Democritus that the real world consists of qualitatively similar atoms of diverse shapes. Lucretius, *De Natura Rerum*. See *Epicurus*. Cf. K. Lasswitz, *Gesch. d. Atomismus*.

(b) As contrasted with the view that certain elements are necessarily connected, or even related at all, the doctrine that some entities are only contingently related or are completely independent. In Russell (*Scientific Method in Philosophy*), Logical Atomism is the view that relations are external and that some true propositions are without simpler constituents in a given system, such propositions are "basic" with respect to that system. In political philosophy, atomism is syn. of particularism.

(c) As contrasted with the view that certain entities are analyzable, the doctrine that some entities are ultimately simple. E.g., Russell's doctrine that there are certain simple, unanalyzable atomic propositions of which other propositions are constituted by compounding or generalization.—*C.A.B.*

A consistent atomistic theory of nature or even of bodily substances is hardly found in medieval texts with the exception of William of Conches' *Philosophia mundi* and the Mutakallemins, a Moslem school of atomists.—*R.A.*

Atomism, psychological: See *Psychological Atomism.*

Atonement: Religious act of expressing consciousness of one's sins, penitence, reconciliation, giving satisfaction. Specifically, a theological doctrine meaning the reconciliation between God and man who had sinned against God, hence given offense to Him. This was effected through the Incarnation of Christ, the Son of God, His sufferings and death on the cross, who consequently is the Saviour and Redeemer of the human race.

This voluntary death and vicarious sacrifice constituted a full reparation for the sins of humanity and satisfied the debt to divine justice, thus making it again possible for men to attain eternal happiness in heaven.—*J.J.R.*

Attention: (Lat. *ad* + *tendere*, to stretch) The concentration of the mind upon selected portions of the field of consciousness thereby conferring upon the selected items, a peculiar vividness and clarity. The field of attention may be divided into two parts:

(a) the focus of attention, where the degree of concentration of attention is maximal and

(b) the fringe of attention, where the degree of attention gradually diminishes to zero at the periphery.

Attention considered with respect to its genesis, is of two types:

(a) involuntary, passive or spontaneous attention, which is governed by external stimulus or internal association of ideas and

(b) voluntary, controlled or directed attention which is guided by the subject's purpose or intention.—*L.W.*

Attention, Span of: The number of simultaneous or successive items or groups of items which can be attended to by a single act of thought; the number varies from individual to individual and for the same individual at different times.—*L.W.*

Attitude: (Ger. *Einstellung*) In Husserl: A habitual positing or neutral intending by the ego. *The natural attitude:* the fundamental protodoxic attitude of the transcendental ego towards the world. The natural attitude underlies and enters into all other positings except those of the transcendental ego in the *transcendental-phenomenological attitude.*—*D.C.*

Attribute: 1. Commonly, what is proper to a thing (Latin, *ad-tribuere*, to assign, to ascribe, to bestow). Loosely assimilated to a quality, a property, a characteristic, a peculiarity, a circumstance, a state, a category, a mode or an accident, though there are differences among all these terms. For example, a quality is an inherent property (the qualities of matter), while an *attribute* refers to the actual properties of a thing only indirectly known (the attributes of God). Another difference between attribute and quality is that the former refers to the characteristics of an infinite being, while the latter is used for the characteristics of a finite being.

2. *In metaphysics*, an *attribute* is what is indispensable to a spiritual or material substance; or that which expresses the nature of a thing; or that without which a thing is unthinkable. As such, it implies necessarily a relation to some substance of which it is an aspect or conception. But it cannot be a substance, as it does not exist by itself. The *transcendental* attributes are those which belong to a being because it is a being: there are three of them, the one, the true and the good, each adding something positive to the idea of being. The word *attribute* has been and still is used more readily, with various implications, by substantialist systems. In the 17th century, for example, it denoted the actual manifestations of substance. [Thus, Descartes regarded extension and thought as the two ultimate, simple and original attributes of reality, all else being modifications

of them. With Spinoza, extension and thought became the only known attributes of Deity, each expressing in a definite manner, though not exclusively, the infinite essence of God as the only substance. The change in the meaning of substance after Hume and Kant is best illustrated by this quotation from Whitehead: "We diverge from Descartes by holding that what he has described as primary attributes of physical bodies, are really the forms of internal relationships between actual occasions and within actual occasions" (*Process and Reality*, p. 471).] The use of the notion of attribute, however, is still favoured by contemporary thinkers. Thus, John Boodin speaks of the five attributes of reality, namely: Energy (source of activity), Space (extension), Time (change), Consciousness (active awareness), and Form (organization, structure).

3. *In theodicy*, the term *attribute* is used for the essential characteristics of God. The *divine attributes* are the various aspects under which God is viewed, each being treated as a separate perfection. As God is free from composition, we know him only in a mediate and synthetic way through his attributes.

4. *In logic*, an *attribute* is that which is predicated of anything, that which is affirmed or denied of the subject of a proposition. More specifically, an *attribute* may be either a category or a predicable; but it cannot be an individual materially. Attributes may be essential or accidental, necessary or contingent.

5. *In grammar*, an *attribute* is an adjective, or an adjectival clause, or an equivalent adjunct expressing a characteristic referred to a subject through a verb. Because of this reference, an *attribute* may also be a substantive, as a class-name, but not a proper name as a rule. An *attribute* is never a verb, thus differing from predicate which may consist of a verb often having some object or qualifying words.

6. *In natural history*, what is permanent and essential in a species, an individual or in its parts.

7. *In psychology*, it denotes the way (such as intensity, duration or quality) in which sensations, feelings or images can differ from one another.

8. *In art*, an *attribute* is a material or a conventional symbol, distinction or decoration.—*T.G.*

Attributes, differentiating: Are special, simple, not essential to a substance, which if they belong to any complex substance as a whole belong also to its parts. (Broad).—*H.H.*

Auctoritas: St. Augustine distinguishes divine from human authority: *Auctoritas autem partim divina est, partim humana: sed vera, firma, summa ea est quae divina nominatur*. Thus God is the highest authority. It is distinctly advantageous to rely on authority: *Auctoritati credere magnum compendium est, nullus labor*. Both authority and reason impel us to learn: *Nulli autem dubium est gemino pondere nos impelli ad discendum, auctoritatis atque rationis.*—*J.J.R.*

Aufklärung: 1. In general, this German word and its English equivalent *Enlightenment* denote the self-emancipation of man from mere authority, prejudice, convention and tradition, with an insistence on freer thinking about problems uncritically referred to these other agencies. According to Kant's famous definition "Enlightenment is the liberation of man from his self-caused state of minority, which is the incapacity of using one's understanding without the direction of another. This state of minority is caused when its source lies not in the lack of understanding, but in the lack of determination and courage to use it without the assistance of another" (*Was ist Aufklärung?* 1784).

2. In its historical perspective, the *Aufklärung* refers to the cultural atmosphere and contributions of the 18th century, especially in Germany, France and England [which affected also American thought with B. Franklin, T. Paine and the leaders of the Revolution]. It crystallized tendencies emphasized by the Renaissance, and quickened by modern skepticism and empiricism, and by the great scientific discoveries of the 17th century. This movement, which was represented by men of varying tendencies, gave an impetus to general learning, a more popular philosophy, empirical science, scriptural criticism, social and political thought.

3. More especially, the word *Aufklärung* is applied to the German contributions to 18th century culture. In philosophy, its principal representatives are G. .E. Lessing (1729-81) who believed in free speech and in a methodical criticism of religion, without being a free-thinker; H. S. Reimarus (1694-1768) who expounded a naturalistic philosophy and denied the supernatural origin of Christianity; Moses Mendelssohn (1729-86) who endeavoured to mitigate prejudices and developed a popular commonsense philosophy; Chr. Wolff (1679-1754), J. A. Eberhard (1739-1809) who followed the Leibnizian rationalism and criticized unsuccessfully Kant and Fichte; and J. G. Herder (1744-1803) who was best as an interpreter of others, but whose intuitional suggestions have borne fruit in the organic correlation of the sciences, and in questions of language in relation to human nature and to national character. The works of Kant and Goethe mark the culmination of the German Enlightenment. Cf. J. G. Hibben, *Philosophy of the Enlightenment,* 1910.—*T.G.*

Augustinianism: The thought of St. Augustine of Hippo, and of his followers. Born in 354 at Tagaste in N. Africa, A. studied rhetoric in Carthage, taught that subject there and in Rome and Milan. Attracted successively to Manicheanism, Skepticism, and Neo-Platonism, A. eventually found intellectual and moral peace with his conversion to Christianity in his thirty-fourth year. Returning to Africa, he established numerous monasteries, became a priest in 391, Bishop of Hippo in 395. Augustine wrote much; *On Free Choice, Confessions, Literal Commentary on Genesis, On the Trinity,* and *City of God,* are his most noted works. He died in 430.

St. Augustine's characteristic method, an inward empiricism which has little in common with later variants, starts from things without, proceeds within to the self, and moves upwards to God. These three poles of the Augustinian dialectic are polarized by his doctrine of moderate illuminism. An ontological illumination is required to explain the metaphysical structure of things. The truth of judgment demands a noetic illumination. A moral illumination is necessary in the order of willing; and so, too, an illumination of art in the aesthetic order. Other illuminations which transcend the natural order do not come within the scope of philosophy; they provide the wisdoms of theology and mysticism. Every being is illuminated ontologically by number, form, unity and its derivatives, and order. A thing is what it is, in so far as it is more or less flooded by the light of these ontological constituents.

Sensation is necessary in order to know material substances. There is certainly an action of the external object on the body and a corresponding passion of the body, but, as the soul is superior to the body and can suffer nothing from its inferior, sensation must be an action, not a passion, of the soul. Sensation takes place only when the observing soul, dynamically on guard throughout the body, is vitally attentive to the changes suffered by the body. However, an adequate basis for the knowledge of intellectual truth is not found in sensation alone. In order to know, for example, that a body is multiple, the idea of unity must be present already, otherwise its multiplicity could not be recognized. If numbers are not drawn in by the bodily senses which perceive only the contingent and passing, is the mind the source of the unchanging and necessary truth of numbers? The mind of man is also contingent and mutable, and cannot give what it does not possess. As ideas are not innate, nor remembered from a previous existence of the soul, they can be accounted for only by an immutable source higher than the soul. In so far as man is endowed with an intellect, he is a being naturally illuminated by God, Who may be compared to an intelligible sun. The human intellect does not create the laws of thought; it finds them and submits to them. The immediate intuition of these normative rules does not carry any content, thus any trace of ontologism is avoided.

Things have forms because they have numbers, and they have being in so far as they possess form. The sufficient explanation of all formable, and hence changeable, things is an immutable and eternal form which is unrestricted in time and space. The forms or ideas of all things actually existing in the world are in the things themselves (as *rationes seminales*) and in the Divine Mind (as *rationes aeternae*). Nothing could exist without unity, for to be is no other than to be one. There is a unity proper to each level of being, a unity of the material individual and species, of the soul, and of that union of souls in the love of the same good, which union constitutes the city. Order, also, is ontologically imbibed by all beings. To tend to being is to tend to order; order secures being, disorder leads to non-being. Order is the distribution which allots things equal and unequal each to its own place and integrates an ensemble of parts in accordance with an end. Hence, peace is defined as the tranquillity of order. Just as things have their being from their forms, the order of parts, and their numerical relations, so too their beauty is not something superadded, but the shining out of all their intelligible co-ingredients.

S. Aurelii Augustini, *Opera Omnia,* Migne, PL 32-47; (a critical edition of some works will be found in the *Corpus Scriptorum Ecclesiasticorum Latinorum,* Vienna). Gilson, E., *Introd. a l'étude de s. Augustin,* (Paris, 1931) contains very good bibliography up to 1927, pp. 309-331. Pope, H., *St. Augustine of Hippo,* (London, 1937). Chapman, E., *St. Augustine's Philos. of Beauty,* (N.Y., 1939). Figgis, J. N., *The Political Aspects of St. Augustine's "City of God,"* (London, 1921).—*E.C.*

Austin, John L.: (1911-1960) British philosopher and advocate of linguistic philosophy at Oxford who was concerned with the connotations, denotations and nuances of language. He distinguished between *locutionary* acts, with a definite reference, from *illocutionary* acts, such as stating, hinting, or exclaiming, and from *perlocutionary* acts, which are performed by means of the previous category. His writings on language and philosophy include *Sense and Sensibilia* (1962) and *How to Do Things With Words* (1962).—*L.L.*

Authenticity: In a general sense, genuineness, truth according to its title. It involves sometimes a direct and personal characteristic (Whitehead speaks of "authentic feelings").

This word also refers to problems of fundamental criticism involving title, tradition, authorship and evidence. These problems are vital in theology, and basic in scholarship with regard to the interpretation of texts and doctrines.—*T.G.*

Authoritarianism: That theory of knowledge which maintains that the truth of any proposition is determined by the fact of its having been asserted by a certain esteemed individual or group of individuals. Cf. H. Newman, *Grammar of Assent*; C.S. Peirce, "Fixation of Belief," in *Chance, Love and Logic,* ed. M. R. Cohen.—*A.C.B.*

Autistic thinking: Absorption in fanciful or wishful thinking without proper control by objective or factual material; day dreaming; undisciplined imagination.—*A.C.B.*

Automaton Theory: Theory that a living organism may be considered a mere machine. See *Automatism.*

Automatism: (Gr. *automatos,* self-moving) (a) *In metaphysics:* Theory that animal and human organisms are automata, that is to say, are machines governed by the laws of physics and mechanics. Automatism, as propounded by Descartes, considered the lower animals to be pure automata (Letter to Henry More, 1649) and man a machine controlled by a rational soul *(Treatise on Man)*. Pure automatism for man as well as animals is advocated by La Mettrie (*Man, a Machine,* 1748). During the Nineteenth century, automatism, combined with epiphenomenalism, was advanced by Hodgson, Huxley and Clifford. (Cf. W. James, *The Principles of Psychology,* Vol. I, ch. V.) Behaviorism, of the extreme sort, is the most recent version of automatism (See *Behaviorism*).

(b) *In psychology:* Psychological automatism is the performance of apparently purposeful actions, like automatic writing without the superintendence of the conscious mind. L. C. Rosenfield, *From Beast Machine to Man Machine,* N. Y., 1941.—*L.W.*

Automatism, Conscious: The automatism and Hodgson, Huxley, and Clifford which considers man a machine to which mind or consciousness is superadded; the mind of man is, however, causally ineffectual. See *Automatism; Epiphenomenalism.*—*L.W.*

Autonomy: (Gr. *autonomia,* independence) Freedom consisting in self-determination and independence of all external constraint. See *Freedom.* Kant defines autonomy of the will as subjection of the will to its own law, the categorical imperative, in contrast to heteronomy, its subjection to a law or end outside the rational will. (*Fundamental Principles of the Metaphysics of Morals,* § 2)—*L.W.*

Autonomy of ethics: A doctrine, usually propounded by intuitionists, that ethics is not a part of, and cannot be derived from, either metaphysics or any of the natural or social sciences. See *Intuitionism, Metaphysical ethics, Naturalistic ethics.*—*W.K.F.*

Autonomy of the will: (in Kant's ethics) The freedom of the rational will to legislate to itself, which constitutes the basis for the autonomy of the moral law.—*P.A.S.*

Autonymy: In the terminology introduced by Carnap, a word (phrase, symbol, expression) is *autonymous* if it is used as a name of itself — for the geometric shape, sound, etc. which it exemplifies, or for the word as a historical and grammatical unit. Autonymy is thus the same as the Scholastic *suppositio materialis (q.v.)* although the viewpoint is different.—*A.C.*

Autotelic: (from Gr. *autos,* self, and *telos,* end) Said of any absorbing activity engaged in for its own sake (cf. German *Selbstzweck*), such as higher mathematics, chess, etc. In aesthetics, applied to creative art and play which lack any conscious reference to the accomplishment of something useful. In the view of some, it may constitute something beneficial in itself of which the person following his art impulse *(q.v.)* or playing is unaware, thus approaching a *heterotelic (q.v.)* conception.—*K.F.L.*

Avenarius, Richard: (1843-1896) German philosopher who expressed his thought in an elaborate and novel terminology in the hope of constructing a symbolic language for philosophy, like that of mathematics—the consequence of his Spinoza studies. As the most influential apostle of pure experience, the positivistic motive reaches in him an extreme position. Insisting on the biologic and economic function of thought, he thought the true method of science is to cure speculative excesses by a return to pure experience devoid of all assumptions. Philosophy is the scientific effort to exclude from knowledge all ideas not included in the given. Its task is to expel all extraneous elements in the given. His uncritical use of the category of the given and the nominalistic view that logical relations are created rather than discovered by thought, leads him to banish not only animism but also all of the categories, substance, causality, *etc.*, as inventions of the mind. Explaining the evolution and devolution of the *problematization* and *deproblematization* of numerous ideas, and aiming to give the natural history of problems, Avenarius sought to show physiologically, psychologically and historically under what conditions they emerge, are challenged and are solved. He hypothesized a *System C,* a bodily and central nervous system upon which consciousness depends. R-values are the stimuli received from the world of objects. E-values are the statements of experience. The brain changes that continually oscillate about an ideal point of balance are termed *Vitalerhaltungs-maximum.* The E-values are differentiated into *elements,* to which the sense-perceptions or the content of experience belong, and *characters,* to which belongs everything which psychology describes as feelings and attitudes. Avenarius describes in symbolic form a series of states from balance to balance, termed *vital series,* all describing a series of changes in System C. Inequalities in the vital balance give rise to *vital differences.* According to his theory there are two vital series. It assumes a series of brain changes because parallel series of conscious states can be observed. The *independent* vital series are physical, and the *dependent* vital series are psychological. The two together are practically covariants. In the case of a process as a dependent vital series three stages can be noted: first, the appearance of the problem, expressed as strain, restlessness, desire, fear, doubt, pain, repentance, delusion; the second, the continued effort and struggle to solve the problem; and finally, the appearance of the solution, characterized by abating anxiety, a feeling of triumph and enjoyment.

Corresponding to these three stages of the dependent series are three stages of the independent series: the appearance of the vital difference and a departure from balance in the System C, the continuance with an approximate vital difference, and lastly, the reduction of the vital difference to zero, the return to stability. By making room for dependent and independent experiences, he showed that physics regards experience as independent of the experiencing individual, and psychology views experience as dependent upon the individual. He greatly influenced Mach and James (*q.v.*). See *Avenarius, Empirio-criticism, Experience, pure.* Main works: *Kritik der reinen Erfahrung*; *Der menschliche Weltbegriff.—H.H.*

Averroës: (Mohammed ibn Rushd) Known to the Scholastic as The Commentator, and mentioned as the author of *il gran commento* by Dante (*Inf.* IV. 68) he was born 1126 at Cordova (Spain), studied theology, law, medicine, mathematics, and philosophy, became after having been judge in Sevilla and Cordova, physician to the khalifah Jaqub Jusuf, and charged with writing a commentary on the works of Aristotle. Almansur, Jusuf's successor, deprived him of his place because of accusations of unorthodoxy. He died 1198 in Morocco. Averroës is not so much an original philosopher as the author of a minute commentary on the whole works of Aristotle. His procedure was imitated

later by Aquinas. In his interpretation of Aristotelian metaphysics Averroës teaches the coeternity of a universe created *ex nihilo.* This doctrine formed together with the notion of a numerical unity of the active intellect became one of the controversial points in the discussions between the followers of Albert-Thomas and the Latin Averroists. Averroës assumed that man possesses only a disposition for receiving the intellect coming from without; he identifies this disposition with the possible intellect which thus is not truly intellectual by nature. The notion of one intellect common to all men does away with the doctrine of personal immortality. Another doctrine which probably was emphasized more by the Latin Averroists (and by the adversaries among Averroës' contemporaries) is the famous statement about "two-fold truth," viz. that a proposition may be theologically true and philosophically false and vice versa. Averroës taught that religion expresses the (higher) philosophical truth by means of religious imagery; the "two-truth notion" came apparently into the Latin text through a misinterpretation on the part of the translators. The works of Averroës were one of the main sources of medieval Aristotelianism, before and even after the original texts had been translated. The interpretation the Latin Averroists found in their texts of the "Commentator" spread in spite of opposition and condemnation. See *Averroism, Latin.* Averroës, *Opera, Venetiis,* 1553. M. Horten, *Die Metaphysik des Averroës,* 1912. P. Mandonnet, *Siger de Brabant et l'Averroisme Latin,* 2d ed., Louvain, 1911.—*R.A.*

Averroism, Latin: The commentaries on Aristotle written by Averroës (Ibn Rushd) in the 12th century became known to the Western scholars in translations by Michael Scottus, Hermannus Alemannus, and others at the beginning of the 13th century. Many works of Aristotle were also known first by such translations from Arabian texts, though there existed translations from the Greek originals at the same time (Grabmann). The Averroistic interpretation of Aristotle was held to be the true one by many; but already Albert the Great pointed out several notions which he felt to be incompatible with the principles of Christian philosophy, although he relied for the rest on the "Commentator" and apparently hardly used any other text. Aquinas, basing his studies mostly on a translation from the Greek texts, procured for him by William of Moerbecke, criticized the Averroistic interpretation in many points. But the teachings of the Commentator became the foundation for a whole school of philosophers, represented first by the Faculty of Arts at Paris. The most prominent of these scholars was Siger of Brabant. The philosophy of these men was condemned on March 7th, 1277 by Stephen Tempier, Bishop of Paris, after a first condemnation of Aristotelianism in 1210 had gradually come to be neglected. The 219 theses condemned in 1277, however, contain also some of Aquinas which later were generally recognized as orthodox. The Averroistic propositions which aroused the criticism of the ecclesiastic authorities and which had been opposed with great energy by Albert and Thomas refer mostly to the following points: The coeternity of the created word; the numerical identity of the intellect in all men, the so-called two-fold-truth theory stating that a proposition may be philosophically true although theologically false. Regarding the first point Thomas argued that there is no philosophical proof, either for the coeternity or against it; creation is an article of faith. The unity of intellect was rejected as incompatible with the true notion of person and with personal immortality. It is doubtful whether Averroës himself held the two-truths theory; it was, however, taught by the Latin Averroists who, notwithstanding the opposition of the Church and the Thomistic philosophers, gained a great influence and soon dominated many universities, especially in Italy. Thomas and his followers were convinced that they interpreted Aristotle correctly and that the Averroists were wrong; one has, however, to admit that certain passages in Aristotle allow for the Averroistic interpretation, especially in regard to the theory of intellect.

Lit.: P. Mandonnet, *Siger de Brabant et l'Averroisme Latin au XIIIe Siecle*, 2d. ed. Louvain, 1911; M. Grabmann, *Forschungen über die lateinischen Aristotelesübersetzungen* des XIII. Jahrhunderts, Münster 1916 (Beitr. z. Gesch. Phil. d. MA. Vol. 17, H. 5-6).—*R.A.*

Avesta: See *Zendavesta*.

Avicebron: (or Avencebrol, Salomon ibn Gabirol) The first Jewish philosopher in Spain, born in Malaga 1020, died about 1070, poet, philosopher, and moralist. His main work, *Fons vitae*, became influential and was much quoted by the Scholastics. It has been preserved only in the Latin translation by Gundissalinus. His doctrine of a spiritual substance individualizing also the pure spirits or separate forms was opposed by Aquinas already in his first treatise *De ente*, but found favor with the medieval Augustinians also later in the 13th century. He also teaches the necessity of a mediator between God and the created world; such a mediator he finds in the Divine Will proceeding from God and creating, conserving, and moving the world. His cosmogony shows a definitely Neo-Platonic shade and assumes a series of emanations. Cl. Baeumker, *Avencebrolis Fons vitae*. Beitr. z. Gesch. d. Philos, d. MA. 1892-1895, Vol. I Joh. Wittman, *Die Stellung des hl. Thomas von Aquino zu Avencebrol*, ibid. 1900. Vol. III.—*R.A.*

Avicenna: (Abu Ali al Hosain ibn Abdallah ibn Sina) Born 980 in the country of Bukhara, began to write in young years, left more than 100 works, taught in Ispahan, was physician to several Persian princes, and died at Hamadan in 1037. His fame as physician survived his influence as philosopher in the Occident. His medical works were printed still in the 17th century. His philosophy is contained in 18 vols. of a comprehensive encyclopedia, following the tradition of Al Kindi and Al Farabi. Logic, Physics, Mathematics and Metaphysics form the parts of this work. His philosophy is Aristotelian with noticeable Neo-Platonic influences. His doctrine of the universal existing *ante res* in God, *in rebus* as the universal nature of the particulars, and *post*

res in the human mind by way of abstraction became a fundamental thesis of medieval Aristotelianism. He sharply distinguished between the logical and the ontological universal, denying to the latter the true nature of form in the composite. The principle of individuation is matter, eternally existent. Latin translations attributed to Avicenna the notion that existence is an accident to essence (see e.g. Guilelmus Parisiensis, *De Universo*). The process adopted by Avicenna was one of paraphrasis of the Aristotelian texts with many original thoughts interspersed. His works were translated into Latin by Dominicus Gundissalinus (Gondisalvi) with the assistance of Avendeath ibn Daud. This translation started, when it became more generally known, the "revival of Aristotle" at the end of the 12th and the beginning of the 13th century. Albert the Great and Aquinas professed, notwithstanding their critical attitude, a great admiration for Avicenna whom the Arabs used to call the "third Aristotle." But in the Orient, Avicenna's influence declined soon, overcome by the opposition of the orthodox theologians. Avicenna, *Opera*, Venetiis, 1495; 1508; 1546. M. Horten, *Das Buch der Genesung der Seele, eine philosophische Enzyklopaedie Avicenna's; XIII. Teil: Die Metaphysik*. Halle a. S. 1907-1909. R. de Vaux, *Notes et textes sur l'Avicennisme Latin*, Bibl. Thomiste XX, Paris, 1934.—*R.A.*

Avidyā: (Skr.) Nescience; ignorance; the state of mind unaware of true reality; an equivalent of *māyā* (*q.v.*); also a condition of pure awareness prior to the universal process of evolution through gradual differentiation into the elements and factors of knowledge.—*K.F.L.*

Avyakta: (Skr.) "Unmanifest," descriptive of or standing for *brahman* (*q.v.*) in one of its or "his" aspects, symbolizing the superabundance of the creative principle, or designating the condition of the universe not yet become phenomenal (*ajā*, unborn).—*K.F.L.*

Awareness: Consciousness considered in its aspect of act, an *act* of attentive awareness such as the sensing of a color patch or the feeling of pain is distinguished from the *content* attended to, the sensed color patch, the felt pain. The psychological theory of intentional act was advanced by F. Brentano (*Psychologie vom empirischen Standpunkte*) and received its epistemological development by Meinong, Husserl, Moore, Laird and Broad. See *Intentionalism*.—*L.W.*

Ayer, Sir Alfred Jules, F.B.A.: (1910–) British philosopher and public figure. Born in London, educated at Eton and Oxford.

Since his return from a stay in Vienna in 1933, where he studied the reigning philosophy of Logical Positivism (*q.v.*) under members of the Vienna Circle (*q.v.*), Ayer has played an important role in shaping the temper, methodology and subject-matter of philosophy in Britain and in the United States. His first book, *Language, Truth and Logic* (1936), written when Ayer was 26, introduced Logical Positivism to the English-speaking world. In it he argued for a redefinition of the scope of philosophical inquiry, turning the argument on a positivist conception of truth and meaning. According to this view, propositions or statements that are non-analytical must be verifiable, in some sense of this term, for them to be considered meaningful (see *Verifiability Principle*). Much of what has traditionally been considered to fall within the domain of philosophy, Ayer argued, is not capable of this sort of verification. Thus metaphysics, he claims, is, while not false, meaningless, as metaphysical statements are incapable of verification and are thus nonsensical. Theology too, as a special case of metaphysics, falls under this rubric, as do the value statements of ethics and aesthetics, which Ayer considers to be expressions only of emotion with imperative overtones. As for the analytical statements of mathematics and logic, Ayer claims that these are empty of factual content and are true by virtue of the conventions governing the use of the words and symbols of which they are composed. Thus having led the retreat from the traditional boundaries of philosophy, Ayer argued that the genuine task of philosophy was the solving by clarification — the problems left untouched by the advance of science.

Language, Truth and Logic (1936), 2nd ed. (1946), which contains an introduction that attempts to give a precise formulation of the principle of verification presented in the 1936 edition; *The Foundations of Empirical Knowledge* (1940); *Thinking and Meaning* (1947); *Philosophical Essays* (1954); *The Problem of Knowledge* (1956); *The Concept of A Person* (1963).

Axiological: (Ger. *axiologisch*) In Husserl: Of or pertaining to value or theory of value (the latter term understood as including disvalue and value-indifference).—*D.C.*

Axiological ethics: Any ethics which makes the theory of obligation entirely dependent on the theory of value, by making the determination of the rightness of an action wholly dependent on a consideration of the value or goodness of something, e.g. the action itself, its motive, or its consequences, actual or probable. Opposed to *deontological ethics*. See also *teleological ethics*.—*W.K.F.*

Axiologic Realism: In metaphysics, theory that value as well as logic, qualities as well as relations, have their being and exist external to the mind and independently of it. Applicable to the philosophy of many though not all realists in the history of philosophy, from Plato to G.E. Moore, A.N. Whitehead, and N. Hartmann.—*J.K.F.*

Axiology: (Gr. *axios*, of like value, worthy, and *logos*, account, reason, theory). Modern term for theory of value (the desired, preferred, good), investigation of its nature, criteria, and metaphysical status. Had its rise in Plato's theory of Forms or Ideas (Idea of the Good); was developed in Aristotle's *Organon, Ethics, Poetics*, and *Metaphysics* (Book Lambda). Stoics and Epicureans investigated the *summum bonum*. Christian philosophy (St. Thomas) built on Aristotle's identification of highest value with final cause in God as "a living being, eternal, most good."

In modern thought, apart from scholasticism and the system of Spinoza (*Ethica*, 1677), in which values are metaphysically grounded, the various values were investigated in separate sciences, until Kant's *Critiques*, in which the relations of knowledge to moral, aesthetic, and religious values were examined. In Hegel's idealism, morality, art, religion, and philosophy were made the capstone of his dialectic. R.H. Lotze "sought in that which should be ground of that which is" (*Metaphysik*, 1879). Nineteenth century evolutionary theory, anthropology, sociology, psychology, and economics subjected value experience to empirical analysis, and stress was again laid on the diversity and relativity of value phenomena rather than on their unity and metaphysical nature. F. Nietzsche's *Also Sprach Zarathustra* (1883-1885) and *Zur Genealogie der Moral* (1887) aroused new interest in the nature of value. F. Brentano, *Vom Ursprung sittlicher Erkenntnis* (1889), identified value with love.

In the twentieth century the term axiology was apparently first applied by Paul Lapie (*Logique de la volonté*, 1902 and E. von Hartmann (*Grundriss der Axiologie*, 1908). Stimulated by Ehrenfels (*System der Werttheorie*, 1897), Meinong (*Psychologisch-ethische Untersuchungen zur Werttheorie*, 1894-1899), and Simmel (*Philosophie des Geldes*, 1900). W.M. Urban wrote the first systematic treatment of axiology in English (*Valuation*, 1909), phenomenological in method under J.M. Baldwin's influence. Meanwhile H. Münsterberg wrote a neo-Fichtean system of values (*The Eternal Values*, 1909).

Among important recent contributions are: B. Bosanquet, *The Principle of Individuality and Value* (1912), a free reinterpretation of Hegelianism; W.R. Sorley, *Moral Values and the Idea of God* (1918, 1921), defending a metaphysical theism; S. Alexander, *Space, Time, and Deity* (1920), realistic and naturalistic; N. Hartmann, *Ethik* (1926), detailed analysis of types and laws of value; R.B. Perry's *magnum opus, General Theory of Value* (1926), "its meaning and basic principles construed in terms of interest"; and J. Laird, *The Idea of Value* (1929), noteworthy for historical exposition. A naturalistic theory has been developed by J. Dewey (*Theory of Valuation*, 1939), for which "not only is science itself *a* value. . . but it is the supreme means of the valid determination of all valuations." A. J. Ayer, *Language, Truth and Logic* (1936) expounds the view of logical positivism that value is "nonsense." J. Hessen, *Wertphilosophie* (1937), provides an account of recent German axiology from a neo-scholastic standpoint.

The problems of axiology fall into four main groups, namely, those concerning (1) *the nature of value*, (2) *the types of value*, (3) *the criterion of value*, and (4) *the metaphysical status of value*.

(1) *The nature of value experience.* Is valuation fulfillment of desire (voluntarism: Spinoza, Ehrenfels), pleasure (hedonism: Epicurus, Bentham, Meinong), interest (Perry), preference (Martineau), pure rational will (formalism: Stoics, Kant, Royce), apprehension of tertiary qualities (Santayana), synoptic experience of the unity of personality (personalism: T.H. Green,

Bowne), any experience that contributes to enhanced life (evolutionism: Nietzsche), or "the relation of things as means to the end or consequence actually reached" (pragmatism, instrumentalism: Dewey). (2) *The types of value*. Most axiologists distinguish between intrinsic (consummatory) values (ends), prized for their own sake, and instrumental (contributory) values (means), which are causes (whether as economic goods or as natural events) of intrinsic values. Most intrinsic values are also instrumental to further value experience; some instrumental values are neutral or even disvaluable intrinsically. Commonly recognized as intrinsic values are the (morally) good, the true, the beautiful, and the holy. Values of play, of work, of association, and of bodily well-being are also acknowledged. Some (with Montague) question whether the true is properly to be regarded as a value, since some truth is disvaluable, some neutral; but love of truth regardless of consequences, seems to establish the value of truth. There is disagreement about whether the holy (religious value) is a unique type (Schleiermacher, Otto), or an attitude toward other values (Kant, Höffding), or a combination of the two (Hocking). There is also disagreement about whether the variety of values is irreducible (pluralism) or whether all values are rationally related in a hierarchy or system (Plato, Hegel, Sorley), in which values interpenetrate or coalesce into a total experience. (3) *The criterion of value*. The standard for testing values is influenced by both psychological and logical theory. Hedonists find the standard in the quantity of pleasure derived by the individual (Aristippus) or society (Bentham), Intuitionists appeal to an ultimate insight into preference (Martineau, Brentano). Some idealists recognize an objective system of rational norms or ideals as criterion (Plato, Windelband), while others lay more stress on rational wholeness and coherence (Hegel, Bosanquet, Paton) or inclusiveness (T.H. Green). Naturalists find biological survival or adjustment (Dewey) to be the standard. Despite differences, there is much in common in the results of the application of these criteria. (4) *The metaphysical status of value*. What is the relation of values to the facts investigated by natural science (Koehler), of *Sein to Sollen* (Lotze, Rickert), of human experience of value to reality independent of man (Hegel, Pringle-Pattison, Spaulding)? There are three main answers: (i) subjectivism (value is entirely dependent on and relative to human experience of it: so most hedonists, naturalists, positivists); (ii) logical objectivism (values are logical essences or subsistences, independent of their being known, yet with no existential status or action in reality); (iii) metaphysical objectivism (values—or norms or ideals—are integral, objective, and active constituents of the metaphysically real: so theists, absolutists, and certain realists and naturalists like S. Alexander and Wieman).—*E.S.B.*

Axiom: See *Mathematics*.

Axiomatic method: That method of constructing a deductive system consisting of deducing by specified rules all statements of the system save a given few from those given few, which are regarded as axioms or postulates of the system.

See *Mathematics*.—*C.A.B.*

Ayam ātmā brahma: (Skr.) "This self is *brahman*," famous quotation from Brhadāranyaka Upanishad 2.5.19, one of many alluding to the central theme of the Upanishads, i.e., the identity of the human and divine or cosmic.—*K.F.L.*

B

Babism: An initially persecuted and later schismatizing religious creed founded in Persia prior to the middle of the last century. International in its appeal the number of its followers increased largely in America. As a development against orthodox Mohammedanism, the Babis deny the finality of any revelation. The sect's former extreme pantheistic tendency and metaphysical hairsplittings have been effectively subordinated to more pronounced ethical imperatives.—*H.H.*

Background: (Ger. *Hintergrund*) In Husserl: The nexus of objects and objective sense explicitly posited along with any object; the objective horizon. The perceptual background is part of the entire background in this broad sense. See *Horizon.*—*D.C.*

Bacon, Francis: (1561-1626) Inspired by the Renaissance, and in revolt against Aristotelianism and Scholastic Logic, proposed an *inductive* method of discovering truth, founded upon empirical observation, analysis of observed data, inference resulting in hypotheses, and verification of hypotheses through continued observation and experiment. The impediments to the use of this method are preconceptions and prejudices, grouped by Bacon under four headings, or *Idols:* (a) *The Idols of the Tribe,* or racially "wishful," anthropocentric ways of thinking, e.g. explanation by final causes, (b) *The Idols of the Cave* or personal prejudices, (c) *The Idols of the Market Place,* or failure to define terms, (d) *The Idols of the Theatre,* or blind acceptance of tradition and authority.

The use of the inductive method prescribes the extraction of the essential from the nonessential and the discovery of the underlying structure or *form* of the phenomena under investigation, through (a) comparison of instances, (b) study of concomitant variations, and (c) exclusion of *negative instances.*

This process is facilitated by the choice of *prerogative,* or, if possible, of *solitary,* instances in which the investigated data are comparatively isolated and unadulterated. But under the most favorable conditions inquiry must be a cautious, laborious, plodding, step by step affair, and results can never be more than provi-

sional because of the possibility of undiscovered negative instances.

Bacon had no system of his own, but openly preferred the Ionians, Atomists and Epicureans.

Bacon's theory of poetry also deserves consideration. Whereas reason adapts the mind to the nature of things, and science conquers nature by obeying her, poetry submits the shows of things to the desires of the mind and overcomes nature by allowing us in our imagination to escape from her. Out of present experience and the record of history, poetry builds its narrative and dramatic fancies. But it may also, in allegory and parable, picture symbolically scientific and philosophic truths and religious mysteries—in which case it creates mythologies. Fr. Bacon, *Works,* 7 vols., 1857, ed. Spedding and Ellis.—*B.A.G.F.*

Bacon, Roger: (1214-1294) Franciscan. He recognized the significance of the deductive application of principles and the necessity for experimental verification of the results. He was keenly interested in mathematics. His most famous work was called *Opus majus,* a veritable encyclopaedia of the sciences of his day.—*L.E.D.*

Baconian Method: The inductive method as advanced by Francis Bacon (1561-1626). The purpose of the method was to enable man to attain mastery over nature in order to exploit it for his benefit. The mind should pass from particular facts to a more general knowledge of forms, or generalized physical properties. They are laws according to which phenomena actually proceed. He demanded an exhaustive enumeration of positive instances of occurrences of phenomena, the recording of comparative instances, in which an event manifests itself with greater or lesser intensity, and the additional registration of negative instances. Then experiments should test the observations. See *Mill's Methods.*—*J.J.R.*

Bahya, ben Joseph Ibn Padudah: (fl. 1050) Philosopher and ethicist. The title of his work, *The Duties of the Heart* (Heb. *Hobot ha-Lebabot*), indicates its purpose, i.e., to teach ethical conduct. First part demonstrates pure conception of God, unity and attributes. His basic principle of ethics is thankfulness to God, for His creating the wonderful world; the goal of religious ethical conduct is love of God. A second work ascribed to him is the *Torot ha-Nefesh*, i.e., *Doctrines of the Soul*, which deals primarily with the soul, but also with other subjects and evinces a strong neo-Platonic strain. See *Jewish Philosophy*.—*M.W.*

Bāhyānumeya-vāda: (Skr.) A Hinayāna Buddhist theory (*vāda*), otherwise known as Sautrāntika, based upon a realist epistemology. It assumes the reality and independence of mind and object, which latter is inferred (*anumeya*) as being outside (*bāhya*) consciousness and apprehended only when the sensory apparatus functions and certain physical conditions are fulfilled. —*K.F.L.*

Bāhyapratyakṣa-vāda: (Skr.) A Hinayāna Buddhist theory (*vāda*) of realism, otherwise known as Vaibhāsika. It holds that objects exist outside (*bāhya*) the mind and consciousness, but that they must be directly (*pratyaksa*) and not inferentially (cf. *Bāhyānumeya-vāda*) known.—*K.F.L.*

Banausic: (Gr. *banausos*) Vulgar; illiberal; applied particularly to arts, sciences, or occupations that deform the body or the mind.—*G.R.M.*

Baptism: A rite of dedication and induction of an individual into a circle of social and religious privilege. The rite is usually of a ceremonious nature with pledges given (by proxy in the case of infants), prayers and accompanied by some visible sign (such as water, symbol of purification, or wine, honey, oil or blood) sealing the bond of fellowship. In its earliest form the rite probably symbolized not only an initiation but the magical removal of some tabu or demon possession (exorcism — see *Demonology*), the legitimacy of birth, the inheritance of privilege, the assumption of a name and the expectancy of responsibility. In Christian circles the rite has assumed the status of a sacrament, the supernatural rebirth into the Divine Kingdom. Various forms include sprinkling with water, immersion, or the laying on of hands. In some Christian circles it is considered less a mystical rite and more a sign of a covenant of salvation and consecration to the higher life.—*V.F.*

Baroque: A style of art, produced especially in the XVIIth century, considered by classicists a type of false art; by romanticists a product of magic imagination.—*L.V.*

Barth, Karl: (1886-1968) Swiss theologian, widely influential among current social pessimists. God, he holds, is wholly other than man, not apprehensible by man's reason nor attainable by human endeavor. Christianity is a revealed and supernatural religion. Man must trust God's plan of salvation or be doomed to utter ruin. God is the sole judge and his judgments are beyond man's attainments. The Barthian position is called "crisis theology" (crisis, the Greek word for judgment) and "dialectical theology" (because of the emphasis upon the contradiction between God and this world). For a summary of Barth's position see *The Knowledge of God and the Service of God* (1939).—*V.F.*

Basic Sentences, Protocol Sentences: Sentences formulating the result of observations or perceptions or other experiences, furnishing the basis for empirical verification or confirmation (see *Verification*). Some philosophers take sentences concerning observable properties of physical things as basic sentences, others take sentences concerning sense-data or perceptions. The sentences of the latter kind are regarded by some philosophers as completely verifiable, while others believe that all factual sentences can be confirmed only to some degree. See *Scientific Empiricism*.—*R.C.*

Bathmism: A name given by the Lamarckian E. D. Cope to a special force, or growth-force, which he regarded as existing and as exhibiting itself in the growth of organic beings.—*W.F.K.*

Baumgarten, Alexander Gottlieb: (1714-1762) A German thinker of the pre-Kantian period and disciple of Christian Wolff whose encyclopaedic work he tried to continue. Among his works the best known is *Aesthetica* in which he analyzes the problem of beauty regarded by him as recognition of perfection by means of the senses. The name of aesthetics, as the philosophy of beauty and art, was introduced by him for the first time.—*R.B.W.*

Becoming: (Medieval) Any kind of change is actualization of potencies. It is often called, following Aristotle, a "movement," because moving is a striking instance of becoming, and because the thing "moves" from the lower level of potentiality to the higher of actuality. Actualization is achieved only by a factor which is act itself. The act is in this sense prior to the potency not only in nature but also in time. See *Being, Dialectic, Hegel.*—*R.A.*

Begging the Question: The logical fallacy of assuming in the premisses of an argument the very conclusion which is to be proved. See *Petitio principii*.—*G.R.M.*

Begriffsgefühl: (Ger. Literally, conceptual feeling) The faculty of eliciting feelings, images or recollections associated with concepts or capable of being substituted for them. Sometimes, the affective tone peculiar to a given concept.—*O.F.K.*

Behaviorism: The contemporary American School of psychology—which abandons the concepts of mind and consciousness, and restricts both animal and human psychology to the study of behavior. The impetus to behaviorism was given by the Russian physiologist, Pavlov, who through his investigation of the salivary reflex in dogs, developed the concept of the conditioned reflex. See *Conditioned Reflex*. The founder of American behaviorism is J. B. Watson, who formulated a program for psychology excluding all reference to consciousness and confining itself to behavioral responses. (*Behavior: An Introduction to Comparative Psychology,* 1914). Thinking and emotion are interpreted as implicit behavior: the former is implicit or subvocal speech; the latter implicit visceral reactions. A distinction has been drawn between methodological and dogmatic behaviorism: the former ignores "consciousness" and advocates, in psychology, the objective study of behavior; the latter denies consciousness entirely, and is, therefore, a form of metaphysical materialism. See *Automatism.*—*L.W.*

Being, hierarchy of: (Scholastic) The Neo-Platonic conception of a hierarchy of "emanations" from the "One" persisted throughout the Middle Ages, though it was given another meaning. Emanationism properly speaking is incompatible with the notion of creation. But the medieval writers agree that there is a hierarchy, comprising within the visible world inanimate beings, plants, animals, and rational beings, men; above them rank the immaterial substances (subsistent forms, angels) and finally God Who, however, is so far distant from any created being that He cannot be placed in line. Whatever is asserted of God is so only "analogically" (see *Analogy*). There is analogy also between the grades of created beings; their various levels are not of one kind, no transition exists between inanimate and animate bodies, or between material and spiritual substances. Though the original meaning has been abandoned, the term "emanation" is still used, even by Aquinas.—*R.A.*

Being: In early Greek philosophy is opposed either to change, or Becoming, or to Non-Being. According to Parmenides and his disciples of the Eleatic School, everything real belongs to the category of Being, as the only possible object of thought. Essentially the same reasoning applies also to material reality in which there is nothing but Being, one and continuous, all-inclusive and eternal. Consequently, he concluded, the coming into being and passing away constituting change are illusory, for that which is-not cannot be, and that which is cannot cease to be. In rejecting Eleatic monism, the materialists (Leukippus, Democritus) asserted that the very existence of things, their corporeal nature, insofar as it is subject to change and motion, necessarily presupposes the other than Being, that is, Non-Being, or Void. Thus, instead of regarding space as a continuum, they saw in it the very source of discontinuity and the foundation of the atomic structure of substance. Plato accepted the first part of Parmenides' argument, namely, that referring to thought as distinct from matter, and maintained that, though Becoming is indeed an apparent characteristic of everything sensory, the true and ultimate reality, that of Ideas, is changeless and of the nature of Being. Aristotle achieved a compromise among all these notions and contended that, though Being, as the essence of things, is eternal in itself, nevertheless it manifests itself only in change, insofar as "ideas" or "forms" have no existence independent of, or transcendent to, the reality of things and minds. The medieval thinkers never revived the controversy as a whole, though at times they emphasized Being, as in Neo-Platonism, at times Becoming, as in Aristotelianism. With the rise of new interest in nature, beginning with F. Bacon, Hobbes and Locke, the problem grew once more in importance, especially to the rationalists, opponents of empiricism. Spinoza regarded change as a characteristic of modal existence and assumed in this connection a position distantly similar to that of Plato. Hegel formed a new answer to the problem in declaring that nature, striving to exclude

contradictions, has to "negate" them: Being and Non-Being are "moments" of the same cosmic process which, at its foundation, arises out of Being containing Non-Being within itself and leading, factually and logically, to their synthetic union in Becoming.—*R.B.W.*

In scholasticism: The English term translates three Latin terms which, in Scholasticism, have different significations. *Ens* as a noun is the most general and most simple predicate; as a participle it is an essential predicate only in regard to God in Whom existence and essence are one, or Whose essence implies existence. *Esse*, though used sometimes in a wider sense, usually means existence which is defined as the *actus essendi*, or the reality of some essence. *Esse quid* or *essentia* designates the specific nature of some being or thing, the "being thus" or the quiddity. *Ens* is divided into real and mental being (*ens rationis*). Though the latter also has properties, it is said to have essence only in an improper way. Another division is into actual and potential being. *Ens* is called the first of all concepts, in respect to ontology and to psychology; the latter statement of Aristotle appears to be confirmed by developmental psychology. Thing *(res)* and *ens* are synonymous; a *res* may be a *res extra mentem* or only *rationis*. Every *ens* is: something, i.e. has quiddity, one, true, i.e. corresponds to its proper nature, and good. These terms, naming aspects which are only virtually distinct from *ens*, are said to be convertible with *ens* and with each other. *Ens* is an analogical term, i.e. it is not predicated in the same manner of every kind of being, according to Aquinas. In Scotism *ens*, however, is considered as univocal and as applying to God in the same sense as to created beings, though they be distinguished as *entia ab alio* from God, the *ens a se*. See *Act, Analogy, Potency, Transcendentals.*—*R.A.*

In Spinoza's sense, that which "is," preëminently and without qualification — the source and ultimate subject of all distinctions. Being is thus divided into that which is "in itself" and "in another" (*Ethica*, I, Ax. 4; see also "substance" and "mode," Defs. 3 and 5). Being is likewise distinguished with respect to "finite" and "infinite," under the qualifications of absolute and relative; thus God is defined (*Ibid.* I, Def. 6) as "Being absolutely infinite." Spinoza seems to suggest that the term, Being, has, in the strict sense, no proper definition (*Cog. Met.*, I, 1). The main characteristics of Spinoza's treatment of this notion are (i) his clear-headed separation of the problems of *existence* and Being, and (ii) his carefully worked out distinction between *ens reale* and *ens rationis* by means of which Spinoza endeavors to justify the ontological argument (*q.v.*) in the face of criticism by the later Scholastics. —*W.S.W.*

Belief: Acquiescence in the existence of objects (*e.g.* external things, other minds, God, etc.) or assent to the truth of propositions (*e.g.* scientific, moral, aesthetic, or metaphysical statements). The belief in objects is frequently immediate and non-inferential; the belief in propositions usually rests on reflection and inference.

Theories of belief may be classified as:

(a) affective
(b) intellectual and
(c) volitional.

Hume's theory that belief is a feeling of vividness attaching to a perception or memory but not to a fiction of the imagination is an example of (a) (*An Enquiry Concerning Human Understanding*, §5 Pt. II). Bain and James Mill represent (b), while W. James represents (c). (*The Will to Believe, Etc.*, 1896).—*L.W.*

In scholasticism: means either faith or opinion. Opinion is a statement lacking evidence. Faith is a supernatural act, due to God's grace, referring to things reason finds beyond its capacity of proof, though not contradicting its principles. Statements capable of experimental proof are not objects of faith.—*R.A.*

Beneke, Friedrich Eduard: (1798-1854) A German thinker of Kantian tradition modified by empiricism; his doctrines exerted considerable influence upon the psychology and educational theory of the 19th century. Main works: *Erfahrungsseelenlehre*, 1820; *Physik d. Sitten*, 1822; *Metaphysik*, 1822; *Logik als Kunstlehre des Denkens*, 1832; *Erziehungslehre*, 1833; *Pragmatische Psychol.*, 1850.—*R.B.W.*

Benthamism: Name conventionally given to the utilitarianism of Jeremy Bentham who regarded the greatest happiness of the greatest number as the supreme ethical goal of human society and individual men. The morality of men's actions is determined experimentally by their utility, which means the power of an action to produce happiness. The moral quality of any action is estimated in accordance with its pleasant or painful consequences; for the sovereign masters of man are pleasure, the only good, and pain, the only evil. Ethics becomes a matter of calculation of consequences. —*J.J.R.*

Bentham, Jeremy: (1748-1832) Founder of the English Utilitarian School of Philosophy. In law, he is remembered for his criticism of Blackstone's views of the English constitution, for his examination of the legal fiction and for his treatment of the subject of evidence. In politics, he is most famous for his analysis of the principles of legislation and, in ethics, for his greatest happiness principle. See *Hedonic Calculus; Utilitarianism*. J. Bentham, *Principles of Morals and Legislation*, 1789; *Outline of a New System of Logic*, 1827; *Deontology*.—*L.E.D.*

Berdyaev, Nikolai Alexandrovitch: (1874-1948) A Russian teacher and writer on the philosophy of religion. He was born in Kiev, exiled to Vologda when twenty-five; threatened with expulsion from the Russian Orthodox Church in 1917, he became professor of philosophy at the Univ. of Moscow. In 1922, he was expelled from the Soviet Union and he went to Berlin, where he established his Academy of Religious Philosophy. He moved his school to Paris and established a Russian review called *Putj* (*The Way*). His thought resembles that of the Christian Gnostics (see *Gnosticism*), and it owes a good deal to German idealism and mysticism (Boehme). He is a trenchant critic of systems as diverse as Communism and Thomistic Scholasticism. His most noted works are: *Smyisl Istorii* (*The Meaning of History*), Berlin, 1923; *Novoye Srednevyekovye* (transl. as *The End of Our Time*, N.Y., 1933), Berlin, 1924; *Freedom and the Spirit*, N.Y., 1935. V. J. Bourke, "The Gnosticism of N. Berdyaev", *Thought*, XI (1936), 409-22.—*V.J.B.*

Bergson, Henri: (1859-1941) As the most influential of modern temporalistic, anti-mechanistic and spiritualistic metaphysics, Bergson's writings (*Les données immédiates de l'expérience, Matière et Mémoire, L'évolution créatrice, Le rire, Introduction à la métaphysique, Les deux sources de la morale et de la religion, etc.*) were aimed against the dogmatic and crude naturalism, and the mechanistic and static materialism which reached their heights in the second half of the last century.

The vital center of his doctrine is duration rather than intuition. Duration is the original thing in itself, the "substance" of philosophic tradition, except that to Bergson it is a specific experience, revealed to the individual in immediate experience. All things, consciousness, matter, time, evolution, motion and the absolute are so many specialized tensional forms of duration. The phrase *élan vital* sums up his vitalistic doctrine that there is an original life force, that it has passed from one generation of living beings to another by way of developed individual organisms, these being the connecting links between the generations. Bergson regards as pseudo-evolutionary the effort to arrange all living beings into a grand uni-linear series. True or creative evolution is pluri-dimensional, *i.e.*, the life force is conserved in every line of evolution of living beings, causing all of the numerous varieties of living forms, creating all new species, and dividing itself more and more as it advances. As the vital impetus is not moving towards any fixed, predetermined and final end, an immanent teleology is within the life force itself.

It is an error to see Bergson's philosophy as being exclusively an intuitive critique of knowledge. Such a mode of exposition constructs of his thought a mere "ism," a species of intuitionalism. Bergson was the first to try to give the term intuition a scientific basis. He transformed and regrounded the static pattern of the older forms of intuitionism by giving it a biogenetic and psychologically dynamic justification. Intuitive knowledge is not limited to the favored few, is not a private, purely solipsistic affair; but is a general property of all thinking minds. Bergson's conception of intuition represents a fusion of scientific objectivity and artistic directness.

Moreover, it is a serious wide-spread error of interpretation to consider Bergson as an anti-intellectualist. His alleged anti-intellectualism should be considered as a protest against taking the static materialism and spatialization of Newton's conception of nature as being anything but a high abstraction, as a rejection of the extreme claims of mechanistic and materialistic science, as an effort of reason to transcend itself in harmony with the greatest idealistic thinkers, as an effort of thinkers to stress the dynamic nature of reality, and as a persistent criticism of reason, a continuation of the Kantian tradition. His much misread conception of intuition may be viewed as akin to Spinoza's *intuitio*, to wit: a completion rather than a rejection of reason.—*H.H.*

Berkeleianism: The idealistic system of philosophy of George Berkeley (1685-1753). He thought that the admission of an extramental world would lead to materialism and atheism. Hence he denied the existence of an independent world of bodies by teaching that their existence consists in perceptibility, *esse* is *percipi*. The cause of the ideas in our mind is not a material substance, but a spiritual being, God, who communicates them to us in a certain order which we call the laws of nature. Things cannot exist unless perceived by some mind. Berkeley acknowledged the existence of other spirits, or minds, besides that of God.—*J.J.R.*

Berkeley, George: (1685-1753) Pluralistic idealist, reflecting upon the spatial attributes of distance, size, and situation, possessed, according to Locke, by external objects in themselves apart from our perception of them, concluded that the discrepancy between the visual and the tactual aspects of these attributes robbed them of all objective validity and reduced them to the status of secondary qualities existing only in and for consciousness. Moreover, the very term "matter," like all other "universals," is found upon analysis to mean and stand for nothing but complexes of experienced qualities. Indeed, "existence" except as presence to consciousness, is meaningless. Hence, nothing can be said to exist except minds (spirits) and mental content (ideas). *Esse = percipi* or *percipere*.

At the same time, Berkeley, trusting the external reference of individual experience, argues from it the existence of a universal mind (God) of which the content is the so-called objective world. Finite spirits are created by God, and their several experiences represent his communication to them, so far as they are able to receive it, of his divine experience. Reality, then, is composed of spirits and ideas. The physical aspects of the world are reducible to mental phenomena. Matter is non-existent. G. Berkeley, *Treatise on the Principles of Human Knowledge,* 1710; *Three Dialogues Between Hylas and Philonous,* 1713; *De Motu* (critique of Newtonian mechanics), 1720; *Alciphron, or the Minute Philosopher,* 1733; *Siris,* 1744.—*B.A.S.F.*

Bernard of Chartres: (died c. 1130) Has been called the "most perfect Platonist of his century" by John of Salisbury (*Metalogicus,* IV, 35, PL 199, 938) but he is known only at second-hand now. He taught in the school of Chartres from 1114-1119 and was Chancellor of Chartres from 1119-1124. According to John of Salisbury, Bernard was an extreme realist in his theory of universals, but he taught that the forms of things (*formae nativae*) are distinct from the exemplary Ideas in the Divine Mind. A treatise, *De expositione Porphyrii* has been attributed to him. He is not to be confused with Bernard Silvestris of Chartres, nor with Bernard of Tours. E. Gilson, "Le platonisme de Ber-

nard de C.," *Revue Néoscolastique,* XXV (1923) 5-19.—*V.J.B.*

Best: The principle of the best of all possible worlds: according to Leibniz, the world which exists is the best possible because God's wisdom makes him know, his goodness makes him choose, and his power always makes him produce the best possible. See *Optimism.*—*J.M.*

Bewusstsein Ueberhaupt: German expression meaning "consciousness in general" that is, consciousness conceived as a real entity over and above individual conscious centers. See *Consciousness.*—*L.W.*

Bhagavad Gītā: (Skr. the song, *gītā,* of the Blessed One), A famed philosophic epic poem, widely respected in India and elsewhere, representing Krishna embodied as a charioteer imparting to the King Arjuna, who is unwilling to fight his kinsmen in battle, comprehension of the mysteries of existence, clearly indicating the relationship between morality and absolute ethical values in a Hindi philosophy of action.—*K.F.L.*

Bhakti: (Skr. division, share) Fervent, loving devotion to the object of contemplation or the divine being itself, the almost universally recognized feeling approach to the highest reality, in contrast to *vidyā* (*q.v.*) or *jñāna* (*q.v.*), sanctioned by Indian philosophy and productive of a voluminous literature in which the names of Rāmānanda, Vallabha, Nānak, Caitanya, and Tulsi Dās are outstanding. It is distinguished as *aparā* (lower) and *parā* (higher) *bhakti,* the former theistic piety, the latter philosophic meditation on the unmanifest *brahman* (cf. *avyakta*).—*K.F.L.*

Bhāsya: (Skr. speaking) Commentary.

Bheda: (Skr. different, distinct) Non-identity, particularly in reference to any philosophy of dualism which recognizes the existence of two opposed principles or admits of a difference between the essentially human and the Absolute.—*K.F.L.*

Bhedābheda: (Skr. "different [yet] not different") A philosophy admitting the point of view of *bheda* (s.v.) as well as that of *abheda* (s.v.), depending on the mental and spiritual attainment of the person.—*K.F.L.*

Bhuta: (Skr. become) The "has-become," or the ultimate element or concrete thing as it has evolved from the abstract, metaphysical unity through a process of infinite particularization and limitation.—*K.F.L.*

Bhutatathātā: (Skr.) "So-ness," the highest state conceivable by the Vijñāna-vāda (s.v.) in which there is a complete *coincidentia oppositorum* of beings and elements of knowledge; directly identified with the Adi-Buddha, or eternal Buddha, in Vajrayāna Buddhism. —*K.F.L.*

Biconditional: The sentential connective ≡, "if and only if." See *Logic, formal,* §1.—*A.C.*

Binomic forces: Extra-biological forces, which influence the direction and development of life, i.e. all physical, chemical and other environmental forces which affect living organisms in any way. The second law of thermo-dynamics seems to vitalists to be an exception to their view that the creative life-force evolves upwards. Nonetheless natural selection is influenced by binomic forces.—*C.K.D.*

Biometry: The scientific application of mathematical analysis to biological problems (also spoken of as "mathematical biophysics" and "mathematical biochemistry"). The journal *Biometrika* was founded by Karl Pearson.—*W.M.M.*

Black, Max: (1909–　) American philosopher, born in Russia and educated in England. Since 1940 Black has been teaching philosophy in the United States, and currently is Professor (Emeritus) of Philosophy at Cornell University.

Black has maintained a wide range of interests throughout his career, which was largely influenced by Moore (*q.v.*), Russell (*q.v.*), Wittgenstein (*q.v.*), Frege (*q.v.*), and Logical Positivism (*q.v.*). The temper of his thought is empirical and analytical. His primary concerns have been with the foundations of logic and mathematics, the theory of knowledge, the philosophy of language and the philosophy of science. He has also done extensive work on induction.

Nature of Mathematics (1933); *Language and Philosophy* (1949); *Problems of Analysis* (1954); *A Companion to Wittgenstein's TRACTATUS* (1964); *Caveats and Critiques: Philosophical Essays in Language, Logic and Art* (1975); *Problems of Choice and Decision* (1975).—*T.P.S.*

Blanshard, Brand: (1892–　) An American philosopher who represents the tradition of classical rationalism, Blanshard maintains, against Hume, that there are necessary connections in the world. Among these causes are the laws of mathematics and logic, connections between property and attribute, and necessary connections in ethics and value. Blanshard's works include *The Nature of Thought* (1939), *The Impasse in Ethics and a Way Out* (1955) and *Reason and Analysis* (1962).—*S.E.N.*

Blondel, Maurice: (1861-1939) A philosopher in the French "spiritualistic" tradition of Maine de Biran and Boutroux, who in his essays *L'Action* (1893), and *Le Procès de l'Intelligence* (1922), defended an activistic psychology and metaphysics. "The Philosophy of Action" is a voluntaristic and idealistic philosophy which, as regards the relation of thought to action, seeks to compromise between the extremes of intellectualism and pragmatism. In his subsequent book *La Pensée* (1934), Blondel retained his earlier activistic philosophy combined with a stronger theological emphasis.—*L.W.*

Bodhidharma: (470-543) According to tradition, Bodhidharma, the founder of Zen (Ch'an) Buddhism, journeyed from India to China in 520 A.D. He is pictured crossing the Yangtze River "on a reed," and rapidly displayed outstanding abilities.

Basing his teachings on the *Lankāvatāra Sūtra,* Bodhidharma proclaimed that: A special transmission (from master to disciple) is possible outside the Scriptures; We should not be dependent upon words or letters as authorities; We should point directly to the soul of man; and We should see into our own nature and thus attain Buddhahood.—*S.E.N.*

Bodhisattva: (Skr.) "Existence (*sattva*) in a state of wisdom (*bodhi*)," such as was attained by Gautama Buddha (*q.v.*); a Buddhist wise and holy man.—*K.F.L.*

Body: Here taken in the sense of the material organized substance of man contrasted with the mind, soul or spirit, thus leading to the problem of the relation between body and mind, one of the most persistent problems of philosophy. Of course, any theory which identifies body and mind, or does not adequately distinguish the psychical from the physical, regarding both as aspects of the same reality, eludes some of the difficulties presented by the problem. Both materialism and idealism may be considered as forms of psychophysical monism. Materialism by denying the real existence of spiritual beings and reducing mind to a function of matter, and spiritualism, or that species called idealism, which regards bodies simply as contents of consciousness, really evade the main issue. All those, however, who frankly acknowledge the empirically given duality of mind and organism, are obliged to struggle with the problem of the relation between them. The two most noted rival theories attempting an answer are interactionism and parallelism. The first considers both body and mind as substantial beings, influencing each other, hence causally related. The second holds that physical processes and mental processes accompany each other without any interaction or interference whatsoever, consequently they cannot be causally related. The Scholastics advance the doctrine of the human composite consisting of body and soul united into one substance and nature, constituting the human person or self, to whom all actions of which man is capable must be ascribed. There can be no interaction, since there is but one agent, formed of two component elements. This theory, like interactionism, makes provision for survival, even immortality, while parallelism definitely precludes it. No known theory can meet all objections and prove entirely satisfactory; the problem still persists. See *Descartes, Spinoza, Mind.*—*J.J.R.*

Boehme, Jacob: (1575-1624) Of Görlitz, was the son of poor parents, received little formal schooling, studied the Bible and the works of Pastor Valentine Weigel assiduously. He became noted as a mystic, theosophist, and in his own day was called the German Philosopher. He wrote in German but his early followers translated his works into Latin, hence it is difficult to distinguish his personal thought from that of his school. He thought that all reality, even God, contains a duality of good and evil, the universe and man's soul are nothing without God. He has had much influence on later German and Russian mysticism. Chief works: *Aurora, Vierzig Fragen von der Seele, Mysterium Magnum, Von der Gnadenwahl.* Deussen, *J. Boehme, über sein Leben u. seine Philos.* (Kiel, 1897).—*V.J.B.*

Boethius: (470-525) An influential commentator on Aristotle and Cicero, who, in his own thinking, reflected a strong influence of Neo-Platonism and Augustinianism. *De Consolatione Philosophiae* (Migne PL, 63-4, 69-70).—*R.B.W.*

Bok, Sissela (Myrdal): (1934–　) American

philosopher, teacher at Harvard, she is author of books on ethics, including *Lying: Moral Choice in Public and Private Life* (1978), a highly influential study.—*S.E.N.*

Bolzano, Bernard: (1781-1848) Austrian philosopher and mathematician. Professor of the philosophy of religion at Prague, 1805-1820, he was compelled to resign in the latter year because of his rationalistic tendencies in theology, and afterwards held no academic position. His *Wissenschaftslehre* of 1837, while it is to be classed as a work on traditional logic, contains significant anticipations of many ideas which have since become important in symbolic logic and mathematics. In his posthumously published *Paradoxien des Unendlichen* (1851) he appears as a forerunner in some respects of Cantor's theory of transfinite numbers.—*A.C.*

W. Dubislav, *Bolzano als Vorläufer der mathematischen Logik*, Philosophisches Jahrbuch der Görres-Gesellschaft, vol. 44 (1931), pp. 448-456. H. Scholz, *Die Wissenschaftslehre Bolzanos*, Abhandlungen der Fries'schen Schule, n. s. vol. 6 (1937), pp. 399-472.

Bonaventure, St.: (1221-1274) Was born at Bagnorea, near Viterbo, and his name originally was John of Fidanza. He joined the Franciscans in 1238, studied at the Univ. of Paris under Alexander of Hales, and took his licentiate in 1248. He taught theology in Paris for seven years and received his doctorate in 1257. In this year he was made Superior-General of his Order and he taught no more. His chief works are: *Commentaria in IV L. Sententiarum, Itinerarium mentis in Deum, Quaestiones Disputatae* (*Opera Omnia*, ed. crit., 10 vol. Quaracchi, 1882-1902). His philosophy is Augustinian, with some Aristotelian modifications in his theory of intellection and matter and form. But his Divine Exemplarism, Illumination theory, and tendency to stress the psychological importance of the human will, derive from St. Augustine. E. Gilson, *La philosophie de S. Bonaventure* (Paris, 1924).—*V.J.B.*

Boodin, John Elof: American philosopher born in Sweden in 1869 who emigrated in 1886 to the United States. Studied at the universities of Colorado, Minnesota, Brown and especially Harvard under Royce with whom he kept a life-long friendship though he was opposed to his idealism. His works (*Time and Reality*, 1904 — *Truth and Reality*, 1912 — *A Realistic Universe*, 1916 — *Cosmic Evolution*, 1925 — *Three Interpretations of the Universe*, 1934 — *God*, 1935 — *The Social Mind*, 1940) form practically a complete system. His philosophy takes the form of a cosmic idealism, though he was interested for a time in certain aspects of pragmatism. It grew gradually from his early studies when he developed a new concept of a real and non-serial time. The structure of the cosmos is that of a hierarchy of *fields*, as exemplified in physics, in organisms, in consciousness and in society. The interpenetration of the mental fields makes possible human knowledge and social intercourse. Reality as such possesses five attributes: *being* (the dynamic stuff of all complexes, the active energy), *time* (the ground of change and transformation), *space* (which accounts for extension), *con-sciousness* (active awareness which lights up reality in spots; it becomes the self when conative tendencies cooperate as one active group), and *form* (the ground of organization and structure which conditions selective direction). God is the spirit of the whole.—*T.G.*

Boole, George: (1815-1864) English mathematician. Professor of mathematics at Queen's College, Cork, 1849-1864. While he made contributions to other branches of mathematics, he is now remembered primarily as the founder of the Nineteenth Century algebra of logic and through it of modern symbolic logic. His *Mathematical Analysis of Logic* appeared in 1847 and the fuller *Laws of Thought* in 1854.—*A.C.*

R. Harley, *George Boole, F. R. S.*, The British Quarterly Review, vol. 44 (1866), pp. 141-181. Anon., *George Boole*, Proceedings of the Royal Society of London, vol. 15 (1867), Obituary notices of fellows deceased, pp. vi-xi. P. E. B. Jourdain, *George Boole*, The Quarterly Journal of Pure and Applied Mathematics, vol. 41 (1910), pp. 332-352.

Boolean algebra: See *Logic, Formal*, § 7.

Bosanquet, Bernard: (1848-1923) Neo-Hegelian idealist, regards Reality as a single individual all-embracing, completely rational experience, combining universality and concreteness. It alone *exists*. All other particulars—minds or things—are only partially concrete, individual and real. The incidental, incomplete, dependent and only partially existent character of finite consciousness is shown by the reaching, seeking character of all its activities, sense-perceptions, thought, moral action, and even aesthetic contemplation — all of which indicate that self-realization means self-abandonment to something larger than the self.

This something larger is the cosmic drama, written, staged, and acted by the Absolute, who is artist and actor as well as a rational intelligence, intent no less upon dramatic than upon intelligible unity and self-expression. The world-process is tragic; witness the sin and suffering and imperfection with which it is fraught. But in the infinite tragedy, as well as in the tragedies composed by men, evil is contributory to the perfection of the whole, and, when seen and accepted as such by the finite individual, not only loses its sting but produces a "catharsis" of his attitude towards it, in which he cheerfully accepts it, battles with it, and finds his triumph over it in nobly enduring it. This "catharsis," identifying him as it does with the meaning of the life of the Absolute, is his peace and his salvation. Main works: *Logic*, 1888; *The Philosophical Theory of the State*, 1899; *Value and Destiny of the Individual*, 1913.—*B.A.G.F.*

Bourgeoisie: (Fr.) In its strict sense in the theory of historical materialism (*q.v.*) the class of urban, commercial, banking, manufacturing and shipping entrepreneurs which, at the close of the middle ages was strong enough, by virtue of its command of developing technics, to challenge the economic power of the predominantly rural and agricultural (manorial) feudal nobility, and to supplant the latter in place of economic and social leadership.—*J.M.S.*

Boutroux, E.: (1845-1921) Teacher of Bergson and M. Blondel, is best known for his defense of radical contingency and indeterminacy in metaphysics. Influenced by French "spiritualism" stemming from Maine de Biran, Boutroux was critical of the current psychological and sociological treatment of religious experience. Main works: *Contingency of the Laws of Nature* (tr. 1920); *Philosophy and War* (tr. 1916); *Science et Religion,* 1908.—*L.W.*

Bowne, Borden Parker: (1847-1910) His influence was not merely confined to the theological world of his religious communion as a teacher of philosophy at Boston University. His philosophy was conspicuous for the combination of theism with an idealistic view which he termed "Personalism" (*q.v.*). He mainly discussed issues of philosophy which had a bearing on religion, ethics, and epistemology. Main works: *Metaphysics,* 1882; *Philosophy of Theism,* 1887; *Theory of Thought and Knowledge,* 1897; *Personalism,* 1908; *Kant and Spencer,* 1912.—*H.H.*

Bradley, Francis Herbert: (1846-1924) Dialectician extraordinary of British philosophy, Bradley sought to purge contemporary thought of the extremely sensationalistic and utilitarian elements embodied in the tradition of empiricism. Though owing much to Hegel, he early repudiated the Hegelian system as such, and his own variety of Absolute Idealism bases itself upon no scheme of categories. His brilliant attack upon the inadequate assumptions of hedonistic ethics (*Ethical Studies,* 1877) was followed in 1883 by *The Principles of Logic* in which his dialectic analysis was applied to the problems of inference and judgment. It was, however, his *Appearance and Reality* (1893) with its famous theory of "the degrees of truth" which first disturbed the somnambulism of modern metaphysics, and led Caird to remark upon "the greatest thing since Kant." In later years, Bradley's growing realization of ultimate difficulties in his version of the coherence theory led him to modify his doctrines in the direction of a Platonic mysticism. See *Essays on Truth and Reality,* the second edition of the *Logic Collected Essays,* etc.—*W.S.W.*

Brahmā: (Skr.) The creator or creative principle of the universe, main figure of the Hindu trinity (see *Trimūrti*).—*K.F.L.*

Brahma eva idam viśvam: (Skr.) "Brahman, indeed, is this world-all," famous passage of Muṇḍaka Upanishad 2.2.11, foreshadowing the complete monism of Śaṅkara's Vedānta (*q.v.*).—*K.F.L.*

Brahman, Brahma: (Skr.) The impersonal, pantheistic world-soul, the Absolute, union with which is the highest goal of the Upanishads (*q.v.*) and Vedic (*q.v.*) thinking in general. It is occasionally identified with *ātman* (*q.v.*) or made the exclusive reality (cf. *brahma eva idam viśvam; sarvam khalv idam brahma*), thus laying the foundation for a deep mystic as well as rational insight into the connaturalness of the human and divine and an uncompromising monism which gave its impress to much of Hindu thinking.—*K.F.L.*

Brāhmaṇa: (Skr.) One of several Vedic (*q.v.*) dictums or treatises of a ritualistic and sacrificial character which prepared the way, sometimes over an Araṇyaka (*q.v.*), for the Upanishads (*q.v.*) by incipient philosophic reflections.—*K.F.L.*

Brahmanism: The predominant form of philosophical, theological, and ethical speculation of India, sponsored by the Brahman caste which traces its doctrines back to the Vedas (*q.v.*) and Upanishads (*q.v.*) without ever having attained uniformity in regard to the main doctrines.—*K.F.L.*

Brahmasûtras: (Skr.) An aphoristic compilation of Bādarāyaṇa's, systematizing the philosophy of the Upanishads (*q.v.*).—*K.F.L.*

Brain: According to Aristotle, it is a cooling organ of the body. Early in the history of philosophy, it was regarded as closely connected with consciousness and with activities of the soul. Descartes contended that mind-body relations are centered in the pineal gland located between the two hemispheres of the brain. Cabanis, a sensualistic materialist, believed that the brain produces consciousness in a manner similar to that in which the liver produces bile. Many have sought to identify it with the seat of the soul. Today consciousness is recognized to be a much more complex phenomenon controlled by the entire nervous system, rather than by any part of the brain, and influenced by the bodily metabolism in general.—*R.B.W.*

Brentano, Franz: (1838-1917) Who had originally been a Roman Catholic priest may be described as an un-orthodox neo-scholastic. According to him the only three forms of psychic activity, representation, judgment and "phenomena of love and hate," are just three modes of "intentionality," *i.e.,* of referring to an object intended. Judgments may be self-evident and thereby characterized as true and in an analogous way love and hate may be characterized as "right." It is on these characterizations that a dogmatic theory of truth and value may be based. In any mental experience the content is merely a "physical phenomenon" (real or imaginary) intended to be referred to; what is psychic is merely the "act" of representing, judging (*viz.* affirming or denying) and valuing (*i.e.* loving or hating). Since such "acts" are evidently immaterial, the soul by which they are performed may be proved to be a purely spiritual and imperishable substance and from these and other considerations the existence, spirituality, as also the infinite wisdom, goodness and justice of God may also be demonstrated. It is most of all by his classification of psychic phenomena, his psychology of "acts" and "intentions" and by his doctrine concerning self-evident truths and values that Brentano, who considered himself an Aristotelian, exercised a profound influence on subsequent German philosophers: not only on those who accepted his entire system (such as A. Marty and C. Stumpf) but also those who were somewhat more independent and original and whom he influenced either directly (as A. Meinong and E. Husserl) or indirectly (as M. Scheler and Nik. Hartmann). Main works: *Psychologie des Aristoteles,* 1867; *Vom Dasein Gottes,* 1868; *Psychologie vom empirischen Standpunkt,* 1874;

Vom Ursprung sittliches Erkenntnis, 1884; *Ueber die Zukunft der Philosophie,* 1893; *Die vier Phasen der Philos.,* 1895.—*H.Go.*

Broad, C. D.: (1887-1971) As a realistic critical thinker Broad takes over from the sciences the methods that are fruitful there, classifies the various propositions used in all the sciences, and defines basic scientific concepts. In going beyond science, he seeks to reach a total view of the world by bringing in the facts and principles of aesthetic, religious, ethical and political experience. In trying to work out a much more general method which attacks the problem of the connection between mathematical concepts and sense-data better than the method of analysis *in situ,* he gives a simple exposition of the method of extensive abstraction, which applies the mutual relations of objects, first recognized in pure mathematics, to physics. Moreover, a great deal can be learned from Broad on the relation of the principle of relativity to measurement.

As an emergent materialist, he holds that everything happens by the blind combination of the elements of matter or energy, without any guidance, excluding the assumption of a non-material component. While he regards primary qualities as physical emergents, he yet considers secondary qualities, such as color, taste, and smell, as transphysical emergents. He favors the emergence of laws, qualities and classes. Psyche, physical in nature, combines with other material factors to make the life of the mind. Broad holds to a generative view of consciousness. Psyche persists after death for some time, floats about in cosmic space indefinitely, ready to combine with a material body under suitable conditions. He calls this theory the "compound theory of materialistic emergency." Sensa, he holds, are real, particular, short-lived existents. They are exclusively neither physical nor mental. He replaces the neo-realistic contrast between existents and subsistents, by a contrast between existents and substracta. Main works: *Scientific Thought,* 1923; *The Mind and Its Place in Nature,* 1925; *Five Types of Ethical Theory,* 1930.—*H.H.*

Brouwer, Luitzen Egbertus Jan: (1881-1966) Dutch mathematician. Professor of Mathematics at the University of Amsterdam, 1909. Besides his work in topology, he is known for important contributions to the philosophy and foundations of mathematics. See *Mathematics* and *Intuitionism (mathematical).*—*A.C.*

Bruno, Giordano: (1548-1600) A Dominican monk, eventually burned at the stake because of his opinions, he was converted from Christianity to a naturalistic and mystical pantheism by the Renaissance and particularly by the new Copernican astronomy. For him God and the universe were two names for one and the same Reality considered now as the creative essence of all things, now as the manifold of realized possibilities in which that essence manifests itself. As God, *natura naturans,* the Real is the whole, the one, transcendent and ineffable. As *natura naturata* the Real is the infinity of worlds and objects and events into which the whole divides itself and in which the one displays the infinite poten-tialities latent within it. The world-process is an ever-lasting going forth from itself and return into itself of the divine nature. The culmination of the outgoing creative activity is reached in the human mind, whose rational, philosophic search for the one in the many, simplicity in variety, and the changeless and eternal in the changing and temporal, marks also the reverse movement of the divine nature re-entering itself and regaining its primordial unity, homogeneity, and changelessness. The human soul, being as it were a kind of boomerang partaking of the ingrowing as well as the outgrowing process, may hope at death, not to be dissolved with the body, which is borne wholly upon the outgoing stream, but to return to God whence it came and to be reabsorbed in him. Cf. Rand, *Modern Classical Philosophers,* selection from Bruno's *On Cause, The Principle and the One.* G. Bruno: *De l'infinito, universo e mundo,* 1584; *Spaccio della bestia trionfante,* 1584; *La cena della ceneri,* 1584; *Deglieroici furori,* 1585; *De Monade,* 1591. Cf. R. Honigswald, *Giordano Bruno;* G. Gentile, *Bruno nella storia della cultura,* 1907.—*B.A.G.F.*

Brunschvicg, Léon: (1869-1944) Professor of Philosophy at the Ecole Normale in Paris. Dismissed by the Nazis (1941). His philosophy is an idealistic synthesis of Spinoza, Kant and Schelling with special stress on the creative role of thought in cultural history as well as in sciences. Main works: *Les étapes de la philosophie mathématique,* 1913; *L'expérience humaine et la causalité physique,* 1921; *De la connaissance de soi,* 1931.

Buber, Martin: (1878-1965) Author of *I and Thou* (1923), an epoch-making book which contrasted an I-Thou attitude, a relationship of mutuality, with an I-It attitude, a relationship in which the I becomes an objective observer operating on a passive object. According to Buber, God is the eternal Thou, neither an observer nor observed, but self-revealing. Buber was born in Vienna and taught at Frankfurt from 1923 to 1933, before fleeing to Palestine to escape from the Nazis.—*S.E.N.*

Buddhism: The multifarious forms, philosophic, religious, ethical and sociological, which the teachings of Gautama Buddha (*q.v.*) have produced. They centre around the main doctrine of *catvāri ārya-satyāni* (*q.v.*), the four noble truths, the last of which enables one in eight stages to reach *nirvāna* (*q.v.*): right views, right resolve, right speech, right conduct, right livelihood, right effort, right mindfulness, right concentration. In the absence of contemporary records of Buddha and Buddhistic teachings, much value was formerly attached to the palm leaf manuscripts in Pāli, a Sanskrit dialect; but recently a good deal of weight has been given also the Buddhist tradition in Sanskrit, Tibetan, and Chinese. Buddhism split into Mahāyānism (*q.v.*) and Hinayānism (Hinayāna is also called Theravada, meaning "the teaching of the elders" by those who practice it, each of which, but particularly the former, blossomed into a variety of teachings and practices. The main philosophic schools are the Madhyamaka or

Śunyavāda, Yogācāra, Sautrāntika, and Vaibhāsika (*q.v.*) The basic assumptions in philosophy are: a causal nexus in nature and man, of which the law of *karma* (*q.v.*) is but a specific application; the impermanence of things; and the illusory notion of substance and soul. Man is viewed realistically as a conglomeration of bodily forms (*rūpa*), sensations (*vedanā*), ideas (*saṅjñā*), latent karma (*sanskāras*), and consciousness (*vijñāna*). The basic assumptions in ethics are the universality of suffering and the belief in a remedy. There is no god; each one may become a Buddha, an enlightened one. Also in art and esthetics Buddhism has contributed much throughout the Far East.—*K.F.L.*

The most influential branch of Buddhism today is Soka Gakkai, the "Value Creating Study Group," with more than ten million members in Japan alone. Based on some of the ideas of Nichiren (1222-1282), the famous prophet of the Mongolian invasion, its current leader is Daisaku Ikeda, who held a sympathetic dialogue with Arnold Toynbee.—*S.E.N.*

"Bundle," Theory of Self: The conception of the self as a mere aggregate of mental states. The designation is an allusion to Hume's famous description of the self as: "a bundle or collection of different perceptions which succeed each other with an inconceivable rapidity, and are in a perpetual flux and movement." (*A Treatise on Human Nature*, Part LV, § 6.)—*L.W.*

Buridan's Ass: The story of the ass, which died of hunger and thirst because incapable of deciding between water and food placed at equal distances from him, is employed to support the free-will doctrine. A man, it is argued, if confronted by a similar situation, would by the exercise of his free-will, be able to resolve the equilibrium of opposing motives. The story of the ass is attributed to John Buridan, a 14th century nominalist who discussed the freedom of the will in his *Quaestiones in decem libros ethicorum Aristotelis*, 1489, Bk. III, quest. I, but is not, in fact, to be found in his writings. (Cf. A. G. Langley, translation of Leibniz's *New Essays Concerning Human Understanding*, p. 116 n.) Dante relates the story in *Paradiso*, IV.—*L.W.*

C

Cabalah (or Kabbalah): (Heb. *gabbalah*, from the verb *kabel,* to receive) General name for the tradition of Jewish mysticism, consisting of the sacred Jewish literature and of the oral traditions which came to be collected in the Mishnah. Also refers specifically to the occult system of Jewish philosophy and theosophy developed in the Middle Ages, whose principal texts include the Sepher Yetzira (Book of Creation), the Sepher Sephiroth (Book of Emanations), and more importantly the Sepher Hazohar (Book of Splendor), usually referred to as Sohar or Zohar.

The Cabalah reflects the history of the Jewish people, which has involved life in a wide range of cultures often hostile to the Jewish religious beliefs and practices. The hostility forced the evolution of an esoteric exegesis of Scripture, involving an elaborate symbolism of letters, names, words and numbers. From the "host" cultures the Cabalah absorbed many elements of philosophical and theological thought. Primary influences came from the ancient Babylonian and Egyptians; from Persian philosophy, both Parsi and Zoroastrian; neo-Pythagorean and neo-Platonic philosophy; and later from Christian and Gnostic thought.

The Cabalistic teachings are principally concerned with the doctrines of God, Creation, Revelation and Redemption. Reinterpreting the literal account of Creation described in Genesis, they consider God to be, not the personal figure portrayed in the "surface" level of the Old Testament story, but rather an infinite Being, whose creation of the world involved the prior creation of a demiurge as an intermediary between Himself and the world. Drawing on neo-Platonic thought, Creation is understood as a series of emanations from God, a hierarchy of spheres of God's spiritual essence. There are ten ascending levels of these spheres or emanations of radiance, which serve to mark the path of the mystic's journey to the divine. Reincarnation and the transmigration of souls are also part of Cabalistic doctrine, as are rewards and punishments after death.

In practice, Cabalistic wisdom has as its goal the spiritual development of individuals, whose ultimate achievement is unification with the divine. This process is facilitated by the use of the divine names, words, and numbers. The higher levels of development entail the attainment of certain psychological or spiritual states, as well as bringing the powers that accompany these states to bear upon the world, particularly in the performance of miracles and in speeding the coming of the Messiah.

The chief sections of the Zohar are available in an English translation by H. Sperling, M. Simon, and P. Levertoff, 5 vols. (1931-34). See also K. Stenring, *The Book of Formation* (1923).—*T.P.S.*

Caitanya: (Skr.) Consciousness, "superconsciousness," a quality near the in-it-self aspect of the Absolute Spirit, and hence sometimes a synonym for it.—*K.F.L.*

Calculus: The name *calculus* may be applied to any organized method of solving problems or drawing inferences by manipulation of symbols according to formal rules. Or an exact definition of a *calculus* may be provided by identifying it with a *logistic system* (*q.v.*) satisfying the requirement of effectiveness.

In mathematics, the word *calculus* has many specific applications, all conforming more or less closely to the above statement. Sometimes, however, the simple phrase "the calculus" is used in referring to those branches of mathematical *analysis* (*q.v.*) which are known more explicitly as the *differential calculus* and the *integral calculus.*—*A.C.*

Calkins, Mary Whiton: (1863-1930) Professor of Philosophy at Wellesley College with which institution she was associated from 1891. She advanced an objective idealism of the Roycean character, styling her views as absolutistic personalism. She endeavored to find psychological justification for her views in the gestalt theory. Her works were in both fields of her interest: *An Introduction to Psychology, The Persistent Problems of Philosophy, The Good Man and the Good,* among others.—*L.E.D.*

Calvinism: A term covering the current of theological thought dating back to John Calvin (1509-1564) whose famous *Institutes* embodies its historic principles. Generally speaking, Calvinistic thought is a system in which God is made the center of all that is and happens, God's will pervading human and cosmic events, and upon whom man is utterly and cheerfully dependent.—*V.F.*

Cambridge Platonists: A small group of 17th century Cambridge thinkers whose views represented a kind of revival of Platonism. Esp. Ralph Cudworth and Henry More. Remembered chiefly, perhaps, for holding that ethics rests on certain absolute and self-evident truths.—*W.K.F.*

Newton was influenced by Henry More, e.g. in viewing space as the sensorium of God. See *Cudworth, Deism*. Cf. M. H. Nicolson, *Conway Papers*.

Cambridge School: A term loosely applied to English philosophers who have been influenced by the teachings of Professor G. E. Moore (mainly in unpublished lectures delivered at the Cambridge University, 1911-1939). In earlier years Moore stressed the need to accept the judgments of "common sense" on such matters as the existence of other persons, of an "external world," etc. The business of the analytical philosopher was not to criticise such judgments but to display the structure of the facts to which they referred. (Cf. "A defense of common-sense in philosophy," *Contemporary British Philosophy*, 2 (1925)—Moore's only discussion of the method.) Such analysis would be directional, terminating in basic or atomic facts, all of whose constituents might be known by acquaintance. The examples discussed were taken largely from the field of epistemology, turning often about the problem of the relation of material objects to sense-data, and of indirect to direct knowledge. In this earlier period problems were often suggested by Russell's discussion of descriptions and logical constructions. The inconclusiveness of such specific discussions and an increasingly critical awareness of the functions of language in philosophical analysis has in later years tended to favor more flexible interpretations of the nature of analysis. (Cf. M. Black, "Relations Between Logical Positivism and the Cambridge School of Analysis," *Journal of Unified Science* (*Erkenntnis*), 8, 24-35 for a bibliography and list of philosophers who have been most influenced by emphasis on directional analysis).—*M.B.*

Campanella, Tommaso: (1568-1639) A Dominican monk in revolt against Aristotelianism, and influenced by the naturalism of Telesio, he arrived at philosophic conclusions in some ways prophetic of Descartes. Distrusting both the reports of the senses and the results of reasoning as indications of the nature of Reality, he found nothing trustworthy except the fact of his own existence, and the inferences drawn from that fact. As certain as his awareness of his own existence was the awareness of an external world to which experience referred and by which it was caused. Again, since the nature of the part is representative of the nature of the whole to which it belongs, the Universe of which the self is part must, like the part, be possessed of knowledge, will, and power. Hence I may infer from my own existence the existence of a God. Again, I must infer other of the divine nature more or less perfect manifesta-

tions than myself descending from the hierarchy of angels above man to the form or structure of the world, the ultimate corporeal elements, and the sensible phenomena produced by these elements of the physical universe, below him in the scale of perfection.

All nature is suffused with a love of God and a desire to return to him, witnessed by the laws of motion governing inanimate bodies, the law of self-preservation in organic life, and by man's conscious search for the divine.

Campanella was a political philosopher. In his *City of the Sun* he conceived a Utopia built on Platonic lines. He was also an ardent champion of the temporal power of the Papacy and of its political as well as its religious sovereignty through the world.—*B.A.G.F.*

Camus, Albert: (1913-1960) Although not a philosopher in the technical sense, Camus was a highly influential French literary leader who popularized the existential mood through vivid images in such major works as *The Stranger* (1946), *The Plague* (*c.* 1947) and *The Myth of Sisyphus* (*c.* 1955).—*S.E.N.*

Canon: (Gr. *kanon,* rule) A term reminiscent of the arts and crafts, sometimes applied, since Epicurus who replaced the ancient dialectics by a canonics (*kanonike*), to any norm or rule which the logical process obeys. Thus John Stuart Mill speaks of five experimental methods as being regulated by certain canons. Kant defined canon as the sum total of all principles a priori of the correct use of our powers of knowledge. See *Baconian method, Mill's methods.*—*K.F.L.*

Cantor, Georg (Ferdinand Ludwig Philipp) 1845-1918 (Russian born) German mathematician. Professor of Mathematics at Halle, 1872-1913. He is known for contributions to the foundations of (mathematical) analysis, and as the founder of the theory of transfinite *cardinal numbers* (*q.v.*) and *ordinal numbers* (*q.v.*) See *Infinite.*–*A.C.*

Gesammelte Abhandlungen Mathematischen und Philosophischen Inhalts, edited by E. Zermelo, and with a life by A. Fraenkel, Berlin, 1932.

Capacity: Any ability, potentiality, power or talent possessed by anything, either to act or to suffer. It may be innate or acquired, dormant or active. The topic of capacity figures, in the main, in two branches of philosophy: (a) in metaphysics, as in Aristotle's discussion of potentiality and actuality, (b) in ethics, where an agent's capacities are usually regarded as having some bearing on the question as to what his duties are.—*W.K.F.*

Capitalism: A mode of economic production which is characterized by the fact that the instruments of production (land, factories, raw materials, etc.) are controlled to a greater or lesser extent by "private" individuals or groups. Since the control an individual can exercise over means of production is never absolute and as a matter of fact fluctuates widely with the ever-changing natural and social environment, "capitalism" is a very loose term which covers a host of actually different economic systems. An implication of this basic notion of individual control is that the individual will control production in his own interests. The ideological counterpart to this fact is the concept of "profit," just as the ideological counterpart to the control itself is the myth of "private property" and "free enterprise."—*M.B.M.*

Capitalists: The economic class (*q.v.*) which owns means of production and hires people at wages to work them, thereby realizing profits.—*J.M.S.*

Cardinal number: Two classes are *equivalent* if there exists a one-to-one correspondence between them (see *One-one*). *Cardinal numbers* are obtained by *abstraction* (*q.v.*) with respect to equivalence, so that two classes have the same cardinal number if and only if they are equivalent. This may be formulated more exactly, following Frege, by defining the cardinal number of a class to be the class of classes equivalent to it.

If two classes *a* and *b* have no members in common, the cardinal number of the logical sum of *a* and *b* is uniquely determined by the cardinal numbers of *a* and *b*, and is called the *sum* of the cardinal number of *a* and the cardinal number of *b*.

0 is the cardinal number of the null class. 1 is the cardinal number of a unit class (all unit classes have the same cardinal number).

A cardinal number is *inductive* if it is a member of *every* class *t* of cardinal numbers which has the two properties, (1) $0 \epsilon t$, and (2) for all *x*, if $x \epsilon t$ and *y* is the sum of *x* and 1, then $y \epsilon t$. In other (less exact) words, the inductive cardinal numbers are those which can be reached from 0 by successive additions of 1. A class *b* is *infinite* if there is a class *a*, different from *b*, such that *a* $\subset b$ and *a* is equivalent to *b*. In the contrary case *b* is *finite*. The cardinal number of an infinite class is said to be infinite, and of a finite class, finite. It can be proved that every inductive cardinal number is finite, and, with the aid of the axiom of choice, that every finite cardinal number is inductive.

The most important infinite cardinal number is the cardinal number of the class of inductive cardinal numbers (0, 1, 2, . . .); it is called aleph-zero and symbolized by a Hebrew letter aleph followed by an inferior 0.

For brevity and simplicity in the preceding account we have ignored complications introduced by the theory of types, which are considerable and troublesome. Modifications are also required if the account is to be incorporated into the Zermelo set theory.—*A.C.*

G. Cantor, *Contributions to the Founding of the Theory of Transfinite Numbers,* translated and with an introduction by P.E.B. Jourdain, Chicago and London, 1915. Whitehead and Russell, *Principia Mathematica,* vol. 2.

Cardinal Point and Value: Psychological terms having to do with relation of stimulus to intensity of sensation. The point at which the proportionate increase of both is in a direct relation.—*C.K.D.*

Cardinal virtues: The cardinal virtues for a given culture are those which it regards as primary, the others being regarded either as derived from them or as relatively unimportant. Thus the Greeks had four, wisdom, courage, temperance, and justice; to which the Chris-

tians added three, faith, hope, and love or charity. —*W.K.F.*

Carlyle, Thomas: (1795-1881) Vigorous Scotch historian and essayist, apostle of work. He was a deep student of the German idealists and did much to bring them before English readers. His forceful style showed marked German characteristics. He was not in any sense a systematic philosopher but his keen mind gave wide influence to the ideas he advanced in ethics, politics and economics. His whimsical *Sartor Resartus* or philosophy of clothes and his searching *Heroes and Hero-worship,* remain his most popular works along with his *French Revolution* and *Past and Present*. He was among the Victorians who displayed some measure of distrust for democracy.—*L.E.D.*

Carnap, Rudolf: (1891-1970) successively Privatdozent at the University of Vienna, Professor of Philosophy at the German University of Prague, Professor of Philosophy at the University of Chicago, one of the leading representatives of the positivism of the Vienna Circle and subsequently of Scientific Empiricism (*q.v.*); co-editor of *The Journal of Unified Science* (previously: *Erkenntnis*).

Carnap's work has been devoted especially to formal logic and its applications to problems of epistemology and the philosophy of science.

His writings in formal logic include a textbook of mathematical logic and a comprehensive monograph devoted to logical syntax, a new branch of logical research to whose development Carnap has greatly contributed.

In his logical work, he has been specially interested in the nature of mathematics and its relation to logic. He has treated these topics in a number of special articles and in a monograph. The latter also includes an introduction to the youngest field of modern logic, semantics.

Carnap's contributions to the study of epistemological and philosophical problems may be characterized as applications of the methods of logical analysis to the languages of everyday life and of science. His books contain applications to the fundamental problems of epistemology, expound the principles of physicalism (*q.v.*) which was developed by Carnap and Neurath and which offers, amongst others, a basis for a more cautious version of the ideas of older behaviorism and for the construction of one common unified language for all branches of empirical science (see *Unity of Science*). Main works: *Logische Aufbau der Welt; Abriss der Logistik; Logische Syntax der Sprache* "Testability and Meaning," *Phil. of Sci.* (1936).—*C.G.H.*

Carneades: (c. 215-125 B.C.) The most prominent head of the Middle Academy and opponent of the Stoics. His most noteworthy contribution to philosophy consisted in the doctrine of logical probabilism as a basis of scepticism.—*R.B.W.*

Cartesianism: The philosophy of the French thinker, René Descartes (Cartesius) 1596-1650. After completing his formal education at the Jesuit College at La Flèche, he spent the years 1612-1621 in travel and military service. The remainder of his life was devoted to study and writing. He died in Sweden, where he had gone in 1649 to tutor Queen Christina. His principal works are: *Discours de la méthode,* (preface to his *Géométric, Méteores, Dieptrique*) *Meditationes de prima philosophia, Principia philosophiae, Passions de l'âme, Regulae ad directionem ingenii, Le monde.* Descartes is justly regarded as one of the founders of modern epistemology. Dissatisfied with the lack of agreement among philosophers, he decided that philosophy needed a new method, that of mathematics. He began by resolving to doubt everything which could not pass the test of his criterion of truth, viz. the *clearness and distinctness of ideas.* Anything which could pass this test was to be readmitted as self-evident. From self-evident truths, he deduced other truths which logically follow from them. Three kinds of ideas were distinguished: (1) innate, by which he seems to mean little more than the mental power to think things or thoughts; (2) adventitious, which come to him from without; (3) factitious, produced within his own mind. He found most difficulty with the second type of ideas. The first reality discovered through his method is the *thinking self.* Though he might doubt nearly all else, Descartes could not reasonably doubt that he, who was thinking, existed as a *res cogitans.* This is the intuition enunciated in the famous aphorism: I think, therefore I am, *Cogito ergo sum.* This is not offered by Descartes as a compressed syllogism, but as an immediate intuition of his own thinking mind. Another reality, whose existence was obvious to Descartes, was God, the Supreme Being. Though he offered several proofs of the Divine Existence, he was convinced that he knew this also by an innate idea, and so, clearly and distinctly. But he did not find any clear ideas of an extra-mental, bodily world. He suspected its existence, but logical demonstration was needed to establish this truth. His adventitious ideas carry the vague suggestion that they are caused by bodies in an external world. By arguing that God would be a deceiver, in allowing him to think that bodies exist if they do not, he eventually convinced himself of the reality of bodies, his own and others. There are, then, three kinds of substance according to Descartes: (1) Created spirits, i.e. the finite soul-substance of each man: these are immaterial agencies capable of performing spiritual operations, loosely united with bodies, but not extended since thought is their very essence. (2) Uncreated Spirit, i.e. God, confined neither to space nor time, All-Good and All-Powerful; though his Existence can be known clearly, his Nature cannot be known adequately by men on earth; He is the God of Christianity, Creator, Providence and Final Cause of the universe. (3) Bodies, i.e. created, physical substances existing independently of human thought and having as their chief attribute, extension. Cartesian physics regards bodies as the result of the introduction of "vortices," i.e. whorls of motion, into extension. Divisibility, figurability and mobility are the notes of extension, which appears to be little more than what Descartes' Scholastic teachers called geometrical space. God is the First Cause of all motion in the physical universe, which is conceived as a mechanical system operated by its Maker. Even the bodies of animals are automata. Sensation is the critical problem in Cartesian psychology; it is viewed by Descartes as a function of the soul, but he was never able to find a satisfactory explanation of the apparent fact that the soul is moved by the body when sensation occurs. The theory of animal spirits provided Descartes with a sort of bridge between mind and matter, since these spirits are supposed to be very subtle matter, half-way, as it were, between thought and extension in their nature. However, this theory of sensation is the weakest link in the Cartesian explanation of cognition. Intellectual error is accounted for by Descartes in his theory of assent, which makes judgment an act of free will. Where the will over-reaches the intellect, judgment may be false. That the will is absolutely free in man, capable even of choosing what is presented by the intellect as the less desirable of two alternatives, is probably a vestige of Scotism retained from his college course in Scholasticism. Common-sense and moderation are the keynotes of Descartes' famous rules for the regulation of his own conduct during his nine years of methodic doubt, and this ethical attitude continued throughout his life. He believed that man is responsible ultimately to God for the courses of action that he may choose. He admitted that conflicts may occur between human passions and human reason. A virtuous life is made possible by the knowledge of what is right and the consequent control of the lower tendencies of human nature. Six primary passions are described by Descartes; wonder, love, hatred, desire, joy and sorrow. These are passive states of consciousness, partly caused by the body, acting through the animal spirits, and partly caused by the soul. Under rational control, they enable the soul to will what is good for the body. Descartes' terminology suggests that there are psychological faculties, but he insists that these powers are not really distinct from the soul itself, which is man's sole psychic agency. Descartes was a practical Catholic all his life and he tried to develop proofs of the existence of God, an explanation of the Eucharist, of the nature of religious faith, and of the operation of Divine Providence, using his philosophy as the basis for a new theology. This attempted theology has not found favor with Catholic theologians in general.

Apart from philosophy, Descartes' contribution to the development of analytical geometry, the theory of music and the science of optics, are noteworthy achievements.

Descartes is one of the fathers of modern philosophy; his general influence is too extensive to be detailed. Leibniz, Spinoza, Malebranche, Clauberg, De La Forge, Geulincx, Placentius, Chouet, Legrand, Cornelio — these and many others spread Cartesianism throughout Europe. (See Boutroux, "Descartes and Cartesianism," *Camb. Mod. Hist.,* IV, ch. 27.) At present, German Phenomenology, French Spiritualism and Positivism, Bergsonism, and certain forms of Catholic thought represented by J. Geyser in Germany and M. Blondel in France, are offshoots of Cartesianism.

Oeuvres complètes, ed. C. Adam et P. Tannery, 13 vols. (Paris, 1896-1911). *The Philos. Works of Descartes,* transl. by Haldane and Ross, 2 vols. (Cambridge, 1911-12). Fischer, K., *Descartes and his School* (London, 1887). Gilson, E., *Le rôle de la pensée médiévale dans la formation du système cartésien* (Paris, 1930). Maritain, J., *Le songe de Descartes* (Paris, 1932). Gemelli, A. (ed.), *Cartesio (symposium)* (Milan, 1937).—*V.J.B.*

Cassirer, Ernst: (1874-1945) Has been chiefly interested in developing the position of the neo-Kantian Philosophy of the Marburg School as it relates to scientific knowledge. Looking at the history of modern philosophy as a progressive formulation of this position, he has sought to extend it by detailed analyses of contemporary scientific developments. Of note are Cassirer's investigations in mathematics, his early consideration of chemical knowledge, and his treatment of Einstein's relativity theory. Main works: *Das Erkenntnisprobleme,* 3 vols. (1906); *Substanz-u-Funktionsbegriff,* 1910 (*tr. Substance and Function*); *Philosophie der Symbolischen Forme* (1923), tr. by Manheim, *Philosophy of Symbolic Forms,* 3 vols., New Haven, 1953, 1955, 1957. *Phänom, der Erkenntnis,* 1929; *Descartes; Leibniz An Essay on Man,* New Haven, 1944.—*C.K.D.*

Casualism: The doctrine that all things and events come to be by chance. E.g., the view of the Epicureans.

Casuistic: Adjective; pertaining to casuistry and casuists, or relating to case histories, especially cases of conduct. In a depreciative sense, sophistical and misleading.—*J.J.R.*

Casuistry: Study of cases of conscience and a method of solving conflicts of obligations by applying general principles of ethics, religion, and moral theology to particular and concrete cases of human conduct. This frequently demands an extensive knowledge of natural law and equity, civil law, ecclesiastical precepts, and an exceptional skill in interpreting these various norms of conduct. It becomes necessary to determine the degree of guilt and responsibility and weigh all the circumstances of the case, especially by taking into account all the conditions affecting motive and consent.—*J.J.R.*

Catechetic: Noun ordinarily employed in the plural, denoting the method and practice of imparting religious instruction orally by means of questions and answers, especially to children.—*J.J.R.*

Categorematic: In traditional logic, denoting or capable of denoting a term, or of standing for a subject or predicate—said of words. Opposite of *syncategorematic* (*q.v.*).—*A.C.*

Categorial: *A priori* or non-empirical elements. (Alexander).—*H.H.*

(Ger. *kategorial*) In Husserl: Of or pertaining to the function or the result of ego-spontaneity as conferring logical form on substrates and producing syntactical objects.—*D.C.*

Categorical Imperative: (Kant. Ger. kategorischer Imperativ) The supreme, absolute moral law of rational, self-determining beings. Distinguished from hypothetical or conditional imperatives which admit of exceptions. Kant formulated the categorical imperative as follows: "Act on maxims which can at the same time have for their object themselves as universal laws of nature." See *Kantianism.*—*O.F.K.*

Categorical (Judgment): (Gr. kategorikos, affirmative, predicative) *Aristotle:* Affirmative; explicit; direct. Commentators on Aristotle emphasized the opposition between *categorical* and *conditional* propositions, although Aristotle did not stress this connotation of the term.—*G.R.M.*

(In Kant) A judgment comprising two concepts related by a copula, typically an attribute (predicate) asserted of a substance or thing (subject). Kant denied that hypothetical and disjunctive propositions can be reduced to categorical ones and insisted that each of the forms of judgment denotes a distinct function of the understanding. See *Logik,* § 24.—*O.F.K.*

Category: (Gr. *kategoria*) In Aristotle's logic (1) the predicate of a proposition; (2) one of the ultimate modes of being that may be asserted in predication, viz.: substance, quantity, quality, relation, place, time, position, state, action, passion.—*G.R.M.*

(In Kant) Any of twelve forms or relating principles of the understanding, constituting necessary conditions of experience. Kant sought to derive an exhaustive list of pure forms of the understanding from the forms of judgment in the traditional logic. His list of categories comprises three each of quantity, quality, relation, and modality. See *Kantianism.*—*O.F.K.*

Category of Unity: *Kant:* The first of three *a priori,* quantitative (so-called "mathematical") categories (the others being "plurality" and "totality") from which is derived the synthetic principle, "All intuitions (appearances) are extensive magnitudes." By means of this principle Kant seeks to define the object of experience *a priori* with reference to its spatial features. See *Crit. of Pure Reason,* B106, B202ff.—*O.F.K.*

Catharsis: (Gr. *katharsis*) Purification; purgation; specifically the purging of the emotions of pity and fear effected by tragedy (Aristotle).—*G.R.M.*

In aesthetics: Purification of and liberation from passions in art (Aristotle). First idea of the distinction between form and sentiments.—*L.V.*

Catvāri ārya-satyāni: (Skr.) "The four noble truths" of Gautama Buddha's (*q.v.*) teaching: Suffering exists; it has a cause; it may cease; there is a path leading to its cessation.—*K.F.L.*

Causa sui: Cause of itself; necessary existence. Causa sui conveys both a negative and a positive meaning. Negatively, it signifies that which is from itself (*a se*), that which does not owe its being to something else; i.e., absolute independence of being, causelessness (God as uncaused). Positively, cause sui means that whose very nature or essence involves existence; i.e., God is the ground of his own being, and regarded as "cause" of his own being, he is, as it were, efficient cause of his own existence (Descartes). Since existence necessarily follows from the very essence of that which is cause of itself, causa sui is defined as that whose nature cannot be conceived as not existing (Spinoza). —*A.G.A.B.*

Causality: (Lat. *causa*) The relationship between a cause and its effect. This relationship has been defined as (1) a relation between events, processes, or entities in the same time series, such that (a) when one occurs, the other necessarily follows (sufficient condition), (b) when the latter occurs, the former must have preceded (necessary condition), (c) both conditions a and b prevail (necessary and sufficient condition), (d) when one occurs under certain conditions, the other necessarily follows (contributory, but not sufficient, condition) (''multiple causality'' would be a case involving several causes which are severally contributory and jointly sufficient); the necessity in these cases is neither that of logical implication nor that of coercion; (2) a relation between events, processes, or entities in the same time series such that when one occurs the other invariably follows (invariable antecedence); (3) a relation between events, processes, or entities such that one has the efficacy to produce or alter the other; (4) a relation between events, processes, or entities such that without one the other could not occur, as in the relation between (a) the material out of which a product is made and the finished product (material cause), (b) structure or form and the individual embodying it (formal cause), (c) a goal or purpose (whether supposed to exist in the future as a special kind of entity, outside a time series, or merely as an idea of the purposer) and the work fulfilling it (final cause), (d) a moving force and the process or result of its action (efficient cause); (5) a relation between experienced events, processes, or entities and extra-experiential but either temporal or non-temporal events, processes, or entities upon whose existence the former depend; (6) a relation between a thing and itself when it is dependent upon nothing else for its existence (self-causality); (7) a relation between an event, process, or entity and the reason or explanation for its being; (8) a relation between an idea and an experience whose expectation the idea arouses because of customary association of the two in this sequence; (9) a principle or category introducing into experience one of the aforesaid types of order; this principle may be inherent in the mind, invented by the mind, or derived from experience; it may be an explanatory hypothesis, a postulate, a convenient fiction, or a necessary form of thought. Causality has been conceived to prevail between processes, parts of a continuous process, changing parts of an unchanging whole, objects, events, ideas, or something of one of these types and something of another. When an entity, event, or process is said to *follow* from another, it may be meant that it must succeed but can be neither contemporaneous with nor prior to the other, that it must either succeed or be contemporaneous with and dependent upon but cannot precede the other, or that one is dependent upon the other but they either are not in the same time series or one is in no time series at all.—*M.T.K.*

Cause: (Lat. *causa*) Anything responsible for change, motion or action. In the history of philosophy numerous interpretations were given to the term. Aristotle distinguished among (1) the material cause, or that out of which something arises; (2) the formal cause, that is, the pattern or essence determining the creation of a thing; (3) the efficient cause, or the force or agent producing an effect; and (4) the final cause, or purpose. Many thinkers spoke also of (5) the first cause, usually conceived as God. During the Renaissance, with the development of scientific interest in nature, cause was usually conceived as an object. Today, it is generally interpreted as energy or action, whether or not connected with matter. According to Newton, ''to the same natural effects we must, as far as possible, assign the same causes.'' But J.S. Mill contended, in his doctrine of the plurality of causes, that an effect, or a kind of effect (e.g. heat or death) may be produced by various causes. The first clear formulation of the principle was given by Leukippus: ''Nothing happens without a ground but everything through a cause and of necessity.''—*R.B.W.*

In scholasticism: Four causes are distinguished, in accordance with Aristotle. Efficient cause, by which any change is brought about in the order of execution, material cause, that out of which a new being arises—prime matter in regard to substantial second matter in regard to accidental forms (Cf. Form, Matter)—formal cause, the act by which a material substratum is determined towards a new being—substantial or accidental—final cause, that because of which something is or becomes. All things tend towards an end by a ''natural appetite.''—*R.A.*

Cause-theory (of mind, body): The influence of mind upon body or body upon mind or both upon each other. This influence may be of any type, e.g., productive, directive, or a stimulus to activity.—*V.F.*

Centre-theory: Ascribes the unity of the mind to a certain particular existent centre, ''which stands in a common asymmetrical relation to all the mental events'' of a certain mind. (Broad).—*H.H.*

Certainty: (Lat. *Certus,* sure) The alleged indubitability of certain truths, especially of logic and mathematics.—*L.W.*

Certitude: Consists in the firmness, by which the mind adheres to any proposition, whereas *evidence,* besides the firmness of adhesion, implies also the quietude (or satisfaction) of the intellect in the thing known either because from a comparison of the terms we immediately know the relation between a subject and predicate, or because, immediately, with the help of deduction we perceive an adequate reason for a thing. Hence for certitude to exist in the mind, it is sufficient that the cause from which it arises be of such a nature as to exclude all fear of the opposite; whereas for evidence, it is required that the intellect fully grasp that which it knows.—*H.G.*

Chance: (Lat. *cadere,* to fall) 1. Property of being undetermined. 2. Property of being predictable according to the laws of probability. (*q.v.*).—*A.C.B.*

Chance events, according to Aristotle, are occurrences purposive in appearance but not actually the result of either conscious or unconscious teleology.—*G.R.M.*

In Cournot, following Aristotle, the co-incidence of two causally determined series of events. In Peirce (*q.v.*), a *vera causa* and metaphysically grounded category. See *Tychism.*

Chang Hêng-ch'ü: (Chang Tsai, Chang Tzŭ-hou, 1021-1077) Was a typical Confucian government official and teacher. When young, he was interested in military strategy. He studied the *Chung Yung* (Golden Mean) at the advice of a prominent scholar, and went on to Taoist and Buddhist works. But he finally returned to the Confucian classics, explored their meanings and discussed them with the Ch'êng brothers. His works called *Chang Hêng-ch'ü Hsien-shêng Ch'üan-chi* (complete works of Master Chang Hêng-ch'ü) are indispensable to the study of the Neo-Confucian (li hsüeh) movement.—*W.T.C.*

Ch'ang: (a) "Invariables" or universal and eternal laws or principles running through the phenomenal change of the universe. (Lao Tzu).

(b) Constant virtues. See *wu ch'ang.*—*H.H.*

Ch'ang Sheng: (a) Everlasting existence, such as that of Heaven and Earth, because of their "not existing for themselves." (Lao Tzu).

(b) Long life, as a result of the nourishment of the soul and rich accumulation of virtue. (Taoist philosophy).

(c) Immortality, to be achieved through internal alchemy and external alchemy (lien tan). (Taoist religion).—*W.T.C.*

Change, Philosophy of: (a) Any philosophical doctrine dealing with the subject of change, e.g., Aristotle's philosophy of change, (b) any philosophy which makes change an essential or pervasive character of reality, e.g., the philosophies of Heraclitus and Bergson.—*W.K.F.*

Ch'an wei: Prognostics in 300 B.C.-400 A.D., a system represented by a group of prophetic writings called ch'an and a group of apocryphal "complements" or "woofs" to the Confucian classics, called wei, in an attempt to interpret the classics in terms of medieval Chinese theology, the theory of correspondence between man and the universe, and the Yin Yang philosophy. (Tung Chung-shu, 177-104 B.C., etc.).—*W.T.C.*

Chaos: (Gr. chaos) The formless, confused, completely disorderly, absolutely lawless.—*H.H.*

Character: (Gr. *character* from *charassein* to engrave) A name for the collective traits, emotional, intellectual and volitional, which constitute an individual mind.—*L.W.*

Characteristic: Pertaining to the starting point of the artist in his quest for beauty. (Goethe).—*L.V.*

Characteristica Universalis: The name given by Leibniz to his projected (but only partially realized) "universal language" for the formulation of knowledge. This language was to be ideographic, with simple characters standing for simple concepts, and combinations of them for compound ideas, so that all knowledge could be expressed in terms which all could easily learn to use and understand. It represents an adumbration of the more recent and more successful logistic treatment of mathematics and science. It is to be distinguished, however, from the "universal calculus," also projected by Leibniz, which was to be the instrument for the development and manipulation of systems *in* the universal language.—*W.K.F.*

L. Couturat, *La Logique de Leibniz* (1901).

Characterology: This name originally was used for types; thus in Aristotle and Theophrastus, and even much later, e.g. in La Bruyère. Gradually it came to signify something individual; a development paralleled by the replacement of "typical" figures on the stage by individualities. There is no agreement, even today, on the definition; confusion reigns especially because of an insufficient distinction between character, personality, and person. But all agree that character manifests itself in the behavior of a person. One can distinguish a merely descriptive approach, one of classification, and one of interpretation. The general viewpoints of interpretation influence also description and classification, since they determine what is considered "important" and lay down the rules by which to distinguish and to classify. One narrow interpretation looks at character mainly as the result of inborn properties, rooted in organic constitution; character is considered, therefore, as essentially unchangeable and predetermined. The attempts at establishing correlations between character and bodybuild (Kretschmer a.o.) are a special form of such narrow interpretation. It makes but little difference if, besides inborn properties, the influence of environmental factors is acknowledged. The rationalistic interpretation looks at character mainly as the result of convictions. These convictions are seen as purely intellectual in extreme rationalism (virtue is knowledge, Socrates), or as referring to the value-aspect of reality which is conceived as apprehended by other than merely intellectual operations. Thus, Spranger gives a classification according to the "central values" dominating a man's behavior. (Allport has devised practical methods of character study on this basis.) Since the idea a person has of values and their order may change, character is conceived as essentially mutable, even if far going changes may be infrequent. Character-education is the practical application of the principles of characterology and thus depends on the general idea an author holds in regard to human nature. Character is probably best defined as the individual's way of preferring or rejecting values. It depends on the innate capacities of value-apprehension and on the way these values are presented to the individual. Therefore the enormous influence of social factors.—*R.A.*

Characters: Statements or E-values like pleasant, true, known; all possible ego attitudes and feelings are so termed. (See *Avenarius*).—*H.H.*

Ch'êng: (a) Honesty; sincerity; absence of fault; actuality.

(b) Reverence; seriousness.

(c) Being one's true self; absolute true self; truth, in the sense of "fulfillment of the self," which "is the beginning and end of material existence," and "without which there is no material existence." "Being true to oneself (or sincerity) is the law of Heaven. To try to be true to oneself is the law of man." "Only those who are their absolute true selves in the world can fulfill their own nature," "the nature of others," "the nature of things," "help Nature in growing and sustaining," and "become equals of Heaven and Earth." (Early Confucianism, Neo-Confucianism.)

Being true to the nature of being (of man and things), which is "the character of the sage," "the basis of the five cardinal moral principles and the source of the moral life." It is "the state of tranquillity without movement." (Chou Lien-hsi, 1017-1073.) "Sincerity (ch'êng) is the way of Heaven, whereas seriousness (ching) is the essence of human affairs. Where there is seriousness, there is sincerity." "Sincerity means 'to have no depraved thought.'" (Ch'êng I-ch'uan, 1033-1107 and Ch'êng Mingtao, 1032-1086.)

"It may also be expressed as the principle of reality." (Chu Hsi, 1130-1200.)—*W.T.C.*

Cheng hsin: Setting one's own heart right or rectifying one's own heart. When one is upset by anger, disturbed by fear, blinded by love, or involved in worries and anxieties, one's mind has lost its balance. It must be rectified before personal cultivation is possible. (Confucianism).—*W.T.C.*

Ch'êng I-ch'üan: (Ch'êng-I, Ch'êng-chêng-shu, 1033-1107) Was younger brother of Ch'êng Ming-tao. He led an active life as a high government official and a prominent teacher. "There was no book which he did not read, and he studied with absolute sincerity. With the *Great Learning,* the *Analects, Works of Mencius* and the *Chung Yung* (Golden Mean) as basis, he penetrated all the six (Confucian) classics." He ranks with his brother as great Neo-Confucians.—*W.T.C.*

Cheng ming: The doctrine of the "rectification of names" which holds that names should correspond to realities, and serve as standards for social organization and personal conduct. The actual must in each case be made to correspond to the name. (Confucius; Hsün Tzu, c. 335-c. 288 B.C.)—*H.H.*

Ch'eng ming: (a) To arrive at understanding from being one's true self. This is due to one's nature, whereas to arrive at being one's true self from understanding is a matter of culture. (Confucianism).

(b) The knowledge that rises above distinctions, attainable only when the human mind completely comprehends Heaven, nature and the moral law. (Chang Hêng-Ch'ü, 1020-1077).—*W.T.C.*

Ch'êng Ming-tao: Ch'êng Hou, Ch'êng Po-tun, 1032-1086) Served as government official both in the capital and in various countries with excellent records in social and educational achievements. For decades he studied Taoism and Buddhism but finally repudiated them. Together with his brother, he developed new aspects of Confucianism and became the greatest Confucian since Mencius and a leader of Neo-Confucianism (li-hsüeh). His works and those of his brother, called *Erh Ch'êng Ch'üan-shu* (complete works of the Ch'êng brothers), number 107 *chüans,* in 14 Chinese volumes.—*W.T.C.*

Chen jen: "The true man," the supreme man, the pure man, the man of supreme inward power, not in the moral sense but in the sense of "pure gold," has limitless inward resources. One who has transcended the self and the non-self, and life and death, and has reached a state of mystical union with the universe. (Chuang Tzǔ between 399 and 295 B.C.)—*H.H.*

Chen ts'a: The true Lord who directs the operation of the universe, to whose existence there is no clue. (Chuang Tzǔ, between 399 and 295 B.C.)—*W.T.C.*

Chên yün: The True Prime Unit, by which the vital force (ch'i) is constituted. It is not mixed with, but nourished and cultivated by, the external force. (Neo-Confucianism).—*W.T.C.*

Chi: The moving power; the subtle beginning of motion; the great Scheme (or germs?) from which all things came and to which all things return (Chuang Tzǔ, d. c. 295 B.C.); a mechanical arrangement according to which heavenly and earthly bodies revolve (Taoist mechanism, especially *Lieh Tzǔ,* third century A.D.); man's pure nature (as in Chuang Tzǔ, between 399 and 295 B.C.)—*W.T.C.*

Ch'i: (a) Breath; the vital fluid.

(b) Force; spirit.

(c) The vital force, as expressed in the operation and succession of the active principle (yang) and the passive principle (yin) and the Five Agents or Elements (wu hsing). To Chou Lien-hsi (1017-1073), this material principle is identical with yin yang and the Five Elements. To Chang Hêng-ch'ü (1020-1077) it is the reality of the Ultimate Vacuity, having the two aspects of yin and yang. It is to the Ultimate Vacuity (Tai Hsü) as ice is to water. Ch'êng I-ch'uan (1033-1107) and Ch'êng Ming-tao (1032-1086) considered all that has physical form to be identical with the vital force. It is the principle of differentiation and individuation. When a thing disintegrates, the vital force is at an end, not to appear again in the creative process. A new entity is constituted of new vital force. Thus it is also the principle of novelty in creation. It is produced by Reason (li). But to the Neo-Confucians, especially Chi Hsi (1130-1200), Reason has no control over it. The two can never be separated; without it, Reason would having nothing to be embodied in.

(d) In aesthetics: Rhythmic vitality; vitalizing spirit; strength of expression or brush stroke.—*W.T.C.*

Ch'i: A material thing; whatever is within the realm of matter; corporeality; whatever has form. (Confucianism and Neo-Confucianism.)—*W.T.C.*

Chia: Specification, a method of appellation or designation. "To say 'a puppy' or 'a dog' is specification." See *chü* and *i.* (Neo-Mohism.)—*W.T.C.*

Chia: The method of hypothesis in argumentation. See *pien.*—*W.T.C.*

Chiao: (a) Teaching; a body of doctrines; a system of morality.

(b) Religion, especially used in tsung chiao, K'ung Chiao (Confucianism) and Tao Chiao (Taoism) may either mean (a) the ethical, political, and philosophical teachings of Confucius and Lao Tzŭ respectively and their followers, or (b) the state cult of the worship of Heaven and ancestors and the folk religion of nature and spirit worship, respectively.—*W.T.C.*

Ch'i chia: Ordering one's home life by the practice of such virtues as filial piety, respect for one's elder brothers, and parental kindness or love, as a necessary condition for the ordering of national life. (Confucianism.)—*W.T.C.*

Chieh hsuan: Emancipation. See *Hsüan chieh*.—*W.T.C.*

Ch'ien: Heaven, symbolized by ☰ in the Eight Trigrams (pa kua); the trigram of the male cosmic principle, yang, opposite of k'un.—*W.T.C.*

Chien ai: The doctrine of "universal love" interpreted wholly in terms of utilitarian standards. (Mo Tzŭ, between 500 and 396 B.C.)—*H.H.*

Chien pai: Solidity (of stone) and whiteness (of a horse), central problems in the dispute over the relationship of substance and quality between the Sophists (pien chê) and the Neo-Mohists (Mo chê) in the third and fourth centuries B.C.—*W.T.C.*

Chih: (a) Memory. (b) Purpose; will.—*W.T.C.*

Chih: Uprightness; straightness; honesty; justice; "exhausting one's sincere heart without any artificiality."—*W.T.C.*

Chih: (a) Wisdom, one of the three Universally Recognized Moral qualities of man (ta tê), the Three Moral Qualities of the superior man (san tê), the Four Fundamentals of the moral life (ssŭ tuan), and the Five Constant Virtues (wu ch'ang). (Confucianism.)

(b) Knowledge; intelligence.

(c) Discriminate knowledge; small knowledge, which is incapable of understanding Tao.

(d) Intuitive knowledge (liang chih). (Wang Yang-ming, 1473-1529.)—*W.T.C.*

Chih: Marks, designation, pointing at (with a finger, chih), an obscure term in the logic of Kung-sun Lung (c. 400-c. 300 B.C.) which can be interpreted as:

(a) Marks or qualities of a thing. All things are marks or predicates.

(b) That which is designated by a name.

(c) An idea or concept which Kung-sun Lung used to designate the universal.—*W.T.C.*

Chih: Basic stuff; essence; solid quality; solid worth. (Confucianism).—*W.T.C.*

Chih chih: Extension of knowledge or achieving true knowledge through the investigation of things (ko wu) and understanding their Reason (li) to the utmost, not necessarily by investigating all things in the world, but by thoroughly investigating one thing and then more if necessary, so that the Reason in that thing, and thereby Reason in general, is understood. In Wang Yang-ming (1473-1529), it means "extension to the utmost of the mind's intuitive knowledge of good—the knowledge of good which Mencius calls the good-evil mind and which all people have." (Neo-Confucianism).—*W.T.C.*

Chih jen: "The perfect man," one who has reached a state of mystical union with the universe, or "one who has not separated from the true." (Chuang Tzŭ between 399 and 295 B.C.)—*H.H.*

Chih kuo: The ordering of the national life, which is the intermediate step between the ordering of one's family life (ch'i chia) and the peace of the world. (Confucianism.)—*W.T.C.*

Chih shan: Highest excellence; perfection; the ultimate good, the goal of Confucian ethics and education.—*W.T.C.*

Ch'i hsueh: The intellectual movement in the state of Ch'i in the third and fourth centuries B.C. where scholars (including Shên Tao, Tsou Yen) gathered under official patronage to write on and to freely discuss philosophy and politics. Seat of learning and freedom of thought at the time.—*W.T.C.*

Chiliasm: Teaching and belief of some Jews and Christians that the Messiah will appear at the end of time to found a glorious kingdom on earth which is to last one thousand years; also called Millenarianism.—*J.J.R.*

Chin: Metal, one of the Five Agents or Elements. See *wu hsing*.—*W.T.C.*

Ch'in: (a) Personal experience, or knowledge obtained through the contact of one's knowing faculty and the object to be known. (Neo-Mohists.)

(b) Parents.

(c) Kinship, as distinguished from the more remote relatives and strangers, such distinction being upheld by Confucians as essential to the social structure but severely attacked by the Mohists and Legalists as untenable in the face of the equality of men.

(d) Affection, love, which it is important for a ruler to have toward his people and for children toward parents. (Confucianism.)—*W.T.C.*

Chinese Philosophy: Confucianism and Taoism have been the dual basis of Chinese thought, with Buddhism presenting a strong challenge in medieval times. The former two, the priority of either of which is still controversial, rivaled each other from the very beginning to the present day. Taoism (tao chia) opposed nature to man, glorifying Tao or the Way, spontaneity (tzŭ jan), "inaction" (wu wei) in the sense of non-artificiality or following nature, simplicity (p'u), "emptiness," tranquillity and enlightenment, all dedicated to the search for "long life and lasting vision" (in the case of Lao Tzŭ, 570 B.C.?), for "preserving life and keeping the essence of our being intact" (in the case of Yang Chu, c. 440-360 B.C.), and for "companionship with nature" (in the case of Chuang Tzŭ, between 399 and 295 B.C.). The notes of the "equality of things and opinions" (ch'i wu) and the "spontaneous and unceasing transformation of things" (tzŭ hua) were particularly stressed in Chuang Tzŭ.

Confucianism (ju chia), on the other hand, advocated true manhood (jên) as the highest good, the superior man (chün tzŭ) as the ideal being, and cultivation of life (hsiu shen) as the supreme duty of man. It was toward this moralism and humanism that Confucius (551-479 B.C.) taught the doctrines of "chung," or being true to the principles of one's nature, and "shu," or the application of those principles in relation to others, as well as the doctrine of the Golden Mean (chung yung), i.e., "to find the central clue of our moral being and to be harmonious with the universe." Humanism was further strengthened by Mencius (371-289 B.C.) who insisted that man *must* develop his nature fully because benevolence (jên) and righteousness (i) are natural to his nature which is originally good, and again reinforced by Hsün Tzŭ. (c. 335-286 B.C.) who, contending that human nature is evil, advocated the control of nature. Amid this antagonism between naturalism and humanism, however, both schools conceived reality as unceasing change (i) and incessant transformation, perpetually in progress due to the interaction of the active (yang) and passive (yin) cosmic principles.

Taoism, however, became too mystical, and Confucianism too formalistic. "Hundred schools" grew and flourished, many in direct opposition to Taoism and Confucianism. There was Mohism (Mo, founded by Mo Tzŭ, between 500 and 396 B.C.) which rejected formalism in favor of "benefit" and "utility" which are to be promoted through universal love (chien ai), practical observation and application, and obedience to the will of Heaven. There was Neo-Mohism (Mo chê, 300 B.C.) which, in trying to prove the thesis of Mohism, developed an intricate system of logic. There was Sophism (ming chia, 400 B.C.) which displayed much sophistry about terms and concepts, particularly about the relationship between substance and quality (chien pai). There was Legalism (fa chia, 500-200 B.C.) which advocated law, statecraft, and authority as effective instruments of government. And finally, there was the Yin Yang school (400-200 B.C.) which emphasized yin and yang as the two fundamental principles, always contrasting but complementary, and underlying all conceivable objects, qualities, situations, and relationships. It was this school that provided a common ground for the fusion of ancient divergent philosophical tendencies in medieval China.

Medieval Chinese philosophy was essentially a story of the synthesis of indigenous philosophies and the development of Buddhism. In the second century B.C., the Yin Yang movement identified itself with the common and powerful movement under the names of the Yellow Emperor and Lao Tzŭ (Huang Lao). This, in turn, became interfused with Confucianism and produced the mixture which was the Eclectic Sinisticism lasting till the tenth century A.D. In both Huai-nan Tzŭ (d. 122 B.C.), the semi-Taoist, and Tung Chung-shu (177-104 B.C.), the Confucian, Taoist metaphysics and Confucian ethics mingled with each other, with yin and yang as the connecting links. As the cosmic order results from the harmony of yin and yang in nature, namely, Heaven and Earth, so the moral order results from the harmony of yang and yin in man, such as husband and wife, human nature and passions, and love and hate. The Five Agents (wu hsing), through which the yin yang principles operate, have direct correspondence not only with the five directions, the five metals,

etc., in nature, but also with the five Constant Virtues, the five senses, etc., in man, thus binding nature and man in a neat macrocosm-microcosm relationship. Ultimately this led to superstition, which Wang Ch'ung (c. 27-100 A.D.) vigorously attacked. He reinstated naturalism on a rational ground by accepting only reason and experience, and thus promoted the critical spirit to such an extent that it gave rise to a strong movement of textual criticism and an equally strong movement of free political thought in the few centuries after him.

In the meantime, Taoism degenerated and identified itself with the lowest forms of religious worship. Its naturalistic philosophy was carried to the point of fatalistic mechanism in *Lieh Tzŭ* (c. 300 A.D.) and was made the theoretical basis for alchemy and the search for longevity in Ko Hung (c. 268-334 A.D.). In Kuo Hsiang (c. 312 A.D.), however, the true spirit of Taoism revived. He restored and developed the Taoist doctrines of naturalism and spontaneous transformation to a position of dignity.

Parallel with these developments was the growth of Buddhism in China, a story too long to relate here. Many Buddhist doctrines, latent in India, were developed in China. The nihilism of Mādhyamika (Sun-lan, c. 450-1000 A.D.) to the effect that reality is Void in the sense of being "devoid" of any specific character, was brought to fullness, while the idealism of Vijñaptimātravada (Yogācāra, Fahsiang, c. 563-1000 A.D.), which claimed that reality in its imaginary, dependent and absolute aspects is "representation-only," was pushed to the extreme. But these philosophies failed because their extreme positions were not consonant with the Chinese ideal of the golden mean. In the meantime, China developed her own Buddhist philosophy consistent with her general philosophical outlook. We need only mention the Hua-yen school (Avatamisaka, 508) which offered a totalistic philosophy of "all in one" and "one in all," the T'ien-t'ai school (c. 550) which believes in the identity of the Void, Transitoriness, and the Mean, and in the "immanence of 3,000 worlds in one moment of thought," and the Chin-t'u school (Pure Land, c. 500) which bases its doctrine of salvation by faith and salvation for all on the philosophy of the universality of Buddha-nature. These schools have persisted because they accepted both noumenon and phenomenon, both *ens* and non-*ens*, and this "both-and" spirit is predominantly characteristic of Chinese philosophy.

The most strange development was Ch'an (Meditation, Zen, c. 500). It is basically a method of "direct intuition into the heart to find Buddha-nature," a method based, on the one hand, on the eightfold negation of production and extinction, annihilation and permanence, unity and diversity, and coming and departing, and, on the other hand, on the affirmation of the reality of the Buddha-nature in all things. Its sole reliance on meditation was most un-Chinese, but it imposed on the Chinese mind a severe mental and spiritual discipline which was invigorating as well as fascinating. For this reason, it exerted tremendous influence not only on Taoism which had much in common with it and imitated it in every way, but also on Neo-Confucianism, which stood in diametrical opposition to it.

Neo-Confucianism developed in three phases, namely the Reason school in the Sung period (960-1279), the Mind school in the Ming period (1388-1644) and the Moral-Law school in the Ch-ing period (1644-1911). The central idea of the movement is focused on the Great Ultimate (T'ai Chi) and Reason (li). The Great Ultimate moves and generates the active principle, yang, when its activity reaches its limit, and engenders the passive principle, yin, when it becomes tranquil. The eternal oscillation of yin and yang gives rise to the material universe through their Five Agents of Water, Fire, Wood, Metal and Earth. Thus, reality is a progressively evolved and a well-coordinated system.

This dynamic and orderly character of the universe is due to Reason and the vital force. As the Ch'êng brothers (I-ch'uan, 1033-1077, and Min-tao, 1032-1086) said, "All things have the same Reason in them." Thus, Reason combines the Many into One, while the vital force differentiates the One into the Many, each with its own "determinate nature." The two principles, however, are not to be sharply contrasted, for neither is independent of the other. Reason operates through, and is embodied in, the vital force. It is this cooperative functioning of theirs that makes the universe a cosmos, a harmonious system of order and sequence. "Centrality is the order of the universe and harmony is its unalterable law." As such the cosmos is a moral order. This is the main reason why the greatest of the Neo-Confucians, Chu Hsi (1130-1200) said that "the Great Ultimate is nothing but the Reason of ultimate goodness."

Furthermore, the universe is a social order, and nothing can stand by itself. At the same time, everything has its opposite. "No two of the productions of creation are alike," and the Taoist doctrine of the equality of things must be rejected. In the eternal sequence of appearance and disappearance every creation is new, and the Buddhist doctrine of transmigration must be rejected.

In order to appreciate fully the meaning of the universe, man must comprehend Reason. This can be done by "investigating things to the utmost" (ko wu), that is, by "investigating the Reason of things to the utmost (ch'iung li)." When sufficient effort is made, and understanding naturally comes, one's nature will be realized and his destiny will be fulfilled, since "the exhaustive investigation of Reason, the full realization of one's nature, and the fulfillment of destiny are simultaneous." When one understands Reason, he will find that "All people are brothers and sisters, and all things are my companions," because all men have the same Reason in them. Consequently one should not entertain any distinction between things and the ego. This is the foundation of the Neo-Confucian ethics of jên, true manhood, benevolence or love. Both the understanding

of Reason and the practice of jên require sincerity (ch'êng) and seriousness (ching) which to the Neo-Confucians almost assumed religious significance. As a matter of fact these have a certain correspondence with the Buddhist dhyāna and prajña or meditation and insight. Gradually the Neo-Confucian movement became an inward movement, the mind assuming more and more importance.

When it came to the Ming period especially in Wang Yang-ming (1473-1529), Reason became identified with Mind. Mencius' doctrine of intuitive knowledge (liang chih) was revived and made the basis of his theory of the identity of knowledge and conduct and the sacred duty of man to "fully exercise his mind" and to "manifest his illustrious virtues."

Wang Yang-ming considered desire as an obstacle to the mind. The Neo-Confucians of the Ch'ing period, especially Tai Tung-yüan (1723-1777), however, argued that since desire is part of our nature, it has its rightful place, just as the vital force has its rightful place beside Reason. The main problem then would be to attain the harmony of human passion (ch'ing) and the originally good human nature (hsing). Thus Neo-Confucianism reasserted the principle of central harmony (chung yung), and central harmony is the Moral Law (tao). This Law finds expression in constant and orderly transformation, the realization of which is Reason.

It will be seen that Neo-Confucianism is essentially compatible with western philosophy and science. It is to be expected, therefore, that both Neo-Confucianism and western thought will play a great role in any future philosophy in China.—*W.T.C.*

References: Alfred Forke, *Geschichte der neueren chinesischen Philosophie*, De Gruyter & Co., Hamburg, 1938; Fung Yu-lan, *A History of Chinese Philosophy* (ancient period), tr. by D. Bodde, Henri Vetch, Peiping, 1937; Hu Shih, *The Development of the Logical Method in Ancient China*, The Oriental Book Co., Shanghai, 1922.

Ching: (a) The classics, whether Confucian or Taoist. Formerly spelled *king*.

(b) Cardinal standards or directions in Confucian ethics and government.—*W.T.C.*

Ching: (a) Reverence. (Ancient Confucianism.)

(b) Seriousness, the inner state of respect or politeness (kung). With respect to daily affairs, it is expressed in care, vigilance, attention, etc., and with respect to the laws of the universe, it is expressed in sincerity (ch'êng), especially toward the Reason (li) of things. "Seriousness is the basis of moral cultivation, the essence of human affairs, just as sincerity is the way of Heaven." It is "to straighten one's internal life and righteousness (i) is to square one's external life." It means "unity of mind and absolute equanimity and absolute steadfastness." (Neo-Confucianism.) —*W.T.C.*

Ching: (a) Essence. "Essence and vital force (ch'i) constitute things."

(b) Purity; the pure nature.

(c) Spirit; intelligence.

(d) Concentration; unity of thought.—*W.T.C.*

Ching: (a) Tranquillity; rest; passivity; inactivity; "the constant feature of the passive principle." See *tung*. (Confucianism.)

(b) Quietude; quiescence; interpreted by the Taoist as absence of desire and unity of thought, by Confucians in general as the original state of human nature, and by Hsün Tzŭ (c. 335-288 B.C.) as the mind not being disturbed by such things as dreams.—*W.T.C.*

Ch'ing: Passions; feelings, emotions, interpreted as:

(a) Human nature (which is originally tranquil) when moved and awakened and expressed in the seven feelings (joy, anger, sorrow, fear, love, hatred, and desire), like and dislike, and the sense of advantage and disadvantage.

(b) The impure side of man, born of the passive (yin) vital force (ch'i) as contrasted with the pure, the nature (hsing) born of the active (yang) vital force and expressed in the Five Constant Virtues (wu ch'ang).

(c) Human nature, or feelings original in or proper to man.—*W.T.C.*

Ch'ing (dynasty) philosophy: See *li hsüeh* and *Chinese philosophy.*—*W.T.C.*

Ching shen: The spirit and soul of man, or "the vital force (ch'i) and the keeper of life of man," which is endowed by Heaven as against the physical form which is endowed by Earth. (Huai-nan Tzŭ, d. 122 B.C.)—*W.T.C.*

Chin hsin: Exerting one's mind to the utmost; complete development of one's mental constitution, by which one knows his nature and thereby Heaven. (Mencius, Wang Yang-ming, 1473-1529, and Tai Tung-yüan, 1723-1777.)—*W.T.C.*

Chin tan: Medicine of immortality. (Taoist alchemy, especially Pao-p'o Tzŭ, c. 268-334 A.D.) See *Wai tan.*—*W.T.C.*

Chiu: Duration, or "what reaches to different times," or "what unites past and present, morning and evening." (Neo-Mohism.)—*W.T.C.*

Chiu ch'ou: The Nine Categories of the Grand Norm (hung fan) of ancient Confucian philosophy, consisting of the Five Elements (wu hsing), the reverent practice of the five functions (of personal appearance, speech, vision, hearing, and thought), the intensive application of the eight governmental measures, the harmonious use of the five regulations of time, the establishment of the royal standard, the orderly practice of the three virtues, the intelligent practice of divination; the thoughtful following of various indications, and the rewarding with five kinds of good and punishment with six forms of evil.—*W.T.C.*

Ch'iung li: Investigation of Reason of things to the utmost. A thing is considered by the Neo-Confucianists to be an event. A perfect understanding of an event can be obtained by investigating to the utmost the Reason underlying it. This does not require the investigation of the Reason of all things. When the Reason in one thing is extensively investigated, the Reason in other things can be understood. (Neo-Confucianism.)—*W.T.C.*

Ch'i wu: The equality of things and opinions; the identity of contraries. "Viewed from the standpoint of Tao, a beam and a pillar are identical. So are ugliness and beauty, greatness, wickedness, perverseness, and strangeness. Separation is the same as construction; construction is the same as destruction." Therefore the sages harmonize the systems of right and wrong, and rest in the equilibrium of nature (t'ien chün). "This is called following two courses at the same time." (Chuang Tzŭ, between 399 and 295 B.C.)—*W.T.C.*

Choice: (a) In ethics the term choice refers to an agent's act of volition in deciding between two or more alternatives. Sometimes it is said that we may choose only between alternative courses of action, sometimes that we may also choose between alternative ends of action. In either case it is said that choice is deliberate and knowing, as compared with preference, which may be spontaneous; and that it is one's choices which both determine and express one's moral character. Two further questions arise: (a) Are our choices free in the sense of not being determined by previous events? and (b) Are our choices simply the determinations of our strongest desires?—*W.K.F.*

See *Cause, Determinism, Will.*

Choice, axiom of, or *Zermelo's axiom,* is the name given to an assumption of logical or logico-mathematical character which may be stated as follows: *Given a class K whose members are non-empty classes, there exists a (one-valued) monadic function f whose range is K, such that f (x) ε x for all members x of K.* This had often been employed unconsciously or tacitly by mathematicians — and is apparently necessary for the proofs of certain important mathematical theorems — but was first made explicit by Zermelo in 1904, who used it in a proof that every class can be well-ordered. Once explicitly stated the assumption was attacked by many mathematicians as lacking in validity or as not of legitimately mathematical character, but was defended by others, including Zermelo.

An equivalent assumption, called by Russell the *multiplicative axiom* and afterwards adopted by Zermelo as a statement of his *Auswahlprinzip,* is as follows: *Given a class K whose members are non-empty classes no two of which have a member in common, there exists a class A* (the *Auswahlmenge*) *all of whose members are members of members of K and which has one and only one member in common with each member of K.* Proof of equivalence of the multiplicative axiom to the axiom of choice is due to Zermelo.—*A.C.*

E. Zermelo, *Beweis, dass jede Menge wohlgeordnet werden kann,* Mathematische Annalen, vol. 59 (1904), pp. 514-516. B. Russell, *On some difficulties in the theory of transfinite numbers and order types,* Proceedings of the London Mathematical Society, ser. 2, vol. 4 (1906), pp. 29-53. E. Zermelo, *Neuer Beweis für die Möglichkeit einer Wohlordnung,* Mathematische Annalen, vol. 65 (1908), pp. 107-128. K. Gödel, *The Consistency of the Axiom of Choice and of the Generalized Continuum Hypothesis with the Axioms of Set Theory,* Princeton, N. J., 1940.

Chou Tun-i: (Chou Lien-hsi, Chou Mao-shu, 1017-1073) Was active in government and was a renowned judge. He was the pioneer of Neo-Confucianism (li hsüeh), anticipating the Ch'êng brothers. He wrote the *T'ung-shu* (explanation of the *Book of Changes*) and the *T'aichi T'ushu* (explanation of the diagram of the Great Ultimate), fundamental texts of Neo-Confucian philosophy.—*W.T.C.*

Chrematistics: (Gr. *chrematistike,* the art of the use of money) A term insisted upon by Ingram (1823-1900) and others in a restricted sense to that portion of the science of political economy which relates to the management and regulation of wealth and property, one of the efforts to indicate more clearly the content of classical economics.—*H.H.*

Christology: The totality of doctrines constituting that part of theology which treats of the nature and personality of Christ. First of all Christology must concern itself with the promise of a Saviour and Redeemer of the human race. It includes the study of the prophecies foretelling the Messiah, as well as their fulfillment. Further it must inquire into the mystery of the Incarnation, of the Word made flesh, and examine all the circumstances of the birth, passion, and resurrection of Christ. Since He acknowledged that He was God, the Son of God, one with the Father, it becomes necessary to examine His credentials, His own prophecies, miracles, and saintly life, which were to serve as evidence that He was sent by God and really possessed all power in heaven and on earth. Christology must deal with the human and Divine nature, their relation to each other, and the hypostatic union of both in one Divine Person, as well as the relation of that Person to the Father and the Holy Ghost. Moreover, the authentic decisions of the Councils of the Church form an exceedingly important portion of all christological theories and doctrines, and also the interpretations of those decisions by theologians.—*J.J.R.*

Chrysippus: (280-209 B.C.) One of the leaders of the Stoic School, whose voluminous writings have been completely lost. In many respects he deviated from the Stoic speculative course; for instance, he combined the principle of natural necessity, or determinism, with the doctrine of Providence.—*R.B.W.*

Chu: Direct appellation, a method of designation. "To call out 'Puppy!' is direct appellation." See *chia* and *i.* (Neo-Mohism.)—*W.T.C.*

Ch'uan: (a) A weight; a standard; a balance.

(b) Power; authority; force.

(c) Expediency, a Confucian ethical concept which justifies deviation from cardinal standards or directions (ching) in ethics and government under certain abnormal circumstances.—*W.T.C.*

Chuang Tzu: (Chuang Chou, Chuang Chi-yüan, between 399 and 295 B.C.) The second greatest Taoist, was once a petty officer in his native state, Mêng, (in present Honan), in the revolutionary and romantic south. A little-travelled scholar, he declined a premiership in favor of freedom and peace. His love of nature, his vivid imagination and subtle logic make his works masterpieces of an exquisite style. Only the first seven and a few other chapters of *Chuang Tzŭ* (English transl. by H. Giles and by Feng Yu-lan) are authentic. —*W.T.C.*

Ch'uan hsing: Preservation of one's original nature. (Taoism.)—*W.T.C.*

Ch'uan sheng: (a) Preservation of life, by the suppression of desires. (Taoism.)

(b) Completeness of life, that is, "all desires reach a proper harmony." (Taoism.)—*W.T.C.*

Chu Hsi: (Chu Hui-an, Chu Yüan-hui, Chu Chung-hui, 1130-1200) Early distinguished himself as a patriot-scholar, having repeatedly petitioned the emperor to practice the principles of "investigation of things" and "extension of knowledge" and not to make peace with the invading enemy. But he preferred a life of peace and poverty, accepted a number of government appointments with a great deal of reluctance. His lectures at the White Deer Grotto attracted all prominent scholars of the time. The works of this leader of Neo-Confucianism (li hsüeh) include the *Chu Tzŭ Ch'üan-shu* ("Complete Works," really Selected Works, partial English transl. by J.P. Bruce: *The Philosophy of Human Nature by Chu Hsi*) of 66 Chinese *chüans* in 25 volumes and the *Yü Lei* (Sayings Arranged by Topics) of 140 *chüans* in 40 volumes.—*W.T.C.*

Chu i wu shih: Unity of mind, with absolute steadfastness or impartiality, a state of reverential seriousness (ching). (Ch'eng I-ch'uan, 1033-1107, and Ch'eng Ming-tao, 1032-1086.)—*W.T.C.*

Chung: (a) The Mean. See *Chung yung.* (Confucius.)

(b) The central self or moral being, in which "the passions such as joy, anger, grief, and pleasure have not awakened," and which exists "in a state of absolute tranquillity without being moved." See *ho.* (Early Confucianism; Neo-Confucianism.)

(c) The central or the proper principle; the Moral Law (tao); the "ultimate principle" of the universe; "the great basis of existence;" "the beginning and the end of the universe."

(d) The principle of centrality, which is observable in everything, that everything should have the proper balance of activity and tranquillity. (Tung Chung-shu, 177-104 B.C.; Ch'eng Ming-tao, 1032-1086.)

(e) Impartiality; the principle of neutrality which is present in every human heart.

(f) The inner life; the inner principle. (Lao Tzŭ.) —*W.T.C.*

Chung: (a) Being true to the principle of the self; being true to the originally good nature of the self; being one's true self; the Confucian "central thread or principle" (i kuan) with respect to the self, as reciprocity (shu) is that principle with respect to others. See *i kuan.*

(b) Exerting one's pure heart to the utmost, to the extent of "not a single thought not having been exhausted;" honesty; sincerity; devotion of soul; conscientiousness. (Confucianism).

"Honesty (chung) is complete realization of one's nature" whereas truthfulness (hsin) is "complete realization of the nature of things." "Honesty (chung) is the subjective side of truthfulness (hsin) whereas truthfulness is the objective side of honesty." (Ch'êng Mingtao, 1032-1086.)

"Honesty is exerting one's heart to the utmost whereas truthfulness is the observance of the Reason of things." (Chu Hsi, 1230-1300.)

(c) Impartiality, especially in love and profit.

(d) Loyalty, especially to one's superiors; faithfulness.—*W.T.C.*

Chung: Identity, one of the proofs of agreement. See *Mo chê.—W.T.C.*

Chung yung: (a) The Golden Mean. See *Chung* and *i kuan.*

(b) Centrality and harmony, a law "from whose operation we cannot for one instant in our existence escape;" the central clue to man's moral being which unites him to the universal order (or to attain central harmony). (Early Confucianism).

(c) The Universal and the Changeless which is the true principle of things and the eternal law of the universe. (Neo-Confucianism.)—*W.T.C.*

Chun tu: (a) The superior man, the perfect man, the moral man, the noble man. "There may have been a superior man who is not a true man (jên), but there has never been an inferior man (hsiao jên) who is a true man." The superior man "makes upward progress," "understands profit," and "despises the ordinances of Heaven, great men, and the words of the sages." (Confucius.)

"The superior man's moral order is on the increase, while the inferior man's moral order is on the decrease." "The superior man abides by what is internal, whereas the inferior man abides by what is external." (Ancient Confucianism.)

"The superior man makes advance in the moral law, whereas the inferior man makes advance in profit." "The superior man enjoys in the fulfillment of the moral law, whereas the inferior man enjoys in the fulfillment of his desires." (Medieval Confucianism.) The superior man "sees what is great and far" and is interested in "helping things to perfection," whereas the inferior man "sees what is small and near" and is interested in destroying things." (Neo-Confucianism.)

(b) A ruler.

(c) Husband (as in the *Odes*).—*W.T.C.*

Cicero: (Marcus Tullius, 106-43 B.C.) Famous for his eclectic exposition of general scientific knowledge and philosophy, by which he aimed to arouse an appreciation of Greek culture in the minds of his countrymen, the Romans.—*M.F.*

Cicero: *De Natura deorum; De officiis; Disputationes Tuscalanae; De finibus bonorum et malorum.*

Circular evidence: (Lat. *circulus in probando*) Proof or evidence involving premises which assume the conclusion which is to be established.—*O.F.K.*

Cit: (Skr.) Awareness. Cf. *sat-cit-ānanda.—K.F.L.*

Citi: (Skr.) Spirit, highest intelligence.—*K.F.L.*

Citta: (Skr.) In the philosophy of the Yogasutras (*q.v.*) the phenomenal form of mind as the first creation of *prakrti* (*q.v.*) which is differentiated into mental states (*vrttis*), such as true and false knowledge, imagination, memory, sleep. These states being of the active, need restraining (*citta-vrtti nirodha;* cf. Yoga) in order to have the true and abiding nature of self *(purusa)* come into its own.—*K.F.L.*

Claims: See *prima facie duties.*

Clarification: (Ger. *Klärung, Aufklärung*) In Husserl: Synthesis of identification, in which the noematic sense is given less clearly in an earlier than in a later intending. The course of potential clarification is predelineated horizonally for every element of sense that is either intended emptily or experienced with less than optimal clarity. The horizonal experiencings in which "the same" would be given more clearly are explicable in phantasy. Thus, the essential dimensions and the range of indeterminacy of the object (and its essential possibility or impossibility) as intended can be grasped in evidence. This is *clarification in the usual sense.* On the other hand, potential experiencings of "the same" may be made actual rather than fictively actual (phantasied) — in which case, the synthesis of clarification is a *synthesis of fulfillment.* See *Fulfillment.—D.C.*

Class: or *set,* or *aggregate* (in most connections the words are used synonymously) can best be described by saying that classes are associated with monadic propositional functions (in intension—i.e., properties) in such a way that two propositional functions determine the same class if and only if they are formally equivalent. A class thus differs from a propositional function in extension only in that it is not usual to employ the notation of application of function to argument in the case of classes (see the article *Propositional function*). Instead, if a class a is determined by a propositional function A, we say that x *is a member of a* (in symbols, $x \in a$) if and only if $A(x)$.

Whitehead and Russell, by introducing classes into their system only as incomplete symbols, "avoid the assumption that there are such things as classes." Their method (roughly) is to reinterpret a proposition about a class determined by a propositional function A as being instead an existential proposition, about *some* propositional function formally equivalent to A.

See also *Logic, formal,* §§ 7, 9.—*A.C.*

Class: (Socio-economic) Central in Marxian social theory (see *Historical materialism*) the term class signifies a group of persons having, in respect to the means of production, such a common economic relationship as brings them into conflict with other groups having a different economic relationship to these means. For example, slaves and masters, serfs and lords, proletariat and capitalists are considered pairs of classes basic respectively to ancient, medieval and modern economies. At the same time many subordinate classes or sub-classes are distinguished besides or within such primary ones. In "Revolution and Counter-Revolution" for instance, Marx applies the term class to the following groups: feudal nobility, wealthy bourgeoisie, petty bourgeoisie, small farmers, proletariat, agricultural laborers, subdividing the class of small farmers into two further "classes," peasant free-holders and feudal tenants. The conflict of interests involved has many manifestations, both economic and non-economic, all of which are considered part of the class struggle (q.v.)—*J.M.S.*

Class concept: A monadic propositional function, thought of as determining a *class* (q.v.).—*A.C.*

Class consciousness: The consciousness on the part of an individual of his membership in a given economic class (q.v.).—*J.M.S.*

Class struggle: Fundamental in Marxian social thought, this term signifies the conflict between classes (q.v.) which, according to the theory of historical materialism (see the entry, Dialectical materialism) may and usually does take place in all aspects of social life, and which has existed ever since the passing of primitive communism (q.v.). The class struggle is considered basic to the dynamics of history in the sense that a widespread change in technics, or a fuller utilization of them, which necessitates changes in economic relations and, in turn, in the social superstructure, is championed and carried through by classes which stand to gain from the change. The economic aspects of the class struggle under capitalism manifest themselves most directly, Marx held, in disputes over amount of wages, rate of profits, rate of interests, amount of rent, length of working day, conditions of work and like matters. The Marxist position is that the class struggle enters into philosophy, politics, law, morals, art, religion and other cultural institutions and fields in various ways, either directly or indirectly, and, in respect to the people involved, consciously or unconsciously, willingly or unwillingly. In any case the specific content of any such field or institution at a given time is held to have a certain effect upon a given class in its conflicts with other classes, weakening or aiding it. Marxists believe that certain kinds of literature or art may inspire people with a lively sense of the need and possibility of a radical change in social relations, or, on the contrary, with a sense of lethargy or complacency, and that various moral, religious or philosophical doctrines may operate to persuade a given class that it should accept its lot without complaint or its privileges without qualms, or may operate to persuade it of the contrary. The Marxist view is that every field or institution has a history, an evolution, and that this evolution is the result of the play of conflicting forces entering into the field, which forces are connected, in one way or another, with class conflicts. While it is thus held that the class struggle involves all cultural fields, it is not held that any cultural production or phenomenon, selected or delimited at random, can be correlated in a one-to-one fashion with an equally delimited class interest.—*J.M.S.*

Classic: A. Art of the first class (Aulus Gellius). B. Greek and Roman art in which perfect balance between body and spirit is achieved (Hegel). Contrasted with Modern and Romantic.—*L.V.*

Classicism: Taste based on the imitation of classic art.—*L.V.*

Classification: 1. Process of grouping objects into clas-

ses on the basis of the discovery of common properties; or the results of such grouping. 2. Process of grouping species into genera, genera into still larger genera, and so on to the *summum genus* (q.v.).—*A.C.B.*

Cleanthes: (c. 310-230 B.C.) Zeno's disciple and one of the most prominent thinkers of the Stoic School. Of his writings only a hymn to Zeus is extant.—*R.B.W.*

Clearness: (Ger. *Klarheit*) In Husserl: Intuitional fullness, whether perceptual, fictively perceptual, memorial, or anticipational. See *Clarification, Distinctness,* and *Intuition.*—*D.C.*

Clement of Alexandria: (150-217) An early Christian thinker and theologian who attempted to raise the attitude of faith to the level of knowledge; he was influenced by Plato, Aristotle, the Stoics, and Philo Judaeus.—*R.B.W.*

Co-conscious, The: (Lat. *co-* + *conscire,* to know) Consciousness which is dissociated from the central core of a personality and of which that personality is unaware. The co-conscious and the unconscious consisting of neural structures and processes are, in the terminology of Morton Prince, the two species of the subconscious. (*The Unconscious,* pp. 247 ff.)—*L.W.*

Coenaesthesis: (Gr. *Koinos,* common + *aisthesis,* feeling) Organic sensation (circulatory, digestive etc.) as distinguished from external sensation (visual, auditory, tactual etc.). See *Somatic Datum.*—*L.W.*

Cogitatio: One of the two attributes (q.v) of God which, according to Spinoza, are accessible to the human intellect (*Ethica,* II, *passim*). Though God is an infinite thinking thing, it is not possible so to *define* him; God is "substance consisting of infinite attributes, etc." (*Ibid,* I, Def. 6), and is thus beyond the grasp of the human mind which can know only thought and extension (*extensio, q.v.*).—*W.S.W.*

Cogito: In Husserl: A collective name for spontaneous acts, acts in which the ego lives.—*D.C.*

"Cogito" Argument, The: (Lat. *cogito,* I think) An argument of the type employed by Descartes (*Meditation II*) to establish the existence of the self. Descartes' *Cogito, ergo sum* ("I think, therefore I exist") is an attempt to establish the existence of the self in any act of thinking, including even the act of doubting. The *cogito ergo sum* is, as Descartes himself insisted, not so much inference as a direct appeal to intuition, but it has commonly been construed as an argument because of Descartes' formulation.—*L.W.*

Cognition: (Lat. *cognoscere,* to know) Knowledge in its widest sense including (a) non-propositional apprehension (perception, memory, introspection, etc.) as well as (b) propositions or judgments expressive of such apprehension. Cognition, along with conation and affection, are the three basic aspects or functions of consciousness. See *Consciousness, Epistemology.*—*L.W.*

In Scholasticism: Whatever is known is, as known, an accident of the knowing soul and therefore caused by an informing agent. All knowledge ultimately is due to an affection of the senses which are informed by the agency of the objects through a medium. The immutation of the sense organ and the corresponding accidental change of the soul are called *species sensibilis impressa*. The conscious percept is the *species expressa*. Intellectual knowledge stems from the phantasm out of which the active intellect disengages the universal nature which as *species intelligibilis impressa* informs the passive intellect and there becomes, as conscious concept, the *species expressa* or *verbum mentis*. Sensory cognition is a material process; but it is not the matter of the particular thing which enters into the sensory faculties; rather they supply the material foundation for the sensible form to become existent within the mind. Cognition is, therefore, "assimilation" of the mind to its object. The cognitive mental state as well as the species by which it originates are "images" of the object, in a metaphorical or analogical sense, not to be taken as anything like a copy or a reduplication of the thing. The senses, depending directly on the physical influence exercised by the object, cannot err; error is of the judging reason which may be misled by imagination and neglects to use the necessary critique.—*R.A.*

Abstractive: That meaning of cognition which lacks one of the two requisites for intuitive knowledge: for in abstractive cognition either we know things through other things, and not through their proper images—or we know things that are not present: e.g., the knowledge we now have of God, through creatures—or the knowledge we have of Adam, a being not present to us.

Comprehensive: Strictly speaking, that which is adequate to or fully commensurate with the object—a knowledge in which the whole object is known completely and in every way in which it can be known — even to all the effects and consequences with which it has an intrinsic connection. This knowledge must be clear, certain, evident, and quidditative, because it is the most perfect type of knowledge corresponding to the object, e.g., God's complete knowledge of Himself.

Intuitive: Requires two things: (1) that it result from the proper species, or the proper image of the object itself, impressed upon the mind by the object or by God; and (2) that it bear upon an object that is really present with the greatest clearness and certitude. Our knowledge of the sun is intuitive while we are looking at the sun, and that knowledge which the blessed have of God is intuitive.

Quidditative: In the strict sense, is that which arises from the proper image of an object, like intuitive knowledge, and besides, penetrates distinctly, with a clear, proper, and positive concept, the essential predicates of a thing even to the last difference. The knowledge which God has of Himself is of this kind. But *quidditative knowledge* in the wide sense is any knowledge of the quiddity or essence of an object, or any definition explaining what a thing is.—*H.G.*

Cognitive Meaning, Cognitive Sentence: See *Meaning, Kinds of,* 1.

Cognoscendum: (pl. *cognoscenda*) (Lat. *cognoscere,* to know) The object of cognition. Cognoscenda may be (a) real and existent, *e.g.* in veridical perception and memory; (b) abstract and ideal, *e.g.* in conception and valuation; (c) fictitious, *e.g.* in imagination and hallucination. See *Object, Objectives.—L.W.*

Cohen, Hermann: (1842-1918) and Paul Natorp (1854-1924) were the chief leaders of the "Marburg School" which formed a definite branch of the Neo-Kantian movement. Whereas the original founders of this movement, O. Liebmann and Fr. A. Lange, had reacted to scientific empiricism by again calling attention to the *a priori* elements of cognition, the Marburg school contended that all cognition was exclusively *a priori*. They definitely rejected not only the notion of "things-in-themselves" but even that of anything immediately "given" in experience. There is no other reality than one posited by thought and this holds good equally for the object, the subject and God. Nor is thought in its effort to "determine the object = x" limited by any empirical data but solely by the laws of thought. Since in Ethics, Kant himself had already endeavored to eliminate all empirical elements, the Marburg school was perhaps closer to him in this field than in epistemology. The sole goal of conduct is fulfillment of duty, *i.e.,* the achievement of a society organized according to moral principles and satisfying the postulates of personal dignity. The Marburg school was probably the most influential philosophic trend in Germany in the last 25 years before the First World War. The most outstanding present-day champion of their tradition is Ernst Cassirer (born 1874). Cohen and Natorp tried to re-interpret Plato as well as Kant. Following up a suggestion first made by Lotze they contended that the Ideas ought to be understood as laws or methods of thought and that the current view ascribing any kind of existence to them was based on a misunderstanding of Aristotle's.—*H.G.*

Cohen, Morris Raphael: (1880-1947) Professor of Philosophy of the College of the City of New York. His contributions have been many in the fields of social, political and legal philosophy. He describes his view in general as realistic rationalism, a view that emphasizes the importance of intellect or reason as applied to what is, rather than *in vacuo*. He has found the principle of polarity a fruitful means of resolving antinomies. His best known works are *Reason and Nature* and *Law and the Social Order.—L.E.D.*

Coherence Theory of Truth: Theory of knowledge which maintains that truth is a property primarily applicable to any extensive body of consistent propositions, and derivatively applicable to any one proposition in such a system by virtue of its part in the system.—*A.C.B.*

Coleridge, Samuel Taylor: (1772-1834) Leading English poet of his generation along with his friend and associate, William Wordsworth. He was for a time a Unitarian preacher and his writings throughout display a keen interest in spiritual affairs. He was among the first to bring the German idealists to the attention of the English reading public. Of greatest philosophic interest among his prose works are: *Biographia Literaria, Aids to Reflection* and *Confessions of an Inquiring Spirit*. His influence was great upon his contemporaries and also upon the American transcendentalists.—*L.E.D.*

Collective and Distributive Properties: A general term is taken in its collective sense when what is predicated of it applies to its designation as a whole, rather than to each of the individual members belonging to it; the distributive properties are those that apply only in the latter way.

Colligation: (Lat. *con + ligare*, to bind) The assimilation of a number of separately observed facts to a unified conception or formula. The term was introduced by Whewell who gives the example of the idea of an eliptical orbit which "unifies all observations made on the positions of a planet" (see *Philosophy of the Inductive Sciences*, I Aphorism 1). J.S. Mill appropriates the term and carefully differentiates it from induction: whereas colligation is a simple "description" of observed facts, induction is an extension to the unknown and to the future. See *Logic*, III, ii, § 4.—*L.W.*

Collingwood, Robin George: (1889–1943) English philosopher and archaeologist. Spent most of his working life in Oxford, first as a student, then as a Fellow of Pembroke College, and subsequently as Professor of Metaphysics. His most influential work is in aesthetics, metaphysics, the philosophy of mind, and the philosophy of history.

Essay on Philosophical Method (1933); *The Principles of Art* (1938); *Autobiography* (1939); *An Essay on Metaphysics* (1940); *Idea of History* (1946).—*T.P.S.*

Combination: (Lat. *combinare*, to join) The process of forming a new whole by the union of parts; also the product of such union. Two types of combination are distinguishable: (a) *Composition* is a union of parts such that the component parts are discernible in the compound. Thus the visual and factual data which combine to form a total percept are recognizable in the resultant percept. (b) *Fusion* is a union of parts into a whole in which the identity of the parts is obliterated. Thus the amalgamation of two sense images to form a new quality would, if this phenomenon were psychologically possible, be an instance of psychic fusion. See *Psychic Fusion*.—*L.W.*

Combination of Ideas: According to Locke and his followers, the process by which the mind forms complex ideas out of the simple ideas furnished to it by experience, and one of the three ways in which the mind by its own activity can get new ideas not furnished to it from without (Locke, *Essay Concerning Human Understanding*, Bk. II, ch. 12, 22). Conceived sometimes as a mechanical, sometimes as a quasi-chemical process. —*W.K.F.*

Combinatory Logic: A branch of mathematical logic, which has been extensively investigated by Curry, and which is concerned with analysis of processes of substitution, of the use of variables generally, and of the notion of a function. The program calls, in particular, for a system of logic in which variables are altogether eliminated, their place being taken by the presence in the system of certain kinds of function symbols. For a more detailed and exact account, reference must be made to the papers cited below.—*A.C.*

M. Schönfinkel, *Über die Bausteine der mathematischen Logik*, Mathematische Annalen, vol. 92 (1924), pp. 305-316. H.B. Curry, *Grundlagen der kombinatorischen Logik*, American Journal of Mathematics, vol. 52 (1930), pp. 509-536, 789-834. H.B. Curry, *The universal quantifier in combinatory logic*, Annals of Mathematics, ser. 2 vol. 32 (1931), pp. 154-180. H.B. Curry, *Apparent variables from the standpoint of combinatory logic*, Annals of Mathematics, ser. 2, vol. 34 (1933), pp. 381-404. H.B. Curry, *Functionality in combinatory logic*, Proceedings of the National Academy of Sciences, vol. 20 (1934), pp. 584-590. J.B. Rosser, *A mathematical logic without variables*, Annals of Mathematics, ser. 2, vol. 36 (1935), pp. 127-150, and Duke Mathematical Journal, vol. 1 (1935), pp. 328-355. H.B. Curry, *A revision of the fundamental rules of combinatory logic*, The Journal of Symbolic Logic, vol. 6 (1941), pp. 41-53. H.B. Curry, *Consistency and completeness of the theory of combinators*, ibid. pp. 54-61.

Comedy: In Aristotle (*Poetics*), play in which chief characters behave worse than men do in daily life, as contrasted with tragedy, where the main characters act more nobly. In Plato's *Symposium*, Socrates argues at the end that a writer of good comedies is able to write good tragedies. See *Comic*. Metaphysically, comedy in Hegel consists of regarding reality as exhausted in a single category. Cf. Bergson, *Le rire* (Laughter).

Commentator, The: Name usually used for Averroës by the medieval authors of the 13th century and later. In the writings of the grammarians (*modistae*, dealing with *modis significandi*) often used for Petrus Heliae.—*R.A.*

Common Sense: In Aristotle's psychology the faculty by which the common sensibles are perceived. It is probable also that Aristotle attributes to this faculty the functions of perceiving what we perceive and of uniting the data of different senses into a single object.—*G.R.M.*

Common Sense Realism: A school of Scottish thinkers founded by Thomas Reid (1710-96) which attempted to set up a theory of knowledge which would support the realistic belief of the man of the street. (See *Naïve Realism*.) The school began a movement of protest against Locke's theory which led to an eventual subjective idealism and skepticism.—*V.F.*

Common Sensibles: (Lat. *sensibilia communia*) In the psychology of Aristotle the qualities of a sense object that may be apprehended by several senses; e.g. motion (or rest), number, shape, size; in distinction from the proper sensibles, or qualities that can be apprehended by only one sense, such as color, taste, smell.—*G.R.M.*

Communication: A term used to refer to a certain feature of sign-situations, viz. the identity, similarity or correspondence of what is understood by the interpreter with what is, or is intended to be, expressed by the speaker.

By a familiar ambiguity the term is used indiscriminately to refer either to the process by which such accordance is brought about, or that with regard to which accord between the speaker and interpreter is achieved.

The definition is intended to cover the communication of attitudes, evaluations, desires, etc., as well as of judgments or assertions. See *Functions of Language, Speech Situation.*—*M.B.*

Communication: (Lat. *communicare*, to share) Intercourse between minds or selves whereby sensations, imagery or conceptional meanings are transferred from one to another. Communication includes: (i) ordinary sense-mediated communication by means of speech, writing, gesture, facial expression and bodily attitude and (ii) allegedly direct contact between minds by mental telepathy and other occult means. See *Telegnosis; Telepathy.*—*L.W.*

Communism: In its fullest sense, that stage of social development, which, following socialism (*q.v.*) is conceived to be characterized by an economy of abundance on a world wide scale in which the state as a repressive force (army, jails, police and the like) is considered unnecessary because irreconcilable class antagonisms will have disappeared, and it will be possible to apply the principle, "from each according to ability, to each according to need" (Marx: "Gotha Program"). It is held that the release of productive potentialities resulting from socialized ownership of the means of production will create a general sufficiency of economic goods which in turn will afford the possibility of educational and cultural development for all, and that under such conditions people will learn to live in accordance with valued standards without the compulsion of physical force represented by a special apparatus of state power. It is considered that by intelligent planning, both economic and cultural, it will then be possible to eradicate the antagonism between town and country and the opposition between physical and mental labor. It is now considered in the U.S.S.R. that the principal features of communist society, with the exception of the "withering away" of the state, may be attained in one country of an otherwise capitalist world. Trotsky considered this a false version of Marxism.—*J.M.S.*

Commutative law: Any law of the form $x o y = y o x$, or with the biconditional, etc., replacing equality—compare *Associative law*. Commutative laws of addition and multiplication hold in arithmetic, also in the theory of real numbers, etc. In the propositional calculus there are commutative laws of conjunction, both kinds of disjunction, the biconditional, alternative denial and its dual; also corresponding laws in the algebra of classes.—*A.C.*

Comparison: (Lat. *com-* + *par*, equal) The act of discerning or describing the common properties possessed by two or more objects; or the result of such discernment or description.—*A.C.B.*

Compathy: (Ger. *Miteinanderfühlen*) Men feel with each other the same sorrow, the same pain. It is a with-each-other feeling. Only psychical suffering can thus be felt, not physical pain.

Completeness: A *logistic system* (*q.v.*) may be called *complete* if there is no formula of the system which is not a theorem and which can be added to the list of primitive formulas (no other change being made) without rendering the system inconsistent, in one of the senses of *consistency* (*q.v.*). The pure propositional calculus—as explained under *logic, formal*, § 1—is complete in this sense.

Given the concept of semantical *truth* (*q.v.*), we may also define a logistic system as *complete* if every true formula of the system is a theorem. This sense of completeness is not, in general, equivalent to the other, and may be the weaker one if formulas containing free variables occur. See *Logic, formal*, §§ 3, 6.—*A.C.*

Complex: (Lat. *complecti*, to entwine around, comprise) 1. Anything that possesses distinguishable parts; or the property of possessing distinguishable parts. 2. Anything that possesses distinguishable parts which are related in such a way as to give unity to the whole; or the property of having parts so related.—*A.C.B.*

Complication: (Lat *com* + *plicatio*, folded together) The union or act of combining more or less disparate elements into a single whole impression or idea. The term usually has reference to the synthesis of sense data in perceptions, or of perceptions in a unifying idea. —*O.F.K.*

Composite: (Scholastic) The existing being as composed of prime matter (*q.v.*) and form (*q.v.*) The human composite: matter informed by the spiritual and rational soul.—*R.A.*

Composite idea: Any idea that consists of a fusion of sentient elements, which together are presumed to pass the threshold of consciousness. In logic, a compound of undefined ideas by way of definition.—*C.K.D.*

Composition: The form of valid inference of the propositional calculus from A ⊃ B and A ⊃ C to A ⊃ BC. The *law of composition* is the theorem of the propositional calculus:

$$[p \supset q] [p \supset r] \supset [p \supset qr].—A.C.$$

Composition and Division, fallacies of: Semi-formal logical fallacies. In the fallacy of composition it is assumed that what characterizes individuals qua individuals will likewise characterize groups of these same individuals qua groups. In that of division what is taken as validly applying to the group as a whole is then assumed to apply with equal validity to the individuals constituting said group. Called semi-formal because they involve passing from the distributive to the collective use of terms and vice versa.—*C.K.D.*

Compossibility: Those things are compossible in Leibniz's philosophy which are literally "co-possible," i.e., which may exist together, which belong to the same possible world. Since metaphysical possibility means for Leibniz simply the absence of contradiction, two or more things are compossible if, and only if, their joint ascription to a single world involves no contradiction. All possible worlds are held by Leibniz to have general laws analogous to those of our own actual world. Compossibility for any set of things, consequently, involves their capacity to be brought under one and the same general system of laws. That this last provision is important follows from the fact that Leibniz affirmed all simple predicates to be compatible.

—F.L.W.

Compound: (Lat. *con* + *ponere,* to place) A complex whole formed by the union of a number of parts in contrast to an element which is a simple unanalyzable part. A *mental* compound is a state of mind formed by the combination (see *Combination*) of simple mental elements, either conscious or unconscious.—*L.W.*

Compound Theory of Mind: The conception of mind as a compound of psychological elements analogous to a chemical compound. See *Psychological Atomism.*—*L.W.*

Comprehension: (Lat. *com* + *prehendere,* to grasp) The act or faculty of understanding, intellectual grasp, or insight. Comprehension may be achieved variously by: (1) unifying and relating manifold facts or ideas; (2) deducing something from premises; (3) accommodating new facts or ideas to established knowledge; (4) seeing a thing or idea in its proper or significant context; (5) relating a fact or idea to something known, universal and subject to law. *Comprehension* carries sometimes the special connotation of thorough understanding. *Logic:* The sum of characteristics which connote a class notion symbolized by a general term. Also, the features common to a number of instances or objects. Thus, the *connotation (q.v.)* or *intension (q.v.)* of a concept. See *Intension.*—*O.F.K.*

Compresence: (Lat: *com praesentia* from *praesse,* to be present) The togetherness of two or more items, for example, the coexistence of several elements in the unity of consciousness. In the terminology of S. Alexander (*Space, Time and Deity*), an unique kind of togetherness which underlies cognition.—*L.W.*

Comte, Auguste: (1798-1857) Was born and lived during a period when political and social conditions in France were highly unstable. In reflecting the spirit of his age, he rose against the tendency prevalent among his predecessors to propound philosophic doctrines in disregard of the facts of nature and society. His revolt was directed particularly against traditional metaphysics with its endless speculations, countless assumptions, and futile controversies. To his views he gave the name of positivism. According to him, the history of humanity should be described in terms of three stages. The first of these was the theological stage when people's interpretation of reality was dominated by superstitions and prejudices; the second stage was metaphysical when people attempted to comprehend, and reason about, reality, but were unable to support their contentions by facts; and the third and final stage was positive, when dogmatic assumptions began to be replaced by factual knowledge. Accordingly, the history of thought was characterized by a certain succession of sciences, expressing the turning of scholarly interest toward the earthly and human affairs, namely: mathematics, astronomy, physics, chemistry, biology, and sociology. These doctrines were discussed in Comte's main work, *Cours de philosophie positive.* —*R.B.W.*

Conation: (Lat. *conatio,* attempt) Referring to voluntary activity.—*V.F.*

Conatus: The drive, force, or urge possessed by a thing which is directed towards the preservation of its own being. Since, for Spinoza, all things are animated, the term is used by him in a broader meaning than that accorded it, for example, in the Stoic philosophy. Spinoza maintains that there is no conatus for self-destruction (*Ethica,* III, 4; see also IV, 20 Schol., etc.); rather, the conatus relates to a thing's "power of existence," and he thus speaks of it as a kind of *amour propre (natuurlyke Liefde)* which characterizes a specific thing. See *Short, Tr.,* App. II.—*W.S.W.*

Conceivability: The quality or condition of taking into and holding an idea in mind. It has come to mean any affection of the mind or any apprehension, imagining or opinion of the mind. It is necessary though not sufficient criterion for the truth of said idea or affection, etc.—*C.K.D.*

Concept: In logic syn. either with *propositional function (q.v.)* generally or with *monadic propositional function.* The terminology associated with the word *function* is not, however, usually employed in connection with the word *concept;* and the latter word may serve to avoid ambiguities which have arisen from loose or variant usages of the word *function (q.v.);* or it may reflect a difference in point of view.—*A.C.*

In scholasticism: the "word of the mind" (*verbum mentis*) by which the possible intellect expresses (therefore also in later writers *species expressa*) the universal nature disengaged by the active intellect from the phantasm and transmitted as *species intelligibilis* to the possible intellect.—*R.A.*

In Kant: In the strict sense, any generic or class term, exclusive or relational terms or categories. Sometimes, loosely, any general or abstract representation. —*O.F.K.*

In Husserl: 1. An expressible sense. 2. An eidos as intended.—*D.C.*

Conception: (Lat. *concipere,* to take together) Cognition of abstracta or universals as distinguished from cognition of concreta or particulars. (See *Abstractum.*) Conception, as a mode of cognition, may or may not posit real or subsistent universals corresponding to the concepts of the mind. See *Conceptualism; Conceptual Realism.*—*L.W.*

Conceptualism: A solution of the problem of universals which seeks a compromise between extreme nominalism (generic concepts are signs which apply indifferently to a number of particulars) and extreme realism (generic concepts refer to subsistent universals). Conceptualism offers various interpretations of conceptual objectivity: (a) the generic concept refers to a class of resembling particulars, (b) the object of a concept is a universal essence pervading the particulars, but having no reality apart from them, (c) concepts refer to abstracta, that is to say, to ideal objects envisaged by the mind but having no metaphysical status.—*L.W.* See *Scholasticism.*

Conceptual Realism: Theory which ascribes objectivity of some sort to conceptual cognition; includes extreme or Platonic realism and conceptualism but excludes nominalism. See *Conceptualism.—L.W.*

Concomitance: (Latin *concomitantia*, accompaniment), literally the act or state of being associated. The term has received wide currency in logic, particularly since John Stuart Mill clearly formulated the method of concomitant variations, as the concurrent existence, appearance or disappearance of certain characters which, under circumstances, admit but do not necessarily postulate causal interrelatedness.—*K.F.L.*

Precise conjunction or accompaniment, spatial or temporal.—*C.A.B.*

Concrete: Anything that is specific or individual. The term is opposed to "general" or "abstract," terms which stress common characteristics or qualities considered apart from their specific setting.—*V.F.*

Concrete Universal: In Hegel's system a category is concrete when it possesses the basic character of the real, *i.e.* tension, change, dialectical opposition. Such a universal comprises a synthesis of two opposite abstractions, and with one exception, it in turn becomes an abstract member of a pair of logical opposites united or "sublated" in a higher category. The lowest of such dynamic or concrete universals is Becoming, which is a dialectical synthesis of Being and Not-Being. The only absolutely concrete universal, however, is Reality itself, the World Whole, conceived as an all-inclusive, organic system of self-thinking Thought.

2. Neo-idealism (*q.v.*) in Italy introduces a second type of concrete universal whose elements lack the character of dialectical opposition and logical abstractness.—*W.L.*

Concretion: (Lat. *concresco*, to grow together) A uniting or growing together.—*V.F.*

Santayana calls universals "concretions of discourse." (*Life of Reason*, vol. I (*Reason in Common Sense*)).

Concupiscence: (Lat. *con + cupere*, to desire wholly or altogether) Desire for pleasure or delight of the senses; as such it is a desire which is natural, necessary and proper to man. But when this desire operates independently of, or contrary to the right rule of reason, then concupiscence is a bad habit or vice, contrary to nature, and thus opposed to the virtue of temperance or "nothing in excess." In an extended sense, concupiscence may apply to desire for objects arousing appetites other than those of the senses.—*L.M.H.*

Concurrence: The doctrine of Augustine that before the Fall it was possible for man not to sin, but he needed God's help, *adjutorium sine quo non*. After the Fall man needs God's grace or concurrence which acts with him, *adjutorium quo*, with which he must cooperate. The term also signifies, concursus, or the general cooperation of God, the primary cause, with the activity of all creatures, as secondary causes.—*J.J.R.*

Concursus dei (or divinus): (Lat. Divine concurrent activity) The divine activity in its relation to the finite causes in the development of the world and the free will of man. The term suggests that divine activity runs parallel with the activity of things and creatures. The concursus dei is differently conceived depending on whether the stress is laid on the divine action or on the action of secondary causes.—*H.H.*

Condignity: A characteristic of merit which implies equality and proportionality between service rendered and its recompense, to which there is a claim on the ground of justice. Merit of this description is called condign merit, or *meritum de condigno.—J.J.R.*

Condillac, Etienne: (1715-1780) French sensationalist. Successor of Locke. In his *Traité des sensations,* he works out the details of a system based on Lockean foundations in which all the human faculties are reduced in essence to a sensory basis. Understanding, in all its phases, is deemed nothing more than the comparison or multiplication of sensations. He is important today for his having followed the lead of Locke in pointing the way to psychology as a way to profit by observation and experience.—*L.E.D.*

E. Condillac, *Traité des systèmes,* 1846; *Traité des sensations,* 1854; *Langue des calculs,* 1858.

Condition: (Lat. *conditio,* agreement, condition)
1. The if-clause in an implicative proposition.
2. Cause (*q.v.*). 3. Necessary cause (*q.v.*) as opposed to sufficient cause.—*A.C.B.*

Conditional: The sentential connective ⊃. See *Logic, formal,* §1.

A sentence of the form A ⊃ B (or a proposition expressed by such a sentence)—verbally, "if A then B"—may be called a *conditional* sentence (or proposition).—*A.C.*

Conditional Immortality: A teaching affirming that immortality is a gift of God conferred on believers in Christ, who become the children of God, and denying that the human soul is immortal by nature.—*J.J.R.*

Conditional Morality: Any system of morals which has for its basic principle what Kant calls a hypothetical imperative, e.g., a system of morals which reasons that we should act in certain ways because such actions will bring us happiness, assuming that we want happiness. See *Hypothetical imperatives.—W.K.F.*

Conditioned Reflex: See *Conditioned Response.*

Conditioned Response: Response of an organism which, originally produced by its "natural" stimulus, is subsequently produced in the absence of the original stimulus by a substitute or "conditioning" stimulus. Thus if *S* represents an original stimulus (in Pavlov's experiment, the presentation of food to a dog) and *R* is the natural response (the salivary flow of the dog) and if *S'* is a conditioning stimulus associated with *S* (the ringing of a bell at the time of presenting food to the dog) then *R,* produced by *S'* in the absence of *S,* is said to be a conditioned or conditional response. See *Behaviorism.—L.W.*

Conditiones sine quibus non: A phrase descriptive of such accompanying conditions without the presence of which it is impossible for a cause to produce an effect; conditions for which there are no substitutes.—*J.J.R.*

Conduct: (Lat *conducere,* to bring together) (a) Voluntary behavior of any sort, actual or intended. Action for which a person may be held responsible. Subject matter of ethics which seeks to determine right and wrong action or proper and improper conduct. Deportment.

(b) In psychology: Behavior of a living organism reacting to environmental stimuli. See Behaviorism.—*A.J.B.*

Configuration: (Lat. *configurare* from, *con*, together and *figurare*, to form) A structural pattern at the physical, physiological or psychological level. The term has been suggested to translate the German *Gestalt*. See *Gestalt Psychology*.—*L.W.*

Configurationism: A suggested English equivalent for *Gestalt Psychology*. See *Gestalt Psychology*.

Confirmation, Confirmable: See *Verification* 3,4.

Conflict: The psychological phenomenon of struggle between competing ideas, emotions or tendencies to action. J.F. Herbart (*Lehrbuch der Psychologie*, 1816) enunciated a doctrine of conflict of ideas in accordance with which ideas opposed to the mind's dominant ideas are submerged below the threshold of consciousness. The doctrine of conflict has been revived by recent psychoanalytic psychology (see *Psychoanalysis*) to account for the relegation to the subconscious of ideas and tendencies intolerable to the conscious mind. —*L.W.*

Confucius: (K'ung Ch'iu, K'ung Chung-ni, K'ung Fu-tzŭ or Grand Master K'ung, 557-479 B.C.) Was born of a poor and common family in the state of Lu (in present Shangtung), a descendant of the people of Sung. His father died soon after his birth. When he grew up, he was put in charge of a granary, then cattle and sheep, and then public works in his native state. Later he became Grand Secretary of Justice and then Chief Minister. He regained some territory lost to a neighboring state purely by his moral force, executed a minister who created disorder, and brought peace to the land to the extent that things lost on the highways were not stolen.

In 496 B.C., he began 14 years of travelling from state to state, offering his service. He was politely consulted by princes and dukes, but no one would put his moral doctrines into practice. He was even sent away from Ch'i, threatened in Sung, driven out of Sung and Wei, and surrounded between Ch'ên and Ts'ai. When in difficulty, he exclaimed, "Heaven has endowed me with a moral destiny. What can Huan Tuei (who threatened him) do to me?" Eventually he retired to Lu to study, teach and write.

He lived in the time when the moral and cultural traditions of Chou were in rapid decline. Attempting to uphold the Chou culture, he taught poetry, history, ceremonies and music to 3,000 pupils, becoming the first Chinese educator to offer education to any who cared to come with or without tuition. He taught literature, human conduct, being one's true self and honesty in social relationships. He wrote the chronicles called *Spring and Autumn*. His tacit judgments on social and political events were such that "unruly ministers and villainous sons were afraid" to repeat their evil deeds.

He severely disciplined himself and practiced what he taught. He loved poetry, ceremonies and music. He was serious, honest, polite, filially pious toward his mother,

stern toward his son, and friendly to his pupils. His most reliable teachings are found in the *Lun Yü* (Analects), aphorisms recorded by his followers.—*W.T.C.*

Confused: (Ger. *verworren*) In Husserl: Not given distinctly, articulately, with respect to implicit components. In Descartes, sensations are confused ideas.—*D.C.*

Confusion: (logical) May be due to the ambiguity which is always a possible accompaniment of the use of words or terms with respect to their several meanings. It may also refer to any logical misapprehension which results in a semi-formal or material fallacy.—*C.K.D.*

Congruity: A characteristic of merit which implies an intrinsic disproportionality between service rendered and its recompense, to which there is no claim on the ground of justice, but on that of equity alone. Merit of this description is called congruous merit, or *meritum de congruo*.—*J.J.R.*

Conjugation: (Lat. *con* + *jungere*, yoke together)

(a) *Grammar:* The inflections of a verb.

(b) *Biology:* The union of male and female plant or animal.

(c) *Logic:* Joining the extreme terms of a syllogism by the middle term; joining dissimilar things by their common characteristics or by analogy.

(d) *Ethics:* Conjugations or pairings of the passions: love and hate, desire and avoidance, pleasure and sadness, etc. Synonymous with *connexio*.

(e) *Metaphysics:* In Aristotle, *De Gen. et Corr.*, the pairings of opposites in the simple bodies: dry and hot (fire), hot and moist (air), moist and cold (water), cold and dry (earth).—*L.M.H.*

Conjunction: See *Logic, formal*, § 1.

Connexity: A dyadic relation R is called *connected* if, for every two different members x, y of its field, at least one of *xRy, yRx* holds.

Connotation: 1. The sum of the constitutive notes of the essence of a concept as it is in itself and not as it is for us. This logical property is thus measured by the sum of the notes of the concept, of the higher genera it implies, of the various essential attributes of its nature as such. This term is synonymous with intension and comprehension; yet, the distinctions between them have been the object of controversies. 2. J. S. Mill identifies connotation with signification and meaning, and includes in it much less than under comprehension or intension. The connotation of a general term (singular terms except descriptions are non-connotative) is the aggregate of all the other general terms necessarily implied by it as an abstract possibility and apart from exemplification in the actual world. It cannot be determined by denotation because necessity does not always refer to singular facts. Logicians who adopt this view distinguish connotation from comprehension by including in the latter contingent characters which do not enter in the former. Comprehension is thus the intensional reference of the concept, or the reference to universals of both general and singular terms. The determination of the comprehension of a concept is helped by its denotation, considering that reference is made also to singular, contingent, or particular objects exhibiting certain characteristics. In short, the connotation of a concept is its intensional reference determined intensionally; while its comprehension is its intensional reference extensionally determined. 3. It may be observed that such a distinction and the view that the connotation of a concept contains only the notes which serve to define it, involves the nominalist principle that a concept may be reduced to what we are actually and explicitly thinking about the several notes we use to define it. Thus the connotation of a concept is much poorer than its actual content. Though the value of the concept seems to be saved by the recognition of its comprehension, it may be argued that the artificial introduction into the comprehension of both necessary and contingent notes, that is of actual and potential characteristics, confuses and perverts the notion of connotation as a logical property of our ideas. See *Intension.—T.G.*

Conscience: (Lat. *conscientia,* knowledge) Any emotionally-toned experience in which a tendency to act is inhibited by a recognition, socially conditioned, that suffering evil consequences is likely to result from acting on the impulse to act.—*A.J.B.*

Conscientalism: The doctrine that contends that the entities we apprehend must be necessarily mental, idealistic; that the real objects are realities of consciousness.—*H.H.*

Conscientialism: (Lat. *conscientia + al,* pertaining to conscience) Originally denoting simple consciousness without ethical bearing, the term conscience came in modern times to mean in contrast to consciousness, viewed either as a purely intellectual function or as a generic term for mind, a function of distinguishing between right and wrong. With the rise of Christianity the term came to be described as an independent source of moral insight, and with the rise of modern philosophy it became an inner faculty, an innate, primeval thing.—*H.H.*

Conscious: (Ger. *bewusst*) In Husserl: 1. Broadest sense: noematically intentional; conscious *of* something. A process may be "conscious" in this sense even if it is not "conscious" in the following sense. 2. Narrower sense: "Actual," belonging to the *cogito*. As living in a process that is "conscious" in this second sense, the *ego* is also said to be "conscious," "awake," and "conscious of" (awake *to*) the intentional object of the process. As objects of processes that are conscious (in either of the first two senses), *objects* are occasionally referred to as "conscious."—*D.C.*

Conscious Illusion Theory: The theory that conscious self-illusion, semblance and deliberate make-believe are constant factors in art and art appreciation which free the individual momentarily from the practical and hum-drum and thus enhance and refresh his life. See Konrad Lange, *Die bewusste Selbsttäuschung als Kern des aesthetischen Genusses,* 1895.—*O.F.K.*

Consciousness: (Lat. *conscire,* to know, to be cognizant of) A designation applied to conscious mind as opposed to a supposedly unconscious or subconscious mind (See *Subconscious Mind; Unconscious Mind*), and to the whole domain of the physical and non-mental. Consciousness is generally considered an indefinable term or rather a term definable only by direct introspective appeal to conscious experiences. The indefinability of consciousness is expressed by Sir William Hamilton: "Consciousness cannot be defined: we may be ourselves fully aware of what consciousness is, but we cannot without confusion convey to others a definition of what we ourselves clearly apprehend. The reason is plain: consciousness lies at the root of all knowledge." (*Lectures on Metaphysics,* I, 191.) Ladd's frequently quoted definition of consciousness succeeds only in indicating the circumstances under which it is directly observable: "Whatever we are when we are awake, as contrasted with what we are when we sink into a profound and dreamless sleep, that is to be conscious."

The analysis of consciousness proceeds in two principal directions: (i) a distinction may be drawn between the *act* of consciousness and the *content* of consciousness and the two may even be considered as separable ingredients of consciousness, and (ii) consciousness is analyzed into its three principal functions: cognition, affection and conation.

Locke, Reid and others restricted consciousness to the reflective apprehension of the mind of its own processes but this usage has been abandoned in favor of the wider definition indicated above and the term introspection is used to designate this special kind of consciousness. See *Behaviorism.—L.W.*

(Ger. *Bewusstsein*) In Husserl: 1. Noematic intentionality in general. The intentional *constituting* of the temporal stream-of-consciousness itself is an instance of "consciousness" in this broad sense, though it is intrinsically prior to the constituted stream. 2. The stream of subjective process, or any part of it, as having the characteristic of noematic intentionality. 3. The stream of "actual" subjective process, or any part of it; the *"ego cogito."—D.C.*

Consciousness, Field of: The sum-total of items embraced within an individual's consciousness at any given moment. The total field consists of: (a) the *focus,* where the concentration of attention is maximal and (b) a *margin, periphery* or *fringe* of a diminishing degree of attention which gradually fades to zero.—*L.W.*

Consciousness-in-general: (Kant's *Bewusstsein Ueberhaupt*) Consciousness conceived as purely logical, objective, universal, necessarily valid, in contrast to the eccentricity, particularity, subjectivity, irrationality, and privacy of the psychological consciousness. See *Kant.—W.L.*

Consectarium: (Lat. *consectarius*) Peculiar to the philosophical vocabulary of Cicero, it means an inference, a conclusion. It is the substantive for the phrase "that follows logically."—*H.H.*

Consensus gentium: (Lat. agreement of people) A criterion of truth: that which is universal among men carries the weight of truth.—*V.F.*

Consent: Agreement or sympathy in feeling or thought.—*V.F.*

Consentience: (Lat. *con* + *sentire*, to feel) Conscious unity existing at the level of sensation after the subtraction of all conceptual and interpretative unity. Consentience includes both: (a) the intra-sensory unity of a single sensory continuum (*e.g.* the visual, tactual or auditory) and (b) the inter-sensory unit embracing the diverse sensory continua. Consentience plays an important rôle in the psychological doctrine of the presentation-continuum of J. Ward and G. F. Stout. An allied concept is the sensory organization of *Gestalt Psychology.* See *Gestalt Psychology.—L.W.*

Consequence: (Ger. *Konsequenz*) In Husserl: The relation of formal-analytic inclusion which obtains between certain noematic senses.

Consequence: See *Valid.*

Consequence-logic: (Ger. *Konsequenzlogik*) Consistency-logic (*Logik der Widerspruchslosigkeit*); pure apophantic analytics (in a strict sense); a level of pure formal logic in which the only *thematic* concepts of validity are consequence, inconsequence, and compatibility. Consequence-logic includes the essential content of traditional syllogistics and the disciplines making up formal-mathematical analysis.—*D.C.*

Consequent: See *Antecedent.*

Consilience: Whewell calls "consilience of inductions" what occurs when a hypothesis gives us the "rule and reason" not only of the class of facts contemplated in its construction, but also, unexpectedly, of some class of facts altogether different.—*C.J.D.*

Consistency: (1) A *logistic system* (*q.v.*) is *consistent* if there is no theorem whose negation is a theorem. See *Logic, formal,* §§, 1, 3, 6; also *Proof theory.*

Since this definition of consistency is relative to the choice of a particular notation as representing negation, the following definition is sometimes used instead: (2) A logistic system is *consistent* if not every formula (not every sentence) is a theorem. In the case of many familiar systems, under the usual choice as to which notation represents negation, the equivalence of this sense of consistency to the previous one is immediate.

Closely related to (2), and applicable to logistic systems containing the pure propositional calculus (see *Logic, formal,* § 1) or an appropriate part of it, is the notion of consistency in the sense of E. L. Post, according to which a system is consistent if a formula composed of a single propositional variable (say the formula *p*) is not a theorem.—*A.C.*

Consistency proofs: See *Proof theory,* and *Logic formal,* §§ 1, 3, 6.

Constant: A *constant* is a symbol employed as an unambiguous name—distinguished from a *variable* (*q. v.*).

Thus in ordinary numerical algebra and in real number theory, the symbols *x, y, z* are variables, while $0, 1, 3, -\frac{1}{2}, \pi, e$ are constants. In such mathematical contexts the term *constant* is often restricted to unambiguous (non-variable) names of *numbers.* But such symbols as $+, =, <$ may also be called constants, as denoting particular functions and relations.

In various mathematical contexts, the term *constant* will be found applied to letters which should properly be called variables (according to our account here), but which are thought of as constant relative to other variables appearing. The actual distinction in such cases, as revealed by logistic formalization, either is between free and bound variables, or concerns the order and manner in which the variables are bound by quantifiers, abstraction operators, etc.

In mathematics, the word *constant* may also be employed to mean simply a *number* ("Euler's constant"), or, in the physical sciences, to mean a *physical quantity* ("the gravitational constant," "Planck's constant").—*A.C.*

Constituted: (Ger. *konstituiert*) In Husserl: Resultant from constitutive synthesis; intentionally synthetized. See *Constitution.—D.C.*

Constitution: (Ger. *Konstitution*) In Husserl: 1. Broader sense: *Intentionally* in its character as producing, on the one hand, intentionally identical and different *objects of consciousness* with more or less determinate objective senses and, on the other hand, more or less abiding *ego-habitudes* (see *Habit*) is said to be "*constitutive;*" its products, "constituted" (*q.v.*). The synthetic *structure* of the constitutive process, regarded either as a static or as a temporally genetic affair, is called the *constitution* of the intentional object. 2. Narrower sense: The structure of intentionality in its character as rational, i.e., as productive of valid objects and correct, justified, habits (convictions, etc.). See *Evidence* and *Reason.—D.C.*

Constitutive: Of the essential nature; internal; component; inherent. Internal relations are *constitutive* because they are integral parts or elements of the natures which they relate; whereas external, non-constitutive relations may be altered without change in the essential natures of the related entities.

In Kant: Whatever enters into the structure of actual experience. Thus, the categories are constitutive of knowledge of nature because they are necessary conditions of any experience or knowledge whatever. In contrast, the transcendent Ideas (God, the total Cosmos, and the immortal Soul) are not constitutive of anything, since they do not serve to define or compose real objects, and must be restricted to a regulative and speculative use. See *Crit. of Pure Reason,* Transc. Dialectic, Bk. II, ch. II, Sec. 8.—*O.F.K.*

Construct, Imaginative: (Lat. *construere,* to build) See *Construction, Psychological.*

Construction: (Lat. *constructio,* from *construere,* to build) The mental process of devising imaginative constructs or the products of such constructional activities. A construction, in contrast to an ordinary hypothesis which professes to represent an actual state of affairs, is largely arbitrary and fictional.—*L.W.*

Construction, Psychological: (In contrast to *Logical*) A framework devised by the common-sense, scientific or philosophical imagination for the integration of diverse empirical data. In contrast to an hypothesis, a construction is not an inference from experience but is an arbitrary scheme which, though presumably not a true picture of the actual state of affairs, satisfies the human imagination and promotes further investigation. Perceptual objects, space and time, physical atoms, electrons, etc. as well as philosophical world-views, have by certain philosophers been called logical constructs. (Cf. B. Russell, *Our Knowledge of the External World*, Ch. IV.)—*L.W.*

Contemplation: (Lat. *contemplare*, to gaze attentively) (a) *In the mystical sense:* Knowledge consisting in the partial or complete identification of the knower with the object of knowledge with the consequent loss of his own individuality. In Hugo of St. Victor (1096-1141), *Contemplatio* is the third and highest stage of knowledge of which *cogitatio* and *meditatio* are the two earlier levels.

(b) *In recent epistemology:* Contemplation is knowledge of an object in contrast to *enjoyment* which is the mind's direct self-awareness. (Cf. S. Alexander, *Space, Time and Deity*, Vol. I, p. 12)—*L.W.*

Content of Consciousness: (Lat. *contentus*, from *continere*, to contain) The totality of qualitative *data* present to consciousness in contrast to the *act* of apprehending such data. See *Act Psychology; Datum.*—*L.W.*

Contextual definition: See *incomplete symbol.*

Contiguity, Association by: A type of association, recognized by Aristotle, whereby one of two states of mind, which have been coexistent or successive, tends to recall the other. This type of association has sometimes been considered the basic type to which all others are reducible. See *Association, Laws of.*—*L.W.*

Continence: In Aristotle's ethics the moral condition of a person able to control his bodily desires by reason. Aristotle distinguishes continence from temperance in that the former implies a conflict between bodily desires and rational choice, whereas in the temperate man there is no such conflict.—*G.R.M.*

Contingency: (Lat. *contingere*, to touch on all sides) In its broadest philosophical usage a state of affairs is said to be contingent if it may and also may not be. A certain event, for example, is contingent if, and only if, it may come to pass and also may not come to pass. For this reason contingency is not quite equivalent in meaning to possibility (*q.v.*), for while a possible state of affairs is one which may be, it may at the same time be necessary, and hence it would be false to say that it may not be.

In this broad sense contingency appears always to imply a reference to some basis in relation to which a given thing may be said to be contingent; and in view of the two referents most commonly employed it is impossible to distinguish two chief types: (1) logical contingency, and (2) physical contingency. The first is contingency with respect to the laws of logic, the second is contingency with respect to the laws of nature. A given state of affairs, e.g., the existence of a snowflake with a given shape, is logically contingent in that the laws of logic do not suffice to establish that such a thing does or does not exist. This same state of affairs would not ordinarily be held to be physically contingent, however, for, although the laws of nature alone do not suffice to determine that there is such a snowflake, still it would be held on the general hypothesis of determinism that, given the specific conditions under which the water was frozen, it was determined by physical laws that a snowflake would exist and that it would have this shape and no other.

A narrower, less philosophical employment of "contingent" emphasizes the aspect of dependence of one state of affairs upon another state of affairs in accordance with the laws of nature. In this usage an event A is said to be contingent upon B when the occurrence of A depends upon the occurrence of B; and it is usually implied that the occurrence of B is itself uncertain.—*F.L.W.*

In metaphysics: The opposite of determinism, which holds that free activity may enter causally into natural processes. See *Boutroux.*—*R.T.F.*

Leibniz distinguished contingent truths (*vérités de fait*) from necessary truths of reason (*vérités de raison*); Hume (*q.v.*) regarded all causal assertions as contingent upon certain habits of the mind. See *Cause, Probability.*

Continuant: "That which continues to exist while its states or relations may be changing" (Johnson, Logic I, p. 199). The continuant is in Johnson's metaphysics a revised and somewhat more precise form of the traditional conception of substance; it includes, according to him, that residuum from the traditional conception of substance which is both philosophically justifiable and indispensable.

A "substantive," or "existent" is defined by Johnson as anything manifested in space or time. The substantives divide into two subclasses, continuants and occurrents: those which continue to exist, and those which cease to exist. Every occurrent is referrable to one or more continuant.

While continuants are collections or sets of occurrents, every collection of occurrents does not constitute a continuant, but only those possessing a certain type of unity. This unity is not an "unknown somewhat" supporting the observable properties; nor does it imply the permanence of any given property. Rather it is a "causal unity of connection between its temporarily or spatially separated manifestations" (*Ibid.*, III, p. 99).

Johnson recognizes two fundamentally distinct types of continuant: physical and psychical,—the "occupant" (of space), and the "experient."—*F.L.W.*

Continuity: A class is said to be *compactly* (or *densely*) ordered by a relation R if it is ordered by R (*see Order*) and, whenever xRz and $x \neq z$, there is a y, not the same as either x or z, such that xRy and yRz. (Compact order may thus be described by saying that between any two distinct members of the class there is always a third, or by saying that no member has a *next* following member in the order.)

If a class b is ordered by a relation R, and $|a \subset b$, we say that z is an *upper bound* of a if, for all x, $x|\epsilon|a$ implies xRz; and that z is a *least upper bound* of a if z is an upper bound of a and there is no upper bound y of a, different from z, such that yRz.

A class b ordered by a relation R is said to have *continuous order* (Dedekindian continuity) if it is compactly ordered by R and every non-empty class a, for which $a \subset b$, and which has an upper bound, has a least upper bound.

An important mathematical example of continuous order is afforded by the real numbers, ordered by the relation *not greater than*. According to usual geometric postulates, the points on a straight line also have continuous order, and, indeed, have the same order type as the real numbers.

The term *continuity* is also employed in mathematics in connection with functions of various kinds. We shall state the definition for the case of a monadic function f for which the range of the independent variable and the range of the dependent variable both consist of real numbers (see the article *Function*).

Let us use R for the relation *not greater than* among real numbers. A *neighborhood* of a real number c is determined by two real numbers m and n—both different from c and such that mRc and cRn—and is the class of real numbers x, other than m and n, such that mRx and xRn. The function f is said to be *continuous at* the real number c if the three following conditions are satisfied: (1) c belongs to the range of the independent variable; (2) in every neighborhood of c there are numbers other than c belonging to the range of the independent variable; (3) corresponding to every neighborhood b of $f(c)$ there is a neighborhood a of c such that, for every real number x belonging to the range of the independent variable, $x \epsilon a$ implies $f(x) \epsilon b$. A function may be called *continuous* if it is continuous at every real number, or at every real number in a certain set determined by the context.—*A.C.*

E. V. Huntington, *The Continuum,* Cambridge, Mass., 1917.

Continuum, Sensory: (Lat. *continuere,* to hold together) The unity of a single sensory field, (visual, tactual, auditory, etc.) or of the total sensory experience of an individual. (Cf. G. F. Stout, *Mind and Matter,* Bk. IV, Ch. III.) See *Consentience.*—*L.W.*

Contraction of a genus or species: (in Scholasticism) Is the determination or application of a genus to some species, or of a species to some individual.—*H.G.*

Contradictio in adjecto: A logical inconsistency between a noun and its modifying adjective. A favorite example is the phrase "round square."—*A.C.*

Contradiction, law of, is given by traditional logicians as "A is B and A is not B cannot both be true." It is usually taken to be the theorem of the propositional calculus, $\sim [p \sim p]$. In use, however, the name often seems to refer to the syntactical principle or precept which may be formulated as follows: A logical discipline containing (an applied) propositional calculus, or a set of hypotheses or postulates to be added to such a discipline, shall not lead to two theorems or consequences of the forms A and $\sim$A. The law is explicitly stated in a syntactical form, e.g. by Ledger Wood in his *The Analysis of Knowledge* (1940).—*A.C.*

Contrapletes: The two opposites or poles of a relationship which while they stand over against each other at the same time fulfill one another. Polarity, Dyadism, Harmony of opposites.—*R.T.F.*

Contraposition: The recommended use of this word is that according to which the contrapositive of $S(x) \supset_x P(x)$ is $\sim P(x) \supset_x \sim S(x)$. This is, however, not quite strictly in accordance with traditional terminology; see *Logic, formal,* § 4.—*A.C.*

Contraries: (a) *Logic:* (i) Terms: According to Aristotle, *Categ.* 11b-18, contrariety is one of the four kinds of opposition between concepts: contradictory, privative, contrary, relative. Those terms are contrary "which, in the same genus, are separated by the greatest possible difference" ib. 6a-17. Thus pairs of contraries belong to the same genus, or contrary sub-genera, or are themselves sub-genera. ib. 14a-18.

Strictly speaking, there are no contraries in the category of substance, since substances are the subject of contraries, nor in the category of quantity, since these are relative. Two contrary states cannot obtain in one and the same individual at the same time and in the same respect; cf. contradiction. Some contraries, e.g. good-bad, black-white, have intermediaries; while others do not, e.g. odd-even. (ii) Propositions: Two universal propositions, having opposite quality (i.e. one affirmative and one negative) are contrary; *De Interpretatione,* 17b-4, See *Logic, formal* § 4, 8.

(b) *Physics:* In Greek philosophy, the ultimate principles of nature and change were contraries: e.g. love-strife; motion-rest; potentiality-actuality. All motion is between contraries. See *Heraclitus, Empedocles, Aristotle.*—*L.M.H.*

Contrast: In aesthetics: the term may refer either to the presence in the object contemplated of contrasting elements (colors, sounds, characters, etc.), or to the principle that the presence of such contrasting elements is a common feature of beautiful objects which, within limits, enhances their beauty.—*W.K.F.*

Contrast: (*contrastare,* to stand opposed to) Relation, complementary to resemblance, obtaining between qualities. In a continuous qualitative series, the contrast increases as the resemblance diminishes.—*L.W.*

Contrast, Association by: (Lat. *contrastare,* to stand opposed to) Association in accordance with the principle proposed by Aristotle but rejected by Hartley, J. S. Mill and other associationists who hold that contrasting qualities tend to reinstate one another in consciousness. See *Association, Laws of.*—*L.W.*

Convention: (Lat. *conveniens,* suitable) Any proposition whose truth is determined not by fact but by social agreement or usage. In Democritus, "Sweet is sweet, bitter is bitter, color is color by convention (*nomoi*)." (Diels, *Frag. de. Vorsokratiker* B. 125) The Sophists (*q.v.*) regarded all laws and ethical principles as conventions.—*A.C.B.*

Conventionalism: Any doctrine according to which *a priori* truth, or the truth of propositions of logic, or the truth of propositions (or of sentences) demonstrable by purely logical means, is a matter of linguistic or postulational convention (and thus not absolute in character). H. Poincare (*q.v.*) regarded the choice of axioms as conventional (cf. *Science et hypothèse,* p. 67).—*A.C.*

Converse: See *logic, formal,* §§ 4, 8.

Coordinates: (from Lat. *co + ordinare,* to regulate) *Logical:* Items of the same order and rank in a scheme of classification. Also, class characteristics serving as indices of order or distinction among the elements of a series or assemblage.—*O.F.W.*

In mathematics, any system of designating points by means of ordered sets of *n* numbers may be called an *n-dimensional coordinate system,* and the *n* numbers so associated with any point are then called its *coordinates.* Coordinates may also be used in like fashion for various other things besides points.—*A.C.*

Copula: The traditional analysis of a proposition into subject and predicate involves a third part, the copula (*is, are, is not, are not*), binding the subject and predicate together into an assertion either of affirmation or of denial. It is now, however, commonly held that several wholly different meanings of the verb to be should be distinguished in this connection, including at least the following: predication of a monadic propositional function of its argument (the sun *is* hot, 7 *is* a prime number, mankind *is* numerous); formal implication (gold *is* heavy, a horse *is* a quadruped, mankind *is* sinful); identity (China *is* Cathay, that *is* the sun, I *am* the State); formal equivalence (lightning *is* an electric discharge between parts of a cloud or a cloud and the earth).—*A.C.*

Corollary: (Lat. *corollarium,* corollary) An immediate consequence of a theorem (*q.v.*).—*A.C.B.*

Corporative State: A type of state in which political and economic life is regulated through the medium of occupational associations. ''Corporations'' in Italy are the central liaison organs through which the employers' and the workers' organizations are brought together.—*W.E.*

Corrective Justice: Justice as exhibited in the rectification of wrongs committed by members of a community in their transactions with each other; distinguished from distributive justice (*q.v.*) (Aristotle's *Ethics*).—*G.R.M.*

Correlation, Sensory: (Lat. *co + relatus,* related) Correspondences between data of different senses, especially visual and tactual, by which the apprehension of perceptual objects is effected. Intersensory correlations depend upon the co-appearance rather than the comparison of data of different senses.—*L.W.*

Correspondence: Suppose there is some determinate relation R between members *a* of a class *A* and members *b* of a class *B*. Consider a subclass *B'* of *B*, consisting of *all* the *b*'s (in *B*) which are related by R to *each* member of some one sub-class A' of A. Then the members of B' may be said to *correspond* to the members of A'. If a class D corresponds to C as so defined (by means of the relation R) and the class C also corresponds to D (by means of the common relation R), the two classes may be said to *correspond to each other*.

If the relation R is such that when C and D so correspond, C must always have exactly k members and D exactly 1 member, the correspondence is termed a *k-1 correspondence*. By an obvious extension it is customary to speak also of *many-one, one-many,* and *many-many* correspondences.

Thus the heads and tails of coins are said to be in one-one correspondence; the square roots of positive integers in two-one correspondence with the positive integers. See *One-one.*—*M.B.*

Correspondence Theory of Truth: The theory that the truth of propositions is determined by the existence of some one-one correspondence between the terms of the proposition and the elements of some fact. Supporters of this view differ as to the nature of the determinate relation by which the alleged correspondence is constituted.

Contrasted with the *Coherence Theory of Truth.* Cf. B. Russell, *An Inquiry into Meaning and Truth,* 1941, for defence, and F. H. Bradley, *Essays on Truth and Reality,* for criticisms of the theory.—*M.B.*

In more general epistemology: Theory of knowledge which maintains that truth attaches to a proposition by virtue of its capacity to represent or portray fact. —*A.C.B.*

Cosmogony: (Gr. *cosmos a. gonia,* producing or creating the world) Is a pictorial treatment of the way in which the world or the universe came into being. In contrast to the most primitive civilizations, the great ethnic stocks of mankind have originated cosmogonies. The basal principles common to all mythological cosmogonies are: They deduce the creation of the world either from the fewest possible elements or from a single material principle such as water, ocean, earth, air, mud of river, slime, two halves of an egg, body of a giant, or from a spiritual or abstract principle such as an anthropomorphic god, deities, chaos, time, night. The genesis being a slow development characterized by an orderly sequence of periods, the creation process is variously divided into definite periods of specified units of years. The process of creation being self-originating, in its final stages the genealogy and origin of deities is a large admixture. There is no apparent ethical import attached to the cosmogonies. Few of them assume the idea of design as underlying the creation. They hold that the world had a beginning in time. The process of creation from less perfect to more perfect, from an original chaos to the final creation of man, the predominance of water in the original condition of the earth, the evolution of a spiritual or luminous principle reacting on the primeval water and the emphasis upon the godlike origin of man or his immediate relation to the deity, are all permeating threads of cosmogonic myths. In dualistic religions the world originates as a result of a hostile conflict of two opposing principles, or as a result of the parallel development of two opposing forces. The conception of creation *ex nihilo* was almost universally unknown in antiquity.—*H.H.*

Cosmological argument: Attempted to prove that God's existence follows from the fact that things exist. It aims to prove that there is a God by showing that causes presuppose causes, no matter how far back we go. The series of causes of causes can only come to an end in a cause which does not depend upon something else for its existence. Being the most basic proof of God's existence as it starts with the existence of anything, it is the favorite of most philosophers and theologians.—*H.H.*

Cosmology: A branch of philosophy which treats of the origin and structure of the universe. It is to be contrasted with *ontology* or *metaphysics*, the study of the most general features of reality, natural and supernatural, and with the *philosophy of nature*, which investigates the basic laws, processes and divisions of the objects in nature. It is perhaps impossible to draw or maintain a sharp distinction between these different subjects, and treatises which profess to deal with one of them usually contain considerable material on the others.

The main topics of cosmology, according to Hegel (*Encyclopedia*, section 35), are the contingency, necessity, eternity, limitations and formal laws of the world, the freedom of man and the origin of evil. Most philosophers would add to the foregoing the question of the nature and interrelationship of space and time, and would perhaps exclude the question of the nature of freedom and the origin of evil as outside the province of cosmology. The method of investigation has usually been to accept the principles of science or the results of metaphysics and develop the consequences. The test of a cosmology most often used is perhaps that of exhibiting the degree of accordance it has with respect to both empirical fact and metaphysical truth. The value of a cosmology seems to consist primarily in its capacity to provide an ultimate frame for occurrences in nature, and to offer a demonstration of where the limits of the spatio-temporal world are, and how they might be transcended.

Most of the basic problems and theories of cosmology seem to have been discussed by the pre-Socratic philosophers. Their views are modified and expanded in the *Timaeus* of Plato, and rehearsed and systematized in Aristotle's *Physics*. Despite multiple divergencies, all these Greek philosophers seem to be largely agreed that the universe is limited in space, has neither a beginning nor end in time, is dominated by a set of unalterable laws, and has a definite and recurring rhythm. The cosmology of the Middle Ages diverges from the Greek primarily through the introduction of the concepts of divine creation and annihilation, miracle and providence. In consonance with the tendencies of the new science, the cosmologies of Descartes, Leibniz and Newton bring the medieval views into closer harmony with those of the Greeks. The problems of cosmology were held to be intrinsically insoluble by Kant. After Kant there was a tendency to merge the issues of cosmology with those of metaphysics. The post-Kantians attempted to deal with both in terms of more basic principles and a more flexible dialectic; their opponents rejected both as without significance or value. The most radical modern cosmology is that of Peirce with its three cosmic principles of chance, law and continuity; the most recent is that of Whitehead, which finds its main inspiration in Plato's *Timaeus*.

Bibliography: Hermann Diels, *Doxographi Graeci;* Duhem, *Le Système du Monde;* Cherniss, *Aristotle's Criticisms of His Predecessors;* O'Neil, *Cosmology;* Burtt's *Metaphysical Foundations of Modern Science.—P.W.*

Cosmopolis: (Cosmopolitan) A type of universalism, derived first from the Cynic doctrine of the cosmopolis which proclaimed that the family and the city were artificial and that the wise man was the cosmopolitan. Taught also by the Cyrenaics. Later with the Stoics it came to mean a franchise of world citizenship with no differences as to class and race, a doctrine not always followed by the Roman Stoics. See *Cynics, Cyrenaics, Stoicism.—E.H.*

Cosmos: (Gr. *kosmos*—in order, duly; hence, good behavior, government; mode or fashion, ornament, dress (cf. cosmetic); a ruler; the world or universe as perfectly arranged and ordered; cf. providence.)

The early Greek notion of the universe as ordered by destiny or fate was gradually refined until the time of Plato and Aristotle who conceived the world as ordered by an intelligent principle (*nous*) of divine justice or harmony; Plato, *Philebus*, 30: ". . . there is in the universe a cause of no mean power, which orders and arranges . . .;" and Aristotle, *Physics*, 252a-12: "nature is everywhere the cause of order." This cosmic view was an essential element of the Stoic metaphysics, and was later incorporated into medieval philosophy and theology as the divine governance or ordering of creation, i.e. providence.

This "widespread instinctive conviction" in the order of nature, without its theological implications, became the basis and primary article of faith of modern natural science, whose aim is to express this rationality of nature as far as possible by the laws of natural science. (Cf. Whitehead, *Science and the Modern World*, p. 5ff). Opposed to *chaos, disorder, absence of law, irrationality.—L.M.H.*

Cosmothetic Idealism: A name given by Hamilton to that form of dualism (held e.g. by Descartes and Locke) which affirms (a) that there are both minds and material objects, and (b) that a mind can have only a mediate or representative perception of material objects.—*W.K.F.*

Counterpoint: Art of combining with a given melody, one or more simultaneous and independent melodies.—*L.V.*

Counting: (Lat. *computare*, to reckon, compute) The process of determining the number of a class of objects by establishing a one-to-one correspondence between the class in question and a portion of the class of natural numbers beginning with 1 and ordered in the usual way.—*A.C.B.*

Courage: In ethical discussions courage is usually regarded as a virtue (it is one of the traditional cardinal virtues), and either enjoined as a duty or praised as an excellence. When thus regarded as a virtue, courage is generally said to be a disposition, not merely instinctive, to exhibit a certain firmness, stopping short of rashness, in the face of danger, threat, temptation, pain, public opinion, etc. (thus including "moral" as well as physical courage, and passive courage or "fortitude" as well as active courage); which disposition, if it is to be a virtue, must, it is thought, be exhibited in the course of what the bearer knows or believes to be his duty, or at least in the support of some cause to which one is seriously committed or which is generally regarded as worthwhile.—*W.K.F.*

Cournot, Antoine Augustin: (1801-1877) French mathematician, economist, and philosopher, is best known for his interest in probability. His philosophical writings, long neglected, reflect disagreement both with the positivism of his own day and with the earlier French rationalism. His place between the two is manifest in his doctrine that order and contingency, continuity and discontinuity, are equally real. This metaphysical position led him to conclude that man, though he cannot attain certain truth of nature, can by increasing the probable truth of his statements approach this truth. Cournot's mathematical investigations into probability and his mathematical treatment of economics thus harmonize with his metaphysics and epistemology. Main works: *Exposition de la théorie des chances et des probabilités*, 1843; *Essai sur les fondements de la connaissance*, 2 vols. 1851; *Consid. sur les marches des idées*, 1872; *Matérialisme, Vitalisme, Rationalism*, 1875; *Traité de l'Enchainement des idées fondamentales dans les sciences et dans l'histoire*, 1881. —*C.K.D.*

Cousin, Victor: (1792-1867) Was among those principally responsible for producing the shift in French philosophy away from sensationalism in the direction of "spiritualism"; in his own thinking, Cousin was first influenced by Locke and Condillac, and later turned to idealism under the influence of Maine de Biran and Schelling. His most characteristic philosophical insights are contained in *Fragments Philosophiques* (1826), in which he advocated as the basis of metaphysics a careful observation and analysis of the facts of the conscious life. He lectured at the Sorbonne from 1815 until 1820 when he was suspended for political reasons, but he was reinstated in 1827 and continued to lecture there until 1832. He exercised a great influence on his philosophical contemporaries and founded the spiritualistic or eclectic school in French Philosophy. The members of his school devoted themselves largely to historical studies for which Cousin had provided the example in his *Introduction á l'Histoire Général de la Philosophie*, 7th ed. 1872.—*L.W.*

Cratylus of Athens: A Heraclitean and first teacher of Plato. Carried the doctrine of irreconcilability of opposites so far that he renounced the use of spoken language. Plato's dialogue of same name criticized the Heraclitean theory of language.—*E.H.*

Creation: (in Scholasticism) Is the production of a thing from nothing either of itself or of a subject which could sustain the finished product. In other words, both the material as well as formal causes are produced *ex nihilo*, or, as in the case of certain doctrines on the *soul*, the formal cause is produced *ex nihilo* without any intrinsic dependence on the material cause of the total entity, man; which material cause in this case would be the body.—*H.G.*

Creative Theory of Perception: The creative theory, in opposition to the selective theory, asserts that the data of

sense are created or constituted by the act of perception and do not exist except at the time and under the conditions of actual perception. (cf. C. D. Broad, *The Mind and its Place in Nature*, pp. 200ff.) See *Selective Theory of Perception*. The theories of perception of Descartes, Locke, Leibniz and Berkeley are historical examples of creative theories; Russell (*Problems of Philosophy*, Ch. II and III) and the majority of the American critical realists defend creative theories.—*L.W.*

Credo quia absurdum est: Literally, I believe because it is absurd. Although these particular words are often wrongly attributed to Tertullian (born middle of the 2nd century) they nevertheless convey the thought of this Latin church father who maintained the rule of faith on the basis of one's trust in the commands and authority of Christ rather than upon the compulsion of reason or truth. To believe in the absurd, in other words, is to reveal a greater faith than to believe in the reasonable.—*V.F.*

Credo ut intelligam: Literally, I believe in order that I may understand. A principle which affirms that after an act of faith a philosophy begins, held by such thinkers as Augustine, Anselm, Duns Scotus and many others.—*V.F.*

Creighton, James Edwin: (1861-1924) Professor of Logic and Metaphysics at Cornell University. He was one of the founders and a president of the American Philosophical Association, American editor of *Kant-Studien* and editor of *The Philosophical Review*. He was greatly influenced by Bosanquet. His *Introductory Logic* had long been a standard text. His basic ideas as expressed in articles published at various times were posthumously published in a volume entitled *Studies in Speculative Philosophy*, a term expressive of his intellectualistic form of objective idealism.—*L.E.D.*

Crescas, Don Hasdai: (1340-1410) Jewish philosopher and theologian. He was the first European thinker to criticize Aristotelian cosmology and establish the probability of the existence of an infinite magnitude and of infinite space, thus paving the way for the modern conception of the universe. He also took exception to the entire trend of the philosophy of Maimonides, namely its extreme rationalism, and endeavored to inject the emotional element into religious contemplation, and make love an attribute of God and the source of His creative activity. He also expressed original views on the problems of freedom and creation. He undoubtedly exerted influence on Spinoza who quotes him by name in the formulation of some of his theories. See *Jewish Philosophy*. Cf. H. A. Wolfson, *Crescas' Critique of Aristotle*, 1929.—*M.W.*

Criterion: Broadly speaking, any ground, basis, or means of judging anything as to its quality. Since validity, truth, goodness, justice, virtue, and beauty are some of the most fundamental qualities for philosophic enquiry, criteria for these are embodied in almost all philosophies and are either assumed or derived. In logic, consistency is a generally recognized criterion; in epistemology, evidence of the senses, comparison, or reason may be regarded as criteria; in metaphysical speculation there have been suggested, as criteria for truth, among others, correspondence, representation, practicability, and coherence; in religion, evidences of faith, revelation or miracle; in ethics, pleasure, desirability, utility, self-determination of the will, duty, conscience, happiness, are among common criteria, while in aesthetics there have been cited interest, satisfaction, enjoyment, utility, harmony.—*K.F.L.*

Criterion ethical: In ethics the main problem is often said to be the finding of a criterion of virtue, or of rightness, or of goodness, depending on which of these concepts is taken as basic; and the quest for a moral standard, or for an ethical first principle, or for a *summum bonum* may generally be construed as a quest for such a criterion (e.g., Kant's first form of the categorical.imperative may be interpreted as a criterion of rightness). Hence to find a criterion of, say, goodness is to find a characteristic whose presence, absence, or degree may be taken as a mark of the presence, absence, or degree of goodness. Thus hedonists hold pleasantness to be such a characteristic. Often, finding a *criterion* of a characteristic is taken as equivalent to finding a *definition* of that characteristic. Strictly, this is not the case, for a characteristic may serve as a criterion of another with which it is not identical. Pleasantness might be a criterion of goodness without being identical with it, if only the above relation held between pleasantness and goodness. However, the discovery of a definition of a characteristic does normally furnish a criterion of that characteristic. *Vide* the definition of a right act as an act conducive to the greatest happiness.

To some minds the ethical quest results in a failure to find and in a denial of the existence of any single moral criterion—this is the position of such intuitionists as G. E. Moore and W. D. Ross and of some relativists.—*W.K.F.*

Critical Idealism: Kant's designation for his theory of knowledge. See *Idealism, Kant*.—*W.L.*

Critical Monism: (a) In ontology: The view of reality which holds that it is one in number but that the unity embraces real multiplicity. Harald Höffding (1843-1931) gave the title of critical monism to the theory that reality, like conscious experience, is one although there are many items within that experience. Another example: both the One and the Many exist and in the closest relation without either merging or cancelling the other. The One is immanent in the Many although transcendent; the Many are immanent in the One although in a sense beyond it.

(b) In epistemology: A variety of "critical realism." The view which holds that in the knowledge-relation the subject or percipient is at one (monism) with the object or the thing objectively existent and perceived; and that the subject contributes qualities not inherent in the object (hence, critical) and the object contains qualities not perceived.—*V.F.*

Critical Realism: A theory of knowledge which affirms an objective world independent of one's perception or conception of it (hence realistic) but critical in the sense of acknowledging the difficulties in affirming that all in the knowing relation is objective. The theory must be distinguished further as follows:

(a) In general, critical realism is distinguished from naïve or uncritical realism.

(b) It may refer to any number of realists, such as those of the Scottish School, critical monism, etc. (See under proper headings.)

(c) A special school called "Critical Realists" arose as a reactionary movement against the alleged extravagant views of another school of realists called the "New Realists" (*q.v.*). According to the "Critical Realists" the objective world, existing independently of the subject, is separated in the knowledge-relation by media or vehicles or essences. These intermediaries are not objects but conveyances of knowledge. The mind knows the objective world not directly (epistemological monism) but *by means of* a vehicle through which we perceive and think (epistemological dualism). For some, this vehicle is an immediate mental essence referring to existences, for some a datum, for some a subsistent realm mediating knowledge, and for one there is not so much a vehicle as there is a peculiar transcendental grasping of objects in cognition. In 1920 *Essays in Critical Realism* was published as the manifesto, the platform of this school. Its collaborators were: D. Drake, A. O. Lovejoy, J. B. Pratt, A. K. Rogers, G. Santayana, R. W. Sellars, and C. A. Strong.—*V.F.*

Criticism: (Kant.) An investigation of the nature and limits of reason and knowledge, conducted in a manner to avoid both dogmatism and skepticism. The term is generally used to designate Kant's thought after 1770. See *Kantianism*.—*O.F.K.*

Critique of Pure Reason: (Ger. *Kritik der reinen Vernunft*) The first of three Critiques written by Immanuel Kant (1781) in which he undertook a critical examination of pure reason, its nature and limits, with a view to exhibiting a criterion for judging the validity of propositions of metaphysics. The first *Critique* was followed by the *Critique of Practical Reason* (1788), and the *Critique of Judgment* (1790). See *Kantianism*.—*O.F.K.*

Croce, Benedetto: (1866-1952) Born at Percaseroli (Abruzzi) Italy, February 25, 1866. Senator, Minister of Public Education. Has influenced every branch of Italian culture.

Considers all human experience an historical experience, philosophy being the methodology of history.

His aesthetics defines art as an expression of sentiment, as a language. His logic emphasizes the distinction of categories, reducing opposition to a derivative of distinction. According to his ethics, economics is an autonomous and absolute moment of spirit. His theory of history regards all history as contemporaneous. His philosophy is one of the greatest attempts at elaboration of pure concepts entirely appropriate to historical experience. B. Croce, *Estetica*, 1902; *Logica*, 1905-1909; *Filosofia della prattica* (1909); *Teoria e storia della storiografia*, 1917; *What is Living and What is Dead of Hegel* (tr. 1915); *Historical Materialism and*

Econ. of K. Marx (tr. 1922); *History as the Story of Liberty* (tr. 1941).—*L.V.*

Cross-Roads Hypothesis: Theory of the relation between the mental and the physical which holds that an identical item (*e.g.* a red color patch) may in one relational context be considered physical and in another context be mental. The neutral entity may accordingly be represented as the point of intersection of the physical and mental cross-roads. Cf. W. James, *Essays in Radical Empiricism*, Chaps. I, II and VIII and *The Meaning of Truth*, pp. 46-50. See *Neutral Monism*.—*L.W.*

Cudworth, Ralph: (1617-1688) Was the leading Cambridge Platonist (*q.v.*). His writings were devoted to a refutation of Hobbesean materialism which he characterized as atheistic. He accepted a rationalism of the kind advanced by Descartes. He found clear and distinct fundamental notions or categories reflecting universal reason, God's mind, the nature and essence of things and the moral laws, which he held to be as binding on God as the axioms of mathematics. His two most important works are *The True Intellectual System of the Universe*, and *A Treatise concerning Eternal and Immutable Morality*.—*L.E.D.*

Culture: (Lat. *cultura,* from *colo,* cultivate) The intrinsic value of society. Syn. with civilization. Employed by Spengler to define a civilization in its creative growth-period. The means, i.e. the tools, customs and institutions, of social groups; or the employment of such means. In psychology: the enlightenment or education of the individual. Some distinguish culture from civilization (*q.v.*): the former being the effect on personal development and expression (art, science, religion) of the institutions, materials and social organization identified with the latter.—*J.K.F.*

Cusa, Nicholas of: (1401-1464) Born in Cusa (family name: Krebs), educated in the mystical school of Deventer, and at the Universities of Heidelberg, Padua and Cologne. He became a Cardinal in 1448, Bishop of Brixen in 1450, and died at Todi. He was interested in mathematics, astronomy, philosophy and ecclesiastical policy. His thought is Neo-Platonic and mystical; he is critical of Aristotelian Scholasticism. His theories of "learned ignorance" and the "concordance of contraries" have been historically influential. Chief works: *De concordantia Catholica, De docta ignorantia, De conjecturis* (*Opera,* Paris, 1514). E. Van Steenberghe, *Le Card. N. de Cuse, Paction, la pensée* (Paris, 1920).—*V.J.B.*

Customs: (a) Behavior patterns participated in by persons as members of a group, contrasted with personal or random group behavior patterns, including folkways, conventions, mores, institutions.

(b) Behavior patterns long established in a group as contrasted with newly enacted laws or newly acquired conduct practices.

(c) Group behavior patterns which are unenforced (folkways) or moderately enforced (conventions) or morally enforced (mores) as contrasted with institutions which are legally enforced.—*A.J.B.*

Cynics: A school of Greek Philosophy, named after the gymnasium Cynosarges, founded by Antisthenes of Athens, friend of Socrates. Man's true happiness, the Cynics taught, lies in right and intelligent living, and this constitutes for them also the concept of the *virtuous* life. For the Cynics, this right and virtuous life consists in a course of conduct which is as much as possible independent of all events and factors external to man. This independence can be achieved through mastery over one's desires and wants. The Cynics attempted to free man from bondage to human custom, convention and institution by reducing man's desires and appetites to such only as are indispensable to life and by renouncing those which are imposed by civilization. In extreme cases, such as that of Diogenes, this philosophy expressed itself in a desire to live the natural life in the midst of the civilized Greek community.—*M.F.*

Cyrenaics: A school of Greek Philosophy founded by Aristippus of Cyrene. The teachings of this school are known as the philosophy of Hedonism, or the doctrine of enjoyment for its own sake. For the Cyrenaics the virtuous or the good life is that which yields the greatest amount of contentment or pleasure derived from the satisfaction of desire. Education and intelligence are necessary so as to guide one to proper enjoyment, that is to such satisfaction of desire as yields most pleasure and is least likely to cause one pain. It also aids one in being master of pleasure and not its slave.—*M.F.*

D

D'Alembert, Jean Le Rond: (1717-1783) Brilliant French geometer. He was for a time an assistant to Diderot in the preparation of the Encyclopaedia and wrote its "Discours Preliminaire." He advanced a noteworthy empirical theory of mathematics in opposition to the stand of Plato or Descartes. He was greatly influenced by Bacon in his presentation of the order and influence of the sciences. He was greatly opposed to organized religion and sceptical as to the existence and nature of God. His ethical views were based on what he characterized as the evidence of the heart and had sympathy as their mainspring.—*L.E.D.*

Damascius: The last head of the Platonic Academy and a commentator on the works of Plato.—*M.F.*

Dance: The art of following musical rhythm with the movement of the human body. It is considered the most elementary art because the product is not detached from the body of the artist.—*L.V.*

Daṇḍanīti: (Skr.) Political science.—*K.F.L.*

Dandyism: A form of aestheticism which pretends to give aesthetic value to a smart life.—*L.V.*

Darśana: (Skr. view) Philosophy, philosophical position, philosophical system. Six systems (*saddarsana*) are recognized as orthodox in Indian philosophy because they fall in line with Vedic tradition (cf. *Indian Philosophy*).—*K.F.L.*

Darwin, Charles: (1809-1882) The great English naturalist who gathered masses of data on the famous voyage of the Beagle and then spent twenty additional years shaping his pronouncement of an evolutionary hypothesis in *The Origin of Species,* published in 1859. He was not the first to advance the idea of the kinship of all life but is memorable as the expositor of a provocative and simple explanation in his theory of natural selection. He served to establish firmly in all scientific minds the fact of evolution even if there remains doubt as to the precise method or methods of evolution. From his premises, he elaborated a subsidiary doctrine of sexual selection. In addition to the biological explanations, there appear some keen observations and conclusions for ethics particularly in his later *Descent of Man.*

Evolution, since his day, has been of moment in all fields of thought. See *Evolutionism, Natural Selection, Struggle for Existence.*—*L.E.D.*

Dasein: (G. in Scheler) Factuality.—*P.A.S.*

Datum: That which is given or presented. (a) In logic: facts from which inferences may be drawn. (b) In epistemology: an actual presented to the mind; the given of knowledge. (c) In psychology: that which is given in sensation; the content of sensation.—*J.K.F.*

Daud, Abraham Ibn: (of Toledo, 1110-1180) Jewish historian and philosopher with distinctly Aristotelian bent. His *Emunah Ramah* (Al-Akidā Al-Rafiā), i.e., Exalted Faith, deals with the principles of both philosophy and religion and with ethics. He also enunciated six dogmas of Judaism to which every Jew must subscribe.—*M.W.*

De Beauvoir, Simone: (1908-   ) Novelist, dramatist, and philosopher, she was the most distinguished woman writer in France at the time. Known for her life-long relationship with the existentialist Jean-Paul Sartre, she wrote *The Second Sex* (1949), *The Ethics of Ambiguity, She Came to Stay, All Men are Mortal, The Mandarins,* and a multi-volume autobiography (including *Memoirs of a Dutiful Daughter* (1958), *The Prime of Life* (1960), *Force of Circumstances* (1963), *All Said and Done* (1974).—*S.E.N.*

Deanthropomorphism: (*de,* a privative; Gr. *anthropos,* man, and *morphe,* form) The philosophic tendency, first cynically applied by Xenophanes ("if cattle and lions had hands to paint. . .") and since then by rationalists and addicts of enlightenment, to get rid of an understandable, if primitive, desire to endow phenomena and the hypostatized objects of man's thought and aspirations with human characteristics. —*K.F.L.*

Decadence: Period of art considered destructive of the aesthetic values of an age previously believed perfect. —*L.V.*

Decision: (Lat. *de + caedere,* to cut) The act of assent in which volition normally culminates. See *Volition.*—*L.W.*

89

Decision problem: See *Logic, formal,* §§ 1, 3.

Decurtate syllogism: A syllogistic enthymeme; a syllogism with one premiss unexpressed.—*C.A.B.*

Dedekind, (Julius Wilhelm) Richard: (1831-1916) German mathematician. Professor of mathematics at Brunswick, 1862-1894. His contributions to the foundations of arithmetic and analysis are contained in his *Stetigkeit und Irrationale Zahlen* (1st edn., 1872, 5th edn., 1927) and *Was Sind und Was Sollen die Zahlen?* (1st edn., 1888, 6th edn., 1930).—*A.C.*

Gesammelte Mathematische Werke, three volumes, Brunswick, 1930-1932.

Dedekind's postulate: If K_1 and K_2 are any two non-empty parts of K, such that every element of K belongs either to K_1 or to K_2 and every element of K_1 precedes every element of K_2, then there is at least one element x in K such that (1) any element that precedes x belongs to K_1, and (2) any element that follows x belongs to K_2. Here *K* is a class ordered by a relation *R* (see *order*), and it is said that *y* precedes *z*, and that *z* follows *y*, if *yRz* and $y \neq z$. If *K* is densely ordered by *R* and in addition satisfies Dedekind's postulate, it is said to have continuous order.—*C.A.B.*

Deduction: (Lat. *deductio,* a leading down) Necessary analytical inference. (a) In logic: inference in which a conclusion follows necessarily from one or more given premisses. Definitions given have usually required that the conclusion be of lesser generality than one of the premisses, and have sometimes explicitly excluded immediate inference; but neither restriction fits very well with the ordinary actual use of the word. (b) In psychology: analytical reasoning from general to particular or less general. The mental drawing of conclusions from given postulates.

Deduction of the Categories: (In Kant: Deduktion der Kategorien) *Transcendental deduction:* An exposition of the nature and possibility of a priori forms and the explanation and justification of their use as necessary conditions of experience. *Empirical deduction:* Factual explanation of how concepts arise in experience and reflection. See *Kantianism.*—*O.F.K.*

Deduction theorem: In a *logistic system (q.v.)* containing propositional calculus (pure or applied) or a suitable part of the propositional calculus, it is often desirable to have the property that if the inference from A to B is a valid inference then A ⊃ B is a theorem, or, more generally, that if the inference from $A_1, A_2, \ldots, A_n$ to B is valid then the inference from $A_1, A_2, \ldots, A_{n-1}$ to $A_n \supset B$ is valid. The syntactical theorem, asserting of a given logistic system that it has this property, is called the *deduction theorem* for that system. (Certain cautions are necessary in defining the notion of valid inference where free variables are present; cf. *Logic, formal,* §§ 1, 3.)—*A.C.*

Definition: In the development of a *logistic system (q. v.)* it is usually desirable to introduce new notations, beyond what is afforded by the primitive symbols alone, by means of *syntactical definitions* or *nominal definitions,* i.e., conventions which provide that certain symbols or expressions shall stand (as substitutes or abbreviations) for particular formulas of the system. This may be done either by particular definitions, each introducing a symbol or expression to stand for some one formula, or by *schemata* of definition, providing that any expression of a certain form shall stand for a certain corresponding formula (so condensing many—often infinitely many—particular definitions into a single schema). Such definitions, whether particular definitions or schemata, are indicated, in article herein by the present writer, by an arrow →, the new notation introduced (the *definiendum*) being placed a the left, or base, of the arrow, and the formula for which it shall stand (the *definiens*) being placed at the right, o head, of the arrow. Another sign commonly employed for the same purpose (instead of the arrow) is the equality sign = with the letters Df, or df, appearing either as a subscript or separately after the definiens.

This use of nominal definition (including contextua definition—see the article *Incomplete symbol*) in con nection with a logistic system is extraneous to the sys tem in the sense that it may theoretically be dispensed with, and all formulas written in full. Practically, how ever, it may be necessary for the sake of brevity o perspicuity, or for facility in formal work.

Such methods of introducing new concepts, func tions, etc. as definition by *abstraction (q.v.),* definitio by *recursion (q. v.),* definition by *composition* (see *Recursiveness*) may be dealt with by reducing them t nominal definitions; i.e., by finding a nominal defini tion such that the definiens (and therefore also the definiendum) turns out, under an intended interpreta tion of the logistic system, to mean the concept, func tion, etc. which is to be introduced.

In addition to syntactical or nominal definition we may distinguish another kind of definition, which i applicable only in connection with *interpreted* logistic systems, and which we shall call *semantical definition* This consists in introducing a new symbol or notation by assigning a *meaning* to it. In an interpreted logistic system, a nominal definition carries with it implicitly a semantical definition, in that it is intended to give to the definiendum the meaning expressed by the definiens but two different nominal definitions may correspond t the same semantical definition. Consider, for example the two following schemata of nominal definition in the propositional calculus (*Logic, formal,* § 1):

$$[A] \supset [B] \to \sim A \vee B.$$
$$[A] \supset [B] \to \sim[A \sim B].$$

As nominal definitions these are inconsistent, since they represent [A] ⊃ [B] as standing for different formulas either one, but not both, could be used in a developmen of the propositional calculus. But the corresponding semantical definitions would be identical if—as would be possible—our interpretation of the propositiona calculus were such that the two definientia had the same meaning for any particular A and B.

In the formal development of a logistic system, since no reference may be made to an intended interpretation semantical definitions are precluded, and must be replaced by corresponding nominal definitions.

Of quite a different kind are so-called *real definitions*, which are not conventions for introducing new symbols or notations—as syntactical and semantical definitions are—but are propositions of equivalence (material, formal, etc.) between two abstract entities (propositions, concepts, etc.) of which one is called the *definiendum* and the other the *definiens*. Not all such propositions of equivalence, however, are real definitions, but only those in which the definiens embodies the "essential nature" (essentia, *ousia*) of the definiendum. The notion of a real definition thus has all the vagueness of the quoted phrase, but the following may be given as an example. If all the notations appearing, including ⊃ $_x$, have their usual meanings (regarded as given in advance), the proposition expressed by

$$(F)(G)[[F(x) \supset _x G(x)] \equiv$$
$$(x)[\sim F(x) \vee G(x)]]$$

is a real definition of formal implication—to be contrasted with the nominal definition of the *notation* for formal implication which is given in the article *Logic, formal*, § 3. This formula, expressing a real definition of formal implication, might appear, e.g., as a primitive formula in a logistic system.

(A situation often arising in practice is that a word—or symbol or notation—which already has a vague meaning is to be given a new exact meaning, which is vaguely, or as nearly as possible, the same as the old. This is done by a nominal or semantical definition rather than a real definition; nevertheless it is usual in such a case to speak either of defining the *word* or of defining the associated *notion*.)

Sometimes, however, the distinction between nominal definitions and real definitions is made on the basis that the latter convey an assertion of *existence*, of the definiendum, or rather, where the definiendum is a concept, of things falling thereunder (Saccheri, 1697); or the distinction may be made on the basis that real definitions involve the *possibility* of what is defined (Leibniz, 1684). Ockham makes the distinction rather on the basis that real definitions state the whole nature of a thing and nominal definitions state the meaning of a word or phrase, but adds that non-existents (as chimaera) and such parts of speech as verbs, adverbs, and conjunctions may therefore have only nominal definition.—*A.C.*

Definition of a term: (in Scholasticism) *Nominal:* Is discourse (language, speech, *oratio*) by which the meaning of a term is explained.

Positive: That which reveals the essence of a thing in positive terms, e.g., man is a rational animal.

Negative: That which states the nature of a thing in negative terms, e.g., God is not mortal, not corporeal, etc. Cf. *La Logique de Port-Royal*, Pt. I, ch. XII.

De Interpretatione: (Gr. *peri hermeneias*) The second treatise in the Aristotelian *Organon*, dealing with the logical analysis of judgments and propositions. See *Aristotelianism.*—*G.R.M.*

Deism: (Lat. *deus*, god) Two uses of the term: (a) By many writers the term covers the view that God has no immediate relation with the world; God indeed is responsible for the world but for reasons unknown or conjectured God has no commerce with it; accordingly, the supplications and hopes of men are illusory and fruitless. This doctrine is sometimes referred to as the "absentee landlord" view. Thomas Hardy's famous poem "God Forgotten" is an illustration.

(b) Deism is a term referring collectively and somewhat loosely to a group of religious thinkers of the 17th (and 18th) century in England and France who in attempting to justify religion, particularly Christianity, began by establishing the harmony of reason and revelation and developed what, in their time, was regarded as extreme views: assaults upon traditional supernaturalism; external revelation and dogmas implying mysteries, and concluding that revelation is superfluous, that reason is the touchstone to religious validity, that religion and ethics are natural phenomena, that the traditional God need hardly be appealed to since man finds in nature the necessary guides for moral and religious living. Not all deists, so called, went toward the more extreme expressions. Among the more important English deists were Toland, Collins, Tindal, Chubb and Morgan. Voltaire (1694-1778), influenced by English thought, is the notable example of deism in France. On the whole the term represents a tendency rather than a school.—*V.F.*

Delusion: (Lat. *de + ludere*, to play) Erroneous or non-veridical cognition. The term is properly restricted to perception, memory and other non-inferential forms of knowledge but is at times extended to include inferential beliefs and theories. See *Veridical*. The two principal types of delusion are: (a) *illusion* or partially delusive cognition, *e.g.*, the ordinary distortions of sense and memory which nevertheless have a basis in fact, and (b) hallucination or totally delusive cognition such as dreams, pseudo-memories, etc., to which nothing corresponds in fact. See *Illusion; Hallucination.*—*L.W.*

Demiurge: (Gr. *demiourgos*) Artisan; craftsman; the term used by Plato in the *Timaeus* to designate the intermediary maker of the world.—*G.R.M.*

Democritus of Abdera: (c. 460-360 B.C.) Developed the first important materialist philosophy of nature, unless we are to count that of Leukippus. His influence was transmitted by Lucretius' poem till the centuries of the Renaissance when scholars' attention began to turn toward the study of nature. He taught that all substance consists of atoms, that is, of indivisible and imperceptibly small particles. The variety of atomic forms corresponds to, and accounts for, the variety of material qualities; the finest, smoothest, and most agile atoms constitute the substance of mind. Human perception is explained by him as an emanation of tiny copies of sensible things (eidola), which, through their impact upon the atoms of mind, leave impressions responsible for facts of memory, Diels, *Fragm der Vorsokr*, 4a; F. A. Lange, *Gesch. der Materialismus*, bd. I.—*R.B.W.*

Demonology: Referring to a study of the widespread religious ideas of hostile superhuman beings called demons. These creatures were generally thought of as inhabiting a super- or under-world and playing havoc with the fortunes of man by bringing about diseases, mental twists and calamities in general. Ridding an individual supposedly held in possession by such a demon was an ancient practice (technically known as "exorcism") and continued in some Christian liturgies even to our own day. Demonology as a theory of demonic behavior throve among the Egyptians, Babylonians, Assyrians, Persians, Post-exilic Hebrews, Jews, Greeks and many scattered peoples including the hoary ancients. Elaborate demonic ideas appear in the Mohammedan religion.—*V.F.*

Demonstration: (Lat *de + monstrare*, to show) Proof of a proposition by disclosure of the deductive processes by which it can be inferred.—*A.C.B.*

De Morgan, Augustus: (1806-1871) English mathematician and logician. Professor of mathematics at University College, London, 1828-1831, 1836-1866. His *Formal Logic* of 1847 contains some points of an algebra of logic essentially similar to that of Boole (*q.v.*), but the notation is less adequate than Boole's and the calculus is less fully worked out and applied. De Morgan, however, had the notion of logical sum for arbitrary classes—whereas Boole contemplated addition only of classes having no members in common. *De Morgan's laws* (*q.v.*)—as they are now known—were also enunciated in this work. The treatment of the syllogism is original, but has since been superseded, and does not constitute the author's real claim to remembrance as a logician. (The famous controversy with Sir William Hamilton over the latter's charge of plagiarism in connection with this treatment of the syllogism may therefore be dismissed as not of present interest.)

Through his paper *On the syllogism, no. IV* in the Transactions of the Cambridge Philosophical Society, vol. 10 (read April 23, 1860), De Morgan is to be regarded as the founder of the logic of relations.—*A.C.*

Sophia Elizabeth De Morgan, *Memoir of Augustus De Morgan,* London, 1882.

De Morgan's laws: Are the two dually related theorems of the propositional calculus,

$$\sim [p \vee q] \equiv [\sim p \ \sim q],$$
$$\sim [pq] \equiv [\sim p \vee \sim q],$$

or the two corresponding dually related theorems of the algebra of classes,

$$-(a \cup b) = -a \cap -b,$$
$$-(a \cap b) = -a \cup -b.$$

In the propositional calculus these laws (together with the law of double negation) make it possible to define conjunction in terms of negation and (inclusive) disjunction, or, alternatively, disjunction in terms of negation and conjunction. Similarly in the algebra of classes logical product may be defined in terms of logical sum and complementation, or logical sum in terms of logical product and complementation.

As pointed out by Łukasiewicz, these laws of the propositional calculus were known already (in verbal form) to Ockham. The attachment of De Morgan's name to the corresponding laws of the algebra of classes appears to be historically more correct.

Sometimes referred to as generalizations or analogues of De Morgan's laws are the two dually related theorems of the functional calculus of first order,

$$\sim (Ex)F(x) \equiv (x)\sim F(x),$$
$$\sim (x)F(x) \equiv (Ex)\sim F(x),$$

and similar theorems in higher functional calculi. These make possible the definition of the existential quantifier in terms of the universal quantifier (or inversely). —*A.C.*

Denial of the antecedent: The *fallacy of denial of the antecedent* is the fallacious inference from $\sim$A and A $\supset$ B to $\sim$B. The *law of denial of the antecedent* is the theorem of the propositional calculus, $\sim p \supset [p \supset q]$.—*A.C.*

Denomination: (Lat. *denominatio*) Literally: a naming of something from some other thing. In Scholastic logic, it is the operation of applying a term to a subject, when the term is derived from something to which the subject is related. Thus a substance may be denominated by deriving a name from its accidents. Extrinsic denomination is dependent upon wholly external relationship. See *Denotation.*—*V.J.B.*

Denotation: The subjects (i.e., those entities which possess attributes) of which a term may be predicated; e.g., the term "man" denotes Socrates, Plato, Aristotle, etc. (J. S. Mill) "Denotation" in this sense should be distinguished from "extension" in the sense in which that signifies the subclasses of the class determined by the term. The former indicates the various *individual instances* in which a common nature is manifested; the latter signifies the variety of *kinds* over which the predication of a term may extend. (H. W. B. Joseph.)—*C.A.B.*

In common usage, "denotation" has a less special meaning, *denote* being approximately synonymous with *designate* (*q.v.*). A proper name may be said to/ denote that of which it is a name. Or, e.g., in the equation 2 + 2 = 4, the sign + may be said to denote addition and the sign = to denote equality (even without necessarily intending to construe these signs as proper names).

Concerning Frege's distinction between sense and denotation see the article *Descriptions.*—*A.C.*

Denotation is a semantical concept, see *Semiotic 2.*—*R.C.*

Dense order: See *Continuity.*

Deontological ethics: Any ethics which does not make the theory of obligation entirely dependent on the theory of value, holding that an action may be known to be right without a consideration of the goodness of anything, or at least that an action may be right and be known to be so even though it does not flow from the agent's best motive (or even from a good one) and does not, by being performed, bring into being as much good as some other action open to the agent. Opposed to axiological ethics. Also called formalism and intuitionism. See *Intuitionism.*—*W.K.F.*

Depersonalization: A personality disorder in which the subject's own words and actions assume for him a character of strangeness or unreality; in its extreme form, the subject is obsessed with the fear of complete dissolution of personality. The English term is an appropriation of the French *dépersonnalization.—L.W.*

Deproblematization: (Ger. *Deproblematisierung*) The gradual cessation of the former problematical tone of any object or idea. (Avenarius.)*—H.H.*

De Sanctis, Francesco: Born at Morra Irpina (Avellino), March 28, 1817. Died at Naples, December 19, 1883. Imprisoned and exiled because liberal, 1848. Professor in Zurich and later in Naples. Minister of Public Education. His *History of Italian Literature* (1870) is still considered fundamental.

Applied Hegel's idealism to literary criticism. Gave a new interpretation to poets' sentiments and ideals, and linked them to the civil history of Italy. New Italian idealism of about 1900 was based on his thought.*—L.V.*

Descartes, René: (1596-1650) The founder of modern philosophy with his method of radical doubt. A rationalist, he used the mathematical method and non-contradiction to establish truth. Born at La Haye, France, his health was so fragile that his existence was threatened, and he was brought to health only by the efforts of a devoted nurse. Educated at the new royal college (by Jesuit teachers) of La Fléche, he also studied law at Poitiers. Joining the army, he saw Europe, returning in the winter of 1619 when he was unexpectedly detained in Ulm by heavy snows. With time to meditate, he received in a dream, according to his account, certain of the ideas that later made him famous. (See also *Cartesianism.*)

His major works include the *Discourse on Method* (1637), *Meditations* (1641), *Principles of Philosophy* (1644), and *Treatise on Passions* (ethics, 1649).

He died in Sweden while tutoring Queen Christina. The early hour which she insisted on, combined with the bitter cold of Swedish winter, proved to be too rigorous for his constitution.*—S.E.N.*

Description, Knowledge by: (Lat. *de* + *scribere*, to write) Knowledge *about* things in contrast to direct acquaintance *with* things. See *Acquaintance, Knowledge by.* Description is opposed to exact definition in the *Port Royal Logic* (Part II, ch. XVI). Among the first to contrast description and acquaintance was G. Grote (*Exploratio Philosophica*, p. 60. See also W. James, *Principles of Psychology*, Vol. I, pp. 221 ff. and B. Russell, *Problems of Philosophy*, ch. V.)*—L.W.*

Descriptions: Where a formula A containing a free variable — say, for example, x — means a true proposition (is true) for one and only one value of x, the notation (ιx) A is used to mean that value of x. The approximately equivalent English phraseology is ''the x such that A''—or simply ''the F,'' where F denotes the concept (monadic propositional function) obtained from A by *abstraction* (*q.v.*) with respect to x. This notation, or its sense in the sense of Frege, is called a *description.*

In *Principia Mathematica* descriptions (or notations serving the same purpose in context) are introduced as *incomplete symbols* (*q.v.*). Russell maintains that descriptions not only may but must be thus construed as incomplete symbols—briefly, for the following reasons. The alternative is to construe a description as a

proper name, so that, e.g., the description *the author of Waverley* denotes the man Scott and is therefore synonymous with the name *Scott*. But then the sentences ''Scott is the author of Waverley'' and ''Scott is Scott'' ought to be synonymous — which they clearly are not (although both are true). Moreover, such a description as *the King of France* cannot be a proper name, since there is no King of France whom it may denote; nevertheless, a sentence such as ''the King of France is bald'' should be construed to have a meaning, since it may be falsely asserted or believed by one who falsely asserts or believes that there is a King of France.

Frege meets the same difficulties, without construing descriptions as incomplete symbols, by distinguishing two kinds of meaning, the sense (Sinn) and the denotation (Bedeutung) of an expression (formula, phrase, sentence, etc.). *Scott* and *the author of Waverley* have the same denotation, namely the man Scott, but not the same sense. *The King of France* has a sense but no denotation; so likewise the sentence, *The King of France is bald*. Two expressions having the same sense must have the same denotation if they have a denotation. When a constituent part of an expression is replaced by another part having the same sense, the sense of the whole is not altered. When a constituent part of an expression is replaced by another having the same denotation, the denotation of the whole (if any) is not altered, but the sense may be. The denotation of an (unasserted) declarative sentence (if any) is a truth-value, whereas the sense is the thought or content of the sentence. But where a sentence is used in indirect discourse (as in saying that so-and-so says that. . ., believes that. . ., is glad that. . ., etc.) the meaning is different: in such a context the denotation of the sentence is that which would be its sense in direct discourse. (In quoting some one in indirect discourse, one reproduces neither the literal wording nor the truth-value, but the sense of what he said.)

Frege held it to be desirable in a formalized logistic system that every formula should have not only a sense but also a denotation—as can be arranged by arbitrary semantical conventions where necessary. When this is done, Frege's *sense of a sentence* nearly coincides with *proposition* (in sense (b) of the article of that title herein). *Alonzo Church*

G. Frege. *Uber Sinn und Bedeutung*, Zeitschrift für Philosophie and philosophische Kritik, n. s., vol. 100 (1892), pp. 25-50. B. Russell, *On denoting*, Mind, n. s., vol. 14 (1905), pp. 479-493.

Designate: A word, symbol, or expression may be said to *designate* that object (abstract or concrete) to which it refers, or of which it is a name or sign. See *Name relation.—A.C.*

Designated values: See *Propositional calculus, many-valued.*

Designatum: The *designatum* of a word, symbol, or expression is that which it *designates* (*q.v.*)*—A.C.*

Destiny: (Fr. *destiner*, to be intended) Future necessity; the legal outcome of actuality. Divine foreordainment, or the predetermined and unalterable course of events.

Defined by Peirce (1839-1914) as the embodiment of generals in existence.—*J.K.F.*

Determination: (Lat. *determinare,* to limit) The limitation of a reality or thought to a narrower field than its original one. In a monistic philosophy the original, single principle must be considered as narrowed down to various genera and species, and eventually to individual existence if such be admitted, in order to introduce that differentiation of reality which is required in a multiple world. In Platonism, the Forms or Ideas are one for each type of thing but are "determined" to multiple existence by the addition of matter (*Timaeus*). Neo-Platonism is even more interested in real determination, since the One is the logical antecedent of the Many. Here determination is effected by the introduction of negations, or privations, into successive emanations of the One. With Boethius, mediaeval philosophy became concerned with the determination of being-in-general to an actual manifold of things. In Boethianism there is a fusion of the question of real determination with that of logical limitation of concepts. In modern thought, the problem is acute in Spinozism: universal substance (substantia, natura, Deus) must be reduced to an apparent manifold through attributes, modes to the individual. Determination is said to be by way of negation, according to Spinoza (Epist. 50), and this means that universal substance is in its perfect form indeterminate, but is thought to become determinate by a sort of logical loss of absolute perfection. The theory is brought to an almost absurd simplicity in the *Ontology* of Chr. Wolff, where being is pictured as successively determined to genera, species and individual. Determination is also an important factor in the development theories of Hegel and Bergson.—*V.J.B.*

Determinism: (Lat. *de + terminus,* end) The doctrine that every fact in the universe is guided entirely by law. Contained as a theory in the atomism of Democritus of Abdera (*q.v.*), who reflected upon the impenetrability, translation and impact of matter, and thus allowed only for mechanical causation. The term was applied by Sir William Hamilton (1788-1856) to the doctrine of Hobbes, to distinguish it from an older doctrine of fatalism. The doctrine holds that all the facts in the physical universe, and hence also in human history, are absolutely dependent upon and conditioned by their causes. In psychology: the doctrine states that the will is not free but determined by psychical or physical conditions. Syn. with fatalism, necessitarianism, destiny.—*J.K.F.*

Deus ex machina: Literally, the god from the machine; an allusion to the device whereby in ancient drama a god was brought on the stage, sometimes to provide a supernatural solution to a dramatic difficulty; hence any person, thing, or concept artificially introduced to solve a difficulty.—*G.R.M.*

Deustua, Alejandro: (1849-1945) Born in Huancayo, Junín (Perú), Professor of Philosophy at the University of San Marcos in Lima, Perú. According to Deustua, there are two kinds of freedom, the Static and the Dynamic. The former accounts for the cosmic order and harmony of phenomena. Dynamic liberty, however, is,

above all, creativity and novelty. The world, not as it is ontologically, but as we experience it, that is, as it comes within the area of consciousness, results from a Hegelian contraposition of the two types of freedom. In this contraposition, the synthesis is always more of the nature of dynamic freedom than it is static. With these presuppositions, Deustua finally works up a kind of practical philosophy leading up to an axiology which he himself finds implied in his concept of freedom. The following are among Deustua's most important works: *Las Ideas de Orden Libertad en la Historia del Pensamiento Humano; Historia de las Ideas Estéticas; Estética General; Estética Aplicada.*—*J.A.F.*

Dewey, John: (1859-1952) Leading American philosopher. The spirit of democracy and an abiding faith in the efficacy of human intelligence run through the many pages he has presented in the diverse fields of metaphysics, epistemology, logic, psychology, aesthetics, religion, ethics, politics and education, in all of which he has spoken with authority. Progressive education owes its impetus to his guidance and its tenets largely to his formulation. He is the chief exponent of that branch of pragmatism known as instrumentalism. Among his main works are: *Psychology,* 1886; *Outline of Ethics,* 1891; *Studies in Logical Theory,* 1903; *Ethics* (Dewey and Tufts), 1908; *How We Think,* 1910; *Influence of Darwin on German Philosophy,* 1910; *Democracy and Education,* 1916; *Essays in Experimental Logic,* 1916; *Reconstruction in Philosóphy,* 1920; *Human Nature and Conduct,* 1922; *Experience and Nature,* 1925; *The Quest for Certainty,* 1929; *Art as Experience,* 1933; *Logic: The Theory of Inquiry,* 1939. Cf. J. Ratner, *The Philosophy of John Dewey,* 1940; M. H. Thomas, *A Bibliography of John Dewey,* 1882-1939; *The Philosophy of John Dewey,* ed. P. A. Schilpp (Evanston, 1940).

Dharma: (Skr.) Right, virtue, duty, usage, law, social as well as cosmic.—*K.F.L.*

Dhyāna: (Skr.) Meditation or the full accord of thinker and thought without interference and without being merged as yet, the last but one stage in the attainment of the goals of Yoga (*q.v.*).—*K.F.L.*

Diagram: A line drawing; commonly used in logic to represent class relationships. See *Euler,* and *Venn.* —*C.A.B.*

Dialectic: (Gr. *dia + legein,* discourse) The beginning of dialectic Aristotle is said to have attributed to Zeno of Elea. But as the art of debate by question and answer, its beginning is usually associated with the Socrates of the Platonic dialogues. As conceived by Plato himself, dialectic is the science of first principles which differs from other sciences by dispensing with hypotheses and is, consequently, "the copingstone of the sciences" —the highest, because the clearest and hence the ultimate, sort of knowledge. Aristotle distinguishes between dialectical reasoning, which proceeds syllogistically from opinions generally accepted, and demonstrative reasoning, which begins with primary and true premises; but he holds that dialectical reasoning, in contrast with eristic, is "a process of criticism wherein lies the path to the principles of all inquiries.'' In modern philosophy, dialectic has two special meanings. Kant uses it as the name of that part of his *Kritik der reinen Vernunft* which deals critically with the special difficulties (antinomies, paralogisms and Ideas) arising out of the futile attempt (transcendental illusion) to apply the categories of the Understanding beyond the only realm to which they can apply, namely, the realm of objects in space and time (Phenomena). For Hegel, dialectic is primarily the distinguishing characteristic of speculative thought—thought, that is, which exhibits the structure of its subject matter (the universal, system) through the construction of synthetic categories (synthesis) which resolve (sublate) the opposition between other conflicting categories (theses and antitheses) of the same subject matter.—*G.W.C.*

Dialectical materialism: The school of philosophy founded by Marx and Engels and developed by many subsequent thinkers.

Ontologically, its materialism means that matter, nature, the observable world is taken ''without reservations,'' as real in its own right, neither deriving its reality from any supernatural or transcendental source, nor dependent for its existence on the mind of man. It is considered scientifically evident that matter is prior to mind both temporally and logically in the sense that mind never appears except as an outgrowth of matter, and must be explained accordingly. Space and time are viewed as forms of the existence of matter.

The term dialectical expresses the dynamic interconnectedness of things, the universality of change and its radical character: everything possessing any sort of reality is in process of self-transformation, owing to the fact that its content is made up of opposing factors or forces the internal movement of which interconnects everything, changes each thing into something else. Mechanism in the sense of non-dialectical materialism as well as metaphysics in the sense of idealistic ontology are thus rejected.

The position taken is that investigation reveals basic, recurrent patterns of change, expressible as laws of materialist dialectics, which are seen as relevant to every level of existence, and, because validated by past evidence, as indispensable hypotheses in guiding further investigation. These are: (1) Law of interpenetration, unity and strife of opposites. (All existences, being complexes of opposing elements and forces, have the character of a changing unity. The unity is considered temporary, relative, while the process of change, expressed by interpenetration and strife, is continuous, absolute.) (2) Law of transformation of quantity into quality and vice versa. (The changes which take place in nature are not merely quantitative; their accumulation eventually precipitates new qualities in a transition which appears as a sudden leap in comparison to the gradualness of the quantitative changes up to that point. The new quality is considered as real as the original quality. It is not mechanically reducible to it: it is not merely a larger amount of the former quality, but something into which that has developed.) (3) Law of negation. (The series of quantitative changes and emerging qualities is unending. Each state or phase of development is considered a synthesis which resolves the contradictions contained in the preceding synthesis and which generates its own contradictions on a different qualitative level.)

These laws, connecting ontology with logic, are contrasted to the formalistic laws of identity, difference and excluded middle of which they are considered qualitatively enriched reconstructions. Against the ontology of the separateness and self-identity of each thing, the dialectical laws emphasize the interconnectedness of all things and self-development of each thing. An A all parts of which are always becoming non-A may thus be called non-A as well as A. The formula, A is A and cannot be non-A, becomes, A is A and also non-A, that is, at or during the same instant: there is no instant, it is held, during which nothing happens. The view taken is that these considerations apply as much to thought and concepts, as to things, that thought is a process, that ideas gain their logical content through interconnectedness with other ideas, out of and into which they develop.

Consequently, the dialectical method means basically that all things must be investigated in terms of their histories; the important consideration is not the state in which the object appears at the moment, but the rate, direction and probable outcome of the changes which are taking place as a result of the conflict of forces, internal and external. The necessity of observation and prediction in every field is thus ontologically grounded, according to dialectical materialism, which not only rejects a priorism, holding that ''nature is the test of dialectics'' (Engels: *Anti-Dühring*), but claims to express with much more fidelity than formal logic, with its emphasis on unmoving form rather than changing content, the basis of the method modern science actually uses. There is an equal rejection of theory without practice and practice without theory.

One may assert that the human brain, capable of forming ideas, does so not prior to or independently of the rest of the natural world, but in relation to it, moved and stimulated by its manifold content. Ideas reflect things, but the reflection, like everything else, is dialectical, not inert, but active. Ideas grow out of and lead back to things, sometimes very circuitously; things may be reflected fancifully, by abstraction or in new combinations as well as directly. While there is a perfectly objective reality to reflect, the reflection is never perfect: truth is absolute, but knowledge relative.

The social theory, termed historical materialism, represents the application of the general principles of materialist dialectics to human society, by which they were first suggested. The fundamental changes and stages which society has passed through in the course of its complex evolution are traced primarily to the influence of changes taking place in its economic base. This base has two aspects: material forces of production (technics, instrumentalities) and economic relations (prevailing system of ownership, exchange, distribution). Growing out of this base is a social superstructure of laws, governments, arts, sciences, religions, philosophies and the like. The view taken is that society evolved as it did primarily because fundamental changes in the economic base resulting from conflicts of interest in respect to productive forces, and involving radical changes in economic relations, have compelled accommodating changes in the social superstructure. Causal action is traced both ways between base and superstructure, but when any "higher" institution threatens the position of those who hold controlling economic power at the base, the test of their power is victory in the ensuing contest. The role of the individual in history is acknowledged, but is seen in relation to the movement of underlying forces. Cf. Plekhanov, *Role of the Individual in History*.

The general direction of social evolution, on this view is from classless, collectivist forms (primitive communism) to class forms (slave-master, serf-lord, worker-capitalist) to classless, socialist, communist forms on the modern level of highly complex technics. Classes are defined as groups having antagonistic economic relationships to the means of production. The resultant conflict of interests is called the class struggle, which, involving the means and ways of life, is carried on in all fields, often unconsciously.

It is held that society has not accomplished many basic transformations peacefully, that fundamental changes in the economic system or the social superstructure, such as that from medieval serf-lord to modern worker-capitalist economy, have usually involved violence wherein the class struggle passes into the acute stage of revolution because the existing law articulates and the state power protects the obsolete forms and minority-interest classes which must be superseded. The evolution of capitalism is considered to have reached the point where the accelerating abundance of which its technics are capable is frustrated by economic relationships such as those involved in individual ownership of productive means, hiring and firing of workers in the light of private profits and socially unplanned production for a money market. It is held that only technics collectively owned and production socially planned can provide employment and abundance of goods for everyone. The view taken is that peaceful attainment of them is possible, but will probably be violently resisted by privileged minorities, provoking a contest of force in which the working class majority will eventually triumph the world over.

The working class, in coming to power, is seen to establish its own state form, based upon the dictatorship of the proletariat, which is maintained so long as a state is necessary, and which is considered to extend democracy to the majority by establishing collective ownership of the means of production. This first stage is defined as socialism, the economic principle of which is, "from each according to ability, to each according to work performed." The second stage is defined as communism, the economic principle of which is, "from each according to ability, to each according to need" (Marx:

"Gotha Program"). In its fullest sense, on a world wide scale, this stage is considered to include an economy of abundance made possible by social utilization of unrestricted production, a disappearance of the antagonism between town and country and that between mental and physical labor, and, because irreconcilable class conflicts will have ceased to exist, a "withering away" (Engels: *Anti-Dühring*) of the state as an apparatus of force. What will remain will be a state-less "administration of things."

The general theory of historical materialism claims to be a methodological basis for all specific social sciences, as well as for aesthetics and ethics. Cf. Trotsky: *Literature and Revolution*.

Art, to dialectical materialism, is an activity of human beings which embodies a reflection of the reality surrounding them, a reflection which may be conscious, unconscious, reconstructive or deliberately fantastic, and which possesses positive aesthetic value in terms of rhythm, figure, color, image and the like. Art is good to the extent that it is a faithful and aesthetic reflection of the reality dealt with. Accordingly, proletarian or socialist realism (*q.v.*) is not photographic, static, but dialectical, conscious that any given period or subject is moving into its future, that class society is becoming classless society. This realism is optimistic, involving a "revolutionary romanticism."

The central ethical conception, called proletarian humanism, sees the source and significance of all values in mankind and, accepting general ends like justice, brotherhood, the principle of all for each and each for all, sees the main problem as that of reconstructing social institutions so as to permit the functioning of such principles in respect to the whole people. It is held that only classless society, where there is productive employment and security for all, will permit all to lead the good life. See *Marx, Engels, Lenin, Soviet philosophy*, also, separate entries for detailed definitions of specific terms.

Bibliography: Marx-Engels *Gesamtausgabe* (complete works of Marx and Engels currently adding to its volumes). Marx, Karl: *Capital. Contribution to the Critique of Political Economy. Value, Price and Profit. Class Struggles in France. Paris Commune* (for extensive bibliography of Marx, see Karl Marx). Engels, Friedrich: *Anti-Dühring. Dialectics of Nature. Ludwig Feuerbach and the Outcome of Classical German Philosophy. Origin of the Family, Private Property and the State.* Marx and Engels: *German Ideology. Communist Manifesto.* Lenin, V. I.: *Collected Works. Selected Works. Materialism and Empirio-Criticism. State and Revolution. Filosofskie Tetrady* (Philosophical Notebooks). Many of Lenin's briefer philosophical writings may be found in *Selected Works*, vol. XI.—*J.M.S.*

Diallelon: A *vicious circle* (*q. v.*) in definition.—*A.C.*

Diallelus: A *vicious circle* (*q.v.*) in proof.—*A.C.*

Dialogic method: The presentation of a thesis or argument in dialogue form.—*C.A.B.*

Dialogism: Inference from one premiss of a (categorical) syllogism to the disjunction of the conclusion and the negation of the other premiss is a *dialogism*. Or, more generally, if the inference from A and B to C is a valid inference, that from A to C v ~B may be called a *dialogism*.—*A.C.*

Dianoetic Virtues: (Gr. *aretai dianoetikai*) In Aristotle's ethics the virtues or excellences of the dianoia; intellectual virtues. The dianoetic virtues are distinguished from the moral virtues in having for their end the explicit apprehension of rational principles, whereas the moral virtues are concerned with the rational control of the sensitive and appetitive life. See *Aristotelianism; Dianoia; Nous; Phronesis.*—*G.R.M.*

Dianoia: (Gr. *dianoia*) The faculty or exercise of thinking, as exhibited especially in the discriminating and conjoining or disjoining of concepts; the discursive understanding (Aristotle).—*G.R.M.*

Diaspora: Literally the Greek word signifies a scattering or dispersion. Name given to the countries through which the Jews were dispersed after being exiled or deported from their homeland and also to the Jews living in those lands. Also applied to converts from Judaism to Christianity of the early Church living outside of Palestine.—*J.J.R.*

Dichotomy: (Gr. *dicha*, in two; *temno*, to cut) Literally, a division into two parts. In a specific example: the view that man consists of soul and body. The earlier view of the Old Testament writers; also, a view found in certain expressions of St. Paul. See also *Trichotomy.*—*V.F.*

Dictum de omni et nullo: The leading principles of the syllogisms in Barbara and Celarent, variously formulated, and attributed to Aristotle. "Whatever is affirmed (denied) of an entire class or kind may be affirmed (denied) of any part." The four moods of the first figure were held to be directly validated by this dictum, and this was given as the motive for the traditional reductions of the last three syllogistic figures to the first. See also *Aristotle's dictum.*—*A.C.*

Didactics: (Gr. *didaktikos*, taught) The branch of education concerned with methods of teaching and instruction. In theology and religion didactics in contradistinction to catechetics, is instruction in fundamentals of religious doctrine.—*L.W.*

Diderot, Denis: (1713-1784) He was editor-in-chief of the French Encyclopaedia and as such had a far reaching influence in the Enlightenment. His own views changed from an initial deism to a form of materialism and ended in a pantheistic naturalism. He displayed a keen interest in science and may be viewed as a forerunner of positivism. He issued severe polemics against the Christian religion. *De la suffisance de la religion naturelle*, 1747 (publ. 1770); *Lettre sur les aveugles* . . . (1749), *Le Rêve d'Alembert*, 1769 (publ. 1830); *La religieuse*, 1760; *Le neveu de Rameau*, 1761; *Jacques les fataliste*, 1773. Cf. J. Morley, *Diderot and the Encyclopedists*, 1878, 2d ed. 1886.—*L.E.D.*

Difference: (in Scholasticism) *Common.* That which makes a distinction (or division) by some separable accident, as when we say that this person is sitting and that one standing. By this difference a person can differ

not only from another but also from himself, as one who is now old differs from himself as he was when young.—*H.G.*

Dilemma: See *Proof by cases*, and *Logic, formal*, § 2.

Dilettantism: Opposite of professionalism. It contributed to art appreciation because it opposed the too intellectual rules of traditional taste, particularly in Rome, 2nd century; in France and England, 18th century.—*L.V.*

Dilthey, Wilhelm: (1833-1911) A devoted student of biography, he constructed a new methodology and a new interpretation of the study of society and culture. He formulated the doctrine of *Verstehungspsychologie*, which is basic to the study of social ends and values. He was the founder of *Lebensphilosophie*. Being the first humanistic philosopher historian of his age, he led in the comprehensive research in the history of intellectual development. Main works: *Einleitung in die Geisteswessenschaften*, 1883; *Der Erlebnis und die Dichtung*, 1905; *Das Wesen der Philosophie*, 1907; *Der Aufbau der geschichtlichen Welt in der Geisteswissenschaften*, 1910; *Die Typen der Weltanschauung*, 1911; *Gesammelte Schriften*, 9 vols., 1922-35.—*H.H.*

Dimension: (scientific) 1. Any linear series or order of elements. 2. Any quantity of a given kind, capable of increase or decrease over a certain range; a variable. 3. In the physical system: mass, length and time.—*A.C.B.*

Dimensions of Consciousness: (Lat. *dimensus*, pp. of *dimentire*, to measure off) Pervasive and mutually irreducible features of conscious processes such as quality, intensity, extent, duration and intentionality. (Cf. E. B. Titchener, *Lectures on the Elementary Psychology of Feeling and Attention*, Lect. IV; E. G. Boring, *The Physical Dimensions of Consciousness*, Ch. 3.)—*L.W.*

Ding an sich: (Ger. thing in itself) A Kantian term referring to what lies beyond human experience and observation. "Things in themselves" are transcendent, not transcendental or applicable to any human experience. The "thing in itself" exists independent of and apart from all knowledge. It has an independent reality apart from the subjectivity of human knowledge.—*H.H.*

Diogenes Laertius: (3^d century B.C.) A late biographical doxographer, to whom is owed most of the biographical and source material of Pre-Socratic philosophy. Cf. R. Hope, *Diog. Laertius*—*E.H.*

Dionysian: The art impulse in which life is relived, in which life's joys and pains are re-experienced. The dynamic and passionate of the will of life and power. (Nietzsche.)—*H.H.*

Diorism: The Greek term in Plato's usage signifies division, distinction; in that of Aristotle, distinction, definition, which is also the meaning today. In mathematics, a statement of the conditions needed in order to solve a problem.—*J.J.R.*

Direct knowledge: A thing is said to be known *directly* when our cognition terminates in and refers immediately to the thing itself; a thing is known *reflexly*, when our cognition terminates in and refers immediately to the image or concept of the thing previously known. E.g. I know man *directly* upon seeing him, but upon seeing his image, I know him *reflexly,* because then I know him through the cognition of the image.—*H.G.*

Direct theories of knowing: Any theories of knowledge which maintain that objects are known directly without the intermediary of percepts, images or ideas.—*A.C.B.*

Discourse: Orderly communication of thought, or the power to think logically.—*C.A.B.*

Discovery: (Lat. *discooperire,* to discover) 1. The act of becoming aware of something previously existing but unknown. 2. The act of insight (usually more or less sudden) by which a scientific hypothesis or explanatory conception comes into consciousness.—*A.C.B.*

Discrepancy: A difference from that which was expected or is required by some datum.—*C.A.B.*

Discrete: A class is said to have discrete order (e.g. the whole numbers), if (1) it satisfies *Dedekind's postulate* (*q.v.*) and (2) every element (except the first if any) has a next predecessor and also (except the last if any) a next successor. Contrasted with "dense" or "compact" order, such as that of the rational numbers, in which no element is next to any other.—*C.J.D.*

Discretion: (Lat. *discretum,* pp. of *discernere,* to discern) The mental capacity for critical discrimination especially in matters of ethics and conduct.—*L.W.*

Discrimination: (Lat. *discriminare,* to separate) (a) subjectively: the rational power to distinguish between objects, real or logical, and between moral right and wrong. In Aristotelianism there is also a function of internal sense (G. kritikon, sensory discrimination; Lat. vis aestimativa or cogitativa) by which men and the higher animals distinguish the good from the bad in their sense experience.

(b) objectively: see *Distinction.*—*V.J.B.*

Discursive Cognition: (Lat. *discurrere,* to run about) Discursive, as opposed to intuitive cognition, is attained by a series of inferences rather than by direct insight. See *Intuitive Cognition.*—*L.W.*

Contrasted with *Intuitive,* and applied to knowledge; also to transitions of thought. Our knowledge of, e.g., the nature of time, is discursive or conceptual if we are able to state what time is; otherwise it is only intuitive. Transitions of thought mediated by verbal or conceptual steps would be called discursive and said to be "reasoning." Immediate transitions, or transitions mediated in subconscious ways, would be called intuitive.—*C.J.D.*

Disjunction: See *Logic, formal,* § 1.

Disjunctive: A sentence of either of the forms A v B, A + B (or a proposition expressed by such a sentence)—see *Logic, formal,* § 1—may be called a *disjunctive sentence* (or proposition).—*A.C.*

Disjunctive syllogism: See *Logic, formal,* § 2.

Disparate: (Lat. *dis + par,* equal) (a) *In psychology and epistemology:* a term descriptive of the qualitative heterogeneity between sensations of different senses. Sensations of the same sense (*e.g.* a red and a green color patch) are dissimilar (see *Similarity; Resemblance*), sensations of different senses (*e.g.* a red patch and a cold surface) are disparate. The criterion of psychological disparity between two sensations is the absence of intermediate sensations by which it is possible to pass continuously from the one to the other. (Wundt, *Physiol. Psychol.,* 4th ed., I, 286.) The disparity of the fields of the several senses divides them into so many watertight compartments and thus raise the epistemological problem of correlation between the disparate data of different senses. See *Correlation.* (b) *In logic:* Disparate terms have been variously defined by logicians:

(i) Boethius defined disparate terms as those which are diverse yet not contradictory. See Prantl, *Geschichte der Logik,* I, 686.

(ii) Leibniz considered two concepts disparate "if neither of the terms contains the other" that is to say if they are not in the relation of genus and species. (Couturat, *Leibniz, Inédits,* pp. 53, 62.)—*L.W.*

Disparity: See *Disparate.*

Disputatio: (Scholastic) Out of the *quaestiones disputatae* developed gradually a rigid form of scholastic disputation. The *defensor theseos* proposed his thesis and explained or proved it in syllogistic form. The *opponentes* argued against the thesis and its demonstration by repeating first the proposition and the syllogism proving it, then either by denying the validity of one or the other premises (*nego maiorem, minorem*) or by making distinctions restricting the proposition (*distinguo maiorem, minorem*). In the disputations of students under the direction of a *magister* the latter used to summarize the disputation and to "determine the question."—*R.A.*

Disputation: (a) A dispute, or the act of disputing. (b) A formal exercise in which some set topic is debated. —*C.A.B.*

Dissimilarity: Difference, unlikeness, heterogeneity. —*C.A.B.*

Dissociation: (Lat. *dis + socius,* a companion) The operation of mind by which the elements of a complex are discriminated. Dissociative discrimination is facilitated when elements which are commonly conjoined are found in new combinations. James calls this the law of "dissociation by varying concomitants." (*Principles of Psychology,* I, 506.)—*L.W.*

Dissociation of Personality: A disorder of personality consisting in the loss of the normally stable and constant integration of the self. Two types of disintegration of personality are distinguishable: (a) The ideas and states dissociated from the central core of the self may float about as detached and depersonalized states. See *Depersonalization.* (b) The dissociated ideas and states may cohere into a secondary or split-off consciousness.—*L.W.*

Distinction: (in Scholasticism) Consists in this, that one thing is not another. *Absolute:* There is an absolute distinction between two things when neither one is a mode of the other, e.g. that between a stone and gold. A *modal distinction* is a distinction between a thing and its mode, *e.g.* that between a body and its shape.

Adequate: A distinction between two *whole* beings, *e.g.* between the sun and the moon. An *inadequate distinction* is a distinction between a whole being and its part, *e.g.* between the hand and one of its fingers.

Of the reasoning reason (rationis ratiocinantis): A distinction in which our mind conceives things *as* distinct when there is no foundation in reality for making such a distinction; the whole distinction is dependent upon the one reasoning. *E.g.,* when in one and the same thing we conceive the nature of subject and predicate as diverse attributes, as when we say: *man is man;* or when we conceive the same thing through synonymous concepts, as if we say: *man is a rational animal,* as though we are distinguishing man from rational animal.

Of the reasoned reason (rationis ratiocinatae): A distinction in which our mind conceives *as* distinct things that are not really distinct, when there is some foundation in reality for making such a distinction, *e.g.* perfections of God.

Real: A distinction belonging to a thing independently of the operation of the intellect, as that between the soul and body of man. A *mental distinction (distinctio rationis)* is one belonging to things through the operation of the intellect conceiving as distinct those things which are not really distinct, *e.g.,* that between the attributes of God.—*H.G.*

Distinctness: (Ger. *Deutlichkheit*) In Husserl: Explicit articulateness with respect to syntactical components. (See *Confused*). Distinctness is compatible with emptiness or obscurity of material content. See *Descartes, Leibniz.*—*D.C.*

Distribution (of terms): In the four traditional Aristotelian propositional forms, the subjects of universal propositions and the predicates of negative propositions are distributed; the other terms are undistributed. —*C.A.B.*

Distributive Justice: Justice as exhibited in the distribution of honor, money, rights and privileges among the members of a community; characterized by Aristotle as requiring equality of proportion between persons and rewards. See *Corrective Justice.*—*G.R.M.*

Distributive law: A name given to a number of laws of the same or similar form appearing in various disciplines—compare *associative law.* A distributive law of multiplication over addition appears in arithmetic:

$$x \times (y + z) = (x \times y) + (x \times z).$$

This distributive law holds also in the theory of real numbers, and in many other mathematical disciplines involving two operations called multiplication and addition. In the propositional calculus there are four distributive laws (two dually related pairs):

$$p[q \vee r] \equiv [pq \vee pr].$$
$$[p \vee qr] \equiv [p \vee q][p \vee r].$$
$$p[q + r] \equiv [pq + pr].$$
$$[p \vee [q \equiv r]] \equiv [[p \vee q] \equiv [p \vee r]].$$

Also four corresponding laws in the algebra of classes.—*A.C.*

Disvalue: Bad. Evil. Opposed to value or goodness. —*A.J.B.*

Divisibility: The property in virtue of which a whole (whether physical, psychical or mathematical) may be divided into parts which do not thereby necessarily sever their relation with the whole. Divisibility usually implies not merely analysis or distinction of parts, but actual or potential resolution into parts. From the beginning philosophers have raised the question whether substances are infinitely or finitely divisible. Ancient materialism conceived of the physical atom as an indivisible substance. Descartes, however, and after him Leibniz, maintained the infinite divisibility of substance. The issue became the basis of Kant's cosmological antinomy (*Crit. of Pure Reason*), from which he concluded that the issue was insoluble in metaphysical terms. In recent decades the question has had to take account of (1) researches in the physical atom, before which the older conception of physical substance has steadily retreated; and (2) the attempt to formulate a satisfactory definition of infinity (*q.v.*).—*O.F.K.*

Division: (Lat *dividere,* to divide) The logical process of indicating the species within a genus, the sub-species within the species, and so on; a classificatory scheme constructed on the principle of genus and species. —*A.C.B.*

Divisionism: Principle of obtaining the effects of light in painting by juxtaposing instead of mixing tints.—*L.V.*

Docta ignorantia: Literally, learned ignorance refers to men's knowledge of God which unavoidably includes a negative element, since He immeasurably surpasses the knowledge of Him gleaned from this phenomenal world, yet for man this is truly a real learning. Title given to one of his philosophical treaties by Nicholas of Cusa (1401-1464) who understood it in the sense of an insight into the incomprehensibility of the infinite.—*J.J.R.*

Doctrinaires: (a) In general: impractical, philosophical theorists, uninterested in views other than their own; dogmatists.

(b) In particular: a group of French political philosophers of the early nineteenth century.—*V.J.B.*

Dogma: The Greek term signified a public ordinance of decree, also an opinion. A present meaning: an established, or generally admitted, philosophic opinion explicitly formulated, in a depreciative sense; one accepted on authority without the support of demonstration or experience. Kant calls a directly synthetical proposition grounded on concepts a dogma which he distinguishes from a *mathema,* which is a similar proposition effected by a construction of concepts. In the history of Christianity dogmas have come to mean definition of revealed truths proposed by the supreme authority of the Church as articles of faith which must be accepted by all its members.—*J.J.R.*

Dogmatism: (Gr. *dogma,* opinion) A term used by many and various philosophers to characterize their opponents' view more or less derogatorily since the word cannot rid itself of certain linguistic and other associations. The Skeptics among Greek philosophers, doubting all, called dogmatism every assertion of a positive nature. More discriminately, dogmatism may be applied to presumptuous statements or such that lack a sufficiently rational ground, while in the popular mind the word still has the affiliation with the rigor of church dogma which, having a certain finality about it, appeals to faith rather than reason. Since Kant, dogmatism has a specific connotation in that it refers to metaphysical statements made without previous analysis of their justification on the basis of the nature and aptitudes of reason, exactly what Kant thought to remedy through his criticism. By this animadversion are scored especially all 17th and 18th century metaphysical systems as well as later ones which cling to *a priori* principles not rationally founded. Now also applied to principles of a generalized character maintained without regard to empirical conditions.—*K.F.L.*

Donatists: Followers of Bishop Donatus, leader of a Christian sect which originated in North Africa in the beginning of the fourth century. They taught the invalidity of sacraments administered by an unworthy minister and that known sinners should be denied membership in the Church. Their most powerful opponent was Saint Augustine.—*J.J.R.*

Donum superadditum: A theological term denoting a gratuitous gift of God superadded to the natural gifts which accompany human nature; hence a supernatural gift, like divine grace.—*J.J.R.*

Double-Aspect Theory: Theory that the mind and the body of an individual are two distinguishable but inseparable aspects of a single underlying substance or process. Spinoza, as a consequence of his metaphysical doctrine that "thinking substance and extended substance are one and the same thing" (*Ethics*, Part II, prop. 7) was committed to the Two-Aspect Theory of the body-mind relation. Cf. C. Lloyd Morgan (*Life, Mind and Spirit*, p. 46); S. Alexander (*Space Time and Deity*) and C. H. Strong are recent advocates of a two-aspect Theory.—*L.W.*

Double negation, law of: The theorem of the propositional calculus, $\sim \sim p \equiv p$.—*A.C.*

Doubt: (Fr. *doute*, from Lat. *dubito*, to be uncertain) Partial disbelief. The denial of a proposition offered or formerly held as true. The withdrawal of belief. In psychology: suspended judgment; the state of hesitation between contradictory propositions. Philosophical doubt has been distinguished as definitive or provisional. Definitive doubt is skepticism (*q.v.*). Provisional doubt is the rule proposed by the Cartesian method (*q.v.*) of voluntary suspension of judgement in order to reach a more dependable conclusion. Opposite of certainty.—*J.K.F.*

Doxa: The positional character common to all modes of believing: not only to believing in simple positive certainty (*protodoxa*, Ger. *Urdoxa*), but to modifications of the latter, such as doubting, disbelieving, affirming, denying, and assuming. Doxa in Husserl's sense includes episteme. It is present not only in syntactical-categorial judging, but in simple pre-categorial perceiving. Moreover, it is present in passive as well as in active synthesis. Non-doxic positionality is present in valuing and willing.—*D.C.*

Drama: a. State of mind characterized by human conflict. b. Literary genre in which conflicts are portrayed on the stage.—*L.V.*

Dravya: (Skr.) Substance, as a substratum of qualities

(see *guna*), accidents, or modes. Various classes are established by Indian philosophers.—*K.F.L.*

Drawing: Essential element of painting, sculpture and architecture. The Florentine Renaissance and all classical epochs in general considered drawing the basis of the aforesaid arts which were called the arts of drawing.—*L.V.*

Driesch, Hans Adolf Eduard: (1867-1940) An experimental biologist turned philosopher, he as a rationalist became the most prominent defender of a renovated vitalism. He excludes the physical-chemical level of reality from his vitalism. He asserts that every organism has its own entelechy. For what he terms phylogenetic development, a more inclusive vitalism of the whole evolutionary process, he postulates a super-personal phylogenetic entelechy. He offers an *a priori* justification of his vitalistic theory, and treats incisively the logic of the psychological. Main works: *Philosophy of the Organism, Ordnungslehre*, 1912, *Wirklichkeitslehre*, 1917; *Alltagsrätsel des Seelenlebens*, 1938; "Kausalität und Vitalismus" in *Jahrbuch der Schopenhauer Gesellschaft*, XVI, 1939.—*H.H.*

Dualism: (Lat. *due*, two) (a) *In metaphysics:* Theory which admits in any given domain, two independent and mutually irreducible substances, *e.g.* the Platonic dualism of the sensible and intelligible worlds, the Cartesian dualism of thinking and extended substances, the Leibnizian dualism of the actual and possible worlds, the Kantian dualism of the noumenal and the phenomenal. The term dualism first appeared in Thomas Hyde, *Historia religionis veterum Persarum* (1700) ch. IX, p. 164, where it applied to religious dualism of good and evil and is similarly employed by Bayle in his Dictionary article "Zoroaster" and by Leibniz in *Theodicée*. C. Wolff is responsible for its use in the psycho-physical sense. (cf. A. Lalande, *Vocabulaire de la Philosophie*, Vol. I, p. 180, note by R. Eucken.)

(b) *In epistemology:* Epistemological dualism is the theory that in perception, memory and other types of non-inferential cognition, there is a numerical duality of the content or datum immediately present to the knowing mind (sense datum, memory image, etc.) and the real object known (the thing perceived or remembered) (cf. A. O. Lovejoy, *The Revolt Against Dualism*, pp. 15-6). Epistemological monism, on the contrary identifies the immediate datum and the cognitive object either by assimilating the content to the object (epistemological realism) or the object to the content (epistemological idealism).—*L.W.*

Duality: See *Logic, formal*, §§ 1, 3, 7, 8.

Ductio per contradictoriam propositionem sive per impossible: (Lat.) A logical argument in which the truth of a proposition is established by showing that its contradictory is untrue or impossible; an application of the principle of excluded middle.—*V.J.B.*

Dühring, Eugen Karl: (1833-1901) Dühring, a German economist and philosopher, started on a legal career which lasted until 1859. He became *docent* at the University of Berlin and taught there until he lost his license in 1874. He was editor of *Der moderne Völkergeist* and of *Personalist und Emancipator*. Philosophically he belonged to the positivistic school. Dühring advocated not the elimination of capitalism, but of its abuses through the medium of a strong labor movement. His literary work is strongly tinged with anti-semitism, and he is probably better known for the attack which Marx and Engels made upon him than for his own work. E. Dühring: *Naturliche Dialektik*, 1863; *Der Wert des Lebens*, 1865; *Kritische Geschichte der Philosophie*, 1869; *Logik und Wissenschaftstheorie*, 1878. —*M.B.M.*

Duns Scotus, John: (1266/74-1308) Doctor Subtilis, was born somewhere in the British Isles, studied at the Franciscan monastery at Dumfries and at Oxford before 1290. He studied at Paris for four years, then taught theology at Oxford from 1300-1302, at Paris from 1302-1303, when he was banished for his opposition to King Philip IV. He received his doctorate at Paris in 1305 and went to Cologne in 1307, where he died. He is the most distinguished medieval defender of the view that universals have "haeccity" (*q.v.*) as well as quiddity. His realism was adopted by Charles Peirce (*q.v.*). Works: *De Primo Principio, Quaestiones in Metaphysicam, Opus Oxoniense, Reportata Parisiensia (Opera Omnia*, Paris, 1891-5).—*V.J.B.*

Duration: A limited extent of existence in time, more or less long, from a fraction of second to countless ages. H. Bergson gives it a special interpretation in regarding it as "time perceived as indivisible," a living present; as such, duration becomes the very essence of creative change, of creative evolution and must be opposed to time as measurable.—*R.B.W.*

Durkheim, Emile: (1858-1917) A French sociological positivist. He stressed the group mind, which for him is the point of reference for all human knowledge. The group mind has an impersonal, non-subjective character that is superior to the individual mind, and acts as a directive force for the individual agents that comprise society. He studied both religion and ethics from his positivistic point of view. E. Durkheim: *De la division du travail sociale*, 1893; *Les règles de la méthode sociologique; Les formes élémentaires de la vie religieuse*, 1912; *Le Socialisme; L'Education morale*.—*H.H.*

Duty: (Ang-Fr. *dueté*, what is due; Ger. *Pflicht*) Whatever is necessary or required; or whatever one is morally obliged to do, as opposed to what one may be pleased or inclined to do. Also, the moral obligation itself and the law or principle in which it is expressed. In ethics, *duty* is commonly associated with *conscience, reason, rightness, moral law,* and *virtue.*

Though Socrates, Plato and Aristotle had propounded doctrines of virtues, they were concerned essentially with *Good* rather than with rightness of action as such. The Stoics were the first to develop and popularize the notion that man has a duty to live virtuously, reasonably and fittingly, regardless of considerations of human happiness. Certain elements in Rabbinical legalism and the Christian Gospel strained in the same direction, notably the concept of the supreme and absolute law of God. But it was Kant who pressed the logic of duty to its final conclusion. The supreme law of duty, the categorical imperative (*q.v.*), is revealed intuitively by the pure rational will and strives to determine the moral agent to obey only that law which can be willed universally without contradiction, regardless of consequences.

Naturalistic interpretations of duty tend to discredit such an intuitionistic basis and seek instead to account for duty and conscience as outgrowths of training, tradition and social custom.—*O.F.K.*

Dyad: (Gr. *duas*, two) A pair of units considered as one. In Pythagoreanism the dyad is the number two, thought of as a substantial essence, or physically, as a line, i.e. two points which do not coincide.—*V.J.B.*

Dyadic: (gr. *duas*, two) Term meaning duality. Human experience is said to be dyadic, *i.e.* man's nature is dual in conflicts between good intentions and bad accomplishments, in oppositional strains and stresses. The personality of God is held to be dyadic in the confronting of difficulties or frustrations to his good will. Reality is spoken of as dyadic when it is said to be characteristically dual, *e.g.* both One and Many, static and dynamic, free and determined, abstract and concrete, universal and particular.—*V.F.*

Dyadic Relation: A two-termed relation (*q.v.*).

Dynamic Vitalism: See *Vitalism*.

Dynamis: (gr. *dynamis*) In Aristotle's philosophy (1) a source of change or power to effect change; faculty; (2) more generally the capacity a thing has of passing to a different state; potentiality. See *Aristotelianism; Energeia*.—*G.R.M.*

Dynamism: (Gr. *dynamis*, power) A term applied to a philosophical system which, in contrast to philosophy of mechanism (*q.v.*), adopts force rather than mass or motion as its basic explanatory concept. In this sense the Leibnizian philosophy is dynamism in contrast to the mechanism of Descartes' physics.—*L.W.*

Dyophysites: A term applied to the Catholics, who held that there are two natures in Christ, the Divine and the human, by the Monophysites, or the followers of Eutyches, who advanced the formula, "one nature after the union."—*J.J.R.*

Dysteleology: (Gr. *dus*, bad; *telos*, end or purpose) The term for the forbidding and frustrating aspects of life (such as unfavorable environmental factors, organic maladaptations, the struggle for existence, disease, death, etc.) which make difficult, if not impossible, the theory that there are good purposes predominantly at work in the world.—*V.F.*

E

E: (C.) Evil, interpreted by the Confucians as "too much or too little," that is, deviation from the Mean (chung yung).—*W.T.C.*

Eckhart, Meister: (1260-1327) Was born in Hochheim (Gotha), may have studied with St. Albert in Cologne, received his doctorate at Paris in 1302. He taught theology at various times, devoted much time to preaching in the vernacular, and filled various administrative posts in the Dominican Order. Mystical, difficult in terminology, his thought appears to contain elements of Aristotelianism, Augustinism, Neoplatonism and Avicennism. Accused of Pantheism and other theological errors, he was the subject of a famous trial in 1326; he abjured publicly any possible religious errors which he may have made. Chief works: *Opus Tripartitum, Quaestiones Parisienses, Deutsche Predigten.* (Pfeiffer, F., *Deutsche Mystiker des* 14 *Jahrh.*, Bd. II, Leipzig, 1857; tr. Evans, London, 1924.) B. J. Muller-Thym, *University of Being in M. Eckhart* (N. Y., 1939).—*V.J.B.*

Eclecticism: The principle, tendency, or practice of combining, or drawing upon, various philosophical or theological doctrines. In its passive form, it is found in many thinkers of no great originality. In its more active form, as a deliberate attempt to create unity among discordant schools of philosophy, eclecticism was practised by the Alexandrien School (*q.v.*), where the Oriental and Occidental thought mingled, and, more recently, by V. Cousin (*q.v.*).—*R.B.W.*

Economic determinism: The theory that the economic base of society determines other social institutions. Dialectical materialists criticise doctrines often designated as economic determinism on the ground that they are too narrow and assert only a one-way causal influence (from economic base to other institutions), whereas causal influence, they hold, proceeds both ways. They refer to their own theory as historical materialism or the materialist conception of history. See *Marxism.*—*J.M.S.*

Economics: (Lat *œconomicus,* domestic economy, from *oikos,* house, + *nomos,* law) That branch of social science which is concerned with the exchange of goods. Employed by Xenophon, Aristotle and Cicero to describe treatises on the proper conduct of the household. In more recent times, combined with politics as political economy, the study of the laws and system of society. Now, more specially, the study of the production, distribution and consumption of material wealth and skills.—*J.K.F.*

Economy: An aspect of the scientific methodology of Ernst Mach (*Die Analyse der Empfindungen,* 5th ed., Jena, 1906); science and philosophy utilize ideas and laws which are not reproductive of sense data as such, but are simplified expressions of the functional relations discovered in the manifold of sense perceptions.—*V.J.B.*

Economy, principle of: Is the modern name for the logical rule known also as Occam's Razor. Its original formula was: *Entia non sunt multiplicanda praeter necessitatem,* i.e. of two or more explanations, which are of equal value otherwise, the one which uses the fewest principles, or suppositions, is true, or at least scientifically preferable.—*V.J.B.*

Ecpyrosis: (Gr. *ekpyrosis*) Conflagration; in Stoic doctrine the periodic resolution of all things into fire.—*G.R.M.*

Ecstasy: (Gr. *ekstasis,* displacement, a trance) The enraptured condition of the mystical spirit which has reached the climax of its intuitive and affective experience. Of brief duration, it is physiologically negative (resembling trance) but, according to some mystics, psychologically very rich. Usually said to be concomitant with a spiritual union of the soul with higher reality. See *Mysticism, Plotinism.*—*V.J.B.*

Ecstasy: (aesthetics) The contemplation of absolute beauty purified of any sensory experience. (Plotinus.)—*L.V.*

Eduction: 1. *In logic,* a term proposed by E. E. Constance Jones as a synonym or substitute for the more usual *immediate inference* (see *Logic, formal,* § 4).—*A.C.*

2. *In cosmology,* the production of the substantial

form out of the potentiality of matter, according to the hylomorphic system.—*T.G.*

Edwards, Jonathan: (1703-1758) American theologian. He is looked upon by many as one of the first theologians that the New World has produced. Despite the formalistic nature of his system, there is a noteworthy aesthetic foundation in his emphasis on "divine and supernatural light" as the basis for illumination and the searchlight to an exposition of such topics as freedom and original sin. Despite the aura of tradition about his pastorates at Northampton and Stockbridge, his missionary services among the Indians and his short lived presidency of Princeton University, then the College of New Jersey, he remains significant in the fields of theology, metaphysics, epistemology, aesthetics and ethics. See *Life and Works of Jonathan Edwards,* 10 vol. (1830) ed. S. E. Dwight.—*L.E.D.*

Effect: (in Scholasticism) Formal: is the effect of a formal cause: a *primary* and *intrinsic formal effect* is a concrete composite, or a designation resulting from form united to an apt subject, (i.e. to a subject capable of receiving that form): e.g. the *formal primary* and *intrinsic effect* of heat by which water is made warm is the warm water itself; so also a holy man is the formal effect of grace united to man. But that which is called *secondary* and *extrinsic* is any effect whether positive or negative, which so results from the union of form with its subject that it may be adequately distinguished from or remain extrinsic to the form, e.g. the driving out of cold from the water.—*H.G.*

Effectiveness: See *Logistic system, and Logic, formal,* § 1.

Effluvium: See *Effluxes, Theory of.*

Effluxes, Theory of: (Lat. *efflux,* from *effluere,* to flow out) Theory of early Greek thinkers that perception is mediated by *effluvia* or *simulacra* projected by physical objects and impinging upon the organs of sense. Thus Empedocles developed the theory of effluxes in conjunction with the principle that "like perceives only like" (similia similibus percipiuntur); an element in the external world can only be perceived by the *same* element in the body. (See *Aristotle, De Gen. et Corr.* I, 8, 324 b 26; *Theophrastus, De Sens.* 7.) Democritus' theory of images is a form of the theory of effluxes.—*L.W.*

Ego-centric Predicament: (Lat. *ego,* self; Gr. *kentrikon,* center) The epistemological predicament of a knowing mind which, confined to the circle of its own ideas, finds it difficult, if not impossible, to escape to a knowledge of an external world (cf. R. B. Perry, *Present Philosophical Tendencies,* pp. 129-30). Descartes is largely responsible for having confronted modern philosophy with the ego-centric predicament. See *Cogito Argument, The.*—*L.W.*

Ego, Empirical: (Lat. *ego,* self) The individual self, conceived as a series of conscious acts and contents which the mind is capable of cognizing by direct introspection. See *Bundle Theory of Self.*—*L.W.*

Ego, Pure: The self conceived as a non-empirical principle, ordinarily inaccessible to direct introspection, but inferred from introspective evidence. See *Ego, empirical.* The principal theories of the pure ego are: (a) the soul theory which regards the pure ego as a permanent, spiritual substance underlying the fleeting succession of conscious experience, and (b) the transcendental theory of Kant which considers the self an inscrutable subject presupposed by the unity of empirical self-consciousness.—*L.W.*

Ego, Transcendental: See *Ego, Pure.*—*L.W.*

Egoism, Ethical: The view that each individual should seek as an end only his own welfare. This principle is sometimes advanced as a separate intuition, sometimes on the ground that an individual's own welfare is the only thing that is ultimately valuable (for him).—*C.A.B.*

Egoism, Psychological: The doctrine that the determining, though perhaps concealed, motive of every voluntary action is a desire for one's own welfare. Often combined with Psychological Hedonism.—*C.A.B.*

Egological: (Ger. *egologisch*) In Husserl: Of or pertaining to the ego or to egology. *Egological reduction:* phenomenological reduction as involving epoché with respect to one's own explicit and implicit positing of concrete egos other than one's own and therefore with respect to one's positing of one's own ego as one *among others.* See *Phenomenology.*—*D.C.*

Ehrenfels, Maria Christian Julius Leopold Karl, Freiherr von: (1859-1932) As one of the leaders of the "Brentano School", he affirmed that the fundamental factor in valuation was desire. His principal interest was to trace the way in which desires and motives generate values. He described for the most part the development, the conflict, the hierarchy, and the obsolescence of values. Having a major influence upon the analytic approach to value theory, his outlook was relativistic and evolutionary. Main works: *Uber Gestaltqualitäten* (1890); *System der Werttheorie* (1897); *Sexualethik* (1907).—*H.H.*

Eidetic: (Ger. *eidetisch*) In Husserl: Of or pertaining to an eidos or to eide. *Eidetic existent:* anything falling as an example within the ideal extension of a valid eidos; e.g., an ideally or purely possible individual. (*Purely*) *eidetic judgments:* judgments that do not posit individual existence, even though they are about something individual. *Eidetic necessity:* an actual state of affairs, so far as it is a singularization of an eidetic universality. E.g., *This color has (this) brightness,* so far as that is a singularization of *All eidetically possible examples of color have brightness. Eidetic possibility:* see *eidos. Eidetic reduction:* see *Phenomenology.*—*D.C.*

Eidetic Imagery: Expression used by the German psychologist E. R. Jaensch, (*Ueber den Aufbau der Wahrnehmungswelt und ihre Struktur im Jugendalter,* 1923) to designate images usually visual which are almost photographic in their fidelity. Eidetic imagery differs from hallucination in that the former are usually recognized by the subject to be "subjective."—*L.W.*

Eidola: (Gr. *eidola*) Images; insubstantial forms; phantoms. Democritus and Epicurus use the term to denote the films, or groups of very fine particles, believed to be thrown off by bodies and to convey impressions to the eye.—*G.R.M.*

Einfühlung: (and Einsfühlung, in Max Scheler) The emotional and dynamic understanding of nature as the operational field of living forces. See *Empathy.* —*P.A.S.*

Eirenicon, epistemological: (Gr. *eirenikos,* peaceful) The purging of the negative claims and the synthesis of subjectivism, objectivism, dualism and relativism in epistemology. (Montague.)—*H.H.*

Eject: (Lat. pp. of *ejicere,* to throw out) Term introduced by W. K. Clifford to designate another conscious subject conceived as an outward projection of the knowing subject.—*L.W.*

Elan vital: Term used by Bergson to denote the source of efficient causation and evolution in nature. See *Bergson.*—*R.T.F.*

Eleatics: See *Parmenides, Zeno*

Election: (Lat. *eligo,* to choose) A choice between alternatives. In psychology: free choice by the will between means proposed by the understanding. An act of volition.—*J.K.F.*

Elements: Are simple constituents, in psychology, of sense perceptions such as sweet and green. Elementary complexes are things of experience. (Avenarius.) In logic: individual members of a class. Also refers to Euclid's 13 books.—*H.H.*

Elenchus: (Gr. *elenchos*) A syllogism establishing the contradictory of a proposition attacked; a refutation. (Aristotle.)—*G.R.M.*

Elijah, Aaron ben: Karaite exegete and philosopher (1300-1369). The *Ez Hayyim,* i.e. Tree of Size, his philosophical work, deals with all problems of philosophy and displays the influence of both Maimonides and of the teachings of the Mutazilites.—*M.W.*

Emanation: Literally, an outpouring or flowing forth, specifically, applied to the process of derivation or mode of origination, immediate or mediate, of the multiplicity of beings whether spiritual or material from the eternal source of all being, God, of Whose being consequently they are a part and in Whose nature they somehow share. It is opposed to creation from nothing. Some writers have not adequately distinguished one from the other.—*J.J.R.*

Emergent Evolution: Generalization of emergent mentalism (*q.v.*) due to S. Alexander (*q.v.*), *Space, Time and Deity.* See Bergson's variation in *L'évolution créatrice.* See *Holism.*

Emergent Mentalism: (Lat. *emergere,* to rise out) The theory of emergent evolutionism considered as an explanation of the genesis of mind or consciousness in the world. Mind is a novel quality emerging from the non-mental when the latter attains a certain complexity of organization. Cf. C. Lloyd Morgan, *Emergent Evolution,* Lect. I, II; *Life, Mind, Spirit,* Ch. V.—*L.W.*

Emerson, Ralph Waldo: (1803-1882) American poet and essayist. His spirit of independence early led him to leave the pulpit for the lecture platform where he earned high rank as the leading transcendentalist and the foremost figure in the famous Concord group. His profound vision, his ringing spirit of individualism and his love of democracy place him among the New World's philosophic pantheon. His "The American Scholar," "The Over-Soul," "Self-Reliance," "Compensation" and the Divinity School Address are perhaps the most famous of his lectures and essays. He edited The Dial, the official organ of the transcendental movement. His several trips to Europe brought him into contact with Coleridge and Wordsworth, but particularly with Carlyle.

R. W. Emerson: *Complete Works,* 12 vols. (Boston, 1903-4).—*L.E.D.*

Emotion: (Lat. *emovere,* to stir up, agitate) In the widest sense emotion applies to all affective phenomena including the familiar "passions" of love, anger, fear, etc. as well as the feelings of pleasure and pain. See *Affect.*—*L.W.*

Emotive Meaning: Emotive, as distinguished from the cognitive, meaning of a statement is its ability to communicate an attitude or emotion, to inspire an act of will without conveying truth. Exclamations, commands and perhaps ethical and aesthetic judgments are emotive but not cognitive.—*L.W.*

Empathic: Adjective of empathy. See *Empathy.*—*L.W.*

Empathy: (Gr. *en + pathein,* to suffer) The projection by the mind into an object of the subjective feeling of bodily posture and attitude which result from the tendency of the body to conform to the spatial organization of the object (*e.g.* the tendency to imitate the outstretched hands of a statue). The phenomenon is of particular significance for aesthetics. See H. S. Langfeld, *The Aesthetic Attitude.* The term was introduced to translate the German *Einfühlung.* See Lipps, *Raumaesthetik und geometrisch-optische Täuschungen.* See *Eject.*—*L.W.*

Empedocles: Of Agrigentum, about 490-430 B.C.; attempted to reconcile the teaching of the permanence of Being of the Eleatics with the experience of change and motion as emphasized by Heraclitus. He taught the doctrine of the four "elements," earth, water, air and fire, out of the mixture of which all individual things came to be; love and hate being the *cause of motion* and therefore of the mixings of these elements. He was thus led to introduce a theory of value into the explanation of Nature since love and hate accounted also for the good and evil in the world.—*M.F.*

Empirical: (Gr. *empeirikos,* experienced) Relating to experience. Having reference to actual facts. (a) In epistemology: pertaining to knowledge gained *a posteriori.* (b) In scientific method: that part of the method of science in which the reference to actuality allows an hypothesis to be erected into a law or general principle. Opposite of: normative.—*J.K.F.*

Empiricism: (1) A proposition about the sources of knowledge: that the sole source of knowledge is experience; or that either no knowledge at all or no knowledge with existential reference is possible independently of experience. Experience (*q.v.*) may be understood as either all conscious content, data of the senses only, or other designated content. Such empiricism may take the form of denial that any knowledge or at least knowledge about existents can be obtained *a priori* (*q.v.*); that is, denial that there are universal and necessary truths; denial that there is knowledge which holds regardless of past, present, or future experience; denial that there is instinctive, innate, or inborn knowledge; denial that the test of truth is clarity to natural reason or self-evidence; denial that one can gain certain knowledge by finding something the opposite of which is inconceivable; denial that there are any necessary presuppositions of all knowledge or of anything known certainly; denial that any truths can be established by the fact that to deny them implies their reaffirmation; or denial that conventional or arbitrary definitions or assumptions yield knowledge.

(2) A proposition about origins of ideas, concepts, or universals: that they or at least those of them having existential reference are derived solely or primarily from experience or some significant part of experience.

(3) A proposition about the nature of meaning, ideas, concepts, or universals: that they (and thus, some contend, knowledge) "consist of" or "are reducible to" references to directly presented data or content of experience; or that signs standing for meanings, ideas, concepts, or universals refer to experienced content only or primarily; or that the meaning of a term consists simply of the sum of its possible consequences in experience; or that if all possible experiential consequences of two propositions are identical, their meanings are identical.

(4) A proposition about the limitations of knowledge: that every possible referent either is something with which one has "direct acquaintance" or consists exclusively of entities with which he is acquainted; or that one can have knowledge of only immediate content of experience; or that although one can have knowledge of existents outside one's own or everyone's experience, that knowledge must always be uncertain, since it is reached through experience.

(5) A proposition about the nature or tests of truth in which proposition some relation or other between experience and truth is taken to be definitive of either the nature of truth or the means of its identification.

(6) A proposition about the existent or the real or both: that experience(s) is (are) the sole existent(s) or reality or both; or the negation of the proposition that nature is a deductive process or is rational through and through; or a proposition that the variable, particular, changing, and contingent are "nearer to the heart of things" than the universal, immutable, and necessary.

(7) A combination of two or more of the above propositions, of approximations to them, of their respective immediate implications, or of their mediate implications when taken together or in conjunction with other premises.

(8) Practice, method, or methodology: relying upon direct observation or immediate experience; or precluding or excluding analysis or reflection; or employing experimentation or systematized induction as opposed to purely discursive, deductive, speculative, transcendental, or dialectical procedures; or relying upon all the ways of mind involved in inquiry.

(9) An assertion, belief, hypothesis, assumption, postulation, or attitude favoring any of the above propositions, practices, methods, or methodologies; or an attitude of dependence upon sense rather than intellect; or an insistence upon fact as against fiction, fancy, or interpretation of fact (supposing fact and interpretation separable); or an attitude favorable to application of scientific attitude or method to inquiry; or a temperament close to common sense and practicality; or a "tough-minded" temperament or attitude involving considerable disillusionment and holding facts (*q.v.*) worthy of utmost intellectual respect; or a tendency to rely on things being as they appear.

The term "empiricism" has been used with extreme looseness and confused with numerous related propositions, practices, and attitudes. Many definitions here listed are themselves ambiguous, but to remove their ambiguity would require misrepresentation of usage of the term. See also *Scepticism, Sensationalism, Pluralism, Phenomenalism, Pragmatism, Positivism, Intuitionalism, Nativism, Rationalism, A Priorism, Intellectualism, Idealism, Transcendentalism, Scientific Empiricism.*—*M.T.K.*

Empiricism, Radical: The theory of knowledge which holds that ideas are reducible to sensations, as in Hume (1711-1776). The doctrine that experience is the final criterion of reality in knowledge. Syn. with sensationalistic empiricism or sensationalism (*q.v.*). See *Avenarius.*

William James, who first adopted this philosophical position, and so named it, described it in *The Meaning of Truth* (Preface, xii-xiii) as consisting "first of a postulate, next of a statement of fact, and finally of a generalized conclusion.

1. "The postulate is that the only things which shall be debatable among philosophers shall be things definable in terms drawn from experience. . . . ."

2. "The statement of fact is that relations between things, conjunctive as well as disjunctive, are as much matters of direct particular experience . . . [as] . . . the things themselves."

3. "The generalized conclusion is that therefore the parts of experience hold together from next to next by relations that are themselves parts of experience. The directly apprehended universe needs, in short, no extraneous trans-empirical connective support, but possesses in its own right a concatenated or continuous structure."

James believed that radical empiricism differed from ordinary or traditional empiricism primarily through the above "statement of fact" (No. 2). By this statement he wished explicitly and thoroughly to reject a common assumption about experience which he found both in the British empiricism and in Kantian and Hegelian idealism, namely, that experience as given is either a collection of disparate impressions or, as Kant would have preferred to say, a manifold of completely unsynthesized representations, and that hence, in order to constitute a world, the material of experience must first be worked over and connective relations established within it either through the principles of the association of ideas (British empiricism) or through a set of trans-empirical categories imposed by the unity of consciousness (Kantian and Hegelian idealism).—*F.L.W.*

Empiricism, Scientific: See *Scientific Empiricism.*—*R.C.*

Empiricists: (Early English) By the beginning of the 17th century, the wave of search for new foundations of knowledge reached England. The country was fast growing in power and territory. Old beliefs seemed inadequate, and vast new information brought from elsewhere by merchants and scholars had to be assimilated. The feeling was in the air that a new, more practicable and more tangible approach to reality was needed. This new approach was attempted by many thinkers, among whom two, Bacon and Hobbes, were the most outstanding. Francis Bacon (1561-1626), despite his busy political career, found enough enthusiasm and time to outline requirements for the study of natural phenomena. Like Descartes, his younger contemporary in France, he felt the importance of making a clean sweep of countless unverified assumptions obstructing then the progress of knowledge. As the first pre-requisite for the investigation of nature, he advocated, therefore, an overthrow of the idols of the mind, that is, of all the preconceptions and prejudices prevalent in theories, ideas and even language. Only when one's mind is thus prepared for the study of phenomena, can one commence gathering and tabulating facts. Bacon's works, particularly *Novum Organum,* is full of sagacious thought and observations, but he seldom goes beyond general advice. As we realize it today, it was a gross exaggeration to call him "the founder of inductive logic." Thomas Hobbes (1588-1679) was an empiricist of an entirely different kind. He did not attempt to work out an inductive method of investigation, but decided to apply deductive logic to new facts. Like Bacon, he keenly understood the inadequacy of medieval doctrines, particularly of those of "form" and "final cause." He felt the need for taking the study of nature anew, particularly of its three most important aspects, Matter, Man and the State. According to Hobbes, all nature is corporeal and all events have but one cause, motion. Man, in his natural state, is dominated by passion which leads him to a "war of all against all." But, contrary to animals, he is capable of using reason which, in the course of time, made him, for self-protection, to choose a social form of existence. The resulting State is, therefore, built on an implicit social contract.—*R.B.W.*

Empirio-criticism: Avenarius' system of pure experience in which all metaphysical additions are eliminated. Opposed to every form of apriorism, it admits of no basic difference between the psychical and the physical, subject and object, consciousness and being. Knowledge consists in statements about contents which are dependent upon System C in man in the form of experience. Ideal of knowledge is the winning of a purely empirical world conception, removal of every dualism and metaphysical category.—*H.H.*

Empty: (Ger. *leer*) In Husserl: Without intuitional fullness; materially indeterminate; obscure. Emptiness is compatible with distinctness. In logic: a class that happens to have no members, but is not a null-class.—*D.C.*

End: (in Scholasticism): That object for the attainment of which the agent moves and acts.

End which (finis qui): That good the agent intends to attain, e.g. health, which a sick man intends. *End for whom (finis cui):* Refers to the person or subject for whom the *end which (finis qui)* is procured, e.g. the sick man himself for whom health is procured.

Formal: Or *end by which (finis quo)* is the actual attainment of the good itself, e.g. beatitude itself in the blessed.

Of the work or of knowledge (finis operis seu scientiae): That to which an act or habit (*habitus*) is ordered through itself and in its proper nature—as the end of logic is the correctness of the actions of the mind. *The end of the one working or knowing (finis operantis seu scientis)* is that which the one acting proposes to his will, in the *exercise* of the action or in the acquisition of knowledge, e.g.—one who learns a science on account of its usefulness.

Simply ultimate: That to which all things are actually or virtually referred;—and which itself is ordered to nothing further, as God. *A relatively ultimate end (finis secundum quid ultimus):* That which terminates some series of acts, in which it is intended ultimately and in itself, but nevertheless can be referred to another end; as health is the end of the art of medicine, but nevertheless it can be ordered to another end, e.g. to working.—*H.G.*

Ends: (in Kant's ethics) (1) Humanity and every rational creature is an end in itself (never merely a means). (2) "The natural end which all men have is their own happiness." (*Kant.*)

Kingdom of ends: Kant's notion of the systematic union of different rational beings by common laws. Cf. also the *Practical Imperative.*—*P.A.S.*

Energeia: (Gr. *energeia,* actuality) In Aristotle's philosophy: (1) the mode of existence of that which possesses to the full its specific essence; actuality; entelechy;—opposed to dynamis, or potentiality; (2) the activity that transforms potentiality into actuality.—*G.R.M.*

Energism: (Lat. *energia,* active) Ethical theory that right action consists in exercising one's normal capacities efficiently. Not happiness or pleasure, but self-realization is the aim of ethical action.—*A.J.B.*

Energy: (Gr. *energos,* at work) The power by which things act to change other things. Potentiality in the physical. Employed by Aristotle as a synonym for actuality or reality. (a) In physics: the capacity for performing work. In modern physics, the equivalent of mass. (b) In axiology: value at the physical level.—*J.K.F.*

Engels, Frederick: Co-founder of the doctrines of Marxism (see *Dialectical materialism*) Engels was the lifelong friend and collaborator of Karl Marx (*q.v.*). He was born at Barmen, Germany, in 1820, the son of a manufacturer. Like Marx, he became interested in communism early in life, developing and applying its doctrines until his death, August 5, 1895. Beside his collaboration with Marx on *Die Heilige Familie, Die Deutsche Ideologie, Manifesto of the Communist Party, Anti-Dühring* and articles for the "New York Tribune" (a selection from which constitutes "Germany: revolution and counter-revolution"), and his editing of Volumes II and III of *Capital* published after Marx's death, Engels wrote extensively on various subjects, from "Condition of the Working Class in England (1844)" to military problems, in which field he had received technical training. On the philosophical side of Marxism, Engels speculated on fundamental questions of scientific methodology and dialectical logic in such books as *Dialectics of Nature* and *Anti-Dühring*. Works like *Ludwig Feuerbach and the Outcome of Classical German Philosophy* and *Origin of the Family, Private Property and the State* are likewise regarded as basic texts. The most extensive collection of Engels' works will be found in Marx-Engels "Gesamtausgabe," to which there is still much unpublished material to be added.—*J.M.S.*

Enjoyment: See *Contemplation.*—*L.W.*

Enlightenment: When Kant, carried by the cultural enthusiasm of his time, explained "enlightenment" as man's coming of age from the state of infancy which rendered him incapable of using his reason without the aid of others, he gave only the subjective meaning of the term. Objectively, enlightenment is a cultural period distinguished by the fervent efforts of leading personalities to make reason the absolute ruler of human life, and to shed the light of knowledge upon the mind and conscience of any individual. Such attempts are not confined to a particular time, or nation, as history teaches; but the term is generally applied to the European enlightenment stretching from the early 17th to the beginning of the 19th century, especially fostered by English, Dutch, French, and German philosophers. It took its start in England from the empiricism of F. Bacon, Th. Hobbes, J. Locke; it found a religious version in the naturalism of Edw. H. Cherbury, J. Toland, M. Tindal, H. Bolingbroke, and the host of "freethinkers," while the Earl of Shaftesbury imparted to it a moral on the "light of reason." Not so constructive but radical in their sarcastic criticism of the past were the French enlighteners, showing that their philosophy got its momentum from the moral corruption at the royal court and abuse of kingly power in France. Descartes' doctrine of the "clear and perspicuous ideas," Spinoza's critical attitude towards religion, and Leibniz-Wolff's "reasonable thinking" prepared the philosophy of P. Bayle, Ch. Montesquieu, F. M. Voltaire, and J. J. Rousseau. The French positive contribution to the subject was the "Encyclopédie ou Dictionaire raisonné des sciences, arts et métiers," 1751-72, in 28 volumes, edited by Diderot, D'Alembert, Helvetius, Holbach, J. L. Lagrane, etc. What, in England and France, remained on the stage of mere ideas and utopic dreams became reality in the new commonwealth of the U.S.A. The "fathers of the constitution" were enlightened, outstanding among them B. Franklin, Th. Jefferson, J. Adams, A. Hamilton, and Th. Paine their foremost literary propagandist.

In Germany, the movement was initiated by G. W. Leibniz whose writings reveal another motive for the cult of pure reason, i.e., the deep disappointment with the Reformation and the bloody religious wars among Christians who were accused of having forfeited the confidence of man in revealed religion. Hence the outstanding part played by the philosophers of "natural law," Grotius, S. Pufendorf, and Chr. Thomasius, their theme being advanced by the contributions to a "natural religion" and tolerance by Chr. Wolff, G. E. Lessing, G. Herder, and the Prussian king Frederik II. Fr. v. Schiller's lyric and dramas served as a powerful commendation of ideal freedom, liberty, justice, and humanity. A group of educators (philanthropists) designed new methods and curricula for the advancement of public education, many of them, *e.g.* Pestalozzi, Basedow, Cooper, A. H. Francke, and Fr. A. Wolf, the father of classic humanism, having achieved international recognition. Although in general agreement with the philosophical axioms of foreign enlighteners, the German philosophy decidedly opposed the English sensism (Hume) and French scepticism, and reached its height in Kant's *Critiques*. The radical rationalism, however, combined with its animosity against religion, brought about a strong philosophical, theological, and literary opposition (Hamann, Jacobi, Lavater) which eventually led to its defeat. The ideals of the enlightenment period, the impassioned zeal for the materialization of the ideal man in an ideal society show clearly that it was basically related to the Renaissance and its continuation. See *Aufklärung*. Cf. J. G. Hibben, *The Philosophy of the Enlightenment*, 1910.—*S.V.F.*

Ens: Being in the most general sense of the term, with the least possible determination, without qualifications.—*J.J.R.*

Ens Parmenideum: (Lat. *ens,* being) The changeless being (existence) ascribed by Parmenides to all things and events. Change was regarded by him as an illogical illusion.—*R.B.W.*

Ens Rationis: (in Scholasticism) A purely objective *ens rationis* is a chimera, or an impossible thing, although in a certain way it is an object of human knowledge, as a triangular circle. A logical *ens rationis* is that which is fashioned by the intellect with some foundation in reality; *e.g.* human nature conceived as one reality because of the likeness of singular natures.—*H.G.*

Entelechy: (Gr. *entelecheia*) In Aristotle's philosophy: (1) the mode of being of a thing whose essence is completely realized, actuality; energeia;—opposed to dynamis, or potentiality; (2) the form or essence. —*G.R.M.*

Enthymeme: (Gr. *enthymema*) In Aristotle's logic a

rhetorical syllogism, usually consisting of probable premisses, and used for persuasion as distinct from instruction. In later logic a syllogism of which one premiss or the conclusion is not explicitly stated. —*G.R.M.*

Entities, neutral: Qualityless elements; simples that are in themselves neither mental nor physical.—*H.H.*

Entity: A real being; also the common element in all individuals belonging to a genus or species, which may be considered apart from the individual characteristics. Sometimes used in the sense of a vague and ill-defined reality.—*J.J.R.*

Entropy: Thermodynamic state approaching a maximum level of zero difference of energy potentials.

Enumerable: A class is *enumerable* if its *cardinal number* (*q.v.*) is aleph O.—*A.C.*

Enumerative Induction: A type of inference from a number of given instances, when these are treated by noting the number of observed coincident happenings of their conditions and their effects, and without attempting to analyze their respective contents or to determine a causal connection between them by means of one or more of the methods of research and verification. The generalization "Every A is B" thus obtained, should be understood with the qualification "Every observed A is B". This process is used especially in statistical methods.—*T.G.*

Epagoge: (Gr. *epagoge*) In Aristotle's logic the process of establishing a general proposition by induction (seeing the universal in the particular).—*G.R.M.*

Epicheirema: (Gr. *epicheirema*) In Aristotle's logic a dialectical as distinct from an apodictic or an eristic syllogism.

In later logic an argument one of whose premisses is established by a prosyllogism expressed in the form of an enthymeme.—*G.R.M.*

Epictetus: (c. 60-100 A.D.) A Stoic philosopher and freed slave, who established his School in Nicopolis, Epirus; his *Discourses* were published by Arrian, his learned disciple; they contain sharp observations of human behavior and pithy sayings on ethical matters.—*R.B.W.*

Epicurean School: Founded by Epicurus in Athens in the year 306 B.C. Epicureanism gave expression to the desire for a refined type of happiness which is the reward of the cultured man who can take pleasure in the joys of the mind over which he can have greater control than over those of a material or sensuous nature. The friendship of gifted and noble men, the peace and contentment that comes from fair conduct, good morals and aesthetic enjoyments are the ideals of the Epicurean who refuses to be perturbed by any metaphysical or religious doctrines which impose duties and thus hinder the freedom of pure enjoyment. Epicurus adopted the atomism of Democritus (*q.v.*) but modified its determinism by permitting chance to cause a swerve (clinamen) in the fall of the atoms. See C. W. Bailey, *Epicurus*. However, physics was not to be the main concern of the philosopher. See *Apathia, Ataraxia, Hedonism.*—*M.F.*

Epicurus: (341-270 B.C.) A native of Samos, founded his School in Athens about 306 B.C., where he instructed his disciples and admirers in the art of rational living. He taught that pleasure and happiness are the natural end of life. But, contrary to later misconceptions, he did not advocate the pursuit of all or any pleasures, but only of those which are consistent with intelligence and moderation. Joys of the mind are superior to pleasures of the body. In his interpretation of nature, he accepted Democritus' atomism, but contended that the element of chance enters into atoms' motions and makes them deviate from their course.—*R.B.W.*

Epiphenomenalism: Theory of the body-mind relation advanced by Clifford, Huxley, Hodgson, etc. which holds that consciousness is, in relation to the neural processes which underlie it, a mere epiphenomenon. See W. James, *Principles of Psychology*, Vol. I, ch. V. See *Epiphenomenon.*—*L.W.*

Epiphenomenon: (Gr. *epi* + *phainomenon*, from phainein, to appear) A by-product of a basic process which exerts no appreciable influence on the subsequent development of the process.—*L.W.*

Epistemic: (Gr. *episteme*, knowledge) Relating to knowledge. See *Epistemological object.*—*L.W.*

Epistemological Dualism: See *Dualism, Epistemological.*

Epistemological Idealism: The form of epistemological monism which identifies the content and the object of knowledge by assimilating the object to the content. Berkeleyan idealism by its rejection of a physical object independent of ideas directly present to the mind is an example of epistemological monism. See *Epistemological Monism.*—*L.W.*

Epistemological Monism: Theory that non-inferential knowledge, (perception, memory, etc.) the object of knowledge, (the thing perceived or remembered) is numerically identical with the data of knowledge (sense data, memory images, etc.). Epistemological monism may be either (a) epistemologically realistic, when it asserts that the data exist independently of the knowing mind, or (b) epistemologically idealistic when it asserts the data to be mind constituted and to exist only when apprehended by the mind. See *Epistemological Dualism, Epistemological Idealism* and *Epistemological Realism.*—*L.W.*

Epistemological Object: The object envisaged by an act of knowledge whether the knowledge be veridical, illusory or even hallucinatory in contrast to ontological object, which is a real thing corresponding to the epistemological object when knowledge is veridical. See C. D. Broad, *The Mind and its Place in Nature*, pp. 141 ff.—*L.W.*

Epistemological Realism: Theory that the object of knowledge enjoys an existence independent of and external to the knowing mind. The theory, though applied most commonly to perception where it is designated perceptual realism, may be extended to other types of knowledge (for example memory and knowledge of other minds). Epistemological realism may be combined either with *Epistemological Monism* or *Epistemological Dualism*. See *Epistemological Monism, Epistemological Dualism.—L.W.*

Epistemology: (Gr. *episteme,* knowledge + *logos,* theory) The branch of philosophy which investigates the origin, structure, methods and validity of knowledge. The term "epistemology" appears to have been used for the first time by J. F. Ferrier, *Institutes of Metaphysics* (1854), who distinguished two branches of philosophy—epistemology and ontology. The German equivalent of epistemology, *Erkenntnistheorie,* was used by the Kantian, K. L. Reinhold, *Versuch einer Neuen Theorie des menschlichen Vorstellungsvermögens* (1789); *Das Fundament des philosophischen Wissens* (1791), but the term did not gain currency until after its adoption by E. Zeller, *Ueber Aufgabe und Bedeutung der Erkenntnisstheorie* (1862). The term *theory of knowledge* is a common English equivalent of epistemology and translation of *Erkenntnistheorie;* the term Gnosiology has also been suggested but has gained few adherents.

The scope of epistemology may be indicated by considering its relations to the allied disciplines: (a) *metaphysics,* (b) *logic,* and (c) *psychology.* (a) Speculative philosophy is commonly considered to embrace metaphysics (see *Metaphysics*) and epistemology as its two coordinate branches, or if the term metaphysics be extended to embrace the whole of speculative philosophy, then epistemology and ontology become the two main subdivisions of metaphysics in the wide sense. Whichever usage is adopted, epistemology as the philosophical theory of knowledge is one of the two main branches of philosophy. The question of the relative priority of epistemology and metaphysics (or ontology) has occasioned considerable controversy: the dominant view fostered by Descartes, Locke and Kant is that epistemology is the prior philosophical science, the investigation of the possibility and limits of knowledge being a necessary and indispensible preliminary to any metaphysical speculations regarding the nature of ultimate reality. On the other hand, strongly metaphysical thinkers like Spinoza and Hegel, and more recently S. Alexander and A. N. Whitehead, have first attacked the metaphysical problems and adopted the view of knowledge consonant with their metaphysics. Between these two extremes is the view that epistemology and metaphysics are logically interdependent and that a metaphysically presuppositionless epistemology is as unattainable as an epistemologically presuppositionless metaphysics. (b) Despite the fact that traditional logic embraced many topics which would now be considered epistemological, the demarcation between logic and epistemology is now fairly clear-cut: logic is the formal science of the principles governing valid reasoning; epistemology is the philosophical science of the nature of knowledge and truth. For example, though the decision as to whether a given process of reasoning is valid or not is a logical question, the inquiry into the nature of validity is epistemological. (c) The relation between psychology and epistemology is particularly intimate since the cognitive processes of perception, memory, imagination, conception and reasoning, investigated by empirical psychology, are the very processes which, in quite a different context, are the special subject matter of epistemology. Nevertheless the psychological and epistemological treatments of the cognitive processes of mind are radically different: scientific psychology is concerned solely with the description and explanation of conscious processes, *e.g.* particular acts of perception, in the context of other conscious events; epistemology is interested in the cognitive pretentions of the perceptions, *i.e.* their apparent reference to external objects. In short, whereas psychology is the investigation of *all* states of mind including the cognitive in the context of the mental life, epistemology investigates only cognitive states and these solely with respect to their cognitive import. Psychology and epistemology are by virtue of the partial identity of their subject matter interdependent sciences. The psychology of perception, memory, imagination, conception, etc. affords indispensable data for epistemological interpretation and on the other hand epistemological analysis of the cognitive processes may sometimes prove psychologically suggestive. The epistemologist must, however, guard against a particularly insidious form of the genetic fallacy: viz. the supposition that the psychological origin of an item of knowledge prejudices either favorably or unfavorably its cognitive validity—a fallacy which is psychologism at its worst.

An examination of the generally recognized *problems of epistemology* and of the representative solutions of these problems will serve to further clarify the nature and scope of epistemological inquiry. The emphasis in epistemology has varied from one historical era to another and yet there is a residuum of epistemological problems which has persisted to the present.

(a) The initial and inescapable problem with which the epistemologist is confronted is that of the very *possibility of knowledge:* Is genuine knowledge at all attainable? The natural dogmatism of the human mind is confronted with the sceptic's challenge: a challenge grounded on the relativity of the senses (sensory scepticism) and the contradictions into which the reason is often betrayed (rational scepticism). An alternative to both dogmatism and extreme scepticism is a tentative or methodological scepticism of which Descartes' systematic doubt, Locke's cautious empiricism and Kant's critical epistemology are instances. See *Dogmatism; Scepticism; Criticism.* Scepticism in modern epistemology is commonly associated with solipsism, since a scepticism regarding knowledge of the external world leads to solipsism and the ego-centric predicament. See *Solipsism; Ego-centric predicament.*

(b) An epistemologist who rejects an extreme or agnostic scepticism, may very properly seek to determine the *limits of knowledge* and to assert that genuine knowledge is, within certain prescribed limits, possible yet beyond those limits impossible. There are, of course, innumerable ways of delimiting the knowable from the unknowable—a typical instance of the sceptical delimitation of knowledge is the Kantian distinction between the phenomenal and noumenal world. See *Phenomenon; Noumenon*. A similar epistemological position is involved in the doctrine of certain recent positivists and radical empiricists that the knowable coincides with the meaningful and the verifiable, the unknowable with the meaningless and unverifiable. See *Positivism, Logical; Empiricism, Radical*.

(c) The traditional problem of the *origin of knowledge*, viz.: By what faculty or faculties of mind is knowledge attainable? It gave rise to the principal cleavage in modern epistemology between rationalism and empiricism (*q.v.*) though both occur in any thinker. The rationalists (Descartes, Spinoza, Leibniz) rely primarily—though not exclusively—on reason as the source of genuine knowledge, and the empiricists (Locke, Berkeley and Hume) rely mainly on experience. A broadly conceived empiricism such as Locke's which acknowledges the authenticity of knowledge derived both from the inner sense (see *Reflection; Introspection*), and the outer senses, contrasts with that type of sensationalism (*q.v.*) which is empiricism restricted to the outer senses. Various attempts, the most notable of which is the critical philosophy of Kant, have been made to reconcile rationalism and empiricism by assigning to reason and experience their respective roles in the constitution of knowledge. Few historical or contemporary epistemologists would subscribe either to a rationalism or an empiricism of an exclusive and extreme sort.

(d) The *methodological problem* bulks large in epistemology and the solutions of it follow in general the lines of cleavage determined by the previous problem. Rationalists of necessity have emphasized deductive and demonstrative procedures in the acquisition and elaboration of knowledge while empiricists have relied largely on induction and hypothesis but few philosophers have espoused the one method to the complete exclusion of the other. A few attempts have been made to elaborate distinctively philosophical methods reducible neither to the inductive procedure of the natural sciences nor the demonstrative method of mathematics—such are the *Transcendental Method* of Kant and the *Dialectical Method* of Hegel though the validity and irreducibility of both of these methods are highly questionable. Pragmatism, operationalism, and phenomenology may perhaps in certain of their aspects be construed as recent attempts to evaluate new epistemological methods.

(e) *The problem of the* A PRIORI, though the especial concern of the rationalist, confronts the empiricist also since few epistemologists are prepared to exclude the *a priori* entirely from their accounts of knowledge. The problem is that of isolating the *a priori* or non-empirical elements in knowledge and accounting for them in terms of the human reason. Three principal theories of the *a priori* have been advanced: (i) *The theory of the intrinsic* A PRIORI which asserts that the basic principles of logic, mathematics, natural sciences and philosophy are self-evident truths recognizable by such intrinsic

traits as clarity and distinctness of ideas. The intrinsic theory received its definitive modern expression in the theory of "innate ideas" (*q.v.*) of Herbert of Cherbury, Descartes, and 17th century rationalism. (ii) *The presuppositional theory* of the *a priori* which validates *a priori* truths by demonstrating that they are presupposed either by their attempted denial (Leibniz) or by the very possibility of experience (Kant). (iii) *The postulational theory of the* A PRIORI, elaborated under the influence of recent postulational techniques in mathematics, interprets *a priori* principles as rules or postulates arbitrarily posited in the construction of formal deductive systems. See *Postulate; Posit*.

(f) The problem of differentiating *the principal kinds of knowledge* is an essential task especially for an empirical epistemology. Perhaps the most elementary epistemological distinction is between (i) *non-inferential apprehension of* objects by perception, memory etc. (see *Knowledge by Acquaintance*), and (ii) *inferential knowledge* of things with which the knowing subject has no direct apprehension. See *Knowledge by Description*. Acquaintance in turn assumes two principal forms: perception or acquaintance with external objects (see *Perception*), and introspection or the subject's acquaintance with the "self" and its cognitive, volitional and affective states. See *Introspection; Reflection*. Inferential knowledge includes *knowledge of other selves* (this is not to deny that knowledge of other minds may at times be immediate and non-inferential), *historical knowledge,* including not only history in the narrower sense but also astronomical, biological, anthropological and archaeological and even cosmological reconstructions of the past and finally *scientific knowledge* in so far as it involves inference and construction from observational data.

(g) The problem of *the structure of the knowledge-situation* is to determine with respect to each of the major kinds of knowledge just enumerated — but particularly with respect to perception — the constituents of the knowledge-situation in their relation to one another. The structural problem stated in general but rather vague terms is: What is the relation between the subjective and objective components of the knowledge-situation? In contemporary epistemology, the structural problem has assumed a position of such preeminence as frequently to eclipse other issues of epistemology. The problem has even been incorporated by some into the definition of philosophy. (See A. Lalande, *Vocabulaire de la Philosophie*, art. *Théorie de la Connaissance*. I. and G. D. Hicks, *Encycl. Brit.* 5th ed. art. *Theory of Knowledge*.) The principal cleavage in epistemology, according to this formulation of its problem, is between a subjectivism which telescopes the object of knowledge into the knowing subject (see *Subjectivism; Idealism, Epistemological*) and panobjectivism which ascribes to the object all qualities perceived or otherwise cognized. See *Panobjectivism*. A compromise between the extremes of subjectivism and objectivism is achieved by the theory of representative perception, which, distinguishing between primary and secondary qualities, considers the former objective, the latter subjective. See *Representative Perception, Theory of; Primary Qualities; Secondary Qualities*.

The structural problem stated in terms of the antithesis between subjective and objective is rather too vague for the purposes of epistemology and a more precise analysis of the knowledge-situation and statement of the issues involved is required. The perceptual situation — and this analysis may presumably be extended with appropriate modifications to memory, imagination and other modes of cognition—consists of a *subject* (the self, or pure act of perceiving), the *content* (sense data) and the *object* (the physical thing perceived). In terms of this analysis, two issues may be formulated: (a) Are content and object identical (epistemological monism), or are they numerically distinct (epistemological dualism)? and (b) Does the object exist independently of the knowing subject (epistemological idealism) or is it dependent upon the subject (epistemological realism)?

(h) *The problem of truth* is perhaps the culmination of epistemological enquiry—in any case it is the problem which brings the enquiry to the threshold of metaphysics. The traditional theories of the nature of truth are: (i) *the correspondence theory* which conceives truth as a relation between an "idea" or a proposition and its object—the relation has commonly been regarded as one of resemblance but it need not be so considered (see *Correspondence theory of truth*); (ii) *the Coherence theory* which adopts as the criterion of truth, the logical consistency of a proposition with a wider system of propositions (see *Coherence theory of truth*), and (iii) *the intrinsic theory* which views truth as an intrinsic property of the true proposition. See *Intrinsic theory of truth.*—*L.W.*

Bibliography: L. T. Hobhouse, *The Theory of Knowledge*, 1896. H. Bergson, *Introduction to Metaphysics*, Eng. trans. 1912. W. P. Montague, *Ways of Knowing*, 1925. J. Dewey, *The Quest for Certainty*, 1929. W. James, *The Meaning of Truth*, 1909. C. I. Lewis, *Mind and the World Order*, 1929. D. Drake and others, *Essays in Critical Realism*, 1920. E. B. Holt, *The Concept of Consciousness*, 1914. W. James, *Essays in Radical Empiricism*, 1912. J. Laird, *A Study in Realism*, 1920. A. O. Lovejoy, *The Revolt against Dualism*, 1930. G. E. Moore, *Philosophical Studies*, 1922, B. Russell, *The Problems of Philosophy*, 1912. B. Russell, *Scientific Method in Philosophy*, 1914. E. G. Spaulding, *The New Rationalism*, 1918, S. Alexander, *Space, Time, and Deity*, 2nd ed., 1928. C. D. Broad, *Perception, Physics, and Reality*. 1914. C. D. Broad, *Scientific Thought*, 1923. C. D. Broad, *Mind and its Place in Nature*, 1925. B. Russell, *The Analysis of Mind*, 1921. N. K. Smith, *Prolegomena to an Idealist Theory of Knowledge*, 1924. H. Vaihinger, *The Philosophy of "As If,"* Eng. trans., 1924. A. N. Whitehead, *Principles of Natural Knowledge*. A. N. Whitehead, *Concept of Nature*. H. H. Price, *Perception*, 1933. W. T. Stace, *The Theory of Knowledge and Existence*, 1932. L. Wood, *The Analysis of Knowledge*.

Episyllogism: Where the conclusion of one (categorical) syllogism is used as one of the premises of another, the first syllogism is called a *prosyllogism* and the second one an *episyllogism.*—*A.C.*

Equality: See *Logic, formal*, §§ 3, 6, 9.

Equipollence: A relation of equivalence between two propositions or propositional forms or symbols for these.

(a) Some writers, following the example of Galen, use it in the sense of material equivalence, i.e., having the same truth value.

(b) Others, following Apuleius, use it in a much more restricted sense such as that of strict equivalence or even reciprocal entailment. In the latter sense the relation holds when and only when the two sentences express the same fact.—*C.A.B.*

Carnap proposes a purely syntactical definition of equipollence by defining two sentences (or two classes of sentences) to be equipollent if they have the same class of non-valid consequences. See the article *Valid.*—*A.C.*

Equivalence: (Lat. *aequivaleo*, have equal power) Identical value. Having the same relation or force. In logic, syn. of *equipollence* (*q.v.*).—*J.K.F.*

Equivocation: Any fallacy arising from ambiguity of a word, or of a phrase playing the role of a single word in the reasoning in question, the word or phrase being used at different places with different meanings and an inference drawn which is formally correct if the word or phrase is treated as being the same word or phrase throughout.—*A.C.*

Erh: (a) The active or male principle (yang) and the passive or female principle (yin), which are the products of Tao and which produce the myriad of things. (Taoism.)

(b) The active or male principle (yang or ch'ien) and the passive or female principle.—*W.T.C.*

Eristic: (Gr. *eristike*) In Aristotle's logic the art of specious reasoning, or of reasoning from specious premises, for the purpose of victory in argument; —opposed to apodictic and to dialectical reasoning. See *Apodictic; Dialectic*.

A kind of polemic, characterized by the use of logical subtleties and oratorical casuistry, for which the Megarian School was particularly famous. See *Megarians:*—*R.B.W.*

Eriugena, Joannes Scottus: (c. 800/815–900 A.D.) Was of Irish birth and early education. He came to the Court of Charles the Bald, son of Charlemagne, as a teacher c. 845. A good linguist, he translated works of Maximus, Gregory of Nyssa and the Pseudo-Dionysius from Greek to Latin. His thought is partly Augustinian, partly a personal development inspired by the Greek Fathers. He has been accused of Pantheism. Chief works: *De Praedestinatione, De divisione Naturae* (PL 122). M. Cappuyns, *Jean S. Erigène, sa vie, son oeuvre, sa pensée* (Louvain-Paris, 1933).—*V.J.B.*

Erlebnis: (Gr. *erleben*, to experience or live through) The mind's identification with its own emotions and feelings when it consciously "lives through"; contrasts with cognition, with its characteristic duality between subject and object.

See *Enjoyment* and *Contemplation.*—*L.W.*

Eros: (Gr.) 1. Possessive desire or love, commonly erotic. 2. In Platonic thought, the driving force of life aspiring to the absolute Good; hence the motive underlying education, fine art, and philosophy. The connotation of aesthetic fascination, impersonality, and intense desire is retained in Plato's use of the term. Hence *Eros* is to be distinguished from the Indian *Bhakti* (selfless devotion), the Buddhist *Metta* (disinterested benevolence), the Confucian *Jên* (humanity, charity), and *Ai* (personal love), and the Christian *Agapáo* (sacrificial, protective brotherly love), and *Philéo* (personal affection or fondness).—*W.L.*

Erotema: (Gr. *erotema*) A question; in Aristotle's logic a premise stated in interrogative form for acceptance or rejection by the respondent; hence, any premise used in dialectical reasoning.—*G.R.M.*

Error: (Lat. *error*, from *errare*, to wander) Distorted or non-veridical apprehension, for example illusory perception and memory. See *Veridical*. The term, although sometimes used as a synonym of falsity, is properly applied to acts of apprehension like perception and memory and not to propositions and judgments.—*L.W.*

Eschatology: (GR. *ta eschata*, death) That part of systematic or dogmatic theology dealing with the last things, namely, death, judgment, heaven and hell, and also with the end of the world. Also applied by philosophers to the complexus of theories relating to the ultimate end of mankind and the final stages of the physical cosmos.—*J.J.R.*

Esoteric: Belonging to the inner circle of initiates, or experts; *e.g.* the esoteric doctrines attributed to the Stoics, or the esoteric members of the Pythagorean brotherhoods; contrasted with exoteric (*q.v.*). —*G.R.M.*

Essence: (Lat. *essentia*, fr. *essens*, participle of *esse*, to be) The being or power of a thing; necessary internal relation or function. The Greek philosophers identified essence and substance in the term, ousia. In classic Latin essence was the idea or law of a thing. But in scholastic philosophy the distinction between essence and substance became important. Essence began to be identified, as in its root meaning, with being or power. For Locke, the being whereby a thing is what it is. For Kant, the primary internal principle of all that belongs to the being of a thing. For Peirce, the intelligible element of the possibility of being. (a) In logic: definition or the elements of a thing; the genus and differentia. See *Definition*. (b) In epistemology: that intelligible character which defines what an indefinite predicate asserts. The universal possibility of a thing. Opposite of existence. Syn. with being, possibility. See Santayana's use of the term in *Realm of Essence,* as a hybrid of intuited datum and scholastic essence (*q.v.*) See *Eternal object.*—*J.K.F.*

Essence, (Scholastic): The essence of a thing is its nature considered independently of its existence. Also nonexistent things and those which cannot exist at all have a proper essence. The definition details all properties making up the essence. It is doubtful whether we can give of any thing a truly essential definition with the one exception of man: man is a rational animal. Most of the definitions have to be content with naming accidental features, because we do not attain a direct knowledge of substances. Synonymously the term "quiddity" is used. The essence implies, in the case of corporeal beings, matter, but not as actually contained, since the essence is individualized by prime matter. But it is of the essence of material things to be material. Thus, Essence is not "form" properly speaking. See *Distinction, Form, Individuation, Matter.*—*R.A.*

Essential Coördination: Term employed by R. Avenarius (*Kritik der reinen Erfahrung,* 1888) to designate the essential solidarity existing between the knowing subject and the object of knowledge. The theory of "essential coördination" is contrasted by Avenarius with the allegedly false theory of introjection. (*q.v.*).—*L.W.*

Esthesis: (Gr. *aisthesis*, sensation or feeling, from *aisthanesthai,* to perceive) A state of pure feeling—sensuous, hedonic or affective—characterized by the absence of conceptual and interpretational elements. Aesthesis at the sensory level consists of pure sense data. See *Sense datum.* Though the existence of pure esthesis is challenged by most psychologists and epistemologists (see C. I. Lewis, *Mind and the World Order,* pp. 54-5), a state of mind approximates pure esthesis when the conceptual, interpretative and constructional elements are reduced to a minimum.—*L.W.*

Esthetic: See *Aesthetic.*

Eternal object: A. N. Whitehead's term essentially synonymous with Plato's "Idea" or Aristotle's "form;" a potential form determining and limiting the qualitative characteristics of actuality; a universal attributed to reality.—*R.B.W.*

Eternal recurrence: The view that as the dynamic energies of nature are finite, whereas time is infinite, only a limited number of combinations is possible, which results in the cyclical recurrence of every situation in infinitely numerous times. The view which assumes that the initial combination of the forces of existence will recur again and again. (Nietzsche.)—*H.H.*

Eternity: An infinite extent of time, in which every event is future at one time, present at another, past at another. As everlastingness, it was formerly divided into two eternities, eternity *a parte ante,* an infinite extent of time before the present, and eternity *a parte post,* an infinite extent of time after the present. Anything can be called "eternal" which is not subject to change, f.i. laws of nature, or which transcends all time. See *Timeless.*—*R.B.W.*

Ethical formalism: (Kantian) Despite the historical over-shadowing of Kant's ethical position by the influence of *The Critique of Pure Reason* upon the philosophy of the past century and a half, Kant's own (declared) major interest, almost from the very beginning, was in moral philosophy. Even the *Critique of Pure Reason* itself was written only in order to clear the ground for dealing adequately with the field of ethics in the *Grundlegung zur Metaphysik der Sitten* (1785), in the *Kritik der Praktischen Vernunft* (1788), and in the *Metaphysik der Sitten* (1797). By the end of the seventeen-sixties Kant was ready to discard every prior ethical theory, from the early Greeks to Baumgarten, Rousseau, and the British moralists, finding all of them, despite the wide divergencies among them, equally dogmatic and unacceptable. Each of the older theories he found covertly to rely upon some dogmatic criterion or other, be it a substantive "principle," an intuition, or an equally substantive "sense." Every such ethical theory fails to deal with ethical issues as genuinely problematic, since it is amenable to some "demonstrative" preconceived criterion.

In harmony with Kant's major concern in his other *Critiques*—namely the establishment of lawfulness in each respective sphere (of scientific knowledge, of moral action, and of artistic and religious hopefulness)—Kant's primary aim in ethics is the unification or synthesis of the field of action. Since, however, action is ever changing and since eternally new and creative possibilities of action are constantly coming into view, Kant saw that lawfulness in the ethical sphere could not be of either a static or predetermined nature.

As against the faulty ethical procedures of the past and of his own day, therefore, Kant very early conceived and developed the more critical concept of "form"—not in the sense of a "mould" into which content is to be poured (a notion which has falsely been taken over by Kant-students from his theoretical philosophy into his ethics)—but as a method of rational (*not* ratiocinative, but inductive) reflection; a method undetermined by, although not irrespective of, empirical data or considerations. This methodologically formal conception constitutes Kant's major distinctive contribution to ethical theory. It is a *process* of rational reflection, creative construction, and transition, and as such is held by him to be the only method capable of coping with the exigencies of the facts of human experience and with the needs of moral obligation. By this method of creative construction the reflective (inductive) reason is able to create, as each new need for a next reflectively chosen step arises, a new object of "pure"—that is to say, empirically undetermined—"practical reason." This makes possible the transition from a present no longer adequate ethical conception or attitude to an untried and as yet "indemonstrable" object. No other method can guarantee the individual and social conditions of progress without which the notion of morality loses all assignable meaning. The newly constructed object of "pure practical reason" is assumed, in the event, to provide a type of life and conduct which, just because it is of my own construction, will be likely to be accompanied by the feeling of self-sufficiency which is the basic prerequisite of any worthy human happiness. It is this theory which constitutes Kant's *ethical formalism*. See also *Autonomy, Categorical Imperative, Duty, End(s), Freedom, Happiness, Law, Moral, Practical Impera-*

tive, Will.—P.A.S.

Ethical Hedonism: See *Hedonism, ethical*.

Ethical relativism: The view that ethical truths are relative—that the rightness of an action and the goodness of an object depend on or consist in the attitude taken towards it by some individual or group, and hence may vary from individual to individual or from group to group. See *Absolutism.—W.K.F.*

Ethical rule: See *Rule*.

Ethics: (Gr. *ta ethika,* from *ethos*) Ethics (also referred to as moral philosophy) is that study or discipline which concerns itself with judgments of approval and disapproval, judgments as to the rightness or wrongness, goodness or badness, virtue or vice, desirability or wisdom of actions, dispositions, ends, objects, or states of affairs. There are two main directions which this study may take. It may concern itself with a psychological or sociological analysis and explanation of our ethical judgments, showing what our approvals and disapprovals consist in and why we approve or disapprove what we do. Or it may concern itself with establishing or recommending certain courses of action, ends, or ways of life as to be taken or pursued, either as right or as good or as virtuous or as wise, as over against others which are wrong, bad, vicious, or foolish. Here the interest is more in action than in approval, and more in the guidance of action than in its explanation, the purpose being to find or set up some ideal or standard of conduct or character, some good or end or *summum bonum,* some ethical criterion or first principle. In many philosophers these two approaches are combined. The first is dominant or nearly so in the ethics of Hume, Schopenhauer, the evolutionists, Westermarck, and of M. Schlick and other recent positivists, while the latter is dominant in the ethics of most other moralists.

Either sort of enquiry involves an investigation into the meaning of ethical statements, their truth and falsity, their objectivity and subjectivity, and the possibility of systematizing them under one or more first principles. In neither case is ethics concerned with our conduct or our ethical judgments simply as a matter of historical or anthropological record. It is, however, often said that the first kind of enquiry is not ethics but psychology. In both cases it may be said that the aim of ethics, as a part of philosophy, is theory not practice, cognition not action, even though it be added at once that its theory is for the sake of practice and its cognition a cognition of how to live. But some moralists who take the second approach do deny that ethics is a cognitive discipline or science, namely those who hold that ethical first principles are resolutions or preferences, not propositions which may be true or false, *e.g.,* Nietzsche, Santayana, Russell.

Ethical judgments fall, roughly, into two classes, (a) judgments of value, i.e., judgments as to the goodness or badness, desirability or undesirability of certain objects, ends, experiences, dispositions, or states of affairs, *e.g.* "Knowledge is good," (b) judgments of obligation, i.e. judgments as to the obligatoriness, rightness or wrongness, wisdom or foolishness of various courses of action and kinds of conduct, judgments enjoining, recommending or condemning certain lines of conduct. Thus there are two parts of ethics, (1) the theory of value or axiology, which is concerned with judgments of value, extrinsic or intrinsic, moral or non-moral, (2) the theory of obligation or deontology, which is concerned with judgments of obligation. In either of these parts of ethics one may take either of the above approaches—in the theory of value one may be interested either in analyzing and explaining (psychologically or sociologically) our various judgments of value or in establishing or recommending certain things as good or as ends, and in the theory of obligation one may be interested either in analyzing and explaining our various judgments of obligation or in setting forth certain courses of action as right, wise, etc.

Historically, philosophers have, in the main, taken the latter approach in both parts of ethics, and we may confine our remaining space to it. On this approach a theory of value is a theory as to what is to be pursued or sought, and a theory of obligation, a theory as to what is to be done. Now, of these two parts of ethics, philosophers have generally been concerned primarily with the latter, busying themselves with the former only secondarily, usually because it seemed to them that one must know what ends are good before one can know what acts are to be performed. They all offer both a theory of value and a theory of obligation, but it was not until the 19th and 20th centuries that value-theory became a separate discipline studied for its own sake—a development in which important roles were played by Kant, Lotze, Ritschl, certain European economists, Brentano, Meinong, von Ehrenfels, W. M. Urban, R. B. Perry, and others.

In the theory of value the first question concerns the meaning of value-terms and the status of goodness. As to meaning the main point is whether goodness is definable or not, and if so, how. As to status the main point is whether goodness is subjective or objective, relative or absolute. Various positions are possible. (a) Recent emotive meaning theories, *e.g.* that of A. J. Ayer, hold that "good" and other value-terms have only an emotive meaning. (b) Intuitionists and non-naturalists often hold that goodness is an indefinable intrinsic (and therefore objective or absolute) property, *e.g.* Plato, G. E. Moore, W. D. Ross, J. Laird, Meinong, N. Hartman. (c) Metaphysical and naturalistic moralists usually hold that goodness can be defined in metaphysical or in psychological terms, generally interpreting "x is good" to mean that a certain attitude is taken toward x by some mind or group of minds. For some of them value is objective or absolute in the sense of having the same locus for everyone, *e.g.*, Aristotle in his definition of the good as that at which all things aim, (*Ethics*, bk. I). For others the locus of value varies from individual to individual or from group to group, i.e. different things will be good for different individuals or groups, *e.g.*, Hobbes, Westermarck, William James, R. B. Perry.

The second question in value-theory is the question "What things are good? What is good, what is the highest good, etc.?" On this question perhaps the main issue historically is between those who say that the good is pleasure, satisfaction, or some state of feeling, and those who say that the good is virtue, a state of will, or knowledge, a state of the intellect. Holding the good to be pleasure or satisfaction are some of the Sophists, the hedonists (the Cyrenaics, the Epicureans, Hobbes, Hume, Bentham, Mill, Sidgwick, Spencer, Schlick). Holding virtue or knowledge or both to be good or supremely good are Plato, Aristotle, the Stoics, the Neo-Platonists, Augustine, Aquinas, Spinoza, Kant, Hegel, G. E. Moore, H. Rashdall, J. Laird, W. D. Ross, N. Hartmann.

In the theory of obligation we find on the question of the meaning and status of right and wrong the same variety of views as obtain in the theory of value: "right," *e.g.*, has only an emotive meaning (Ayer); or it denotes an intuited indefinable objective quality or relation of an act (Price, Reid, Clarke, Sidgwick, Ross, possibly Kant); or it stands for the attitude of some mind or group of minds towards an act (the Sophists, Hume, Westermarck). But it is also often defined as meaning that the act is conducive to the welfare of some individual or group—the agent himself, or his group, or society as a whole. Many of the teleological and utilitarian views mentioned below include such a definition.

On the question as to what acts are right or are to be done, ethical theories fall into two groups: (1) Axiological theories seek to determine what is right entirely by reference to the *goodness* or *value* of something, thus making the theory of obligation dependent on the theory of value. For a philosopher like Martineau it is the comparative goodness of its motive that determines which act is right. For a teleologist it is the comparative amount of good which it brings or probably will bring into being that determines which act is right—the egoistic teleologist holding that the right act is the act which is most conducive to the good of the agent (some Sophists, Epicurus, Hobbes), and the universalistic teleologist holding that the right act is the act which is most conducive to the good of the world as a whole (see *Utilitarianism*). (2) On deontological theories see *Deontological ethics* and *Intuitionism*.

Historically, one may say that, in general, Greek ethics was teleological, though there are deontological strains in Plato, Aristotle, and the Stoics. In Christian moralists one finds both kinds of ethics, according as the emphasis is on the will of God as the source of duties (the ordinary view) or on the goodness of God as somehow the end of human life (Augustine and Aquinas), theology and revelation taking a central role in either case. In modern philosophical ethics, again, both kinds of ethics are present, with the opposition between them coming out into the open. Starting in the 17th and 18th centuries in Britain are both "intuitionism" (Cambridge Platonists, Clarke, Butler, Price, Reid, Whewell, McCosh, etc.) and utilitarianism (*q.v.*), with British ethics largely a matter of controversy between the two, a controversy in which the teleological side has lately been taken by Cambridge and the deontological side by Oxford. Again, in Germany, England, and elsewhere there have been, on the one hand, the formalistic deontologism of Kant and his followers, and, on the other, the axiological or teleological ethics of the Hegelian self-realizationists and the *Wertethik* of Scheler and N. Hartmann.

Ethical theories are also described as metaphysical, naturalistic, and non-naturalistic or intuitionistic. See *Intuitionism, Non-naturalistic ethics, Metaphysical ethics, Naturalistic ethics, Autonomy of ethics.*

Histories of Ethics: H. Sidgwick, *Outlines of the History of Ethics,* Rev. Ed. 1931. Gives titles of the classical works in ethics in passing. C. D. Broad, *Five Types of Ethical Theory,* 1930.

Elementary Texts: J. Dewey and J. H. Tufts, *Ethics,* Rev. Ed. 1932. W. M. Urban, *Fundamentals of Ethics,* 1930.

Treatises: H. Sidgwick, *Methods of Ethics,* 7th Ed. 1907. G. E. Moore, *Principia Ethica,* 1903. W. D. Ross, *Foundations of Ethics,* 1939. N. Hartmann, *Ethics,* 3 vol., trans. 1932. M. Schlick, *Problems of Ethics,* trans. 1939. R. B. Perry, *General Theory of Value,* 1926. —*W.K.F.*

Ethics, Absolute: A phrase which is sometimes used to designate an ethics which is put forth as absolute, see *Absolutism,* and sometimes, as by H. Spencer, to designate the formulation of the ideal code of conduct of an ideal man in the ideal society. See *Relative Ethics.* —*W.K.F.*

Ethics, Relative: A term due to H. Spencer and used to designate any attempt to apply the ideal code of conduct formulated by Absolute Ethics to actual men in actual societies. See *Absolute Ethics.* —*W.K.F.*

Ethos: (Gr. *ethos*) Character; moral purpose; distinguished by Aristotle from thought or intelligence as a source of dramatic action; hence that element in a dramatic composition which portrays character as distinct from the portrayal of thought or suffering. —*G.R.M.*

Etiology: (1) The science or philosophical discipline which studies causality; (2) The science of the causes of some particular phenomenon, *e.g.* in medicine the science of the causes of disease. —*A.C.B.*

Eucken, Rudolf: (1846-1926) Being a writer of wide popularity, winner of the Nobel Prize for literature in 1908, Eucken defends a spiritualistic-idealistic metaphysics against materialistic naturalism, positivism and mechanism. Spiritual life, not being an oppositionless experience, is a struggle, a self-asserting action by resistance, a matter of great alternatives, either-ors between the natural and the spiritual, a matter of vital choice. Thus all significant oppositions are, within spiritual life itself, at once created and overcome. Immanence and transcendence, personalism and absolutism are the two native spiritual oppositions that agitate Eucken's system. Reconciliation between the vital dualities therefore depends not on mere intellectual insight, but on personal effort, courageous, heroic, militant and devoted action. He handles the basic oppo-

sitions of experience in harmony with the activist tenor of liberal Protestantism. Eucken sought to replace the prevailing intellectualistic idealism by an activistic idealism, founded on a comprehensive and historical consideration of culture at large. He sought to interpret the spiritual content of historical movements. He conceived of historical facts as being so many systematized wholes of life, for which he coined the term *syntagma.* His distinctive historical method consists of the reductive and the noological aspects. The former considers the parts directly in relation to an inward whole. The latter is an inner dialectic and immanent criticism of the inward principles of great minds, embracing the cosmological and psychological ways of philosophical construction and transcending by the concept of spiritual life the opposition of the world and the individual soul. Preaching the need of a cultural renewal, not a few of his popularized ideas found their more articulated form in the philosophical sociology of his most eminent pupil, Max Scheler; in the cultural psychology of both Spranger and Spengler. His philosophy is essentially a call to arms against the deadening influences of modern life. —*H.H.*

Euclid: (c. 400 B.C.) Of Megara, founder of the Megarian School. He was chiefly interested in the theory of refutation. See *Megarians.*

Euclid of Megara identified the good and the One. The many are unreal. Not to be confused with the great geometer who lived at Alexandria (c. 300 B.C.), author of the *Elements* in 13 books. —*M.F.*

Eudaemonia: (Gr. *eudaimonia*) Happiness, or well-being, acclaimed by Aristotle as the universally recognized chief good, and described by him as consisting in the active exercise (*energeia*) of the soul's powers in accordance with reason. See *Aristotelianism.* —*G.R.M.*

Eudaemonism: (Gr. *eu,* well + *daimon,* spirit) Theory that the aim of right action is personal well-being or happiness, often contrasted with hedonism's aim at pleasure. —*A.J.B.*

Euhemerism: The view that explains religious myths as traditional and partially distorted accounts of historical events and personages; from Euhemerus, Cyrenaic philosopher (c. 300 B.C.), who advanced the theory that the gods of mythology were deified heroes. —*G.R.M.*

Euler diagram: The elementary operations upon and relations between classes—complementation, logical sum, logical product, class equality, class inclusion—may sometimes advantageously be represented by means of the corresponding operations upon and relations between regions in a plane. (Indeed, if regions are considered as classes of points, the operations and relations for regions become particular cases of those for classes.) By using regions of simple character, such as interiors of circles or ellipses, to stand for given classes, convenient diagrammatic representations are obtained of the possible logical relationships between two or more classes. These are known as *Euler diagrams,* although their employment by Euler in his *Letters to a German Princess* (vol. 2, 1772) was not their first appearance. Or the diagram may be so drawn as to show all possible intersections (2^n intersections in the case of n classes), and then intersections known to be empty may be crossed out, and intersections known not to be empty marked with an asterisk or otherwise (*Venn diagram*).—*A.C.*

Eusebius of Caesarea: (265-340) Is one of the first great historians of the Christian Church. He was born at Caesarea, in Palestine, studied at the school of Pamphilus, became Bishop of Caesarea in 313. His works are in Greek and include a *Chronicle, Ecclesiastical History,* and a treatise *On Theophanies* (PG 19-24). His philosophical views are those of a Christian Platonist and he contributed to the development of the allegorical method of Scriptural exegesis.—*V.J.B.*

Evaluation: Quantitative comparison of values. The appraisal of value; the estimation of worth. See *Value.*—*J.K.F.*

E-values: Every descriptive value is as far as it is a statement of another individual. E-values divide into elements and characters. They are basic values independent of the System C whose function they are. (Avenarius.)—*H.H.*

Event: (Lat. *evenire*, to happen, come out) Anything which happens, usually something which exhibits change and does not endure over a long time; hence opposed to *object* (*q.v.*) or thing.—*A.C.B.*

Event-particle: A. N. Whitehead's term meaning a material event with all its dimensions ideally restricted.—*R.B.W.*

Evidence: (Lat. *e+videre*, to see) Any supposed fact which is considered as supporting the truth of a given proposition.—*A.C.B.*

Evidence: (Ger. *Evidenz*) In Husserl: 1. Usual (strict) sense: consciousness of an intended object as itself (more or less fully) given; experience in the broadest sense. Contrasted with empty intending. *Perfect evidence* is a regulative idea: In any particular evidence the object is also emptily intended as the object of further, confirmative, evidence. Evidence is either *original* ("perceptual" in the broadest sense) or directly *reproductive* ("memorial" in the broadest sense); again, it is either *impressional* or *retentional evidence*. *Empirical evidence*, in general, is the category of evidence of real individual objects; within this category, sensuous perceiving is *original evidence* of sensible real individuals and their sensible real individual determinations. For every other category of objects there is a corresponding category of *evidence* in general and *original evidence* in particular. 2. In a broader sense, "evidence" may be either immediate (evidence in the first sense) or mediate. E.g., an intended fact is *mediately evident* if (and only if) there is immediate evidence of its entailment as the consequence of an immediately evident fact. 3. In a still broader sense, evidence of an intended object may be *indirect*, i.e., by way of direct evidence (evidence in the first or second sense) of evidence of the intended object in some other consciousness, perhaps the consciousness belonging to another ego. The concept of *original evidence* is accordingly relativized and broadened to include all kinds of consciousness in which the intended object is given in the most original manner possible for an object of its kind and status. Thus, *e.g.*, clear direct remembering is original evidence of one's own retained past, qua past, and perceptive empathy is original evidence of another's consciousness. Evidence of every kind (and in each of the above-defined senses) has its parallel in phantasy (fictive consciousness). Fictive empirical evidence involves non-fictive *evidence of the essential possibility* of an individual having the fictively presented determinations. The evident incompatibility of fictively experienced determinations is *evidence of the essential impossibility* of any individual having such determinations. *Apodictic evidence* is evidence together with the further evidence that no conflicting evidence is essentially possible. Essential possibilities, impossibilities, and necessities, admit of apodictic evidence. The only actual individual object that can be an object of apodictic evidence is one's own subjectivity. Evidence is not to be confounded with certainty of positing (see *Modality*) nor conceived as restricted to apodictic evidence. Furthermore, it is evident that no evidence is a talisman against error. What is evident in one process may evidently conflict with what is evident in another; or, again, the *range of evidence* may be overestimated. Evidence is exemplified in valuing and willing as well as in believing. It is the source of all objective sense (see *Apperception* and *Genesis*) and the basis of all rationality (see *Reason*).—*D.C.*

Evident: (Ger. *evident*) In Husserl: Both evidence and the object of evidence are called "evident."—*D.C.*

Evil: (AS. *yfel*) Negation of the extrinsic elections of things. In practice, the positive effects of such negation. The morally bad. Hostility to the welfare of anything. Absence of the good. Opposite of goodness. See *Ethics.*—*J.K.F.*

Evolution: The development of organization. The working out of a definite end; action by final causation. For Comte, the successive stages of historical development are necessary. In biology, the series of phylogenetic changes in the structure or behavior of organisms, best exemplified by Charles Darwin's *Origin of Species*. In cosmology, cosmogony is the theory of the generation of the existing universe in space and time. Opposite of: epigenesis. See *Emergent evolution, Evolutionism.* Cf. T. Osborn, *From the Greeks to Darwin.*—*J.K.F.*

Evolution, creative: The conserved pluri-dimensional life force causing all the numerous varieties of living forms, dividing itself more and more as it advances. (Bergson.)—*H.H.*

Evolutionary ethics: Any ethical theory in which the doctrine of evolution plays a leading role, as explaining the origin of the moral sense, and, more especially, as contributing importantly to the determination of the moral standard, *e.g.* the ethics of Charles Darwin, H. Spencer, L. Stephen. Typical moral standards set up by evolutionists are adaptation, conduciveness to life, social health. Cf. H. Spencer, *The Data of Ethics.*—*W.K.F.*

Evolutionism: This is the view that the universe and life in all of their manifestations and nature in all of its aspects are the product of development. Apart from the religious ideas of initial creation by fiat, this doctrine finds variety of species to be the result of change and modification and growth and adaptation rather than from some form of special creation of each of the myriads of organic types and even of much in the inorganic realm. Contrary to the popular notion, evolution is not a product of modern thought. There has been an evolution of evolutionary hypotheses from earliest Indian and Greek speculation down to the latest pronouncement of scientific theory. Thales believed all life to have had a marine origin and Anaximander, Anaximenes, Empedocles, the Atomists and Aristotle all spoke in terms of development and served to lay a foundation for a true theory of evolution. It is in the work of Charles Darwin, however, that clarity and proof is presented for the explanation of his notion of natural selection and for the crystallization of evolution as a prime factor in man's explanation of all phases of his mundane existence. The chief criticism leveled at the evolutionists, aside from the attacks of the religionists, is based upon their tendency to forget that not all evolution means progress. See *Charles Darwin, Herbert Spencer, Thomas Henry Huxley, Natural Selection, Evolutionary Ethics.* Cf. A. Lalande, *L'Idée de dissolution opposée á celle de l'évolution* (1899); revised ed. (1930): *Les Illusions évolutionistes.—L.E.D.*

Exact: Opposite of *vague* (*q.v.*).—*A.C.*

Excluded middle, law of: or *tertium non datur*, is given, by traditional logicians as "*A* is *B* or *A* is not *B*." This is usually identified with the theorem of the propositional calculus, $p \vee \sim p$, to which the same name is given. The general validity of the law is denied by the school of mathematical *intuitionism* (*q.v.*).—*A.C.*

Exclusive particularity, fallacy of: The unwarranted belief that a particular term belongs only to one system of terms; that it can function in only one relationship.—*H.H.*

Exemplarism: (Lat. *exemplum*, a pattern or copy) The theological doctrine that finite things are copies of originals existing in the divine mind.—*L.W.*

Exemplary cause: (Lat. *exemplum*, pattern or example) A form of causality resembling that exercised by the Ideas in Platonism, the *rationes aeternae* in Augustinianism and Thomism. The rôle of an archetypal, or "pattern" cause is much discussed in Scholastic metaphysics because of the teaching that the universe was created in accord with a Divine Plan consisting of the eternal ideas in the Mind of God.—*V.J.B.*

Exemplification: (Ger. *Exemplifizierung*) In Husserl: The relation of an entity to any eidos or any universal type under which it falls as an instance or as containing a part which is an instance of the eidos or the type. Exemplification is distinguished from (*a*) the relation of species to genus, (*b*) the relation of a more detailed syntactical form to a less detailed, and (*c*) the relation of real embodiment to embodied ideal individual.—*D.C.*

Exercite: (in Scholasticism) The exercise (*exercitium*) of, for example, understanding, walking, or doing something, indicates the act itself of understanding, of walking, or of doing something. Opposed to *signate* (signately) (*q.v.*).—*H.G.*

Existence: (Lat. *existere*: to emerge) The mode of being which consists in interaction with other things. For Aristotle, matter clothed with form. Essences subjected to accidents; the state of things beyond their causes. The state of being actual, the condition of objectivity. In epistemology: that which is experienced. In psychology: the presence of a given datum in the physical universe at some date and place. Sometimes identified with truth or reality. Opposite of essence. See *Actuality.—J.K.F.*

Existence: (Ger. *Dasein, Existenz*) In Husserl's writings the terms *Dasein* and *Existenz* are not given different senses nor restricted to the sphere of personal being, except with explicit reference to other writers who use them so. In Husserl's usage, "existence" means being (*q.v.*) of any kind or, more restrictedly, individual being.—*D.C.*

Existential import: See *Logic, formal* § 4.

Existential Philosophy: Determines the worth of knowledge not in relation to truth but according to its biological value contained in the pure data of consciousness when unaffected by emotions, volitions, and social prejudices. Both the source and the elements of knowledge are sensations as they "exist" in our consciousness. There is no difference between the external and internal world, as there is no natural phenomenon which could not be examined psychologically; it all has its "existence" in states of the mind. See *Kierkegaard, Heidegger, Jaspers, Sartre.*

Existential Philosophy arose from disappointment with Kant's "thing-in-itself" and Hegel's metaphysicism whose failure was traced back to a fundamental misrepresentation in psychology. It is strictly nonmetaphysical, anti-hypothetical, and contends to give only a simple description of existent psychological realities. "Existence" is therefore not identical with the metaphysical correlative of "essence." Consciousness is influenced by our nervous system, nutrition, and environment; these account for our experiences. Such terms as being, equal, similar, perceived, represented, have no logical or truth-value; they are merely biological "characters;" a distinction between physical and psychological is unwarranted. Here lies the greatest weakness of the Existential Philosophy, which, however, did not hinder its spreading in both continents.

Resuming certain ideas of Locke and Berkeley, it was first propounded by the physicist Kirchhoff, and found its best representation by Richard Avenarius (1843-96) in *Menschlicher Weltbegriff,* and, independently, by Ernst Mach (1838-1916) in *Anal. d. Empfindungen.* Many psychologists (Wm. Wundt, O. Kuelpe, Harold Hoeffding, E. B. Titchener) approved of it, while H. Rickert and W. Moog discredited it forcefully. Charles Peirce (Popular Science Monthly, Jan. 1878) and Wm. James (Principles of Psych. 1898) applied Avenarius' ideas, somewhat roughly though, for the foundation of "Pragmatism." John Dewey (*Reconstruction in*

Philos.) used it in his "Instrumentalism," while F. C. S. Schiller (Humanism) based his ethical theory on it.—*S.V.F.*

Existential proposition: Traditionally, a proposition which directly asserts the existence of its subject, as, *e.g.*, Descartes's "ergo sum" or the Christian's "Good exists." Expressed in symbolic notation, such a proposition has a form like (*Ex*)M.

By an extension of this, a proposition expressible in the functional calculus of first order may be called *existential* if the prenex normal form has a prefix containing an existential quantifier (see *Logic, formal*, § 3).

Brentano (*Psychologie*, 1874) takes an existential proposition (Existentialsatz) to be one that directly affirms *or denies* existence, and shows that each of the four traditional kinds of categorical propositions is reducible (i.e., equivalent) to an existential proposition in this sense; thus, *e.g.*, "all men are mortal" becomes "immortal men do not exist." This definition of an existential proposition and the reduction of categorical propositions to existential appears also in Keynes's *Formal Logic*, 4th edn. (1906).—*A.C.*

Existential Psychology: A school of introspective psychology represented in America by E. B. Titchener (1867-1927) which conceived the task of psychology to be the description, analysis and classification of the experiences of an individual mind considered as *existences*. Also called Existentialism. A characteristic doctrine of the school is the denial of imageless thought.—*L.W.*

Existential quantifier: See *Quantifier*.

Exoteric: External; belonging to or suited for those who are not initiates or experts. The *exoterikoi logoi* referred to in Aristotle are popular arguments or treatises, as contrasted with strictly scientific expositions. —*G.R.M.*

Expectation: 1. In general, the act or state of looking forward to an event about to happen. The grounds on which something is believed to happen. A supposition, an anticipation, a reasonable hope, a probable occurrence.

2. A *mathematical expectation* is the value of any chance which depends upon some contingent event. Thus, if a person is to receive an amount of money upon the occurrence of an event which has an equal chance of happening or failing, the expectation is worth half that amount. The mathematical *expectation of life* is the average duration of life (of an individual or a group) after a given age, as determined by computation from the mortality tables.

3. The term *actuarial expectation* is used analogically by Lloyd Morgan to denote the qualitative probability of the emergence of a genuine or primary novelty.—*T.G.*

Experience: (Lat. *Experientia*, from experiri: to test) The condition or state of subjectivity or awareness. (The term differs from Consciousness by emphasizing the temporal or passing character of affective undergoing. Usage, however, is not uniform, since its definition involves a theoretical standpoint. Thus Bradley identified it with Consciousness, while W. James used it to mean neutral phenomenon, a That or Given, without implications of either subjectivity or objectivity.) —*W.L.*

Experience, pure: The elimination of all presuppositions of thought. See *Avenarius, Experientialism*. —*H.H.*

Experientialism: The resort to concrete experience, whether perceptual, intuitive, activistic, axiological, or mystical, as the source of truth. The opposite of Intellectualism. Experientialism is a broader term than Empiricism.—*W.L.*

Experiment: (Lat. *experiri*, to try) Any situation which is deliberately set up by an investigator with a view to verifying a theory or hypothesis.—*A.C.B.*

Experimental Psychology: (1) Experimental psychology in the widest sense is the application to psychology of the experimental methods evolved by the natural sciences. In this sense virtually the whole of contemporary psychology is experimental. The experimental method consists essentially in the prearrangement and control of conditions in such a way as to isolate specific variables. In psychology, the complexity of subject matter is such that direct isolation of variables is impossible and various indirect methods are resorted to. Thus an experiment will be repeated on the same subjects with all conditions remaining constant except the one variable whose influence is being tested and which is varied systematically by the experimenter. This procedure yields *control data* within a single group of subjects. If repetition of the experiment with the same group introduces additional uncontrolled variables, an equated *control group* is employed. Systematic rotation of variables among several groups of subjects may also be resorted to. In general, however, psychologists have designed their experiments in accordance with what has frequently been called the "principle of the one variable."

A distinction is frequently drawn between two observational methods in psychology: (a) *introspection* which appeals to private data, accessible to a single observer (see *Introspection*), and (b) *objective observation* of public data, accessible to a number of observers among whom there is substantial agreement (see *Behaviorism*). These two methods, though they are often regarded as disparate, may perhaps be more properly regarded as the extremes of a continuum of observational objectivity, many varying degrees of which can be found in psychological experimentation.

(2) The term experimental psychology is also used in a more restricted sense to designate a special branch of psychology consisting of laboratory studies conducted on normal, human adults as distinguished from such branches as child, abnormal, differential, animal or comparative, social, educational and applied psychology. This restricted sense is employed in the titles of text-books and manuals of "experimental psychology." Included in this field are such topics as sensory phenomena, perception, judgment, memory, learning, reaction-time, motor phenomena, emotional responses,

motivation, thinking and reasoning. This identification of experimental psychology with a specific type of content is largely a result of historical accident; the first experimental psychologists were preoccupied with these particular topics.

The historical antecedents of experimental psychology are various. From British empiricism and the psychological philosophy of Locke, Berkeley and Hume came associationism (see *Associationism*), the psychological implications of which were more fully developed by Herbart and Bain. Associationism provided the conceptual framework and largely colored the procedures of early experimental psychology. Physics and physiology gave impetus to experiments on sensory phenomena while physiology and neurology fostered studies of the nervous system and reflex action. The names of Helmholtz, Johannes Müller, E. H. Weber and Fechner are closely linked with this phase of the development of experimental psychology. The English biologist Galton developed the statistical methods of Quetelet for the analysis of data on human variation and opened the way for the mental testing movement; the Russian physiologist Pavlov, with his researches on "conditioned reflexes," contributed an experimental technique which has proved of paramount importance for the psychologist. Even astronomy made its contribution; variations in reaction-time of different observers having long been recognized by astronomers as an important source of error in their observations.

The first laboratory of experimental psychology was founded at Leipzig in 1879 by Wundt, who has been called "the first professional psychologist." With such research as that of Stumpf on sound; G. E. Müller on psycho-physics, color and learning; Ebbinghaus on memory; and Külpe and the Würzburg school on the "higher thought processes," experimental psychology made rapid strides within the next two decades. In America, the chief standard bearer of Wundtian psychology was Titchener. Among the others who were instrumental in the introduction and development of experimental psychology in America, may be mentioned James, Hall, Münsterberg, Cattell, and Watson.

Johannes Müller, *Elements of Physiology*, 1834-40. E. H. Weber, *De Tractu*, 1851. G. T. Fechner, *Elemente der Psychophysik*, 1860. W. Wundt, *Principles of Physiological Psychology*, 1873-4. G.T. Fechner, *In Sachen der Psychophysik*, 1877. G. E. Müller, *Zur Grundlegung der Psychophysik*, 1878, G.E. Müller, *Die Gesichtspunkte und die Tatsachen der Psychophysichen Methodik*, 1904. E. B. Titchener, *Experimental Psychology*, 1905. Fröbes, *Lehrbuch· der Experimentellen Psychologie*, 3rd, ed., 1923. E. G. Boring, *History of Experimental Psychology*, 1929.—*L.W.*

Explanation: In general: (1) the process, art, means or method of making a fact or a statement intelligible, (2) the result and the expression of what is made intelligible; (3) the meaning attributed to anything by one who makes it intelligible; (4) a genetic description, causal development, systematic clarification, rational exposition, scientific interpretation, intelligible connection, ordered manifestation of the elements of a fact or a statement.

A. More technically, the method of showing discursively that a phenomenon or a group of phenomena obeys a law, by means of causal relations or descriptive connections; or briefly, the methodical analysis of a phenomenon for the purpose of stating its cause. The process of explanation suggests the real preformation or potential presence of the consequent in the antecedent; so that the phenomenon considered may be evolved, developed, unrolled out of its conditioning antecedents. The process and the value of a scientific explanation involve the question of the relation between cause and law, as these two terms may be identified (Berkeley) or distinguished (Comte). Hence modern theories range between extreme idealism and logical positivism. Both these extremes seem to be unsatisfactory: the former would include too much into science, while the latter would embrace a part of it only, namely the knowledge of the scientific laws. Taking into account Hume's criticism of causality and Mill's reasons for accepting causality, Russell proposes what seems to be a middle course, namely (a) that regular sequences suggest causal relations, (b) that causal relations are one special class of scientific generalization, that is one-way sequences in time, and (c) that causal relations as such should not be used in the advanced stages of scientific generalization, functional relations being sufficient in all cases. However satisfactory in methodology, this view may not cover all the implications of the problem.

B. There are three specific types of causal explanation, and their results may be combined: (1) *genetic* or in terms of the direct and immediate conditions or causes producing a phenomenon (formal and efficient cause); (2) *descriptive*, or in terms of the material elements of the phenomenon (material cause); (3) *teleological*, or in terms of the ultimate end to be attained (final cause), either in accordance with the nature of the event or with the intention of the agent. The real causes of a phenomenon cannot be identified always, because the natural process of change or becoming escapes complete rationalization. But the attempt to rationalize the real by causal explanation, need not be abandoned in favor of a limited genetic description (postulational or functional) of the laws which may account for the particular phenomenon.

C. More formally, explanation is a step towards generalization or the establishment of a theory. It is the process of linking a statement of fact to its logical implications and consequences; or the process of fitting a statement of fact into a coherent system of statements extending beyond the given fact; or the construction of a logically related body of statements including the statement of fact to be justified. In the most general terms, explanation is the search for generalizations whose variables are functionally related in such a way that the value of any one variable is calculable from the value of the others, whether or not causal relations are noticeable or ultimately involved in the elements of the generalization.—*T.G.*

Explication: (Ger. *Auslegung*) In Husserl: Synthesis of identification between a confused, non-articulated (internally indistinct, unseparated) sense and a subsequently intended distinct, articulated, sense. The latter is the *explicate (Explikat)* of the former. See *Explanation.—D.C.*

Explicative judgment: (Lat. *explicatio*, unfolding) A mental action which explains a subject by mentally dissecting it; (Kant) a judgment in which the predicate is obtained by analysis of the subject. See *Analytic judgment.—V.J.B.*

Exponible: Employed as a noun and as an adjective, applied to an obscure proposition which needs an exposition or explanation owing to a hidden composition. Kant applied it to propositions including an affirmation and a concealed negation, which an exposition makes apparent.—*J.J.R.*

Exportation is the form of valid inference of the propositional calculus from AB ⊃ C to A ⊃ [B ⊃ C]. The *law of exportation* is the theorem of the propositional calculus:

$$[pq \supset r] \supset [p \supset [q \supset r]].—A.C.$$

Expression: (Ger. *Ausdruck*) In Husserl: A symbol that embodies and signifies the noematic-objective sense of an act of thinking. The sense is *expressed;* the act, *manifested.—D.C.*

Expressionism: In aesthetics, the doctrine that artistic creation is primarily an expressive act, a process of clarifying and manifesting the impressions, emotions, intuitions, and attitudes of the artist. Such theories hold that art has its foundation in the experiences and feelings of its creator; it is a comment on the artist's soul, not on any external object, and its value depends on the freshness and individuality of this creative spirit. The artist is he who feels strongly and clearly; his art is a record of what he has felt. It is maintained that the artist has no responsibility to respect reality nor to please an audience, and the primary synonyms of beauty become sincerity, passion, and originality.—*I.J.*

Expressive Meaning: See *Meaning, Kinds of*, 4.

Extension: (Lat. *ex* + *tendere*, to stretch) Physical space, considered as a single concrete continuum as contrasted with the abstract conceptual space of mathematics. The distinction between extension and "space" in the abstract sense is clearly drawn by Descartes (1596-1650) in *The Principles of Philosophy*, part II, Princ. IV-XV.—*L.W.*

One of the two attributes *(q.v.)* of God which, according to Spinoza, are accessible to the human intellect *(Ethica*, II, *passim)*. While the attribution of thought *(cogitatio, q.v)* to God was a medieval commonplace, the attribution of extension to God was, in the tradition, highly heretical. Spinoza, however, was at great pains to show *(Ibid*, I, 14-18) that unless such attribution was made, all theories of God's causality were rendered either nonsensical or explicitly contradictory.—*W.S.W.*

Extension: See *Intension and Extension.*

Extensionality, axiom of: See *Logic, formal*, § 9.

Extensity: A rudimentary spatiality alleged to characterize all sensation. See J. Ward, article "Psychology" in *Encyclopaedia Britannica*, 9th, Ed. pp. 46, 53. —*L.W.*

Extensive quantity: Any quantity such that there exists some physical process of addition by which a greater quantity of the kind in question may be produced from a lesser one; opposed to intensive quantity *(q.v.)*. —*A.C.B.*

Exteriority: (Lat. *exterior* comp. of *exter*, without) The character of externality ascribed to physical objects by common sense and by realistic epistemology.—*L.W.*

External: (Fr. *externe*, outer) Outside a thing. Independent of opinion. Capable of pressure or resistance. Used by Peirce (1839-1914) in contradistinction to mental.—*J.K.F.*

External Reference: The tendency of the mind to objectify sensory data and construe them as referring to a real external world. See *Intentionality.—L.W.*

External relations, Doctrine of: Neo-realistic view that relations are not grounded in the nature of their terms, that relations are independent of the terms, that terms can pass in and out of relations without being modified.—*H.H.*

External sense: In Kant, intuition of spatial properties, as contrasted with the internal sense which is that of the *a priori* form of time.

External World: The ideally envisaged totality of objects of actual or possible perception conceived as constituting a unified system.—*L.W.*

Externalization: (Lat. *externus*, external from *exter*, without) The mental act by which sensory data originally considered to be internal are projected into the external world. See *Introjection*. The problem of externalization was formulated by Condillac in these words: "If one admits that sensations are only modifications of the mind, how does it come about that the mind apprehends them as objects independent of and external to it?" *Traité de sensations*, Part III.—*L.W.*

Exteroceptor: See *Receptor.*

Extramental: (Lat. *extra* + *mens*, mind) Possessing a status external to and independent of the knowing mind. Extramental status is attributed to physical objects by physical realists and to universals by Platonic realists.—*L.W.*

Extraspective situations: "Situations in which we seem to be in direct cognitive contact with other minds and their states." (Broad.)—*H.H.*

Extrinsic: (Lat. *exter*, out + *secus*, beside) Having external value. Value in the relation of wholes to other wholes.—*J.K.F.*

Extrojection: (Lat. *extra* + *jacere*, to throw) The tendency of the mind to externalize sensuous qualities and even affective states. See *External Reference.—L.W.*

Ezra, Abraham Ibn: Jewish exegete and philosopher (1093-1167). Born in Spain he wandered in many lands, sojourned for a time in Italy and Provence. His philosophy is expressed largely in his commentaries but also in several short treatises, such as the *Yesod Mora*, i.e., Foundation of the Knowledge of God, and the *Shaar ha-Shamayyim*, i.e., The Gate to Heaven. Main problems he deals with are that of the right conception of the universe and its becoming and that of knowledge.

He was influenced by teachings of neo-Platonism and Gabirol.—*M.W.*

F

Fa chia: The Legalists School, the Philosophers of Law, also called hsing ming chia, who "had absolute faithfulness in reward and punishment as support for the system of correct conduct," and made no distinction between kindred and strangers and no discrimination between the honorable and the humble, but treated them as equals before the law. They emphasized the power natural to the position of a ruler (shih, especially Kuan Tzŭ, sixth century B.C. and Shên Tao, 350-275 B.C.?), statecraft (shu, especially Shên Pu-hai, 400-337 B.C.?) and law (fa, especially Shang Chün, 390-338 B.C.?), with Han Fei Tzŭ (280-233 B.C.) synthesizing all the three tendencies.—*W.T.C.*

Fact: In Husserl: 1. State of affairs (*Sachverhalt*): an object having categorial-syntactical structure. 2. matter of fact (*Tatsache, Faktum*): (*a*) that which simply is, as contrasted with that which is necessarily; (*b*) that which is actual, as contrasted with that which is merely possible; (*c*) that which is, regardless of its value; (*d*) that which is non-fictive.—*D.C.*

Fact: (Lat. *factus,* pp. of *facio,* do) Actual individual occurrence. An indubitable truth of actuality: A brute event. Syn. with actual event.—*J.K.F.*

Factual: See *Meaning, Kins of,* 2.

Faculty: (Scholastic) Medieval psychology distinguishes several faculties of the soul which are said to be really distinct from each other and from the substance of the soul. According to Aquinas the distinction is based on objects and operations. The faculties are conceived as accidents of the soul's substance, but as pertaining essentially to its nature, therefore "proper accidents." The soul operates by means of the faculties. Much misunderstood and deteriorated, this theory remained alive until recent times and is still maintained, in its original and pure form, by Neo-Scholasticism. A certain *rapprochement* to the older notion may be observed in the modern theory of "general factors." Most of the criticisms directed against the faculty-psychology are based on modern experimental and nominalistic approaches. The faculties listed by Aquinas are: 1. The sensory faculties, which to operate need a bodily organ; (a) The external senses, (b) The internal senses, *sensus communis,* memory, imagination, *vis aestimativa* (in animals) or *cogitativa* (in man), (c) The sensory appetites, subdivided in the concupiscible appetite aiming at the attainable good or fleeing the avoidable evil, the irascible appetite related to good and evil whose attainment or avoidance encounters obstacles. 2. The vegetative faculties, comprising the achievements of nutrition, growth and procreation. While the sensory appetites are common to man and animals, the vegetative are observed also in plants. 3. The locomotive faculty, characteristic of animals and, therefore, also of man. 4. The rational faculties, found with man alone; (a) Intellect, whose proper object is the universal nature of things and whose achievements are abstraction, reasoning, judging, syllogistic thought; (b) Rational Will, directed towards the good as such and relying in its operation on particulars of the cooperation of the appetites, just as intellect needs for the formation of its abstract notions the phantasm, derived from sense impressions and presented to the intellect by imagination. The *vis cogitativa* forms a link between rational universal will and particular strivings; it is therefore also called *ratio particularis.*

Ch. A. Hart, *The Thomistic Theory of Mental Faculties,* Washington, D. C., 1930.—*R.A.*

Faculty Psychology: (Lat. *facultas,* faculty or ability) The conception of mind as the unity in a number of special faculties, like sensibility, intelligence, volition, by reference to which individual processes of sensation, thought or will are explained. Faculty psychology, which originated in Plato's division of the soul into the appetitive, the spirited and the rational faculties, was the dominant psychology of the Middle Ages and received its most influential modern statement by C. Wolff (1679-1754) in his *Rational Psychology,* 1734. Faculty psychology is usually associated with the Soul Substance Theory of Mind. See *Soul Substance.* The common criticism of the theory is its circularity in attempting to explain individual mental processes in terms of a faculty which is merely the hypostatization

122

of those processes. See. J. Locke, *Essay Concerning Human Understanding,* 1690. Bk. II, Ch. xxi, § 17.—*L.W.*

Faith: (Kant. Ger. *Glaube*) The acceptance of ideals which are theoretically indemonstrable, yet necessarily entailed by the indubitable reality of freedom. For Kant, the Summum Bonum, God, and immortality are the chief articles of faith or "practical" belief. See *Kantianism*. Cf. G. Santayana, *Skepticism and Animal Faith*, where faith is the non-rational belief in objects encountered in action.—*O.F.K.*

In religious use, faith refers to trust, especially trust in God, particularly in God's reliability, rather than simply to belief in various doctrines.—*S.E.N.*

Fallacy is any unsound step or process of reasoning, especially one which has a deceptive appearance of soundness or is falsely accepted as sound. The unsoundness may consist either in a mistake of formal logic, or in the suppression of a premiss whose unacceptability might have been recognized if it had been stated, or in a lack of genuine adaptation of the reasoning to its purpose. Of the traditional names which purport to describe particular kinds of fallacies, not all have a sufficiently definite or generally accepted meaning to justify notice. See, however, the following: *affirmation of the consequent; amphiboly; denial of the antecedent; equivocation; ignoratio elenchi; illicit process of the major; illicit process of the minor; many questions; non causa pro causa; non sequitur; petitio principii; post hoc ergo propter hoc; quaternio terminorum; secundum quid; undistributed middle; vicious circle.*—*A.C.*

Fan or fu: The greatest of all the laws underlying phenomenal change, that if any one thing moves to an extreme direction, a change must bring about an opposite result, called "reversion" or "return." Reminds one of Hegel's antithesis. (Lao Tzŭ.)—*H.H.*

Fang hsin: The lost heart, i.e., the originally good mind which has turned away from the principles of benevolence and righteousness. (Mencius.)—*W.T.C.*

Fang shih: "Scholars with formulae," or priests and magicians who flourished in the Ch'in and Han dynasties (249 B.C.—220 A.D.) and who offered divination, magic, herbs, charms, alchemy, breath technique, and other crafts (fang shu) and superstitions in terms of Yin Yang and Taoist philosophies, as means to immortality, inward power, restored youth, and superhuman ability.—*W.T.C.*

Fang shu: Divination and magic. See *Fang shih*. —*W.T.C.*

Fantastic: (Art) Product of an arbitrary imagination without any claim to reality.—*L.V.*

Fatalism: (Lat. *fatalis,* fatal) Determinism, especially in its theological form which asserts that all human activities are predetermined by God. See *Determinism*.—*L.W.*

Fechner, Gustav Theodor: (1801-1887) Philosophizing during the ascendency of modern science and the wane of metaphysical speculation, Fechner though a physicist believing in induction, analogy, history and pragmatic procedure, expounded a pure, objective idealism of Berkeley's type. With Oken and Schelling as spiritual guides, he held that everything is in consciousness; there are no substances, no things-in-themselves; everything, including animals, plants, earth, and heavens, shares the life of the soul *(alles ist beseelt)*. In a consequent psycho-physicalism he interpreted soul (which is no substance, but the simplifying power in contrast to the diversifying physical) as appearance to oneself, and matter as appearance to others, both representing the same reality differentiated only in point of view. He applied the law of threshold to consciousness, explaining thus its relative discontinuity on one level while postulating its continuity on another, either higher or lower level. In God, as the highest rung of existence, there is infinite consciousness without an objective world. Evil arises inexplicably from darker levels of consciousness. With poetic imagination Fechner defended the "day-view" of the world in which phenomena are the real content of consciousness, against the "night-view" of science which professes knowledge of the not-sensation-conditioned colorless, soundless world.

Main works: *Nanna o.d. Seelenleben d. Pflanzen,* 1848; *Ueber die physikalische u. philos. Atomenlehre,* 1855; *Elemente der Psychophysik,* 1860; *Drei Motiven des Glaubens,* 1863; *Vorschule der Aesthetik,* 1876. See K. Lasswitz, *G. Th. Fechner,* 1876.—*K.F.L.*

Feeling: (Ger. *Gefühl*) In Husserl: 1. Noetic processes of valuing (e.g., liking, disliking, preferring). 2. Non-intentional, "hyletic," processes or states, immanent in the stream of consciousness. See *Hyle* and *Noesis*.—*D.C.*

Feeling: (Kant. Ger. *Gefühl*) A conscious, subjective impression which does not involve cognition or representation of an object. Feelings are of two kinds: pleasures and pains. These represent nothing actual in objects, but reveal the state or condition of the subject. Kant saw in pleasure and pain, respectively, life-promoting and life-destroying forces; pleasure results from the harmony of an object with the subjective conditions of life and consciousness, while pain is the awareness of disharmony. See *Kantianism*.—*O.F.K.*

Felicific: Making happy; conducive to happiness or pleasure.—*G.R.M.*

Feuerbach, Ludwig Andreas: (1804-1872) Was one of the earliest thinkers manifesting the trend toward the German materialism of the 19th century. Like so many other thinkers of that period, he started with the acceptance of Hegel's objective idealism, but soon he attempted to resolve the opposition of spiritualism and materialism. His main contributions lay in the field of the philosophy of religion interpreted by him as "the dream of the human spirit," essentially an earthly dream. He publicly acknowledged his utter disbelief in immortality, which act did not fail to provoke the ire of the authorities and terminated his academic career.

L. A. Feuerbach, *Das Wesen des Christentums,* 1840; *Philosophie u. Christentum,* 1859. See *Engels*.—*R.B.W.*

Fichte, Johann Gottlieb: (1762-1814) Skillful in framing the general conception of a few great ideas, Fichte's thought centered in a passionate espousal of Kant's practical reason or of autonomous good will as the creative source of all that is distinctive in personality. He sought to discern the method of the psychogenetic process of the acceptance of the moral law as supreme. He assumed that consciousness, including the representations of physical objects that make up the outer world, is the product of one ultimate cause in the universe. The world in which each individual lives is his own world, brought into being through the creative agency of the ultimate.

Thinking was to Fichte a wholly practical affair, a form of action. Since experience is given in the form of consciousness, the origin and nature of consciousness is the key to all problems. The ego is the point at which the creative activity of the Absolute emerges in the individual consciousness. The world means nothing of itself. It has no independent self-existence. It exists for the sole purpose of affording man the occasion for realizing the ends of his existence. It is merely the material for his duty. Fichte sought to bring out the structural principles of the knowing act.

His popular works, influential in the German uprising against Napoleon, have been interpreted as being a source of Pan-Germanism.

J. G. Fichte, *Versuch einer Kritik aller Offenbarung*, 1792; *Grundlage der gesamten Wissenschaftslehre*, 1794; *Grundlage des Naturrechts*, 1798; *System der Sittenlehre; Die Bestimmung des Menschen*, 1800; *Der Geschlossene Handelsstaat*, 1800; *Grundzüge d. Gegenwärtigen Zeitalters*, 1804-5; *Die Anweisung zum seligen Leben*, 1806.—*H.H.*

Ficino, Marsilio: Of Florence (1433-99). Was the main representative of Platonism in Renaissance Italy. His doctrine combines NeoPlatonic metaphysics and Augustinian theology with many new, original ideas. His major work, the *Theologia Platonica* (1482) presents a hierarchical system of the universe (God, Angelic Mind, Soul, Quality, Body) and a great number of arguments for the immortality of the soul. Man is considered as the center of the universe, and human life is interpreted as an internal ascent of the soul towards God. Through the Florentine Academy Ficino's Platonism exercised a large influence upon his contemporaries. His theory of "Platonic love" had vast repercussions in Italian, French and English literature throughout the sixteenth century. His excellent Latin translations of Plato (1484), Plotinus (1492), and other Greek philosophers provided the occidental world with new materials of the greatest importance and were widely used up to the beginning of the nineteenth century.—*P.O.K.*

Fiction: Whenever a symbol, as part of an utterance, occurs in such a context that the truth of any utterance of the same form would normally guarantee the existence of an individual denoted by that symbol, whereas in the case considered no such implication holds, the symbol may be said to *occur fictitiously in that context*. Thus in the utterance "The average man is six feet tall" the phrase "the average man" occurs fictitiously. For "X is less than six feet tall" normally implies that there is an individual denoted by "X." But there is no individual denoted by "the average man."

If "S" occurs fictitiously it is customary to say that S is a fictitious entity or a fiction. (The language is unfortunate as falsely suggesting that in such case there is a special kind of entity denoted by S and having the property of being fictitious.)

It is to be noted that a symbol "S" occurs fictitiously only if the complex token "C(S)," containing "S," does not fully display the logical form of the utterance. In such cases the fictitious character of the occurrence of S is revealed by translation of the utterance (e.g. by translating remarks about the average man in such a way as to remove any apparent reference to a specific person).

The definition is suggested by that of Jeremy Bentham. Reference: C. K. Ogden, *Bentham's Theory of Fictions*, 12. See also *Incomplete Symbol, Construction*.—*M.B.*

(Lat. *fictio*, from *fingere*, to devise, or form) A logical or imaginative construction framed by the mind to which nothing corresponds in reality. See *Construction, Imaginative*.—*L.W.*

Fictionism: An extreme form of pragmatism or instrumentalism according to which the basic concepts and principles of natural science, mathematics, philosophy, ethics, religion and jurisprudence are pure fictions which, though lacking objective truth, are useful instruments of action. The theory is advanced under the influence of Kant, by the German philosopher H. Vaihinger in his *Philosophie des Als Ob*, 1911; Philosophy of the "As If." English translation by C. K. Ogden. See *Fiction, Construction*.—*L.W.*

Fideism: A doctrine of Abbé Bautain which attempted to justify the teachings of Christianity by the theory that all knowledge rested upon premises accepted by faith. The premises of religion are to be found in the tradition of the Synagogue and Church. This tradition needs no rational criticism because it is self-critical. The doctrine was condemned in 1840 by Gregory XVI.—*G.B.*

Fides: Faith, according to St. Augustine, means to believe that which one does not see: *Fides ergo est, quod non vides credere*. That is the reason why faith is praiseworthy. *Haec est enim laus fidei, si quod creditur non videtur*.—*J.J.R.*

Figure (syllogistic): The moods of the categorical syllogism (see *Logic, formal*, § 5) are divided into four figures, according as the middle term is subject in the major premiss and predicate in the minor premiss (first figure), or predicate in both premisses (second figure), or subject in both premisses (third figure), or predicate in the major premiss and subject in the minor premiss (fourth figure). Aristotle recognized only three figures, including the moods of the fourth figure among those of the first. The separation of the fourth figure from the first (ascribed to Galen) is accompanied by a redefinition of "major" and "minor"—so that the major premiss is that involving the predicate of the conclusion, and the minor premiss is that involving the subject of the conclusion.—*A.C.*

Filioque: See *Trinitarianism.*

Final Causes, the doctrine of: The view that things and events in the world can be explained, and ultimately can best be explained, by reference to some end or purpose or good or final cause to which they are conducive. Held, *e.g.*, by Aristotle and Leibniz.—*W.K.F.*

Finalism: The theory that purpose is present in all the events of the physical order. Teleology.—*R.T.F.*

Fine Arts: Opposite of mechanical arts. Distinction of the arts whose principle is based on beauty (poetry, painting, sculpture, architecture, music).—*L.V.*

Finite: For the notion of finiteness as applied to classes and cardinal numbers, see the article *cardinal number.* An ordered class (see *order*) which is finite is called a *finite sequence* or *finite series.* In mathematical analysis, any fixed real number (or complex number) is called *finite,* in distinction from "infinity" (the latter term usually occurs, however, only as an incomplete symbol, in connection with *limits, q.v.*). Or *finite* may be used to mean *bounded,* i.e., having fixed real numbers as lower bound and upper bound. Various physical and geometrical quantities, measured by real numbers, are called finite if their measure is finite in one of these senses.—*A.C.*

First Heaven: The outermost sphere in the Aristotelian cosmology, the sphere of the fixed stars.—*G.R.M.*

First Mover: See *Prime Mover.*

First Philosophy: (Gr. *prote philosophia*) The name given by Aristotle (1) to the study of the principles, first causes and essential attributes of being as such; and (2) more particularly to the study of transcendent immutable being; theology.—*G.R.M.*

Fischer, Kuno: (1824-1907) Is one of the series of eminent German historians of philosophy, inspired by the impetus which Hegel gave to the study of history. He personally joined in the revival of Kantianism in opposition to rationalistic, speculative metaphysics and the progress of materialism.

K. Fischer, *Gesch. der neueren Philosophie,* 10 vols. 1854-1877.—*H.H.*

Fiske, John: (1842-1901) Harvard librarian and philosopher. He is best known as an historian of the colonial period. He was a voluminous writer in many fields. His *Outlines of Cosmic Philosophy* is his best known work as a pioneer in America of the evolutionary theories. He claimed an original contribution to these speculations in his studies of the period of infancy. His works on God and on immortality were widely read in his day although he later expressed doubts about them. Nevertheless his constant emphasis on the theistic as opposed to the positivistic implications of evolution served to influence the current theories of creative and emergent evolution. See *Evolutionism.*—*L.E.D.*

Florentine Academy: It was a loose and informal circle of scholars and educated persons which gathered in Florence around the Platonic philosopher Marsilio Ficino. Its activities consisted in regular lectures on Platonic philosophy as well as informal discussions and parties. "Platonic" love or friendship was considered as the spiritual link between the members of the group which was organized and named after the model of Plato's Academy. The main documents describing it are Ficino's correspondence and a number of dialogues like Ficino's commentary on Plato's *Symposium, Landino's Disputationes Camaldulenses,* and Benedetto Colucci's *Declamationes.* Outstanding members or associates of the Academy were Cosimo, Piero, and Lorenzo de'Medici, Angelo Poliziano, and Giovanni Pico della Mirandola. The Academy which was first founded in 1462, dissolved after the revolution in Florence (1494) and after Ficino's death (1499), but the tradition of Platonic philosophy was continued in other private circles as well as at the universities of Florence and Pisa throughout the sixteenth century.—*P.O.K.*

Flux: The characteristic of time, by virtue of which all things change inevitably. In Heraclitus' view, who brought the problem into prominence, "all things flow; nothing abides."—*R.B.W.*

Foerster, Friedrich Wilhelm: (1869-1966) A German ethicist and pedagogical authority. He was born in Berlin and taught at the Universities of Vienna and Munich. In 1927 he went to Paris and Zurich. He is most noted for his forthright criticism of the moral tenets of German National Socialism. His principal works are: *Jugendlehre* (1904), *Schule und Charakter,* 14th ed. (1930), *Politische Ethik und Pädagogik,* 4th ed. (1920).—*V.J.B.*

Folk-Art: A fragmentary art in which the artistic elements are not bound together by an artistic personality.—*L.V.*

Folkways: (AS *folc*) Customs. Conventions. Mores. Traditional group behavior patterns. Cf. Sumner, *Falkways.*—*A.J.B.*

Foreknowledge: Knowledge of the future of which two types may be distinguished: (a) anticipation or prescience which professes to be immediate and non-inferential and (b) expectation, which is inferential prediction of the future on the basis of the remembered or recorded past. See *Anticipation, Prescience, Expectation.*—*L.W.*

Foreordination: The doctrine that events of one's life, even one's eternal destiny, are determined beforehand by Deity. See *Predestination.*—*V.F.*

Foreshortening: Application of perspective to plastic bodies, occupying space in depth.—*L.V.*

Form: (Gr. *eidos*) The intelligible structure, characters constituting a substance or species of substances, as distinguished from the matter in which these characters are embodied; essence; formal cause. See *Aristotelianism.*—*G.R.M.*

In Art: a. Opposite of content. The conclusive aspect of art, the surpassing of emotions, taste, matter; the final imprint of the personality of the artist. b. Opposite of color. The plastic form achieved by drawing and chiaroscuro.—*L.V.*

Form: (in Kant) That *a priori* element in experience in virtue of which the manifold of sense is synthesized and unified into meaningful perceptions and judgments.

Kant attributed the form of experience to mind and reason, the matter to sensuous intuition. See *Kantianism.—O.F.K.*

In Scholasticism. *Accidental*: That which comes to a subject already substantially complete, *e.g.* roundness or whiteness.

Substantial form: Substance distinct from matter, ordered in itself in such a way that with prime matter it constitutes a natural body; for—since matter is indifferent to any composite, it is determined by the form united to itself, so that it may be, *e.g.*, a stone, or a dog, or wood. There are as many substantial forms as there are different bodies.

Metaphysical: Is the substantial essence of the whole thing—as rational animal is said to be the metaphysical form of man.—*H.G.*

Form, logical: See *Logic, formal.*

Forma: Latin noun meaning shape, figure, appearance, image; also plan, pattern, stamp, mold. As a philosophic term used by Cicero and Augustine in the sense of *species,* and similarly by Scotus Eriugena. Boethius and the medieval writers employed it in the Aristotelian sense of a constituent of being, synonymous with *causa formalis.* Generally speaking it is an intrinsic, determining, perfective principle of existence of any determinate essence. More strictly it is a *forma substantialis,* or that constitutive element of a substance which is the principle or source of its activity, and which determines it to a definite species, or class, and differentiates it from any other substance. It is distinguished from a *forma accidentalis* which confers a sort of secondary being on a substance already constituted in its proper species and determines it to one or other accidental mode, thus a man may become a musician. A *forma corpereitatis* is one by which a being is a body, on which its corporeal nature and essence depend and which is its principle of life. A *forma non-subsistense* or *materialis* is one whose existence depends on matter without which it cannot exist and be active. It is distinguished from a *forma subsistens* or *immaterialis* which can exist and act separately from matter. An immaterial form may be an incomplete substance, like the human soul, which is created to be united with a body to complete its own species, or a complete substance, a pure spirit, which is not destined to be united with matter to which it cannot communicate its being, hence it is also called a *forma separata.—J.J.R.*

Formal: 1. In the traditional use: valid independently of the specific subject matter; having a merely logical meaning (see *Meaning, Kinds of,* 3). 2. Narrower sense, in modern logic: independent of, without reference to meaning (compare *Semiotic,* 3).—*R.C.*

Formal Cause: See *Form; Aristotelianism.*

Formalism: (a) In ethics: the term is sometimes used as equivalent to intuitionism in the traditional sense. See *Intuitionism.* Also used to designate any ethical theory, such as Kant's, in which the basic principles for determining our duties are purely formal. See *Ethics, formal.—W.K.F.*

(b) In art: A form for form's sake, lacking in content.—*L.V.*

Formalism (mathematical) is a name which has been given to any one of various accounts of the foundations of mathematics which emphasize the formal aspects of mathematics as against content or meaning, or which, in whole or in part, deny content to mathematical formulas. The name is often applied, in particular, to the doctrines of Hilbert (see *Mathematics*), although Hilbert himself calls his method axiomatic, and gives to his syntactical or metamathematical investigations the name Beweistheorie (*proof theory, q.v.*).—*A.C.*

Formalization: (Ger. *Formalisierung*) In Husserl: 1. (objective) Ideational "abstraction" from the determination of an object as belonging in some material region. The residuum is a pure eidetic *form.* 2. (noematic) Substitution, in a noematic-objective sense, *e.g.*, the sense signified by a sentence, of the moment "what you please" for every materially determinate core of sense, while retaining all the moments of categorial form. Noematic formalization reduces a determinate objective sense to a materially indeterminate categorial sense-form. See *Algebraization, Generalization,* and *Ideation.—D.C.*

Formally: (in Scholasticism) Is sometimes taken for mentally, i.e. according to the formalities which we distinguish by the mind alone. When *formally* is so understood, it has as its correlative *really.* Thus the omnipotence and the wisdom of God are not *really* but *formally* distinct.

It is also said of the thing considered in itself or in its proper entity. It then has various correlatives as the aspects of the thing compared vary:

(1) If compared with an effect, its correlative will be *efficiently*: *e.g.* food is the life of man not *formally* but *efficiently.*

(2) If compared with an object, its correlative will be *objectively*: *e.g.* God is said to be the hope of a just man not *formally but objectively,* i.e. God is not the hope of man, but the object of that hope.

(3) If compared with an exemplar, a likeness in accordance with which a thing is made, the correlative will be *exemplarily*: *e.g.* the image of Caesar existing in the painter's imagination concurs with the picture of Caesar's image not *formally* but *exemplarily.*

(4) If compared with an end, the correlative is *finally*: *e.g.* eternal happiness is said to move man to act rightly not *formally* but *finally,* as an end to be attained.

(5) If compared with another thing connected with it, whose existence is inferred from or simply accompanies it, its correlative will be *illatively connectively*: *e.g.* in smoke we recognize fire not *formally* but *illatively.*

(6) If compared with a thing whose existence is imputed to it, its correlative will be *imputatively.*

(7) If compared with a thing of which it is the root, the correlative will be *radically*: *e.g.* we say that almost all evils consist in a disordered self-love not *formally* but *radically.*

(8) If compared with those qualities which constitute a disposition for having that thing, the correlative will be *dispositively.* Thus the dryness of wood will result in

fire not *formally* but *dispositively*.

(9) If compared with a thing from which it receives some denomination (or designation) its correlative will be *denominatively*: *e.g.* when some part of the body is formally ill, man himself or the whole man is said to be *denominatively* ill.

Meaning the same as *truly* and *properly*—then it has as correlatives: *apparently*, *metaphorically*.

Meaning the same as *essentially*, so that the predicate which is said to belong to the subject *formally*, enters into the essence and definition of the subject. Thus man is *formally* animal. *Formally*, so understood has various correlatives, according to the various aspects under which the essence of a thing can be considered:

(1) An essence can be compared with accidental predicates and then its correlative is *accidentally*: *e.g.* a man is said to be not *formally*, but *accidentally* white.

(2) An essence can be compared with the attributes or parts of a thing which like the matter of a subject may indifferently constitute that thing or another, and then the correlative is *materially*: *e.g.* man is said to be *materially* flesh.

When said of an effect: An effect is taken *formally* when it is looked at according to itself; but it is taken *radically* or *fundamentally* when it is looked at according to its cause, root, or foundation. Thus visibility taken *formally* is a property of man, and is distinguished by the mind from rationality; but taken *radically,* it is the same as rationality, inasmuch as rationality is the root of visibility.

When referring to causes containing the perfection of their effect. *Formally, virtually,* and *eminently* are said of causes according as they contain the perfection of their effect. For an effect is said to be contained *formally* in its cause, when the nature of the effect which is produced, is found in the cause itself; thus heat is contained *formally* in fire, because fire also contains in itself the heat which it produces. An effect is contained *virtually* in its cause when the cause can indeed produce such an effect, but the nature of the effect is not found in the cause itself, *e.g.* the statue is contained *virtually* in the artist. Lastly, an effect is contained *eminently* in its cause, when the cause is much more perfect than the effect and is without the imperfections which are found in the effect. *E.g.* God *eminently* contains the perfections of creatures.—*H.G.*

Founded: (Ger. *fundiert*) In Husserl: 1. The character of one noetic-noematic stratum as presupposing the presence of another, the *founding* stratum. 2. The character of an act or an act-correlate as containing founded and founding strata. E.g., intending something as a tool is *founded* in intending "the same" as a material thing; correlatively, the tool-sense is *founded* in the mere-thing-sense.—*D.C.*

Four Elements: The four primary kinds of body recognized by the Greek philosophers, viz. fire, air, water, and earth.—*G.R.M.*

Frank, Philipp: (1884-1966) A member of the "Vienna Circle," who has made his home in the U.S. He has been avowedly influenced by Mach. His major work lies on the borderline between philosophy and physics and he makes an effort "to employ only concepts which will not lose their usefulness outside of physics."

Ph. Frank, *Between Physics and Philosophy* (Harvard, 1941).—*R.B.W.*

Freedom: (Kant. Ger. *Freiheit*) The autonomy or self-determination of rational beings. Kant considers the reality of freedom an indubitable, albeit an inexplicable, fact, and places it at the fulcrum of his entire system, theoretical as well as practical. See *Kantianism.*—*O.F.K.*

Freedom, Sense of: The subjective feeling of an agent either at the moment of decision or in retrospect that his decision is free and that he might, if he had chosen, have decided differently. This feeling is adduced by Free-Willists as empirical evidence for their position but is interpreted by their opponents as a subjective illusion. See *Free-Will.*—*L.W.*

Free-will: The free-will doctrine, opposed to determinism, ascribes to the human will freedom in one or more of the following senses:

(a) The freedom of indeterminacy is the will's alleged independence of antecedent conditions, psychological and physiological. A free-will in this sense is at least partially uncaused or is not related in a uniform way with the agent's character, motives and circumstances.

(b) *The freedom of alternative* choice which consists in the supposed ability of the agent to choose among alternative possibilities of action and

(c) The freedom of self-determination consisting in decision independent of external constraint but in accordance with the inner motives and ideals of the agent. See *Determinism, Indeterminism.*—*L.W.*

Frege, (Friedrich Ludwig) Gottlob, 1848-1925, German mathematician and logician. Professor of mathematics at the University of Jena, 1879-1918. Largely unknown to, or misunderstood by, his contemporaries, he is now regarded by many as "beyond question the greatest logician of the Nineteenth Century" (quotation from Tarski). He must be regarded—after *Boole* (*q.v.*)—as the second founder of symbolic logic, the essential steps in the passage from the algebra of logic to the logistic method (see the article *Logistic system*) having been taken in his *Begriffsschrift* of 1879. In this work there appear for the first time the *propositional calculus* in substantially its modern form, the notion of *propositional function*, the use of *quantifiers*, the explicit statement of primitive *rules of inference*, the notion of an *hereditary property* and the logical analysis of proof by mathematical induction or *recursion* (*q.v.*). This last is perhaps the most important element in the definition of an inductive *cardinal number* (*q.v.*) and provided the basis for Frege's derivation of arithmetic from logic in his *Grundlagen der Arithmetik* (1884) and *Grundgesetze der Arithmetik,* *vol. 1* (1893), and vol. 2 (1903). The first volume of *Grundgesetze der Arithmetik* is the culmination of Frege's work, and we find here many important further ideas. In particular, there is a careful distinction between *using* a formula to express something else and *naming* a formula in order to make a syntactical statement about it, quotation marks being used in order to distinguish the name of a formula from the formula itself. In an appendix to the second volume of *Grundgesetze*, Frege acknowledges the presence of an inconsistency in his system through what is now known as the Russell paradox (see *Paradoxes, logical*), as had been called to his attention by Russell when the book was nearly through the press.—*A.C.*

P. E. B. Jourdain, *Gottlob Frege*, The Quarterly Journal of Pure and Applied Mathematics, vol. 43 (1912), pp. 237-269. H. Scholz, *Was ist ein Kalkül und was hat Frege für eine pünktliche Beantwortung dieser Frage geleistet?*, Semester-Berichte (Münster i. W.), summer 1935, pp. 16-47.Scholz and Bachmann, *Der wissenschaftliche Nachlass von Gottlob Frege*, Actes du Congrès International de Philosophie Scientifique (Paris, 1936), section VIII, pp. 24-30.

Freud, Sigmund: (1856-1939) Founder of the Psycho-analytic school (see *Psycho-Analysis*), studied medicine at the University of Vienna, and becoming interested in the treatment of neuroses, went to Paris in 1885 to study under Charcot and later examined the methods employed by the Nancy school. In his own practice, he employed hypnotic methods of treatment (see *Hypnosis, Hypnotism*) in combination with his own techniques of free association and dream interpretation. (*The Interpretation of Dreams*, German ed., 1900; *Psychopathology of Everyday Life*, German ed. 1901.) Freud not only developed a therapeutic technique for the treatment of hysteria and neuroses but advanced an elaborate psychological theory of which the main tenets are the predominance of sex and the doctrine of the subconscious.

Freud's writings in addition to those already cited include: *Wit and its Relation to the Unconscious*, 1905; *General Introduction to Psycho-Analysis*, Eng. Trans., 1920-1.—*L.W.*

Fries, Jakob Friedrich: (1773-1843) Eminent German philosopher. The contribution of Fries lies in the continuation of Kant's work as offered in *New or Anthropological Criticism of Reason* and by his system of philosophy as exact science.

J. F. Fries, *Rechtslehre*, 1804; *Wissen, glauben, u. Ahnung*, 1805; *Neue Kritik der reinen Vernunft*, 1807; *System der Logik*, 1811; *Psychische Anthropologie*, 1821.—*J.K.*

Fringe, Psychical: See *Consciousness, Field of*.

Frui: St. Augustine distinguished *frui*, to enjoy, from *uti*, to use. We use the things of this world; we are to enjoy God, of whom St. Augustine writes: *Ista temporalia dedit ad utendum, se ad fruendum.*—*J.J.R.*

Fu: Correspondence, especially that between man and the Universe in the macrocosm-microcosm relationship. (Tung Chung-shu, 177-104 B.C.)—*W.T.C.*

Fulfilment: (Ger. *Erfüllung*) In Husserl: Synthesis of identification, based on conscious processes, in the earlier of which the intended object is intended emptily or is given less evidently than it is in the later. The more evident conscious process is said to fulfil (or to fill) and clarify the noematic-objective sense of the less evident.

Positive fulfilment: Fulfilment in which the objective senses of the fulfilled and fulfilling processes harmonize.

Negative fulfilment: Fulfilment in which the objective senses of the fulfilled and fulfilling processes conflict. Fulfilment cannot be completely negative, since that would preclude synthesis of identification.—*D.C.*

Fulguration: Is a lightning flash of the mind. To Leibniz, the monads are God's perpetual fulguration, *Monadology* 47.—*J.M.*

Function: In mathematics and logic, an *n-adic function* is a law of correspondence between an ordered set of *n* things (called *arguments* of the function, or *values of the independent variables*) and another thing (the value of the function, or *value of the dependent variable*), of such a sort that, given any ordered set of *n* arguments which belongs to a certain domain (the *range* of the function), the value of the function is uniquely determined. The value of the function is spoken of as obtained by *applying* the function to the arguments. The domain of all possible values of the function is called the *range of the dependent variable*. If F denotes a function and $X_1, X_2, \ldots, X_n$ denote the first argument, second argument, etc., respectively, the notation $F(X_1, X_2, \ldots, X_n)$ is used to denote the corresponding value of the function; or the notation may be $[F](X_1, X_2 \ldots, X_n)$, to provide against ambiguities which might otherwise arise if F were a long expression rather than a single letter.

In particular, a *monadic function* is a law of correspondence between an *argument* (or *value of the independent variable*) and a *value* of the function (or *value of the dependent variable*), of such a sort that, given any argument belonging to a certain domain (the *range* of the function, or *range of the independent variable*), the value of the function is uniquely determined. If F denotes a monadic function and X denotes an argument, the notation $F(X)$ is used for the corresponding value of the function.

Instead of a *monadic* function, *dyadic* function, etc., one may also speak of a function *of one variable*, a function *of two variables*, etc. The terms *singularly* or *unary* (= monadic), *binary* (= dyadic), etc., are also in use. The phrase, "function from *A* to *B*," is used in the case of a monadic function to indicate that *A* and *B* (or some portion of *B*) are the ranges of the independent and dependent variables respectively—in the case of a polyadic function to indicate that *B* (or some portion of *B*) is the range of the dependent variable while the range of the function consists of ordered sets of *n* things out of *A*.

It is sometimes necessary to distinguish between functions in intension and functions in extension, the distinction being that two *n*-adic functions in extension are considered identical if they have the same range and the same value for every possible ordered set of *n* arguments, whereas some more severe criterion of identity is imposed in the case of functions in intension. In most mathematical contexts the term *function* (also the roughly synonymous terms *operation, transformation*) is used in the sense of function in extension.

(In the case of *propositional functions*, the distinction between intension and extension is usually made somewhat differently, two propositional functions in extension being identical if they have materially equivalent values for every set of arguments.)

Sometimes it is convenient to drop the condition that the value of a function is unique and to require rather that an ordered set of arguments shall determine a set of values of the function. In this case one speaks of a *many-valued function*.

Often the word *function* is found used loosely for what would more correctly be called an ambiguous or undetermined value of a function, an expression containing one or more free variables being said, for example, to denote a function. Sometimes also the word *function* is used in a syntactical sense—*e.g.*, to mean an expression containing free variables.

See the article *Propositional function*.—*Alonzo Church*

Functional calculus: See *Logic, formal*, §§ 3, 6.

Functional Psychology: (Lat. *functio* from *fungor*, I execute) A tendency in American psychology represented by W. James, G. T. Ladd, G. S. Hall, J. Dewey, and J. R. Angell which considered the mental processes of sense perception, emotion, volition and thought as functions of the biological organism in its adaptation to and control of its environment. Functionalism arose as a protest against structural psychology for which the task of psychology is the analysis and description of consciousness. The functional theory of mind is characteristic of the pragmatism and instrumentalism of C. S. Peirce, W. James, G. H. Mead and J. Dewey. See C. H. Morris, *Six Theories of Mind*, Ch. VI.—*L.W.*

Functional Theory of Mind: See *Functional Psychology*.

Functionalism: See *Functional Psychology*.

Functor: In the terminology of Carnap, a *functor* is a sign for a (non-propositional) *function* (*q.v.*). The word is thus synonymous with *(non-propositional) function symbol*.—*A.C.*

Fundamentum divisionis: (Lat.) Principle according to which a genus is subdivided into species.—*A.C.B.*

Fung Yu-lan: (1895-   ) Prominent contemporary Chinese philosopher, educated at Peking (A.B. 1918) and Columbia (Ph.D. 1923). Author of *History of Chinese Philosophy* (1931). *A Short History of Chinese Philosophy* (1948, not a condensation of the first work, but an entirely new production), "I Discovered Marxism-Leninism" in *People's China* (1950), and "Problems in the Study of Confucius" in *People's China* (1957).—*S.E.N.*

Fusion, Psychic: See *Psychic Fusion*.

Future: That part of time which includes all the events which will happen; these events may be conceived as determined in advance, though unknown, or as an indefinite potentiality, not fixed in advance, but subject to chance, free choice, statistical determination, or Divine interference. In Aristotle, assertions about the future are always contingent or non-apodeictic.—*R.B.W.*

G

Gabirol, Solomon Ibn: Known to scholastics as Avicebron (*q.v.*), but not identified as such until the discovery by the French scholar, Munk. See *Jewish Philosophy.*—*M.W.*

Galen, Claudius: Famous physician; died about the year 200 A.D.; an Eclectic philosopher who combined the Peripatetic and Stoic teachings.

Galen was the chief authority in medicine practically until the time of Vesalius (c. 1543). He is responsible for the fourth figure in the syllogism. His voluminous works remain untranslated.—*M.F.*

Galenian Figure: See *Figure, syllogistic.*

Garbha: (Skr. seed) The creative power that lies at the bottom of the world, hypostatized in or symbolized by the germ or seed. In cosmologico-metaphysical conception it is allied to such *termini technici* as *hiranyagarbha* (golden germ), *bīja* (seed), *retas* (semen), *yoni* (womb), *anda* (egg, world-egg), *jan* (to give birth to), *srj* (to pour out), etc. descriptive of psycho-cosmogony from the earliest days of Indian philosophy (*q.v.*). —*K.F.L.*

Gassendi, Pierre: (1592-1655) Was a leading opponent of Cartesianism and of Scholastic Aristotelianism in the field of the physical sciences. Though he was a Catholic priest, with orthodox views in theology, he revived the materialistic atomism of Epicurus and Lucretius. Born in Provence, and at one time Canon of Dijon, he became a distinguished professor of mathematics at the Royal College of Paris in 1645. He seems to have been sincerely convinced that the Logic, Physics and Ethics of Epicureanism were superior to any other type of classical or modern philosophy. His objections to Descartes' *Meditationes,* with the Cartesian responses, are printed with the works of Descartes. His other philosophical works are: *Commentarius de vita, moribus et placitis Epicuri* (Amsterdam, 1659), *Syntagma philosophiae Epicuri* (Amsterdam, 1684).—*V.J.B.*

Gautama Buddha: (Skr. *Gautama,* a patronymic, meaning of the tribe of *Gotama; Buddha,* the enlightened one) The founder of Buddhism, born about 563 B.C. into a royal house at Kapilāvastu. As Prince Sid-dhārtha (Siddhattha) he had all worldly goods and pleasures at his disposal, married, had a son, but was so stirred by sights of disease, old age, and death glimpsed on stolen drives through the city that he renounced all when but 29 years of age, became a mendicant, sought instruction in reaching an existence free from these evils and tortures, fruitlessly however, till at the end of seven years of search while sitting under the Bodhi-tree, he became the Buddha, the Awakened One, and attained the true insight. Much that is legendary and reminds one of the Christian mythos surrounds Buddha's life as retold in an extensive literature which also knows of his former and future existences. Māra, the Evil One, tempted Buddha to enter *nirvāna,* (*q.v.*) directly, withholding thus knowledge of the path of salvation from the world; but the Buddha was firm and taught the rightful path without venturing too far into metaphysics, setting all the while an example of a pure and holy life devoted to the alleviation of suffering. At the age of 80, having been offered and thus compelled to partake of pork, he fell ill and in dying attained *nirvāna.*—*K.F.L.*

Gay, John: (1669-1745) English scholar and clergyman, not to be confused with his contemporary, the poet and dramatist of the same name. He is important in the field of ethics for his *Dissertation Concerning the Fundamental Principle of Virtue or Morality.* This little work influenced David Hartley in his formulation of Associationism in Psychology and likewise served to suggest the foundation for the later English Utilitarian School.—*L.E.D.*

Gegenstandstheorie: (Ger. the theory of objects). It is the phenomenological investigation of various types of objects, existential and subsistential—an object being defined in the widest sense as the *terminus ad quem* of any act of perceiving, thinking, willing or feeling. The theory was developed by H. Meinong under the influence of F. Brentano and is allied with the phenomenology of E. Husserl. See *Phenomenology.*—*L.W.*

Geist: (Ger. Kant) That quality in a beautiful object which animates the mind (Gemüt) and gives life to the work of art. It is best translated "soul" or "spirit." See

Kantianism, Hegel.—O.F.K.

Gemara: (Heb. completion) Is the larger and latter part of the Talmud (*q.v.*) discussing the Mishnah, and incorporating also vast materials not closely related to the Mishnah topics. The 1812 authorities of the gemara are known as *Amoraim* (speakers). Its contents bear on Halaeha (law) and Aggadah (tale), i.e., non-legal material like legends, history, science, ethics, philosophy, biography, etc. There are two gemaras better known as Talmuds: the Jerusalem (i.e. Palestinian) Talmud and the Babylonian Talmud.—*H.L.G.*

General Will: Term used by Jean Jacques Rousseau in *The Social Contract* (1761) to refer to the ideal of a collective will or consensus among the governed, which Rousseau viewed as the locus point of all political authority. This differs from the position taken by Hobbes (*q.v.*), who saw human nature as so corrupt that ultimate authority must reside in an absolute monarch so as to guarantee the benefits of a collective or social existence without which human beings cannot flourish. Also differs from Locke (*q.v.*), who held ultimate sovereignty to reside in Natural Law (*q.v.*).—*T.P.S.*

Generalization: (Lat. *genus*, class, kind) 1. Process of arriving at a general notion or concept from individual instances. 2. Any general notion or concept. 3. A proposition stating an order or relation of events which holds without exception; universal proposition.—*A.C.B.*

Generalization, rule of: See *Logic, formal*, § 3.

Generative Theory of Data: (Lat. *generatus*, pp. of *generare*, to beget) Theory of sense perception asserting that sense data or sensa are generated by the percipient organism or by the mind and thus exist only under the conditions of actual perception. The Theory which is common to subjective idealism and representational realism is opposed to the Selective Theory of Data. See *Representationism, Selective theory of Data.*—*L.W.*

Generic Image: (Lat. *genus*, kind) A mental image which is sufficiently vague and indeterminate to represent a number of different members of a class and thus to provide the imaginal basis of a concept. A generic image is thus intermediate between a concrete image and a generic concept. The vagueness of the generic image contrasts with the specificity of the concrete image, yet the generic image lacks the fullness of meaning requisite to a genuine concept. The doctrine of the generic image was introduced by Francis Galton who drew the analogy with composite photography (*Inquiries into Human Faculty*, 1883 appendix on Generic Images) and is adopted by Huxley (*Hume*, Ch. IV). The existence of non-specific or generic images would be challenged by most contemporary psychologists.—*L.W.*

Genesis: (Gr. *genesis*) Coming into being, particularly the coming into being of a substance through the taking on of form by matter (Aristotle). The biblical account of creation (*Book of Genesis*).—*G.R.M.*

Genetic: (Gr. *genesis*, origin) Having to do with the origin and the development of anything.—*V.F.*

Genetic Fallacy: The misapplication of the genetic method resulting in the depreciatory appraisal of the product of an historical or evolutionary process because of its lowly origin.—*L.W.*

Genetic Method: Explanation of things in terms of their origin or genesis.—*L.W.*

Genius: Originally the word applied to a demon such as Socrates' inner voice. During the 17th century it was linked to the Platonic theory of inspiration and was applied to the rejection of too rigid rules in art. It defined the real artist and distinguished his creative imagination from the logical reasoning of the scientist. In Kant (*Critique of Judgment*), genius creates its own rules.—*L.V.*

Genres: Types of art to which special rules and independent developments were attributed. For example: in poetry—epic, lyric, dramatic; in painting—historic, portrait, landscape; in music—oratorial, symphonic, operatic.—*L.V.*

Gentile, Giovanni: (1875-1944) Born in Castelvetrano (Sicily) Professor of Philosophy and History of Philosophy at universities in Palermo, Pisa, and Rome. Minister of Public Education 1922-1924. Senator 1922-1944. Reformed the school system of Italy.

A pupil of late followers of Hegel, he emphasized the unity of spirit which he recognized in the *pure act*. His philosophy is therefore called *actualism*. He is responsible for the philosophic theory of Fascism with the conception of the Ethic State to which the individual must be totally sacrified.

G. Gentile, *La filosofia di Marx*, 1899; *Il concetto della storia della fiosofia*, 1908; *L'atto del pensare como atto pure*, 1912; *Sistema di logica come teoria del conoscere*, 1917; *Discorsi di Religione*, 1920; *La filosofía dell'Arte*, 1931; *Introd. alla filosofía*, 1933.—*L.V.*

Genus: (Gr. *genos*) In Aristotle's logic: (1) that part of the essence of anything which belongs also to other things differing from it in species; (2) a class of objects possessing an identical character and consisting of two or more subclasses or species. See *Species.*—*G.R.M.*

Genus, summum: (Lat.) In a classificatory scheme the largest and most inclusive genus which is not itself a species to any larger genus.—*A.C.B.*

Geometry: Originally abstracted from the measurement of, and the study of relations of position among material objects, geometry received in Euclid's *Elements* (c. 300 B.C.) a treatment which (despite, of course, certain defects by modern standards) became the historical model for the abstract deductive development of a mathematical discipline. The general nature of the subject of geometry may be illustrated by reference to the *synthetic* geometry of Euclid, and the *analytic* geometry which resulted from the introduction of coordinates into Euclidean geometry by *Descartes* (1637) (*q.v.*). In the mathematical usage of today the name *geometry* is given to any abstract mathematical discipline of a certain general type, as thus illustrated, without any requirement of applicability to spatial relations among physical objects or the like.

See *Mathematics*, and *Non-Euclidean geometry*. For a very brief outline of the foundations of plane Euclidean geometry, both from the synthetic and the analytic viewpoint, see the Appendix to Eisenhart's book cited below. A more complete account is given by Forder.—*A.C.*

L. P. Eisenhart, *Coordinate Geometry*, 1939. H. G. Forder, *The Foundations of Euclidean Geometry*, Cambridge, England, 1927. T. L. Heath, *The Thirteen Books of Euclid's Elements*, *translated from the text of Heiberg, with introduction and commentary*, 3 vols., Cambridge, England, 1908.

Gerbert of Aurillac: (Pope Sylvester II, died 1003) Was one of the greatest scholars of the 10th century. He studied at Aurillac with Odo of Cluny, learned something of Arabian science during three years spent in Spain. He taught at the school of Rheims, became Abbot of Bobbio (982), Archbishop of Rheims (991), Archbishop of Ravenna (998), Pope in 999. A master of the seven liberal arts, he excelled in his knowledge of the quadrivium, i.e. logic, math., astron. and music. His works, the most important of which are on mathematics, are printed in PL 139, 57-338.—*V.J.B.*

Gerson, Levi ben: (Gersonides) Bible commentator, astronomer, and philosopher (1288-1340). He invented an instrument for astronomical observation which is described in his *Sefer ha-Tekunah* (Hebr.) Book on Astronomy. His philosophy embodied in the *Milhamot Elohim* i.e., The Wars of God, is distinguished by its thoroughgoing Aristotelianism and by its general free spirit. His theory of the soul teaches that the passive or material intellect is only a potentiality for developing pure thought which is accomplished through the influence of the Universal Active Intellect, and that it is that part of the soul which contains the sum total of the exalted thoughts which remains immortal, thus making intellectuality a condition of immortality. He also teaches that God knows things from their general aspect but does not know the particulars in their infinite ramifications.—See *Jewish Philosophy*.—*M.W*

Gestalt Psychology: (German, *Gestalt*, shape or form) A school of German psychology, founded about 1912 by M. Wertheimer, K. Koffka and W. Köhler. Gestalt psychology reacted against the psychic elements of analytic or associationist psychology (see *Associationism*) and substituted the concept of *Gestalt* or organized whole. The parts do not exist prior to the whole but derive their character from the structure of the whole. The *Gestalt* concept is applied at the physical and physiological as well as the psychological levels and in psychology both to the original sensory organization and to the higher intellectual and associative processes of mind. Configuration has been suggested as an English equivalent for *Gestalt* and the school is accordingly referred to as Configurationism.—*L.W.*

Geulincx, Arnold: (1625-1669) Was born in Antwerpen but later, when he became a Protestant, he moved to Holland. His work lay along Cartesian lines, but he felt dissatisfied with Descartes' solution of the mind-body problem. As a result, he developed the doctrine of occasionalism according to which interaction between mind and body is impossible, but God effects bodily motions "on occasion" of each mental process.

A. Geulincx: *Ethica*, 1655; *Metaphysica*, 1695. Complete works in 3 vols. ed. by J. P. Land, 1891-3.—*R.B.W.*

Geyser, Joseph: (1869-1948) Is a leader of Catholic psychological and metaphysical thought in present-day Germany. Born in Erkelenz, he has taught at the Universities of Freiburg, Münster and Munich (1924-33). His criticism of materialistic tendencies in modern psychology, his Aristotelian views on causality, and his espousal of a semi-Cartesian position in epistemology, are noteworthy. He has written: *Lehrbuch der allgem. Psychologie*, 3rd ed. (1920), *Erkenntnistheorie d. Aristoteles* (1917), *Das Prinzip vom zurelchenden Grunde* (1930). See *Philosophia Perennis* (Geyser Festg.), II vol. (Regensburg, 1930).—*V.J.B.*

Gioberti, Vincenzo: Born in Turin (Italy) April 5, 1801. Died in Paris, October 26, 1852. Ordained priest 1825. Exiled to Paris, 1833, because too liberal. Triumphantly returned to Italy 1848. Served as Minister and Ambassador.

His fundamental problem was the relation between sensibility and intelligibility. Being creates existence. The universal spirit becomes individual by its own creation. Thus, the source of individuality is not subjective but divine. And individuality returns to universality when it attains the state of intelligibility from the state of sensibility.

Main works: *Teoria della sovranaturale*, 1838; *Del bello*, 1841; *Del buono*, 1842; *Della filosofia della rivelazione*, 1856 (posth.); *Della protologia*, 1857 (posth.). See B. Spaventa, *La filosofia di G.*, 1863.—*L.V.*

Given, The: Whatever is immediately present to the mind before it has been elaborated by inference, interpretation or construction. See *Datum*.—*L.W.*

Gnosiology: (Gr. *gnosis*, knowledge + *logos*, discourse) Theory of knowledge in so far as it relates to the origin, nature, limits and validity of knowledge as distinguished from methodology, the study of the basic concepts, postulates and presuppositions of the special sciences.—*L.W.*

Gnosis: (Gr. knowledge) Originally a generic term for knowledge, in the first and second centuries A.D. it came to mean an esoteric knowledge of higher religious and philosophic truths to be acquired by an élite group of intellectually developed believers. Philo Judaeus (30 B.C. to 50 A.D.) is a fore-runner of Jewish Gnosticism; the allegorical interpretation of the Old Testament, use of Greek philosophical concepts, particularly the Logos doctrine, in Biblical exegesis, and a semi-mystical number theory characterize his form of gnosis. Christian gnostics (Cerinthus, Menander, Saturninus, Valentine, Basilides, Ptolemaeus, and possibly Marcion) maintained that only those men who cultivated their spiritual powers were truly immortal, and they adopted the complicated teaching of a sphere of psychic intermediaries (*aeons*) between God and earthly things. There was also a pagan gnosis begun before Christ as a reformation of Greek and Roman religion. Philosophically, the only thing common to all types of gnosis is the effort to transcend rational, logical thought processes by means of intuition.

De Faye, E., *Gnostiques et Gnosticisme*, 2me. éd., (Paris, 1925).—*V.J.B.*

Gobineau, Arthur de: (1816-1882) A French nobleman and author of *Essay on the Inequality of Human Races,* in which he propounds the doctrine of "nordic supremacy." According to him, "the white race originally possessed the monopoly of beauty, intelligence and strength. By its union with other varieties hybrids were created, which were beautiful without strength, strong without intelligence, or, if intelligent, both weak and ugly."—*R.B.W.*

God: In metaphysical thinking a name for the highest, ultimate being, assumed by theology on the basis of authority, revelation, or the evidence of faith as absolutely necessary, but demonstrated as such by a number of philosophical systems, notably idealistic, monistic and dualistic ones. Proofs of the existence of God fall apart into those that are based on facts of experience (desire or need for perfection, dependence, love, salvation, etc.), facts of religious history (*consensus gentium*, etc.), postulates of morality (belief in ultimate justice, instinct for an absolute good, conscience, the categorical imperative, sense of duty, need of an objective foundation of morality, etc.), postulates of reason (cosmological, physico-theological, teleological, and ontological arguments), and the inconceivableness of the opposite. As to the nature of God, the great variety of opinions are best characterized by their several conceptions of the attributes of God which are either of a non-personal (pantheistic, etc.) or personal (theistic, etc.) kind, representing concepts known from experience raised to a superlative degree ("omniscient," "eternal," etc.). The reality, God, may be conceived as absolute or as relative to human values, as being an all-inclusive one, a duality, or a plurality. Concepts of God calling for unquestioning faith, belief in miracles, and worship or representing biographical and descriptive sketches of God and his creation, are rather theological than metaphysical, philosophers, on the whole, utilizing the idea of God or its linguistic equivalents in other languages, despite popular and church implications, in order not to lose the feeling-contact with the rather abstract world-ground. See *Religion, Philosophy of.*—*K.F.L.*

According to the common teaching of the Schoolmen, philosophy is able to demonstrate the existence of God, though any statement of his essence is at best only analogical. See *Analogy.* Aquinas formulated the famous five ways by which to demonstrate God's existence: as prime mover, first cause, pure act to be assumed because there has to be act for anything to come into existence at all, necessary being in which existence and essence are one, as set over against contingent beings which may be or not be, as summit of the hierarchy of beings. A basic factor in these demonstrations is the impossibility of infinite regress. God is conceived as the first cause and as the ultimate final cause of all beings.

He is pure act, *ens realissimum* and *summum bonum*. Thomism and later Scholasticism denied that any adequate statement can be made on God's essence; but earlier thinkers, especially Anselm of Canterbury indulged in a so-called "Christian Rationalism" and believed that more can be asserted of God by "necessary reasons." Anselm's proof of God's existence has been rejected by Aquinas and Kant. See *Ontological argument.*—*R.A.*

Godhead: In general, the state of being a god, godhood, godness, divinity, deity. More strictly, the essential nature of God, especially the triune God, one in three Persons.—*J.J.R.*

Gödel, Kurt: (1906-1978) Austrian mathematician and logician — educated at Vienna, and member (1941) at the Institute for Advanced Study in Princeton, N. J. — is best known for his important incompleteness theorem, the closely related theorem on the impossibility (under certain circumstances) of formalizing a consistency proof for a logistic system within that system, and the essentially simple but far-reaching device of *arithmetization of syntax* which is employed in the proof of these theorems (see *Logic, formal*, § 6). Also of importance are his proof of the completeness of the functional calculus of first order (see *Logic, formal*, § 3), and his work on the consistency of the axiom of choice (*q.v.*) and of Cantor's *continuum hypothesis.*—*A.C.*

Good: (AS *god*) (a) In ethics, morally praiseworthy character, action, or motive.

(b) In axiology, two types of good, goodness, or value: intrinsic and extrinsic or instrumental.

Extrinsic or instrumental goodness depends for its existence upon some object, end or purpose which it serves. It derives its being from its service as an instrument in promoting or sustaining some more ultimate good and finally some ultimate or intrinsic good. It is good which is good for something.

Intrinsic goodness, or that which is good in itself without depending upon anything else for its goodness (though it may for its existence), is conceived in many ways: Realists, who agree that goodness is not dependent upon persons for its existence, say good is (1) anything desirable or capable of arousing desire or interest, (2) a quality of any desirable thing which can cause interest to be aroused or a capacity for being an end of action, (3) that which ought to be desired, (4) that which ought to be. Subjectivists, who agree that goodness is dependent upon persons for existence, hold views of two sorts: (1) good is partially dependent upon persons as (a) anything desired or "any object of any interest" (R. B. Perry), (b) "a quality of any object of any interest" causing it to be desired (A. K. Rogers); (2) good is completely dependent upon persons as (a) satisfaction of any desire or any interest in any object (DeW. H. Parker), (b) pleasant feeling (Hedonism). See *Value.* Opposed to bad, evil, disvalue.—*A.J.B.*

Good, Highest: (sometimes the greatest, or supreme, good. Lat. *summum bonum*) That good which transcends yet includes all the others. According to Augustine, Varro was able to enumerate 288 definitions. For Plato, the supreme Idea, the totality of being. For Aristotle, eudemonism (*q.v.*), which consists in the harmonious satisfaction of all rational powers. For the Epicureans, pleasure. For Aquinas, obedience to and oneness with God. The all-inclusive object of desire. —*J.K.F.*

Goodness: (AS. *god*) The extrinsic elections of things. The positive object of desire. For Plato, coextensive with being. For the Romans, duty. For Kant, that which has value. For Peirce, the adaptation of a subject to its end. In psychology, the characteristic actions which follow moral norms. Opposite of evil. See *Ethics*.—*J.K.F.*

Gorgias: (c. 480—375 B.C.) Celebrated orator, rhetorician and philosopher from Leontini in Sicily. He was numbered among the leading Sophists. He spent the major part of his long life in Greece, particularly in Athens. The Platonic dialogue bearing his name indicates in some measure the high esteem in which he was held.—*L.E.D.*

Gotama: The founder of the Nyāya (*q.v.*), also known as Gautama and Aksapāda.—*K.F.L.*

Gothic: A style in architecture, sculpture and painting between the 12th and the 16th century.

During the neo-classical 18th century, a syn. for the barbarous and lawless; the "romanticists" who reacted against the 18th century classicism, reverted to a love for the medieval Gothic styles.—*L.V.*

Government: This term is used in two senses. Sometimes it is used to indicate the particular administrative institutions or agencies of a society whose function it is to control individual action, safeguard individual and national rights, and, in general, promote the public welfare; all in accordance with the methodological principles and for the sake of the ends decreed to be legitimate by the sovereign. A government is, consequently, purely instrumental, and cannot rightly create sanctions for its own activities. It may, however, persist through change of personnel. In another less common use the word indicates the person or persons who hold office in these institutions, rather than the institutions themselves. This second use is more common in Europe than in America, and corresponds to the American term "the administration."—*M.B.M.*

Grabmann, Martin: (1875-1949) One of the most capable historians of medieval philosophy. Born in Wintershofen (Oberpfalz), he was ordained in 1898. He has taught philosophy and theology at Eichstätt (1906), Vienna (1913), and Munich (1918-). An acknowledged authority on the chronology and authenticity of the works of St. Thomas, he is equally capable in dealing with the thought of St. Augustine, or of many minor writers in philosophy and theology up to the Renaissance. *Aus d. Geisteswelt d. Mittelalters* (Festg. Grabmann) Münster i. W. 1935, lists more than 200 of his articles and books, published before 1934. Chief works: *Die Geschichte der scholastischen Methode* (1909), *Mittelalterliches Geistesleben* (1926), *Werke des hl. Thomas v. Aq.* (1931).—*V.J.B.*

Grand style: A style based on antique statues and Italian art of the Renaissance, flourishing in France during the 17th century, and in England during the 18th century.—*L.V.*

"Greatest Happiness": In ethics, the basis of ethics considered as the highest good of the individual or of the greatest number of individuals. The feeling-tone of the individual, varying from tranquility and contentment to happiness, considered as the end of all moral action, as for example in Epicurus, Lucretius and Rousseau. The welfare of the majority of individuals, or of society as a whole, considered as the end of all moral action, as for example in Plato, Bentham and Mill. The greatest possible surplus of pleasure over pain in the greatest number of individuals. Although mentioned by Plato in the *Republic* (IV, 420), the phrase in its current form probably originated in the English translation, in 1770, of Beccaria's *Dei delitti e delle pene,* where it occurs as *"la massima felicità divisa nel maggior numero,"* which was rendered as "the greatest happiness of the greatest number," a phrase enunciated by Hutcheson in 1725. One of a number of ethical ideals or moral aims. The doctrine with which the phrase is most closely associated is that of John Stuart Mill, who said in his *Utilitarianism* (ch. II) that "the happiness which forms the . . . standard of what is right in conduct, is not the agent's own happiness, but that of all concerned." —*J.K.F.*

Green, Thomas Hill: (1836-1882) Neo-Hegelian idealist, in revolt against the fashionable utilitarian ethics and Spencerian positivism and agnosticism of his time, argued the existence of a rational self from our inability to derive from sense-experience the categories in which we think and the relations that pertain between our percepts. Again, since we recognize ourselves to be part of a larger whole with which we are in relations, those relations and that whole cannot be created by the finite self, but must be produced by an absolute all-inclusive mind of which our minds are parts and of which the world-process in its totality is the experience.

An examination of desire and will leads to the same conclusion. These, too, betoken a self which fulfills itself in attaining an ideal. This ideal can be found only in the Absolute, revealed now not only as an absolute mind but as an absolute moral person, enshrining goodness and beauty as well as truth—that is as God. —*B.A.G.F.*

T. H. Green: *Prolegomena to Ethics,* 1883.

Grotesque: (It. *grottesca,* from *grotta, grotto*) The idealized ugly. In aesthetics, the beauty of fantastic exaggeration, traditionally achieved by combining foliate and animal or human figures, as for example those found in the classic Roman and Pompeiian palaces and reproduced by Raphael in the Vatican.—*J.K.F.*

Grotius, Hugo: (1583-1645) Dutch jurist. In his celebrated *De jure belli et pacis* (1625) he presents a theory of natural rights, based largely upon Stoicism and Roman legal principles. A sharp distinction is made between inviolable natural law and the ever changing positive or civil law. His work has been basic in the history of international law.

Other works: *De mari libero,* 1609; *De veritate religionis christianae,* 1622.—*L.E.D.*

Guilt: In ethics, conduct involving a breach of moral law. The commission of a moral offense considered as the failure of duty. Defection from obligation or responsibility. In the psychology of ethics, the sense of guilt is the awareness of having violated an ethical precept or law. Opposite of innocence, merit.—*J.K.F.*

Guṇa: (Skr. thread, cord) Quality; that which has substance (see *dravya*) as substratum. It is variously conceived in Indian philosophy and different enumerations are made. The Vaiśeṣika, e.g., knows 24 kinds, along with subsidiary ones; the Sānkhya, Trika, and others recognized three: *sattva, rajas, tamas* (*q.v.*).—*K.F.L.*

Guru: (Skr.) Teacher.

H

Habermas, Jürgen: (1929-   ) Author of *Communication and the Evolution of Society* (1979), *Knowledge and Human Interests* (*Erkenntnis and Interesse,* 1968) and other works on the theory of society. He is interested in the thought of Schelling and debates against Marcuse.—*S.E.N.*

Habit: (Lat. *habitus* from *habere,* to have) *In psychology:* An acquired mental function reinforced by repetition.

In metaphysics, one of Aristotle's 10 categories, Hume's ground for causality ("custom of the mind") and Peirce's leading principle or basis of natural law.—*L.W.*

Habit Memory: The retention and reproduction of something learned *e.g.* a poem, a geometrical demonstration—without the recognition characteristic of memory proper. See *Memory.*—*L.W.*

Hades: (Gr. *Haides*) In Greek mythology the god of the underworld, the son of Cronos and Rhea and the brother of Zeus; hence the kingdom ruled over by Hades, or the abode of the dead.—*G.R.M.*

Haeberlin, Paul: (1878-1960) A well known Swiss thinker whose major contributions until recent years were in the field of education. In his hands phenomenology has become existential philosophy. A transcendental-idealistic tone pervades his philosophy. He combines in theory the advantages of existential phenomenology with those of psychologism.—*H.H.*

Haecceity: (Lat. *haecceitas,* literally thisness) A term employed by Duns Scotus to express that by which a quiddity, or general essence, becomes an individual, particular nature, or being. That incommunicable nature which constitutes the individual difference, or individualizes singular beings belonging to a class; hence his principle of individuation.—*J.J.R.*

Haeckel, Ernst Heinrich: (1834-1919) Was a German biologist whose early espousal of Darwinism led him to found upon the evolutionary hypothesis a thoroughgoing materialistic monism which he advanced in his numerous writings particularly in his popular *The Riddle of the Universe.* Believing in the essential unity of the organic and the inorganic, he was opposed to revealed religions and their ideals of God, freedom and immortality and offered a monistic religion of nature based on the true, the good and the beautiful. See *Darwin, Evolutionism, Monism.*—*L.E.D.*

Ha-Levi, Judah: (b. ca. 1080, d. ca. 1140) Poet and philosopher. His Kuzari (Arabic Kitab Al-Khazari), written in dialogue form, has a double purpose. First, as its subtitle, A Book of Proofs and Arguments in Defense of the Humiliated Religion, indicates, it aims to prove the dignity and worth of Judaism. Secondly, he endeavors to show the insufficiency of philosophy and the superiority of the truths of revealed religion to those arrived at by logic. The admission of both Christianity and Islam that Judaism is their source proves the first. The exaltation of intuition as a means of certainty in matters of religion, and the claim that the prophet is the highest type of man rather than the philosopher purposes to substantiate the second. He endows the Jewish people with a special religio-ethical sense which is their share only and constitutes a quasi-biological quality. He assigns also a special importance to Palestine as a contributory factor in the spiritual development of his people, for only there can this religio-ethical sense come to full expression.—*M.W.*

Hallucination: (Lat. *hallucinatio,* from *hallucinari,* to wander in mind) A non-veridical or delusive perception of a sense object occurring when no object is in fact present to the organs of sense. See *Delusion, Illusion.*—*L.W.*

Hallucination, Negative: The failure to perceive an object which is in fact present to the organs of sense. See *Hallucination.*—*L.W.*

Hamann, Johann Georg: (1730-1788) Kant's extreme pietist friend, and, like him, a native of Königsberg, he saw in the critical philosophy of Kant an unsuccessful attempt to make reason independent of all tradition, belief and experience.—*H.H.*

Han Fei Tzŭ: (d. 233 B.C.) Was a pupil of Hsün Tzŭ. The greatest Chinese philosopher of law (fa chia), he advocated government by law and statecraft. Delegated by his native state, he appealed to the king of Chin (Shih Huang-ti) not to invade his country. At first he was cordially entertained but later was ordered to commit suicide by the premier of Chin, his former schoolmate, Li Ssŭ, who became jealous of him. (*Han-fei Tzŭ*, Eng. tr. by W.K. Liao: *Han Fei Tzŭ, Complete Works.*) —*W.T.C.*

Happiness: (in Kant's ethics) Kant is more concerned with happiness in terms of its ideal possibility than with its realization in actual human experience. Its ideal possibility rests on the a priori laws of intelligible freedom *(vide)*, by which the individual through self-determination achieves unity: the self-sufficiency and harmony of his own being. "Real happiness rests with my free volition, and real contentment consists in the consciousness of freedom" (Kant).—*P.A.S.*

Harmony, Pre-Established: The perfect functioning of mind and body, as ordained by God in the beginning. The dualism of Descartes (1596-1650) had precluded interaction between mind or soul and body by its absolute difference and opposition between *res cogitans* and *res extensa*. How does it happen, then, that the mind perceives the impressions of the body, and the body is ready to follow the mind's will? The Cartesians, in order to correct this difficulty, introduced the doctrine of "occasionalism," whereby when anything happens to either mind or body, God interferes to make the corresponding change in the other. Leibniz (1646-1716) countered by suggesting that the relation between mind and body is one of harmony, established by God before their creation. Earlier than mind or body, God had perfect knowledge of all possible minds and bodies. In an infinite number of creations all possible combinations are possible, including those minds whose sequence of ideas perfectly fits the motions of some bodies. In the latter, there is a perfect and pre-ëstablished harmony. A parallelism between mind and body exists, such that each represents the proper expression of the other. Leibniz compares their relation to that of two clocks which have been synchronized once for all and which therefore operate similarly without the need of either interaction or intervention. Expressed by Leibniz' follower, C. Wolff (1679-1754) as "that by which the intercourse of soul and body is explained by a series of perceptions and desires in the soul, and a series of motions in the body, which are harmonic or accordant through the nature of soul and body."—*J.K.F.*

Harris, William Torrey: (1835-1909) American philosopher who founded the *Journal of Speculative Philosophy*, was connected with the St. Louis School of philosophy, later worked with the Concord summer school of philosophy, and then was appointed U.S. Commissioner of Education. He wrote *Hegel's Logic, a Book on the Genesis of the Categories of the Mind* (1890).—*S.E.N.*

Hart, H.L.A.: (1907-   ) Former principal of Brasenose College, Oxford, former Professor of Jurisprudence, and author of *The Concept of Law* (1961), *Punishment and Responsibility*, and *Law, Liberty, and Morality* (1963). He argues against "legal moralism,"

holding that there is no necessary connection between law and morality.—*S.E.N.*

Hartley, David: (1705-1757) Was an English physician most noted as the founder of the associationist school in psychology. His theory of the association of ideas was prompted by the work of John Gay to which he gave a physiological emphasis and which, in turn, influenced the Utilitarians, Bentham and the Mills. See *Bentham, Gay, James Mill, John Stuart Mill* and *Utilitarians*.

D. Hartley, *Observations of man: his frame, his duty and his expectations*, 1749.—*L.E.D.*

Hartmann, Eduard von: (1842-1906) Hybridizing Schopenhauer's voluntarism with Hegel's intellectualism, and stimulated by Schelling, the eclectic v.H. sought to overcome irrationalism and rationalism by postulating the Unconscious, raised into a neutral absolute which has in it both will and idea in co-ordination. Backed by an encyclopedic knowledge he showed, allegedly inductively, how this generates all values in a conformism or correlationism which circumvents a subjective monistic idealism no less than a phenomenalism by means of a transcendental realism. Writing at a time when vitalists were hard put to synthesize the new natural sciences and teleology he endeavored to by assigning to mechanistic causality a special function in the natural process under a more generalized and deeper purposiveness. Dispensing with a pure rationalism, but without taking refuge in a vital force, v.H. was then able to establish a neo-vitalism. In ethics he transcended an original pessimism, flowing from the admittance of the alogical and disteleological, in a qualified optimism founded upon an evolutionary hypothesis which regards nature with its laws subservient to the logical, as a species of the teleogical, and to reason which, as product of development, redeems the irrational will once it has been permitted to create a world in which existence means unhappiness.

E. von Hartmann, *Philos. des Unbewussten*, 3 vol. 1869 (Eng. tr. *Philosophy of the Unconscious*, 1931); *Die Religion des Geistes*, 1882; *Aesthetik*, 1886; *Kategorienlehre*, 1897; *Geschichte der Metaphysik*, 1900; *Das Problem des Lebens*, 1906; *System der Philosophie in Grundriss*, 1906-10.—*K.F.L.*

Hartmann, Nicolai: (1882-1951) A realist in metaphysics, he refutes nineteenth century idealism and monism, and attacks medieval super-naturalism and the various forms of theism. As exponent of a philosophic humanism, he made extensive contributions to ethics.

N. Hartmann, *Platos Lehre vom Sein*, 1909; *Grundzüge einer Metaphysik der Erkenntnis*, 1921; *Ethik*, 1926 (Eng. tr. 1932); *Die Philosophie des Deutschen Idealismus* I, 1923; II, 1929; *Zur Grundlegung der Ontologie*, 1935; *Möglichkeit u. Wirklichkeit*, 1938. See his own exposition of his views in *Deutsch Syst. Philos. nach ihr. Gestalten*, 1931. —*H.H.*

Hauber's law: Given a set of conditional sentences $A_1 \supset B_1, A_2 \supset B_2, \ldots, A_n \supset B_n$, we may infer each of the conditional sentences $B_1 \supset A_1, B_2 \supset A_2, \ldots, B_n \supset A_n$, provided we know that $A_1, A_2, \ldots, A_n$ are exhaustive and B$_1$, B$_2$, . . . , Bn are mutually exclusive—i.e., provided we have also A$_1$ v A$_2$ v . . . v An *and* ~ [B$_1$B$_2$], ~ [B$_1$B$_3$], . . . , ~ [Bn-$_1$Bn]. This form (or set of forms) of valid inference of the propositional calculus is *Hauber's law.*—*A.C.*

Hedonic: Possessing pleasurable or painful affective quality. See *Algedonic.*—*L.W.*

Hedonic Calculus: View, ascribed to Jeremy Bentham, that the ends of mankind may be calculated by determining the preponderance of the pleasurable over the painful in order to evaluate the useful. See *Utilitarianism.*—*L.F.D.*

Hedonism, Ethical: (Gr. *hedone,* pleasure) A doctrine as to what entities possess intrinsic value. According to it pleasure or pleasant consciousness, and this alone, has positive ultimate value, that is, is intrinsically good and has no parts or constituents which are not intrinsically good. The contrary hedonic feeling tone, displeasure or unpleasant consciousness, and this alone has negative ultimate value, that is, is intrinsically bad and has no parts or constituents which are not intrinsically bad. The intrinsic value of all other entities is precisely equivalent to the intrinsic value of their hedonic components. The total value of an action is the net intrinsic value of all its hedonic consequences. According to pure hedonism either there are no differences of quality among pleasures or among displeasures or else such differences as exist do not affect the intrinsic values of the different hedonic states. These values vary only with the intensity and duration of the pleasure or displeasure.

Ethical Hedonism is usually combined with a teleological view of the nature of right action. It may be combined with Ethical Egoism as in the view of Epicurus, or with Ethical Universalism, as in the views of J. Bentham, J. S. Mill, and H. Sidgwick.—*C.A.B.*

Hedonism, Psychological: (Gr. *hedone,* pleasure) Theory that psychological motivation is to be explained exclusively in terms of desire for pleasure and aversion from pain. (See W. James' criticism of psychological hedonism, *The Principles of Psychology,* II pp. 549 ff.) Psychological hedonism, as a theory of human motivation in contrast with ethical hedonism which accepts as the criterion of morality, the pleasure-pain consequences of an act.—*L.W.*

Hedonistic Aesthetics: Theories reducing beauty to the pleasure of seeing, hearing and playing, to the satisfaction of sensual enjoyment.—*L.V.*

Hedonistic Paradox: A paradox or apparent inconsistency in hedonistic theory arising from (1) the doctrine that since pleasure is the only good, one ought always to seek pleasure, and (2) the fact that whenever pleasure itself is the object sought it cannot be found. Human nature is such that pleasure normally arises as an accompaniment of satisfaction of desire for any end except when that end is pleasure itself. The way to attain pleasure is not to seek for it, but for something else which when found will have yielded pleasure through the finding. Likewise, one should not seek to avoid pain, but only actions which produce pain.—*A.J.B.*

Hegel, Georg Wilhelm Friedrich: Born at Stuttgart in 1770 and died at Berlin in 1831. He studied theology, philosophy and the classics at Tübingen, 1788-93, occupied the conventional position of tutor in Switzerland and Frankfort on the Main, 1794-1800, and went to Jena as Privatdocent in philosophy in 1801. He was promoted to a professorship at Jena in 1805, but was driven from the city the next year by the incursion of the French under Napoleon. He then went to Bamberg, where he remained two years as editor of a newspaper. The next eight years he spent as director of the Gymnasium at Nürnberg. In 1816 he accepted a professorship of philosophy at Heidelberg, from which position he was called two years later to succeed Fichte at the University of Berlin. While at Jena, he cooperated with Schelling in editing the *Kritisches Journal der Philosophie,* to which he contributed many articles. His more important volumes were published as follows: *Phänomenologie des Geistes,* 1807; *Wissenschaft der Logik,* 1812-16; *Encyklopädie der philosophischen Wissenschaften im Grundrisse,* 1817; *Grundlinien der Philosophie des Rechts,* 1820. Shortly after his death his lectures on the philosophy of religion, the history of philosophy, the philosophy of history, and aesthetics were published from the collated lecture notes of his students. His collected works in nineteen volumes were published 1832-40 by a group of his students.—*G.W.C.*

Hegelianism: As expounded in the writings of Hegel, Hegelianism is both a doctrine and a method. The two are held to be logically inseparable: the method is precisely the formulation of the doctrine, and the doctrine is precisely the detailed expression of the method. This integration of the two aspects of the philosophy presents a formidable obstacle to interpretation and to summary presentation of Hegelianism as conceived by its founder.

The method is, of course, the dialectic. On its formal side, it is constituted by the triadic dialectic of thesis, antithesis and synthesis. In his logical writings Hegel is very fond of manipulating this formal apparatus, which he does in great detail. From his practice here one might be led to suppose that in his opinion the dialectic itself constitutes the essence of the method. In his other writings, however, little if any use is made of the schematism, except for the purpose of presenting the larger patterns of the subject matter; and in his remarks on method its formal aspect is hardly referred to. In these remarks Hegel is concerned with emphasizing the logical structure underlying the machinery, namely, the relationship of contrariety and its resolution. Everywhere, the method is grounded in system; and the transition from thesis and antithesis to synthesis is held to be necessitated by the structure of the system within which it is grounded. Consequently the dialectical advance exhibits *pari passu* the structure of the system which is its matrix; the synthesis is positive throughout. This characteristic of the method, its "holding fast the positive in the negative," is what Hegel calls its *negativity;* and this characteristic is to him the essence of the dialectic.

The sort of system which grounds the method is not the sort within which the principle of contradiction obtains. Contradictories cannot be dialectically resolved; between them there is no ground of synthesis. But such systems are abstract, that is, exemplified only in formal deductions; they are lacking in factual content. Dialectical analysis is possible only within systems which are factual, that is, constituted by statements of fact and statements of possibility grounded in fact. Here the principle of contrariety, not the principle of contradiction, obtains; and dialectical analysis is identical with the resolution of contraries. Here, and here alone, is the dialectical method applicable; and it alone is applicable here.

Thus the method is the delineation of systems which are real, and the doctrine of reality nothing other than a detailed statement of the result. Such a statement is the final category of dialectical analysis, the *Absolute Idea;* this is the "truth" of *Being.* What this category is in detail can be specified only by the method whereby it is warranted. In general it is the structure of fact, possibility and value as determined by dialectical negation. It is the all-comprehensive system, the "whole," which harmoniously includes every statement of fact, possibility and value by "sublating" (through dialectical negation) every such statement within its own structure. It is also of the nature of "subject" in contradistinction to "substance" as defined by Spinoza; Hegel sometimes speaks of it as *Absolute Spirit.* If this doctrine is to be called absolute idealism, as is customary, its distinguishing characteristic should not be submerged in the name: the system which is here identified with reality is structured precisely as disclosed in the process of dialectical negation which exhibits it.

The later thinkers commonly referred to in the histories as Hegelians fall mainly into two groups. One is the group more or less indifferent to the method of Hegel and interested primarily in the ramifications of his doctrine; the other is the group committed in principle to the method, to its "negativity" and not to its categories, and concerned by its means to build independently. The early Hegelians in Germany belong to the former group; outstanding representatives of the latter are the recent British and American philosophers sometimes called neo-Hegelians.

See *Hegel-Archiv,* ed. G. Lasson; K. Fischer, *Hegel's Leben, Werke und Lehre,* 2 vols. (1901, 1911); W. Dilthey, *Gesamm Schr.* IV; B. Croce, *What is Living and What is Dead of Hegel,* 1915; G. Lasson, *Hegel als Geschichtsphilosoph,* 1920; Th. Haering, *Hegel sein Wollen u. s. Werk,* I (1929); II (1939); H. Glockner, *Hegel;* S. Hook, *From Hegel to Marx,* 1938.—*G.W.C.*

Heidegger, Martin: (1889-1976) Trained in Husserl's radical structural analysis of pure consciousness, Heidegger shares with phenomenology the effort to methodically analyze and describe the conceptual meanings of single phenomena. He aimed at a phenomenological analysis of human existence in respect to its temporal and historical character. Concen-trating on the Greek tradition, and endeavoring to open a totally different approach from that of the Greek thinkers to the problem of being, he seeks to find his way back to an inner independence of philosophy from the special sciences.

Before a start can be made in the radical analysis of human existence, the road has to be cleared of the objections of philosophical tradition, science, logic and common sense. As the moderns have forgotten the truths the great thinkers discovered, have lost the ability to penetrate to the real origins, the recovery of the hard-won, original, uncorrupted insights of man into metaphysical reality is only possible through a "destructive" analysis of the traditional philosophies. By this recovery of the hidden sources, Heidegger aims to revive the genuine philosophizing which, notwithstanding appearances, has vanished from us in the Western world because of autonomous science serious disputing of the position of philosophy. As human reality is so structured that it discloses itself immediately, he writes really an idealistic philosophy of *homo faber.* But instead of being a rationalistic idealist reading reason into the structure of the really real, he takes a more avowedly emotional phenomenon as the center of a new solution of the *Seinsfrage.*

Under Kierkegaard's influence, he pursues an "existential" analysis of human existence in order to discuss the original philosophical question of being in a new way. He explores many hitherto unexplored phenomena which ontology disregarded. *Sorge* (concern), being *par excellence* the structure of consciousness, is elevated to the ultimate. Concern has a wholly special horizon of being. Dread *(Angst),* the feeling of being on the verge of nothing, represents an eminently transcendental instrument of knowledge. Heidegger gives dread a content directed upon the objective world. He unfolds the essence of dread to be *Sorge* (concern). As concern tends to become obscured to itself by the distracted losing of one's selfhood in the cares of daily life, its remedy is in the consideration of such experiences as conscience, forboding of death and the existential consciousness of time. By elevating *Sorge* to the basis of all being, he raised something universally human to the fundamental principle of the world. It is only after an elementary analysis of the basic constitution of human existence that Heidegger approaches his ultimate problem of *Being and Time,* in which more complicated structures such as the existential significance of death, conscience, and the power of resolute choice explain the phenomena of man's position in daily life and history.—*H.H.*

When the Nazis took control of the education apparatus of the state, Heidegger collaborated with them. He was put in charge of the university. He made extravagant and exaggerated speeches in praise of Hitler, and was showered with the highest honors. Although he later resigned, the disgrace and shame of his actions followed him to the end of his days.—*S.E.N.*

Main works: *Kategorien— u. Bedentungslenre d. Duns Scotus,* 1916; *Sein u. Zeit,* 1927; *Was ist*

Metaphysik?; Kant u.d. Probl. d. Meta; 1929, *Vom Wesen des Grundes,* 1929. See J. Kraft, *Von Husserl zu H.,* 1932.—*H.H.*

Helvétius, Claude Adrien: (1715-1771) A French philosopher, he developed on the basis of Condillac's sensationalism his superficial materialistic philosophy. His theories of the original mental equality of individuals, of egoism or self-interest as the sole motive of human action, and of the omnipotence of education, stress the basic determining influence of circumstances.

C. A. Helvétius, *De l'Esprit,* 1758; *De l' Homme, de ses facultés et de son éducation,* 1772.—*H.H.*

Heraclitus: ("The Obscure") Of Ephesus, about 536-470 B.C. In opposition to the Milesians, from whom he is separated by a generation, he held that there is nothing abiding in the world. All things and the universe as a whole are in constant, ceaseless flux; nothing is, only change is real, all is a continuous passing away. For this reason the world appeared to him to be an ever-living fire, a consuming movement in which only the orderliness of the succession of things, or as Heraclitus called it, the "reason" or "destiny" of the world remains always the same. Heraclitus thus foreshadowed the modern conception of the uniformity of natural law. Cf. Diels, *Frag. d. Vor,* I, ch. 12.—*M.F.*

Herbart, Johann Friedrich: (1776-1841) Best known as the "father" of scientific pedagogy centrally based upon psychology, a general tenet that still has weight today, Herbart occupies as educational philosophical theorist a position strikingly similar to that of John Dewey, the nestor of American philosophy.

Objecting to Fichte, his master's method of deducing everything from a single, all-embracing principle, he obstinately adhered to the axiom that everything is what it is, the principle of identity. He also departed from him in the principle of idealism and freedom. As man is not free in the sense of possessing a principle independent of the environment, he reverted to the Kantian doctrine that behind and underlying the world of appearance there is a plurality of real things in themselves that are independent of the operations of mind upon them. Deserving credit for having developed the realism that was latent in Kant's philosophy, he conceived the "reals" so as to do away with the contradictions in the concepts of experience. The necessity for assuming a plurality of "reals" arises as a result of removing the contradictions in our experiences of change and of things possessing several qualities. Herbart calls the method he applies to the resolution of the contradictions existing between the empirically derived concepts, the method of relations, that is the accidental relation between the different "reals" is a question of thought only, and inessential for the "reals" themselves. It is the changes in these relations that form the process of change in the world of experience. Nothing can be ultimately real of which two contradictory predicates can be asserted. To predicate unity and multiplicity of an object is to predicate contradictions. Hence ultimate reality must be absolutely unitary and also without change. The metaphysically interpreted

abstract law of contradiction was therefore central in his system. Incapability of knowing the proper nature of these "reals" equals the inability of knowing whether they are spiritual or material. Although he conceived in his system that the "reals" are analogous with our own inner states, yet his view of the "reals" accords better with materialistic atomism. The "reals" are simple and unchangeable in nature.

Metaphysics and psychology are not distinct in Herbart's view. In his day psychology was also philosophy. It was still a metaphysical science in the sense that it is differentiated from physical science. It was only later that psychology repudiated philosophy. Accepting Kant's challenge to make psychology a mathematical science, he developed an elaborate system of mathematical constructions that proved the least fruitful phase of his system. As a mathematical science psychology can use only calculation, not experiment. The mind or soul is unitary, indivisible; science, including philosophy, is neither analytical nor experimental. By denying analysis to psychology, Herbart combatted the division of mind into separate faculties. Psychology is not the mere description of the mind, but the working out of its mathematical laws.

Ideas, he argued, arise originally from the collision between "reals" or things. As centers of force, they were always in mind and determined by it by their energies. Once they come to mind through the senses, they are never lost. Explaining ideas as forces acting very much as the electrons of modern physics, the ideas already in consciousness play an important role with regard to new ideas just appearing. The ideas already present are the apperceiving ideas and the new ideas are to be apperceived, i.e. incorporated with the old ideas to form knowledge. Herbert himself made less of apperception, even though most famous for the term "apperceiving mass." He became famous because the term is a psychological factor in the process of education.

J. F. Herbart, *Hauptpunkte d. Logik,* 1808; *Hauptpunkte d. Metaphysik,* 1806-1808; *Allgem. prakt. Philos.,* 1808; *Lehrb. z. Psychologie,* 1816; *Psychol. als Wissensch. neu gegründet auf Erfahrung, Metaphysik u. Mathematik,* 1824; *Allgemeine Metaphysik,* 1828-9. See *Sämmtliche Werke,* 19 vols. (ed. Fluegel, 1887-1912).—*H.H.*

Herbartianism: The philosophical, but particularly the psychological and pedagogical doctrines of Johann Friedrich Herbart *(q.v.)* as expounded in modified and developed form by his disciples, notably M. Lazarus and H. Steinthal in psychology, T. Ziller and W. Rein in pedagogy, M. Drobisch in religious philosophy and ethics. In America, the movement was vigorous and influential, but shortlived (about 1890-1910) and confined mainly to education (Charles De-Garmo and Charles A. McMurry). Like Herbart, his disciples strove for a clarification of concepts with special emphasis on scientific method, the doctrine of apperception, and the efficacy of a mathematical approach even in their psychology which was dominated by associational thinking; yet they discarded more or less the master's doctrine of reals.—*K.F.L.*

Herder, Johann Gottfried: (1744-1803) A founder of modern religious humanism, he explained human history as a consequence of the nature of man and of man's physical environment. Held implicitly to the view that society is basically an organic whole. Accounted for the differences in culture and institutions of different peoples as beng due to geographical conditions. Although history is a process of the education of the human species, it has no definite goal of perfection and development. The vehicle of living culture is a distinct *Volk* or *Nation* with its distinct language and traditions. As a child of the Enlightenment, Herder had a blind faith in nature, in man and in the ultimate development of reason and justice.

   J. G. Herder, *Ideen z. Philos. d. Gesch. d. Menschheit*, 1784-91; *Gott. Gespräche über Spinoza's System*, 1787; *Briefe z. Beförderung d. Humanität*, 1793; *Metakritik*, 1799; *Kalligone*, 1800; last two works directed against Kant's *Critiques* (*q.v.*).—*H.H.*

Hereditary property: See *Recursion, proof by*.

Hermeneutics: The art and science of interpreting the meaning of texts, for example in application to sacred scripture, and equivalent to exegesis.—*K.F.L.*

Herrenmoral: (German) A concept popularly used as a blanket term for any ruthless, non-Christian type of morality justly and unjustly linked with the ethical theories of Friedrich Nietzsche (*q.v.*) as laid down by him especially in the works of his last productive period fraught as it was with iconoclast vehemence against all plebeian ideals and a passionate desire to establish a new and more virile aristocratic morality, and debated by many writers, such as Kaftan, Kronenberg, Staudinger, and Hilbert. Such ideas as will to power, the conception of the superman, the apodictic primacy of those who with strong mind and unhindered by conventional interpretations of good and evil, yet with lordly lassitude, are born to leadership, have contributed to this picture of the morality of the masters (*Herren*) whom Nietzsche envisaged as bringing about the revaluation of all values and realizing the higher European culture upon the ruins of the fear-motivated, passion-shunning, narrowly moral world of his day.—*K.F.L.*

Heschel, Abraham Joshua: (1907-1972) Jewish theologian and educator at the Jewish Theological Seminary of America in New York (beginning in 1945), he wrote many influential books, including *Man's Quest for God: Studies in Prayer and Symbolism* (1954), *God in Search of Man: a Philosophy of Judaism* (1955), *Man is Not Alone: A Philosophy of Religion* (1951), *Between God & Man, an Interpretation of Judaism* (1965), *The Earth Is the Lord's* (1978), *The Insecurity of Freedom: Essays on Human Existence* (1972), *Israel: An Echo of Eternity* (1969), *A Passion for Truth* (1973), *Prophets* (1969, 1971), *The Sabbath* (1975), *Theology of Ancient Judaism* (1973), and *Who Is Man?* (1965).—*S.E.N.*

Heterogeneity: (Lat. *Heterogeneitas*) The condition of having different parts; diversity of composition; distinc-

tion of kind. Hamilton's law: "that every concept contains other concepts under it; and therefore, when divided proximately, we descend always to other concepts, but never to individuals; in other words, things the most homogenous—similar—must in certain respects be heterogeneous—dissimilar." Employed by H. Spencer (1820-1903) to denote the presence of differentiation in the cosmic material. Opposite of: homogeneity (*q.v.*).—*J.K.F.*

Heteronomy: (Gr. *hetero*, other + *nomos*, law) See *Autonomy*.

Heteronomy of Ends: (Kant) Just as autonomy of the will is that state of affairs in the life of a rational being in which the will is determined in its choices by no ends other than itself, so heteronomy of the will is the state in which the will is determined by ends other than itself, *e.g.* happiness or gain either for self or others. In autonomy the will is its own end, and is determined only by its own laws. Autonomy of the will is the supreme principle of morality, Kant affirms, and heteronomy is the source of all spurious principles of morality. For in heteronomy the will, being attracted by external ends, is obeying laws not of its own making. In autonomy, however, the will obeys only its own laws; it makes only those choices of action which may also be regarded as instances of laws of its own choosing. The principle of the Autonomy of the Will, and the Categorical Imperative, are thus one and the same thing.—*F.L.W.*

Hetero-psychological Ethics: Ethics based on mental categories other than the conscience, as contrasted with idio-psychological ethics, or ethics based on the inner facts of conscience. Introduced as terms into ethics by J. Martineau (1805-1899) in 1885.—*J.K.F.*

Heterotelic: (from Gr. *heteros*, another, and *telos*, end) Said of any activity having a conscious or implied reference to the accomplishment of some end. In aesthetics applied to creative art and play in which a useful purpose may be discerned or may constitute the motive. See also *Autotelic*.—*K.F.L.*

Heterozetesis: (Gr. *heteros*, other + *zetein*, inquiry) In logic, *ignoratio elenchi*, and argument which does not prove the conclusion wanted. The fallacy of irrelevant conclusion; the general name for fallacies due to irrelevancy.—*J.K.F.*

Heuristic: (Gr. *heuriskein*, to discover) Serving to find out, helping to show how the qualities and relations of objects are to be sought. In Kant's philosophy, applying to ideas of God, freedom and immortality, as being undemonstrable but useful in the interpretation of things and events in time and space. In methodology, aiding in the discovery of truth. The heuristic method is the analytical method. Opposite of: ostensive.—*J.K.F.*

Hexis: (Gr. *hexis*) In Aristotle's philosophy a state or condition of a thing; particularly an acquired disposition or habit, not easily changed, and affecting the welfare of its possessor, such as the moral virtues and the intellectual skills.—*G.R.M.*

Hierarchy of types: See *Logic, formal*, § 6.

Hilbert, David: (1862-1943) German mathematician. Professor of mathematics at the University of Göttingen,

1895-. A major contributor to many branches of mathematics, he is regarded by many as the greatest mathematician of his generation. His work on the foundations of Euclidean geometry is contained in his *Grundlagen der Geometrie* (1st edn., 1899, 7th edn., 1930). Concerning his contributions to mathematical logic and mathematical philosophy, see the articles *mathematics,* and *proof theory.—A.C.*

Gesammelte Abhandlungen, three volumes, with an account of his work in mathematical logic by P. Bernays, and a life by O. Blumenthal, Berlin, 1932-1935.

Hillel of Verona: (1220-1295) Physician and philosopher. His principal philosophic work, the *Tagmulé ha-Nefesh* (Heb.) The Reward of the Soul, is devoted to two problems, that of the soul and that of reward and punishment. In his theory of the soul he follows partly Averroes (*q.v.*) and assumes with him that the universal Active Intellect acts upon the soul of the individual and helps to realize its powers. He rejects, though, the former's view of immortality which consists of a union of the human intellect with the universal Active Intellect.—*M.W.*

Hindu Ethics: See *Indian Ethics.*

Hindu Aesthetics: See *Indian Aesthetics.*

Hindu Philosophy: See *Indian Philosophy.*

Historical materialism: The social philosophy of dialectical materialism. The application of the general principles of dialectical materialism to the specific field of human history, the development of human society. One of the chief problems Marx dealt with was that of the basic causal agent in the movement of human history. He states his thesis as follows:

"In the social relations which men carry on they enter into definite relations that are indispensible and independent of their will. These relations of production correspond to a definite stage of development of their material powers of production . . . . At a certain stage of their development the material forces of production in society come in conflict with the existing relations of production, or—what is but a legal expression for the same thing—with the property relations within which they had been at work before. From forms of development of the forces of production these relations turn into their fetters. Then comes the period of social revolution. With the change of the economic foundation the entire immense superstructure is more or less rapidly transformed. In considering such transformations the distinction should always be made between the material transformation of the economic conditions of production which can be determined with the precision of natural science, and the legal, political, religious, aesthetic or philosophic—in short, ideological forms in which men become conscious of this conflict and fight it out." (Marx: *Contribution to the Critique of Political Economy,* p. 12.)—*J.M.S.*

Historicism: The view that the history of anything is a sufficient explanation of it, that the values of anything can be accounted for through the discovery of its origins, that the nature of anything is entirely comprehended in its development, as for example, that the properties of the oak tree are entirely accounted for by an exhaustive description of its development from the acorn. The doctrine which discounts the fallaciousness of the historical fallacy. Applied by some critics to the philosophy of Hegel and Karl Marx.—*J.K.F.*

Historiography: (Gr. *histor* + *graphein,* to write) The art of recording history (*q.v.*).

History: (Gr. *histor,* learned) Ambiguously used to denote either (a) events or (b) records of the past. The term historiography (*q.v.*) is used for (b). Also ambiguous in denoting natural as well as human events, or records of either.

History of Art: Vasari (16th century) began the history of the artists. Winckelmann (18th century) began the history of art, that is of the development of the elements comprised in works of art. The history of art today is directed towards a synthesis of the personalities of the artists and of their reaction to tradition and environment.—*L.V.*

History, Philosophy of: History investigates the theories concerning the development of man as a social being within the limits of psychophysical causality. Owing to this double purpose the philosophy of history has to study the principles of historiography, and, first of all, their background, their causes and underlying laws, their meaning and motivation. This can be called the metaphysics of history. Secondly, it concerns itself with the cognitive part, i.e. with historic understanding, and then it is called the logic of history. While in earlier times the philosophy of history was predominantly metaphysics, it has turned more and more to the methodology or logic of history. A complete philosophy of history, however, ought to consider the metaphysical as well as the logical problems involved.

I. *Logic of History*: The historical objects under observation (man, life, society, biological and geological conditions) are so diverse that even slight mistakes in evaluation of items and of the historical whole may lead to false results. This can be seen from the modern logic of history. In the 18th century, G. B. Vico contended, under the deep impression of the lawfulness prevailing in natural sciences, that historical events also follow each other according to unswerving natural laws. He assumed three stages of development, that of fantasy, of will, and of science. The encyclopedists and Saint-Simon shared his view. The individual is immersed, and driven on, by the current of social tendencies, so that Comte used to speak of an *histoire sans noms.* His three stages of development were the theological, metaphysical, and scientific stage. H. Spencer and A. Fouillée regard social life as an organism unfolding itself according to immanent laws, either of racial individuality (Gobineau, Vocher de Lapauge) or of a combination of social, physical, and personal forces (Taine). The spirit of a people and of an age outweigh completely the power of an individual personality which can work only along socially conditioned tendencies. The development of a nation always follows the same laws, it may vary as to time and whereabouts but never as to the form Burkhardt, Lamprecht). To this group of historians belong also O Spengler and K. Marx: "Fate" rules the civilization of peoples and pushes them on to their final destination. Idealists regard such an equalization of physical laws and psychological, historical laws as untenable. The "typical case" with which physics or chemistry analyzes is a result of logical abstraction; the object of history, however, is not a unit with universal traits but something individual, in a singular space and at a particular time, never repeatable under the same circumstances. Therefore no physical laws can be formed about it. What makes it a fact worthy of historical interest, is just the fullness of live activity in it; it is a "value," not a "thing." Granted that historical events are exposed to influences from biological, geological, racial and traditional sources, they are always carried by a human being whose singularity of character has assimilated the forces of his environment and surmounted them. There is a reciprocal action between man and society, but it is always personal initiative and free productivity of the individual which account for history. Denying, therefore, the logical primacy of physical laws in history, does not mean lawlessness, and that is the standpoint of the logic of history in more recent times. Windelband and H. Rickert established another kind of historical order of laws. On their view, to understand history one must see the facts in their relation to a universally applicable and transcendental system of values. Values "are" not, they "hold;" they are not facts but realities of our reason; they are not developed but discovered. According to Max Weber historical facts form an ideally typical, transcendental whole which, although seen, can never be fully explained G. Simmel went further into metaphysics: "life" is declared an historical category; it is the indefinable, last reality ascending to central values which shaped cultural epochs, such as the medieval idea of God, or the Renaissance idea of Nature, only to be tragically disappointed, whereupon other values rise up, as humanity, liberty, technique, evolution and others.

This opposition of natural sciences *(Naturwissenschaften)* and cultural or socio-historical sciences *(Geisteswissenschaften)* is characteristic of idealistic philosophies of history, especially of the modern German variety. See Max Weber, *Gesamm. Aufrätze z. Sozio u Sozialpolitik,* 1922; W. Windelband, *Geschichte u. Naturwissenschaft,* 1894; H. Rickert, *Die Grenzen d. Naturwiss. Begriffsbildung, eine logische Einleitung i. d. histor. Wissenschaften,* 1899; Dilthey *(q.v.);* E. Troeltsch, *Der Historismus, u. s. Probleme,* 1922; E. Spranger, *Die Grundlagen d. Geschichteswissench,* 1905.

For the opposing, more empirical approach and criticisms of the idealistic, organismic philosophies of history, see M. Mandelbaum, *The Problem of Historical Knowledge,* 1939; F. J. E. Teggart, *The Method of History;* Ph. P. Wiener, "Methodology in the Philos. of Hist.". *Jour. of Philos.* (June 5, 1941).

II. *Metaphysics of History*: The metaphysical interpretations of the meaning of history are either supra-mundane or intra-mundane (secular). The oldest extra-mundane, or theological interpretation, has been given by St. Augustine *(Civitas Dei),* Dante *(Divina Commedia)* and J. Milton *(Paradise Lost* and *Regained).* All historic events are seen as having a bearing upon the redemption of mankind through Christ which will find its completion at the end of this world. Owing to the secularistic tendencies of modern times the Enlightenment Period considered the final end of human history as the achievement of public welfare through the power of reason. Even the ideal of "humanity" of the classic humanists, advocated by Schiller, Goethe, Fichte, Rousseau, Lord Byron, is only a variety of the philosophy of the Enlightenment, and in the same line of thought we find A. Comte, H. Spencer ("human moral"), Engels and K. Marx. The German Idealism of Kant and Hegel saw in history the materialization of the "moral reign of freedom" which achieves its perfection in the "objective spirit of the State." As in the earlier systems of historical logic man lost his individuality before the forces of natural laws, so, according to Hegel, he is nothing but an instrument of the "idea" which develops itself through the three dialectic stages of thesis, anti-thesis, and synthesis. (Example: *Absolutism, Democracy, Constitutional Monarchy.*) Even the great historian L.v. Ranke could not break the captivating power of the Hegelian mechanism. Ranke places every historical epoch into a relation to God and attributes to it a purpose and end for itself. Lotze and Troeltsch followed in his footsteps. Lately, the evolutionistic interpretation of H. Bergson is much discussed and disputed. His "vital impetus" accounts for the progressiveness of life, but fails to interpret the obvious setbacks and decadent civilizations. According to Kierkegaard and Spranger, merely human ideals prove to be too narrow a basis for the tendencies, accomplishments, norms, and defeats of historic life. It all points to a supramundane intelligence which unfolds itself in history. That does not make superfluous a natural interpretation; both views can be combined to understand history as an endless struggle between God's will and human will, or non-willing, for that matter.—*S.v.F.*

Ho: (a) Harmony; being "neither too weak nor too strong." "When the passions, such as joy, anger, grief, and pleasure, have not awakened, that is our central self, or moral being (chung). When these passions awaken and each and all attain due measure and degree, that is harmony, or the moral order (ho). Our central self or moral being is the great basis of existence, and harmony or moral order is the universal law in the world." See *Chung.*

(b) Change and transformation in the proper order.

(c) Peace; meekness; amiability.—*W.T.C.*

Ho: Co-existence, one of the proofs of agreement. See *Mo chê.—W.T.C.*

Hobbes, Thomas: (1588-1679) Considering knowledge empirical in origin and results, and philosophy inference of causes from effects and *vice versa,* regarded matter and motion as the least common denominators of all our percepts, and bodies and their movements as the only subject matter of philosophy. Consciousness in its sensitive and cognitive aspects is a jarring of the nervous system; in its affectional and volitional, motor aspects, a kick-back to the jar. Four subdivisions of philosophy cover all physical and psychological events: *geometry* describing the spatial movements of bodies; *physics,* the effects of moving bodies upon one another; *ethics,* the movements of nervous systems; *politics,* the effects of nervous systems upon one another. The first law of motion appears in every organic body in its tendency, which in man becomes a natural *right,* to self-preservation and self-assertion. Hence the primary condition of all organic as of all inorganic bodies is one of collision, conflict, and war. The second law of motion, in its organic application, impels men to relinquish a portion of their natural right to self-assertion in return for a similar relinquishment on the part of their fellows. Thus a component of the antagonistic forces of clashing individual rights and wills is established, embodied in a social contract, or treaty of peace, which is the basis of the *state.* To enforce this social covenant entered into, pursuant to the second law of motion, by individuals naturally at war in obedience to the first, *sovereignty* must be set up and exercised through *government.* Government is most efficient when sovereignty, which has in any case to be delegated in a community of any size, is delegated to one man—an absolute monarch—rather than to a group of men, or a parliament.

Main works: *De corpore (On bodies); De homine (On Man); De cive (On the state); The Elements of Law,* 1640; *Leviathan,* 1650.—*B.A.G.F.*

Hocking, William Ernest: (1873-1966) Professor in the Department of Philosophy at Harvard. Has endeavored to blend idealism with pragmatism while making some concessions to realism, even as in current theory he strives for a reconciliation between laissez faire liberalism and collectivism through a midground found in the worth of the individual in a "commotive union in the coagent state," a notion comparable to the "conjunct self" of George Herbert Palmer only with a more individualistic emphasis and a current flavor. Among his works are: *The Meaning of God in Human Experience, Man and the State, Types of Philosophy, Lasting Elements of Individualism,* and *Living Religions and a World Faith.*—*L.E.D.*

Hodgson, Shadworth: (1852-1913) English writer who had no profession and who held no public office. He displayed throughout a long life a keen devotion to philosophy. He was among the founders of the Aristotelian Society and served as its president for fourteen years. His earlier work was reshaped in a monumental four volume treatise called *The Metaphysic of Experience.* He viewed himself as correcting and completing the Kantian position in his comparatively materialistic approach to reality with a recognition of the unseen world prompted by a practical, moral compulsion rather than speculative conviction.—*L.E.D.*

Höffding, Harald: (1843-1931) Danish philosopher at the University of Copenhagen and brilliant author of texts in psychology, history of philosophy and the philosophy of religion. He held that the world of reality as a whole is unknowable although we may believe that conscious experience and its unity afford the best keys to unlock the metaphysical riddle. His system of thought is classified on the positive side as a cautious idealistic monism (his own term is "critical monism").

Main works: *Philosophy of Religion,* 1901; *Kierkegaard; Rousseau; History of Modern Philosophy.*—*V.F.*

Holbach, Paul Henri Thiry, Baron d': (1723-1789) One of the Encyclopedists (*q.v.*) and a prominent materialist. He is the probable author of *Le Système de la Nature,* known as "the Bible of Atheism."—*R.B.W.*

Holism: See *Emergent Evolutionism.*

Holmes, Oliver Wendell: (1841-1935) Justice of the United States Supreme Court and philosopher of law, author of *The Common Law* (1881) and advocate of judicial restraint. He argued that the only acceptable basis for limiting the freedom of speech would depend upon demonstration of "a clear and present danger."—*S.E.N.*

Holy: (AS. *halig*) The symbolically universal value of things. That aspect of value which reflects the totality, or God. The totality of value.—*J.K.F.*

Hominism: (Lat. *homo,* Man) German term (proposed by Windelband) for pragmatic humanism or psychologism.—*W.L.*

Homoeomeries: (Gr. *homoiomere*) In Aristotle's philosophy those bodies that are divisible into parts qualitatively identical with one another and with the whole, such as the metals and the tissues of living organisms; in distinction from bodies whose parts are qualitatively unlike one another and the whole, such as the head of an animal or the leaf of a plant.—*G.R.M.*

See *Anaxagoras.*

Homogeneity: (Lat. *homogeneitas*) The condition of having similar parts; uniformity of composition; identity of kind. Hamilton's Law of, "that however different any two concepts may be, they both are subordinate to some higher concept—things most unlike must in some respects be like." Employed by H. Spencer (1820-1903) to denote the absence of differentiation in the cosmic material. Opposite of heterogeneity (*q.v.*). —*J.K.F.*

Homotheism: (Lat. *homo,* man; Gr. *theos,* god) another name for anthropomorphism (*q.v.*) coined by Ernst Häckel.

Hook, Sidney: (1902-   ) Influenced by Marxism in early years, finding in it important parallels with Pragmatism, Hook soon became disenchanted with communism and opposed the Leninist-Stalinist wing.

Born in New York City December 20, 1902, Hook was educated at CCNY (under Cohen) and Columbia (under Dewey), receiving his Ph.D. in 1927. He taught in the New York City public schools, at Columbia's summer session, and at the Washington Square College of NYU.

He is an empiricist because "empiricism is more likely to be critical, socially, than intuitionism." He insists that "every philosopher has a set of value judgments." His philosophical work illustrates his own firmly held set of such judgments.

He is the author of many books, including *The Metaphysics of Pragmatism* (1927), *From Hegel to Marx* (1936), *Reason, Social Myths and Democracy* (1940), *The Hero in History* (1943), *Education for Modern Man* (1946), *The Paradoxes of Freedom* (1962), *The Place of Religion in a Free Society* (1968), *The Idea of a Modern University* (1974), *Revolution, Reform, and Social Justice: Studies in the Theory and Practice of Marxism* (1975), *Philosophy and Public Policy* (1980).—*S.E.N.*

Howison, George Holmes: (1834-1916) A teacher at the University of California. He regarded the tendency of monistic thinking as the most vicious in contemporary philosophy. Opposed absolute idealism or cosmic theism for its thoroughgoing monism because of its destruction of the implications of experience, its reduction to solipsism and its resolution into pantheism. His "personalistic idealism," unlike absolute idealism, did not negate the uniqueness and the moral nature of finite selves. Moreover, *a priori* consciousness is a human, not a divine original consciousness within the individual mind.—*H.H.*

Hsiang: (a) Phenomenon.

(b) Form or image.

(c) Secondary Modes (or Forms), namely, Major Yang, Minor Yang, Major Yin, and Minor Yin, which are engendered by the Two Primary Modes, Yin and Yang, products of the Great Ultimate (T'ai Chi).

(d) Hexagram, which, in the system of changes (i), is a symbol representing a phenomenon noted or perceived in nature, and suggestive of an idea or form according to which a thing or an activity may be realized.—*W.T.C.*

Hsiao: Filial piety; love of parents; serving and supporting one's parents in the best way. It is "the standard of Heaven, the principle of Earth, and the basis for the conduct of Man," "the basis of morality and the root of culture." "It begins with serving one's parents, extends to the duties towards one's sovereign, and ends in the establishment of one's personal character." "It is the beginning of morality, as respect for elders (ti) is the order of morality;" it is "the actuality of benevolence (jên)" as respect for elders is "the actuality of righteousness (i)." As such "it involves loving kindness to relatives, respect to associates, benevolence to friends, and good faith to acquaintances." "True manhood (jên) means to make filial piety the basis of manhood; righteousness (i) means to give it proper application; being true to the nature of the self (chung) means to make it the central moral ideal; moral order (li) is to put it to actual practice, and truthfulness (hsin) means to make it strong."—*W.T.C.*

Hsiao i: "The little unit" is the smallest that has nothing within itself. See *Pien chê*. (Sophists.)—*H.H.*

Hsiao jen: (a) The inferior man, the small man, the mean man, the vulgar man. The opposite of the superior man. See *Chün tzǔ*.

(b) Common man; little man; uneducated man; particularly as distinguished from the ruling class and the literati.—*W.T.C.*

Hsiao ku: Minor cause. See *Ku*.

Hsiao t'i: The senses which man shares with animals are "the part of man which is small," making him not merely an inferior man, but a mere animal. Not man's nature, but his animal nature. (Mencius.)—*H.H.*

Hsiao t'ung i: The little similarity-and-difference; a great similarity differs from a little similarity. See *Pien chê*. (Sophists.)—*H.H.*

Hsiao yao yu: The happy excursion, that is, roaming outside of the realm of matter, following nature, and drifting in the Infinite, resulting in transcendental bliss. (Chuang Tzǔ, between 399 and 295 B.C.)—*W.T.C.* .

Hsi ch'ang: Practicing the Eternal; i.e., "seeing what is small," "preserving one's weakness," "employing the light," and "reverting to enlightenment to avoid disaster to life." (Lao Tzǔ.)—*W.T.C.*

Hsien: The Confucians and Mohists demand that people of "superior moral character" should be rewarded and put in power, irrespective of their previous achievements; or "better," someone above the normal level of human capacity, almost a sage.—*H.H.*

Hsin: (a) Heart; mind.

(b) The original or intuitive mind of man which is good (Mencius).

(c) Human desires (the hsin of man as different from the hsin of the Confucian Moral Law or tao).

(d) The Mind which is identical with the Great Ultimate (T'ai Chi). (Shao K'ang-chieh, 1011-1077.)

(e) One aspect of the Nature (hsing). "When the Nature is viewed from its goodness, it is the Moral Law (tao); when it is viewed from its essence, it is the Destiny (ming); when it is viewed from its natural state of spontaneity, it is Heaven (T'ien); and when it is viewed from its manifestations, it is the Mind (hsin.)" (Ch'eng I-ch'uan, 1033-1107.)

(f) "the pure and refined portion of the vital force, ch'i." Being such it "has the Great Ultimate as its Reason (li) and Yin and Yang as its passivity and activity." It is the spiritual faculty or consciousness of man. (Chu Hsi, 1130-1200.)

(g) The mind conceived as identical with the Universe and Reason (li). (Lu Hsiangshan, 1139-1193.)

(h) The mind conceived as identical with Reason (li) and intuition. (Wang Yang-ming, 1473-1529.)—*W.T.C.*

Hsin: (a) Good faith, one of the Five Cardinal Confucian Virtues (wu ch'ang); honesty; sincerity; truthfulness; truth. (Confucianism.) "Actualization of honesty (chung)." (Ch'êng Ming-tao, 1032-1086.) See *Chung*.

(b) Belief; trust.

(c) Power, or the efficacy of the essence of Tao. (Lao Tzǔ.)—*W.T.C.*

Hsin chai: "Fasting of the mind" is a state of pure experience in which one has no intellectual knowledge, in which there is immediate presentation; the attainment of the mystical state of unity. (Chuang Tzǔ between 399 and 295 B.C.)—*H.H.*

Hsing: The nature of man and things, especially human nature, understood as "what is inborn," or "what is created." It is what is imparted by Heaven, whereas what is received by man and things is fate (ming). The original state of the nature is tranquil. In its aroused state, when it comes into contact with the external world, it becomes feelings (ch'ing).

To Kao Tzŭ, contemporary of Mencius, human nature is capable of being good or evil; to Mencius (c. 371—289 B.C.), good; to Hsün Tzŭ (c. 355—238 B.C.) evil; to Tung Chung-shu (c. 177—104 B.C.), potentially good; to Yang Hsiung (d. 18 B.C.), both good and evil; to Han Yü (676—824 A.D.), good in some people, mixed in some, and evil in others; to Li Ao (d. c. 844), capable of being "reverted" to its original goodness. To the whole Neo-Confucian movement, what is inborn is good, but due to external influence, there is both goodness and evil. Chang Hêng-ch'ü (1020-1077) said that human nature is good in all men. The difference between them lies in their skill or lack of skill in returning to accord with their original nature. To Ch'êng I-ch'uan (1033-1107) and Ch'êng Ming-tao (1032-1193), man's nature is the same as his vital force (ch'i). They are both the principle of life. In principle there are both good and evil in the vital force with which man is involved. Man is not born with these opposing elements in his nature. Due to the vital force man may become good or evil. Chu Hsi (1130-1200) regarded the nature as identical with Reason (li). Subjectively it is the nature; objectively it is Reason. It is the framework of the moral order (tao), with benevolence, righteousness, propriety, and wisdom (ssŭ) tuan) inherent in it. Evil is due to man's failure to preserve a harmonious relation between his nature-principles. Wang Yang-ming (1473-1529) identified the nature with the mind, which is Reason and originally good.—*W.T.C.*

Hsing (erh) hsia: What is within the realm of corporeality. See *Hsing (erh) shang*.

Hsing li hsueh: Philosophy of the Nature and Reason of man and things. See *Li hsüeh.—W.T.C.*

Hsing ming (chia): The school which advocated government by law (which includes punishment, hsing) and insisted on the correspondence of names (ming) to reality, as represented by Shên Tzŭ (fourth century B.C.), Han Fei Tzŭ (d. 233 B.C.), etc. Another name for the Legalist School (fa chia). When hsing is interpreted in the sense of shape to which names must correspond, the term is also applied to the Sophists (ming chia). —*W.T.C.*

Hsing (erh) shang: What is above corporeality, such as The Moral Law (tao), Reason (li), etc., the general principle of which is the Great Ultimate (T'ai Chi), as contrasted with what is within the realm of corporeality, such as the vital force (ch'i), a material thing (ch'i), etc., the general principles of which are the active (yang) and passive (yin) cosmic forces. (Confucianism and Neo-Confucianism.)—*W.T.C.*

Hsiu shen: Cultivating one's personal life, which involves investigation of things, extension of knowledge, sincerity of the will, and rectification of the heart, and which results in the harmony of family life, order in the state, and world peace. (Confucianism.)—*W.T.C.*

Hsu: (a) Emptiness; non-existence, a major characteristic of Tao.

(b) Emptiness of mind in the sense of absolute peace and purity (Taoism), and also in the sense of "not allowing what is already in the mind to disturb what is coming into the mind." (Hsün Tzŭ, c. 335—288 B.C.)—*W.T.C.*

Hsuan: (a) Mysterious; profound; abstruse.

(b) Another name for Tao, understood in the sense of "Mystery of mysteries, the gate to all existence." (Lao Tzŭ.)

(c) The Supremely Profound Principle. See *T'a hsüan.*

(d) The heavens.—*W.T.C.*

Hsuan chiao: The Doctrine of Mystery, another name for the Taoist religion.—*W.T.C.*

Hsuan chieh: Emancipation, to let nature take its course, to be at home with pleasant situations and at ease with misfortune, and not to be affected by sorrow and joy. (Chuang Tzŭ, between 399 and 295 B.C.) —*W.T.C.*

Hsuan hsueh: The system of profound and mysterious doctrines, with special reference to Taoism from the third to the fifth centuries A.D.—*W.T.C.*

Hsuan te: (Profound Virtue) "The Way produces things but does not take possession of them. It does its work but does not take pride in it. It rules over things but does not dominate them. This is called Profound Virtue." (Lao Tzŭ.)

Profound Virtue and Mysterious Power, through the cultivation of one's original nature and the returning to the character of Tao. Thus one "becomes identified with the Beginning, attains emptiness and vastness, and enters into mystic union with the Universe." (Chuang Tzŭ, between 399 and 295 B.C.)—*W.T.C.*

Hsuan tsung: The Religion of Mystery, another name for the Taoist religion—*W.T.C.*

Hsuen men: The School of Mystery, another name for the Taoist religion.—*W.T.C.*

Hsün Tzŭ: (Hsün Ch'ing, Hsün Kuan, c. 335—286 B.C.) For thirty years travelled, offered his service to the various powerful feudal states, and succeeded in becoming a high officer of Ch'i and Ch'u. A great critic of all contemporary schools, he greatly developed Confucianism, became the greatest Confucian except Mencius. Both Han Fei, the outstanding Legalist, and Li Ssŭ, the premier of Ch'in who effected the first unification of China, were his pupils. (*Hsün Tzŭ*, Eng. tr. by H. H. Dubs: *The Works of Hsun Tze*.)—*W.T.C.*

Hsu wu: (a) Emptiness and non-existence referring to Tao which is so full and real that it appears to be empty and non-existent. "It is in the empty and the non-existent where Tao is found." (Huai-nan Tzŭ, d. 122 B.C.)

(b) Absence of desire and egotism. (Taoism)—*W.T.C.*

Hua: Change, whether natural or infra-natural; transformation; the culmination of the process of change (pien); change from non-*ens* to *ens;* sudden change. —*W.T.C.*

Huai-nan Tzŭ: (Liu An, Prince of Huai-nan, d. 122 B.C.) Grandson of the founder of the Han dynasty, was a man of Confucian traditions with Taoist inclinations. Thousands of scholars, experts and Taoist magician-priests gathered around him. When his rebellion failed, he committed suicide, leaving *Huai-nan Hung-lieh* (partial Eng. tr. by E. Morgan:*Tao the Great Luminant*) and other works now extinct.—*W.T.C.*

Huang Lao: The teachings of the Yellow Emperor and Lao Tzu which emphasized the nourishing of one's original nature and which were very influential in the Han dynasty (206 B.C.—220 A.D.).—*W.T.C.*

Huang T'ien: August Heaven, identical with *Shang Ti.*

Hugo of St. Victor: (1096-1141) He was among the leading mystics and presented his summary of theological arguments in his contribution to the popular summa of the so-called summists in his "Summa sententiarum."—*L.E.D.*

Huizinga, Johan: (1872-1945) Professor of Philosophy at the University of Leyden, Holland. He has been a pronounced exponent of the philosophy of culture which he describes as a condition of society in which there is a harmonious balance of material and spiritual values and a harmonious ideal spurring the community's activities to a convergence of all efforts toward the attainment of that ideal. His best known work is *Homo Ludens.*—*L.E.D.*

Humanism: (Lat. *humanus,* human*)* (a) Any view in which the welfare and happiness of mankind in this life is primary.

(b) The Renaissance revolt against religious limitations on knowledge, with a revival of classical learning and a stress on man's enjoying this existence to the utmost.

(c) A twentieth-century philosophy — naturalistic Humanism — or religion that rejects belief in all forms of the supernatural; that considers the greater good of all humanity on this earth as the supreme ethical goal; and that relies on the methods of reason, science and democracy for the solution of human problems. Auguste Comte's Positivism and British Utilitarianism were forerunners of naturalistic Humanism, which in its general position is close to Naturalism and Materialism. In the United States, Humanism receives organizational support through the American Humanist Association, and in the world at large through the International Humanist and Ethical Union.

(d) An outmoded form of Pragmatism propounded by the Oxford don, F. C. S. Schiller, and emphasizing subjective elements. See *Pragmatism.*

(e) Academic or Literary Humanism founded in the early 1930s by Professors Irving Babbitt and Paul Elmer More. This short-lived movement urged a return to the classics in education and expounded a stilted morality of "decorum."—*C.L.*

Humanitarianism: (Lat. *humanus,* human) (a) Any view in which interest in human values is central.

(b) Any moral or social program seeking to lessen suffering and increase welfare of human beings, often involving intense emotional devotion to social reform, sometimes extending to prevention of cruelty to animals. Philanthropy. Altruism.

(c) Worship of Humanity. Comtean doctrine, based on positivistic science, that Humanity, rather than God or Nature is the Great Being worthy of worship.

(d) Theological doctrine denying the divinity of Christ.—*A.J.B.*

Human nature: The limited range of human possibilities. The human tendency toward, or the human capacity for, only those actions which are common in all societies despite their acquired cultural differences. See *Primitivism.*—*J.K.F.*

Hume, David: Born 1711, Edinburgh; died at Edinburgh, 1776. Author of *A Treatise of Human Nature, Enquiry Concerning the Human Understanding, Enquiry Concerning the Passions, Enquiry Concerning Morals, Natural History of Religion, Dialogues on Natural Religion, History of England,* and many essays on letters, economics, etc. Hume's intellectual heritage is divided between the Cartesian Occasionalists and Locke and Berkeley. From the former, he obtained some of his arguments against the alleged discernment or demonstrability of causal connections, and from the latter his psychological opinions. Hume finds the source of cognition in impressions of sensation and reflection. All simple ideas are derived from and are copies of simple impressions. Complex ideas may be copies of complex impressions or may result from the imaginative combination of simple ideas. Knowledge results from the comparison of ideas, and consists solely of the intrinsic resemblance between ideas. As resemblance is nothing over and above the resembling ideas, there are no abstract general ideas: the generality of ideas is determined by their habitual use as representatives of all ideas and impressions similar to the representative ideas. As knowledge consists of relations of ideas in virtue of resemblance, and as the only relation which involves the connection of different existences and the inference of one existent from another is that of cause and effect, and as there is no resemblance necessary between cause and effect, causal inference is in no case experientially or formally certifiable. As the succession and spatio-temporal contiguity of cause and effect suggests no necessary connection and as the constancy of this relation, being mere repetition, adds no new idea (which follows from Hume's nominalistic view), the necessity of causal connection must be explained psychologically. Thus the impression of reflection, i.e., the felt force of association, subsequent to frequent repetitions of conjoined impressions, is the source of the idea of necessity. Habit or custom sufficiently accounts for the feeling that everything which begins must have a cause and that similar causes must have similar effects. The arguments which Hume adduced to show that no logically necessary connection between distinct existences can be intuited or demonstrated are among his most signal contributions to philosophy, and were of great importance in influencing the speculation of Kant.

Hume explained belief in external existence (bodies) in terms of the propensity to feign the independent and continued existence of perceptual complexes during the interruptions of perception. This propensity is determined by the constancy and coherence which some perceptual complexes exhibit and by the transitive power of the imagination to go beyond the limits afforded by knowledge and ordinary causal belief. The sceptical principles of his epistemology were carried over into his views on ethics and religion. Because there are no logically compelling arguments for moral and religious propositions, the principles of morality and religion must be explained naturalistically in terms of human mental habits and social customs. Morality thus depends on such fundamental aspects of human nature as self-interest and altruistic sympathy. Hume's views on religion are difficult to determine from his Dialogues, but a reasonable opinion is that he is totally sceptical concerning the possibility of proving the existence or the nature of deity. It is certain that he found no connection between the nature of deity and the rules of morality.—*J.R.W.*

Humor: (a) Jocose imagination; sympathetic wit.

(b) Romantic irony, equivalent of the triumph of the creative power of the artist's soul over all content and all form (Hegel).—*L.V.*

Hun: (C.) The active, positive, or heavenly (yang) part of the soul, as contrasted with the passive, negative, or earthly (yin) part of the soul called p'o. Hun is the soul of man's vital force (ch'i) which is expressed in man's intelligence and power of breathing, whereas p'o is the spirit of man's physical nature which is expressed in bodily movements. In heavenly spirits, hun predominates, whereas in earthly spirits, p'o predominates. When hun is separated from p'o in man or things, change ensues.—*W.T.C.*

Hung fan: The Grand Norm. See *Chiu ch'ou*.

Hun mang: The Taoist conception of the Golden Age, in which there was in the beginning, in the time of the primeval chaos, a state of absolute harmony between man and his surroundings, a life as effortless and spontaneous as the passage of the seasons, the two cosmic principles of yin and yang worked together instead of in opposition—*H.H.*

Husserl, Edmund: 1859-1938. See *Phenomenology*.

Main works of Husserl: *Philosophie der Arithmetik,* 1891; *Logische Untersuchungen,* 1900; *Ideen z. e. reinen Phänomenologie u. Phenomologische Philos.,* 1913; *Vorlesungen z. Phänom. d. inneren Bewusstseine,* 1928; *Formale u. transz. Logik,* 1929; *Méditations Cartésiennes Introd. à la Phénoménologie,* 1931; *Die Krisis der europäischen Wissensch u.d. fransz. Phänomenologie, I,* 1936; *Erfahrung u. Urteil. Untersuch. z. Genealogie der Logik,* 1939.

Hussism: The Reformatory views of John Hus (1370-1415). A popular agitator and finally martyr, Hus stood between Wycliffe and Luther in the line of continental Protestant Reformers. He rested authority upon Scripture and defied ecclesiastical bans. The Hussite wars (1419-1432) following his death epitomized the grow-

ing nationalism and desire for religious reform.—*V.F.*

Hutcheson, Francis: (1694-1746) A prominent Scottish philosopher. Born in Drumalig, Ulster, educated at Glasgow, died in Dublin. The influence of his doctrine of "moral sense," stressing inborn conscience or "moral feeling," was very wide; he was also the original author of the phrase "the greatest happiness for the greatest number," utilized by J. Bentham (*q.v.*) for the development of utilitarianism (*q.v.*) His principal work is *Inquiry into the Origin of Our Ideas of Beauty and Virtue.*—*R.B.W.*

Huxley, Thomas Henry: (1825-1895) Was a renowned English scientist who devoted his mastery of expository and argumentative prose to the defense of evolutionism. An example of his scintillating style can be found in his famous essay on "A Piece of Chalk." His works touched frequently on ethical problems and bore much of the brunt of the raging controversy between religion and science. He is credited with having invented the word "agnosticism," adopted by Herbert Spencer. See *Evolutionism.*—*L.E.D.*

Cf. H. Peterson, *Thomas Huxley,* for biography and bibliography.

Hyle: See *Matter*.

Hylomorphism: (also *hylemorphism*. Gr. *hyle,* matter; and *morphē,* contour, form) A theory that all physical things are constituted of two internal principles: the one of which remains the same throughout all change and is the passive basis of continuity and identity in the physical world, called *prime matter;* the other of which is displaced, or removed from actuation of its matter, in every substantial change, called *substantial form*. See *Aristotelianism, Thomism, Suarezianism.*—*V.J.B.*

Hylons: This name (combining the Greek words *hyle,* matter, and *on,* being) was given by Mitterer to the heterogeneous subatomic and subelemental particles of matter (electrons, neutrons, protons, positrons) which enter into the composition of the elements without being elements themselves. The natural elements represent distinct types or species of natural bodies, while the hylons do not. These matter-particles have an important role in the exposition of the cosmological doctrine of hylosystemism.—*T.G.*

Hylosis: The material states concomitant with a psychosis. (Montague.)—*H.H.*

Hylosystemism: A cosmological theory developed by Mitterer principally, which explains the constitution of the natural inorganic body as an atomary energy system. In opposition to hylomorphism which is considered inadequate in the field of nuclear physics, this system maintains that the atom of an element and the molecule of a compound are really composed of subatomic particles united into a dynamic system acting as a functional unit. The main difference between the two doctrines is the *hylomeric* constitution of inorganic matter: the plurality of parts of a particle form a whole which is more than the sum of the parts, and which gives to a body its specific essence. While hylomorphism contends that no real substantial change can occur in a hylomeric constitution besides the alteration of the specific form, hylosystemism maintains that in substantial change more remains than primary matter and more changes than the substantial form.—*T.G.*

Hylotheism: (Gr. *hyle* matter, and *theism, q.v.*). A synonym for either pantheism or materialism in that this doctrine identifies matter and god, or has the one merge into the other.—*K.F.L.*

Hylozoism: Gr. *hyle,* matter, *zoe,* life) The doctrine that life is a property of matter, that matter and life are inseparable, that life is derived from matter, or that matter has spiritual properties. The conception of nature as alive or animated, of reality as alive. The original substance as bearing within itself the cause of all motion and change. The early Greek cosmologists of the Milesian school made statements which implied a belief in life for their primary substances. For Straton of Lampsacus each of the ultimate particles of matter possesses life. For the Stoics the universe as a whole is alive. For Spinoza different kinds of things possess life in different grades.—*J.K.F.*

Hyperaesthesia: (Gr. *hyper* + *aesthesis,* sensation) Excessive sensitivity, either sensory or affective. —*L.W.*

Hyperbole: (Gr. *hyperbole,* over-shooting, excess) In rhetoric, that figure of speech according to which expressions gain their effect through exaggeration. The representation of things as greater or less than they really are, not intended to be accepted literally. Aristotle relates, for example, that when the winner of a mule-race paid enough money to a poet who was not anxious to praise half-assess, the poet wrote, "Hail, daughters of storm-footed steeds" (*Rhetoric,* III. ii. 14).—*J.K.F.*

Hypnosis: (Gr. *hypnos,* sleep) A trance-like state characterized by an exaggerated suggestibility and an alteration of the normal functions of memory, of personality and perhaps also of perception. The state is ordinarily induced by another person, but may also be self-induced and then the phenomenon is called autohypnosis.—*L.W.*

Hypnotism: A general term used to designate hypnotic phenomena including the techniques for inducing hypnosis (see *Hypnosis*), the therapeutic uses of hypnotic suggestion, etc.—*L.W.*

Hypostasis: Literally the Greek word signifies that which stands under and serves as a support. In philosophy it means a singular substance, also called a supposite, *suppositum,* by the Scholastics, especially if the substance is a completely subsisting one, whether non-living or living, irrational or rational. However, a rational hypostasis has the same meaning as the term, person.—*J.J.R.*

Hypothesis: 1. *In general,* an assumption, a supposition, a conjecture, a postulate, a condition, an antecedent, a contingency, a possibility, a probability, a principle, a premiss, a ground or foundation, a tentative explanation, a probable cause, a theoretical situation, an academic question, a specific consideration, a conceded statement, a theory or view for debate or action, a likely relation, the conditioning of one thing by another.

2. *In logic,* the conditional clause or antecedent in a hypothetical proposition. Also a thesis subordinate to a more general one.

3. *In methodology,* a principle offered as a conditional explanation of a fact or a group of facts; or again, a provisional assumption about the ground of certain phenomena, used as a guiding norm in making observations and experiments until verified or disproved by subsequent evidence. A hypothesis is conditional or provisional, because it is based on probable and insufficient arguments or elements; yet, it is not an arbitrary opinion, but a justifiable assumption with some foundation in fact; this accounts for the expectation of some measure of agreement between the logical conclusion or implications drawn from a hypothesis, and the phenomena which are known or which may be determined by further tests. A scientific hypothesis must be: (1) proposed after the observations it must explain (a posteriori), (2) compatible with established theories, (3) reasonable and relevant, (4) fruitful in its applications and controllable, (5) general in terms and more fundamental than the statements it has to explain. A hypothesis is descriptive (forecasting the external circumstances of the event) or explanatory (offering causal accounts of the event). There are two kinds of explanatory hypotheses: (1) the *hypothesis of law* (or genetic hypothesis) which attempts to determine the manner in which the causes or conditions of a phenomenon operate and (2) the *hypothesis of cause* (or causal hypothesis) which attempts to determine the causes or conditions for the production of the phenomenon. A *working hypothesis* is a preliminary assumption based on few, uncertain or obscure elements, which is used provisionally as a guiding norm in the investigation of certain phenomena. Often, the difference between a working hypothesis and a scientific hypothesis is one of degree; and in any case, a hypothesis is seldom verified completely with all its detailed implications.

4. The Socratic *Method of Hypothesis,* as developed by Plato in the *Phaedo* particularly, consists in positing an assumption without questioning its value, for the purpose of determining and analyzing its consequences: only when these are clearly debated and judged, the assumption itself is considered for justification or rejection. Usually, a real condition is taken as a ground for inferences, as the aim of the method is to attain knowledge or to favor action. Plato used more specially the word "hypothesis" for the assumptions of geometry (postulates and nominal definitions); Aristotle extended this use to cover the immediate principles of mathematics. It may be observed that the modern *hypothetico-deductive method* in logical and mathematical theories, is a development of the Socratic method stripped of its ontological implications and purposes.—*T.G.*

Hypothetical sentence or proposition is the same as a *conditional* (*q.v.*) sentence or proposition.—*A.C.*

Hypothetical dualism: In epistemology, the theory that the external world is known only by inference. Absolute dualism of mind and external world. Opposite of presentational realism—*J.K.F.*

Hypothetical imperatives: Term due to Kant which designates all statements of the form, "If you desire so and so, you must, should, or ought to do such and such." In such cases the obligatoriness of the action enjoined depends on the presence in the agent of the desire mentioned. See *Categorical imperative*. —*W.K.F.*

Hypothetical morality: In ethics, any moral imperative stated in hypothetical form. For instance, if thou dost not desire certain consequences, thou shalt not commit adultery. Kant's categorical imperative, stated in hypothetical form. See *Hypothesis, Morality.*—*J.K.F.*

Hypothetical syllogism: See *Logic, formal,* § 2.

Hysteron proteron: (Gr. *hysteron proteron*) Literally, making the consequent an antecedent; inverting the logical order by explaining a thing in terms of something which presupposes it.—*G.R.M.*

I

I: (C.) (a) The One, which is engendered by Tao and which in turn engenders the Two (yin and yang). (Lao Tzŭ) "The Formless is the One. The One has no compare in the universe. . . It is the Great Infinite and forms the Unity. It is the life of myriad generations, everlasting without beginning, and most mysterious. It enfolds the universe and opens the portal of Tao. . . When the One is established and the myriad things are engendered, there is Tao." (Huai-nan Tzŭ, d. 112 B.C.)

(b) Unity of mind, "not allowing one impression to harm another." (Hsün Tzŭ c. 335—288 B.C.)

(c) The number for Heaven, as two is the number for Earth. See *Ta i and T'a i.—W.T.C.*

I: The method of difference in Neo-Mohist logic, which includes duality, absence of generic relationship, separateness, and dissimilarity. "Duality means that two things necessarily differ. Absence of generic relationship means to have no connection. Separateness means that things do not occupy the same space. Dissimilarity means having nothing in common." See *Mo chê. —W.T.C.*

I: Transference, a method of appellation or designation. "To name a puppy a dog is transference." See *Chü* and *Chia* (Neo-Mohism.)—*W.T.C.*

I: Change (often spelled yi), a fundamental principle of the universe, arising out of the interaction of the two cosmic forces of yin and yang, or passive and active principles, and manifested in natural phenomena, human affairs, and ideas. According to Confucian and Neo-Confucian cosmology, "In the system of Change, there is the Great Ultimate (T'ai Chi) which engenders the Two Modes (i). The Two Modes engender the Four Secondary Modes (hsiang), which in turn give rise to the Eight Trigrams (pa kua). These Eight Trigrams (or Elements) determine all good and evil and the great complexity of life." Thus it involves in the first place, the meaning of i, or simplicity from which complexity is evolved; in the second place, the meaning of hsiang, that is, phenomenon, image, form; and in the third place, the idea of "production and reproduction."—*W.T.C.*

I: (a) Subjective opinion; preconceived notion. (Confucius, Neo-Confucianism.)

(b) The will; purpose; motive; idea; which is "operation of" and "emanation from" the mind with an objective in view (Chu Hsi, 1130-1200). It is called will "when the intuitive faculty, with its pure intelligence and clear understanding, is moved and becomes active." (Wang Yang-ming, 1473-1529.) See *Ch'eng i.—W.T.C.*

I: Righteousness, justice; one of the four Confucian Fundamentals of the Moral Life (ssŭ tuan) and the Five Constant Virtues (wu ch'ang). It is the virtue "by which things are made proper," "by which the world is regulated." It means the proper application of filial piety. It means, as in Han Yü (767-824), "the proper application of the principle of true manhood (jên)." It also means the removal of evil in the world. Mencius (371-289 B.C.) said that "righteousness is man's path, whereas true manhood is man's mind." Tung Chung-shu (177-104 B.C.) regarded it as the cardinal virtue by which one's self is rectified, whereas benevolence (jên) is the virtue by which others are pacified. To the Neo-Confucians, "seriousness (ching) is to straighten one's internal life and righteousness is to square one's external life." It is to regulate things and affairs by Reason (li).—*W.T.C.*

Ich: (Ger. I; myself; me; the ego (*q.v.*)) In the German idealistic movement from *Kant* through *Schopenhauer,* the *Ich,* the final, ultimate conscious subject, plays a central and dynamic role. Kant discredited the traditional Cartesian conception of a simple, undecomposable, substantial I, intuitively known. On his view, the *Ich* is not a substance, but the functional, dynamic unity of consciousness—a necessary condition of all experience and the ultimate subject for which all else is object. This "transcendental unity of apperception," bare consciousness as such, is by its very nature empty; it is neither a thing nor a concept. For the pure transcendental I, my empirical self is but one experience among others in the realm of phenomena, and one of which Kant does not seek an adequate definition. The stress on the pure I as opposed to the empirical self is carried over into his practical philosophy, where the moral agent becomes, not the concrete personality, but a pure rational will, i.e., a will seeking to act in accordance with an absolute universal law of duty, the categorical imperative (*q.v.*).

Fichte conceives the ultimate *Ich* as an absolute, unconditioned, simple ego which "posits" itself and its not-self in a series of intellectual acts. He emphasizes the dynamic, creative powers of the ego, its capacity for self-determination, the act in which the absolute subject creates the I. Self and not-self are products of the original activity of the conscious subject. *Schelling* conceives the I as a creation of the Absolute Idea. *Hegel*, however, treats the *Ich* as thought conceived as subject, as thinking, abstracted from all things perceived, willed or felt—in short abstracted from all experience. As such it is universal abstract freedom, an ideal unity.

From this point the notion of *Ich* in the German idealistic tradition passes into (1) voluntaristic channels, with emphasis on the dynamic will, as in Schopenhauer, Eduard von Hartmann and Nietzsche; (2) the pragmatic-psychologic interpretation, typified by Lotze and other post-idealists; and (3) such reconstructions of the transcendental I as are to be found in the school of Husserl and related groups.—*O.F.K.*

Icon: (Gr. *eikon*, image) Any sign which is like the thing it represents.—*A.C.B.*

Iconoclasm: Religious struggle against images (8th and 9th centuries) and towards symbolic art.—*L.V.*

Iconology: Studies in history of art concerned with the interpretation of the matter or subject treated by artists without consideration of their personalities.—*L.V.*

Idantā: (Skr. "this-ness") Thingness, the state of being a *this*, an object of knowledge.—*K.F.L.*

Idea: (Gr. *idéa*) This term has enjoyed historically a considerable diversity of usage.

1. In pre-Platonic Greek: form, semblance, nature, fashion or mode, class or species.

2. Plato (and Socrates?): The Idea is a timeless essence or universal, a dynamic and creative archetype of existents. The Ideas comprise a hierarchy and an organic unity in the Good, and are ideals as patterns of existence and as objects of human desire.

3. The Stoics: Ideas are class concepts in the human mind.

4. Neo-Platonism: Ideas are archetypes of things considered as in cosmic Mind (*Nous* or *Logos*).

5. Early Christianity and Scholasticism: Ideas are archetypes eternally subsistent in the mind of God.

6. 17th Century: Following earlier usage, Descartes generally identified ideas with subjective, logical concepts of the human mind. Ideas were similarly treated as subjective or mental by Locke, who identified them with all objects of consciousness. Simple ideas, from which, by combination, all complex ideas are derived, have their source either in sense perception or "reflection" (intuition of our own being and mental processes).

7. Berkeley: Ideas are sense objects or perceptions,

considered either as modes of the human soul or as a type of mind-dependent being. Concepts derived from objects of intuitive introspection, such as activity, passivity, soul, are "notions."

8. Hume: An Idea is a "faint image" or memory copy of sense "impressions."

9. Kant: Ideas are concepts or representations incapable of adequate subsumption under the categories, which escape the limits of cognition. The ideas of theoretical or Pure Reason are ideals, demands of the human intellect for the absolute, i.e., the unconditioned or the totality of conditions of representation. They include the soul, Nature and God. The ideas of moral or Practical Reason include God, Freedom, and Immortality. The ideas of Reason cannot be sensuously represented (possess no "schema"). Aesthetic ideas are representations of the faculty of imagination to which no concept can be adequate.—*W.L.*

Ideal: 1. Pertaining to ideas (*q.v.*).

2. Mental.

3. Possessing the character of completely satisfying a desire or volition. A state of perfection with respect to a standard or goal of will or desire.

4. A norm, perfect type, or goal, an object of desire or will, whether or not conceived as attainable.—*W.L.*

Idealism: Any system or doctrine whose fundamental interpretative principle is ideal. Broadly, any theoretical or practical view emphasizing mind (soul, spirit, life) or what is characteristically of pre-eminent value or significance to it. Negatively, the alternative to Materialism. (Popular confusion arises from the fact that Idealism is related to either or both uses of the adjective "ideal," *i.e.*, (a) pertaining to ideas, and (b) pertaining to ideals. While a certain inner bond of sympathy can be established between these two standpoints, for theoretical purposes they must be clearly distinguished.) Materialism emphasizes the spatial, pictorial, corporeal, sensuous, non-valuational, factual, and mechanistic. Idealism stresses the supra- or non-spatial, non-pictorial, incorporeal, suprasensuous, normative or valuational, and teleological. The term Idealism shares the unavoidable expansion of such words as Idea, Mind, Spirit, and even Person; and in consequence it now possesses usefulness only in pointing out a general direction of thought, unless qualified, *e.g.*, Platonic Idealism, Personal Idealism, Objective Idealism, Moral Idealism, etc.

The term appeared in the later 17th century to name (a) the theory of archetypal Ideas, whether in the original Platonic teaching or as incorporated into Christian Platonic and Scholastic theism; (b) the epistemological doctrine of Descartes and Locke, according to which "ideas," *i.e.*, direct objects of human apprehension, are subjective and privately possessed. Since this latter view put in doubt the very existence of a material world, the term began to be used in the early 18th century for acosmism (according to which the external world is only the projection of our minds), and immaterialism (doctrine of the non-existence of material being). Its use was popularized by Kant, who named his theory of knowledge Critical or Transcendental Idealism, and by his metaphysical followers, the Post-Kantian Idealists.

Metaphysics. *Pure Idealism* or Immaterialism identifies ontological reality (substance, substantives, concrete individuality) exclusively with the ideal, *i.e.*, Mind, Spirit, Soul, Person, Archetypal Ideas, Thought. See *Spiritualism, Mentalism, Monadism, Panpsychism, Idealistic Phenomenalism*. With respect to the metaphysical status of self-consciousness and purposeful activity, Idealism is either impersonalistic or personalistic. See *Personalism*.

Impersonalistic Idealism identifies ontological reality essentially with non-conscious spiritual principle, unconscious psychic agency, pure thought, impersonal or "pure" consciousness, pure Ego, subconscious Will, impersonal logical Mind, etc. *Personalistic Idealism* characterizes concrete reality as personal selfhood, *i.e.*, as possessing self-consciousness. With respect to the relation of the Absolute or World-Ground (*q.v.*) to finite selves or centers of consciousness, varying degress of unity or separateness are posited. The extreme doctrines are radical monism and radical pluralism. *Monistic Idealism* (pantheistic Idealism) teaches that the finite self is a part, mode, aspect, moment, appearance or projection of the One. *Pluralistic Idealism* defends both the inner privacy of the finite self and its relative freedom from direct or causal dependence upon the One. With respect to Cosmology, pure idealism is either subjective or objective. *Subjective Idealism* (acosmism) holds that Nature is merely the projection of the finite mind, and has no external, real existence. (The term "Subjective Idealism" is also used for the view that the ontologically real consists of subjects, *i.e.*, possessors of experience.) *Objective Idealism* identifies an externally real Nature with the thought or activity of the World Mind. (In Germany the term "Objective Idealism" is commonly identified with the view that finite minds are parts—modes, moments, projections, appearances, members—of the Absolute Mind.) *Epistemological Idealism* derives metaphysical idealism from the identification of objects with ideas. In its nominalistic form the claim is made that "To be is to be perceived." From the standpoint of rationalism it is argued that there can be no Object without a Subject. Subjects, relations, sensations, and feelings are mental; and since no other type of analogy remains by which to characterize a non-mental thing-in-itself, pure idealism follows as the only possible view of Being.

Realistic Idealism recognizes the reality of non-ideal types of being, but relegates them to a subordinate status with respect either to quantity of being or power. This view is either atheistic or theistic. *Realistic theism* admits the existence of one or more kinds of non-mental being considered as independently co-eternal with God, eternally dependent upon Deity, or as a divine creation. *Platonic Idealism,* as traditionally interpreted, identifies absolute being with timeless Ideas or disembodied essences. These, organically united in the Good, are the archetypes and the dynamic causes of existent, material things. The Ideas are also archetypes of rational thought, and the goal of fine art and morality. *Axiological Idealism,* a modern development of Platonism and Kantianism, maintains that the category of Value is logically and metaphysically prior to that of Being.

The idealistic doctrine known as *Conceptual Realism* identifies the logical (and at times the perceptual) content of experience with universals (essences, objectives, subsistents, etc.) considered as non-mental, *i.e.* as essentially independent of cognitive subjects.

Epistemology. *Theistic Platonism* maintains that the archetypes of existent things are eternal ideas in the mind of God. *Epistemological Idealism* teaches that all entities other than egos or subjects of experience are exclusively noetic objects, *i.e.* have no existence or reality apart from the relation of being perceived or thought. *Transcendental Idealism* (Critical Idealism) is Kant's name for his doctrine that knowledge is a synthetic, relational product of the logical self (transcendental unity of apperception). *Phenomenology* is Husserl's name for the science that investigates the essences or natures of objects considered apart from their existential or metaphysical status.

Ethics. Any system of moral theory may be called *Ethical Idealism,* whether teleological or formal in principle, which accepts several of the following: (a) a scale of values, moral principles, or rules of action; (b) the axiological priority of the universal over the particular; (c) the axiological priority of the spiritual or mental over the sensuous or material; (d) moral freedom rather than psychological or natural necessity. In popular terminology a moral idealist is also identified with the doctrinaire, as opposed to the opportunist or realist; with the Utopian or visionary as opposed to the practicalist; with the altruist as opposed to the crass egoist.

Aesthetics. Any system or program of fine art emphasizing the ideal (*q.v.*) is *Aesthetic Idealism*. 1. The view that the goal of fine art is an embodiment or reflection of the perfections of archetypal Ideas or timeless essences (Platonism). 2. The view of art which emphasizes feeling, sentiment, and idealization (as opposed to "literal reproduction" of fact). 3. The view of art which emphasizes cognitive content (as opposed to abstract feeling, primitive intuition, formal line or structure, mere color or tone).

Psychology. The doctrine that ideas or judgments are causes of thought and behavior, and not mere effects or epiphenomena, is *Psychological Idealism*.

History. Inasmuch as pure or basic Materialism has been an infrequent doctrine among major thinkers, the history of philosophy broadly understood, is largely the history of Idealism.

India. Intimations of advanced theism, both in a deistic and immanentistic form, are to be found in the *Rig Veda*. The early *Upanishads* in general teach variously realistic deism, immanent theism, and, more characteristically, mystical, impersonal idealism, according to which the World Ground (*brahman*) is identified with the universal soul (*ātman*) which is the inner or essential self within each individual person.

The *Bhagavad Gītā*, while mixing pantheism, immanent theism, and deism, inclines towards a personalistic idealism and a corresponding ethics of *bhakti* (selfless devotion). Jainism is atheistic dualism, with a personalistic recognition of the reality of souls. Many of the schools of Buddhism (see *Buddhism*) teach idealistic doctrines. Thus a monistic immaterialism and subjectivism (the Absolute is pure consciousness) was expounded by Maitreya, Asaṅga, and Vasubandhu. The *Laṅkāvatārasūtra* combined monistic, immaterialistic idealism with non-absolutistic nihilism. Subjectivistic, phenomenalistic idealism (the view that there is neither absolute Pure Consciousness nor substantial souls) was taught by the Buddhists Sāntarakṣita and Kamalaśīla. Examples of modern Vedāntic idealism are the *Yogavāsiṣtha* (subjective monistic idealism) and the monistic spiritualism of Guadapāda (duality and plurality are illusion). The most influential Vedāntic system is the monistic spiritualism of Śaṅkara. The Absolute is pure indeterminate Being, which can only be described as pure consciousness or bliss. For the different Vedāntic doctrines see *Vedānta* and the references there. Vedāntic idealism, whether in its monistic and impersonalistic form, or in that of a more personalistic theism, is the dominant type of metaphysics in modern India. Idealism is also pronounced in the reviving doctrines of Shivaism (which see).

China. The traditional basic concepts of Chinese metaphysics are ideal. Heaven (*T'ien*), the spiritual and moral power of cosmic and social order, that distributes to each thing and person its alloted sphere of action, is theistically and personalistically conceived in the *Shu Ching* (Book of History) and the *Shih Ching* (Book of Poetry). It was probably also interpreted thus by Confucius and Mencius, assuredly so by Motze. Later it became identified with Fate or impersonal, immaterial cosmic power. *Shang Ti* (Lord on High) has remained through Chinese history a theistic concept. *Tao*, as cosmic principle, is an impersonal, immaterial World Ground. Mahayana Buddhism introduced into China an idealistic influence. Pure metaphysical idealism was taught by the Buddhist monk Hsüan Ch'uang. Important Buddhist and Taoist influences appear in Sung Confucianism (*Ju Chia*), a distinctly idealistic movement. Chou Tun I taught that matter, life and mind emerge from *Wu Chi* (Pure Being). Shao Yung espoused an essential objective idealism: the world is the content of an Universal Consciousness. The Brothers Ch'eng Hsao and Ch'eng I, together with Chu Hsi, distinguished two primordial principles, an active, moral, aesthetic, and rational Law (*Li*), and a passive ether stuff (*Ch'i*). Their emphasis upon *Li* is idealistic. Lu Chiu Yuan (Lu Hsiang Shan), their opponent, is interpreted both as a subjective idealist and as a realist with a strong idealistic emphasis. Similarly interpreted is Wang Yang Ming of the Ming Dynasty, who stressed the spiritual and moral principle (*Li*) behind nature and man.

Persia. The theology of Zarathustra was a realistic and dualistic personalism. Nature is assumed to be a plastic order controlled by Ahura Mazda, personalized spirit of Good, against whom struggles in vain Ahriman, the personalized spirit of Evil.

Israel. In the period of the written prophets Jewish thought moved to a personalistic and realistic theism, reaching maturity in Jeremiah and Genesis I. The cosmic "I am" is a personal and righteous World Ground who fashions and controls both Nature and human history.

Greece. Homeric thought centered in *Moîra* (Fate), an impersonal, immaterial power that distributes to gods and men their respective stations. While the main stream of pre-Socratic thought was naturalistic, it was not materialistic. The primordial Being of things, the *Physis*, is both extended and spiritual (hylozoism). Soul and Mind are invariably identified with *Physis*. Empedocles' distinction between inertia and force (Love and Hate) was followed by Anaxagoras' introduction of Mind (*Noûs*) as the first cause of order and the principle of spontaneity or life in things. Socrates emphasized the teleological principle and introduced the category of Value as primary both in Nature and Man. He challenged the completeness of the mechanical explanation of natural events. Plato's theory of Ideas (as traditionally interpreted by historians) is at once a metaphysics, epistemology, and axiology. Ideas, forming a hierarchy and systematically united in the Good, are timeless essences comprising the realm of true Being. They are archetypes and causes of things in the realm of Non-Being (Space). Aristotle, while moving in the direction of common-sense realism, was also idealistic. Forms or species are secondary substances, and collectively form the dynamic and rational structure of the World. Active reason (*Noûs Poiétikos*), possessed by all rational creatures, is immaterial and eternal. Mind is the final cause of all motion. God is pure Mind, self-contained, self-centered, and metaphysically remote from the spatial World. The Stoics united idealism and hylozoistic naturalism in their doctrine of dynamic rational cosmic law (*Logos*), World Soul, *Pneuma*, and Providence (*Pronoia*).

Alexandrian-Roman Period. Fed by Eastern ideas, later Alexandrian-Roman thought was essentially idealistic. In Neo-Pythagorean, Neo-Platonic and Alexandrian Christianity, matter was identified with non-being, and placed at the metaphysical antipodes with respect to God or the Absolute. Early Christianity identified itself with the personalistic theism of Israel, Pauline spiritualism, and the Neo-Platonism of Alexandria.

Medieval Period. Medieval Christian thought, axiomatically idealistic, united the personalism of Israel and the speculative idealism of Neo-Platonism and Aristotle. Similarly, Islamic thought, centering at Bagdad and Cordova, attached Mohammedan religious idealism to Neo-Platonism and Aristotelianism.

Modern Period. In the 17th century the move towards scientific materialism was tempered by a general reliance on Christian or liberal theism (Galileo, Bacon, Descartes, Hobbes, Gassendi, Toland, Hartley, Priestley, Boyle, Newton). The principle of gravitation was regarded by Newton, Boyle, and others, as an indication of the incompleteness of the mechanistic and materialistic account of the World, and as a direct proof of the existence of God. For Newton, space was the "divine sensorium." The road to pure modern idealism was laid by the epistemological idealism (epistemological subjectivism) of Campanella and Descartes. The theoretical basis of Descartes' system was God, upon whose moral perfection reliance must be placed ("God will not deceive us") to insure the reality of the physical world. Spinoza's impersonalistic pantheism is idealistic to the extent that space or extension (with modes of Body and Motion) is merely one of the infinity of attributes of Being. Leibniz founded pure modern idealism by his doctrine of the immateriality and self-active character of metaphysical individual substances (monads, souls), whose source and ground is God. Locke, a theist, gave chief impetus to the modern theory of the purely subjective character of ideas. The founder of pure objective idealism in Europe was Berkeley, who shares with Leibniz the creation of European immaterialism. According to him perception is due to the direct action of God on finite persons or souls. Nature consists of (a) the totality of percepts and their order, (b) the activity and thought of God. Hume, later an implicit Naturalist, earlier subscribed ambiguously to pure idealistic phenomenalism or scepticism. Kant's epistemological, logical idealism (Transcendental or Critical Idealism) inspired the systems of pure speculative idealism of the 19th century. Knowledge, he held, is essentially logical and relational, a product of the synthetic activity of the logical self-consciousness. He also taught the ideality of space and time. Theism, logically undemonstrable, remains the choice of pure speculative reason, although beyond the province of science. It is also a practical implication of the moral life. In the *Critique of Judgment* Kant marshalled facts from natural beauty and the apparent teleological character of the physical and biological world, to leave a stronger hint in favor of the theistic hypothesis. His suggestion that reality, as well as Mind, is organic in character is reflected in the idealistic pantheisms of his followers: Fichte (abstract personalism or "Subjective Idealism"), Schelling (aesthetic idealism, theism, "Objective Idealism"), Hegel (Absolute or logical Idealism), Schopenhauer (voluntaristic idealism), Schleiermacher (spiritual pantheism), Lotze ("Teleological Idealism"). Nineteenth century French thought was grounded in the psychological idealism of Condillac and the voluntaristic personalism of Biran. Throughout the century it was essentially "spiritualistic" or personalistic (Cousin, Renouvier, Revaisson, Boutroux, Lachelier, Bergson). British thought after Hume was largely theistic (A. Smith, Paley, J. S. Mill, Reid, Hamilton). In the latter 19th century, inspired largely by Kant and his metaphysical followers, it leaned heavily towards semimonistic personalism (E. Caird, Green, Webb, Pringle-Pattison) or impersonalistic monism (Bradley, Bosanquet). Recently a more pluralistic personalism has developed (F. C. S. Schiller, A. E. Taylor, McTaggart, Ward, Sorley). Recent American idealism is represented by McCosh, Howison, Bowne, Royce, Wm. James (before 1904), Baldwin. German idealists of the past century include Fechner, Krause, von Hartmann, H. Cohen, Natorp, Windelband, Rickert, Dilthey, Brentano, Eucken. In Italy idealism is represented by Croce and Gentile; in Spain, by Unamuno and Ortega y Gasset; in Russia, by Lossky; in Sweden, by Boström; in Argentina, by Aznar. (For other representatives of recent or contemporary personalism, see *Personalism.*)—*W.L.*

Ideality: Condition of being mental.—*W.L.*

Ideal of Reason: (Ger. *Ideal der Vernunft*) Kant: The idea of an all-comprehending reality, God, containing the determination of all finite existence. In the *Cr. of Pure Reason* Kant shows how and why the mind hypostaszes this Ideal, the source of "transcendental illusion" (*q.v.*). He concluded that while the traditional proofs of God's existence were all fallacious, the idea of God had a regulative use for reason, and was a necessary postulate for practical reason (*q.v.*). See *Kantianism.*—*O.F.K.*

Ideal Utilitarianism: See *Utilitarianism.*

Idealization: In art, the process of generalizing and abstracting from specifically similar individuals, in order to depict the perfect type of which they are examples; the search for real character or structural form, to the neglect of external qualities and aspects. Also, any work of art in which such form or character is exhibited; i.e. any adequate expression of the perfected essence inadequately manifested by the physical particular. In classical theory, the object so discovered and described is a Form or Idea; in modern theory, it is a product of imagination.—*I.J.*

Ideas of Pure Reason: (Kant. Ger. *Ideen der reinen Vernunft*) Ideas, expounded and criticized in the "Transcendental Dialectic" of the *Cr. of Pure Reason*, in which an absolute whole determines the parts in an aggregate or as series. For Kant there were three such Ideas: the soul, the world, and God. He maintained that these Ideas did not constitute "objects," but claimed for them a regulative use in pure reason, and asserted their reality as postulates of practical reason. See *Kantianism.*—*O.F.K.*

Ideatum: Noun denoting the object of an idea, or that which is represented in the mind by the idea. Also applied to really existing things outside the mind corresponding to the concepts in consciousness.—*J.J.R.*

Identity: (Lat. *identicus,* from *identidem,* repeatedly) In psychology: personal identity, or the continuous existence of the personality despite physiological and psychological changes. See: *Identity, law of.*—*J.K.F.*

Identity, law of: Given by traditional logicians as "*A* is *A*." Because of the various possible meanings of the *copula* (*q.v.*) and the uncertainty as to the range of the variable *A,* this formulation is ambiguous. The traditional law is perhaps best identified with the theorem $x = x$, either of the functional calculus of first order with equality, or in the theory of types (with equality defined), or in the algebra of classes, etc. It has been, or may be, also identified with either of the theorems of the propositional calculus, $p \supset p$, $p \equiv p$, or with the theorem of the functional calculus of first order, $F(x) \supset_x F(x)$. Many writers understand, however, by the law of identity a semantical principle—that a word or other symbol may (or must) have a fixed referent in its various occurrences in a given context (so, e.g., Ledger Wood in his *The Analysis of Knowledge*). Some, it would seem, confuse such a semantical principle with a proposition of formal logic.—*A.C.*

Identity-philosophy: In general the term has been applied to any theory which failed to distinguish between spirit and matter, subject and object, regarding them as an undifferentiated unity; hence such a philosophy is a species of monism. In the history of philosophy it usually signifies the system which has been called *Identitätsphilosophie* by Friedrich Wilhelm Schelling, who held that spirit and nature are fundamentally the same, namely, the Absolute. Neither the ego nor the non-ego are the ultimate principles of being; they are both relative concepts which are contained in something absolute. This is the supreme principle of Absolute Identity of the ideal and the real. Reasoning does not lead us to the Absolute which can only be attained by immediate intellectual intuition. In it we find the eternal concepts of things and from it we can derive everything else. We are obliged to conceive the Absolute Identity as the indifference of the ideal and the real. Of course, this is God in Whom all opposites are united. He is the unity of thought and being, the subjective and the objective, form and esssence, the general and infinite, and the particular and finite. This teaching is similar to that to Spinoza.—*J.J.R.*

Ideogenetic Theory: (Gr. *eidos*, idea + *genesis*, origin) Theory of Brentano (see *Brentano, Franz*) and other phenomenologists (see *Phenomenology*) which holds that judgment is an original act of consciousness directed towards presentations. The term is a translation of the German *ideogenetische Urteile*.—*L.W.*

Ideological: 1. Pertaining to the school of Condillac and his French followers of the early 19th century.

2. Pertaining to theories determined by cultural environment or non-rational interests.

3. Idle, unrealistic, fanciful.—*W.L.*

Ideology: A term invented by Destutt de Tracy for the analysis of general ideas into the sensations from which he believed them to emanate. The study was advocated as a substitute for metaphysics.

The term was used in a derogatory sense by Napoleon to denominate all philosophies whose influence was republican. In recent times the English equivalent has come to mean: (1) in some economic determinists, ineffectual thoughts as opposed to causally efficacious behavior, (2) any set of general ideas or philosophical program.—*G.B.*

Ideo-motor Action: (Gr. *eidos*, idea + *motus*, motion) Bodily action directly induced by the prevalence of an idea in the mind and considered by W. James as the basis of volition. (See W. James, *The Principles of Psychology*, Vol. II, pp. 522 ff.)—*L.W.*

Idio-psychological Ethics: Ethics based on the inner facts of conscience, as contrasted with hetero-psychological ethics, or ethics based on mental categories other than the conscience. Introduced as terms into ethics by J. Martineau (1805-1899) in 1885.—*J.K.F.*

Idol: (Gr. *eidolon* and Lat. *idolum*, image or likeness) Democritus (5th c. B.C.) tried to explain sense perception by means of the emission of little particles (*eidola*) from the sense object. This theory and the term, *idolum*, are known throughout the later middle ages, but in a pejorative sense, as indicating a sort of "second-hand" knowledge. G. Bruno is usually credited with the earliest Latin use of the term to name that which leads philosophers into error, but this is an unmerited honor. The most famous usage occurs in F. Bacon's *Novum Organum*, I, 39-68, where the four chief causes of human error in philosophy and science are called: the Idols of the Tribe (weakness of understanding in the whole human race), of the Cave (individual prejudices and mental defects), of the Forum (faults of language in the communication of ideas), and of the Theatre (faults arising from received systems of philosophy). A very similar teaching, without the term, idol, had been developed by Grosseteste and Roger Bacon in the 13th century.—*V.J.B.*

Ignorance: (Lat. *in*, not + *noscere*, to become acquainted with) Partial or complete absence of knowledge.—*A.C.B.*

Ignoratio elenchi: The fallacy of irrelevance, i.e., of proving a conclusion which is other than that required or which does not contradict the thesis which it was undertaken to refute.—*A.C.*

I kuan: The "one thread" or central principle that runs through the teachings of Confucius. See *Chung yung*. This is interpreted as:

(a) The Confucian doctrine of being true to the principles of one's nature (chung) and the benevolent exercise of them in relation to others (shu), by Confucius' pupil, Tseng Tzǔ.

(b) The central principle of centrality and harmony (chung yung) by which all human affairs and natural phenomena may be understood. (Early Confucianism).

(c) "Man and things forming one organic unity," there being no discrimination between the self and the non-self. (Ch'êng I-ch'uan 1033-1107).

(d) Sincerity (ch'êng), which is the way of Heaven, indestructible, by which all things are in their proper places. Sincerity is the thread that runs through all affairs and things; and being true to the principles of one's nature and the benevolent exercise of them in relation to others is the way to try to be sincere. (Chu Hsi, 1130-1200).

(e) The "one" is the Great Ultimate in general and the "thread" is the Great Ultimate in each thing. (Chu Hsi).—*W.T.C.*

Illative: Having to do with inference.—*A.C.*

Illicit importance, fallacy of: The mistake of assuming that because a proposition is self-evident, it is therefore important.—*H.H.*

Illicit process of the major: In the categorical syllogism (*Logic, formal*, § 5), the conclusion cannot be a proposition *E* or *O* unless the major term appears in its premiss as *distributed*—i.e., as subject of a proposition *A* or *E*, or the predicate of a proposition *E* or *O*. Violation of this rule is the fallacy of *illicit process of the major*.—*A.C.*

Illicit process of the minor: In the categorical syllogism (*logic, formal*, § 5), the conclusion cannot be a proposition *A* or *E* unless the minor term appears in its premiss as *distributed*.—i.e., as the subject of a proposition *A* or *E*, or the predicate of a proposition *E* or *O*. Violation of this rule is the fallacy of *illicit process of the minor*.—*A.C.*

Illumination: Source of contemplation; transfiguration of emotional life for the attainment of measure and harmony (Schleiermacher).—*L.V.*

Illusion: (Lat. *in + ludere*, to play) An illusion of sense is an erroneous perception arising from a misinterpretation of data of sense because they are produced under unusual conditions of perception, physical, physiological or psychological. Illusion contrasts with hallucination in which the sensuous ingredients are totally absent. See *Delusion; Hallucination*.—*L.W.*

Illusionism: The view that the spatial-temporal external world is merely a veil of māyā, a phantasmagoria. Not only is everything illusion, deception, appearance, but existence itself has no real value. (Schopenhauer.)—*H.H.*

Image: (Lat. *imago*, likeness) A sensory quality reinstated by the mind in the absence of sensory stimulation.—*L.W.*

Medieval: Image and *Similitude* are frequently used by the medieval scholars. Neither of them needs mean copy. Sometimes the terms are nearly synonymous with sign in general. The alteration of the sense organs when affected by some external object is an image of the latter (*species sensibilis*); so is the memory image or phantasm. The intelligible species resulting from the operation of the active intellect on the phantasm is not less an image of the universal nature than the concept and the word expressing the latter is. Images in the strict sense of copies or pictures are only a particular case of image or similitude in general. The idea that Scholasticism believed that the mind contains literally "copies" of the objective world is mistaken interpretation due to misunderstanding of the terms.—*R.A.*

Imageless Thought: Conceptual meanings not embodied in sensuous imagery. The existence of imageless thought was a subject of controversy among American and German psychologists about 1910; imageless thought was affirmed by Külpe, and Bühler, but was rejected by Titchener.—*L.W.*

Imagination: Imagination designates a mental process consisting of: (a) The revival of sense images derived from earlier perceptions (the reproductive imagination), and (b) the combination of these elementary images into new unities (the creative or productive imagination.) The creative imagination is of two kinds: (a) the fancy, which is relatively spontaneous and uncontrolled, and

(b) the constructive imagination, exemplified in science, invention and philosophy which is controlled by a dominant plan or purpose.—*L.W.*

Imitation: In aesthetics, the general theory that artistic creation is primarily an imitative or revelatory process, and the work of art an imitation or representation. Such theories hold that the artist discovers, and in his work imitates, real Forms, and not physical objects; art is conceived as a revelation of a spiritual realm, and so as the exhibition of the essential character of the particular object represented. The work of art reveals adequately the essence which the physical thing manifests inadequately. In modern expressionistic theory, imitation is conceived as servile reproduction of obvious external qualities, a mere copying of a particular, and so is denounced.—*I.J.*

Immanence: (late Lat. *Immanere*, to remain in) The state of being immanent, present, or indwelling. 1. In medieval Scholasticism a cause is immanent whose effects are exclusively within the agent, as opposed to transient. 2. For Kant the immanent is experiential as opposed to non-experiential or transcendent. 3. In modern metaphysics and theology immanence signifies presence (of essence, being, power, etc.), as opposed to absence. According to pantheism the essence of God or the Absolute is completely immanent in the world, *i.e.* is identical with it. According to Deism God is essentially absent or transcendent from the world. According to immanent theism He is both immanent (in presence and activity) and transcendent (in essence) with respect to it. Mysticism in its broadest sense posits the mutual immanence of the human and the divine.—*W.L.*

Immanence philosophy: In Germany an idealistic type of philosophy represented by Wilhelm Schuppe (1836-1913), which combines elements of British empiricism, Kant, and Fichte. It rejects any non-conscious thing-in-itself, and identifies the Real with consciousness considered as an inseparable union of the "I" and its objects. The categories are restricted to identity-difference and causality. To the extent that the content of finite consciousness is common to all or "trans-subjective" it is posited as the object of a World Consciousness or *Bedwusstsein Ueberhaupt*. Consequently the World is "immanent" in each finite consciousness rather than essentially transcendent.—*W.L.*

Immanent and Transient Activity: In logic, the activity of the mind which produces no effect upon the object of knowledge is called immanent; that which does have such an effect is called transient (or transitive). According to Kant, the immanent use of the understanding is valid since it deals only with subject-matter furnished by the senses; while the transcendent effort to conceive of things as they are in themselves is illegitimate. In Christian theology, Jesus was created by an immanent act, and the world by a transient act.—*J.K.F.*

Immanent Theism: Doctrine that God is both immanent and transcendent with respect to the World. This view differs from Pantheism (*q.v.*) by denying that God's essence is identical with that of the World.—*W.L.*

Immaterialism: Doctrine of the non-existence of material or corporeal reality. Pure Idealism.—*W.L.*

Immateriality: (Scholastic) Immaterial substances are the human soul and the subsistent forms, the angels. The rational faculties of the human soul, intellect and will are called immaterial and believed to need no bodily organ for their performances, although they depend on the senses for their activities. Their immateriality is proved by their capacity of becoming cognizant of the universals and by reflection on their own performances.—*R.A.*

Immediacy: (Lat. *in* + *medius,* middle) Immediacy is used in two senses:

(a) Contrasted with representation, immediacy is the direct presence to the mind of the object of knowledge. See *Presentational immediacy.*

(b) Contrasted with mediation, immediacy consists in the absence or minimal and submerged presence of inference, interpretation and construction in any process of knowledge. In this sense perception and memory are relatively immediate whereas scientific and philosophical theories are mediate.—*L.W.*

Immediate inference: See *Logic, formal,* § 4.

Immoralism: Moral indifference; in general the combating of traditional morality. (Nietzsche.)—*H.H.*

Immortality: (Lat. *in* + *mortalis,* mortal) The doctrine that the soul or personality of man survives the death of the body. The two principal conceptions of immortality are: (a) *temporal immortality,* the indefinite continuation of the individual mind after death and (b) *eternity,* ascension of the soul to a higher plane of timelessness.

Immortality is properly speaking restricted to post-existence (survival after death) but is extended by the theory of transmigration of souls. (See *Metempsychosis*) to include pre-existence (life before birth).

The arguments for immortality fall into four groups:

(a) *Metaphysical arguments* which attempt to deduce immortality from properties of the soul such as simplicity, independence of the body, its knowledge of eternal truth, etc.

(b) *Valuational and moral arguments* seek to derive the immortality of the soul from its supreme worth or as a presupposition of its moral nature.

(c) *Empirical arguments* which adduce as evidence of immortality, automatic writing, mediumship and other spiritualistic phenomena.—*L.W.*

Immutability: Changelessness, or the state or quality of not being susceptible to any alteration. An attribute of God denoting that His nature is essentially incapable of any internal change whatsoever.—*J.J.R.*

Impersonalism: The mechanist conception of the unconditional regularity of nature in mechanics, physics, and the sciences of the living organism. Opposite of Personalism.—*R.T.F.*

Implication: See *Logic, formal,* §§ 1, 3; *Strict implication.*

Importation: The form of valid inference of the propositional calculus from A ⊃ [B ⊃ C] to AB ⊃ C. The *law of importation* is the theorem of the propositional calculus:

$$[p \supset [q \supset r]] \supset [pq \supset r].—A.C.$$

Imposition: In Scholastic logic, grammatical terms such

as *noun, pronoun, verb, tense, conjugation* were classed as terms of second imposition, other terms as of first imposition. The latter were subdivided into terms of first and second *intention* (*q.v.*).—*A.C.*

Impredicative definition: Poincaré, in a proposed resolution (1906) of the paradoxes of Burali-Forti and Richard (see *Paradoxes, logical*), introduced the principle that, in making a definition of a particular member of any class, no reference should be allowed to the totality of members of that class. Definitions in violation of this principle were called *impredicative* (*non prédicatives*) and were held to involve a vicious circle.

The prohibition against impredicative definition was incorporated by Russell into his ramified theory of types (1908) and is now usually identified with the restriction to the remified theory of types *without the axiom of reducibility.* (Poincaré, however, never made his principle exact and may have intended, vaguely, a less severe restriction than this—as indeed some passages in later writings would indicate.)—*A.C.*

H. Poincaré, *Les mathématiques et la logique,* Revue de Métaphysique et de Morale, vol. 14 (1906), pp. 294-317. R. Carnap, *The Logical Syntax of Language,* New York and London, 1937.

Impression: Act or process of affecting; effect or influence of such, especially psychological; immediate or momentary effect; stimulation of neural processes apart from its effect; immediate effect in consciousness of neural stimulation; immediate, uninterpreted datum of consciousness, especially of aesthetic objects; sensuous image; relatively vivid perceptual datum as against a fainter idea. See *Hume.*—*M.T.K.*

Impressionism: As a general artistic movement, the theory that art should strive only to reveal the *felt quality* of an object, scene, or event; i.e. the total effect that it creates in the artist. Specifically in painting, the general idea underlying practice is to render the immediate visual appearance of the object, independently of its physical structure and its meaning for the mind. Emphasis is placed on capturing ephemeral surface aspects of things as disclosed by changes in light, neglecting any supposed real thing which undergoes these changes and underlies these aspects.—*I.J.*

In and for itself: (Ger. *an und für sich*) *An sich* is the given primary, latent, undeveloped immediacy. The bare intrinsic and inherent essence of an object. *Für sich* is a greater, developed intensity of immediacy; an object genuinely independent either of consciousness or of other things; something for itself. In and for itself belongs to the Absolute alone. Its asserted independence is the developed result of its nature and as a system of internal relations it is independent of external relations.—*H.H.*

Incomplete symbol: A symbol (or expression) which has no meaning in isolation but which may occur as a constituent part in, and contribute to the meaning of, an expression which does have a meaning. Thus—as ordinarily employed—a terminal parenthesis) is an incomplete symbol; likewise the letter λ which appears in the notation for functional *abstraction* (*q.v.*); etc.

An expression A introduced by *contextual definition*–i.e., by a definition which construes particular kinds of expressions containing A, as abbreviations or substitutes for certain expressions not containing A, but provides no such construction for A itself—is an incomplete symbol in this sense. In *Principia Mathematica,* notations for classes, and descriptions (more correctly, notations which serve some of the purposes that would be served by notations for classes and by descriptions) are introduced in this way by contextual definition.—*A.C.*

Whitehead and Russell, *Principia Mathematica,* vol. I.

Inconceivability: The property of being something that is unthinkable. Having self-contradictory properties such that mental representation is impossible. In metaphysics, Herbert Spencer's criterion of truth, that when the denial of a proposition is incapable of being conceived the proposition is to be accepted as necessary or true. Syn. with *Inconceptible.*—*J.K.F.*

Inconsistency: As applied to logistic systems, the opposite of *consistency* (*q.v.*)

A set of propositional functions is *inconsistent* if there is some propositional function such that their conjunction formally implies (see *Logic, formal,* § 3) both it and its negation.

A set of sentences is *inconsistent* if there is some sentence A such that there is a valid inference from them to A and also from them to ~ A.

If the notion of possibility is admitted, in the sense of a modality (see *Modality,* and *Strict implication*), a set of propositions may be said to be *inconsistent* if their conjunction is impossible.—*A.C.*

Incontinence: (Gr. *akrasia*) Moral condition of a person unable to control his bodily desires by rational principles. The incontinent man is distinguished from the licentious in that in the one case there is a conflict between bodily desires and rational choice and in the other case not (Aristotle).—*G.R.M.*

Indefinite potentiality, error of: Inadequate analysis of causation.—*H.H.*

Independence: In a set of postulates for a mathematical discipline (see *Mathematics*), a particular postulate is said to be *independent* if it cannot be proved as a consequence of the others. A non-independent postulate is thus superfluous, and should be dropped.

In a *logistic system* (*q.v.*), a primitive formula or a primitive rule of inference may be said to be *independent* if there are theorems upon omission of the primitive formula or primitive rule of inference.—*A.C.*

Indeterminism: (Lat. *in* + *determinatus,* pp. of *determinare*) Theory that volitional decisions are in certain cases independent of antecedent physiological and psychological causation. See *Free-Will, Determinism.*—*L.W.*

Index: (Lat. *indicare,* to indicate) A directing sign; that which indicates. Employed by C.S. Peirce (1839-1914) in logic, or semiotic, as that sign which refers to an object by virtue of being affected by it. See: *Sign.*—*J.K.F.*

Indian Aesthetics: Art in India is one of the most diversified subjects. Sanskrit *śilpa* included all crafts, fine art, architecture and ornament, dancing, acting, music and even coquetry. Behind all these endeavors is a deep rooted sense of absolute values derived from Indian philosophy (*q.v.*) which teaches the incarnation of the divine (Kṛṣṇa, Shiva, Buddha), the transitoriness of life (cf. *saṁsāra*), the symbolism and conditional nature of the phenomenal (cf. *māyā*). Love of splendor and exaggerated greatness, dating back to Vedic (*q.v.*) times, mingled with a grand simplicity in the conception of ultimate being and a keen perception and nature observation. The latter is illustrated in examples of verisimilous execution in sculpture and painting, the detailed description in a wealth of drama and story material, and the universal love of simile. With an urge for expression, the metaphysical associated itself in its practical and seemingly other-worldly aspects and, aided perhaps by the exigencies of climate, yielded the grotesque as illustrated by the cave temples of Ellora and Elephanta, the apparent barbarism of female ornament covering up all organic beauty, the exaggerated, symbol-laden representations of divine and theanthropic beings, a music with minute subdivisions of scale, and the like. As Indian philosophy is dominated by a monistic, Vedāntic (*q.v.*) outlook, so in Indian esthetics we can notice the prevalence of an introvert unitary, soul-centric, self-integrating tendency that treats the empirical suggestively and by way of simile, trying to stylize the natural in form, behavior, and expression. The popular belief in the immanence as well as transcendence of the Absolute precludes thus the possibility of a complete naturalism or imitation. The whole range of Indian art therefore demands a sharing and re-creation of absolute values glimpsed by the artist and professedly communicated imperfectly. Rules and discussions of the various aspects of art may be found in the Silpa-śāstras, while theoretical treatments are available in such works as the Daśarūpa in dramatics, the Nrtya-śāstras in dancing, the Sukranītisāra in the relation of art to state craft, etc. Periods and influences of Indian art, such as the Buddhist, Kushān, Gupta, etc., may be consulted in any history of Indian art.—*K.F.L.*

Indian Ethics: Ethical speculations are inherent in Indian philosophy (*q.v.*) with its concepts of *karma, moksa, ānanda* (*q.v.*). Belief in salvation is universal, hence optimism rather than pessimism is prevalent even though one's own life is sometimes treated contemptuously, fatalism is embraced or the doctrine of non-attachment and desirelessness is subscribed to. Social institutions, thoughts, and habits in India are interdependent with the theory of *karma* and the belief in universal law and order (cf. *dharma*). For instance, caste exists because *dharma* is inviolable; man is born into his circumstances because he reaps what he has sown. Western influence, in changing Indian institutions, will eventually also modify Indian ethical theories. All the same, great moral sensitiveness is not lacking, rather much the contrary, as is proven by the voluminous story and didactic fable literature which has also acted on the West. Hindu moral conscience is evident from the ideals of womanhood (symbolized in Sitā), of loyalty (symbolized in Hanumān), of kindness to all living beings (cf. *ahimsā*), of tolerance (the racial and religious hotchpotch which is India being an eloquent witness), the great respect for the *samnyāsin* (who, as a member of the Brahman caste has precedence over the royal or military). Critics confuse—and the wretched conduct of some Hindus confirm the indistinction—practical morality with the fearless statements of metaphysics pursued with relentless logic "beyond good and evil."

Periods of despondency and inactivity or even degeneracy and depravity in India have kept pace with disastrous political developments. But a joy in life's pursuits is evident from the earliest Vedic period and is to be traced in the multifariousness of Indian culture and the colorful Indian history itself which has left the Hindus one of the ancient races still virile among nations and capable of assimilation without itself becoming extinct. Happiness may be enjoyed even in the severest penance and asceticism for which India is noted, while a certain concomitant heroism seems undeniable.

The ethical teachings of the Bhagavad Gītā (*q.v.*), of the various religio-philosophical groups, of the Buddhists and Jainas of Greater India, are high; but if such ideals have not been attained generally in practice, or even if repulsive and cruel rituals and *linga* worship are prevalent, such phenomena are understandable if we consider the 340 millions of teeming humanity within the fold of Hinduism, from aborigines to a Gandhi, Tagore, and Sir Raman. Treatises dealing with practical morality are very numerous. They may be classed into those of a purely religious leaning among which we might count all religio-philosophical literature of the Vedic and non-Vedic tradition, including drama and epic literature, and those that deal specifically with practices of the nature of self-culture (cf. Yoga), religious observances (sacrifice, priest-craft, rites, ceremonies, etc.), household affairs and duties (Gṛhyasūtras), and the science of polity and government (Arthaśāstras).—*K.F.L.*

Indian Philosophy: General name designating a plethora of more or less systematic thinking born and cultivated in the geographic region of India among the Hindus who represent an amalgamation of adventitious and indigenous peoples, but confined at first exclusively to the caste conscious Indo-germanic conquerors of the lands of the Indus and Ganges. Its beginnings are lost in the dim past, while a distinct emergence in tangible form is demonstrable from about 1000 B.C. Hindu idiosyncrasies are responsible for our inability to date with any degree of accuracy many of the systems, schools, and philosophers, or in some cases even to refer to the latter by name. Inasmuch as memory, not writing, has been universally favored in India, an aphoristic form (cf. *sūtra*), subtended by copious commentaries, gives Indian Philosophy its distinctive appearance. The medium is Sanskrit and the dialects derived from it. There are translations in all major Asiatic and European languages. The West became familiar with it when philologists discovered during last century the importance of Sanskrit. As a type of thinking employing unfamiliar conceptions and a terminology fluctuating in meaning (cf. e.g., *rasa*), it is distinct from Western speculations. Several peaks have been reached in the past, yet Indian Philosophy does not cease to act fructifyingly upon the present mind in India as elsewhere. Various factions advance conflicting claims as to the value of Indian speculation, because interpretations have not as yet become standardized. Textual criticism is now making strides, but with varying successes. Among larger histories of Indian Philosophy may be mentioned those of Deussen, Das Gupta, Belvalkar and Ranade, and Radhakrishnan.

Philosophic speculations, heavily shrouded by "pre-logical" and symbolic language, started with the poetic, ritualistic Vedas (*q.v.*), luxuriating in polytheism and polyanthropoism, was then fostered by the Brahman caste in treatises called Aranyakas (*q.v.*) and Brāmanas (*q.v.*) and strongly promoted by members of the ruling caste who instituted philosophic congresses in which peripatetic teachers and women participated, and of which we know through the Upanishads (*q.v.*). Later, the main bulk of Indian Philosophy articulated itself organically into systems forming the nucleus for such famous schools as the Mīmāṁsā and Vedānta, Sāṅkhya, and Yoga, Nyaya and Vaiśesika, and those of Buddhism and Jainism (all of which see). Numerous other philosophic and quasi philosophic systems are found in the epic literature and elsewhere (cf., e.g., Shaktism, Shivaism, Trika, Vishnuism), or remain to be discovered. Much needs to be translated by competent philosophers.

All Indian doctrines orient themselves by the Vedas, accepting or rejecting their authority. In ranging from materialism to acosmism and nihilism, from physiologism to spiritualism, realism to idealism, monism to pluralism, atheism and pantheism, Hindus believe they have exhausted all possible philosophic attitudes (cf. *darśana*), which they feel supplement rather than exclude each other. A universal feature is the fusion of religion, metaphysics, ethics and psychology, due to the universal acceptance of a psychophysicalism, further exemplified in the typical doctrines of *karma* and *samsāra* (*q.v.*). Rigorous logic is nevertheless applied in theology where metaphysics passes into eschatology (cf., e.g., *īs*) and the generally accepted belief in the cyclic nature of the cosmos oscillating between *sṛṣṭi* ("throwing out") and *pralaya* (dissolution) of the absolute reality (cf. *ābhāsa*), and in psychology, where epistemology seeks practical outlets in Yoga (*q.v.*). With a genius for abstraction, thinkers were and are almost invariably hedonistically motivated by the desire to overcome the evils of existence in the hope of attaining liberation (cf. *moksa*) and everlasting bliss (cf. *ānanda, nirvāṇa*).—*K.F.L.*

Indifferents: (Gr. *adiaphora*) In Stoic ethics those things which are in themselves neither good nor bad, as producing neither virtue nor vice; such as life, health, pleasure, beauty, wealth, noble birth, and their contraries. The Stoics further distinguished between indifferents that are to be preferred (proegmena) and those that are not to be preferred (apoproegmena). The former, though not goods, have a certain value and are the objects of natural inclination.—*G.R.M.*

Indirect proof: See *Reductio ad absurdum*.

Indiscernibles, Principle of:(Lat. *indiscernibilis*, indistinguishable) In the philosophy of Leibniz (*Monadologie*, IX; *Nouv. Essais*, II, 22), no two monads can be exactly alike.—*V.J.B.*

Individual: In formal logic, the *individuals* form the first or lowest type of Russell's hierarchy of types. In the *Principia Mathematica* of Whitehead and Russell, individuals are "defined as whatever is neither a proposition nor a function." It is unnecessary, however, to give the word any such special significance, and for many purposes it is better (as is often done) to take the individuals to be an arbitrary—or an arbitrary infinite—domain; or any particular well-defined domain may be taken as the domain of individuals, according to the purpose in hand. When used in this way, the term *domain of individuals* may be taken as synonymous with the term *universe of discourse* (in the sense of Boole) which is employed in connection with the algebra of classes. See *Logic, formal*, §§ 3, 6, 7.—*A.C.*

Individualism: The doctrine that emphasizes the reality of the individual and concrete. Differs from Personalism (*q.v.*).—*R.T.F.*

In political philosophy, the doctrine that the state exists for the individual, not *vice versa*. In political economy, *laissez faire* system of competition.

Individual Psychology: (a) In the widest sense, individual psychology is one of the major departments of psychology, comparable to such other major subdivisions as experimental psychology, abnormal psychology, comparative psychology, etc. It is the branch of psychology devoted to the investigation of mental variations among individuals and includes such topics as: character and temperament (see *Characterology*) mental types, genius, criminality, intelligence, testing, etc. Attention was first directed to individual differences by Francis Galton (*Hereditary Genius*, 1869). Galton's method was applied to mental deficiency by Dugdale (*The Jukes*, 1877) and Galton himself extended the same type of inquiry to free association and imagery in *Inquiries into Human Faculty*, 1883. A more recent contribution to individual psychology is Cattell's *American Men of Science* (1906).

(b) In a somewhat more restricted sense, individual psychology, in contrast to folk psychology, group psychology or social psychology is the investigation of the individual considered—so far as possibly—apart from the influence of the social group of which he is a member.

(c) Finally the term "individual" psychology has been appropriated by a special school of analytic psychology (see *Psychoanalysis*), namely that of Alfred Adler. See A. Adler, *Problems of Neurosis*; E. Wexberg, *Individual Psychology*.—*L.W.*

Individuation: The constitution of a reality as a singular member of a species. In the context of the matter and form theory it is difficult to explain how either prime matter (which is in itself the same in all physical things), or substantial form (which is the same in all members of the same species), can be the cause or principle of individuality. See *Thomism, Scotism, Suarezianism*, for various explanations.—*V.J.B.*

Indriya: (Skr.) One of five or more sensory functions or "senses," conceived generally in Indian philosophy kinetically as powers subservient to *manas* (*q.v.*). A common division is into the quintads of *karmendriyas* (*q.v.*) and *jñānendriyas* (*q.v.*).—*K.F.L.*

Induction: (Lat. *in* and *ducere*, to lead in) i.e., to lead into the field of attention a number of observed particular facts as ground for a general assertion. "Perfect" induction is assertion concerning all the entities of a collection on the basis of examination of each and every one of them. The conclusion sums up but does not go beyond the facts observed. Ordinarily, however, "induction" is used to mean ampliative inference as distinguished from explicative; i.e., it is the sort of inference which attempts to reach a conclusion concerning all the members of a class from observation of only some of them. Conclusions inductive in this sense are only probable, in greater or less degree according to the precautions taken in selecting the evidence for them. Induction is conceived by J.S. Mill, and generally, as essentially an *evidencing* process; but Whewell conceives it as essentially *discovery*, viz., discovery of some conception, not extracted from the set of particular facts observed, but nevertheless capable of "colligating" them, i.e., of expressing them all at once, (or, better stated, of making it possible to deduce them). For example, Kepler's statement that the orbit of Mars is an ellipse represented the discovery by him that the conception of the ellipse "colligated" all the observed positions of Mars. Mill's view of induction directly fits the process of empirical generalization; that of Whewell, rather the theoretical, explanatory part of the task of science. Charles Peirce, viewing induction as generalization, contrasts it not only with inference from antecedent to consequent ("deduction") but also with inference from consequent to antecedent, called by him "hypothesis" (also called by him "abduction" (*q.v.*), but better termed "diagnosis").—*C.J.D.*

Induction, complete or mathematical. See *Recursion*.

In esse, in intellectu, in re: Medieval Latin expressions of which the first signifies, in being, in existence; the second, in the intellect, especially as a general idea formed by the process of abstraction; the third, in a really existing thing outside the mind. One may add that *in the matter of* is the commonly known signification of the third.—*J.J.R.*

Inference: (Lat. *in* + *ferre*, to bear) The process of reasoning whereby starting from one or more propositions accepted as true, the mind passes to another proposition or propositions whose truth is believed to be involved in the truth of the former. Inference is a

psychological process connecting propositions asserted to be true and is to be distinguished from implication, the logical relation which holds between the same propositions when the inference is valid. An inference is valid when a genuine implicative relation holds between the propositions; invalid when there is no such implicative relation. Inference is deductive or inductive according as the underlying logic is deduction (see *Deduction*) or induction (see *Induction*). W.B. Joseph, *An Introduction to Logic*. L.S. Stebbing, *Modern Introduction to Logic*. J. Cook Wilson, *Statement and Inference*. B. Bosanquet, *Implication and Linear Inference*.—*L.W.*
   See *Logic, formal* and *Valid inference*.

In fieri: (in Scholasticism) A thing is said to be *in fieri* when it is beginning to be, but is not yet complete. It is said to be *in facto* when it exists *completely* in the nature of things with those constituent parts with which it remains. Thus a picture is *in fieri*, when the painter is painting the canvas, but it is said to be *in facto* when the picture has already been painted.—*H.G.*

Infima species: The lowest species of a classification. In Aristotle, the individual.—*R.B.W.*

Infinite: Opposite of *finite* (*q.v.*), as applied to classes, cardinal and ordinal numbers, sequences, etc. See further *Cardinal number*; *Limit*.—*A.C.*

Infinitesimal: In a phraseology which is logically inexact but nevertheless common, an *infinitesimal* is a quantity, or a variable, whose limit is 0. Thus in considering the limit of $f(x)$ as x approaches c, if this limit is 0 the "quantity" $f(x)$ may be said to be an infinitesimal; or in considering the limit of $f(x)$ as x approaches 0, the "quantity" x may be said to be an infinitesimal. (See the article *limit*.)—*A.C.*

Infinity: An endless extent of space, time, or any series. Is usually conceived negatively, as having no termination; may be conceived positively, in respect to reality as actually extending without end.—*R.B.W.*

Infinity, axiom of: See *Logic, formal*, §§ 6, 9.

Ingression: According to A.N. Whitehead, participation of potentialities in the creation of complex actualities; "a concretion—that is, a growing together—of diverse elements."—*R.B.W.*

Innate Ideas: (Lat. *innatis*, inborn) The power of understanding given in the very nature of mind. Such ideas are spoken of as *a priori*. Ideas which are inborn and come with the mind at birth, such as God or immortality. More generally, ideas which all men as human and rational, necessarily and universally possess.
   Locke's arguments against Descartes' belief in innate ideas (cf. *Essay on the Human Understanding*, bk. I) were the target of Leibniz's *Nouveaux Essais*, 1701 (publ. in 1765).—*M.F.*

Innatism: (Lat. *in* + *natus*, inborn) A theory of philosophy in which ideas, or principles, are considered to be present in the mind at birth, either fully formed or requiring some additional experience for their complete formulation.—*V.J.B.*

Inner sense: The capacity of feeling immediately, (i.e. unconditioned by the knowledge of principles, causes, or advantages) the beauty and harmony (or their opposites) of material objects. (Francis Hutcheson).—*K.E.G.*

Innervation, Sensation of: (Lat. *in* + *nervus*, nerve) Sensation accompanying the efferent nerve currents which discharge from the central nervous system into the muscles. The existence of such a sensation has been much disputed by psychologists. (See W. James, *The Principles of Psychology*, Vol. II, pp. 498 ff.)—*L.W.*

Insolubilia: See *Paradoxes, logical*.

Inspection: (Lat. *inspection*, from *inspectus*, pp. of *inspicere*, to look into) Rudimentary knowledge of qualities and relations between qualities as given in immediate experience, (see *Presentational Immediacy*) in contradistinction to perception, memory, introspection and other higher cognitive processes which are conversant not with qualities but with objects.—*L.W.*

Institutions: (Lat. *instituere*, to cause to stand)
   (a) Establishments. Relatively permanent group behavior patterns or established social practices, as distinguished from temporary practices or patterns.
   (b) Socially established behavior patterns, authoritatively or legally enforced, as distinguished from Folkways which are merely taken-for-granted common but uncompelled ways of behavior and as distinguished from "mores" which are enforced by group opinion rather than by legally authorized means.—*A.J.B.*

Instrumentalism: See *Pragmatism*.

Instrumental theory: The mind is a substance existentially independent of the body, either existing prior to the body, or after the destruction of the body. (Broad.)—*H.H.*

Instrumental value: See *Value, Instrumental*.

Integral: A whole composed of parts. Belonging to a whole as one of its parts. Anything composed of distinguishable parts. Complete, untouched. In mathematics, related to integers; the result of integration.—*J.K.F.*

Integration: (Lat. *integrare*, to make whole) The act of making a whole out of parts. In mathematics, a limiting process which may be described in vague terms as summing up an infinite number of infinitesimals, part of the calculus. In psychology, the combination of psycho-physical elements into a complex unified organization. In cosmology, the synthetic philosophy of Spencer holds that the evolutionary process is marked by two movements: integration and differentiation. Integration consists in the development of more and more complex organizations. Inverse of: differentiation (*q.v.*).—*J.K.F.*

Intellect: (Lat. *intellectus*, from *intellegere*, to understand) The cognitive faculty of the mind as it operates at higher abstract and conceptual levels.—*L.W.*

   St. Augustine distinguished the intellect from reason; *aliud est intellectus, aliud ratio*. Intellection would be impossible without reason: *Intelligere non valemus, nisi rationem habeamus*. The intellect is the soul itself: *Non enim aliquid aliud est quam anima, sed aliquid animae est intellectus*. It rules the soul: *Intellectus animam regit, ad ipsam animam pertinens*. Sometimes the *intellectus* is called *intelligentia*. Both the intellect and reason are innate in the mind; *mens cui ratio et intel-*

ligentia naturaliter inest. Reason seeks knowledge or science, *scientia,* while the intellect, which is higher, aims at wisdom, *sapientia,* or the contemplation of eternal things, and especially God.—*J.J.R.*

Whence, in the typical Scholastic or medieval notion, intellect is an immaterial faculty of the soul, that is, its operations are performed without a bodily organ, though they depend on the body and its senses for the material from which they receive their first impulse. Nothing is in the intellect that has not been previously in the senses. The impressions received by the external senses are synthesized by the internal *sensus communis* which forms an image or phantasm; the phantasm is presented to the intellect by imagination, memory and the *vis cogitativa* cooperating. The internal senses are conceived as being bound to organic functions of the brain. The intellect operates in a two-fold manner, but is only one. As active intellect (*intellectus agens*) it "illuminates" the phantasm, disengaging there from the universal nature; as passive intellect (*int. possibilis*) it is informed by the result of this abstractive operation and develops the concept. Concepts are united into judgments by combination and division (assertion and negation). Judgments are related to each other in syllogistic reasoning or by the abbreviated form of enthymeme. Aquinas denies to the intellect the capacity of becoming aware of particulars in any direct way. The intellect knows of them (e.g. when asserting: Socrates is a man) only indirectly by reflecting on its own operations and finally on the phantasm which served as starting point. Propositions, however, have no directly corresponding phantasm. Later Scholastics credit the intellect with a direct knowledge of particulars (Suarez). See *Abstraction, Faculty.*—*R.A.*

Intellectualism: (esthetics) a. The "Intellectual Principle" is supreme beauty (Plotinus).

b. "Intellectual Intuition" turned objective is esthetic intuition (Schelling).—*L.V.*

Intellectual virtues: See *Dianoetic virtues.*

Intelligence: (Lat. *intelligentia,* from *intellegere,* to understand) The capacity of the mind to meet effectively—through the employment of memory, imagination and conceptual thinking—the practical and theoretical problems with which it is confronted. Intelligence is more inclusive than intellect which is primarily conceptual. See *Intellect.*

In Dewey (*q.v.*), intelligence is the basic instrument, to be contrasted with fixed habit, traditional customs, and the sheer force of political or bureaucratic power as means of settling social issues.—*L.W.*

Intelligence, creative: A term denoting the presence of self-consciousness, self-direction and purpose in the creative processes of the world. Syn. in Personalism for God, *élan vital,* but in naturalism of Dewey, divorced from such association.—*R.T.F.*

Intelligible: (1) Understandable; comprehensible; knowable; meaningful; (2) Orderly; logical; coherent; rational; (3) Communicable; expressible; (4) Having unity of principle; capable of complete rational explanation or understanding; capable of causal explanation; (5)

Clear to natural or pure reason; apprehensible by the intellect (*q.v.*) only as against apprehensible through the senses; conceptual as against perceptual; conceptually describable or explainable; (6) Capable of being known synoptically or as it is in itself or in essence; capable of being known through itself as against by agency of something else; graspable by intuition; self-explanatory; (7) Capable of being appreciated or sympathized with; (8) Supersensible; of the nature of mind, reason, or their higher powers.—*M.T.K.*

Intension and extension: The *intension* of a concept consists of the qualities or properties which go to make up the concept. The *extension* of a concept consists of the things which fall under the concept; or, according to another definition, the *extension* of a concept consists of the concepts which are subsumed under it (determine subclasses). This is the old distinction between intension and extension, and coincides approximately with the distinction between a monadic *propositional function* (*q.v.*) in intension and a *class* (*q.v.*). The words *intention* and *extension* are also used in connection with a number of distinctions related or analogous to this one, the adjective *extensional* being applied to notions or points of view which in some respect confine attention to truth-values of propositions as opposed to meanings constituting propositions. In the case of (interpreted) calculi of propositions or propositional functions, the adjective *intensional* may mean that account is taken of modality, *extensional* that all functions of propositions which appear are truth-functions. The extreme of the extentional point of view does away with propositions altogether and retains only truth-values in their place.—*A.C.*

The Port-Royal Logic, translated by T.S. Baynes (see *Introduction by the translator*).

Lewis and Langford, *Symbolic Logic,* New York and London, 1932. R. Carnap, *The Logical Syntax of Language,* New York and London, 1937.

Intensive quantity: Any quantity which is such that there exists no known physical process of addition by which a greater quantity of the kind in question could be produced from a lesser quantity; opposed to extensive quantity (*q.v.*).—*A.C.B.*

Intent: (Lat. *intensus,* pp. of *intendere,* to stretch) The act of directing the mind towards an object. See *Intentionality.*—*L.W.*

Intention: In Scholastic logic, first intentions were properties or classes of, and relations between, concrete things. Second intentions were properties or classes of, and relations between, first intentions.

This suggests the beginning of a simple heirarchy of types (see *Logic, formal,* § 6), but actually is not so, because no "third intentions" were separated out or distinguished from second. Thus the general concept of *class* is a second intention, although some particular classes may also be second intentions.

Thomas Aquinas (*q.v.*) defined logic as the science of second intentions applied to first intentions.—*A.C.*

Intentionalism: Theory of mind and knowledge which considers intentionality a distinctive if not the defining characteristic of mind and the basis for mind's cognitive and conative functions. See *Intentional Theory of Mind.*—*L.W.*

Intentionality: (Lat. *intentio*, from *intendere*, to stretch) The property of consciousness whereby it refers to or intends an object. The intentional object is not necessarily a real or existent thing but is merely that which the mental act is *about*. Intentionality is the modern equivalent of the Scholastic *intentio.*—*L.W.*

(Ger. *Intentionalität*) In Husserl: 1. (broadest sense) The character of anything as "intending" or pointing beyond itself; self-transcendence. 2. (most frequent sense) The character of consciousness as pointing beyond itself, as consciousness *of* something, and as having its horizon of co-intendings: *noetic* intentionality. 3. The character of an object other than consciousness itself as pointing beyond itself, e.g., to its objective background or to something that it represents or indicates: *objective* intentionality. 4. The character of a modality as pointing back to the original of which it is intrinsically a modification. See *phenomenology.*—*D.C.*

Intentionally: (in Scholasticism) Same as mentally. —*H.G.*

Intentional Theory of Mind: The definition of mind in terms of intentionality (See *Intentionality*) which originated in the Scholastic doctrine of *intentio*, was revived by F. Brentano (*Psychologie vom empirischen standpunkte*, 1874), through his influence has become a characteristic theory of German phenomenology. See *Phenomenology.*—*L.W.*

Interactionism: See *Interaction Theory*.

Interaction Theory:(Lat. *inter* + *actio*, action) A dualistic theory of the body-mind relation, advanced by Descartes (1596-1650), which asserts a two directional causal influence between mind and body. See *Mind-Body Relation.*—*L.W.*

Interest: (Lat. *interest*, it concerns, 3rd pers. sing of *interesse*, to be between) The characteristic attitude of the mind toward any object which attracts and absorbs its attention. See *Attention.*—*L.W.*

Internal: Inside a thing (or person). Of the thing itself. The relation of part to whole or of whole to part. (a) In logic: compare intension. (b) In metaphysics: the doctrine of internal relations, that all relations are internal, that is, monism. (c) In epistemology: subjective. Opposite of external.—*J.K.F.*

Interoceptor: See *Receptor*.

Intersubjective: Used and understood by, or valid for different subjects. Especially, i. language, i. concepts, i. knowledge, i. confirmability (see *Verification*). The i. character of science is especially emphasized by Scientific Empiricism (*q.v.*).—*R.C.*

Intersubjective cognition: See *Intersubjective Intercourse*.

Intersubjective intercourse: (Lat. *inter* + *subiectus*) Knowledge by one subject of another subject or the other's conscious states. (See J. Ward, *Naturalism and Agnosticism*, pp. 164-70).—*L.W.*

Intra-ordinal Laws: Connecting properties of aggre-

gates of the same order. Laws connecting the characteristics of living organisms. (Broad.)—*H.H.*

Intrinsic: (Lat. *inter*, between + *secus*, beside) Having internal value. Value in the relation of parts to whole. —*J.K.F.*

Intrinsic goodness: The property of being good in itself or good as an end (and not as a means merely) or desirable for its own sake. Sometimes identified with the property of being desired for its own sake. According to G.E. Moore a thing is intrinsically good if it would be good even if it existed quite alone.—*W.K.F.*

Introception: (in Personalism) The coalescence of the world of objective values with his own substance by which a person attains reality.—*R.T.F.*

Introjection: (Lat. *intro.* within + *jacere*, to throw) In Epistemology, theory of the knowledge process, that objects of knowledge are represented in consciousness by images. A name given by R. Avenarius (1843-1896) to the doctrine of perception which he rejected. The doctrine of representative perception. In psychology, the ascription to material objects of some of the properties of life. More specifically, in psycho-analysis, the act of absorbing other personalities into one's own, of assuming that external events are internal. Opposite of projection.—*J.K.F.*

Epistemological theory of Descartes, Locke, Berkeley that the individual mind is confined to the circle of its ideas, and that it cognizes an external world and other minds only by an outward projection of its inner representations. The term was employed by Avenarius, (*Kritik der reinen Erfahrung*, 1888) who criticized the theory and proposed as an alternative his own theory of pure experience which emphasizes the essential solidarity between knowing subject and object known and has been introduced into English philosophy by Ward, Stout and others.—*L.W.*

Introspection: (Lat. *intro*, within + *spicere*, to look) Observation directed upon the self or its mental states and operations. The term is the modern equivalent of "reflection" and "inner sense" as employed by Locke and Kant. Two types of introspection may be distinguished: (a) the direct scrutiny of conscious states and processes at the time of their occurrence (See *Inspection*), and (b) the recovery of past states and processes by a retrospective act.—*L.W.*

Introspectionism: The standpoint in psychology which advocates the employment of the introspective method. —*L.W.*

Introspective Method: The method in psychology, which, in opposition to the objective method of Behaviorism (See *Behaviorism*) relies largely upon introspective observation. See *Introspection.*—*L.W.*

Intuitio: A term generally employed by Spinoza in a more technical sense than that found in the Cartesian philosophy (see *Reg. ad Dir. Ing.*, III). It is primarily used by Spinoza in connection with "*scientia intuitiva*" or knowledge "of the third kind" (*Ethica*, II, 40, Schol. 2). Intuition of this sort is absolutely certain and infallible; in contrast to reason (*ratio, q.v.*), it produces the highest peace and virtue of the mind (*Ibid*, V, 25 and

27). Also, as over against *ratio*, it yields an adequate knowledge of the essence of things, and thus enables us to know and love God, through which knowledge (*Ibid*, V, 39) the greater part of our mind is rendered eternal.—*W. S. W.*

Intuition: (Lat. *intuere*, to look at) The direct and immediate apprehension by a knowing subject of itself, of its conscious states, of other minds, of an external world, of universals, of values or of rational truths.—*L. W.*

Intuitionism (mathematical): The name given to the school (of mathematics) founded by L. E. J. Brouwer (*q.v.*) and represented also by Hermann Weyl, Hans Freudenthal, Arend Heyting, and others. In some respects a historical forerunner of intuitionism is the mathematician Leopold Kronecker (1823-1891). Views related to intuitionism (but usually not including the rejection of the law of excluded middle) have been expressed by many recent or contemporary mathematicians, among whom are J. Richard, Th. Skolem, and the French semi-intuitionists—as Heyting calls them—E. Borel, H. Lebesque, R. Baire, N. Lusin (Lusin is Russian but has been closely associated with the French school).

For the account given by Brouwerian intuitionism of the nature of mathematics, and the asserted priority of mathematics to logic and philosophy, see the article *Mathematics*. This account, with its reliance on the intuition of ordinary thinking and on the immediate evidence of mathematical concepts and inferences, and with its insistence on intuitively understandable construction as the only method for mathematical existence proofs, leads to a rejection of certain methods and assumptions of classical mathematics. In consequence, certain parts of classical mathematics have to be abandoned and others have to be reconstructed in different and often more complicated fashion.

Rejected in particular by intuitionism are: (1) the use of *impredicative definition* (*q.v.*); (2) the assumption that all things satisfying a given condition can be united into a set and this set then treated as an individual thing—or even the weakened form of this assumption which is found in Zermelo's *Aussonderungsaxiom* or axiom of subset formation (see *logic, formal*, § 9); (3) the law of excluded middle as applied to propositions whose expression requires a quantifier for which the variable involved has an infinite range.

As an example of the rejection of the law of excluded middle, consider the proposition, "Either every even number greater than 2 can be expressed as the sum of two prime numbers or else not every even number greater than 2 can be expressed as the sum of two prime numbers." This proposition is intuitionistically unacceptable, because there are infinitely many even numbers greater than 2 and it is impossible to try them all one by one and decide of each whether or not it is the sum of two prime numbers. An intuitionist would accept the disjunction only after a proof had been given of one or other of the two disjoined propositions—and in the present state of mathematical knowledge it is not certain that this can be done (it is not certain that the mathematical problem involved is solvable). If, however, we replace "greater than 2" by "greater than 2 and less than 1,000,000,000," the resulting disjunction becomes intuitionistically acceptable, since the number of numbers involved is then finite.

The intuitionistic rejection of the law of excluded middle is not to be understood as an assertion of the negation of the law of excluded middle; on the contrary, Brouwer asserts the negation of the negation of the law of excluded middle, i.e., $\sim \sim [p \vee \sim p]$. Still less is the intuitionistic rejection of the law of excluded middle to be understood as the assertion of the existence of a third truth-value intermediate between truth and falsehood.

The rejection of the law of excluded middle carries with it the rejection of various other laws of the classical propositional calculus and functional calculus of first order, including the law of double negation (and hence the method of indirect proof). In general the double negation of a proposition is weaker than the proposition itself; but the triple negation of a proposition is equivalent to its single negation. Noteworthy also is the rejection of $\sim (x) F (x) \supset (Ex) \sim F (x)$; but the reverse implication is valid. (The sign $\supset$ here does not denote material implication, but is a distinct primitive symbol of implication.)—*A. C.*

L.E.J. Brouwer, *De onbetrouwhaarheid der logische principes*, Tijdschrift voor Wijsbegeerte, vol. 2 (1908), pp. 152-158; reprinted in Brouwer's *Wiskunde, Waarheid, Werkelijkheid*, Groningen, 1919. L.E.J. Brouwer, *Intuitionism and formalism*, English translation by A. Dresden, Bulletin of the American Mathematical Society, vol. 20 (1913), pp. 81-96. H. Weyl, *Consistency in mathematics,* The Rice Institute Pamphlet, vol. 16 (1929), pp. 245-265. A. Heyting, *Mathematische Grundlagenforschung, Intuitionismus, Beweistheorie*, Berlin, 1934.

Intuitionism (philosophical): (1) In general: any philosophy in which intuition is appealed to as the basis of knowledge, or at least of philosophical knowledge.

(2) In ethics: (a) in the narrower traditional sense, intuitionism is the view that certain actions or kinds of action may be known to be right or wrong by a direct intuition of their rightness or wrongness, without any consideration of the value of their consequences. In this sense intuitionism is opposed to utilitarian and teleological ethics, and is most recently represented by the neo-intuitionists at Oxford: H.A. Prichard, E.F. Carritt, W.D. Ross. It is sometimes said to involve the view that the organ of ethical insight is non-rational and even unique. It takes, according to Sidgwick, three forms. Perceptual intuitionism holds that only judgments relating to the rightness or wrongness of particular acts are intuitive. Dogmatic intuitionism holds that some general material propositions relating to the rightness or wrongness of kinds of acts may also be intuited, e.g. that promises ought to be kept. Philosophical intuitionism holds that it is only certain general propositions about what is right or wrong that are intuitive, and that these are few and purely formal.

(b) In the wider more recent sense, intuitionism includes all views in which ethics is made to rest on intuitions, particular or general, as to the rightness, obligatoriness, goodness, or value of actions or objects. Taken in this sense, intuitionism is the dominant point of view in recent British ethics, and is represented in Europe by the phenomenological ethics of M. Scheler and N. Hartmann, having also proponents in America. That is, it covers not only the deontological intuitionism to be found at Oxford, but also the axiological and even teleological or utilitarian intuitionism to be found in J. Martineau, H. Sidgwick, H. Rashdall, G.E. Moore, J. Laird. Among earlier British moralists it is represented by the Cambridge Platonists, the Moral Sense School, Clarke, Cumberland, Butler, Price, Reid, Whewell, etc.

By saying that the basic propositions of ethics (i.e. of the theory of obligation, of the theory of value, or of both) are intuitive, the intuitionists mean at least that they are ultimate and underivative, primitive and uninferable, as well as synthetic, and sometimes also that they are self-evident and *a priori*. This implies that one or more of the basic notions of ethics (rightness, goodness, etc.) are indefinable, i.e. simple or unanalyzable and unique; and that ethics is autonomous. Intuitionists also hold that rightness and goodness are objective and non-natural. Hence their view is sometimes called objectivism or non-naturalism. The views of Moore and Laird are also sometimes referred to as realistic.

See *Deontological ethics, Axiological ethics, Teleological ethics, Utilitarianism, Objectivism, Realism, Autonomy of ethics, Non-naturalistic ethics.—W.K.F.*

Intuitive cognition: Intuitive cognition is the apprehension of an object (*e.g.* the hearing of a bell) in contrast to thinking about an object (*e.g.* "thinking about a bell"). (See C.D. Broad, *The Mind and its Place in Nature,* p. 144). See *Acquaintance, Knowledge by.—L.W.*

Invariant: A constant quantity. In mathematics, a quantity which remains the same under a group of transformations.—*J.K.F.*

Invention: As a practical activity is distinguished from creation as an artistic activity.—*L.V.*

Irregularity: (Theory of): In art as in nature all beauty is irregular (Renoir).—*L.V.*

Irrelevant: Not bearing upon, or logically related to, the point under discussion, or the case in hand.—*G.R.M.*

Irony, Socratic: See *Socratic method.*

Is, Isa, Isana, Isvara: (Skr.) "Lord," an example of the vacillating of Indian philosophy between theology and metaphysics. They often use such theistic nomenclature for the Absolute without always wishing to endow it as such with personal attributes except as may be helpful to a lower intelligence or to one who feels the need of worship and *bhakti* (*q.v.*).—*K.F.L.*

Islam: Name of the religion founded by Mohammed, embracing all sects found among his followers. Etymologically the term means "to resign oneself". The word means not fatalistic submission to the deity, but striving after righteousness, the practice of the law, obedience to rules and formal performance of outward duties. Meaning the acceptance of the divine will, Islam stresses the legal and external performance of religion.—*H.H.*

Isolation by Varying Concomitants: In the logic of scientific method, the fourth of the five experimental methods of J.S. Mill (1806-1873), whereby cause can be determined in any actual case. Known also as the Method of Concomitant Variation. Stated by Mill as follows: "Whatever phenomenon varies in any manner whenever another phenomenon varies in some particular manner, is either a cause or an effect of that phenomenon, or is connected with it through some fact of causation".—*J.K.F.*

Isomorphism: (Gr. *isos,* equal + *morphe,* form) Similarity of structure. In *Gestalt* psychology, structural similarity between fields in the brain and the content of consciousness.

In logic and mathematics, a relation between two systems such that there exists a one-one correspondence between their elements and an identity of some relation that holds between any of the elements in one system and the corresponding elements in the other system.—*J.K.F.*

I Yuan: The One-Prime which is the supreme beginning. It is One and is identical with the Origin. "The Prime is the root of the myriad things, in which there is also the origin of Man." (Tung Chung-shu, c. 177—104 B.C.)—*W.T.C.*

J

Jacobi, Friedrich Heinrich: (1743-1819) German philosopher of "feeling" who opposed the Kantian tradition. He held that the system of absolute subjective idealism, to which he reduced Kant, could not grasp ultimate reality. He was equally opposed to a dogmatic rationalism such as the Spinozistic. He based his view upon feeling, belief or faith by which he purported to find truth as immediately revealed in consciousness. Main works: *Ueber die Lehre des Spinoza in Briefen an Moses Mendelsohn*, 1785; *David Hume über den Glauben*, 1787; *Sendschreiben an Fichte*, 1799.—*L.E.D.*

Jainism: An Indian religion claiming great antiquity, the last of the great teachers (*tirthankara*) being Mahāvira (6th cent. B.C.), embracing many philosophical elements of a pluralistic type of realism. It rejects Vedic (*q.v.*) authority and an absolute being, gods as well as men partaking of mortality, and holds the mythologically conceived world to be eternal and subject only to the fixed sequence of six ages, good and bad, but not periodic creation and destruction. There is an infinitude of indestructible individual souls or spiritual entities, each possessing by nature many properties inclusive of omniscience, unlimited energy and bliss which come to the fore upon attaining full independence. The non-spiritual substances are space and time, rest and motion, and matter composed of atoms and capable of being apprehended by the senses and combining to form the world of infinite variety. Matter also penetrates spiritual substance like a physician's pill, changing to *karma* and producing physical attachments. The good life consists in the acquisition of the three gems (*triratna*) of right faith (*samyag-darśana*), right knowledge (*samyag-jñāna*), right conduct (*samyag-cāritra*). Salvation, i.e., becoming a *kevalin* (cf. *kevala*), is an arduous task achieved in 14 stages of perfection, the last being bodiless existence in bliss and complete oblivion to the world and its ways.—*K.F.L.*

Jamblicus: (c. 270-330 A.D.) A Syrian Neo-Platonist, who wrote extensive commentaries on Hellenic and Oriental theology and transformed Plotinus' teachings into a dogmatic theology of metaphysical pantheism.—*R.B.W.*

James, William: (1842-1910) Unquestionably one of the most influential of American thinkers, William James began his career as a teacher shortly after graduation (MD, 1870) from Harvard University. He became widely known as a brilliant and original lecturer, and his already considerable reputation was greatly enhanced in 1890 when his *Principles of Psychology* made its appearance. Had James written no other work, his position in American philosophy and psychology would be secure; the vividness and clarity of his style no less than the keenness of his analysis roused the imagination of a public in this country which had long been apathetic to the more abstract problems of technical philosophy. Nor did James allow this rising interest to flag. Turning to religious and moral problems, and later to metaphysics, he produced a large number of writings which gave ample evidence of his amazing ability to cut through the cumbersome terminology of traditional statement and to lay bare the essential character of the matter in hand. In this sense, James was able to revivify philosophical issues long buried from any save the classical scholars. Such oversimplifications as exist, for example, in his own "pragmatism" and "radical empiricism" must be weighed against his great accomplishment in clearing such problems as that of the One and the Many from the dry rot of centuries, and in rendering such problems immediately relevant to practical and personal difficulties.—*W.S.W.*

Other main works: *The Will to Believe and Other Essays in Popular Philosophy*, 1897; *Varieties of Religious Experience: A Study in Human Nature*, 1902; *Pragmatism: A New Name for Some Old Ways of Thinking*, 1907; *A Pluralistic Universe*, 1909; *Some Problems of Philosophy*, 1911; *Essays in Radical Empiricism*, 1912. Cf. R. B. Perry, *Thought and Character of William James*, 2 vols., 1935.

Jansenism: The teaching of Cornelius Jansen, latinized Jansenius (1585-1638), Bishop of Ypres, and his followers in France and Holland. Its most significant doctrines were the total corruption of human nature owing to original sin, man's inability to resist either concupiscence or grace implying the denial of free will, predestination, and the denial that Christ died for all men without exception. The Jansenists were characterized by an unusual harshness, severity of manners, and moral rigorism. The doctrine was condemned by the Church.—*J.J.R.*

Jaspers, Karl: (1883-1969) Inspired by Nietzsche's and Kierkegaard's psychology, but aiming at a strictly scientific method, the "existentialist" Jaspers analyzes the possible attitudes of man towards the world; the decisions which the individual must make in inescapable situations like death, struggle, change, guilt; and the various ways in which man meets these situations. Motivated by the boundless desire for clarity and precision, Jaspers earnestly presents as his main objective to awaken the desire for a fuller, more genuine philosophy, these three methods of philosophizing which have existed from the earliest times to the present: *Philosophical world orientation* consisting in an analysis of the limitations, incompleteness and relativity of the researches, methods, world pictures of all the sciences; *elucidation of existence* consisting of a cognitive penetration into reality on the basis of the deepest inner decisions experienced by the individual, and striving to satisfy the deepest demands of human nature; the *way of metaphysics,* the never-satisfied and unending search for truth in the world of knowledge, conduct of life and in the seeking for the one being, dimly seen through antithetic thoughts, deep existential conflicts and differently conceived metaphysical symbols of the past. Realizing the decisive problematic relation between philosophy and religion in the Middle Ages, Jaspers elevates psychology and history to a more important place in the future of philosophy. Main works: *Allgem. Psychopath.,* 1913; *Psych. d. Weltan.,* 1919; *Die geistige Situation d. Zeit,* 1931; *Vernunft u. Existenz,* 1935; *Nietzsche,* 1936; *Descartes,* 1937; *Existenzphilosophie,* 1938.—*H.H.*

Jefferson, Thomas: (1743-1826) Third president of the United States. He was the author of the Declaration of Independence, which remains as one of the monuments to his firm faith in democratic principles. His opposition to Hamiltonian centralization of power placed him at one extreme of the arc described by the pendulum of political theory that has swayed through the history of this country. He had firm faith in free speech and education and his life long efforts stand uppermost among those who struggled for tolerance and religious freedom. In addition to politics, he was keenly interested in the science and mathematics of his day. Cf. *Writings of T.J.,* 10*vols.* (N.Y. 1892-9), ed. P. L. Ford.—*L.E.D.*

Jehovah: (Hebrew *Yahveh,* of doubtful origin and meaning) Personal name of God or the supreme being in Hebrew theological and philosophical writings, commonly only since the 14th century; the national god of Israel since Mosaic times. Neither name was originally pronounced as written on account of its holiness, but was replaced by Elohim and Adonai.—*K.F.L.*

Jen: (a) Man.

(b) Goodness; virtue in general; the moral principle; the moral ideal of the superior man (chün tzŭ); the fundamental as well as the sum total of virtues, just as the Prime (yüan) is the origin and the vital force of all things— jên consisting of "man" and "two" and yüan consisting of "two" and "man." (Confucianism.)

(c) True manhood; man's character; human-heartedness; moral characters, being man-like; "that by which a man is to be a man;" "realization of one's true self and the restoration of the moral order." (Confucius and Mencius.) "The active (yang) and passive (yin) principles are the way of Heaven; the principles of strength and weakness are the way of Earth; and true manhood and righteousness (i) are the way of Man." "True manhood is man's mind and righteousness is man's path." It is one of the three Universally Recognized Moral Qualities of man (ta tê), the four Fundamentals of the Moral Life (ssŭ tuan), and the five Constant Virtues (wu ch'ang). True manhood and righteousness are the basic principles of Confucian ethics and politics (Confucianism).

(d) The golden rule; "Being true to the principles of one's nature (chung) and the benevolent exercise of them in relation to others (shu)." "The true man, having established his own character, seeks to establish the character of others; and having succeeded, seeks to make others succeed." (Confucius.)

(e) Love; benevolence; kindness; charity; compassion; "the character of the heart and the principle of love;" "love towards all men and benefit towards things." (Confucianism.) "Universal love without the element of self." (Chuang Tzŭ, between 399 and 295 B.C.) "Universal Love." (Han Yü, 767-824.)

(f) The moral principle with regard to others. "True manhood is the cardinal virtue by which others are pacified, whereas righteousness is the cardinal principle by which the self is rectified." It means "to love others and not the self." (Tung Chung-shu, 177-104 B.C.)

(g) Love of all men and things and impartiality and justice towards all men and things, this virtue being the cardinal virtue not only of man but also of the universe. "Love means to devote oneself to the benefit of other people and things." "Love implies justice, that is, as a man, treating others as men." "The true man regards the universe and all things as a unity. They are all essential to himself. As he realizes the true self, there is no limit to his love." (Ch'êng Ming-tao, 1032-1068.) "Love is the source of all laws, the foundation of all phenomena." "What is received from Heaven at the beginning is simply love, and is therefore the complete substance of the mind." "Love is the love of creating in the mind of Heaven and Earth, and men and other creatures receive it as their mind." (Chu Hsi, 1130-1200.)—*W.T.C.*

Jesuitism: Noun applied rather loosely to the teachings and practices of the Jesuits, a religious order of men of the Roman Catholic Church engaged in missionary and educational work. Originally it was called the Company, but in the Bull of Pope Paul III approving it in

1540, the Society of Jesus. Besides the three usual vows the members take a fourth of special obedience to the Pope, who may send them on missions anywhere in the world. They depend on alms and gifts for support. The word is frequently used in the depreciative and opprobrious sense of craftiness, deceit, duplicity, and equivocation.—*J.J.R.*

Jewish Philosophy: Jewish philosophy is primarily a religious philosophy.

Its first manifestation took place in Egypt where Judaism came in contact with Hellenic culture, and the result was the development of an extensive speculation among the Jews of Alexandria, the most important representative of which was Philo (*q.v.*). With the disappearance of the Egyptian Diaspora its philosophy vanished and only slight vestiges of its teachings can be traced in the early Agadic literature.

Speculation in Jewry rose again in the ninth century in the lands of the East, particularly in Babylonia, when Judaism once more met Greek philosophy, this time dressed in Arabic garb. The philosophic tradition of the ancients transmitted through the Syrians, to the young Arabic nation created a disturbance in the minds of the devotees of the Koran who, testing its principles by the light of the newly acquired wisdom, found them often wanting. As a result, various currents of thought were set in motion. Of these, the leading was the Kalamitic or the Mutazilite philosophy (*q.v.*) of several shades, the general aim of which was both to defend doctrines of religion against heresies and also to reconcile them with the principles of reason.

On the whole, there can be distinguished two currents in the entire stream of Jewish philosophy which flowed for about five hundred years, the Oriental and the Occidental. The first was limited to the lands of the East, such as Babylonia and the neighboring countries, and the leading representatives of which were Saadia (*q.v.*) among the Rabbanites and Aaron ben Elijah (*q.v.*) among the Karaites. The second developed primarily in Spain and the Provence, and among its leading thinkers were Bahya (*q.v.*), Gabirol (*q.v.*), Maimonides (*q.v.*), Gersonides (*q.v.*), and Crescas (*q.v.*). Since Jewish philosophy, during a large part of its existence, was developed within the Arabic world, it consequently reflects the influence of the various systems of thought dominant within that sphere.

Almost all Jewish philosophers with the exception of Gabirol, ha-Levi, and Gersonides produce proofs for the existence of God. These proofs are based primarily on principles of physics. In the case of the Western philosophers, they are Aristotelian, while in the case of the Eastern, they are a combination of Aristotelian and those of the Mutazilites. The Eastern philosophers, such as Saadia and others and also Bahya of the Western prove the existence of God indirectly, namely that the world was created and consequently there is a creator. The leading Western thinkers, such as Ibn Daud (*q.v.*) and Maimonides employ the Aristotelian argument from motion, even to positing hypothetically the eternity of the world. Ha-Levi considers the conception of

the existence of God an intuition with which man is endowed by God Himself. Crescas, who criticized Aristotle's conception of space and the infinite, in his proof for the existence of God, proves it by positing the need of a being necessarily existent, for it is absurd to posit a world of possibles.

The next step is to demonstrate God's unity for which various proofs are given. Saadia and the followers prove it from the conception of creator; the others, including Maimonides, deduce it from the concept of an unmoved mover from which His incorporeality is also deduced. The argument that harmony of the universe is due to one creator or one first cause is also frequently employed.

The problem of attributes gave rise to extensive discussions. In general, the attempt is made to convey some knowledge about God and yet maintain that His essence is inconceivable. The number of attributes varies with individual philosophers, from three of Bahya to eight of Ibn Daud. Saadia counts one, living, potent and wise as essential attributes; Bahya one, existent, and eternal. Ha-Levi substitutes living for existent. Ibn Daud adds to those of Saadia and Bahya three more: true, willing, and potent. Maimonides considers living, potent, wise, and willing as those agreed upon by philosophers. The difficulty, however, does not consist in the number but in their content, or in other words, how to speak of essential attributes and not to impair the simplicity of God's essence. Bahya was the first to assert that their content is negative, e.g., existent means not non-existent. He was followed in this by all others. Maimonides is especially insistent upon the negative meaning and asserts that they are to be applied to God and man in an absolute homonymic manner, i.e., there is no possible relation between God and other beings. Gersonides and Crescas, on the other hand, believe that the essential attributes are positive though we cannot determine their content. There are, of course, other attributes which are descriptive of His action, but these are not essential.

The relation of God to the world includes, as we have seen, a number of problems. The general conception of the world with almost all Jewish philosophers is mainly Aristotelian. All, not excluding Saadia, who was to a considerable degree under the influence of the Mutazilites, accept Aristotle's theory of matter and form, i.e., that all bodies are composed of two elements, the substratum or the *hylé* and the particular form with which it is endowed. They all speak of primal matter which was the first creation, and all accept his view of the four elements, i.e., fire, air, water, and earth which are the components of all things in the lower world. They also accept his cosmogony, namely, the division of the universe of the upper world of the spheres and the lower or sublunar world, and also posit the influence of the spheres upon the course of events in this world. On the other hand, all oppose his view of the eternity of the world and champion creation *de novo* with slight variations.

The differences begin when the questions of the mode of creation and mediators between God and the world are dealt with. In these matters there are to be noted three variations. Saadia rejected entirely the theory of the emanation of separate intelligences, and teaches God's creation from nothing of all beings in the sublunar and upper worlds. He posits that God created first a substratum or the first air which was composed of the *hylé* and form and out of this element all beings were created, not only the four elements, the components of bodies in the lower world, but also the angels, stars, and the spheres. Bahya's conception is similar to that of Saadia. The Aristotelians, Ibn Daud, Maimonides, and Gersonides accepted the theory of the separate intelligences which was current in Arabic philosophy. This theory teaches that out of the First Cause there emanated an intelligence, and out of this intelligence another one up to nine, corresponding to the number of spheres. Each of these intelligences acts as the object of the mind of a sphere and is the cause of its movement. The tenth intelligence is the universal intellect, an emanation of all intelligences which has in its care the sublunar world. This theory is a combination of Aristotelian and neo-Platonic teachings; Ibn Daud posits, however, in addition to the intelligences also the existence of angels, created spiritual beings, while Maimonides seems to identify the angels with the intelligences, and also says that natural forces are also called angels in the Bible.

As for creation, Ibn Daud asserts that God created the *hylé* or primal matter and endowed it with general form from which the specific forms later developed. Maimonides seems to believe that God first created a substance consisting of primal matter and primal form, and that He determined by His will that parts of it should form the matter of the spheres which is imperishable, while other parts should form the matter of the four elements. These views, however, are subject to various interpretations by historians. Gabirol and Gersonides posit the eternal existence of the *hylé* and limit creation to endowing it with form and organization — a view close to the Platonic.

Divine providence is admitted by all Jewish philosophers, but its extent is a matter of dispute. The conservative thinkers, though admitting the stability of the natural order and even seeing in that order a medium of God's providence, allow greater latitude to the interference of God in the regulation of human events, or even in disturbing the natural order on occasion. In other words, they admit a frequency of miracles. The more liberal, though they do not deny the occurrence of miracles, attempt to limit it, and often rationalize the numerous miraculous events related in the Bible and bring them within the sphere of the rational order. Typical and representative is Maimonides' view of Providence. He limits its extent in the sublunar world to the human genus only on account of its possession of mind. As a result he posits a graded Providence, namely, that the one who is more intellectually perfect receives more attention or special Providence. This theory is also espoused, with certain modifications, by Ibn Daud and Gersonides. Divine providence does by no means impair human freedom, for it is rarely direct, but is exerted through a number of mediate causes, and human choice is one of the causes.

There is, however, greater difficulty in making freedom of the will compatible with divine prescience of human action. The question arises, does God know beforehand what man will do or not? If he does, it follows that the action is determined, or if man can choose, His knowledge is not true. Various answers were proposed by Jewish philosophers to this difficult problem. Saadia says that God's knowledge is like gazing in a mirror of the future which does not influence human action. He knows the ultimate result. Maimonides says that God's knowledge is so totally different from human's that it remains indefinable, and consequently He may know things beforehand, and yet not impair the possibility of man to choose between two actions. Ibn Daud and Gersonides limit God's knowledge and say that He only knows that certain actions will be present to man for choice but not the way he will choose. Crescas is more logical and comes to the conclusion that action is possible only per se, i.e., when looked upon singly, but is necessary through the causes. Free will is in this case nominal and consists primarily in the fact that man is ignorant of the real situation and he is rewarded and punished for his exertion to do good or for his neglecting to exert himself.

The origin, nature, and the continued existence or immortality of the soul is widely discussed in Jewish philosophy. As to origin, Saadia believes that each individual soul is created by God — considering, of course, creation a continuous process — and that it is of a fine spiritual substance. As to its faculties, he accepts the Aristotelian-Platonic division of the soul into three parts, namely, the appetitive, emotional, and cognitive. Ibn Daud thinks that the soul exists prior to the body potentially, i.e., that the angels endow the body with form; he further considers it a substance but says that it undergoes a process of development. The more it thinks the more perfect it becomes, and the thoughts are called acquired reason, it is this acquired reason, or being perfected which remains immortal. Maimonides does not discuss the origin of the soul, but deals more with its parts. To the three of Saadia he adds the imaginative and the conative. Gersonides' view resembles somewhat that of Ibn Daud, except that he does not speak of its origin and limits himself to the intellect. The intellect, says he, is only a capacity residing in the lower soul, and that capacity is gradually developed with the help of the Active Intellect into an acquired and ultimately into an active reason. All thinkers insist on immortality, but with Saadia and ha-Levi it seems that the entire soul survives, while the Aristotelians assert that only the intellect is immortal. Maimonides is not explicit on the subject, yet we may surmise that even the more liberal thinkers did not subscribe to Averroes' theory of *unitas intellectus,* and they believed that the immortal intellect is endowed with consciousness of personality. To this trend of connecting immortality with rational reflection Crescas took exception, and asserts that it is not pure thought which leads to survival, but that the soul is immortal because it is a spiritual being, and it is perfected by its love for God and the doing of good.

The view of freedom of the will and the soul influenced to a great extent the ethics of the Jewish philosophers. A large number of thinkers accepted the Aristotelian norm of the golden mean as the rule of conduct, but considered that the laws and precepts of the Torah help towards obtaining right conduct. Maimonides, however, stated that the norm of the mean is only for the average man, but that the higher man should incline towards an extreme good way in conduct. Crescas' view of the good way follows from the theory of the soul, he stresses the emotional element, namely the necessity of the love of the Good and the desire to actualize it in life.

Of the many theological doctrines included in this philosophy, there are to be noted those of the Torah and prophecy. The Torah is considered by all philosophers divinely revealed. The Sinaitic revelation was accomplished by means of a specially created voice which uttered the commandments. The Torah is therefore immutable and is eternal. Its purpose is to train men for a good life. According to Maimonides, the Torah aims at both the improvement of the soul and of the body. The first is accomplished by inculcating right conceptions about God, and the second by numerous laws which regulate the life of the individual and society.

Another means of revelation is prophecy. The authenticity of prophecy, says Saadia, is not based on the miracles by which it is demonstrated but on its intrinsic worth. Maimonides says the prophet must possess great intellectual ability, rich phantasy, and perfect ethical conduct; only then he may be called by the divine spirit.

Literature. I. Husik, *A History of Jewish Philosophy*, New York, 1918; D. Neumark, *Geschichte der Jüdischen Philosophie*, Vols. I, II, Berlin, 1907, 1910; Julius Guttmann, *Philosophie des Judentums*, Berlin, 1935; M. Waxman, *The Philosophy of Don Hasdai Crescas*, New York, 1920; *A History of Jewish Literature*, Vols. I, II, Chapters on Jewish Philosophy, New York, 1930, 1933; H. A. Wolfson, *Crescas' Critique of Aristotle*, Cambridge, 1929.—*M.W.*

Jīva: (Skr.) Life; also the individual, conscious soul as distinguished from the universal soul or the Absolute.—*K.F.L.*

Jīvanmukta: (Skr.) One who has attained salvation while in this present life: all but a remainder of *prārabdha karma* (*q.v.*) has been neutralized and no new *karma* is accumulated in virtue of the person's having gained insight, *jñāna* (*q.v.*).—*K.F.L.*

Jñāna: (Skr.) Cognition, knowledge, wisdom, philosophic understanding, insight, believed by some Indian philosophers to effect *moksa* (*q.v.*).–*K.F.L.*

Jñānendriya: (Skr.) One of the five *indriyas* (*q.v.*) of knowledge, the cognitive senses or powers of hearing, seeing, feeling, smelling, and tasting.—*K.F.L.*

Jodl, Friedrich: (1848-1914) His central interest was research in the field of ethics; engaged in developing a humanistic and naturalistic ethic. Made his most nota-

ble contribution in the history of ethical theories. Following the positivists Feuerbach, Comte and Mill, he projected a new religion of national culture. Main works: *Gesch. der Ethik*, 1906; *Wissensch u. Religion*, 1909; *Der Monismus u.d. Kulturprobleme*, 1911.—*H.H.*

John of Salisbury: (c. 1115-1180) From the works of this Englishman, much can be learned about the schoolmen of his day for he presents cogent criticism of their views which he characterizes as fruitless. In his *Metalogicus* he advocates reform in logic. He was among the earliest adherents of absolute separation of church and state, a view which he advanced in *Policraticus*. He adopted a practical attitude toward knowledge, seeking the rejection of what was useless and contrary to a pious life, even though proof positive could not be advanced for what was found favorable to the true good.—*L.E.D.*

Joseph, Albo: (1380-1444) Jewish philosopher. His *Ikkarim*, i.e., *Dogmas* is devoted primarily to the problem of dogmatics. He differs with Maimonides who fixed the Articles of Creed at thirteen, and posits only three fundamental dogmas.

(1) Belief in the existence of God; (2) Divine origin of the Torah; (3) Reward and punishment. The others are of secondary importance. See *Jewish Philosophy*. —*M.W.*

Jou: Weakness; the principle of weakness, opposite of the principle of strength; the outstanding characteristic of the Earthly Principle (k'un) and corresponding to the passive cosmic principle (Yin). See *Kang*.—*W.T.C.*

Ju: (a) Confucianists.

(b) Scholars who were versed in the six arts, namely, the rules of propriety, music, archery, charioteering, writing, and mathematics.

(c) Priest-teachers in the Chou period (1122-249 B.C.) who clung to the dying culture of Shang (1765-1122 B.C.), observed Shang rules of conduct, became specialists on social decorum and religious rites. —*W.T.C.*

Ju chia: The Confucian School, which "delighted in the study of the six Classics and paid attention to matters concerning benevolence and righteousness. They regarded Yao and Shun (mythological emperors) as founders whose example is to be followed, King Wen (1184-1135 B.C.?) and King Wu (1121-1116 B.C.?) as illustrious examples, and honored Confucius (551-479 B.C.) as the exalted teacher to give authority to their teaching." "As to the forms of proper conduct which they set up for prince and minister, for father and son, or the distinctions they make between husband and wife and between old and young, in these not even the opposition of all other philosophers can make any change."

Confucius taught that "it is man that can make truth great, and not truth that can make man great." Consequently he emphasized moral perfection, true manhood (jên), moral order (li) the Golden Mean (Chung Yung) and the superior man (chün tzü). To this end, knowledge must be directed, names must be rectified (chêng ming), and social relationships harmonized (wu lun). The whole program involved the investigation of things, the extension of knowledge, sincerity of the will, rectification of the heart, cultivation of the personal life, regulation of family life, national order, and finally, world peace. Mencius (371-289 B.C.) carried this further, holding that we not only should be good, but must be good, as human nature is originally good. True manhood (jên) and righteousness (i) are considered man's mind and path, respectively. Government must be established on the basis of benevolence (jên cheng) as against profit and force. Hsun Tzŭ (c. 335-288 B.C.) believing human nature to be evil, stressed moral accumulation and education, especially through the rectification of names, music, and the rule of propriety (li). In the book of *Chung Yung* (Central Harmony, the Golden Mean, third or fourth century B.C.), the doctrine of central harmony is set forth. Our central self or moral being is conceived to be the great basis of existence and harmony or moral order is the universal law in the world. From then on, the relationship between man and the universe became one of direct correspondence. The idea of macrocosmos-microcosmos relationship largely characterized the Confucianism of medieval China. The most glorious development of Confucianism is found in Neo-Confucianism, from the eleventh century to this day. For a summary of medieval Confucianism and Neo-Confucianism, see *Chinese philosophy.—W.T.C.*

Ju chiao: The teachings of the Confucian school, which are based on the Confucian classics with the chief emphasis on ethics and polity. Since the establishment of Confucianism as the state cult in the second century A.D., the term has also been used to designate the traditional system of worship of Shang Ti, ancestors, etc., which the Confucians followed.—*W.T.C.*

Judgment: (a) The mental act of asserting (affirming or denying) an assertible content. Traditionally a judgment is said to affirm or to deny a predicate of a subject. As generalized by modern logicians this becomes affirmation or denial of a relation (not necessarily that of predication) among certain terms (not necessarily two). One classification of judgments lists them as problematic, assertoric, or apodeictic, depending on whether they are asserted as probable (or improbable or possible), true (or false), or necessary (or impossible). Since a judgment in this sense always involves a truth claim it is either correct or erroneous.

(b) That which is asserted in an act of judgment, often called a belief or a proposition. That which is judged may merely be contemplated or considered instead of being affirmed or denied. Opinions differ as to the ontological status of propositions. Some regard them as mental, some as neutral, some as verbal.—*C.A.B.*

Judgment of Taste: The assertion that an object is beautiful, or aesthetically pleasing. Such propositions are traditionally classified as judgments of value, as distinguished from judgments of fact, and are regarded as making assertions about the subjective reaction and interest that the object has aroused, and not about any intrinsic property of the object. Hence, generally interpreted as having no claim to universality. Kant, and others, have sought to establish their universality on the ground that they assert a necessary subjective reaction.—*I.J.*

Jung, C. G.: (1875-1961) Exponent of a type of psychoanalysis (see *Psychoanalysis*) known as "analytic psychology," which has close affinities with Freudianism (see *Freud, Sigmund*) and with individual psychology (see *Adler, Alfred*). Jung employed Freud's methods of free association and dream analysis but emphasized his own method of word-association. He differed from Freud in (a) minimizing the rôle of sex, and (b) emphasizing *present* conflict rather than childhood complexes in the explanation of neuroses. Jung is also known for his classification of psychological types as introverts and extroverts. Cf. Jung's *Psychological Types.—L.W.*

Jurisprudence: English term for the study of philosophical questions in law, which in the United States are often subsumed under the headings "Philosophy of Law" or "Legal Philosophy" (*q.v.*).—*T.P.S.*

Justice: (L. justitia; OF justise) In the Western philosophical tradition justice has been viewed as the first virtue of societies and individuals. Plato held justice to be the harmonious arrangement of the three major virtues, wisdom, courage and temperance, where in the individual and by analogy in the state all of the components, as in the workings of a well-built machine, are in their proper place and performing the particular function for which they were designed. Aristotle echoes this view when he says that "in justice is every virtue comprehended" (*Nic. Ethics*, v. 1). Justice is a complex concept, traditionally linked to moral, legal, social and political philosophy, and is generally understood in terms of fairness, reciprocity, impartiality, equatability, or legality.

Justice can be divided into two major categories. The first, Distributive justice, concerns the proper ordering of the social, legal, economic and political institutions of a society such that there is a just or equatable distribution of the benefits and burdens entailed by the social order. Included under this heading are economic factors such as income, taxation, goods and services, as well as less tangible commodities such as citizenship, honors, rights and duties. Distributive justice presupposes that there is a limit to the resources available to the members of society, for without scarcity the question of justice would not arise. Distributive justice may be organized in accordance with three major principles, each with attendant complications: (a) arithmetical equality; (b) merit; (c) need. Distribution according to the principle of arithmetical equality presents difficulties when we consider that, in certain circumstances, some individuals may be more deserving than others to receive particular rewards that society may bestow. We consider it just to award a gold medal, not to each contestant, but to the winner of the race. Distribution according to merit raises the question of how we are to judge merit, and what qualities or achievements we are to consider meritorious. Similarly, distribution according to need demands the establishment of criteria by which need is to be judged, a complicated process even in a small social unit such as a family.

The second category of justice is Commutative or Rectificatory justice, that involving transactions between persons. Aristotle groups this into two main headings, the first involving voluntary transactions such as the establishment of a just price or a fair wage, the second involving involuntary transactions such as harm done by one person to another.

Both categories of justice are subsumed under the wider questions that concern the status of justice, particularly the relationship between justice, society and the law. The sociological argument that claims justice to be a creation of society, or of a particular segment or strata of society, has its roots in ancient Greek thought. In Book I of Plato's *Republic* Thrasymachus argues that justice is the advantage of the stronger, a view held in modified form by Machiavelli in *The Prince* and many modern Marxists. In Book II Glaucon portrays justice as a matter of social convention, a position which David Hume explored in the 18th century. According to Hume, conventions overseeing human cooperation arise naturally, in a manner analogous to the way in which two persons rowing on opposite sides of a boat gradually discover that they will each achieve their individual goals of getting across the lake more efficiently if they row in consort with each other. These conventions regulating social life, without which, according to Hobbes, the life of man would be "solitary, poor, nasty, brutish, and short," eventually are codified into law, and justice consists of following these laws which establish the social order. Later, says Hume, a moral feeling or sentiment for mankind underpins the existing laws, so that justice takes on a moral as well as a legal sanction.

The positivistic view of justice as a function of the laws of society is opposed by a long tradition of natural law that holds there to be a court of appeals beyond the ken of extant social and political institutions with the power to adjudicate fundamental disputes in the name of justice. This view of the "Law behind the law" passes through the Greeks to the Roman concept, articulated by Cicero, of the universal law of nature, eternal and unchangable, equally accessable to all by the use of reason. The concept was Christianized by Aquinas (*Summa Theologia,* Q90ff, "Treatise on Law"), who distinguished four levels of law: (1) eternal law, or the law of God; (2) natural law, or what humans by the light of reason can see of the eternal law; (3) divine law, or the law of God as revealed by Scripture; and (4) positive law, or the existing laws of society. The concept of natural law as the ultimate arbiter of justice was central also to Locke and other exponents of traditional social contract theory. Recently, John Rawls' *A Theory of Justice* (1970) is an attempt to find a contemporary equivalent of natural law, drawing on an updated version of the "state of nature" of social contract theory to formulate a set of principles of justice which "free and rational persons would accept in an initial position of equality."

Plato, *Republic;* Aristotle, *Nicomachean Ethics* (especially Book V); Aquinas, *Summa Theologica,* Part I; Hobbes, *Leviathan;* Hume, *Treatise of Human Nature,* Book III, *Enquiry Concerning The Principles of Morals;* Rousseau, *The Social Contract;* Mill, *Utilitarianism, On Liberty;* Hart, *The Concept of Law;* Rawls, *A Theory of Justice.* See also *Political Philosophy, Legal Philosophy, Natural Law, Plato, Aristotle, Locke, Hume, Hobbes, Rousseau, Social Contract.—T.P.S.*

Justin Martyr: (c. 100-160) A prominent Christian Apologist, who taught that Divine truth appears in two forms, first, in man's power of reasoning, and second, in special revelation expressed by philosophers, prophets, and especially Christ. Cf. Justin's *Apologia.—R.B.W.*

K

Kafka, Franz: (1883-1924) Influential literary figure in existentialism, Kafka's main works include *The Castle* and *The Trial,* describing the human situation as one in which a man is on trial without ever knowing why.—*S.E.N.*

Kalā: (Skr.) Art-creation, authorship, *e.g.,* as one of the aspects of Shiva's progressive world creation. See *Kañcuka.*—*K.F.L.*

Kāla: (Skr.) Time, variously conceived in India philosophy. See *e.g., Astikaya, Dravya, Kañcuka.*—*K.F.L.*

Kalanos; (Grecized from Skr. *kalyāna*) A Hindu philosopher who lived at the court of Alexander the Great while in India and finally mounted his own funeral pile.—*K.F.L.*

Kalology: The study of the beauties of sensible objects and of character combined. (Montague).—*H.H.*

Kames, Henry Home: (1696-1782) He was a well known Scotch lawyer of his day who later became one of the lords of justiciary and sat as a judge in the court of session. He became entangled in a free will controversy after the publication of his "Principles of Morality and Natural Religion." His "Elements of Criticism" is a widely known classic in the field of aesthetics. —*L.E.D.*

Kami: (Japanese) Originally denoting anything that inspires and overawes man with a sense of holiness, the word assumed a meaning in Japanese equivalent to spirit (also ancestral spirit), divinity, and God. It is a central concept in the pre-Confucian and pre-Buddhistic native religion which holds the sun supreme and still enjoys national support, while it may also take on a more abstract philosophic significance.—*K.F.L.*

Kant, Immanuel: (1724-1804), born and died in Königsberg. Studied the Leibniz-Wolffian philosophy under Martin Knutzen. Also studied and taught astronomy (see *Kant-Laplace hypothesis*), mechanics and theology. The influence of Newton's physics and Lockean psychology vied with his Leibnizian training. Kant's personal life was that of a methodic pedant, touched with Rousseauistic piety and Prussian rigidity. He scarcely travelled 40 miles from Königsberg in his life-time, disregarded music, had little esteem for women, and cultivated few friends apart from the Prussian officials he knew in Königsberg. In 1755, he became tutor in the family of Count Kayserling. In 1766, he was made under-librarian, and in 1770 obtained the chair of logic and metaphysics at the University of Königsberg. Heine has made classical the figure of Kant appearing for his daily walk with clock-like regularity. But his very wide reading compensated socially for his narrow range of travel, and made him an interesting conversationalist as well as a successful teacher.

Kantianism: The philosophy of Immanuel Kant (1724-1804); also called variously, the critical philosophy, criticism, transcendentalism, or transcendental idealism. Its roots lay in the Enlightenment; but it sought to establish a comprehensive method and doctrine of experience which would undercut the rationalistic metaphysics of the 17th and 18th centuries.

In an early "pre-critical" period, Kant's interest centered in evolutionary, scientific cosmology. He sought to describe the phenomena of Nature, organic as well as inorganic, as a whole of interconnected natural laws. In effect he elaborated and extended the natural philosophy of Newton in a metaphysical context drawn from Christian Wolff and indirectly from Leibniz.

But Kant's versatile, analytical mind could not rest here; and gradually his ideas underwent a radical transformation. He questioned the assumption, common to dogmatic metaphysics, that reality can be apprehended in and through concepts. He was helped to this view by the study of Leibniz's *Nouveaux Essais* (first published in 1765), and the skepticism and empiricism of Hume, through which, Kant stated, he was awakened from his "dogmatic slumbers." He cast about for a method by which the proper limits and use of reason could be firmly established. The problem took the form: By what right and within what limits may reason make synthetic, a priori judgments about the data of sense?

By 1770, the beginning of his "critical" period, Kant had an answer which he confidently expected would revolutionize philosophy. First dimly outlined in the *Inaugural Dissertation* (1770), and elaborated in great detail in the *Critique of Pure Reason* (1781 and 1787), the answer consisted in the critical or transcendental method. The typical function of reason, on Kant's view, is relating or synthesizing the data of sense. In effecting any synthesis, the mind relies on the validity of certain principles, such as causality, which, as Hume had shown, cannot be inductive generalizations from sense data, yet are indispensable in any account of "experience" viewed as a connected, significant whole. If the necessary, synthetic principles cannot be derived from sense data proper, then, Kant argued, they must be "a priori"—logically prior to the materials which they relate. He also called these formal elements "transcendental," by which he meant that, while they are indubitably *in* experience viewed as a connected whole, they transcend or are distinct from the sensuous materials in source and status. In the *Critique of Pure Reason*—his "theoretical philosophy"—Kant undertakes a complete inventory and "deduction" of all synthetic, a priori, transcendental forms employed in the knowledge of Nature. The first part, the "Transcendental Aesthetic," exhibits the two forms or "intuitions" *(Anschauungen)* of the *sensibility:* space and time. Knowledge of Nature, however varied its sense content, is necessarily always of something in space and time; and just because these are necessary conditions of any experience of Nature, space and time cannot be objective properties of things-in-themselves, but must be formal demands of reason. Space and time are "empirically real," because they are present in actual experience; but they are "transcendentally ideal," since they are forms which the mind "imposes" on the data of sense.

In the second part, the "Transcendental Logic," Kant treats of the synthetic forms of the *understanding* (Verstand), which he calls "categories" or "pure principles of the understanding." Of these he recognizes twelve in all, arranged in groups of threes under the heads: quantity, quality, relation and modality. The sensuous materials embedded in the forms of sensibility constitute percepts, while reason, through the understanding, supplies the concepts and principles by means of which percepts are synthesized into meaningful judgments of Nature. In the celebrated "deduction of the categories," Kant shows that without these forms there could be no knowledge or experience of Nature. Just therein and only therein lies their validity.

But by the same token, as Kant now shows in the third part on "Transcendental Dialectic," the forms of *sensibility* and *understanding* cannot be employed beyond experience in order to define the nature of such metaphysical entities as God, the immortal soul, and the World conceived as a totality. If the forms are valid *in* experience only because they are necessary conditions *of* experience, there is no way of judging their applicability to objects transcending experience. Thus Kant is driven to the denial of the possibility of a science of metaphysics. But though judgments of metaphysics are indemonstrable, they are not wholly useless. The "Ideas of Pure Reason" *(Vernunft)* have a "regulative use," in that they point to general objects which they cannot, however, constitute. Theoretical knowledge is limited to the realm of experience; and within this realm we cannot know *"things-in-themselves,"* but only the way in which things appear under a priori forms of reason; we know things, in other words, as *"phenomena."*

But reason is not limited to its theoretical use. Besides objects of cognition and thought, there are also those of will and feeling. Kant's "practical philosophy," the real foundation of his system of transcendental idealism, centers in a striking doctrine of freedom. Even in its theoretical use, reason is a lawgiver to Nature, in that the data of sense must conform to the forms of the sensibility and understanding if Nature is to be known at all. But in moral experience, as Kant shows in the *Critique of Practical Reason* (1788), the will of a rational being is directly autonomous—a law unto itself. but the unconditional moral law, "duty" or "categorical imperative," the validity of which Kant does not question, is possible only on the supposition that the will is really free. As *phenomenal* beings we are subject to the laws of nature and reason; but as pure rational wills we move in the free, *noumenal* or intelligible realm, bound only by the self-imposed rational law "to treat humanity in every case as an end, never as a means only."

The influence of Pietism and of Rousseau's gospel of Nature are apparent in the essentially Christian and democratic direction in which Kant develops this rigorous ethics. The reality of God and the immortality of souls—concerning which no theoretical demonstration was possible—emerge now as *postulates* of practical reason; God, to assure the moral governance of a world in which virtue is crowned with happiness, the *"summum bonum;"* immortality, so that the pursuit of moral perfection may continue beyond the empirical life of man. These postulates, together with moral freedom and popular rights, provide the basis for Kant's assertion of the *primacy of practical reason.*

Finally, intellect and will are brought into meaningful relation (*Critique of Judgment,* 1789-1793) in the feelings of aesthetic (i.e., "artistic") enjoyment and natural purposiveness. The appreciation of beauty, "aesthetic judgment," arises from the harmony of an object of cognition with the forms of knowledge; the perfect compatibility, in other words, of Nature and freedom, best exemplified in genius. Natural purposiveness, on the other hand, is not necessarily a real attribute of Nature, but an a priori, heuristic principle, an irresistible hypothesis, by which we regard Nature as a supreme end or divine form in order to give the particular contents of Nature meaning and significance.

The influence of Kant has penetrated more deeply than that of any other modern philosopher. His doctrine of freedom became the foundation of idealistic metaphysics in Fichte, Schelling and Hegel, but not without sacrifice of the strict critical method.

Schopenhauer based his voluntarism on Kant's distinction between phenomena and things-in-themselves. Lotze's teleological idealism was also greatly indebted to Kant. Certain psychological and pragmatic implications of Kant's thought were developed by J. F. Fries, Liebmann, Lange, Simmel and Vaihinger. More recently another group in Germany, reviving the critical methods, sought a safe course between metaphysics and psychology; it includes Cohen, Natorp, Riehl, Windelband, Rickert, Husserl, Heidegger, and E. Cassirer. Until recent decades English and American idealists such as Caird, Green, Bradley, Howison, and Royce, saw Kant for the most part through Hegel's eyes. More recently the study of Kant's philosophy has come into its own in English-speaking countries through such commentaries as those of N. K. Smith and Paton. In France the influence of Kant was most apparent in Renouvier's "Phenomenism."—*O.F.K.*

Kant-Laplace hypothesis: Theory of the origin of the solar system, formulated first by Kant (*Natural History and Theory of the Heavens,* 1755) and later by Laplace (*Exposition of the System of the World,* 1796). According to this theory the solar system evolved from a rotating mass of incandescent gas which by cooling and shrinking, and thus increasing its rate of spin, gradually flattened at its poles and threw off rings from its equator. These rings became the planets, which by the operation of the same laws developed their own satellites. While Laplace supposed the rotating nebula to have been the primordial stuff, Kant maintained that this was itself formed and put into rotation by gravitational action on the original atoms which through their impact with one another generated heat.—*A.C.B.*

Kapila: Founder of the Sāṅkhya (*q.v.*).—*K.F.L.*

Kāraṇa: Skr. Cause; *causa efficiens.*—*K.F.L.*

Karma, Karman: (Skr.) Action, movement, deed, a category *e.g.* in the Vaiśeṣika (*q.v.*). In Indian philosophy generally thought of as a metaphysical entity carried by the individual along in *saṃsāra* (*q.v.*). As law, *karma* would be identical with physical causation or causality while working with equal rigor in man's psychic and thought life. As such it is the unmitigated law of retribution working with equal precision in "good" and "evil" deeds and thoughts, thus determining the nature and circumstances of incarnation. *Karma* is classified into *prārabdha* (effects determining the unavoidable circumstances of man's life), *saṃcita* (effects able to be expiated or neglected, *e.g.,* through *jñāna*), and *āgāmi* (effects currently generated and determining the future). Jainas (*q.v.*) enumerate 148 kinds of *karma*.—*K.F.L.*

Karmakānda: (Skr., see *Karma* above) That portion of the Veda (*q.v.*) with which the priests are concerned.—*K.F.L.*

Karmendriya: (Skr.) One of the five *indriyas* (*q.v.*) or powers of action, reactive or muscular senses, corresponding to the physiological capacities of expression or speech, seizing or handling, locomotion, excretion, and sexual activity.—*K.F.L.*

Kathenotheism: A term invented by Max Müller which literally denotes one at a time—theism. It symbolizes the Vedic monotheistic practice according to which the position of the gods is so arranged that each God is supreme in turn, in which the titular god is always changing without entailing a denial that the other gods exist.—*H.H.*

Kempen, Thomas Hemerken van: (1380-1471) Also called Thomas á Kempis, was born at Kempen in Holland, received his early education and instruction in music at the monastery of the Brethren of the Common Life, at Deventer. He attended no university but attained a high degree of spiritual development. His *Imitation of Christ* is one of the most famous and most used books of Catholic spiritual meditation; it has been printed in nearly all languages and is found in innumerable editions. There seems to be no valid reason for questioning his authorship of the work.—*V.J.B.*

Kenotism: The doctrine of Kenosis; literally the Greek term Kenosis means an emptying. The doctrine arose from the discussion of Phil. ii, 7, where we read that Christ "emptied himself, taking the form of a servant." Some have interpreted the text in the sense that the Son of God in becoming man put aside some of His divine attributes, while others, notably the Catholics, maintain that the abasement referred to signifies only the occultation of the Divinity when the Word was made flesh.—*J.J.R.*

Kevala: (Skr. alone) A predicate or synonym of the Absolute in its unitary, free, autonomous, all-inclusive and universal aspect. The condition or state of being absolute and independent is *kevalatva,* one who meditates on or has attained personal experience of it, is a *kevalin.*—*K.F.L.*

Kierkegaard, Søren: (1813-1855) Danish philosopher, founder of existentialism (*q.v.*). Born in Copenhagen, the son of a wealthy and successful businessman, he studied at the University of Copenhagen and devoted his life to writing, both under his own name (the "direct" works) and under various pen names (the "indirect," or pseudonymous works). His works include *The Concept of Irony* (1841), *Either/or* (1843), *Fear and Trembling* (1844), *The Concept of Dread* (1844), *Stages on Life's Way* (1845), *Concluding Unscientific Postscript* (1846), *Works of Love* (1847), *The Sickness Unto Death* (1849), *Training in Christianity* (1850), and (when the articles from the *Fatherland,* a newspaper, were collected together), *Attack Upon Christendom.*

Kierkegaard's main thought is a reaction against Hegelian rationalism: "Abstract thought . . . ignores the concrete and the temporal . . . For the abstract thinker himself, since he is an existing individual he must in one way or another be suffering from absent-mindedness." Existence, he holds, is passionate and even comic, but it is not rational.

Truth is subjectivity, the only truth possible for existing individuals. Kierkegaard does not deny the possibility of objective truth, but only that human beings may know it.

Every generation is equidistant from eternity. History does not improve our ability to know the truth, or to be related to it.

The standard Danish edition of his works is *Samlede Vaerker* (Gyldendal, 1964).—*S.E.N.*

Kind: (a) A class or collection of entities having a common character that differentiates members of this class from non-members. (b) J. S. Mill *(System of Logic)* limits the term to natural classes, such as biological species, where members have, in addition to the defining property, an unlimited number of other properties in common.—*C.A.B.*

Kinesis: (Gr. *kinesis*) Motion; change. In Aristotle's philosophy three kinds of kinesis are distinguished: (1) quantitative change, i.e., increase and diminution; (2) change of quality; and (3) change of place, or locomotion. Among the forms of kinesis Aristotle also sometimes reckons the two forms of substantial change, viz. generation, or coming-to-be, and destruction, or passing away. See *Aristotelianism.*—*G.R.M.*

Knower, The: The subject of knowledge, conceived either as a mental act, an empirical self or a pure ego. See *Subject.* The knower in contrast to the object known. See *Epistemological object.*—*L.W.*

Knowledge: (As. *cnawan,* know) Relations known. Apprehended truth. Opposite of opinion. Certain knowledge is more than opinion, less than truth. Theory of knowledge, or epistemology (*q.v.*), is the systematic investigation and exposition of the principles of the possibility of knowledge. In epistemology: the relation between object and subject. See *Epistemology.*

Cf. E. Cassirer, *Das Erkenntnisprobleme,* 1906.—*J.K.F.*

K'o chi: Conquering, controlling oneself or self-cultivation, Chinese scholars are divided in interpretation. By the first interpretation it means "restoring the moral order" and being a true man (jên), avoiding, in particular, partiality and selfish desires. By the second interpretation it means self realization.—*W.T.C.*

Köhler, Wolfgang: (1887-1967) An associate of Wertheimer and Koffka at Frankfort, was one of the co-founders of *Gestalt* psychology. He was later Professor of Psychology at the University of Berlin and Professor of Psychology at Swarthmore College. His *Gestalt Psychology* (1929), contains an excellent statement in English of the theoretical foundations of *Gestalt.*—*L.W.*

Koffka, Kurt: (1896-1941) Along with Wertheimer and Köhler, one of the original triumvirate of *Gestalt* psychologists. See *Gestalt Psychology.* Koffka, relying on the results of Köhler's study of learning in apes, has, in opposition to the current attempts to treat learning exclusively in terms of trial and error, emphasized the essential role of insight in learning. See *The Growth of the Mind,* 1925, pp. 153-230.—*L.W.*

Koran: *(Qoran)* The name for the sacred book of the Mohammedans. Its contents consist largely of warnings, remonstrances, assertions, arguments in favor of certain doctrines, narratives for enforcing morals. It stresses the ideal of the day of judgment, and abounds in realistic description of both the pains of hell and the delights of paradise. As a collection of command-ments, it resembles juristic rescripts (answers to special questions), mentioning the contradictory rulings on the same subjects. It also resembles a diary of the prophet, consisting of personal addresses by the deity to Mohammed.—*H.H.*

Korn, Alejandro: Born in San Vicente, Buenos Aires in 1860. Died in Buenos Aires, 1936. Psychiatrist in charge of Melchor Romero Hospital for the Insane and Professor of Anatomy at the National College of La Plata. Professor of Ethics and Metaphysics in the Universities of Buenos Aires and La Plata, from 1906-1930, and one time Dean of the Faculty of Philosophy and Letters of Buenos Aires. Director of his own review, *Valoraciones,* and patriarch of the modern philosophical tradition of Argentine. The following may be considered his most important works: *Influencias Filosoficas en la Evolucion Nacional,* 1919; *La Libertad Creadora,* 1922; *Esquema Gnoseologico,* 1924; *El Concepto de Ciencia,* 1926; *Axiología,* 1930; *Apuntes Filosoficos,* 1935.

Korn's philosophy represents an attack against naïve and dogmatic positivism, but admits and even assimilates an element of Positivism which Korn calls *Native Argentinian Positivism.* Alejandro Korn may be called The Philosopher of Freedom. In fact, freedom is the keynote of his thought. He speaks of human liberty as the indissoluble union of economic and ethical liberties. The free soul's knowledge of the world of science operates mainly on the basis of intuition. In fact, intuition is the basis of all knowledge. "Necessity of the objective world order," "Freedom of the spirit in the subjective realm," "Identity," "Purpose," "Unity of Consciousness," and other similar concepts, are "expressions of immediate evidence and not conclusions of logical dialectics." The experience of freedom, according to Korn, leads to the problem of evaluation, which he defines as "the human response to a fact," whether the fact be an object or an event. Valuation is an experience which grows out of the struggle for liberty. Values, therefore, are relative to the fields of experience in which valuation takes place. The denial of an absolute value or values, does not signify the exclusion of personal faith. On the contrary, personal faith is the common ground and point of departure of knowledge and action. See *Latin-American Philosophy.*—*J.A.F.*

Kośa: (Skr.) "Sheath," one of the envelopes of the soul or self concealing its real nature, which is pure consciousness. The Vedānta knows three: the *ānandamaya, vijñānamaya,* and *annamaya kośas,* i.e., the sheaths of pleasure, intellect, and food, composing respectively the *kāraṇa, sūksma,* and *sthūla śarīra,* meaning the causal, subtile, and gross frame or body.—*K.F.L.*

Ko wu: (a) Investigation of things. (Confucianism.)

(b) Investigation of the Reason (li) of things and affairs to the utmost. (Chu Hsi, 1130-1200.)

(c) "Rectification" of things and affairs by the extension of one's intuitive knowledge so that what is not correct in things, and therefore evil, may be corrected and made good. (Wang Yang-ming, 1473-

1529.)—*W.T.C.*

Kratocracy: (Gr. *krateros,* strong) Government by those who are strong enough to seize power through force or cunning. (Montague).—*H.H.*

Krause, Karl Christian Friedrich: (1781-1832) Kant's younger contemporary, who attempted to formulate a speculative reconciliation of theism and pantheism, or "panentheism." Main works: *Grundl. d. Naturrechts,* 1803; *System d. Sittenlehre,* 1810; *Das Urbild d. Menschheit,* 1811; *Vorles. u.d. Grundwahrheiten d. Wissenschaften,* 1829.—*R.B.W.*

Kripke, Saul: (1941-) American philosopher, teacher at Rockefeller University and Princeton, author of "Naming and Necessity" (1972), arguing that reference, not description, gives proper names their meaning. He also argues that the materialist idea that mental states are identical with brain states is mistaken.—*S.E.N.*

Ksanika-vāda: (Skr.) The Buddhistic theory *(vāda)* asserting that everything exists only momentarily *(kṣaṇika),* hence changes continually.—*K.F.L.*

Ku: Cause, "that with the obtaining of which a thing becomes." "A minor cause is that the obtaining of which a thing may not necessarily be so but without the obtaining of which a thing will never be so." "A major cause is that with the obtaining of which a thing is necessarily so but without the obtaining of which a thing is necessarily not so." (Neo-Mohism.)—*W.T.C.*

Kua: Trigram. See *Pa kua.*

Kuei: Man's spirit after death; earthly spirits coexisting with heavenly spirits (shên); the passive or negative (yin) aspect of the soul as against the active or positive (yang) aspect which is called hun; the operation of the passive cosmic principle, yin, (in Neo-Confucianism).—*W.T.C.*

Külpe, Oswald: (1862-1915) Opposing idealistic Neo-Kantianism, he is the most typical pioneer of philosophical realism in Germany. He characterized the method of the sciences, himself a leading psychologist, as a procedure which he terms *Realizierung.* He affirms the existence of the real in sharp contrast to every conscientialism and objective idealism. He defends the possibility and justification of physical realism. He recognizes neither purely rational nor purely empirical arguments for the existence of the external world in itself. Main works: *Grundriss d. Psychol.,* 1893; *Einleitung i.d. Philos.,* 1895 (Eng. tr. *Introd. to Philosophy); Kant,* 1907; *Erkenntnistheorie u. Wissensch.,* 1910; *Die Realisierung,* 3 vols. 1912-1922; *Vorlesungen über Logik,* 1923.—*H.H.*

K'un: (a) The trigram of the element earth of the eight trigrams (pa kua).

(b) The trigram of the female principle of the universe. See *Ch'ien.*—*H.H.*

Kung: Accomplishment "which is of benefit to the people." (Mohism.)—*W.T.C.*

Kung: Respect; courtesy; politeness; expression of reverence and seriousness (chin). Kung refers to expression, whereas chin refers to action. (Confucianism, Neo-Confucianism.)—*W.T.C.*

Kuo Hsiang: (Kuo Tzŭ-hsüan, c. 312. A.D.) The outstanding Taoist in medieval China, wrote the standard commentary on *Chuang Tzŭ* based on the notes of his senior contemporary Hsiang Hsiu.—*W.T.C.*

L

Lachelier, J.: (1831-1918) A French philosopher who, though he wrote little, exerted a considerable direct personal influence on his students at the Ecole Normale Supérieure; he was the teacher of both E. Boutroux and H. Bergson. His philosophical position was a Kantian idealism modified by the French "spiritualism" of Maine de Biran and Ravaisson.

Main works: *Le fondement de l'induction,* 1871; *Psychologie et métaphysique,* 1885; *Etudes sur le syllogisme,* 1907; *Note sur le pari de Pascal.—L.W.*

Lamaism: (from Tibetan *b La-ma,* honorable title of a monk) The religious beliefs and institutions of Tibet, derived from Mahāyāna Buddhism (*q.v.*) which was first introduced in the 7th century by the chieftain Sron-tsan-gampo, superimposed on the native Shamaistic Bon religion, resuscitated and mixed with Tantric (*q.v.*) elements by the mythic Hindu Padmasambhava, and reformed by the Bengalese Atīśa in the 11th and Tsong-kha-pa at the turn of the 14th century. The strong admixture of elements of the exorcismal, highly magically charged and priest-ridden original Bon, has given Buddhism a turn away from its philosophic orientation and produced in Lamaism a form that places great emphasis on *mantras* (*q.v.*)—the most famous one being *om mani padme hum*—elaborate ritual, and the worship of subsidiary tutelary deities, high dignitaries, and living incarnations of the Buddha. This worship is institutionalized, with a semblance of the papacy, in the double incarnation of the Bodhisattva (*q.v.*) in the Dalai-Lama who resides with political powers at the capital Lhasa, and the more spiritual head Tashi-Lama who rules at Tashi-lhum-po. Contacts with Indian and Chinese traditions have been maintained for centuries and the two canons of Lamaism, the Kan-jur of 108 books and the Tan-jur of 225 books represent many translations as well as original works, some of great philosophical value.—*K.F.L.*

Lambert, J. H: (1728-1777) Was one of Kant's correspondents. He was of the Leibniz-Wolffian school which attempted an eclectic reconciliation between rationalism and empiricism and thus laid a foundation for the later Kantian critical philosophy. As such, he is viewed as an important forerunner of Kant.—*L.E.D.*

Lambert is known also for important contributions to mathematics, and astronomy; also for his work in logic, in particular his (unsuccessful, but historically significant) attempts at construction of a mathematical or symbolic logic. Cf. C. I. Lewis, *Survey of Symbolic Logic.—A.C.*

Lamennais, R.: (1782-1854) Leader of a Platonic-Christian movement in the Catholic clergy of France. He advanced the idea of "inspired mankind." He attacked the eighteenth century for its principles and its method. In finding dissolution and destruction as its aftermath, he advocated a return to the Catholic Church as the solution.

Main works: *Paroles d'un croyant,* 1834; *Esquisse d'une philosophie,* 1841-46.—*L.E.D.*

Lamettrie, Julien Offroy de: (1709-1751) A French materialist and author of *L'homme machine,* in which he expresses his belief that the soul is a product of bodily growth; he maintains that the brain has its "thought muscles" just as the leg has its "walk muscles."

Main works: *Histoire naturelle de l'âme,* 1745; *L'homme-machine,* 1747; *L'homme-plante,* 1748; *Discours sur le bonheur,* 1748; *Le système d' Epicure,* 1750.—*R.B.W.*

Lange, Friedrich Albert: (1828-1875) Celebrated for his *History of Materialism,* based upon a qualified Kantian point of view, he demonstrated the philosophical limitations of metaphysical materialism, and his appreciation of the value of materialism as a stimulus to critical thinking. He worked for a greater understanding of Kant's work and anticipated fictionalism.—*H.H.*

Langer, Susanne K.: (1895-   ) Famous American philosopher and teacher at Connecticut College, author of *Philosophy in a New Key* (1942) and *Mind: an Essay on Human Feeling,* Vol. I (1967), II (1972), and III(1981). A student of Alfred North Whitehead, she writes that music expresses a knowledge of life patterns which ordinary language cannot express.—*S.E.N.*

Language, Functions of: Some utterances (a) are produced by a speaker, (b) induce effects in an interpreter, (c) are related to a certain subject matter (which may, but in general will not, include either the speaker or interpreter). According as one or other of the relations in which the utterance stands to the several factors of such speech-situations is selected for attention, the (token) utterance may be said to have expressive, evocative and referential functions. The utterance *expresses* thoughts, desires, attitudes of the speaker; *evokes* reactions (thoughts, evaluations, tendencies to action) in the hearer; *designates* or *refers to* its reference.

While all three functions are normally distinguishable in any given utterance, typesentences (and, derivatively, words) may be classified according as one or the other of the functions normally predominates in the occurrence of the corresponding tokens. (Thus exclamations are predominantly expressive, commands evocative, scientific generalizations referential.) Such distinctions may, in turn, be made the basis for distinguishing different types of linguistic systems.

While most writers on language agree as to the value of making some such distinctions, there is little agreement as to the number and kinds of functions which may usefully be recognized. There is even less agreement about nomenclature. The account given follows that of Kretschmer (*Sprache*, 61 ff. in Gercke and Norden, *Einleitung in die Altertumswissenschaft*, I) and Bühler (*Sprachtheorie*, passim). Ogden and Richards distinguish five functions (*Meaning of Meaning*, 357 ff.). The broad distinction between "referential" and "emotive" uses of language, due to the same authors, has been widely accepted.—*M.B.*

Language, Philosophy of: Any philosophical investigation arising from study of concrete, actualized, languages, whether "living" or "dead." By "language" is here to be understood a system of signs (whether words or ideograms) used in regular modes of combination, in accordance with conventionally established rules, for the purpose of communication.

Philosophers have in the past been concerned with two questions covered by our definition, though attempts to organize the subject as an autonomous department of philosophy are of recent date.

(1) Enquiries into the *origin* of language (*e.g.* in Plato's *Kratylos*) once a favorite subject for speculation, are now out of fashion, both with philosophers and linguists.

(2) Enquiries as to the *nature* of language (as in Descartes, Leibniz, and many others) are, however, still central to all philosophical interest in language. Such questions as "What are the most general characters of symbolism?," "How is 'Language' to be defined?," "What is the essence of language?," "How is communication possible?," "What would be the nature of a perfect language?," are indicative of the varying modulations which this theme receives in the works of contemporaries.

Current studies in the philosophy of language can be classified under five heads:

(a) *Questions of method, relation to other disci-*

plines, etc. Much discussion turns here upon the proposal to establish a science and art of symbolism, variously styled semiotic, semantics or logical syntax.

(b) *The analysis of meaning*. Problems arising here involve attention to those under the next heading.

(c) *The formulation of general descriptive schemata*. Topics of importance here include the identification and analysis of different ways in which language is used, and the definition of such crucial notions as "symbol," "grammar," "form," "convention," "metaphor," etc.

(d) *The study of fully formalized language systems or "calculi"*. An increasingly important and highly technical division which seeks to extend and adapt to all languages the methods first developed in "metamathematics" for the study of mathematical symbolism.

(e) *Applications to problems in general philosophy*. Notably the attempt made to show that necessary propositions are really verbal; or again, the study of the nature of the religious symbol. Advance here awaits more generally acceptable doctrine in the other divisions.

References: K. Bühler, *Sprachtheorie*. R. Carnap, *Logical Syntax of Language*. E. Cassirer, *Philosophie der symbolischen Formen*. A. H. Gardiner, *The Theory of Speech and Language*. C. W. Morris, *Foundations of the Theory of Signs*. C. K. Ogden and I. A. Richards, *The Meaning of Meaning*. C. S. Peirce, *Collected Papers*.

See also *Communication, Meaning, Referent, Semiotic, Sign, Symbol, Functions of Language, Scientific Empiricism*.—*M.B.*

Language of Science: See *Scientific Empiricism II B* 1.

Lao Tzŭ: Whether the founder of Taoism (tao chia) was the same as Li Erh and Li An, whether he lived before or after Confucius, and whether the *Tao Tê Ching* (Eng. trans.: *The Canon of Reason and Virtue* by P. Carus, *The Way and Its Power* by A. Waley, etc.) contains his teachings are controversial. According to the *Shih Chi* (Historical Records), he was a native of Chu (in present Honan), land of romanticism in the south, and a custodian of documents whom Confucius went to consult on rituals. Thus he might have been a priest-teacher who, by advocating the doctrine of "inaction," attempted to preserve the declining culture of his people, the suppressed people of Yin, while Confucius worked hard to promote the culture of the ruling people of Chou.—*W.T.C.*

Lassalle, Ferdinand: (1825-1864) Was influenced in his thought by Fichte and Hegel but soon assumed a distinctly materialist position. His main interest and activity lay in the field of political and economic philosophy; he advocated, and worked for, the formation of trade unions in Germany and adhered to socialism.

Main works: *Die Philosophie Herakleitos d. Dunklen*, 1858; *System d. Erworbenen Rechte*, 1861; and political speeches and pamphlets in *Collected Works* (Leipzig, 1899-1901).—*R.B.W.*

Latency: (Lat. *latere*, to be hidden) (a) *In metaphysics*, the term latency is equivalent to potency or potentiality. See *Potentiality*.

(b) *In epistemology and psychology*, the term is applied to knowledge, *e.g.* memory, which lies dormant in the mind but is capable of becoming actual and explicit (see W. Hamilton, *Lectures on Metaphysics*, xviii, cited by J. M. Baldwin, *Dictionary of Philosophy and Psychology*, Vol. I, p. 628). Latency in this restricted sense, designates phenomena now embraced by the term subconscious. See *Subconscious*.—*L.W.*

Latin-American Philosophy: Philosophy in Latin America may be divided into three periods.

(1) The *scholastic* period begins with the *Recognitio summularum* of Alonso de la Vera-cruz (1554) and continues to the dawn of the nineteenth century. According to Ueberweg, the influence of Duns Scotus during this period was greater than that of Thomas Aquinas.

(2) The predominantly *naturalistic and positivistic* period coincides roughly with the nineteenth century. The wars of independence were accompanied by revolt from scholasticism. In the early part of the century, liberal eclectics like Cousin and P. Janet were popular in South America, but French eighteenth century materialism exerted an increasing influence. Later, the thought of Auguste Comte and of Herbert Spencer came to be dominant especially in Mexico, Brazil, Argentina, and Chile. Even an idealistically inclined social and educational philosopher like Eugenio Maria de Hostos (1839-1903), although rejecting naturalistic ethics, maintains a positivistic attitude toward metaphysics.

(3) The *predominantly idealistic* period of the twentieth century was initiated by the work of the Argentine Alejandro Korn (1860-1936), who introduced modern German philosophy to his fellow-countrymen. Francisco Romero, also an Argentine, has brought about the translation of many European philosophical classics into Spanish. Leibniz, Kant, Hegel, and the more recent neo-Kantians and phenomenologists have exerted wide influence in Latin America. North American personalism has also attracted attention. In Mexico, José Vasconcelos and Pedro Gringoire reflect in their own syntheses the main streams of idealistic metaphysics, ethics, esthetics. Puerto Rico, with its recent publication of the writings of Hostes, is also a center of philosophic activity. There are signs of growing philosophical independence throughout Latin America.—*J.F., E.S.B.*

Latitudinarianism: (1) A party in the Church of England (middle of the 17th century) aiming to reconcile contending parties by seeking a broad basis in common doctrines. (2) A term applied to a liberal opinion which allows diversity in unity. (3) A term used derisively as meaning indifference to religious doctrines.—*V.F.*

Law: (in Kant) "Every formula which expresses the necessity of an action is called a law" (*Kant*).—*P.A.S.*

Law, Chinese School of: See *Fa chia* and *Chinese philosophy*.

Law of Population: In economics, the tendency of population to encroach upon the means of subsistence. First announced by Malthus (1766-1834), the Law asserts that the increase of unchecked population is in geometric ratio while the increase of the means of subsistence is in arithmetic ratio, so that population must always press upon the limits of the means of subsistence.—*J.K.F.*

Laws of thought: See *Logic, traditional*.

Leading principle: The general statement of the validity of some particular form of valid inference (see *Logic, formal*) may be called its *leading principle*.

Or the name may be applied to a proposition or sentence of logic corresponding to a certain form of valid inference. E.g., the law of *exportation* (*q.v.*) may be called the *leading principle* of the form of valid inference known as exportation.—*A.C.*

Legal Philosophy: Deals with the philosophic principles of law and justice. The origin is to be found in ancient philosophy. The Greek Sophists criticized existing laws and customs by questioning their validity: All human rules are artificial, created by enactment or convention, as opposed to natural law, based on nature. The theory of a law of nature was further developed by Aristotle and the Stoics. According to the Stoics the natural law is based upon the eternal law of the universe; this itself is an outgrowth of universal reason, as man's mind is an offshoot of the latter. The idea of a law of nature as being innate in man was particularly stressed and popularized by Cicero, who identified it with "right reason" and already contrasted it with written law that might be unjust or even tyrannical. Through Saint Augustine these ideas were transmitted to medieval philosophy and by Thomas Aquinas built into his philosophical system. Thomas considers the eternal law the reason existing in the divine mind and controlling the universe. Natural law, innate in man, participates in that eternal law.

A new impetus was given to Legal Philosophy by the Renaissance. Natural Jurisprudence, properly so-called, originated in the XVII century. Hugo Grotius, Thomas Hobbes, Benedictus Spinoza, John Locke, Samuel Pufendorf were the most important representatives of this line of thought. Grotius, continuing the Scholastic tradition, particularly stressed the absoluteness of natural law (it would exist even if God did not exist) and, following Jean Bodin, the sovereignty of the people.

The idea of the social contract (*q.v.*) traced all political bodies back to a voluntary compact by which every individual gave up his right to self-government, or rather transferred it to the government, abandoning a state of nature which according to Hobbes must have been a state of perpetual war. The theory of the social compact more and more accepts the character of a "fiction" or of a regulative idea (Kant). In this sense the theory means that we ought to judge acts of government by their correspondence to the general will (Rousseau) and to the interests of the individuals who by transferring their rights to the commonwealth intended to establish their real liberty. Natural law, by putting the emphasis on natural rights, takes on a revolutionary character. It played a part in shaping the bills of rights, the constitutions of the American colonies and of the Union, as well as of the French declaration of the rights of men and of citizens. Natural jurisprudence in the teachings of Christian Wolff and Thomasius undergoes a kind of petrification in the vain attempt to outline an elaborate system of natural law not only in the field of international or public law, but also in the detailed regulations of the law of property, of contract, etc. This sort of dogmatic approach towards the problems of law evoked the opposition of the Historic School (Gustav Hugo and Savigny) which stressed the natural growth of laws and customs, originating from the mysterious "spirit of the people." On the other hand Immanuel Kant tried to overcome the old natural law by the idea of a "law of reason," meaning an a priori element in all existing or positive law. In his definition of law ("the ensemble of conditions according to which everyone's will may coëxist with the will of every other in accordance with a general rule of liberty"), however, as in his legal philosophy in general, he still shares the attitude of the natural law doctrine, confusing positive law with the idea of just law. This is also true of Hegel whose panlogism seemed to lead in this very direction.

Under the influence of epistemological positivism (Comte, Mill) in the later half of the nineteenth century, legal philosophy, especially in Germany, confined itself to a "general theory of law." Similarly John Austin in England considered philosophy of law concerned only with positive law, "as it necessarily is," not as it ought to be. Its main task was to analyze certain notions which pervade the science of law (Analytical Jurisprudence). In recent times the same tendency to reduce legal philosophy to logical or at least methodological tasks was further developed in attempting a pure science of law (Kelsen, Roguin). Owing to the influence of Darwinism and natural science in general the evolutionist and biological viewpoint was accepted in legal philosophy: comparative jurisprudence, sociology of law, the Freirecht movement in Germany, the study of the living law, "Realism" in American legal philosophy, all represent a tendency against rationalism. On the other hand there is a revival of older tendencies: Hegelianism, natural law — especially in Catholic philosophy—and Kantianism (beginning with Rudolf Stammler). From here other trends arose: the critical attitude leads to relativism (f.i. Gustav Radbruch); the antimetaphysical tendency towards positivism—though different from epistemological positivism—and to a pure theory of law. Different schools of recent philosophy have found their applications or repercussions in legal philosophy: Phenomenology, for example, tried to intuit the essences of legal institutions, thus coming back to a formalist position, not too far from the real meaning of analytical jurisprudence. Neo-positivism, though so far not yet explicitly applied to legal philosophy, seems to lead in the same direction.—*W.E.*

Plato, *Republic, Statesman;* Aristotle, *Nicomachean Ethics;* Cicero, *De Re Publica, De Legibus;* Augustine, *City of God;* Hobbes, *Leviathan;* Locke, *Second Treatise on Government;* Mill, *Utilitarianism, On Liberty;* Hart, *The Concept of Law, Punishment and Responsibility;* Wasserstrom, *The Judicial Decision;* Dworkin, ''The Model of Rules;'' Feinberg and Gross, eds., *Philosophy of Law.*

Legalism, ethical: The insistence on a strict literal or overt observance of certain rules of conduct, or the belief that there are rules which must be so obeyed. Opposed on the one hand by the view which emphasizes the spirit over the letter of the law, and on the other by the view which emphasizes a consideration of the value of the consequences of actions and rules of action. Deontological ethics is often said to be legalistic. Cf. F. Cohen, *Legal Ideals and Ethical Systems.—W.K.F.*

Lei: (a) Generic name. "All similar substances necessarily bear the same name." (Neo-Mohism)

(b) Generic relationship or partial relationship. See *Mo chê.—W.T.C.*

Leibniz, Gottfried Wilhelm: (1646-1716) Born in Leipzig, where his father was a professor in the university, he was educated at Leipzig, Jena, and Altdorf University, where he obtained his doctorate. Jurist, mathematician, diplomat, historian, theologian of no mean proportions, he was Germany's greatest 17th century philosopher and one of the most universal minds of all times. In Paris, then the centre of intellectual civilization (Molière was still alive, Racine at the height of his glory), where he had been sent on an official mission of state, he met Arnauld, a disciple of Descartes who acquainted him with his master's ideas, and Huygens who taught him as to the higher forms of mathematics and their application to physical phenomena. He visited London, where he met Newton, Boyle, and others. At the Hague he came face to face with the other great philosopher of the time, Spinoza. One of Liebniz's cherished ideas was the creation of a society of scholars that would investigate all branches of scientific truth so as to combine them into one great system of truth. His philosophy, the work "of odd moments," bears, in content and form, the impress of its haphazard origin and its author's cosmopolitan mode of life. There is no systematic exposition, only a large number of letters, essays, memoranda, etc., published in various scientific journals. Universality and individuality characterized him both as a man and philosopher.

Leibniz's philosophy was the dawning consciousness of the modern world (Dewey). So gradual and continuous, like the development of a monad, so all-inclusive was the growth of his mind, that his philosophy, as he himself says, "connects Plato with Democritus, Aristotle with Descartes, the Scholastics with the moderns, theology and morals with reason." The reform of all science was to be effected by the use of two instruments, a universal scientific language and a calculus of reasoning. He advocated a universal language of ideographic symbols in which complex concepts would be expressed by combinations of symbols representing simple concepts or by new symbols defined as equivalent to such a complex. He believed that analysis would enable us to limit the number of undefined concepts to a few simple primitives in terms of which all other concepts could be defined. This is the essential notion back of modern logistic treatments.

In contributing some elements of a "universal calculus" he may be said to have been the first serious student of symbolic logic. He devised a symbolism for such concepts and relations as "and," " or," implication between concepts, class inclusion, class and conceptual equivalence, etc. One of his sets of symbolic representations for the four standard propositions of traditional logic coincides with the usage of modern logic. He anticipated in the principles of his calculus many of the important rules of modern symbolic systems. His treatment, since it was primarily intensional, neglected important extensional features of recent developments, but, on the other hand, called attention to certain intensional distinctions now commonly neglected.

Leibniz is best known in the history of philosophy as the author of the Monadology and the theory of the Preestablished Harmony both of which see.

Main works: *De arte combinatoria,* 1666; *Theoria motus concreti et abstracti,* 1671; *Discours de la métaphysique,* 1686; *Système nouveau de la nature,* 1695; *Nouveaux Essais sur l'entendement humain,* 1701 (publ. 1765, criticism of Locke's *Essay*); *Théodicée,* 1710; *Monadologie,* 1714 (letter to Prince Eugene of Savoy). No complete edition of L. exists, but the Prussian Academy of Sciences began one and issued 4 vols. to date. Cf. Gerhardt's edition of L's philosophical works (7 vols., 1875-90) and mathematical works (1849-63), Foucher de Careil's edition, 7 vols. (1859-75), O. Klopp's edition of L.'s historico-political works, 10 vols. (1864-77), L. Couturat's *Opuscules et fragments inédits de L.,* 1903.—*K.F.L.*

Lemma: (Gr. *lemma*) In Aristotle's logic a premiss of a syllogism.—*G.R.M.*

In mathematics, a theorem proved for the sake of its use in proving another theorem. The name is applied especially in cases where the lemma ceases to be of interest in itself after proof of the theorem for the sake of which it was introduced.—*A.C.*

Lenin, V. I.: (Ulianov, Vladimir Ilyich) Lenin is generally regarded as the chief exponent of dialectical materialism (*q.v.*) after Marx and Engels. He was born April 22, 1870, in Simbirsk, Russia, and received the professional training of a lawyer. A Marxist from his student days onward, he lived many years outside of Russia as a political refugee, and read widely in the social sciences and philosophy. In the latter field his "Philosophical Note Books" (as yet untranslated into English) containing detailed critical comments on the works of many leading philosophers, ancient and modern, and in particular on Hegel, indicate his close study of texts. In 1909, Lenin published his best known philosophic work "Materialism and Empirio-Criticism" which was directed against "a number of writers, would-be Marxists" including Bazarov, Bogdanov, Lunacharsky, Berman, Helfond, Yushkevich, Suvorov and Valentinov, and especially against a symposium of this group published under the title, "Studies in the Philosophy of Marxism" which in general adopted the "positivistic" position of Mach and Avenarius.

In his economic and political writings, Lenin extended and developed the doctrines of Marx and Engels especially in their application to a phase of capitalism which emerged fully only after their death—imperialism. In the same fashion Lenin built upon and further extended the Marxist doctrine of the state in his "State and Revolution," written just before the revolution of 1917. In this work Lenin develops a concept like the dictatorship of the proletariat which Marx treated only briefly and generally, elaborates a distinction like that between socialism and communism, only implicit in Marx's work, and asserts a thesis like the possibility of socialism in one country, towards which Marx was negative in the light of conditions as he knew them. After the Bolsheviks came to power, Lenin headed the government until his death on January 21, 1924. In Russian, Lenin's "Collected Works" comprise thirty volumes, with about thirty additional volumes of miscellaneous writings ("Leninskie Sborniki"). The principal English translations are the "Collected Works," to comprise thirty volumes (of which five in eight books have been published to date), the "Selected Works" comprising twelve volumes (for philosophical materials, see especially Volume XI, "Theoretical Principles of Marxism"), and the Little Lenin Library, made up mostly of shorter works, comprising 27 volumes to date.—*J.M.S.*

Lessing, Gotthold Emphraim: (1729-1781) German dramatist and critic. He is best known in the philosophic field for his treatise on the limitations of poetry and the plastic arts in the famous "Laokoon." In the drama, "Nathan the Wise," he has added to the world's literature a profound plea for religious toleration.—*L.E.D.*

Leucippus: (c. 450 B.C.) A contemporary of Empedocles and Anaxagoras and founder of the School of Abdera, developed the fruitful principle that all qualitative differences in nature may be reduced to quantitative ones. Thus Leucippus breaks up the homogeneous "Being" of Parmenides into an infinity of equally homogeneous parts or atoms and he distributes these, in an infinite variety of forms, through infinite space. These small particles of "Being" are separated from one another by that which is not-Being, i.e. by empty space. "Becoming," or the coming into being of things, is essentially the result of the motion of these atoms in space and their accidental coming together.—*M.F.*

Level: A grade or type of existence or being which entails a special type of relatedness or of organization, with distinctive laws. The term has been used primarily in connection with theories of emergent evolution where certain so-called higher levels, *e.g.* life, or mind, are supposed to have emerged from the lower levels, *e.g.* matter, and are considered to exhibit features of novelty not predictable from the lower levels.—*A.C.B.*

Lévy-Bruhl, Lucien: (1857-1939) Professor of Philosophy at the Sorbonne 1899-1939, represents a sociological and anthropological approach to philosophy; his chief contribution is an anthropological study of primitive religion which emphasizes the "prelogical" or mystical character of the thinking of primitive peoples. *La Mentalité primitive* (1922), Eng. trans., 1923; *L'Ame Primitive* (1927). His other writings include: *History of Modern Philosophy in France* (Eng. trans., 1899); *The Philosophy of Auguste Comte* (1900, Eng. trans., 1903).—*L.W.*

Lewis, Clarence Irving: (1883-1964) Professor of Philosophy at Harvard. In Logic, Lewis has originated and defended *strict implication* (*q.v.*) in contrast to *material implication,* urging that formal inference should be based on a relation which can be known to hold without knowing what is true or false of this particular universe. See his *Survey of Symbolic Logic,* and his and C. H. Langford's *Symbolic Logic,* esp. Ch. VIII. Lewis has argued also for "queer logics," that is abstract systems somewhat different from the abstract system usually interpreted as logic. Lewis raises the question how "queer" a system can be and still be interpretable properly as a system of logic.

In Epistemology (See his *Mind and the World-Order*) Lewis has presented a "conceptualistic pragmatism" based on these theses: (1) "A priori truth is definitive in nature and rises exclusively from the analysis of concepts." (2) "The choice of conceptual systems for . . . application [to particular given experiences] is . . . pragmatic." (3) "That experience in general is such as to be capable of conceptual interpretation . . . could not conceivably be otherwise."—*C.A.B.*

Li: Reason; Law; the Rational Principle. This is the basic concept of modern Chinese philosophy. To the Neo-Confucians, especially Ch'êng I-ch'uan (1033-1107), Ch'êng Ming-tao (1032-1086) and Chu Hsi (1130-1200), Reason is the rational principle of existence whereas the vital force (ch'i) is the material principle. All things have the same Reason in them, making them one reality. By virtue of their Reason, Heaven and Earth and all things are not isolated. The Reason of a thing is one with the Reason of all things. A thing can function easily if it follows its own Reason. Everything can be understood by its Reason. This Reason of a thing is the same as its nature (hsing). Subjectively it is the nature, objectively it is Reason. Lu Hsiang shan (1139-1193) said that there is only one mind and there is only one Reason, which are identical. It fills the universe, manifesting itself everywhere. To Wang Yang-ming (1473-1529), the mind itself is the embodiment of Reason. To say that there is nothing existing independent of Reason is to say that there is nothing apart from the mind. See *Li hsüeh, Chinese philosophy,* and *ch'i.*—*W.T.C.*

Li: Propriety; code of proper conduct; rules of social contact; good manners; etiquette; mores; rituals; rites; ceremonials. In Confucius, it aims at true manhood (jên) through self-mastery, and central harmony (ho). "Propriety regulates and refines human feelings, giving them due allowance, so as to keep the people within bounds." It is "to determine human relationships, to settle suspicions and doubts, to distinguish similarity and difference, and to ascertain right and wrong." "The rules of propriety are rooted in Heaven, have their correspondences in Earth, and are applicable to spiritual beings." "Music unites, while rituals differentiate. . . . Music comes from the inside, while rituals come from the outside. Because music comes from the inside, it is characterized by quiet and calm. And because rituals come from the outside, they are characterized by formalism. . . . Truly great music shares the principles of harmony with the universe, and truly great ritualism shares the principles of distinction with the universe. Through the principles of harmony, order is restored in the physical world, and through the principles of distinction, we are enabled to offer sacrifices to Heaven and Earth. . . . Music expresses the harmony of the universe, while rituals express the order of the universe. Through harmony all things are influenced, and through order all things have a proper place. Music rises from Heaven, while rituals are patterned on Earth. . . ." (Early Confucianism.) "The code of propriety has three sources: Heaven and Earth gave birth to it—this is a source; our ancestors made it fit the situation—this is a source; the princes and teachers formed it—this is a source." (Hsün Tzŭ; c. 335 — 238 B.C.)—*W.T.C.*

Li: (a) Profit, the principle of gain in contrast with the principle of righteousness (i). (Mencius, etc.)

(b) Benefit, "that which, when obtained, gives pleasure," or the largest amount of happiness for the greatest number of people, as a result of Universal Love (chien ai). Righteousness, loyalty, filial piety, and accomplishment are forms of li. (Mohism and Neo-Mohism.)—*W.T.C.*

Libertarianism: (Lat. *libertas,* freedom) Theory of the freedom of the will. See *Free-Will.*—*L.W.*

Liberty: (in Scholasticism) *Of exercise:* Is the same as liberty of contradiction: a potentiality for either one of two contradictories, as to do good or not to do good, to act or not to act.

Of specification: Is the same as liberty of contrariety: a potentiality for either one of two contraries, as to do good or to do evil.—*H.G.*

Liberum Arbitrium: The freedom of indifference *(liberum arbitrium indifferentiae)* is the ability of the will to choose independently of antecedent determination. See *Free-Will.*—*L.W.*

Lichtenberg, Georg Christoph: (1742-1799) Influential German satirist. Made discoveries in physics. He leaned towards theoretical materialism, and yet had a strong religious (Spinozistic) element.—*H.H.*

Main works: *Briefe aus England,* 1776-8; editor of *Göttingisches Mag. d. Literatur u. Wissensch.,* 1780-2; *Ausführliche Erklärung d. Hogarthschen Kupferstiche,* 1794-9.

Lieh Tzŭ: Nothing is known of Lieh Tzŭ (Lieh Yü-k'ou, c. 450-375 B.C.) except that he was a Taoist. The book *Lieh Tzŭ* (partial Eng. tr. by L. Giles: *Taoist Teachings from the Book of Lieh Tzŭ*) which bears his name is a work of the third century A.D.—*W.T.C.*

Li hsueh: The Rational Philosophy or the Reason School of the Sung dynasty (960-1279) which insisted on Reason or Law (li) as the basis of reality, including such philosophers as Chou Lien-hsi (1017-1073), Shao K'ang-chieh (1011-1077), Chang Hêng-ch'ü (1020-1077), Ch'êng I-ch'uan (1033-1107), Ch'êng Ming-tao (1032-1086), Chu Hsi (1130-1200), and Lu Hsiang-shan (1139-1193). It is also called Hsing-li Hsüeh (Philosophy of the Nature and Reason) and Sung Hsüeh (Philosophy of the Sung Dynasty). Often the term includes the idealistic philosophy of the Ming dynasty (1368-1644), including Wang Yang-ming (1473-1529), sometimes called Hsin Hsüeh (Philosophy of Mind). Often it also includes the philosophy of the Ch'ing dynasty (1644-1911), called Tao Hsüeh, including such philosophers as Yen Hsi-chai (1635-1704) and Tai Tung-yüan (1723-1777). For a summary of the Rational Philosophy, see *Chinese philosophy*. For its philosophy of Reason (li), vital force (ch'i), the Great Ultimate (T'ai Chi), the passive and active principles (yin yang), the nature of man and things (hsing), the investigation of things to the utmost (ch'iung li), the extension of knowledge (chih chih), and its ethics of true manhood or love (jên), seriousness (ching) and sincerity (ch'êng), see articles on these topics. —*W.T.C.*

Limit: We give here only some of the most elementary mathematical senses of this word, in connection with real numbers. (Refer to the articles *Number* and *Continuity*.)

The *limit* of an infinite sequence of real numbers a_1, a_2, a_3, . . . is said to be (the real number) b if for *every* positive real number ϵ there is a positive integer N such that the difference between b and a_n is less than ϵ whenever n is greater than N. (By the difference between b and a_n is here meant the non-negative difference, i.e., b-a_n if b is greater than a_n, a_n-b if b is less than a_n and O if b equal to a_n.)

Let f be a monadic function for which the range of the independent variable and the range of the dependent variable both consist of real numbers; let b and c be real numbers; and let g be the monadic function so determined that $g(c) = b$, and $g(x) = f(x)$ if x is different from c. (The range of the independent variable for g is thus the same as that for f, with the addition of the real number c if not already included.) The *limit* of $f(x)$ as x approaches c is said to be b if g is continuous at c. —More briefly but less accurately, the *limit* of $f(x)$ as x approaches c is the value which must be assigned to f for the argument c in order to make it continuous at c.

The *limit* of $f(x)$ as x approaches *infinity* is said to be b, if the *limit* of $h(x)$ as x approaches O is b, where h is the function so determined that $h(x) = f(1/x)$.

In connection with the infinite sequence of real numbers a_1, a_2, a_3, . . ., a monadic function a may be introduced for which the range of the independent variable consists of the positive integers 1, 2, 3, . . . and $a(1) = a_1$, $a(2) = a_2$, $a(3) = a_3$, ... It can then be shown that the limit of the infinite sequence as above defined is the same as the limit of $a(x)$ as x approaches infinity.

(Of course it is not meant to be implied in the preceding that the limit of an infinite sequence or of a function always exists. In particular cases it may happen that there is no limit of an infinite sequence, or no limit of $f(x)$ as x approaches c, etc.)—*A.C.*

Limitative: Tending to restrict; pertaining to the limit-value. In logic, and affirmative infinitated judgment, often employed as a third quality added to affirmative and negative. More specifically used by Kant to denote judgments of the type, ''Every A is not-B,'' and since Kant, applied to the judgments known to the older logicians as indefinite.—*J.K.F.*

Limiting Notion: The notion of the extreme applicability of a universal principle considered as a limit. Employed by Kant (1724-1804) in his *Kritik der Reinen Vernunft*, A 255, to indicate the theory that experience cannot attain to the noumenon.—*J.K.F.*

Limits of Sensation: The two limiting sensations in the sensory continuum of any given sense: (a) the lower limit is the just noticeable sensation which if the stimulus producing it were diminished, would vanish altogether or—in the view of some psychologists—would pass into the unconscious. See *Threshold of Consciousness*. (b) The upper limit is the maximum sensation such that if the producing stimulus were increased the resultant sensation would again vanish.—*L.W.*

Line of Beauty: Title given by Wm. Hogarth to an undulating line supposedly containing the essence of the graphically beautiful, and so regarded as both the cause and the criterion of beauty; particular lines and paintings become beautiful as and because they exhibit this line. According to Hogarth, such lines must express ''symmetry, variety, uniformity, simplicity, intricacy, and quantity.'' (*Analysis of Beauty,* London, 1753, p. 47.)—*I.J.*

Lipps, Theodor: (1851-1914) Eminent German philosopher and psychologist. The study of optical illusions led him to his theory of empathy. Starts with the presupposition that every aesthetic object represents a living being, and calls the psychic state which we experience when we project ourselves into the life of such an object, an empathy *(Einfühlung)* or ''fellow-feeling.'' He applied this principle consistently to all the arts. The empathic act is not simply kinaesthetic inference but has exclusively objective reference. Being a peculiar source of knowledge about other egos, it is a blend of inference and intuition. Main works: *Psychol. Studien*, 1885; *Grundzüge d. Logik*, 1893; *Die ethische Grundfragen*, 1899; *Aesthetik*, 2 vols., 1903-06; *Philos. u. Wirklichkeit*, 1908; *Psychol. Untersuch.*, 2 vols., 1907-12.—*H.H.*

Localization, Cerebral: (Lat. *locus*, place) The supposed correlation of mental processes, sensory and motor, with definite areas of the brain. The theory of definite and exact brain localization has been largely disproven by recent physiological investigations of Franz, Lashley and others.–*L.W.*

Locke, John: (1632-1704) The first great British

empiricist, denied the existence of innate ideas, categories, and moral principles. The mind at birth is a *tabula rasa*. Its whole content is derived from sense-experience, and constructed by reflection upon sensible data. Reflection is effected through memory and its attendant activities of contemplation, distinction, comparison in point of likeness and difference, and imaginative recomposition. Even the most abstract notions and ideas, like infinity, power, cause and effect, substance and identity, which seemingly are *not* given by experience, are no exceptions to the rule. Thus "infinity" confesses our inability to limit in fact or imagination the spatial and temporal extension of sense-experience; "substance," to perceive or understand why qualities congregate in separate clumps; "power" and "cause and effect," to perceive or understand why and how these clumps follow, and seemingly produce one another as they do, or for that matter, how our volitions "produce" the movements that put them into effect. Incidentally, Locke defines freedom as liberty, not of choice, which is always sufficiently motivated, but of action in accordance with choice. "Identity" of things, Locke derives from spatial and temporal continuity of the content of clumps of sensations; of structure, from continuity of arrangement in changing content; of person, from continuity of consciousness through memory, which, incidentally, permits of alternating personalities in the same body or of the transference of the same personality from one body to another.

In these circumstances real knowledge is very limited. "Universals" register superficial resemblances, not the real essences of things. Experience directly "intuits" identity and diversity, relations, coexistences and necessary connections in its content, and aided by memory, "knows" the agreements and disagreements of ideas in these respects. We also feel directly (sensitive knowledge) that our experience comes from without. Moreover, though taste, smell, colour, sound, etc. are internal to ourselves (secondary qualities) extension, shape, rest, motion, unity and plurality (primary qualities) seem to inhere in the external world independently of our perception of it. Finally, we have "demonstrative knowledge" of the existence of God. But of anything other than God, we have no knowledge except such as is derived from and limited by the senses.

Locke also was a political, economic and religious thinker of note. A "latitudinarian" and broad churchman in theology and a liberal in politics, he argued against the divine right of kings and the authority of the Bible and the Church, and maintained that political sovereignty rests upon the consent of the governed, and ecclesiastical authority upon the consent of reason. He was also an ardent defender of freedom of thought and speech. Main works: *Two Treatises on Gov't*, 1689; *Reasonableness in Christianity*, 1695; *Some Thoughts on Education*, 1693; *An Essay on Human Understanding*, 1690.—*B.A.G.F.*

Logic, formal: Investigates the structure of propositions and of deductive reasoning by a method which abstracts from the *content* of propositions which come under consideration and deals only with their logical *form*. The distinction between form and content can be made definite with the aid of a particular language or symbolism in which propositions are expressed, and the formal method can then be characterized by the fact that it deals with the objective form of *sentences* which express propositions and provides in these concrete terms criteria of meaningfulness and validity of inference. This formulation of the matter presupposes the selection of a particular language which is to be regarded as logically exact and free from the ambiguities and irregularities of structure which appear in English (or other languages of everyday use)—i.e., it makes the distinction between form and content relative to the choice of a language. Many logicians prefer to postulate an abstract form for propositions themselves, and to characterize the logical exactness of a language by the uniformity with which the concrete form of its sentences reproduces or parallels the form of the propositions which they express. At all events it is practically necessary to introduce a special logical language, or symbolic notation, more exact than ordinary English usage, if topics beyond the most elementary are to be dealt with (see *logistic system*, and *semiotic*.).

Concerning the distinction between form and content see further the articles *formal*, and *syntax*, *logical*.

1. THE PROPOSITIONAL CALCULUS formalizes the use of the sentential connectives *and, or, not, if . . . then*. Various systems of notation are current, of which we here adopt a particular one for purposes of exposition. We use juxtaposition to denote conjunction ("pq" to mean "p and q"), the sign ∨ to denote inclusive disjunction ("$p \vee q$" to mean "p or q or both"), the sign $+$ to denote exclusive disjunction ("$p + q$" to mean "p or q but not both"), the sign $\sim$ to denote negation ("$\sim p$" to mean "not p"), the sign ⊃ to denote the conditional ("$p \supset q$" to mean "if p then q," or "not both p and not-q"), the sign $\equiv$ to denote the biconditional ("$p \equiv q$" to mean "p if and only if q," or "either p and q or not-p and not-q"), and the sign | to denote alternative denial ("$p \mid q$" to mean "not both p and q").—The word *or* is ambiguous in ordinary English usage between inclusive disjunction and exclusive disjunction, and distinct notations are accordingly provided for the two meanings of the word. The notations "$p \supset q$" and "$p \equiv q$" are sometimes read as "p implies q" and "p is equivalent to q" respectively. These readings must, however, be used with caution, since the terms implication and equivalence are often used in a sense which involves some relationship between the logical forms of the propositions (or the sentences) which they connect, whereas the validity of $p \supset q$ and of $p \equiv q$ requires no such relationship. The connective ⊃ is also said to stand for "material implication," distinguished from *formal implication* (§ 3 below) and *strict implication* (*q.v.*). Similarly the connective $\equiv$ is said to stand for "material equivalence."

It is possible in various ways to define some of the sentential connectives named above in terms of others.

In particular, if the sign of alternative denial is taken as primitive, all the other connectives can be defined in terms of this one. Also, if the signs of negation and inclusive disjunction are taken as primitive, all the others can be defined in terms of these; likewise if the signs of negation and conjunction are taken as primitive. Here, however, for reasons of naturalness and symmetry, we prefer to take as primitive the three connectives, denoting negation, conjunction, and inclusive disjunction. The remaining ones are then defined as follows:

$$A \mid B \rightarrow \sim A \vee \sim B.$$
$$A \supset B \rightarrow \sim A \vee B.$$
$$A \equiv B \rightarrow [B \supset A] [A \supset B].$$
$$A + B \rightarrow [\sim B]A \vee [\sim A]B.$$

The capital roman letters here denote arbitrary formulas of the propositional calculus (in the technical sense defined below) and the arrow is to be read "stands for" or "is an abbreviation for."

Suppose that we have given some specific list of propositional symbols, which may be infinite in number, and to which we shall refer as the *fundamental propositional symbols*. These are not necessarily single letters or characters, but may be expressions taken from any language or system of notation; they may denote particular propositions, or they may contain variables and denote ambiguously any proposition of a certain form or class. Certain restrictions are also necessary upon the way in which the fundamental propositional symbols can contain square brackets [ ]; for the present purpose it will suffice to suppose that they do not contain square brackets at all, although they may contain parentheses or other kinds of brackets. We call *formulas* of the propositional calculus (relative to the given list of fundamental propositional symbols) all the expressions determined by the four following rules: (1) all the fundamental propositional symbols are formulas; (2) if A is a formula, ~ [A] is a formula; (3) if A and B are formulas [A] [B] is a formula; (4) if A and B are formulas [A] v [B] is a formula. The formulas of the propositional calculus as thus defined will in general contain more brackets than are necessary for clarity or freedom from ambiguity; in practice we omit superfluous brackets and regard the shortened expressions as abbreviations for the full formulas. It will be noted also that, if A and B are formulas, we regard [A] | [B], [A] ⊃ [B], [A] ≡ [B], and [A] + [B], not as formulas, but as abbreviations for certain formulas in accordance with the above given definitions.

In order to complete the setting up of the propositional calculus as a *logistic system* (*q.v.*) it is necessary to state primitive formulas and primitive rules of inference. Of the many possible ways of doing this we select the following.

If A, B, C are any formulas, each of the seven following formulas is a primitive formula:

$[A \vee A] \supset A.$	$A \supset [B \supset AB].$
$A \supset [A \vee B].$	$AB \supset A.$
$[A \vee B] \supset [B \vee A].$	$AB \supset B.$

$$[A \supset B] \supset [[C \vee A] \supset [C \vee B]].$$

(The complete list of primitive formulas is thus infinite, but there are just seven possible forms of primitive formulas as above.) There is one primitive rule of inference, as follows: *Given* A *and* A ⊃ B *to infer* B. This is the inference known as *modus ponens* (see below, § 2).

The *theorems* of the propositional calculus are the formulas which can be derived from the primitive formulas by a succession of applications of the primitive rule of inference. In other words, (a) the primitive formulas are theorems, and (b) if A and A ⊃ B are theorems then B is a theorem. An inference from premisses A_1, A_2, . . ., A_n to a conclusion B is a *valid inference* of the propositional calculus if B becomes a theorem upon adding A_1, A_2, . . ., A_n to the list of primitive formulas. In other words, (a) the inference from A_1, A_2, . . ., A_n to B is a valid inference if B is either a primitive formula or one of the formulas A_1, A_2, . . ., An, and (b) if the inference from A_1, A_2, . . ., A_n to C and the inference from A_1, A_2, . . ., A_n to C⊃B are both valid inferences then the inference from A_1, A_2, . . ., A_n to B is a valid inference. It can be proved that the inference from A_1, A_2, . . ., A_n to B is a valid inference of the propositional calculus if (obviously), and only if (the *deduction theorem*), $[A1 \supset [A_2 \supset \ldots [A_n \supset B] \ldots]]$ is a theorem of the propositional calculus.

The reader should distinguish between theorems *about* the propositional calculus—the deduction theorem, the principles of duality (below), etc.—and theorems *of* the propositional calculus in the sense just defined. It is convenient to use such words as *theorem*, *premiss*, *conclusion* both for propositions (in whatever language expressed) and for formulas representing propositions in some fixed system or calculus.

In the foregoing the list of fundamental propositional symbols has been left unspecified. A case of special importance is the case that the fundamental propositional symbols are an infinite list of variables, p, q, r, . . ., which may be taken as representing ambiguously any proposition whatever— or any proposition of a certain class fixed in advance (the class should be closed under the operations of negation, conjunction, and inclusive disjunction). In this case we speak of the *pure propositional calculus*, and refer to the other cases as *applied propositional calculus* (although the application may be to something as abstract in character as the pure propositional calculus itself, as, *e.g.*, in the case of the pure functional calculus of first order (§ 3), which contains an applied propositional calculus).

In formulating the pure propositional calculus the primitive formulas may (if desired) be reduced to a finite number, *e.g.*, to the seven listed above with A, B, C taken to be the particular variables p, q, r. A second primitive rule of inference, the *rule of substitution*, is then required, allowing the inference from a formula A to the formula B for a particular variable in A (the same formula B must be substituted for all occurrences of that variable in A). The definition of a theorem is then given in the same way as before, allowing for the additional primitive rule; the definition of a valid inference must, however, be modified.

In what follows (to the end of § 1) we shall, for convenience of statement, confine attention to the case of the pure propositional calculus. Similar statements hold, with minor modifications, for the general case.

The formulation which we have given provides a means of *proving* theorems of the propositional calculus, the proof consisting of an explicit finite sequence of formulas, the last of which is the theorem proved, and each of which is either a primitive formula or inferable from preceding formulas by a single application of the rule of inference (or one of the rules of inference, if the alternative formulation of the pure propositional calculus employing the rule of substitution is adopted). The test of whether a given finite sequence of formulas is a proof of the last formula of the sequence is *effective* — we have the means of always determining of a given formula whether it is a primitive formula, and the means of always determining of a given formula whether it is inferable from a given finite list of formulas by a single application of *modus ponens* (or substitution). Indeed our formulation would not be satisfactory otherwise. For in the contrary case a proof would not necessarily carry conviction, the proposer of a proof could fairly be asked to give a proof that it was a proof — in short the formal analysis of what constitutes a proof (in the sense of a cogent demonstration) would be incomplete.

However, the test of whether a given formula is a theorem, by the criterion that it is a theorem if a proof of it exists, is not effective—since failure to find a proof upon search might mean lack of ingenuity rather than non-existence of a proof. The problem to give an effective test by means of which it can always be determined whether a given formula is a theorem is the *decision problem* of the propositional calculus. This problem can be solved either by the process of reduction of a formula to *disjunctive normal form*, or by the *truth-table decision procedure*. We state the latter in detail.

The three primitive connectives (and consequently all connectives definable from them) denote *truth-functions* — i.e., the *truth-value* (truth or falsehood) of each of the propositions $\sim p$, pq, and $p \vee q$ is uniquely determined by the truth-values of p and q. In fact, $\sim p$ is true if p is false and false if p is true; pq is true if p and q are both true, false otherwise; $p \vee q$ is false if p and q are both false, true otherwise. Thus, given a formula of the (pure) propositional calculus an assignment of a truth-value to each of the variables appearing, we can reckon out by a mechanical process the truth-value to be assigned to the entire formula. If, for all possible assignments of truth-values to the variables appearing, the calculated truth-value corresponding to the entire formula is truth, the formula is said to be a *tautology*. The test of whether a formula is a tautology is effective, since in any particular case the total number of different assignments of truth-values to the variables is finite, and the calculation of the truth-value corresponding to the entire formula can be carried out separately for each possible assignment of truth-values to the variables.

Now it is readily verified that all the primitive formulas are tautologies, and that for the rule of *modus ponens* (and the rule of substitution) the property holds that if the premisses of the inference are tautologies the conclusion must be a tautology. It follows that every theorem of the propositional calculus is a tautology. By a more difficult argument it can be shown also that every tautology is a theorem. Hence the test whether a formula is a tautology provides a solution of the decision problem of the propositional calculus.

As corollaries of this we have proofs of the *consistency* of the propositional calculus (if A is any formula, A and $\sim$A cannot both be tautologies and hence cannot both be theorems) and of the *completeness* of the propositional calculus (it can be shown that if any formula not already a theorem, and hence not a tautology, is added to the list of primitive formulas, the calculus becomes inconsistent on the basis of the two rules, substitution and *modus ponens*).

As another corollary of this, or otherwise, we obtain also the following theorem about the propositional calculus: If A $\equiv$ B is a theorem, and D is the result of replacing a particular occurrence of A by B in the formula C, then the inference from C to D is a valid inference.

The *dual* of a formula C of the propositional calculus is obtained by interchanging conjunction and disjunction throughout the formula, i.e., by replacing AB everywhere by A $\vee$ B, and A $\vee$ B by AB. Thus, *e.g.*, the dual of the formula $\sim[pq \vee \sim r]$ is the formula $\sim[[p \vee q]\sim r]$. In forming the dual of a formula which is expressed with the aid of the defined connectives, $|, \supset, \equiv, +$, it is convenient to remember that the effect of interchanging conjunction and (inclusive) disjunction is to replace A|B by $\sim$A $\sim$B, to replace A $\supset$ B by $\sim$A B, and to interchange $\equiv$ and $+$.

It can be shown that the following *principles of duality* hold in the propositional calculus (where A* and B* denote the duals of the formulas A and B respectively): (1) if A is a theorem, then $\sim$ A* is a theorem; (2) if A $\supset$ B is a theorem, then B* $\supset$ A* is a theorem; (3) if A $\equiv$ B is a theorem, then A* $\equiv$ B* is a theorem.

Special names have been given to certain particular theorems and forms of valid inference of the propositional calculus. Besides § 2 following, see: *absorption; affirmation of the consequent; assertion; associative law; commutative law; composition; contradiction, law of; De Morgan's laws; double negation, law of; excluded middle, law of; exportation; Hauber's law; identity, law of; importation; Peirce's law; proof by cases; reductio ad absurdum; reflexivity; tautology; transitivity; transposition.*

Names given to particular theorems of the propositional calculus are usually thought of as applying to laws embodied in the theorems rather than to the theorems as formulas; hence, in particular, the same name is applied to theorems differing only by alphabetical changes of the variables appearing; and frequently the name used for a theorem is used also for one or more forms of valid inference associated with the theorem. Similar remarks apply to names given to particular theorems of the functional calculus of first order, etc.

Whitehead and Russell, *Principia Mathematica,* 2nd edn., vol. 1, Cambridge, England, 1925. E. L. Post, *Introduction to a general theory of elementary propositions,* American Journal of Mathematics, vol. 43 (1921), pp. 163-185. W.V. Quine, *Elementary Logic,* Boston and New York, 1941. J. Herbrand, *Recherches sur la Théorie de la Demonstration,* Warsaw, 1930. Hilbert and Ackermann, *Grundzüge der Theoretischen Logik,* 2nd edn., Berlin, 1938. Hilbert and Bernays, *Grundlagen der Mathematik,* vol. 1, Berlin, 1934; also Supplement III to vol. 2, Berlin, 1939.

2. HYPOTHETICAL SYLLOGISM, DISJUNCTIVE SYLLOGISM, DILEMMA are names traditionally given to certain forms of inference, which may be identified as follows with certain particular forms of valid inference of the propositional calculus (see § 1)

The hypothetical syllogism has two kinds or moods. *Modus ponens* is the inference from a major premiss A ⊃ B and a minor premiss A to the conclusion B. *Modus tollens* is the inference from a major premiss A ⊃ B and a minor premiss ~B to the conclusion ~A.

The disjunctive syllogism has also two moods. *Modus tollendo ponens* is any one of the four following forms of inference:

from A v B and ~B to A;
from A v B and ~A to B;
from A + B and ~B to A;
from A + B and ~A to B.

Modus ponendo tollens is either of the following forms of inference:

from A + B and A to ~B;
from A + B and B to ~A.

In each case the first premiss named is the major premiss and the second one the minor premiss.

Of the dilemma four kinds are distinguished. The simple constructive dilemma has two major premisses A ⊃ C and B ⊃ C, minor premiss A v B, conclusion C. The simple destructive dilemma has two major premisses A ⊃ B and A ⊃ C, minor premiss ~B v ~C, conclusion ~A. The complex constructive dilemma has two major premisses A ⊃ B and C ⊃ D, minor premiss A v C, conclusion B v D. The complex destructive dilemma has two major premisses A ⊃ B and C ⊃ D, minor premiss ~B v ~D, conclusion ~A v ~C. (Since the conclusion of a complex dilemma must involve inclusive disjunction, it seems that the traditional account is best rendered by employing inclusive disjunction throughout.)

The inferences from A ⊃ B and C ⊃ A to C ⊃ B, and from A ⊃ B and C ⊃ ~B to C ⊃ ~A are called pure hypothetical syllogisms, and the above simpler forms of the hypothetical syllogism are then distinguished as mixed hypothetical. Some recent writers apply the names, *modus ponens* and *modus tollens* respectively, also to these two forms of the pure hypothetical syllogism. Other variations of usage or additional forms are also found. Some writers include under these heads forms of inference which belong to the functional calculus of first order rather than the propositional calculus.

F. Ueberweg, *System der Logik,* 4th edn., Bonn, 1874. H. W. B. Joseph, *An Introduction to Logic,* 2nd edn., Oxford, 1916. R. M. Eaton, *General Logic,* New York, 1931. S. K. Langer, *An Introduction to Symbolic Logic,* 1937, Appendix A.

3. THE FUNCTIONAL CALCULUS OF FIRST ORDER is the next discipline beyond the propositional calculus, according to the usual treatment. It is the first step towards the hierarchy of types (§ 6) and deals, in addition to unanalyzed propositions, with *propositional functions* (*q.v.*) of the lowest order. It employs the sentential connectives of § 1, and in addition the universal *quantifier* (*q.v.*), written (X) where X is any individual variable, and the existential *quantifier,* written (*EX*) where X is any individual variable. (The *E* denoting existential quantification is more often written inverted, as by Peano and Whitehead-Russell, but we here adopt the typographically more convenient usage, which also has sanction.)

For the interpretation of the calculus we must presuppose a certain domain of *individuals.* This may be any well-defined non-empty domain, within very wide limits. Different possible choices of the domain of individuals lead to different interpretations of the calculus.

In order to set the calculus up formally as a logistic system, we suppose that we have given four lists of symbols, as follows: (1) an infinite list of *individual variables* $x, y, z, t, x', y', z', t', x'', \ldots$, which denote ambiguously any individual; (2) a list of *propositional variables* $p, q, r, s, p', \ldots$, representing ambiguously any proposition of a certain appropriate class; (3) a list of *functional variables* $F_1, G_1, H_1, \ldots, F_2, G_2, H_2, \ldots, F_3, G_3, H_3, \ldots$, a variable with subscript n representing ambiguously any n-adic propositional function of individuals; (4) a list of *functional constants,* which denote particular propositional functions of individuals. There shall be an effective notational criterion associating with each functional constant a positive integer n, the functional constant denoting an n-adic propositional function of individuals. One or more of the lists (2), (3), (4) may be empty, but not both (3) and (4) shall be empty. The list (1) is required to be infinite, and the remaining lists may, some or all of them, be infinite. Finally, no symbol shall be duplicated either by appearing twice in the same list or by appearing in two different lists; and no functional constant shall contain braces [ ] (or either a left brace or a right brace) as a constituent part of the symbol.

When (2) and (3) are complete—i.e., contain all the variables indicated above (an infinite number of propositional variables and for each positive integer n an infinite number of functional variables with subscript n)—and (4) is empty, we shall speak of the *pure* functional calculus of first order. When (2) and (3) are empty and (4) is not empty, we shall speak of a *simple applied* functional calculus of first order.

Functional variables and functional constants are

together called *functional symbols* (the adjective *functional* being here understood to refer to *propositional* functions). Functional symbols are called *n-adic* if they are either functional variables with subscript *n* or functional constants denoting *n-adic* propositional functions of individuals. The *formulas* of the functional calculus of first order (relative to the given lists of symbols (1), (2), (3), (4)) are all the expressions determined by the eight following rules: (1) all the propositional variables are formulas; (2) if F is a monadic functional symbol and X is an individual variable, [F](X) is a formula; (3) if F is an *n*-adic functional symbol and $X_1, X_2, \ldots,$ X_n are individual variables (which may or may not be all different), [F]$(X_1, X_2, \ldots, X_n)$ is a formula; (4) if A is a formula, $\sim$[A] is a formula; (5) if A and B are formulas, [A][B] is a formula; (6) if A and B are formulas, [A] v [B] is a formula; (7) if A is a formula and X is an individual variable, (X) [A] is a formula; (8) if A is a formula and X is an individual variable, (EX) [A] is a formula. In practice, we omit superfluous brackets and braces (but not parentheses) in writing formulas, and we omit subscripts on functional variables in cases where the subscript is sufficiently indicated by the form of the formula in which the functional variable appears. The sentential connectives |, $\supset$, $=$, $+$, are introduced as abbreviations in the same way as in § 1 for the propositional calculus. We make further the following definitions, which are also to be construed as abbreviations, the arrow being read "stands for:"

[A] $\supset_x$ [B] $\rightarrow$ (X) [[A] $\supset$ [B]].

[A] $\equiv_x$ [B] $\rightarrow$ (X) [[A] $\equiv$ [B]].

[A] $\wedge_x$ [B] $\rightarrow$ (EX) [[A] [B]].

(Here A and B are any formulas, and X is any individual variable. Brackets may be omitted when superfluous.) If F and G denote monadic propositional functions, we say that F(X) $\supset_x$ G (X) expresses *formal implication* of the function G by the function F, and F(X) $\equiv$x G (X) expresses *formal equivalence* of the two functions (the adjective *formal* is perhaps not well chosen here but has become established in use).

A *sub-formula* of a given formula is a consecutive constituent part of the given formula which is itself a formula. An occurrence of an individual variable X in a formula is a *bound* occurrence of X if it is an occurrence in a subformula of either of the forms (X)[A] or (EX)[A]. Any other occurrence of a variable in a formula is a *free* occurrence. We may thus speak of the *bound variables* and the *free variables* of a formula. (Whitehead and Russell, following Peano, use the terms *apparent variables* and *real variables,* respectively, instead of *bound variables* and *free variables.*)

If A, B, C are any formulas, each of the seven following formulas is a primitive formula:

[A v A] $\supset$ A.   A $\supset$ [B $\supset$ AB].

A $\supset$ [A v B].   AB $\supset$ A.

[A v B] $\supset$ [B v A].   AB $\supset$ B.

[A $\supset$ B] $\supset$ [[C v A] $\supset$ [C v B]].

If X is any individual variable, and A is any formula not containing a free occurrence of X, and B is any formula, each of the two following formulas is a primitive formula:

[A $\supset_x$ B] $\supset$ [A $\supset$ (X) B].

[B $\supset_x$ A] $\supset$ [(EX) B $\supset$ A].

If X and Y are any individual variables (the same or different), and A is any formula such that no free occurrence of X in A is in a sub-formula of the form (Y)[C], and B is the formula resulting from the substitution of Y for all the free occurrences of X in A, each of the two following formulas is a primitive formula:

(X)A $\supset$ B.   B $\supset$ (EX)A.

There are two primitive rules of inference: (1) *Given* A *and* A $\supset$ B to infer B (the rule *of modus ponens*). (2) *Given* A *to infer* (X)A, *where* X *is any individual variable* (the rule of *generalization*). In applying the rule of generalization, we say that the variable X is *generalized upon*.

The *theorems* of the functional calculus of first order are the formulas which can be derived from the primitive formulas by a succession of applications of the primitive rules of inference. An inference from premisses $A_1, A_2, \ldots, A_n$ to a conclusion B is a valid *inference* of the functional calculus of first order if B becomes a theorem upon adding $A_1, A_2, \ldots, A_n$ to the list of primitive formulas and at the same time restricting the rule of generalization by requiring that the variable generalized upon shall not be any one of the free individual variables of $A_1, A_2, \ldots, A_n$. It can be proved that the inference from $A_1, A_2, \ldots, A_n$ to B is a valid inference of the functional calculus of first order if (obviously), and only if (the *deduction theorem*), $[A_1 \supset [A_2 \supset \ldots [[A_n \supset B] \ldots]]$ is a theorem of the functional calculus of first order.

It can be proved that if A $\equiv$ B is a theorem, and D is the result of replacing a particular occurrence of A by B in the formula C, then the inference from C to D is a valid inference.

The *consistency* of the functional calculus of first order can also be proved without great difficulty.

The *dual* of a formula is obtained by interchanging conjunction and (inclusive) disjunction throughout and at the same time interchanging universal quantification and existential quantification throughout. (In doing this the different symbols, *e.g.,* functional constants, although they may consist of several characters in succession rather than a single character, shall be treated as units, and no change shall be made inside a symbol. A similar remark applies at all places where we speak of occurrences of a particular symbol or sequence of symbols in a formula, and the like.) It can be shown that the following *principles of duality* hold (where A* and B* denote the duals of the formulas A and B respectively): (1) if A is a theorem, then $\sim$A* is a theorem; (2) if A $\supset$ B is a theorem, then B* $\supset$ A* is a theorem; (3) if A $\equiv$ B is a theorem, then A* $\equiv$ B* is a theorem.

A formula is said to be in *prenex normal form* if all the quantifiers which it contains stand together at the beginning, unseparated by negations (or other sentential connectives), and the *scope* of each quantifier (i.e., the extent of the bracket [ ] following the quantifier) is to the end of the entire formula. In the case of a formula in prenex normal form, the succession of quantifiers at the beginning is called the *prefix;* the remaining portion contains no quantifiers and is the *matrix* of the formula. It can be proved that for every formula A there is a formula B in prenex normal form such that A ≡ B is a theorem; and B is then called a *prenex normal form of* A.

A formula of the pure functional calculus of first order which contains no free individual variables is said to be *satisfiable* if it is possible to determine the underlying non-empty domain of individuals and to give meanings to the propositional and functional variables contained—namely to each propositional variable a meaning as a particular proposition and to each n-adic functional variable a meaning as an n-adic propositional function of individuals (of the domain in question)—in such a way that (under the accepted meanings of the sentential connectives, the quantifiers, and application of function to argument) the formula becomes *true*. The meaning of the last word, even for abstract, not excluding infinite, domains, must be presupposed—a respect in which this definition differs sharply from most others made in this article.

It is not difficult to find examples of formulas A, containing no free individual variables, such that both A and ~A are satisfiable. A simple example is the formula $(x)F(x)$. More instructive is the following example,

$$[\ (x)\ (y)\ (z)\ [\ \sim\!F(x,\ x)\ ]\ [\ F(x,\ y)\ F(y,\ z)$$
$$\supset F(x,\ z)\ ]\ ]\ ]\ [(x)(Ey)F\ (x,\ y)\ ],$$

which is satisfiable in an infinite domain of individuals but no t in any finite domain— the negation is satisfiable in any non-empty domain.

It can be shown that all theorems A of the pure functional calculus of first order which contain no free individual variables have the property that ~ A is not satisfiable. Hence the pure functional calculus of first order is not complete in the strong sense in which the pure propositional calculus is complete. Gödel has shown that the pure functional calculus of first order is complete in the weaker sense that if a formula A contains no free individual variables and ~A is not satisfiable then A is a theorem.

The *decision problem* of the pure functional calculus of first order has two forms (1) the so-called prooftheoretic decision problem, to find an effective test (decision procedure) by means of which it can always be determined whether a given formula is a theorem; (2) the so-called set-theoretic decision problem, to find an effective test by means of which it can always be determined whether a given formula containing no free individual variables is satisfiable. It follows from Gödel's completeness theorem that these two forms of the decision problem are equivalent: a solution of either would lead immediately to a solution of the other.

Church has proved that the decision problem of the pure functional calculus of first order is unsolvable. Solutions exist, however, for several important special cases. In particular a decision procedure is known for the case of formulas containing only *monadic* function variables (this would seem to cover substantially every-

thing considered in traditional formal logic prior to the introduction of the modern logic of relations).

Finally we mention a variant form of the functional calculus of first order, the *functional calculus of first order with equality,* in which the list of functional constants includes the dyadic functional constant $=$, denoting equality or identity of individuals. The notation $[X] = [Y]$ is introduced as an abbreviation for $[=]\,(X, Y)$, and primitive formulas are added as follows to the list already given: if X is any individual variable, X $= X$ is a primitive formula; if X and Y are any individual variables, and B results from the substitution of Y for a particular free occurrence of X in A, which is not in a sub-formula of A of the form $(Y)[C]$, then $[X = Y] \supset [A \supset B]$ is a primitive formula. We speak of the *pure* functional calculus of first order with equality when the lists of propositional variables and functional variables are complete and the only functional constant is $=$; we speak of a *simple applied* functional calculus of first order with equality when the lists of propositional variables and functional variables are empty.

The addition to the functional calculus of first order of *individual constants* (denoting particular individuals) is not often made—unless symbols for functions from individuals to individuals (so-called "mathematical" or "descriptive" functions) are to be added at the same time. Such an addition is, however, employed in the two following sections as a means of representing certain forms of inference of traditional logic. The addition is really non-essential, and requires only minor changes in the definition of a formula and the list of primitive formulas (allowing the alternative of individual constants at certain places where the above given formulation calls for free individual variables).

Whitehead and Russell, *Principia Mathematica*, 2nd edn., vol. 1, Cambridge, England, 1925. J. Herbrand, *Recherches sur la Théorie de la Démonstration*, Warsaw, 1930. K. Gödel, *Die Vollständigkeit der Axiome des logischen Funktionenkalküls*, Monatshefte für Mathematik und Physik, vol. 37 (1930), pp. 349-360. Hilbert and Ackermann, *Grundzüge der theoretischen Logik*, 2nd edn., Berlin, 1938. Hilbert and Bernays, *Grundlagen der Mathematik*, vol. 1, Berlin, 1934, and vol. 2, Berlin, 1939.

4. OPPOSITION, IMMEDIATE INFERENCE. The four traditional kinds of categorical propositions—all S is P, no S is P, some S is P, some S is not P—customarily designated by the letters *A, E, I, O,* respectively—may conveniently be represented in the functional calculus of first order (§ 3) by the four forms $S\,(x) \supset_x P\,(x)$, $S\,(x) \supset_x \sim P\,(x)$, $S\,(x) \wedge_x P\,(x)$, $S\,(x) \wedge_x \sim P\,(x)$, S and P being taken as functional constants. (For brevity, we shall use the notations S, P, $S\,(x) \supset_x P\,(x)$, etc., alike for certain formulas and for the propositional functions or propositions expressed by these formulas.)

This representation does not reproduce faithfully all particulars of the traditional account. The fact is that the traditional doctrine, having grown up from various sources and under an inadequate formal analysis, is not altogether coherent or even self-consistent. We here select what seems to be the best representation, and simply note the four following points of divergence:

(1) We have defined the connectives $\supset_x$ and $\wedge_x$ in terms of universal and existential quantification, whereas the traditional account might be thought to be more closely reproduced if they were taken as primitive notations. (It would, however, not be difficult to reformulate the functional calculus of first order so that those connectives would be primitive and the usual quantifiers defined in terms of them.)

(2) The traditional account associates the negation in E and O with the *copula* (*q.v.*), whereas the negation symbol is here prefixed to the sub-formula $P(x)$. (Notice that this subformula represents ambiguously a proposition and that, in fact, the notation of the functional calculus of first order provides for applying negation only to propositions.)

(3) The traditional account includes under A and E, respectively, also (propositions denoted by) P(A) and ~P(A), where A is an individual constant. These *singular* propositions are ignored in our account of opposition and immediate inference, but will appear in § 5 as giving variant forms of certain syllogisms.

(4) Some aspects of the traditional account require that A and E be represented as we have here, others that they be represented by $[(Ex) S(x)] [S(x) \supset_x P(x)]$ and $[(Ex) S(x)] [S(x) \supset_x \sim P(x)]$ respectively. The question concerning the choice between these two interpretations is known as the problem of *existential import* of propositions. We prefer to introduce $(Ex) S(x)$ as a separate premiss at those places where it is required.

Given a fixed subject S and a fixed predicate P, we have, according to the *square of opposition*, that A and O are *contradictory*, E and I are *contradictory*, A and E are *contrary*, I and O are *subcontrary*, A and I are *subaltern*, E and O are *subaltern*. The two propositions in a contradictory pair cannot be both true and cannot be both false (one is the exact negation of the other). The two propositions in a subaltern pair are so related that the first one, together with the premiss $(Ex) S(x)$, implies the second *(subalternation)*. Under the premiss $(Ex)S(x)$, the contrary pair, A, E, cannot be both true, and the subcontrary pair, I, O, cannot be both false.

Simple conversion of a proposition, A, E, I, or O, consists in interchanging S and P without other change. Thus the converse of $S(x) \supset_x P(x)$ is $P(x) \supset_x S(x)$, and the converse of $S(x) \supset_x \sim P(x)$ is $P(x) \supset_x \sim S(x)$. In mathematics the term *converse* is used primarily for the simple converse of a proposition A; loosely also for any one of a number of transformations similar to this (*e.g.*, $F(x) G(x) \supset_x H(x)$ may be said to have the converse $F(x) H(x) \supset_x G(x)$. Simple conversion of a proposition is a valid inference, in general, only in the case of E and I.

Conversion per accidens of a proposition A, i.e., of $S(x) \supset_x P(x)$, yields $P(x) \wedge_x S(x)$.

Obversion of a proposition A, E, I, or O consists in replacing P by a functional constant p which denotes the negation of the propositional function (property) denoted by P, and at the same time inserting ~ if not already present or deleting it if present. Thus the obverse of $S(x) \supset_x P(x)$ is

$S(x) \supset_x \sim P(x)$ (the obverse of "all men are mortal" is "no men are immortal"). The obverse of $S(x) \supset_x \sim P(x)$ is $S(x) \supset_x p(x)$; the obverse of $S(x) \wedge_x P(x)$ is $S(x) \wedge_x \sim p(x)$; the obverse of $S(x) \wedge_x \sim P(x)$ is $S(x) \wedge_x p(x)$.

The name *immediate inference* is given to certain inferences involving propositions A, E, I, O. These include obversion of A, E, I, or O, simple conversion of E or I, conversion *per accidens* of A, subalternation of A, E. The three last require the additional premiss (Ex) $S(x)$. Other immediate inferences (for which the terminology is not wholly uniform among different writers) may be obtained by means of sequences of these: *e.g.*, given that all men are mortal we may take the obverse of the converse of the obverse and so infer that all immortals are non-men (called by some the contrapositive, by others the obverted contrapositive).

The immediate inferences not involving obversion can be represented as valid inferences in the functional calculus of first order, but obversion can be so represented only in an extended calculus embracing functional *abstraction* (*q.v.*). For the p used above in describing obversion is, in terms of abstraction,

$$\lambda x[\sim P(x)].$$

F. Ueberweg, *System der Logik*, 4th edn., Bonn, 1874. H. W. B. Joseph, *An Introduction to Logic*, 2nd edn., Oxford, 1916. R. M. Eaton, *General Logic*, New York, 1931. Bennett and Baylis, *Formal Logic*, New York, 1939.

5. CATEGORICAL SYLLOGISM is the name given to certain forms of valid inference (of the functional calculus of first order) which involve as premisses two (formulas representing) categorical propositions, having a term in common—the middle term. Using S, M, P as minor term, middle term, and major term, respectively, we give the traditional classification into figures and moods. In each case we give the major premiss first, the minor premiss immediately after it, and the conclusion last; in some cases we give a third (existential) premiss which is suppressed in the traditional account. Because of the admission of singular propositions under the heads, A, E, two different forms of valid inference appear in some cases under the same figure and mood—these singular forms are separately listed.

First Figure

Barbara: $M (x) \quad \supset_x \quad P(x), \quad S (x) \quad \supset_x \quad M (x),$ $S (x) \supset_x P (x)$.

Celarent: $M (x) \quad \supset_x \quad \sim P (x), \quad S (x) \quad \supset_x \quad M (x),$ $S (x) \supset_x \sim P (x)$.

Darii: $M (x) \quad \supset_x \quad P (x), \quad S (x) \quad \wedge_x \quad M (x), \quad S (x)$ $\wedge_x P (x)$.

Ferio: $M (x) \quad \supset_x \quad \sim P (x), S (x) \quad \wedge_x \quad M (x), \quad S (x)$ $\wedge_x \sim P (x)$.

Second Figure

Cesare: $P (x) \quad \supset_x \quad \sim M (x), \quad S (x) \quad \supset_x \quad M (x),$ $S (x) \supset_x \sim P (x)$.

Camestres: $P (x) \quad \supset_x \quad M (x), \quad S (x) \quad \supset_x \quad \sim M (x),$ $S (x) \supset_x \sim P (x)$.

Festino: $P (x) \quad \supset_x \quad M (x), \quad S (x) \quad \wedge_x \quad M (x),$ $S (x) \quad \wedge_x \sim P (x)$.

Baroco: $P(x) \supset_x M(x)$, $S(x) \wedge_x \sim M(x)$, $S(x) \wedge_x \sim P(x)$.

Third Figure

Darapti: $M(x) \supset_x P(x)$, $M(x) \supset_x S(x)$, $(Ex) M(x)$, $S(x) \wedge_x P(x)$.

Disamis: $M(x) \wedge_x P(x)$, $M(x) \supset_x S(x)$, $S(_x) \wedge_x P(x)$.

Datisi: $M(x) \supset_x P(x)$, $M(x) \wedge_x S(x)$, $S(x) \wedge_x P(x)$.

Felapton: $M(x) \supset_x \sim P(x)$, $M(x) \supset_x S(x)$, $(Ex) M(x)$, $S(x) \wedge_x \sim P(x)$.

Bocardo: $M(x) \wedge_x \sim P(x)$, $M(x) \supset_{xx} S(x)$, $S(x) \wedge_x \sim P(x)$

Feriso or Ferison: $M(x) \supset_x \sim P(x)$, $M(x) \wedge_x S(x)$, $S(x) \wedge_x \sim P(x)$.

Fourth Figure

Bamalip or Bramantip: $P(x) \supset_x M(x)$, $M(x) \supset_x S(x)$, $(Ex) P(x)$, $S(x) \wedge_x P(x)$.

Calemes or Camenes: $P(x) \supset_x M(x)$, $M(x) \supset_x \sim S(x)$, $S(x) \supset_x \sim P(x)$.

Dimatis or Dimaris: $P(x) \wedge_x M(x)$, $M(x) \supset_x S(x)$, $S(x) \wedge_x P(x)$.

Fesapo: $P(x) \supset_r \sim M(x)$, $M(x) \supset_x S(x)$, $(Ex) M(x)$, $S(x) \wedge_x \sim P(x)$.

Fresison: $P(x) \supset_x \sim M(x)$, $M(x) \wedge_x S(x)$, $S(x) \wedge_x \sim P(x)$.

Singular Forms in the First and Second Figures

Barbara: $M(x) \supset_x P(x)$, $M(A)$, $P(A)$.

Celarent: $M(x) \supset_x \sim P(x)$, $M(A)$, $\sim P(A)$.

Cesare: $P(x) \supset_x \sim M(x)$, $M(A)$, $\sim P(A)$.

Camestres: $P(x) \supset_x M(x)$, $\sim M(A)$, $\sim P(A)$.

The five moods of the fourth figure are sometimes characterized instead as indirect moods of the first figure, the two premisses (major and minor) being interchanged, and the names being then given respectively as Baralipton, Celantes, Dabitis, Fapesmo, Frisesomorum. (Some add the five "weakened" moods, Barbari, Celaront, Cesaro, Camestros, Calemos, to be obtained respectively from Barbara, Celarent, Cesare, Camestres, Calemes, by subalternation of the conclusion.) Other variations in the names of the moods are also found. These names have a mnemonic significance, the first three vowels indicating whether the major premiss, minor premiss, and conclusion, in order, are *A, E, I,* or *O;* and some of the consonants indicating the traditional reductions of the other moods to the four direct moods of the first figure.

The Port-Royal Logic, translated by T. S. Baynes, 2nd edn., London, 1851. F Ueberweg, *System der Logik,* 4th edn., Bonn, 1874. H.W.B. Joseph, *An Introduction to Logic,* 2nd edn., Oxford, 1916. R. M. Eaton, *General Logic,* New York, 1931. H. B. Curry, *A mathematical treatment of the rules of the syllogism,* Mind, vol. 45 (1936), pp. 209-216, 416. Hilbert and Ackermann, *Grundzüge der Theorestischen Logik,* 2nd edn., Berlin, 1938. Bennett and Baylis, *Formal Logic,* New York, 1939.

6. THEORY OF TYPES. In the functional calculus of first order, variables which appear as arguments of propositional functions or which are bound by quantifiers must be variables which are restricted to a certain limited range, the domain of individuals. Thus there are certain kinds of propositions about propositional functions which cannot be expressed in the calculus. The uncritical attempt to remove this restriction, by introducing variables of unlimited range (the range covering both non-functions and functions of whatever kind) and modifying accordingly the definition of a formula and the lists of primitive formulas and primitive rules of inference, leads to a system which is formally inconsistent through the possibility of deriving in it certain of the logical *paradoxes* (*q.v.*). The functional calculus of first order may, however, be extended in another way, which involves separating propositional functions into a certain array of categories (the *hierarchy of types*), excluding propositional functions which do not fall into one of these categories, and— besides propositional and individual variables—admitting only variables having a particular one of these categories as range.

For convenience of statement, we confine attention to the pure functional calculus of first order. The first step in the extension consists in introducing quantifiers such as (F_1), (EF_1), (F_2), (EF_3), etc. binding *n*-adic functional variables. Corresponding changes are made in the definition of a formula and in the lists of primitive formulas and primitive rules of inference, allowing for these new kinds of bound variables. The resulting system is the *functional calculus of second order*. Then the next step consists in introducing new kinds of functional variables; namely for every finite ordered set k, l, m, . . ., p of i non-negative integers ($i = 1, 2, 3, . . .$) an infinite list of functional variables $F^{klm \cdots p}$, $G^{klm \cdots p}$, . . ., each of which denotes ambiguously any i-adic propositional function for which the first argument may be any $(k-1)$-adic propositional function of individuals, the second argument any $(l-1)$-adic propositional function of individuals, etc. (if one of the integers $k, l, m, . . ., p$ is 1 the corresponding argument is a proposition—if 0, an individual). Then quantifiers are introduced binding these new kinds of functional variables; and so on. The process of alternately introducing new kinds of functional variables (denoting propositional functions which take as arguments propositional functions of kinds for which variables have already been introduced) and quantifiers binding the new kinds of functional variables, with appropriate extension at each stage of the definition of a formula and the lists of primitive formulas and primitive rules of inference, may be continued to infinity. This leads to what we may call the *functional calculus of order omega*, embodying the (so-called *simple*) *theory of types*.

In the functional calculi of second and higher orders, we may introduce the definitions:

$$X = Y \rightarrow (F)[F(X) \supset F(Y)],$$

where X and Y are any two variables of the same type and F is a monadic functional variable of appropriate type. The notation X = Y may then be interpreted as denoting equality or identity.

The functional calculus of order omega (as just described) can be proved to be *consistent* by a straightforward generalization of the method employed by Hilbert and Ackermann to prove the consistency of the functional calculus of first order.

For many purposes, however, it is necessary to add to the functional calculus of order omega the *axiom of infinity*, requiring the domain of individuals to be infinite.—This is most conveniently done by adding a single additional primitive formula, which may be described by referring to § 3 above, taking the formula, which is there given as an example of a formula satisfiable in an infinite domain of individuals but not in any finite domain, and prefixing the quantifier (EF) with scope extending to the end of the formula. This form of the axiom of infinity, however, is considerably stronger (in the absence of the axiom of choice) than the "Infin ax" of Whitehead and Russell.

Other primitive formulas (possibly involving new primitive notations) which may be added correspond to the axiom of *choice* (*q.v.*) or are designed to introduce *classes* (*q.v.*) or *descriptions* (*q.v.*). Functional *abstraction* (*q.v.*) may also be introduced by means of additional primitive formulas or primitive rules of inference, or it may be defined with the aid of descriptions. Whitehead and Russell employ the axiom of infinity and the axiom of choice but avoid the necessity of special primitive formulas in connection with classes and descriptions by introducing classes and description as incomplete symbols.

With the aid of the axiom of infinity and a method of dealing with classes and descriptions, the non-negative integers may be introduced in any one of various ways (*e.g.*, following Frege and Russell, as finite cardinal numbers), and arithmetic (elementary number theory) derived formally within the system. With the further addition of the axiom of choice, analysis (real number theory) may be likewise derived.

No proof of *consistency* of the functional calculus of order omega (or even of lower order) with the axiom of infinity added is known, except by methods involving assumptions so strong as to destroy any major significance.

According to an important theorem of Gödel, the functional calculus of order omega with the axiom of infinity added, if consistent, is *incomplete* in the sense that there are formulas A containing no free variables, such that neither A nor ~A is a theorem. The same thing holds of any logistic system obtained by adding new primitive formulas and primitive rules of inference, provided only that the effective (recursive) character of the formal construction of the system is retained. Thus the system is not only incomplete but, in the indicated sense, incompletable. The same thing holds also of a large variety of logistic systems which could be considered as acceptable substitutes for the functional calculus of order omega with axiom of infinity; in particular the Zermelo set theory (§ 9 below) is in the same sense incomplete and incompletable.

The formalization as a logistic system of the functional calculus of order omega with axiom of infinity leads, by a method which cannot be given here, to a (definite but quite complicated) proposition of arithmetic which is equivalent to—in a certain sense, expresses—the consistency of the system. This proposition of arithmetic can be represented within the system by a formula A containing no free variables, and the following second form of Gödel's incompleteness theorem can then be proved: If the system is consistent, then the formula A, although its meaning is a true proposition of arithmetic, is not a theorem of the system. We might, of course, add A to the system as a new primitive formula—we would then have a new system, whose consistency would correspond to a new proposition of arithmetic, represented by a new formula B (containing no free variables), and we would still have in the new system, if consistent, that B was not a theorem.

Whitehead and Russell, *Principia Mathematica*, 3 vols., Cambridge, England, 1st edn. 1910-13, 2nd edn. 1925-27. R. Carnap, *Abriss der Logistik*, Cambridge, Vienna, 1929. W. V. Quine, *A System of Logistic*, Cambridge Mass., 1934. Hilbert and Ackermann, *Grundzüge der theoretischen Logik*, 2nd edn., Berlin, 1938. A Church, *A formulation of the simple theory of types*, The Journal of Symbolic Logic, vol. 5 (1940), pp. 56-68.—A. Tarski, *Einige Betrachtungen über die Begriffe der ω-Widerspruchsfreiheit und der ω-Vollstandigkeit*, Monatshefte für Mathematik und Physik, vol. 40 (1933), pp. 97-112. G. Gentzen, *Die Widerspruchsfreiheit der Stufenlogik*, Mathematische Zeitschrift, vol. 41 (1936), pp. 357-366. — K. Gödel, *Über formal unentscheidbare Sätze der Principia Mathematica und verwandter Systeme*, Monatshefte für Mathematik und Physik, vol. 38 (1931), pp. 173-198. J. B. Rosser, *Extensions of some theorems of Gödel and Church*, The Journal of Symbolic Logic, vol. 1 (1936), pp. 87-91. J. B. Rosser, *An informal exposition of proofs of Gödel's theorems and Church's theorem*, The Journal of Symbolic Logic, vol. 4 (1939), pp. 53-60. Hilbert and Bernays, *Grundlagen der Mathematik*, vol. 2, Berlin, 1939.

7. ALGEBRA OF CLASSES deals with *classes* (*q.v.*) whose members are from a fixed non-empty class called the *universe of discourse*, and with the operations of complementation, logical sum, and logical product upon such classes. (The classes are to be thought of as determined by propositional functions having the universe of discourse as the range of the independent variable.) The universal class V comprises the entire universe of discourse. The null (or empty) class Λ has no members. The *complement*— a of a class a has as members all those elements of the universe of discourse which are not members of a (and those only). In particular the null class and the universal class are each the complement of the other. The *logical sum* $a \cup b$ of two classes a and b has as members all those elements which are members either of a or b, not excluding elements which are members of both a and b (and those only). The *logical product* $a \cap b$ of two classes a and b has as members all those elements which are members of both

a and b (and those only—in other words the logical product of two classes is their common part. The *expressions* of the algebra of classes are built up out of *class variables* a, b, c, . . . and the symbols for the universal class and the null class by means of the notations for complementation, logical sum, and logical product (with parentheses). A *formula* of the algebra of classes consists of two expressions with one of the symbols $=$ or $\neq$ between. ($a = b$ means that a and b are the same class, $a \neq b$ that a and b are not the same class.)

While the algebra of classes can be set up as an independent logistic system, we shall here describe it instead by reference to the functional calculus of first order (§ 3), using two monadic functional constants, V and Λ, and an infinite list of monadic functional variables F_1, G_1, H_1, . . . corresponding in order to the class variables a, b, c, . . . respectively. Given any expression A of the algebra of classes, the corresponding formula A ‡ of the functional calculus is obtained by replacing complementation, logical sum, and logical product respectively by negation, inclusive disjunction, and conjunction, and at the same time replacing V, Λ, a, b, c, . . . respectively by $V(x)$, $\Lambda(x)$, $F_1(x)$, $G_1(x)$, $H_1(x)$, . . . Given any formula A = B of the algebra of classes the corresponding formula of the functional calculus is A‡ $\equiv_x$ B‡. Given any formula A $\neq$ B of the algebra of classes, the corresponding formula of the functional calculus is $\sim[A‡ \equiv_x B‡]$. A formula C is a *theorem* of the algebra of classes if and only if the inference from (x) $V(x)$ and $(x){\sim}\Lambda(x)$ to C‡ (where C‡ corresponds to C) is a valid inference of the functional calculus. The inference from premisses D_1, D_2, . . . , D_n to a conclusion C is a *valid inference* of the algebra of classes if and only if the inference from $(x)V(x)$, $(x) \sim \Lambda(x)$, D_1‡, D_2‡, . . . , Dn‡ to C‡ is a valid inference of the functional calculus.

This isomorphism between the algebra of classes and the indicated part of the functional calculus of first order can be taken as representing a parallelism of meaning. In fact, the meanings become identical if we wish to construe the functional calculus *in extension* (see the article *propositional function*); or, inversely, if we wish to construe the algebra of classes *in intension*, instead of the usual construction.

If we deal only with formulas of the algebra of classes which are *equations* (i.e., which have the form A = B), the above description by reference to the functional calculus may be replaced by a simpler description using the applied propositional calculus (§ 1) whose fundamental propositional symbols are $x \epsilon V$, $x \epsilon \Lambda$, $x \epsilon a$, $x \epsilon b$, $x \epsilon c$, . . . , Given an equation C of the algebra of classes, the corresponding formula C† of the propositional calculus is obtained by replacing equality ($=$) by the biconditional ($\equiv$), replacing complementation, logical sum, and logical product respectively by negation, inclusive disjunction, and conjunction, and at the same time replacing V, Λ, a, b, c, . . . respectively by $x \epsilon V$, $x \epsilon \Lambda$, $x \epsilon a$, $x \epsilon b$, $x \epsilon c$, . . . , *An equation C is a theorem* of the algebra of classes if and only if the inference from

$x \epsilon V$, $\sim x \epsilon \Lambda$ to C† is a valid inference of the propositional calculus; analogously for *valid inferences* of the algebra of classes in which the formulas involved are equations.

As a corollary of this, every theorem of the pure propositional calculus (§ 1) of the form A $\equiv$ B has a corresponding theorem of the algebra of classes obtained by replacing the principal occurrence of $\equiv$ by $=$, elsewhere replacing negation, inclusive disjunction, and conjunction respectively by complementation, logical sum, and logical product, and at the same time replacing propositional variables by class variables. Likewise, every theorem A of the pure propositional calculus has a corresponding theorem B = V of the algebra of classes, where B is obtained from A by replacing negation, inclusive disjunction, and conjunction respectively by complementation, logical sum, and logical product, and replacing propositional variables by class variables.

The *dual* of a formula or an expression of the algebra of classes is obtained by interchanging logical sum and logical product, and at the same time interchanging V and Λ. The *principle of duality* holds, that the dual of every theorem is also a theorem.

The relation of class inclusion, $\subset$, may be introduced by the definition:

$$A \subset B \rightarrow A \supset\!\!— B = \Lambda.$$

Instead of *algebra of classes*, the term *Boolean algebra* is used primarily when it is intended that the formal system shall remain uninterpreted or that interpretations other than that described above shall be admitted. For the related idea of a *Boolean ring* see the paper of Stone cited below.

E. Schröder, *Algebra der Logik*, vol. 1, vol. 2 part 1, and vol. 2 part 2, Leipzig, 1890, 1891, 1905. E. V. Huntington, *Sets of independent postulates for the algebra of logic*, Transactions of the American Mathematical Society, vol. 5 (1904), pp. 288-309. S. K. Langer, *An Introduction to Symbolic Logic*, 1937. M. H. Stone, *The representation of Boolean algebras*, Bulletin of the American Mathematical Society, vol. 44 (1938), pp. 807-816.

8. ALGEBRA OF RELATIONS or *algebra of relatives* deals with *relations* ($q.v.$) in extension whose domains and converse domains are each contained in a fixed *universe of discourse* (which must be a class having at least two members), in a way similar to that in which the algebra of classes deals with classes. Fundamental ideas involved are those of the universal relation and the null relation; the relations of identity and diversity; the contrary and the converse of a relation; the logical sum, the logical product, the relative sum, and the relative product of two relations.

The *universal relation* V can be described by saying that xVy holds for every x and y in the universe of discourse. The *null relation* Λ is such that $x\Lambda y$ holds for no x and y in the universe of discourse. The *relation of identity I* is such that xIx holds for every x in the universe of discourse and xIy fails if x is not identical with y. The *relation of diversity J* is such that xJx fails for every x in the universe of discourse and xJy holds if x is not identical with y.

The *contrary*— $\bar{R}$ of a relation R is the relation such that x— $\bar{R}y$ holds if and only if xRy fails (x and y being in the universe of discourse). In particular, the universal relation and the null relation are each the contrary of the other; and the relations of identity and diversity are each the contrary of the other.

The *converse* of a relation R is the relation $\breve{S}$ such that $x\breve{S}y$ if and only if yRx. The usual notation for the converse of a relation is obtained by placing a breve ⌣ over the letter denoting the relation. A relation is said to be *symmetric* if it is the same as its converse. In particular, the universal relation, the null relation, and the relations of identity and diversity are symmetric.

The *logical sum* $R \cup S$ of two relations R and S is the relation such that $x R \cup S y$ holds if and only if at least one of xRy and xSy holds. The *logical product* $R \cap S$ of two relations R and S is the relation such that $x R \cap S y$ if and only if both xRy and xSy. The *relative product* $R|S$ of two relations R and S is a relation such that $x R|S y$ if and only if there is a z (in the universe of discourse) such that xRz and zSy. The *relative sum* of two relations R and S is the relation which holds between x and y if and only if for every z (in the universe of discourse) at least one of xRz and zSy holds. The *square* of a relation R is $R|R$.

The signs $=$ and $\neq$ are used to form equations and inequations in the same way as in the algebra of classes. An isomorphism between the algebra of relations and an appropriately chosen part of the functional calculus of first order can also be exhibited in the same way as was done in § 7 above for the algebra of classes. A *principle of duality* also holds, where duality consists in interchanging logical sum and logical product, relative sum and relative product, V and Λ, I and J.

The portion of the algebra of relations which involves, besides relation variables, only the universal relation and the null relation, and the operations of contrary, logical sum, and logical product, and $=$, $\neq$, is isomorphic with (formally indistinguishable from) the algebra of classes.

Relative inclusion, $\subset$, may be introduced by the definition:

$$R \subset S \to R \cap -S = \Lambda.$$

When $R \subset S$, we say that R *is contained in* S, or that S contains R.

A relation is *transitive* if it contains its square, *reflexive* if it contains I, *irreflexive* if it is contained in J, *asymmetric* if its square is contained in J.

E. Schröder, *Algebra der Logik*, vol. 3, Leipzig, 1895. A. Tarski, *On the calculus of relations*, The Journal of Symbolic Logic, vol. 6 (1941), pp. 73.

9. ZERMELO SET THEORY. The attempt to devise a system which deals with the logic of classes in a more comprehensive way than is done by the algebra of classes (§ 7), and which, in particular, takes account of the relation ϵ between classes (see the article *class*), must be carried out with caution in order to avoid the Russell paradox and similar logical *paradoxes* (*q.v.*)

There are two methods of devising such a system

which (so at least it is widely held or conjectured) do not lead to any inconsistency. One of these involves the theory of types, which was set forth in § 6 above, explicitly for propositional functions, and by implication for classes (classes being divided into types according to the types of the monadic propositional functions which determine them). The other method is the Zermelo *set theory*, which avoids this preliminary division of classes into types, but imposes restrictions in another direction.

Given the relation (dyadic propositional function) ϵ, the relations of equality and class inclusion may be introduced by the following definitions:

$$Z\epsilon Y \to \epsilon(Z, Y).$$
$$Z = Y \to Z\epsilon X \supset_x Y\epsilon X.$$
$$Z \subset Y \to X\epsilon Z \supset_x X\epsilon Y.$$

Here X, Y, and Z are to be taken as individual variables ("individual" in the technical sense of § 3), and X is to be determined according to an explicit rule so as to be different from Y and Z.

The Zermelo set theory may be formulated as a simple applied functional calculus of first order (in the sense of § 3), for which the domain of individuals is composed of classes, and the only functional constant is ϵ, primitive formulas (additional to those given § 3) being added as follows:

$[x\epsilon z \equiv_x x\epsilon y] \supset z = y$. (Axiom of extensionality)

(Et) $[x\epsilon t \equiv_x [x = y \lor x = z]]$. (Axiom of pairing)

(Et) $[x\epsilon t \equiv_x (Ey) [x\epsilon y] [y\epsilon z]]$. (Axiom of summation)

(Et) $[x\epsilon t \equiv_x x \subset z]$. (Axiom of the set of subsets)

(Et) $[x\epsilon t \equiv_x [x\epsilon z] A]$. (Axiom of subset formation)

$[y\epsilon z \supset_y [y'\epsilon z \supset_{y'} [[x\epsilon y] [x\epsilon y'] \supset_x y = y']]] \supset$
(Et) $[y\epsilon z \supset_y [x''\epsilon y \supset_{x''} (Ex') [[x\epsilon y] [x\epsilon t] \equiv_x$
$x = x']]]$. (Axiom of choice)

(Et) $[z\epsilon t][x'\epsilon t \supset_{x'} (Ey) [y\epsilon t] [x\epsilon y \equiv_x x = x']]$.
(Axiom of infinity)

$[y\epsilon z \supset_y (Ex') [A \equiv_x x = x']] \supset$
(Et) $[x\epsilon t \equiv_x (Ey) [y\epsilon z] A]$.
(Axiom of replacement)

In the axiom of subset formation, A is any formula not containing t as a free variable (in general, A will contain x as a free variable). In the axiom of replacement, A is any formula which contains neither t nor x' as a free variable (in general, A will contain x and y as free variables). These two axioms are thus represented each by an infinite list of primitive formulas—the remaining axioms each by one primitive formula.

The axiom of extensionality as above stated has (incidentally to its principal purpose) the effect of excluding non-classes entirely and assuming that everything is a class. This assumption can be avoided if desired, at the cost of complicating the axioms somewhat—one method would be to introduce an additional functional constant, expressing the property *to be a class* (or *set*), and to modify the axioms accordingly, the domain of individuals being thought of as possibly containing other things besides sets.

The treatment of sets in the Zermelo set theory differs from that of the theory of types in that all sets are "individuals'' and the relation ϵ (of membership in a set) is significant as between any two sets—in particular, $x \epsilon x$ is not forbidden. (We are here using the words *set* and *class* as synonymous.)

The restriction which is imposed in order to avoid paradox can be seen in connection with the axiom of subset formation. Instead of this axiom, an uncritical formulation of axioms for set theory might well have included $(Et) [x \epsilon t \equiv_x A]$, asserting the existence of a set whose members are the sets x satisfying an arbitrary condition A expressible in the notation of the system. This, however, would lead at once to the Russell paradox by taking A to be $\sim x \epsilon x$ and then going through a process of inference which can be described briefly by saying that x is put equal to t. As actually proposed, however, the axiom of subset formation allows the use of the condition A only to obtain a set t whose members are the sets x which *are members of a previously given set z* and satisfy A. This is not known to lead to paradox.

The notion of an ordered pair can be introduced into the theory by definition, in a way which amounts to identifying the ordered pair (x, y) with the set z which has two and only two members, x' and y', x' being the set which has x as its only member, and y' being the set which has x and y as its only two members. (This is one of various similar possible methods.) Relations in extension may then be treated as sets of ordered pairs.

The Zermelo set theory has an adequacy to the logical development of mathematics comparable to that of the functional calculus of order omega (§ 6). Indeed, as here actually formulated, its adequacy for mathematics apparently exceeds that of the functional calculus; however, this should not be taken as an essential difference, since both systems are incomplete, in accordance with Gödel's theorem (§ 6), but are capable of extension.

Besides the Zermelo set theory and the functional calculus (theory of types), there is a third method of obtaining a system adequate for mathematics and at the same time—it is hoped—consistent, proposed by Quine in his book cited below (1940).—The last word on these matters has almost certainly not yet been said.

Alonzo Church

A. Fraenkel. *Einleitung in die Mengenlehre*, 3rd edn., Berlin, 1928. W. V. Quine, *Set-theoretic foundations for logic*, The Journal of Symbolic Logic, vol. 1 (1936), pp. 45-57. Wilhelm Ackermann, *Mengentheoretische Begründung der Logik*, Mathematische Annalen, vol. 115 (1937), pp. 1-22. Paul Bernays, *A system of axiomatic set theory*, The Journal of Symbolic Logic, vol. 2 (1937), pp. 65-77, and vol. 6 (1941), pp. 1-17. W. V. Quine, *Mathematical Logic*, New York, 1940.

Logic, symbolic, or *mathematical logic,* or *logistic,* is the name given to the treatment of formal logic by means of a formalized logical language or calculus whose purpose is to avoid the ambiguities and logical inadequacy of ordinary language. It is best characterized, not as a separate subject, but as a new and powerful method in formal logic. Foreshadowed by ideas of Leibniz, J. H. Lambert, and others, it had its substantial historical beginning in the Nineteenth Century *algebra of logic (q.v.)*, and received its contemporary form at the hands of Frege, Peano, Russell, Hilbert, and others. Advantages of the symbolic method are greater exactness of formulation, and power to deal with formally more complex material. See also *logistic system.—A.C.*

C. I. Lewis, *A Survey of Symbolic Logic*, Berkeley, Cal., 1918. Lewis and Langford, *Symbolic Logic,* New York and London, 1932. S. K. Langer, *An Introduction to Symbolic Logic*, Boston and New York, or London, 1937. W. V. Quine, *Mathematical Logic,* New York, 1940. A. Tarski, *Introduction to Logic and to the Methodology of Deductive Sciences,* New York, 1941. W. V. Quine, *Elementary Logic,* Boston and New York, 1941. A. Church, *A bibliography of symbolic logic,* The Journal of Symbolic Logic, vol. 1 (1936), pp. 121-218, and vol. 3 (1938), pp. 178-212. I. M. Bochenski, *Nove Lezioni di Logica Simbolica,* Rome, 1938. R. Carnap, *Abriss der Logistik,* Vienna, 1929. H. Scholz, *Geschichte der Logik,* Berlin, 1931. Hilbert and Ackermann, *Grundzüge der theoretischen Logik,* 2nd edn., Berlin, 1938.

Logic, traditional: the name given to those parts and that method of treatment of formal logic which have come down substantially unchanged from classical and medieval times. Traditional logic emphasizes the analysis of propositions into subject and predicate and the associated classification into the four forms, *A, E, I, O;* and it is concerned chiefly with topics immediately related to these, including opposition, immediate inference, and the syllogism (see *logic, formal*). Associated with traditional logic are also the three so-called laws of thought—the laws of *identity (q.v.), contradiction (q.v.),* and *excluded middle (q.v.)*—and the doctrine that these laws are in a special sense fundamental presuppositions of reasoning, or even (by some) that all other principles of logic can be derived from them or are mere elaborations of them. *Induction (q.v.)* has been added in comparatively modern times (dating from Bacon's *Novum Organum*) to the subject matter of traditional logic.—*A.C.*

A. Arnauld and others, *La Logique ou l'Art de Penser,* better known as the Port-Royal Logic, 1st edn., Paris, 1662; reprinted, Paris, 1878; English translation by T. S. Baynes, 2nd edn., London, 1851. F. Ueberweg, *System der Logik und Geschichte der logischen Lehren,* 1st edn., Bonn, 1857; 4th edn., Bonn, 1874. C. Prantl, *Geschichte der Logik im Abendlande,* 4 vols., Leipzig, 1855-1870; reprinted, Leipzig, 1927. H. W. B. Joseph, *An Introduction to Logic,* 2nd edn., Oxford, 1916. F. Enriques, *Per la Storia della Logica,* Bologna, 1922; English translation by J. Rosenthal, New York, 1929. H. Scholz, *Geschichte der Logik,* Berlin, 1931.

Logical Empiricism: See *Scientific Empiricism I.*

Logical machines: Mechanical devices or instruments designed to effect combinations of propositions, or premisses, with which the mechanism is supplied, and derive from them correct logical conclusions. Both premisses and conclusions may be expressed by means of conventional symbols. A contrivance devised by William Stanley Jevons in 1869 was a species of logical abacus. Another constructed by John Venn in 1881 consisted of diagrams which could be manipulated in such a manner that appropriate consequences appeared. A still more satisfactory machine was designed by Allan Marquand in 1882. Such devices would indicate that the inferential process is mechanical to a notable extent.—*J.J. R.*

Logical meaning: See *meaning, kinds of,* 3.

Logical Positivism: See *Scientific Empiricism.*

Logical truth: See *Meaning, kinds of,* 3; and *Truth, semantical.*

Logistic: The old use of the word *logistic* to mean the art of calculation, or common arithmetic, is now nearly obsolete. In Seventeenth Century English the corresponding adjective was also sometimes used to mean simply *logical.* Leibniz occasionally employed *logistica* (as also *logica mathematica*) as one of various alternative names of his *calculus ratiocinator.* The modern use of *logistic* (French *logistique*) as a synonym for symbolic *logic* (*q.v.*) dates from the International Congress of Philosophy of 1904, where it was proposed independently by Itelson, Lalande, and Couturat. The word *logistic* has been employed by some with special reference to the Frege-Russell doctrine that mathematics is reducible to logic, but it would seem that the better usage makes it simply a synonym of *symbolic logic.*—*A.C.*

L. Couturat, *IIme Congres de Philosophie,* Revue de Métaphysique et de Morale, vol. 12 (1904), see p. 1042.

Logistic system: The formal construction of a logistic system requires: (1) a list of *primitive symbols* (these are usually taken as marks but may also be sounds or other things—they must be capable of *instances* which are, recognizably, the same or different symbols, and capable of *utterance* in which instances of them are put forth or arranged in an order one after another); (2) a determination of a class of *formulas,* each formula being a finite sequence of primitive symbols, or, more exactly, each formula being capable of instances which are finite sequences of instances of primitive symbols (generalizations allowing two-dimensional arrays of primitive symbols and the like are non-essential); (3) a determination of the circumstances under which a finite sequence of formulas is a *proof* of the last formula in the sequence, this last formula being then called a *theorem* (again we should more exactly speak of proofs as having instances which are finite sequences of instances of formulas); (4) a determination of the circumstances under which a finite sequence of formulas is a *proof* of the last formula of the sequence *as a consequence of* a certain set of formulas (when there is a proof of a formula B as a consequence of the set of formulas $A_1, A_2, \ldots, A_n$, we say that the *inference* from the *premisses* $A_1, A_2, \ldots, A_n$ to the *conclusion* B is a *valid inference* of the logistic system). It is not excluded that the class of proofs in the sense of (3) should be empty. But every proof of a formula B as a consequence of an empty set of formulas,

in the sense of (4), must also be a proof of B in the sense of (3), and conversely. Moreover, if to the proof of a formula B as a consequence of $A_1, A_2, \ldots, A_n$ are prefixed in any order proofs of $A_1, A_2, \ldots, A_n$, the entire resulting sequence of formulas must be a proof of B; more generally, if to the proof of a formula B as a consequence of $A_1, A_2, \ldots, A_n$ are prefixed in any order proofs of a subset of $A_1, A_2, \ldots, A_n$ as consequences of the remainder of $A_1, A_2, \ldots, A_n$, the entire resulting sequence must be a proof of B as a consequence of this remainder.

The determination of the circumstances under which a sequence of formulas is a proof, or a proof as a consequence of a set of formulas, is usually made by means of: (5) a list of *primitive formulas;* and (6) a list of *primitive rules of inference* each of which prescribes that under certain circumstances a formula B shall be an *immediate consequence* of a set of formulas $A_1, A_2, \ldots, A_n$. The list of primitive formulas may be empty—this is not excluded. Or the primitive formulas may be included under the head of primitive rules of inference by allowing the case $n=0$ in (6). A *proof* is then defined as a finite sequence of formulas each of which is either a primitive formula or an immediate consequence of preceding formulas by one of the primitive rules of inference. A *proof as a consequence* of a set of formulas $A_1, A_2, \ldots, A_n$ is in some cases defined as a finite sequence of formulas each of which is either a primitive formula, or one of $A_1, A_2, \ldots, A_n$, or an immediate consequence of preceding formulas by one of the primitive rules of inference; in other cases it may be desirable to impose certain restrictions upon the application of the primitive rules of inference (*e.g.,* in the case of the functional calculus of first order— *logic, formal,* § 3—that no free variable of $A_1, A_2, \ldots, A_n$ shall be generalized upon).

A logistic system need not be given any meaning or interpretation, but may be put forward merely as a formal discipline of interest for its own sake; and in this case the words *proof, theorem, valid inference,* etc., are to be dissociated from their every-day meanings and taken purely as technical terms. Even when an interpretation of the system is intended, it is a requirement of rigor that no use shall be made of the interpretation (as such) in the determination whether a sequence of symbols is a formula, whether a sequence of formulas is a proof, etc.

The kind of an interpretation, or assignment of meaning, which is normally intended for a logistic system is indicated by the technical terminology employed. This is namely such an interpretation that the formulas, some or all of them, mean or express propositions; the theorems express true propositions; and the proofs and valid inferences represent proofs and valid inferences in the ordinary sense. (Formulas which do not mean propositions may be interpreted as names of things other than propositions, or may be interpreted as containing free variables and having only an ambiguous denotation—see *variable.*) A logistic system may thus be regarded as a device for obtaining—or, rather stating—an objective, external criterion for the validity of proofs and inferences (which are expressible in a given notation).

A logistic system which has an interpretation of the kind in question may be expected, in general, to have more than one such interpretation.

It is usually to be required that a logistic system shall provide an *effective* criterion for recognizing formulas, proofs, and proofs as a consequence of a set of formulas; i.e., it shall be a matter of direct observation, and of following a fixed set of directions for concrete operations with symbols, to determine whether a given finite sequence of primitive symbols is a formula, or whether a given finite sequence of formulas is a proof, or is a proof as a consequence of a given set of formulas. If this requirement is not satisfied, it may be necessary— *e.g.*—given a particular finite sequence of formulas, to seek by some argument adapted to the special case to prove or disprove that it satisfies the conditions to be a *proof* (in the technical sense); i.e., the criterion for formal recognition of proofs then presupposes, in actual application, that we already know what a valid deduction is (in a sense which is stronger than that merely of the ability to follow concrete directions in a particular case). See further on this point *logic, formal,* § 1.

The requirement of effectiveness does not compel the lists of primitive symbols, primitive formulas, and primitive rules of inference to be finite. It is sufficient if there are effective criteria for recognizing formulas, for recognizing primitive formulas, for recognizing applications of primitive rules of inference, and (if separately needed) for recognizing such restricted applications of the primitive rules of inference as are admitted in *proofs as a consequence* of a given set of formulas.

With the aid of Gödel's device of representing sequences of primitive symbols and sequences of formulas by means of numbers, it is possible to give a more exact definition of the notion of effectiveness by making it correspond to that of *recursiveness* (*q.v.*) of numerical functions. E.g., a criterion for recognizing primitive formulas is effective if it determines a general recursive monadic function of natural numbers whose value is 0 when the argument is the number of a primitive formula, 1 for any other natural number as argument. The adequacy of this technical definition to represent the intuitive notion of effectiveness as described above is not immediately clear, but is placed beyond any real doubt by developments for details of which the reader is referred to Hilbert-Bernays and Turing (see references below).

The requirement of effectiveness plays an important role in connection with logistic systems, but the necessity of the requirement depends on the purpose in hand and it may for some purposes be abandoned. Various writers have proposed non-effective, or non-constructive, logistic systems; in some of these the requirement of finiteness of length of formulas is also abandoned and certain infinite sequences of primitive symbols are admitted as formulas.

For particular examples of logistic systems (all of which satisfy the requirement of effectiveness) see the article *logic, formal,* especially §§ 1, 3, 9.

Alonzo Church

R. Carnap, *The Logical Syntax of Language,* New York and London, 1937. H. Scholz, *Was ist ein Kalkül und was hat Frege für eine pünktliche Beantwortung dieser Frage geleistet?,* Semester-Berichte, Münster i. W., summer 1935, pp. 16-54. Hilbert and Bernays, *Grundlagen der Mathematik,* vol. 2, Berlin, 1939. A. M. Turing, *On computable numbers, with an application to the Entscheidungsproblem,* Proceedings of the London Mathematical Society, ser. 2 vol. 42 (1937), pp. 230-265, and *Correction,* ibid., ser. 2 vol. 43 (1937), pp. 544-546. A. M. Turing, *Computability and λ-definability,* The Journal of Symbolic Logic, vol. 2 (1937). pp. 153-163.

Logomachy: (Gr. *logos,* word + *mache,* battle) A contention in which words are involved without their references. A contention which lacks the real grounds of difference, or one in which allegedly opposed views are actually not on the same level of discourse. A battle of words alone, which ignores their symbolic character.—*J.K.F.*

Logos: (Gr. *logos*) A term denoting either reason or one of the expressions of reason or order in words or things; such as word, discourse, definition, formula, principle, mathematical ratio. In its most important sense in philosophy it refers to a cosmic reason which gives order and intelligibility to the world. In this sense the doctrine first appears in Heraclitus, who affirms the reality of a Logos analogous to the reason in man that regulates all physical processes and is the source of all human law. The conception is developed more fully by the Stoics, who conceive of the world as a living unity, perfect in the adaptation of its parts to one another and to the whole, and animated by an immanent and purposive reason. As the creative source of this cosmic unity and perfection the world-reason is called the seminal reason (logos spermatikos), and is conceived as containing within itself a multitude of logoi spermatikoi, or intelligible and purposive forms operating in the world. As regulating all things, the Logos is identified with Fate (heimarmene); as directing all things toward the good, with Providence (pronoia); and as the ordered course of events, with Nature (physis). In Philo of Alexandria, in whom Hebrew modes of thought mingle with Greek concepts, the Logos becomes the immaterial instrument, and even at times the personal agency, through which the creative activity of the transcendent God is exerted upon the world. In Christian philosophy the Logos becomes the second person of the Trinity and its functions are identified with the creative, illuminating and redemptive work of Jesus Christ. Finally the Logos plays an important role in the system of Plotinus, where it appears as the creative and form-giving aspect of Intelligence (Nous), the second of the three Hypostases.—*G.R.M.*

Lombard, Peter: (c. 1100—c. 1160) Was the author of the *Four Books of Sentences,* i.e. a compilation of the opinions of the Fathers and early teachers of the Catholic Church concerning various points in theology. He was born at Lumello in Lombardy, studied at Bologna, Rheims and the School of St. Victor in Paris. He was made Bishop of Paris in 1159. The *Libri IV Sententiarum* was used as a textbook in Catholic theology for more than two centuries, hence it has been commented by all the great theologians of the 13th and 14th centuries. The Franciscans of Quaracchi have published a critical edition in 2 vols. (Quaracchi, 1916).—*V.J.B.*

Lotze, Rudolph Hermann: (1817-1881) Empiricist in science, teleological idealist in philosophy, theist in religion, poet and artist at heart, Lotze conceded three spheres: Necessary truths, facts, and values. Mechanism holds sway in the field of natural science; it does not generate meaning but is subordinated to value and reason which evolved a specific plan for the world. Lotze's psycho-physically oriented medical psychology is an applied metaphysics in which the concept soul stands for the unity of experience. Science attempts the demonstration of a coherence in nature; being is that which is in relationship; ''thing'' is not a conglomeration of qualities but a unity achieved through law; mutual effect or influence is as little explicable as being: It is monistic Absolute working upon itself. The ultimate, absolute substance, God, is the good and is personal, personality being the highest value, and the most valuable is also the most real. Lotze disclaimed the ability to know all answers: they rest with God. Unity of law, matter, force, and all aspects of being produce beauty, while aesthetic experience consists in *Einfühlung*. Main works: *Metaphysik*, 1841; *Logik*, 1842; *Medezinische Psychologie*, 1842; *Gesch. der Aesthetik im Deutschland*, 1868; *Mikrokosmos*, 3 vols., 1856-64 (Eng. tr. 1885); *Logik* 1874; *Metaphysik*, 1879 (Eng. tr. 1884).—*K.F.L.*

Love: (in Max Scheler) Giving one's self to a ''total being'' *(Gesamtwesen);* it therefore discloses the essence of that being; for this reason love is, for Scheler, an aspect of phenomenological knowledge.—*P.A.S.*

Lovejoy, Arthur O.: (1873-1962) Professor of Philosophy of Johns Hopkins University. He was one of the contributors to ''Critical Realism.'' He wrote the famous article on the thirteen pragmatisms *(Jour. Philos.*, Jan. 16, 1908). Also critical of the behavioristic approach. His best known works are *The Revolt against Dualism* and *The Great Chain of Being*, 1936. The latter exemplified L's method of tracing the history of a ''unit-idea.'' A. O. L. was the first editor of the *Journal of the History of Ideas* (1940-), an authority on Primitivism *(q.v.)* and Romanticism *(q.v.).—L.E.D.*

Löwenheim's theorem: The theorem, first proved by Löwenheim, that if a formula of the pure functional calculus of first order (see *Logic, formal*, § 3), containing no free individual variables, is *satisfiable* (see ibid.) at all, it is satisfiable in a domain of individuals which is at most enumerable. Other, simpler, proofs of the theorem were afterwards given by Skolem, who also obtained the generalization that, if an enumerable set of such formulas are simultaneously satisfiable, they are simultaneously satisfiable in a domain of individuals at most enumerable.

There follows the existence of an interpretation of the Zermelo set theory (see *Logic, formal*, § 9) — consistency of the theory assumed—according to which the domain of sets is only enumerable; although there are theorems of the Zermelo set theory which, under the *usual interpretation*, assert the existence of the non-enumerable infinite.

A like result may be obtained for the functional calculus of order omega (theory of types) by utilizing a representation of it within the Zermelo set theory.

It is thus in a certain sense impossible to postulate the non-enumerable infinite: any set of postulates designed to do so will have an unintended interpretation within the enumerable. Usual sets of mathematical postulates for the real number system (see *number*) have an appearance to the contrary only because they are incompletely formalized (i.e., the mathematical concepts are formalized, while the underlying logic remains unformalized and indefinite).

The situation described in the preceding paragraph is sometimes called *Skolem's paradox*, although it is not a paradox in the sense of formal self-contradiction, but only in the sense of being unexpected or at variance with preconceived ideas.—*A.C.*

Th. Skolem, *Sur la portée du théorème de Löwenheim-Skolem*, Les Entretiens de Zurich sur les Fondements et la Méthode des Sciences Mathématiques, Zurich 1941, pp. 25-52.

Lucretius, Carus: (c. 98-54 B.C.) Noted Roman poet, author of the famous didactic poem *De Natura Rerum*, in six books, which forms an interesting exposition of the philosophy of Epicureanism.—*M.F.*

Lu Hsiang-shan: (Lu Chiu-yüan, Lu Tzŭ-ching, 1139-1192) Questioned Ch'êng I-ch'üan's interpretation of Confucianism when very young, later often argued with Chu Hsi, and claimed that ''the six (Confucian) classics are my footnotes.'' This official-scholar served as transition from the Reason School (li hsüeh) of Neo-Confucianism. His complete works, *Lu Hsiang-shan Ch'üan-chi*, number 36 *chüans* in four volumes.—*W.T.C.*

Lullic art: The *Ars Magna* or *Generalis* of Raymond Lully (1235-1315), a science of the highest and most general principles, even above metaphysics and logic, in which the basic postulates of all the sciences are included, and from which he hoped to derive these fundamental assumptions with the aid of an ingenious mechanical contrivance, a sort of logical or thinking machine.—*J.J.R.*

Lumen naturale: Natural light, equivalent to *lumen naturalis rationis*, in medieval philosophy and theology denoted the ordinary cognitive powers of human reason unaided by the supernatural light of grace, *lumen gratiae*, or divine revelation, *lumen fidei*.—*J.J.R.*

The phrase ''natural light of reason'' occurs also in the scientific writings of Galileo *(q.v.)* and Descartes *(q.v.).—P.P.W.*

Lutheranism: An ecclesiastical school of thought

claiming Martin Luther (1483-1546) as its source and inspiration. See *Reformation*. The Protestant doctrine of salvation by faith, the free grace of God, wholly without earned merit and institutional sanctions, is emphasized. The essence of the church-community is held to revolve about the pure, revealed Word of God and the sacraments of baptism and communion. Varieties of Lutheranism range from a liberal acknowledg-

ment of the Augsburg Confession of 1530 to a more strict adherence to the several Lutheran documents collectively known as the *Book of Concord*.—*V.F.*

Lyric: a. Literary genre pertaining to the absolute uniqueness of poets' sensations.

    b. Identified with art in general because it symbolizes expression of sentiment (Croce).—*L.V.*

M

Machiavellism: A political principle according to which every act of the state (or statesman) is permissible — especially with reference to foreign relations — which might be advantageous for one's own country. The word refers to Niccolo di Bernardo Machiavelli, born May 3, 1469 in Florence, died June 22, 1527. Author of *Discorsi sopra la prima deca di Tito Livio* (*Discourses about the first ten books of Titus Livius*), *Il Principe* (*The Prince*).—*W.E.*

Macrocosm: (vs. Microcosm) The universe as contrasted with some small part of it which epitomizes it in some respect under consideration or exhibits an analogous structure; any large "world" or complex or existent as contrasted with a miniature or small analogue of it, whether it be the physical expanse of the universe as against an atom, the whole of human society as against a community, district, or other social unit, or any other large scale existent as contrasted with a small scale representation, analogue, or miniature of it; sometimes God as against man, or the universe as against man; or God or the universe as against a monad, atom, or other small entity.—*M.T.K.*

Madhva: An Indian dualistic philosopher of the 13th century A.D., a Vedāntist and Vishṇuite who held that world and soul, as well as the highest reality are entities different in their essence, and non-commutable.—*K.F.L.*

Madhyamaka: Another name for the Buddhist school of Sūnyavāda (*q.v.*) so-called because it assumes a middle path (*madhyama*) between theories clinging to the knowableness of the noumenal and the sufficiency of the phenomenal.—*K.F.L.*

Maecenatism: Patronage of the arts (from Maecenas, the patron of Horace and Virgil).—*L.V.*

Mahābhārata: (Skr. "the great [war of the] *Bharatas*"). An Indian epic of 100,000 verses, ascribed to Vyāsa, incorporating many philosophical portions, such as the Bhagavad Gītā (*q.v.*)—*K.F.L.*

Mahābhūta: (Skr.) A physical element; in the Sāṅkhya (*q.v.*) one of the five gross elements contrasted with the *tanmātras* (*q.v.*).—*K.F.L.*

Mahat: (Skr. great, mighty) The first great principle produced by *prakrti* (*q.v.*) according to the Sāṅkhya (*q.v.*), ideation, spirit, idea.—*K.F.L.*

Mahātma, mahātman: (Skr. great soul) Term of respect, as applied to Gandhi, for instance. In philosophy, the super-individual or transcendental self, or the Absolute.—*K.F.L.*

Mahāyāna Buddhism: "Great Vehicle Buddhism," the Northern, Sanskrit, Tibetan, and Chinese form of Buddhism (*q.v.*), extending as far as Korea and Japan, whose central theme is that Buddhahood means devotion to the salvation of others and thus manifests itself in the worship of Buddha and Bodhisattvas (*q.v.*). Apart from absorbing beliefs of a more primitive strain, it has also evolved metaphysical and epistemological systems, such as the Śūnyavāda (*q.v.*) and Vijñāna-vāda (*q.v.*).—*K.F.L.*

Maieutic: Adjective derived from the Greek *maia*, midwife; hence pertaining to the art of assisting at childbirth, and to the positive aspect of the Socratic method. Socrates pretended to be a midwife, like his mother, since he assisted at the birth of knowledge by eliciting correct concepts by his process of interrogation and examination.—*J.J.R.*

Maimon, Moses ben: (better known as Maimonides) (Abu Imram Musā Ibn Maimun Ibn Abdallah) (1135-1204) Talmud commentator and leading Jewish philosopher during the Middle Ages. Born in Cordova, left Spain in 1160, settled in Fez, N. Africa, whence he migrated to Palestine in 1165 and ultimately settled in Fostat, Egypt. His *Guide for the Perplexed* (*More Nebukim* in Heb.; *Dalalat al-hairin*, in Arab.) contains the *summa* of Jewish philosophic thought up to his time. It is written in the spirit of Aristotelianism and is divided into three parts. The first is devoted to the problems of Biblical anthropomorphisms, Divine attributes, and exposition and criticism of the teachings of the Kalam; the second to the proof of the existence of God, matter and form, *creatio de novo,* and an exposition of prophecy; the third to God and the world including problems of providence, evil, prescience and freedom of the will, teleology, and rationality of the precepts of the Torah. Maimonides exerted great influence not only on the course of subsequent Jewish speculation but also on the leaders of the thirteenth century scholastic philosophy. Albertus Magnus and Thomas Aquinas.—*M.W.*

Maimon, Salomon: (1754-1800) A Jewish philosophical writer, versed in rabbinical literature, in whom Kant found his acknowledged most astute critical opponent. He wrote historical works on philosophy, attempted to expound a system of symbolic logic, and originated a speculative monism which influenced the leading Post-Kantians.—*H.H.*

Works: *Versuch einer Transzendentalphilosophie*, 1790-92; *Versuch einer neuen Logik oder Theorie des Denkens*, 1794.

Maine de Biran, F. P. Gonthier: (1766-1824) French philosopher and psychologist, who revolted against the dominant sensationalistic and materialistic psychology of Condillac and Cabanis and developed, under the influence of Kant and Fichte, an idealistic and voluntaristic psychology. The mind directly experiences the activity of its will and at the same time the resistance offered to it by the "non-moi." Upon this basis, Maine de Biran erected his metaphysics which interprets the conceptions of force, substance, cause, etc. in terms of the directly experienced activity of the will. This system of psychology and metaphysics, which came to be known as French *spiritualism*, exerted considerable influence on Cousin, Ravaisson and Renouvier. His writings include: *De la Décomposition de la Pensée* (1805); *Les Rapports du Physique et du Moral de l'Homme* (1834); *Essai sur les Fondements de la Psychologie* (1812); *Oeuvres Philosophiques*, ed. by V. Cousin (1841).—*L.W.*

Major premiss: See *figure (syllogistic)*.

Major term: (Gr. *meizon horos*) That one of the three terms in a syllogism which appears as predicate of the conclusion; so called by Aristotle because in the first, or perfect, figure of the syllogism it is commonly the term of greatest extension, the middle term being included in it, and the minor term in turn coming under the middle term. See *Aristotelianism; Logic, formal*, § 5. —*G.R.M.*

Malebranche, Nicolas: (1638-1715) Was born in Paris and, on his maturity, embraced the doctrines of the Cartesian school. Like Geulincx, he was particularly interested in the problem of mind-body relation which he interpreted in the spirit of occasionalism. Believing that the mind and body cannot possibly interact, he concluded that God enacts bodily movements "on occasion" of corresponding mental processes. In general, he believed that God works in all things and is the only real cause of events.—*R.B.W.*

Main works: *Recherche de la vérité*, 1674-5; *Conversations Chrétiennes*, 1676; *Traité de la Nature et de la Grace*, 1680; *Traité de Morale*, 1683; *Entretiens sur la métaphysique et la religion*, 1688; *Traité de l'Amour de Dieu*, 1697; *Réflexions sur la prémotion physique*, 1714.

Malevolence: Ill or evil will or disposition—the will or disposition to do wrong or to harm others. The vice opposed to the virtue of benevolence or good will.—*W.K.F.*

Mana: An impersonal power or force believed to reside in natural objects contact with which infuses benefits of power, success, good or evil. A belief held by the Melanesians.—*V.F.*

Manas: (Skr.) Mind, mentality, the unifying principle involved in sensation (cf. *indriya*), perception, conation, conception, always thought of in Indian philosophy as a kinetic entity, will and desire being equally present with thinking.—*K.F.L.*

Manicheism, a religio-philosophical doctrine which spread from Persia to the West and was influential during the 3rd and 7th century, was instituted by Mani (Grk. Manes, Latinized: Manichaeus), a Magian who, upon conversion to Christianity, sought to synthesize the latter with the dualism of Zoroastrianism (*q.v.*), not without becoming a martyr to his faith. To combat the powers of darkness, the mother of light created the first man. As Buddha (*q.v.*) and Zoroaster he worked illumination among men; as Jesus, the Son of Man, he had to suffer, become transfigured and symbolize salvation by his apparent death at the cross; as spirit of the sun he attracts all connatural light particles to himself. But final salvation from the throes of evil demons is accomplished by ascetic living, reminding of the Hindu code of ethics (see *Indian Ethics*), and belief in Mani as the prophesied paraclete (John 14.16-17). Revived once more in the Occident during the crusades by the Cathari.—*K.F.L.*

Manifold of Sense: (A.S. *manig*, many + *feold*, fold) The sensuous ingredients of experience (colors, sounds, etc.) considered as a multiplicity of discrete items. See I. Kant, *Critique of Pure Reason*, A. 77-9-B. 102-5.—*L.W.*

Mantra: (Skr.) Pious thought couched in repeated prayerful utterances, for meditation or charm. Also the poetic portion of the Veda (*q.v.*). In Shaktism (*q.v.*) and elsewhere the holy syllables to which as manifestations of the eternal word or sound (cf. *śabda, vāc, aksara*) is ascribed great mystic significance and power.—*K.F.L.*

Many questions: The name given to the fallacy—or, rather, misleading device of disputation—which consists in requiring a single answer to a question which either involves several questions that ought to be answered separately or contains an implicit assertion to which any unqualified answer would give assent. —*A.C.*

Many-valued logic: See *propositional calculus, many-valued*.

Mao Zedong: (Tse-tung in the Wade-Giles system of transcription) (1893-1976) Chinese political leader who exercised great cultural impact through social organization. Author of the "little red book", *Quotations from Chirman Mao* (1964). Some of the better-known quotations are: "Political power grows out of the barrel of a gun" (—V. "War and Peace"), and "Our principle is that the Party commands the gun, and the gun must never be allowed to command the Party"

(—IX. "The People's Army").—*S.E.N.*

Marburg School: Founded by Herman Cohen (1842-1918) and Paul Natorp (1854-1924) and supported by Ernst Cassirer (1874-1945), the noteworthy historian of philosophy, and Rudolf Stammler (1856-1938), the eminent legal philosopher, the school revived a specialized tendency of critical idealism. Stress is laid on the *a priori*, non-empirical, non-psychological and purely logical nature of all certain knowledge. Cohen and Natorp register an emphatic opposition to psychologism, and sought to construct a system upon pure thought on the basis of Kant and the Kantian reconstruction of Platonism. The logical and *a priori* in aesthetics, ethics, psychology and law is, being also independent of experience, the essential basis of these fields. Cf. Natorp, *Kant u.d. Marburger Schule*, 1915.—*H.H.*

Marcus Aurelius: (121-180 A.D.) The Roman Emperor who as a Stoic endowed chairs in Athens for the four great philosophical schools of the Academy, the Lyceum, The Garden and the Stoa. Aurelius' Stoicism, tempered by his friend Fronto's humanism, held to a rational world-order and providence as well as to a notion of probable truth rather than of the Stoic infallibilism. In the famous 12 books of Meditations, the view is prominent that death was as natural as birth and development was the end of the individual and should elicit the fear of no one. His harsh treatment of the Christians did not coincide with his mild nature which may have reflected the changed character of Stoicism brought on by the decadence of Rome. Cf. *Meditations* (Eng. tr. of *Ta Eis Héauton*) of A.—*M.F.*

Marcuse, Herbert: (1898-1981) Ideological leader of the new left, arguing that every political and social system, regardless of its type, needs to be overthrown. Born in Berlin and educated at Berlin and Freiburg, he fled to the United States and taught at Columbia, Harvard, Brandeis, and the University of California at San Diego. He has written *Reason and Revolution* (1941), *Eros and Civilization, a Philosophical Inquiry into Freud* (1955), *One-Dimensional Man: Studies in the Ideology of Advanced Industrial Society* (1964), *A Critique of Pure Tolerance* (1965), *Negations* (1968), *An Essay on Liberation* (1969), and *Counterrevolution and Revolt* (1972).—*S.E.N.*

Maritain, Jacques: (1882-1973) Was born in Paris, educated at the Lycée Henri IV and the Sorbonne, where he studied with H. Bergson. He was converted to Catholicism in 1906. Then he studied biology with H. Driesch for two years, and the philosophy of St. Thomas with Father Clérissac. He became an ardent advocate of Thomistic philosophy, stressing its applicability to modern problems. He was a professor at the Institut Catholique (1914) and the Institute of Med. Studies, Toronto (1933). Chief works: *Philos. Bergsonienne* (1914), *Distinguer pour Unir* (1932), *Sept Lecons sur l'Etre* (1934). G. B. Phelan, *Jacques Maritain* (N. Y., 1937).—*V.J.B.*

Marx, Karl: Was born May 5, 1818 in Trier (Trèves), Germany, and was educated at the Universities of Bonn and Berlin. He received the doctorate in philosophy at Berlin in 1841, writing on *The Difference between the Democritean and Epicurean Natural Philosophy*, which theme he treated from the Hegelian point of view. Marx early became a Left Hegelian, then a Feuerbachian. In 1842-43 he edited the "Rheinische Zeitung," a Cologne daily of radical tendencies. In 1844, in Paris, Marx, now calling himself a communist, became a leading spirit in radical groups and a close friend of Friedrich Engels (*q.v.*). In 1844 he wrote articles for the "Deutsch-Französische Jahrbücher," in 1845 the *Theses on Feuerbach* and, together with Engels, *Die Heilige Familie*. In 1846, another joint work with Engels and Moses Hess, *Die Deutsche Ideologie* was completed (not published until 1932). 1845-47, Marx wrote for various papers including "Deutsche Brüsseler Zeitung," Westphälisches Dampfbot," Gesellschaftsspiegel" (Elberfeld), "La Réforme" (Paris). In 1847 he wrote (in French) *Misère de la Philosophie*, a reply to Proudhon's *Système des Contradictions économiques, ou, Philosophie de la Misère*. In 1848 he wrote, jointly with Engels, the "Manifesto of the Communist Party," delivered his "Discourse on Free Trade" in Brussels and began work on the "Neue Rheinische Zeitung" which, however, was suppressed like its predecessor and also its successor, the "Neue Rheinische Revue" (1850). For the latter Marx wrote the essays later published in book form as *Class Struggles in France*. In 1851 Marx did articles on foreign affairs for the "New York Tribune," published *The 18th Brumaire of Louis Bonaparte* and the pamplet "Enthülungen über den Kommunistenprozess in Köln." In 1859 Marx published *Zur Kritik der politischen Okonomie*, the foundation of "Das Kapital," in 1860, "Herr Vogt" and in 1867 the first volume of *Das Kapital*. In 1871 the "Manifesto of the General Council of the International Workingmen's Association on the Paris Commune," later published as *The Civil War in France* and as *The Paris Commune* was written. In 1873 there appeared a pamphlet against Bakunin and in 1875 the critical comment on the "Gotha Program." The publication of the second volume of *Capital* dates from 1885, two years after Marx's death, the third volume from 1894, both edited by Engels. The essay "Value Price and Profit" is also posthumous, edited by his daughter Eleanor Marx Aveling. The most extensive collection of Marx's work is to be found in the Marx-Engels *Gesamtausgabe*.

It is said by the Marx-Engels-Lenin Institute (Moscow) that the as yet unpublished work of Marx, including materials of exceptional theoretical significance, is equal in bulk to the published work. Marx devoted a great deal of time to practical political activity and the labor movement, taking a leading rôle in the founding and subsequent guiding of the International Workingmen's Association, The First International. He lived the life of a political refugee in Paris, Brussels and finally London, where he remained for more than thirty years until he died March 14, 1883. He had seven children and at times experienced the severest want. Engels was a partial supporter of the Marx household for the better part of twenty years. Marx, together with Engels, was the founder of the school of philosophy known as dialectical materialism (*q.v.*). In the writings of Marx and Engels this position appears in a relatively general form. While statements are made within all fields of philosophy, there is no systematic elaboration of doctrine in such fields as ethics, aesthetics or epistemology, although a methodology and a basis are laid down. The fields developed in most detail by Marx, besides economic theory, are social and political philosophy (see *Historical materialism,* and entry, *Dialectical materialism*) and, together with Engels, logical and ontological aspects of materialist dialectics.—*J.M.S.*

Marxism: The philosophical, social and economic theories developed by Karl Marx and Friedrich Engels. A concise statement of the general Marxist position is to be found in the *Communist Manifesto.*

The philosophical aspect of Marxism is known as dialectical materialism (*q.v.*); in epistemology it adopts empiricism; in axiology, an interest theory of value strongly tinged, in places, with humanitarianism. The social theory of Marxism centers around the concepts of basic (but not complete) economic determinism (*q.v.*), and the class character of society. In economics it maintains a labor theory of value (*q.v.*) which involves the concept of surplus value (*q.v.*) in the capitalistic mode of production. Upon the basis of its analysis of capitalism, Marxism erects the ethical conclusion that capitalism is unjust and ought to be supplanted by socialism. It predicts for the more or less immediate future the decay of capitalism, an inevitable and victorious revolution of the workers, and the establishing of socialism under the dictatorship of the proletariat. It looks forward to the ultimate goal of the "withering away of the state" leading to a classless society, communistic in economy and self-regulatory in politics.—*M.B.M.*

Material a priori: (in Max Scheler) Intuitively given essences (relation of ideas).—*P.A.S.*

Materialism: (1) A proposition about the existent or the real: that only matter (*q.v.*) is existent or real; that matter is the primordial or fundamental constituent of the universe; atomism; that only sensible entities, processes, or content are existent or real; that the universe is not governed by intelligence, purpose, or final causes; that everything is strictly caused by material (inanimate, non-mental, or having certain elementary physical powers) processes or entities (mechanism); that mental entities, processes, or events (though existent) are caused solely by material entities, processes, or events and themselves have no causal effect (epiphenomenalism); that nothing supernatural exists (naturalism); that nothing mental exists; (2) a proposition about explanation of the existent or the real: that everything is explainable in terms of matter in motion or matter and energy or simply matter (depending upon conception of matter entertained); that all qualitative differences are reducible to quantitative differences; that the only objects science can investigate are the physical or material (that is, public, manipulable, nonmental, natural, or sensible); (3) a proposition about values: that wealth, bodily satisfactions, sensuous pleasures, or the like are either the only or the greatest values man can seek or attain; (4) a proposition about explanation of human history: that human actions and cultural change are determined solely or largely by economic factors (economic determinism or its approximation); (5) an attitude, postulate, hypothesis, assertion, assumption, or tendency favoring any of the above propositions; a state of being limited by the physical environment or the material elements of culture and incapable of overcoming, transcending, or adjusting properly to them; preoccupation with or enslavement to lower or bodily (non-mental or non-spiritual) values. Confusion of epiphenomenalism or mechanism with other conceptions of materialism has caused considerable misunderstanding.—*M.T.K.*

Materialization: (in Scholasticism) The function of matter when it receives form and with it constitutes a body, as distinguished from *information,* which is the function of form when it perfects the matter united to it so as to constitute a specific body.—*H.G.*

Materially: (in Scholasticism) A predicate is said to belong to a subject materially when it belongs to it by reason of its matter or subject—but *formally* when it belongs to it by reason of its form, e.g. fire is *materially* wasteful or destructive, but *formally warm.*—*H.G.*

Material Mode of Speech: A description introduced by Carnap and based upon his distinction between "object-sentences" and "syntactical sentences." A sentence is syntactical if it can be translated into (is materially equivalent to) another sentence of the same language which refers only to signs or formal properties of and relations between signs. *All non-syntactical sentences are said to be object sentences.*

In a fully symbolized language (a "calculus") any sentence can be assigned to one of these classes by inspecting the formal properties of the sentence-token. In a "natural" language such as English, the formal properties of a sentence-token may indicate that it is an object-sentence when it is *in fact* syntactical. Such a sentence (also said to be *quasi-syntactical*) is expressed in the *material mode of speech.* When translated into an overtly syntactical sentence it is then said to be expressed in the *formal mode of speech.*

R. Carnap, *Logical Syntax of Language,* 284 ff. (for a more exact account).—*M.B.*

Mathematics: The traditional definition of mathematics as "the science of quantity" or "the science of discrete and continuous magnitude" is today inadequate, in that modern mathematics, while clearly in some sense a single connected whole, includes many branches which do not come under this head. Contemporary accounts of the nature of mathematics tend to characterize it rather by its method than by its subject matter.

According to a view which is widely held by mathematicians, it is characteristic of a mathematical discipline that it begins with a set of undefined elements, properties, functions, and relations, and a set of unproved propositions (called *axioms* or *postulates*) involving them; and that from these all other propositions (called *theorems*) of the discipline are to be derived by the methods of formal logic. On its face, as thus stated, this view would identify mathematics with *applied logic*. It is usually added, however, that the *undefined terms,* which appear in the rôle of names of undefined elements, etc., are not really names of particulars at all but are variables, and that the theorems are to be regarded as proved for *any* values of these variables which render the postulates true. If then each theorem is replaced by the proposition embodying the implication from the conjunction of the postulates to the theorem in question, we have a reduction of mathematics to *pure logic*. (For a particular example of a set of postulates for a mathematical discipline see the article *Arithmetic, foundations of.*)

There is also another sense in which it has been held that mathematics is reducible to logic, namely that in the expressions for the postulates of a mathematical discipline the undefined terms are to be given definitions which involve logical terms only, in such a way that postulates and theorems of the discipline thereby become propositions of pure logic, demonstrable on the basis of logical principles only. This view was first taken, as regards arithmetic and analysis, by Frege, and was afterwards adopted by Russell, who extended it to all mathematics.

Both views require for their completion an exact account of the nature of the underlying logic, which, it would seem, can only be made by formalizing this logic as a *logistic system* (*q.v.*). Such a formalization of the underlying logic was employed from the beginning by Frege and by Russell, but has come into use in connection with the other—*postulational* or *axiomatic*—view only comparatively recently (with, perhaps, a partial exception in the case of Peano).

Hilbert has given a formalization of arithmetic which takes the shape of a logistic system having primitive symbols some of a logical and some of an arithmetical character, so that logic and arithmetic are formalized together without taking logic as prior; similarly also for analysis. This would not of itself be opposed to the Frege-Russell view, since it is to be expected that the choice as to which symbols shall be taken as primitive in the formalization can be made in more than one way. Hilbert, however, took the position that many of the theorems of the system are *ideale Aussagen,* mere formulas, which are without meaning in themselves but are added to the *reale Aussagen* or genuinely meaningful formulas in order to avoid formal difficulties otherwise arising. In this respect Hilbert differs sharply from Frege and Russell, who would give a meaning (namely as propositions of logic) to all formulas (sentences) appearing.—Concerning Hilbert's associated program for a consistency proof see the article *Proof theory.*

A view of the nature of mathematics which is widely different from any of the above is held by the school of mathematical *intuitionism* (*q.v.*). According to this school, mathematics is "identical with the exact part of

our thought." "No science, not even philosophy or logic, can be a presupposition for mathematics. It would be circular to apply any philosophical or logical theorem as a means of proof in mathematics, since such theorems already presuppose for their formulation the construction of mathematical concepts. If mathematics is to be in this sense presupposition-free, then there remains for it no other source than an intuition which presents mathematical concepts and inferences to us as immediately clear. . . . [This intuition] is nothing else than the ability to treat separately certain concepts and inferences which regularly occur in ordinary thinking." This is quoted in translation from Heyting, who, in the same connection, characterizes the intuitionistic doctrine as asserting the existence of mathematical objects (Gegenstände), which are immediately grasped by thought, are independent of experience, and give to mathematics more than a mere formal content. But to these mathematical objects no existence is to be ascribed independent of thought. Elsewhere Heyting speaks of a relationship to Kant in the apriority ascribed to the natural numbers, or rather to the underlying ideas of *one* and the process of *adding one* and the *indefinite repetition* of the latter. At least in his earlier writings, Brouwer traces the doctrine of intuitionism directly to Kant. In 1912 he speaks of "abandoning Kant's apriority of space but adhering the more resolutely to the apriority of time" and in the same paper explicitly reaffirms Kant's opinion that mathematical judgments are *synthetic* and *a priori*.

The doctrine that the concepts of mathematics are empirical and the postulates elementary experimental truths has been held in various forms (either for all mathematics, or specially for geometry) by J. S. Mill, H. Helmholtz, M. Pasch, and others. However, the usual contemporary view, especially among mathematicians, is that the propositions of mathematics say nothing about empirical reality. Even in the case of *applied* geometry, it is held, the geometry is used to organize physical measurement, but does not receive an interpretation under which its propositions become unqualifiedly experimental or empirical in character; a particular system of geometry, applied in a particular way, may be wrong (and demonstrably wrong by experiment), but there is not, in significant cases, a *unique* geometry which, when applied in the particular way, is right.

M. Bôcher, *The fundamental conceptions and methods of mathematics,* Bulletin of the American Mathematical Society, vol. 11 (1904), pp. 115-135. J. W. Young, *Lectures on Fundamental Concepts of Algebra and Geometry,* New York, 1911. Veblen and Young, *Projective Geometry,* vol. 1, 1910 (see the Introduction). C. J. Keyser, *Doctrinal functions,* The Journal of Philosophy, vol. 15 (1918), pp. 262-267. —— G. Frege, *Die Grundlagen der Arithmetik,* Breslau, 1884; reprinted, Breslau, 1934. G. Frege, *Grundgesetze der Arithmetik,* vol. 1, Jena, 1893, and vol. 2, Jena, 1903. B. Russell, *The Principles of Mathematics,* Cambridge, England, 1903; 2nd edn., London, 1937, and New York, 1938. B. Russell, *Introduction to Mathematical Philosophy*, London, 1919. —— R. Carnap, *Die logizistische Grundlegung der Mathematik*, Erkenntnis, vol. 2 (1931), pp. 91-105, 141-144, 145. A Heyting, *Die intuitionistische Grundlegung der Mathematik*, ibid., pp. 106-115. J. v. Neumann, *Die formalistische Grundlegung der Mathematik*, ibid., pp. 116-121, 144-145, 146, 148. R. Carnap, *The Logical Syntax of Language*, New York and London, 1937. —— L. E. J. Brouwer, *Intuitionisme en Formalisme*, Groningen, 1912; reprinted in *Wiskunde, Waarbeid, Werkelijkheid*, Groningen, 1919; English translation by A. Dresden, Bulletin of the American Mathematical Society, vol. 20 (1913), pp. 81-96. H. Weyl, *Die heutige Erkenntnislage in der Mathematik*, Symposion, vol. 1 (1926), pp. 1-32. D. Hilbert, *Die Grundlagen der Mathematik*, Abhandlungen aus dem Mathematischen Seminar der Hamburgischen Universität, vol. 6 (1928), pp. 65-85; reprinted in Hilbert's *Grundlagen der Geometrie*, 7th edn. A. Heyting, *Mathematische Grundlagenforschung, Intuitionismus, Beweistheorie*, Berlin, 1934. —— H. Poincaré, *The Foundations of Science*, English translation by G. B. Halsted, New York, 1913. —— E. Nagel, *The formation of modern conceptions of formal logic in the development of geometry*, Osiris, vol. 7 (1939), pp. 142-224. —— A. N. Whitehead, *An Introduction to Mathematics*, London, 1911, and New York, 1911. —— G. H. Hardy, *A Mathematician's Apology*, London, 1940.

Histories: Moritz Cantor, *Vorlesungen über Geschichte der Mathematik*, 4 vols., Leipzig, 1880-1908; 4th edn., Leipzig, 1921. Florian Cajori, *A History of Mathematics*, 2nd edn., New York and London, 1922. Florian Cajori, *A History of Elementary Mathematics*, revised edn., New York and London, 1917. Florian Cajori, *A History of Mathematical Notations*, 2 vols., Chicago, 1928-1929. D. E. Smith, *A Source Book in Mathematics*, New York and London, 1929. T. L. Heath, *A History of Greek Mathematics*, 2 vols., Oxford, 1921. Felix Klein, *Vorlesungen über die Entwicklung der Mathematik im 19. Jahrhundert*, 2 vols., Berlin, 1926-1927. J. L. Coolidge, *A History of Geometrical Methods*, New York, 1940.

Mathesis universalis: Universal mathematics. One major part of Leibniz's program for logic was the development of a universal mathematics or universal calculus for manipulating, i.e. performing deductions in, the universal language (*characteristica universalis*). This universal language, he thought, could be constructed on the basis of a relatively few simple terms and, when constructed, would be of immense value to scientists and philosophers in reasoning as well as in communication. Leibniz's studies on the subject of a universal mathematics are the starting point in modern philosophy of the development of symbolic, mathematical logic.—*F.L.W.*

Matrix: See *Logic, formal*, § 3.

Matrix method: Synonymous with *truth-table method*, (*q.v.*)—*A.C.*

Matter: (1) That the defining characteristic of which is extension, occupancy of space, mass, weight, motion, movability, inertia, resistance, impenetrability, attraction and repulsion, or their combinations; these characteristics or powers themselves; the extra-mental cause of sense experience; what composes the "sensible world;" the manipulable; the permanent (or relatively so); the public (accessible to more than one knower; non-private); (2) the physical or nonmental; (3) the physical, bodily, or nonspiritual; the relatively worthless or base; (4) the inanimate; (5) the worldly or natural (non-supernatural); (6) the wholly or relatively indeterminate; potentiality for receiving form or what has that potentiality; that which in union with form constitutes an individual; differentiating content as against form; the particular as against the universal; (7) the manifold of sensation; the given element in experience as against that supplied by mind; (8) that of which something consists; that from which a thing develops or is made; (9) the first existent or primordial stuff; (10) what is under consideration. Philosophers conceive matter as appearance or privation of reality, as one or the only reality; as the principle of imperfection and limitation, as potentially or sometimes good; as substance, process, or content; as points, atoms, substrata, or other media endowed with powers mentioned above.—*M.T.K.*

Matter, prime: (Scholastic) Though the notion of prime matter or hyle is not unknown to the Schoolmen previous to the 13th century, a consistent philosophical view has been developed only after the revival of Aristotelian philosophy. In accordance with the Stagirite, Aquinas considers prime matter as pure potentiality, lacking all positive characteristics. Matter becomes the principle of individuation; by being united to matter, the form is "contracted," that is narrowed from its universal and specific being to existence in a particular. Consequently, individuality is denied to the Angels who are free of matter, subsistent forms; every angel is a species of his own. The individuating principle is, however, not prime matter as such but *materia signata quantitate;* this means that a still indefinite relation to quantity is added. What is now commonly called matter is defined by Aquinas as *materia secunda;* the material thing owes its existence to the information of prime matter by a substantial form.—*R.A.*

Maxim, ethical: In general any rule of conduct which an individual may adopt, or which he may be advised to follow as a good guide for action, e.g., Descartes' maxim to try always to conquer himself rather than fortune. The formulation of such rules is often recommended as a help in deciding what to do in particular cases, especially if time is short, in resisting temptation, etc. Kant held (1) that each voluntary act proceeds according to a maxim or "subjective principle of action," e.g., in breaking a promise one has as one's maxim, "When it is to my advantage, I will make a promise and not keep it," (2) that one can tell whether an act is right or not by asking whether one can will its maxim to be a universal law.—*W.K.F.*

Māyā: (Skr.) The power of obscuring or state producing error and illusion; the "veil" covering reality, the experience of manifoldness when only the One is real; *natura naturans;* appearance or phenomenon, as opposed to reality and noumenon. A condition generally acknowledged in Indian philosophy and popular Hindu thinking due to the ascendency of the Vedānta (*q.v.*) which can be overcome principally by knowledge or insight. See *Jñāna.—K.F.L.*

McDougall, William: (1871-1938) Formerly of Oxford and later of Harvard and Duke Universities, was the leading exponent of purposive or "hormic" (from Gr. horme, impulse) psychology. "Purposive psychology . . . asserts that active striving towards a goal is a fundamental category of psychology, and is a process of a type that cannot be mechanistically explained or resolved into mechanistic sequences." *Psychologies of* 1930, p. 4. In his epoch-making book, *Introduction to Social Psychology* (1908), McDougall developed a purposive theory of the human instincts designed to serve as an adequate psychological foundation for the social sciences. His social psychology listed among the primary instincts of man: flight, repulsion, curiosity, self-abasement, self-assertion and the parental instinct. McDougall's teleological theory is psychological rather than metaphysical, but he believed that the psychological fact of purpose was a genuine instance of teleological causation. (*Modern Materialism and Emergent Evolution*, 1929.) He was also led by his psychological studies to adopt a metaphysical dualism and interactionism which he designated "animism." See *Body and Mind*, 1911.—*L.W.*

Mead, George Herbert: (1863-1931) Professor of Philosophy at Chicago University. One of the leading figures in the Deweyan tradition. He contributed an important article to the volume, *Creative Intelligence*. He emphasized the relationship between the individual and his formulation and testing of hypotheses, on the one hand, as against the organic relationship of the individual with the society which is responsible for him.—*L.E.D.*

Main works: *Philosophy of the Present*, 1932; *Mind, Self, and Society*, 1934; *Movements of Thought in the Nineteenth Century*, 1936; *Philosophy of the Act*, 1938.

Mean: (1) In general, that which in some way mediates or occupies a middle position among various things or between two extremes. Hence (especially in the plural) that through which an end is attained; in mathematics the word is used for any one of various notions of average; in ethics it represents moderation, temperance, prudence, the middle way.

(2) In mathematics:

(A) The *arithmetic mean* of two quantities is half their sum; the *arithmetic mean* of n quantities is the sum of the n quantities, divided by n. In the case of a function $f(x)$ (say from real numbers to real numbers) the *mean value* of the function for the values $x_1, x_2, \ldots, x_n$ of x is the arithmetic mean of $f(x_1), f(x_2), \ldots, f(x_n)$. This notion is extended to the case of infinite sets of values of x by means of integration; thus the *mean value* of $f(x)$ for values of x between a and b is $\int f(x) \, dx$, with a and b as the limits of integration, divided by the difference between a and b.

(B) The *geometric mean* of or between, or the *mean proportional* between, two quantities is the (positive) square root of their product. Thus if b is the geometric mean between a and c, c is as many times greater (or less) than b as b is than a. The geometric mean of n quantities is the nth root of their product.

(C) The *harmonic mean* of two quantities is defined as the reciprocal of the arithmetic mean of their reciprocals. Hence the harmonic mean of a and b is $2ab/(a + b)$.

(D) The *weighted mean* or *weighted average* of a set of n quantities, each of which is associated with a certain number as weight, is obtained by multiplying each quantity by the associated weight, adding these products together, and then dividing by the sum of the weights. As under A, this may be extended to the case of an infinite set of quantities by means of integration. (The weights have the rôle of estimates of relative importance of the various quantities, and if all the weights are equal the weighted mean reduces to the simple arithmetic mean.)

(E) In statistics, given a population (i.e., an aggregate of observed or observable quantities) and a variable x having the population as its range, we have: (a) The *mean value* of x is the weighted mean of the values of x, with the probability (frequency ratio) of each value taken as its weight. In the case of a finite population this is the same as the simple arithmetic mean of the population, provided that, in calculating the arithmetic mean, each value of x is counted as many times over as it occurs in the set of observations constituting the population. (b) In like manner, the *mean value* of a function $f(x)$ of x is the weighted mean of the values of $f(x)$, where the probability of each value of x is taken as the weight of the corresponding value of $f(x)$. (c) The *mode* of the population is the most probable (most frequent) value of x, provided there is one such. (d) The *median* of the population is so chosen that the probability that x be less than the median (or the probability that x be greater than the median) is $\frac{1}{2}$ (or as near $\frac{1}{2}$ as possible). In the case of a finite population, if the values of x are arranged in order of magnitude—repeating any one value of x as many times over as it occurs in the set of observations constituting the population—then the middle term of this series, or the arithmetic mean of the two middle terms, is the median.—*A.C.*

3. *In cosmology*, the fundamental means (arithmetic, geometric, and harmonic) were used by the Greeks in describing or actualizing the process of becoming in nature. The Pythagoreans and the Platonists in particular made considerable use of these means (see the *Philebus* and the *Timaeus* more especially). These ratios are among the basic elements used by Plato in his doctrine of the mixtures. With the appearance of the qualitative physics of Aristotle, the means lost their cosmological importance and were thereafter used chiefly in mathematics. The modern mathematical

theories of the universe make use of the whole range of means analyzed by the calculus of probability, the theory of errors, the calculus of variations, and the statistical methods.

4. *In ethics,* the 'Doctrine of the Mean' is the moral theory of moderation, the development of the virtues, the determination of the wise course in action, the practice of temperance and prudence, the choice of the middle way between extreme or conflicting decisions. It has been developed principally by the Chinese, the Indians and the Greeks; it was used with caution by the Christian moralists on account of their rigorous application of the moral law.

A) In Chinese philosophy, the *Doctrine of the Mean* or of the *Middle Way* (the *Chung Yung,* literally 'Equilibrium and Harmony') involves the absence of immoderate pleasure, anger, sorrow or joy, and a conscious state in which those feelings have been stirred and act in their proper degree. This doctrine has been developed by Tzu Shu (V. C. B.C.), a grandson of Confucius who had already described the virtues of the 'superior man' according to his aphorism "Perfect is the virtue which is according to the mean." In matters of action, the superior man stands erect in the middle and strives to follow a course which does not incline on either side.

B) In Buddhist philosophy, the *System of the Middle Way* or *Madhyamaka* is ascribed more particularly to Nagarjuna (II c. A.D.). The Buddha had given his revelation as a mean or middle way, because he repudiated the two extremes of an exaggerated asceticism and of an easy secular life. This principle is also applied to knowledge and action in general, with the purpose of striking a happy medium between contradictory judgments and motives. The final objective is the realization of the *nirvana* or the complete absence of desire by the gradual destruction of feelings and thoughts. But while orthodox Buddhism teaches the unreality of the individual (who is merely a mass of causes and effects following one another in unbroken succession), the Madhyamaka denies also the existence of these causes and effects in themselves. For this system, "Everything is void," with the legitimate conclusion that "Absolute truth is silence." Thus the perfect mean is realized.

C) In Greek Ethics, the doctrine of the *Right Mean* has been developed by Plato (*Philebus*) and Aristotle (*Nic. Ethics* II. 6-8) principally, on the Pythagorean analogy between the sound mind, the healthy body and the tuned string, which has inspired most of the Greek Moralists. Though it is known as the "Aristotelian Principle of the Mean," it is essentially a Platonic doctrine which is performed in the *Republic* and the *Statesman* and expounded in the *Philebus,* where we are told that all good things in life belong to the class of the mixed (26*D*). This doctrine states that in the application of intelligence to any kind of activity, the supreme wisdom is to know just where to stop, and to stop just there and nowhere else. Hence, the "right-mean" does not concern the quantitative measurement of magnitudes, but simply the qualitative comparison of values

with respect to a standard which is the appropriate (prepon), the seasonable (kairos), the morally necessary (deon), or generally the moderate (metrion). The difference between these two kinds of metretics (metretike) is that the former is extrinsic and relative, while the latter is intrinsic and absolute. This explains the Platonic division of the sciences into two classes: those involving reference to relative quantities (mathematical or natural), and those requiring absolute values (ethics and aesthetics). The Aristotelian analysis of the "right mean" considers moral goodness as a fixed and habitual proportion in our appetites and tempers, which can be reached by training them until they exhibit just the balance required by the right rule. This process of becoming good develops certain habits of virtues consisting in reasonable moderation where both excess and defect are avoided: the virtue of temperance (sophrosyne) is a typical example. In this sense, virtue occupies a middle position between extremes, and is said to be a *mean;* but it is not a static notion, as it leads to the development of a stable being, when man learns not to over-reach himself. This qualitative conception of the mean involves an adaptation of the agent, his conduct and his environment, similar to the harmony displayed in a work of art. Hence the aesthetic aspect of virtue, which is often overstressed by ancient and neopagan writers, at the expense of morality proper.

D) The ethical idea of the mean, stripped of the qualifications added to it by its Christian interpreters, has influenced many positivistic systems of ethics, and especially pragmatism and behaviourism (e.g., A. Huxley's rule of *Balanced Excesses*). It is maintained that it is also involved in the dialectical systems, such as Hegelianism, where it would have an application in the whole dialectical process as such: thus, it would correspond to the synthetic phase which blends together the thesis and the antithesis by the meeting of the opposites.—*T.G.*

Mean, Doctrine of the: In Aristotle's ethics, the doctrine that each of the moral virtues is an intermediate state between extremes of excess and defect.—*G.R.M.*

Meaning: A highly ambiguous term, with at least four pivotal senses, involving (a) intention or purpose, (b) designation or reference, (c) definition or translation, (d) causal antecedents or consequences. Each of these provides overlapping families of cases generated by some or all of the following types of systematic ambiguity.—

(i) Arising from a contrast between the standpoints of speaker and interpreter.

(ii) arising from contrast between the meaning of specific utterances (tokens) and that of the general (type) symbol.

(iii) arising from attention to one rather than another use of language (e.g., to the expressive rather than the evocative or referential uses).

Some of these ambiguities are normally eliminated by attention to the context in which the term 'meaning' occurs. Adequate definition, would, accordingly, involve a detailed analysis of the types of context which are most common.

The following is a preliminary outline.

A. *"What does X (some event, not necessarily linguistic) mean?"* =

(1) "Of what is X an index?"

(2) "Of what is X a sign?"

B. *"What does S (a speaker) mean by X (an utterance)?"* =

(1) "What are S's interests, intentions, purposes in uttering X?"

(2) "To whom (what) is he referring?"

(3) "What effect does he wish to produce in the hearer?"

(4) "What *other* utterance could he have used to express the same interest, make the same reference, or produce the same effect?"

C. *"What does X (an utterance of a speaker) mean to an interpreter I?"* =

(1) "What do I take S to have meant by X (in any of the senses listed under B)?"

D. *"What does X (a type symbol) mean in language L?"*

(1) "What symbols (in L) can be substituted for X (in specified contexts) without appreciable loss of expressive, evocative or referential function?"

(2) "In a translation from L into another language M, either of X or of a more complex symbol containing X as part, what portion of the end-product corresponds to X?"

In addition to the above, relatively non-technical senses, many writers use the word in divergent special ways based upon and implying favored theories *about* meaning.

See also: *Index, Sign, Types of Language.*

Reference: Ogden and Richards, *Meaning of Meaning,* Chs. 8 and 9.—*M.B.*

Meaning, Kinds of: In semiotic (*q.v.*) several kinds of meaning, i.e. of the function of an expression in language and the content it conveys, are distinguished. 1. An expression (sentence) has *cognitive* (or theoretical, assertive) meaning, if it asserts something and hence is either true or false. In this case, it is called a cognitive sentence or (cognitive, genuine) statement; it has usually the form of a declarative sentence. If an expression (a sentence) has cognitive meaning, its truth-value (*q.v.*) depends in general upon both (a) the (cognitive, semantical) meaning of the terms occurring, and (b) some facts referred to by the sentence. 2. If it does depend on both (a) and (b), the sentence has *factual* (synthetic, material) meaning and is called a factual (synthetic, material) sentence. 3. If, however, the truth-value depends upon (a) alone, the sentence has a (merely) *logical* meaning (or formal meaning, see Formal 1). In this case, if it is true, it is called *logically true* or *analytic* (*q.v.*); if it is false, it is called *logically false* or *contradictory*. 4. An expression has an *expressive meaning* (or function) in so far as it expresses something of the state of the speaker; this kind of meaning may for instance contain pictorial, emotive, and volitional components (e.g. lyrical poetry, exclamations, commands).

An expression may or may not have, in addition to its expressive meaning, a cognitive meaning; if not, it is said to have a merely expressive meaning. 5. If an expression has a merely expressive meaning but is mistaken as being a cognitive statement, it is sometimes called a *pseudo-statement*. According to logical positivism (see *Scientific Expiricism,* IC) many sentences in metaphysics are pseudo-statements (compare *Anti-metaphysics,* 2).—*R.C.*

Measurement: (Lat. *metiri,* to measure) The process of ascribing a numerical value to an object or quality either on the basis of the number of times some given unit quantity is contained in it, or on the basis of its position in a series of greater and lesser quantities of like kind. See *Intensive, Extensive Quantity.*—*A.C.B.*

Mechanism: (Gr. *mechane,* machine) Theory that all phenomena are totally explicable on mechanical principles. The view that all phenomena is the result of matter in motion and can be explained by its law. Theory of total explanation by efficient, as opposed to final, cause (*q.v.*). Doctrine that nature, like a machine, is a whole whose single function is served automatically by its parts. In cosmology, first advanced by Leucippus and Democritus (460 B.C.-370 B.C.) as the view that nature is explicable on the basis of atoms in motion and the void. Held by Galileo (1564-1641) and others in the seventeenth century as the mechanical philosophy. For Descartes (1596-1650), the essence of matter is extension, and all physical phenomena are explicable by mechanical laws. For Kant (1724-1804), the necessity in time of an occurrence in accordance with causality as a law of nature. In biology, theory that organisms are totally explicable on mechanical principles. Opposite of: vitalism (*q.v.*). In psychology, applied to associational psychology, and in psychoanalysis to the unconscious direction of a mental process. In general, the view that nature consists merely of material in motion, and that it operates automatically. Opposite of: all forms of super-naturalism. See also *Materialism, Atomism.*—*J.K.F.*

Mechanics: The science of motion, affording theoretical description by means of specification of position of particles bound by relations to other particles, usually having no extension but possessing mass. This involves space and time and frames of reference (in a relative fashion). Particles are assumed to traverse continuous paths. Auxiliary kinematical concepts are displacement, velocity, acceleration. The dynamical concept of forces (F's) acting independently of one another is coupled with mass (M) in a defining law, as $F = Ma$, where a = acceleration. Explicit reference to causation is avoided and is held to be unnecessary. Classical mechanics is restricted to the use of central forces (along the lines joining particles and a function of the length of those lines). This with a knowledge of boundary conditions leads to complete mechanistic determinism. The entire system of mechanics may also be developed by starting with other concepts such as energy and a stationary principle (usually that of "least action") in either an integral or differential form —*W.M.M.*

Mediation: (Lat. *mediatio*) The act or condition in which an intermediary is supplied between heterogeneous terms. (a) *In philosophy*: Mediation is necessary in systems in which two forms of reality are held to be so different that immediate interaction is impossible; this is the case in later Neo-Platonism, and particularly in the Cartesianism of Malebranche, Geulincx and Spinoza, where mind and matter cannot directly interact; God supplies the principle of mediation in these latter systems. (b) *In theology*: Mediation is an important aspect of the doctrine and practice of many religions; particularly in Judaism and Christianity because of the Transcendency of God and the imperfection of men. Mediation is an important function of Christ; as the God-Man, He is eminently fitted to form the connecting link between God and creatures; His Incarnation is considered as supplying the means (i.e. *media*) of salvation to man.—*V.J.B.*

Meinong, Alexius: (1853-1920) Was originally a disciple of Brentano, who however emphatically rejected many of Meinong's later contentions. He claimed to have discovered a new *a priori* science, the "theory of objects" (to be distinguished from metaphysics which is an empirical science concerning reality, but was never worked out by Meinong). Anything "intended" by thought is an "object." Objects may either "exist" (such as physical objects) or "subsist" (such as facts which Meinong unfortunately termed "objectives," or mathematical entities), they may either be possible or impossible and they may belong either to a lower or to a higher level (such as "relations" and "complexions," "founded" on their simple terms or elements). In the "theory of objects," the existence of objects is abstracted from (or as Husserl later said it may be "bracketed") and their essence alone has to be considered. Objects are apprehended either by self-evident judgments or by "assumptions," that is, by "imaginary judgments." In the field of emotions there is an analogous division since there are also "imaginary" emotions (such as those of the spectator in a tragedy). Much of Meinong's work was of a psychological rather than of a metaphysical or epistemological character.—*H.G.*

   Main works: *Psychol-ethische Untersuch. z Werttheorie*, 1894; *Ueber Annahmen*, 1907; *Ueber d. Stellung d. Gegenstandstheorie im Syst. d. Wissensch.*, 1907; *Ueber Möglichkeit u. Wahrscheinlichkeit*, 1915. Cf. *Gesammelte Abh.* 3 vols., 1914.

Meliorism: (Lat. *melior,* better) View that the world is neither completely evil nor completely good, but that the relative amounts of good and evil are changeable, that good is capable of increase. Human effort to improve the world can be effective in making the world better and probably the trend of biological and social evolution tends in that direction. Opposed to Optimism and Pessimism. The term was coined by George Eliot.—*A.J.B.*

Melissus: (c. 450 B.C.) Of Samos. He advanced a positive proof of the Eleatic doctrine of being as one and eternal, motionless and without change. The senses deceive us. He wrote in the Ionic dialect.—*L.E.D.*

Memory: (Lat. *memoria*) Non-inferential knowledge of past perceptual objects (perceptual memory) or of past emotions, feelings and states of consciousness of the remembering subject (introspective memory). See *Introspection*. Memory is psychologically analyzable into three functions: (a) *revival or reproduction* of the memory image, (b) *recognition* of the image as belonging to the past of the remembering subject, and (c) *temporal localization* of the remembered object by reference to a psychological or physical time-scheme.—*L.W.*

Mencius: (*Mêng Tzŭ, Mêng K'o,* 371-289 B.C.) A native of Tsao (in present Shantung), studied under pupils of Tzŭ Ssŭ, grandson of Confucius, became the greatest Confucian in Chinese history. He vigorously attacked the "pervasive teachings" of Yang Chu and Mo Tzŭ. Like Confucius, he travelled for many years, to many states, trying to persuade kings and princes to practice benevolent government instead of government by force, but failed. He retired to teach and write. (*Mêng Tzŭ,* Eng. tr. by James Legge: *The Works of Mencius.*)—*W.T.C.*

Mendelsohn, Moses: (1729-1786) A German Jewish popular philosopher, holding an admired position in German literature. He was the first to advocate the social emancipation of the Jews, to plead in Germany for the separation of the Church and the State and for freedom of belief and conscience. He is philosophically best known for his adduced proofs of the immortality of the soul and of the existence of a personal God.

   Schriften z. Philos., Aesthetik u. Apologetik (ed. Brasch, 1880).—*H.H.*

Mental: (Lat. *mens,* mind) Pertaining to the mind either in its functional aspect (perceiving, imagining, remembering, feeling, willing, etc.) or in its contential aspects (sense data, images and other contents existing "in" the mind). See *Mind.*—*L.W.*

Mental Chemistry: Psychological procedure, analogous to chemical analysis and synthesis, consisting in the attempted explanation of mental states as the products of the combination and fusion of psychic elements. See *Associationism.*—*L.W.*

Mentalism: Metaphysical theory of the exclusive reality of individual minds and their subjective states. The term is applied to the individualistic idealism of Berkeley and Leibniz rather than to the absolutistic Idealism of Hegel and his followers.—*L.W.*

Mental tests: Measurement of independent variables in a person to specific situations controlled by the medium of the instrument, expressing measurable differences in individuals. Chief form: intelligence test.—*J.E.B.*

Mesmerism: A term formed from the name of F. Mesmer (1734-1815) to designate hypnotic phenomena (see *Hypnotism*) but now little used.—*L.W.*

Metalanguage: A language used to make assertions about another language; any language whose symbols refer to the properties of the symbols of another language. (Formed by analogy with "metamathematics," the study of formalized mathematical systems.)—*M.B.*

Metalogical: That which belongs to the basis of logic.

Metalogical truths are the laws of thought, the formal conditions of thinking inherent in reason. (Schopenhauer.)—*H.H.*

The same word is now commonly used in quite a different sense, as a synonym of *syntactical*. See *syntax, logical*.—*A.C.*

Metamathematics: See *Proof theory*, and *Syntax, logical*.

Metaphor: a. Rhetorical figure transposing a term from its original concept to another and similar one. b. In its origin, all language was metaphoric; so was poetry. Metaphor is a short fable (Vico).—*L.V.*

Metaphysical deduction: An examination of the logical functions of thought that there are certain *a priori* forms of synthesis which belong to the very constitution, the bare, purely formal machinery of the understanding.—*H.H.*

Metaphysical essence: (in Scholasticism) The complexus of notes which are in a thing, as it is conceived by us—i.e. the principle and primary notes by which that thing is sufficiently understood and distinguished from other things.—*H.G.*

Metaphysical ethics: Any view according to which ethics is a branch of metaphysics, ethical principles being derived from metaphysical principles and ethical notions being defined in terms of metaphysical notions.—*W.K.F.*

Metaphysics: (Gr. *meta ta Physika*) Arbitrary title given by Andronicus of Rhodes, circa 70 B.C. to a certain collection of Aristotelian writings.

Traditionally given by the oracular phrase: "The science of being as such." To be distinguished from the study of being under some particular aspect; hence opposed to such sciences as are concerned with *ens mobile, ens quantum*, etc. The term, "science," is here used in its classic sense of "knowledge by causes," where "knowledge" is contrasted with "opinion" and the term cause has the full signification of the Greek *aitia*. The "causes" which are the objects of metaphysical cognition are said to be "first" in the natural order (first principles), as being founded in no higher or more complete generalizations available to the human intellect by means of its own natural powers.

Secondary and derivative meanings: (a) Anything concerned with the supra-physical. Thus "metaphysical healing," "metaphysical poetry," etc. (b) Any scheme of explanation which transcends the inadequacies or inaccuracies of ordinary thought.—*W.S.W.*

Metempsychosis: (Gr. *meta,* over + *empsychoun,* to animate) The doctrine that the same soul can successively reside in more than one body, human or animal. See *Immortality*. The doctrine was part of the Pythagorean teaching incorporated in mythical form in the Platonic philosophy (see *Phaedrus,* 249; *Rep.* X, 614). The term metempsychosis was not used before the Christian era.—*L.W.*

Method: (Gr. *methodos,* method) 1. Any procedure employed to attain a certain end. 2. Any knowing techniques employed in the process of acquiring knowledge of a given subject matter. 3. The science which formulates the rules of any procedure.—*A.C.B.*

Methodic Doubt: The suspension of judgment in regard to possible truths until they have been demonstrated to be either true or false; in Cartesianism the criterion is the clearness and distinctness of ideas.—*V.J.B.*

Method of simple enumeration: Inductive process by which the initial probability of a generalization is increased by more instances exactly the same as those previously observed.—*A.C.B.*

Method of trial and error: Method of solving a problem, or of accomplishing an end, by putting the hypotheses or means to direct test in actuality rather than by considering them imaginatively in terms of foreseen consequences; opposed to reflection.—*A.C.B.*

Methodology: The systematic analysis and organization of the rational and experimental principles and processes which must guide a scientific inquiry, or which constitute the structure of the special sciences more particularly. Methodology, which is also called *scientific method,* and more seldom *methodeutic,* refers not only to the whole of a constituted science, but also to individual problems or groups of problems within a science. As such it is usually considered as a branch of logic; in fact, it is the application of the principles and processes of logic to the special objects of the various sciences; while science in general is accounted for by the combination of deduction and induction as such. Thus, methodology is a generic term exemplified in the specific method of each science. Hence its full significance can be understood only by analyzing the structure of the special sciences. In determining that structure, one must consider (a) the proper object of the special science, (b) the manner in which it develops, (c) the type of statements or generalizations it involves, (d) its philosophical foundations or assumptions, and (e) its relation with the other sciences, and eventually its applications. The last two points mentioned are particularly important: methods of education, for example, will vary considerably according to their inspiration and aim. Because of the differences between the objects of the various sciences, they reveal the following principal methodological patterns, which are not necessarily exclusive of one another, and which are used sometimes in partial combination. It may be added that their choice and combination depend also in a large degree on psychological motives. In the last resort, methodology results from the adjustment of our mental powers to the love and pursuit of truth.

I. There are various *rational methods* used by the speculative sciences, including theology, which adds certain qualifications to their use. More especially, philosophy has inspired the following procedures: (1) The *Socratic method* of analysis by questioning and dividing until the essences are reached; (2) the *synthetic method* developed by Plato, Aristotle and the Medieval thinkers, which involves a demonstrative exposition of the causal relation between thought and being; (3) the *ascetic method* of intellectual and moral purification leading to an illumination of the mind, as proposed by Plotinus, Augustine and the mystics; (4) the *psycholog-*

ical method of inquiry into the origin of ideas, which was used by Descartes and his followers, and also by the British empiricists; (5) the *critical* or *transcendental method,* as used by Kant, and involving an analysis of the conditions and limits of knowledge; (6) the *dialectical method* proceeding by thesis, antithesis and synthesis, which is promoted by Hegelianism and Dialectical Materialism; (7) the *intuitive method,* as used by Bergson, which involves the immediate perception of reality, by a blending of consciousness with the process of change; (8) the *reflexive method* of metaphysical introspection aiming at the development of the immanent realities and values leading man to God; (9) the *eclectic method* (historical-critical) of purposive and effective selection as proposed by Cicero, Suarez and Cousin; and (10) the *positivistic method* of Comte, Spencer and the logical empiricists, which attempts to apply to philosophy the strict procedures of the positive sciences.

II. The *axiomatic* or *hypothetico-deductive method* as used by the theoretical and especially the mathematical sciences. It involves such problems as the selection, independence and simplification of primitive terms and axioms, the formalization of definitions and proofs, the consistency and completeness of the constructed theory, and the final interpretation.

III. The *nomological or inductive method* as used by the experimental sciences, aims at the discovery of regularities between phenomena and their relevant laws. It involves the critical and careful application of the various steps of induction: observation and analytical classification; selection of similarities; hypothesis of cause or law; verification by the experimental canons; deduction, demonstration and explanation; systematic organization of results; statement of laws and construction of the relevant theory.

IV. The *descriptive method* as used by the natural and social sciences, involves observational, classificatory and statistical procedures (see art. on statistics) and their interpretation.

V. The *historical method* as used by the sciences dealing with the past involves the collation, selection, classification and interpretation of archeological facts and exhibits, records, documents, archives, reports and testimonies.

VI. The *psychological method,* as used by all the sciences dealing with human behaviour and development. It involves not only introspective analysis, but also experimental procedures, such as those referring to the relations between stimuli and sensations, to the accuracy of perceptions (specific measurements of intensity) to gradation (least noticeable differences), to error methods (average error in right and wrong cases), and to physiological and educational processes.—*T.G.*

Miao:(a) Mystery of existence, which is unfathomable. (Lao Tzŭ.) (b) Subtlety, such as the subtle presence of the Omnipotent Creative Power (shên) in the myriad things.—*W.T.C.*

Middle Term: (Gr. *mesos horos*) That one of the three terms in a syllogism which appears in both premisses; so called by Aristotle because in the first, or perfect, figure of the syllogism it is commonly intermediate in extension between the Major Term and the Minor Term. See *Aristotelianism; Major Term; Minor Term.* See *Logic, formal,* § 5.—*G.R.M.*

Mill, James: (1773-1836) Father of John Stuart Mill and close associate of Jeremy Bentham as a member of the Utilitarian School of Philosophy. His chief original contributions were in the field of psychology where he advanced an associational view and he is likewise remembered for his *History of India.* See *Utilitarianism.*

Main work: *Analysis of the Phenomena of the Human Mind;* 1829.—*L.E.D.*

Mill, John Stuart: (1806-1873) The son of James Mill, was much influenced by his father and Jeremy Bentham. Principal philosophical works: *Logic,* 1843; *Liberty,* 1859; *Utilitarianism,* 1861. In logic and epistemology he was a thorough empiricist, holding that all inference is basically induction on the basis of the principle of the uniformity of nature from one particular event to another or a group of others. Syllogistic reasoning, he holds always involves a *petitio,* the conclusion being included in the premises, with knowledge of those in turn resting on empirical inductions. Mill defines the cause of an event as the sum total of its necessary conditions positive and negative.

In ethics his *Utilitarianism* has been very influential in popularizing universalistic hedonism, albeit with certain confusions (see *Hedonism*). His essay on *Liberty* is authoritative as concerns liberty of thought and discussion, stimulating as concerns liberty of action in general.—*C.A.B.*

Mill's methods: Inductive methods formulated by John Stuart Mill for the discovery of causal relations between phenomena.

1. Method of Agreement: If two or more instances of the phenomenon under investigation have only one circumstance in common, the circumstance in which alone all the instances agree, is the cause (or effect) of the given phenomenon.

2. Method of Difference: If an instance in which the phenomenon under investigation occurs, and an instance in which it does not occur, have every circumstance in common save one, that one occurring in the former; the circumstance in which alone the two instances differ, is the effect, or the cause, or an indispensable part of the cause, of the phenomenon.

3. Joint Method of Agreement and Difference: If two or more instances in which the phenomenon occurs have only one circumstance in common, while two or more instances in which it does not occur have nothing in common save the absence of that circumstance; the circumstance in which alone the two sets of instances differ, is the effect, or the cause, or an indispensable part of the cause, of the phenomenon.

4. Method of Concomitant Variations: Whatever phenomenon varies in any manner whenever another phenomenon varies in some particular manner, is either a cause or an effect of that phenomenon, or is connected

with it through some fact of causation.

5. Method of Residues: Subduct from any phenomenon such part as is known by previous inductions to be the effect of certain antecedents, and the residue of the phenomenon is the effect of the remaining antecedents.

See Mill's *System of Logic*, bk. III, ch. VIII. —*A.C.B.*

Mīmāṁsā: Short for Purva-Mīmāṁsā, one of the six major systems of Indian philosophy (*q.v.*), founded by Jaimini, rationalizing Vedic ritual and upholding the authority of the Vedas by a philosophy of the word (see *vāc*). In metaphysics it professes belief in the reality of the phenomenal, a plurality of eternal souls, but is indifferent to a concept of God though assenting to the superhuman and eternal nature of the Vedas. There is also an elaborate epistemology supporting Vedic truths, an ethics which makes observance of Vedic ritual and practice a condition of a good and blissful life.—*K.F.L.*

Mimpathy: (Ger. *Nachfühlen*) The suffering of another must already be given in some form before it is possible for anyone to become a fellow sufferer. Pity and sympathy as experienced are always subsequent to the already apprehended and understood experience of another person who is pitied. One may share another's feeling about a matter, and yet have no sympathy for that one. The historian, novelist, dramatic artist must possess in high degree the gift of "after-experiencing" or mimpathizing, but they do not in the least need to have sympathy with their objects and persons. See *Sympathy*.—*H.H.*

Mind: (Lat. *mens*) Mind is used in two principal senses: (a) The individual mind is the self or subject which perceives, remembers, imagines, feels, conceives, reasons, wills, etc. and which is functionally related to an individual bodily organism. (b) Mind, generically considered, is a metaphysical substance which pervades all individual minds and which is contrasted with matter or material substance.—*L.W.*

Mind-body relation: Relation obtaining between the individual mind and its body. Theories of the mind-body relation are monistic or dualistic according as they identify or separate the mind and the body. Monistic theories include: (a) the theory of mind as bodily function, advanced by Aristotle and adhered to by thinkers as divergent as Hobbes, Hegel, and the Behaviorists, (b) the theory of body as mental appearance held by Berkeley, Leibniz, Schopenhauer and certain other idealists, (c) the two-aspect theory of Spinoza and of recent neutral monism which considers mind and body as manifestations of a third reality which is neither mental nor bodily. The principal dualistic theories are: (a) two sided interactionism of Descartes, Locke, James and others. See *Interactionism*. (b) psycho-physical parallelism. See *Parallelism, Psycho-physical*. (c) Epephenomenalism. See *Epephenomenalism*.—*L.W.*

Mind-Dust Theory: Theory that individual minds result from the combination of particles of mind which have always existed in association with material atoms. The rival theory is emergent evolution which assumes that mind is a novel emergent in the process of biological evolution.—*L.W.*

Mind-Stuff Theory: Theory that individual minds are constituted of psychic particles analogus to physical atoms. Differs from mind-dust theory in its emphasis on the constitution rather than the genesis of mind. See *Mind-Dust Theory*.—*L.W.*

Ming: Name, or "that which designates a thing." This includes "designations of things and their qualities," "those referring to fame and disrepute," and "such descriptive appellations as 'intelligence' and 'stupidity' and 'love' and 'hate.'" "Names are made in order to denote actualities so as to make evident the honorable and the humble and to distinguish similarities and differences." For Rectification of Names, see *Chêng ming*.—*W.T.C.*

Ming: Fate; Destiny; the Decree of Heaven. The Confucians and Neo-Confucians are unanimous in saying that the fate and the nature (hsing) of man and things are two aspects of the same thing. Fate is what Heaven imparts; and the nature is what man and things received from Heaven. For example, "whether a piece of wood is crooked or straight is due to its nature. But that it should be crooked or straight is due to its fate." This being the case, understanding fate (as in Confucius), establishing fate (as in Mencius, 371-289 B.C.), and the fulfillment of fate (as in Neo-Confucianism) all mean the realization of the nature of man and things in accordance with the principle or Reason (li) of existence. "That which Heaven decrees is true, one, and homogeneous . . . Fate in its true meaning proceeds from Reason; its variations (i.e., inequalities like intelligence and stupidity) proceed from the material element, the vital force (ch'i) . . . 'He who understands what fate is, will not stand beneath a precipitous wall.' If a man, saying 'It is decreed,' goes and stands beneath a precipitous wall and the wall falls and crushes him, it cannot be attributed solely to fate. In human affairs when a man has done his utmost he may talk of fate." The fate of Heaven is the same as the Moral Law (tao) of Heaven. The "fulfillment of fate" consists of "the investigation of the Reason of things to the utmost (ch'iung li)" and "exhausting one's nature to the utmost (chin hsing)"—the three are one and the same." In short, fate is "nothing other than being one's true self (ch'êng)."—*W.T.C.*

Ming chia: Sophists or Dialecticians, also called hsing-ming chia, including Têng Hsi Tzŭ (545-501 B.C.?), Hui Shih (390-305 B.C.?), and Kung-sun Lung (between 400 and 250 B.C.), at first insisted on the correspondence between name and reality. The school later became a school of pure sophistry which Chuang Tzŭ and the Neo-Mohists strongly attacked. See *Chien pai*.—*W.T.C.*

Ming (dynasty) philosophy: See *Li hsüeh* and *Chinese philosophy*.

Ming te: (a) Illustrious virtue; perfect virtue. (Early Confucianism.)

(b) Man's clear character; the virtuous nature which man derives from Heaven. (Neo-Confucianism.)—*W.T.C.*

Minor Arts: Empirically distinguished from sculpture and painting. They are: jewelry, miniature, textiles, pottery, etc.—*L.V.*

Minor premiss: See *figure (syllogistic)*.

Minor Term: (Gr. *elatton horos*) That one of the three terms in a syllogism that appears as subject of the conclusion; so called by Aristotle because it is commonly the term of least extension. See *Aristotelianism; Major Term; Middle Term; Logic, formal,* § 5. —*G.R.M.*

Mishnah: (Heb., repetition) Older part of the Talmud (*q.v.*) containing traditions from the close of the Old Testament till the end of the second century A.D. when it was compiled (in several revisions) by R. Judah Hanasi (the prince), known also as *Rabbi* (my master) and *Rabbênu Nakkadosh* (our saintly master) who died between 193-215 A.D. It is divided in 6 *sedarim* (orders), 63 *massektot* (tractates) and 524 *perakim* (chapters).

Here is a very brief summary of the Mishnah according to its *sedarim:*

Seder I, zeraim (seeds), 11 tractates: liturgy, tithes, inhibited mixtures of plants, animals and textiles, sabbatical year, produce offerings, first fruits.

Seder II, Moed (feast), 12 tractates: observance of sabbath, feasts and fasts.

Seder III, Nashim (women)—7 tractates: laws of marriage, divorce, forced marriage, adultery, asceticism.

Seder IV, Nezikin (damages), 10 tractates—laws of damages, injuries, property, buying, selling, lending, hiring, renting, heredity, court proceedings, fines and punishment, cities of refuge, oaths. Special tractates on ethics (Abot) and idolatry and testimonials of special decisions.

Seder V, Kodashim (holy things), 11 tractates: sacrifices, slaughter of animals, ritual dietetics, first born animals, vows, excommunication, sacrilege, temple architecture and rituals.

Seder VI, Toharot (purification)—12 tractates: lay and levitical purity and impurity.

Oldest complete manuscript of the Mishna, of the XIIIth century, is preserved in the Library of Parma, Italy.

First complete printed edition of the Mishnah appeared in Naples, 1492.

An excellent one-volume English translation of the entire Mishnah, with introduction and copious notes was made by Herbert Danby, D.D. (Oxford, 1933).—*H.L.G.*

Mishnah, authorities of: The authorities cited in the *Mishnah* as rings in "golden chain" of the Jewish *masorah* (tradition) are:

a. Sopherim (scribes) known also as *Anshe Keneseth Hagedolah* (men of the great synod), beginning with Ezra of the Bible and terminating with Simeon the Just.

b. Five Zugoth (duumviri) the last pair being the noted Hillel and Shamai. The former was according to E. Renan's hypothesis, a teacher of Jesus.

c. Tannaim (repeaters) — They numbered 277 and are divided in 5 generations. In the first generation where men who still held office in the temple of Jerusalem and witnessed its destruction (70 A.D.).

The second generation counts the celebrated Nasi Rabban Gamaliel II and R. Eliezer ben Hyrcanus, excommunicated for opposing the rule of the majority, R. Ishmael who was held hostage in Rome, and R. Akiba, supporter of Bar Koheba who suffered a martyr's death by the Romans, Elisha b. Abuiah, the heretic.

The third generation consisted of the disciples of R. Ishmael and R. Akiba: R. Meir, Simeon b. Johai to whom the authorship of the Zohar is ascribed.

R. Juda Hanasi, compiler of the Mishnah and possibly friend of Marcus Aurelius (161-180), belonged to the fourth generation, while R. Hiyya, author of the Tosephta, belonged to the fifth and last generation.—*H.L.G.*

Mishnah, extra canonical: R. Juda Hanasi included in his Mishnah (now *the* Mishnah *par excellence*) selected materials from the older Mishnah-collections, particularly from that of R. Akiba (d. 135 A.D.) and his disciple, R. Meir. In fact, it is assumed that any anonymous statement in the Mishnah is R. Meir's (setam mathnithin R. Meir).

The vast traditions not included in the official Mishnah are known as Baraitha (extraneous). These Baraithas were ultimately collected in separate works.

Misology: (Gr. *miseo:* to hate; *logia:* proposition) A contempt for logic.—*V.F.*

Misoneism: A term derived from the Greek, *miso*, I hate, and *neos*, new, employed by Lombroso (1836-1909) to express a morbid hatred of the new, or the dread of a new situation.—*J.J.R.*

Mneme: (Gr. *Mnēmē,* memory) Term proposed by Semon (*Die Mneme,* 1904; *Die mnemeschen Empfindungen,* 1909) and adopted by B. Russell (*Analysis of Mind*) to designate the conservation in a living organism of the effects of earlier stimulation. Ordinary memory is interpreted as an instance of mnemic conservation.—*L.W.*

Mnemic Causation: (Gr. *mneme,* memory) Type of causation of which memory is an instance, in which a present phenomenon (*e.g.* a present memory) is explained not only by its immediate antecedents but by a remote event in time (*e.g.* an earlier experience). See *Mneme.*—*L.W.*

Mnemonics: (Gr. *mnemonikos,* pertaining to memory) An arbitrary framework or device for assisting the memory, *e.g.* the mnemonic verses summarizing the logically valid moods and figures of the syllogism. See J. M. Baldwin, *Dictionary of Philosophy and Psychology,* II, pp. 87-9.—*L.W.*

Mo: Sometimes spelled Moh. (a) Mo Tzŭ. (b) Mohism. See *Mo chia.* (c) Followers of Mo Tzŭ. See *Mo chê.*—*W.T.C.*

Mo che: Neo-Mohists, followers of Mo Tzŭ in the third century B.C., probably organized as a religious or fraternal order, who continued the utilitarian humanism of

Mo Tzŭ wrote the *Mo Ching* (Mohist Canons) which now form part of *Mo Tzŭ;* developed the seven methods of argumentation, namely, the methods of possibility, hypothesis, imitation, comparison, parallel, analogy, and induction; discovered the "method of agreement," which includes "identity, generic relationship, co-existence, and partial resemblance," the "method of difference," which includes "duality, absence of generic relationship, separateness, and dissimilarity," and the "joint method of differences and similarities;" refuted the Sophists, (pien chê) theory of distinction of quality and substance; and became the outstanding logical school in Chinese philosophy.—*W.T.C.*

Mo chia: The School of Mo Tzŭ (Moh Tzŭ, Mo Ti, between 500 and 396 B.C.) and his followers. This utilitarian and scientific minded philosopher, whose doctrines are embodied in *Mo Tzŭ,* advocated: (1) "benefit" (li), or the promotion of general welfare and removal of evil, through the increase of population and wealth, the elevation of conduct, the regulation of benevolence and righteousness toward this practical objective, the elimination of war, and the suppression of wasteful musical events and elaborate funerals; (2) "universal love" (chien ai), or treating others, their families, and their countries as one's own, to the end that the greatest amount of benefit will be realized; (3) agreement with the superiors (shang t'ung); (4) a method of reasoning which involves a foundation, a survey, and application (san piao); (5) the belief in Heaven and the spirits both as a religious sanction of governmental measures and as an effective way of promotion of peace and welfare. For the development of his teachings by his followers, see *Mo chê.*—*W.T.C.*

Modalism: (Lat. *modus,* mode) A theological doctrine, of the second and third centuries A.D., affirming the unity of substance and personality in God. The Son and the Holy Ghost are but "modes" of God the Father. Also known as Monarchism; adherents of this position were Patripassians or Sabellians.—*V.J.B.*

Modality: (Kant. Ger. *Modalität*) Concerning the mode—actuality, possibility or necessity—in which anything exists. Kant treated these as a priori categories or necessary conditions of experience, though in his formulation they are little more than definitions. See *Kantianism.*—*O.F.K.*

Modality is the name given to certain classifications of propositions which are either supplementary to the classification into true and false or intended to provide categories additional to truth and falsehood—namely to classifications of propositions as possible, problematical, and the like. See *Strict implication,* and *Propositional calculus, Many-valued.*

Or, as in traditional logic, modality may refer to a classification of propositions according to the kind of assertion which is contained, rather than have the character of a truth-value. From this point of view propositions are classed as *assertoric* (in which something is asserted as true), *problematic* (in which something is asserted as possible), and *apodeictic* (in which something is asserted as necessary).—*A.C.*

Mode: (Lat. *modus,* measure, standard, manner) (a) In Augustinism: a measure imprinted upon human minds by God, enabling man to know what is good and true.

(b) In medieval Aristotelianism: a determination of being-in-general to some limited condition; also, in Neo-Thomism, an entitative component of a composite being, as "union" is called a mode combining matter and form in a thing (Olivi and Suarez).

(c) In Spinoza: "that which exists in, and is conceived through, something other than itself." These modes are determinations of the infinite Attributes of Divine Substance; of the attribute, Thought, the two chief modes are intellect and will; of the attribute, Extension, the chief modes are motion and rest. These modes are nothing apart from God's Substance; they are infinite from one point of view *(natura naturans)* and finite from another *(natura naturata).*

(d) In Locke: the simple mode of an idea is the manner of thinking in which one idea is taken several times over, e.g. a dozen; mixed modes of ideas are those types of ideation in which various non-similar simple ideas are combined by the mind so as to produce a complex idea which does not represent a substance: e.g. obligation, drunkenness.

(e) In statistics: see *Mean.*—*V.J.B.*

Moderate Realism: See *Realism.*

Modus tollens: See *Logic, formal,* § 2.

Moha: (Skr.) Distraction, perplexity, delusion, beclouding of the mind rendering it unfit to perceive the truth, generally explained as attachment to the phenomenal; in Buddhism, ignorance, as a source of vice.—*K.F.L.*

Mohammedanism: The commonly applied term in the Occident to the religion founded by Mohammed. (See Islam) It sought to restore the indigenous monotheism of Arabia, Abraham's uncorrupted religion. Its essential dogma is the belief in the absolute unity of Allah. Its chief commandments are: profession of faith, ritual prayer, the payment of the alms tax, fasting and the pilgrimage. It has no real clerical caste, no church organization, no liturgy, and rejects monasticism. Its ascetic attitude is expressed in warnings against woman, in prohibition of nudity and of construction of splendid buildings except the house of worship; condemns economic speculation; praises manual labor and poverty; prohibits music, wine and pork, and the portrayal of living beings.—*H.H.*

Mohism: See *Mo chia* and *Chinese philosophy.*

Moksa: (Skr.) Liberation, salvation from the effects of *karma* (*q.v.*) and resulting *samsāra* (*q.v.*). Theoretically, good *karma* as little as evil *karma* can bring about liberation from the state of existence looked upon pessimistically. Thus, Indian philosophy early found a solution in knowledge *(vidyā, jñāna)* which, disclosing the essential oneness of all in the metaphysical world-ground, declares the phenomenal world as *maya* (*q.v.*). Liberation is then equivalent to identification of oneself with the ultimate reality, eternal, changeless, blissful, or in a state of complete indifference either with or without loss of consciousness, but at any rate beyond good and evil, pleasure and pain. Divine grace is also recognized by some religious systems as effecting *mokṣa*. No generalization is possible regarding the many theories of *mokṣa*, its nature, or the mode of attaining it. See *Nirvāna, Samādhi, Prasāda.—K.F.L.*

Molecule: A complex of atoms, which may be of the same kind or different. Thus there may be molecules of elements and molecules which are compounds. So far no single molecule has been synthesized larger than the wave length of light so that it could be rendered visible. Molecular aggregates, however, exist, which may be looked upon in a sense as giant molecules visible under the microscope.—*W.M.M.*

Monad: (Gr. *Monás*, a unit) 1. In Greek usage, originally the number one. Later, any individual or metaphysical unit.

2. Bruno named his metaphysical units monads to distinguish them from the Democritean atoms. The monads, centers of the world life, are both psychic and spatial individuals.

3. Leibniz (borrowing the term possibly from Augustine, Bruno or Protestant scholastics) identified the monads with the metaphysical individuals or souls, conceived as unextended, active, indivisible, naturally indestructible, teleological substances ideally related in a system of pre-established harmony.

4. By extension of Leibnizian usage, a soul, self, metaphysical unit, when conceived as possessing an autonomous life, and irrespective of the nature of its relations to beings beyond it.—*W.L.*

Monadology: (also Monadism) The doctrine of monads, the theory that the universe is a composite of elementary units. A monad may also be a metaphysical unit. The notion of monad can be found in Pythagoras, Ecphantus, Aristotle, Euclid, Augustine, *et. al.* Plato refers to his ideas as monads. Nicolaus Cusanus regards individual things as units which mirror the world. Giordano Bruno seems to have been the first to have used the term in its modern connotation. God is called monas monadum; each monad, combining matter and form, is both corporeal and spiritual, a microcosm of the whole. But the real founder of monadology is Leibniz. To him, the monads are the real atoms of nature, the elements of things. The monad is a simple substance, completely different from a material atom. It has neither extension, nor shape, nor divisibility. Nor is it perishable. Monads begin to exist or cease to exist by a decree of God. They are distinguished from one another in character, they "have no windows" through which anything can enter in or go out, that is, the substance of the monad must be conceived as force, as that which contains in itself the principle of its changes. The universe is the aggregate, the ideal bond of the monads, constituting a harmonious unity, pre-established by God who is the highest in the hierarchy of monads. This bond of all things to each, enables every simple substance to have relations which express all the others, every monad being a perpetual living mirror of the universe. The simple substance or monad, therefore, contains a plurality of modifications and relations even though it has no parts but is unity.

The highest monad, God, appears to be both the creator and the unified totality and harmony of self-active and self-subsistent monads.—*J.M.*

Monadology, The New: Expression used by Renouvier for his type of personalism.—*R.T.F.*

Monergism: The view that the human will contributes nothing to its regeneration but that this is the work of one factor, the Divine.—*V.F.*

Monism: (Gr. *mones,* single) (a) Metaphysical: The view that there is but one fundamental Reality; first used by Wolff. (A Universe.) Sometimes spoken of as Singularism. The classical ancient protagonist of an extreme monism is Parmenides of Elea; a modern exponent is Spinoza. Christian Science is an example of a popular contemporary religion built on an extreme monistic theory of reality. Most metaphysical monists hold to a modified or soft monistic theory (*e.g.* the metaphysics of Royce).

(b) Epistemological: The view that the real object and the idea of it (perception of conception) are one in the knowledge relation. (*e.g.* the school known as New Realism; extreme mystics.)—*V.F.*

Monism, neutral: The doctrine that regards neither mind nor matter as ultimates.—*H.H.*

Mono-personalism: A term ascribed by Kohnstamm to Stern's doctrine of an impersonal-God.—*R.T.F.*

Monosyllogism: See *Polysyllogism.*

Montague, William Pepperell: (1873-1953) Professor of Philosophy at Columbia University. He was among the early leaders of the neo-realist group. He developed views interpreting consciousness, variation and heredity in mechanical terms. He has characterized his view as animistic materialism. Among his best known works are: *The Ways of Knowing or the Methods of Philosophy, Belief Unbound, A Promethean Religion for the Modern World* and his most recent, *Knowledge, Nature and Value.* See *Neo-Realism.—L.E.D.*

Montaigne, Michel De: (1533-1592) French essayist whose renowned *Essays* are famous for his tolerant study of himself and through himself of mankind as a whole. He doubts the possibility of certain knowledge and recommends a return to nature and revelation. He was a keen observer of the frailties of human nature and has left among the essays crowned masterpieces of insight and delight.—*L.E.D.*

Montanism: A Christian movement dated about the middle of the second century centering about the teachings of the prophet Montanus and two women, Prisca and Maximilla. They distinguished between mortal and venial sins, practiced ascetic ideals and believed themselves to possess the pure type of Christian living on the authority of a special revelation from the Holy Spirit. The movement faded out about the 4th century. Tertullian, famous Latin churchman, was for a time a member.—*V.F.*

Montesquieu, Charles De Secondat: (1689-1755) French historian and writer in the field of politics. His *Lettres persanes,* thinly disguise trenchant criticism of the decadence of French society through the letters of two Persian visitors. His masterpiece, *L'Esprit des*

Lois, gives a political and social philosophy in pointing the relation between the laws and the constitution of government. He finds a relation between all laws in the laws of laws, the necessary relations derived from the nature of things. In his analysis of the English constitution, he stressed the separation of powers in a manner that has had lasting influence though based on historical inaccuracy.—*L.E.D.*

Monumentality: Artistic character suggesting the sense of grandeur, even though small in size.—*L.V.*

Moods of the syllogism: See *figure (syllogistic),* and *logic, formal,* § 5.

Moore, George Edward: (1873-1958) One of the leading English realists. Professor of Mental Philosophy and Logic at Cambridge. Editor of "Mind." He has been a vigorous opponent of the idealistic tradition in metaphysics, epistemology and in ethics. His best known works are: *Principia Ethica,* and *Philosophical Studies.* Belief in external things having the properties they are normally experienced to have. Founder of neo-realistic theory of epistemological monism. See *Neo-Realism.*—*L.E.D.*

Moral Argument for God: Basing the belief upon the fact of man's moral nature which compels him to make moral assertions about the world and destiny. The argument assumes many forms. Kant held, *e.g.* that the moral consciousness of man is *a priori* and compels him willy nilly to assert three great affirmatives: his freedom, immortality, and the existence and high character of God.—*V.F.*

Moral Judgment: (a) good or bad judgment in moral matters, (b) any ethical judgment, especially judgments of good and bad, right, wrong and duty (see *ethics*). For Kant a moral judgment or imperative as contrasted with the hypothetical imperatives of skill and prudence. —*W.K.F.*

Moral Law: (in Kant's ethics) That formula which expresses the necessity of an action done from duty in terms of one's own reflection.—*P.A.S.*

Moral Optimism: See *Religious meliorism.*

Moral Order: The phrase may refer to the order or harmony which is often said to be an essential part of the good or virtuous life, but it is generally used in such expressions as "the moral order" or "belief in the existence of a moral order," which refer either (a) to a conceived transcendental order of what ought to be, an intelligible moral universe or realm of values or ends, an a priori system of objective ethical truth—which somehow underlies this natural or existential order as its basis or overarches it as its pattern and law-giver, or (b) to a belief that there is a moral direction in the affairs of the world.—*W.K.F.*

Moral Philosophy: See *Ethics.*

Morals: The term is sometimes used as equivalent to "ethics." More frequently it is used to designate the codes, conduct, and customs of individuals or of groups, as when one speaks of the morals of a person or of a people. Here it is equivalent to the Greek word *ethos* and the Latin *mores.*—*W.K.F.*

Moral Sense School, The: The phrase refers primarily

to a few British moralists of the late 17th and early 18th centuries, notably Shaftesbury and Hutcheson, who held the organ of ethical insight to be, not reason, but a special "moral sense," akin to feeling in nature.—*W.K.F.*

Moral Virtues: (Gr. *aretai ethikai*) In Aristotle's philosophy those virtues, or excellences, which consist in the habitual control of conduct by rational principle; as distinct from the intellectual virtues, whose end is the knowledge of principles. See *Aristotelianism; Dianoetic Virtues.*—*G.R.M.*

More, Paul Elmer: An American literary critic and philosopher (1864-1937), who after teaching at Bryn Mawr and other colleges, edited *The Nation* for several years before retiring to lecture at Princeton University and write *The Greek Tradition,* a series of books in which he argues for orthodox Christianity on the basis of the Platonic dualism of mind-body, matter-spirit, God-man. In *The Sceptical Approach to Religion* he gave his final position, as ethical theism grounded on man's sense of the good and consciousness of purpose, and validated by the Incarnation of God in Christ.—*W.N.P.*

More, Thomas: (1478-1535) Lord chancellor of England. One of the leading humanists along with his friends Colet and Erasmus. He was beheaded for his refusal to recognize the king as the head of the church. In his classic, *Utopia,* he has left a vision of an ideal state in which war and all glories connected with it were abhorrent. The prince and all magistrates were elected. Nothing is private. All work and all enjoyment are shared. There is no oppression, neither industrial nor religious. The work gives no philosophical analysis of the nature of the state, but merely an exposition of what the author conceived to be and what we have since come to call utopian.—*L.E.D.*

Mores: (Lat. *mos,* usage) Customs, Folkways, Conventions, Traditions.—*A.J.B.*

Motion: (Lat. *moveo,* move) Difference in space. Change of place. Erected into a universal principle by Heraclitus. Denied as a possibility by Parmenides and Zeno. Subdivided by Aristotle into alteration or change in shape, and augmentation or diminution or change in size. In realism: exclusively a property of actuality.—*J.K.F.*

Motion: (in Scholasticism) The passing of a subject from potency to act.—*H.G.*

Motivation: Designation of the totality of motives operative in any given act of volition or of the mechanism of the operation of such motives. See *Motive.*—*L.W.*

Motive: (Lat. *motus,* from *movere,* to move) An animal drive or desire which consciously or unconsciously operates as a determinant of an act of volition.—*L.W.*

Mo Tzŭ: (Mo Ti, between 500 and 396 B.C.) Founder of Mohism (Mo chia), studied Confucianism, later repudiated it, especially its doctrines of Fate and elaborate rituals. As a high officer in the state of Sung (in present Honan, most probably his native state) he "skillfully carried out military defense and practiced economy." He vigorously defended religious beliefs and practices, became the chief promoter, if not the only founder, of religion in ancient China. His pupils became an organized religious group, or possibly a society of people who had been punished with branding and had become slaves, which is what the word *mo* in one sense meant. *Mo Tzŭ* (Eng. tr. by Y. P. Mei: *The Ethical and Political Works of Motse*) contains his teachings recorded by his followers.—*W.T.C.*

Mou: The method of parallel in argumentation. See *Pien.*—*W.T.C.*

Mukti: (Skr.) Liberation. Same as *moksa* (*q.v.*) —*K.F.L.*

Multiple Inherence, Theory of: The view that qualities, secondary qualities in particular can inhere in a triadic or multiple relationship. (Broad.)—*H.H.*

Multiplicative axiom: See *choice, axiom of.*

Multiplicity: The doctrine of the plurality of beings, or the manifoldness of the real, denied by the Eleatics, who contended that the multiplicity of things was but an illusion of the senses, was defended by Aristotle who maintained that the term, being, is only a common predicate of many things which become out of that which is relatively not-being by making the transition from the potential to the actual.—*J.J.R.*

Mundus intelligibilis: (Lat.) The world of intelligible realities; Plato's realm of Ideas, or St. Augustine's *rationes aeternae* in the Divine Mind. Each species of things is represented here by one, perfect exemplar, the pattern for the many, imperfect copies in the world of sense. See *Mundus sensibilis.*—*V.J.B.*

Mundus sensibilis: (Lat.) The world of things perceived by the human senses. In Platonism, Neo-Platonism, Augustinism, and some Renaissance thought (Ficino) this realm of sensible objects was regarded as an imitation of the superior world of intelligible realities. See *Mundus intelligibilis.*—*V.J.B.*

Muni: (Skr.) A philosopher, sage, especially one who has taken upon himself observance of silence.—*K.F.L.*

Münsterberg, Hugo: (1863-1916) German-born philosopher and psychologist, for many years professor of psychology at Harvard University. One of the advance guard of present axiological development, he is affiliated with the teleological criticism stemming from Fichte. Agrees that pure reason is endowed with *a priori* principles which enable it to achieve objective super-individual affirmations which transcend and which can neither be confirmed nor denied by psychological investigation. Main works: *Der Ursprung d. Sittlichkeit,* 1889; *Beiträge z. Experim. Psychol.,* 1889-92; *Psychol. u. Lehre,* 1906; *Philos. der Werte,* 1908 (Eng. tr. *The External Values); Grundzüge d. Psychotechnik,* 1914.—*H.H.*

Mutazilite: (Ar. seceders) Member of a Shiite sect of Islam dating from the 8th century, which stood for free will and against divine predestination.

Mysticism: Mysticism in its simplest and most essential meaning is a type of religion which puts the emphasis on immediate awareness of relation with God, direct and intimate consciousness of Divine Presence. It is religion in its most acute, intense and living stage. The word owes its origin to the Mystery Religions. The initiate who had the "secret" was called a *mystes.* Early Christians used the word "Contemplation" for mystical experience. The word "mystical" first came into use in the Western World in the writings ascribed to "Dionysius the Areopagite," which appeared at the end of the fifth century.

"Dionysius" used the word to express a type of "Theology" rather than an experience. For him and for many interpreters since his day, Mysticism stands for a religious theory or system, which conceives of God as absolutely transcendent, beyond reason, thought, intellect and all approaches of mind. The way up is a *via negativa.* It is *Agnostia,* unknowing knowing." This type of Mysticism, which emerged from the Neo-Platonic stream of thought might be defined as Belief in the possibility of Union with the Divine by means of ecstatic contemplation.

The word, furthermore, has been loosely used for esoteric, gnostic, theosophical types of "knowledge," not capable of verification. It has been used, too, for the whole area of psychic phenomena and occult happenings, borderland phenomena. The result of this confusion has been that in scientific laboratories the word mysticism often connotes spurious knowledge, occult lore or abnormal phenomena. The Germans use the word *Mysticismus* for this dubious type of knowledge and *Mystik* for the loftier types of experience.

It is not historically sound to find the *essentia* of Mysticism in ecstacy, or in a *via negativa,* or in some kind of esoteric *knowledge,* or in mysterious "communications." The *essentia* of Mysticism is the experience of direct communion with God.

Henri Delacroix, *Etude d'Histoire et de Psychologie du Mysticisme* (Paris, 1908); Baron Friedrich von Hügel, *The Mystical Element of Religion* (London, 1908); Evelyn Underhill, *Mysticism* (London, 1911); William James, *Varieties of Religious Experience* (New York, 1902); Rufus M. Jones, *Studies in Mystical Religion* (London, 1909).—*R.M.J.*

Myth: (Gr. *mythos,* legend) The truth, symbolically, or affectively, presented. Originally, the legends of the Gods concerning cosmogonical or cosmological questions. Later, a fiction presented as historically true but lacking factual basis; a popular and traditional falsehood. A presentation of cosmology, employing the affective method of symbolic representation in order to escape from the limitations of literal meaning.—*J.K.F.*

N

Na chia: The coordination and interlocking of the Ten Celestial Stems with the Eight Elements (pa kua), to the end that the first Stem, which is the embodiment of the active or male cosmic force, and the second Stem, which is the reservoir of the passive or female cosmic force, gather in the center and the highest point in the universe. Taoist religion.—*W.T.C.*

Naive Realism: The view of the man in the street. This view is an uncritical belief in an external world and the ability to know it.—*V.F.*

Nakamura, Hajime: (1912—   ) Contemporary Japanese philosopher and author of *Ways of Thinking of Eastern Peoples: India, China, Tibet, Japan* (1964), *Parallel Developments: A Comparative History of Ideas* (1975), and *Buddha* (1977). He relates the language and thought of East and West, showing how thought patterns influence perception. The key to the process is Buddhism, beginning in India and then spreading to Tibet, China and Japan. What each culture selected indicates their characteristic ways of thinking.—*S.E.N.*

Name: A word or symbol which denotes (designates) a particular thing is called a *proper name* of that particular thing.

In English and other natural languages there occur also *common names* (common nouns), such a common name being thought of as if it could serve as a name of anything belonging to a specified class or having specified characteristics. Under usual translations into symbolic notation, common names are replaced by proper names of classes or of class concepts; and this would seem to provide the best logical analysis. In actual English usage, however, a common noun is often more nearly like a *variable* (*q.v.*) having a specified range.—*A.C.*

Name relation or *meaning relation:* The relation between a symbol (formula, word, phrase) and that which it denotes or of which it is the name.

Where a particular (interpreted) system does not contain symbols for formulas, it may be desirable to employ Gödel's device for associating (positive integral) numbers with formulas, and to consider the relation between a number and that which the associated formula denotes. This we shall call the *numerical name relation* and distinguish it from the relation between a formula and that which it denotes by calling the latter the *semantical name relation*.

In many (interpreted) logistic systems — including such as contain, with their usual interpretations, the Zermelo set theory, or the simple theory of types with axiom of infinity, or the functional calculus of second order with addition of Peano's postulates for arithmetic — it is impossible without contradiction to introduce the numerical name relation with its natural properties, because Grelling's paradox or similar paradoxes would result (see *paradoxes, logical*). The same can be said of the semantical name relation in cases where symbols for formulas are present.

Such systems may, however, contain partial name relations which function as name relations in the case of some but not all of the formulas of the system (or of their associated Gödel numbers).

In particular, it is normally possible — at least it does not obviously lead to contradiction in the case of such systems as the Zermelo set theory or the simple theory of types (functional calculus of order omega) with axiom of infinity — to extend a system L_1 into a system L_2 (the semantics of L_1 in the sense of Tarski), so that L_2 shall contain symbols for the formulas of L_1, and for the essential syntactical relations between formulas of L_1, and for a relation which functions as a name relation as regards all the formulas of L_1 (or, in the case of the theory of types, one such relation for each type), together with appropriate new primitive formulas. Then L_2 may be similarly extended into L_3, and so on through a hierarchy of systems each including the preceding one as a part.

Or, if L_1 contains symbols for positive integers, we may extend L_1 into L_2 by merely adding a symbol for a relation which functions as a numerical name relation as regards all numbers of formulas of L_1 (or one such relation for each type) together with appropriate new primitive formulas; and so on through a hierarchy of systems $L_1, L_2, L_3, \ldots$

See further *Semantics; Semiotic* 2; *Truth, Semantical.—A.C.*

Nāma-rūpa: (Skr.) "Name and form," a stereotyped formula for the phenomenal world, or its conceptual and material aspects; also: "word and beauty," as forms of manifestation. See *Rupa.—K.F.L.*

Nascency: (Lat. *nascens,* ppr. of *nasci,* to be born) A potency which is in process of actualization. See *Potency; Potentiality.* The term may be applied generally to anything in process of coming into being but it is particularly appropriate to psychological states and feelings.—*L.W.*

Nascent: A term applied to a thing or a state of mind at an early stage of its development when it is as yet scarcely recognizable. See *Nascency.* The term, as applied by H. Spencer (*Psychology,* § 195) to psychological states, foreshadowed the later theory of the subconscious. See *Subconscious; Latency.—L.W.*

Nāstika: (Skr.) "Not orthodox," not acknowledging the authority of the Veda (*q.v.*).—*K.F.L.*

Nativism: Theory that mind has elements of knowledge not derived from sensation. Similar to the common sense theory of T. Reid (1710-1796) and the Scotch School. Introduced as a term by Helmholtz (1821-1894) for the doctrine that there are inherited items in human knowledge which are, therefore, in each and every individual independently of his experience. The doctrine of innate ideas. Opposed to: radical empiricism. See *Transcendentalism.—J.K.F.*

Natorp, Paul: (1854-1924) Collaborating with Cohen, Natorp applied the transcendental method to an interpretation of Plato, to psychology and to the methodology of the exact sciences. Like Cohen, Natorp really did not contribute to the scientific development of critical philosophy but prepared the way for philosophical mysticism. Cf. *Platos Ideenlehre,* 1903; *Kant u. d. Marburger Schule,* 1915.—*J.K.*

Natural: (in Scholasticism) As opposed to supernatural, is that which belongs to (or is due to) a thing according to its nature, as it is natural to man to know; as opposed to voluntary and free, it is that which is done without the command and the advertence of the will, but of nature's own accord, *e.g.* to sleep; as opposed to chance, it is that which happens through natural causes, as the falling of a stone. Sometimes it is used to refer to a physical body composed of matter and form.—*H.G.*

Natural election: The inherent desire of all things for all other things in a certain order. First employed by Francis Bacon (1561-1626) in a passage quoted by A.N. Whitehead (1861-1947) from the *Silva Silvarum:* "there is a kind of election to embrace that which is agreeable and to exclude or expel that which is ingrate." First erected into a philosophical principle by John Laird in *The Idea of Value,* following a suggestion in Montaigne's *Essays.* Value, considered as a larger category than human value, an ingredient of the natural world but regarded without its affective content. Syn. with objective value, as independent of the cognitive

process.—*J.K.F.*

Naturalism: Naturalism, challenging the cogency of the cosmological, teleological, and moral arguments, holds that the universe requires no supernatural cause and government, but is self-existent, self-explanatory, self-operating, and self-directing; that the world-process is not teleological and anthropocentric, but purposeless, deterministic (except for possible tychistic events), and only incidentally productive of man; that human life, physical, mental, moral and spiritual, is an ordinary natural event attributable in all respects to the ordinary operations of nature; and that man's ethical values, compulsions, activities, and restraints can be justified on natural grounds, without recourse to supernatural sanctions, and his highest good pursued and attained under natural conditions, without expectation of a supernatural destiny.—*B.A.G.F.*

The general philosophical position which has as its fundamental tenet the proposition that the natural world is the whole of reality. "Nature" and "natural world" are certainly ambiguous terms, but this much is clear: in thus restricting reality, naturalism means to assert that there is but one system or level of reality; that this system is the totality of objects and events in space and time; and that the behavior of this system is determined only by its own character and is reducible to a set of causal laws. Nature is thus conceived as self-contained and self-dependent, and from this view spring certain negations that define to a great extent the influence of naturalism. First, it is denied that nature is derived from or dependent upon any transcendent, supernatural entities. From this follows the denial that the order of natural events can be intruded upon. And this in turn entails the denial of freedom, purpose, and transcendent destiny.

Within the context of these views there is evidently allowance for divergent doctrines, but certain general tendencies can be noticed. The metaphysics of naturalism is always monistic and if any teleological element is introduced it is emergent. Man is viewed as coordinate with other parts of nature, and naturalistic psychology emphasizes the physical basis of human behavior; ideas and ideals are largely treated as artifacts, though there is disagreement as to the validity to be assigned them. The axiology of naturalism can seek its values only within the context of human character and experience, and must ground these values on individual self-realization or social utility; though again there is disagreement as to both the content and the final validity of the values there discovered. Naturalistic epistemologies have varied between the extremes of rationalism and positivism, but they consistently limit knowledge to natural events and the relationships holding between them, and so direct inquiry to a description and systematization of what happens in nature. The beneficent task that naturalism recurrently performs is that of recalling attention from a blind absorption in theory to a fresh consideration of the facts and values exhibited in nature and life.

In aesthetics: The general doctrine that the proper

study of art is nature. In this broad sense, artistic naturalism is simply the thesis that the artist's sole concern and function should be to observe closely and report clearly the character and behavior of his physical environment. Similar to philosophical naturalism, aesthetic naturalism derives much of its importance from its denials and from the manner in which it consequently restricts and directs art. The artist should not seek any "hidden" reality or essence; he should not attempt to correct or complete nature by either idealizing or generalizing; he should not impose value judgments upon nature; and he should not concern himself with the selection of "beautiful" subjects that will yield "aesthetic pleasure." He is simply to dissect and describe what he finds around him. Here, it is important to notice explicitly a distinction between naturalism and romanticism (*q.v.*): romanticism emphasizes the felt quality of things, and the romanticist is primarily interested in the experiences that nature will yield; naturalism emphasizes the objective character of things, and is interested in nature as an independent entity. Thus, romanticism stresses the intervention of the artist upon nature, while naturalism seeks to reduce this to a minimum.

Specifically, naturalism usually refers to the doctrines and practices of the 19th century school of realism which arose as the literary analogue of positivism, and whose great masters were Flaubert, Zola, and de Maupassant. The fundamental dogma of the movement, as expressed by Zola in "Le Roman expérimental" and "Les Romanciers naturalistes," states that naturalism is "the scientific method applied to literature." Zola maintains that the task of the artist is to report and explain what happens in nature; art must aim at a literal transcript of reality, and the artist attains this by making an analytic study of character, motives, and behavior. Naturalism argues that all judgments of good and bad are conventional, with no real basis in nature; so art should seek to understand, not to approve or condemn. Human behavior is regarded as largely a function of environment and circumstances, and the novelist should exhibit these in detail, with no false idealizing of character, no glossing over the ugly, and no appeal to supposed hidden forces.—*I.J.*

Naturalistic ethics: Any view according to which ethics is an empirical science, natural or social, ethical notions being reduced to those of the natural sciences and ethical questions being answered wholly on the basis of the findings of those sciences.—*W.K.F.*

Naturalistic fallacy, the: The procedure involved in metaphysical and naturalistic systems of ethics, and said by G. E. Moore and his followers to be a fallacy, of deriving ethical conclusions from non-ethical premises or of defining ethical notions in non-ethical terms. See *Naturalistic ethics, Metaphysical ethics.—W.K.F.*

Natural law: (in legal philosophy) A "higher law" as opposed to the positive law of a state. The rules of natural law were supposed to be universally valid and therefore natural. They are discoverable by reason alone (rationalism). Natural law theories originated in ancient Greek philosophy. From the Renaissance on they were used as an argument for liberal political doctrines. There is a marked tendency in recent legal philosophy to revive the natural law doctrine.—*W.E.*

Nature Philosophers: Name given to pre-Socratic "physiologers" and to Renaissance philosophers who revived the study of physical processes. Early in the 16th century, as a result of the discovery of new lands, the revival of maritime trade, and the Reformation, there appeared in Europe a renewed interest in nature. Rationalism grown around the authorities of the Bible and Aristotle was challenged and the right to investigate phenomena was claimed. Interest in nature was directed at first toward the starry heaven and resulted in important discoveries of Copernicus, Galileo and Kepler. The scientific spirit of observation and research had not yet matured, however, and the philosophers of that time blended their interest in facts with much loose speculation. Among the nature philosophers of that period three deserve to be mentioned specifically, Telesio, Bruno and Campanella, all natives of Southern Italy. Despite his assertions that thought should be guided by the observation of the external world, Bernardino Telesio (1508-1588) confined his works to reflections on the nature of things. Particularly significant are two of his doctrines, first, that the universe must be described in terms of matter and force, the latter classified as heat and cold, and second, that mind is akin to matter. Giordano Bruno (1548-1600), a Dominican monk and a victim of the Inquisition, was greatly influenced by the Copernican conception of the universe regarded by him as a harmonious unity of which the earth was but a small and not too important part. The concept of unity was not a condition of human search for truth but a real principle underlying all things and expressing the harmonious order of Divine wisdom. Deity, in his view, was the soul of nature, operating both in the human minds and in the motion of bodies. Consequently, both living beings and material objects must be regarded as animated. Tomaso Campanella (1568-1639), another Dominican monk, was also persecuted for his teachings and spent 27 years in prison. He contended that observations of nature were not dependent on the authority of reason and can be refuted only by other observations. His interests lay largely along the lines previously suggested by Telesio, and much of his thought was devoted to problems of mind, consciousness and knowledge. He believed that all nature was permeated by latent awareness, and he may therefore be regarded as an animist or perhaps pantheist. Today, he is best known for his *City of the Sun,* an account of an imaginary ideal state in which existed neither property nor nobility and in which all affairs were administered scientifically.—*R.B.W.*

Natural Realism: In epistemology, the doctrine that sensation and perception can be relied upon to give indubitable evidence of the real existence of the external world. Theory that realism is part of the inherent common sense of mankind. First advanced by T. Reid (1710-1796) and held by his followers of the Scotch school. Also known as the common-sense philosophy.

See *Realism*.—*J.K.F.*

Natural Selection: This is the corner stone of the evolutionary hypothesis of Charles Darwin. He found great variation in and among types as a result of his extensive biological investigations and accounted for the modifications, not by some act of special creation or supernatural intervention, but by the descent, generation after generation, of modified species selected to survive and reproduce the more useful and the more successfully adapted to the environmental struggle for existence. He elaborated a corollary to this general theory in his idea of sexual selection. See *Evolutionism, Charles Darwin, Herbert Spencer*.— *L.E.D.*

Natural Theology: In general, natural theology is a term used to distinguish any theology based upon the fundamental premise of the ability of man to construct his theory of God and of the world out of the framework of his own reason and of reasonable probability from the so-called "revealed theology" which presupposes that God and divine purposes are not open to unaided human understanding but rest upon a supernatural and not wholly understandable basis. See *Deism; Renaissance*. During the 17th and 18th centuries there were attempts to set up a "natural religion" to which men might easily give their assent and to offset the extravagant claims of the supernaturalists and their harsh charges against doubters. The classical attempt to make out a case for the sweet reasonableness of a divine purpose at work in the world of nature was given by Paley in his *Natural Theology* (1802). Traditional Catholicism, especially that of the late Middle Ages developed a kind of natural theology based upon the metaphysics of Aristotle. Descartes, Spinoza and Leibniz developed a more definite type of natural theology in their several constructions of what now may well be called philosophical theology wherein reason is made the guide. Natural theology has raised its head in recent times in attempts to combat the extravagant declarations of theologians of human pessimism. The term, however, is unfortunate because it is being widely acknowledged that so-called "revealed theology" is natural (recent psychological and social studies) and that natural theology need not deny to reason its possible character as the bearer of an immanent divine revelation.—*V.F.*

Nature: A highly ambiguous term, of which the following meanings are distinguished by A. O. Lovejoy:

1. The objective as opposed to the subjective.

2. An objective standard for values as opposed to custom, law, convention.

3. The general cosmic order, usually conceived as divinely ordained, in contrast to human deviations from this.

4. That which exists apart from and uninfluenced by man, in contrast with art.

5. The instinctive or spontaneous behavior of man as opposed to the intellective.

Various normative meanings are read into these, with the result that the "natural" is held to be better than the "artificial," the "unnatural," the "conventional" or customary, the intellectual or deliberate, the subjec-

tive.—*G.B.*

In *Aristotle's philosophy*: (1) the internal source of change or rest in an object as such, in distinction from art, which is an external source of change. Natural beings are those that have such an internal source of change. Though both matter and form are involved in the changes of a natural being, its nature is ordinarily identified with the form, as the active and intelligible factor. (2) The sum total of all natural beings. See *Aristotelianism*.—*G.R.M.*

Nature "naturing": (*Natura naturans;* in Scholasticism) God. Nature "natured" (*Natura naturata*) is the complexus of all created things. Sometimes *nature* is used for the essence of a thing or for natural causes, and in this sense it is said: nature does nothing in vain; for the generation and birth of living beings; for substantial form; and for the effective or passive principle of motion and rest.—*H.G.*

Necessary: According to distinctions of *modality* (*q.v.*), a proposition is *necessary* if its truth is certifiable on *a priori* grounds, or on purely logical grounds. Necessity is thus, as it were, a stronger kind of truth, to be distinguished from the *contingent truth* of a proposition which might have been otherwise. (As thus described, the notion is of course vague, but it may in various ways be given an exact counterpart in one logistic system or another.)

A proposition may also be said to be necessary if it is a consequence of some accepted set of propositions (indicated by the context), even if this accepted set of propositions is not held to be *a priori*. See *Necessity*.

That a propositional function F is necessary may mean simply $(x)F(x)$, or it may mean that $(x)F(x)$ is necessary in one of the preceding senses.—*A.C.*

Necessary condition: F is a *necessary condition* of G if $G(x) \supset x F(x)$. F is a *necessary and sufficient condition of* G if $G(x) \equiv_x F(x)$.—*A.C.*

Necessitarianism: (Lat. *necessitas*, necessity) Theory that every event in the universe is determined by logical or causal necessity. The theory excludes both physical indeterminacy (chance) and psychical indeterminacy (freedom). Necessitarianism, as a theory of cosmic necessity, becomes in its special application to the human will, determinism. See *Determinism*.—*L.W.*

Necessity: A state of affairs is said to be necessary if it cannot be otherwise than it is. Inasmuch as the grounds of an assertion of this kind may in general be one of three very distinct kinds, it is customary and valuable to distinguish the three types of necessity affirmed as (1) logical or mathematical necessity, (2) physical necessity, and (3) moral necessity. The distinction between these three was first worked out with precision by Leibniz in his *Thodicée*.

Logical, physical, and moral necessity are founded in logical, physical, and moral laws respectively. Anything is logically necessary the denial of which would violate a law of logic. Thus in ordinary commutative algebra the implication from the postulates to *ab-ba* is logically necessary, since its denial would violate a logical law (viz. the commutative rule) of this system.

Similarly, physically necessary things are those whose denial would violate a physical or natural law. The orbits of the planets are said to be physically necessary. Circular orbits for the planets are logically possible, but not physically possible, so long as certain physical laws of motion remain true. Physical necessity is also referred to as "causal" necessity.

As moral laws differ widely from logical and physical laws, the type of necessity which they generate is considerably different from the two types previously defined. Moral necessity is illustrated in the necessity of an obligation. Fulfillment of the obligation is morally necessary in the sense that the failure to fulfill it would violate a moral law, where this law is regarded as embodying some recognized value. If it is admitted that values are relative to individuals and societies, then the laws embodying these values will be similarly relative, and likewise the type of thing which these laws will render morally necessary.

While these three types of necessity are generally recognized by philosophers, the weighing of the distinctions is a matter of considerable divergence of view. Those who hold that the distinctions are all radical, sharply distinguish between logical statements, statements of fact, and so-called ethical or value statements. On the other hand, the attempt to establish an a priori ethics may be regarded as an attempt to reduce moral necessity to logical necessity; while the attempt to derive ethical evaluations from the statements of science, *e.g.* from biology, is an attempt to reduce moral necessity to physical or causal necessity.—*F.L.W.*

Negation: The act of denying a proposition as contrasted with the act of affirming it. The affirmation of a proposition *p*, justifies the negation of its contradictory, *p'*, and the negation of *p* justifies the affirmation of *p'*. Contrariwise the affirmation of *p'* justifies the negation of *p* and the negation of *p'* justifies the affirmation of *p*.—*C.A.B.*

The negation of a proposition *p* is the proposition ~*p* (see *Logic, formal,* § 1). The negation of a monadic propositional function *F* is the monadic propositional function $\lambda x[\sim F(x)]$; similarly for dyadic propositional functions, etc.

Or the word *negation* may be used in a syntactical sense, so that the negation of a sentence (formula) A is the sentence ~ A.—*A.C.*

Negative proposition: See *affirmative proposition*.

Negative Sensation: Term used by Wundt to designate sensations produced by stimuli below the threshold of positive sensation. See *Limits of Sensation*. The term has largely been discarded because the existence of such sensations is now generally denied.—*L.W.*

Nei sheng: Often used as referring to the man who attained to complete self-cultivation, sagehood. (Confucius.)—*H.H.*

Nei tan: Internal alchemy, as a means of nourishing life, attaining Tao and immortality, including an elaborate system of breathing technique, diet, and the art of preserving unity of thought (tsün i, tsün hsiang, tsün ssŭ).

Also called t'ai hsi. For external alchemy, see *Wai tan*. (Taoist religion.)—*W.T.C.*

Neo-Confucianism: See *Li hsüeh* and *Chinese philosophy*.

Neo-Criticism: The designation of his philosophy used by Cournot, and in the early stage of his thought by Renouvier, who later changed to Personalism as the more fitting title. See also *Monadology, The New*.—*R.T.F.*

Neo-Hegelianism: The name given to the revival of the Hegelian philosophy which began in Scotland and England about the middle of the nineteenth century and a little later extended to America. Outstanding representatives of the movement in England and Scotland are J. H. Stirling, John and Edward Caird, T. H. Green (perhaps more under the influence of Kant), F. H. Bradley, B. Bosanquet, R. B. Haldane, J. E. McTaggart and, in America, W. T. Harris and Josiah Royce. Throughout, the representatives remained indifferent to the formal aspects of Hegel's dialectic and subscribed only to its spirit—what Hegel himself described as "the power of negation" and what Bosanquet named the *argumentum a contingentia mundi*.—*G.W.C.*

Neo-Idealism: Primarily a name given unofficially to the Italian school of neo-Hegelianism headed by Benedetto Croce and Giovanni Gentile, founded on a basic distinction that it proposes between two kinds of "concrete universals" (*q.v.*). In addition to the Hegelian concrete universal, conceived as a dialectical synthesis of two abstract opposites, is posited a second type in which the component elements are "concretes" rather than dialectical abstracts, *i.e.* possess relative mutual independence and lack the characteristic of logical opposition. The living forms of Mind, both theoretical and practical, are universal in this latter sense. This implies that fine art, utility, and ethics do not comprise a dialectical series with philosophy at their head, *i.e.* they are not inferior forms of metaphysics. Thus neo-Idealism rejects Hegel's panlogism. It also repudiates his doctrine of the relative independence of Nature, the timeless transcendence of the Absolute with respect to the historical process, and the view that at any point of history a logically final embodiment of the Absolute Idea is achieved.—*W.L.*

Neo-intuitionism: See *Intuitionism*.

Neo-Kantianism: A group of Kantian followers who regard the thing-in-itself or noumenal world as a limiting concept rather than, as did Kant, an existent, though unknowable realm. Reality is for the Neo-Kantians a construct of mind, not another realm. Even Kant's noumenal world is a construct of mind. The phenomenal world is the real and it is the realm of ideas. Hence Neo-Kantianism is a form of idealism. Hermann Cohen, a Neo-Kantian, spoke of the world as the creative act of thought. This idealism is sometimes termed "positivistic."—*V.F.*

Neology: Literally, the introduction of new words or new meanings. In theology the neologist is the heretic who introduces a new doctrine. In the latter sense, the rationalist was called a neologist by the traditional theologian.—*V.F.*

Neo-Mohism: See *Mo chê* and *Chinese philosophy*.

Neo-Platonism: New Platonism, i.e. a school of philosophy established perhaps by Ammonius Saccus in the second century A.D., in Alexandria, ending as a formal school with Proclus in the fifth century. See *Plotinism.*—*V.J.B.*

Neo-Pythagoreanism: A school of thought initiated in Alexandria, according to Cicero, by Nigidius Figulus, a Roman philosopher who died in 45 B.C. It was compounded of traditional Pythagorean teachings, various Platonic, Aristotelian and Stoic doctrines, including some mystical and theosophical elements.—*J.L.R.*

Neo-Realism: A school of thought which dates from the beginning of the twentieth century. It began as a movement of reaction against the wide influence of idealistic metaphysics. Whereas the idealists reduce everything to mind, this school reduced mind to everything. For the New Realists Nature is basic and mind is part and parcel of it. How nature was conceived (whether materialistic, neutralistic, etc.) was not the important factor. New Realists differed here among themselves. Their theory of knowledge was strictly monistic, the subject and object are one since there is no fundamental dualism. Two schools of New Realists are recognized:

(a) English New Realists: Less radical in that mind was given a status of its own character although a part of its objective environment. Among distinguished representatives were: G. E. Moore, Bertrand Russell, S. Alexander, T. P. Nunn, A. Wolf, G. F. Stout.

(b) American New Realists: More radical in that mind tended to lose its *special* status in the order of things. In psychology this school moved toward behaviorism. In philosophy they were extreme pan-objectivists. Distinguished representatives: F. J. E. Woodbridge, G. S. Fullerton, E. B. McGilvary and six platformists (so-called because of their collaboration in a volume *The New Realism*, published 1912): E. B. Holt, W. T. Marvin, W. P. Montague, R. B. Perry, W. B. Pitkin, E. G. Spaulding. The American New Realists agreed on a general platform but differed greatly among themselves as to theories of reality and particular questions.—*V.F.*

Neo-Scholasticism: See *Scholasticism*.

Nescience: (Lat. *nesciens,* ignorant) A state of ignorance such as is professed by the agnostic. See *Agnosticism.*—*L.W.*

Nestorians: A Christian sect dating from the 5th century. Nestorius, a patriarch of Constantinople (428-431) opposed the designation "Mother of God" (a declaration of Origen's) applied to Mary, the mother of Jesus. He said that Christ had two distinct natures and that Mary, a human being, could not have delivered anyone but a human. The emphasis is upon the genuine human nature and the exemplary value of Christ. Nestorianism was not only a Christological viewpoint and the only cause for much theological dispute; it was also a part of a political and ecclesiastical feud between bishops east and west. The council of Ephesus in 431 declared the view heretical. Nevertheless the Nestorian churches spread widely and continue until our present time in Asiatic Turkey and Persia.—*V.F.*

Neti, neti: (Skr.) "Not this, not that," famous passage in the Brhadāranyaka Upanishad 2.3.6 *et al. loc.*, giving answer to questions as to the nature of *brahman* (*q.v.*), thus hinting its indefinability.—*K.F.L.*

Neutralism: A type of monism which holds that reality is neither mind nor matter but a single kind of stuff of which mind and matter are but appearances or aspects. Spinoza is the classical representative.—*H.H.*

Neutral Monism: Theory of American New Realism, derived from W. James' essay "Does Consciousness Exist?," *Journal of Philosophy,* 1904, which reduces the mental as well as physical to relations among neutral entities (*i.e.* entities which are in themselves neither mental nor physical). The theory is qualitatively monistic in its admission of only one kind of ultimate reality *viz.* neutral or subsistent entities but is numerically pluralistic in acknowledging a multiplicity of independent reals.—*L.W.*

New Academy: Name commonly given to what is also called the Third Academy, started by Carneades (215-125 B.C.) who substituted a theory of probability for the principle of doubt which had been introduced into Plato's School by Arcesilaus, the originator of the Second or Middle Academy. The Academy later veered toward eclecticism and eventually was merged with Neo-Platonism.—*J.J.R.*

Newton's Method: The method of procedure in natural philosophy as formulated by Sir Isaac Newton, especially in his Rules of Reasoning in Philosophy (*Mathematical Principles of Natural Philosophy*, Book III). These rules are as follows: "I. We are to admit no more causes of natural things than such as are both true and sufficient to explain their appearances. II. Therefore to the same natural effects we must, as far as possible, assign the same causes. III. The qualities of bodies, which admit neither intension nor remission of degrees, and which are found to belong to all bodies within the reach of our experiments, are to be esteemed the universal qualities of all bodies whatsoever. IV. In experimental philosophy we are to look upon propositions collected by general induction from phaenomena as accurately or very nearly true, notwithstanding any contrary hypotheses that may be imagined, till such time as other phaenomena occur, by which they may either be made more accurate, or liable to exceptions." To this passage should be appended another statement from the closing pages of the same work: "I do not make hypotheses; for whatever is not deduced from the phaenomena is to be called an hypothesis; and hypotheses, whether metaphysical or physical, whether of occult qualities or mechanical, have no place in experimental philosophy."—*A.C.B.*

Nichiren: (Risshō daishi, 1222-1282): Nichiren (which means "sun-lotus," *nichi* meaning sun, the sunlight of the true faith, and also for Japan; *ren* meaning lotus, also referring to the *Lotus Sūtra*) practiced the Amidist *nembutsu,* calling on the name of Amida for assistance, but after a while began to doubt whether it would work.

Spending ten years in the monastery at Mount Hiei, he decided that the old-fashioned Tendai doctrine of Saicho was better than Amidist. Nichiren's attempts to purify Tendai resulted in his expulsion.

Rather than calling on the name of one single Buddha alone, according to Nichiren, a better nembutsu would be to call upon the entire *Lotus Sūtra*, which taught the essential oneness of the three bodies of the Buddha (transformation, bliss, and law). The devout believer was counseled to say: "reverence to the wonderful Law of the *Lotus*" (*namu myōhō renge-kyō*). This became the slogan of the Nichiren movement.

Buddhist history, he taught, divides into (1) *shōbō*, the True Law, Hinayana, lasting a thousand years from the time of Buddha's death, which he reckoned on the Chinese fashion to be 947 B.C.; (2) *zōbō*, the Image Law, Mahayana; and (3) *mappō*, the End of the Law, beginning around 1050 A.D.

The most outstanding Buddhist group today is Sōka Gakkai ("Value Creating Study Group"). It claims more than ten million members in Japan alone, making it the largest single religious organization in the land. Sōka Gakkai is based on the Nichiren True Sect branch.—*S.E.N.*

Nicht-Ich: (Ger. *non-ego*) Anything which is not the subjective self. Fichte accounted for the not-self in terms of the ontologically posited subjective self. The not-self is the external, outer world opposed to the ego.—*H.H.*

Nicolai, Friedrich: (1733-1811) Was one of the followers of Leibniz-Wolffian school which developed an eclectic reconciliation of rationalism and empiricism in a popular form that served to lay a foundation for the Kantian critical philosophy.—*L.E.D.*

Nicomachus: Of Gerasa in Arabia, a Neo-Pythagorean (*q.v.*) philosopher of the second century.—*M.F.*

Nidrā: (Skr.) Sleep. In Indian philosophy, particularly the Yoga (*q.v.*), not considered void of mental activity.—*K.F.L.*

Nietzsche, Friedrich: (1844-1900) Nietzsche's discovery and description of "resentment," to mention only one of his major achievements, stamps him as one of the philosophical psychologists of the last century. His critique of the antiquated and false values of the educated middle class led pre-war generations to the pursuit of an ethics of more realistic ideals. See *Superman*.

He was the first to recognize a fundamental critical difference between the philosopher and the scientist. He found those genuine ideals in the pre-Socratic period of Greek culture which he regarded as essential standards for the deepening of individuality and real culture in the deepest sense, towards which the special and natural sciences, and professional or academic philosophers failed to contribute. Nietzsche wanted the philosopher to be prophetic, originally forward-looking in the clarification of the problem of existence. Based on a comprehensive critique of the history of Western civilization, that the highest values in religion, morals and philosophy have begun to lose their power, his philosophy gradually assumed the will to power, self-aggrandizement, as the all-embracing principle in inorganic and organic nature, in the development of the mind, in the individual and in society. More interested in developing a philosophy of life than a system of academic philosophy, his view is that only that life is worth living which develops the strength and integrity to withstand the unavoidable sufferings and misfortunes of existence without flying into an imaginary world.

His major works are: *Thus Spake Zarathustra, Beyond Good and Evil*, and *Genealogy of Morals*.—*H.H.*

Nihil est in intellectu quod non prius fuerit in sensu: (Lat.) Nothing is in the intellect which was not first in sense. All the materials, or content, of higher, intellectual cognition are derived from the activity of lower, sense cognition. A principle subscribed to by Aristotle, St. Thomas and Locke; opposed by Plato, St. Augustine and Leibniz (who qualified the proposition by adding: *nisi intellectus ipse*, i.e. except for what is already present as part of the innate nature of the intellect, thus making it possible for Kant to suggest that certain forms of sensibility and reason are prior to sense experience).—*V.J.B.*

Nihil ex nihilo: (Lat.) Nothing comes from nothing; a negative statement of the principle of sufficient reason.—*V.J.B.*

Nihilism: The doctrine that nothing, or nothing of a specified and very general class, exists, or is knowable, or is valuable. Thus Gorgias held that (1) Nothing exists; (2) Even if something did exist it could not be known; (3) Even if it were known this knowledge could not be communicated. Schopenhauer's pessimism and denial of the Will expresses a nihilistic attitude toward the so-called values of the world. As a social doctrine Nihilism is the belief that progress is possible only through the destruction of all social and political organizations. See *Anarchism*.—*C.A.B.*

Nihilism, ethical: The denial of the validity of all distinctions of moral value. As this position involves in effect the denial of possibility of all ethical philosophy, it has seldom been taken by philosophers. In the history of thought, however, a less pure ethical nihilism sometimes appears as an intermediate stage in a philosophy which wishes to deny the validity of all *previous* systems of value as a preliminary to substituting a new one in their places.—*F.L.W.*

Nimbārka: An Indian thinker and theologian of the 12th century A.D., of Vedāntic (*q.v.*), Vishnuite persuasion, who assumed the world and the human soul to be essentially and eternally different from Vishnu, yet constituting a certain unity with him because of complete dependence.—*K.F.L.*

Nirguna: (Skr.) "Devoid of qualities" (cf. *guna*), predicated as early as the Upanishads (*q.v.*) of the Absolute as its in-it-self aspect (cf. *saguna*). The highest reality is conceived to be of such fulness, such transcendence that it has no part in the manifold of the phenomenal which is mere *māyā* (*q.v.*) in Śaṅkara's (*q.v.*) philosophy in so far as it is esoteric.—*K.F.L.*

Nirvana: (Skr. blown out) The complete extinction of

individuality, without loss of consciousness, in the beatific rejoining of the liberated with the metaphysical world-ground. A term used principally by Buddhists though denoting a state the attainment of which has been counselled from the Upanishads (q.v.) on as the *summum bonum*. It is invariably defined as a condition in which all pain, suffering, mental anguish and, above all, *saṁsāra* (q.v.) have ceased. It is doubtful that complete extinction of life and consciousness or absolute annihilation is meant.—*K.F.L.*

Nisus: The creative principle of emergent evolution. See *Emergent Evolution.*—*R.B.W.*

Nitya-vāda: (Skr.) The Vedāntic (q.v.) theory (*vāda*) which asserts that reality is eternal (*nitya*), change being unreal.—*K.F.L.*

Niyama: (Skr.) The imposing on oneself of good and kind habits, including bathing, eating clean food, steeling the body, contentedness, cheerfulness, study, and piety.—*K.F.L.*

Noema: (Ger. *Noema*) In Husserl: The objective sense of a noesis, together with the character of the sense as posited in a certain manner, as given or emptily intended in a certain manner, etc. For every dimension of the noesis there is a corresponding dimension of the noema. See note under *noesis*.—*D.C.*

Noematic: (Ger. *noematisch*) In Husserl: Of or pertaining to noema. *Noematic sense:* see *Sense*.—*D.C.*

Noesis: (Gr. *Noesis*) In Husserl: 1. That current in the stream of consciousness which is intrinsically intentional in that it points to an object as beyond itself. The noesis animates the intrinsically non-intentional hyletic current in the stream. (see *Hyle*). 2. A particular instance of the *ego cogito. Note*: In Husserl's usage, *noesis* and *noema* are very rarely restricted to the sphere of "thinking" or "intellect" (however defined) but are rather extended to all kinds of consciousness.—*D.C.*

In Greek philosophers: The exercise of nous, or reason; the activity of intellectual apprehension and intuitive thought. See *Nous; Aristotelianism*.—*G.R.M.*

Noetic: The character some entities have due to their resulting from the activity of *nous* or reason. Thus those concepts which are nonsensuous and non-empirical but are conceived by reason alone are noetic; the noetic aspects of reality are those which are knowable by reason. In a more general sense, "noetic" is equivalent to "cognitive."—*C.A.B.*

(Ger. *noetisch*) In Husserl: Of or pertaining to noesis. See note under *noesis*.—*D.C.*

Nolition: (Lat. *nolo*, I am unwilling) The state or act of negative volition.—*V.J.B.*

Nominal: Having to do with names, nouns, words, or symbols rather than with that which would ordinarily be regarded as symbolized by these verbal forms. See *Nominalism*.—*C.A.B.*

Nominalism: (Lat. *nominalis*, belonging to a name) In scholastic philosophy, the theory that abstract or general terms, or universals, represent no objective real existents, but are mere words or names, mere vocal utterances, "*flatus vocis*." Reality is admitted only to actual physical particulars. Universals exist only *post res*. Opposite of *Realism* (q.v.) which maintains that universals exist *ante res*. First suggested by Boethius in his 6th century Latin translation of the *Introduction to the Categories* (of Aristotle) by Porphyry (A.D. 233-304). Porphyry had raised the question of how Aristotle was to be interpreted on this score, and had decided the question in favor of what was later called nominalism. The doctrine did not receive any prominence until applied to the Sacrament of the Eucharist by Berengar in the 11th century. Berengar was the first scholastic to insist upon the evidence of his senses when examining the nature of the Eucharist. Shortly after, Roscellinus, who had broadened the doctrine to the denial of the reality of all universals and the assertion of the sole reality of physical particulars, was forced by the Council of Soissons to recant. Thereafter, despite Abelard's unsuccessful attempt to reconcile the doctrine with realism by finding a half-way position between the two, nominalism was not again explicitly held until William of Occam (1280-1349) revived it and attempted to defend it within the limits allowed by Church dogma. In the first frankly nominalistic system Occam distinguished between the real and the grammatical meanings of terms or universals. He assigned a real status to universals in the mind, and thus was the first to see that nominalism can have a subjective as well as an objective aspect. He maintained that to our intellects, however, everything real must be some particular individual thing. After Occam, nominalism as an explicitly held doctrine disappeared until recently, when it has been restated in certain branches of *Logical Positivism*.—*J.K.F.*

Non-Being: (1) Non-existence or the non-existent; absence or privation of existence or the existent; (2) absence of determinateness or what is thus indeterminate; (3) unreality or the unreal—either lack of any reality or what is so lacking (absence, negation, or privation of reality), or lack of a particular kind of reality or what is so lacking; otherness or existents of another order of reality than a specified type; failure to fulfill the defining criteria of some category, or what so fails; (4) a category encompassing any of the above. Confusion of non-existence and unreality renders paradoxical the question whether non-being is.—*M.T.K.*

Non causa pro causa, or *false cause*, is the fallacy, incident to the method of proof by *reductio ad absurdum* (q.v.), when a contradiction has been deduced from a number of assumptions, of inferring the negation of one of the assumptions, say M, where actually it is one or more of the other assumptions which are false and the contradiction could have been deduced without use of M. This fallacy was committed, e.g., by Burali-Forti in his paper of 1897 (see *Paradoxes, logical*) when he inferred the existence of ordinal numbers, *a*, *b* such that *a* is neither less than, equal to, nor greater than *b*, upon having deduced what is now known as Burali-Forti's paradox from the contrary assumption: he had used without question the assumption that there is a class of all ordinal numbers.—*A.C.*

Non-centre theory: Ascribes the unity of mind to the fact a number of contemporary mental events are directly interrelated in certain characteristic ways. (Broad).—*H.H.*

Non-contradiction, law of: Same as *Contradiction, law of (q.v.).—A.C.*

Non-ego: The outer world that has no independent self-existence. (Fichte).—*H.H.*

Non-Euclidean geometry: Euclid's postulates for geometry included one, the *parallel postulate,* which was regarded from earliest times (perhaps even by Euclid himself) as less satisfactory than the others. This may be stated as follows (not Euclid's original form but an equivalent one): *Through a given point P not on a given line l there passes at most one line, in the plane of P and l, which does not intersect l.* Here "line" means a straight line extended infinitely in both directions (not a line segment).

Attempts to prove the parallel postulate from the other postulates of Euclidean geometry were unsuccessful. The undertaking of Saccheri (1733) to make a proof by *reductio ad absurdum* of the parallel by deducing consequences of its negation did, however, lead to his developing many of the theorems of what is now known as hyperbolic geometry. The proposal that this hyperbolic geometry, in which Euclid's parallel postulate is replaced by its negation, is a system equally valid with the Euclidean originated with Bolyai and Lobachevsky (independently, c. 1825). Proof of the self-consistency of hyperbolic geometry, and thus of the impossibility of Saccheri's undertaking, is contained in results of Cayley (1859) and was made explicit by Klein in 1871; for the two-dimensional case another proof was given by Beltrami in 1868.

The name *non-Euclidean geometry* is applied to hyperbolic geometry and generally to any system in which one or more postulates of Euclidean geometry are replaced by contrary assumptions. (But geometries of more than three dimensions, if they otherwise follow the postulates of Euclid, are not ordinarily called non-Euclidean.)

Closely related to the hyperbolic geometry is the elliptic geometry, which was introduced by Klein on the basis of ideas of Riemann. In this geometry lines are of finite total length and closed, and every two coplanar lines intersect in a unique point.

Still other non-Euclidean geometries are given an actual application to physical space — or rather, space-time — in the General Theory of Relativity.

Contemporary ideas concerning the abstract nature of *mathematics (q.v.)* and the status of applied geometry have important historical roots in the discovery of non-Euclidean geometries.—*A.C.*

G. Saccheri, *Euclides Vindicatus,* translated into English by G. B. Halsted, Chicago and London, 1920. H. P. Manning. *Non-Euclidean Geometry,* 1901, J. L. Coolidge, *The Elements of Non-Euclidean Geometry,* Oxford, 1909.

Non-Naturalistic ethics: Any ethical theory which holds that ethical properties or relations are non-natural.

See *Non-natural properties, Intuitionism.—W.K.F.*

Non-Natural Properties: A notion which plays an important part in recent intuitionistic ethics. A non-natural property is one which is neither natural, as yellow and pleasantness are, nor metaphysical, as absoluteness and being commanded by God are. It is, then, a property which is apprehended, not by sensation or by introspection, but in some other way, and which is somehow non-descriptive, non-expository, or non-existential. It is also said sometimes, *e.g.* by G. E. Moore and W. D. Ross, to be a consequential property, i.e. a property which a thing has in virtue of its having another property, as when an experience is good in virtue of being pleasant. See *Intuitionism.—W.K.F.*

Non sequitur is any fallacy which has not even the deceptive appearance of valid reasoning, or in which there is a complete lack of connection between the premisses advanced and the conclusion drawn. By some, however, *non sequitur* is identified with Aristotle's *fallacy of the consequent,* which includes the two fallacies of *denial of the antecedent* (q.v.) and *affirmation of the consequent (q.v.).—A.C.*

Noology: (Gr. *nous,* Mind; *logos,* Science) A term variously used, but without common acceptance, for the science of mind or of its noetic function. According to several 17th century German writers (Colovius, Mejerus, Wagnerus, Zeidlerus) it is the science of the first principles of knowledge. Crusius identified it with psychology. According to Kant it is the rationalistic theory of innate ideas. For Bentham "noological" is a synonym of logical. Noology is the field of mental science in which the will does not function in the production of mental events; that branch of psychology concerned with the field of purely mental change. For Hamilton it is the science of the noetic, *i.e.* the function and content of intellectual intuition or pure reason. Eucken distinguished noological method from the psychological and cosmological. Its object is the Spiritual Life, *i.e.* the source of Reality, and the self-contained goal in which man participates. For H. Gomperz it is the science that mediates between logic and psychology.—*W.L.*

Norm: (Lat. *norma,* rule) (a) General: Standard for measure. Pattern. Type. (b) In ethics: Standard for proper conduct. Rule for right action. (c) In axiology: Standard for judging value or evaluation. (d) In aesthetics: Standard for judging beauty or art. Basis for criticism. (e) In logic: Rule for valid inference. (f) In psychology: Class average test score.—*A.J.B.*

Normative: (Lat. *normatus,* pp. of *normo,* square) Constituting a standard; regulative. Having to do with an established ideal. In scientific method: concerning those sciences which have subject matters containing values, and which set up norms or rules of conduct, such as ethics, aesthetics, politics. The ideal formulation of any science. Opposite of empirical.—*J.K.F.*

Nota notae est nota rei ipsius: (Lat.) That which falls within the comprehension of a "note," i.e. a known component of a thing, also falls within the comprehension of the thing; an attempted formulation of the supreme principle of syllogistic reasoning on the basis of comprehension rather than extension; Kant is said to have offered this principle in place of the famous extensivist rule, the *dictum de omni et nulio* (*q.v.*).—*V.J.B.*

Notations, logical: There follows a list of some of the logical symbols and notations found in contemporary usage. In each case the notation employed in articles in this dictionary is given first, afterwards alternative notations, if any.

PROPOSITIONAL CALCULUS (see *Logic, formal*, § 1, and *strict implication*):

pq, the conjunction of p and q, "p and q." Instead of simple juxtaposition of the propositional symbols, a dot is sometimes written between, as $p \cdot q$. Or the common abbreviation for *and* may be employed as a logical symbol, $p \& q$. Or an inverted letter v, usually from a gothic font, may be used. In the Łukasiewicz notation for the propositional calculus, which avoids necessity for parentheses, the conjunction of p and q is Kpq.

$p \vee q$, the inclusive disjunction of p and q, "p or q." Frequently the letter v is from a gothic font. In the Łukasiewicz notation, Apq is employed.

$\sim p$, the negation of p, "not p." Instead of $\sim$, a dash — may be used, written either before the propositional symbol or above it. Heyting adds a short downward stroke at the right end of the dash (a notation which has come to be associated particularly with the intuitionistic propositional calculus and the intuitionistic concept of negation). Also employed is an accent ' after the propositional symbol (but this more usual as a notation for the complement of a class). In the Łukasiewicz notation, the negation of p is Np.

$p \supset q$, the material implication of q by p, "if p then q." Also employed is a horizontal arrow, $p \rightarrow q$. the Łukasiewicz notation is Cpq.

$p \equiv q$, the material equivalence of p and q, "p if and only if q." Another notation which has sometimes been employed is $p \supset \subset q$. Other notations are a double horizontal arrow, with point at both ends; and two horizontal arrows, one above the other, one pointing forward and the other back. The Łukasiewicz notation is Epq.

$p + q$, the exclusive disjunction of p and q, "p or q but not both." Also sometimes used is the sign of material equivalence $\equiv$ with a vertical or slanting line across it (non-equivalence). In connection with the Łukasiewicz notation, Rpq has been employed.

$p \mid q$, the alternative denial of p and q, "not both p and q." —For the dual connective, joint denial ("neither p nor q"), a downward arrow has been used.

$p \, 3 \, q$, the strict implication of q by p, "p strictly implies q."

$p = q$, the strict equivalence of p and q, "p strictly implies q and q strictly implies p." Some recent writers employ, for strict equivalence, instead of Lewis's $=$, a sign similar to the sign of material equivalence, $\equiv$, but with four lines instead of three.

Mp, "p is possible." This is Łukasiewicz's notation and has been used especially in connection with his three-valued propositional calculus. For the different notion of possibility which is appropriate to the calculus of strict implication, Lewis employs a diamond.

CLASSES (see *class,* and *logic, formal*, §§ 7, 9):

$x \epsilon a$, "x is a member of the class a," or, "x is an a." For the negation of this, sometimes a vertical line across the letter epsilon is employed, or a $\sim$ above it.

$a \subset b$, the inclusion of the class a in the class b, "a is a subclass of b." This notation is usually employed in such a way that $a \subset b$ does not exclude the possibility that $a = b$. Sometimes, however, the usage is that $a \subset b$ ("a is a proper subclass of b") does exclude that $a = b_i$ and in that case another notation is used when it is not meant that $a = b$ is excluded, the sign $=$ being either surcharged upon the sign $\subset$ or written below it (or a single horizontal line below the $\subset$ may take the place of $=$).

$\exists \mid a$, "the class a is not empty [has at least one member]," or, "a's exist."

ιx, or $\iota' x$, or $[x]$—the unit class of x, i.e., the class whose single member is x.

V, the universal class. Where the algebra of classes is treated in isolation, the digit 1 is often used for the universal class.

Λ, the null or empty class. Where the algebra of classes is treated in isolation, the digit 0 is often used.

$-a$, the complement of a, or class of non-members of the class a. An alternative notation is a'.

$a \cup b$, the logical sum, or union, of the classes a and b. Alternative notation, $a + b$.

$a \cap b$, the logical product, or intersection, or common part, of the classes a and b. Alternative notation, ab.

RELATIONS (see *Relation,* and *Logic, formal,* § 8) (where a notation used in connection with relations is here given as identical with a corresponding notation for classes, the relational notation will also often be found with a dot added to distinguish it from the one for classes):

xRy, "x has [or stands in, or bears] the relation R to y."

$R \subset S$, "the relation R is contained in [implies] the relation S."

$\exists ! R$, "the relation R is not null [holds in at least one instance]."

A downward arrow placed between (*e.g.*) x and y denotes the relation which holds between x and y (in that order) and in no other case.

V, the universal relation. Schröder uses 1.

Λ, the null relation. Schröder uses 0.

$-R$, the contrary, or negation, of the relation R. The dash may also be placed over the letter R (or other symbol denoting a relation) instead of before it.

$R \cup S$, the logical sum of the relations R and S, "R or S." Schröder uses $R + S$.

$R \cap S$, the logical product of the relations R and S, "R and S." Schröder uses $R \cdot S$.

I, the relation of identity—so that xIy is the same as $x = y$. Schröder uses 1'.

J, the relation of diversity—so that xJy is the same as $x \neq y$. Schröder uses 0'.

A breve $\smile$ is placed over the symbol for a relation to denote the converse relation. An alternative notation for the converse of R is $\mathrm{Cnv}\,{}^{\backprime}R$.

$R + S$, the relative sum of R and S. Schröder adds a leftward hook at the bottom of the vertical line in the sign $+$.

$R \mid S$, the relative product of R and S. Schröder uses a semicolon to symbolize the relative product, but the vertical bar, or sometimes a slanted bar, is now the usual notation.

R^2, the square of the relation R, i.e., $R \mid R$. Similarly for higher powers of a relation, as R^3, etc.

$R{}^{\backprime}y$, the (unique) x such that xRy, "the R of y." Frequently the inverted comma is of a bold square (bold gothic) style.

$R``b$, the class of $x$'s which bear the relation $R$ to at least one member of the class $b$, "the $R$'s of the $b$'s." Then $R``\iota y$, or $R``\iota{}^{\backprime}y$, is the class of x's such that xRy, "the R's of y."

A forward pointing arrow is placed over $(e.g.)$ R to denote the relation of $R``\iota y$ to y. Similarly a backward pointing arrow placed over R denotes the relation of *the class of y's such that xRy* to x.

An upward arrow placed between $(e.g.)$ a and b denotes the relation which holds between x and y if and only if $x \epsilon a$ and $y \epsilon b$.

The left half of an upward arrow placed between $(e.g.)$ a and R denotes the relation which holds between x and y if and only if $x \epsilon a$ and xRy, in other words, the relation R with its domain limited to the class a.

The right half of an upward arrow placed between $(e.g.)$ R and b denotes the relation which holds between x and y if and only if xRy and $y \epsilon b$; in other words the relation R with its converse domain limited to b.

The right half of a double—upward and downward—arrow placed between $(e.g.)$ R and a denotes the relation which holds between x and y if and only if xRy and both x and y are members of the class a; in other words, the relation R with its field limited to a.

$D{}^{\backprime}R$, the domain of R.

$\mathfrak{C}{}^{\backprime}R$, the converse domain of R.

$C{}^{\backprime}R$, the field of R.

R_{po}, the proper ancestral of R—ie., the relation which holds between x and y if and only if x bears the first or some higher power of the relation R to y (where the first power of R is R).

R_* the ancestral of R—i.e., the relation which holds between x and y if and only if x bears the zero or some higher power of the relation R to y (where the zero power of R is taken to be, either I, or I with its field limited to the field of R).

QUANTIFIERS (see *Quantifiers*, and *Logic, formal*, §§ 3, 6):

(x), universal quantification with respect to x — so that $(x)M$ may be read "for every x, M." An alternative notation occasionally met with, instead of (x), is $(\forall x)$, usually with the inverted A from a gothic or other special font. Another notation is composed of a Greek capital pi with the x placed either after it, or before it, or as a subscript. — Negation of the universal quantifier is

sometimes expressed by means of a dash, or horizontal line, over it.

(Ex), existential quantification with respect to x — so that $(Ex)M$ may be read "there exists an x such that M." The E which forms part of the notation may also be inverted; and, whether inverted or not, the E is frequently taken from a gothic or other special font. An alternative notation employs a Greek capital sigma with x either after it or as a subscript.—Negation of the existential quantifier is sometimes expressed by means of a dash over it.

$\supset_x$, formal implication with respect to x. See definition in the article *logic, formal*, § 3.

$\equiv_x$, formal equivalence with respect to x. See definition in *logic, formal*, § 3.

Λ_x. See definition in *logic, formal*, § 3.

$\supset_{xy}$, or $\supset_{x,y}$—formal implication with respect to x and y. Similarly for formal implication with respect to three or more variables.

$\equiv_{xy}$, or $\equiv_{x,y}$—formal equivalence with respect to x and y. Similarly for formal equivalence with respect to three or more variables.

ABSTRACTION, DESCRIPTIONS (see articles of those titles):

λx, functional abstraction with respect to x—so that $\lambda x{}^{\backprime}M$ may be read "the (monadic) function whose value for the argument x is M."

$\hat{x}$, class abstraction with respect to x — so that $\hat{x}\,M$ may be read "the class of x's such that M." An alternative notation, instead of $\hat{x}$, is $x\exists$.

$\hat{x}\hat{y}$, relation abstraction with respect to x and y — so that $\hat{x}\hat{y}M$ may be read "the relation which holds between $\hat{x}$ and $\hat{y}$ if and only if M."

(ιx), description with respect to x—so that $(\iota x)M$ may be read "the x such that M."

$E!$ is employed in connection with descriptions to denote existence, so that $E!(\iota x)M$ may be read "there exists a unique x such that M."

OTHER NOTATIONS:

$F(x)$, the result of application of the (monadic, propositional or other) function F to the argument x—the value of the function F for the argument x—"F of x." Sometimes the parentheses are omitted, so that the notation is Fx.—See the articles *function*, and *propositional function*.

$F(x, y)$ the result of application of the (dyadic) function F to the arguments x and y. Similarly for larger numbers of arguments.

$x = y$, the identity or equality of x and y, "x equals y." See *logic, formal*, §§ 3, 6, 9.

$x \neq y$, negation of $x = y$.

$\vdash$ is the assertion sign. See *assertion, logical*.

Dots (frequently printed as bold, or bold square, dots) are used in the punctuation of logical formulas, to avoid or replace parentheses. There are varying conventions for this purpose.

$\rightarrow$ is used to express definitions, the definiendum being placed to the left and the definiens to the right. An alternative notation is the sign $=$ (or, in connection with the propositional calculus, $\equiv$) with the letters Df, or df, written above it, or as a subscript, or separately after the definiens.

Quotation marks, usually single quotes, are employed as a means of distinguishing the name of a symbol or formula from the symbol or formula itself (see *syntax, logical*). A symbol or formula between quotation marks is employed as a name of that particular symbol or formula. E.g., *'p'* is a name of the sixteenth letter of the English alphabet in small italic type.

The reader will observe that this use of quotation marks has not been followed in the present article, and in fact that there are frequent inaccuracies from the point of view of strict preservation of the distinction between a symbol and its name. These inaccuracies are of too involved a character to be removed by merely supplying quotation marks at appropriate places. But it is thought that there is no point at which real doubt will arise as to the meaning intended.—*Alonzo Church*

Nothing: Literally, not a thing. According to Kant, emptiness of concept, object or intuition. According to Hegel, the immediate, indeterminate notion of being. According to Peirce, that which possesses contrary attributes.—*J.K.F.*

In translation into logical notation, the word *nothing* is usually to be represented by the negation of an existential quantifier. Thus "nothing has the property F" becomes "$\sim(Ex)F(x)$."—*A.C.*

Notion: (Ger. *Begriff*) This is a technical term in the writings of Hegel, and as there used it has a dual reference. On one side, it refers to the essence or nature of the object of thought; on the other side, it refers to the true thought of that essence or nature. These two aspects of the Notion are emphasized at length in the third part of the *Logic* (The Doctrine of the Notion), where it is dialectically defined as the synthesis of Being and Essence under the form of the Idea *(Die Idee)*.—*G.W.C.*

Notiones communes: Cicero's translation of the phrase *koinai ennoiai,* by which the Stoics designated such notions as good, evil, and the existence of God, which they regarded as common to all men, and as, in some sense, natural (*physikai*) or implanted (*emphytai*), though not, perhaps, in the sense of being literally innate.—*W.K.F.*

Noumenal World: The real world as opposed to the appearance world. Kant said of the noumenal realm that it cannot be known.—*V.F.*

Noumenon: (Gr. *noumenon*) In Kant: An object or power transcending experience whose existence is theoretically problematic but must be postulated by practical reason. In theoretical terms Kant defined the noumenon positively as "the object of a non-sensuous intuition," negatively as "not an object of the sensuous intuition;" but since he denied the existence of any but sensuous intuitions, the noumenon remained an unknowable "x." In his practical philosophy, however, the postulation of a noumenal realm is necessary in order to explain the possibility of freedom. See *Kantianism.*—*O.F.K.*

Noun: In English and other natural languages, a word serving as a proper or common *name* (*q.v.*).—*A.C.*

Nous: (Gr. *nous*) Mind, especially the highest part of mind, viz. reason; the faculty of intellectual (as distinct from sensible) apprehension and of intuitive thought. In its restricted sense nous denotes the faculty of apprehending the first principles of science, the forms, and the eternal intelligible substances, and is thus distinguished from discursive thought. In this sense nous is regarded as the essence of the divine being. In man Aristotle distinguishes between the nous *pathetikos,* or passive reason, and a higher active reason, called by the commentators nous *poietikos,* which alone is truly divine and eternal, and which is related to the nous *pathetikos* as form to matter. See *Aristotelianism.*—*G.R.M.*

Null class: See *Logic, formal,* § 7.

Number: The number system of mathematical analysis may be described as follows—with reference, not to historical, but to one possible logical order.

First are the *non-negative integers* 0, 1, 2, 3, . . ., for which the operations of addition and multiplication are determined. They are ordered by a relation *not greater than*—which we shall denote by R—so that e.g., $0R0$, $0R3$, $2R3$, $3R3$, $57R218$, etc.

These are extended by introducing, for every pair of non-negative integers a, b, with b different from 0, the fraction a/b, subject to the following conditions (which can be shown to be consistent): (1) $a/1 = a$; (2) $a/b = c/d$ if and only if $ad = bc$; (3) $a/b\,R\,c/d$ if and only if $ad\,R\,bc$; (4) $a/b + c/d = (ad + bc)/bd$; (5) $(a/b)\,(c/d) = ac/bd$. The resulting system is that of the *non-negative rational numbers,* which are compactly ordered but not continuously ordered (see *continuity*) by the relation R (as extended).

Then the next step is to introduce, for every non-negative rational number r, a corresponding negative rational number $-r$, subject to the conditions: (1) $-r = -s$ if and only if $r = s$; (2) $-r = s$ if and only if $r = 0$ and $s = 0$; (3) $-r\,R\,-s$ if and only if $s\,R\,r$; (4) $-r\,R\,s$; (5) $s\,R\,-r$ if and only if $r = 0$ and $s = 0$; (6) $-r + s = s + -r = $ either t, where $r + t = s$, or $-t$ where $s + t = r$; (7) $-r + -s = -(r + s)$; (8) $(-r)\,s = s(-r) = -(rs)$; (9) $(-r)\,(-s) = rs$. Here r, s, t are variables whose range is the non-negative rational numbers. The extended system, comprising both non-negative rational numbers and negative rational numbers is the system of *rational numbers*—which are compactly ordered but not continuously ordered by the relation R (as extended).

If we make the *minimum* extension of the system of rational numbers which will render the order continuous, the system of *real numbers* results. Addition and multiplication of real numbers are uniquely determined by the meanings already given to addition and multiplication of rational numbers and the requirement that addition of, or multiplication by, a fixed real number (on right or left) shall be a continuous function (see *continuity*). Subtraction and division may be introduced as inverses of addition and multiplication respectively.

Finally, the *complex numbers* are introduced as numbers $a + bi$, where a and b are real numbers. There is no ordering relation, but addition and multiplication are determined as follows:

$$(a+bi) + (c+di) = (a + c) + (b + d)i.$$
$$(a + bi)(c + di) = (ac - bd) + (ad + bc)i.$$

In particular i (i.e., $0 + 1i$) multiplied by itself is -1. A number of the form $a + 0i$ may be identified with the real number a; other complex numbers are called *imaginary numbers*, and those of the form $0 + bi$ are called *pure imaginaries*.

(It is, of course, not possible to *define i* as "the square root of -1." The foregoing statement corresponds to taking i as a new, undefined, symbol. But there is an alternative method, of *logical construction*, in which the complex numbers are defined as ordered pairs (a, b) of real numbers, and i is then defined as $(0, 1)$.)

In a mathematical development of the real number system or the complex number system, an appropriate set of postulates may be the starting point. Or the non-negative integers may first be introduced (by postulates or otherwise — see *arithmetic, foundations of*) and from these the above outlined extensions may be provided for by successive logical constructions, in any one of several alternative ways.

The important matter is not the definition of *number* (or of particular numbers), which may be made in various ways more or less indifferently, but the internal structure of the number *system*.

For the notions of *cardinal number, relation-number*, and *ordinal number*, see the articles of these titles.—*Alonzo Church*

R. Dedekind, *Essays on the Theory of Numbers*, translated by W. W. Beman, Chicago, 1901. E. V. Huntington, *A set of postulates for real algebra*, Transactions of the American Mathematical Society, vol. 6 (1905), pp. 17-41. E. V. Huntington, *A set of postulates for ordinary complex algebra*, ibid., pp. 209-229. E. Landau, *Grundlagen der Analysis,* Leipzig 1930.

Numinous: A word coined from the Latin "numen" by Rudolf Otto to signify the absolutely unique state of mind of the genuinely religious person who feels or is aware of something mysterious, terrible, awe-inspiring, holy and sacred. This feeling or awareness is a *mysterium tremendum*, beyond reason, beyond the good or the beautiful. This numinous is an *a priori* category and is the basis of man's cognition of the Divine. See his book *The Idea of the Holy* (rev. ed., 1925).—*V.F.*

Nuñez Regüeiro, Manuel: (1880-1952) Born in Uruguay, Professor of Philosophy at the National University of the Litoral in Argentina. Author of about twenty-five books, among which the following are the most important from a philosophical point of view: *Fundamentos de la Anterosofía*, 1925; *Anterosofía Racional*, 1926; *De Nuevo Hablo Jesús*, 1928; *Filosofía Integral*, 1932; *Del Conocimiento y Progreso de Sí Mismo*, 1934; *Tratado de Metalogica, o Fundamentos de Una Nueva Metodología*, 1936; *Suma Contra Una Nueva Edad Media*, 1938; *Metafísica y Ciencia*, 1941; *La Honda Inquietud*, 1915; *Conocimiento y Creencia*, 1916.

Three fundamental questions and a tenacious effort to answer them run throughout the entire thought of Núñez Regüeiro, namely the three questions of Kant: What can I know? What must I do? What can I expect? Science as such does not write finis to anything. We experience in science the same realm of contradictions and inconsistencies which we experience elsewhere. Fundamentally, this chaos is of the nature of dysteleology. At the root of the conflict lies a crisis of values. The problem of doing is above all a problem of valuing. From a point of view of values, life ennobles itself, man lifts himself above the trammels of matter, and the world becomes meaningful. Is there a possibility for the realization of this ideal? Has this plan ever been tried out? History offers us a living example: The Fact of Jesus. He is the only possible expectation. In him and through him we come to fruition and fulfilment. Núñez Regüeiro's philosophy is fundamentally religious.—*J.A.F.*

Nyāya: (Skr.) One of the great systems of Indian philosophy (*q.v.*) going back to the Nyāyasutras of Gotama (*q.v.*) and dealing with the logical approach to reality in a science of reasoning and epistemology designed to accomplish the practical aims of all Indian speculation. Having established perception (*pratyakṣa*), inference (*anumāna*), comparison (*upamāna*), and testimony (*śabda*) as sources of valid knowledge or truth, a doctrine of logical realism is arrived at in which the objective world is conceived independent of thought and mind.—*K.F.L.*

O

Object: (Lat. *objectus,* pp. of *objicere,* to throw over against) In the widest sense, object is that towards which consciousness is directed, whether cognitively or conatively. The cognitive or epistemological object of mind is anything perceived, imagined, conceived or thought about. See *Epistemological Object.* The conative object is anything desired, avoided or willed.—*L.W.*

Objectivation: See *Objectivize.*

Objective: (a) Possessing the character of a real object existing independently of the knowing mind in contrast to subjective. See *Subjective.* (b) In Scholastic terminology beginning with Duns Scotus and continuing into the 17th and 18th centuries, objective designated anything existing as idea or representation in the mind without independent existence. (cf. Descartes, *Meditations,* III; Spinoza, *Ethics,* I, prop. 30; Berkeley's *Siris,* § 292). The change from sense (b) to (a) was made by Baumgarten. See R. Eucken, *Geschichte der Philosophischen Terminologie,* p. 68.—*L.W.*

Objective idealism: A name for that philosophy which is based on the theory that both the subject and the object of knowledge are equally real and equally manifestations of the absolute or ideal. Earlier employed to described Schelling's philosophy. Used independently by Charles S. Peirce (1839-1914) and A. N. Whitehead (1861-1947) to describe their varieties of realism. Subjective idealism supposes the world to consist of exemplifications of universals which have their being in the mind. Objective idealism supposes the world to consist of exemplifications of universals which have their being independent of the mind.—*J.K.F.*

Objective Reference: The self-transcendence of an immediately given content whereby it is directed toward an object. See *Object.*—*L.W.*

Objective Relativism: Epistemological theory which ascribes real objectivity to all perspectives and appearances of an object of perception. (See A. E. Murphy, "Objective Relativism in Dewey and Whitehead," *Philosophical Review,* Vol. XXXVI, 1927)—*L.W.*

Objective rightness: An action is objectively right if it is what the agent really should do, and not merely what he thinks he should do. See *Subjective rightness.*—*W.K.F.*

Objective test: Any test, whether standardized or not, which meets the requirements of a measuring instrument, permitting no reasonable doubt as to the correctness or incorrectness of the answers given.—*J.E.B.*

Objectivism: 1. Realism (*q.v.*)

2. Objective Idealism (*q.v.*)

3. Logic, Aesthetics, Ethics: The view that the mind possesses objects, norms, or meanings of universal validity. The opposite of subjectivism, psychologism, solipsism, individualism (*q.v.*).—*W.L.*

Objectivism, epistemological: Doctrine maintaining that everything apprehended is independent of the apprehender. (Montague.)—*H.H.*

Objectivistic ethics: The view that ethical truths are not relative, that there are certain actions which are right or certain objects which are good for all individuals alike. See *Relativism.*—*W.K.F.*

Objectivize: The mental process whereby a sensation which is in the first instance, a subjective state, is transformed into the perception of an object. See *Introjection.*—*L.W.*

Object language: A language or logistic system *L* is called *object language* relatively to another language (metasystem) *L'* containing notations for formulas of *L* and for syntactical properties of and relations between formulas of *L* (possibly also semantical properties and relations). The language *L'* is called a *syntax language* of *L.*

See *Name relation; Syntax, Logical; Truth, semantical.*—*A.C.*

Obligation: This may be said to be present whenever a necessity of any kind is laid upon any one to do a certain thing. Here the term "obligation" may refer either to the necessity of his doing the act or to the act which it is necessary for him to do. Always, in any case of obligation, there is a kind of necessity for someone to do something. This is true in all cases in which one says, "I was obliged to do that," "I have an obligation to him,"

"You ought to do so and so," "It is our duty to do such and such." It follows that obligation involves a relational structure. One never has an obligation simply, one always has an obligation to do a certain thing. An act is never simply obligatory, it is always obligatory for someone to do.

The necessity involved in an obligation may be of various kinds—sheer physical compulsion, social pressure, prudential necessity, etc. Thus not all obligation is moral, e.g. when one says, "The force of the wind obliged me to take cover." The question is: what sort of necessity is involved in moral obligation? Is moral obligation hypothetical or is it categorical? Hypothetical obligation is expressed in such sentences as "If you want so and so, e.g. happiness, then you must or should do such and such." Here the necessity or obligatoriness is conditional, depending on whether or not one desires the end to which the action enjoined is conducive. Categorical obligation is expressed by simple sentences of the form, "You ought to do such and such." Here the necessity of doing such and such is unconditional.

Many moralists deny that there are any categorical obligations, and maintain that moral obligations are all hypothetical. E.g., John Gay defines obligation as "the necessity of doing or omitting any action in order to be happy." On such views one's obligation to do a certain deed reduces to one's desire to do it or to have that to which it conduces. Obligation and motivation coincide. Hence J.S. Mill identifies sanctions, motives, and sources of obligation.

Other moralists hold that hypothetical obligations are merely pragmatic or prudential, and that moral obligations are categorical (Kant, Sidgwick). On this view obligation and motivation need not coincide, for obligation is independent of motivation. There is, it is said, a real objective necessity or obligation to do certain sorts of action, independently of our desires or motives. Indeed, it is sometimes said (Kant, Sidgwick) that there is no obligation for one to do an action unless one is at least susceptible to an inclination to do otherwise.

This categorical necessity or obligation is regarded by the moralists in question as something peculiar. It is not to be identified with physical, causal, or metaphysical necessity. It is compatible with and even requires freedom to do otherwise. It is a "moral" necessity. "Duty," says Kant, "is the necessity of acting from respect for the (moral) law." It is a unique and indefinable kind of necessity, and the relational structure which is involved cannot be explained in any other terms; it must be intuited to be understood (T. Reid, Sidgwick, W. D. Ross). See *Ethics, Value, Sanctions.—W.K.F.*

Oblivescence: (Lat. *oblivesci,* to forget) The gradual obliteration of a memory.—*L.W.*

Observation: (Lat. *ob + servare,* to save, keep, observe) The act of becoming aware of objects through the sense organs and of interpreting them by means of concepts. See *Sensation.—A.C.B.*

Observational Judgment: Any judgment, particular or general, which is based on observation or experience, but especially, and more strictly, any particular judg-

ment based on sense-perception, e.g. "That is a round tower."—*W.K.F.*

Obversion: See *Logic, formal* § 4.

Occasion: (Lat. *occasio,* a happening) The agency of action. The proximate or historical cause. Any actual thing or event considered as the historical cause of another. The occasion of anything is its antecedent reference; the cause, its logical reference. Syn. with actual. See *Cause, Chance.—J.K.F.*

Occasional causes, the doctrine of: The doctrine that in some or in all cases of apparent causal connection, the apparent cause does not itself actually bring about the apparent effect, but only serves as the occasion on which some other agent or force brings about that effect. Thus Malebranche and the other Occasionalists held that in all cases where mind and body seem to be causally connected, the truth is not that the one is acting on the other (which is impossible because they differ essentially in kind), but that an event in the one is taken by God as an occasion for his producing an event in the other. Again, Schopenhauer maintained that every natural cause is only an occasional cause for the manifestation of the Will.—*W.K.F.*

Occasionalism: A theory of knowledge and of voluntary control of action, in which mind and matter are noninteractive but events in one realm occur in correspondence with events in the other realm. Thus, God sees to it that an idea of noise occurs in a mind on the occasion of the occurrence of a physical noise; or, He makes a physical event happen when a mind wishes it. See *Psycho-Physical Parallelism.—V.J.B.*

Ockhamism: A term in common use since the early 15th century, indicating doctrines and methods associated with those of the English Franciscan theologian William of Ockham (died 1349). It is currently applied by neoscholastic writers as a blanket designation for a great variety of late medieval and early modern attitudes such as are destructive of the metaphysical principles of Thomism, even though they may not be directly traceable to Ockham's own writings.

Three senses of "Ockhamism" may be distinguished: (1) *Logical,* indicating usage of the terminology and technique of logical analysis developed by Ockham in his *Summa totius logicae;* in particular, use of the concept of supposition *(suppositio)* in the significative analysis of terms. (2) *Epistemological,* indicating the thesis that universality is attributable only to terms and propositions, and not to things as existing apart from discourse. (3) *Theological,* indicating the thesis that no theological doctrines, such as those of God's existence or of the immortality of the soul, are evident or demonstrable philosophically, so that religious doctrine rests solely on faith, without metaphysical or scientific support. It is in this sense that Luther is often called an Ockhamist.

Bibliography: B. Geyer, *Ueberwegs Grundriss d. Gesch. d. Phil.,* Bd. II (11th ed., Berlin 1928), pp. 571-612 and 781-786; N. Abbagnano, *Guglielmo di Ockham* (Lanciano, Italy, 1931); E. A. Moody, *The Logic of William of Ockham* (N.Y. & London, 1935); F.

Ehrle, Peter von Candia (Muenster, 1925); G. Ritter, *Studien zur Spaetscholastik*, I-II (Heidelberg, 1921-1922).—*E.A.M.*

Om, aum: (Skr.) Mystic, holy syllable as a symbol for the indefinable Absolute. See *Akṣara, Vāc, Śabda.* —*K.F.L.*

Omniscience: In philosophy and theology it means the complete and perfect knowledge of God, of Himself and of all other beings, past, present, and future, or merely possible, as well as all their activities, real or possible, including the future free actions of human beings. —*J.J.R.*

One: Philosophically, not a number but equivalent to unit, unity, individuality, in contradistinction from multiplicity and the manifoldness of sensory experience. In metaphysics, the Supreme Idea (Plato), the absolute first principle (Neo-platonism), the universe (Parmenides), Being as such and divine in nature (Plotinus), God (Nicolaus Cusanus), the soul (Lotze). Religious philosophy (*q.v.*) has favored the designation of the One for the metaphysical world-ground, the ultimate reality, the world-soul, the principle of the world conceived as reason, *nous,* or more personally. The One may be conceived as an independent whole or as a sum, as analytic or synthetic, as principle or ontologically. Except by mysticism, it is rarely declared a fact of sensory experience, while its transcendent or transcendental, abstract nature is stressed, *e.g.,* in epistemology where the ''I'' or self is considered the unitary background of personal experience, the identity of self-consciousness, or the unity of consciousness in the synthesis of the manifoldness of ideas (Kant).—*K.F.L.*

One-one: A relation *R* is *one-many* if for every *y* in the converse domain there is a unique *x* such that *xRy*. A relation *R* is *many-one* if for every *x* in the domain there is a unique *y* such that *xRy*. (See the article *relation*.) A relation is *one-one,* or *one-to-one,* if it is at the same time one-many and many-one. A one-one relation is said to be, or to determine, a *one-to-one correspondence* between its domain and its converse domain.—*A.C.*

On-handedness: (Ger. *Vorhandenheit*) Things exist in the mode of thereness, lying passively in a neutral space. A ''deficient'' form of a more basic relationship, termed at-handedness (Zuhandenheit). (Heidegger.)—*H.H.*

Ontological argument: Name by which later authors, especially Kant, designate the alleged proof for God's existence devised by Anselm of Canterbury. Under the name of God, so the argument runs, everyone understands that greater than which nothing can be thought. Since anything being the greatest and lacking existence is less then the greatest having also existence, the former is not really the greater. The greatest, therefore, has to exist. Anselm has been reproached, already by his contemporary Gaunilo, for unduly passing from the field of logical to the field of ontological or existential reasoning. This criticism has been repeated by many authors, among them Aquinas. The argument has, however, been used, if in a somewhat modified form, by

Duns Scotus, Descartes, and Leibniz.—*R.A.*

Ontological Object: (Gr. *onta,* existing things + *logos,* science) The real or existing object of an act of knowledge as distinguished from the epistemological object. See *Epistemological Object.*—*L.W.*

Ontologism: (Gr. *on,* being) In contrast to psychologism, is called any speculative system which starts philosophizing by positing absolute being, or deriving the existence of entities independently of experience merely on the basis of their being thought, or assuming that we have immediate and certain knowledge of the ground of being or God. Generally speaking any rationalistic, *a priori* metaphysical doctrine; specifically the philosophies of Rosmini-Serbati and Vincenzo Gioberti. As a philosophic method censured by skeptics and critics alike, as a scholastic doctrine formerly strongly supported, revived in Italy and Belgium in the 19th century, but no longer countenanced.—*K.F.L.*

Ontology: (Gr. *on,* being + *logos,* logic) The theory of being *qua* being. For Aristotle, the First Philosophy, the science of the essence of things. Introduced as a term into philosophy by Wolff. The science of fundamental principles; the doctrine of the categories. Ultimate philosophy; rational cosmology. Syn. with metaphysics. See *Cosmology, First Principles, Metaphysics, Theology.*—*J.K.F.*

Operation: (Lat. *operari,* to work) Any act, mental or physical, constituting a phase of the reflective process, and performed with a view to acquiring knowledge or information about a certain subject matter.—*A.C.B.*

In logic, see *Operationism.*

In philosophy of science, see *Pragmatism, Scientific Empiricism.*

Operationism: The doctrine that the meaning of a concept is given by a set of operations.

1. The operational meaning of a term (word or symbol) is given by a semantical rule relating the term to some concrete process, object or event, or to a class of such processes, objects or events.

2. Sentences formed by combining operationally defined terms into propositions are operationally meaningful when the assertions are testable by means of performable operations. Thus, under operational rules, terms have semantical significance; propositions have empirical significance.

Operationism makes explicit the distinction between *formal* (*q.v.*) and *empirical* sentences. Formal propositions are signs arranged according to syntactical rules but lacking operational reference. Such propositions, common in mathematics, logic and syntax, derive their sanction from convention, whereas an empirical proposition is acceptable (1) when its structure obeys syntactical rules and (2) when there exists a concrete procedure (a set of operations) for determining its truth or falsity (*cf. Verification*). Propositions purporting to be empirical are sometimes amenable to no operational test because they contain terms obeying no definite semantical rules. These sentences are sometimes called pseudo-propositions and are said to be operationally meaningless. They may, however, be ''meaningful'' in other ways, *e.g.* emotionally or aesthetically (*cf. Meaning*).

Unlike a formal statement, the "truth" of an empirical sentence is never absolute and its operational confirmation serves only to increase the degree of its validity Similarly, the semantical rule comprising the operational definition of a term never has absolute precision. Ordinarily a term denotes a *class* of operations and the precision of its definition depends upon how definite are the rules governing inclusion in the class.

The difference between Operationism and Logical Positivism (*q.v.*) is one of emphasis. Operationism's stress of empirical matters derives from the fact that it was first employed to purge physics of such concepts as absolute space and absolute time, when the theory of relativity had forced upon physicists the view that space and time are most profitably defined in terms of the operations by which they are measured. Although different methods of measuring length at first give rise to different concepts of length, wherever the equivalence of certain of these measures can be established by other operations, the concepts may legitimately be combined.

In psychology the operational criterion of meaningfulness is commonly associated with a behavioristic point of view. See *Behaviorism*. Since only those propositions which are testable by *public* and *repeatable* operations are admissible in science, the definition of such concepts as mind and sensation must rest upon observable aspects of the organism or its behavior. Operational psychology deals with experience only as it is indicated by the operation of differential behavior, including verbal report. Discriminations, or the concrete differential reactions of organisms to internal or external environmental states, are by some authors regarded as the most basic of all operations.

For a discussion of the role of operational definition in physics, see P. W. Bridgman, *The Logic of Modern Physics,* (New York, 1928) and *The Nature of Physical Theory* (Princeton, 1936). The extension of operationism to psychology is discussed by C. C. Pratt in *The Logic of Modern Psychology* (New York, 1939).

For a discussion and annotated bibliography relating to Operationism and Logical Positivism, see S. S. Stevens, Psychology and the Science of Science, *Psychol. Bull.,* 36, 1939, 221, 263.—*S.S.S*

Ophelimity: Noun derived from the Greek, *ophelimos* (useful), employed by Vilfredo Pareto (1848-1923) in economics as the equivalent of utility, or the capacity to provide satisfaction.—*J.J.R.*

Opinion: (Lat. *opinio,* from *opinor,* to think) An hypothesis or proposition entertained on rational grounds but concerning which doubt can reasonably exist. A belief. See *Hypothesis, Certainty, Knowledge.*—*J.K.F.*

Opposition: (Lat. *oppositus,* pp. of *oppono,* to oppose) Positive actual contradiction. One of Aristotle's Postpredicaments. In logic any contrariety or contradiction, illustrated by the "Square of Opposition." Syn. with: conflict. See *Logic, formal,* § 4.—*J.K.F.*

Optimism: (Lat. *optimus,* the best) The view inspired by wishful thinking, success, faith, or philosophic reflection, that the world as it exists is not so bad or even the best possible, life is good, and man's destiny is bright. Philosophically most persuasively propounded by Leibniz in his *Théodicée,* according to which God in his wisdom would have created a better world had he known or willed such a one to exist. Not even he could remove moral wrong and evil unless he destroyed the power of self-determination and hence the basis of morality. All systems of ethics that recognize a supreme good (Plato and many idealists), subscribe to the doctrines of progressivism (Turgot, Herder, Comte, and others), regard evil as a fragmentary view (Josiah Royce *et al.*) or illusory, or believe in indemnification (Henry David Thoreau) or melioration (Emerson), are inclined optimistically. Practically all theologies advocating a plan of creation and salvation, are optimistic though they make the good or the better dependent on moral effort, right thinking, or belief, promising it in a future existence. Metaphysical speculation is optimistic if it provides for perfection, evolution to something higher, more valuable, or makes room for harmonies or a teleology. See *Pessimism.*—*K.F.L.*

Order: A class is said to be *partially ordered* by a dyadic relation *R* if it coincides with the field of *R,* and *R* is transitive and reflexive, and xRy and yRx never both hold when x and y are different. If in addition *R* is connected, the class is said to be *ordered* (or simply ordered) by *R,* and *R* is called an *ordering relation.*

Whitehead and Russell apply the term *serial relation* to relations which are transitive, irreflexive, and connected (and, in consequence, also asymmetric). However, the use of serial relations in this sense, instead ordering relations as just defined, is awkward in connection with the notion of order for unit classes.

Examples: The relation *not greater than* among real numbers is an ordering relation. The relation *less than* among real numbers is a serial relation. The real numbers are simply ordered by the former relation. In the algebra of classes (*logic, formal* § 7), the classes are partially ordered by the relation of class inclusion.

For explanation of the terminology used in making the above definitions, see the articles *connexity, reflexivity, relation, symmetry, transitivity.*—*A.C*

Order type: See *relation-number.*

Ordinal number: A class *b* is *well-ordered* by a dyadic relation *R* if it is ordered by *R* (see *order*) and, for every class *a* such that $a \subset b$, there is a member *x* of *a,* such that xRy holds for *every* member *y* of *a;* and *R* is then called a *well-ordering relation.* The *ordinal number* of a class *b* well-ordered by a relation *R,* or of a well-ordering relation *R,* is defined to be the *relation-number* (*q.v.*) of *R.*

The ordinal numbers of finite classes (well-ordered by appropriate relations) are called *finite* ordinal numbers. These are 0, 1, 2, . . . (to be distinguished, of course, from the finite cardinal numbers 0, 1, 2, . . .).

The first non-finite (transfinite or infinite) ordinal number is the ordinal number of the class of finite ordinal numbers, well-ordered in their natural order, 0, 1, 2, . . ; it is usually denoted by the small Greek letter omega.—*A.C.*

G. Cantor, *Contributions to the Founding of the Theory of Transfinite Numbers*, translated and with an introduction by P. E. B. Jourdain, Chicago and London, 1915. (new ed. 1941) Whitehead and Russell, *Principia Mathematica*, vol. 3.

Ordinary Language Philosophy: A contemporary school of thought so called because its adherents maintain that ordinary language is adequate to carry on philosophical analysis, and that it is not necessary to construct artificial languages first. The names associated with this viewpoint include John L. Austin (*q.v.*), Ludwig Wittgenstein (*q.v.*), Gilbert Ryle (*q.v.*), and John Wisdom (*q.v.*). Believing that metaphysical statements are meaningless, they try to solve philosophical puzzles by using natural language which, they hold, functions correctly so long as it remains within the limits of its proper use. If people will learn to use the words of ordinary language properly, they will not create metaphysical nonsense. Close similarities to Analytic Philosophy.—*S.E.N.*

Orexis: (Gr. *orexis*) Striving; desire; the conative aspect of mind, as distinguished from the cognitive and emotional (Aristotle).—*G.R.M.*

Organicism: A theory of biology that life consists in the organization or dynamic system of the organism. Opposed to mechanism and vitalism.—*J.K.F.*

Organism: An individual animal or plant, biologically interpreted. A. N. Whitehead uses the term to include also physical bodies and to signify anything material spreading through space and enduring in time. —*R.B.W.*

Organismic Psychology: (Lat. *organum*, from Gr. *organon*, an instrument) A system of theoretical psychology which construes the structure of the mind in organic rather than atomistic terms. See *Gestalt Psychology; Psychological Atomism*.—*L.W.*

Organization: (Lat. *organum*, from Gr. *organon*, work) A structured whole. The systematic unity of parts in a purposive whole. A dynamic system. Order in something actual.—*J.K.F.*

Organon: (Gr. *organon*) The title traditionally given to the body of Aristotle's logical treatises. The designation appears to have originated among the Peripatetics after Aristotle's time, and expresses their view that logic is not a part of philosophy (as the Stoics maintained) but rather the instrument (organon) of philosophical inquiry. See *Aristotelianism*.—*G.R.M.*

In Kant. A system of principles by which pure knowledge may be acquired and established.

Cf. Fr. Bacon's *Novum Organum*.—*O.F.K.*

Oriental Philosophy: A general designation used loosely to cover philosophic tradition exclusive of that grown on Greek soil and including the beginnings of philosophical speculation in Egypt, Arabia, Iran, India, and China, the elaborate systems of India, Greater India, China, and Japan, and sometimes also the religion-bound thought of all these countries with that of the complex cultures of Asia Minor, extending far into antiquity. Oriental philosophy, though by no means presenting a homogeneous picture, nevertheless shares one characteristic, i.e., the practical outlook on life (ethics linked with metaphysics) and the absence of clear-cut distinctions between pure speculation and religious motivation, and on lower levels between folklore, folk-etymology, practical wisdom, prescientific speculation, even magic, and flashes of philosophic insight. Bonds with Western, particularly Greek philosophy have no doubt existed even in ancient times. Mutual influences have often been conjectured on the basis of striking similarities, but their scientific establishment is often difficult or even impossible. Comparative philosophy (see especially the work of Masson-Oursel) provides a useful method. Yet a thorough treatment of Oriental Philosophy is possible only when the many languages in which it is deposited have been more thoroughly studied, the psychological and historical elements involved in the various cultures better investigated, and translations of the relevant documents prepared not merely from a philological point of view or out of missionary zeal, but by competent philosophers who also have some linguistic training. Much has been accomplished in this direction in Indian and Chinese Philosophy (*q.v.*). A great deal remains to be done however before a definitive history of Oriental Philosophy may be written. See also *Arabian*, and *Persian Philosophy*.—*K.F.L.*

Origen: (185-254) The principal founder of Christian theology who tried to enrich the ecclesiastic thought of his day by reconciling it with the treasures of Greek philosophy. Cf. Migne *PL.*—*R.B.W.*

Ormazd: (New Persian) Same as Ahura Mazdāh (*q.v.*), the good principle in Zoroastrianism, and opposed to Ahriman (*q.v.*).—*K.F.L*

Orphic Literature: The mystic writings, extant only in fragments, of a Greek religious-philosophical movement of the 6th century B.C., allegedly started by the mythical Orpheus. In their mysteries, in which mythology and rational thinking mingled, the Orphics concerned themselves with cosmogony, theogony, man's original creation and his destiny after death which they sought to influence to the better by pure living and austerity. They taught a symbolism in which, *e.g.*, the relationship of the One to the many was clearly enunciated, and believed in the soul as involved in reincarnation. Pythagoras, Empedocles, and Plato were influenced by them.—*K.F.L.*

Ortega y Gasset, José: (1883-1955) Born in Madrid, May 9, 1883. Son of Ortega y Munillo, the famous Spanish journalist. Studied at the College of Jesuits in Miraflores and at the Central University of Madrid. In the latter he presented his Doctor's dissertation, *El Milenario*, in 1904, thereby obtaining his Ph.D. degree. After studies in Leipzig, Berlin, Marburg, under the special influence of Hermann Cohen, the great exponent of Kant, who taught him the love for the scientific method and awoke in him the interest in educational philosophy, Ortega came to Spain where, after the death of Nicolás Salmeron, he occupied the professorship of metaphysics at the Central University of Madrid. The following may be considered the most important works of Ortega y Gasset: *Meditaciones del Quijote*, 1914; *El Espectador*, I-VIII, 1916-1935; *El Tema de Nuestro Tiempo*, 1921; *España Invertebrada*, 1922; *Kant*, 1924; *La Deshumanizacion del Arte*, 1925; *Espíritu de la Letra*, 1927; *La Rebelion de las Masas*, 1929; *Goethe desde Adentro*, 1934; *Estudios sobre el Amor*, 1939; *Ensimismamiento y Alteracion*, 1939; *El Libro de las Misiones*, 1940; *Ideas y Creencias*, 1940; and others.

Although brought up in the Marburg school of thought, Ortega is not exactly a neo-Kantian. At the basis of his *Weltanschauung* one finds a denial of the fundamental presuppositions which characterized European Rationalism. It is life and not thought which is primary. Things have a sense and a value which must be affirmed independently. *Things*, however, are to be conceived as the totality of situations which constitute the circumstances of a man's life. Hence, Ortega's first philosophical principle: "I am myself plus my circumstances." Life as a problem, however, is but one of the poles of his formula. Reason is the other. The two together function, not by dialectical opposition, but by necessary coexistence. Life, according to Ortega, does not consist in being, but rather, in coming to be, and as such it is of the nature of direction, program building, purpose to be achieved, value to be realized. In this sense the future as a time dimension acquires new dignity, and even the present and the past become articulate and meaningful only in relation to the future. Even history demands a new point of departure and becomes militant with new visions.—*J.A.F.*

Orthodoxy: Beliefs which are declared by a group to be true and normative. Heresy is a departure from and relative to a given orthodoxy.—*V.F.*

Orthos Logos: See *Right Reason*.

Ostensible Object: (Lat. *ostendere*, to show) The object envisaged by cognitive act irrespective of its actual existence. See *Epistemological Object*.—*L.W.*

Ostensive: (Lat. *ostendere*, to show) Property of a concept or predicate by virtue of which it refers to and is clarified by reference to its instances.—*A.C.B.*

Ostwald, Wilhelm: (1853-1932) German chemist. Winner of the Nobel prize for chemistry in 1909. In *Die Uberwindung des wissenschaftlichen Materialismus* and in *Naturphilosophie*, his two best known works in the field of philosophy, he advocates a dynamic theory in opposition to materialism and mechanism. All properties of matter, and the psychic as well, are special forms of energy.—*L.E.D.*

Other Minds: The philosophical problem, much discussed by contemporary British philosophers such as P. F. Strawson and John Wisdom, or how we can know that anyone besides ourselves is a conscious being. What we think are intelligent beings might be merely automatons acting as if they were conscious. The usual argument to establish the existence of other minds, by analogy, fails when arguments by analogy are attacked in general. Ayer (*q.v.*) defends such arguments. Strawson argues that it is impossible to have a proper notion of mental attributes unless that notion also includes others besides oneself. Wisdom says that every statement has its own logic, but that these logics are to some degree like other logics. He argues that our customary ways of thinking are the source of the philosophical difficulties which arise with this and other topics.—*S.E.N.*

Oupnekhat: Anquetil Duperron's Latin translation of the Persian translation of 50 Upanishads (*q.v.*), a work praised by Schopenhauer as giving him complete consolation.—*K.F.L.*

Outness: A term employed by Berkeley to express the experience of externality, that is the ideas of space and things placed at a distance. Hume used it in the sense of distance. Hamilton understood it as the state of being outside of consciousness in a really existing world of material things.—*J.J.R.*

Overindividual: Term used by H. Münsterberg to translate the German *überindividuell*. The term is applied to any cognitive or value object which transcends the individual subject.—*L.W.*

Owen, Robert: (1771-1858) English socialist and author of *A New View of Society*, advocating a reform of education, society, and the humane treatment of factory workers.—*S.E.N.*

P

Paganism: (Lat. *pagus,* village) The term probably reverts to the designation of villagers who had not yet been reached by the missionary propaganda emanating from populous centers. Fourth-century Christians employed the term to refer to those faiths and practices outside the circumference of the Christian faith.—*V.F.*

Pai chia: The "Hundred Schools," referring to the various tendencies of thought in philosophy, logic, ethics, law, politics, diplomacy, economics, agriculture, military science, etc., in the third and fourth centuries B.C. with Chi Hsia as a center.—*W.T.C.*

Pain: See *Pleasure.*

Painting: A plane surface covered with colors assembled in a given order (M. Denis, 1890).—*L.V.*

Paley, William: (1743-1805) Was an English churchman well known for a number of works in theology. He is also widely remembered in the field of ethics. His *Principles of Moral and Political Philosophy* passed through many editions and served as a text book at Cambridge for many years. As an advocate of the doctrine of expediency, he gave impetus to the later Utilitarian School. He maintained that the beneficial tendency is what makes an action right. See *Utilitarianism.* Cf. W. Paley, *Horae Pauline,* 1790; *View of the Evidences of Christianity,* 1794; *Natural Theology,* 1802.—*L.E.D.*

Palingenesis: (Gr. *palin,* again; *genesis,* birth) Literally, a new birth or regeneration. A rebirth of ideas and events (in a philosophy of history); a new birth of individuals (in theology).—*V.F.*

Panaetius: (180-110 B.C.) A prominent Stoic philosopher whose thought was influenced by the Skeptics; in his attempt to adapt Stoicism to practical needs of life, he abandoned some of the more speculative notions current among his predecessors. Influenced Cicero and Augustine.—*R.B.W.*

Pancaratra: (Skr.) A quasi philosophical system of Vishnuism (*q.v.*) based upon the Agamas (*q.v.*)—*K.F.L.*

Pan-entheism: (Gr. *pan,* all; *en,* in; *theos,* god) The term for the view that God interpenetrates everything without cancelling the relative independent existence of the world of entities; moreover, while God is immanent, this immanence is not absolute (as in pantheism); God is more than the world, transcendent, in the sense that though the created is dependent upon the Creator the Creator is not dependent upon the created. God thus is held to be the highest type of Unity, viz., a Unity in Multiplicity. The term is employed to cover a mediating position between pantheism with its extreme immanence and a theism of the type which tends to extreme transcendence.—*V.F.*

Panlogism: (Gr. *pan,* all + *logos,* word) The doctrine that the world is the actualization of Mind or Logos. Term applied to Hegel's theory of Reality. See *Hegel.*—*L.W.*

Pan-objectivism: (Gr. *pan,* all + Lat. *objectus,* pp. of *objicere,* to throw over against) An extreme form of epistemological realism which attributes real objectivity to all objects of knowledge, veridical and non-veridical alike. See *Epistemological Realism.*—*L.W.*

Panpneumatism: According to Ed. v. Hartmann (*q.v.*) a synthesis of panlogism and pantheism (*q.v.*).—*K.F.L.*

Panpsychism: (Gr. *pan,* all; *psyche,* soul) A form of metaphysical idealism, of which Leibniz's theory of monads is the classical example, according to which the whole of nature consists of psychic centers similar to the human mind.—*L.W.*

Pan-Satanism: The vague belief that the world is somehow identified with the devil. Name given to pantheism by Herbart. Otto Liebmann (1840-1912) regarded Schopenhauer's philosophy as a sort of Pan-Satanism.—*J.J.R.*

Pantheism: (Gr. *Pan,* all; *Theos,* God) 1. The doctrine that reality comprises a single being of which all things are modes, moments, members, appearances, or projections.

2. As a religious concept Pantheism is to be distinguished from Immanent Theism and Deism by asserting the essential immanence of God in the creatures. See *Monism, Idealism.*—*W.L.*

Pantheism, medieval: True pantheistic ideas are rare in

medieval literature. The accusation raised against Scotus Eriugena seems unfounded and was caused more by his writings being quoted as authorities by the followers of Amalric of Bène (1206-7) whose views were condemned in 1210. His writings are lost; he apparently taught the identity of Creator and creature and called God the essence of all beings. A contemporary was David of Dinant of whom still less is known; he identified, as it seems, God with prime matter. Master Eckhardt too has been accused of pantheism and some modern authors are believed to find confirmation in his writings. A more thorough study of them, especially of the Latin texts, shows this to be a misinterpretation.—*R.A.*

Pantheistic Personalism: The doctrine that reality consists of a Supreme Personality of which the world of persons are parts. The Divine Personality having no separate existence from its creation. See also *Critical Personalism, Mono-Personalism.*—*R.T.F.*

Paracelsus, Theophrastus Bombast: (1493-1541) Of Hohenheim, was a physician who endeavored to use philosophy as one of the "pillars" of medical science. His philosophy is a weird combination of Neo-Platonism, experimentalism, and superstitious magic. He rejected much of the traditional theory of Galen and the Arab physicians. His works (*Labyrinthus, Opus paramirum, Die grosse Wundarznei, De natura rerum*) were written in Swiss-German, translated into Latin by his followers; recent investigators make no attempt to distinguish his personal thought from that of his school. Thorndyke, L., *Hist. of Magic and Experimental Science* (N. Y., 1941), V, 615-651.—*V.J.B.*

Paraclete: (Gr. *parakaleo*, to call to one's aid) One who is called to assistance. More specifically: the designation of the function of the Holy Spirit, the third embodiment of the Christian Trinity.—*V.F.*

Paradigm: A term first used by T. S. Kuhn in *The Structure of Scientific Revolutions* (1962) to refer to constellations of "law, theory, application and instrumentation" which, taken together, "provide models from which spring particular coherent traditions of scientific research," *e.g.,* Ptolemaic astronomy, Newtonian mechanics.

It is generally agreed that paradigms undergo some sort of historical change, as in the shift from Newtonian to Quantum mechanics. The exact mechanism of paradigm transformation in the history of science, however, or more generally of "conceptual change" and the growth of knowledge, has emerged as a subject of contention in a major philosophical debate, whose leading participants include Kuhn, Sir Karl Popper (*q.v.*), Stephen Toulmin (*q.v.*), Frederick L. Will (*q.v.*), and others.

F. L. Will, *Induction and Justification: An Investigation of Cartesian Procedure in the Philosophy of Knowledge* (1974); Stephen Toulmin, *Human Understanding*, Vol I (1972); Sir Karl Popper, *The Logic of Scientific Discovery* (1959).—*T.P.S.*

Paradigma: The Latin form of the Greek noun, which denotes model. Plato called his ideas in the world of ideas, models on which were patterned the things of the phenomenal world.—*J.J.R.*

Paradoxes, logical: The ancient paradox of Epimenides the Cretan, who said that all Cretans were liars (i.e., absolutely incapable of telling the truth), was known under numerous variant forms in ancient and medieval times. The medieval name for these was *insolubilia*.

A form of this paradox due to Jourdain (1913) supposes a card upon the front of which are written the words, "On the other side of this card is written a true statement"—and nothing else. It seems to be clear that these words constitute a significant statement, since, upon turning the card over one must either find some statements written or not, and, in the former case, either there will be one of them which is true or there will not. However, on turning the card over there appear the words, "On the other side of this card is written a false statement"—and nothing else. Suppose the statement on the front of the card is true; then the statement on the back must be true; and hence the statement on the front must be false. This is a proof by *reductio ad adsurdum* that the statement on the front of the card is false. But if the statement on the front is false, then the statement on the back must be false, and hence the statement on the front must be true. Thus the paradox.

A related but different paradox is Grelling's (1908). Let us distinguish adjectives — i.e., words denoting properties — as *autological* or *heterological* according as they do or do not have the property which they denote (in particular, adjectives denoting properties which cannot belong to words at all will be heterological). Then, *e.g.,* the words *polysyllabic, common, significant, prosaic* are autological, while *new, alive, useless, ambiguous, long* are heterological. On their face, these definitions of *autological* and *heterological* and unobjectionable (compare the definition of *onomatopoetic* as *similar in sound to that which it denotes*). But paradox arises when we ask whether the word *heterological* is autological or heterological.

That paradoxes of this kind could be relevant to mathematics first became clear in connection with the paradox of the greatest ordinal number, published by Burali-Forti in 1897, and the paradox of the greatest cardinal number, published by Russell in 1903. The first of these had been discovered by Cantor in 1895, and communicated to Hilbert in 1896, and both are mentioned in Cantor's correspondence with Dedekind of 1899, but were never published by Cantor.

From the paradox of the greatest cardinal number Russell extracted the simpler paradox concerning the class t of all classes x such that $\sim x \epsilon x$. (Is it true or not that $t \epsilon t$?) At first sight this paradox may not seem to be very relevant to mathematics, but it must be remembered that it was obtained by comparing two mathematical proofs, both seemingly valid, one leading to the conclusion that there is no greatest cardinal number, the other to the conclusion that there is a greatest cardinal number.—Russell communicated this simplified form of the paradox of the greatest cardinal number to Frege in 1902 and published it in 1903. The same paradox was discovered independently by Zermelo before 1903 but not published.

Also to be mentioned are König's paradox (1905) concerning the least undefinable ordinal number and Richard's paradox (1905) concerning definable and undefinable real numbers.

Numerous solutions of these paradoxes have been proposed. Many, however, have the fault that while they purport to find a flaw in the arguments leading to the paradoxes, no effective criterion is given by which to discover in the case of other (*e.g.*, mathematical) proofs whether they have the same flaw.

Russell's solution of the paradoxes is embodied in what is now known as the *ramified theory of types*, published by him in 1908, and afterwards made the basis of *Principia Mathematica*. Because of its complication, and because of the necessity for the much-disputed *axiom of reducibility*, this has now been largely abandoned in favor of other solutions.

Another solution — which has recently been widely adopted—is the *simple theory of types* (see *Logic, formal*, § 6). This was proposed as a modification of the ramified theory of types by Chwistek in 1921 and Ramsey in 1926, and adopted by Carnap in 1929.

Another solution is the Zermelo set theory (see *Logic, formal*, § 9), proposed by Zermelo in 1908, but since considerably modified and improved.

Unlike the ramified theory of types, the simple theory of types and the Zermelo set theory both require the distinction (first made by Ramsey) between the paradoxes which involve use of the *name relation* (*q.v.*) or the semantical concept of *truth* (*q.v.*), and those which do not. The paradoxes of the first kind (Epimenides, Grelling's, König's, Richard's) are solved by the supposition that notations for the name relation and for truth (having the requisite formal properties) do not occur in the logistic system set up — and in principle, it is held, ought not to occur. The paradoxes of the second kind (Burali-Forti's, Russell's) are solved in each case in another way.—*A.C.*

G. Frege, *Grundgesetze der Arithmetik* vol. 2, Jena 1903 (see Appendix). B. Russell, *The Principles of Mathematics*, Cambridge, England, 1903; 2nd edn., London 1937, and New York, 1938. Grelling and Nelson, *Bemerkungen zu den Paradoxieen von Russell und Burali-Forti*, Abhandlungen der Fries'schen Schule, n.s. vol. 2 (1908), pp. 301-334. A. Rüstow, *Der Lügner* (Dissertation Erlangen 1908), Leipzig, 1910, P. E. B. Jourdain *Tales with philosophical morals*, The Open Court, vol. 27 (1913), pp. 310-315.

Parallelism: (philosophical) A doctrine advanced to explain the relation between mind and body according to which mental processes vary concomitantly with simultaneous physiological processes. This general description is applicable to all forms of the theory. More strictly it assumes that for every mental change there exists a correlated neural change, and it denies any causal relation between the series of conscious processes and the series of processes of the nervous system, acknowledging, however, causation within each series. It was designed to obviate the difficulties encountered by the diverse interaction theories. Moreover, no form of parallelism admits the existence of a spiritual substance or a substantial soul. Some regard consciousness as the only reality, the soul which is but an actuality, as the sum of psychic acts whose unity consists in their coherence. Others accept the teaching of the fundamental identity of mind and body, regarding the two corresponding series of psychical and physical processes as aspects of an unknown series of real processes. Thus mind and body are but appearances of a hidden underlying unity. Finally there are those who hold that the series of conscious states which constitute the mind is but an epiphenomenon, or a sort of by-product of the bodily organism. See *Mind-body relation*.—*J.J.R.*

Parallelism, psychophysical: (Gr. *parallelos*, from *para*, beside + *allelon*, of one another) A dualistic solution of the mind-body problem (see *Mind-body relation*) which asserts, in its extreme form, a perfect one-to-one correlation between the system of physical events in nature and the system of psychical events in mind. In its more moderate and restricted form, parallelism asserts only a correlation between all psychoses (mental events in an individual mind) and all or some neuroses (neural events in the individual's body). Thus there may exist physico-chemical and even neural processes in the body having no psychical correlates. The term parallelism was introduced by Fechner (*Zend-Avesta*, Bk. III, ch. XIX, D) but the doctrine appeared in Spinoza (*Ethics*, Bk. II; prop. 7 schol. and props. 11 and 12).—*L.W.*

Paralogism: (Gr. *paralogismos*) A fallacious syllogism; an error in reasoning. See *Sophism*.—*G.R.M.*

In Kant's system the paralogisms are arguments alleging to prove the substantivity, simplicity and eternality of the soul or pure ego. See *Kantianism*.—*O.F.K.*

Paramâṇu: (Skr.) An exceedingly (*parama*) or infinitely small or magnitudeless thing (cf. *aṇu*), a discrete physical entity playing a similar rôle in Indian philosophy as ions, electrons, or protons in modern physics.—*K.F.L.*

Pāramârthika: (Skr.) Relating to spiritual, essential, or absolute matters.—*K.F.L.*

Parapsychology: (Gr. *para*, at the side of + *psychē*, soul + *logia* from logein, to speak) The investigation of prescience, telepathy and other alleged psychical phenomena which seem to elude ordinary physical and physiological explanation. The term was proposed by Boirac (1893) and was adopted by Florunay and Oesterreich. See A. Lalande, *Vocabulaire de la philosophie*, Vol. II, p. 646. See *Prescience, Telepathy*.—*L.W.*

Pariṇâma-vâda: (Skr.) Theory of evolution expounded by the Sānkhya (*q.v.*), according to which the disturbed equilibrium between two primary substances (*prakṛti* and *puruṣa*) is responsible for change.—*K.F.L.*

Parmenides: 6th-5th century B.C., head of the Eleatic School of Greek Philosophy; developed the conception of "Being" in opposition to the "Becoming" of Heraclitus. To think at all we must postulate something which *is;* that which is *not* cannot be thought, and cannot be. Thought without being or being without thought are impossible, and the two are therefore identical. At the same time the "Being" of Parmenides is that which fills space; non-being is empty space. Empty space therefore cannot be, and if empty space or the "Void" cannot be then the plurality of individual things is equally not real since this results from the motion of the "full" in the "void." There is thus for Parmenides only one "Being" without inner differentiation; this alone really *is*, while the particularity of individual things is appearance, illusion. Homogeneous and unchangeable "Being" is the only reality.—*M.F.*

Parmenides' main extant work is a poem "On Truth."

Parousia: (Gr. presence) In Plato's philosophy, the presence of the Idea in the thing which, in turn, partakes of the Idea; in theology, the presence of Christ after his prophesied return to earth.—*K.F.L.*

Parsimony, Law of: Name given to various statements of a general regulative principle of economy of thought, or effort, in the use of means to attain a purpose; like that of William of Ockham (died about 1349), called Ockham's razor: *Entia non sunt multiplicanda praeter necessitatem.* It is interpreted in the sense that the least possible number of assumptions are to be made in the attempt to explain ascertained facts. It has been supposed that the same principle of simplicity prevails in the physical cosmos, since apparently nature employs the fewest possible means effectively to attain the ends which are intended.—*J.J.R.*

Particular: (Lat. *pars,* a part) A member of a class as opposed to the property which defines the class; an individual as opposed to a universal.—*A.C.B.*

Particular proposition: In traditional logic, propositions *A, E* (excepting singular forms, according to some) were called *universal and I, O, particular.* See *Logic, formal,* § 4.—*A.C.*

Particulate: An adjective which means having the form of minute particles, or assuming such a form. Also a verb now almost obsolete which signified, to divide into parts mentally, or to separate into really existing particles. Formerly it also meant, to particularize.—*J.J.R.*

Parva Naturalia: The name traditionally given to a series of short treatises by Aristotle on psychological and biological topics: viz. *De Sensu et Sensibili, De Memoria et Reminiscentia, De Somno, De Somniis, De Divinatione per Somnium, De Longitudine et Brevitate Vitae, De Vita et Morte, De Respiratione.*—*G.R.M.*

Pascal, Blaise: (1623-1662) French philosopher, mathematician and scientist. He conducted scientific researches including experiments on atmospheric pressure and invented an ingenious calculating machine. He turned from preoccupation with the scientific to the study of man and his spiritual problems and found faith as a sounder guide than reason. At this stage of his thought, theology becomes central. These thoughts are developed in his *Provincial Letters* and in his posthumously published masterpieces of style, the *Pensées.*—*L.E.D.*

Passive Empiricism: The doctrine that knowledge comes by way of experience with the emphasis upon the negative character of the mind. The mind can act only upon the stimulus of contact with the world outside itself. John Locke furnishes an example of this view. See *Tabula rasa.*—*V.F.*

Past: That part of time, continuously growing, which includes all the events which have already happened. Their relationship with other past events is generally regarded as fixed.—*R.B.W.*

Past-Time: All the extent of time preceding a given event or experience; the term is occasionally confined to that extent of preceding time which is relevant to a given event or experience. Obviously enough, past-time is not a permanent condition unrelated to the succession of events: anything that is past has been present and also future before it became present. The ontological status of the past is uncertain, insofar as it has no existence at the moment when it is called past yet cannot be designated as unconditionally non-existent in the sense applicable to fiction or untruth.—*R.B.W.*

Patanjali: The author of the Yogasutras (*q.v.*), not identical with the famous Hindu grammarian by the same name.—*K.F.L.*

Patripassianism: (Lat. *pater,* father; *patior* suffer) The teaching that God suffers. In Christian thought this view was held by Sabellius (fl. first half of third century) in connection with the sufferings of Jesus conceived to be God manifested.—*V.F.*

Patristic Philosophy: The advent of Christian revelation introduced a profound change in the history of philosophy. New facts about God, the world and man were juxtaposed to the conclusions of pagan philosophy, while reason was at once presented with the problem of reconciling these facts with the pagan position and the task of constructing them into a new science called theology.

In general, patristic philosophy is differentiated from medieval and modern philosophies in that it failed to distinguish adequately between the conclusions of reason and the facts of revelation. Philosophy, theology and the truths of religion made one amorphous body of truth. However, three stages mark the development of patristic thought. (1) *From dawn of Christian Era to 200:* The Father of this period, most of them converts from paganism, proclaimed the Christian religion as "the true philosophy." Their works were mostly apologetic in nature, directed either against pagan prejudices and misconceptions or the religious speculations of Gnosticism. (2) *From 200 to circa 450:* With the catechetic school of Alexandria and in particular with Clement and Origen, the work of reconciliation between Hellenistic philosophy and the Christian religion formally begins. This period is characterized by the *formulation* of Christian truths in the terminology and framework of Greek thought. It ends with the gigantic synthesis of Augustine (354-430), whose fusion of Neo-Platonic thought and Christian truth molded society and furnished the tradition, culture and mental background for Christian Europe up to the end of the

14th century. (3) *From 450 to the 8th century:* During this period there is a general decline until the Carlovingian renaissance. Great names are not lacking, such as those of Pseudo-Denis the Areopagite, John Damascene, Boethius and Isidore of Seville; however, the originality and spiritual elevation of an Augustine are not to be found. The period is generally characterized by the *elaboration* and *systematization* of truths already formularized. Platonic and Neo-Platonic influences predominate, though Aristotle's *logic* holds an honored place throughout this pre-Scholastic era. Cf. Migne's *Patrologiae Latinae.—H.Gu.*

Patterns of learning: Reaction modes, physiological habit systems.—*J.E.B.*

Peano, Giuseppe: (1858-1932), Italian mathematician. Professor of Mathematics at the University of Turin, 1890-1932. His work in mathematical logic marks a transition stage between the old algebra of logic and the newer methods. It is inferior to Frege's by present standards of rigor, but nevertheless contains important advances, among which may be mentioned the distinction between class inclusion ($\subset$) and class membership (ϵ)— which had previously been confused —and the introduction of a notation for formation of a class by *abstraction* (*q.v.*). His logical notations are more convenient than Frege's, and many of them are still in common use.

Peano's first publication on mathematical logic was the introduction to his *Calcolo Geometrico,* 1888. His postulates for arithmetic (see *arithmetic, foundations of*) appeared in his *Arithmetices Principia* (1889) and in revised form in *Sul concetto di numero* (Rivista di Matematica, vol. 1 (1891)), and were repeated in successive volumes (more properly, editions) of his *Formulaire de Mathématiques* (1894-1908). The last-named work, written with the aid of collaborators, was intended to provide a reduction of all mathematics to symbolic notation, and often the encyclopedic aspect was stressed as much as, or more than, that of logical analysis.

Peano is known also for other contributions to mathematics, including the discovery of the area-filling curve which bears his name, and for his advocacy of *Latino sine flexione* as an international language.—*A.C.*

P. E. B. Jourdain, *Giuseppe Peano,* The Quarterly Journal of Pure and Applied Mathematics, vol. 43 (1912), pp. 270-314. *Giuseppe Peano,* supplement to Schola et Vita, Milan, 1928. U. Cassina, *Vita et opera de Giuseppe Peano,* Schola et Vita, vol. 7 (1932), pp. 117-148. e. Stamm, *Józef Peano,* Wiadomości Matematyczne, vol. 36 (1933). pp. 1-56. U. Cassina, *L'opera scientifica de Giuseppe Peano,* Rendiconti del Seminario Matematico e Fisico di Milano, vol. 7 (1933), pp. 323-389. U. Cassina. *L'oeuvre philosophique de G. Peano,* Revue de Métaphysique et de Morale, vol. 40 (1933), pp. 481-491.

Peirce, Charles Sanders: (1839-1914) American philosopher. Born in Cambridge, Mass on September 10th, 1839. Harvard M.A. in 1862 and Sc. B. in 1863.

Except for a brief career as lecturer in philosophy at Harvard, 1864-65 and 1869-70, and in logic at Johns Hopkins, 1879-84, he did no formal teaching. Longest tenure was with the United States Coast and Geodetic Survey for thirty years beginning in 1861. Died at Milford, Pa. in 1914. He had completed only one work, *The Grand Logic,* published posthumously (*Coll. Papers*). Edited *Studies in Logic* (1883). No volumes published during his lifetime but author of many lectures, essays and reviews in periodicals, particularly in the *Popular Science Monthly,* 1877-78, and in *The Monist,* 1891-93, some of which have been reprinted in *Chance, Love and Logic* (1923), edited by Morris R. Cohen, and, together with the best of his other work both published and unpublished, in *Collected Papers of Charles Sanders Peirce* (1931-35), edited by Charles Hartshorne and Paul Weiss. He was most influenced by Kant, who had, he thought, raised all the relevant philosophical problems but from whom he differed on almost every solution. He was excited by Darwin, whose doctrine of evolution coincided with his own thought, and disciplined by laboratory experience in the physical sciences which inspired his search for rigor and demonstration throughout his work. Felt himself deeply opposed to Descartes, whom he accused of being responsible for the modern form of the nominalistic error. Favorably inclined toward Duns Scotus, from whom he derived his realism. Philosophy is a sub-class of the science of discovery, in turn a branch of theoretical science. The function of philosophy is to explain and hence show unity in the variety of the universe. All philosophy takes its start in logic, or the relations of signs to their objects, and phenomenology, or the brute experience of the objective actual world. The conclusions from these two studies meet in the three basic metaphysical categories: quality, reaction, and representation. Quality is firstness or spontaneity; reaction is secondness or actuality; and representation is thirdness or possibility. Realism (*q.v.*) is explicit in the distinction of the modes of being: actuality as the field of reactions; possibility as the field of quality (or values) and representation (or relations). He was much concerned to establish the realism of scientific method: that the postulates, implications and conclusions of science are the results of inquiry yet presupposed by it. He was responsible for pragmatism as a method of philosophy: that the sum of the practical consequences which result by necessity from the truth of an intellectual conception constitutes the entire meaning of that conception. Author of the ethical principle that the limited duration of all finite things logically demands the identification of one's interests with those of an unlimited community of persons and things. In his cosmology the flux of actuality left to itself develops those systematic characteristics which are usually associated with the realm of possibility. There is a logical continuity to chance events which through indefinite repetition beget order, as illustrated in the tendency of all things to acquire habits. The desire of all things to come together in this certain order renders love a kind of evolutionary force. Exerted a strong influence both on the American pragmatist, William James (1842-1910), the instrumentalist, John Dewey (1859-1952), as well as on the idealist, Josiah Royce (1855-1916), and many others.—*J.K.F.*

Peirce's law: The theorem of the propositional calculus,

$$[[p \supset q] \supset p] \supset p.—A.C.$$

Pelagianism: The teaching of Pelagius of Britain who was active during the first quarter of the fifth century in Rome, North Africa, and Palestine. He denied original sin and the necessity of baptism in order to be freed from it. Death was a punishment for sin, and men can be saved without the aid of divine grace. By justification men are purged of their sins through faith alone. Pelagius was notably influenced by Stoic doctrines. He and his followers refused to submit to the decisions of the Church, which repeatedly condemned their tenets, largely owing to the efforts of Augustine.—*J.J.R.*

Perception: (Lat. *perceptio*, from *percipere*, to perceive) (a) *In contemporary psychology and epistemology:* Perception is the apprehension of ordinary sense-objects, such as trees, houses, chairs etc., on the occasion of sensory stimulation. Perception is distinguished, on the one hand, from sensation (the apprehension of isolated sense qualities) and on the other hand, from higher ideational processes of imagination, remembrance, conception and reasoning. The percept or vehicle of perception consists of actually given sense qualities supplemented by imaginatively supplied qualities which on the basis of earlier experience are ascribed to the perceived object.

(b) *In early modern philosophy*, perception was used in a much wider sense than (a). Thus, for Bacon, perception designated the mind's subjection to external influence and its adaptive reaction to such influence.(*De Augmentis*, IV, 3.) Descartes and Spinoza designated by perception intellectual rather than sensuous apprehension (see Descartes, *Principles*, I, 32 and Spinoza's *Ethics*, II, prop. 40 schol. 2) and Leibniz understood by perceptions the internal state of one monad whereby it takes cognizance of other monads. *Monadology*, § 21.—*L.W.*

Perception, non-sensory: As the opposite of imagining, it lacks the sensory content. Space and time have this characteristic as experienced by man. (Montague.)—*H.H.*

Perception, pure: Is a form of action rather than a form of cognition. Involves an actual presence of external objects to the sense organs; is the reflection of the body's virtual or possible action upon these objects, or of the object's possible action upon the body. The consciousness of perception is a measure of its indetermination. (Bergson.)—*H.H.*

Percepts: The abbreviation for perceptual data.

Perfectibility: The optimistic belief in the ability of man to attain an eventual complete realization of his moral possibilities. Opposed to the various philosophies and theologies of moral pessimism (e.g., the sinfulness and moral impotence of man, original sin, in Augustinianism, Lutheranism, Barthianism, et. al.).—*V.F.*

See *Condorcet, Enlightenment*.

Perfectionism: The ethical theory that perfection, our own or that of others or both, is the end at which we ought to aim, where perfection involves virtue chiefly and sometimes also the cultivation of one's talents or endowments.—*W.K.F.*

Peripatetics: See *Aristotelianism*.

Peripety: (Gr. *peripeteia*) A sudden reversal of condition or fortunes; considered by Aristotle as an essential element in the plot of a tragedy.—*G.R.M.*

Perry, Ralph Barton: (1876-1957) Professor of Philosophy at Harvard University. He was one of the founders of the new realist movement. His classic biography of William James won the Pulitzer Prize for 1936. During the first World War he served as a major with the War Department Committee on Education and Special Training and this service has evidenced itself in his fervent advocacy of a militant democracy. Among his works are: *Present Philosophical Tendencies; Philosophy of the Recent Past; General Theory of Value*, 1926; *Thought and Character of Wm. James*, 2 vols., 1935; *Shall Not Perish From the Earth*, 1941. See *Neo-Realism*.—*L.E.D.*

Perseity: (Lat. *per se*) The condition of being *per se*, by itself, that is being such as it is from its very nature. Perseity must not be confused with aseity. The former implies independence of a subject in which to inhere, whereas the latter demands a still higher degree of independence of any efficient or producing agency whatsoever; it is predicated of God alone. Thomas Aquinas held: *Quod est per se, semper est prius eo quod est per aliud*. That which exists *per se* is always a substance. This mode of existence is distinguished from that which is *per accidens*, that is something which is not essential, but only belongs to a subject more or less fortuitously. A thing is *per se* owing to its internal constitution, or essence, but that which is *per accidens* is due rather to external or non-essential reasons. Thomas Aquinas taught that that which is *per accidens, non potest esse semper et in omnibus*, whereas that which belongs to something *per se, de necessitate et semper et inseparabiliter ei inest*. Duns Scotus held that *per se esse* may be understood in the sense of being incommunicable, *incommunicabiliter esse*, or *per se subsistere*, subsisting by itself, not by another. In human acts that which is directly intended is *per se*, while that which is *per accidens* is *praeter intentionem*. Rational beings tend toward the good, or that which is regarded as good. If the good is intended for itself it is *bonum per se*, otherwise it is a *bonum per accidens* or *secundum quid*, that is relatively good.—*J.J.R.*

Persian Philosophy: Persia was a vast empire before the time of Alexander the Great, embracing not only most of the oriental tribes of Western Asia but also the Greeks of Asia Minor, the Jews and the Egyptians. If we concentrate on the central section of Persia, three philosophic periods may be distinguished: (1) Zoroastrianism (including Mithraism and Magianism), (2) Manichaeanism, and (3) medieval Persian thought. Zarathustra (Gr. Zoroaster) lived before 600 B.C. and wrote the *Avesta*, apparently in the Zend language. It is primarily religious, but the teaching that there are two ultimate principles of reality, *Ormazd*, the God of Light and Goodness, and *Ahriman*, God of Evil and Darkness, is of philosophic importance. They are eternally fighting. Mitra is the intermediary between Ormazd and man. In the third century A.D., Mani of Ecbatana (in Media) combined this dualism of eternal principles with some of the doctrines of Christianity. His seven books are now known only through second-hand reports of Mohammedan (Abu Faradj Ibn Ishaq, 10th c., and Sharastani, 12th c.) and Christian (St. Ephrem, 4th c., and Bar-Khoni, 7th c.) writers. St. Augustine of Hippo (354-430 A.D.) has left several works criticizing Manichaeism, which he knew at first-hand. From the ninth century onward, many of the great Arabic philosophers are of Persian origin. Mention might be made of the Epicureanism of the *Rubaiyat* of the Persian poet, Omar Khayyám, and the remarkable metaphysical system of Avicenna, i.e. Ibn Sina (11th c.), who was born in Persia.—*V.J.B.*

Persistence: The condition of enduring in time, with or without change.—*R.B.W.*

Person: (in Max Scheler) The concrete unity of acts. Individual person, and total person, with the former not occupying a preferential position.—*P.A.S.*

In scholasticism: The classic definition is given by Boethius: person is an individual substance of rational nature. As individual it is material, since matter supplies the principle of individuation. The soul is not person, only the composite is. Man alone is among the material beings person, he alone having a rational nature. He is the highest of the material beings, endowed with particular dignity and rights.—*R.A.*

Personal Equation: (a) Discrepancy between the chronological measurements of different scientific observers due to their differing reaction times. The error was first discovered in astronomical measurements but is a recognized source of error in all scientific measurements.

(b) The term has been extended to include all observational error due to the intrusion of idiosyncrasies of individual observers.—*L.W.*

Personal Idealism: The affirmation of reality in the person and the personal nature of the World-Ground. Synonymous with Absolutistic Personalism.—*R.T.F.*

Personal Identity: (Lat. *persona*) Personal identity is individual identity as possessed by a person or self. Any individual, whether an inanimate thing, a living organism or a conscious self, is identical in so far as it preserves from moment to moment a similarity of structure. Personality identity involves in addition the conscious recognition of sameness.—*L.W.*

Personalism: (Lat. *persona*, actor's mask) A modern term applied to any philosophy which considers personality the supreme value and the key to the meaning of reality.

Typical or original Personalism was theistic, the term being first used in America (1863) by Bronson Alcott for "the doctrine that the ultimate reality of the world is a Divine Person who sustains the universe by a continuous act of creative will." (Odell Shepard: *Pedlar's Progress*, p.494.)

Theistic Personalism was given systematic form in America by Borden Parker Bowne (1847-1910) for whom it implied:

Metaphysically, the personal nature of the World Ground;

Epistemologically, a knowledge validated by the common source of thought and thing in the World Ground and mediated through personality;

Logically, the pragmatic assumption that life is superior to logical form;

Ethically, that values are real and based in the Cosmic Nature.

While the term Personalism is modern it stands for an old way of thinking which grows out of the attempt to interpret the self as a part of phenomenological experience. Personalistic elements found expression in Heraclitus' (536-470 B.C.) statement: "Man's own character is his daemon" (Fr. 119), and in his assertion of the Logos as an enduring principle of permanence in a world of change. These elements are traceable likewise in the cosmogony of Anaxagoras (500-430 B.C.), who gave philosophy an anthropocentric trend by affirming that mind "regulated all things, what they were to be, what they were and what they are;" the force which arranges and guides (Fr. 12). Protagoras (cir. 480-410 B.C.) emphasized the personalistic character of knowledge in the famous dictum: "Man is the measure of all things."

The doctrine of the person reached its high point in Greek philosophy in Socrates (469-399 B.C.) who recognized the soul or self as the center from which sprang all man's actions.

Plato (427-347 B.C.) recognized the person in his doctrine of the soul, but turned the direction of thought toward dominance by the abstract Idea.

Aristotle (384-322 B.C.) made his contribution by insisting that only the concrete and individual could be real.

St. Augustine (354-430 A.D.) asserted that thought, and therefore the thinker, was the most certain of all things.

To Boëthius (475-525) it was given to furnish the philosophy and definition of the person that held for the Middle Ages: "A person is the individual substance of a rational nature."

The importance of the person in Scholastic thought insured the personalistic concepts until they found expression in the word of Thomas Aquinas (1225-1274).

The renewal of philosophy signalized by Descartes introduced a long line of personalistic thinkers in France who under various classifications offered the main opposition to naturalism, materialism and positivism. Among these were Geulincx (1625-1669), Occasionalism; Malebranche (1638-1715), Activism; de Lignac (1710-1769), Theistic Personalism; de Biran (1766-1824), Philosophy of Effort; Cournot (1801-1877), Probabilism, Vitalism; Ravaisson (1813-1900),

Spiritual Realism; Renouvier (1815-1903), Neo-criticism, Personalism; Lachelier (1832-1918), Spiritual Realism; Boutroux (1845-1921), Philosophy of Discontinuity; Bergson (1859-1941), Philosophy of Change, Intuitionism.

In Germany the first use of the word personalism seems to have been by Schleiermacher (1768-1834) and later by Hans Dreyer, Troeltsch, and Rudolf Otto. Among German Personalists would be included G. H. Leibniz (1646-1716), Monadism; R. H. Lotze (1817-1881), Teleological Personalism; Rudolf Eucken (1846-1926), Theistic Personalism, Vitalism; Max Scheler (1874-1928), Phenomenological Personalism; William Stern (1871-1939), Critical Personalism, Pantheistic Personalism.

In England many Theistic Personalists have appeared since Bishop Berkeley (1710-1796), Subjectivism, Subjective Idealism; including A. C. Frazer (1819-1914); T. H. Green (1836-1882); Edward Caird (1835-1908); James Ward (1843-1925), Singularism; A. J. Balfour (1848-1930); J. Cook Wilson (1849-1915); W. R. Sorley (1855-1935). Also English were H. W. Carr (1857-1931), Monadistic Personalism; F. C. S. Schiller (1864-1937), Humanism, Personalism; J. M. E. McTaggart (1866-1925), Atheistic Personalism.

In America we have among Theistic Personalists in addition to Bowne, G. T. Ladd (1842-1921); J. W. Buckham (1864-1962); Mary Whiton Calkins (1863-1930), Personal Idealism, Absolutistic Personalism; G. A. Wilson (1864-1941); H. A. Youtz (1867-); R. T. Flewelling (1871-1960), Personal Realism; A. C. Knudson (1873-1962); E. S. Brightman (1884-1953). "The Given." Though probably rejecting the term personalism, a view of American Personalism would be incomplete without mention of W. T. Harris (1835-1909); G. W. Howison (1834-1916); Josiah Royce (1855-1916); G. T. W. Patrick (1857-); J. E. Boodin (1869-1950); J. A. Leighton (1870-1948); W. E. Hocking (1873-1966); J. B. Pratt (1875-1944), Personal Realism. Among contemporary Personalists abroad mention should be made of Ph. Kohnstamm, Holland, Critical Personalism; N. Losski (1870-1975), Prague, Organismic Personalism; N. Berdyaev (1874-1948), Paris; Maurice Blondel (1861-1939), Paris, Activism; Ch. Baudouin (1893-); Geneva; Radelescu-Motru, Bucharest. In France also should be noted the leader of the Personalistic movement which might be denominated Political Personalism, E. Mounier.—*R.T.F.*

Personalism, Critical: The term used by William Stern to define his concept of person as applied to the organic whole of existence. See *Pantheistic Personalism, Mono-Personalism.*—*R.T.F.*

Personalistics: Term used by William Stern in psychology to indicate a study of the facts that are true of man as a meaningful living whole — a fundamental science of the human person. *The Personalist*, XVIII, p. 50.—*R.T.F.*

Personality: The totality of mental traits characterizing an individual personality or self. See *Self.*—*L.W.*

Personal Realism: That type of Personalism which

emphasizes the metaphysical nature of personality, its continuous activity in natural phenomena, and its unanalyzable or realistic character as experienced fact, the ultimate real, the object of immediate knowledge.—*R.T.F.*

Perspective: (Lat. *perspectus*, pp. of *perspicio*, to look through) The determination of inclusiveness of what can be actual for any organization. The point of view of an individual on the rest of existence. (a) In epistemology: the perspective predicament, the limited though real viewpoint of the individual; the plight of being confined to the experience of only part of actuality. (b) In psychology: the perception of relative distance by means of the apparent differences in the size of objects.

In aesthetics: The sense of depth and distance in painting as in poetry. Term used also for time elapsed.—*J.K.F.*

Pessimism: (Lat. *pessimus*, the worst) The attitude gained by reflection on life, man, and the world (psychiatrically explained as due to neurotic or other physiological conditions, economically to over-population, mechanization, rampant utilitarianism; religiously to lack of faith; etc.) which makes a person gloomy, despondent, magnifying evil and sorrow, or holding the world in contempt. Rationalizations of this attitude have been attempted before Schopenhauer (as in Hesiod, Job, among the Hindus, in Byron, Giacomo Leopardi, Heine, Musset, and others), but never with such vigor, consistency, and acumen, so that since his *Welt als Wille und Vorstellung* we speak of a 19th century philosophic literature of pessimism which considers this world the worst possible, holds man to be born to sorrow, and thinks it best if neither existed. Buddhism (*q.v.*) blames the universal existence of pain, sorrow, and death; Schopenhauer the blind, impetuous will as the very stuff life and the world are made of; E. V. Hartmann the alogical or irrational side of the all-powerful subconscious; Oswald Spengler the Occidental tendency toward civilization and hence the impossibility of extricating ourselves from decay as the natural terminus of all organic existence. All pessimists, however, suggest compensations or remedies; thus, Buddhism looks hopefully to *nirvāna* (*q.v.*), Schopenhauer to the Idea, V. Hartmann to the rational, Spengler to a rebirth through culture. See *Optimism.*—*K.F.L.*

Petites Perceptions: (Fr. little perceptions) Term by which Leibniz designates confused and unconscious perceptions. (Cf. *the Monadology*, Sects. 21, 23.) The Leibnizian theory of *petites perceptions* anticipates the modern theory of unconscious mind. See *Unconscious Mind.*—*L.W.*

Petitio principii, or *begging the question*, is a fallacy involving the assumption as premises of one or more propositions which are identical with (or in simple fashion equivalent to) the conclusion to be proved, or which would require the conclusion for their proof, or which are stronger than the conclusion and contain it as a particular case or otherwise as an immediate consequence. There is a fallacy, however, only if the premisses assumed (without proof) are illegitimate for some other reason than merely their relation to the conclusion — *e.g.,* if they are not among the avowed presuppositions of the argument, or if they are not admitted by an opponent in a dispute.—*A.C.*

Phala: (Skr.) "Fruit," result, effect.—*K.F.L.*

Phantasm: (Gr. *phantasma,* appearance) Term used by Hobbes to designate an image or representation directly given to the percipient. See *Elements of Philosophy Concerning Body,* Part IV, ch. XXV.—*L.W.*

Phantasy: (in Scholasticism) The internal sense perception of objects, even of absent objects, previously perceived by the external sense. The *phantasm* is the species of the object perceived by an internal sense and retained in the phantasy.—*H.G.*

Pharisaism: The most characteristic type of Palestinian Judaism at the time of Christ. This group is to be thought of as the remnant of the traditional culture of the ancient Hebrews. Scorched by the memory of the long struggle between their fathers' and other cultures which resulted in the unhappy Captivity, these descendants took on a more militant nationalism and a more rigid loyalty to traditional customs, teaching their children in schools of their own (the Synagogue) the religion of the ancient sacred covenant. Since their ways separated sharply from their brethren in the dispersion and from the less nationalistic minded at home they acquired the party name (from the second century B.C.) "Pharisees." Their leaders were devout students of the written and oral traditions which they regarded as the Divine Will (Torah). To this tradition they added detailed codes of rigorous religious living. Popular among the masses they were comparatively few in number although powerful in influence. Pharisaism was a book-centered religion, strongly monotheistic, intensely legalistic, teaching a national and social gospel of redemption by an expectant supernatural visitation. The term "Pharisaic" unfortunately has acquired a sinister meaning, probably due to certain N.T. statements linking Pharisees with hypocrites. R. T. Herford in his *Pharisaism* (1912) and *The Pharisees* (1924) has shown that this religious party was preeminently spiritually minded even though legalistic and not sufficiently understood by Christian traditionalists.—*V.F.*

Phase: (chemical, physical) A term referring to a *homogeneous* composition of matter, either solid, liquid, or gaseous. All three phases of a single substance may co-exist.—*W.M.M.*

Phase Rule: (chemical, physical) A relationship between the number of components (C), phases (P), and degrees of freedom (F) (variability) of a heterogeneous system with respect to pressure and temperature and similar intensive variables when in equilibrium: $P + F = C + 2$. Discovered by J. W. Gibbs (1839-1903). —*W.M.M.*

Phenomena: See *Appearances.*

Phenomenalism: (gr. *phainomenon,* from *phainesthai,* to appear) Theory that knowledge is limited to phenomena including (a) physical phenomena or the totality of objects of actual and possible perception and (b) mental phenomena, the totality of objects of introspection. Phenomenalism assumes two forms according as it: (a) denies a reality behind the phenomena (Renouvier, Shadworth, Hodgson), or (b) expressly affirms the reality of things-in-themselves but denies their knowability. (Kant, Comte, Spencer.) See *Hume.* —*L.W.*

Phenomenal World: The world of appearance as opposed to the world as-it-is-in-itself. The only world we know, said Kant, is the world-we-know, (appearance). The real world is beyond our knowledge. —*V.F.*

Phenomenological Personalism: Applied to the system of Max Scheler.—*R.T.F.*

Phenomenology: Since the middle of the Eighteenth Century, "*Phänomenologie,* like its English equivalent, has been a name for several disciplines, an expression for various concepts. Lambert, in his *Neue Organon* (1764), attached the name "*Phänomenologie*" to the theory of the appearances fundamental to all empirical knowledge. Kant adopted the word to express a similar though more restricted sense in his *Metaphysische Anfangsgründe der Naturwissenschaft* (1786). On the other hand, in Hegel's *Phänomenologie des Geistes* (1807) the same word expresses a radically different concept. A precise counterpart of Hegel's title was employed by Hamilton to express yet another meaning. In "The Divisions of Philosophy" (*Lectures on Metaphysics,* 1858), after stating that "Philosophy properly so called" is "conversant about Mind," he went on to say: "If we consider the mind merely with the view of observing and generalizing the various phenomena it reveals, . . . we have . . . one department of mental science; and this we may call the *Phaenomenology of Mind.*" Similarly Moritz Lazarus, in his *Leben der Seele* (1856-57), distinguished *Phänomenologie* from *Psychologie:* The former describes the phenomena of mental life; the latter seeks their causal explanation.

Edmund Husserl (1859-1938) was the first to apply the name "*Phänomenologie*" to a whole philosophy. His usage, moreover, has largely determined the senses commonly attached to it and cognate words in the Twentieth Century. In his *Logische Untersuchungen* (1900-01), Husserl gave the name to such investigations and theories as make up most of that work and of the only published volume of his *Philosophie der Arithmetik* (1891). This established what was to remain the primary denotation of the term in all his later writings. On the other hand — owing to changes in his concept of his unchanging theme — the explicit connotation of the term, as used by him, underwent development and differentiation.

In the first edition of the *Logische Untersuchungen,* phenomenology was defined (much as it had been by Hamilton and Lazarus) as descriptive analysis of subjective processes *Erlebnisse.* Thus its theme was unqualifiedly identified with what was commonly taken to be the central theme of psychology; the two disciplines were said to differ only in that psychology sets up causal or genetic laws to explain what phenomenology merely describes. Phenomenology was called "pure" so far as the phenomenologist distinguishes the subjective from the objective and refrains from looking into either the genesis of subjective phenomena or their relations to somatic and environmental circumstances. Husserl's *"Prolegomena zur reinen Logik,"* published as the first part of the *Logische Untersuchungen,* had elaborated the concept of pure logic, a theoretical science independent of empirical knowledge and having a distinctive theme: the universal categorical forms exemplified in possible truths, possible facts, and their respective components. The fundamental concepts and laws of this science, Husserl maintained, are genuine only if they can be established by observing the matters to which they apply. Accordingly, to test the genuineness of logical theory, *"wir wollen auf die 'Sachen selbst' zurückgehen:"* we will go, from our habitual empty understanding of this alleged science, back to a seeing of the logical forms themselves. But it is then the task of pure phenomenology to test the genuineness and range of this "seeing," to distinguish it from other ways of being conscious of the same or other matters. Thus, although pure phenomenology and pure logic are mutually independent disciplines with separate themes, phenomenological analysis is indispensible to the critical justification of logic. In like manner, Husserl maintained, it is necessary to the criticism of other alleged knowledge; while, in another way, its descriptions are prerequisite to explanatory psychology. However, when Husserl wrote the *Logische Untersuchungen,* he did not yet conceive phenomenological analysis as a method for dealing with metaphysical problems.

The most radical changes in this concept of phenomenology and its relations to other disciplines had taken place before Husserl wrote his *Ideen zu einer reinen Phänomenologie und phänomenologischen Philosophie,* of which the only published volume, "General Introduction to Pure Phenomenology," appeared in 1913. They resulted from a development having two main aspects.

1. Phenomenological analyses, partly summarized in the *Logische Untersuchungen,* had led Husserl to the view that material (generic and specific) as well as logically formal universals or essences are themselves observable, though non-individual, objects. Further analyses showed that awareness of an essence as itself presented might be based on either a clear experiencing or a clear phantasying (fictive experiencing) of an example. In either case, the evidence of the essence or eidos involves evidence of some example as ideally possible but not as actual. Consequently, a science like pure logic, whose theme includes nothing but essences and essential possibilities, — in Husserl's later terminology, as *eidetic* science—involves no assertion of actual existence. Husserl used these views to redefine phenomenology itself. The latter was now conceived explicitly as the eidetic science of the material essences exemplified in subjective processes, qua pure possibilities, and was accordingly said to be pure *also* in the

way pure logic is pure. A large proportion of the emendations in the second edition of the *Logische Untersuchungen* serve to clarify this freedom of phenomenology from all presuppositions of actual individual existence — particularly, psychic existence.

2. Under the influence of Franz Brentano (1838-1917), Husserl coined the name *"Intentionalität"* for what he saw as the fundamental character of subjective processes. The reflectively experiencable part of one's stream of consciousness is, on the one hand, consciousness of subjective processes as immanent in the stream itself and, on the other hand, consciousness of other objects as transcending the stream. This character of subjective processes as consciousness *of,* as processes in which something is intended, is a property they have intrinsically, regardless of whether what is intended in them exists. Seeing intentionality as the fundamental attribute of subjective processes, Husserl held that phenomenology must describe them not only with respect to their immanent components but also with respect to their intended objects, as intended; in the language of his *Ideen,* phenomenological description must be "noematic," as well as "noetic" and "hyletic."

Every conscious process intends its objects as *in a context with others,* some intended as presented, others intended as to become presented if intended future consciousness takes a particular course. In other words, consciousness is always an intentional predelineating of processes in which objects will be intended, as the same or different within an all-inclusive objective context: the world. A pure phenomenology should therefore describe not only particular intended objects but also the intended world, as intended — as part of the "noematic-objective" sense belonging to consciousness by virtue of the latter's intrinsic intentionality. To be sure, in such noematic-objective description the phenomenologist must still disregard the actual relations of the described subjective processes to other entities in the world. But, Husserl contended, when one disregards everything except the intrinsic nature of subjective processes, one still can see their intentionality; therefore all the entities and relations from which one has abstracted can — and should — reappear as noematic-intentional objects, within one's isolated field. In particular, the disregarded status of the observed stream of consciousness itself, its status as related to other entities in the world, reappears — as a noematic-objective sense which the observed consciousness intends. Moreover, as purely eidetic, phenomenology finds that the intrinsic character of any actual consciousness, as intending a world and itself as in that world, is an essentially necessary determination of any possible consciousness.

Husserl noted, however, that even when one's analyses are thus pure, both abstractively and eidetically, one naturally takes it for granted that possible consciousness is possible in some (otherwise indefinite) possible world. That is to say, besides finding "the world" as part of the intentional objective sense posited in the consciousness under investigation, the investigator continues to apprehend this consciousness as essentially worldly, even though he successfully disregards even its possible relations to other worldly objects. At this point, what Husserl considered as the philosophically decisive change in his concept of phenomenology ensues.

Before writing the *Ideen*, he had come to believe that, as the reflective observer of one's subjective processes, one can establish and maintain the attitude of a mere onlooker, who does not participate even in his own natural attitude of believing in a possible world and apprehending his consciousness as essentially possible in that world. If this attitude of self-restraint (epoché) is consistently maintained, one can discriminate a status of one's consciousness more fundamental than its actuality or its possibility *in* a world and one can see that this essential worldliness of consciousness is a reflexive consequence of its more fundamental character as consciousness *of* a world. One can then see, furthermore, that every intendable object is essentially, and most fundamentally, a noematic-intentional object (a phenomenon) and has its being and nature because consciousness — regardless of the latter's secondary status as in the world — is intrinsically an (actual or potential) intending of that object, in a certain manner, as having certain determinations. Such was Husserl's contention.

In the *Ideen* and in later works, Husserl applied the epithet "transcendental" to consciousness as it is aside from its (valid and necessary) self-apperception as in a world. At the same time, he restricted the term "psychic" to subjectivity (personal subjects, their streams of consciousness, etc.) in its status as worldly, animal, human subjectivity. The contrast between transcendental subjectivity and worldly being is fundamental to Husserl's mature concept of pure phenomenology and to his concept of a universal phenomenological philosophy. In the *Ideen*, this pure phenomenology, defined as the eidetic science of transcendental subjectivity, was contrasted with psychology, defined as the empirical science of actual subjectivity in the world. Two antitheses are involved, however, eidetic *versus* factual, and transcendental *versus* psychic. Rightly, they yield a four-fold classification, which Husserl subsequently made explicit, in his *Formale und Transzendentale Logik* (1929), *Nachwort zu Meinen Ideen* (1930), and *Méditations Cartésiennes* (1931). In these works, he spoke of psychology as including all knowledge of worldly subjectivity while, within this science, he distinguished an empirical or matter-of-fact pure psychology and an eidetic pure psychology. The former is "pure" only in the way phenomenology, as explicitly conceived in the first edition of the *Logische Untersuchungen*, is pure: actual psychic subjectivity is abstracted as its exclusive theme; objects intended in the investigated psychic processes are taken only as the latter's noematic-intentional objects. Such an abstractive and self-restraining attitude, Husserl believed, is necessary, if one is to isolate the psychic in its purity and yet preserve it in its full intentionality. The instituting and maintaining of such an attitude is called "psychological epoché;" its effect on the objects of psychic consciousness is called "psychological reduction." As empiricism, this pure psychology describes the experienced typical structures of psychic processes and the typical noematic objects belonging inseparably to the latter by virtue of their intrinsic intentionality. Description of typical personalities and of their habitually intended worlds also lies within its province. Having acquired empirical knowledge of the purely psychic, one may relax one's psychological epoche and inquire into the extrapsychic circumstances under which, *e.g.*, psychic processes of a particular type actually occur in the world. Thus an empirical pure intentional psychology would become part of a concrete empirical science of actual psychophysical organisms.

If the psychologist, having isolated some instance of subjectivity, considers it only as a purely possible example of subjectivity in some possible world, he is effecting a further, so-called eidetic, reduction of the psychic and is in the position to develop an *eidetically* pure phenomenological psychology or (as Husserl also called it) an eidetic psychological phenomenology. He can discover, not merely empirical types but essential psychic possibilities, impossibilities, and necessities, in any possible world. Moreover, eidetic reduction can be performed, not only on the psychic but also on any other abstractible region of the world, *e.g.*, the physical, the concretely psychophysical, the cultural. We can develop purely eidetic sciences of every material region (material ontologies), an eidetic science of the formally universal region, "something or other" (formal ontology, the formal logic of possible being), and finally an all-embracing science of the essential (formal and material) compossibilities and non-compossibilities in any possible concrete world. An eidetic psychological phenomenology would thus become coordinated in a universal eidetic science of worldly being.

There is yet a third kind of epoché that allegedly enables one to discriminate subjectivity qua transcendental — by effecting yet another kind of reduction, which Husserl eventually called "transcendental-phenomenological." (In his *Ideen* he called it simply "phenomenological.") By refraining from participation in one's inveterate (and justifiable) natural attitude of presupposing the world and the status of one's subjectivity in the world, one can see the world (and whatever else one may intend) as fundamentally a noematic-intentional object for transcendental subjectivity — for one's individual self, the subject whose life is one's own transcendental stream of consciousness, and for other transcendental subjects. As one can describe one's actual *psychic* subjectivity, so one can describe one's actual *transcendental* subjectivity and thus produce an empirical transcendental phenomenology. Again, as in the case of the purely psychic, so in the case of the purely transcendental, an eidetic reduction enables one to produce a purely eidetic science — here an *eidetic transcendental phenomenology,* the theme of which is the absolutely universal domain of transcendental subjectivity in general, including the latter's noematic-objective sense: the entire world and all its possible variants. This eidetic transcendental phenomenology is what Husserl ordinarily meant when, in the *Ideen* or subsequent works, he spoke simply of "phenomenology."

Because the difference between phenomenological pure psychology and transcendental phenomenology depends on a difference in attitude towards "the same" subject-matter, their contents are widely analogous. Husserl maintained, however, that genuine philosophy is possible only as transcendental phenomenology, because it alone is knowledge of that non-worldly nucleus of subjectivity in which everything intendable as immanent or as transcendent is constituted (produced, generated) as an essentially intentional object. As envisaged in the *Ideen* and later works, phenomenological analysis is chiefly "transcendental-constitutional" analysis of the subjective structures in which the concrete individual world is built up as an intersubjectively valid transcendent sense for transcendental subjectivity. In the course of such analysis, every legitimate philosophical problem must find its definitive solution. From the transcendental-phenomenological standpoint, however, one traditional problem, namely the relation between what are essentially objects of consciousness and "things-in-themselves" that are not essentially objects of consciousness, is seen to be spurious. On the one hand, it is evidently false that all directly presented objects of consciousness are immanent in the mind; on the other hand, the concept of an entity that is not an intentionally constituted object of transcendental consciousness is evidently self-contradictory. This is the central thesis of what Husserl called his "transcendental-phenomenological idealism."

The diversity of concepts that Husserl himself expressed by the word "phenomenology" has been a source of diverse usages among thinkers who came under his influence and are often referred to as "the phenomenological school." Husserl himself always meant by "phenomenology" a science of the subjective and its intended objects qua intentional; this core of sense pervades the development of his own concept of phenomenology as eidetic, transcendental, constitutive. Some thinkers, appropriating only the psychological version of this central concept, have developed a descriptive intentional psychology — sometimes empirical, sometimes eidetic — under the title "phenomenology." On the other hand, Husserl's broader concept of eidetic science based on seeing essences and essentially necessary relations — especially his concept of material ontology — has been not only adopted but made central by others, who define phenomenology accordingly. Not uncommonly, these groups reject Husserl's method of transcendental-phenomenological reduction and profess a realistic metaphysics. Finally, there are those who, emphasizing Husserl's cardinal principle that evidence — seeing something that is itself presented — is the only ultimate source of knowledge, conceive their phenomenology more broadly and etymologically, as explication of that which shows itself, whatever may be the latter's nature and ontological status.—*D.C.*

Phenomenon: (Gr. *phainomenon,* Ger. *Phaenomenon*) In Kant: Broadly, appearance or that which appears. More specifically, any presentation, cognition or experience whose form and other depends upon the synthetic forms of the sensibility and categories of the understanding. In contrast to noumenon and thing-in-itself which lie outside the conditions of possible experience, and remain, therefore, theoretically unknowable. See *Kantianism* and *Noumenon.*—*O.F.K.*

Philo of Alexandria: (30 B.C.—50 A.D.) Jewish theologian and Neo-Platonic philosopher. He held that Greek thought borrowed largely from Mosaic teachings and therefore justified his use of Greek philosophy for the purpose of interpreting Scripture in a spiritual sense. For Philo, the renunciation of self and, through the divine Logos in all men, the achievement of immediate contact with the Supreme Being, is the highest blessedness for man.—*M.F.*

Philosopheme: (Gr. *philosophema*) An apodictic syllogism (Aristotle).—*G.R.M.*

Philosopher, The: Generally used name for Aristotle by medieval authors after the "reception of Aristotle" from the early 13th century onwards. In earlier writers the name may refer to any head of a school; *e.g.* to Abelard in the writings of his pupils.—*R.A.*

Philosophes: French 18th century philosophers, *e.g.* Condorcet, Condillac, Rousseau, Voltaire (*q.v.*).

Philosopher King: In Plato's theory of the ideal state rulership would be entrusted to philosopher kings. These rulers would reach the top by sheer talent and merit after a long period of training in the school of everyday work and leadership and by a prescribed pattern of formal discipline and study. The final test of leadership lay in the ability to see the truth of the Platonic vision of a reality governed by universal ideas and ideals.—*V.F.*

Philosophical Anthropology: A broad and loosely unified philosophical discipline which seeks to give the philosophical study of man and his place in the world a scientific, empirical basis, coordinating philosophy and in some instances theology with biology, psychology and anthropology. It arose in Germany in the 1940s as a new development of the *Geisteswissenschaften,* or science of man, counting among its intellectual predecessors such late-18th and 19th century European thinkers as Pascal, Goethe, Kant, Herder, Hegel, Kierkegaard, Marx and Nietzsche. Since World War II its influence has spread to Holland, France, and recently to the United States. Its leading figures include Arnold Gehlen and Max Scheler.—*T.P.S.*

Philosophical Psychology: Philosophical psychology, in contrast to scientific or empirical psychology, is concerned with the more speculative and controversial issues relating to mind and consciousness which, though arising in the context of scientific psychology, have metaphysical and epistemological ramifications. The principal topics of philosophical psychology are (a) the criteria of mentality (see *Mental*), (b) the relation between mind and consciousness (see *Consciousness*), (c) the existence of unconscious or subconscious mind (see *Unconscious mind*), (d) the structure of the mind (see *Mind-stuff Theory, Gestalt Psychology*), (e) the genesis of mind (see *Mind-Dust, Emergent Mentalism*), (f) the nature of the self (see *Ego, Self, Personal Identity, Soul*), (g) the mind-body relation (see *Mind-Body Relation*), (i) the Freedom of the Will (see *Determinism, Freedom*), (j) psychological methodology (see *Behaviorism, Introspection*), (k) mind and cognition. See *Cognition, Perception, Memory.*—*L.W.*

Philosophy: (Gr. *philein*, to love, — *sophia*, wisdom) The most general science. Pythagoras is said to have called himself a lover of wisdom. But philosophy has been both the seeking of wisdom and the wisdom sought. Originally, the rational explanation of anything; the general principles under which all facts could be explained; in this sense, indistinguishable from science. Later, the science of the first principles of being; the presuppositions of ultimate reality. Now, popularly, private wisdom or consolation; technically, the science of sciences, the criticism and systematization or organization of all knowledge, drawn from empirical science, rational learning, common experience, or wherever. Philosophy includes metaphysics, or ontology and epistemology, logic, ethics, aesthetics, etc. (all of which see.)—*J.K.F.*

Concerning the task of philosophy. See also *Science of Science, Epistemology.*

Philosophy of Change: The theory that change itself is the only enduring principle and therefore the fundamental reality. Applied to the views of Heraclitus, and in modern times to those of Henri Bergson.—*R.T.F.*

Philosophy of Discontinuity: The theory that the principle of change is the fundamental basis of reality; that natural law is but the outward aspect of what is internally habit. Being as an irreducible synthesis of possibility and action. God and Creator and Essence of things. Applied to the thought of Renouvier, Boutroux, and Lachelier.—*R.T.F.*

Philosophy of Effort: The theory that in the self-consciousness of effort the person becomes one with reality. Consciousness of effort is self-consciousness. Used by Maine de Biran.—*R.T.F.*

Philosophy of Mind: Philosophical theory of the nature of mind and its place in the world. See *Philosophical Psychology.*—*L.W.*

Philosophy of Religion: An inquiry into the general subject of religion from the philosophical point of view, *i.e.*, and inquiry employing the accepted tools of critical analysis and evaluation without a predisposition to defend or reject the claims of any particular religion. Among the specific questions considered are: the nature, function and value of religion; the validity of the claims of religious knowledge; the relation of religion and ethics; the character of ideal religion; the nature of evil; the problem of theodicy; revealed *versus* natural religion; the problem of the human spirit (soul) and its destiny; the relation of the human to the divine as to the freedom and responsibility of the individual and the character (if any) of a divine purpose; evaluation of the claims of prophecy, mystic intuitions, special revelations, inspired utterances; the value of prayers of petition; the human hope of immortality; evaluation of institutional forms of expressions, rituals, creeds, ceremonies, rites, missionary propaganda; the meaning of human existence; the character of value, its status in the world of reality; the existence and character of deity; the nature of belief and faith; etc.

The subject of the philosophy of religion is regarded in conservative circles not as a discipline given to free philosophical inquiry but as a particular religion's philosophy. In this form it is a more or less disguised apologetics or defense of an already accepted religious faith. While the data for this subject include the so-called classical religions, philosophy of religion, in the genuinely philosophical sense, takes for its material religious expressions of all types, whether classical or not, together with all the psychological material available on the nature of the human spirit and man's whole cultural development.—*V.F.*

Phoronomy: Noun derived from the Greek, *phorein* used by Plato and Aristotle in the sense of motion, and *nomos*, law; signifies kinematics, or absolute mechanics, which deals with motion from the purely theoretical point of view. According to Kant it is that part of natural philosophy which regards motion as a pure quantum, without considering any of the qualities of the moving body.—*J.J.R.*

Phronesis: (Gr. *phronesis*) Practical wisdom, or knowledge of the proper ends of conduct and the means of attaining them; distinguished by Aristotle both from theoretical knowledge or science, and from technical skill. See *Aristotelianism.*—*G.R.M.*

Physical essence: (or physical composition; in Scholasticism) Consists in the composition of the parts by which that composite truly is. Of these parts, that which indifferently consitutes this or that, is called matter, as the body in man, but that which determines and perfects matter is called form, as soul.—*H.G.*

Physicalism: The thesis, developed within Scientific Empiricism (*q.v.*, II B), that every descriptive term in the language of science (in the widest sense, including social science) is connected with terms designating observable properties of things. This connection is of such a kind that a sentence applying the term in question is intersubjectively (*q.v.*) confirmable by observations (see *Verification*). The application of physicalism to psychology is the logical basis for the method of behaviorism (*q.v.*). See papers by O. Neurath, R. Carnap, C. G. Hempel, in Erkenntnis, 2, 1931; 3, 1932; 4, 1934; Scientia 50, 1931; Rev. de Sythèse 10, 1935; Phil. Science 3, 1936; S. S. Stevens in Psych. Bull. 36, 1939.—*R.C.*

Physico-Theological Argument: Kant's (*q.v.*) term for the teleological proof of the existence of God.—*O.F.K.*

Physico-Theology: A theology which finds corroboration in natural philosophy. A term now in general disuse.—*V.F.*

Physics: (Gr. *physis,* nature) In Greek philosophy, one of the three branches of philosophy, Logic and Ethics being the other two among the Stoics (*q.v.*). In Descartes, metaphysics is the root and physics the trunk of the "tree of knowledge." Today, it is the science (overlapping chemistry, biology and human physiology) of the calculation and prediction of the phenomena of motion of microscopic or macroscopic bodies, *e.g.* gravitation, pressure, heat, light, sound, magnetism, electricity, radio-activity, etc. Philosophical problems arise concerning the relation of physics to biological and social phenomena, to pure mathematics, and to metaphysics. See *Mechanism, Physicalism.*

Physis: See *Nature, Physics.*

Picturesque: A modification of the beautiful in English aesthetics, 18th century.—*L.V.*

Pieh Mo: Neo-Mohists; heretical Mohists. See *Mo chê* and *Chinese philosophy.*

Pien: Argumentation or dialectics, which "is to make clear the distinction between right and wrong, to ascertain the principles of order and disorder, to make clear the points of similarity and difference,to examine the laws of names and actualities, to determine what is beneficial and what is harmful, and to decide what is uncertain and doubtful. It describes the ten thousand things as they are, and discusses the various opinions in their comparative merits. It uses names to specify actualities, propositions to express ideas, and explanations to set forth reasons, including or excluding according to classes." It involves seven methods: "The method of possibility is to argue from what is not exhausted. The method of hypothesis is to argue from what is not actual at present. The method of imitation is to provide a model. What is imitated is taken as the model. If the reason agrees with the model, it is correct. If it does not agree with the model it is incorrect. This is the method of imitation. The method of comparison is to make clear about one thing by means of another. The method of parallel is to compare two propositions consistently throughout. The method of analogy says, 'You are so. Why should I not be so?' The method of induction is to grant what has not been accepted on the basis of its similarity to what has already been accepted. For example, when it is said that all the others are the same, how can I say that the others are different?" (Neo-Mohism.)—*W.T.C.*

Pien: Transformation or change in process; change from *ens* to non-*ens;* gradual change. See *Hua.*—*W.T.C.*

Pien che: Sophists or Dialecticians. See *Ming chia.*

Pien hua che: The evolutionary transformation, which of effortless power is the greatest. (Sophism.)—*H.H.*

Pietism: In general, an emphasis upon the individual appropriation of religious truth as over against its formal acceptance. As a movement, the term refers specifically to the reaction against the cold orthodoxies within German Protestantism of the late 17th and 18th centuries. Philip Spener (1635-1705) is regarded as the father of German Pietism. Under Spener's influence August

Franke (1663-1727) became one of the most vigorous champions of the movement toward a more genuine Christian living. Franke was a preacher of power and founder of charitable organizations. Spener's *Pia Desideria,* "The Thing, Religiously Desired" (1675) is regarded as the Manifesto of the movement. Pietism also carries a derogatory connotation: a person is said to be "pietistic" if the seriousness of his religious practices lead him to extremes, even to the point of asceticism and fanaticism. See *Puritanism.*—*V.F.*

Ping t'ien hsai: World peace, the ultimate goal of Confucian moral training and education.—*W.T.C.*

Pistology: A noun derived from the Greek, *pistis,* faith; hence in general the science of faith or religious belief. A branch of theology specially concerned with faith and its restricted scope, as distinguished from reason. —*J.J.R.*

Pity: A more or less condescending feeling for other living beings in their suffering or lowly condition, condoned by those who hold to the inevitability of class differences, but condemned by those who believe in melioration or the establishment of more equitable relations and therefore substitute sympathy (*q.v.*). Synonymous with "having mercy" or "to spare" in the Old Testament (the Lord is "of many bowels"), Christians also are exhorted to be pitiful (*e.g.,* 1. Pet. 3.8). Spinoza yet equates it with commiseration, but since this involves pain in addition to some good if alleviating action follows, it is to be overcome in a life dictated by reason. Except for moral theories which do not recognize feeling for other creatures as a fundamental urge pushing into action, such as utilitarianism in some of its aspects and Hinduism which adheres to the doctrine of *karma* (*q.v.*), however far apart the two are, pity may be regarded a prime ethical impulse but, due to its coldness and the possibility of calculation entering, is no longer countenanced as an essentially ethical principle in modern moral thinking.—*K.F.L.*

Planck, Max: (1858-1947) A German physicist who taught at the University of Kiel and later at the University of Berlin. He is world-famous for his theory of quanta, according to which all energy travels in units comparable to atoms of matter. See *Planck's constant.* —*R.B.W.*

Planck's constant: In *quantum mechanics* (*q.v.*), a fundamental physical constant, usually denoted by the letter h, which appears in many physical formulas. It may be defined by the law that the *quantum* (*q.v.*) of radiant energy of any frequency is equal to the frequency multiplied by h. See further *Uncertainty principle.*—*A.C.*

Plastic: The effect of relief obtained by the nuance of light and shade.—*L.V.*

Plato: (428-7 — 348-7 B.C.) Was one of the greatest of the Greek philosophers. He was born either in Athens or on the island of Aegina, and was originally known as Aristocles. Ariston, his father, traced his ancestry to the last kings of Athens. His mother, Perictione, was a descendant of the family of Solon. Plato was given the best elementary education possible and he spent eight years, from his own twentieth year to the death of

Socrates, as a member of the Socratic circle. Various stories are told about his supposed masters in philosophy, and his travels in Greece, Italy, Sicily and Egypt, but all that we know for certain is that he somehow acquired a knowledge of Pythagoreanism, Heraclitanism, Eleaticism and other Pre-Socratic philosophies. He founded his school of mathematics and philosophy in Athens in 387 B.C. It became known as the Academy. Here he taught with great success until his death at the age of eighty. His career as a teacher was interrupted on two occasions by trips to Sicily, where Plato tried without much success to educate and advise Dionysius the Younger. His works have been very well preserved; we have more than twenty-five authentic dialogues, certain letters, and some definitions which are probably spurious. For a list of works, bibliography and an outline of his thought, see *Platonism.—V.J.B.*

Platonic Realism: See *Realism*.

Platonism: The philosophy of Plato marks one of the high points in the development of Greek philosophical genius. Platonism is characterized by a partial contempt for sense knowledge and empirical studies, by a high regard for mathematics and its method, by a longing for another and better world, by a frankly spiritualistic view of life, by its use of a method of discussion involving an accumulation of ever more profound insights rather than the formal logic of Aristotle, and, above all, by an unswerving faith in the capacity of the human mind to attain absolute truth and to use this truth in the rational direction of human life and affairs.

The works of Plato are chiefly in the form of dialogues, remarkable for their literary as well as for their philosophic qualities. The following list includes all the dialogues recognized as authentic by modern authorities. Early period: *Ion, Charmides, Hippias I* and *II* (doubtful), *Laches, Lysis, Euthyphro, Euthydemus, Gorgias, Protagoras, Meno, Apology, Crito, Phaedo, Menexenus.* Middle period: *Symposium, Phaedrus, Republic, Theaetetus, Cratylus.* Late period: *Timaeus, Critias, Sophistes, Politicus, Philebus, Parmenides, Laws, Epinomis* (doubtful). Thirteen *Letters* have also been preserved, of which two (VII-VIII), at least, are probably authentic.

Plato's theory of knowledge can hardly be discussed apart from his theory of reality. Through sense perception man comes to know the changeable world of bodies. This is the realm of opinion (*doxa*); such cognition may be more or less clear but it never rises to the level of true knowledge, for its objects are impermanent and do not provide a stable foundation for science. It is through intellectual, or rational, cognition that man discovers another world, that of immutable essences, intelligible realities, Forms or Ideas. This is the level of scientific knowledge (*episteme*); it is reached in mathematics and especially in philosophy (*Repub.* VI, 510). The world of intelligible Ideas contains the ultimate realities from which the world of sensible things has been patterned. Plato experienced much difficulty in regard to the sort of existence to be attributed to his Ideas. Obviously it is not the crude existence of physical things; nor can it be merely the mental existence of logical constructs. Interpretations have varied from the theory of the Christian Fathers (which was certainly not that of Plato himself) viz., that the Ideas are exemplary Causes in God's Mind, to the suggestion of Aristotle (*Metaphysics,* I) that they are realized, in a sense, in the world of individual things, but are apprehended only by the intellect. The Ideas appear, however, particularly in the dialogues of the middle period, to be objective essences, independent of human minds, providing not only the foundation for the truth of human knowledge but also the ontological bases for the shadowy things of the sense world. Within the world of Forms, there is a certain hierarchy. At the top, the most noble of all, is the Idea of the Good (*Repub.* VII); it dominates the other Ideas and they participate in it. Beauty, symmetry and truth are high-ranking Ideas; at times they are placed almost on a par with the Good (*Philebus* 65; also *Sympos,* and *Phaedrus* passim). There are, below these, other Ideas, such as those of the major virtues (wisdom, temperance, courage, justice and piety) and mathematical terms and relations, such as equality, likeness, unlikeness and proportion. Each type or class of being is represented by its perfect Form in the sphere of Ideas; there is an ideal Form of man, dog, willow tree, of every kind of natural object and even of artificial things like beds (*Repub.* 596). The relationship of the "many" objects, belonging to a certain class of things in the sense world, to the "One," i.e. the single Idea which is their archetype, is another great source of difficulty to Plato. Three solutions, which are not mutually exclusive, are suggested in the dialogues: (1) that the many *participate* imperfectly in the perfect nature of their Idea; (2) that the many are made in *imitation* of the One; and (3) that the many are composed as a *mixture* of the *Limit* (Idea) with the *Unlimited* (matter).

The human soul is considered by Plato to be an immaterial agent, superior in nature to the body and somewhat hindered by the body in the performance of the higher, psychic functions of human life. The tripartite division of the soul becomes an essential teaching of Platonic psychology from the *Republic* onward. The rational part is higher and is pictured as the ruler of the psychological organism in the well-regulated man. Next in importance is the "spirited" element of the soul, which is the source of action and the seat of the virtue of courage. The lowest part is the concupiscent or acquisitive element, which may be brought under control by the virtue of temperance. The latter two are often combined and called irrational in contrast to the highest part. Sensation is an active function of the soul, by which the soul "feels" the objects of sense through the instrumentality of the body. Particularly in the young, sensation is a necessary prelude to the knowledge of Ideas, but the mature and developed soul must learn to rise above sense perception and must strive for a more direct intuition of intelligible essences. That the soul exists before the body (related to the Pythagorean and, possibly, Orphic doctrine of transmigration) and knows the world of Ideas immediately in this anterior condition, is the foundation of the Platonic theory of *reminiscence* (*Meno, Phaedo, Republic, Phaedrus*). Thus the soul is born with true knowledge in it, but the soul, due to the encrustation of bodily cares and interests, cannot easily recall the truths innately, and we might say now, subconsciously present in it. Sometimes sense perceptions aid the soul in the process of reminiscence, and again, as in the famous demonstration of the Pythagorean theorem by the slave boy of the *Meno,* the questions and suggestions of a teacher provide the necessary stimuli for recollection. The personal immortality of the soul is very clearly taught by Plato in the tale of Er (*Repub.* X) and, with various attempts at logical demonstration, in the *Phaedo*. Empirical and physiological psychology is not stressed in Platonism, but there is an approach to it in the descriptions of sense organs and their media in the *Timaeus* 42 ff.

The Platonic theory of education is based on a drawing out (*educatio*) of what is already dimly known to the learner (*Meno, Repub.* II-VII, *Theaetetus, Laws.*). The training of the philosopher-ruler, outlined in the *Republic,* requires the selection of the most promising children in their infancy and a rigorous disciplining of them in gymnastic, music (in the Greek sense of literary studies), mathematics and dialectic (the study of the Ideas). This training was to continue until the students were about thirty-five years of age; then fifteen years of practical apprenticeship in the subordinate offices of the state were required; finally, at the age of fifty, the rulers were advised to return to the study of philosophy. It should be noted that this program is intended only for an intellectual élite; the military class was to undergo a shorter period of training suited to its functions, and the masses of people, engaged in production, trading, and like pursuits, were not offered any special educational schedule.

Platonism as a political philosophy finds its best known exposition in the theory of the ideal state in the Republic. There, Plato described a city in which social justice would be fully realized. Three classes of men are distinguished: the philosopher-kings, apparently a very small group whose education has been alluded to above, who would be the rulers because by nature and by training they were the best men for the job. They must excel particularly in their rational abilities: their special virtue is philosophic wisdom; the soldiers, or guardians of the state, constitute the second class; their souls must be remarkable for the development of the spirited, warlike element, under the control of the virtue of courage; the lowest class is made up of the acquisitive group, the workers of every sort whose characteristic virtue is temperance. For the two upper classes, Plato suggested a form of community life which would entail the abolition of monogamous marriage, family life, and of private property. It is to be noted that this form of semi-communism was suggested for a minority of the citizens only (*Repub.* III and V) and it is held to be a practical impossibility in the *Laws* (V, 739-40), though Plato continued to think that some form of community life is theoretically best for man. In Book VIII of the Republic, we find the famous classification of five types of political organization, ranging from *aristocracy* which is the rule of the best men, *timocracy,* in which the rulers are motivated by a love of honor, *oligarchy,* in which the rulers seek wealth, *democracy,* the rule of the masses who are unfit for the task, to *tyranny,* which is the rule of one man who may have started as the champion of the people but who governs solely for the advancement of his own, selfish interests.

The Platonic philosophy of art and aesthetics stresses, as might be expected, the value of the reasonable imitation of Ideal realities rather than the photographic imitation of sense things and individual experiences. All beautiful things participate in the Idea of beauty (*Symposium* and *Phaedrus*). The artist is frequently described as a man carried away by his inspiration, akin to the fool; yet art requires reason and the artist must learn to contemplate the world of Ideas. Fine art is not radically distinguished from useful art. In both the *Republic* and the *Laws,* art is subordinated to the good of the state, and those forms of art which are effeminate, asocial, inimical to the morale of the citizens, are sternly excluded from the ideal state.

The ethics of Platonism is intellectualistic. While he questions (*Protagoras,* 323 ff.) the sophistic teaching that ''virtue is knowledge,'' and stresses the view that the wise man must *do* what is right, as well as *know* the right, still the cumulative impetus of his many dialogues on the various virtues and the good life, tends toward the conclusion that the learned, rationally developed soul is the good soul. From this point of view, wisdom is the greatest virtue (*Repub.* IV). Fortitude and temperance are necessary virtues of the lower parts of the soul and justice in the individual, as in the state, is the harmonious co-operation of all parts, under the control of reason. Of pleasures, the best are those of the intellect (*Philebus*); man's greatest happiness is to be found in the contemplation of the highest Ideas (*Repub.,* 583 ff.).

In the field of the philosophy of religion, Platonism becomes obscure. There is little doubt that Plato paid only lip-service to the anthropomorphic polytheism of Athenian religion. Many of the attributes of the Idea of the Good are those of an eternal God. The *Republic* (Book II) pictures the Supreme Being as perfect, unchangeable and the author of truth. Similar rationalizations are found throughout the Laws. Another current of religious thought is to be found in the *Timaeus, Politicus* and *Sophist*. The story of the making of the universe and man by the *Demiurgus* is mythic and yet it is in many points a logical development of his theory of Ideas. The World-Maker does not create things from nothing; he fashions the world out of a pre-existing chaos of matter by introducing patterns taken from the sphere of Forms. This process of formation is also explained, in the *Timaeus* (54 ff.), in terms of various mathematical figures. In an early period of the universe, God (*Chronos*) exercised a sort of Providential care over things in this world (*Politicus,* 269-275), but eventually man was left to his own devices. The tale of Er, at the end of the *Republic,* describes a judgment of souls after death, their separation into the good and the bad, and the assignment of various rewards and punishments.

H. Stephanus et J. Serranus (ed.), *Platonis Opera* (Parris, 1578), has provided the standard pagination, now used in referring to the text of Plato; it is not a critical edition. J. Burnet (ed.), *Platonis Opera,* 5 vol. (Oxford, 1899-1907). Platon, *Oeuvres complètes,* texte et trad., Collect. G. Budé (Paris, 1920 ff.). *The Dialogues of Plato,* transl. B. Jowett, 3rd ed. (Oxford, 1920). W. Pater, *Plato and Platonism* (London, 1909). A. E. Taylor, *Plato, the Man and his Work* (N. Y., 1927). P. Shorey, *What Plato Said* (Chicago, 1933). A. Diès, *Autour de Platon,* 2 vol. (Paris, 1927). U. von Wilamowitz-Moellendorf, *Platon,* 2 vol. (Berlin, 1919). John Burnet, *Platonism* (Berkeley, 1928). Paul Elmer More, *Platonism* (Oxford, 1931). Walter Pater, *Plato and Platonism.* Constantin Ritter, *Essence of Plato's Philosophy* (London, 1933). Léon Robin, *Platon* (Paris 1935). Paul Shorey, *Platonism, Ancient and Modern* (Berkeley, 1938). A. E. Taylor, *Platonism and Its Influence* (London, 1924). F. J. E. Woodbridge, *The Son of Apollo* (Boston, 1929). C. Bigg, *The Christian Platonists of Alexandria* (Oxford, 1913). T. Whittaker, *The Neo-Platonists* (Cambridge, 1918, 2nd ed.). John H. Muirhead, *The Platonic Tradition in Anglo-Saxon Philosophy* (New York, 1931). F. J. Powicke, *The Cambridge Platonists* (Boston, 1927.)—*V.J.B.*

The Academy continued as a school of philosophy until closed by Justinian in 529 A.D. The early scholars (Speusippus, Xenocrates, Polemo, Crates) were not great philosophers; they adopted a Pythagorean interpretation of the Ideas and concentrated on practical, moral problems. Following the Older Academy (347-247 B.C.), the Middle and New Academies (Arcesilaus and Carneades were the principal teachers) became sceptical and eclectic. Aristotle (384-322 B.C.) studied with Plato for twenty years and embodied many Platonic views in his own philosophy. Platonism was very highly regarded by the Christian Fathers (Ambrose, Augustine, John Damascene and Anselm of Canterbury, for instance) and it continued as the approved philosophy of the Christian Church until the 12th century. From the 3rd century on, Neo-Platonism (see *Plotinism*) developed the other-worldly, mystical side of Plato's thought. The School of Chartres (Bernard, Thierry, Wm. of Conches, Gilbert of Poitiers) in the 12th century was a center of Christian Platonism, interested chiefly in the cosmological theory of the *Timaeus.* The Renaissance witnessed a revival of Platonism in the Florentine Academy (Marsilio Ficino and the two Pico della Mirandolas). In England, the Cambridge Platonists (H. More, Th. Gale, J. Norris) in the 17th century started an interest in Plato, which has not yet died out in the English Universities. Today, the ethical writings of A. E. Taylor, the theory of essences developed by G. Santayana, and the metaphysics of A. N. Whitehead, most nearly approach a contemporary Platonism.—*V.J.B.*

Platonism, medieval: Plato's works were not accessible to the medieval writers previous to the 13th century. They possessed only part of the Timaeus in the translation and commentary by Chalcidius. Nor were they acquainted with the writings of the Neo-Platonists. They had the logical texts by Porphyrius; little besides. St. Augustine, the greatest authority in these ages, was well acquainted with the teachings of the "Academy" of his time and became a source for Neo-Platonic influences. Furthermore, there were the writings of Pseudo-Dionysius of which first Alcuin had made a rather insufficient, later Scotus Eriugena a readable translation. Scotus himself was thoroughly Neo-Platonic in his philosophy, however "Christianized" his Platonism may have been. The medieval "Platonists" held, among some propositions of minor importance, that universals were existent substances (Realism, *q.v.*), that body and soul were two independent substances, united more or less accidentally; they assumed accordingly a "plurality of forms" in one substance. Some believed that Plato had been given a peculiar insight even in the mysteries of Christian faith. Thus they went so far as to identify the *anima mundi,* which they believed to be a Platonic notion, with the Holy Ghost (*e.g.* Abelard). Even after the revival of Aristotelian philosophy, against which the "Platonists" reacted violently, Platonism, or as they afterwards preferred to call it, Augustinianism persisted in many schools, especially in those depending on the Franciscans.—*R.A..*

Pleasure and pain: In Philosophy these terms appear mostly in ethical discussions, where they have each two meanings not always clearly distinguished. "Pleasure" is used sometimes to refer to a certain hedonic quality of experiences, viz. pleasantness, and sometimes as a name for experiences which have that quality (here "pleasures" are "pleasant experiences" and "pleasure" is the entire class of such experience). *Mutatis mutandis,* the same is true of "pain." Philosophers have given various accounts of the nature of pleasure and pain. E.g., Aristotle says that pleasure is a perfection supervening on certain activities, pain the opposite. Spinoza defines pleasure as the feeling with which one passes from a lesser state of perfection to a greater, pain as the feeling with which one makes the reverse transition. Again, philosophers have raised various questions about pleasure and pain. Can they be identified with good and evil? Are our actions always determined by our own pleasure and pain actual or prospective? Can pleasures and pains be distinguished quantitatively, qualitatively? See *Bentham, Epicureanism.—W.K.F.*

Pleasures of the imagination: The moderate, healthful, and agreeable stimulus to the mind, resulting (in the primary class) from the properties of greatness, novelty, and beauty (kinship, color, proportionality, etc.) in objects actually seen; (in the secondary class) from the processes of comparison, association, and remodelling set up in the mind by the products of art or by the recollection of the beauties of nature. (Addison.) —

K.E.G.

Plekhanov, George Valentinovich: (1856-1918) Was a Russian Marxist who became the philosophical leader of the Menshevik faction of the pre-Revolutionary Russian Social Democratic Workers' Party, opposing Lenin, the leader of the Bolshevik wing. In spite of what are regarded as his political errors, such as his support of the war of 1914-1918 and his negative attitude to the Revolution of October, 1917, contemporary Soviet thinkers regard Plekhanov's works as containing valuable expositions of Marxist philosophy. Among his writings in this field are, *Our Disputes* (1885), *On the Problem of the Development of the Monistic View of History* (1895), *Essays on the History of Materialism* (1896), *On the Materialist Conception of History* (1897), *On the Problem of the Role of the Individual in History* (1898).—*J.M.S.*

Pleroma: Literally the Greek term means a filling up; it was used by the Gnostics to denote the world of light, or the spiritual world of aeons full of divine life.—*J.J.R.*

Plotinism: The philosophic and religious thought of Plotinus (205-270). His writings were published by Porphyry in six books of nine sections, *Enneads,* each. All reality consists of a series of emanations, from the *One,* the eternal source of all being. The first, necessary emanation is that of *Nous* (mind or intelligence), the second that of *Psyche* (soul). At the periphery of the universe is found matter. Man belongs partly in the realm of spirit and partly in the sphere of matter.

Plotinism offers a well-developed theory of sensation. The objects of sensation are of a lower order of being than the perceiving organism. The inferior cannot act upon the superior. Hence sensation is an *activity* of the sensory agent upon its objects. Sensation provides a direct, realistic perception of material things, but, since they are ever-changing, such knowledge is not valuable. In internal sense perception, the imagination also functions actively, memory is attributed to the imaginative power and it serves not only in the recall of sensory images but also in the retention of the verbal formulae in which intellectual concepts are expressed. The human soul can look either upward or downward; up to the sphere of purer spirit, or down to the evil regions of matter. Rational knowledge is a cognition of intelligible realities, or Ideas in the realm of Mind which is often referred to as Divine. The climax of knowledge consists in an intuitive and mystical union with the One; this is experienced by few.

The Idea of Beauty is one and perfect according to Plotinus. All lesser beauties, spiritual and physical, are participations in the one, supreme Beauty. The attribute of the beautiful which is most stressed is *splendor;* it consists of a shining-forth of the spiritual essence of the beautiful thing.

Characteristically Plotinian is the teaching that man must first turn his mind away from the inferior things of sense toward the inner reality of his own soul. He must learn to regard his soul as part of the World-Soul. He must transcend the multiple things of the realm of Mind and endeavor to achieve that communion with the One, which is his ultimate good. There is no question of personal immortality and so the goal of human life is a merging with universal Spirit. In his politics, Plotinus favored a sort of community life incorporating many of the idealistic suggestions to be found in Plato's *Republic.*

Plotinism is a theocentric form of thought. As reality becomes more intelligible, it becomes more spiritual and Divine. The Ideas in the sphere of *Nous* are Divine and in later Neo-Platonism become gods; hence the system is polytheistic.

As a school of Greek and Latin philosophers, Plotinism lasted until the fifth century. Porphyry, Apuleius, Jamblichus, Julian the Apostate, Themistius, Simplicius, Macrobius andd Proclus are the most important representatives. Through St. Augustine, Dionysius the Pseudo-Areopagite, John Scotus Eriugena, and the Greek Fathers, Plotinian thought has been partly incorporated into Christian intellectualism. Nearly all prominent Arabian philosophers before Averroës are influenced by Plotinus; this is particularly true of Avicenna and Algazel. In the Jewish tradition Avicebron's *Fons Vitae* is built on the frame of the emanation theory. Meister Eckhart and Nicholas of Cusa continue the movement. It is spiritually related to some modern anti-intellectualistic and mystical currents of thought.

Plotin, *Ennéades,* (Greek text and French transl.) by E. Bréhier, (Budé) 6 vol., Paris, 1930-40. Mackenzie, S., *The Enneads of Plotinus,* London, 1917-1919. Heinemann, F., *Plotin,* Leipzig, 1921. Bréhier, E., *La Philosophie de Plotin,* Paris, 1928. Inge, W. R., *The Philosophy of Plotinus,* 2 vol. 2nd ed., London and N. Y., 1929.—*V.J.B.*

Pluralism: This is the doctrine that there is not one (Monism), not two (Dualism) but many ultimate substances. From the earliest Ionian fundamentals of air, earth, fire and water, to the hierarchy of monads of Leibniz, the many things-in-themselves of Herbart and the theory of the many that "works" in the latter day Pragmatism of James and others, we get a variety of theories that find philosophic solace in variety rather than in any knowable or unknowable one. See *Dualism, Idealism, Materialism, Monism, Political Philosophy* (Laski).—*L.E.D.*

Plurality of causes: The doctrine according to which identical events can have two or more different causes. "It is not true that the same phenomenon is always produced by the same causes," declared J. S. Mill, author of the doctrine. Quite the contrary, "many causes may produce some kind of sensation; many causes may produce death." Mill's position was not taken in support of the doctrine of free will or of that of chance, but rather in opposition to an old contention of the physicists, among whom Newton stated that "to the same natural effect we must, as far as possible, ascribe the same cause." The subsequent controversy has shown that Mill's position was based on the confusion between "the same phenomenon" and "the same kind of phenomena." It is doubtless true that the same kind of phenomena, say death, can be produced by many causes, but only because we take the phenomenon broadly; nevertheless, it may remain true that each particular phenomenon can be caused only by a very definite cause or by a very definite combination of causes. In other words, the broader we conceive the phenomenon, the more causes are likely to apply to it. —*R.B.W.*

Plutarch of Athens: (5th century A.D.) Founder of Athenian Neo-Platonism, author of commentaries on Platonic and Pythagorean writings.

Plutarch of Chaeronea: (about 100 A.D.) Famous biographer and author of several philosophical treatises. —*M.F.*

Parallel Lives; Opera moralia (tr. Bolin's Classical Libr.).

Pneuma: (Gr. *pneuma*, breath) A Stoic, also Epicurean, concept signifying spirit, vital force, or creative fire in its penetration into matter. Sometimes understood as psychic energy, or distinguished as the formative fire-mind and the divinely inspired rational part of man from the more emotional, physical aspect of soul. In early Christian, particularly Gnostic philosophy, *pneuma*, as spirit, is differentiated from *psyche*, or soul. See *Pneuma Hagion*, the Holy Ghost.—*K.F.L.*

Pneumatology: (Gr. *pneuma*, spirit + *logos*, theory) In the most general sense pneumatology is the philosophical or speculative treatment of spirits or souls, including human, divine and those intermediate between God and man. D'Alembert restricted pneumatology to human souls. *Discours préliminaire de l'Encyclopédie*, § 73; he considered pneumatology, logic and ethics the three branches of the philosophical science of man. The term has also been considered to *exclude* man and to apply only to God and the angelic hierarchy. (See article by Bersot in Franck's *Dict. des Sci. Philos.*) The wide sense in which pneumatology embraces first, God, second, the angels and third, man is perhaps the most convenient and justifiable usage.—*L.W.*

Poiesis: (Gr. *poiesis*) Activity of creating or making; artistic production (Aristotle).—*G.R.M.*

Poietic: Relating to production or the arts of production; *e.g.* poietic knowledge, as distinguished from practical and from theoretical knowledge. See *Aristotelianism*. —*G.R.M.*

Poincaré, Henri: (1854-1912) French mathematician and mathematical physicist to whom many important technical contributions are due. His thought was occupied by problems on the borderline of physics and philosophy. His views reflect the influence of positivism and seem to be closely related to pragmatism. Poincaré is known also for his opposition to the logistic method in the foundations of mathematics, especially as it was advocated by Bertrand *Russell* (*q.v.*) and Louis Couturat, and for his proposed resolution of the logical *paradoxes* (*q.v.*) by the prohibition of *impredicative definition* (*q.v.*). Among his books, the more influential are *Science and Hypothesis, Science and Method,* and *Dernières Pensées*.—*R.B.W.*

Point-event: A. N. Whitehead's term signifying an event with all its dimensions ideally restricted. —*R.B.W.*

Poissons Law: This rule, which is also called Poisson's Law of Small Numbers, is an elaboration of Bernouilli's Theorem dealing with the difference between the actual and the most probable number of occurrences of an event. 1. In cases of Random Sampling, the Poisson Exponential Limit is used in place of the Normal Probability Function or the strict application of the Bernouilli Theorem, when considering events which happen rarely. 2. In cases of Dispersion of Statistical Ratios, a Bernouilli Distribution is used when the probability of an event is constant; and a Poisson Distribution is used when that probability is variable. In both cases, there is a maximum involved which will not be surpassed; and the values obtained by Poisson's Law are smaller than those obtained in the other cases.—*T.G.*

Polarity, philosophy of: Philosophies that make the concept of polarity one of the systematic principles according to which opposites involve each other when applied to any significant realm of investigation. Polarity was one of the basic concepts in the philosophy of Cusanus and Schelling. Morris R. Cohen made use of the principle of polarity in scientific philosophy, in biology, in social and historical analysis, in law and in ethics. (Cf. *Reason and Nature*).—*H.H.*

Political Personalism: The doctrine that the state is under obligation to provide opportunity to each citizen for the highest possible physical, mental, and spiritual development, because personality is the supreme achievement of the social order. A movement in France represented by the journal *Esprit*.—*R.T.F.*

Political Philosophy: That branch of philosophy which deals with political life, especially with the essence, origin and value of the state. In ancient philosophy politics also embraced what we call ethics. The first and most important ancient works on Political Philosophy were Plato's *Politeia (Republic)* and Aristotle's *Politics*. The *Politeia* outlines the structure and functions of the ideal state. It became the pattern for all the Utopias (see *Utopia*) of later times. Aristotle, who considers man fundamentally a social creature i.e. a political animal, created the basis for modern theories of government, especially by his distinction of the different forms of government. Early Christianity had a rather negative attitude towards the state which found expression in St. Augustine's *De Civitate Dei*. The influence of this work, in which the earthly state was declared to be civitas diaboli, a state of the devil, was predominant throughout the Middle Ages. In the discussion of the relation between church and empire, the main topic of medieval political philosophy, certain authors foreshadowed modern political theories. Thomas Aquinas stressed the popular origin of royal power and the right of the people to restrict or abolish that power in case of abuse; William of Ockham and Marsiglio of Padua held similar views. Dante Alighieri was one of the first to recognize the intrinsic value of the state; he considered the world monarchy to be the only means whereby peace, justice and liberty could be secured.

But it was not until the Renaissance that, due to the rediscovery of the individual and his rights and to the formation of territorial states, political philosophy began to play a major rôle. Niccolo Machiavelli and Jean Bodin laid the foundation for the new theories of the state by stressing its independence from any external power and its indivisible sovereignty. The theory of popular rights and of the right of resistance against tyranny was especially advocated by the "Monarchomachi" (Huguenots, such as Beza, Hotman, Languet, Danaeus, Catholics such as Boucher, Rossaeus, Mariana). Most of them use the theory of an original contract (see *Social Contract*) to justify limitations of monarchical power. Later, the idea of a Natural Law, independent from divine revelation (Hugo Grotius and his followers), served as an argument for liberal — sometimes revolutionary — tendencies. With the exception of Hobbes, who used the contract theory in his plea for absolutism, almost all the publicists of the 16th and 17th century built their liberal theories upon the idea of an original covenant by which individuals joined together and by mutual consent formed a state and placed a fiduciary trust in the supreme power (Roger Williams and John Locke). It was this contract which the Pilgrim Fathers translated into actual facts, after their arrival in America, in November, 1620, long before John Locke had developed his theory. In the course of the 17th century in England the contract theory was generally substituted for the theory of the divine rights of kings. It was supported by the assumption of an original "State of Nature" in which all men enjoyed equal reciprocal rights. The most ardent defender of the social contract theory in the 18th century was J. J. Rousseau who deeply influenced the philosophy of the French revolution. In Rousseau's conception the idea of the sovereignty of the people took on a more democratic aspect than in 17th century English political philosophy which had been almost exclusively aristocratic in its spirit. This tendency found expression in his concept of the "general will" in the moulding of which each individual has his share. Immanuel Kant, who made these concepts the basis of his political philosophy, recognized more clearly than Rousseau the fictitious character of the social contract and treated it as a "regulative idea," meant to serve as a criterion in the evaluation of any act of the state. For Hegel the state is an end in itself, the supreme realization of reason and morality. In marked opposition to this point of view, Marx and Engels, though strongly influenced by Hegel, visualized a society in which the state would gradually fade away. Most of the 19th century publicists, however, upheld the juristic theory of the state. To them the state was the only source of law and at the same time invested with absolute sovereignty: there are no limits to the legal omnipotence of the state except those which are self-imposed. In opposition to this doctrine of unified state authority, a pluralistic theory of sovereignty has been advanced recently by certain authors, laying emphasis upon corporate personalities and professional groups (Duguit Krabbe, Laski). Out-

spoken anti-stateism was advocated by anarchists such as Kropotkin, etc., by syndicalists and Guild socialists. —*W.E.*

Recent political theory includes the argument by Robert J. Nozick (*Anarchy, State, and Utopia*) for the minimal state, which is morally legitimate, and against any more extensive state, which will violate the rights of individuals. Hannah Arendt (*On Revolution*) remarks that one of the most important negative liberties we have enjoyed since the end of the ancient world is the freedom *from* politics. In Melvin J. Lasky's brilliant study, *Utopia and Revolution* (1976), he observes that human beings seem to value intense pleasures over steady ones, ecstasy over contentment, the excitement of war over the possession of peace. Playing on this, the revolutionary despises reform in favor of complete transformation. All present things will be destroyed at once. Revolutionaries have no guilt and no conscience, and say that we must give up all present values in the name of future values, which remain to be disclosed. The revolution itself is the utopia.—*S.E.N.*

Politics: (Gr. *polis,* city) The normative science which treats of the organization of social goods. The branch of civics concerned with government and state affairs. See *Political Philosophy.*—*J.K.F.*

Polysyllogism: A chain of syllogisms arranged to lead to a single final conclusion, the conclusion of each syllogism except the last serving as premiss of a later syllogism.

In contrast, an argument consisting of a single syllogism is called a *monosyllogism.*—*A.C.*

Polytheism: (Gr. *polus,* many; and *theos,* god) A theory that Divine reality is numerically multiple, that there are many gods; opposed to monotheism. See *Plotinism.* —*V.J.B.*

Pompanazzi, Pietro or Pereto: (1462-1524) Was born in Mantua, in Italy, and studied medicine and philosophy at Padua. He taught philosophy at Padua, Ferrara and Bologna. He is best known for his *Tractatus de immortalitate animae* (ed. C. G. Bardili, Tübingen, 1791) in which he denied that Aristotle taught the personal immortality of the human soul. His interpretation of Aristotle follows that of the Greek commentator, Alexander of Aphrodisias (3rd c. A.D.) and is also closely related to the Averroistic tradition.—*V.J.B.*

Pons asinorum: The literal meaning of the Latin expression, asses' bridge, has been figuratively applied to a diagram constructed by Petrus Tartaretus about 1480, whose purpose was to aid the student of logic in finding the middle term of a syllogism and disclose its relations. It was assumed that it was as difficult to persuade students to do this as to get asses to pass over a bridge. Hence expression has also been applied to any relatively easy test. Euclid's proposition, that if two sides of a triangle are equal the angles opposite to those sides must also be equal, has been called a *pons asinorum* for students of geometry.—*J.J.R.*

Popper, Sir Karl R.: (1902-) Viennese philosopher of science and politics who moved from Austria to New Zealand and later on to London. His tenets in philosophy hold that as a scientific philosopher we should aim towards the elimination of that which is false rather than the search for that which is true, and so too as a political philosopher our aim must be not the establishment of good but rather the elimination of evil. His writings include *The Open Society and Its Enemies* (1945), *The Poverty of Historicism* (1957) and The *Logic of Scientific Discovery* (1959.)—*L.L.*

Porphyry: (c. 232-304 A.D.) A disciple of Plotinus, who adapted Aristotelian logic to Neo-Platonic philosophy. His method of classification by means of dichotomy is known as the "Tree of Porphyry." Cf. *Isagoge* (tr. by Boethius, *q.v.*).—*R.B.W.*

Port Royal Logic: See *Logic, traditional*.

Port Royalists: Name applied to a group of thinkers, writers, and educators, more or less closely connected with the celebrated Cistercian Abbey of Port Royal near Paris, which during the seventeenth century became the most active center of Jansenism and, to a certain extent, of Cartesianism in France. The Port Royalists were distinguished by the severity and austerity of their moral code and by their new educational methods which greatly promoted the advance of pedagogy. The most noted among them were Jean Duvergier de Hauranne, abbot of Saint Cyran (1581-1643), Antoine-*le grand* Arnauld (1612-1694), and Pierre Nicole (1625-1695). Cf. Sainte-Beuve, *Port-Royal*.—*J.J.R.*

Posidonius of Rhodes: (c. 135-50 B.C.) An eclectic philosopher of the Stoic School, who incorporated into his thought many doctrines of Plato and Aristotle.—*R.B.W.*

Posit: (Lat. *ponere,* to put or place) (a) *In logic and epistemology,* positing is the act of entertaining or asserting a proposition immediately *i.e.* without recourse to inference. A proposition may be posited either because it is regarded as (1) a self-evident truth or (2) a postulate arbitrarily assumed. The postulational sense of positing is the more common at present. See *Postulate*.

(b) *In idealistic metaphysics:* positing, in the philosophy of G. Fichte is the initial act by which the Ego creates itself: "The positing of the Ego through itself is therefore, the pure activity of the Ego." (Fichte, *The Science of Knowledge,* Trans. by A.F. Kroeger, p. 68.)—*L.W.*

Positional: The characters of perception are positional. The positional character of the thought is the idea. (Avenarius.)—*H.H.*

Positionality: (Ger. *Positionalität*) In Husserl: The character common to conscious processes of positing or setting an object, whether believingly, or in valuing or willing. *Doxic* positionality is common to processes involving belief, disbelief, doubt, etc. (see *Doxa*); *axiological* positionality, to processes of loving, hating, or otherwise valuing; *volitional,* to those involving inclination, disinclination, voluntary doing, etc. *Positionality* in all its forms is contrasted with *quasi-positionality* (see *Phantasy*) and *neutrality*.—*D.C.*

Positive Theology: A term referring to doctrines alleged to be grounded upon a "positive" revelation and not upon the alleged "negative" conclusions of liberal and rationalistic speculations. The term was used to characterize Scriptural theologies from the freer deistic and rationalistic expositions of doctrines; also, it was used to oppose the conclusions of the so-called "higher critics" of the New and Old Testaments. The term has still another meaning: a theology is said to be positive if it is "constructive," by which is meant that it is apologetic of the spirit, if not the letter, of Protestant faith. In the latter sense positive theology is said to be distinguished from a philosophical theology.—*V.F.*

Positivism: First associated with the doctrine of Auguste Comte that the highest form of knowledge is simple description presumably of sensory phenomena. The doctrine was based on an evolutionary "law of three stages," believed by Comte to have been discovered by him in 1822 but anticipated by Turgot in 1750. The three stages were the *theological,* in which anthropomorphic wills were resorted to in order to explain natural events; the *metaphysical,* in which these wills were depersonalized and became forces and essences; and finally the *positive.* It should be noted that positivistic description was supposed to result in mathematical formulas, not in introspective psychology. See *Scientific Empiricism I*.—*G.B.*

In legal philosophy (*q.v.*): That trend in Legal Philosophy which confines itself to positive law, i.e. the law that actually is valid in a certain country at a certain time. It excludes any higher law such as natural law, sometimes even any evaluation of positive law. The Algemeine Rechtslehre (general theory of law) in Germany, analytical jurisprudence in England, the "pure theory of law" and American legal realism are types of legal positivism. See *Legal Philosophy*.—*W.E.*

Positivism, Logical: See *Scientific Empiricism* I.

Possibility: According to distinctions of *modality* (*q.v.*), a proposition is *possible* if its negation is not necessary. The word *possible* is also used in reference to a state of knowledge rather than to modality; as a speaker might say, "It is possible that 486763 is a prime number," meaning that he had no information to the contrary (although this proposition is impossible in the sense of modality).

A propositional function F may also be said to be *possible*. In this case the meaning may be either simply $(Ex) F(x)$; or that $(Ex) F(x)$ is possible in one of the senses just described; or that $F(x)$ is permitted under some particular system of conventions or code of laws. As an example of the last we may take: "It is possible for a woman to be President of the United States." Here F is $\lambda x[x$ is a woman and x is a President of the United States], and the code of laws in question is the Constitution of the United States.—*A.C.*

Possible: (Gr. *endechomenon*) According to Aristotle that which happens usually but not necessarily; hence distinguished both from the necessary and from the impossible.—*G.R.M.*

Post hoc, ergo propter hoc: (Lat. after this, therefore on account of this) A logical fallacy in which it is argued that a consequent is caused by an antecedent, simply because of the temporal relationship.—*V.J.B.*

Postpredicament: Noun generally applied since the time of Abelard to any particular one of the five conceptions, or relations, examined in detail in the tenth and following chapters of the treatise on the Categories, or Predicaments, ascribed to Aristotle, which, however, was very probably written by others after his death.—*J.J.R.*

Postulate: (Lat. *postulatum;* Ger. *Postulat*) In Kant: (1) An indemonstrable practical or moral hypothesis, such as the reality of God, freedom, or immortality, belief in which is necessary for the performance of our moral duty. (2) Any of three principles of the general category of modality, called by Kant "postulates of empirical thought." See *Modality* and *Kantianism.*—*O.F.K.*

Postulate: See *Mathematics.*

Potency: (Scholastic) Potency is opposed to act as asserted of being. It means the capacity of being or of being thus. Prime matter (*q.v.*) is pure potency, indetermined in regard to actual corporeal being. Any change or development or, generally, becoming presupposes a corresponding potency. Some potencies belong to the nature of a thing, others are merely passive and consist in non-repugnance. Thus to be thrown is not due to a potency strictly speaking in the stone which has, in regard to this a "merely obediential" potency. The first kind is also called operative potency.—*R.A.*

Potentiality: See *Dynamis.*

Power: In general: (1) the physical, mental and moral ability to act or to receive an action; (2) the general faculty of doing, making, performing, realizing, achieving, producing or succeeding; (3) ability, capacity, virtue, virtuality, potency, potentiality, faculty, efficacy, efficacity, efficiency, operative causality, process of change or becoming; (4) natural operative force, energy, vigor, strength, or effective condition applied or applicable to work; (5) person, agent, body, institution, government or state, having or exercising an ability to act in accordance with its nature and functions; (6) spirit, divinity, deity, superhuman agent, supernatural principle of activity; (7) an attribute or name of God; (8) in theology, an order of angels; (9) in law the authority, capacity or right to exercise certain natural and legal prerogatives also, the authority vested in a person by law; (10) influence, prerogative, force.

A. *In psychology,* power is sometimes synonymous with *faculty* (*q.v.*). It also means a quality which renders the nature of an individual agent apt to elicit certain physical and moral actions. Hence, power is a natural endowment enabling the intellect to condition the will and thus create habits and virtues; in a higher degree, power is a moral disposition enabling the individual to cultivate his perfectibility. The distinction between powers is given by the distinction of their actions. Powers are active or operative, and passive or receptive; they are immediate or remote. Even impotence and incapacity are not different in kind from power, but simply in degree. These Aristotelian views on power, including its ontological interpretation, have held the

ground for centuries; and we find them partly also in Hobbes and Locke who defined power as the ability to make or to receive change. Hume's analysis of power showed it to be an illusion; and with the advent of positivism and experimental psychology, this concept lost much of its value. The notion of power has been used by Fechner in his doctrine and law concerning the relation between stimuli and sensations.

B. *In ontology,* power is often synonymous with *potency* (*q.v.*) Aristotle, who is mainly responsible for the development of this notion (*Metaph.* IV, (5) 12), distinguishes three aspects of it: as a source of change, as a capacity of performing, and as a state in virtue of which things are unchangeable by themselves. Hobbes accepts only the first of these meanings, namely that power is the source of motion. Various questions are involved in the analysis of the notion of power; as, for example, whether power is an accident or a perfection of substance, and whether it is distinct from it.

C. *In natural philosophy,* power corresponds to effort, to the force applied to overcome resistance. More technically, it is the time rate of the performance of work, or the transfer of energy. In optics, power is the degree to which an optical instrument magnifies.

D. *In mathematics,* (1) it is a numerical or algebraical index showing the number of times the element it affects must be multiplied by itself; concurrently, it denotes the product arising from the continued multiplication of a quantity by itself. (2) In the theory of aggregates, the power of a class is the number of its elements, its cardinal number (*q.v.*).—*T.G.*

Practical: (Ger. *praktisch*) In Husserl: Of or pertaining to such conscious processes as reach fulfillment in behavior.—*D.C.*

Practical: Relating to praxis, or conduct.—*G.R.M.*

Practical Imperative: (in Kant's ethics) Kant's famous dictum: "So act as to treat humanity, whether in thine own person or in that of any other, in every case as an end withal, never as means only."—*P.A.S.*

Practical Reason: (Kant. Ger. *praktische Vernunft*) Reason or reflective thought concerned with the issues of voluntary decision and action. Practical reason includes "everything which is possible by or through freedom." In general, practical reason deals with the problems of ethics. Kant asserted the primacy of practical reason over theoretical reason; and also asserted as practical postulates (*q.v.*) certain conceptions which were not theoretically demonstrable. See *Kantianism.*—*O.F.K.*

Practical Theology: A special department of conventional theological study, called "practical" to distinguish it from general theology, Biblical, historical and systematic studies. As the term denotes, subjects which deal with the application of the theoretical phases of the subject come under this division: church policy (ecclesiology), the work of the minister in worship (liturgics and hymnology), in preaching (homiletics), in teaching (catechetics), in pastoral service (poimenics), and in missionary effort (evangelistics). For further discussion see *Theological Propaedeutic* (9th ed.,

1912), Philip Schaff.—*V.F.*

Practice: (Lat. *practica,* business) The deliberate application of a theory. Formerly, an established custom; the pursuance of some traditional action. Now, the organization of actuality according to some general principle. Sometimes, opposed to, sometimes, correlative with, theory (*q.v.*).—*J.K.F.*

Praedicabilia: (Lat. that which is able to be predicated) Since Greek philosophic thinking, the modes of predicating or the concepts to be affirmed of any subject whatsoever, usually enumerated as five: genus, species, difference, property (or characteristic), and accident. They assumed an important rôle in the scholastic discussions of universals. According to Kant, they are pure, yet derived concepts of the understanding.—*K.F.L.*

Praedicamenta: (Scholastic) The ten praedicaments are, according to Aristotle (Met. V.) and the Schoolmen: substance, quantity, quality, relation, habitus, when, where, location, action, passion.—*R.A.*

Pragmatic theory of truth: Theory of knowledge which maintains that the truth of a proposition is determined by its practical consequences. See *Pragmatism.*—*A.C.B.*

Pragmatic Realism: The doctrine that knowledge comes by way of action; that to know is to act by hypotheses which result in successful adaption or resolve practical difficulties. According to pragmatic realism, the mind is not outside the realm of nature; in experience the organism and the world are at one; the theories of knowledge which follow the alleged dualism between the objective and subjective worlds are false. Ideas and knowledge are instruments for activity and not spectators of an outside realm.—*V.F.*

Pragmaticism: Pragmatism in Peirce's sense. The name adopted in 1905 by Charles S. Peirce (1839-1914) for the doctrine of pragmatism (*q.v.*) which had been enunciated by him in 1878. Peirce's definition was as follows: "In order to ascertain the meaning of an intellectual conception one should consider what practical consequences might conceivably result by necessity from the truth of that conception; and the sum of these consequences will constitute the entire meaning of the conception." According to Peirce, W. James had interpreted pragmatism to mean "that the end of man is action," whereas Peirce intended his doctrine as "a theory of logical analysis, or true definition," and held that "its merits are greatest in its application to the highest metaphysical conceptions." "If one can define accurately all the conceivable experimental phenomena which the affirmation or denial of a concept could imply, one will have therein a complete definition of the concept, and there is absolutely nothing more in it." Peirce hoped that the suffix, -icism, might mark his more strictly defined acception of the doctrine of pragmatism, and thus help to distinguish it from the extremes to which it had been pushed by the efforts of James, Schiller, Papini, and others.—*J.K.F.*

Pragmatics: The study of the relations between signs and their interpreters in abstraction from relations to their designata or to other signs. A department of Semiotic (*q.v.*).—*M.B.*

Pragmatism: (Gr. *pragma,* things done) Owes its inception as a movement of philosophy to C. S. Peirce and William James, but approximations to it can be found in many earlier thinkers, including (according to Peirce and James) Socrates and Aristotle, Berkeley and Hume. Concerning a closer precursor, Shadworth Hodgson, James says that he "keeps insisting that realities are only what they are 'known as.' " Kant actually uses the world "pragmatic" to characterize "counsels of prudence" as distinct from "rules of skill" and "commands of morality" (*Fundamental Principles of the Metaphysic of Morals,* p. 40). His principle of the primacy of practical reason is also an anticipation of pragmatism. It was reflection on Kant's *Critique of Pure Reason* which originally led Peirce to formulate the view that the muddles of metaphysics can be cleared up if one attends to the *practical consequences of ideas.* The pragmatic maxim was first stated by Peirce in 1878 (*Popular Science Monthly*): "Consider what effects, that might conceivably have practical bearings, we conceive the object of our conception to have. Then, our conception of these effects is the whole of our conception of the object." A clearer formulation by the same author reads: *"In order to ascertain the meaning of an intellectual conception one should consider what practical consequences might conceivably result by necessity from the truth of that conception; and the sum of these consequences will constitute the entire meaning of the conception."* This is often expressed briefly, viz.: The meaning of a proposition is its logical (or physical) consequences. The principle is not merely logical. It is also admonitory in Baconian style: "Pragmatism is the principle that every theoretical judgment expressible in a sentence in the indicative mood is a confused form of thought whose only meaning, if it has any, lies in its tendency to enforce a corresponding practical maxim expressible as a conditional sentence having its apodosis in the imperative mood" (*Collected Papers of Charles Sanders Peirce,* edited by Charles Hartshorne and Paul Weiss, 5.18). Although Peirce's maxim has been an inspiration not only to later pragmatists, but to operationalists as well, Peirce felt that it might easily be misapplied, so as to eliminate important doctrines of science — doctrines, presumably, which have no ascertainable practical consequences.

James' definition of pragmatism, written for *Baldwin's Dictionary of Philosophy,* is simply a restatement, or "exegesis," of Peirce's definition (see first definition listed above) appearing in the same place. The resemblance between their positions is illustrated by their common insistence upon the feasibility and desirability of resolving metaphysical problems by practical distinctions, unprejudiced by dogmatic presuppositions, their willingness to put every question to the test. "The pragmatic method," says James, "tries to interpret each notion by tracing its respective practical consequences. . . . If no practical difference whatever can be traced," between two alternatives, they "mean practically the same thing, and all dispute is idle'' (*Pragmatism,* p. 45. See also Chapters III and IV).

But while Peirce thought of pragmatism as akin to the mathematical method, James' motivation and interest was largely moral and religious. Thus in his *Will to Believe* (*New World,* 1896) he argues, in line with Pascal's wager, that "we have the right to believe at our own risk any hypothesis that is live enough to tempt our will,'' i.e. if it is not resolvable intellectually. Speaking of religious scepticism, he says: "We cannot escape the issue by remaining sceptical . . . because, although we do avoid error in that way *if religion be untrue,* we lose the good, *if it be true,* just as certainly as if we positively choose to disbelieve.'' The position of the religious skeptic is: *"Better risk loss of truth than chance of error. . . .''* Later, in 1907 in the Lowell Lectures he stated that "on pragmatistic principles, if the hypothesis of God works satisfactorily in the widest sense of the word, it is true,'' and took a position between absolutism and materialism which he called "pragmatistic or melioristic'' theism. In the same lectures he announces that " 'the true,' to put it briefly, is only the expedient in the way of thinking. . . .'' James also identifies truth with verifiability, thus anticipating both the experimentalism of Dewey and the operationalism of Bridgman and the logical positivists.

Pragmatism is first and always a doctrine of meaning, and often a definition of truth as well, but as to the latter, not all pragmatists are in complete agreement. Neither Peirce nor Dewey, for example, would accept James' view that if the hypothesis of God works satisfactorily for the individual, it is true. Pragmatism is also a method of interpreting ideas in terms of their consequences. James, however, apparently does not believe that this method entails his specific philosophical doctrines — his pluralism, individualism, neutralism, indeterminism, meliorism, pragmatic theism, "crass'' supernaturalism, etc. In fact, he states that pragmatism is independent of his new philosophy of "radical empiricism'' and agrees with the anti-intellectualist bent of the Italian pragmatist, Papini, who sees the pragmatic method available to the atheist, the praying penitent, the investigating chemist, the metaphysician and the anti-metaphysician ('What Pragmatism Means''). On the other hand, insofar as pragmatism is practically identified with the scientific method (as is allegedly the case with Dewey) it appears that the pragmatic method might be expected to yield much the same conclusions for one philosopher as for another. In general, pragmatism as a method does not seem to imply any final philosophical conclusions. It may imply a general direction of thought, such as empiricism. Although pragmatists (Peirce, James, Dewey) frequently attack older forms of empiricism, or crude empiricism, and necessarily reject truth as a simple or static correspondence of propositions with sense data, they nevertheless continue to describe themselves as empiricists, so that today pragmatism (especially in Dewey's case) is often regarded as a synonymous with empiricism. See *Empiricism.*

F. C. S. Schiller, the Oxford pragmatist or humanist, is, if anything, more hostile to rationalism, intellectualism, absolute metaphysics and even systematic and rigorous thinking than James himself. In his *Humanism* (1903) and his most important book *Studies in Humanism* (1907), he attempts to resolve or deflate metaphysical issues and controversies by practical distinctions of terms and appeal to personal, human factors, supposedly forgotten by other philosophers. Schiller wrote about many of the topics which James treated: absolute metaphysics, religion, truth, freedom, psychic research, etc., and the outcome is similar. His spirited defense of Protagoras, "the humanist," against Socrates and his tireless bantering critique of all phases of formal logic are elements of novelty. So also is his extreme activism. He goes so far as to say that "In validating our claims to 'truth'. . . we really *transform* them [realities] by our cognitive efforts, thereby proving our desires and ideas to be real forces in the shaping of the world'' (*Studies in Humanism,* 1906, p. 425). Schiller's apparent view that desires and ideas can transform both truth and reality, even without manipulation or experiment, could also be found in James, but is absent in Dewey and later pragmatists.

John Dewey prefers to call his philosophy experimentalism, or even instrumentalism, but the public continues to regard him as the leading exponent of pragmatism. Dewey's pragmatism (like that of Peirce and James) is (1) a theory of meaning, and of truth or "warranted assertibility," and (2) a body of fairly flexible philosophical doctrines. The connection between (1) and (2) requires analysis. Joseph Ratner (editor of volumes of Dewey's philosophy), claims that if Dewey's analysis of experimentalism is accepted almost everything that is fundamental in his philosophy follows (*Intelligence in the Modern World, John Dewey's Philosophy,* ed. Joseph Ratner, N. Y., 1939), but on the other hand it might also be claimed that Dewey's method, whatever name is given to it, can be practiced by philosophers who have important doctrinal differences.

In *Reconstruction in Philosophy* (New York, 1920, p. 156), Dewey states: "When the claim or pretension or plan is acted upon *it guides us truly or falsely;* it leads us to our end or away from it. Its active, dynamic function is the all-important thing about it, and in the quality of activity induced by it lies all its truth and falsity. The hypothesis that works is the *true* one; *truth* is an abstract noun applied to the collection of cases, actual, foreseen and desired, that receive confirmation in their work and consequences.'' The needs and desires which truth must satisfy, however, are not conceived as personal and emotional (as with James) but rather as "public" in some not altogether explicit sense. Although Dewey emphasizes the functional rôle of propositions and laws (and even of sensations, facts and objects), and describes these materials of knowledge as means, tools, instruments or operations for the transformation of an indeterminate situation into a determinate one in the process of inquiry (*Logic, The Theory of*

Inquiry, N. Y., 1938), he does not clearly deny that they have a strictly cognitive rôle as well, as he once states that "the essence of pragmatic instrumentalism is to conceive of *both* knowledge and practice as means of making goods — excellencies of all kinds — secure in experienced existence" (*The Quest for Certainty,* N. Y., 1929, p. 37). Indeed, in his *Logic* (p. 345), he quotes with approval Peirce's definition: "truth is that concordance of an abstract statement with the ideal limit towards which endless inquiry would tend to bring scientific belief. . . ." Here truth seems to be represented as progressive approximation to reality, but usually it is interpreted as efficacy, verification or practical expediency.

Experimentalism: Since Dewey holds that "experimentation enters into the determination of every warranted proposition" (*Logic,* p. 461), he tends to view the process of inquiry as experimentation. Causal propositions, for example, become prospective, heuristic, teleological; not retrospective, revelatory or ontological. Laws are predictions of future occurrences provided certain operations are carried out. Experimentalism, however, is sometimes interpreted in the wider Baconian sense as an admonition to submit ideas to tests, whatever these may be. If this is done, pseudo-problems (such as common epistemological questions) either evaporate or are quickly resolved.

Operationalism: Scientific propositions are, roughly speaking, predictions and a prediction is an if-then proposition: "If certain operations are performed, then certain phenomena having determinate properties will be observed. Its hypothetical character shows that it is not final or complete but intermediate and instrumental" (*Logic,* p. 456). P. W. Bridgman's very influential formulation of operationalism is comparable: "In general, we mean by any concept nothing more than a set of operations; *the concept is synonymous with the corresponding set of operations*" (*The Logic of Modern Physics,* p. 5). If the operation is (or can be), carried out, the proposition has meaning; if the consequences which it forecasts occur, it is true, has "warranted assertibility" or probability.

The question of whether the operations must be specified or merely conceivable for the proposition to have meaning (which is analogous to the constructibility problem in mathematical discussions) has occasioned considerable criticism, for there appeared to be a danger that important scientific propositions might be excluded as meaningless. To this and other problems of operationalism the logical positivists (or empiricists) have contributed formulary modifications and refinements. See *Logical Empiricism*. In spite of their frequent difference with regard to the empirical foundation of logic and mathematics, pragmatism has received some support from the strict logicians and mathematical philosophers. One of the most important instances historically was C. I. Lewis' paper, "The Pragmatic Element in Knowledge" (*University of California Publications in Philosophy,* 1926). Here he stated: "that the truth of experience must always be relative to our cho-

sen conceptual systems," and that our choice between conceptual systems "will be determined consciously or not, on pragmatic grounds."

Instrumentalism: In the philosophy of Dewey, instrumentalism is scarcely distinguishable from experimentalism or operationalism although it is used to characterize his earlier philosophy, and is, in its associations, more closely related to evolutionary philosophy, and more influenced by biological, than by physical or social science.

On the continent of Europe philosophers as far removed from Dewey as Hans Vaihinger are sometimes called pragmatists (Ueberweg). The similarities are of doubtful importance.—*V.J.M.*

Prajāpati: (Skr.) "Lord of creatures," originally applied to various Vedic (*q.v.*) gods, it assumed as early as the Rig Veda the importance of a first philosophical principle of creation, and later in time was suggestive of gestation and productive periodicity.—*K.F.L.*

Prajñā: (Skr.) Realization, insight into the true and abiding nature of the self, *ātman, puruṣa,* etc.—*K.F.L.*

Prakrti: (Skr.) Primary matter or substance, nature, with *puruṣa* (*q.v.*) one of the two eternal bases of the world according to the Sāṅkhya and the Yogasutras. It is the unconscious yet subtle cause of all material phenomena having three *gunas* (*q.v.*), *sativa, rajas, tamas*. Modifications of this view may be met throughout Indian philosophy.—*K.F.L.*

Pramā: (Skr.) In its philosophical sense equivalent to *pramāṇa* (*q.v.*).—*K.F.L.*

Pramāṇa: (Skr. measure) A standard of action or reasoning; knowledge as such or as a logical criterion having validity; a mode of proof, a criterion of truth, such as authority, perception, inference, customarily acknowledged at the outset by all Indian philosophic systems, according to predelection.—*K.F.L.*

Prameya: (Skr. to be measured, measurable) The proposition or thing to be proved; the object of knowledge.—*K.F.L.*

Prāna: (Skr.) Originally meaning "breath," the word figures in early Indian philosophy as "vital air" and "life" itself. Subspecies of it are also recognized, such as *apāna, udāna,* etc.—*K.F.L.*

Prāṇāyāma: (Skr.) Breath (*prāṇa*) exercise considered, like *āsana* (*q.v.*), a necessary accessory to proper functioning of mind, *manas* (*q.v.*).—*K.F.L.*

Prasāda: (Skr. inclining towards) Favor, grave, recognized by some Indian religio-metaphysical systems as divine recompense for *bhakti* (*q.v.*).—*K.F.L.*

Pratyabhijñā: (Skr.) "Recognition," particularly the rediscovery or realization that the divine and ultimate reality is within the human soul or self. One phase of the philosophy of the Trika (*q.v.*).—*K.F.L.*

Pratyāhāra: (Skr.) Withdrawal of the senses from external objects, one of the psycho-physical means for attaining the object of Yoga (*q.v.*). For the theory of the senses conceived as powers, see *Indriya*.—*K.F.L.*

Pratyakṣa: (Skr.) Perception; evidence of the senses.—*K.F.L.*

Praxis: (Gr. *praxis*) Activity that has its goal within itself; conduct; distinguished from poiesis, or production, which aims at bringing into existence something distinct from the activity itself.—*G.R.M.*

Preception: (Lat. *prae + perceptio,* a taking) The anticipatory representation of an object which guides and facilitates the perception of it.—*L.W.*

Pre-critical: This adjective is commonly applied to all Kant's works prior to the Critique of Pure Reason since they all dogmatically assume knowledge of things-in-themselves to be possible. It is also applied to the sections of the Critique which are thought to have been written earliest, whether or not they imply this assumption. See *Kantianism.—A.C.E.*

Predestination: The doctrine that all events of man's life, even one's eternal destiny, are determined beforehand by Deity. Sometimes this destiny is thought of in terms of an encompassing Fate or Luck (Roman and Greek), sometimes as the cyclic routine of the wheel of Fortune (Indian), sometimes as due to special gods or goddesses (Clotho, Lachesis and Atropos in Hesiod), sometimes as the Kismet or mysterious Fate (Mohammedanism), as due to rational Necessity (Stoicism) and more often in terms of the sheer will of a sovereign Deity (Hebrew, Jewish and Christian). In historic Christianity utterances of Paul are given as the authority for the doctrine (Eph. 1:11; Rom. 8:30; Rom. 9: 18). St. Augustine believed that man's own sinfulness made his salvation utterly dependent upon the sheer grace and election of God. Extreme expressions of Calvinism and Lutheranism held that man does absolutely nothing toward his salvation apart from the grace and good will of the Divine. Classical examples of theological determinism are the views of Bucer (1491-1551), Calvin (see *Calvinism*), and the American theologian, Jonathan Edwards (1703-1758). The two classic theories concerning the place of the alleged Fall of man are: supralapsarianism, the view that the Fall itself was predetermined; infralapsarianism, the view that man's predestination was set up subsequent to the Fall, the Fall itself only being permitted.—*V.F.*

Predetermination: Purpose set up beforehand.—*V.F.*

Predicables: (Lat.*praedicabilia*) In Aristotle's logic the five types of predicates that may be affirmed or denied of a subject in a logical proposition, viz. definition, genus, differentia, property, and accident. The list of predicables as formulated by Porphyry and later logicians omits definition and includes species. See *Definition: Genus; Species; Differentia; Property; Accident.—G.R.M.*

Predicament: (Ger. from Lat. *praedicamentum,* a category) The Kantian name for the innate *a priori* forms of the understanding; since each category is a way of predicating something of a subject, and since there are twelve types of judgment, Kant enumerated twelve praedicaments: totality, plurality, unity, reality, negation, limitation, substantiality-inherence, causality-dependence, reciprocity, possibility-impossibility, being and non-being, necessity-contingency.—*V.J.B.*

Predicate: The four traditional kinds of categorical propositions (see *Logic, formal,* § 4) are: all S is P, no S

is P, some S is P, some S is not P. In each of these the concept denoted by S is the *subject* and that denoted by P is the *predicate.*

Hilbert and Ackermann use the word *predicate* for a propositional function of one or more variables; Carnap uses it for the corresponding syntactical entity, the name or designation of such a propositional function (i.e., of a property or relation).—*A.C.*

Preformationism: (Lat. *pre + formare,* to form before) The doctrine, according to which, the organs and hereditary characters of living creatures are already contained in the germ either structurally or by subsequent differentiation. Cf. Leibniz (*q.v.*) (*Monadology,* sect. 74) who was influenced by Leeuwenhoek's microscopic discoveries and theory of the *homunculus* (little human contained in the sperm).

Prediction: 1. The process and the expression of an inference made with respect to a future event.

2. According to Plato, a *prophetic prediction* is a form of inspired "frenzy" which produces a good result which could not be obtained in a normal state of mind (*Phaedrus*). The other two forms of this abnormal activity are poetic inspiration and religious exaltation. This concept has been exalted by Christian theology which gave to it a divine origin: the *gift of prediction* is an attribute of a saint, and also of the biblical prophets.

3. In mathematical theory, prediction is an inference regarding an unknown or future event, from calculations involving probabilities and in particular the computation of correlations. Statistical predictions are usually made by means of regression coefficients and regression lines, which indicate the amount of change of one variable which accompanies a given amount of change in the other variable. The process of predicting values within the range of known data is called *interpolation;* and the process of predicting values beyond the range of known data is called *extrapolation.* The reliability of these predictions varies on the basis of the known variables, and of their limits.—*T.G.*

Preestablished Harmony: A theory expounded by Leibniz and adopted in modified form by other thinkers after him, to refute the theories of interactionism, occasionalism, and the parallelism of the Spinozistic type, in psycho-physics. According to its dynamism, matter and spirit, body and soul, the physical and the moral, each a "windowless," perfect monad (*q.v.*) in itself, are once and for all not only corresponding realities, but they are also synchronized by God in their changes like two clocks, thus rendering the assumption of any mutual or other influences nugatory.—*K.F.L.*

Prehension: (Lat. *prehensus,* from *prehendere,* to seize) In the terminology of A. N. Whitehead, prehension is the process of feeling whereby data are grasped or prehended by a subject. See *Process and Reality,* Part III.—*L.W.*

Prehension, Span of: The maximum number of items or groups of items which an individual mind is capable of embracing within the unity of attention. See J. Ward, *Psychological Principles,* pp. 222 ff. See *Attention, Span of.—L.W.*

Prehistory: That part of history of which we have no written records, documents or oral accounts, but which is reconstructed from material remains by archeologists and anthropologists.

Premiss: A proposition, or one of several propositions, from which an inference is drawn; or the sentence expressing such a proposition. Following C. S. Peirce, we here prefer the spelling *premiss,* to distinguish from the word *premise* in other senses (in particular to distinguish the plural from the legal term *premises*).—*A.C.*

Prenex normal form: See *Logic, formal,* § 3.

Prescience: Supposedly direct acquaintance with the future in contrast to fore-knowledge which is usually considered to be descriptive and inferential (see *Fore-Knowledge*) Prescience is usually attributed only to God.—*L.W.*

Present: That momentary and transient part of time in which all events and experiences take place. Is usually conceived as having no duration ("knife-edge") or small duration ("saddleback").—*R.B.W.*

Presentation: (Lat. *praesentatio,* a showing, representation) (a) In the narrow sense: anything directly present to a knowing mind such as sense data, images of memory and imagination, emotional and hedonic states, etc. See *Datum.* (b) In the wider sense: any object known by acquaintance rather than by description, for example, an object of perception or memory. See *Acquaintance, Knowledge by.*—*L.W.*

Presentational continuum: (Lat. *praesentare,* to present) The conception of an individual mind as an originally undifferentiated continuum which becomes progressively differentiated in the course of experience. See article *Psychology* by J. Ward in *Encyclopaedia Britannica,* 9th ed.; also J. Ward *Psychological Principles,* Ch. IV.—*L.W.*

Presentational Immediacy: (Lat. *praesens* ppr. of *praeesse;* and *in* + *medius,* middle) Presentational immediacy characterizes any items which are in the direct cognitive presence of the mind such as sense data, images, emotional and affective data. Immediacy is ascribed by some epistemologists to higher levels of knowledge, *e.g.* perception and memory and by the mystic to the knowledge of God.—*L.W.*

Presentationism: The epistemological theory that the mind is in perception and perhaps also memory and other types of cognition directly aware of its object (see *Epistemological Monism*). Although the term is ordinarily applied to realistic theories of perception (see *Epistemological Realism; Naïve Realism*), it is equally applicable to idealistic and phenomenalistic theories (see *Epistemological Idealism*). Presentationism, whether realistic or idealistic, is opposed to representationalism. See *Representationalism.*—*L.W.*

Presupposition: (a) That which must antecedently be assumed if a desired result is to be derived, thus, a postulate.

(b) That which is logically necessary; thus, that which is implied, an implicate.

(c) That which is causally necessary; thus, a condition or result.—*C.A.B.*

Prevarication: A deviation from truth or fact; an evasion or equivocation; a quibble, a lie.—*C.A.B.*

Prima facie duties: A phrase used by W. D. Ross to indicate the nature of the general material rules of duty which he regarded as self-evident. Promise-keeping is a *prima facie* duty, one among others; i.e., if I have made a promise, I have a *prima facie* duty to keep it, which means that I will have an actual duty to keep it, if no higher *prima facie* duty is incumbent upon me. What Ross calls *"prima facie* duties" H. A. Prichard calls "claims" and E. F. Carritt "responsibilities." The notion is central to the recent neo-intuitionism of Oxford, constituting its reply to the usual objection to intuited general material propositions about duty on the score that these may conflict and must admit of exceptions.—*W.K.F.*

Primary Qualities: The inherent qualities of bodies: solidity, extension, figure, motion, rest, number. These qualities are conceived to be utterly inseparable from objects; they are constant. John Locke made classic the distinction of primary and secondary qualities made by Galileo and Descartes.—*V.F.*

Primary truth: (Lat. *primus,* first) A conception or proposition which is dependent for its truth on no other principle in the same order of thought; it may be considered self-evident from common experience, special intuitive insight, or even by postulation; but it is not demonstrated.—*V.J.B.*

Prime Matter: See *Matter.*

Prime Mover: In Aristotle's philosophy that which is the first cause of all change and, being first, is not subject to change by any prior agent. See *Aristotelianism.*—*G.R.M.*

Primitive Communism: That stage of primitive society in which there is some form of socialized ownership of the basic means of production (the land, fisheries, natural resources and the like), an absence of economic classes (*q.v.*) and of the state as a special apparatus of internal force.—*J.M.S.*

Primitivism: A modern term for a complex of ideas running back in classical thought to Hesiod. Two species of primitivism are found, (1) *chronological primitivism,* a belief that the best period of history was the earliest; (2) *cultural primitivism,* a belief that the acquisitions of civilization are evil. Each of these species is found in two forms, *hard* and *soft.* The hard primitivist believes the best state of mankind to approach the ascetic life; man's power of endurance is eulogized. The soft primitivist, while frequently emphasizing the simplicity of what he imagines to be primitive life, nevertheless accentuates its gentleness. The Noble Savage is a fair example of a hard primitive; the Golden Race of Hesiod of a soft.—*G.B.*

Cf. *Studies in Primitivism,* ed. Lovejoy and Boas.

Primum cognitum: (Lat. *primus,* first; *cognitus* pp. of *cognoscere,* to know) In Scholastic philosophy the most primitive intellectual cognition of the mind, in contrast to mere sensible cognition.—*L.W.*

Principium individuationis: (Lat.) Principle of individuation (*q.v.*); the intrinsic, real factor in an existing singular thing which causes the individuality of the thing.—*V.J.B.*

Principle: (Lat.*principe*, from*principium*, a beginning) A fundamental cause or universal truth; that which is inherent in anything. That which ultimately accounts for being. According to Aristotle, the primary source of all being, actuality and knowledge. (a) In ontology: first principles are the categories or postulates of ontology. (b) In epistemology: as the essence of being, the ground of all knowledge. Syn. with essence, universal, cause.—*J.K.F.*

Principle of non-sufficient reason: According to this law, the probabilities of two propositions may be said to be equal, if there is no adequate ground for declaring them unequal. When applied without qualification, this principle may lead to unwarranted results. Such a difficulty may be avoided by an adequate formulation of the Principle of Indifference.—*T.G.*

Principle of Organic Unities: A principle enunciated by G. E. Moore to the effect that the intrinsic value of a whole need not be equal to the sum of the intrinsic values of its parts. See *Intrinsic value.*—*W.K.F.*

Principle of sufficient reason: According to Leibniz, one of the two principles on which reasoning is founded, the other being the principle of Contradiction. While the latter is the ground of all necessary truths, the Principle of Sufficient Reason is the ground of all contingent and factual truths. It applies especially to existents, possible or factual; hence its two forms: actual sufficient reasons, like the actual volitions of God or of the free creatures, are those determined by the perception of the good and exhibit themselves as final causes involving the good; and possible sufficient reasons are involved, for example, in the perception of evil as a possible aim to achieve. Leibniz defines the Principle of Sufficient Reason as follows: It is the principle "in virtue of which we judge that no fact can be found true or existent, no judgment veritable, unless there is a sufficient reason why it should be so and not otherwise, although these reasons cannot more than often be known to us. . . . There must be a sufficient reason for contingent truths or truths of fact, that is, for the sequence of things which are dispersed throughout the universe of created beings, in which the resolution into particular reasons might go into endless detail" (*Monadology,* 31, 32, 33, 36). And again, "Nothing happens without a sufficient reason; that is nothing happens without its being possible for one who should know things sufficiently to give a reason showing why things are so and not otherwise" (*Principles of Nature and of Grace*). It seems that the account given by Leibniz of this principle is not satisfactory in itself, in spite of the wide use he made of it in his philosophy. Many of his disciples vainly attempted to reduce it to the Principle of Contradiction. See *Wolff.*

Kant also developed the Leibnizian principles with some modifications in his early writing *Principiorum Primorum Cognitionis Metaphysicae Nova Dilucidatio* (1755), where the Principle of Sufficient Reason becomes the Principle of Determining Reason (*Ratio Determinans*). Two forms of this principle are distinguished by Kant: the *ratio cur* or *antecedenter determinans* identified with the *ratio essendi vel fiendi,* and the *ratio quod* or *consequenter determinans* identified with the *ratio cognoscendi*. It has been defended under these forms against *Crusius* and the argument that it destroys human freedom.—*T.G.*

Principal coordination: (Ger. *prinzipialkoordination*) The ego and the environment are the two central links in the originally given. The restoration of the natural world conception in which the perceived environmental fragments are no more viewed as ideas in us. It forms the correlative functioning of object and subject. (Avenarius.)—*H.H.*

Priority: The condition of being earlier in a succession of events. This condition is meaningful only in the past-present-future series relative to a given event or experience. In its logical sense, the term signifies a condition without which something else cannot be understood, explained, or thought of.—*R.B.W.*

Privacy, Epistemic: (Lat. *privatus,* from *privus,* private) Status of data of knowledge, *e.g.* somatic sensations, hedonic and emotional states, and perhaps even sense data, in so far as they are directly accessible to a single knowing subject. See *Publicity, Epistemic.*—*L.W.*

Privation: (Lat. *privatis*) In Aristotle's philosophy the condition of a substance that lacks a certain quality which it is capable of possessing and normally does possess.—*G.R.M.*

Proaeresis: (Gr. *proairesis*) Reflective choice, especially of means to an end; deliberate desire (Aristotle).—*G.R.M.*

Probabilism: The doctrine of the ancient Skeptics that certainty is unattainable, and that probability is the only guide to belief and action; especially characteristic of the New Academy. See *Peirce.*—*G.R.M.*

Probability: In general (1) Chance, possibility, contingency, likelihood, likeliness, presumption, conjecture, prediction, forecast, credibility, relevance; (2) the quality or state of being likely true or likely to happen; (3) a fact or a statement which is likely true, real, operative or provable by future events; (4) the conditioning of partial or approximate belief or assent; (5) the motive of a presumption or prediction; (6) the conjunction of reasonable grounds for presuming the truth of a statement or the occurrence of an event; (7) the field of knowledge between complete ignorance and full certitude; (8) an approximation to fact or truth; (9) a qualitative or numerical value attached to a probable inference; and (10) by extension, the systematic study of chances or relative possibilities as forming the subject of the theory of probability.

A. *The Foundation of Probability.* We cannot know everything completely and with certainty. Yet we desire to think and to act as correctly as possible: hence the necessity of considering methods leading to reasonable approximations, and of estimating their results in terms of the relative evidence available in each case. In D VI-VII (*infra*) only, is probability interpreted as a property of events or occurrences as such: whether necessary or contingent, facts are simply conditioned by other facts, and have neither an intelligence nor a will to realize their certainty or their probability. In other views, probability requires ultimately a mind to perceive it as such: it arises from the combination of our partial ignorance of the extremely complex nature and conditions of the phenomena, with the inadequacy of our means of observation, experimentation and analysis, however searching and provisionally satisfactory. Thus it may be said that probability exists formally in the mind and materially in the phenomena as related between themselves. In stressing the one or the other of these two aspects, we obtain: (1) *subjective probability,* when the psychological conditions of the mind cause it to·evaluate a fact or statement with fear of possible error; and (2) *objective probability,* when reference is made to that quality of facts and statements, which causes the mind to estimate them with a conscious possibility of error. Usually, methods can be devised to objectify technically the subjective aspect of probability, such as the rules for the elimination of the *personal equation* of the inquirer. Hence the methods established for the study and the interpretation of chances can be considered independently of the state of mind as such of the inquirer. These methods make use of rational or empirical elements. In the first case, we are dealing with *a priori* or *theoretical probability,* which considers the conditions or occurrences of an event hypothetically and independently of any direct experience. In the second case, we are dealing with *inductive* or *empirical probability.* And when these probabilities are represented with numerals or functions to denote measures of likelihood, we are concerned with *quantitative* or *mathematical probability.* Methods involving the former cannot be assimilated with methods involving the latter; but both can be logically correlated on the strength of the general principle of explanation, that similar conjunctions of moral or physical facts demand a general law governing and justifying them.

B. *The Probability-Relation.* Considering the general grounds of probability, it is pertinent to analyze the proper characteristics of this concept and the valid conditions of its use in inferential processes. Probability presents itself as a special relation between the premises and the conclusion of an argument, namely when the premises are true but not completely sufficient to condition the truth of the conclusion. A probable inference must however be logical, even though its result is not certain; for its premises must be a true sign of its conclusion. The probability-relation may take three aspects: it is inductive, probable or presumptive. In strict induction, there is an essential connection between the facts expressed in the premises and in the conclusion, which almost forces a factual result from the circumstances of the predication. This type of probability-relation is prominent in induction proper and in statistics. In strict probability, there is a logical connection between the premises and the conclusion which does not entail a definite factual value for the latter. This type of probability-relation is prominent in mathematical probability and circumstantial evidence. In strict presumption, there is a similarity of characteristics between the fact expressed in the conclusion and the real event if it does or did exist. This type of probability-relation is prominent in analogy and testimony. A presumptive conclusion should be accepted provisionally, and it should have definite consequences capable of being tested. The results of an inductive inference and of a probable inference may often be brought closer together when covering the same field, as the relations involved are fundamental enough for the purpose. This may be done by a qualitative analysis of their implications, or by a quantitative comparison of their elements, as it is done for example in the methods of correlation. But a presumptive inference cannot be reduced to either of the other two forms without losing its identity; because the connection between its elements is of an indefinite character. It may be said that inductive and probable inferences have an intrinsic reasonableness; while presumptive inferences have an extrinsic reasonableness. The former involve determinism within certain limits; while the latter display indeterminacy more prominently. That is why very poor, misleading or wrong conclusions are obtained when mathematical methods are applied to moral acts, judiciary decisions or indirect testimony. The activity of the human will has an intricate complexity and variability not easily subjected to calculation. Hence the degree of probability of a presumptive inference can be estimated only by the character and circumstances of its suggested explanation. In moral cases, the discussion and application of the probability-relation leads to the consideration of the doctrines of Probabilism and Probabiliorism which are qualitative. The probability-relation as such has the following general implications which are compatible with its three different aspects, and which may serve as general inferential principles: (1) Any generalization must be probable upon propositions entailing its exemplification in particular cases; (2) Any generalization or system of generalizations forming a theory, must be probable upon propositions following from it by implication; (3) The probability of a given proposition on the basis of other propositions constituting its evidence, is the degree of logical conclusiveness of this evidence with respect to the given proposition; (4) The empirical probability ($p = S/E$) of a statement S increases as verifications accrue to the evidence E, provided the evidence is taken as a whole; and (5) Numerical probabilities may be assigned to facts or statements only when the evidence includes statistical data or other numerical information which can be treated by the methods of mathematical probability.

C. *Mathematical Probability.* The mathematical theory of probability, which is also called the theory of chances or the theory of relative possibilities, is concerned with the application of mathematical methods to the determination of the likelihood of any event, when there are not sufficient data to determine with certainty its occurrence or failure. As Laplace remarked, it is nothing more than common sense reduced to calculation. But its range goes far beyond that of common sense: for it has not only conditioned the growth of various branches of mathematics, such as the theory of errors, the calculus of variations and mathematical statistics; but it has also made possible the establishment of a number of theories in the natural and social sciences, by its actual applications to concrete problems. A distinction is usually made between direct and inverse probability. The determination of a *direct* or *a priori probability* involves an inference from given situations or sets of possibilities numerically characterized, to future events related with them. By definition, the *direct probability* of the occurrence of any particular form of an event, is the ratio of the number of ways in which that form might occur, to the whole number of ways in which the event may occur, all these forms being equiprobable or equally likely. The basic principles referring to *a priori* probabilities are derived from the analysis of the various logical alternatives involved in any hypothetical questions such as the following: (a) To determine whether a cause, whose exact nature is or is not known, will prove operative or not in certain circumstances; (b) To determine how often an event happens or fails. The comparison of the number of occurrences with that of the failures of an event, considered in simple or complex circumstances, affords a basis for several cases of probable inference. Thus, theorems may be established to deal with the *probability of success* and the *probability of failure* of an event with the probability of *the joint occurrence* of several events, with the *probability of the alternative occurrence* of several events, with the different conditions of *frequency* of occurrence of an event, with *mathematical expectation,* and with similar questions. The determination of an *a posteriori* or *inverse probability* involves an inference from given situations or events, to past conditions or causes which may have contributed to their occurrence. By definition, an *inverse probability* is the numerical value assigned to each one of a number of possible causes of an actual event that has already occurred; or more generally, it is the numerical value assigned to hypotheses which attempt to explain actual events or circumstances. If an event has occurred as a result of any one of *n* several causes, the probability that *C* was the actual cause is $Pp/\mathrm{E}\ (P_n\ p_n)$, when *P* is the probability that the event could be produced by *C* if present, and *p* the probability that *C* was present before the occurrence of that event. Inverse probability is based on general and special assumptions which cannot always be properly stated; and as there are many different sets of such assumptions, there cannot be a coercive reason for making a definite choice. In particular, the condition of the equiprobability of causes is seldom if ever fulfilled. The distinction between the two kinds of probability, which has led to some confusion in interpreting their grounds and their relations, can be technically ignored now as a result of the adoption of a statistical basis for measuring probabilities. In particular, it is the statistical treatment of correlation which led to the study of probabilities of concurrent phenomena irrespective of their direction in time. This distinction may be retained, however, for the purpose of a general exposition of the subject. Thus, a number of probability theorems are obtained by using various cases of direct and inverse probability involving permutations and combinations, the binomial theorem, the theory of series, and the methods of integration. In turn, these theorems can be applied to concrete cases of the various sciences.

D. *Interpretations of Probability.* The methods and results of mathematical probability (and of probability in general) are the subject of much controversy as regards their interpretation and value. Among the various theories proposed, we shall consider the following: (1) Probability as a measure of belief, (2) probability as the relative frequency of events, (3) probability as the truth-frequency of types of argument, (4) probability as a primitive notion, (5) probability as an operational concept, (6) probability as a limit of frequencies, and (7) probability as a physical magnitude determined by axioms.

I. *Probability as a Measure of Belief:* According to this theory, probability is the measure or relative degree of rational credence to be attached to facts or statements on the strength of valid motives. This type of probability is sometimes difficult to estimate, as it may be qualitative as well as quantitative. When considered in its mathematical aspects, the measure of probable inference depends on the preponderance or failure of operative causes or observed occurrences of the case under investigation. This conception involves axioms leading to the classic rule of Laplace, namely: The measure of probability of any one of mutually exclusive and apriori equiprobable possibilities, is the ratio of the number of favorable possibilities to the total number of possibilities. In probability operations, this rule is taken as the definition of direct probability for those cases where it is applicable. The main objections against this interpretation are: (1) that probability is largely subjective, or at least independent of direct experience; (2) that equiprobability is taken as an a priori notion, although the ways of asserting it are empirical; (3) that the conditions of valid equiprobability are not stated definitely; (4) that equiprobability is difficult to determine actually in all cases; (5) that it is difficult to attach an adequate probability to a complex event from the mere knowledge of the probabilities of its component parts; and (6) that the notion of probability is not general, as it does not cover such cases as the inductive derivation of probabilities from statistical data.

II. *Probability as a Relative Frequency:* This interpretation is based on the nature of events, and not on any subjective considerations. It deals with the rate with which an event will occur in a class of events. Hence, it considers probability as the ratio of frequency of true results to true conditions; and it gives as its measure the relative frequency leading from true conditions to true results. What is meant when a set of calculations predict that an experiment will yield a result A with probability P, is that the relative frequency of A is expected to approximate the number P in a long series of such experiments. This conception seems to be more concerned with empirical probabilities, because the calculations assumed are mostly based on statistical data or material assumptions suggested by past experiments. It is valuable in so far as it satisfies the practical necessity of considering probability aggregates in such problems. The main objections against this interpretation are: (1) that it does not seem capable of expressing satisfactorily what is meant by the probability of an event being true; (2) that its conclusions are more or less probable, owing to the difficulty of defining a proper standard for comparing ratios; (3) that neither its rational nor its statistical evidence is made clear; (4) that the degree of relevance of that evidence is not properly determined, on account of the theoretical indefiniteness of both the true numerical value of the probability and of the evidence assumed; and (5) that it is operational in form only, but not in fact, because it involves the infinite without proper limitations.

III. *Probability as Truth-Frequency of Types of Arguments:* In this interpretation, which is due mainly to Peirce and Venn, probability is shifted from the events to the propositions about them; instead of considering types and classes of events, it considers types and classes of propositions. Probability is thus the ability to give an objective reading to the relative truth of propositions dealing with singular events. This ability can be used successfully in interpreting definite and indefinite numerical probabilities, by taking statistical evaluations and making appropriate verbal changes in their formulation. Once assessed, the relative truth of the propositions considered can be communicated to facts expressed by these propositions. But neither the propositions nor the facts as such have a probability in themselves. With these assumptions, a proposition has a degree of probability, only if it is considered as a member of a class of propositions; and that degree is expressed by the proportion of true propositions to the total number of propositions in the class. Hence, probability is the ratio of true propositions to all the propositions of the class examined, if the class is finite; or to all the propositions of the same type in the long run, if the class is infinite. In the first case, fair sampling may cover the restrictions of a finite class; in the second case, the use of infinite series offers a practical limitation for the evidence considered. But in both cases, probability varies with the class or type chosen; and probability-inferences are limited by convention to those cases where numerical values can be assigned to the ratios considered. It will be observed that this interpretation of probability is similar to the relative frequency theory. The difference between these two theories is more formal than material: in both cases the probability refers ultimately to kinds of evidence based on objective matters of fact. Hence the Truth-Frequency theory is open to the same objections as the Relative-Frequency theory, with proper adjustments. An additional difficulty of this theory is that the pragmatic interpretation of truth it involves has yet to be proved, and the situation is anything but improved by assimilating truth with probability.

IV. *Probability as a Primitive Notion:* According to this interpretation, which is due particularly to Keynes, probability is taken as ultimate or undefined, and it is made known through its essential characteristics. Thus, probability is neither an intrinsic property of propositions like truth, nor an empty concept; but a relative property linking a proposition with its partial evidence. It follows that the probability of the same proposition varies with the evidence presented; and that even though a proposition may turn out to be false, our judgment that it is probable upon a given evidence can be correct. Further, since probability belongs to a proposition only in its relation to other propositions, probability-inferences cannot be the same as truth-inferences: as they cannot break the chain of relations between their premises, they lack one of the essential features usually ascribed to inference. That is why, in particular, the conclusions of the natural sciences cannot be separated from their evidence, as it may be the case with the deductive sciences. With such assumptions, probability is the group name given to the processes which strengthen or increase the likelihood of an analogy. The main objection to this interpretation is the arbitrary character of its primitive idea. There is no reason why there are relations between propositions *such that p is probable upon q*, even on the assumption of the relative character of probability. There must be conditions determining which propositions are probable upon others. Hence we must look beyond the primitive idea itself and place the ground of probability elsewhere.

V. *Probability as an Operational Concept:* In this interpretation, which is due particularly to Kemble, probability is discussed in terms of the mental operations involved in determining it numerically. It is pointed out that probability enters the postulates of physical theories as a useful word employed to indicate the manner in which results of theoretical calculations are to be compared with experimental data. But beyond the usefulness of this word, there must be a more fundamental concept justifying it; this is called *primary probability* which should be reached by an instrumentalist procedure. The analogy of the thermometer, which connects a qualitative sensation with a number, gives an indication for such a procedure. The expectation of the repetition of an event is an elementary form of belief which can be strengthened by additional evidence. In collecting such evidence, a selection is naturally made, by accepting the relevant data and rejecting the others. When the selected data form a pattern which does not involve the event as such or its negative, the event is considered as probable. The rules of collecting the data and of comparing them with the theoretical event and its negative, involve the idea of correspondence which leads to the use of numbers for its expression. Thus, probability is a number computed from empirical data according to given rules, and used as a metric and a corrective to the sense of expectation; and the ultimate value of the theory of probability is its service as a guide to action. The main interest of this theory lies in its psychological analysis and its attempt to unify the various conceptions of probability. But it is not yet complete; and until its epistemological implications are made clear, its apparent eclecticism may cover many of the difficulties it wishes to avoid.—*T.G.*

VI. *Probability as a Limit of Frequencies.* According to this view, developed especially by Mises and by Wald, the probability of an event is equal to its total frequency, that is to the limit, if it exists, of the frequency of that event in *n* trials, when *n* tends to infinity. The difficulty of working out this conception led Mises to propose the notion of a *collective* in an attempt to evolve conditions for a true random sequence. A collective is a random sequence of supposed results of trials when (1) the total frequency of the event in the sequence exists, and (2) the same property holds with the same limiting value when the sequence is replaced by any sequence derived from it. Various methods were devised by Copeland, Reichenbach and others to avoid objections to the second condition: they were generalized by Wald who restricted the choice of the "laws of selection" defining the ranks of the trials forming one of the derived sequences, by his postulate that these laws must form a denumerable set. This modification gives logical consistency to this theory at the expense of its original simplicity, but without disposing of some fundamental shortcomings. Thus, the probability of an event in a collective remains a relative notion, since it must be known to which denumerable set of laws of selection it has been defined relatively, in order to determine its meaning, even though its value is not relative to the set. Controversial points about the axiomatization of this theory show the possibility of other alternatives.

VII. *Probability as a Physical Magnitude determined by Axioms.* This theory, which is favored mainly by the Intuitionist school of mathematics, considers probability as a physical constant of which frequencies are measures. Thus, any frequency is an approximate measure of one physical constant attached to an event and to a set of trials: this constant is the probability of that event over the set of trials. As the observed frequencies differ little for large numbers of trials from their corresponding probabilities, some obvious properties of frequencies may be extended to probabilities. This is done without proceeding to the limit, but through general approximation as in the case of physical magnitudes. These properties are not constructed (as in the axiomatization of Mises), but simply described: as such, they form a set of axioms defining probability. The classical postulates involved in the treatises of Laplace; Bertrand or Poincaré have been modified in this case, under the joint influence of the discovery of measure by Borei, and of the use of abstract sets. Their new form has been fully stated by Kolmogoroff and interpreted by Frechet who proposes to call this latest theory the 'modernized axiomatic definition' of probability. Its interpretation requires that it should be preceded by an inductive synthesis, and followed by numerical verifications.

Bibliography. The various theories outlined in this article do not exhaust the possible definitions and problems concerning probability; but they give an idea of the trend of the discussions. The following works are selected from a considerable literature of the subject. Laplace, *Essai sur les Probabilités.* Keynes, *A Treatise on Probability.* Jeffreys, *Theory of Probability.* Uspensky, *Introduction to Mathematical Probability.* Borel, *Traité dé Calcul des Probabilités* (especially the last volume dealing with its philosophical aspects). Mises, *Probability, Statistics and Truth.* Reichenbach, *Les Fondements Logiques du Calcul des Probabilités.* Fréchet, *Recherches sur le Calcul des Probabilités.* Ville, *Essai sur la Théorie des Collectifs.* Kolmogoroff, *Grundbegriffe der Wahrscheinlichkeitsrechnung.* Wald, *Die Widerspruchsfreiheit des Kollektivbegriffes.* Nagel, *The Theory of Probability.*—*T.G.*

Problem: (Gr. *problema,* anything thrown forward) 1. Any situation, practical or theoretical, for which there is no adequate automatic or habitual response, and which therefore calls up the reflective processes. 2. Any question proposed for solution.—*A.C.B.*

Problematic knowledge: Knowledge of what might occur or is capable of occurring as opposed to knowledge of what is actual or of what must occur; opposed to *assertoric knowledge* and *apodictic knowledge.*—*A.C.B.*

In Kant, the domain of things beyond possible experience is completely problematic because of the *a priori* limitations of human knowledge (cf. J. Loewenberg, *Calif. Studies in Philosophy*). See *Modality.*

Process: (Lat. *processus,* pp. of *procedo,* to go before) A series of purposive actions, generally tending toward the production of something. A systematic forward movement, resulting in growth or decay. As employed by Whitehead (1861-1947), the course of actuality in its cosmological aspects. Syn. with action, becoming, existence.—*J.K.F.*

Process Theory of Mind: The conception of mind in terms of process in contrast to substance. A mind, according to the process theory, is a relatively permanent pattern preserved through a continuously changing process. Leibniz's doctrine of the self-developing monad signalizes the transition from the substance to the process theory of mind and such philosophers as Bradley, Bosanquet, Bergson, James, Whitehead, Alexander and Dewey are recent exponents of the process theory. See C. W. Morris, *Six Theories of Mind,* Ch. II.—*L.W.*

Proclus: (411-485) A prominent Neo-Platonist and theological commentator, who taught that man becomes united with God through the practice of love, truth and faith. Main works: *Commentaries on Timaeus, on Republic, on Parmenides; Instit. Theol.; In Platonis Theol.; Comment on First Book of Euclid.*—*R.B.W.*

Projection: (Lat. *projectio,* from *projicere,* to throw forward) The mental act of attributing to sensations or sense qualia, an external and independent existence. The projection theory of Condillac and other sensationalists (see *Sensationalism*) asserts that sensations are first experienced as subjective states and are subsequently externalized by a special act of mind. Helmholtz restricted projection to spatial projection (the localization of sensations in space at a certain distance from the body) but the more general usage is preferable.—*L.W.*

Project method: An education method which makes use of practical activities, organizing the scholastic work of the child about complex enterprises, such as making a garden, planning a circus.—*J.E.B.*

Prolegomena: (Gr. *pro,* before; *lego,* say) Introductory material. (Singular form: prolegomenon.) Cf. *Prolegomena to Every Future Scientific Metaphysic,* by Kant (*q.v.*).—*V.F.*

Prolepsis: (Gr. *prolepsis*) Notion; preconception. The term is used by the Stoics and Epicureans to denote any primary general notion that arises spontaneously and unconsciously in the mind, as distinguished from concepts that result from conscious reflection. These prolepses are regarded by the Stoics as common to all men as rational beings, and are sometimes called innate (symphytoi), though in general they were looked upon as the natural outgrowth of sense-perception.—*G.R.M.*

Proof by cases: Represented in its simplest form by the valid inference of the propositional calculus, from A $\supset$ C and B $\supset$ C and A v B to C. More complex forms involve multiple disjunctions, e.g., the inference from A $\supset$ D and B $\supset$ D and C $\supset$ D and [A v B] v C to D. The simplest form of proof by cases is thus the same as the simple constructive dilemma (see *Logic, formal,* § 2), the former term deriving from mathematical usage and the latter from traditional logic. For the more complex forms of proof by cases, and like generalizations of the other kinds of dilemma to the case of more than two major premisses, logicians have devised the names trilemma, tetralemma, polylemma — but these are not much found in actual use.—*A.C.*

Proof theory: The formalization of mathematical proof by means of a *logistic system* (*q.v.*) makes possible an objective theory of proofs and probability, in which proofs are treated as concrete manipulations of formulas (and no use is made of meanings of formulas). This is Hilbert's *proof theory,* or *metamathematics.*

A central problem of proof theory, according to Hilbert, is the proof of consistency of logistic systems adequate to mathematics or substantial parts of mathematics. A logistic system is said to be consistent, relatively to a particular notation in the system called negation, if there is no formula A such that both A and the negation of A are provable (i.e., are theorems). The systems with which Hilbert deals, and the notations in them which he wishes to call negation, are such that, if a formula A and its negation were once proved, every propositional formula could be proved; hence he is able to formulate the consistency by saying that a particular formula (*e.g.,* $\sim[0 = 0]$) is not provable.

A consistency proof evidently loses much of its significance unless the methods employed in the proof are in some sense less than, or less dubitable than, the methods of proof which the logistic system is intended to formalize. Hilbert required that the methods employed in a consistency proof should be *finitary*—a condition more stringent than that of intuitionistic acceptability. See *Intuitionism* (*mathematical*).

Gödel's theorems (see *Logic, formal,* § 6) are a difficulty for the Hilbert program because they show that the methods employed in a consistency proof must also be in some sense more than those which the logistic system formalizes. Gödel himself remarks that the difficulty may not be insuperable.

Other problems of proof theory are the *decision problem,* and the problem of proving *completeness* (in one of various senses) for a logistic system. Cf. *Logic, formal,* §§ 1, 3.—*A.C.*

Hilbert and Bernays, *Grundlagen der Mathematik,* vol. 1, Berlin, 1934, and vol. 2, Berlin, 1939. P. Bernays, *Sur le platonisme dans les mathématiques,* and *Quelques points essentiels de la metamathematique,* l'Enseignement Mathématique, vol. 34 (1935), pp. 52-95. W. Ackermann, *Zur Widerspruchsfreiheit der Zahlentheorie,* mathematische Annalen, vol. 117 (1940), pp. 162-194.

Propensity: (Lat. *propensio,* from *propendere,* to hang forth) A term used to designate a mental appetite or desire. See *Appetition.* Hume applied the term to the tendency of the mind to pass from one to the other of two associated ideas.—*L.W.*

Proper sensible: (in Scholasticism) That which through itself, or through its proper species is perceived by only one external sense without error, as light is perceived by the eyes, sound by the ear. *Common sensible* is that which is perceived by several external senses through modified species of the proper sensibles, e.g. quantity, distance. *Accidental sensible* (*sensibile per accidens*) is that which falls under the external senses neither through its proper species nor through the modified species of another, but only through another with which it is joined, e.g. material substance.—*H.G.*

Property: (Gr. *idion;* Lat. *proprium*) In Aristotle's logic (1) an attribute common to all members of a species and peculiar to them; (2) an attribute to the above sort not belonging to the essence of the species, but necessarily following from it.—*G.R.M.*

Propitiation: The attempt by act or intent of gaining the favor of a god, removing one's guilt and the divine displeasure. Such acts have taken on innumerable forms: sacrifice of precious possessions, even of human life, of animals, by pilgrimages, tithing, self-imposed asceticism of one kind or another, fastings, rituals, tortures, contrition, etc. The substitution of some one else as an act of voluntary propitiation has found classic expression in Christian tradition in the estimation of Jesus' life and death as the supreme Ransom, Substitute and Mediator.—*V.F.*

Proposition: This word has been used to mean: (a) a declarative sentence (in some particular language); (b) the content of meaning of a declarative sentence, i.e., a postulated abstract object common not only to different occurrences of the same declarative sentence but also to different sentences (whether of the same language or not) which are synonymous or, as we say, mean the same *thing;* (c) a declarative sentence associated with its content of meaning. Often the word proposition is used ambiguously between two of these meanings, or among all three.

The Port-Royal Logic defines a proposition to be the same as a judgment but elsewhere speaks of propositions as denoting judgments. Traditional logicians generally have defined a proposition as a judgment expressed in words, or as a sentence expressing a judgment, but some say or seem to hold in actual usage that synonymous or intertranslatable sentences represent the same proposition. Recent writers in many cases adopt or tend towards (b).

In articles in this dictionary by the present writer the word proposition is to be understood in sense (b) above. This still leaves an element of ambiguity, since common usage does not always determine of two sentences whether they are strictly synonymous or merely logically equivalent. For a particular language or logistic system, this ambiguity may be resolved in various ways.—*A.C.*

Propositional calculus: See *Logic, formal,* § 1.

Propositional calculus, many-valued: The truth-table method for the classical (two-valued) propositional calculus is explained in the article *logic, formal,* § 1. It depends on assigning truth-tables to the fundamental connectives, with the result that every formula—of the pure propositional calculus, to which we here restrict ourselves for the sake of simplicity—has one of the two truth-values for each possible assignment of truth-values to the variables appearing. A formula is called a *tautology* if it has the truth-value truth for every possible assignment of truth-values to the variables; and the calculus is so constructed that a formula is a theorem if and only if it is a tautology.

This may be generalized by arbitrarily taking n different truth-values, $t_1, t_2, \ldots, t_m, f_1, f_2, \ldots, f_{n-m}$, of which the first m are called *designated* values—and then setting up truth-tables (in terms of these n truth-values) for a set of connectives, which usually includes connectives notationally the same as the fundamental connectives of the classical calculus, and may also include others. A formula constructed out of these connectives and variables is then called a *tautology* if it has a designated value for each possible assignment of truth-values to the variables, and the theorems of the n-valued propositional calculus are to coincide with the tautologies.

In 1920, Lukasiewicz introduced a three-valued propositional calculus, with one designated value (interpreted as *true*) and two non-designated values (interpreted as *problematical* and *false* respectively). Later he generalized this to n-valued propositional calculi with one designated value (first published in 1929). Post introduced n-valued propositional calculi with an arbitrary number of designated values in 1921. Also due to Post (1921) is the notion of *symbolic completeness*—an n-valued propositional calculus is symbolically complete if every possible truth-function is expressible by means of the fundamental connectives.

The case of infinitely many truth-values was first considered by Lukasiewicz.—*A.C.*

J. Lukasiewicz, *O logice trójwartościowej,* Ruch Filozoficzny, vol. 5 (1920), pp. 169-171. E. L. Post, *Introduction to a general theory of elementary propositions,* American Journal of Mathematics, vol. 43 (1921), pp. 163-185. Lukasiewicz and Tarski, *Untersuchungen über den Aussagenkalkül,* Comptes Rendus des Séances de la Société des Sciences et des Lettres de Varsovie, Classe III, vol. 23 (1930), pp. 30-50. J. Lukasiewicz, *Philosophische Bemerkungen zu mehrwertigen Systemen des Aussagenkalkuls,* ibid., pp. 51-77. Lewis and Langford. *Symbolic Logic,* New York and London, 1932.

Propositional function is a *function (q.v.)* for which the range of the dependent variable is composed of *propositions (q.v.).* A monadic propositional function is thus in substance a *property* (of things belonging to the range of the independent variable), and a dyadic propositional function a *relation.* If F denotes a propositional function and $X_1, X_2, \ldots, X_n$ denote arguments, the notation $F(X_1, X_2, \ldots, X_n)$—or $[F] (X_1, X_2, \ldots, X_n)$—is used for the resulting proposition, which is said to be the *value* of the propositional function for the given arguments, and to be obtained from the propositional function by *applying* it to, or *predicating* it of the given arguments.

Often, however, the assumption is made that two propositional functions are identical if corresponding values are materially equivalent, and in this case we speak of propositional functions *in extension* (the definition in the preceding paragraph applying rather to propositional functions *in intension*). The values of a propositional function in extension are *truth-values (q.v.)* rather than propositions. A monadic propositional function in extension is not essentially different from a *class (q.v.).*

Whitehead and Russell use the term *propositional function* in approximately the sense above described, but qualify it by holding, as a corollary of Russell's doctrine of *descriptions (q.v.),* that propositional functions are the fundamental kind from which other kinds of functions are derived—in fact that non-propositional ("descriptive") functions do not exist except as incomplete symbols. For details of their view, which underwent some changes between publication of the first and the second edition of *Principia Mathematica,* the reader is referred to that work.

Historically, the notion of a function was of gradual growth in mathematics. The word *function* is used in approximately its modern sense by John Bernoulli (1698, 1718). The divorce of the notion of a function from that of a particular kind of mathematical expression (analytic or quasi-algebraic) is due to Dirichlet (1837). The general logical notion of a function, and in particular the notion of a propositional function, were introduced by Frege (1879). *Alonzo Church*

Proprioceptor: See *Receptor.*

Prosyllogism: See *Episyllogism.*

Protagoras of Abdera: (about 480-410 B.C.) A leading Sophist, renowned for his philosophical wisdom; author of many treatises on grammar, logic, ethics and politics; visited Athens on numerous occasions and was finally forced to flee after having been convicted of impiety. His famous formula that man is the measure of all things is indicative of his relativism which ultimately rests upon his theory of perception according to which we know only what we perceive but not the *thing* perceived.—*M.F.*

Protasis: (Gr. *protasis,* placed first) In Aristotle's logic a proposition; more particularly a proposition used as a premiss in a syllogism.—*G.R.M.*

Protensity: (Lat. *protensum* from *protendere,* to stretch forth) Duration-spread considered as a primary characteristic of all conscious experience. This usage was introduced by Kant (*Critique of Pure Reason,* A 805—B 833) where the protensive is distinguished from the extensive and the intensive and this usage has been adopted by recent psychologists.—*L.W.*

Protocol Sentences: See *Basic Sentences.*

Proximum genus: (Lat. nearest kind) In Aristotelian theory of definition (*q.v.*), must be used with differentia.—*R.B.W.*

Pseudo-Statement: See *Meaning, Kinds of,* 5.

Psyche: (Gr. soul, World-Soul, spirit) In Plotinism, it is the name of the second emanation from the One. See *Soul.*—*V.J.B.*

Psychic or psychical: (Gr. *psychikos,* from *psyche,* the soul) (a) In the general sense, psychic is applied to any mental phenomenon. See *Psychosis, Mental.* (b) In the special sense, psychic is restricted to unusual mental phenomena such as mediumship, telepathy, prescience, etc. which are the subjects of "Psychic Research." See *Telepathy, Prescience, Parapsychology.*—*L.W.*

Psychic Fusion: The supposed merging of a number of separate psychic states to form a new state. The possibility of psychic fusion is highly questionable and alleged instances of it may be interpreted as the associative revival of images based on the memory of physical mixture.—*L.W.*

Psychic Summation: See *Psychic Fusion.*

Psychoanalysis: The psychological method and therapeutic technique developed by Freud (see *Freud, Sigmund*). This method consists in the use of such procedures as free association, automatic writing and especially dream analysis to recover forgotten memories, suppressed desires and other subconscious items which exert a disturbing influence on the conscious life of an individual. The cure of the psychic disturbances is effected by bringing the suppressed items into the full of consciousness of the individual. Psychoanalytic theory has posited a subconscious mind as a repository for the suppressed elements. Freud exaggerated the sexual origin of the suppressed desires but other psychoanalysts, notably Jung and Adler, corrected this exaggeration. The psychoanalytical school has developed its terminology in which the following are characteristic:

(a) *Free association* is the method of encouraging the patient to recall in random fashion experiences, particularly of childhood.

(b) A *"complex"* is a more or less permanent emotional system or mechanism responsible for the mental disturbances of the patient.

(c) *Libido* designates the underlying sexual drive or impulse, the suppression of which is responsible for the psychic disturbance.

(d) *Suppression* or *repression* is the rejection from consciousness of desires and urges which it finds intolerable.

(e) *Sublimation* is the transference of a suppressed desire to a new object.

These terms are only a few samples of the elaborate and at times highly mythological terminology of psychoanalysis.—*L.W.*

Psychoid: Term applied by the German neo-vitalist, H. Driesch to the psychic factor which guides the growth of organisms.—*L.W.*

Psychological Atomism: Theory of the structure of mind: any mental state is analyzable into simple, discrete components and that the total mental state was produced by fusion and composition of the atomic states. See *Associationism; Mind-Stuff Theory.*—*L.W.*

Psychological Egoism: See *Egoism, Psychological.*—*C.A.B.*

Psychologism: (Ger. *Psychologismus*) The tendency of such philosophers as Hume, J. S. Mill and William James to approach philosophical problems, whether ethical, logical, aesthetic or metaphysical, from the stand-point of psychology. *Psychologismus* is used by Husserl and other German writers as a term of reproach which suggests the exaggeration of the psychological to the neglect of the logical and epistemological considerations.—*L.W.*

Psychologists' Fallacy: The confusion of the standpoint of the psychologist with that of the subject upon whose introspective report the psychologist relies. See Wm. James, *The Principles of Psychology,* Vol. I, p. 196. —*L.W.*

Psychology: (Gr. *psyche,* mind or soul + *logos,* law) The science of the mind, its functions, structure and behavioral effects. In Aristotle, the science of mind (*De Anima*) emphasizes mental functions; the Scholastics employed a faculty psychology. In Hume and the Mills, study of the data of conscious experience, termed association psychology. In Freud, the study of the unconscious (depth psychology). In behaviorism, the physiological study of physical and chemical responses. In Gestalt psychology, the study of organized psychic activity, revealing the mind's tendency toward the completion of patterns. Since Kant, psychology has been able to establish itself as an empirical, natural science without *a priori* metaphysical or theological commitments. The German romanticists (*q.v.*) and Hegel, who had developed a metaphysical psychology, had turned to cultural history to illustrate their theories of how the mind, conceived as an absolute, must manifest itself. Empirically they have suggested a possible field of exploration for the psychologist, namely, the study of mind in its cultural effects, viz. works of art, science, religion, social organization, etc. which are customarily studied by anthropologists in the case of "primitive" peoples. But it would be as difficult to separate anthropology from social psychology as to sharply distinguish so-called "primitive" peoples from "civilized" ones.

The various branches of psychology depend on the class of problems studied: (a) physiological psychology is the most experimentally exact in so far as specific physiological processes and effects (vision, hearing, reaction-time, learning curves, fatigue, effects of drugs, etc.) are measurable and controllable. Wundt established the first laboratories of experimental psychology in Germany, Pavlov in Russia, James and Cattell in the U.S.; (b) pathological or abnormal psychology deals with cases of extreme deviations of behavior from what is regarded as "normal" (a statistical term often treated as a value); (c) social psychology deals with the behavior of groups as reflected in the behavior of individuals. Cf. Le Bon's law that the mentality of a crowd or mob tends to descend to the level of a least common denominator, the lowest intelligence present.

Bibliography: H. Siebeck, *Gesch. der Psychol.* (goes from Aristotle to Aquinas); E. G. Boring, *History of Experimental Psychology;* Wm. James, *Principles of Psychology,* 1890; W. McDougall, *Intro. to Social Psychology;* J. B. Watson, *Psychology as Science of Behavior;* R. Woodworth, *Psychology;* Koffka, *Gestalt Psychology;* Köhler, *Mentality of Apes;* Pavlov, *The Conditioned Reflex;* E. L. Thorndike, *Human Nature and the Social Order.* See *Freud, Gestalt, Introspection, Mind, Subconscious.*

Psychology of Religion: A scientific, descriptive study of mental life and behavior with special reference to religious activities. The aim of this study is not to criticize or evaluate religion (see *Philosophy of Religion*) but to *describe* its forms as they reflect the mental processes of men. As an extended chapter in the field of general psychology, psychology of religion reflects the various types of psychology now current. As a scientific study this subject began its fruitful career at the beginning of this century, making illuminating disclosures on the nature of conversion, varieties of religious experience, the origin and character of beliefs in God and immortality, the techniques of mystics, types of worship, etc. Due to the confused state of psychology in general and especially to the recent vogue of behaviorism this subject has fallen somewhat into an eclipse—at least for the present. Cf. Wm. James: *Varieties of Religious Experience,* 1902.—*V.F.*

Psycho-Physical Parallelism: See *Parallelism, Psycho-Physical.*

Psycho-Physical Problem: (Gr. *psyché,* soul — *physikos,* physical) See *Mind-Body Problem.*

Psychosis: (Gr. *psychosis,* a giving of life or soul) (a) *In the general sense,* psychosis designates any mental or psychical process, just as a neurosis, in the wide sense is any neural process. (b) *In the restricted sense,* psychosis designates a pathological condition of mind, just as "neurosis" is an abnormal condition of the nervous system.—*L.W.*

P'u: "Unwrought simplicity;" the Taoist symbol of man's natural state, when his inborn powers have not been tampered with by knowledge or circumscribed by morality.—*H.H.*

Publicity, Epistemic: (a) In the strict sense, publicity pertains to such data of knowledge as are directly and identically accessible to more than one knowing subject. Thus epistemological monism may assert the publicity of sense data, of universals, of moral and aesthetic values and even of God. See *Epistemological Monism.* (b) In a less exact sense, publicity is ascribed to any object of knowledge which may be known either directly or indirectly by more than one mind, such as physical objects, public space, etc. in contrast to feelings, emotions, etc. which can be directly known only by a single subject.—*L.W.*

Pudgala: (Skr. beautiful, lovely) The soul, or personal entity, admitted by some thinkers even though belonging to the schools of Buddhism (*q.v.*); they hold that at least a temporary individuality must be assumed as vehicle for *karma* (*q.v.*).—*K.F.L.*

Pu jen: Early kings, being of "unbearing," commiserating mind, unable to bear and see others suffer, exemplified a virtuous government, (Mencius.)—*H.H.*

Punishment, Theory Of: Theories of punishment normally attempt to establish justification for the institution of criminal punishment, though their principles may also be extended to other forms of punishment by authority, such as parent to child or teacher to student.

Typically, theories of punishment fall into one of two groups. The first are "Retributive" theories, which hold punishment to be the just desert of the wicked. In its extreme form retribution becomes the law of retaliation, exemplified by the "eye for an eye" passage in the Old Testament. The second can be broadly classed as "Utilitarian" theories, which view punishment as justified in so far as it promises to exclude some greater evil. We punish, therefore, so that worse consequences will not befall us. Under this heading lie theories that view punishment as a means of deterring potential offenders and /or reforming the corrupt criminal.

Apart from establishing the justifying aim(s) of punishment, there are a number of further considerations which these theories must address. There is first the problem of the severity of punishment. How are we to construe the dictum that the punishment must somehow "fit the crime," or the Constitutional guarantees against cruel and unusual punishment? The second is the problem of responsibility. Should persons be punished for what they cannot help? Both internal and external factors serve to mitigate against the individual's responsibility. Internal factors include such things as insanity and ignorance of fact, while external factors may include extreme poverty, beatings incurred as a child, and other concomitant liabilities of a radically disadvantaged position in society.

Acton, H. B., ed., *The Philosophy of Punishment*

(1969); Bentham, Jeremy, *Introduction to the Principles of Morals and Legislation* (1789); Hart, H.L.A., *Law, Liberty and Morality* (1963), "Prolegomenon to the Principles of Punishment" (1959), *Punishment and Responsibility: Essays in the Philosophy of Law* (1968); Kant, "Metaphysische Anfangsgrunde Der Rechtslehre" (1797); Pincoffs, E.L., *The Rationale of Legal Punishment* (1966); Ross, W.D., *The Right and the Good* (1930).—*T.P.S.*

Purāṇa: (Skr. ancient) One of 18 or more treatises, mainly cosmological, mythological, or legendary in character and composed in *p.Ch.n.* times. Interspersed are ethical, philosophical and scientific observations.—*K.F.L.*

Pure: (Ger. *rein*) In Kant: Strictly, that which is unmixed with anything sensuous or empirical. Loosely, whatever pertains to the form instead of the matter of our cognition. See *Kantianism.*—*O.F.K.*

Pure Ego: See *Ego, Pure.*

Pure Experience: (Lat. *purus*, clean) (a) The qualitative ingredients of experience, *e.g.* sense data, feelings, images, etc., which remain after the ideal elimination of conceptual, interpretational and constructional factors. (b) The world of ordinary immediate experience which constitutes the point of departure for science and philosophy. See Avenarius, *Kritik der reinen Erfahrung.*—*L.W.*

Pure Theory of Law: An attempt to introduce the "critical" method of Kant to the understanding of positive law. Kelsen, who coined the expression, intended to create "a geometry of the totality of legal phenomena." All legal phenomena are to be reduced to norms which have the form: "If A is, then B ought to be;" all norms are to be derived from one basic norm (Grundnorm). It is the task of a theory of law to establish the unity of all legal phenomena.—*W.E.*

Purism: Taste tending towards archaistic and simplified form, prevailing chiefly at the beginning of the 19th century.—*L.V.*

Puritanism: A term referring, in general, to a purification of existing religious forms and practices. More specifically, Puritanism refers to that group of earnest English Protestants who broke with the Roman system more completely in objection to traditional ceremonies, formalities and organization. This moral earnestness at reformation led to the emphasis upon such commendable virtues as self-reliance, thrift, industry and initiative but it led also to unnatural self-denials and overly austere discipline. In this last respect Puritanism has come to mean an ascetic mode of living, an over-sensitive conscience and an undue repression of normal human enjoyments. Milton was Puritanism at its best. New England Puritanism in its most extreme expressions of Spartan discipline and its censorious interference with the behavior of others was Puritanism at its worst.—*V.F.*

Pūrṇa: (Skr.) The plenum, a synonym for the Absolute, *brahman*, used by Ajātaśatru in Kauṣītaki Upanishad 4.8. See also *Bṛhadāraṇyaka Up.* 5.1.—*K.F.L.*

Pūrṇatva: (Skr.) Fullness, as descriptive of real-

ity.—*K.F.L.*

Purpose: (Lat. *propositus* from *pro*, before + *ponere*, to place) An ideally or imaginatively envisaged plan or end of action.—*L.W.*

Purposiveness: (in Kant's philosophy: *die Zweckmassigkeit*) Adaptation whether in the body of an animal or plant to its own needs or in a beautiful object to the human intelligence. We must not say dogmatically, Kant contends, that there is a purpose behind the phenomena, but we can say that they occur as if there were, though we cannot bring the purpose under definite concepts.—*A.C.E.*

Puruṣa: (Skr.) "Man," a symbol for the world in the Veda (*q.v.*). One of the two cardinal principles of the Sāṅkhya (*q.v.*) and Yoga (*q.v.*), representing pure spirituality, consciousness, and self. Various theories prevail in Indian philosophy, some semi-physical, others psycho-physical, or logical, taking the term to denote a real self or an entity produced by *māyā* (*q.v.*).—*K.F.L.*

Puruṣārtha: (Skr.) Object (*artha*) or man's (*puruṣa*) pursuits, enumerated as four: *kāma* (desire), *artha* (wealth), *dharma* (duty), *mokṣa* (liberation). Also, a statement of aims with which Indian philosophers traditionally preface their works.—*K.F.L.*

Pūrvapakṣa: (Skr.) "The prior view," the first step in a logical argument, stating the view to which exception is taken.—*K.F.L.*

Pu tung hsin: The state of unperturbed mind, as a result of "maintaining firm one's will and doing no violence to the vital force" which pervades the body. (Mencius.)—*H.H.*

Pyrrho of Elis: (c. 365-275 B.C.) A systematic skeptic who believed that it is impossible to know the true nature of things and that the wise man suspends his judgment on all matters and seeks to attain imperturbable happiness (ataraxy) by abstaining from all passion and curiosity. See *Timon of Phlius*, pupil of Pyrrho.—*R.B.W.*

Pythagoreanism: The doctrines (philosophical, mathematical, moral, and religious) of Pythagoras (c. 572-497 B.C.) and of his school which flourished until about the end of the 4th century B.C. The Pythagorean philosophy was a dualism which sharply distinguished thought and the senses, the soul and the body, the mathematical forms of things and their perceptible appearances. The Pythagoreans supposed that the substances of all things were numbers and that all phenomena were sensuous expressions of mathematical ratios. For them the whole universe was harmony. They made important contributions to mathematics, astronomy, and physics (acoustics) and were the first to formulate the elementary principles and methods of arithmetic and geometry as taught in the first books of Euclid. But the Pythagorean sect was not only a philosophical and mathematical school (cf. K. von Fritz, *Pythagorean Politics in Southern Italy*, 1941), but also a religious brotherhood and a fellowship for moral reformation. They believed in the immortality and transmigration (see *Metempsychosis*) of the soul which they defined as the harmony of the body. To restore harmony which was confused by the senses was the goal of their Ethics and Politics. Their religious ideas were closely related to those of the Greek mysteries which sought by various rites and abstinences to purify and redeem the soul. The attempt to combine this mysticism with their mathematical philosophy led the Pythagoreans to the development of an intricate and somewhat fantastic symbolism which collected correspondences between numbers and things and for example identified the antithesis of odd and even with that of form and matter, the number 1 with reason, 2 with the soul, etc. Through their ideas the Pythagoreans had considerable effect on the development of Plato's thought and on the theories of the later Neo-platonists.

Bibliography: John Burnet, *Early Greek Philosophy*, 3rd ed. (1920). E. Zeller-R. Mondolfo, *La Filosofia dei Greci*, vol. I (1932-1938). E. Frank, *Plato und die sogenannten Pythagoreer* (1923). T. L. Heath, *A History of Greek Mathematics*, vol. I (1921).—E.F.

Q

Quadrivium: (Lat. *quatuor,* and *viae,* four ways) The second, and more advanced group of liberal arts studies in the middle ages; arithmetic, geometry, astronomy and music.—*V.J.B.*

See *Trivium* for the other three of the seven liberal arts, first proposed for education by Plato, *Republic,* III.

Quaestio: (Scholastic) A subdivision or chapter of some treatise. Later, the special form, imitating or actually reproducing a discussion, in which a thesis is proposed, then the arguments against it are listed, next the objections or *argumenta contra* are exposed, and the question is solved in the so-called *corpus articuli,* usually introduced by the standing phrase *respondeo dicendum;* finally the objections against the thesis and the response or solution are taken up one by one and answered. This is the *quaestio disputata.* The *quaestio quodlibetalis* stems from disputations in which all kind of problems were brought up and the leader had to arrange them somehow and to answer all of them.—*R.A.*

Quakerism: The name given to that Christian group officially known as the Society of Friends founded by George Fox (1624-1691). Central principles include: guidance by an inner light; freedom from institutional or outward sanctions; the sanctity of silence; the simplicity of living; and commitment to peaceful social relations. Three American groups are: orthodox, Hicksites (liberal) and Wilburites (formalists).—*V.F.*

Quale: (Pl. qualia) (Lat. from *qualis,* of what kind) A quality considered as an independent entity rather than as a quality of a thing. A quale is usually conceived as a universal essence (like redness, sweetness, etc.) but the term may also be applied to individual qualities (this red, this sweet taste).—*L.W.*

Qualities, extensional: Qualities which characterize certain complex wholes composed of point-instants related to each other in virtue of their different positional qualities. (Broad.)—*H.H.*

Qualities, immaterial: Instances of non-positional qualities that are not characterized by any determinable form of quality of spatial position. (Broad.)—*H.H.*

Qualities, material: Instances of non-positional qualities characterized by the determinable qualities of spatial position. (Broad.)—*H.H.*

Qualities, non-positional: Qualities like color, temperature, *etc.* to which no spatial or temporal position can be assigned. (Broad.)—*H.H.*

Qualities, positional: Temporal and spatial positions. (Broad.)—*H.H.*

Qualities, structural: Positional and extensional qualities classed together. (Broad.)—*H.H.*

Quality: The four traditional kinds of categorical propositions (see *logic, formal,* § 4) were distinguished according to *quality* as affirmative or negative, and according to *quantity* as particular, singular, or universal. See the articles *Affirmative Proposition* and *Particular Proposition.*—*A.C.*

Quantifier: *Universal quantifier* is the name given to the notation (*x*) prefixed to a logical formula A (containing the free variable *x*) to express that A holds for *all* values of *x*—usually, for all values of *x* within a certain range or domain of values, which either is implicit in the context, or is indicated by the notation through some convention. The same name is also given to variant or alternative notations employed for the same purpose. And of course the same name is given when the particular variable appearing is some other letter than *x.*

Similarly, *existential quantifier* is the name given to the notation (*Ex*) prefixed to a logical formula A (containing the free variable *x*) to express that A holds for *some* (i.e., at least one) value of *x*—usually, for some value of *x* within a certain range or domain. The *E* which forms part of the notation is often inverted, and various alternative notations also occur.

It may also be allowed to prefix the quantifiers (*x*) and (*Ex*) to a formula (sentence) A not containing *x* as a free variable, (*x*)A and (*Ex*)A then having each the same meaning as A.

See *logic, formal,* § 3.—*A.C.*

W. V. Quine, *Elementary Logic,* Boston and New York, 1941.

Quantity: In Aristotle and Kant (*q.v.*), one of the

categories (*q.v.*) of judgment. See *Quality*.

Quaternio terminorum: In the categorical syllogism (*logic, formal*, § 5), the major and minor premisses must have a term in common, the middle term. Violation of this rule is the fallacy of *quaternio terminorum*, or of *four terms*. It is most apt to arise through *equivocation* (*q.v.*), an ambiguous word or phrase playing the rôle of the middle term, with one meaning in the major premiss and another meaning in the minor premiss; and in this case the fallacy is called the fallacy of *ambiguous middle*.—*A.C.*

Quantum: An indivisible unit, or atom, of any physical quantity. *Quantum mechanics* (*q.v.*) is based on the existence of quanta of energy, the magnitude of the quantum of radiant energy (light) of a given frequency—or of the energy (light) of a given frequency—or of the energy of a particle oscillating with given frequency—being equal to *Planck's constant* (*q.v.*) multiplied by the frequency.—*A.C.*

Quantum mechanics: An important physical theory, a modification of classical mechanics, which has arisen from the study of atomic structure and phenomena of emission and absorption of light by matter; embracing the matrix mechanics of Heisenberg, the wave mechanics of Schrödinger, and the transformation theory of Jordan and Dirac. The wave mechanics introduces a duality between waves and particles, according to which an electron, or a photon (quantum of light), is to be considered in some of its aspects as a wave, in others as a particle. See further *quantum* and *uncer-*

tainty principle.—*A.C.*

F. A. Lindemann, *The Physical Significance of the Quantum Theory*. Oxford, 1932. J. Frenkel, *Wave Mechanics, Elementary Theory*, Oxford, 1932. Louis de Broglie, *Matter and Light, The New Physics*, translated by W. H. Johnson, New York, 1939.

Quiddity: (Lat. *quidditas*, whatness) Essence; that which is described in a definition.—*V.J.B.*

Quieting: The pacification of mind is the initial point of departure as well as the endpoint of a vital series. (Avenarius.)—*H.H.*

Quine, Willard V.O.: (1908-   ) Professor of Philosophy at Harvard University, distinguished mathematical logician. Quine's most influential work has been the development of an improved version of the reduction of mathematics to logic first formulated by Russell and Whitehead in *Principia Mathematica*. Also established a theoretical perspective on the possibility and nature of translation between languages. Coined the well-known slogan, ''To be is to be the value of a variable.''

Methods of Logic (1950); *From A Logical Point of View* (1953); *Word and Object* (1960).—*T.P.S.*

Quintessence: (Lat. *quinta essentia*, the fifth essence) the purest, most highly concentrated form of a nature or essence; originally, in Aristotelianism, the fifth element, found in celestial bodies, distinguished from the four earthly elements.—*V.J.B.*

Quotation marks, syntactical use of: See *Notations, logical*.

R

Radhakrishnan, Sarvepalli: (1888-   ) One of the main Indian philosophers interested in the East/West dialogue, Radhakrishnan wrote *Eastern Religions and Western Thought* (1939), *East and West; Some Reflections* (1956), *Education, Politics and War* (1944) and edited *The Concept of Man; a Study in Comparative Philosophy* (1960).—*S.E.N.*

Rāmānuja: A renowned Indian thinker and theologian of the 11th cent. A.D. who restated within the tradition of Vishnuism (*q.v.*) the doctrines of the Vedānta (*q.v.*) in that he assumed world and soul to be a transformation of God variously articulated.—*K.F.L.*

Rāmāyana: (Skr.) An epic poem, ascribed to Vālmīki, celebrating in about 24,000 verses the doings of Rāma and his wife Sītā and containing ethical and philosophic speculations.—*K.F.L.*

Ramified theory of types: See *impredicative definition,* and *paradoxes, logical.*

B. Russell, *Mathematical logic as based on the theory of types,* American Journal of Mathematics, vol. 30 (1908), pp. 222-262. L. Chwistek, *The theory of constructive types,* Annales de la Société Polonaise de Mathématique, vol. 2 (1924), pp. 9-48, and vol. 3 (1925), pp. 92-141. W. V. Quine, *On the axiom of reducibility,* Mind, n. s. vol. 45 (1936), pp. 498-500. F. B. Fitch, *The consistency of the ramified Principia,* The Journal of Symbolic Logic, vol. 3 (1938), pp. 140-149.

Ramsey, Frank Plumpton: (1903-1930) In the light of Wittgenstein's work, he proposed several modifications in the *Principia Mathematica* treatment of functions. These, he urged, made possible the omission of the Axiom of Reducibility, a simplification of the Theory of Types and an improved definition of identity. In stimulating philosophical papers he denied any ultimate distinction between particulars and universals, defended a Wittgensteinian interpretation of general propositions, proposed a subjective theory of probability and a pragmatic view of induction, and offered a theory of theories and a theory of the nature of causal propositions. Most of his work is included in *The Foundations of Mathematics,* London, Kegan Paul,
1931.—*C.A.B.*

Rand, Ayn: (1905-1982) American philosopher and writer, born in St. Petersburg, lecturer at Yale, Princeton, and Columbia (1960). Author of *The Virtue of Selfishness* (1965), *Atlas Shrugged* (1957), *The Fountainhead* (1943), and other books on ethics.—*S.E.N.*

Rasa: (Skr. sap, juice, nectar, essence, flavor, etc.) In Indian aesthetics (*q.v.*), pleasure, enjoyment, love, charm, grace, elegance, taste, emotion, sentiment, spirit, passion, beauty etc.—*K.F.L.*

Ratio: (Lat. *ratio,* reason) According to St. Augustine, reason is the mind's capacity of distinguishing and connecting the things that are learned. *Ratio est mentis motio ea quae discuntur distinguendi et connectendi potens.* He also calls it an *aspectus animi, quo per seipsum, non per corpus verum intuetur.* It precedes the exercise of the intellectual capacity. He says of man: *Nam ideo vult intelligere, quia ratio praecedit.* Reason is, however, inferior to the intellect. Man possesses reason before he begins the activity of intellection, which is a contemplation. Action is rather the province of reason.—*J.J.R.*

For Spinoza: Knowledge "of the second kind" (*Ethica,* II, 40, Schol. 2; cf. also *De Em. Int., passim*), to be distinguished from *opinio* or *imaginatio* and from *scientia intuitiva* (*q.v.*). This second type of knowledge is knowledge in the strict sense of the word since, as opposed to *opinio,* it is certain and true (*Ethica,* II, 41), and since by means of it, we perceive "under a certain form of eternity" (*sub quadam aeternitatis specie; Ibid,* II, 42, Cor. 2). Likewise, by means of reason (*ratio*), we are enabled to distinguish truth from falsity (*Ibid,* 42), and to master the emotions (*Ibid,* IV, *passim*). The objects cognized by reason are (primarily) "common notions" and their derivatives; reason cannot, however, accomplish or bring about the highest virtue of the mind, as can *scientia intuitiva* by which blessedness and true liberty are conferred (*Ibid,* V, 36, Schol.).—*W.S.W.*

Ratiocination: (Lat. *ratiocinatio,* reasoning) Discursive reasoning, the third act of the intellect in the Aristotelian theory of knowledge; a process of intellectual demonstration involving the use of three terms.—*V.J.B.*

Rationalism: A method, or very broadly, a theory of philosophy, in which the criterion of truth is not sensory but intellectual and deductive. Usually associated with an attempt to introduce mathematical methods into philosophy, as in Descartes, Leibniz and Spinoza.—*V.J.B.*

The history of rationalism begins with the Eleatics (*q.v.*), Pythagoreans and Plato (*q.v.*) whose theory of the self-sufficiency of reason became the *leitmotif* of neo-Platonism and idealism (*q.v.*).

Rationalization: (Lat. *rationalis,* from *ratio,* reason) A psychological term to describe the mind's fabrication of rational argument to justify conduct of which one is really ashamed.—*L.W.*

Rational Psychology: A speculative and metaphysical treatment of the soul, its faculties and its immortality in contrast to a descriptive, empirical psychology.—*L.W.*

Ravaisson-Mollien, Jean Gaspard Félix: (1813-1900) French idealistic philosopher who studied under Schelling at Munich, became Professor of Philosophy at Rennes in 1838 and later inspector of Higher Education. Although he wrote little, he profoundly influenced French thought in the direction of the "dynamic spiritualism" of Maine de Biran. He explored the spiritual implications of individual personality especially in the domains of art and morals. See *Morale et Métaphysique in Revue de Mét. et de Mor.* 1893.—*L.W.*

Real: (Lat. *realis,* of the thing itself) Absoluteness of being. The immediate object of that which is true. Invented in the 13th century to signify having characters sufficient to identify their subject, whether attributed by men or not. Sometimes, the existential as opposed to mere possibility, or the physical as opposed to consciousness. Syn. with external (*q.v.*), actual. Opposite of figment.—*J.K.F.*

Realism: Theory of the reality of abstract or general terms, or universals, which are held to have an equal and sometimes a superior reality to actual physical particulars. Universals exist before things, *ante res.* Opposed to *nominalism* (*q.v.*) according to which universals have a being only after things, *post res.* Realism means a) in ontology: that no derogation of the reality of universals is valid, the realm of essences, or possible universals, being as real as, if not more real than, the realm of existence, or actuality; b) in epistemology: that sense experience reports a true and uninterrupted, if limited, account of objects; that it is possible to have faithful and direct knowledge of the actual world. While realism was implicit in Egyptian religion, where truth was through deification distinguished from particular truths, and further suggested in certain aspects of Ionian philosophy, it was first explicitly set forth by Plato in his doctrine of the ideas and developed by Aristotle in his doctrine of the forms. According to Plato, the ideas have a status of possibility which makes them independent both of the mind by which they may be known and of the actual world of particulars in which they may take place. Aristotle amended this, so that his forms have a

being only in things, *in rebus.* Realism in its Platonic version was the leading philosophy of the Christian Middle Ages until Thomas Aquinas (1225-1274) officially adopted the Aristotelian version. It has been given a new impetus in recent times by Charles S. Peirce (1839-1914) in America and by G. E. Moore (1873-1958) in England. Moore's realism has been responsible for many of his contemporaries, in both English-speaking countries. Roughly speaking, the American realists, Montague, Perry, and others, in *The New Realism* (1912) have directed their attention to the epistemological side, while the English have constructed ontological systems. The most comprehensive realistic systems of the modern period are *Process and Reality* by A. N. Whitehead (1861-1947) and *Space, Time and Deity* by S. Alexander (1859-1939). The German, Nicolai Hartmann, should also be mentioned, and there are others.—*J.K.F.*

Realism in Legal Philosophy: No connection with epistemological realism. Theory that law is not a system of rules but in flux, and part of actual social process.—*W.E.*

Realm of ends: The cosmic order viewed as the means for the achievement by a Supreme Person of higher or spiritual purposes. Teleological Personalism.—*R.T.F.*

Reals: Are atomic or monadic beings which underlie the phenomenal world. Alike in quality, not being points of self-directive force, they are conceived to be in a state of mechanical interaction, not in the realm of phenomenal space but in the realm of intelligible space. (Herbart).—*H.H.*

Reason: (Lat. *ratio,* Ger. *Vernunft*) In Kant: (1) The special mental faculty (distinct from sensibility and understanding) which in thinking Ideas of absolute completeness and unconditionedness transcends the conditions of possible experience. See *Ideas of Pure Reason.* (2) All those mental functions and relations characterized by spontaneity rather than receptivity. In this sense, reason includes both reason (1) and the understanding, but excludes the sensibility. (3) The source of all a priori synthetic forms in experience. In this sense, reason includes elements of sensibility, understanding and reason (1). When Kant says, "reason is a lawgiver to Nature," he employs the term in the third sense. See *Kantianism, Understanding, Ratio.*—*O.F.K.*

Reasoning: 1. Discursive thought. Faculty of connecting ideas consciously, coherently and purposively. Thinking in logical form. Drawing of inferences. Process of passing from given data or premises to legitimate conclusions. Forming or discovering rightly relations between ideas. Deriving properly statements from given assumptions or facts. Power, manifestation and result of valid argumentation. Ordering concepts according to the canons of logic. Legitimate course of a debate.

2. *In psychology,* the act or process of exercising the mind; the faculty of connecting judgments; the power and fact of using reason; the thought-processes of discussion, debate, argumentation or inference; the man-

ifestation of the discursive property of the mind; the actual use of arguments with a view to convince or persuade; the art and method of proving or demonstrating; the orderly development of thought with a view to, or the attainment of a conclusion believed to be valid.—The origin, nature and value of reasoning are debated questions, with their answers ranging from spiritualism (reasoning as the exercise of a faculty of the soul) to materialism (reasoning as an epiphenomenon depending on the brain), with all the modern schools of psychology ordering themselves between them. A few points of agreement might be mentioned here: (1) reasoning follows judgment and apprehension, whichever of the last two thought-processes comes first in our psychological development; (2) reasoning proceeds according to four main types, namely deductive, inductive, presumptive and deceptive; (3) reasoning assumes a belief in its own validity undisturbed by doubt, and implies various logical habits and methods which may be organized into a logical doctrine; (4) reasoning requires a reference to some ultimate principles to justify its progress.

3. *In logic,* Reasoning is the process of inference; it is the process of passing from certain propositions already known or assumed to be true, to another truth distinct from them but following from them; it is a discourse or argument which infers one proposition from another, or from a group of others having some common elements between them. The inference is necessary in the case of deductive reasoning; and contingent, probable or wrong, in the case of inductive, presumptive or deceptive reasoning respectively.—There are various types of reasoning, and proper methods for each type. The definition, discussion, development and evaluation of these types and methods form an important branch of logic and its subdivisions. The details of the application of reasoning to the various sciences form the subject of methodology. All these types are reducible to one or the other of the two fundamental processes of reasoning, namely deduction and induction. It must be added that the logical study of reasoning is normative: logic does not analyze it simply in its natural development, but with a view to guide it towards coherence, validity or truth.—*T.G.*

Receptivity: (Lat. *recipere,* to take back) The collective name for receptive or sensory functions of the mind in contrast to its active or motor functions. In the Kantian terminology, receptivity is defined as the faculty of receiving representations in contrast to spontaneity, the faculty of knowing an object by means of concepts. See Kant, *Critique of Pure Reason,* A 50—B 74.—*L.W.*

Receptor: The organ of sense considered as part of the total response mechanism of a human or animal organism. Receptors are classified as: a) *exteroceptors* or receptors at the surface of the body, and b) *proprioceptors* or receptors embedded in the muscles and bodily tissues themselves. The term *interoceptors* is sometimes applied to receptors embedded in the vital organs especially those of the digestive tract.—*L.W.*

Recognition: (Lat. *re + cognitio,* knowledge) The knowledge of an object along with the realization that the same object has been previously known. Recognition may, but need not be, effected by a comparison of a memory image with recurring objects. See *Familiarity, Feeling of; Memory.*—*L.W.*

Recursion, definition by: A method of introducing, or "defining," functions from non-negative integers to non-negative integers, which, in its simplest form, consists in giving a pair of equations which specify the value of the function when the argument (or a particular one of the arguments) is 0, and supply a method of calculating the value of the function when the argument (that particular one of the arguments) is $x + 1$, from the value of the function when the argument (that particular one of the arguments) is x. Thus a monadic function f is said to be defined by *primitive recursion* in terms of a dyadic function g—the function g being previously known or given—by the pair of equations,

$$f(0) = A,$$
$$f(S(x)) = g(x, f(x)),$$

where A denotes some particular non-negative integer, and S denotes the *successor* function (so that $S(x)$ is the same as $x+1$), and x is a variable (the second equation being intended to hold for all non-negative integers x). Similarly the dyadic function f is said to be defined by *primitive recursion* in terms of a triadic function g and a monadic function h by the pair of equations,

$$f(a, 0) = h(a),$$
$$f(a, S(x)) = g(a, x, f(a, x)),$$

the equations being intended to hold for all non-negative integers a and x. Likewise for functions f of more than two variables.—As an example of definition by primitive recursion we may take the "definition" of addition (i.e., of the dyadic function *plus*) employed by Peano in the development of arithmetic from his postulates (see the article *Arithmetic, foundations of*):

$$a+0 = a,$$
$$a + S(x) = S(a + x)$$

This comes under the general form of definition by primitive recursion, just given, with h and g taken to be such functions that $h(a) = a$ and $g(a, x, y) = S(y)$. Another example is Peano's introduction of multiplication by the pair of equations:

$$a \times 0 = 0,$$
$$a \times S(x) = (a \times x)+a.$$

Here addition is taken as previously defined, and $h(a) = 0$, $g(a, x, y) = y+a$.

More general kinds of definition by recursion allow sets of recursion equations of various forms, the essential requirement being that the equations specify the value of the function being introduced (or the values of the functions being introduced), for any given set of arguments, either absolutely, or in terms of the value (values) for preceding sets of arguments. The word *preceding* here may refer to the natural order or order of magnitude of the non-negative integers, or it may refer to some other method of ordering arguments or sets of arguments; but the method of ordering shall be such that *infinite* descending sequences of sets of arguments (in which each set of arguments is *preceded* by the next set) are impossible.

The notion of definition by recursion may be extended to functions whose ranges consist of only a portion of the non-negative integers (in the case of monadic functions) or of only a portion of the ordered sets of n non-negative integers (in the case of n-adic functions); also to functions for which the range of the dependent variable may consist wholly or partly of other things than non-negative integers (in particular, propositional functions — properties, relations — of integers may receive definition by recursion).

The employment of definition by recursion in the development of arithmetic from Peano's postulates, or in the Frege-Russell derivation of arithmetic from logic, requires justification, which most naturally takes the form of finding a method of replacing a definition by recursion by a nominal definition, or a contextual definition, serving the same purpose. In particular it is possible, by a method due to Dedekind or by any one of a number of modifications of it, to prove the existence of a function f satisfying the conditions expressed by an admissible set of recursion equations; and f may then be given a definition employing descriptions, as *the function f such that* the recursion equations, with suitable quantifiers prefixed, hold. See the paper of Kalmár cited below.

See also the article *Recursiveness*..—*A.C.*

L. Kalmár, *On the possibility of definition by recursion,* Acta Scientiarum Mathematicarum(Szeged), vol. 9 (1940), pp. 227-232.

Recursion, proof by, or, as it is more often called, proof by *mathematical induction* or *complete induction,* is in its simplest form a proof that every non-negative integer possesses a certain property by showing (1) that 0 possesses this property, and (2) that, on the hypothesis that the non-negative integer x possesses this property, then $x + 1$ possesses this property. (The condition (2) is often expressed, following Frege and Russell, by saying that the property is *hereditary* in the series of non-negative integers.) The name *proof by recursion,* or *proof by mathematical* or *complete induction,* is also given to various similar but more complex forms.

In Peano's postulates for arithmetic (see *Arithmetic, foundation of*) the possibility of proof by recursion is secured by the last postulate, which, indeed, merely states the leading principle of the simplest form of proof by recursion. In the Frege-Russell derivation of arithmetic from logic, the non-negative integers are identified with the inductive *cardinal numbers* (*q.v.*), the possibility of proof by recursion being implicit in the definition of *inductive.*—*A.C.*

Recursiveness: The notion of definition by recursion, and in particular of definition by primitive recursion, is explained in the article *recursion, definition by.* An n-adic function f (from non-negative integers to non-negative integers) is said to be defined by *composition* in terms of the m-adic function g and the n-adic functions $h_1, h_2, \ldots, h_m$ by the equation:

$$f(x_1, x_2, \ldots, x_n) = g(h_1(x_1, x_2, \ldots, x_n), h_2(x_1, x_2, \ldots, x_n), \ldots, h_m(x_1, x_2, \ldots, x_n)).$$ (The case is

not excluded that $m = 1$, or $n = 1$, or both.)

A function from non-negative integers to non-negative integers is said to be *primitive recursive* if it can be obtained by a succession of definitions by primitive recursion and composition, from the following list of initial functions: the successor function S, the function C such that $C(x) = 0$ for every non-negative integer x, and the functions U_{in} ($i \leqq n$, $n = 1, 2, 3, \ldots$) such that $U_{in}(x_1, x_2, \ldots, x_n) = x_i$. Each successive definition by primitive recursion or composition may employ not only the initial functions but also any of the functions which were introduced by previous definitions.

More general notions of recursiveness result from admitting, in addition to primitive recursion, also more general kinds of definition by recursion, including those in which several functions are introduced simultaneously by a single set of recursion equations. The most general such notion is that of *general recursiveness*—see the first paper of Kleene cited below. Notions of recursiveness may also be introduced for a function whose range consists of only a portion of the non-negative integers (in the case of a monadic function) or of only a portion of the ordered sets of n non-negative integers (in the case of an n-adic function)—see the second paper of Kleene cited.

Concerning the relationship between general recursiveness and the notion of effectiveness, see the article *logistic system.*—*A.C.*

R. Péter, a series of papers (in German) in the Mathematische Annalen, vol. 110 (1934), pp. 612-632; vol. 111 (1935), pp. 42-60; vol. 113 (1936), pp. 489-527. S. C. Kleene, *General recursive functions of natural numbers,* Mathematische Annalen, vol. 112 (1936), pp. 727-742. S. C. Kleene, *On notation for ordinal numbers,* The Journal of Symbolic Logic, vol. 3 (1938), pp. 150-155.

Redintegration: (Lat. *re* + *integratio,* from *integer,* whole) The integral reproduction of a total state of consciousness when an element of it is reproduced.—*L.W.*

Reducibility, axiom of: An axiom which (or some substitute) is necessary in connection with the *ramified theory of types* (*q.v.*) if that theory is to be adequate for classical mathematics, but the admissibility of which has been much disputed (see *Paradoxes, logical*). An exact statement of the axiom can be made only in the context of a detailed formulation of the ramified theory of types—which will not here be undertaken. As an indication or rough description of the axiom of reducibility, it may be said that it cancels a large part of the restrictive consequences of the prohibition against *impredicative definition* (*q.v.*) and, in approximate effect, reduces the ramified theory of types to the *simple theory of types* (for the latter see *Logic, formal,* § 6).—*A.C.*

Reductio ad absurdum: The method of proving a proposition by deducing a contradiction from the negation of the proposition taken together with other propositions which were previously proved or are granted. It may thus be described as the valid inference of the propositional calculus from three premisses, B and B[~A] ⊃ C and B[~A]⊃~C, to the conclusion A (this presupposes the *deduction theorem, q.v.*). Such an argument may be rearranged so that the element of *reductio ad absurdum* appears in the inference from ~A ⊃ A to A.

The name *reductio ad absurdum* is also given to the method of proving the negation of a proposition by deducing a contradiction from the proposition itself, together with other propositions which were previously proved or are granted.

The first of the two kinds of *reductio ad absurdum*, but not the second, is called *indirect proof*.

Whitehead and Russell give the name *principle of reductio ad absurdum* to the theorem of the propositional calculus:

$$[p \supset \sim p] \supset \sim p. —A.C.$$

Reductio ad impossibile: The method of establishing a proposition by showing that its contradictory involves impossible consequences; also of disproving a proposition by showing that its consequences are absurd; reductio ad absurdum (*q.v.*). *See Apagoge.—G.R.M.*

Reduction: (Ger. *Reduktion*) In Husserl: See *Egological* and *Phenomenology.—D.C.*

Reduplicatively: (in Schol.) A term is taken reduplicatively or there is reduplication when to a term there is added *as, just as, as though, inasmuch as,* or some similar expression, either in order to double the same term, or in order to add another so as to indicate the meaning in which the first term is to be taken, or so as to indicate a reason why the predicate belongs to the subject. E.g. *animal as animal cannot reason; Christ as man has suffered; Paul as a priest is worthy of honor.—H.G.*

Referend: The vehicle or instrument of an act of reference. Thus a percept functions as a referend in relation to the perceptual object (the referent). There still exists some confusion in the terminology of reference, and the term referend is used by some authors to denote the "object" instead of the "instrument" of the referential act. This usage, though it has some etymological justification does not seem likely to prevail: See *Reference, Referent.—L.W.*

Referent: The object towards which an act of reference is directed. See *Referend.—L.W.*

(1) That which is denoted by a word, sentence, utterance or judgment.

(2) A term used by adherents of a certain causal theory of meaning. That event to which a symbol is actually used to refer.

More explicitly: — Let "context" be used to mean a set of events such that events of the same kind and in the same relations recur "nearly uniformly." Let *a* be an event such that the complex event *a + b* would be a context of character C. Let it be granted that a certain utterance (or expectation) is caused jointly by the occurrence of *a* and residual traces in the speaker of previous adaptations to contexts of character C. Then that event which, in conjunction with *a* constitutes a context of character C is called the *referent* of the utterance in question. (This covers only true utterances.

The 'referents' of false expectations and general beliefs requires a separate account.) See: Ogden and Richards, *Meaning of Meaning,* passim.

(3) In any proposition of form 'aRb,' where R is a propositional function of two variables, a is termed the referent by contrast with the relatum b. (Due to Whitehead and Russell, *Principia Mathematica*).—M.B.

Referential: Relating to an act of reference. See *Referent.—L.W.*

Reflection: (Lat. *reflectio,* from *re + flectere,* to bend) The knowledge which the mind has of itself and its operations. The term is used in this sense by Locke (cf. *Essay,* II, 1, § 4), Spinoza (cf. *On the Improvement of the Understanding* 13) and Leibniz (cf. *Monadology,* and *New Essays,* Preface, § 4) but has now largely been supplanted by the term introspection. See *Intelligence, Introspection.—L.W.*

In Scholasticism: Reflexion is a property of spiritual or immaterial substances only. It is, therefore, a capacity of the human intellect which not only operates, but knows of its operating and may turn back on itself to know itself and its performances (*reditio completa*). A particular kind of reflexion is, in Thomism, the *reflexio super phantasma,* by which the intellect retraces its steps until it reaches the phantasm from which it originally derived the universal; this is, according to Aquinas, the way the intellect comes to know the particular which, because material, is otherwise inaccessible to an immaterial faculty.—R.A.

Reflexivity: A dyadic relation *R* is called *reflexive* if *xRx* holds for all *x* within a certain previously fixed domain which must include the field of *R* (cf. *logic, formal,* § 8). In the propositional calculus, the *laws of reflexivity* of material implication and material equivalence (the conditional and biconditional) are the theorems,

$$p \supset p, \qquad\qquad p \equiv p,$$

expressing the reflexivity of these relations. Other examples of reflexive relations are equality; class inclusion, ⊂ (see *logic, formal,* § 7); formal implication and formal equivalence (see *logic, formal,* § 3); the relation *not greater than* among whole numbers, or among rational numbers, or among real numbers; the relation *not later than* among instants of time; the relation *less than one hour apart* among instants of time.

A dyadic relation *R* is *irreflexive* if *xRx* never holds (e.g., the relation *less than* among whole numbers).—A.C.

Reformation: The Protestant Reformation may be dated from 1517, the year Martin Luther (1483-1546), Augustinian monk and University professor in Wittenberg, publicly attacked the sale of indulgences by the itinerant Tetzel, Dominican ambassador of the Roman Church. The break came first in the personality of the monk who could not find in his own religious and moral endeavors to win divine favor the peace demanded by a sensitive conscience; and when it came he found to his surprise that he had already parted company with a whole tradition. The ideology which found a response in his inner experience was set forth by Augustine, a troubled soul who had surrendered himself completely to divine grace and mercy. The philosophers who legitimized man's endeavor to get on in the world, the church which demanded unquestioned loyalty to its codes and commands, he eschewed as thoroughly inconsonant with his own inner life. Man is wholly dependent upon the merits of Christ; the miracle of faith alone justifies before God. Man's conscience, his reason, and the Scriptures together became his only norm and authority. He could have added a fourth: patriotism, since Luther became the spokesman of a rising tide of German nationalism already suspect of the powers of distant Rome. The humanist Erasmus (see *Renaissance*) supported Luther by his silence, then broke with him upon the reformer's extreme utterances concerning man's predestination. This break with the humanists shows clearly the direction which the Protestant Reformation was taking: it was an enfranchised religion only to a degree. For while Erasmus pleaded for tolerance and enlightenment the new religious movement called for decision and faith binding men's consciences to a new loyalty. At first the Scriptures were taken as conscience permitted; then conscience became bound by the Scriptures. Luther lacked a systematic theology for the simple reason that he himself was full of inconsistencies. A reformer is often not a systematic thinker. Lutheran princes promoted the reconstruction of institutions and forms suggested by the reformer and his learned ally, Melanchthon, and by one stroke whole provinces became Protestant. The original reformers were reformed by new reformers. Two of such early reformers were Ulrich Zwingli (1484-1531) in Switzerland and John Calvin (1509-1564) who set up a rigid system and rule of God in Geneva. Calvinism crossed the channel under the leadership of John Knox in Scotland. The English (Anglican) Reformation rested on political rather than strictly religious considerations. The Reformation brought about a Counter-Reformation within the Roman Church in which abuses were set right and lines against the Protestants more tightly drawn (Council of Trent, 1545-1563).—*V.F.*

Regressive: See *Sorites*.

Regulative Principles: (*regulative Prinzipien*) Though this term, in Kant's philosophy, is in one passage applied to the analogies in general, it is reserved for ideas of reason as opposed to the categories. They cannot be proved like the latter, but though not known, theoretically at least, to be true of anything, serve to regulate our thought and action.—*A.C.E.*

Reichenbach, Hans: (1891-1953) Born Sept. 26, 1891, Hamburg, Germany. Successively Privatdozent at the College of Engineering at Stuttgart, Professor of philosophy in the universities of Berlin, Istanbul (1933-1938), University of California at Los Angeles (after 1938); the leading figure of the Berlin group in the development of recent logical empiricism.

Reichenbach's work has been devoted mainly to the Philosophy of empirical science; for a brief general survey of the problems which have particularly attracted his attention, and of his conception of an adequate method for their solution, cf. his *Raum. Zeit Lehre*. His contributions center around (I) the problems of space and time, and (II) those of causality, induction and probability. His studies of the first group of problems include thorough analyses of the nature of geometry and of the logical structure of relativistic physics; these researches led Reichenbach to a rejection of the aprioristic theory of space and time. Reichenbach's contributions to the second group of problems pivot around his general theory of probability which is based on a statistical definition of the probability concept. In terms of this probabilistic approach, Reichenbach has carried out comprehensive analyses of methodological and epistemological problems such as those of causality and induction. He has also extended his formal probability theory into a probability logic in which probabilities play the part of truth values.—*C.G.H.*

Other works: *Atom and Cosmos; Wahrscheinlichkeitslehre; Experience and Prediction*.

Reid, Thomas: (1710-1796) Scotch philosopher. In his *An Inquiry into the Human Mind on the Principles of Common Sense*, he opposed the tradition of Berkeley and Hume and emphasized the common consciousness of mankind as basic. These ideas on the importance of self-evidence were further elaborated in "Essays on the Intellectual Powers of Man" and "Essays on the Active Powers of Man." He was founder of the so-called Common Sense School, employing that term as here indicated and not in its present acceptation.—*L.E.D.*

Relation: The same as dyadic *propositional function* (*q.v.*). The distinction between relations *in intension* and relations *in extension* is the same as that for propositional functions.—Sometimes the word *relation* is used to mean a propositional function of *two or more* variables, and in this case one distinguishes *binary* (dyadic) relations, *ternary* (triadic) relations, etc.

If R denotes a (binary) relation, and X and Y denote arguments, the notation XRY may be used, instead of R(X, Y), to mean that the two arguments stand in the relation denoted by R. The *domain* of a relation R is the class of things x for which there exists at least one y such that xRy holds. The *converse domain* of a relation R is the class of things y for which there exists at least one x such that xRy. The *field* of a relation is the logical sum of the domain and the converse domain.

See also *Logic, formal*, § 8.—*A.C.*

Whitehead and Russell, *Principia Mathematica,* 2nd edn., vol. 1, Cambridge, England, 1925.

Relation-number: Dyadic relations R and R' are said to be *similar* (or *ordinally similar*) if there exists a one-one relation S whose domain is the field of R and whose converse domain is the field of R', such that, if aSa' and bSb', then aRb if and only if $a'R'b'$. The *relation-number* of a dyadic relation may then be defined as the class of relations similar to it—cf *cardinal number*.

The relation-number of an ordering relation (see *order*) is called also an *ordinal type* or *order type*.

The notion of a relation-number may be extended in a straightforward way to polyadic relations.—*A.C.*

Whitehead and Russell, *Principia Mathematica,*

vol. 2.

Relational Theory of Mind: The conception of mind as a relation between neutral entities (i.e. entities which are intrinsically neither mental nor physical) which was foreshadowed by Hume and developed by British and American New Realism. See C. W. Morris, *Six Theories of Mind*, Ch. III. See *Neutral Monism.*—*L.W.*

Relative: A concept is *relative* if it is—a word, if it denotes—a polyadic propositional function, or relation, rather than a monadic propositional function. The term *relative* is applied especially to words which have been or might be thought to denote monadic propositional functions, but for some reason must be taken as denoting relations. Thus the word *short* or the notion of shortness may be called relative because as a monadic propositional function it is vague, while as a relation (*shorter than*) it is not vague.

Analogously, the term *relative* may be applied to words erroneously thought of or used as if denoting binary relations, but which actually must be taken as denoting ternary or quaternary relations; etc. E.g., the Special Theory of Relativity is said to make simultaneity relative because, according to it, simultaneity is a function of two events *and a coordinate system or frame of reference*—instead of a function merely of two events, as in the Newtonian or classical theory.

The adjective *relative* is also used in a less special way, to mean simply *relational* or *pertaining to relations*.

In connection with the algebra of relations (see *logic, formal*, § 8), Peirce and Schröder use *relative* as a noun, in place of *relation*. For Schröder, a relative (Relativ) is a relation in extension. Peirce makes a distinction between *relative* and *relation*, not altogether clear; many passages suggest that *relative* is a syntactical term, but others approximate the usage adopted by Schröder.—*A.C.*

Relativism: The view that truth is relative and may vary from individual to individual, from group to group, or from time to time, having no objective standard. See *Ethical relativism.*—*W.K.F.*

Relativism, Epistemological: The theory that all human knowledge is relative to the knowing mind and to the conditions of the body and sense organs. Relativism is usually combined with a subjectivistic theory of knowledge (see *Subjectivism*) but, in recent epistemology, a realistic or objectivistic relativism has been advanced. See *Objective Relativism*. Ethical relativism.—*L.W.*

Relativism, Psychological: The psychological principle that the character of any present conscious content is relative to and influenced by past and contemporaneous experiences of the organism. The law of psychological relativity was prominent in the psychology of Wundt, and has recently been emphasized by *Gestalt* Psychology.—*L.W.*

Relativity of Knowledge: See *Relativism, Epistemological*.

Relevance or Relevancy: (Fr. *relevant*) Relation between concepts which are capable of combining to form meaningful propositions or between propositions belonging to the same "universe of discourse."—*L.W.*

Relativity, theory of: A mathematical theory of *space-time (q.v.)*, of profound epistemological as well as physical importance, comprising the special theory of relativity (Einstein, 1905) and the general theory of relativity (Einstein, 1914-16). The name arises from the fact that certain things which the classical theory regarded as absolute—e.g., the simultaneity of spatially distant events, the time elapsed between two events (unless co-incident in space-time), the length of an extended solid body, the separation of four-dimensional space-time into a three-dimensional space and a one-dimensional time—are regarded by the relativity theory as *relative (q.v.)* to the choice of a coordinate system in space-time, and thus relative to the observer. But on the other hand the relativity theory represents as absolute certain things which are relative in the classical theory—e.g., the velocity of light in empty space. See *Non-Euclidean geometry.*—*A.C.*

Albert Einstein, *Relativity, The Special & The General Theory, A Popular Exposition*, translated by R. W. Lawson, London, 1920. A. S. Eddington, *Space, Time, and Gravitation*, Cambridge, England, 1920. A. V. Vasiliev, *Space, Time, Motion*, translated by H. M. Lucas and C. P. Sanger, with an introduction by Bertrand Russell, London, 1924, and New York, 1924.

Religion, Philosophy of: The methodic or systematic investigation of the elements of religious consciousness, the theories it has evolved and their development and historic relationships in the cultural complex. It takes account of religious practices only as illustrations of the vitality of beliefs and the inseparableness of the psychological from thought reality in faith. It is distinct from theology in that it recognizes the priority of reason over faith and the acceptance of creed, subjecting the latter to a logical analysis. As such, the history of the Philosophy of Religion is coextensive with the free enquiry into religious reality, particularly the conceptions of God, soul, immortality, sin, salvation, the sacred (Rudolf Otto), etc., and may be said to have its roots in any society above the pre-logical, mythological, and custom-controlled level, first observed in Egypt, China, India, and Greece. Its scientific treatment as a subsidiary philosophic discipline dates from about Kant's *Religion innerhalb der Grenzen der reinen Vernunft* and Hegel's *Philosophie der Religion*, while in the history of thought based on Indian and Greek speculation, sporadic sallies were made by all great philosophers, especially those professing an idealism, and by most theologians.

With reference to the approach to the central reality of religion, God, and man's relation to it, types of the Philosophy of Religion may be distinguished, leaving out of account negative (atheism), skeptical and cynical (Xenophanes, Socrates, Voltaire), and agnostic views, although assertions by them are not to be separated from the history of religious consciousness. *Fundamentalism*, mainly a theological and often a Church phenomenon of a revivalist nature, philosophizes on the basis of unquestioning faith, seeking to buttress it by logical argument, usually taking the form of proofs of the existence of God (see *God*). Here belong all historic religions, Christianity in its two principal forms, Catholicism with its Scholastic philosophy and Protestantism with its greatly diversified philosophies, the numerous religions of Hinduism, such as Brahmanism, Shivaism and Vishnuism, the religion of Judaism, and Mohammedanism. *Mysticism,* tolerated by Church and philosophy, is less concerned with proof than with description and personal experience, revealing much of the psychological factors involved in belief and speculation. Indian philosophy is saturated with mysticism since its inception, Sufism is the outstanding form of Arab mysticism, while the greatest mystics in the West are Plotinus, Meister Eckhart, Tauler, Ruysbroek, Thomas a Kempis, and Jacob Böhme. *Metaphysics* incorporates religious concepts as thought necessities. Few philosophers have been able to avoid the concept of God in their ontology, or any reference to the relation of God to man in their ethics. So, e.g., Plato, Spinoza, Leibniz, Schelling, and especially Hegel who made the investigation of the process of the Absolute the essence of the Philosophy of Religion.

With respect to the concept of God, a specific philosophy of religion may be a theism with its many forms of henotheism, monotheism, etc., a deism, pantheism, anthropomorphism, animism, panpsychism (all of which see), or the like; or it may fall into the general philosophic classification of a transcendentalism, immanentalism, absolutism, etc. By the term modernism is meant the tendency, subtended by the recent interest of science in religion (Sirs J. H. Jeans and A. S. Eddington, A. Carrell *et al.*) to interpret religious experience in close contact with physical and social reality, thus transforming the age-old personalism into a thoroughgoing humanism, thereby accomplishing an even greater attachment to social thinking and practical ethics and a trend away from metaphysical speculation toward a psychologizing in the Philosophy of Religion.

Practically all philosophers of religion (to name in addition to those above only Schleiermacher, Lotze, Pfleiderer, Höffding, Siebeck, Galloway, Ladd, Wundt, Josiah Royce, W. E. Hocking, Barth, and Hauer) are carried by an ethical idealism, being interested in the good life as the right relation between God and man, conforming by and large to the ethical categories of determinism, indeterminism, mechanism, rationalism, etc. Buddhists, though not believing in God, profess an ethics religiously motivated and supported philosophically.

The scientific study of primitive religions, with such well-known names as E. B. Tylor, F. B. Jevons, W. M. R. Rivers, J. G. Frazer, R. H. Codrington, Spencer and Gillen, E. Westermarck, E. Durkheim, L. Lévy-Bruhl; the numerous outlines of the development of religion since Hume's *Natural History of Religion* and E. Caird's *Evolution of Religion;* the prolific literature dealing with individual religions of a higher type; the science of comparative religion with such names as that of L. H. Jordan; the many excellent treatises on the

psychology of religion including Wm. James' *Varieties of Religious Experience;* the sacred literature of all peoples in various editions together with a voluminous theological exegesis; Church history and, finally, the history of dogma, especially the monumental work of von Harnack, all are contributing illustrative material to the Philosophy of Religion which became stimulated to scientific efforts through the positivism of Spencer, Huxley, Lewes, Tyndall, and others, and is still largely oriented by the progress in science; as may be seen, e.g., by the work of Emile Boutroux, S. Alexander (*Space, Time and Deity*), and A. N. Whitehead.

See, apart from the works of the authors named, George Trumbull Ladd, *The Philosophy of Religion;* Edwin A. Burtt, *Types of Religious Philosophy*, Edgar S. Brightman, *A Philosophy of Religion.*—*K.F.L.*

Religion, Promethean: An anarchistic piety which refrains from making past or present revolutionary doctrine the basis of new tyranny. (Montague).—*H.H*

Religious A Priori: A separate, innate category of the human consciousness, religious in that it issues certain insights and indisputable certainties concerning God or a Superhuman Presence. Man's religious nature rests upon the peculiar character of his mind. He possesses a native apprehension of the Divine. God's existence is guaranteed as an axiomatic truth. For Ernst Troeltsch (1865-1923) this *a priori* quality of the mind is both a rational intuition and an immediate experience. God is present as a real fact both rationally and empirically. For Rudolf Otto this *a priori* quality of the mind is a nonrational awareness of the holy, mysterious and awe-inspiring divine Reality. Man possesses a kind of eerie sense of a Presence which is the basis of the genuinely religious feeling. See *Numinous.*—*V.F.*

Religious Phenomenology: (in Max Scheler) The doctrine of the essential origin and forms of the religious, and of the essence of the divine, as well as of its revelation.—*P.A.S.*

Renaissance: (Lat. *re* + *nasci,* to be born) Is a term used by historians to characterize various periods of intellectual revival, and especially that which took place in Italy and Europe during the 15th and 16th centuries. The term was coined by Michelet and developed into a historical concept by J. Burckhardt (1860) who considered individualism, the revival of classical antiquity, the "discovery" of the world and of man as the main characters of that period as opposed to the Middle Ages. The meaning, the temporal limits, and even the usefulness of the concept have been disputed ever since. For the emphasis placed by various historians on the different fields of culture and on the contribution of different countries must lead to different interpretations of the whole period, and attempts to express a complicated historical phenomenon in a simple, abstract definition are apt to fail. Historians are now inclined to admit a very considerable continuity between the "Renaissance" and the Middle Ages. Yet a sweeping rejection of the whole concept is excluded, for it expresses the view of the writers of the period itself, who considered their century a revival of ancient civilization after a period of decay. While Burckhardt had paid no attention to philosophy, others began to speak of a "philosophy of the renaissance," regarding thought of those centuries not as an accidental accompaniment of renaissance culture, but as its characteristic philosophical manifestation. As yet this view has served as a fruitful guiding principle rather than as a verified hypothesis. Renaissance thought can be defined in a negative way as the period of transition from the medieval, theological to the modern, scientific interpretation of reality. It also displays a few common features, such as an emphasis on man and on his place in the universe, the rejection of certain medieval standards and methods of science, the increased influence of some newly discovered ancient sources, and a new style and literary form in the presentation of philosophical ideas. More obvious are the differences between the various schools and traditions which cannot easily be brought to a common denominator: Humanism, Platonism, Aristotelianism, scepticism and natural philosophy, to which may be added the group of the founders of modern science (Copernicus, Kepler, Galileo).—*P.O.K.*

Cf. "Study of the Renaissance Philosophies." P.O Kristeller and J. H. Randall, Jr. in *Jour. History of Ideas*, II, 4 (Oct. 1941).

Renouvier, Charles: (1818-1903) a thinker strongly influenced by Leibniz and Kant. His philosophy has been called 'phenomenological neo-criticism', and its peculiar feature is that·it denies the existence of all transcendental entities, such as thing-in-itself, the absolute, and the noumenon.—*R.B.W.*

Main works: *Uchronie*, 1857; *Philos. analytique de l'histoire*, 4 vols., 1896-98; *La nouvelle monadologie*, 1899; *Le Personnalisme*, 1903; *Essais de critique générale*, 1851-64.

Representative Ideas, Theory of: Theory that the mind in perception, memory and other types of knowledge, does not know its objects directly but only through the mediation of ideas which represent them. The theory was advanced by Descartes and the expression, representative ideas, may have been suggested by his statement that our ideas more or less adequately "represent" their originals. See *Meditations*, III. Locke, Hobbes, Malebranche, Berkeley subscribed to the theory in one form or another and the theory has supporters among contemporary epistemologists (*e.g.* Lovejoy and certain other Critical Realists). The theory has been severely criticized ever since the time of Arnauld. (See *Des vrais et de fausses idées*) and has become one of reproach. See *Epistemological Dualism*.—*L.W.*

Representative Realism: The view that in the knowing process our ideas are representations or ambassadors of the real external world. (E.g. the view of John Locke.)—*V.F.*

Res Cogitans: (Lat. *res*, thing + *cogitans* from *cogitare*, to think) Descartes' designation for thinking substance which along with extended substance (res extensa) constitute his dualism. The term presumably designates not only the individual mind which thinks but also the substance which pervades all individual minds.—*L.W.*

Retentiveness: (Lat. *re* + *tendere*, to hold) The mind's capacity to retain and subsequently revive earlier experiences. See *Memory*.—*L.W.*

Revelation: The communication to man of the Divine Will. This communication has taken, in the history of religions, almost every conceivable form, e.g., the results of lot casting, oracular declaration, dreams, visions, ecstatic experiences (induced by whatever means, such as intoxicants), books, prophets, unusual characters, revered traditional practices, storms, pestilence, etc. The general conception of revelation has been that the divine communication comes in ways unusual, by means not open to the ordinary channels of investigation. This, however, is not a necessary corollary; revelation of the Divine Will may well come through ordinary channels, the give-and-take of everyday experience, through reason and reflection and intuitive insight.—*V.F.*

Rhetoric: (Gr. *Rhetor*, public speaker) Art turned to the practical purpose of persuading and impressing.—*L.V.*

Rhythm: (a) Harmonious correlation of parts in a work of art. (b) (Music) Systematic grouping of notes according to duration.—*L.V.*

Rickert, Heinrich: (1863-1936) Believing that only in system philosophy achieves its ends, Rickert established under the influence of Fichte a transcendental idealism upon an epistemology which has nothing to do with searching for connections between thought and existence, but admits being only as a being in consciousness, and knowledge as an affirming or negating, approving or disapproving of judgments. Hence, philosophy is one of norms in which the concept of reality dissolves into a concept of value, while consciousness ceases to be an individual phenomenon and becomes impersonal and general. Value exists not as a physical thing but in assent and our acknowledging its validity. In this we are guided by means and obligated by the ought. Method distinguishes history as the discipline of the particular from science which must advance beyond fact-gathering to the discovery of general laws, and from philosophy which seeks absolute cultural values through explanation, understanding, and interpretation.

Main works: *Die Grenzen d. naturwiss. Begriffsbildung*, 1896; *Kultur u. Naturwissenschaften*, 1899; *Philos. d. Lebens*, 1920.—*K.F.L.*

Ricoeur, Paul: (1913-   ) Contemporary French philosopher, teacher at the Sorbonne and at The University of Chicago. Bridging phenomenology and contemporary language analysis through the theory of metaphor, myth, and scientific model, he is one of the leading philosophers in France today. His early phenomenology of mind-body is a fruitful way of overcoming the troublesome mind-body distinction. Author of *The Conflict of Interpretations: Essays on Hermeneutics* (1974), *Freud and Philosophy: An Essay on Interpretation* (1970), *The Contribution of French Historiography to French History* (1980), *Freedom & Nature: The Voluntary and the Involuntary* (trans. E.V.

Kohák, 1966), *History & Truth* (1965), *Husserl: An Analysis of His Phenomenology* (1967), *Interpretation Theory: Discourse & the Surplus of Meaning* (1976), *Main Trends in Philosophy* (1979), *Political & Social Essays* (1974), *The Rule of Metaphor: Multi-Disciplinary Studies of the Creation of Meaning in Language* (1977), and *Symbolism of Evil* (1969).—*S.E.N.*

Right: In an ethical sense an *action* conforming to the moral law. Also the correlative of duty.

In a legal sense, any claim against others, recognized by law. Political rights, the capacity of exercising certain functions in the formation and administration of government—the right to vote, to be elected to public office, etc. Natural rights, as against positive rights, those claims or liberties which are not derived from positive law but from a "higher law," the law of nature. The right to live, the right to work, the "pursuit of happiness," the right to self-development are sometimes considered natural rights.—*W.E.*

Right action: (a) Teleologically defined as action such that no alternative possible under the circumstances is better. Cf. G. E. Moore, *Princ. Ethica.*—*C.A.B.*

(b) Formalistically (or deontologically) regarded as not equivalent to the above, as perhaps, indefinable. For example, C. D. Broad holds that the rightness or wrongness of an action in a given situation is a function of its "fittingness" in that situation and of its utility in that situation. W. D. Ross holds that in given circumstances that action is right whose *prima facie* rightness in the respects in which it is *prima facie* right outweighs its *prima facie* wrongness in the respects in which it is *prima facie* wrong to a greater degree than is the case with any possible alternative action.—*C.A.B.*

Right Reason: (Gr. *orthos logos;* L. *recta ratio*) The law or order exhibited in the constitution of the world, to which, according to the Stoics, human law and human action should conform; the Law of Nature.—*G.R.M.*

Rigorism: Any view according to which the ethical life involves a rigorous treatment of the more natural or physical desires, feelings, and passions.—*W.K.F.*

Ritschlianism: A celebrated school of 19th century Christian thought inaugurated by Albrecht Ritschl (1822-89). This school argued for God upon the basis of what is called the religious value-judgment. Two kinds of judgments are said to characterize man's reaction to his world of experience: (1) dependent or concomitant, those dependent upon perceived facts, such as the natural sciences; (2) independent or religious, those which affirm man's superior worth independent of the limitations of the finite world and man's dependence upon a superhuman order of reality, God. God is not reached by speculation, nor by the "evidences" in nature, nor by intuitions or mystic experience, nor by a rational *a priori* or intimate feeling. God is implied in the religous value judgment: "though he slay me will I trust him." That man needs God as a deliverer from his bonds is the assertion of the independent religious value judgment; the consequences following this judgment of need and worth sustain him with courage and victory over every obstacle. Ritschlianism is notable in the emphasis it placed upon the category of value, an emphasis which has grown stronger in contemporary theistic belief.—*V.F.*

Romanism: (Lat. *Roma*, Rome, the seat of Papal authority) The doctrines and practices of the Roman Catholic Church; tendencies in members of other churches to favor Catholicism.—*V.J.B.*

Romantic art: (a) Artistic era between the end of the 18th and middle of the 19th centuries. (b) A form closer to and less independent of emotions than classic form.—*L.V.*

Romanticism: As a general philosophical movement, romanticism is best understood as the initial phase of German Idealism, serving as a transition from Kant to Hegel, and flourishing chiefly between 1775 and 1815. It is associated primarily with the Schlegel brothers, Novalis, Fried, Schelling, and Schleiermacher, with Schelling as its culmination and most typical figure. The philosophical point of departure for romanticism is the Kantian philosophy, and romanticism shares with all German Idealism both the fundamental purpose of extending knowledge to the realm of noumena, and the fundamental doctrine that all reality is ultimately spiritual, derivative from a living spirit and so knowable by the human spirit. The essence of philosophical romanticism as expressed by Schelling, that which differentiates it from other types of Idealism, resides in its conception of Spirit; upon this depend its metaphysical account of nature and man, and its epistemological doctrine of the proper method for investigating and understanding reality. Romanticism holds that Spirit, or the Absolute, is essentially creative; the ultimate ground of all things is primarily an urge to self-expression, and all that it has brought into being is but a means to its fuller self-realization. If the Absolute of Fichte is a moralist, and that of Hegel a logician, then that of the romanticists is primarily an artist. From this basic view there springs a metaphysic that interprets the universe in terms of the concepts of evolution, process, life, and consciousness. The world of nature is one manifestation of Spirit; man is another and a higher such manifestation, for in man Spirit seeks to become conscious of its own work. The metaphysical process is the process by which the Absolute seeks to realize itself, and all particular things are but phases within it. Hence, the epistemology of romanticism is exclusively emotional and intuitive, stressing the necessity for fullness of experience and depth of feeling if reality is to be understood. Reason, being artificial and analytical, is inadequate to the task of comprehending the Absolute; knowing is living, and the philosopher must approach nature through inspiration, longing, and sympathy.

Romanticism was a healthy and necessary influence in reasserting the dignity of nature, in stressing the emotional factor in knowledge, and in emphasizing the concepts of process and evolution. It was an inadequate doctrine, in that it did not clarify the detailed movement of the process it posited, and could offer no positive advice for discovering this, other than to be inspired and intuit it. Romanticism is metaphysical expressionism, and like any expressionistic doctrine it is unable to give any concrete meaning to the concept of causality; it can therefore provide no categories under which to comprehend things, but can only say that things *are* because they have been expressed, and can be understood only by being re-expressed; i.e., only by re-living the experience of their creator.

(In Aesthetics): A movement in both art and general aesthetic theory which was particularly widespread and influential in the last years of the 18th and the first half of the 19th centuries. So interpreted, it is especially associated with Novalis, the Schlegels, and Jean Paul Richter in Germany; Rousseau, Chateaubriand, Hugo, Lamartine in France; Blake, Scott, the Lake Poets, Shelley, and Byron in England. As a general attitude toward art and its function, as an interpretation of the goodness, beauty, and purpose of life, romanticism has always existed and can be confined to no one period.

The essence of romanticism, either as an attitude or as a conscious program, is an intense interest in nature, and an attempt to seize natural phenomena in a direct, immediate, and naive manner. Romanticism thus regards all forms, rules, conventions, and manners as artificial constructs and as hindrances to the grasp, enjoyment, and expression of nature; hence its continual opposition to any kind of classicism (*q.v.*), whose formalities it treats as fetters. Romanticism stresses the values of sincerity, spontaneity, and passion, as against the restraint and cultivation demanded by artistic forms and modes. It reasserts the primacy of feeling, imagination, and sentiment, as opposed to reason. It maintains that art should concern itself with the particular and the concrete, observing and reporting accurately the feelings aroused by nature, with no idealization or generalization. It commands the artist to feel freely and deeply, and to express what he has felt with no restraints, either artistic or social. It seeks in works of art a stimulus to imagination and feeling, a point of departure for free activity, rather than an object that it can accept and contemplate.

Such a general attitude and purpose of course allow for vast specific differences, and under the term *romantics* must be included artists and theorists who stress varying aspects of nature and man. All have in common a rejection of formal restraints, an obsession with their experience of nature, and the conviction that this felt quality of things is of ultimate value in its immediacy.

On the ambiguities of the term, as well as an analysis of one of its meanings as the characteristics of thought shared by some German thinkers from about 1790 to 1830, cf. A. O. Lovejoy, "Meaning of Romanticism for the Historian of Ideas," *Jour. Hist. Ideas* (Jan. 1941), which refers also to Lovejoy's now famous articles on the subject.—*I.J.*

Romero, Francisco: (1891-1962) Professor of Philosophy at the Universities of Buenos Aires, La Plata, and the National Institute for Teachers. Director of the Philosophical Library of the Losada Publishing House, and distinguished staff member of various cul-

tural magazines and reviews in Latin America. Francisco Romero is one of the most important figures in the philosophical movement of South America. He is the immediate successor of Korn, and as such he follows on the footsteps of his master, doing pioneer work, not only striving towards an Argentinian philosophy, but also campaigning for philosophy in the nations of Latin America through a program of cultural diffusion. Among his most important writings, the following may be mentioned: *Vieja y Nueva Concepción de la Realidad,* 1932; *Los Problemas de la Filosofía de la Cultura,* 1936; *Filosofía de la Persona,* 1938; *Lógica* (In collaboration with Pucciarelli), 1936; *Programa de una Filosofía,* 1940; *Un Filósofo de la Problematicidad,* 1934; *Descartes y Husserl,* 1938; *Contribución al Estudio de las Relaciones de Comparación,* 1938; *Teoría y Práctica de la Verdad,* 1939. Three characteristic notes may be observed in the philosophy of Romero: (a) Aporetics or Problematics, (b) Philosophy of *Weltanschauungen,* (c) Philosophy of the *Person.* The first has to do with his criterion of knowledge. Justice to all the facts of experience, over against mere system building, seems to be the watchword. The desirability and gradual imposition of *Structuralism* as the modern *Weltanschauung,* over against outworn world conceptions such as Evolution, Mechanism, Rationalism, etc., is the emphasis of the second principle of his philosophy. Personality as a mere function of transcendence, with all that transcendence implies in the realm of value and history, carries the main theme of his thought. See *Latin American Philosophy.*—*J.A.F.*

Roscelin: (c. 1050—1120) born at Compiègne, France, probably studied in Soissons and Rheims. He taught as Canon of Compiène, and at Tours, Loches (where Abelard was his pupil) and Besancon. Noted in philosophy for his extremely nominalistic solution to the problem of universals. Theologically, he was accused of tritheism. No major works are extant and his views are known only through possibly biased accounts in John of Salisbury, (*Metalogicus,* II, 17, PL 199, 874), St. Anselm, Abailard and Otto of Freising.

J. Reiners, *Der Nominalismus in der Frühscholastik,* BGPM VIII, 5, 25-41 (Münster, 1910).—*V.J.B.*

Rosmini-Serbati, (Antonio): Born in Rovereto (Trento), March 24, 1797; died in Stresa (Milan), July 1, 1855. Ordained priest 1821. Founded the Institute for Charity. Influenced Italian Risorgimento, impelling Pope Pius IX towards liberalism.

His philosophy is a fusion of idealism and scholasticism, adhering to human experience. He maintained there is a distinction between the natural and the supernatural order, but emphasized that the supreme principle uniting all knowledge is universal being.—*L.V.*

Cf. T. Davidson, *Rosmini's Philosophical System,* 1882.

Ross, (William) David: (1877-1940) Is principally known as an Aristotelian scholar. He served first as joint editor, later as editor of the Oxford translation of Aristotle. In this series he himself translated the *Metaphysics* and the *Nicomachean Ethics.* In addition he published critical texts with commentaries of the *Metaphysics* and the *Physics,* and also an edition of Theophrastus's *Metaphysics.* Besides enjoying a reputation as Aristotelian interpreter, Sir David has gained repute as a writer on morality and ethics.—*C.K.D.*

Rousseau, Jean Jacques: (1712-1778), a native of Geneva, Switzerland, whose influence in France and throughout Europe was enormous for many a decade, thanks to his timely ideas and colorful and lucid style of writing. Particularly influential were his *Emile,* a book on education, and *Social Contract,* a work reviving an old political doctrine concerning the origin of human society, into which he introduced novel democratic ideas. His thought was characterized by skepticism and criticism of the Western civilization regarded by him as a sad deviation from natural conditions of existence, described imaginatively in his *New Heloise.*—*R.B.W.*

Royce, Josiah: (1855-1916) Born in California, taught philosophy at Harvard. Neo-Hegelian idealist, conceives Reality as the career of an all-inclusive absolute mind, of which our minds are fragmentary manifestations. Nothing short of such a mind can terminate the quest of each finite consciousness for the true and final object of its experience, which is found always in more experience fulfilling and giving significance to the experience in question. In an absolute experience alone, to which all things are present and by which all things are understood, can the ultimate explanation and meaning of any and all finite experience be revealed, all error be corrected, all imperfection be overcome.

Though fragments of the absolute experience, our minds somehow remain separate selves and persons. Though infinite and all-comprehensive in extent, and reviewing *ad infinitum* its own infinity in knowing that it knows that it knows, the Absolute is nevertheless a finished and closed whole. Though shot through and through with error and evil and sin and suffering, the Absolute is nevertheless perfect, and perfect because of them, since struggle with them and triumph over them is of the essence of its perfection. Though a temporal process, it nevertheless overarches that process in a single act of comprehension in which past, present, and future are grasped, even as the successive notes of a musical phrase are grasped, as an eternally present completed fact.

The will, like the intellect, reaches after and finds its peace in the Absolute. The moral life lies in seeking the ever widening meaning of our individual lives and identifying ourselves with it. This self-identification with larger meaning is loyalty—the basis and the essence of all human virtue.—*B.A.G.F.*

Main works: *The Religious Aspect of Philosophy,* 1885; *The Spirit of Modern Philosophy,* 1892; *The World and the Individual,* 1900; *Lectures on Modern Idealism,* 1919.

Rule, ethical or moral: Any general ethical proposition enjoining a certain kind of action in a certain kind of situation, e.g., one who has made a promise should keep it. Rules figure especially in "dogmatic" types of deontological or intuitionistic ethics, and teleological ethics is often described as emphasizing ends rather than rules. Even a teleologist may, however, recommend certain rules, such as the above, as describing kinds of action which are generally conducive to good ends.—*W.K.F.*

Rule of Faith: In general, an authoritative statement of belief. In historic Christianity such statements appeared out of existing formulae (e.g., the early baptismal confessions) or were formulated to meet existing heresies. In Catholic Christianity the Rule of Faith (Regula Fidei) includes the whole of apostolic teaching and its further elaborations.—*V.F.*

Rule of inference: See *logic, formal,* §§ 1, 3, and *logistic system.*

Russell, Bertrand A. W.: (1872-1970) Fellow Trinity College, Cambridge, 1895; lecturer in philosophy, University of Cambridge, 1910-1916. Author of *The Philosophy of Leibniz,* 1900; *The Principles of Mathematics,* 1903; *Principia Mathematica* (in collaboration with A. N. Whitehead), 3 vols. 1910-13, (second edition, 1925-27); *The Problems of Philosophy,* 1912; *Our Knowledge of the External World,* 1914; *Introduction to Mathematical Philosophy,* 1918; *The Analysis of Mind,* 1921; *The Analysis of Matter,* 1927; *An Outline of Philosophy,* 1928; *An Inquiry into Meaning and Truth,* 1940. Also numerous other works on philosophy, politics and education, outrageously attacked by reactionaries.

Two aspects of Russell's work are likely to remain of permanent importance, (1) his major part in the twentieth century renaissance of logic, (2) his reiterated attempts to identify the methods of philosophy with those of the sciences.

(1) While the primary objective of *Principia* was to prove that pure mathematics could be derived from logic, the success of this undertaking (as to which hardly any dissenting opinion persists) is overshadowed by the importance of the techniques perfected in the course of its prosecution. Without disrespect to other pioneers in the field, it is sufficient to point out that a knowledge of the symbolic logic of Russell and Whitehead is still a necessary prerequisite for understanding contemporary studies in logic, in the foundations of mathematics, and the philosophy of science.

(2) Flirtations with realism, neutral monism, positivism or behaviorism have never seriously interfered with Russell's attempt to establish philosophy as a science. The empirical data being supplied by the experimental scientist, the specifically philosophical task becomes the *analysis* of such deliverances (with the full resources of modern logistic). Unlike certain of his followers, Russell has never been strenuously antimetaphysical. He has never held pragmatic, still less conventional, views with regard to the nature of logic itself. And his general empirical approach has been constantly modified by rationalistic views concerning the subsistence of universals.—*M.B.*

Ryle, Gilbert: (1900–   ) British Analytic philosopher. Formerly Waynflete Professor of Metaphysical Philosophy in the University of Oxford.

In his most influential work, *Concept of Mind*, Ryle argues against the traditional conception of mind as a spiritual or non-physical substance residing in the physical body. His claim is that this view, which he labels "the ghost in the machine," rests on what he calls a "category mistake," analogous to the mistake involved in asking where one can find the *University* at Oxford, which is in fact a collection of separate and autonomous colleges.—*T.P.S.*

S

Saadia, ben Joseph: (Arabic Sa'id Al-Fayyumi) (892-942) Born and educated in Egypt, he left his native country in 915 and settled in Babylonia where he was appointed in 928 Gaon of the Academy of Sura. He translated the Bible into Arabic and wrote numerous works, both in Hebrew and Arabic, in the fields of philology, exegesis, Talmudics, polemics, Jewish history, and philosophy. His chief philosophical work is the *Kitab Al-Amanat wa'l-Itikadat,* better known by its Hebrew title, *Emunot we-Deot,* i.e., Doctrines and Religious Beliefs. Its purpose is to prove the compatibility of the principles of Judaism with reason and to interpret them in such a way that their rationality becomes evident. The first nine sections establish philosophically the ten fundamental articles of faith, and the tenth deals with ethics. Philosophically, Saadia was influenced by the teachings of the Mutazilia. See *Jewish Philosophy.—Q.V.*

Sabda: (Skr.) Sound, an Indian metaphysical concept; word, particularly the cosmic or divine word (see *vāc*); testimony, a valid source of knowledge in some philosophic systems.—*K.F.L.*

Sabellianism: The view of Sabellius who taught in the first half of the third century the doctrine that there is one God but three (successive) modes or manifestations of God: as creator and governor God is Father, as redeemer God is the Son, as regenerator and sanctifier God is the Holy Spirit — one and the same God. The view approximated the later orthodox Trinitarian conception (see *Trinitarianism*) but was too harsh to be maintained. Further clarification was needed. Sabellianism has been called by several names, Modalism, Modalistic Monarchianism and Patripassianism (Father suffering).—*V.F.*

Sacerdotalism: (Lat. *sacerdotalis:* pertaining to a priest) A religious system revolving about a priestly order. The term, when employed in a derogatory sense, means the unwholesome preference for ecclesiastical and sacramental observances in contrast to the more valid personal and moral values.—*V.F.*

Sadducee-ism: Both a party and a belief so named after the Zadokites, sons of Zadok, the family and temple hierarchy, advocates of the written Torah (teaching) in Judaism, the party and attitude opposite to the Pharisees and scribes, who prized oral and developing thought as well as the Torah. In general, Sadducee-ism, holding the Law (Pentateuch) to be explicit and its language straight-forward, rejected the Messianic doctrine as regards the House of David, but not as regards a priestly source, and also that of resurrection of the body, but not that of the soul. On the whole, however, Jesus and Paul both proved to be the enemies of Phariseeism and in effect sided with the Sadduccees against traditional law.—*F.K.*

Saguna: (Skr.) "possessed of qualities" (see *guna*), predicated of the Absolute from the exoteric point of view of the worshipper, according to Saṅkara (*q.v.*; see *Nirguna*).—*K.F.L.*

Saint-Simon, Claude Henry, Count De: (1760-1825) French philosopher who fought with the French army during the American Revolution. He supported the French Revolution. He advocated what he termed a new science of society to do away with inequalities in the distribution of property, power and happiness. Love for the poor and the lowly was basic for the reform he urged. He greatly influenced Comte and Positivism.—*L.E.D.*

Main work: *L'Industrie on discussions politiques, morales, et philosophiques, dans l'intérèt de tous les hommes livrés a des travaux utiles et indépendants,* 1817. Cf. *Oeuvres de Saint-Simon,* 46 vols., 1865-77.

Sakti: (Skr.) Strength, might, of feminine gender, the word designates in Tantric (see *Tantra*) literature the female generative power of energy in the universe, worshipped by the religious as the wife of some deity or other, e.g., as *Durgā,* wife of Shiva. See *Shaktism.—K.F.L.*

Samādhi: (Skr.) The final stage in the practice of Yoga (*q.v.*) according to the Yogasūtras (*q.v.*) in which individuality is given up while merging with the object of meditation, thus producing a state of unqualified blissfulness and unperturbed consciousness, which is *mokṣa* (q.v.).—*K.F.L.*

Sāmanya: (Skr. similar, generic, etc.) Generality, universality; the universal in contrast to the particular. The universal is understood in the realist manner by the Nyāya-Vaiśeṣika to be eternal and distinct from, yet inherent in the particular; in the nominalist manner, by the Buddhists, to have no intrinsic existence; in the manner of *universalia in re* by the Jainas and Advaita Vedānta.—*K.F.L.*

Same and Other: One of the "persistent problems" of philosophy which goes back at least to Parmenides and Heraclitus (*q.v.*). In its most general form it raises the question: Is reality explicable in terms of one principle, ultimately the same in all things (monism), or is reality ultimately heterogeneous, requiring a plurality of first principles (pluralism)? Plato really developed the problem (in the *Sophist, Parmenides* and *Timaeus*) by suggesting that both sameness and otherness are required for a complete explanation of things. It is closely related to the problems of One and Many, Identity and Difference, of Universal and Individual in Mediaeval Scholasticism. With Hegel and Fichte the problem becomes fused with that of Spirit and Matter, or of Self and Not-self.—*V.J.B.*

Samnyāsin: (Skr.) A wise man, philosopher.—*K.F.L.*

Saṁsāra: (Skr.) "Going about," the passage of the soul in the cycle of births and deaths; the round of existence; transmigration, a universally accepted dogma in India, early justified philosophically on the basis of *karma* (*q.v.*). and the nature of *ātman* (*q.v.*), but its *modus operandi* variously explained. It is the object of practically every Indian philosophy to find a way to escape from *saṁsāra* and attain *mokṣa* (*q.v.*).—*K.F.L.*

Samskāra: (Skr. putting together) Mental impression, memory. Also the effects of *karma* (*q.v.*) as shaping one's life.—*K.F.L.*

San cheng: The Three Rectifications, also called san t'ung, which means that in the scheme of the macrocosmos — microcosmos relationship between man and the universe, the vital force (ch'i) underlying the correspondence should be so directed and controlled that, first of all, the germination of things, its symbolic color, black, and all governmental and social functions corresponding to it; secondly, the sprouting of things together with its symbolic color, white, and social and political correspondences; and, thirdly, the movement of things and its color, red, and correspondence in human affairs — all become correct. Applied to the interpretation of history, this theory means that the Hsia dynasty (2207-1766 B.C.?) was the reign of Man, the Shang dynasty (1765-1122 B.C.?) that of Earth, and the Chou dynasty (1122?-249 B.C.) that of Heaven. (Tung Chung-shu, 177-104 B.C.)—*W.T.C.*

San chiao: The three systems, doctrines, philosophies, or religions of Confucianism, Buddhism, and Taoism.—*W.T.C.*

Sanction: A sanction is anything which serves to move (and, in *this* sense, to oblige) a man to observe or to refrain from a given mode of conduct, any source of motivation, and hence, on a hedonistic theory, any source of pleasure or pain. Gay and Bentham distinguished four such sanctions: (1) the natural or physical sanction, i.e., the ordinary course of nature, (2) the virtuous or moral sanction, i.e., the ordinary actions and judgments of one's fellows, (3) the civil or political sanction, i.e., the threat of punishment or the promise of reward made by the government, (4) the religious sanction, i.e., the fear of God, etc. J. S. Mill labelled these external, and added an internal sanction, viz., the desire or the feeling of obligation to do the kind of conduct in question. See *Obligation.*—*W.K.F.*

Sanga: (Skr. sticking to) Attachment, especially to material things, or entanglement in earthly cares, considered an impediment to spiritual attainment or *moksa* (*q.v.*).—*K.F.L.*

San kang: The Three Standards, i.e., the sovereign is the standard of the minister; the father the standard of the son, and the husband the standard of the wife; on the ground that the active or male cosmic principle of the universe (yang), to which the sovereign, the father, and the husband correspond, is the standard of the passive or female cosmic principle (yin) to which is his commentary on the Vedānta (*q.v.*) respond. (Tung Chung-shu, 177-104 B.C.)—*W.T.C.*

Sankara: One of the greatest of Indian philosophers, defender of Brahamism, who died about 820 A.D., after having led a manysided, partly legendary life as peripatetic teacher and author of numerous treatises, the most influential of which is his commentary on the Vedānta (*q.v.*) in which he established the doctrine of *advaita* (*q.v.*).—*K.F.L.*

Sānkhya: Perhaps the oldest of the major systems of Indian philosophy (*q.v.*), founded by Kapila. Originally not theistic, it is realistic in epistemology, dualistic in metaphysics, assuming two moving ultimates, spirit (*puruṣa, q.v.*) and matter (*prakṛti, q.v.*) both eternal and uncaused. *Prakṛti* possesses the three qualities or principles of *sativa, rajas, tamas* (see these and *guṇa*), first in equipoise. When this is disturbed, the world in its multifariousness evolves in conjunction with *puruṣa* which becomes the plurality of selves in the process. The union (*saṁyoga*) of spirit and matter is necessary for world evolution, the inactivity of the former needing the verve of the latter, and the non-intelligence of that needing the guidance of conscious *puruṣa*. Successively, *prakṛti* produces *mahat* or *buddhi, ahaṁkāra, manas,* the ten *indriyas,* five *tanmātras* and five *mahābhūtas* (all of which see).—*K.F.L.*

Sānkhya-kārikā: (Skr.) The earliest extant text of the Sānkhya by Iśvarakrṣṇa; a famous commentary on it is that of Gauḍeapāda.—*K.F.L.*

San piao: The three laws in reasoning and argumentation, namely, that "there must be a basis or foundation" which can be "found in a study of the experiences of the wisest men of the past," that "there must be a general survey" by "examining (its compatibility with) the facts of the actual experience of the people," and that "there must be practical application" by "putting it into law and governmental policies, and see whether or not it is conducive to the welfare of the state and of the people." (Mo Tzŭ, between 500 and 396 B.C.)—*W.T.C.*

Santayana, George: For Santayana (1863-1952), one of the most eminent of contemporary naturalists, consciousness, instead of distorting the nature of Reality immediately reveals it. So revealed, Reality proclaims itself an infinity of *essences* (Platonic Ideas) *subsisting* in and by themselves, some of which are entertained by minds, and some of which are also enacted in and by a non-mental substratum, *substance* or *matter*, which adds concrete *existence* to their *subsistence*. The presence of this substratum, though incapable of rational proof, is assumed in action as a matter of *animal faith*. Furthermore, without it as a selective principle, the concrete enactment of some essences but not of others is inexplicable.

Matter, among other things, is external to and independent of consciousness, spatially extended, unequally distributed (corporeal), subject to locomotion and perhaps to intrinsic alteration in its parts, and capable of becoming conscious. Its selective and progressive enactment of essences is not teleological or intelligent, but is actuated by efficient causation and predetermined by antecedent situations.

In organic bodies matter may become conscious. Mind, being an activity of the body, and unsubstantial, is not causally effective, but simply entertains and contemplates essences both enacted and unenacted. Its registration of the natural functions and drives of the body of which it is the aura, is desire, which gives values like truth, goodness, and beauty to the essences entertained. The desire to know, satisfied by intelligibility, creates science, which is investigation of the world of enacted essences, where alone the explanation of things is to be found. The natural desire to experience social harmony and to contemplate beauty creates morality, art, poetry and religion, which entertain in imagination and seek to make concrete by action, combinations of essences, often unenacted and purely *ideal*.

These desires and drives, however, tend to stray beyond their proper provinces and to become intermingled and confused in attempts to identify truth, goodness, and beauty, to turn justifications into explanations, to regard subsistent ideals as concretely existent facts, and to distort facts into accordance with desired ideals. It is the business of reason and philosophy to clear up this confusion by distinguishing human drives and interests from one another, indicating to each its proper province and value, and confining each to the field in which it is valid and in which its appropriate satisfaction may be found. By so doing, they dispel the suspicion and antagonism with which the scientist, the moralist, the artist, and the theologian are wont to view one another, and enable a mind at harmony with itself to contemplate a world in which the subsistent and the existent form a harmonious whole.

Main works: *Sense of Beauty*, 1896; *Interpret. of Poetry and Religion*, 1900; *Life of Reason*, 5 vols., 1905-6 (*Reason in Common Sense, Reason in Society, Reason in Religion, Reason in Art, Reason in Science*);

Winds of Doctrine, 1913; *Egotism in German Philosophy*, 1915; *Character and Opinion in the U.S.*, 1920; *Skepticism and Animal Faith*, 1923; *Realms of Being*, 4 vols., 1927-40 (*Realm of Essence, Realm of Matter, Realm of Truth, Realm of Spirit*).—*B.A.G.F.*

Sartre, Jean-Paul: (1905-1980) The leading and most radical of the French Existentialists, born on the 21st of June, 1905. He was brought up by his grandfather, grandmother, and mother, who considered him a child prodigy.

He was educated at the École Normale Supériere in Paris. By the age of twenty-four, he had earned a Ph. D. in Philosophy.

He taught at the Lycée at Le Havre, at the Lycée Henri IV, and at the Institute Francais in Berlin (1934) before joining the staff of the Lycée Condorcet (1935). He resigned in 1942 to devote himself to literary work.

He served in the army from 1939 to 1941, was captured and spent nine months as a prisoner of war in Germany. When released, he returned to Paris where, with Camus and Francois Mauriac, he joined the resistance movement (1941-1944) and was finally caught and imprisoned by the Nazis. These experiences taught Sartre that freedom is "total responsibility in total solitude," for a member of the resistance, if caught, had no redress. He had to learn for himself how much torture he could stand. In such a world of intrigue and deception, there was no hope from the outside. The only support was internal. Our capacity for resisting torture and death, under those conditions, became the limits of freedom.

It is possible to group Sartre's philosophical thought into four periods, corresponding with four of his most important works. A development may be traced from one stage to the next.

(1) First is the stage of *solipsistic despair*. Unable to prove the existence of other persons, one is marooned within himself. The novel *Nausea* is most representative of this stage of thought.

(2) Next is the *negative spirit of resistance*, typified by the major work, *Being and Nothingness*. The first attitude toward others, he declares, is love, language, and masochism. The second attitude toward others is indifference, desire, hate, and sadism.

(3) The third stage is the optimistic humanism of *Existentialism is a Humanism*. Self-assured and certain of the basis for his thought, this stage, immediately following the second World War, was tremendously influential at the time.

(4) The fourth stage is Sartre's development of sociological doctrine in *Critique of Dialectical Reason*. He attempts to combine the concepts of existentialism with marxism, dropping marxist determinism as anachronistic and suggesting existentialism as a humanizing influence within the marxist system.

Sartre's autobiography, *The Words* (*Les Mots*, 1964) won the Nobel Prize for literature, which he refused on the grounds that it was "a literary bribe."

Active in opposing the Algerian War, he was called a traitor and his apartment was bombed. He was only kept out of prison by his prestige.

When he died in Paris at the age of 74, fifty thousand mourners formed a funeral procession through the Left Bank in his honor.—*S.E.N.*

'Man is nothing else than his plan; he exists only to the extent that he fulfills himself; he is therefore nothing else than the ensemble of his acts; nothing else than his life.''—Sartre, *Essays in Existentialism,* 47.

Sarva-darsana-sangraha: (Skr.) A work by Mādhvavācarya, professing to be a collection (*sangraha*) of all (*sarva*) philosophic views (*darśana*) or schools. It includes systems which acknowledge and others which reject Vedic (*q.v.*) authority, such as the Cārvāka, Buddhist and Jaina schools (which see).—*K.F.L.*

Sarvakartrtva: (Skr.) "All-makingness," descriptive of the ultimate principle in the universe, conceived dynamically.—*K.F.L.*

Sarvam khalv idam brahma: (Skr.) "Indeed, all this is *brahman,"* a famous dictum of Chāndogya Upanishad 3.14.1, symptomatic of the monistic attitude later elaborated in Śaṅkara's Vedānta (*q.v.*).—*K.F.L.*

Sarvāsti-vāda: (Skr.) The doctrine (*vāda*) of Hīnayāna Buddhism according to which "all is" (*sarvam asti*), or all is real, that which was, currently is, and will be but now is, potentially.—*K.F.L.*

Śāstra: (Skr.) A Sanskrit textbook.—*K.F.L.*

Sat: (Skr.) Being, a metaphysical concept akin to Eleatic thinking, which a school of thinkers regards as fundamental, as in Chāndogya Upanishad 6.2.1: "In the beginning . . . this world was just being, one only, without a second." It refutes the theory of non-being. (See *asat*).—*K.F.L.*

Sat-cit-ānanda, saccidānanda: (Skr.) "Being-awareness-bliss," a Vedāntic (*q.v.*) definition of the highest, all-inclusive reality, also of the *ātman* (*q.v.*) insofar as it has attained its full realization.—*K.F.L.*

Sattva: (Skr. "be-ness") Being, existence, reality, etc. Also one of the three *guṇas* (*q.v.*) of the Sāṅkhya (*q.v.*) and as such the quality of buoyancy, pleasure, and goodness of matter or *prakṛti* (*q.v.*).—*K.F.L.*

Satya: (Skr.) Actual, real, true, valid; truth, reality; the real.—*K.F.L.*

Sautrāntika: A Buddhist school of representationalism, same as Bāhyanumeya-vāda (*q.v.*).—*K.F.L.*

Scepticism: 1) a proposition about the limitations of knowledge: that no knowledge at all or that no absolute, unquestionable, trustworthy, certain, complete, or perfect knowledge (or rationally justifiable belief) is attainable by man or that such is not attainable by any knower; or that none of these kinds of knowledge, if attained, would be recognizable as such; or that no such knowledge is attainable about certain subjects, e.g., questions about existence, ultimate reality, certain religious beliefs, or the existence or nature of certain entities (e.g., God, one's self, other selves, values, an external world, or causal connections); or that one or more or all of these types of knowledge is not attainable by certain methods or media, e.g., reason, inference, revelation, any non-empirical method, direct observation, or immediate experience (hence identification of scepti-

cism variously with anti-rationalism, anti-supernaturalism, or doctrines of relativity of the senses or relativity of all knowledge); 2) a proposition about a method of obtaining knowledge: that every hypothesis should be subjected to continual testing; that the only or the best or a reliable method of obtaining knowledge of one or more of the above kinds is to doubt until something indubitable or as nearly indubitable as possible is found; that wherever evidence is indecisive, judgment should be suspended; that knowledge of all or certain kinds at some point rests on unproved postulates or assumptions; 3) a proposition about values: that morality is entirely a matter of individual preference; or that there are no fixed and eternal values; or that all values are relative to time, place, or other circumstance (these propositions, properly or improperly, have been called scepticism because of their association with certain other propositions here mentioned); 4) a method of: intellectual caution; systematic suspension of judgment on the basis of some criteria of certainty or truth; criticism, particularly in absence of conclusive evidence; questioning or doubting as a means to gaining absolute or relative certainty; 5) an attitude, belief, postulate, assumption, assertion, or tendency favoring any of the above propositions or methods; an attitude of complete or dogmatic disbelief; an attitude involving greater inclination to disbelief than to belief; an attitude involving no greater inclination to belief than to disbelief nor to disbelief than to belief, but favoring dispassionate consideration. Scepticism may be treated as such attitudes, beliefs, etc., as applied to all or only certain particular propositions; 6) a proposition negating the sincerity, rectitude, or existence of motives of human conduct other than selfish or at least negating their significance in human affairs; or a proposition expressing lack of confidence in the worth or hope of success of any one or all of man's enterprises (cynicism); or an attitude, belief, postulate, assumption, assertion, or tendency favoring such propositions; or moroseness, surliness, or pessimism growing out of cynicism or any of the aforesaid attitudes, beliefs, etc. Confusion of cynicism with other conceptions of scepticism may result in great misunderstanding and harm. See *Pyrrhonism, agnosticism.—M.T.K.*

Scepticism, Fourteenth Century: At the beginning of the 14th century, Duns Scotus adopted a position which is not formally sceptical, though his critical attitude to earlier scholasticism may contain the germs of the scepticism of his century. Among Scotistic presceptical tendencies may be mentioned the stress on self-knowledge rather than the knowledge of extra-mental reality, psychological voluntarism which eventually made the assent of judgment a matter of will rather than of intellect, and a theory of the reality of universal essences which led to a despair of the intellect's capacity to know such objects and thus spawned Ockhamism. Before 1317, Henry of Harclay noticed that, since the two terms of efficient causal connection are mutually distinct and absolute things, God, by his omnipotent will, can cause anything which naturally (*naturaliter*) is caused by a finite agent. He inferred from this that neither the present nor past existence of a finite external agent is necessarily involved in cognition (Pelstex p. 346). Later Petrus Aureoli and Ockham made the same observation (Michalski, p. 94), and Ockham concluded that natural knowledge of substance and causal connection is possible only on the assumption that nature is pursuing a uniform, uninterrupted course at the moment of intuitive cognition. Without this assumption, observed sequences might well be the occasion of direct divine causal action rather than evidence of natural causation. It is possible that these sceptical views were suggested by reading the arguments of certain Moslem theologians (Al Gazali and the Mutakallimun), as well as by a consideration of miracles. The most influential sceptical author of the fourteenth century was Nicholas of Autrecourt (fl. 1340). Influenced perhaps by the Scotist conception of logical demonstration, Nicholas held that the law of non-contradiction is the ultimate and sole source of certainty. In logical inference, certainty is guaranteed because the consequent is identical with part or all of the antecedent. No logical connection can be established, therefore, between the existence or non-existence of one thing and the existence or non-existence of another and different thing. The inference from cause to effect or conversely is thus not a matter of certainty. The existence of substance, spiritual or physical, is neither known nor probable. We are unable to infer the existence of intellect or will from acts of intellection or volition, and sensible experience provides no evidence of external substances. The only certitudes properly so-called are those of immediate experience and those of principles known *ex terminis* together with conclusions immediately dependent on them. This thoroughgoing scepticism appears to have had considerable influence in its time, for we find many philosophers expressing, expounding, or criticizing it. John Buridan has a detailed criticism in his commentary on Aristotle's Physics (in 1. I, q. 4), Fitz-Ralph, Jacques d'Eltville, and Pierre d'Ailly maintain views similar to Nicholas', with some modifications, and there is at least one exposition of Nicholas' views in an anonymous commentary on the Sentences (British Museum, Ms. Harley 3243) These sceptical views were usually accompanied by a kind of *probabilism*. The condemnation of Nicholas in 1347 put a damper on the sceptical movement, and there is probably no continuity from these thinkers to the French sceptics of the 16th century. Despite this lack of direct influence, the sceptical arguments of 14th century thinkers bear marked resemblances to those employed by the French Occasionalists, Berkeley and Hume.

Michalski, C., *Les sources du criticisme et du scepticisme dans la philosophie, du XIV e s.,* (Cracovie, 1924).

Pelster, F., *Heinrich v. Harclay u. seine Quaestionen, Miscel. Fr. Ehrle,* I, 307-355.

Rashdall, H., "Nicholas de Ultricuria, a medieval Hume,"*Proc. Aristotel. Soc.* (Lond. 1907) N. S. VIII, 1-27.—*V.J.B.*

Scheler, Max (1874-1928) was originally a disciple of Rudolf Eucken, but joined early—at the University of Munich—the Husserl circle of phenomenologists, of which school he became one of the leading exponents. Moving from Kantianism and Eucken-personalism into phenomenology, he later espoused successively positions which may be called a synthesis between phenomenology and Catholic philosophy, sociological dynamism, and ideo-realistic humanism. He was the psychologist, ethicist, and religious and social philosopher of the phenomenological movement. In common with other phenomenologists, Scheler's doctrine begins with the assertion of an inherent correlation of the essences of objects with the essences of intentional experience. His unique contributions lie in the comprehensiveness of his vision; in his interpretation of the value-qualities of being; of emotional experience, especially love, as the key for the disclosure of being; of a hierarchy of concrete ("material" as against formal) values; of an analysis of "resentment" as a thorough grudge (rancour) perverted emotional attitude towards the values of life; of his definition of "person" as the concrete unity of acts; of his acknowledgment of total personality beyond individual persons; of his definition of "ethos" as a preferential system of values determinative for the validity of any specific thought-form; of hi development of the sociology of knowledge as a distinc discipline within cultural sociology; and of his working out of a philosophical anthropology showing man's position in and towards the whole of being. His most important works include: *Die transzendentale und die psychologische Methode* (1900); *Der Formalismus in der Ethik und die materiale Wertethik* (1916); *Vom Ewigen in Menschen* (1921); *Wesen und Formen der Sympathie* (1923); *Schriften zur Soziologie und Weltanschauungslehre* (3 vols., 1923-1924); *Die Wissensformen und die Gesellschaft* (1926); *Die Stellung des Menschen in Kosmos* (1928); *Philosophische Weltanschauung* (1929); *Zur Ethik und Erkenntnislehre* (1933).—*P.A.S.*

Schelling, Friedrich Wilhelm Joseph von (1775-1854): Founder of the philosophy of identity which holds that subject and object coincide in the Absolute, a state to be realized in intellectual intuition. Deeply involved in romanticism, Schelling's philosophy of nature culminates in a transcendental idealism where nature and spirit are linked in a series of developments by unfolding powers or potencies, together forming one great organism in which nature is dynamic visible spirit and spirit invisible nature. Freedom and necessity are different refractions of the same reality. Supplementing science—which deals with matter as extinguished spirit and endeavors to rise from nature to intelligence—philosophy investigates the development of spirit, theoretically, practically, and artistically, converts the subjective into the objective, and shows how the world soul or living principle animates the whole. Schelling's monism recognizes nature and spirit as real and ideal poles respectively, the latter being the positive one. It is pantheistic and aesthetic in that it allows the world process to create with free necessity unconsciously at first in the manner of an artist. Art is perfect union of freedom and necessity, beauty reflects the infinite in the finite. History is the progressive revelation of the Absolute. The ultimate thinking of Schelling headed toward mysticism in which man, his personality expanded into the infinite, becomes absorbed into the absolute self, free from necessity, contingency, consciousness, and personality. *Sämmtliche Werke,* 14 vols. (1856, re-edited 1927). Cf. Kuno Fischer, *Schellings Leben, Werke und Lehre;* E. Bréhier, *Schelling,* 1912: V. Jankelevitch, *L'Odysée de la conscience dans la derniére philosophie de Schelling,* 1933.—*K.F.L.*

Schema: (Gr. *schema*) Figure; external form or structural plan; specifically, in Aristotle's logic, a syllogistic figure.—*G.R.M.*

In Kant's *Critique of Pure Reason* (Tr. Analytic): The procedure of the imagination by which the categories of the understanding are applied to the manifold of sensuous intuitions. Imagination, working with the pure form of time, connects sense and understanding. This is possible because the imagination contains an element of both sense and understanding, and thus is capable of formulating the rules and procedures by means of which sensuous representations may be subsumed under pure concepts. See *Kantianism.—O.F.K.*

Schiller, Ferdinand Canning Scott: (1864-1937), unwilling to accept the idealism current at Oxford in his day on grounds that it was "absolutist," sought by a metaphysical pluralism not only to account for the unity and multiplicity of things, but also to furnish the basis for evolution theory. His developed philosophical position was generally known as "personal idealism," or "humanism," though it was closely akin to the pragmatism of William James. The kinship may be seen in Schiller's thesis that a theory of knowledge cannot be formed by abstracting from man's total experience, and may be seen further in his advocacy of the "logic of discovery" over the "logic of proof." Main works: *Riddles of the Sphinx,* 1891; *Humanism,* 1903; *Logic For Use,* 1930.—*C.K.D.*

Schism: The withdrawal of a party from an established group and its inclination to form a new order. The term may also mean "dissension." The former meaning, however, is the usual one. Thus, the separation of the Greek and the Roman Catholic churches (culminating in 1054) is known as the "Great Schism."—*V.F.*

Schleiermacher, Friedrich Ernst Daniel (1768-1834): Religion, in which Schleiermacher substitutes for a theology (regarded impossible because of the unknowableness of God) the feeling of absolute dependence, is sharply delineated from science as the product of reason in which nature may ultimately attain its unity. Schleiermacher, a romanticist, exhibits Fichtean and Schellingean influence, and transcends Kant by proclaiming an ideal realism. Nature, the totality of existence, is an organism, just as knowledge is a system: Through the unity of the real and the ideal, wisdom, residing with the Absolute as the final unity, arises and is ever striven for by man. A determinism is evident in religion where sin and grace provide two poles and sin is regarded partly avoidable, partly unreal, and in ethics where freedom is admitted only soteriologically as spontaneous acknowledgment of identity with the divine in the person of Christ. However, the right to uniqueness and individuality in which each attains his real nature, is stressed. An elaborate ethics is based on four goods: State, Society, School, and Church, to which accrue virtues and duties. An absolute good is lacking, except insofar as it lies in the complete unity of reason and nature.—*K.F.L.*

Complete works: *Werke* 32 vols., 1835-64. Cf. W. Dilthey: *Das Leben Schleiermachers.*

Schlick, Moritz: (1882-1936) Taught at Rostock, Kiel, Vienna, also visit. prof., Stanford, Berkeley. Founder of the Vienna Circle (see *Scientific empiricism.*) Called his own view "Consistent Empiricism." Main contributions: A logically revised correspondence view of the nature of truth. A systematic epistemology based on the distinction of (immediate) experience and (relational) knowledge. Clarified the analystic-a priori character of logic and mathematics (by disclosing the "implicit definitions" in postulate systems). Repudiation of Kantian and phenomenological (synthetic) apriorism. Physicalistic, epistemological solution of the psychophysical problem in terms of a double language theory. Earlier critical-realistic views were later modified and formulated as Empirical Realism. Greatly influenced in this final phase by Carnap and especially Wittgenstein, he considered the logical clarification of meanings the only legitimate task of a philosophy destined to terminate the strife of systems. Important special applications of this general outlook to logic and methodology of science (space, time, substance, causality, probability, organic life) and to problems of ethics (meaning of value judgments, hedonism, free-will, moral motivation). An optimistic, poetic view of the meaning of life is expressed in only partly published writings on a "Philosophy of Youth."

Major publications: *Allgemeine Erkenntnislehre,* Berlin 1925; *Gesammelte Aufsätze,* Wien 1938; *Problems of Ethics* (Rynin, transl.), New York 1939. —*S.S.S.*

Scholasticism: Scholasticism is both a method and system of thought. The name is derived from its proponents who were called *doctores scholastici.* This term, in turn, came from scholazein, which originally meant *to have leisure* or spare *time* but later, as in Xen. *Cyr.* 7. 5, 39, took the meaning *to denote oneself* to pupils or, conversely, to a master. The term Skolastikos is used for the first time by Theophrastus as recorded by Diog. L. 5. 37 (or V. 50 according to Ueberweg). From Roman antiquity the expression was handed down to the ninth century, when *doctores scholastici* came into general usage and was applied indifferently to those who taught the seven liberal arts or theology in the cloister and cathedral schools.

Hence in its widest sense Scholasticism embraces all the intellectual activities, artistic, philosophical and theological, carried on in the medieval schools. Any attempt to define its narrower meaning in the field of philosophy raises serious difficulties, for in this case, though the term's comprehension is lessened, it still has to cover many centuries of many-faced thought. However, it is still possible to list several characteristics sufficient to differentiate Scholastic from non-Scholastic philosophy. 1) While ancient philosophy was the philosophy of a people and modern thought that of individuals, Scholasticism was the philosophy of *Christian society* which transcended the characteristics of individuals, nations and peoples. It was the corporate product of social thought, and as such its reasoning respected authority in the forms of tradition and revealed religion. 2) *Tradition* consisted primarily in the systems of Plato and Aristotle as sifted, adapted and absorbed through many centuries. 3) It was natural that religion, which played a paramount role in the culture of the middle ages, should bring influence to bear on the medieval, rational view of life. Revelation was held to be at once a norm and an aid to reason. Since the philosophers of the period were primarily scientific theologians, their rational interests were dominated by religious preoccupations. Hence, while in general they preserved the formal distinctions between reason and faith, and maintained the relatively autonomous character of philosophy, the *choice of problems and the resources of science were controlled by theology*. 4) The most constant characteristic of Scholasticism was its *method*. This was formed naturally by a series of historical circumstances. a) The need of a medium of communication, of a consistent body of technical language tooled to convey the recently revealed meanings of religion, God, man and the material universe led the early Christian thinkers to adopt the means most viable, most widely extant, and nearest at hand, viz. Greek scientific terminology. This, at first purely utilitarian employment of Greek thought soon developed under Justin, Clement of Alexandria, Origen, and St. Augustine into the "Egyptian-spoils" theory; Greek thought and secular learning were held to be propaedeutic to Christianity on the principle: "Whatever things were rightly said among all men are the property of us Christians." (Justin, *Second Apology,* ch. XIII). Thus was established the first characteristic of the Scholastic method: *philosophy is directly and immediately subordinate to theology*. b) Because of this subordinate position of philosophy and because of the sacred, exclusive and total nature of revealed wisdom, the interest of early Christian thinkers was focused much more on the form of Greek thought than on its content and, it might be added, much less of this content was absorbed by early Christian thought than is generally supposed. As practical consequences of this specialized interest there followed two important factors in the formation of Scholastic philosophy: a) Greek logic *en bloc* was taken over by Christians; b) from the beginning of the Christian era to the end of the XII century, no provision was made in Catholic centers of learning for the formal teaching of philosophy. There was a faculty to teach logic as part of the *trivium* and a faculty of theology. For

these two reasons, what philosophy there was during this long period of twelve centuries, was dominated first, as has been seen, by theology and, second, by logic. In this latter point is found rooted the second characteristic of the Scholastic method: *its preoccupation with logic, deduction, system, and its literary form of syllogistic argumentation*. 3) The third characteristic of the Scholastic method follows directly from the previous elements already indicated. It adds, however, a property of its own gained from the fact that philosophy during the medieval period became an important instrument of pedagogy. It existed in and for the schools. This new element coupled with the domination of logic, the tradition-mindedness and social-consciousness of the medieval Christians, produced opposition of authorities for or against a given problem and, finally, disputation, where a given doctrine is syllogistically defended against the adversaries' objections. This third element of the Scholastic method is its most original characteristic and accounts more than any other single factor for the forms of the works left us from this period. These are to be found as commentaries on single or collected texts; *summae,* where the method is dialectical or disputational in character.

The main sources of Greek thought are relatively few in number: all that was known of Plato was the *Timaeus* in the translation and commentary of Chalcidius. Augustine, the pseudo-Areopagite, and the *Liber de Causis* were the principal fonts of Neoplatonic literature. Parts of Aristotle's logical works (*Categoriae* and *de Interpre.*) and the *Isagoge* of Porphyry were known through the translations of Boethius. Not until 1128 did the Scholastics come to know the rest of Aristotle's logical works. The golden age of Scholasticism was heralded in the late XIIth century by the translations of the rest of his works (*Physics, Ethics, Metaphysics, De Anima,* etc.) from the Arabic by Gerard of Cremona, John of Spain, Gundisalvi, Michael Scot, and Hermann the German, from the Greek by Robert Grosseteste, William of Moerbeke, and Henry of Brabant. At the same time the Judae-Arabian speculation of Alkindi, Alfarabi, Avencebrol, Avicenna, Averroes, and Maimonides together with the Neoplatonic works of Proclus were made available in translation. At this same period the Scholastic attention to logic was turned to metaphysics, even psychological and ethical problems and the long-discussed question of the universals were approached from this new angle. Philosophy at last achieved a certain degree of autonomy and slowly forced the recently founded universities to accord it a separate faculty.

Though the roots of Scholasticism are to be found in the preoccupation of the Patristical (vide) period, its proper history does not begin until the Carolingian renaissance in the ninth century. From that date to the present day, its history may be divided into seven divisions. 1, *Period of Preparation* (9-12 cent.). Though he does not belong in time to this period, the most dominant figure in Christian thought was St. Augustine (+430), who constructed the general framework within which all subsequent Scholastic speculation operated. Another influential figure was Boethius (+525) whose *opuscula sacra* established the Scholastic method and who furnished many of the classical definitions and axioms. The first great figure of this period was John Scottus Erigena (+c. 877) who introduced to Latin thought the works of Denis the Pseudo-Areopagite, broadened the Scholastic method by his glossary on Boethius' *opuscule sacra* and made an unfruitful attempt to interest his contemporaries in natural philosophy by his semi-pantheistic *De Divisione Naturae*. Other figures of note: Gerbert (+1003) important in the realm of mathematics and natural philosophy; Fulbert of Chartres (+1028) influential in the movement to apply dialectics to theology; Berengar of Tours (+1088) Fulbert's disciple, who, together with Anselm the Peripatetic, was a leader in the movement to rationalize theology. Peter Damiani (+1072), preached strongly against this rationalistic spirit. More moderate and more efficacious in his reaction to the dialectical spirit of his age was Lawfranc (+1089), who strove to define the true boundaries of faith and reason.

II. *Early Scholastics* (12 cent.) St. Anselm of Canterbury (+1109) did more than anyone else in this early period to codify the spirit of Scholasticism. His motto: *credo, ut intelligam*, taken from St. Augustine, expressed the organic relation that existed between the supernatural and the natural during the Middle Ages and the interpretative and the directive force which faith had upon reason. In this period a new interest was taken in the problem of the universals. For the first time a clear demarcation was noted between the *realistic* and the *nominalistic* solutions to this problem. William of Champeaux (+1121) proposed the former and Roscelin (+c. 1124) the latter. A third solution, *conceptualistic* in character, was proposed by Abelard (+1142) who finally crystallized the Scholastic method. He was the most subtle dialectician of his age. Two schools of great importance of this period were operating at Chartres and the Parisian Abbey of St. Victor. The first, founded by Fulbert of Chartres in the late tenth century, was characterized by its leanings toward Platonism and distinguished by its humanistic tendencies coupled with a love of the natural sciences. Many of its Greek, Arabian and Jewish sources for studies in natural sciences came from the translations of Constantine the African (+c. 1087) and Adelard of Bath. Worthy to be noted as members of or sympathizers with this school are: Bernard and Thierry of Chartres (+c. 1127; c. 1150); William of Conches (+1145) and Bernard Silvestris (+1167). The two most important members of the School were Gilbert de la Porrée (+1154) and John of Salisbury (+1180). The latter was a humanistic scholar of great stylistic skill and calm, balanced judgment. It is from his works, particularly the *Metalogicus*, that most of our knowledge of this period still derives. Juxtaposed to the dialectic, syllogistic and rationalistic tendencies of this age was a mystical movement, headed by St. Bernard of Clairvaux (+1153). This movement did not oppose itself to dialectics in the uncompromising manner of Peter Damiani, but sought rather to experience and interiorize truth through contemplation and practice. Bernard found a close follower and friend in William of St. Thierry (+1148 or 1153). An attempt to synthesize the mystic and dialectical movements is found in two outstanding members of the Victorine School: Hugh of St. Victor (+1141) who founded its spirit in his *omnia disce, videbis postea nihil esse supervuum* and Richard of St. Victor (+1173), his disciple, who introduced the *a posteriori* proof for God's existence into the Scholastic current of thought. Finally, this century gave Scholasticism its principal form of literature which was to remain dominant for some four centuries. While the method came from Abelard and the formulas and content, in great part, from the *Didascalion* of Hugh of St. Victor, it was Robert of Melun (+1167) and especially Peter the Lombard (+i164) who fashioned the great *Summae sententiarum*.

III. *Golden Age* (13 cent.). The sudden elevation of and interest in philosophy during this period can be attributed to the discovery and translation of Aristotelian literature from Arabian, Jewish and original sources, together with the organization of the University of Paris and the founding of the Franciscan and Dominican Orders. Names important in the introduction and early use of Aristotle are: Dominic Gundisalvi, William of Auvergne (+1149), Alexander Neckam (+1217), Michael Scot (+c. 1234) and Robert Grosseteste (+1253). The last three were instrumental in interesting Scholastic thought in the natural sciences; while the last (Robert), if not the author of, was, at least, responsible for the first *Summa philosophiae* of Scholasticism. Scholastic philosophy has now reached the systematizing and formularizing stage and so on the introduction of Aristotle's works breaks up into two camps: *Augustinianism*, comprising those who favor the master theses of Augustine and look upon Aristotle with varying degrees of hostility; *Aristotelianism*, comprising those who favor Aristotle, without altogether abandoning the Augustinian framework. *Augustinianism*: Alexander of Hales (+1245) is the founder of this line and the first great Scholastic to utilize all of Aristotle's works, whose terminology and concepts he adopted rather than the spirit. Others worthy of mention are: John de la Rochelle (+1145), Adam of Marsh (+1258) and Thomas of York (+1260). The *Metaphysica* of this latter constitutes a milestone in philosophy's fight for autonomy. The outstanding representative of this group is Bonaventure (+1274), who combined great constructive ability with profound psychological and mystical insight. Prominent among his pupils were Matthew of Aquasparta (+1302), John Peckham (+1292), William de la Mare (+1298) and Walter of Brügge (+1306). Also prominent in this line are Roger of Marston, Richard of Middleton (+1308), a forerunner of Duns Scotus, William of Ware, Duns Scotus' master, and Peter Johannis Olivi (+1298). Among the Dominicans who belonged to this group should be mentioned Roland of Cremona, Peter of Tarantaise (+1276), Richard Fitzacre (+1248) and Robert Kilwardby (+1279). Among the secular clergy, although more independent in their allegiance, we may place here Gerard of Abbeville and Henri of Ghent (1293). *Aristotelianism*: In this group there are two broad currents of thought. The first attempted to harmonize Aristotle with St. Augustine and the Church's dogmas. This line was founded by St. Albert the Great (+1280), who amassed the then known Aristotelian literature but failed to construct any coherent synthesis. His pupil, St. Thomas Aquinas (+1274) succeeded to a remarkable degree. From the standpoint of clarity and formularization, St. Thomas marks the apex of medieval Scholasticism. Pupils and adherents worthy of note: among Albert's, Hugo and Ulrich of Strassburg, this latter (+c. 1277), together with Dietrich of Freiberg (+c. 1310) revealing marked Neoplatonic tendencies; among Thomas,' Aegidius of Lessines (+1304), Herveus Natalis (Hervé Nédélec, +1318), John (de Regina) of Naples (+c. 1336), Aegidius Romanus (+1-316), Godfrey of Fontaines (+1306 or 1309), quite independent in his allegiance, and the great Dante Alighieri (+1321). The second broad current of thought is Latin Averroism. This movement, accepting Averroes' interpretation of Aristotle and his doctrine of separated orders of truth, gave birth to the two-third theory which eventually led to rationalism and which together with nominalism brought about the first decline of Scholasticism. The main proponents of this period were: Siger of Brabant (+1282); Boece of Dacie and perhaps Bernier of Nivelles. Another movement of thought worthy of note was Neoplatonism. Grounded by Ulrich of Srassburg on texts found in Albert the Great, this movement gathered momentum, particularly in Germany under Dietrich of Freiberg until it ended in the mysticism of Meister Eckhart (+1327). Other figures worthy of mention who fit wholly into none of the above currents of thought are Raymond Lull (+1315), an active opponent of Averroism and the inventor of the famous *Ars magna* which intrigued young Leibniz; Roger Bacon (+c. 1293) who under the influence of Platonism, furthered the mathematical and experimental methods; William of Moerbeke (+1286), one of the greatest philologists of the M.A., who greatly improved the translations of Aristotelian and Neoplatonic literature by consulting directly Greek sources; the first proponents of the *via moderna* doctrine in Logic, William Shyreswood (+1249) and Petrus Hispanus (+1277). Finally the period ends with the great John Duns Scotus (+1308), whose thought is characterized by great acuteness and a fine critical sense. In opposition to that of St. Thomas, his synthesis lays greater stress on the traditional Augustinian theses. IV. *First Decline*. (14-16 cent.) St. Thomas' position in many points had been so radical a departure from the traditional thought of Christendom that many masters in the late XIII and early XIV centuries were led to reexamine philosophy in the light of Aristotle's works. This gave rise to a critical and independent spirit which multiplied systems and prepared for the individualism of the Renaissance. Noteworthy in this movement are: James of Metz, Durand de St. Pourcain (+1334), Peter Aureoli (+1322) and Henry of Harclay (+1317). The greatest figure, however, is William of Occam (+1349), founder of modern thought, who renewed the Nominalism of the XI and XII cent., restricted the realm of reason but made it quite independent in its field. In reaction to this critical and independent movement, many thinkers gathered about the two great minds of the past century. Thomas and Duns Scotus, contenting themselves with merely reproducing their masters' positions. Thus Scholasticism broke up into three camps: Thomism, Scotism and Nominalism or Terminism; the first two stagnant, the third freelance. *Nominalism:* critical and skeptical, this is the largest and most influential school of the period. Important members are, first, Occam's pupils: Adam Wodham (+1358), Walter Chatton, and Robert Holcot (+1349), then come Gregory of Rimini (+1358), John of Mirecourt, Nicholas of Autrecourt, a medieval Hume, John Buridan (+c. 1360) and Nicholas of Oresme (+1382), two forerunners of modern physics and astronomy, Albert of Sachsen (+1390), first Rector of University of Vienna, Peter d'Ailly (+1420), John Gerson (+1429), Marsilius of Inghen (+1396), first Rector of Heidelberg, and Gabriel Biel (+1495), who introduced Luther to Occamism. *Scotism:* from the standpoints of number and influence, this was the next most important school of this period. Among the pupils of Duns Scotus, may be mentioned: Anthony Andreas (+1320), Francis of Meyronnes (de Mayronis) (+1325) and John de Bassolis (+1347). Walter Burleigh (+1343) was a vigorous opponent of Nominalism; Thomas Bradwardine (+1349), a mathematician and philosopher whose determinism influenced John Wiclif (+1384), John Hus and the German reformers. In the XV cent., this school is represented by William of Vaurouillon (+1464), Nicholas of Orbellis (+1455), John Anglicus, Thomas Bricot and the great Peter Tartaret (+1494). *Thomists:* John Capreolus, *Thomistarum princeps,* (+1444), Denis the Carthusian (+1471) and Peter Nigri (+c. 1484). Two other important schools of this period are the Latin Averroists and the Mystics. In the first group we find Peter d'Abano (+1315) who made Padua the center of this movement, John of Jandun (+1328), John Baconthorp (+1348), *Averroistarum princeps,* Paul of Perusio, Paul of Venice (+1429), Cajetan of Tiene (+1465) The mystical school, dominated by Eckhart, and the famous Peter Pomponazzi (+1525). is represented by Tauler (+1361) and Seuse (+1366), who tried to conform the Master's teaching with the Church's dogmas, and Jan van Ruysbroeck (+1381). From this school stemmed the anonymous "Deutsche Theologie" which Luther edited (1516). Gerson belonged to this group and also Nicholas of Cusa (+1464), the first systematic philosopher of modern times. V. *Spanish Renaissance* (16-17 cent.). This renaissance took place in the Thomistic school and was remotely prepared for by such figures as Thomas del Vio (Cajetan) (+1534), Peter Crockaert (+1514), Francis de Sylvestris

(+1528), Conrad Koellin (1536) and Chrysostom Javellus (+1550). It began as a concerted movement under Francis Victoria (+1566) at Salamanca and Ignatius Loyola (+1556), founder of the Society of Jesus. Dominicans of note were: Dominic Soto (1560), Melchior Cano (+1560), de Medina (+1581), and Bañez (+1604). Jesuits: Francis Toledo (+1596), Fonseca (+1599), Molina (+1600), Vasquez (+1604), Lessius (+1623), de Valentia (+1603), Bellarmine (+1625), Francis Suarez (+1617), and greatest philosopher and jurist of this period, whose *Disputationes Metaphysicae* constitutes perhaps the greatest philosophical work produced by Scholasticism. Others worthy of mention: Cosmas de Lerma (+1642), John a S. Thoma (+1644), Goudin (+1695), Philip a SS. Trinitate (+1671), Ruiz de Montoya (+1632), Cosmas Alamannus (+1634), Hurtado de Mendoza (+1651), De Lugo (+1660), Arriaga (+1667), Sylvester Maurus (+1687). Among the *Scotists* active during this period: Maurice a Portu (+1513), Francis Lychetus a Brixia (+1520), John Poncius (+1660), Bellutus (+1671) and Mastrius (+1673). In the second half of the XVII cent., a group of Scholastics attempted to modify the traditional system by adopting some of the modern theses particularly from Cartesianism. This tendency, together with the conservative reaction which accompanied it, brought about the second decline of Scholasticism. Two leaders in this movement were Emmanuel Maignau (+1676) and Honoratus Fabri (+1688). VI. *Second Decline* (18-19 cent.). This group and its tendencies were continued by Du Hamel (+1706), Tolomei (+1726), Fortunatus a Brixia (+1754), Steinmeyer (+1797) and Reuss (+1798). Among the conservatives: Louis de Lossada (+1748). In 1773 the Society of Jesus was suppressed. This disaster completed the downfall of Scholasticism. Not until its restoration in 1814 did the Church's traditional philosophy revive. Prominent in preparing for this second renaissance was the Jesuit-trained Vincent Bruzzetti (+1824). Others: Taparelli (+1862), Liberatore (+1872), Sanseverino (+1865), Kleutgen (+1883), Zigliara (+1893) and Gonzalez (+1895). For the first time in the modern period, history began to play an important part in Scholasticism. Karl Werner (+1888) and Al. Stoeckl (1895) were the first figures in this movement. VII. *Leonine Restoration* (1879). The Encyclical *Aeterni Patris* of Leo XIII gave this new movement a conscious direction. Since Leo XIII's time to the present day, Catholic Scholars have been active both in the fields of speculation and history. Numerous reviews have been founded and Scholasticism has raised its voice even in the non-sectarian Universities of America.—*H.G.*

Schopenhauer, Arthur: (1788-1860) Brilliant, many-sided philosopher, at times caustic, who attained posthumously even popular acclaim. His principal work, *The World as Will and Idea,* starts with the thesis that the world is my idea, a primary fact of consciousness implying the inseparableness of subject and object (refutation of materialism and subjectivism). The object underlies the principle of sufficient reason whose four-fold root Schopenhauer had investigated previously in his doctoral dissertation as that of becoming (causality), knowing, being, and acting (motivation). But the world is also obstinate, blind, impetuous will (the word taken in a larger than the dictionary meaning) which objectifies itself in progressive stages in the world of ideas beginning with the forces of nature (gravity, etc.) and terminating in the will to live and the products of its urges. As thing-in-itself, the will is one, though many in its phenomenal forms, space and time serving as *principia individuationis.* The closer to archetypal forms the ideas (Platonic influence) and the less revealing the will, the greater the possibility of pure contemplation in art in which Schopenhauer found greatest personal satisfaction. Propounding a determinism and a consequential pessimism (*q.v.*), Schopenhauer concurs with Kant in the intelligible character of freedom, makes compassion (*Mitleid;* see *Pity*) the foundation of ethics, and upholds the Buddhist ideal of desirelessness as a means for allaying the will. Having produced intelligence, the will has created the possibility of its own negation in a calm, ascetic, abstinent life.

Sämmtliche Werke, ed. P. Deussen, 14 vols. —*K.F.L.*

Schröder, (Friedrich Wilhelm Karl) Ernst: (1841-1902), German mathematician. Professor of mathematics at Karlsruhe, 1876-1902. His three-volume *Algebra der Logik* (1890-1895, with a posthumous second part of vol. 2 published in 1905) is an able compendium and systematization of the work of his predecessors, with contributions of his own, and may be regarded as giving in nearly all essentials the final form of the Nineteenth Century *algebra of logic* (*q.v.*), including the algebra of relatives (or relations).—*A.C.*

J. Lüroth, *Ernst Schröder,* Jahresbericht der Deutschen Mathematiker-Vereinigung, vol. 12 (1903), pp. 249-265; reprinted in Schröder's *Algebra der Logik,* vol. 2, part 2.

Science of Science: The analysis and description of science from various points of view, including logic, methodology, sociology, and history of science. One of the chief tasks of the science of science is the analysis of the language of science (see *Semiotic*). *Scientific empiricism* (*q.v.*) emphasizes the rôle of the science of science, and tries to clarify the different aspects. Some empiricists believe that the chief task of philosophy is the development of the logic and methodology of science, and that most of the problems of traditional philosophy, as far as they have cognitive meaning (see *Meaning, Kinds of,* 1, 5), may be construed as problems of the science of science.—*R.C.*

Science, philosophy of: That philosophic discipline which is the systematic study of the nature of science, especially of its methods, its concepts and presuppositions, and its place in the general scheme of intellectual disciplines.

No very precise definition of the term is possible since the discipline shades imperceptibly into *science,* on the one hand, and into *philosophy* in general, on the other. A working division of its subject-matter into three fields is helpful in specifying its problems, though the three fields should not be too sharply differentiated or separated.

1. A critical study of the method or methods of the sciences, of the nature of scientific symbols, and of the logical structure of scientific symbolic systems. Presumably such a study should include both the empirical and the rational sciences. Whether it should also include the methods of the valuational studies (e.g., ethics, esthetics) and of the historical studies, will depend upon the working definition of science accepted by the investigator. Valuational studies are frequently characterized as "normative" or "axiological" sciences. Many of the recognized sciences (e.g., anthropology, geology) contain important historical aspects, hence there is some justification for the inclusion of the historical method in this aspect of the philosophy of science. As a study of method, the philosophy of science includes much of the traditional *logic* and *theory of knowledge*. The attempt is made to define and further clarify such terms as *induction, deduction, hypothesis, data, discovery* and *verification*. In addition, the more detailed and specialized methods of science (e.g., *experimentation, measurement, classification* and *idealization*) (*q.v.*) are subjected to examination. Since science is a symbolic system, the general theory of *signs* plays an important role in the philosophy of science.

2. The attempted clarification of the basic *concepts, presuppositions* and *postulates* of the sciences, and the revelation of the empirical, rational, or pragmatic grounds upon which they are presumed to rest. This aspect of the philosophy of science is closely related to the foregoing but includes, in addition to the logical and epistemological subject-matter, a large portion of *metaphysics*. Roughly, the task here is two-fold. On the one hand it involves the critical analysis of certain basic notions, such as *quantity, quality, time, space, cause* and *law,* which are used by the scientist but not subjected to examination. On the other hand it includes a similar study of certain presupposed beliefs, such as the belief in an external world, the belief in the uniformity of nature, and the belief in the rationality of natural processes.

3. A highly composite and diverse study which attempts to ascertain the limits of the special sciences, to disclose their interrelations one with another, and to examine their implications so far as these contribute to a theory either of the universe as a whole or of some pervasive aspect of it. This aspect of the philosophy of science is the least precise and definite of the three, and employs the more speculative methods. One of the most characteristic of its problems is that of the classification of the sciences. This involves the attempt to construct a general table, or diagram, or map of the sciences which will properly integrate the sciences according to method, subject-matter, or some other principle of organization. Another characteristic problem is that of the implications of science for some general theory of the universe, e.g., *idealism, materialism, positivism,* *mechanism, teleology, monism,* or *pluralism*. In recent years a new type of problem has appeared which, if it is properly part of the philosophy of science at all, belongs to this aspect of the subject. This is the problem of the social relations of science. It examines such problems as the place of science in a given cultural scheme, e.g., its relations to government, business, art, religion and morality.

Bibliography: Karl Pearson, *Grammar of Science,* 1892. Henri Poincaré, *Science and Hypothesis,* 1905. W. S. Jevons, *Principles of Science,* 1907. J. A. Thomson, *An Introduction to Science,* 1911. N. Campbell, *What is Science?,* 1921. C. D. Broad, *Scientific Thought,* 1923. A. D. Ritchie, *Scientific Method,* 1923. E. W. Hobson, *Domain of Natural Science,* 1923. A. S. Eddington, *Nature of the Physical World,* 1929. M. R. Cohen, *Reason and Nature,* 1931. A. C. Benjamin, *An Introduction to the Philosophy of Science,* 1937. W. H. Werkmeister, *A Philosophy of Science,* 1940.—*A.C.B.*

Scientific Empiricism; Unity of Science Movement: A philosophical movement originated by the movement of Logical Positivism but including many other groups and persons (see II below).

I. *Vienna Circle; Logical Positivism; Logical Empiricism.*

A. The *Vienna Circle,* founded by M. Schlick (*q.v.*) in 1924, ending with his death in 1936. Among its members: G. Bergmann, R. Carnap (*q.v.*), H. Feigl, Ph. Frank (*q.v.*), K. Gödel (*q.v.*), H. Hahn (d. 1934), O. Neurath, F. Waismann.

B. Seen historically, the movement shows influences from three sides: (1) the older empiricism and positivism, especially Hume, Mill, Mach; (2) methodology of empirical science, as developed by scientists since about the middle of the 19th century, e.g., Helmholtz, Mach, Poincaré, Duhem, Boltzmann, Einstein; (3) symbolic logic and logical analysis of language as developed especially by Frege, Whitehead and Russell, Wittgenstein. Russell (*q.v.*) was the first to combine these trends and therefore had an especially strong influence.

C. The views developed in the V. C. have been called *Logical Positivism* (A. E. Blumberg and H. Feigl, J. Phil. 28, 1931); many members now prefer the term "*Logical Empiricism.*" Among the characteristic features: emphasis on scientific attitude and on cooperation; hence emphasis on intersubjective (*q.v.*) language and unity of science. Empiricism: every knowledge that is factual (see *Meaning, Kinds of,* 1), is connected with experiences in such a way that verification or direct or indirect confirmation is possible (see *Verification*).

The emphasis on logical analysis of language (see *Semiotic*) distinguishes this movement from earlier empiricism and positivism. The task of philosophy is analysis of knowledge, especially of science; chief method: analysis of the language of science (see *Semiotic; Meaning, Kinds of*).

D. Publications concerning the historical development of this movement and its chief views: *Wis-*

senschaftliche Weltauffassung: Der Wiener Kreis, Wien 1929 (with bibliography). O. Neurath, *Le Développement du Cercle de Vienne, et l'Avenir de l'Empirisme Logique,* 1935. C. W. Morris, *Logical Positivism, Pragmatism, and Scientific Empiricism,* Paris 1937. E. Nagel, "Impressions and Appraisals of Analytic Philosophy in Europe," I, II, tic Empiricism in Germany, and the Present State of its Problems. Ibid. E. Nagel, "The Fight for Clarity: Logical Empiricism," *Amer. Scholar,* 1938. Many papers by members of the group have been published in "Erkenntnis" since 1930, now continued as "Journal of Unified Science."

Compare M. Black, "Relations between Logical Positivism and the Cambridge School of Analysis," J. Un. Sc. 8, 1940.

II. *Scientific Empiricism.* A wider movement, comprising besides Logical Empiricism other groups and individuals with related views in various countries. Also called *Unity of Science Movement.*

Among its members: W. Dubislav (1937), K. Grelling, O. Helmer, C. G. Hempel, A. Herzberg, K. Korsch, H. Reichenbach (*q.v.*), M. Strauss.

A. Many members of the following groups may be regarded as adherents of Scientific Empiricism: the Berlin Society for Scientific Philosophy, the Warsaw School, the Cambridge School for Analytic Philosophy (*q.v.*), further, in U.S.A., some of the representatives of contemporary Pragmatism (*q.v.*), especially C. W. Morris, of Neo-Realism (*q.v.*), and of Operationalism (*q.v.*).

Among the individual adherents not belonging to the groups mentioned: E. Kaila (Finland), J. Jörgensen (Denmark), A. Ness (Norway); A. J. Ayer, J. H. Woodger (England); M. Boll (France); K. Popper (now New Zealand); E. Brunswik, H. Gomperz, Felix Kaufmann, R. V. Mises, L. Rougier, E. Zilsel (now in U.S.A.); E. Nagel, W. V. Quine, and many others (in U.S.A.).

B. The general attitude and the views of Scientific Empiricism are in essential agreement with those of Logical Empiricism (see above, I). Here, the *unity of science* is especially emphasized, in various respects (1) There is a logical unity of the language of science; the concepts of different branches of science are not of fundamentally different kinds but belong to one coherent system. The unity of science in this sense is closely connected with the thesis of *Physicalism* (*q.v.*). (2) There is a practical task in the present stage of development, to come to a better mutual adaptation of ter minologies in different branches of science. (3) There is today no unity of the laws of science. It is an aim of the future development of science to come, if possible, to a simple set of connected, fundamental laws from which the special laws in the different branches of science, including the social sciences, can be deduced.

C. Here also, the *analysis of language* is regarded as one of the chief methods of the science of science. While logical positivism stressed chiefly the logical side of this analysis, it is here carried out from various directions, including an analysis of the biological and sociological sides of the activities of language and knowledge, as they have been emphasized earlier by Pragmatism (*q.v.*), especially C. S. Peirce and G. H. Mead. Thus the development leads now to a comprehensive general theory of signs or *semiotic* (*q.v.*) as a basis for philosophy.

D. The following publications and meetings may be regarded as organs of this movement. 1. The Periodical "Erkenntnis," since 1930, now continued as "*Journal of Unified Science.*" 2. The "*Encyclopedia of Unified Science,*" its first part ("Foundations of the Unity of Science," 2 vols.) consisting of twenty monographs (eight appeared by 1940). Here, the foundations of various fields of science are discussed, especially from the point of view of the unity of science and scientific procedure, and the relations between the fields. Thus, the work intends to serve as an introduction to the science of science (*q.v.*). 3. A series of *International Congresses* for the Unity of Science was started by a preliminary-conference in Prague 1934 (see *report, Erkenntnis* 5, 1935). The congresses took place at Paris in 1935 ("Actes," Paris 1936; Erkenntnis 5, 1936); at Copenhagen in 1936 (Erkenntnis 6, 1937); at Paris in 1937; at Cambridge, England, in 1938 (Erkenntnis 7, 1938); at Cambridge, Mass., in 1939 (J. Unif. Sc. 9, 1941); at Chicago in 1941.

Concerning the development and the aims of this movement, see O. Neurath and C. W. Morris (for both, see above, I D), further H. Reichenbach, Ziele and Wege der heutigen Naturphilosophie, 1931; S. S. Stevens, "Psychology and the Science of Science," *Psych. Bull.* 36, 1939 (with bibliography). Bibliographies in "Erkenntnis": 1, 1931, p. 315, p. 335 (Polish authors); 2, 1931, p. 151, p. 189; 5, 1935, p. 185, p. 195 (American authors), p. 199 (Polish authors), p. 409, larger bibliography: in Encycl. Unif. Science, vol. II, No. 10 (to appear in 1942).—*R.C.*

Scotism: The philosophical and theological system named after John Duns Scotus (1266?-1308), *Doctor Subtilis,* a Franciscan student and later professor at Oxford and Paris and the most gifted of the opponents of the Thomist school. The name is almost synonymous with subtlety and the system generally is characterized by excessive criticism, due to Duns Scotus' predilection for mathematical studies—the influence, perhaps, of his Franciscan predecessor, Roger Bacon, upon him. This spirit led Scotus to indiscriminate attack upon all his great predecessors in both Franciscan and Dominican Schools, especially St. Thomas, upon the ground of the inconclusiveness of their philosophical arguments. His own system is noted especially for its constant use of the so-called Scotist or formal distinction which is considered to be on the one hand less than real, because it is not between thing and thing, and yet more than logical or virtual, because it actually exists between various thought objects or "formalities" in one and the same individual prior to the action of the mind—*distinctio formalis actualis ex natura rei;* e.g., the distinction between the essence and existence, between the animality and rationality in a man, between the principle of individuation in him and his matter and form, and between the divine attributes in God, are all formal distinctions. This undoubtedly leaves the system open to the charge of extreme realism and a tendency generally to consider the report of abstract thought with little regard for sense experience. Further, by insisting also upon a formal unity of these formalities which exists apart from conception and is therefore apparently real, the system appears to lead logically to monism, e.g., the really distinct materiality in all material things is *formally one* apart from the abstracting and universalizing activity of the mind. By insisting that this formal unity is less than real unity, the Scotists claim to escape the charge.

The general superiority of theology in this system over the admittedly distinct discipline of philosophy, makes it impossible for unaided reason to solve certain problems which Thomism claims are quite within the province of the latter, e.g., the omnipotence of God, the immortality of the soul. Indeed the Scotist position on this latter question has been thought by some critics to come quite close to the double standard of truth of Averroes, (*q.v.*) namely, that which is true in theology may be false in philosophy. The univocal assertion of being in God and creatures; the doctrine of universal prime matter (*q.v.*) in all created substances, even angels, though characteristically there are three kinds of prime matter; the plurality of forms in substances (e.g., two in man) giving successive generic and specific determinations of the substance; all indicate the opposition of Scotistic metaphysics to that of Thomism despite the large body of ideas the two systems have in common. The denial of real distinction between the soul and its faculties; the superiority of will over intellect; the attainment of perfect happiness through a willful act of love; the denial of the absolute unchangeableness of the natural law in view of its dependence on the will of God, acts being good because God commanded them; indicate the further rejection of St. Thomas who holds the opposite on each of these questions. However, the opposition is not merely for itself but that of a voluntarist against an intellectualist. This has caused many students to point out the affinity of Duns Scotus with Immanuel Kant (*q.v.*). But unlike the great German philosopher who relies entirely upon the supremacy of moral consciousness, Duns Scotus makes a constant appeal to revelation and its order of truth as above all philosophy. In his own age, which followed immediately upon the great constructive synthesis of Saints Albert, Bonaventure, and Thomas, this lesser light was less a philosopher because he and his School were incapable of powerful synthesis and so gave themselves to analysis and controversy. The principal Scotists were Francis of Mayron (d. 1327) and Antonio Andrea (d. 1320); and later John of Basoles, John Dumbleton, Walter Burleigh, Alexander of Alexandria, Lychetus of Brescia and Nicholas de Orbellis. The complete works with a life of Duns Scotus were published in 1639 by Luke Wadding (Lyons) and reprinted by Vives in 1891 (Paris).—*C.A.H.*

Scottish philosophy: Name applied to the current of thought originated by the Scottish thinker, Thomas Reid (1710-1796), and disseminated by his followers as a reaction against the idealism of Berkeley and empiricism and skepticism of Hume. Its most salient characteristic is the doctrine of common sense, a natural instinct by virtue of which men are prompted to accept certain fundamental principles as postulates without giving a reason for their truth. Reason is subordinated to the rôle of a servant or able assistant of common sense. Philosophy must be grounded on common sense, and skepticism is a consequence of abandoning its guidance.—*J.J.R.*

Secondary Qualities: Those sensible qualities which are "nothing in the objects themselves, but powers to produce various sensations in us by their primary qualities." This is the definition of John Locke. Such qualities (colors, sounds, tastes, smells) are distinguishable from primary in that they are highly variable, less constant. They appear in human consciousness in various forms; whereas the primary ones remain the same. See *Primary Qualities.*—*V.F.*

Secunda Petri: Literally, the second of Peter, that is the second part of a work on logic, *Institutiones Dialecticae,* of Pierre de la Ramée, latinized Petrus Ramus (1515-1572), which treated of judgments, *de iudicio.* Hence a stupid person was said to be deficient in *secunda Petri,* or sound judgment.—*J.J.R.*

Secundi adjacentis: Latin expression employed to describe a proposition which consists solely of a subject and a predicate without even a copula.—*J.J.R.*

Secundum quid: (Lat.) Relatively, in some respect, in a qualified sense; contrasted with *simpliciter,* absolutely.—*V.J.B.*

Secundum quid, or more fully, *a dicto simpliciter ad dictum secundum quid,* is any fallacy arising from the use of a general proposition without attention to tacit qualifications which would invalidate the use made of it.—*A.C.*

Selective Theories of Sensa: A selective in contrast to a creative theory, holds that sensa experienceable by any mind under all possible conditions of perception; preexists the act of sensing and that, consequently the function of the mind in relation to the sensa is selective rather than creative. The selective theory has been advanced by such contemporary Realists as B. Russell (*The Analysis of Mind*), E. B. Holt (*The Concept of Consciousness*), J. Laird (*A Study in Realism*). See *Creative Theory of Sensa.*—*L.W.*

Self: 1. Ego, subject, I, me, as opposed to the object or to the totality of objects; may be distinguished from "not-me," as in W. James' statement (*Principles of Psychology,* I, 289) "One great splitting of the whole universe into two halves is made by each of us, and for each of us almost all of the interest attaches to one of the halves; but we all draw the line of division between them in a different place. When I say that we all call the two halves by the same name, and that those names are 'me' and 'not-me' respectively, it will at once be seen what I mean."

2. The quality of uniqueness and persistence through changes (Lat. *ipse*), by virtue of which any person calls himself I and leading to the distinction among selves, as implied in such words as myself, yourself, himself, etc. (By transfer, this applies to the uniqueness of anything, as in 'itself').

3. The metaphysical principle of unity underlying subjective experience, which may be conceived as dependent upon the given organism or as distinct in nature; sometimes identified with the soul.

Some philosophers doubted or even denied the existence of the self. Thus, Hume pointed out (*Treatise of Human Nature*, I, pt. 4) that, apart from the bundle of successive perceptions, nothing justifying the concept of self can be discerned by introspection.

The meaning of self, with its metaphysical, linguistic and psychological distinction, has become so ambiguous that it may be useful to distinguish between:

(a) the self as applied to the bearer of subjective experience, or the *physical* or *somatic* self; (G. S. Hall, *The American Journal of Psychology*, 1897-1898) and

(b) the self as applied to the contents of that experience, or the *psychological* self, which is "an organization of experiences in a dynamic whole." (W. Pillsbury, *Attention*, 217).—*R.B.W.*

Self-Consciousness: The knowledge by the self of itself. The term is usually restricted to empirical self-consciousness. (See *Empirical Ego*)—*L.W.*

Self-determination.: (a) In political theory: the working out by a people or nation of its own problems and destiny, free from interference from without. It is often said that peoples and nations have a right to self-determination, at least under certain conditions.

(b) In ethics the notion of self-determination is used by self-determinists to solve the free-will problem. H. Rashdall, e.g., uses the notion of a "causality of a permanent spiritual self" as mediating between the indeterminists on the one hand and the mechanical determinists on the other, his view being that our actions are indeed determined but determined by "the nature or character of the self" and not just mechanically, and that it is in this determination by the self that our moral freedom consists.—*W.K.F.*

Self-Evidence: That property of a proposition by which its truth is open to direct inspection and requires no appeal to other evidence. See *Intuition*.—*A.C.B.*

Selfhood: The unique individuality possessed by a self or person.—*L.W.*

Self-love: The term may be used to denote self-complacency or self-admiration (see Spinoza, *Ethics*, Book III, Prop. 55, note), but in ethical discussions it usually designates concern for one's own individual interest, advantage, or happiness. Taking the term in this latter sense philosophers have debated the question whether or not all of our actions, approvals, etc., are motivated entirely by self-love. Hobbes holds that they are. Spinoza, similarily, holds that the endeavor to conserve oneself is the basis of all of one's actions and virtues. Shaftesbury, Hutcheson, Butler, and Hume, in opposition to Hobbes, argued that benevolence or sympathy and the moral sense or conscience are springs of action which are not reducible to self-love. Butler also pointed out that self-love itself presupposes the existence of certain primary desires, such as hunger, with whose satisfaction it is concerned, and which therefore cannot be subsumed under it. See *Egoism*.—*W.K.F.*

Self-Realization: A notion central to the ethics of recent Idealism, e.g., T. H. Green, F. H. Bradley, J. Seth, J. H. Muirhead. These writers hold that self-realization is the end, and that right action is action which conduces to self-realization.—*W.K.F.*

Selves, Knowledge of other: The knowledge by one self of another. See *Intersubjective Intercourse*.—*L.W.*

Semantics: (1) "The study of the relation of signs to the objects to which the signs are applicable" (C. W. Morris). A department of semiotic.

(2) The study of signs and symbolism. In this sense equivalent to *semiotic* (*q.v.*).—*M.B.*

The theory of the relation between the formulas of an *interpreted logistic system* (*semantical system* in Carnap's terminology) and their meanings. See *Name relation; Semiotic* 2; and Truth, semantical.—*A.C.*

C. W. Morris, *Foundations of the Theory of Signs*, International Encyclopedia of Unified Science, vol. 1, no. 2, Chicago, 1938. R. Carnap, *Foundations of Logic and Mathematics*, International Encyclopedia of Unified Science, vol. 1, no. 3, Chicago, 1939.

Semasiology: Noun derived from the Greek, *semasia*, signification of a term; the equivalent of semantics, the science of the meanings of words.—*J.J.R.*

Semiosis: The process in which something functions as a sign. It involves that which acts as a sign (the *sign vehicle*), that to which the sign refers (the *designatum*), and that effect upon some interpreter in virtue of which the thing in question is a sign to that interpreter. See also *Semiotic*.

Semiotic; Theory of Signs: A general theory of signs and their applications, especially in language; developed and systematized within Scientific Empiricism (*q.v.* II C). Three branches: pragmatics, semantics, syntactics.

1. *Pragmatics*. Theory of the relations between signs and those who produce or receive and understand them. This theory comprehends psychology, sociology, and history of the use of signs, especially of languages. 2. *Semantics*. Theory of the relations between signs and what they refer to (their "designata" or "denotata"). This theory contains also the theory of truth (*q.v.*, semantical definition) and the theory of logical deduction. 3. *Syntactics*. Theory of the formal relations (see *Formal* 2) among signs. *Logical Syntax* is syntactics applied to theoretical language (language of science); it contains the theory of formal calculi (*q.v.*), including formalized logic. Compare C. W. Morris, Foundations of the Theory of Signs, 1938; R. Carnap, Foundations of Logic and Mathematics, 1939.—*R.C.*

Semi-Pelagianism: A movement in Christian theology which attempted to find a middle ground between the extreme doctrine of total depravity and predestination as over against the doctrine of the determinative character of the human will in the matter of salvation. The Semi-Pelagian view held that regeneration was the result of the cooperation of divine grace and the human will. Although the view was condemned by church councils in favor of predestination (*q.v.*), Semi-Pelagianism has continually reappeared in Christian theology without its label.—*V.F.*

Sempiternal: (Lat. *semper*, always; *aeternus*, eternal) Everlasting, endless, having no beginning and no ending.—*V.F.*

Sempiternity: (Lat. *semper*, always) Eternity conceived as everlasting existence or perpetuity. May have a beginning, but no end; an end, but no beginning; neither a beginning nor end.—*R.B.W.*

Seneca: (4-65 A.D.) A Roman Stoic and instructor of Nero, who emphasized the distinction between the soul and body and developed the ethical elements of Stoicism.—*R.B.W.*

Main works: *Naturalium quaestionum libri septem; Dialogorum libri duodecim.*

Sensa: Plural of *sensum* (*q.v.*). The transitory particulars or objective constituents of perceptual situations that have spatial characteristics, colors, shapes, sizes, privacy and are body-dependent. (Broad)—*H.H.*

Sensationalism: (Lat. *sensatio*, from *sentire*, to feel or perceive) Subvariety of empiricism which asserts that all knowledge is ultimately derived from sensations. Hobbes (*De Corpore*, 1655) is considered the founder of modern sensationalism and Condillac (*Traité des Sensations*, 1754) is its most typical exponent. Sensationalism is usually combined with associationism. See *Associationism.*—*L.W.*

Sensation: (Ger. *Empfindung*) In Kant: The content of sensuous intuition, or the way in which a conscious subject is modified by the presence of an object. Kant usually employs the term to designate the content sensed instead of the process of sensing. The process he calls 'intuition' (*q.v.*); the faculty he names 'sensibility' (*q.v.*). See *Kantianism.*—*O.F.K.*

Sense and denotation: See *Descriptions.*

Sense Datum (pl. sense data: Lat. *sensus*, a feeling—*datum*, a gift from dare, to give). A datum conditioned by one of the outer senses. See *Datum.*—*L.W.*

Sense, internal: The mind's supposed ability to scrutinize reflectively its own inner operations. The term was suggested by J. Locke (*Essay Concerning Human Understanding*, 1690, Bk. II, ch. 1, 4.)—*L.W.*

Sense Manifold: See *Manifold of Sense.*

Sensibility: (Kant. Ger. *Sinnlichkeit*) The faculty by means of which the mind receives sensuous intuitions (*q.v.*). The sensibility is *receptive* (passive), while understanding and reason are spontaneous (active). See *Kantianism.*—*O.F.K.*

Sensing: The mental act of apprehending a sensum or sense datum. See *Sense Datum.*—*L.W.*

Sensum (Pl. *sensa*: Lat. *sensus*, pp. of *sentiore* to feel or discern by sense) Equivalent to sense datum. See *Sense Datum.*—*L.W.*

Sensum-Theory: Epistemological theory which explains perception and other higher forms of knowledge by means of inferences and constructions from sensa. See *Sensum.*—*L.W.*

Sentence: Denotes a certain class of complex symbols in a language. Which combinations of symbols are to be regarded as sentences in the language is normally determined (a) by certain specifiable formation rules (e.g. in English, that any proper name followed by a verb in the singular constitutes a sentence), (b) by the presence of certain specific "morphemes" or symbolic features indicating form (e.g., the characteristic falling intonation-pattern of English declarative sentences).

There is little agreement as to the correct analytical definition. To define a sentence as a complete utterance (Bloomfield, *Language*, 27) merely shifts the difficulty to that of deciding when symbols are not incomplete. A similar objection applies to Gardiner's definition (*Speech and Language*, 182): "those single words or combinations of words which taken as complete in themselves give satisfaction by shadowing forth the intelligible purpose of a speaker."

An exact definition is of some importance in view of the tendency of some contemporary logicians to replace the use of the term proposition by that of sentence.

Like all designations of symbols, the term is subject to *Type-Token Ambiguity* (*q.v.*).

References: J. Ries, *Was ist ein Satz?* 208, ff. (for quoted definitions). R. Carnap, *Logical syntax of Language*, 26.—*M.B.*

In connection with logic, and logical syntax, the word *sentence* is used for what might be called more explicitly a *declarative sentence*—thus for a sequence of words or symbols which (in some language or system of notation, as determined by the context) expresses a *proposition* (*q.v.*), or which can be used to convey an assertion. A sequence of words or symbols which contains free variables and which expresses a proposition when values are given to these variables (see the article *variable*) may also be called a sentence.

In connection with logistic systems, *sentence* is often used as a technical term in place of *formula* (see the explanation of the latter term in the article *logistic system*). This may be done when, under the intended interpretation of the system, sentences in this technical or formal sense become sentences in the sense of the preceding paragraph.—*A.C.*

Sentences (Scholastic): *Sententiae* were originally collections of various propositions and explanations thereof; e.g., the *Sententiae divinitatis* of Anselm of Laon. Peter Lombardus condensed the main theological and philosophical ideas of his time into the famous *Quattuor libri sententiarum* which became the textbook for the medieval universities and had to be studied and expounded by everyone aspiring to higher academic honors. The student had to pass the degree of *sententiarius*, and as such he had to read on the sentences. From these expositions developed the many commentaries on the four books of sentences. Practically every scholar of renown has left such a commentary. Peter's books are divided into "distinctions" which division is conscientiously followed by the commentators.—*R.A.*

Sentential calculus: Same as *propositional calculus* (see *logic, formal,* § 1).—*A.C.*

Sentential function has been used by some as a syntactical term, to mean a *sentence* (*q.v.*) containing free variables. This notion should not be confused with that of a *propositional function* (*q.v.*); the relationship is that a propositional function may be obtained from a sentential function by *abstraction* (*q.v.*).—*A.C.*

Sentience: (Lat. *sentiens,* from *sentire,* to feel) Consciousness at a rudimentary sensory level.—*L.W.*

Sentimentalism: An exaggerated and distorted expression of sentiment, revealing a lack of, or a superficiality of feeling.—*L.V.*

Sextus Empiricus: A physician who lived about 200 A.D. His writings contain numerous arguments of a sceptical empiricistic variety drawn from Pyrrho (*q.v.*) and directed against dogmatic claims to absolute truth, especially in the sciences and ethics. His *Adversus Mathematicos* (*Against the Mathematicians*) is an important source for the history of the sciences of astronomy, geometry, and grammar as well as of the Stoic theology of the period.—*M.F.*

Shaftesbury, Anthony Ashley Cooper, Third Earl of: (1671-1713) He was a pupil and later a patron of Locke although in the field of morals, for which he remains best known, he was opposed to the Lockean position. He advocated the so-called moral sense view which finds a sense of right and wrong in man, guiding him with social or natural affections to the good of the species rather than to self-interest. He was a lover of liberty in thought and in political affairs. He was numbered among the deists but remained a churchman throughout his life. His most famous work was his *Characteristics of Men, Manners, Opinions, Times.*—*L.E.D.*

Shaktism, Saktism: The philosophy, supported by liturgy and ritual of various degrees of purity, of the believers in the Tantra (*q.v.*). It explains Brahma as absolute spirit which, on becoming Shiva and Shakti, the male and female principles, produces through *māyā* (*q.v.*) from itself as the One in a series of 36 *tattvas* (*q.v.*) the Many, a process which at the end of the world is made to retrogress and again progress periodically.—*K.F.L.*

Shamanism: (from Tungusic *shaman*) A type of religion common in Siberia and neighboring regions without systematic beliefs but entirely inspired by the shaman (priest or priestess) who, working up a frenzy by dancing, puts himself in touch with the spirits of animals or deceased humans for purposes of magic or divination.—*K.F.L.*

Shan: Goodness, "the practice of virtue." (Confucianism). It is antecedent to the Great Ultimate (T'ai Chi) and motion, although it is involved in the Reason of the universe. (Neo-Confucianism)—*W.T.C.*

Shang ti: Anthropomorphis, Supreme Emperor or Ruler on High, who as the highest authority, presides over an elaborate hierarchy of spirits; the supreme object of veneration used interchangeably with the above. Also called Heaven (Tien'ien), August Heaven (Huang T'ien), and Sovereign (Ti).—*H.H.*

Shang t'ung: 'The principle of agreement with the superior' by Mo Tzǔ that all people must without the slightest divergence put themselves in agreement with their superior.—*H.H.*

Shao K'ang-chieh: Shao K'ang-chieh (Shao Yung, Shao Yao-fu, 1011-1077) was son of a scholar (Ch'êng I-ch'üan's teacher). Although he served in the government in a few minor capacities, in general, his life was that of quietude and poverty. But his reputation of integrity and scholarship grew so high that scholars far and near regarded him as their "teacher," and people "warned one another to refrain from evil for fear that Master Shao might know." His *Huang-chi Ching-shih,* (Supreme Principles for the States and for Society) is a standard Neo-Confucian (li hsüeh) work.—*W.T.C.*

Shao yang: The Minor Mode of Activity. See: *T'ai Chi.*

Shao yin: The Minor Mode of Passivity. See: *T'ai Chi.*

Shen: (a) In religion: Spirits; heavenly spirits as against earthly spirits (kuei); spiritual power which is unfathomable in the movement of yin and yang or passive and active cosmic forces; the active or yang aspect of the soul (hun) as against the passive aspect (p'o).

(b) In philosophy: god-like power, spiritual power, or creative power; mystery; the divine man; a spirit man, god-like man, a sage who is beyond our knowledge; vital force; the mind; the animal spirit; energy; the operation of the active cosmic principle yang (as in Neo-Confucianism).

(c) In aesthetics: Rhythmic vitality; expression; wonderful quality; style full of spirit, energy or vivacity.—*W.T.C.*

(d) What is given by nature.—*W.T.C.*

Sheng (jen): (a) A person of the highest wisdom.

(b) A sage (Confucianism). A great man who exercises a transforming influence (as in Mencius).

(c) Confucius.

(d) The ideal ruler. (Lao Tzǔ).

(e) One who "regards nature as the essential, the character of Tao (tê) as the basis, Tao as the way, and follows the indications of changes." (Taosim)—*W.T.C.*

Shen Jen: 'The spiritual man,' one who has reached a state of mystical union with the universe, or "who has not separated from the pure and the mysterious." (Chuang Tzǔ, between 399 and 295 B.C.)—*H.H.*

Shen tu: Being watchful over himself when one is alone. This is important in Confucian moral training, because "there is nothing more evident than that which cannot be seen by the eyes and nothing more palpable than that which cannot be perceived by the senses." It is a way of "making one's will sincere," and of exhausting one's heart and nature.—*W.T.C.*

Shih: Actuality, substance, to which a name must correspond.—*W.T.C.*

Shih: (a) Authority and power natural to the position of a ruler, especially the power of reward and punishment as in Han Fei Tzǔ (d. 233 B.C.). See: *fa chia.* (Legalists).

(b) External force; tending force; circumstances; such as that which completes things after Tao engenders them and the Individual Principle (tê) develops them. (Lao Tzŭ).

(c) Movement; tendency.—*W.T.C.*

Shih fei: Right and wrong, with reference to both opinion and conduct, a distinction strongly stressed by the Confucians, Neo-Confucians, Mohists, Neo-Mohists, Sophists, and Legalists alike, except the Taoists who repudiated such distinction as superficial, relative, subjective, unreal in the eyes of Tao, and inconsistent with the Taoist idea of the absolute equality of things and opinions. To most of the ancient Chinese schools, correspondence of name to actuality, both in the social sense and the logical sense, served as the standard of right and wrong. The Sophists often employed the result of argumentation as the standard. The one who won was right and the one who lost was wrong. The Neo-Mohists emphasized logical consistency, whereas the Legalists insisted on law. The early Confucians emphasized conformity with the moral order. "Whatever conforms with propriety is right and whatever does not conform with propriety is wrong." As Hsün Tzŭ (c. 335—288 B.C.) put it, "Whatever conforms with the system of the sage-kings is right and whatever does not conform with the system of the sage-kings is wrong." To the Neo-Confucians, "Whatever is in accord with Reason (li) is right." "The right is the expression of justice and impartiality based on the Universal Reason, and the wrong is the expression of selfishness and partiality based on human desire."—*W.T.C.*

Shiites: A collective name for countless groups of an Islamic sect, small in number, whose basic dogma is that Ali and his descendants are the sole legitimate successors of Mohammed. They are the rallying point for all revolutionary and heterodox tendencies among Islamic peoples outside Arabia.—*H.H.*

Shiva, Siva: (Skr. the kind one) Euphemistic name of the God Rudra, the ultimate destructive principle in the philosophies of Shivaism (q.v.). One of the *trimūrti* (q.v.).—*K.F.L.*

Shivaism, Sivaism, Saivism: One of the major groups of Hinduism which has evolved, in addition to religious doctrines and observances, also philosophical systems of note, based upon certain Agamas (q.v.). Shiva, as one aspect of the *trimūrti* (q.v.), has inspired cosmological speculations no less than psychological and logical ones. As philosophy it attained its greatest flower in the Kashmirian Trika (q.v.).—*K.F.L.*

Shu: "The benevolent exercise of the principle of human nature in relation to others;" "the extension of the principle of the self to other people and things;" "the application of the principle of true manhood (jên);" "the application of the principle of the central self (chung);" "putting oneself in the position of others;" "measuring others by oneself;" consideration; altruism; reciprocity; the Confucian "central thread" (i kuan) with respect to social relationship, as being true to the principles of one's nature (chung) is with respect to the self.—*W.T.C.*

Shu: (a) Statecraft, craft, tact, or method for a ruler to keep the ministers and the people under control, "to

award offices according to their responsibilities, to hold actualities in accordance with their names, to exercise the power of life and death, and to make use of the ability of the ministers." See: *fa chia*. (Legalists).

(b) Magic: See *shu* and *shu shu*.—*W.T.C.*

Shu: Number, which gives rise to form (hsiang) according to which things become. This philosophy was based on the *I Ching* (Book of Changes), developed in the medieval interpretation of it (chan wei), and culminated in Neo-Confucianism, especially in Shao K'ang-chieh (1011-1077). According to this philosophy, to Heaven belong the odd numbers which represent the active principle (yang) and are characterized by the tendency to increase, and to Earth the even numbers, which represent the passive principle (yin) and are characterized by the tendency to decrease, forming two series of five numbers. The numbers of Heaven add up to twenty-five and those of Earth to thirty, making a total of fifty-five. It is by these that the changes and transformation are effected and the heavenly and earthly spirits have their movements. The system of numbers begins with 1, which represents the Great Ultimate ('ai Chi) and is completed with 5, which corresponds to the Five Elements (wu hsing) out of the interplay of which all things are what they are. Thus, in the final analysis, everything comes from number, by which it can be understood, evaluated, and adjusted to other things with a corresponding number.—*W.T.C.*

Shuo: Inference, one of the methods of knowledge of the Neo-Mohists (Mo chê).—*W.T.C.*

Shu shu: (a) Divination and magic in ancient China, including astrology, almanacs, the art of coordinating human affairs by the active and passive principles of the universe (yin yang) and the Five Elements (wu hsing), fortune telling by the use of the stalks of the divination plant and the tortoise shell, and miscellaneous methods such as dream interpretation, the regulation of forms and shapes of buildings, etc.

(b) The method of enforcing law and maintaining the order of the state.—*W.T.C.*

Sibylline Books: These were allegedly ancient, mythical and inspired utterances of prophecy consulted in times of calamity. Their destruction led to composite and forged versions. The so-called Sibylline Oracles were a group of Jewish and Christian writings dating from the 2nd century B.C. to the 3rd century A.D., written in Homeric style, and in imitation of the lost Sibylline Books. They included prophecies of future events, of the fate of eminent persons, of cities and kingdoms.—*V.F.*

Siddhi: (Skr.) Reaching of the aim, success, particularly the attainment of supernatural powers, such as clairvoyance, clairaudience, levitation, the penetration of matter, etc., claimed for the Yogin (q.v.) in the highest stage of the practice of Yoga (q.v.).—*K.F.L.*

Sidgwick, Henry: (1838-1900) Last of the leading utilitarians, remembered principally for his work in ethics. He was an advocate of college education for women and one of the founders of the Society for Psychical Research. See: *Utilitarianism.*—*L.E.D.*

Main works: *Method of Ethics,* 1875; *Outlines of the History of Ethics* (5th ed. 1902); *Scope and Method of Economic Science,* 1885; *Lect. on Philosophy of Kant,* 1905.

Sign: (Lat. *signum,* sign) Logic has been called the science of signs. In psychology: that which represents anything to the cognitive faculty. That which signifies or has significance; a symbol. Semasiology or sematology is the science of signs. See *Logic, symbolic; Symbolism.*

For Theory of Signs, see *Semiotic.—J.K.F.*

Any event of character A whose occurrence is invariably accompanied by another event of character B may be said to be an *index* of that event. Any index which is recognized as being such may be said to function as a *sign.* Thus, as contrasted with 'index,' the use of 'sign' presupposes a triadic relation.—*M.B.*

Sign-Language: A system of signs established either traditionally (primitive tribes) or technically (deaf-mutes) for the purpose of communicating concepts or sentences, rather than letters or sounds or words as in signalling. The question of the priority of vocal and gesture speech is much debated; but there is no doubt that primitive peoples used signs for communicating intensions and expressing their needs, especially when dealing with tribes with a different tongue. This is almost a psychological reflex, as it may be noted in the elementary improvised mimic of travellers among people they do not understand, and also in the vivid gestures accompanying the utterances of even civilized people like those of the Mediterranean shores. Sign-languages have a psychological, sociological and ethnological importance, as they may reveal the fundamental trains of thought, the sociological status, the race peculiarities, the geographical segregation, and even the beliefs and rituals of those who use them. Their study would also give material for various syntactical, semantical and logical problems.

Note on the Indian Sign-Language. Certain general principles concerning gesture speech may be established, by considering the sign-language of the North American Indian which seems to be the most developed. (1) A sign-language is established when equally powerful tribes of different tongues come into contact. (2) Better gestures are composed and undesirable ones are weeded out, partly as a result of tribal federations and partly through the development of technical skills and crafts. (3) Signs come into being, grow and die, according to the needs of the time and to the changes in practical processes. (4) Stimulus of outside intercourse is necessary to keep alive the interest required for the maintenance and growth of a gesture speech; without it, the weaker tribe is absorbed in the stronger, and the vocal language most easily acquired prevails. (5) Sign-languages involve a basic syntax destined to convey the fundamental meanings without refinement and in abbreviated form. Articles, prepositions and conjunctions are omitted; adjectives follow nouns; verbs are used in the present tense; nouns and verbs are used in the singular, while the idea of plurality

is expressed in some other way. The use of signals with the smoke, the pony, the mirror, the blanket and the drum (as is also the case with the African tam-tams) may be considered as an extension of the sign-language, though they are related more directly to the general art of signalling.—*T.G.*

Signate: (In Schol). Refers to the intention or direction of the agent; as distinguished from *exercite,* which refers to the effects of the work or the exercise. Eg., one who studies mathematics, *signate* intends to acquire the knowledge of truths concerning quantity,—but *exercite,* or in the exercise itself of studying, renders the mind more able and apt for reasoning rightly.—*H.G.*

Significs: Theory of *Meaning* (*q.v.*). See *Peirce, Semiotic.*

Signification: *Signify* may be synonymous with *designate* (*q.v.*), or it may be used rather for the meaning of words which are not or are not thought of as proper names, or it may be used to indicate the intensional rather than the extensional meaning of a word.—*A.C.*

Similarity, Law of: (Lat. *similis,* like) Association depending upon resemblance between the associated ideas. See *Association, Laws of.—L.W.*

Similia similibus percipiuntur: (Lat. like things are apprehended through like things) Like knows like; the basic principle of nearly all epistemologies, viz., that knowledge involves an assimilation of subject to object, or vice versa.—*V.J.B.*

Similitudo (Scholastic): *Similitudo* may be called anything which stands for another so that the second may be known by the first. Aquinas uses the term as a translation of symbol in Aristotle. It does not necessarily imply any resemblance.—*R.A.*

Simmel, Georg: (1858-1918) Occupying himself mostly with the reciprocal effects between individuals, he practically ignored the problem of the individual to the group. Calling attention to the psychical interactions as constituting the real foundation of community life, he stressed the reciprocity of relations. As alleged founder of the "formalistic" sociology, he regards the forms of socialization, the kinds of interactions of individuals upon each other as the distinctive subject of sociology. He defended in his earlier years a descriptive and relative, as opposed to a normative, absolutistic ethics. Subscribing to a metaphysics of life, he characterizes life as ceaseless self-transcendence.—*H.H.*

Main works: *Problem d. Geschichtsphilosophie,* 1892; *Philosophie des Geldes,* 1900; *Soziologie,* 1908; *Goethe,* 1913; *Lebensanschauung,* 1918.

Simple Enumeration: (Bacon) The name given by F. Bacon to the Aristotelian and the Scholastic process of induction which advances to the knowledge of laws from the knowledge of facts established by observation and experiment and clearly arranged. This type of induction treats instances by noting the number of observed coincident happenings of the antecedent and the consequent under investigation, and then formulating a causal connection between them. Bacon considers that Simple Enumeration lacks the methodological characteristics which he conceived (rather than determined and applied) for the process of induction. It may be added that the ancient and medieval logicians were fully aware of this type of induction.—*T.G.*

Simplicius: (6th cent.) A prominent commentator on Aristotelian works in the closing years of the New Academy of Plato.—*M.F.*

Main works: Commentaries on Aristotle's *De Caelo, Physica, De Anima,* and *Categoriae.*

Simulacrum: (pl. *simulacra*) (Lat. likeness, image) A likeness or copy of an original; applied especially to a perceptual image which copies its object. See *Effluxes, Theory of*—*L.W.*

Simultaneity: The condition of belonging to the same time. As two or more events observed as simultaneous may actually take place at different moments, it is useful to distinguish between subjective and objective simultaneity. See *Relativity, theory of.*—*R.B.W.*

Singular proposition: See *logic, formal,* §§ 4, 5.

Skepticism: See *Scepticism.*

Skolem paradox: See *Löwenheim's theorem.*

Smith, Adam: (1723-1790) Professor of Moral Philosophy and Logic at Glasgow. He is best known for his *The Wealth of Nations,* but he is not to be forgotten for his contributions to the study of ethics, expressed principally in his "The Theory of Moral Sentiments." He finds sympathy as the fundamental fact of the moral consciousness and he makes of sympathy the test of morality, the sympathy of the impartial and well-informed spectator.—*L.E.D.*

Social Contract: The original covenant by which, according to certain philosophers of modern times—Hooker, Hobbes, Althusius, Spinoza, Locke, Pufendorf, etc.—individuals have united and formed the state. This theory was combined with the older idea of the governmental contract by which the people conferred the power of government upon a single person or a group of persons. This theory goes back to ancient philosophy and was upheld by medieval thinkers, such as Thomas Aquinas, Marsilius of Padova. Though most of the philosophers of the seventeenth and eighteenth century realized that no such original compact as the idea of the Social Contract called for, had actually occurred, the idea, nevertheless, served as a criterion to determine whether any act of the government was just or not, i.e., whether the consent of the governed might be assumed (especially Rousseau, Kant). The theory of the Social Contract had a remarkable influence upon the political philosophy of the American colonies. See *Political Philosophy.*—*W.E.*

Socialism, Marxian: Early in their work, Marx and Engels called themselves communists (e.g., the "Communist Manifesto"). Later they found it more accurate, in view of the terminology of the day, to refer to themselves as socialists. During the war of 1914—18, when socialists split into two camps, one supporting and the other opposing participation in the war, Lenin proposed for the latter group, which became the Third International, a return to the name communist, so far as a party designation was concerned, which proposal was adopted. Those who remained connected with the Sec-ond International retained the name socialist as a party designation. This split not only involved the problem of the war, but crystallized other fundamental divergences. For example, among "socialists," there was a widespread belief in gradualism—the doctrine that the socialist society could be attained by piecemeal reform within the capitalist system, and that no sudden change or contest of force need be anticipated. These beliefs were rejected by the "communists."

By way of connoting different types of society, many contemporary Marxists, especially in the U.S.S.R., building upon Marx's analysis of the two phases of "communist society" ("Gotha Program") designate the first or lower phase by the term socialism, the second or higher by the term communism (*q.v.*). The general features of socialist society (identified by Soviet thinkers with the present phase of development of the U.S.S.R.) are conceived as follows: 1) Economic: collective ownership of the means of production, such as factories, industrial equipment, the land, and of the basic apparatus of distribution and exchange, including the banking system; the consequent abolition of classes, private profit, exploitation, surplus value, (*q.v.*) private hiring and firing and involuntary unemployment; an integrated economy based on long time planning in terms of needs and use. It is held that only under these economic conditions is it possible to apply the formula, "from each according to ability, to each according to work performed," the first part of which implies continuous employment, and the second part, the absence of private profit. 2) Political: a state based upon the dictatorship of the proletariat (*q.v.*) 3) Cultural: the extension of all educational and cultural facilities through state planning; the emancipation of women through unrestricted economic opportunities; the abolition of race discrimination through state enforcement; a struggle against all cultural and social institutions which oppose the socialist society and attempt to obstruct its realization.

Marx and Engels held that socialism becomes the inevitable outgrowth of capitalism because the evolution of the latter type of society generates problems which can only be solved by a transition to socialism. These problems are traced primarily to the fact that the economic relations under capitalism, such as individual ownership of productive technics, private hiring and firing in the light of profits and production for a money market, all of which originally released powerful new productive potentialities, come to operate, in the course of time, to prevent full utilization of productive technics, and to cause periodic crises, unemployment, economic insecurity and consequent suffering for masses of people. Marx and Engels regarded their doctrine of the transformation of capitalist into socialist society as based upon a scientific examination of the laws of development of capitalism and a realistic appreciation of the role of the proletariat (*q.v.*). Unlike the utopian socialism (*q.v.*) of St. Simon, Fourier, Owen (*q.v.*) and others, their socialism asserted the necessity of mass political organization of the working classes for the purpose of gaining political power in order to effect the transition from capitalism, and also foresaw the probability of a contest of force in which, they held, the working class majority would ultimately be victorious. The view taken is that Marx was the first to explain scientifically the nature of capitalist exploitation as based upon surplus value and to predict its necessary consequences. "These two great discoveries, the materialist conception of history and the revelation of the secret of capitalist production by means of surplus value we owe to Marx. With these discoveries socialism became a science. . ." (Engels: *Anti-Dühring*, pp. 33-34.) See *Historical materialism.—J.M.S.*

Socinians: Followers of the 16th century Italian, humanistic Christians, Socinus (Sozzini), Laelius and Faustus. They advocated freedom of thought over against the orthodox expressions of Christianity. The *Racovian Catechism* (1605) states their method and doctrines. In general, they were anti-Trinitarians (see *Trinitarianism*), anti-Augustinian (opposing the doctrines or original sin, depravity, predestination), anti-Catholic institutionalism; their interpretation of Christianity was that it is a religion of the attainment of eternal life, Jesus being the revealer of God, and the Scriptures giving a supernatural revelation which is necessary and rationally defensible. A strong ethical note pervaded their theology. They opposed the view of sacramental mysteries. Although condemned by the Protestant churches, the Socinians exerted a tremendous influence even after their formal dissolution as a party.—*V.F.*

Sociology: The word "sociologie" was coined by the French philosopher, Auguste Comte, (1798-1857).

The study of society, societal relations. Originally called Social Physics, meaning that the methods of the natural sciences were to be applied to the study of society. Whereas the pattern originally was physics and the first sociologists thought that it was possible to find laws of nature in the social realm (Quetelet, Comte, Buckle), others turned to biological considerations. The "organic" conception of society (Lilienfeld, Schaeffle) treated society as a complex organism, the evolutionists, Gumplowicz, Ratzenhofer, considered the struggle between different ethnic groups the basic factor in the evolution of social structures and institutions. Other sociologists accepted a psychological conception of society; to them psychological phenomena (imitation, according to Gabriel Tarde, consciousness of kind, according to F. H. Giddings) were the basic elements in social interrelations (see also W. McDougall, Alsworth Ross, etc.). These relations themselves were made the main object of sociological studies by G. Simmel, L. Wiese, Howard Becker. A kind of sociological realism was fostered by the French sociologist, Emile Durkheim, and his school. They considered society a reality, the group-mind an actual fact, the social phenomena "choses sociales." The new "sociology of knowledge," inaugurated by these French sociologists, has been further developed by M. Scheler, K. Mannheim and W. Jerusalem. Recently

other branches of social research have separated somewhat from sociology proper: Anthropogeography, dealing with the influences of the physical environment upon society, demography, social psychology, etc. Problems of the methodology of the social sciences have also become an important topic of recent studies.—*W.E.*

Sociology of Law: The sociology of law is a comparatively infant type of investigation and consequently exhibits, to an even greater degree than most fields of sociology (*q.v.*), confusion and variety in methods and results. It can be defined, then, only in terms of its subject matter, which is neither the metaphysical and ethical bases of the law nor law as a separate field of social fact. It is, rather, all aspects of the law considered in their relation to all other social institutions and processes.—*M.B.M.*

Socrates: (c. 470-399 B.C.) Was one of the most influential teachers of philosophy. The son of an Athenian stone cutter, named Sophroniscus, and of a midwife, Socrates learned his father's trade, but, in a sense, practised his mother's. Plato makes him describe himself as one who assists at the birth of ideas. With the exception of two periods of military service, he remained in Athens all his life. He claimed to be guided by a *daimon* which warned him against what was wrong, and Plato suggests that Socrates enjoyed mystic experiences. Much of his time was spent in highminded philosophic discussion with those he chanced to meet in the public places of Athens. The young men enjoyed his easy methods of discussion and delighted in his frequent quizzing of the Sophists. He was eventually charged in the Athenian citizen court with being irreligious and corrupting the young. Found guilty, he submitted to the court and drank the poison which ended the life of one of the greatest of Athenians. He wrote nothing and is known through three widely divergent contemporary accounts. Aristophanes has caricatured him in the *Clouds;* Xenophon has described him, with personal respect but little understanding of his philosophical profundity; Plato's dialogues idealize him and probably develop the Socratic philosophy far beyond the original thought of his master. Socrates personifies the Athenian love of reason and of moderation; he probably taught that virtue is knowledge and that knowledge is only true when it reaches the stage of definition. See: *Socratic method.—V.J.B.*

Socratic method: (from Socrates, who is said by Plato and Xenophon to have used this method) is a way of teaching in which the master professes to impart no information, (for, in the case of Socrates, he claimed to have none), but draws forth more and more definite answers by means of pointed questions. The method is best illustrated in Socrates' questioning of an unlearned slave boy in the *Meno* of Plato. The slave is lead, step by step, to a demonstration of a special case of the Pythagorean theorem. Socrates' original use of the method is predicated on the belief that children are born with knowledge already in their souls but that they cannot recall this knowledge without some help, (theory of *anamnesis*). It is also associated with Socratic Irony, i.e., the profession of ignorance on the part of a questioner, who may be in fact quite wise.—*V.J.B.*

Solipsism: (Lat. *solus*, alone + *ipse*, self)

(a) *Methodological:* The epistemological doctrine which considers the individual self and its states the only possible or legitimate starting point for philosophical construction. See *Cogito, ergo sum; Ego-centric predicament, Subjectivism.*

(b) *Metaphysical:* Subvariety of idealism which maintains that the individual self of the solipsistic philosopher is the whole of reality and that the external world and other persons are representations of that self having no independent existence.—*L.W.*

Soma: One of the three important gods of the Vedic religion, about whom the ninth book of the Rig-Veda centers. This god is associated with the plant growing in northern India which was made into an intoxicating liquor. The effects of this drink became associated with supernatural powers.—*V.F.*

Somatic: (Gr. *somatikos*, from *soma*, body) Pertaining to the bodily organism.—*L.W.*

Somatic Datum: Somatic data are those originating within the bodily organism (*e.g.*, feelings of muscular tension, fatigue, organic and circulatory sensations, etc.) in contrast to sense data, which are conditioned by the organs of outer sense. See *Datum, Sense Datum.*—*L.W.*

Some: It is now recognized that to construe such a phrase as, e.g., ''some men'' as a name of an undetermined [non-empty] part of the class of men (thus as a sort of variable) constitutes an inadequate analysis. In translation into an exact logical notation the word ''some'' is usually to be represented by an existential *quantifier.* (*q.v.*).—*A.C.*

Sophia: (Gr. *sophia*) Theoretical as distinguished from practical wisdom; specifically, in Aristotle, knowledge of first principles, or first philosophy.—*G.R.M.*

Sophism: An eristic or contentious syllogism; distinguished from paralogism by the intent to deceive (Aristotle).—*G.R.M.*

Sophistic: (Gr. *sophistike*) The art of specious reasoning pursued for pay, according to Aristotle; thus distinguished from eristic, whose end is simply victory in disputation.—*G.R.M.*

Sophistici Elenchi: (Gr. *sophistikoi elenchoi*) The last of the logical treatises of Aristotle, dealing with fallacies in argumentation.—*G.R.M.*

Sophists: (5th Cent. B.C.) Wandering teachers who came to Athens from foreign cities, and sought to popularize knowledge. They filled a need felt in Greece at this time for a general dissemination of that scientific knowledge which had previously been more or less privately cultivated in learned societies. Nowhere was this need more widespread than in Athens where a political career necessitated an acquaintance with the intellectual attainments of the race. The Sophists came to Athens to assist young men in achieving political success. Before long, this brought with it the subordination of purely theoretical learning to its practical useful-

ness, and the Sophists, far from teaching what is most likely to be true, instructed the youth in what is most likely to bear political fruit. Thus, eloquent public appeal and the art of rhetoric soon took the place of pure science and philosophy. In this very desire, however, to persuade and refute, the problem presented itself as to whether among the various conflicting opinions which the Sophists had taught their pupils to defend and to oppose, there was anything of permanent value which could claim the assent of all men everywhere. This quest of the universal in knowledge and in conduct forms the basis of the Socratic Quest.—*M.F.*

Sophocracy: (Gr. *sophos*, wise) Government by the wisest. (Montague).—*H.H.*

Sorge: (Ger. *concern*) The most essential structure of human consciousness and of the world; the basis of all 'being'. (Heidegger).—*H.H.*

Sorites: A chain of (categorical) syllogisms, the conclusion of each forming a premiss of the next—traditionally restricted to a chain of syllogisms in the first figure (all of which, with the possible exception of the first and last, must then be syllogisms in Barbara).

In the statement of a sorites all conclusions except the last are suppressed, and in fact the sorites may be thought of as a single valid inference independently of analysis into constituent syllogisms. According to the order in which the premisses are arranged, the sorites is called *progressive* (if in the analysis into syllogisms each new premiss after the first is a major premiss, and each intermediate conclusion serves as a minor premiss for the next syllogism) or *regressive or Goclenian* (if each new premiss after the first is a minor premiss, and each intermediate conclusion a major premiss).—*A.C.*

Soul: (Gr. *psyche*) In Aristotle the vital principle; the formal cause, essence, or entelechy of a natural organic body.—*G.R.M.*

Soul (Scholastic): With few exceptions (e.g., Tertullian) already the Fathers were agreed that the soul is a simple spiritual substance. Some held that it derived from the souls of the parents (Traducianism), others that it is created individually by God (Creationism), the latter view being generally accepted and made an article of faith. Regarding the union with the body, the early Middle-Ages, following St. Augustine, professed a modified Platonic Dualism: the body is a substance in itself to which the soul is added and with which it enters a more or less accidental union. With the revival of Aristotelianism, the hylemorphic theory became general: the soul is the substantial form of the body, the only origin of all vital and mental performances, there is no other form besides. This strictly Aristotelian-Thomistic view has been modified by later Scholastics who assume the existence of a *forma corporeitatis* distinct from the soul. (See *Form*)—The soul is simple but not devoid of accidents; the "faculties" (*q.v.*) are its proper accidents; every experience adds an accidental form to the soul. Though a substance in itself, the soul is naturally ordained towards a body; separated, it is an ''incomplete'' substance. It is created in respect to the body it will inform, so that the inheritance of bodily features and of mental characteristics insofar as they depend on organic functions is safeguarded.—As a simple and spiritual substance, the soul is immortal. It is not the total human nature, since person is the composite of matter informed by the soul.—Animals and plants too have souls, the former a sensitive, the latter a vegetative soul, which function as the principles of life. These souls are perishable; they too are substantial forms. The human soul contains all the powers of the two other souls and is the origin of the vegetative and sensitive performances in man.—*R.A.*

Soul-Substance Theory: Theory that the unity of the individual mind is constituted by a single, permanent, and indivisible spiritual substance. (See *Ego, Pure*). The theory is usually combined with a faculty psychology. See *Faculty Psychology.*—*L.W.*

Soviet philosophy: The contemporary development of the philosophy of dialectical materialism in the U.S.S.R.

There are two major points of reference for tracing the path that Soviet philosophy has taken—the successive controversies around the issues of mechanism and idealism. The first began in the early twenties as a discussion centering on the philosophy of science, and eventually spread to all phases of philosophy. The central issue was whether materialism could be identified with mechanism. Those who answered in the affirmative, among them Timiriazev, Timinski, Axelrod and Stepanov, were called mechanistic materialists. Their position tended to an extreme empiricism which was suspicious of generalization and theory, saw little if any value in Hegel's philosophy, or in dialectical as distinguished from formal logic, and even went so far, in some cases, as to deny the necessity of philosophy in general, resting content with the findings of the specific sciences. It was considered that they tended to deny the reality of quality, attempting to reduce it mechanically to quantity, and to interpret evolution as a mere quantitative increase or decrease of limited factors, neglecting the significance of leaps, breaks and the precipitation of new qualities. In opposition to their views, a group of thinkers, led by Deborin, asserted the necessity of philosophic generalization and the value of the dialectical method in Hegel as a necessary element in Marxian materialism. In 1929, at a conference of scientific institutions attended by 229 delegates from all parts of the country, the issues were discussed by both sides. A general lack of satisfaction with the mechanist position was expressed in the form of a resolution at the close of the conference. However, the Deborin group was also criticized, not only by the mechanists, but by many who were opposed to the mechanists as well. It was felt by Mitin, Yudin and a group of predominantly younger thinkers that neither camp was really meeting the obligations of philosophy. While they felt there was much that was valuable in Deborin's criticism of mechanism, it seemed to them that he had carried it too far and had fallen over backward into the camp of the idealists. They called his group menshevizing idealists, that is to say, people who talked like the Mensheviks, a pre-revolutionary faction of the Russian Social Democratic Party. By this was meant that they were unduly abstract, vague and tended to divorce theory from practice. In particular, they seemed to accept Hegelian dialectics as such, overlooking the deeper implications of the materialist reconstruction of it which Marx insisted upon. Moreover, they had neglected the field of social problems, and consequently made no significant philosophic contribution to momentous social issues of the times such as collectivization of the land, abandonment of NEP, the possibility of a Five Year Plan. At a three day conference in 1930, the situation was discussed at length by all interested parties. Deborin, Karev and Sten leading the discussion on one side, Mitin and Yudin on the other. The sense of the meetings was that the criticisms made of the Deborin group were valid.

In respect to the field of ethics in general, Soviet philosophers have lately been developing the doctrine known as socialist or proletarian humanism. As distinguished from "bourgeois humanism," this term signifies that system of social institutions and personal values designed to insure that there be no underprivileged group or class de facto excluded from full participation in the good life conceived in terms of the educational and cultural development of the individual and the full enjoyment of the things of this world. Such objectives, it is held, are only possible to attain in a classless society where there is economic security for all. The view taken is that the freedoms and liberties proclaimed by "bourgeois humanism" represented a great historical advance, but one that was, in general, limited in application to the emancipation of the bourgeoisie (*q.v.*) from the restrictions of feudalism while retaining and making use, to greater or lesser extent, of slavery, serfdom and a system of private capitalism involving the precarious economic existence and cultural darkness of large proletarian masses. While it is held that there is an absolute right binding upon all, vaguely expressed in such formulations as, each for all and all for each, it is asserted that in class society, the position and class interest of one class may motivate it to oppose a genuine application of this right, whereas the class interest of another class may coincide with such an application. It is held that the proletariat is in this latter position, for its class interest as well as its moral obligation is considered to lie in abolishing itself as a proletariat, which is taken to mean, abolishing classes generally.

Lenin, V. I.: *Materialism and Empirio-Criticism; State and Revolution; Karl Marx; Leo Tolstoy as Mirror of the Russian Revolution.* (These works, with the exception of *State and Revolution,* appear in Lenin: *Selected Works,* vol. XI.—*J.M.S.*

Space: In Aristotle, the container of all objects. In the Cambridge Platonists, the sensorium of God. In Kant: the a priori form of intuition of external phenomena. In modern math., name for certain abstract, invariant groups or sets. See *Space-Time.*—*P.P.W.*

Space, homogeneous: A form of sensibility; an intuition peculiar to man which enables him to externalize his concepts in relation to one another; reveals the objectivity of things; foreshadows and prepares the way for social life. (Bergson).—*H.H.*

Space-perception: (Lat. *spatium*) The apprehension of the spatial properties and relations of the concrete objects of ordinary sense perception in contrast to the conceptual knowledge of the abstract spaces of physics and mathematics. Theories of space-perception are: a) *nativistic,* where they endow the mind with a primitive intuition of space which becomes qualitatively differentiated through sense experience; b) *empirical,* when they assume that perceptual space emerges from the correlation of the spatial features of the different senses.—*L.W.*

Space-Time: The four-dimensional continuum including the three dimensions of space (length, width and height) and one of time; the unity of space and time. The concept was first suggested by H. Minkowski and immediately afterward incorporated by A. Einstein into his (special) theory of relativity. The former contended that nothing can exist or be conceived of as physical apart from space-time; for every object must have not only length, width and height, but also duration in time. As a result, a complete description and location of an object must be given in terms of four coordinates. Space-Time is mathematically grounded in world-points, or durationless geometrical points, as the foundation of all four-dimensional measurement, and in world-lines, or geometrical lines cutting across the four dimensions. An enduring geometrical point thus becomes a geometrical line (or possibly a curve) in space-time. Space-Time is physically conceived of as a general structure determined by the relationship among world-events, or four-dimensional events. The universe of four dimensions (the omniverse, as it may be called) includes space with all of its events and objects as well as time with its changes and motions. As such, this four-dimensional universe must be changeless and motionless, insofar as things move and change only when taken in abstraction from time, or rather when space and time are regarded as separate.

According to the classical or Newtonian theory, space-time is separable in an absolute way into the two elements, space and time; on the other hand, according to either the special or the general theory of relativity, this separation is not possible in an absolute sense but is relative to a choice of a coordinate system.

A somewhat different, metaphysical, interpretation of Space-Time was formed by S. Alexander and C. L. Morgan. According to their doctrine of Emergent Evolution, space-time is the matrix of the world, out of which have emerged matter, life, mind, and Deity. The world as we know it has evolved out of the original space-time.—*R.B.W.*

Species: A relatively narrow class—or better, class concept—thought of as included (in the sense of class inclusion, ⊂) within a wider class—or class concept—the *genus.*—*A.C.*

In Scholasticism: 1. In logic: the subdivision of genus, comprising several individuals, constituted by the *differentia specifica.* 2. In ontology: the common

nature or essence, individualized by some agent. This agent is in Thomism conceived as matter, in Scotism as a form of "thisness" (*haecceitas*). No agreement has been reached on the number of ontological species; some hold that there is an indefinite number, others that the number is limited. 3. In psychology of cognition: (a) regarding sensory cognition: The senses are affected by the object through the medium; this affection results in the *species impressa* which, however, is not merely the immutation of the sense organ or the nervous apparatus belonging thereto, but implies a "psychic immutation." As conscious percept the ultimate effect of sense affection in the mind becomes the *species expressa.* (b) regarding intellectual cognition: the active intellect, by "illuminating" the phantasm disengages therefrom the *species intelligibilis impressa* which in turn actuates, through informing it, the passive intellect and becomes theory, as the known concept, the *species intelligibilis expressa,* also called *verbum mentis.* This "word" is not of the "inner language," but belongs to preverbal thought and becomes, when given verbal form, the "meaning" of the spoken word, which refers primarily to the mental concept and, by this, secondarily to the object.—*R.A.*

Specificative: (in Schol.) Any concrete thing is taken specificatively or denominatively when the predicate which is attributed to it belongs to it by reason of the concrete subject itself: if we say, *the philosopher sleeps, philosopher* is taken specificatively, for he sleeps *as* man.—*H.G.*

Specious Present: (Lat. *speciosus,* from species, look or apprehend) The psychological or felt present is a spread of duration embraced within the mind's momentary experience. Contrasts with the physical present which is an ideal limit or boundary between the past and the future.—*L.W.*

Speculative Idealism: Doctrine, founded on the coherence theory of truth, that Reality comprises one Self, Mind, or spiritual principle. See *Coherence, Internal Theory of Relations, Pantheism, Organicism, Dialectic, W. T. Harris.*—*W.L.*

Speculum: (Lat. mirror) In ordinary language: a mirror. Special meanings in optics, astronomy, surgery, and in ornithology. In medieval philosophy, mind is the *speculum* of nature and God.—*V.F.*

Speech Situation: (1) A situation in which a complete utterance is made by a speaker and correctly interpreted by a hearer to whom it is addressed, as referring to some feature of the immediate environment.

(2) More generally: the circumstances attending any use of speech from which some of the defining characteristics of a primary speech situation are absent. See *Language.*—*M.B.*

Spencer, Herbert: (1820-1903) was the great English philosopher who devoted a lifetime to the formulation and execution of a plan to follow the idea of development as a first principle through all the avenues of human thought. A precursor of Darwin with his famous notion of all organic evolution as a change "from homogeneity to heterogeneity," from the simple to the complex, he nevertheless was greatly influenced by the Darwinian hypothesis and employed its arguments in his monumental works in biology, psychology, sociology and ethics. He aimed to interpret life, mind and society in terms of matter, motion and force. In politics, he evidenced from his earliest writings a strong bias for individualism. See: *Evolutionism, Charles Darwin.—L.E.D.*

Main works: *System of Synthetic Philosophy (First Principles of Biology, Psychology, Sociology, Ethics),* 1862-92; *On Moral and Physical Education,* 1861.

Spens, Will: (1882-1962) An English educator who as Master of Corpus Christi College in Cambridge wrote widely on educational theory. In philosophy and theology, he developed a theory of Christian doctrine as based on religious experience, which it generalizes and states in terms whose adequacy is determined by their capacity to nourish and develop that experience (*Belief and Practice*); he has also written on sacramental theology, including several essays (chiefly in the symposium *Essays, Catholic and Critical*) on the Eucharist; here his view is that by the "real presence" is meant the congeries of opportunities of experiencing through material means the spiritual reality of Christ.—*W.N.P.*

Sphaeriker: (German) A term used by Friedrich Froebel to designate those, including himself and Pestalozzi, who believe in or realize in practice the totality or wholeness of man in whom all polarities, such as mind and emotion, spirit and soul, are unified, the sphere with centre being the symbol of this attitude.—*K.F.L.*

Spinoza, Baruch or Benedict: (1632-1677) The great rationalist, born in Amsterdam, was given a rabbinic education until he was expelled from the synagogue for disturbing them by asking too many unorthodox questions. He survived an assassination attempt when the dagger was deflected by a button. Living in Amsterdam, Rijnsburg and Voorburg, he supported himself by grinding lenses. When offered an appointment to the faculty at the University of Heidelberg, he turned it down on the grounds that he would be deprived of his freedom to seek the truth in his own way and on its own terms. He is the author of *Principles of Descartes' Philosophy (Renati Descartes Principiorum Philosophiae, Pars I et II,* 1663), *Treatise on Theology and Politics (Tractatus Theologico-politicus,* published anonymously in 1670), *Ethics (Ethica,* published posthumously), *Treatise on the Correction of the Intellect (Tractatus de Intellectus Emendatione,* not published until the late eighteenth century).

His philosophy is based on the thought that the universe is one fundamental unity, which can be called either God or Nature. All we know about it is mental or physical, but these are only two of what must be an infinite number of attributes. We can know the truth by a deductive, mathematical, geometric system of investigation.—*S.E.N.*

Spinozism: The philosophic doctrine of Baruch Spinoza. Described by Hegel as the philosophy of Substance. Spinoza denies the possibility of a plurality of substances, and reserves the term for absolute reality.

Hence Spinozism is sometimes used as equivalent to Monism. It is also identified with Pantheism, although this is a highly misleading characterization.

In his chief work, the *Ethica,* Spinoza's teaching is expressed in a manner for which geometry supplies the model. This expository device served various purposes. It may be interpreted as a clue to Spinoza's ideal of knowledge. So understood, it represents the condensed and ordered expression, not of 'philosophy' alone, but rather of all knowledge, 'philosophy' and 'science,' as an integrated system. In such an ideal ordering of ideas, (rational) theology and metaphysics provide the anchorage for the system. On the one hand, the theology-metaphysics displays the fundamental principles (definitions, postulates, axioms) upon which the anchorage depends, and further displays in deductive fashion the primary fund of ideas upon which the inquiries of science, both "descriptive" and "normative" must proceed. On the other hand, the results of scientific inquiry are anchored at the other end, by a complementary metaphysico-theological development of their significance. Ideally, there obtains, for Spinoza, both an initial theology and metaphysics — a necessary preparation for science — and a culminating theology and metaphysics, an interpretative absorption of the conclusions of science.

The fixity of this theoretical structure is not to be interpreted as incompatible with the continuous movement of discovery. The function of philosophy as such, in any age, is that of attempting to effect the theoretical ordering of the available fund of knowledge. There is implicit in Spinoza's conception of this function the recognition of the two-fold character of the task of philosophy. The task, on the one hand, is reflection upon the available fund of insight and ideas, upon all the fruits of reflection and inquiry, with the purpose of coherent ordering and expression of the fund. In this sense, 'philosophy' is that which can be displayed in the geometrical fashion. It is equally the task of philosophy, however, to prepare for this display and ordering. Paradoxically, philosophy must prepare for itself. Philosophy, in this function, is reflection upon the conditions of all inquiry, the discovery of the grounds of method, of the proper and indispensable assumptions of inquiry as such, and of the basic ideas within whose domain inquiry will move. If inquiry is to be undertaken at all, then mind must discover within itself, and disclose to itself, whatever authoritative guidance can be assured for the enterprise. The competence of the mind to know, the determination of the range of that competence, the rational criteria of truth, the necessities revealed to mind by the very reflections of mind—these and related questions define the task of philosophy as propaedeutic both to philosophy itself and to science. In this recognition of the two-fold character of philosophy, and of its relation to science, Spinoza is re-stating the spirit of Descartes.

The precipitates of the propaedeutical effort are to be found, for Spinoza, in the definitions, axioms, postulates, and within the structural plan expressed in the geometrical ordering. It is highly probable that Spinoza would have admitted the tentative character of at least some of the definitions, axioms, and postulates formulated by him. He doubtless saw the possibility that the process of inquiry, revising, augmenting, and re-coordinating the fund of knowledge, might demand alteration in the structural bases of systematic expression as well as in the knowledge to be ordered. Such changes, however, would occur within limits set by the propaedeutical disclosures and the general framework. Advance might require the abandonment of an older metaphysical element, and the substitution of a new one. But with equal likelihood, the advance of knowledge would make possible a richer and deeper apprehension of the content of fixed principles. To illustrate: The first definition of the *Ethica*, that of *Causa sui*, might well be for Spinoza a principle that awakened reason must accept, a truth whose priority and validity could not be undermined. He might regard it as a minimal definition of reality, of the nature of the ultimate object of inquiry. On the other hand, Spinoza, it may be conjectured, would not claim for every element of his system a similar finality. Just as he recognizes the role of hypothesis in science, in a similar way, he would recognize the tentative character of some metaphysical and theological elements.

The structural nature of this ideal ordering reflects, of course, the Spinozistic view of the real. Ultimate reality, as *Causa sui* and as substance, is all-inclusive. Causality is immanent causality, and every determinative being lies within the one substantial being. Spinoza's doctrine of attributes, infinite and finite modes, serve to express both the all-encompassing and systematic nature of the one ultimate reality and to distinguish and to determine the status of finite beings within this reality. In its immanentism as well as in its rational mysticism, the doctrine of Spinoza is not improperly regarded as Plotinism re-directed by the influence of Descartes and invigorated by the enterprise of modern science.—*A.G.A.B.*

Main works: *Exposition more geometrico of Descartes' Principles*, 1663; *Tract. Theol.-Politicus*, 1670 (only two books published during Spinoza's lifetime); *Ethics, demonstrated in geometrical order*, 1677; *Political Treatise*, 1677; *De intellectus emendatione*, 1677 (*On the Improvement of the Human Mind*). Cf. Vloten and Land, 2 vol. edition of Spinoza's works.

Spir, African: (1837-1890) A native of Russia, whose philosophy was influenced by Spinozistic and Kantian traditions. The main thesis of his philosophy is that sensory experience and reasoning are basically contradictory, insofar as the former informs us of constant change, whereas the latter is characterized by the *a priori* principle of identity.—*R.B.W.*

Main works: *Denken u. Wirklichkeit*, 1873; *Moralität u. Religion*, 1874; *Empirie u. Philosophie*, 1876.

Spirit: (L. Spiritus: breath, life, soul, mind, spirit).
1. Originally, the Stoic fire-like, animating and

energizing principle (*pneūma*) of the Cosmos.
2. A being capable of consciousness and commonly considered as possessing will and intelligence.
3. Immaterial being.
4. A disembodied or incorporeal conscious being.
5. The supersensuous, ideal order of being or realm of mind: the intellectual, rational, noetic, aesthetic, moral, holy, divine.
6. Medieval and alchemic: A subtle stuff; an element.—*W.L.*

Spiritism: 1. Doctrine that ancestral or other spirits can communicate with man; also the practice of contacting them.
2. Belief in the existence of conscious, voluntary beings other than of the organic, corporeal type represented by animals and man, such as souls connected with inorganic Nature, disembodied nature spirits, manes or ancestral spirits, demons, celestial beings, angelic beings, deities. See *Animism, Demonism, Spiritualism* (4).—*W.L.*

Spiritual Realism: The theory that only the truly good will is free. Causality based on spiritual activity. Self-forgetfulness as the way to a supreme realization of personality. Ravaisson expressed it in the phrase: "To simplify one's self."—*R.T.F.*

Spiritualism: Spiritualism (1) is the doctrine that the ultimate reality in the universe is Spirit, (Pneuma, Nous, Reason, Logos) an Over-Mind akin to human spirit, but pervading the entire universe as its ground and rational explanation. It is opposed to materialism.

Spiritualism (2) is sometimes used to denote the Idealistic view that nothing but an absolute Spirit and finite spirits exist. The world of sense in this view is a realm of ideas.

Spiritualism (3) is used in religious terminology to emphasize the direct influence of the Holy Spirit in the sphere of religion and especially to indicate the teaching of St. John's Gospel that God is Spirit and that worship is direct correspondence of Spirit with spirit.

Spiritualism (4) means the faith that spirits of the dead communicate with the living through persons who are "mediums" and through other forms of manifestation. The word *Spiritism* is more properly used for this faith.—*R.M.J.*

Spiritus rector: Literally in Latin, the ruling or master spirit; some sort of subtle natural force in corporeal beings. The alchemists applied the expression to some substance, or distilled product, said to be capable of transmuting metals into gold, and also to an elixir which was supposed to prolong life indefinitely.—*J.J.R.*

Spontaneity: (Lat. *sponte*, of free will) The supposed ability of the will to act on its own initiative (*sua sponte*) and in independence of antecedent conditions. See *Free-Will.*—*L.W.*

Spranger, Eduard: (1882-1963) Developed Dilthey's thought, favoring like him, descriptive instead of explanatory psychology. As leading exponent of the *Verstehungspsychologie*, he postulates ideal types representing ultimate categories of value. These types of personality represent merely "schemata of comprehensibility,'' theoretical guides or aids in understanding people.—*H.H.*

Main works: *Grundl. d. Geschichtswiss.*, 1905; *Lebensformen*, 1914; *Die Geisteswiss. u. d. Schule*, 1920; *Die wissensch. Grundl. d. Schulverfassungslehre u.d. Schulpolitik*, 1925; *Das deutsche Bildungsideal*, 1928; *Volk, Staat, Erziehung*, 1930; *Die Magieder Seele*, (1947).

Ssu: (a) Partiality, selfishness.

(b) A private name. "Only a particular substance bears the name." (Neo-Mohism).—*W.T.C.*

Ssu: (a) Deliberation, thinking.

(b) Wish.

(c) Idea.—*W.T.C.*

Ssu chiao: The four things which Confucius taught his pupils, namely, letters, personal conduct, being one's true self (chung), and good faith in social relationships (hsin).—*W.T.C.*

Ssu te: The Four Virtues:

(a) Being attentive to the fundamentals, penetrative, beneficial, and unflinching — the virtues of the trigram ch'ien (Heaven, male, yang) and therefore ethical ideals of the superior man.

(b) Filial piety, respect for elders, loyalty to superiors (chung), and good faith in social relationship (hsin).

(c) Lady-like conduct, speech, skill, and appearance. Also called ssŭ hsing.—*W.T.C.*

Ssu tuan: All men possess the 'four beginnings' of benevolence (jên), righteousnèss (ī), propriety (li), and wisdom (chih). (Mencius).—*H.H.*

St. Louis School of Philosophy: Started with the first meeting between Henry Brokmeyer and Wm. Torrey Harris (*q.v.*) in 1858, it became one of the most important and influential movements in America to die in the early 1880's with the dispersion of the members who included among others Denton J. Snider, Adolph E. Kroeger, George H. Howison, and Thomas Davidson. It engendered the St. Louis Philosophical Society (founded in Feb., 1866) and the *Journal of Speculative Philosophy*. Cf. D. S. Snider, *St. Louis Movement*, and Charles M. Perry, *St. Louis Movement in Philosophy*.—*K.F.L.*

State: (Lat. *status*, Ital. *stato*; the term introduced by Machiavelli) A political organization based upon a common territory and exercising control over the inhabitants of that territory. Essential for a state is the existence of a government, and in the "legal state," a written or unwritten constitution. By the pure theory of law (Kelsen), the state is identified with law. By others (Duguit) considered a mere fiction, devised to conceal the matter of fact preponderance of particular persons or groups. The state is sometimes explained as the positive or actual organization of the legislative or judicial powers. (In America also: one of the commonwealths which form the United States of America, Brazil, Mexico).—*W.E.*

State of Nature: The state of man as it would be if there were no political organization or government. The concept was used by many philosophers of the seventeenth and eighteenth centuries as a criterion of what man's natural condition might be and as to what extent that condition has been spoiled or corrupted by civilization. It was used as an argument for man's original rights to liberty and equality (Hooker, Locke, Rousseau), but occasionally also as an argument for the necessity of the state and its right to control all social relations (Hobbes).—*W.E.*

Statement: See *Meaning, Kinds of,* 1.

Statistics: The systematic study of quantitative facts, numerical data, comparative materials, obtained through description and interpretation of group phenomena. 2. The method of using and interpreting processes of classification, enumeration, measurement and evaluation of group phenomena. 3. In a restricted sense, the materials, facts or data referring to group phenomena and forming the subject of systematic computation and interpretation.

The Ground of Statistics. Statistics have developed from a specialized application of the inductive principle which concludes from the characteristics of a large number of parts to those of the whole. When we make generalizations from empirical data, we are never certain of having expressed adequately the laws connecting all the relevant and efficient factors in the case under investigation. Not only have we to take into account the personal equation involved and the imperfection of our instruments of observation and measurement, but also the complex character of physical, biological, psychological and social phenomena which cannot be subjected to an exhaustive analysis. Statistics reveals precisely definite trends and frequencies subject to approximate laws, in these various fields in which phenomena result from many independently varying factors and involve a multitude of numerical units of variable character. Statistics differs from probability insofar as it makes a more consistent use of empirical data objectively considered, and of methods directly inspired by the treatment of these data.

The Method of Statistics. The basic principle of statistical method is that of simplification, which makes possible a concise and comprehensive knowledge of a mass of isolated facts by correlating them along definite lines.

A) The various stages of this method are: (1) precise definition of the problem or field of inquiry; (2) collection of material required by the problem; (3) tabulation and measurement of material in a manner satisfying the purpose of the problem; (4) clear presentation of the significant features of tabulated material (by means of charts, diagrams, symbols, graphs, equations and the like); (5) selection of mathematical methods for application to the material obtained; (6) necessary conclusion from the facts and figures obtained; (7) general interpretation within the limits of the problem and the procedure used.

B) The special methods of treating statistical data are: collecting, sampling, selecting, tabulating, classifying, totaling or aggregating, measuring, averaging, relating and correlating, presenting symbolically. Each one of these methods uses specialized experimental or mathematical means in its actual application.

C) The special *methods of interpreting* statistical data already treated are: analyzing, estimating, describing, comparing, explaining, applying and predicting.

D) In order to be conclusive, the various stages and types of the statistical method must avoid (1) loose definitions, (2) cross divisions resulting from conflicting interpretations of the problem, (3) data which are not simultaneous or subject to similar conditions, (4) conclusions from poor or incomplete data, (5) prejudices in judging, even when there is no corruption of evidence.

E) The philosophy of statistics is concerned in general with the discussion and evaluation of the mathematical principles, methods and results of this science; and in particular with a critical analysis of the fitness of biological, psychological, educational, economic and sociological materials, for various types of statistical treatment. The purpose of such an inquiry is to integrate its results into the general problems and schemes of philosophy proper. Cf. Richard von Mises, *Statistics, Probability, and Truth.*—*T.G.*

Steiner, Rudolph: (1861-1925) An evolutionary materialist who converted to mysticism and the occult sciences. Founder of the Anthroposophical Society in Switzerland and author of the book, *On the Riddle of Man* (1916).—*S.E.N.*

Stern, William: (1871-1938) Psychologist and philosopher who has contributed extensively to individual psychology (see *Individual Psychology*), child psychology and applied psychology. He was an innovator in the field of intelligence testing, having suggested the use of intelligence quotient (I.Q.) obtained by dividing an individual's mental age by his chronological age and recognized that this quotient is relatively constant for a given individual (*The Psychological Methods of Testing Intelligence*). Stern's psychology with its emphasis on individual differences affords the foundation for his personalistic philosophy, the main contention of which is that the person is a psychophysical unity, characterized by purposiveness and individuality. See *Die Psychologie und der Personalismus* (1917) *Person and Sache*, 3 Vols. *Die Philosophie der Gegenwart in Selbstdarstellung*, Vol. 6.—*L.W.*

Sthenic: An adjective derived from the Greek, Sthenos, strength. It was applied by Dr. John Brown (1735-1788), a British physician, to diseases distinguished by a usual or excessive accumulation of vital power, or nervous energy. Kant applied it to vigorous or exciting emotions.—*J.J.R.*

Stirner, Max: Pen name of Johann Caspar Schmidt (1806-1856) Most extreme and thoroughgoing individualist in the history of philosophy. In his classic, *The Ego and his Own,* he regards everything except the individual as minor; family, state and society all disappear before the individual, the ego, as the primary power for life and living.—*L.E.D.*

Stoic School: Founded by Zeno (of Citium, in Cyprus) in the year 308 B.C. in Athens. For Stoicism, virtue alone is the only good and the virtuous man is the one who has attained happiness through knowledge, as Socrates had taught. The virtuous man thus finds happiness in himself and is independent of the external world which he has succeeded in overcoming by mastering himself, his passions and emotions. As for the Stoic conception of the universe as a whole, their doctrine is *pantheistic.* All things and all natural laws follow by a conscious determination from the basic World-Reason, and it is this rational order by which, according to Stoicism, the wise man seeks to regulate his life as his highest *duty.*—*M.F.*

Strato: of Lampsacus, head of the Peripatetic School of Greek philosophy from 287-269 B.C.—*M.F.*

Strauss, David Friedrich: (1808-1874) German philosopher who received wide popularity and condemnation for his *Life of Jesus*. He held that the unity of God and man is not realized in Christ but in mankind itself and in its history. This relation, he believed, was immanent and not transcendent. His numerous writings displayed many currents from Hegelianism and Darwinism to a pantheism that approaches atheism and then back to a naturalism that clings devoutly to an inward religious experience. Main works: *Das Leben Jesu,* 1835; *Die Christlische Dogmatik,* 1840; *Der alte u. d. neue Glaube,* 1872.—*L.E.D.*

Strawson , Peter F.: (1919-) Waynflete Professor of Metaphysical Philosophy in the University of Oxford, Fellow of Magdalen College, Oxford. He has made important contributions to the theory of truth and has been instrumental in leading linguists to a more thorough examination of Kantian metaphysics. He attracted a good deal of attention by criticizing Russell's theory of descriptions. Among his works are "On Referring" (in *Mind,* 1950), *Introduction to Logical Theory* (1952), *Individuals: An Essay in Descriptive Metaphysics* 1959 and *The Bounds of Sense.*—*L.L.*

Stream of Consciousness or Thought: Thought considered as a process of continuous change. The metaphor of the stream was suggested by W. James. See *The Principles of Psychology,* Vol. 1, ch. IX, entitled "The Stream of Thought" especially p. 239.—*L.W.*

Strict implication: As early as 1912, C. I. Lewis projected a kind of implication between propositions, to be called *strict implication,* which should more nearly accord with the usual meaning of "implies" than does *material implication* (see *logic, formal,* § 1), should make "*p* implies *q*" synonymous with "*q* is deducible from *p,*" and should avoid such so-called paradoxes of material implication as the theorem $[p \supset q] \vee [q \supset p]$. The first satisfactory formulation of a calculus of propositions with strict implication appeared in 1920, and this system, and later modified forms of it, have since been extensively investigated. An essential feature is the introduction of modalities through the notation (say) $M[p]$, to mean "*p* is possible" (Lewis uses a diamond instead of M). The strict implication of q by p is then identified with $\sim M[p \sim q]$, whereas the material implication $p \supset q$ is given by $\sim [p \sim q]$. In 1932 Lewis, along with other modifications, added a primitive formula (involving the binding of propositional variables by existential quantifiers) which renders definitively impossible an interpretation of the system which would make Mp the same as p and strict implication the same as material implication. Consistency of the system, including this additional primitive formula, may be established by means of an appropriate four-valued propositional calculus, the theorems of the system being some among the tautologies of the four-valued propositional calculus.—*A.C.*

Lewis and Langford, *Symbolic Logic,* New York and London, 1932. E. V. Huntington, *Postulates for assertion, conjunction, negation, and equality,* Proceedings of the American Academy of Arts and Sciences, vol. 72, no. 1, 1937. W. T. Parry, *Modalities in the Survey system of strict implication,* The Journal of Symbolic Logic, vol. 4 (1939), pp. 137-154.

Structuralism: (Lat. *structura,* a building) The conception of mind in terms of its structure whether this structure be interpreted: a) atomistically. See *Psychological Atomism; Structural Psychology;* or b) configurationally. (*Gestalt Psychology*).—*L.W.*

Structural Psychology: A tendency in American psychology, represented by E. B. Titchener. (*A Textbook of Psychology,* 1909-10) which in opposition to Functional Psychology (see *Functional Psychology; Functionalism*) adopted as the method of psychology the analysis of mental states into component sensations, images and feelings; the structure of consciousness is for structural psychology atomistic.—*L.W.*

Structural Theories of Mind: See *Structuralism.*

Struggle For Existence: This is given by Charles Darwin as a premise for his evolutionary hypothesis of natural selection. There is constant struggle in a species resultant from the over production of offspring. This notion is an outgrowth of the influence of Malthus on Darwin. Darwin does not mean actual or necessary combat at all stages, but requisite dependence of one upon another and of each upon all factors in the environment leading to the natural selection of the fittest: See *Evolutionism, Natural Selection, Charles Darwin, Herbert Spencer, Thomas Henry Huxley.*—*L.E.D.*

Stuff, Neutral: A reality posited by certain philosophers which is neither mental nor physical, but which underlies both. See *Neutral Monism.*—*L.W.*

Stumpf, Carl: (1848-1936) A life long Platonic realist, he was philosophically awakened and influenced by Brentano. His most notable contributions were in the psychology of tone and music, and in musicology. Metaphysics is, in his opinion, best constructed inductively as a continuation of the sciences.—*H.H.*

Main works: *Tonpsychologie,* 2 vols. 1883-90; *Die Anfänge der Musik,* 1911; *Empfindung u. Vorstellung,* 1918; *Gefühl u. Gefühlsempfinding,* 1928; *Erkenntnislehre,* I, 1939.

Sturm und Drang: (German, "Storm and Stress"), a period sweeping the German countries about 1770-1785, in which men like Hamann, Herder, the young Goethe, Schiller, Wagner, Christian Schubart, and Friedrich Maximilian Klinger (from whose play the movement got its name) advocated, in a flush of creative enthusiasm, the forces of native talent, the value of emotion, and the power of genius as a conscious reaction against the enlightenment which had spread from France.—*K.F.L.*

Su: 'Unadornment,' (p'u) 'unadorned simplicity;' (ching) 'quiescence' bespeaking all the complete absence of desires, but really meaning that the desires should be made fewer. (Lao Tzŭ) Seeking for the *tao,* emptiness, singleness, concentrated attention (tu), quiescence are all rules for man's conduct. (Hsün Tzŭ c. 355—288 B.C.).—*H.H.*

Suarezianism: A school of philosophy and theology founded by Francisco Suarez, of the Society of Jesus, Spain, 1548-1617. His philosophic position is, in general, that of Christian Aristotelianism. The immediate background of his thought is to be found in Albertinism, Thomism, Scotism and Nominalism.

The *Disputationes Metaphysicae* (no Eng. translation) forms a complete exposition of Suarez's general metaphysics, psychology, theory of knowledge, cosmology and natural theology. Basic is the rejection of the Thomistic real distinction between essence and existence in finite things. Physical substances are individuated, neither by their matter nor their form, but by their total entities. Their components, matter and form, are individual entities united in the composite of physical substance by a "mode" (*unio*) which has itself no reality apart from the composite. Except in the case of the human form which is the soul, matter and form in the natural order cannot exist in isolation. Accidental "modes" are used to explain the association of accidents with their subjects. Spiritual creatures (angels and human souls) are not specific natures as in Thomism, but are individuals, constituted as such by their own entities.

The soul is the principle of all vital actions and, though these vital operations on the biological, sensory and intellectual levels are attributed to various "faculties," these faculties are not really distinct from the essence of the soul. In this life the human intellect cannot operate without the aid of images supplied by sense perception. An intellectual concept of a single individual thing may be formed directly and then a universal concept of the common nature of many sensible things within a class may be developed by the intellect through the process of abstraction. The will is the faculty of rational appetite; it is free in the ultimate choice of its object, which is called a "good." Suarez emphasizes the psychological and moral supremacy of the will. The Suarezian theory of knowledge is what would be called naïve realism today.

As a free creature, man is responsible for his freely performed actions. Man knows the basic principles of the Divine Law through the natural use of his intellect. Thus known, the Divine Law is called the natural moral law. It is immutable. Suarez' ethics provides a rational justification for most of the accepted moral standards of Christianity. The individual has rights and duties in regard to other creatures and himself; he has duties toward his Creator. The political theory of Suarez is most noted for its opposition to the divine right of kings. He held that a ruler derives his authority *immediately* from the consent of the people, *ultimately* from God. Suarez maintained that there are several forms of political organizations in which social justice may be secured.

According to Suarez, theology is not a part of philosophy, but a supreme science having a supernatural justification and deriving its principles from Divine revelation. However, in this natural theology, Suarez examined the arguments for the existence of God. The attributes of God can be but dimly known by the unaided reason of man.

Suarezianism is systematic, orderly, easy to teach; it has become the framework of many Catholic textbooks in philosophy, particularly of those by Jesuit authors. Schopenhauer, Spinoza, Leibniz and Descartes mention their reading of the *Disputations*. See: Grabmann, M., "Die *Disp. Metaph*. F. Suarez in ihrer methodischen Eigenart und Fortwirkung," in *Franz Suarez, S. J.*, (Innsbruck, 1917). (Pedro Descoqs, S. J., is an outstanding contemporary Suarezian).

Opera Omnia, ed C. Berton, (Paris, 1856-1878), 30 vols. (not quite complete).

De Scorraille, R., *F. Suarez, de la Compagnie de Jesus*, 2 vols. (Paris, 1912).

A Symposium on Suarez (Five papers and a good bibliography by American Jesuit scholars),*Proc. Jesuit Educat. Assoc.*, (Chicago, 1931) pp. 153-214.

Jesuit Thinkers of the Renaissance, ed. G. Smith, S. J., (Milwaukee, 1939).—*V.J.B.*

Subalternation: See *Logic, formal*, § 4.

Subclass: A class *a* is a *subclass* of a class *b* if *a* ⊂ *b*. See *Logic, formal* § 7.

A class *a* is a *proper subclass* of a class *b* if *a* ⊂|*b*|and *a* ≠ *b*.—*A.C.*

Subconscious Mind: (Lat. *sub*, under — *cum* together + *scire* to know) A compartment of the mind alleged by certain psychologists and philosophers (see *Psychoanalysis*) to exist below the threshold of consciousness. The subconscious, though not directly accessible to introspection (see *Introspection*), is capable of being tapped by special techniques such as random association, dream-analysis, automatic writing, etc. The doctrine of the subcounscious was foreshadowed in Leibniz's doctrine of *petites perceptions* (*Monadology*, Sections 21, 23) and received philosophical expression by A. Schopenhauer, *The World as Will and Idea*, and E. von Hartmann, *Philosophy of the Unconscious* and has become an integral part of Freudian psychology. See Freud, *The Interpretation of Dreams*, esp. pp. 425-35, 483-93.—*L.W.*

Subcontrary: See *Logic, formal* § 4.

Subject: (Lat. *subjicere*, to pace under)

a) *In Epistemology:* The subject of knowledge is the individual knower considered either as a pure ego (see *Ego, Pure*), a transcendental ego (see *Ego, Transcendental*) or an act of awareness. (See *Awareness*).

b) *In Psychology:* The psychological subject is the individual subjected to observation. Thus the introspective psychologist may either rely on the report of another subject or he may self-introspect, i.e., serve as his own subject. (See *Introspection*).—*L.W.*

For the use of this word in traditional logic, see *Predicate*.

Subjective Idealism: Sometimes referred to as psychological idealism or subjectivism. The doctrine of knowledge that the world exists only for the mind. The only world we know is the-world-we-know shut up in the realm of ideas. To be is to be perceived: *esse est percipi*. This famous doctrine (classically expressed by Bishop Berkeley, 1685-1753) became the cornerstone of modern metaphysical idealism. Recent idealists tend to minimize its significance for metaphysics.—*V.F.*

Subjective rightness: An action is subjectively right if it is done in the belief that it is objectively right. See *objective rightness*.—*W.F.K.*

Subjectivism: a) *In Epistemology:* The restriction of knowledge to the knowing subject and its sensory, affective and volitional states and to such external realities as may be inferred from the mind's subjective states. See *Solipsism, Ego-centric Predicament*.

b) *In Axiology:* The doctrine that moral and aesthetic values represent the subjective feelings and reactions of individual minds and have no status independent of such reactions. Ethical subjectivism finds typical expression in Westermarek's doctrine that moral judgments have reference to our emotions of approval and disapproval. See *The Origin and Development of Moral Ideas*, Vol. 1, Ch. 1.—*L.W.*

Subjectivism, epistemological: Doctrine contending that every object apprehended is created, constructed by the apprehender. (Montague).—*H.H.*

Sublimation: (Lat. *sublimatio*, from *sublimare*, to elevate, lift up) The psychological mechanism, described by Freudians, which consists in the discovery of a substitute object for the expression of a basic instinct or feeling e.g., the sublimation of the sex impulses in aesthetic creation.—*L.W.*

Subliminal: (Lat. *sub*. under + *limen*, the threshold) Term popularized by F. Myers to describe allegedly unconscious mental processes, especially sensations which lie below the threshold of consciousness. See *Unconscious Mind*.—*L.W.*

Subsistents: Abstract and eternal entities, values, universals in a non-mental and non-physical world.—*H.H.*

Substance: (Lat. *sub* + *stare* = Gr. *hypo* + *stasis*, to stand under. Also from Lat. *quod quid est*, or *quod quid erat esse* = Gr. *to ti en einai*, i.e., that by virtue of which a thing has its determinate nature, which makes it *what* it is, as distinguished from something else. See *ousia, natura, subsistentia, essentia*. Thus Augustine writes (De Trin. VII, ch. 4, # 7) "essence (ousia) usually means nothing else than substance in our language, i.e., in Latin").

Substance is the term used to signify that which is sought when philosophers investigate the primary being of things. Thus Plato was primarily concerned with investigating the being of things from the standpoint of their intelligibility. Hence the Platonic dialectic was aimed at a knowledge of the essential nature (ousia) of things. But science is knowledge of universals; so the essence of things considered as intelligible is the universal common to many; i.e., the universal Form or Idea, and this was for Plato the substance of things, or what they are primarily.

Besides the universal intelligible being of things, Aristotle was also primarily concerned with an investigation of the being of things from the standpoint of their generation and existence. But only individual things are generated and exist. Hence, for him, substance was primarily the individual: a "this" which, in contrast with the universal or secondary substance, is not communicable to many. The Aristotelian meaning of substance may be developed from four points of view:

a) *Grammar:* The nature of substance as the ultimate subject of prediction is expressed by common usage in its employment of the noun (or substantive) as the subject of a sentence to signify an individual thing which "is neither present in nor predicable of a subject." Thus substance is grammatically distinguished from its (adjectival) properties and modifications which "are present in and predicable of a subject."

Secondary substance is expressed by the universal term and by its definition, which are "not present in a subject but predicable of it." See *Categoriae*, ch. 5.

b) *Physics:* Independence of being emerges as a fundamental characteristic of substance in the analysis of change. Thus we have:

1) Substantial change: Socrates comes to be (Change simply).

2) Accidental change; in a certain respect only: Socrates comes to be 6 feet tall (*Quantitative*). Socrates comes to be musical (*Qualitative*). Socrates comes to be in Corinth (*Local*).

As substantial change is prior to the others and may occur independently of them, so the individual substance is prior in being to the accidents; i.e., the accidents cannot exist independently of their subject (Socrates), but can *be* only in him or in another primary substance, while the reverse is not necessarily the case.

c) *Logic:* Out of this analysis of change there also emerges a division of being into the schema of categories, with the distinction between the category of substance and the several accidental categories, such as quantity, quality, place, relation, etc. In a corresponding manner, the category of substance is first; i.e., prior to the others in being, and independent of them.

d) *Metaphysics:* The character of substance as that which is present in an individual as the cause of its being and unity is developed in Aristotle's metaphysical writings; see especially Bk. Z, ch. 17, 1041b. Primary substance is not the matter alone, nor the universal form common to many, but the individual unity of matter and form. For example, each thing is composed of parts or elements, as an organism is composed of cells; yet it is not merely its elements, but has a being and unity over and above the sum of its parts. This something more which causes the cells to be this organism rather than a

malignant growth, is an example of what is meant by substance in its proper sense of first substance (*substantia prima*).

Substance in its secondary sense (*substantia secunda*) is the universal form (idea or species) which is individuated in each thing.

For the later development of the conception of substance, see *Thomas Aquinas,* especially *De Ente et Essentia,* ch. 2.

Note that according to Aristotle, the substance of a thing is always intelligible. Thus there are sensible substances, but the substance of these things is itself neither sensible nor capable of being apprehended by the senses alone, but only when the activity of the intellect is added. In later scholastic philosophy this point was missed, so the Aristotelian doctrine of substance quite naturally ceased to be any longer intelligible.

In modern thought, two general types of usage are discernible. In the empirical tradition, the notion of thing and properties continues the meaning of independence as expressed in first substance. Under the impact of physical science, the notion of thing and its properties tends to dissolve. Substance becomes substratum as that in which properties and qualities inhere. The critique of Berkeley expressed the resultant dilemma: either sub-stratum is property-less and quality-less, and so is nothing at all; or else it signifies the systematic and specific coherence of properties and qualities, and so substance or sub-stratum is merely the thing of common sense. Within science 'first substance' persists as the ultimate discrete particle with respect to which spatial and temporal coordinates are assigned. Within empirical philosophical thought the element of meaning described as 'independence' tends to be resolved into the order and coherence of experience.

In the rationalistic tradition, Descartes introduces a distinction between finite and infinite substance. To conceive of substance is to conceive of an existing thing which requires nothing but itself in order to exist. Strictly speaking, God alone is substance. Created or finite substances are independent in the sense that they need only the concurrence of God in order to exist. "Everything in which there resides immediately, as in a subject, or by means of which there exists anything that we perceive, i.e., any property, quality, or attribute, of which we have a real idea, is called a *Substance*." (Reply to Obj. II, Phil. Works, trans. by Haldane and Ross, vol. II, p. 53; see Prin. of Phil. Pt. I, 51, 52). Substance is that which can exist by itself without the aid of any other substance. Reciprocal exclusion of one another belongs to the nature of substance. (Reply to Obj. IV). Spinoza brings together medieval Aristotelian meanings and the Cartesian usage, but rejects utterly the notion of finite substance, leaving only the infinite. The former is, in effect, a contradiction in terms, according to him. Spinoza further replaces the Aristotelian distinction between substance and accident with that between substance and mode (See *Wolfson, The Phil. of Spinoza,* vol. I, ch. 3). "By substance, I understand that which is in itself and is conceived through itself; in other words, that, the conception of which does not need the conception of another thing from which it must be formed.'' (Ethics, I, Def. III). Substance is thus ultimate being, self-caused or from itself (*a se*), and so absolutely independent being, owing its being to itself, and eternally self-sustaining. It is in itself (*in se*), and all things are within it. Substance is one and there can be but one substance; God is this substance. For Descartes, every substance has a principal attribute, an unchangeable essential nature, without which it can neither be nor be understood. The attribute is thus constitutivus of substance, and the latter is accessible to mind only through the former. By virtue of having different constitutive essences or attributes, substances are opposed to one another. Spinoza, rejecting the idea of finite substance, necessarily rejects the possibility of a plurality of substances. The attributes of the one substance are plural and are constitutive. But the plurality of attributes implies that substance as such cannot be understood by way of any one attribute or by way of several. Accordingly, Spinoza declares that substance is also *per se*, i.e., conceived through itself. The infinite mode of an attribute, the all pervasive inner character which defines an attribute in distinction from another, is Spinoza's adaptation of the Cartesian constitutive essence.

The critique of Kant resolves substance into the a priori category of Inherence-and-subsistence, and so to a necessary synthetic activity of mind upon the data of experience. In the dialectic of Hegel, the effort is made to unify the logical meanings of substance as subject and the meaning of absolute independent being as defined in Spinoza.—*L.M.H. & A.G.A.B.*

In Scholasticism: The nature of substance is that it exists in itself, independently from another being. While accidents are in another, substance is in itself. It is what underlies the accidents, persists even if these are changing; insofar as its being in itself is considered, it is spoken of as subsistence (*subsistentia*). Substances are either material, and as such dependent on matter informed by a substantial form, or spiritual, free of any kind of matter (even a spiritual one, as Aquinas points out in *De Ente* against Avencebron, i.e., Ibn Gebirol), and as such is called *forma subsistens*. Substantial forms are not substances, with the one exception of the human soul (*q.v.*) which, however, is when separated from the body only an incomplete substance. See *Form, Matter.*—*R.A.*

Substance Theory of Mind: The conception of the individual mind as a permanent, self-identical substance. (See *Soul-Substance Theory*). The Substance Theory is distinguished from the substantive theory by C. W. Morris, (*Six Theories of Mind*, Chs. I and V) but the distinction is difficult to maintain.—*L.W.*

"Substantive States": (Lat. *substantivus*, self-existent) Substantive states of mind in contrast to transitive or relational states are the temporary resting-places in the flow of the stream of thought. The term was introduced by W. James (*The Principles of Psychology*, Vol. I, pp. 243-8).—*L.W.*

Substantive Theory of Mind: A diluted form of the Substance Theory of mind which asserts that the mind, while not strictly a substance, possesses a substantial character. See *Substance Theory of Mind*.—*L.W.*

Substitution, rule of: See *logic, formal*, § 1.

Substratum: (Gr. *hypokeimenon*) That in which an attribute inheres, or of which it is predicated; substance; subject. In Aristotle's philosophy *hypokeimenon* sometimes means matter as underlying form, sometimes the concrete thing as possessing attributes, sometimes the logical subject of predication.—*G.R.M.*

Subsumption: Noun signifying that the subject of a proposition is taken under the predicate. Also the inclusion of the species under the genus, and the individual under the species. The minor premiss which applies a general law stated by the major premiss of a syllogism is called a subsumption.—*J.J.R.*

Succession and Duration: These concepts are inseparable from the idea of 'flowing' time in which every event endures relatively to a succession of other events. In Leibniz's view, succession was the most important characteristic of time defined by him as ''the order of succession.'' Some thinkers, notably H. Bergson, regard duration (*durée*) as the very essence of time, ''time perceived as indivisible,'' in which the vital impulse (*élan vital*) becomes the creative source of all change comparable to a snow-ball rolling down a hill and swelling on its way. According to A. N. Whitehead, duration is 'a slab of nature' possessing temporal thickness; it is a cross-section of the world in its process, or ''the immediate present condition of the world at some epoch.''—*R.B.W.*

Sufficient condition: F is a *sufficient condition of G* if $F(x) \supset_x G(x)$. See *Necessary condition.*—*A.C.*

Sufficient Reason, Principle of: Consists in the necessary relation of every object or event to every other. Time, space, causality, ground of knowledge and motivation are so many forms of this most basic principle of the relatedness of phenomena. (Schopenhauer). In Leibniz, see *Principle of Sufficient Reason.*—*H.H.*

Sufism: A classical development of mysticism and a reaction from the legalism and rigidity of orthodox Islam. Being a sect seeking to attain a nearer fellowship with God by scrupulous observation of the religious law, it represents an infiltration into Islam of the Christian-gnostic type of piety with its charismatic and ascetic features. Gained many of its converts from the heterodox Moslems in Persia.—*H.H.*

Sui generis: (Lat.) Alone of its kind; the condition of a subject which is unique; applied particularly to God.—*V.J.B.*

Sukha-duhkha: (Skr.) Pleasure and pain, to which is often added *moha* (*q.v.*), a stereotyped expression for the involvement in activity and thought preventing *moksa* (*q.v.*).—*K.F.L.*

Summa (Scholastic): Name of comprehensive treatises, subdivided in *tractatus* or *quaestiones*, which in their turn may contain several articles or *membra*. The classical procedure is that of the *quaestio disputata* (see *quaestio*) which developed from the method adopted first by the students of Canon Law (Yves of Chartres, a.o.) and applied to philosophical and theological discussion by Abelard (*Sic et Non*). The 12th century produced some works entitled *Summa* but not yet showing the strictly logical and systematic structure of the later works (e.g. *Summa sacramentorum*, attributed (?) to Hugh of St. Victor). The 13th century gave birth to the classical form.—*R.A.*

Summation, Psychic: (Lat. *summa*, sum) Fusion or combination of separate states of mind to form a new whole. See *Fusion, Psychic*.—*L.W.*

Summists: (Lat. *Summa*, a compendium) A group of writers in the 12th to 14th centuries who produced compendiuous, encyclopedic works known as *Summae*. Beginnings of the summa form are to be found in Peter Abaelard's *Sic et Non* (early 12th C.) and Peter Lombard's *Libri IV Sententiarum* (mid 12th C.). Theological *Summae* consisted of collections of opinions (*sententiae*) from earlier authorities, particularly Patristic, with some attempt at a resolution of the conflicts in such opinions. Hugh of St. Victor may have been the first to use the name *Summa*. Wm. of Auxerre (*Summa Aurea*), Alexander of Hales and his fellow Franciscans (*Summa universae theologiae*), John of La Rochelle (*S. de anima*), St. Albert (*S. de Creaturis*, and an incomplete *S. Theologiae*), and St. Thomas Aquinas (*S. contra Gentiles*, and *S. Theologiae*), are important 13th C. Summists. There were philosophical *Summae*, also, such as the *S. Logicae* of Lambert of Auxerre, the *S. modorum significandi* of Siger of Courtrai (14th C.), and the *Summa philosophiae* of the Pseudo-Grosseteste (late 13th C).—*V.J.B.*

Summum Bonum: (Lat. the supreme good) A term applied to an ultimate end of human conduct the worth of which is intrinsically and substantively good. It is some end that is not subordinate to anything else. Happiness, pleasure, virtue, self-realization, power, obedience to the voice of duty, to conscience, to the will of God, good will, perfection have been claimed as ultimate aims of human conduct in the history of ethical theory. Those who interpret all ethical problems in terms of a conception of good they hold to be the highest ignore all complexities of conduct, focus attention wholly upon goals towards which deeds are directed, restrict their study by constructing every good in one single pattern, center all goodness in one model and thus reduce all other types of good to their model.—*H.H.*

Summum Genus: The highest genus in a division; a genus which is not a species of a higher genus. —*G.R.M.*

Sunnites: Denotes the orthodox, traditionalist, by far the larger numbered Islamic sect which denies the Shiite claim that Ali and his descendants are alone entitled to the caliphate.—*H.H.*

Sûnya-vâda: A Buddhist theory (*vâda*) holding the world to be void (*sunya*) or unreal. Otherwise known as Madhyamaka (*q.v.*), this Mahāyāna (*q.v.*) school as founded by Nāgārjuna and elaborated in the Madhyamakaśāstra, is hardly correctly translated by nihilism. To be sure, the phenomenal world is said to

have no reality; yet the world underlying it defies description, also because of our inability to grasp the thing-in-itself (svabhāva). All we know is its dependence on some other condition, its so-called "dependent origination." Thus, nothing definite being able to be said about the real, it is, like the apparent, as nothing, in other words, *sunya*, void.—*K.F.L.*

Supererogation: (Lat. *super*, above; and *erogare*, to spend public funds) The act or condition of doing more than is strictly required by law; in Catholic moral terminology, an act of supererorogation consists in doing more than one's duty, a practice of special virtue.—*V.J.B.*

Superman: The name given by Nietzsche to what he deems a higher type of humanity; viewed as the goal of evolution.—*H.H.*

Supernatural: That which surpasses the active and exactive powers of nature—or that which natural causes can neither avail to produce nor require from God as the compliment of their kind.—*H.G.*

Suppositio: In medieval logic, the kind of meaning in use which belongs to nouns or substantives; opposed to *copulatio*, belonging to adjectives and verbs. A given noun having a fixed *signification* might nevertheless have different *suppositions* (stand for different things). Various kinds of *suppositio*, i.e., various ways in which a noun may stand for something, were distinguished.—*A.C.*

Petri Hispani Summulae Logicales cum Versorii Parisiensis clarissima expositione, editions e.g. Venice 1597, 1622. J. Maritain, *Petite Logique, Paris*, 1933.

Suppositio discreta: The kind of *suppositio* belonging to a proper name; opposed to *suppositio communis*.—*A.C.*

Suppositio materialis: The use of a word autonymously, or as a name for itself (see *autonymy*)—"Homo est disyllabum;" opposed to *suppositio formalis*, the use of a noun in its proper or ordinary signification.—*A.C.*

Suppositio naturalis: The use of a common noun to stand collectively for everything to which the name applies—"Homo est mortalis." It would now usually be held that this involves an inadequate or misleading analysis—see *copula*.—*A.C.*

Suppositio personalis: The use of a common noun, or class name, to stand for a particular member of the class—"Homo currit." Contemporary logical usage would supply, in such a case, either a description (corresponding in English to the definite article *the*) or an existential quantifier (corresponding to the indefinite article *a*).

Suppositio personalis confusa (opposed to the preceding as *suppositio personalis determinata*) was further ascribed to a common noun used for the subject or predicate of a universal affirmative proposition. The relation of this to *suppositio naturalis* and *suppositio simplex* is not clear, and not uniform among different writers.—*A.C.*

Suppositio simplex: The use of a common noun to stand for the class concept to which it refers—"Homo est species." *Suppositio simplex* was also ascribed to a common noun used for the predicate of an affirmative proposition.—*A.C.*

Supposititious: (Lat. *suppositicius,* put in the place of, substituted) Epistemological expression applying to any object which is assumed or posited by the mind without being actually given by experience.—*L.W.*

Supralapsarianism: (Lat. *supra,* before; and *lapsus,* the Fall of man) The theological view that God positively decreed the Fall of man as a means to the manifestation of His Power of salvation; attributed to Calvinism but opposed by some "Infralapsarian" Calvinists. See: *Predestination.—V.J.B.*

Su p'u: "Unadorned simplicity," being the state of original nature, is a state of desirelessness, of total absence of knowledge distinctions, of pure instinctivity. (Chuang Tzŭ, between 399 and 295 B.C.).—*H.H.*

Surrealism: a. Spiritualistic trend of art.

b. An artistic school representing dreams interpreted according to Freud's theories.—*L.V.*

Artistic movement which maintains that there exists, and seeks access to, a "real" world that lies behind the artificial world of ordinary objects given in normal awareness. Argues that what is found on the conscious level is an arbitrary construct of mind, determined by habit and custom, and that the function of art is to recover and report the world as originally experienced and felt. Seeks to disintegrate the clear logical life of intellect, so as to search for its materials on the subconscious level, and discover there the true and primitive meanings that things have for us prior to the forms that we impose on them.—*I.J.*

Sūtra: (Skr. string) An aphorism, the earliest form chosen for mnemonic reasons, in which philosophic thought was couched in India, necessitating often elaborate commentaries (*bhāṣya*) which frequently differ widely in their interpretation of the original and have occasioned various schools.—*K.F.L.*

Svabhāva: (Skr.) being-in-itself, essence, natural state, inherent or innate nature; the thing-in-itself aspect of anything; independent being; in the view of some Indian philosophers, the principle governing the universe through the spontaneity and individual character of the various substances.—*K.F.L.*

Svarāj: (Skr.) self-rule, self-determination, currently a designation of the home rule movement in India. —*K.F.L.*

Svatantra: (Skr. "what has itself as basis") Presuppositionless, absolute, free, said of the ultimate in its in-itself aspect.—*K.F.L.*

Svetāmbara: (Skr. "white-robed") A branch of the Jainas (*q.v.*) differing with the Digambaras (*q.v.*) in doctrine and habits.—*K.F.L.*

Swedenborgianism: A highly developed religious philosophy arising from Emanuel Swedenborg (Jan. 29, 1688-March 29, 1772). Swedenborg claimed direct spiritual knowledge. He recognized three descending levels or "degrees of being in God;" Love the Celestial, Spirit or the End; then Wisdom, the Spiritual or Soul, Cause; and finally the degree of Use, the Natural and Personal, the realm of Effects. Swedenborgism was formally launched in London in 1783 and is often called the New (or New Jerusalem) Church.—*F.K.*

Syādvāda: (Skr.) The theory of "somehow" (*syāt*), a theory of judgment of the Jainas (*q.v.*) which takes full account of the partiality of the judged reality and the idiosyncracy of the one who is judging in the world of discourse.—*K.F.L.*

Syllogism: See *Antilogism; Figure (syllogistic);* and *Logic, formal,* §§ 2, 5.

Symbol: (1) Used by some writers as synonymous with *sign* (*q.v.*).

(2) A *conventional* sign, i.e., a sign which functions as such in virtue of a *convention,* explicit or implicit, between its users. In this sense 'symbol' is sometimes opposed to 'natural sign'.—*M.B.*

Symbolism: An artistic trend flourishing at the end of the XIXth century in reaction to faith in the beauty of nature, and endeavoring to represent spiritual values by means of abstract signs.—*L.V.*

Symmetry: A dyadic relation R is *symmetric* if, for all x and y in the field of R, $xRy \supset yRx$; it is *asymmetric* if, for all x and y in the field of R, $xRy \supset \sim yRx$; *non-symmetric* if there are x and y in the field of R such that $[xRy]$ $[\sim yRx]$. An n-adic propositional function F is *symmetric* if $F(x_1, x_2, \ldots, x_n)$ is materially equivalent to the proposition obtained from it by permuting $x_1, x_2, \ldots, x_n$ among themselves in any fashion—for all sets of n arguments $x_1, x_2, \ldots, x_n$ belonging to the range of F.

A dyadic function f, other than a propositional function, is *symmetric* if, for all pairs of arguments, $x, y,$ belonging to the range of f, $f(x, y) = f(y, x)$. An n-adic function f is symmetric if, for any set of n arguments belonging to the range of f, the same value of the function is obtained no matter how the arguments are permuted among themselves (i.e., if the value of the function is independent of the order of the arguments).

In geometry, a figure is said to be *symmetric* with respect to a point P if the points of the figure can be grouped in pairs in such a way that the straight-line segment joining any pair has P as its mid-point. A figure is *symmetric* with respect to a straight line l if the points can be grouped in pairs in such a way that the straight-line segment joining any pair has l as a perpendicular bisector. These definitions apply in geometry to any number of dimensions. Similar definitions may be given of symmetry with respect to a plane, etc.—*A.C.*

Sympathy: On psychological levels, a participation in and feeling for other living beings in adversity or other emotional phases, not always painful, which may or may not lead to participating or alleviating action, explained naturalistically as a general instinct inherent in all creatures, ethically sometimes as an original altruism, sociologically as acquired in the civilisatory process through needs of co-operation, mutual aid, and fellow-feeling in family and group action. Stressed particularly in Hinduism, fostered along with pity (*q.v.*) in Christianity, discussed and recommended as a shrewd social expedient by such men as Hobbes, Bentham, and Adam Smith, Schopenhauer raised sympathy (*Mitleid*), as an equivalent to love, into an ethical principle which

Nietzsche repudiated because to him it increases suffering and through weakness hinders development. Sympathy, as a cultural force, becomes progressively more evident in the increasing establishment of benevolent institutions, such as hospitals, asylums, etc., a more general altruism and ejection (Clifford), an extension of kindness even to animals (first taught by Buddhism; see *Ahimsā*), reform and relief movements of all kinds, etc. Still regarded highly as a praise-worthy virtue, it has been gradually rid of its dependence on individual ethical culture by scientific conditioning in social planning on a large scale. See v. Orelli, *Die philosophischen Auffassungen des Mitleids* (1912); Scheler, *Wesen und Formen der Sympathie* (1926).—*K.F.L.*

Synaesthesia: (Gr. *syn.* with + *aesthesis,* sensation) A connection between sensation of different senses which is independent of association established by experience. For example, the capacity of certain musical notes to induce color-images.—*L.W.*

Syncategorematic (word): Approximately a synonym of *incomplete symbol* (*q.v.*), but usually applied to words of such a language as English rather than to symbols or expressions in a fully formalized logistic system. —*A.C.*

Syncretism: (Gr. *syn.,* with; and either *kretidzein,* or *kerannynai,* to mix incompatible elements) A movement to bring about a harmony of positions in philosophy or theology which are somewhat opposed or different. Earliest usage (Plutarch) in connection with the Neo-Platonic effort to unify various pagan religions in the 2nd and 4th centuries A.D. Next used in Renaissance (Bessarion) in reference to the proposed union of the Eastern and Western Catholic Churches, also denoted the contemporary movement to harmonize the philosophies of Plato and Aristotle; again in 17th century used by Georg Calixt in regard to proposed union of the Lutheran with other Protestant bodies and also with Catholicism.—*V.J.B.*

Synderesis: (Late Gr. *synteresis,* spark of conscience; may be connected with syneidesis, conscience) In Scholastic philosophy: the habitus, or permanent, inborn disposition of the mind to think of general and broad rules of moral conduct which become the principles from which a man may reason in directing his own moral activities. First used, apparently, by St. Jerome (*In Ezekiel.,* I, 4-15) as equivalent to the *scintilla conscientiae* (spark of conscience), the term became very common and received various interpretations in the 13th century. Franciscan thinkers (St. Bonaventure) tended to regard synderesis as a quality of the human will, inclining it to embrace the good-in-general. St. Thomas thought synderesis a habitus of the intellect, enabling it to know first principles of practical reasoning; he distinguished clearly between synderesis and conscience, the latter being the action of the practical intellect deciding whether a particular, proposed operation is good or bad, here and now. Duns Scotus also considered synderesis a quality belonging to intellect rather than will.—*V.J.B.*

Syndicalism: This social and political theory, usually considered as the creation of Georges Sorel, is philosophically rooted in a radical anti-intellectualism. Will, faith and action are the basic and creative realities of human nature, whereas all ideological factors are but creatures of these realities—they are 'myths.' Working upon this metaphysical assumption and upon the Marxist concept of the class struggle, Syndicalism argues that the ills and vices of bourgeois society can be eliminated only if that class which possesses the most creative power (such a class is known as the 'elite') destroys the present form of society by direct action and violence guided by the 'myth of the general strike.' The working class is, of course, taken to be this elite, and hence the trade unions, or 'syndicates,' become the center of revolution. The economic aim of the revolution is to substitute collectivism for capitalism; its political aim, to substitute 'proletarian management' through the instrumentality of the various syndicates (which represent functional interests) for political control through the instrumentality of the State. Some features of Syndicalism have been consciously incorporated into the ideology of Italian Fascism.—*M.B.M.*

Synechism: (Gr. *syn,* with; and *echein,* to hold) A theory of philosophical explanation developed, and first named by C. S. Peirce (*Monist,* II, 534). He defined the theory as: "That tendency of philosophical thought which insists upon the idea of continuity as of prime importance in philosophy, and in particular, upon the necessity of hypothesis involving true continuity" (Baldwin, *Dict. of Philos. and Psych.,* N.Y. 1902, II, 657). Continuity seems to have been the name chosen by Peirce for the complete interdependence and interrelationship of all things. An explanation is not good which relies upon an inexplicable ultimate. In this he was reacting, possibly, to such contemporary principles of explanation as Spencer's *Unknown,* and the *Absolute* of German and English Hegelianism. Synechism was no doubt an important forerunner of the Pragmatic theory of explanation, but Peirce, in describing synechism, stressed the value of generalization ("the form under which alone anything can be understood is the form of generality, which is the same thing as continuity"), much more than modern pragmatism does.—*V.J.B.*

Synechology: The doctrine that simple conscious functions correspond to composite physical events, the psycho-physical view of Fechner (*q.v.*).—*K.F.L.*

Synergism: (Gr. *syn.,* with; and *ergein,* to work) The theological position that there is more than one principle actively working in the salvation of man; the term became common in the 16th century disputes of Melancthon against the "Monergism" of Luther; Melancthon held that the Holy Spirit, the Word of God, and the human will are three co-operating principles in conversion.—*V.J.B.*

Synkatathesis: Greek noun derived from *syn,* together, and *katathesis,* to put down; hence Synkatathesis, to deposit together. In the passive voice the verb means, to assent to, to agree with. Used by the Stoics in the sense of agreement, or conviction. In general it signifies, the acknowledgment of the truth of a proposition, or consent given to it with someone else.—*J.J.R.*

Syntactics: See *Syntax, logical,* and *Semiotic* 3.

Syntagma: The systematized wholes of life views, of life tendencies such as aestheticism, naturalism and intellectualism. (Eucken).—*H.H.*

Syntax language: See *object language.*

Syntax, logical: "By the *logical syntax* of a language," according to Carnap, "we mean the formal theory of the linguistic forms of that language—the systematic statement of the formal rules which govern it together with the development of the consequences which follow from these rules. A theory, a rule, a definition, or the like is to be called *formal* when no reference is made in it either to the meaning of the symbols or to the sense of the expressions, but simply and solely to the kinds and order of the symbols from which the expressions are constructed."

This definition would make logical syntax coincide with Hilbertian *proof theory* (*q.v.*), and in fact the adjectives *syntactical, metalogical, metamathematical* are used nearly interchangeably. Carnap, however, introduces many topics not considered by Hilbert, and further treats not only the syntax of particular languages but also *general syntax,* i.e., syntax relating to all languages in general or to all languages of a given kind.

Concerning Carnap's contention that philosophical questions should be replaced by, or reformulated as syntactical questions, see *scientific empiricism* I C, and Carnap's book cited below.—*A.C.*

R. Carnap, *The Logical Syntax of Language,* New York and London, 1937. Review by S. MacLane, Bulletin of the American Mathematical Society, vol. 44 (1938), pp. 171-176. Review by S. C. Kleene, The Journal of Symbolic Logic, vol. 4 (1939), pp. 82-87.

Synthesis: 1. *In logic,* the general method of deduction or deductive reasoning, which proceeds from the simple to the complex, from the general to the particular, from the necessary to the contingent, from a principle to its application, from a general law to individual cases, from cause to effect, from an antecedent to its consequent, from a condition to the conditioned, from the logical whole to the logical part.

2. The logical composition or combination of separate elements of thought; and also the result of this process. A judgment is considered as a synthesis when its predicate is accidental or contingent with respect to the subject: as the ground of such a synthesis is experience, synthetic judgments are *a posteriori.* The Kantian doctrine of synthetic judgments *a priori* involves a synthesis between two terms, prior to experience and through the agency of the forms of our intuition or of our understanding.

3. The logical process of adding some elements to the comprehension of a concept in order to obtain its 'logical division' in contradistinction to the 'real division' which breaks up a composition by analysis.

4. The third phase in the dialectical process, combining the thesis and the antithesis for the emergence of a new level of being.

5. *In natural philosophy,* the process of combining various material elements into a new substance. The art of making or building up a compound by simpler compounds or by its elements. Also, the complex substance so formed.—*T.G.*

Synthetic Judgment: (Kant. Ger. *synthetische Urteil*) A judgment relating a subject concept with a predicate concept not included within the subject proper. The validity of such a judgment depends on its 'ground.' Kant's central question was: "Are synthetic a priori judgments possible?" See *Kantianism, Scientific Empricism.* See also *Meaning, kinds of,* 2.—*O.F.K.*

Ta: General name. "All substances necessarily call for such a name." (Neo-Mohism).—*W.T.C.*

Taboo or Tabu: Anthropological term of Polynesian origin applied to persons or things with which contacts are forbidden under severe social and religious penalties. The primitive belief in taboos, affording as it does religious sanctions for moral prohibitions, is of great ethical significance and has even been considered by some to be the origin of morality and ethics.—*L.W.*

Tabula rasa: (Literally, a blank tablet.) John Locke (1632-1704) held that human knowledge came by way of experience. The mind is like a slate upon which experience records impressions. This is a denial of innate, *a priori* knowledge.—*V.F.*

Ta i: 'The great unit,' the greatest with nothing beyond itself. (Sophism).—*H.H.*

Ta i: The Great Unit. See *t'ai i*.

T'ai Chi: (a) The Great Ultimate or Terminus, which, in the beginning of time, "engenders the Two Primary Modes (i), which in turn engender the Four Secondary Modes or Forms (hsiang), which in their turn give rise to the Eight Elements (pa kua) and the Eight Elements determine all good and evil and the great complexity of life." (Ancient Chinese philosophy).

(b) The Great Ultimate which comes from, but is originally one with, the Non-Ultimate (wu chi). Its movement and tranquillity engender the active principle, yang, and the passive principle, yin, respectively (the Two Primary Modes), the transformation and the union of which give rise to the Five Agents (wu hsing) of Water, Fire, Wood, Metal, and Earth, and thereby the determinate things. (Chou Lien-hsi, 1017-1073).

(c) The Great Ultimate which is One and unmoved, and which, when moved, becomes the Omnipotent Creative Principle (shên) which engenders Number, then Form, and finally corporeality. Being such, the Great Ultimate is identical with the Mind; it is identical with the Moral Law (tao). (Shao K'ang-chieh, 1011-1077).

(d) The Great Ultimate which is identical with the One (1), or the Grand Harmony (T'ai Ho). (Chang Hêng-ch'ü, 1020-1077).

(e) The Great Ultimate which is identical with the Reason (li) of the universe, of the two (yin and yang) vital forces (ch'i), and of the Five Elements (wu hsing). It is the Reason of ultimate goodness. "Collectively there is only one Great Ultimate, but there is a Great Ultimate in each thing." (Chu Hsi, 1130-1200).—*W.T.C.*

T'ai ch'u: At the 'great beginning' there was non-being, which had neither being nor name. (Chuang Tzu, between 399 and 295 B.C.). The great origin, or the beginning of the vital force (ch'i). (Lieh Tzŭ, third century A.D.).—*H.H.*

T'ai Ho: Grand Harmony of Infinite Harmony, the state and totality of being anterior to, but inclusive of, the Ultimate Vacuity (T'ai Hsü) and the vital force (ch'i); identical with the One (I) or the Great Ultimate (T'ai Chi). (Chang Hêng-ch'ü, 1020-1077).—*W.T.C.*

T'ai Hsu: The Ultimate Vacuity, the course, the basis and the being of the material principle, ch'i, or the universal vital force the concentration and extension of which is to the Ultimate Vacuity as ice is to water. (Chang Hêng-ch'ü, 1020-1077).—*W.T.C.*

T'ai Hsuan: The Supremely Profound Principle, "extending to and covering the myriad things without assuming any physical form, which created the universe by drawing its support from the Void, embraces the divinities, and determines the course of events." (Yang Hsiung, d. 18 B.C.).—*W.T.C.*

T'ai I: The Great Indeterminate, the state of existence before the emergence of the vital force (ch'i). (*Lieh Tzŭ*, third century A.D.).—*W.T.C.*

T'ai i: (a) The Great Unit, the Prime Force before the appearance *of* Heaven and Earth. Also called *ta i*. (Ancient Confucianism).

(b) Ultimate Oneness, which involves both Being (yu) and Non-Being (wu) (as in Chuang Tzŭ, between 399 and 295 B.C.); or "which pervades Heaven and Earth, indeterminate but simple, existing but uncreated," (As in Huainan Tzŭ, d. 122 B.C.).

(c) The Lord of Heaven (Huain-nan Tzŭ).—*W.T.C.*

T'ai Shih: The Great Beginning, the first appearance of material form.—*W.T.C.*

T'ai Su: The Great Element, the beginning of qualities of things. (*Lieh Tzŭ,* third century A.D.).—*W.T.C.*

T'ai yang: The Major Mode of Activity. See *T'ai Chi.*

T'ai yin: The Major Mode of Passivity. See: *T'ai Chi.*

Tai Tung-yüan: (Tai Chên, Tai Shên-hsiu, 1723-1777) came from a poor family, self-made to be a leader in outstanding intellectual activities of the time, and became an authority in philosophy, mathematics, and geography as well as philosophy. By reinterpreting the teachings óf Mencius, he attempted to rediscover the original meanings of Confucius and Mencius. His *Tai-shih I-shu* (works) consists of 31 *chüans* in several volumes.—*W.T.C.*

Ta Ku: Major cause. See: *ku.*

Talmud; (Learning) An encyclopedic work in Hebrew-Aramaic produced during 800 years (300 B.C.-500 A.D.) in Palestine and Babylon. Its six *sedarim* (orders) subdivided in 63 massektot (tractates) represent the oral traditional of Judaism expounding and developing the religious ideas and civil laws of the written special hermeneutic *middot* (measures) of law (i.e., the Hebrew Bible) by means of Rabbi Hillel, 13 of R. Ishmael and 32 of R. Eliezer of Galilee.

However, more than a mere commentary on the old testament, it is a veritable storehouse of ancient Jewish philosophy, theology, history, ethics, sciences, folklore, etc., that accumulated during those eventful eight centuries. The Talmud consists of an older layer, the *Mishnah* (*q.v.*) compiled in Palestine (200 A.D.) and younger layer—*the Gemara* (*q.v.*) as commentary on the former. The Gemara produced in Palestine together with the Mishnah is known as the Jerusalem Talmud (*q.v.*) and the Gemara produced in Babylon together with the same Mishnah is known as the Babylonian Talmud.

﹒Contemporary with the Talmud developed a somehow similar literature closely related to the text of the Hebrew Bible and known as Midrash (interpretation), containing both halakah (law) and aggada (homily).—*H.L.G.*

Talmud, Babylonian: The Palestine Mishna was carried to Babylon and studied by seven generations of Amoraim in the Academies of Nehardea (under Samuel).—*H.L.G.*

Talmud, Palestinian: Was arranged first by Rabbi Johanan (d. 279 A.D.) and finally compiled early in the 5th century. It is based on the Mishnah of R. Judah as interpreted in the academies of Lydda, Caesaria, Sepphoris and Tiberias (closed 425 A.D.). Its Gemaras extend presently only over 39 of the 63 tractates of the Mishnah, but it is assumed that many Gemaras were lost during the many persecutions.

In the latest edition, the Palestine Talmud occupies ca. 2663 pages.

Wherever opinions differ, it is the Babylonian Talmud that is considered as authoritative for the Jews.

A complete manuscript of the Palestinian Talmud is found in the Leiden Library, and from it was printed its first edition by Bomberg, Venice, 1523-24.—*H.L.G.*

Tamas: (Skr.) One of the three *guṇas* (*q.v.*) of the Sāṅkhya (*q.v.*), representing the principle of inactivity, sluggishness. and indifference in matter or *prakṛti* (*q.v.*).—*K.F.L.*

T'an: The opposite of 'grossness;' remaining detached from all outside things; the climax of fineness. It is to have in oneself no contraries; the climax of purity, in the sense of 'unmixedness.' (Chuang Tzŭ, between 399 and 295 B.C.).—*H.H.*

Tanmātra: (Skr.) One of the five "subtile elements" in the philosophy of the Sāṅkhya (*q.v.*) and other systems, corresponding to the matter apprehended in the sensation of sound, touch, color, taste, and smell; generally, the manifold of sensory experience, perhaps also the "reals," or sensation-generals, equivalent to *bhūtamātra* (*q.v.*).—*K.F.L.*

Tantra: (Skr.) One of a large number of treatises reflecting non-indogermanic Hindu and Mongolian influence, composed in the form of dialogues between Shiva (*q.v.*) and Durgā (see *Śakti*) on problems of ritual, magic, philosophy, and other branches of knowledge. The Tantras, outside the main current of Vedic (*q.v.*) thinking yet sharing many of the deepest speculations, stress cult and teach the supremacy of the female principle as power or *śakti* (see *Shaktism*).—*K.F.L.*

Tantric: Adjective to Tantra (*q.v.*).

Tao: (a) The Way; principle; cosmic order; nature. "The Tao that can be expressed in words is not the eternal Tao." It is "vague and eluding," "deep and obscure," but "there is in it the form" and "the essence." "In it is reality." It "produced the One; the One produced the two; the two produced the three; and the three produced all things." Its "standard is the Natural." (Lao Tzŭ).

"Tao has reality and evidence but no action nor form. It may be transmitted, but cannot be received. It may be attained, but cannot be seen. It is its own essence, and its own root." "Tao operates, and results follow." "Tao has no limit." "It is in the ant," "a tare," "a potsherd," "ordure." (Chuang Tzŭ, between 399 and 295 B.C.).

(b) The Confucian "Way;" the teachings of the sage; the moral order; the moral life; truth; the moral law; the moral principle. This means "the fulfillment of the law of our human nature." It is the path of man's moral life. "True manhood (jên) is that by which a man is to be a man. Generally speaking, it is the moral law." (Mencius, 371-289 B.C.). "To proceed according to benevolence and righteousness is called the Way." (Han Yü, 767-824).

(c) The Way, which means following the Reason of things, and also the Reason which is in everything and which everything obeys. (Neo Confucianism).

(d) The Way or Moral Law in the cosmic sense, signifying "what is above the realm of corporeality," and the "successive movement of the active (yang) and the passive principles (yin)." In the latter sense as understood both in ancient Confucianism and in Neo-Confucianism, it is interchangeable with the Great Ultimate (T'ai Chi). Shao K'ang-chieh (1011-1077) said that "The Moral Law is the Great Ultimate." Chang Hêng-ch'ü (1022-1077) identified it with the Grand Harmony (Ta Ho) and said that "from the operation of the vital force (ch'i) there is the Way." This means that the Way is the principle of being as well as the sum total of the substance and functions of things. To Ch'eng I-ch'uan (1033-1107) "There is no Way independent of the active (yang) principle and the passive (yin) principle. Yet it is precisely the Way that determines the active and passive principles. These principles are the constituents of the vital force (ch'i), which is corporeal. On the other hand, the Way transcends corporeality." To Chu Hsi (1130-1200), the Way is "the Reason why things are as they are." Tai Tung-yüan (1723-1777) understood it to mean "the incessant transformation of the universe," and "the operation of things in the world, involving the constant flow of the vital force (ch'i) and change, and unceasing production and reproduction."—W.T.C.

Tao chia: The Taoist school, the followers of Lao Tzu, Chuang Tzu, Lieh Tzu, etc., who "urged men to unity of spirit, teaching that all activities should be in harmony with the unseen (Tao), with abundant liberality toward all things in nature. As to method, they accept the orderly sequence of nature from the Yin Yang school, select the good points of Confucianists and Mohists, and combine with these the important points of the Logicians and Legalists. In accordance with the changes of the seasons, they respond to the development of natural objects."

"By studying the principles of success and failure, preservation and destruction, calamity and prosperity from ancient to recent times, they learn how to hold what is essential and to grasp the fundamental. They guard themselves with purity and emptiness, in humility and weakness they maintain themselves . . . Afterwards those who act without restraint desired to reject learning and the rules of propriety, and at the same time, discard benevolence and righteousness. They said that the world could be governed simply by purity and emptiness."

"To regard the fundamental as the refined essence and to regard things as its coarse embodiment; to regard accumulation as deficiency; to dwell quietly and alone with the spiritual and the intelligent; these were some aspects of the system of Tao of the ancients . . . They built their system upon the principle of the eternal Non-Being and centered it upon the idea of Ultimate Unity. Their outward expression was weakness and humility. Pure emptiness without injury to objective things was for them true substance. Kuan Yin said, 'Establish nothing in regard to oneself. Let things be what they are; move like water; be tranquil like a mirror; respond like an echo. Pass quickly like the non-existent; be quiet like purity. . .'Lao Tan (Lao Tzŭ) said, 'Know manhood (active force), and preserve womanhood (passive force); become the ravine of the world. Know whiteness (glory); endure blackness (disgrace); become a model of the world.' Men all seek the first; he alone took the last . . . Men all seek for happiness; he alone

sought contentment in adaptation . . . He regarded the deep as the fundamental; moderation as the rule. . ."

"Silent and therefore formless, changing and therefore impermanent, now dead, now living, equal with Heaven and Earth, moving with the spiritual and the intelligent, disappearing—where? Suddenly—whither? . . . These were some aspects of the system of Tao of the ancients. Chuang Chow (Chuang Tzŭ) heard of them and was delighted . . . He had personal communion with the spirit of Heaven and Earth but no sense of pride in his superiority to all things. He did not condemn either right or wrong, so he was at ease with the world . . . Above he roams with the Creator; below he makes friends of those who transcend beginning and end and make no distinctions between life and death . . ."—W.T.C.

Tao chiao: The Taoist religion, or the religion which was founded on the exotic interpretation of the teachings of the Yellow Emperor and Lao Tzŭ (Huang Lao) that flourished in the Han dynasty (206 B.C.-220 A.D.), which assimilated the Yin Yang philosophy, the practice of alchemy, and the worship of natural objects and immortals, and which became highly elaborated through wholesale imitation of the Buddhist religion.—W.T.C.

Tao Hsueh: The "Moral Law" School, See: li hüeh. —W.T.C.

Taoism: See Tao chia and Chinese philosophy.

Tao shu: The essence of Tao, or the axis of Tao at the center of which all Infinities converge and all distinctions disappear. (Chuang Tzŭ, between 399 and 295 B.C.).—W.T.C.

Tapas: (Skr. heat) Austerity, penance; intense application of Yoga (q.v.).—K.F.L.

Tarka: (Skr.) Reasoning, logic; also a name for the Nyāya (q.v.).—K.F.L.

Ta shun: Complete harmony, as a result of the Profound Virtue or Mysterious Power. See hsüan tê.—W.T.C.

Taste: a. The faculty of judging art without rules, through sensation and experience.

b. The ensemble of preferences shown by an artist in his choice of elements from nature and tradition, for his works of art.—L.V.

Ta te: Universally recognized moral qualities of man, namely, wisdom (chih), moral character (jên), and courage (yung). (Confucianism).—W.T.C.

Ta t'i: "The part of man which is great." (Mencius).—H.H.

Tattva: (Skr.) "Thatness," "whatness," one of the principles ranging from abstract factors of conscious life to relations and laws governing natural facts. The Trika (q.v.), knows 36 tattvas which come into play when the universe "unfolds," i.e., is created by Shiva in an act variously symbolized by the awakening of his mind, or a "shining forth" (see ābhāsea).—K.F.L.

Tat tvam asi: (Skr.) "That art thou," the sum and substance of the instruction which Śvetaketu received from his father Uddālaka Aruni, according to the Chāndogya Upanishad. It hints the identity of the self, ātman, with the essence of the world as the real, satya.—K.F.L.

Ta t'ung: (a) The period of Great Unity and Harmony; the Confucian Utopia. (Early Confucianism; K'ang Yu-wei, 1858-1929).

(b) The Great Unity, Heaven and Earth and all things forming an organic unity. (Ancient Chinese philosophy).—*W.T.C.*

Ta t'ung i: The great similarity-and-difference; all things are in one way all similar, in another way all different (Sophists).—*H.H.*

Tauler, Johannes: (1300-1361) was an outstanding German mystic and preacher. Born in Strassburg, he entered the Dominican Order and did his philosophical and theological studies at Cologne, where he was probably influenced by Eckhart. He was most interested in the ethical and religious aspects of mysticism, and, like Eckhart, he concentrated on an analytical intuition of his own consciousness in his endeavor to grasp the immanent reality of God. *Die Predigten Taulers;* ed. F. Vetter, (Berlin, 1910) is the most recent edition of his sermons.—*V.J.B.*

Tautology: As a syntactical term of the propositional calculus this is defined in the article on *logic, formal* (*q.v.*). Wittgenstein and Ramsey proposed to extend the concept of a tautology to disciplines involving quantifiers, by interpreting a quantified expression as a multiple (possibly infinite) conjunction or disjunction; under this extension, however, it no longer remains true that the test of a tautology is effective.

The name *law of tautology* is given to either of the two dually related theorems of the propositional calculus,

$$[p \vee p] \equiv p, \qquad pp \equiv p,$$

or either of the two corresponding dually related theorems of the algebra of classes,

$$a \cup a = a, \qquad a \cap a = a.$$

Whitehead and Russell reserve the name *principle of tautology* for the theorem of the propositional calculus, $[p \vee p] \supset p$, but use *law of tautology* in the above nses.—*A.C.*

L. Wittgenstein, *Tractatus Logico-Philosophicus,* New York and London, 1922. F. P. Ramsey, *The foundations of mathematics,* Proceedings of the London Mathematical Society, ser. 2, vol. 25 (1926), pp. 338-384; reprinted in his book of the same title, New York and London, 1931.

Taylor, Alfred Edward: (1869-1945) Professor of philosophy at St. Andrews and Edinburgh, after teaching for many years at Oxford. Taylor's metaphysics were predominantly Hegelian and idealist (as in *Elements of Metaphysics*) during his early years; in later years (as in numerous essays in *Mind,* and his Gifford Lectures *Faith of a Moralist*) he has become something of a neo-scholastic, although he follows no school exclusively. In his Gifford Lectures he argues from moral experience to God; in other essays, he declares that grounds for belief are found in cosmology, in conscience and in religious experience. As an Anglo-Catholic, he has given (in volume two of his Giffords) a learned apologia for this position, on philosophical grounds.—*W.N.P.*

Te: (a) Virtue; power; character; efficacy—The Individual Principle, Tao particularized or inherent in a thing, the "abode of Tao," through "the obtaining of which" a thing becomes what it is.

(b) Virtue, moral character, "that which obtains in a person;" "that which is sufficient in the self without depending on any external help," referring particularly to benevolence and righteousness which are natural to man (Han Yü, 767-824 A.D.).

(c) Kindness.

Techne: (Gr. *techne*) The set of principles, or rational method, involved in the production of an object or the accomplishment of an end; the knowledge of such principles or method; art. Techne resembles episteme in implying knowledge of principles, but differs in that its aim is making or doing, not disinterested understanding.—*G.R.M.*

Teichmüller, Gustav: (1832-1888) Strongly influenced by Leibniz and Lotze and anticipating some recent philosophic positions, taught a thoroughgoing personalism by regarding the "I," given immediately in experience as a unit, as the real substance, the world of ideas a projection of its determinations (perspectivism). Nature is appearance, substantiality being ascribed to it only in analogy to the "I." Consciousness and knowledge are clearly separated, the latter being specific and semiotic. Reality is interpreted monadologically.—*K.F.L.*

Teilhard de Chardin, Pierre: (1881-1955) French Jesuit scientist whose research in China led to the discovery of Peking man, he wrote *The Phenomenon of Man* (*Le Phénomène humain,* 1938-40), which argues for the reality of a spiritual evolution in which humanity and the whole universe aim toward an "omega point." That is, a thinking layer has been imposed upon the biological layer. A world culture will develop and a super-personal psychic consciousness will emerge through the influence of love.—*S.E.N.*

Telegnosis: (Gr. *tēle,* at a distance—*gnosis,* knowledge) Knowledge of another mind which is presumably not mediated by the perception of his body nor by any other physical influence by which communication between minds is ordinarily mediated. See *Intersubjective Intercourse, Telepathy.*—*L.W.*

Telegnostic situations: "Cognitive situations in which a mental event belonging to another mind is the sole objective constituent." (Broad).—*H.H.*

Telegram Argument: Argument for the efficacy of mind resting on a radical difference of response to two slightly differing stimuli because of their difference of meaning. The Telegram Argument is so called because of the illustration of two telegrams: "Our son has been killed" and "Your son has been killed" received by parents whose son is away from home and whose difference of reading depends only on the presence or absence of the letter "Y." See C. D. Broad, *The Mind and its Place in Nature,* pp. 118 ff.

Teleoklin: Adjective meaning, tending toward a purpose; used in German by Oskar Kohnstamm, born in 1871. He held that *Teleoklise,* the inclination toward purposive activity, is a characteristic of all life.—*J.J.R.*

Teleological Argument for God: (Gr. *telos,* end or purpose) Sometimes referred to as the argument from design. Events, objects, or persons are alleged to reveal a kind of relationship which suggests a purpose or end toward which they move. Such ends reveal a Fashioner or Designer who guides and directs toward the fulfillment of their functions. This Architect is God. Paley (1745-1805) in his *Natural Theology* is a classic expositor of the argument. Kant favored the argument, but held that it leaned too heavily upon the cosmological argument which in turn rested upon the ontological, both of which crumbled when critical analysis was applied.—*V.F.*

Teleological ethics: A species of axiological ethics which makes the determination of the rightness of an action wholly dependent on an estimate of its actual probable conduciveness to some end or of its actual or probable productiveness, directly or indirectly, of the maximum good. E.g., utilitarianism.—*W.K.F.*

Teleological Idealism: Name given by Lotze for his system of semi-monistic personalism.—*W.L.*

Teleological Personalism: The doctrine that God is to be thought of not as First, but as Final Cause. Applied to Lotze and Howison.—*R.T.F.*

Teleology: (Gr. *telos,* end, completion) The theory of purpose, ends, goals, final causes, values, the Good (*q.v.*). The opposite of Mechanism. As opposed to mechanism, which explains the present and the future in terms of the past, teleology explains the past and the present in terms of the future. Teleology as such does not imply personal consciousness, volition, or intended purpose (*q.v.*).

1. Physics, Biology: See *Vitalism.*

2. Psychology: See *Hormic, Instinct, Hedonism, Voluntarism.*

3. Epistemology: the view that mind is guided or governed by purposes, values, interests, "instinct," as well as by "factual," "objective" or logical evidence in its pursuit of truth (see *Fideism, Voluntarism, Pragmatism, Will-to-believe, Value judgment*).

4. Metaphysics: The doctrine that reality is ordered by goals, ends, purposes, values, formal or final causes (*q.v.*).

5. Ethics: The view that the standard of human life is value, the Good, rather than duty, law, or formal decorum.—*W.L.*

Teleosis: Noun used in German by Ernst Haeckel (1834-1919) denoting organic improvement or perfection.—*J.J.R.*

Telepathy: (Gr. *tēle,* at a distance + *pathein,* to experience) The phenomenon of direct communication between two minds separated by a great distance and without the normal operation of the organs of sense. Telepathy is a subvariety of telegnosis (see *Telegnosis*) which is characterized by its felt directness or immediacy.—*L.W.*

Telesio, Bernardino: (1508-1588) was one of the Fathers of the scientific movement of the Renaissance. He was born at Cosenza, near Naples, studied philosophy and mathematics at Padua, and natural science at Rome. The Academia Telesiana, which he founded at Naples, stressed empirical methods and Telesio tried to explain all physical phenomena in terms of heat and cold, as expanding and contracting forces in matter. He wrote: *De Natura rerum juxta propria principia* (1570), ed. V. Spampanato, 2 vol. (Moderna-Genoa, 1911-13).—*V.J.B.*

Telos: (Gr. *telos*) The end term of a process; specifically, in Aristotle, the purpose of final cause. See *Aristotelianism.*—*G.R.M.*

Temple, William: (1881-1944) For many years Archbishop of York, Temple has written extensively on the philosophy of religion. In *Mens Creatrix* and most recently in *Nature Man and God,* he has argued for a universe of levels, culminating in value, and pointing to God as Supreme Value and hence Ultimate Reality. Recent work on the nature of revelation has given him the definition of revelation as "coincidence of divinely guided event and divinely guided apprehension;" in this setting he places (see *Christ the Truth*) the Incarnation as central and most significant event apprehended by the Christian community. He is a Platonist in tendency, although within recent years this has been modified by scholasticism, and a study of Marxian philosophy. —*W.N.P*

Tension: Since normal mental life oscillates between two extremes: a plane of action in which sensori-motor functions occur, and a plane of dream, in which we live our imaginative life, of which memory is a major part, there are as many corresponding intermediate planes as there are degrees of 'attention to life,' adaptation to reality. The mind has a power *sui generis* to produce contractions and expansions of itself. Calling attention to the need of distinguishing various heights of tension or 'tones' in psychic life, Bergson interprets the life of the universe and the life of human personality in terms of tension.—*H.H.*

Term: In common English usage the word "term" is syntactical or semantical in character, and means simply a word (or phrase), or a word associated with its meaning. The phrase "undefined term" as used in mathematical postulate theory (see *mathematics*) is perhaps best referred to this common meaning of "term." In traditional logic, a term is a concept appearing as *subject* or *predicate* (*q.v.*), of a categorical proposition; also, a word or phrase denoting such a concept. The word "term" has also been employed in a syntactical sense in various special developments of *logistic systems* (*q.v.*), usually in a way suggested by the traditional usage.

The mathematical use of the word "term" appears in such phrases as "the terms of a sum" (i.e., the separate numbers which are added to form the sum, or the expressions for them), "the terms of a polynomial," "the terms of a proportion," "the terms of an infinite series," etc. Similarly one may speak of "the terms of a logical sum," and the like.—*A.C.*

Terminism: See *Nominalism.*

Tertiary Qualities: Those qualities which are said to be imparted to objects by the mind. In contrast to primary and secondary qualities which are directed toward the objects (primary being thought of distinctly a part of objects) tertiary qualities are the subject's reactions to them. A thing, for example, is said to be good: The good points to the subject's reaction rather than to the object itself.—*V.F.*

Tertii adjacentis: Latin expression employed to describe a proposition in which the subject, predicate, and copula are clearly distinguishable.—*J.J.R.*

Tertium comparationis: (Lat.) A basis of comparison.—*V.J.B.*

Tertium non datur: See *Excluded middle, law of*.

Tertium quid: (Lat.) A third something; a term to be discovered in addition to two original ones.—*V.J.B.*

Tertullian: (165-220) A prominent Christian Apologist, later the leader of the sect of the Montanists. He took an excessively dogmatic position toward faith, regarded it as standing above reason, and expressed the attitude in his famous statement "Credo quia absurdum est." Cf. Migne PL (vols. 1, 2).—*R.B.W.*

Tetractys: Literally the Greek term signifies, an aggregate of four; specifically it was applied to the Pythagorean perfect number, ten, which is the sum of one, two, three, and four.—*J.J.R.*

Thales: 6th Cent. B.C.; of the Milesian School of Greek Philosophy; is said to have predicted the eclipse of 585; had probably been to Egypt and was proficient in mathematics and physics. Thales, along with the other cosmological thinkers of the Ionian school, presupposed a single elementary cosmic matter at the base of the transformations of nature and declared this to be water.—*M.F.*

Thanatism: A term employed by Ernst Haeckel (1834-1919) to express his doctrine of the mortality and annihilation of the human soul; the contrary of athanatism, immortality.—*J.J.R.*

Theism: (Gr. *theos,* god) Is in general that type of religion or religious philosophy (see *Religion, Philosophy of*) which incorporates a conception of God as a unitary being, thus may be considered equivalent to monotheism. The speculation as to the relation of God to world gave rise to three great forms: God identified with world in pantheism (rare with emphasis on God); God, once having created the world, relatively disinterested in it, in deism (mainly an 18th cent. phenomenon); God working in and through the world, in theism proper. Accordingly, God either coincides with the world, is external to it (*deus ex machina*), or is immanent. The more personal human-like God, the more theological the theism, the more appealing to a personal adjustment in prayer, worship, etc., which presuppose either that God, being like man, may be swayed in his decision, has no definite plan, or subsists in the very stuff man is made of (humanistic theism). Immanence of God entails agency in the world, presence, revelation, involvement in the historic process; it has been justified by Hindu and Semitic thinkers, Christian apologetics, ancient and modern metaphysical idealists, and by natural science philosophers. Transcendency of God removes him from human affairs, renders fellowship and communication in Church ways ineffectual, yet preserves God's majesty and absoluteness such as is postulated by philosophies which introduce the concept of God for want of a terser term for the ultimate, principal reality. Like Descartes and Spinoza, they allow the personal in God to fade and approach the age-old Indian pantheism evident in much of Vedic and post-Vedic philosophy in which the personal pronoun may be the only distinguishing mark between metaphysical logic and theology, similarly as in Hegel. The endowment postulated of God lends character to a theistic system of philosophy. Much of Hindu and Greek philosophy stresses the knowledge and reason aspect of the deity, thus producing an epistemological theism; Aristotle, in conceiving him as the prime mover, started a teleological one; mysticism is psychologically oriented in its theism, God being a feeling reality approachable in appropriate emotional states. The theism of religious faith is unquestioning and pragmatic in its attitude toward God; theology has often felt the need of offering proofs for the existence of God (see *God*), thus tending toward an ontological theism; metaphysics incorporates occasionally the concept of God as a thought necessity, advocating a logical theism. Kant's critique showed the respective fields of pure philosophic enquiry and theistic speculations with their past in historic creeds. Theism is left a possibility in agnosticism (*q.v.*). —*K.F.L.*

In discussions of religion, syn. for the belief in a personal God. God is here usually conceived of as Creator, as having brought into existence realities *other than* himself which, though he is not completely (although for certain purposes, partly) dependent upon them, nevertheless are dependent upon him. Theism has characteristically held to a combination of both the transcendence and immanence of God.—*V.F.*

Theistic Personalism: The theory most generally held by Personalists that God is the ground of all being, immanent in and transcendent over the whole world of reality. It is pan-psychic but avoids pantheism by asserting the complementary nature of immanence and transcendence which come together in and are in some degree essential to all personality. The term used for the modern form of theism. Immanence and transcendence are the contraplates of personality.—*R.T.F.*

Thelematism: Noun derived from the Greek, *thelema*, will. The equivalent of voluntarism, employed in German, scarcely, if at all, in English.—*J.J.R.*

Thelematology: (from Gr. *thelema*, will) The doctrine of the nature and phenomenology of the will.—*K.F.L.*

Thema: A term proposed by *Burgersdicius* to indicate a sign which signifies its object directly as a result of a convention or intellectual insight without the necessity of factual connection in previous experience.—*C.A.B.*

Theocracy: (Gr. *theos*, god; *kratos*, government, power) A view of political organization in which God is sole ruler. All political laws come under what is held to be the Divine Will. Church and State become one. Examples: the development of the Hebrew ideal and Judaism;

Mohammedan politics; Calvinism in Geneva; Puritan New England.—*V.F.*

Theocrasy: (Gr. *theos* god; *krasis* a mixture)

a) A mixture of the worship of different gods.

b) The intimate union of the soul with God in contemplation as in Neo-Platonism.—*V.F.*

Theodicy: (Gr. *theos,* god; *dike,* justice) The technical term for the problem of justifying the character of a good, creative and responsible God in the face of such doubts as arise by the fact of evil. If God is good, why evil?—*V.F.*

Title of Leibniz's essay on evil (*Essai de Théodicée*).

Theology: (Gr. *theos,* god; *logos,* study) Simply stated, theology is a study of the question of God and the relation of God to the world of reality. Theology, in the widest sense of the term, is a branch of philosophy, *i.e.,* a special field of philosophical inquiry having to do with God. However, the term is widely employed to mean the theoretical expression of a particular religion. In the latter sense, theology becomes "Christian," "Jewish," "Presbyterian," "Reformed," etc. When thus employed, theology becomes in a narrow sense "historic," "systematic," "polemic," "ecclesiastical," "apologetic," etc.,—phases of theoretical discussions within a particular religious faith. Theology need not have any necessary reference to religion; it may be a purely theoretical discussion about God and God's relation to the world on a disinterested plane of free inquiry.—*V.F.*

Theomachy: (Gr. *theoi, machein,* battle against the gods), a term implying opposition to the divine will.—*K.F.L.*

Theophany: (Gr. *theos,* God; *phaino,* to appear) The manifestation of God to man by actual appearance.—*V.F.*

Theophrastus: (370-287 B.C.), the most important disciple and friend of Aristotle, left voluminous writings of which only fragments are extant; they dealt with many topics of philosophy and science (notably, botany) and defended his master's philosophy against rival schools of thought, particularly against Stoics. Cf. *Characters of Theophrastus.*—*R.B.W.*

Theorem: (Gr. *theorema,* a sight, theory, theorem) Any proposition which is demonstrated in terms of other more basic propositions.—*A.C.B.*

Theoretical Reason: (Kant. Ger. *Theoretische Vernunft*) Reflective thought dealing with cognition, knowledge and science. Contrasted with practical reason (*q.v.*) which is concerned with moral and religious intuitions. See *Kantianism.*—*O.F.K.*

Theory: (Gr. *theoria,* viewing) The hypothetical universal aspect of anything. For Plato, a contemplated truth. For Aristotle, pure knowledge as opposed to the practical. An abstraction from practice. The principle from which practice proceeds. Opposite of: practice.—*J.K.F.*

(1) Hypothesis. More loosely: supposition, whatever is problematic, verifiable but not verified.

(2) (As opposed to practice): systematically organized knowledge of relatively high generality. (See *"the theory of light"*).

(3) (As opposed to laws and observations): explanation. The deduction of the axioms and theorems of one system from assertions (not necessarily verified) from another system and of a relatively less problematic and more intelligible nature.

(Note: Since criteria of what is 'intelligible' and 'problematic' are subjective and liable to fluctuation, any definition of the term is bound to be provisional. It might be advisable to distinguish between *laws* (general statements in a system), *principles* (axioms), and *theories* (methods for deriving the axioms by means of appropriate definitions employing terms from other systems).—*M.B.*

Theosis: The ultimate absorption of the soul into Deity.—*V.F.*

Theosophy: (Gr., lit. "divine wisdom") is a term introduced in the third century by Ammonius Saccas, the master of Plotinus, to identify a recurring tendency prompted often by renewed impulses from the Orient, but implicit in mystery schools as that of Eleusis, among the Essenes and elsewhere. Theosophy differs from speculative philosophy in allowing validity to some classes of mystical experience as regard soul and spirit, and in recognizing clairvoyance and telepathy and kindred forms of perception as linking the worlds of psyche and body. Its content describes a transcendental field as the only real (approximating to Brahman, Nous, and Pleroma) from which emerge material universes in series, with properties revealing that supreme Being. Two polarities appear as the first manifesting stage, consciousness or spirit (Brahma, Chaos, Holy Ghost), and matter or energy (Śiva, Logos, Father). Simultaneously, life appears clothed in matter and spirit, as form or species (Vishnu, Cosmos, Son). In a sense, life is the direct reflection of the transcendent supreme, hence biological thinking has a privileged place in Theosophy. Thus, cycles of life are perceived in body, psyche, soul and spirit. The lesser of these is reincarnation of impersonal soul in many personalities. A larger epoch is "the cycle of necessity," when spirit evolves over vast periods.—*F.K.*

Thesis: (Gr. *thesis*) In Aristotle's logic (1) an undemonstrated proposition used as a premiss in a syllogism, sometimes distinguished from axiom in that it need not be self-evident or intrinsically necessary; (2) any proposition contrary to general opinion but capable of being supported by reasoning. See *Antithesis, Dialectic, Synthesis.*—*G.R.M.*

Thetics: (from Grk. *Thetikos*) According to Kant the sum total of all affirmations.—*K.F.L.*

Theurgy: (Gr. *Theos,* god; *ergon,* work) The work of some divine, supernatural agency in the affairs of men, generally by direct intervention.—*V.F.*

Thnetopsychite: (Gr.) One who confesses the doctrine that the soul dies when the body dies and rises when it is resurrected.—*K.F.L.*

Thought-Transference: Equivalent to Telegnosis. See *Telegnosis.*—*L.W.*

Thoreau, Henry David: (1817-1862) One of the leading American transcendentalists, of the Concord group.

He was a thoroughgoing individualist, most famous for the attempts to be self-sufficient that he recounts so brilliantly in his diaries, lectures, essays and expositions, such as the famous "Walden."—*L.E.D.*

Ti: (a) The Confucian anthropomorphic Lord or Supreme Lord (Shang Ti), almost interchangeable with Heaven (T'ien) except that Ti refers to the Lord as the directing and governing power whereas Heaven refers to the Lord in the sense of omnipresence and all-inclusiveness.

(b) The world-honored deities (such as those of the four directions and the Five Elements).

(c) Mythological sovereigns whose virtues approximate those of Heaven and Earth.—*W.T.C.*

Ti: Also t'i.

(a) Respect for elders. See: *hsiao*.

(b) Brotherliness.

(c) Younger brother.—*W.T.C.*

T'i: Generic relationship or part and whole relationship, one of the proofs of agreement. See: *Mo chê.*—*W.T.C.*

Ti chih tse: 'The pattern of the Lord', by which is meant the political and social regulations instituted by the supreme ruler or emperor on high. (Taoism).—*H.H.*

T'ien: A material or physical sky, spoken in opposition to earth; a ruling or presiding Heaven, anthropomorphic by nature; a fatalistic heaven, one equivalent to Nature; an ethical heaven, one having a moral principle and which is the highest primordial principle of the universe.—*H.H.*

T'ien chü: The 'evolution of nature' is the change things undergo from one form to another, the beginning and end of whose changes are like a circle, in which no part is any more the beginning than another part. (Chuang Tzǔ, between 399 and 295 B.C.). The mind is the 'natural ruler'. (Hsün Tzǔ, c. 335—288 B.C.).—*H.H.*

T'ien i: The evolution of nature is the 'boundary of nature'. (Chuang Tzǔ, between 399 and 295 B.C.).—*H.H.*

T'ien jen: The heavenly man, one "who is not separated from The Natural." (Taoism).—*W.T.C.*

T'ien li: (a) Heaven-endowed nature.

(b) The Reason of Heaven; the Divine Law; the moral principle of Heaven which is embodied in benevolence, righteousness, propriety, and wisdom (ssŭ tuan) (Chu Hsi, 1130-1200); the Law of Nature, which is the Reason (li) in all things and is impartial. (Tai Tung-yüan, 1723-1777).—*W.T.C.*

T'ien ti: Heaven and Earth:

(a) as the universe;

(b) as the origin of life;

(c) as the consolation of the pure and impure vital forces (ch'i) respectively;

(d) as the active or male (yang) and the passive or female (yin) phases of the universe, respectively.—*W.T.C.*

Timarchy: (Gr.) A type of government characterized by voluntary or acclamatory rule of worthy and competent men, not aristocrats.—*K.F.L.*

Time: The general medium in which all events take place in succession or appear to take place in succes-

sion. All specific and finite periods of time, whether past, present or future, constitute merely parts of the entire and single Time. Common-sense interprets Time vaguely as something moving toward the future or as something in which events point in that direction. But the many contradictions contained in this notion have led philosophers to postulate doctrines purporting to eliminate some of the difficulties implied in common-sense ideas. The first famous but unresolved controversy arose in Ancient Greece, between Parmenides, who maintained that change and becoming were irrational illusions, and Heraclitus, who asserted that there was no permanence and that change characterized everything without exception. Another great controversy arose centuries later between disciples of Newton and Leibniz. According to Newton, time was independent of, and prior to, events; in his own words, "absolute time, and mathematical time, of itself, and from its own nature, flows equably without regard to anything external." According to Leibniz, on the other hand, there can be no time independent of events: for time is formed by events and relations among them, and constitutes the universal order of succession. It was this latter doctrine which eventually gave rise to the doctrine of space-time, in which both space and time are regarded as two systems of relations, distinct from a perceptual standpoint, but inseparably bound together in reality. All these controversies led many thinkers to believe that the concept of time cannot be fully accounted for, unless we distinguish between perceptual, or subjective, time, which is confined to the perceptually shifting 'now' of the present, and conceptual, or objective, time, which includes all periods of time and in which the events we call past, present and future can be mutually and fixedly related. See *Becoming, Change, Duration, Persistence, Space-Time.*—*R.B.W.*

Time-Arrow: The general direction of change in time; is supposed to point toward the future. The concept was suggested by A. S. Eddington.—*R.B.W.*

Timeless: Having no end in time, pertaining to no time, or transcending time.—*R.B.W.*

Time-perception: The apprehension of the protensive or durational character of the data of experience. See *Dimensions of Consciousness; Protensity.*—*L.W.*

Timology: (Gr. *time,* esteem, dignity; *logos,* study of) A term meaning a study of excellence or worth. More particularly, the term refers to a theory of value which holds that value has an intrinsic worth apart from considerations of any particular point of view. Opposed, e.g., to the view that value is relative to an individual. A notable expounder of the timological view in theory of value is G. E. Moore.—*V.F.*

Timon of Phlius: (320-230 B.C.) A sceptic who held that an ultimate knowledge of things was beyond man's capacity. Author of *Silloi.* See *Pyrrho,* teacher of Timon.—*M.F.*

Tone: (Music) The larger intervals in diatonic scale.

(Painting) The modification of colors through the general effect of light and shade.—*L.V.*

Topics: (Gr. *Topika*) The title of a treatise by Aristotle on dialectical reasoning, so named because the material is grouped into convenient topoi, or common-places of argument, useful in examining an opponent's assertions. See *Dialectic*.—*G.R.M.*

Totemism: (*Totem*, of Ojibway origin) A feature of primitive social organization whereby the members of a tribe possess group solidarity by virtue of their association with a class of animals or in some cases plants or inanimate objects. The primitive conception of the totem as the essential unity and solidarity among the different members of a class of men and of animals may have prepared the way for the philosophical doctrine of substantival universals and of the participation of many individuals in a single universal.—*L.W.*

Totum divisum: Latin expression denoting a whole having some kind of unity, which is to be divided, or is capable of division. Thus a logical whole, some general idea, may be broken up into smaller classes, or members, according to some principle of division, or point of view.—*J.J.R.*

Toulmin, Stephen Edelston: (1922–) Born in England. Formerly Professor of Philosophy at the University of Leeds. Currently Professor of Social Thought, of Philosophy, and in the Divinity School at The University of Chicago.

Toulmin has had an extremely varied career, writing on a wide range of subjects. His early work, *Place of Reason in Ethics* (1950), was the first book on ethics to present the viewpoint of modern linguistic analysis. His later book, *Human Understanding*, Vol. I (1972), is an attempt to adapt the categories of the theory of biological evolution to the problem of the evolution of conceptual systems (see *Paradigm*).

Place of Reason in Ethics (1950); *Philosophy of Science: An Introduction* (1953); *The Uses of Argument* (1958); *Human Understanding*, Vol. I (1972).—*T.P.S.*

Trace Theory of Memory: Physiological explanation of memory through the conservation of traces in the nervous system. Opposed to the theory of Mnemic causation. See *Mnemic Causation*.—*L.W.*

Traditionalism: In French philosophy of the early nineteenth century, the doctrine that the truth—particularly religious truth—is never discovered by an individual but is only to be found in "tradition." It was revealed in potentia at a single moment by God and has been developing steadily through history. Since truth is an attribute of ideas, the traditionalist holds that ideas are super-individual. They are the property of society and are found embedded in language which was revealed to primitive man by God at the creation. The main traditionalists were Joseph de Maistre, the Vicomte de Bonald, and Bonetty.—*G.B.*

Traducianism: The view that the soul (as well as the body) is generated from the souls of parents. A doctrine dating back to Tertullian (200 A.D.). The process of natural propagation procreates the soul.—*V.F.*

Transcendent: (L. *transcendere*: to climb over, surpass, go beyond) That which is beyond, in any of several senses. The opposite of the immanent (*q.v.*).

1. In Scholasticism, notions are transcendent which cannot be subsumed under the Aristotelian categories. The definitive list of transcendentia comprises *ens, unum, bonum, verum, res*, and *aliquid*.

2. For Kant whatever is beyond possible experience is transcendent, and hence unknowable.

3. Metaphysics and Theology: God (or the Absolute) is said to be transcendent in the following senses: (a) perfect, *i.e.*, beyond limitation or imperfection (*Scholasticism*); b) incomprehensible (negative theology, mysticism); c) remote from Nature (Deism); d) alienated from natural man (Barthianism). Pluralism posits the essential mutual transcendence of substances or reals.

4. Epistemology: Epistemological dualism (*q.v.*) holds that the real transcends apprehending consciousness, *i.e.*, is directly inaccessible to it. Thought is said to be "self-transcendent" when held to involve essentially reference beyond itself (s. intentionality).

5. Ethics: Moral idealism posits the transcendence of the will over Nature (see *Freedom*).—*W.L.*

Transcendent Reference: The reference of a mental state to something beyond itself. See *Reference*.—*L.W.*

Transcendental: (Ger. *transzendental*) In Kant's Philosophy: Adjective applied to the condition of experience or anything relating thereto. Thus transcendental knowledge is possible while transcendent knowledge is not. In the Dialectic, however, the term transcendental is often used where one would expect transcendent.—*A.C.E.*

Transcendental analytic: The first part of Kant's Logic; its function is "the dissection of the whole of our *a priori* knowledge into the elements of the pure cognition of the understanding," (*Kritik d. reinen Vernunft*, Part II, div. I, tr. M. Müller, 2nd ed., pp. 50-1); to be distinguished from (1) Transcendental Aesthetic, which studies the *a priori* forms of sensation, and (2) Transc. Dialectic, which attempts to criticize the illusory and falsifying arguments based on *a priori* principles.—*V.J.B.*

Transcendental idealism: See *Idealism*.—*A.C.E.*

Transcendental Illusion: (Kant. Ger. *transzendentaler Schein*) An illusion resulting from the tendency of the mind to accept the *a priori* forms of reason, valid only in experience, as constituting the nature of ultimate reality. Thus we are led, according to Kant, to *think* Ideas, such as God, World, and Soul, though we cannot *know* them. See *Kantianism*.—*O.F.K.*

Transcendental method: (In Kant) The analysis of the conditions (*a priori* forms of intuition, categories of the understanding, ideals of reason) that make possible human experience and knowledge. See *Kantianism*.

Transcendental Object: (Kant. Ger. *Transzendentale Objekt*) The pure rational 'x' which Kant defines as the general form of object or the object as such. It is not a particular concrete object, but the ideal objective correlate of pure consciousness as such. It is the object which the mind seeks to know in each empirical cognition. See *Kantianism*.—*O.F.K.*

Transcendental Philosophy: 1. Kant's name for his proposed *a priori* science of pure science ("pure reason'') which would include both a detailed analysis of its fundamental concepts and a complete list of all derivative notions. Such a study would go beyond the purpose and scope of his *Critique of Pure Reason*.

2. Name given to Kant's philosophy.

3. Schelling's term for his science of Mind, as opposed to the science of Nature.

4. Transcendentalism (*q.v.*).—*W.L.*

Transcendental proof: In Kant's Philosophy: Proof by showing that what is proved is a necessary condition without which human experience would be impossible and therefore valid of all phenomena.—*A.C.E.*

Transcendentalism: Any doctrine giving emphasis to the transcendent or transcendental (*q.v.*).

1. Originally, a convenient synonym for the "transcendental philosophy" (*q.v.*) of Kant and Schelling.

2. By extension, post-Kantian idealism.

3. Any idealistic philosophy positing the immanence of the ideal or spiritual in sensuous experience.

4. The philosophy of the Absolute (*q.v.*), the doctrine of: a) the immanence of the Absolute in the finite; b) the transcendence of the Absolute above the finite conceived as illusion or ''unreality.''

5. A name, originally pejorative, given to and later adopted by an idealistic movement in New England centering around the informal and so-called ''Transcendental Club,'' organized at Boston in 1836. An outgrowth of the romantic movement, its chief influences were Coleridge, Schelling, and Orientalism. While it embodied a general attitude rather than a systematically worked out philosophy, in general it opposed Lockean empiricism, materialism, and middle-class commercialism. Its metaphysics followed that of Kant and post-Kantian idealism, positing the immanence of the divine in finite existence, and tending towards pantheism (Emerson's ''Nature,'' ''Oversoul,'' ''The Transcendentalist''). Its doctrine of knowledge was idealistic and intuitive. Its ethics embraced idealism, individualism, mysticism, reformism, and optimism regarding human nature. Theologically it was autosoteric, unitarian, and broady mystical (Theo Parker's ''The Transient and Permanent in Christianity'').

6. Popularly, a pejorative term for any view that is ''enthusiastic,'' ''mystical,'' extravagant, impractical, ethereal, supernatural, vague, abstruse, lacking in common sense.—*W.L.*

Transcendentals (Scholastic): The *transcendentalia* are notions which apply to any being whatsoever. They are: Being, Thing, Something, One, True, Good. While thing (*res*) and being (*ens*) are synonymous, the other four name properties of being which, however, are only virtually distinct from the concept to which they apply.—*R.A.*

Transfinite induction: A generalization of the method of proof by mathematical induction or recursion (see *recursion, proof by*), applicable to a well-ordered class of arbitrary ordinal number—especially one of ordinal number greater than omega (see *ordinal number*)—in a way similar to that in which mathematical induction is

applicable to a well-ordered class or ordinal number omega.—*A.C.*

Transfinite ordinals: See *ordinal number*.

Transformator: In R. Reininger's philosophy, the agent or factor bringing about the change from the physical sensation or perception to experience as something psychic.—*K.F.L.*

''Transitive States'': (Lat. *transire*, to pass over) W. James' term which designates those parts of the stream of thought which effect a transition from one substantive state to another. See *Substantive States*.—*L.W.*

Transitivity: A dyadic relation R is *transitive* if, whenever xRy and yRz both hold, xRz also holds. Important examples of transitive relations are: the relation of identity or equality; the relation *less than* among whole numbers, or among rational numbers, or among real numbers; the relation *precedes* among instants of time (as usually taken); the relation of class inclusion, $\subset$ (see *logic, formal*, § 7); the relations of material implication and material equivalence among propositions; the relations of formal implication and formal equivalence among monadic propositional functions. In the propositional calculus, the *laws of transitivity* of material implication and material equivalence (the conditional and biconditional) are:

$$[p \supset q] [q \supset r] \supset [p \supset r].$$
$$[p \equiv q] [q \equiv r] \supset [p \equiv r].$$

Similar laws of transitivity may be formulated for equality (e.g., in the functional calculus of first order with equality), class inclusion (e.g., in the Zermelo set theory), formal implication (e.g., in the pure functional calculus of first order), etc.—*A.C.*

Transmigration of Souls: See *Metempsychosis*.

Trans-ordinal laws: Connecting properties of aggregates of different orders. Laws connecting the characteristics of inorganic things with living things. (Broad).—*H.H.*

Transpathy: (Lat. *trans*, across + *pathos*, feeling) As distinct from sympathy is feeling engendered by 'contagion.' In sympathy the function of 'after-experiencing' is so interwoven with true sympathy that an experienced separation of the two never occurs. In the case of transpathy, the two functions are distinctly separated from each other in experience. Transpathy takes place between emotional states, presupposes no knowledge of the other's joy or sorrow. One detects afterwards that an emotion which one finds in oneself derives from 'contagion,' which took place in an earlier gathering. See *Sympathy*.—*H.H.*

Transposition: The form of valid inference of the propositional calculus from A ⊃ B to ~B ⊃ ~A. The *law of transposition* is the theorem of the propositional calculus,

$$[p \supset q] \supset [\sim q \supset \sim p].—A.C.$$

Transubjective Reference: (Lat. trans, across + *subjectivus* from *subjicere*) The reference of an item of thought to an object independent of the knowing subject.—*L.W.*

Transvaluation of values: Nietzsche's proposal of revolutionizing the reigning tendencies and sentiments of one's age.—*H.H.*

Trendelenburg, Friedrich Adolf: (1802-1872) A German idealist who attempted to substitute the concept of 'motion' for Hegel's dialectics; the central theme of his writings is the notion of purpose.—*R.B.W.*

Main works: *Logische Untersuchungen,* 1840; *Die sittliche Idee des Rechts,* 1849; *Naturrecht auf dem Grunde der Ethik,* 1860.

Trichotomy: (Gr. *tricha,* threefold; *temno,* to cut) Literally, a division into three parts. More specifically, the doctrine that man consists of soul, body and spirit. This view appears as a later doctrine in the Old Testament, in Stoic thought and was held by St. Paul.—*V.F.*

Trika: An Indian philosophic system founded by Vasugupta in the 9th cent. A.D., having flourished among the Shivaites of Kashmir till the 14th cent., and now reviving along with the Southern, Tamil, offshoot of the Shaivasiddhānta. Its aim is the recognition of Shiva as one's own inmost nature (see *pratyabhijñā*) from which ensues progressive dissolution of manifoldness and reduction of the threefold (*trika*) reality of Shiva, *śakti* (*q.v.*), and soul to Oneness, thus reversing the "unfolding" of the universe through the 36 *tattvas* (*q.v.*).—*K.F.L.*

Trilemma: See *Proof by cases.*

Trilling, Lionel: (1905-1975) Teacher at Columbia University, literary critic and philosopher, author of *The Liberal Imagination* (1950), *Freud and the Crisis of Our Culture* (1955), *Beyond Culture: Essays on Literature and Learning* (1965), *Sincerity and Authenticity* (1972) and *Mind in the Modern World* (1972).—*S.E.N.*

Trimūrti: (Skr. having three shapes) The Hindu trinity, religiously interpreted as the three gods Brahmā-Vishnu-Shiva, or metaphysically as the three principles of creation-maintenance-destruction operative in cosmo-psychology.—*K.F.L.*

Trinitarianism: a) Referring to a Roman Catholic order founded in 1198 to redeem Christian captives from Mohammedans.

b) The usual meaning of the term: the doctrine of the Trinitarians who hold that the nature of God is one in substance and three in embodiment (Latin: persona). Upon the basis of Platonic realism (*q.v.*) which makes the universal fundamental and the particulars real in terms of the universal, the Christian Trinitarians made philosophically clear their doctrine of one Godhead and three embodiments, Father, Son and Holy Spirit: three and yet one. The doctrine was formulated to make religiously valid the belief in the complete Deity of Jesus and of the Holy Spirit (referred to in the New and the Old Testaments) and to avoid the pitfalls of polytheism. Jesus had become the object of Christian worship and the revealer of God and thus it was felt necessary to establish (together with the H.S.) his real Deity along with monotheistic belief. A long controversy over the relationship of the three led to the formulation by the Council of Nicea in 325, and after further disputes, by the Council of Constantinople in 381 of the orthodox Trinitarian creed (the Niceno-Constantinopolitan). Roman and Greek Catholicism

split on the doctrine of the status of the H.S. The Western church added the expression "filioque" (the H.S. proceeding "and from the Son") making more explicit the complete equality of the three; the Eastern church maintained the original text which speaks of the H.S. as "proceeding from the Father." Orthodox Protestantism maintains the Trinitarian conception.—*V.F.*

Tripitaka: "The Three Baskets," the Buddhistic Canon as finally adopted by the Council of Sthaviras, or elders, held under the auspices of Emperor Aśoka, about 245 B.C., at Pātaliputra, consisting of three parts: "The basket of discipline," "the basket of (Buddha's) sermons," and "the basket of metaphysics."—*K.F.L.*

Tritheism: Name given to the opinions of John Philoponus, the noted commentator on Aristotle, Conon, Bishop of Tarsus, and Eugenius, Bishop of Seleucia in Isauria, leaders of a group of Monophysites of the sixth century, which were understood in the sense that the Father, Son, and Holy Spirit are three partial substances and distinct individuals, consequently three *Gods.* Any similar doctrine is usually called Tritheism.—*J.J.R.*

Trivium: (Lat. *tres,* and *viae,* three ways) The first three disciplines in the mediaeval educational system of seven liberal arts. The trivium includes: grammar, rhetoric and dialectic. See *Quadrivium.*—*V.J.B.*

Truth: See also *Semiotic* 2.

Truth: A characteristic of some propositional meanings, namely those which are true. Truth (or falsity) as predicated of "ideas" is today normally restricted to those which are propositional in nature, concepts being spoken of as being exemplified or not rather than as being true or false. Truth is predicable indirectly of sentences or symbols which express true meanings. (See *Truth, semantical.*)

It is customary to distinguish between the *nature* of truth and the *tests* for truth. There are three traditional theories as to the nature of truth, each finding various expression in the works of different exponents. (1) According to the correspondence theory, a proposition (or meaning) is true if there is a fact to which it corresponds, if it expresses what is the case. For example, "It is raining here now" is true if it is the case that it is raining here now; otherwise it is false. The nature of the relation of correspondence between fact and true proposition is variously described by different writers, or left largely undescribed. Russell in *The Problems of Philosophy* speaks of the correspondence as consisting of an identity of the constituents of the fact and of the proposition.

(2) According to the coherence theory (see H. H. Joachim: *The Nature of Truth*), truth is *systematic coherence.* This is more than logical consistency. A proposition is true insofar as it is a necessary constituent of a systematically coherent whole. According to some (e.g., Brand Blanshard, *The Nature of Truth*), this whole must be such that every element in it necessitates, indeed entails, every other element. Strictly, on this view, truth, in its fullness, is a characteristic of only the one systematic coherent whole, which is the absolute. It

attaches to propositions as we know them and to wholes as we know them only to a degree. A proposition has a degree of truth proportionate to the completeness of the systematic coherence of the system of entities to which it belongs.

(3) According to the pragmatic theory of truth, a proposition is true insofar as it *works* or *satisfies,* working or satisfying being described variously by different exponents of the view. Some writers insist that truth characterizes only those propositions (ideas) whose satisfactory working has actually verified them; others state that only verifiability through such consequences is necessary. In either case, writers differ as to the precise nature of the verifying experiences required. See *Pragmatism, Verifiability Principle—C.A.B.*

Truth, semantical: Closely connected with the *name relation (q.v.)* is the property of a propositional formula (sentence) that it expresses a true proposition (or if it has free variables, that it expresses a true proposition for all values of these variables). As in the case of the name relation, a notation for the concept of truth in this sense often cannot be added, with its natural properties, to an (interpreted) logistic system without producing contradiction. A particular system may, however, be made the beginning of a hierarchy of systems each containing the truth concept appropriate to the preceding one.

The notion of truth should be kept distinct from that of a theorem, the true formulas being in general only some among the theorems (in view of Gödel's result, *Logic, formal,* § 6).

The first paper of Tarski cited below is devoted to the problem of finding a definition of semantical truth for a logistic system *L*, not in *L* itself but in another system (metasystem) containing notations for the formulas of *L* and for syntactical relations between them. This is attractive as an alternative to the method of introducing the concept of truth by arbitrarily adding a notation for it, with appropriate new primitive formulas, to the metasystem; but in many important cases it is possible only if the metasystem is in some essential respect logically stronger than *L*.

Tarski's concept of truth, obtained thus by a syntactical definition, is closely related to Carnap's concept of *analyticity.* According to Tarski, they are the same in the case that *L* is a "logical language." See further *semiotic* 2.—*A.C.*

A. Tarski, *Der Wahrheitsbegriff in den formalisierten Sprachen,* Studia Philosophica, vol. 1 (1935), pp. 261-405. A. Tarski, *On undecidable statements in enlarged systems of logic and the concept of truth,* The Journal of Symbolic Logic, vol. 4 (1939), pp. 105-112. R. Carnap, *The Logical Syntax of Language,* New York and London, 1937.

Truth-Frequency: (Prob.) See *Probability,* sec. D (III).

Truth-function is either: (1) a *function (q.v.)* from propositions to propositions such that the truth-value of the value of the function is uniquely determined by the *truth-values alone* of the arguments; or (2) simply a function from truth-values to truth-values.—*A.C.*

Truth-table method: See *logic, formal,* § 1, and *prop-ositional calculus, many-valued.*

C. S. Peirce, *On the algebra of logic,* American Journal of Mathematics, vol. 7 (1885), pp. 180-202; reprinted in his *Collected Papers,* vol. 3. J. Lukasiewicz, *Logika dwuwartościowa,* Przeglad Filozohecny, vol. 23 (1921), pp. 189-205. E. L. Post, *Introduction to a general theory of elementary propositions,* American Journal of Mathematics, vol. 43 (1921), pp. 163-185.

Truth-value: On the view that every proposition is either true or false, one may speak of a proposition as having one of two *truth-values,* viz. *truth* or *falsehood.* This is the primary meaning of the term *truth-value,* but generalizations have been considered according to which there are more than two truth-values—see *propositional calculus, many-valued.—A.C.*

Tsa chia: The "Miscellaneous" or "Mixed" School, which "drew from the Confucians and the Mohists and harmonized the Logicians and the Legalists," including Shih Tzŭ (fourth century B.C.), Lu Pu-wei (290-235 B.C.), and Huai-nan Tzŭ (d. 122 B.C.).—*W.T.C.*

Ts'ai: a) This means that when a man is not good, it is not because he is actually lacking in the basic 'natural powers,' 'natural endowment,' or 'raw material,' whereby to be good. His badness results simply from the fact that he has not developed the beginnings of virtue, which is not the fault of his 'natural powers.' (Mencius).

b) Power. Heaven. Earth, and Man are the three Powers or Forces of Nature.—*H.H.*

Tsao hua: (a) Creator, also called tsao wu (chê).

(b) Heaven and Earth; the Active or Male Cosmic Principle (yang) and the Passive or Female Cosmic Principle (yin).—*W.T.C.*

Tsao wu (che): Creator. Also called tsao hua.—*W.T.C.*

Tsao Yen: Nothing is known of this founder of the Yin Yang School except that he was a scholar in the state of Ch'i in the third century B.C., who "inspected closely the rise and fall of the passive and active principles and wrote essays totalling more than one hundred thousand words." His works are now lost.—*W.T.C.*

Ts'e yin: The feeling of commiseration. (Mencius).—*H.H.*

Tso wang: 'Sitting in forgetfulness;' that state of absolute freedom, in which the distinctions between others and self is forgotten, in which life and death are equated, in which all things have become one. A state of pure experience, in which one becomes at one with the infinite. (Chuang Tzŭ, between 399 and 395 B.C.).—*H.H.*

Ts'un hsin: Preserving one's native mind, that is, preserving in one's heart benevolence and propriety which are natural to man. (Mencius).—*W.T.C.*

Ts'un hsing: Putting the desires into proper harmony by restraint; the way to achieve 'complete preservation of one's nature.' (Yang Chŭ, c. 440—360 B.C.).—*H.H.*

Ts'un sheng: 'Completeness of living,' which is the best, is the enjoyment of life not to excess, a life in which all desires reach a proper harmony. While advocating restraint of the desires, Yang Chu (c.

440—360 B.C.) at the same time maintains the fulfillment of these.—*H.H.*

Tsung heng: Diplomatists in ancient China.—*W.T.C.*

Tu: Steadfastness in quietude, in order to comprehend Fate, The Eternal, and Tao (Lao Tzŭ).—*W.T.C.*

T'u: Earth, one of the Five Agents or Elements. See: *wu hsing.*—*W.T.C.*

Tuan: Human nature is innately good insofar as all men possess the 'beginnings' of the virtues, which if completely developed, make a man a sage. (Mencius).—*H.H.*

Tufts, James Hayden: (1862-1942) Professor of Philosophy, the University of Chicago. He was strongly influenced by Kant. He collaborated with Dewey in the standard, "Ethics," and among his other writings are: "Ethics of Cooperation," "Education and Training for Social Work" and *America's Social Morality.*—*L.E.D.*

Tu hua: Spontaneous transformation, the universal law of existence, the guiding principle of which is neither any divine agency or any moral law but Tao. (Kuo Hsiang, d. 321 A.D.).—*W.T.C.*

Tui: The opposite. Everything has its opposite. "When there is the active force (yang), there is the passive force (yin). When there is good, there is evil. As yang increases, yin decreases, and as goodness is augmented, evil is diminished." (Ch'êng Ming-tao, 1032-1086).—*W.T.C.*

T'ui: The method of induction or extension in argumentation. See: *pien.*—*W.T.C.*

Tuism: (from Latin *tu,* thou) In ethics the doctrine which puts the emphasis on the well-being of one's fellow-men. Another name for *altruism,* which see.—*K.F.L.*

Tung: (a) Activity; motion; "the constant feature of the active or male cosmic principle (yang)" of the universe, just as passivity is the constant feature of the passive or female cosmic principle (yin). According to Chou Lien-hsi 1017-1173), "the Great Ultimate (T'ai Chi) moves, becomes active, and generates the active principle (yang). When its activity reaches its limit, it becomes tranquil, engendering the passive principle (yin). When the Great Ultimate becomes completely tranquil, it begins to move again. Thus, movement and tranquility alternate and become the occasion of each other, giving rise to the distinction of yin and yang, and the Two Primary Modes are thus established." To the entire Neo-Confucian school, activity is potential tranquility (ching).

(b) Being moved, being awakened, in the sense that it is the nature of man to be tranquil, but when man comes into contact with external things, his nature is moved, and desires and passions follow. (Confucianism).—*W.T.C.*

T'ung: (a) Mere identity, or sameness, especially in social institutions and standards, which is inferior to harmony (ho) in which social distinctions and differences are in complete concord. (Confucianism).

(b) Agreement, as in "agreement with the superiors" (shang t'ung).

(c) The method of agreement, which includes identity, generic relationship, co-existence, and partial resemblance. "Identity means two substances having one name. Generic relationship means inclusion in the same whole. Both being in the same room is a case of co-existence. Partial resemblance means having some points of resemblance." See: *Mo Chê.*

T'ung i: The joint method of similarities and differences, by which what is present and what is absent can be distinguished. See: *Mo chê.*—*W.T.C.*

Tung Chung-shu: (177-104 B.C.) was the leading Confucian of his time, premier to two feudal princes, and consultant to the Han emperor in framing national policies. Firmly believing in retribution, he strongly advocated the "science of catastrophies and anomalies," and became the founder and leader of medieval Confucianism which was extensively confused with the Yin Yang philosophy. Extremely antagonistic towards rival schools, he established Confucianism as basis of state religion and education. His best known work, *Ch-un-ch'iu Fan-lu,* awaits English translation.—*W.T.C.*

Turro y Darder, Ramon: Spanish Biologist and Philosopher. Born in Malgrat, Dec. 8, 1854. Died in Barcelona, June 5, 1926. As a Biologist, his conclusions about the circulation of the blood, more than half a century ago, were accepted and verified by later researchers and theorists. Among other things, he showed the insufficiency and unsatisfactoriness of the mechanistic and neomechanistic explanations of the circulatory process. He was also the first to busy himself with endocrinology and bacteriological immunity. As a philosopher Turró combated the subjectivistic and metaphysical type of psychology, and circumscribed scientific investigation to the determination of the conditions that precede the occurrence of phenomena, considering useless all attempts to reach final essences. Turró does not admit, however, that the psychical series or conscious states may be causally linked to the organic series. His formula was: Physiology and Consciousness are phenomena that occur, not in connection, but in conjunction. His most important work is *Filosofia Critica,* in which he has put side by side two antagonistic conceptions of the universe, the objective and the subjective conceptions. In it he holds that, at the present crisis of science and philosophy, the business of intelligence is to realize that science works on philosophical presuppositions, but that philosophy is no better off with its chaos of endless contradictions and countless systems of thought. The task to be realized is one of coming together, to undo what has been done and get as far as the original primordial concepts with which philosophical inquiry began.—*J.A.F.*

Tychism: A term derived from the Greek, *tyche* fortune, chance, and employed by Charles Sanders Peirce (1839-1914) to express any theory which regards chance as an objective reality, operative in the cosmos. Also the hypothesis that evolution occurs owing to fortuitous variations.—*J.J.R.*

Types, theory of: See *Logic, formal,* § 6; *Paradoxes, logical; Ramified theory of types.*

Type-token ambiguity: The words *token* and *type* are

used to distinguish between two senses of the word *word*.

Individual marks, more or less resembling each other (as "cat" resembles "cat" and "CAT") may (1) be said to be "the same word" or (2) so many "different words." The apparent contradiction thereby involved is removed by speaking of the individual marks as tokens, in contrast with the one type of which they are instances. And *word* may then be said to be subject to *type-token ambiguity*. The terminology can easily be extended to apply to any kind of symbol, e.g. as in speaking of token- and type-sentences.

Reference: C. S. Peirce, *Collected Papers*, 4.537.—*M.B.*

Tz'u: (a) Parental love, kindness, or affection, the ideal Confucian virtue of parents.

(b) Love, kindness in general.—*W.T.C.*

Tzu hua: Self-transformation or spontaneous transformation without depending on any divine guidance or external agency, but following the thing's own principle of being, which is Tao. (Taoism).—*W.T.C.*

Tzu jan: The natural, the natural state, the state of Tao, spontaneity as against artificiality. (Lao Tzŭ; Huai-nan Tzŭ, d. 122 B.C.)—*W.T.C.*

U

Ubicatio: (Lat. *ubi*, where) Whereness, the condition of being located in space.—*V.J.B.*

Ueberweg, Friedrich: (1826-1871) Is mainly known for his exhaustive studies in the history of philosophy.—*R.B.W.*

Main works: *System d. Logik u. Gesch. d. logischen Lehre*, 1857; *Grundriss d. Gesch. d. Philosophie*, 1863-66.

Ultimate Value: See: Value, ultimate.

Ultramontanism: (Lat. *ultra*, beyond; and *montanus*, pertaining to mountains, i.e., the Alps) Extreme theory of the absolute supremacy of the Pope, not only in religious but in political matters.—*V.J.B.*

Unamuno y Jugo, Miguel de: Spanish Professor and writer. Born at Bilbao, Spain, September 29, 1864. Died 1936. First and secondary education in Bilbao. Philosophical studies and higher learning at the Central University of Madrid since 1880. Private instructor in Bilbao, 1884-1891. Professor of Greek language and literature at the University of Salamanca after 1891. President of the University of Salamanca and at the same time Professor of the History of the Spanish Language, in 1901. Madariaga considers him "The most important literary figure of Spain." If he does not embody, at least it may be asserted that Unamuno very well symbolizes the character of Spain. His conflict between faith and reason, life and thought, culture and civilization, depicts for us a clear picture of the Spanish cultural crisis.

Unamuno conceives of every individual man as an end in himself and not a means. Civilization has an individual responsibility towards each man. Man lives in society, but society as such is an abstraction. The concrete fact is the individual man "of flesh and blood." This doctrine of man constitutes the first principle of his entire philosophy. He develops it throughout his writings by way of a soliloquy in which he attacks the concepts of "man," "Society," "Humanity," etc. as mere abstractions of the philosophers, and argues for the "Concrete," "experiential" facts of the individual living man. On his doctrine of man as an individual fact

ontologically valid, Unamuno roots the second principle of his philosophy, namely, his theory of Immortality. Faith in immortality grows out, not from the realm of reason, but from the realm of facts which lie beyond the boundaries of reason. In fact, reason as such, that is, as a logical function is absolutely disowned by Unamuno, as useless and unjustified. The third principle of his philosophy is his theory of the *Logos* which has to do with man's intuition of the world and his immediate response in language and action.—*J.A.F.*

Among his most important works the following must be mentioned: *Paz en la Guerra*, 1897; *De la Enseñanza Superior en España*, 1899; *En Torno al Casticismo*, 1902; *Amor y Pedagogia*, 1902; *Vida de Don Quijote y Sancho*, 1905; *Mi Religion y Otros Ensayos*, 1910; *Soliloquios y Conversaciones*, 1912; *Contra Esto y Aquello*, 1912; *Ensayos*, 7 vols., 1916-1920; *Del Sentimiento Trágico de la Vida en los Hombres y en los Pueblos*, 1914; *Niebla*, 1914; *La Agonia del Cristianismo*, 1930; etc.

Unanimism: A term invented by Jules Romains to mean (1) a belief "in a certain reality of a spiritual nature," and (2) a belief that the human soul can enter into direct, immediate, and intuitive communication with the universal soul.—*G.B.*

Uncertainty principle: A principle of *quantum mechanics* (*q.v.*), according to which complete quantitative measurement of certain states and processes in terms of the usual space-time coordinates is impossible. Macroscopically negligible, the effect becomes of importance on the electronic scale. In particular, if simultaneous measurements of the position and the momentum of an electron are pressed beyond a certain degree of accuracy, it becomes impossible to increase the accuracy of either measurement except at the expense of a decrease in the accuracy of the other; more exactly, if a is the uncertainty of the measurement of one of the coordinates of position of the electron, and b is the uncertainty of the measurement of the corresponding component of momentum, the product ab (on principle) cannot be less than a certain constant h (namely

Planck's constant, q.v.). On the basis that quantities in principle unobservable are not to be considered physically real, it is therefore held by quantum theorists that simultaneous ascription of an exact position and an exact momentum to an electron is meaningless. This has been thought to have a bearing on, or to limit or modify, the principle of determinism in physics.—*A.C.*

C. G. Darwin, *The uncertainty principle,* Science, vol. 73 (1931), pp. 653-660.

Unconscious: According to Ed. v. Hartmann (*q.v.*) the united unconscious will and unconscious idea.—*K.F.L.*

Unconscious Mind: A compartment of the mind which lies outside the consciousness, existence of which has frequently been challenged. See for example W. James, *The Principles of Psychology,* Vol. I, pp. 162 ff. See *Subconscious Mind.*—*L.W.*

Understanding: (Kant. Ger. *Verstand*) The faculty of thinking the object of sensuous intuition; or the faculty of concepts, judgments and principles. The understanding is the source of concepts, categories and principles by means of which the manifold of sense is brought into the unity of apperception. Kant suggests that understanding has a common root with sensibility. See *Kantianism.*—*O.F.K.*

Undistributed middle: In the categorical syllogism (*logic, formal,* § 5), the middle term must appear in at least one of the two premisses (major and minor) as *distributed*—i.e., as denoting the subject of a proposition *A* or *E*, or the predicate of a proposition *E* or *O*. Violation of this rule is the fallacy of *undistributed middle.*—*A.C.*

Uniformity of Nature: Principle that what happens once in nature will, under a sufficient degree of similarity of circumstances, happen again and as often as the same circumstances recur.—*A.C.B.*

Unio mystica: (Lat.) Mystical union; the merging of the individual consciousness, cognitively or affectively, with a superior, or supreme consciousness. See *Mysticism.*—*V.J.B.*

Union: (in Scholasticism) Is often designated from the effect which united parts manifest, as an *essential* union by which parts constituting the essence of a thing are united,—or *accidental* union by which an accident is united to a substance.—*H.G.*

Unipathy: (Ger. *Einsfühlung*) Is a form of emotional identification, close to the term "participation" of Levy-Bruhl. There are two types of unipathy: idiopathic and heteropathic. In the one the alter is absorbed by the ego, and in the other the ego is absorbed by the alter. See *Sympathy.*—*H.H.*

Unit class: A class having one and only one member. Or, to give a definition which does not employ the word *one,* a class *a* is a *unit class* if there is an *x* such that $x \epsilon a$ and, for all *y,* $y \epsilon a$ implies $y = x$.—*A.C.*

Unitarianism: The name for the theological view which emphasizes the oneness of God in opposition to the Trinitarian formula (*q.v.*). Although the term is modern, the idea underlying Unitarianism is old. In Christian theology any expression of the status of Jesus as being less than a metaphysical part of Deity is of the spirit of Unitarianism (e.g., Dynamistic Monarchianists, Adoptionists, Socinians, and many others). Unitarians hold only the highest regard for Jesus but refuse to bind that regard to a Trinitarian metaphysics. In general, their views of the religious life have been prophetic of liberal thought. Today there are numbers of liberal Christian ministers who are Unitarian in thought but not in name. The British and Foreign Unitarian Association dates formally to 1825. Manchester College, Oxford, was claimed Unitarian. Leading theologians were Joseph Priestly (1733-1804), James Martineau (1805-1900), James Drummond and J. E. Carpenter. American Unitarianism was given expression in King's Chapel, Boston (1785), in a number of associations, in Meadville Theological School (1844) and Harvard Divinity School (the chief seat of the movement prior to 1878). Channing (1780-1842) and Theodore Parker (1810-1860) directed the movement into wider liberal channels.—*V.F.*

Unity of Science, Unified Science: See *Scientific Empiricism* IIB.

Universal: (Lat. *universalia,* a universal) That term which can be applied throughout the universe. A possibility of discrete being. According to Plato, an idea (which see). According to Aristotle, that which by its nature is fit to be predicated of many. For medieval realists, an entity whose being is independent of its mental apprehension or actual exemplification. (See: *Realism*). For medieval nominalists, a general notion or concept having no reality of its own in the realm of being (see *Nominalism*). In psychology: a concept. See *Concept, General, Possibility.* Opposite of: particular.—*J.K.F.*

In Scholasticism: Until the revival of Aristotelianism in the 13th century, universals were considered by most of the Schoolmen as real "second substances." This medieval Realism (see *Realism*), of those who *legebant in re,* found but little opposition from early Nominalists, *legentes in voce,* like Roscellin. The latter went to the other extreme by declaring universal names to be nothing but the breath of the voice—*flatus vocis.* Extreme realism as represented by William of Champeaux, crumbled under the attacks of Abelard who taught a modified nominalism, distinguishing, however, sharply between the mere word, *vox,* as a physical phenomenon, and the meaningful word, *sermo.* His interests being much more in logic than in ontology, he did not arrive at a definite solution of the problem. Aquinas summarized and synthetisized the ideas of his predecessors by stating that the universal had real existence only as creative idea in God, *ante rem,* whereas it existed within experienced reality only in the individual things, *in re,* and as a mental fact when abstracted from the particulars in the human mind, *post rem.* A view much like this had been proposed previously by Avicenna to whom Aquinas seems to be indebted. Later Middle-Ages saw a rebirth of nominalistic conceptions. The new school of Terminists, as they called themselves, less crude in its ideas than Roscellin, asserted that universals are only class names. Occam is usually considered as the most prominent of the Terminists. To Aquinas, the universal was still more than a mere name; it corresponded to an ontological fact; the definition of the universal reproduces the essence of the things. The universals are with Occam indeed natural signs which the mind cannot help forming, whereas the terms are arbitrary, *signa ad placitum*. But the universal is only a sign and does not correspond to anything ontological.—*R.A.*

Universal class: See *logic, formal*, § 7.

Universal proposition: See *particular proposition*.

Universal quantifier: See *quantifier*.

Universalism: The doctrine that each individual should seek as an end the welfare of all. Usually advanced on the basis of the principle that the intrinsic value of an entity, e.g., pleasure, does not vary with the individual possessing it.—*C.A.B.*

In Theology: Unless otherwise defined, the term refers to the Christian denomination which emphasizes the universal fatherhood of God and the final redemption and salvation of all. The doctrine is that of optimism in attaining an ultimate, ordered harmony and stands in opposition to traditional pessimism, to theories of damnation and election. Universalists look back to 1770 as an organized body, the date of the coming to America of John Murray. Unitarian thought (see *Unitarianism*) was early expressed by Hosea Ballou (1771-1852), one of the founders of Universalism.—*V.F.*

Universe: (a) Metaphysics: (1) The complete natural world; (2) That whole comprised of all particulars and of all universals; (3) The Absolute. (b) Logic: The universe of discourse in any given treatment is that class such that all other classes treated are subclasses of it and consequently such that all members of any class treated are members of it. See *logic, formal*, §§ 7, 8.—*C.A.B.*

Universe of discourse: See *individual;* and *logic, formal*, §§ 7, 8.

Upādhi: (Skr. substitute, disguise) One of many conditions of body and mind obscuring the true state of man or his self which Indian philosophies try to remove for the attainment of *mokṣa* (*q.v.*).—*K.F.L.*

Upamāna: (Skr.) Comparison, a valid source of knowledge and truth in some Indian philosophical systems.—*K.F.L.*

Upanishad, Upaniṣad: (Skr.) One of a large number of treatises, more than 100. Thirteen of the oldest ones (Chāndogya, Bṛhadāraṇyaka, Aitareya, Taittirīya, Katha, Iśa, Muṇḍaka, Kauṣītaki, Kena, Praśna, Śvetāśvatara, Māṇḍukya, Maitrī) have the distinction of being the first philosophic compositions, antedating for the most part the beginnings of Greek philosophy; others have been composed comparatively recently. The mode of imparting knowledge with the pupil sitting opposite (*upa-ni-sad*) the teacher amid an atmosphere of reverence and secrecy, gave these originally mnemonic treatises their name. They are remarkable for ontological, metaphysical, and ethical problems, investigations into the nature of man's soul or self (see *ātman*), God, death, immortality, and a symbolic interpretation of ritualistic materials and observances. Early examples of universal suffrage, tendencies to break down caste, philosophic dialogues and congresses, celebrated similes, succession of philosophic teachers, among other things, may be studied in the more archaic, classical Upanishads. See *ayam ātemā brahma, aham brahma asmi, tat tvam asi, net neti.—K.F.L.*

Upāsana: (Skr. sitting near) Worship, reverential attitude.—*K.F.L.*

Upāsanakānda: (Skr.) That portion of the Veda (*q.v.*) dealing with worship.—*K.F.L.*

Usiologie: A German term apparently not used in English, derived from the Greek, Ousia, essence, hence the science of essence.—*J.J.R.*

Uti: St. Augustine holds that the verbs *uti* and *frui* have not the same meaning. We use things because we need them, whereas we enjoy that which causes pleasure; *utimur pro necessitate, fruimur pro iucunditate.—J.J.R.*

Utilitarianism: (a) Traditionally understood as the view that the right act is the act which, of all those open to the agent, will actually or probably produce the greatest amount of pleasure or happiness in the world at large (this is the so-called Principle of Utility). This view has been opposed to intuitionism in the traditional sense in a long and well-known controversy. It received its classical form in Bentham and the two Mills. Earlier it took a theological form in Gay and Paley, later an evolutionistic form in Spencer, and an intuitionistic form (in the wider sense) in Sidgwick.

(b) More recently understood, especially in England, as the view that the right act is the act which will actually or probably produce at least as much intrinsic good, directly or indirectly, as any other action open to the agent in question. On this interpretation, traditional utilitarianism is one species of utilitarianism—that which regards pleasure as the good. Ideal utilitarianism, on the other hand, holds that other things besides pleasure are good (see *G.E. Moore, H. Rashdall, J. Laird*). In America utilitarianism is chiefly associated with voluntaristic or "interest" theories of value, e.g., in the pragmatic ethics of James and Dewey, and R. B. Perry. See *intuitionism, deontological ethics, teleological ethics.—W.K.F.*

Utopia: (Gr. *ou-topos*, the Land of Nowhere) An expression used by Sir Thomas More in his book "De optimo reipublicae statu deque nova insular Utopia," 1516, which in the form of a novel described an ideal state. Plato's Politeia is the first famous Utopia. Plato, however, had several predecessors and followers in this type of literature. From the Renaissance on the most famous Utopias besides Thomas More's book were: Tommaso Campanella: *The City of the Sun*, 1612; Francis Bacon, *New Atlantis*, 1627; Cabet, *Voyage en Icarie*, 1842; Bellamy, *Looking Backward*, 1888.—*W.E.*

Utopian socialism: Given wide currency by the writings of Marx and Engels, this term signifies the socialist ideas of thinkers like Owen, St. Simon and Fourier who protested against the sufferings of the masses under capitalism and who saw in social ownership of the means of production a remedy which would eliminate unemployment and afford economic security to all, but who at the same time felt that socialism could be attained by persuading the ruling classes to give up voluntarily their privileged positions and extensive holdings. Marx and Engels criticized such a conception

of method and tactics as utopian, naive, unhistorical, and opposed to it their own "scientific socialism." See *Socialism, Marxian.—J.M.S.*

Uttara-Mīmāmsā: Same as Vedānta (*q.v.*).

Uttarapakṣa: (Skr.) "Subsequent view," the second or the thinker's own view, stated after the refutation (*Khaṇḍana*) of the opponent's view (see *prvapak-ṣa*).—*K.F.L.*

V

Vāc: (Skr.) Speech, voice, word. In Vedic (*q.v.*) philosophy *vāc* and *śabda* (*q.v.*) have a similar rôle as the Logos in Greek philosophy (see e.g. Rigveda 10.125). It appears personified (feminine) and close to primeval reality in the hierarchy of emanations.—*K.F.L.*

Vāda: (Skr.) Theory.

Vague: A word (or the idea or notion associated with it) is vague if the meaning is so far not fixed that there are cases in which its application is in principle indeterminate — although there may be other cases in which the application is quite definite. Thus *longevity* is vague because, although a man who dies at sixty certainly does not possess the characteristic of longevity and one who lives to be ninety certainly does, there is doubt about a man who dies at seventy-five. On the other hand, *octogenarian* is not vague, because the precise moment at which a man becomes an octogenarian may (at least in principle) be determined. Of course, the vagueness of *longevity* might be removed by specifying exactly at what age longevity begins, but the meaning of the word would then have been changed. (See further the article *Relative*.).

Similarly a criterion or test, a convention, a rule, a command is vague if there are cases in which it is in principle indeterminate what the result of the test is, or whether the convention has been followed, or whether the rule or command has been obeyed.—*A.C.*

Vagueness: A term may be said (loosely) to be vague if there are "borderline cases" for its applicability, i.e. cases for which the rules of the language containing the term do not specify either that the term shall or that it shall not apply. Thus certain shades of reddish-orange in the spectrum are borderline cases for the application of the term "red." And "red" is vague in the English language.

More precisely: Let "S" be a symbol (simple or complex) in the language L. and let "f(S)" be any sentence containing "S" and constructed in conformity with the syntactical rules of L. Let "e_1" be any experiential sentence of L. Then "S" may be said to be *vague in the context* "$f(. .)$" if, for at last one "e_1" the rules of L do not provide that f(S) be either consistent or inconsistent with e_1. And "S" may be said to be *vague in L* if it is vague in at least one context of L.

Vagueness needs to be distinguished from *Generality* and *Ambiguity* (*q.v.*). See also *Vague*.

References: B. Russell, "Vagueness," Australasian J. of Phil. I, 88. M. Black, "Vagueness: An exercise in logical analysis" Phil. of Sci. 4,427.—*M.B.*

Vaibhāṣika: (Skr.) A Buddhist school of realism so named after a commentary (*vibhāṣā*) on one of their standard texts; same as Bāhyapratyakṣavāda (*q.v.*).—*K.F.L.*

Vairāgya: (Skr.) Disgust, aversion; renunciation of worldly things, recommended for the attainment of *mokṣa* (*q.v.*).—*K.F.L.*

Vaiśeṣika: One of the major systems of Indian philosophy (*q.v.*) founded by Ulaka, better known by his surname Kaṇāda. It is a pluralistic realism, its main insistence being on *viśeṣa* or particularity of the ultimate reality, incidental to an atomism. There are theistic implications. Reality falls into seven categories: nine substances (*dravya, q.v.*), 24 qualities (*guṇa, q.v.*), action (*karma, q.v.*), universality (*sāmānya, q.v.*), particularity (*viśeṣa*), inherence (*samavāya*), and non-existence (*abhāva*).—*K.F.L.*

Valid: In the terminology of Carnap, a sentence (or class of sentences) is *valid* if it is a consequence of the null class of sentences, *contra-valid* if every sentence is a consequence of it. The notion of consequence here refers to a full set of primitive formulas and rules of inference for the language or *logistic system* (*q.v.*) in question, known as *c-rules,* and including (in general) non-effective rules. If the notion of consequence is restricted to depend only on the *d-rules*—i.e., the subclass of the c-rules which are effective—it is then called *d-consequence* or *derivability,* and the terms corresponding to *valid* and *contravalid* are *demonstrable* and *refutable* respectively.

The formulas and the c-rules of the language in question may include some which are extralogical in character — corresponding, e.g., to physical laws or to matters of empirical fact. Carnap makes an attempt (which, however, has been questioned) to define in purely syntactical terms when a relation of consequence is one of *logical consequence*. If the notion of consequence is restricted to that of logical consequence, the terms corresponding to *valid* and *contravalid* are *analytic* and *contradictory* respectively. If the c-rules are purely logical in character, the class of analytic sentences coincides with that of valid sentences, and the class of contradictory sentences with that of contravalid sentences.

The explicit definition of analyticity (etc.) for a particular language of course requires statement of the c-rules. Actually, in the case of his "Language II," Carnap prefers to define *analytic* and *contradictory* first, and *consequence* in terms of these.

Part of the purpose of the definition of analyticity is to secure that every logical sentence is either analytic or contradictory. (The corresponding situation with demonstrability and refutability is impossible in many significant cases in consequence of Gödel's theorem— see *logic, formal,* § 6.)

Refer further to the article *syntax, logical* where references to the literature are given.—*A.C.*

Valid inference: In common usage an inference is said to be *valid* if it is permitted by the laws of logic. It is possible to specify this more exactly only in formal terms, with reference to a particular *logistic system* (*q.v.*).

The question of the validity of an inference from a set of premises is, of course, independent of the question of the truth of the premises.—*A.C.*

Vallabha: An Indian thinker and theologian of the 15th century A.D., a follower of the Vedānta (*q.v.*) and of Vishṇuism (*q.v.*), who interpreted all to be the divine reality with its threefold aspect of *sat-cit-ānanda,* the human soul *ānanda.*—*K.F.L.*

Valuation: The process, act or attitude of assigning value to something, or of estimating its value. See *Value; Evaluation.*—*R.B.W.*

Value: The contemporary use of the term "value" and the discipline now known as the theory of value or axiology are relatively recent developments in philosophy, being largely results of certain 19th and 20th century movements. See *Ethics.* "Value" is used both as a noun and as a verb. As a noun it is sometimes abstract, sometimes concrete. As an abstract noun it designates the property of value or of being valuable. In this sense "value" is often used as equivalent to "worth" or "goodness," in which case evil is usually referred to as "disvalue." But it is also used more broadly to cover evil or badness as well as goodness, just as "temperature" is used to cover both heat and cold. Then evil is referred to as negative value and goodness as positive value.

As a concrete noun, singular ("a value") or plural ("values"), our term refers either to things which have this property of value or to things which are valued (see below).

There is also a use of the terms "a value" and "values" which is intermediate between the two uses so far indicated, and which appears mainly in German writings. Here they refer to specific value-qualities (Werte) analogous to colors.

When used as a verb ("to value") our term denotes a certain mental act or attitude of valu*ing* or valu*ation*.

Now value-theory is concerned both with the property of value and with the process of valuing. About the former it asks various questions. What is its nature? Is it a quality or a relation? Is it objective or subjective? Is it a single property, or is it several properties, value being an ambiguous term? Is its presence in a thing dependent on or reducible to the fact that the thing is valued by someone? About the latter it also has various questions. Is it a mere feeling or desire? Or does it involve judgment and cognition? And if so, is this a cognition of a value already there independently of the act of valuing or of knowing?

A distinction is often drawn between two kinds of value, namely: intrinsic value and extrinsic or instrumental value. By extrinsic value is meant the character of being good or of having value as a means to something. By intrinsic value is meant the character of being good or valuable in itself or as an end or for its own sake. See *Intrinsic goodness.* Value-theorists have been mainly concerned with intrinsic value. The term "worth" has sometimes been used as equivalent to intrinsic value (Kant). But the distinction has often been criticized, e.g., by Dewey and Laird.

Two contrasts in which the term "value" occurs remain to be mentioned. (1) "Value" is sometimes contrasted with "fact" or "existence." Here the contrast intended is that of the "ought" versus the "is," and the term "value" is used to cover not only the various kinds of goodness, but also beauty and rightness. And the main problem is that of the relation of value and existence. (2) "Value" is also used more narrowly, being contrasted with rightness. Here the distinction intended is within the "ought" as opposed to the "is," and is between the "good" and the "right," with "value" taken as equivalent to "goodness." Then the main problem concerns the relation of value and obligation. In the sense of value involved in the former, contrast value-theory will include ethics. In the latter it will not. See *Axiology, Ethics, Obligation.*—*W.K.F.*

Value, contributive: The value an entity has insofar as its being a constituent of some whole gives value to that whole. (G.E. Moore).—*C.A.B.*

Value, instrumental: The value an entity possesses in virtue of the value of the consequences it produces; an entity's value as means. Sometimes the term is applied with reference only to the actual consequences, sometimes with reference to the potential consequences. —*C.A.B.*

Value, intrinsic: Sometimes defined as (a) the value an entity would have even if it were to have no consequences. In this sense, an entity's intrinsic value is equivalent to its total value less its instrumental value; it would include its contributive value.

Sometimes defined as (b) the value an entity would have were it to exist quite alone. In this sense, an entity's intrinsic value would be equivalent to its total value less the sum of its instrumental and contributive values.—*C.A.B.*

Values, Hierarchy of: (in Max Scheler) A scale of values and of personal value-types, based on "essences" (saint, genius, hero, leading spirit, and virtuoso of the pleasures of life, in descending scale).—*P.A.S.*

Value, Ultimate: The intrinsic value of an entity possessing intrinsic value throughout. For example, a hedonist might say that a pleasant evening at the opera has intrinsic value and yet maintain that only the hedonic tone of the evening has ultimate value, because it alone has no constituents which fail to have intrinsic value (G. E. Moore).—*C.A.B.*

Variable: A letter occurring in a mathematical or logistic formula and serving, not as a name of a particular, but as an ambiguous name of any one of a class of things—this class being known as the *range* of the variable, and the members of the class as *values* of the variable.

Where a formula contains a variable, say x, as a *free variable*, the meaning of the formula is thought of as depending on the meaning of x. If the formula contains no other free variables than x, then it acquires a particular meaning when x is *given a value*—i.e., when a name of some one value of x is substituted for all free occurrences of x in the formula—or, what comes to the same thing for this purpose, when the free occurrences of x are taken as denoting some one value.

Frequently an (interpreted) *logistic system* (*q.v.*) is so constructed that the theorems may contain free variables. The interpretation of such a theorem is that, for *any* set of values, of the variables which occur as free variables, the indicated proposition is true. I.e., in the interpretation the free variables are treated as if bound by universal *quantifiers* (*q.v.*) initially placed.

A *bound variable*, or *apparent variable*, in a given formula, is distinguished from a free variable by the fact that the meaning of the formula does not depend on giving the variable a particular value. (The same variable may be allowed, if desired, to have both bound occurrences and free occurrences in the same formula, and in this case the meaning of the formula depends on giving a value to the variable only at the places where it is free.) For examples, see *Abstraction,* and *Logic, formal,* § 3.

For the terminology used in connection with functions, see the article *function.* Cf. also the articles *Constant,* and *Combinatory logic.*—*A.C.*

Variable error: The average departure or deviation from the average between several given values. In successive measurements of magnitudes considered in the natural sciences or in experimental psychology, the observed differences are the unavoidable result of a great number of small causes independent of each other and equally likely to make the measurement too small or too large. In experimental psychology in particular, the real magnitude is known in some cases, but its evaluation tends to be on average too large or too small. The *average error* is the average departure from the true magnitude; while the *variable error* is the deviation as already defined.—*T.G.*

Veda, plural Vedas: (Skr. knowledge) Collectively the ancient voluminous, sacred literature of India (in bulk prior to 1000 B.C.), composed of Rigveda (hymns to gods), Sāmaveda (priests' chants), Yajurveda (sacrificial formulae), and Atharvaveda (magical chants), which among theosophic speculations contain the first philosophic insights. Generally recognized as an authority even in philosophy, extended and supplemented later by *sutras* (*q.v.*) and various accessory textbooks on grammar, astronomy, medicine, etc., called *Vedāṅgas* ("members of the Veda") and the philosophical treatieses, such as the Upanishads (*q.v.*).—*K.F.L.*

Vedānta: The "end of the Veda" (*q.v.*), used both in the literal sense and that of final goal, or meaning. Applied to the Upanishads (*q.v.*) and various systems of thought based upon them. Specifically the doctrine elaborated in the Brahmasutras of Bādarāyaṇa, restated, reinterpreted, and changed by later philosophers, notably Śankara, Rāmānuja, Nimbārka, Madhva, and Vallabha (which see). The central theme is that enunciated in the Upanishads of the relation between world soul and individual soul or self. Within the Vedānta , a number of solutions were found and taught with varying success. Śankara supposed God and soul identical (see *advaita*), Madhva different (see *dvaita*), Rāmānuja different yet identical (see *viśiṣṭādvaita*), Vallabha had a theory of obscuration, etc.—*K.F.L.*

Vedāntasūtras: See Brahmasutras.

Vedāntic: Adjective, "belonging to the Vedānta" (*q.v.*).

Vedic: (Skr.) Adjective, referring to the Vedas (*q.v.*) or the period that generated them, considered closed about 500 B.C.—*K.F.L.*

Vedic Religion: Or the Religion of the Vedas (*q.v.*). It is thoroughly cosmological, inspirational and ritualistic, priest and sacrifice playing an important rôle. It started with belief in different gods, such as Indra, Agni, Surya, Vishnu, Ushas, the Maruts, usually interpreted as symbolizing the forces of nature; but with the development of Hinduism it deteriorated into a worship of thousands of gods corresponding to the diversification of function and status in the complex social organism. Accompanying there was a pronounced tendency toward magic even in Vedic times, while the more elevated thoughts which have found expression in magnificent praises of the one or the other deity finally became crystallized in the philosophic thought of the Upanishads (*q.v.*). There is a distinct break, however, between Vedic culture with its free and autochthonous religious consciousness and the rigidly caste and custom controlled religion as we know it in India today, as also the religion of *bhakti* (*q.v.*).—*K.F.L.*

Venn diagram: See *Euler diagram.*

Verbal: Consisting of or pertaining to words. Having to do (merely) with the use and meaning of words.—*A.C.*

Verbum mentis: (Lat. mental word) The concept; the

intra-mental product of the act of intellection.—*V.J.B.*

Veridicity: A property of certain perceptions, memories and other acts of cognition which, though not in the strictest sense true—since truth is usually considered an exclusive property of propositions and judgments—tend to form true propositions. Non-veridical cognitions including illusions and hallucinations though not in themselves false are deceptive and foster falsity and error.—*L.W.*

Verification: (Ger. *Bewährung*) In Husserl: Fulfilment; especially, fulfilment of the sense of a doxic thesis.—*D.C.*

Verification, Confirmation: 1. *Verification:* the procedure of finding out whether a sentence (or proposition) is true or false. 2. A sentence is *varifiable* (in principle) if a (positive or negative) verification of it is possible under suitable conditions, leaving aside technical difficulties. 3. Many philosophical doctrines (e.g. Scientific Empiricism, *q.v.*) hold that a verification is replaced here by the concept of *confirmation*. A certain hypothesis is said to be confirmed to a certain degree by a certain amount of evidence. The concept of *degree of confirmation* is closely connected or perhaps identical (Reichenbach) with the statistical concept of probability (*q.v.*). 4. A sentence is *confirmable* if suitable (possible, not necessarily actual) experiences could contribute positively or negatively to its confirmation. 5. Many empiricists (see e.g. *Scientific Empiricism* 1C) regard either verifiability (e.g. Wittgenstein, the Vienna Circle in its earlier phase) or confirmability as a *criterion of meaningfulness* (in the sense of factual meaning, see *Meaning, Kinds of*, 2). This view leads to a rejection of certain metaphysical doctrines (see *Anti-metaphysics*, 2).—*R.C.*

Verifiability Principle: A term introduced by members of the Vienna Circle (*q.v.*). According to this school, a sentence can be considered cognitively meaningful if and only if it is analytically or empirically verifiable. Thus the verifiability principle seeks to establish criteria by which sentences may in fact be considered meaningful. Statements which are incapable of this sort of verification may be meaningful in other sentences, especially as utterances of emotion or sentiment. The first explicit formulation of the verifiability principle was made by Friedrich Waismann in "Logische Analyse des Wahrscheinlinchkeitsbegriffs" (1930). In 1936 it was brought to the English-speaking world with the publication of A.J. Ayer's (*q.v.*) *Language, Truth and Logic*. See especially Ayer's introduction to the second edition (1946), where he attempts to give a more precise formulation of the verifiability principle sketched out in the first edition.

Rudolf Carnap, "Testability and Meaning" (1936); Friedrich Waismann, "Language Strata" (1953); G.J. Warnock, "Verification and the Use of Language" (1951).—*T.P.S.*

Verité de fait (Verité de raison): There are two kinds of truth, according to Leibniz, truths of fact and truths of reason (or reasoning). These two classes of truths are exhaustive, and also, with the single exception of the existence of God, which has a logically anomalous position of being a necessary truth about existence, completely exclusive. Truths of reason are completely certain and necessary, for their denial involves a contradiction and is hence impossible. Truths of fact, on the other hand, are not completely certain and necessary. Their denial involves no contradiction; they rest upon experience; and they have, hence, only a limited inductive certainty. The truth of inductive inferences which go beyond the evidence of immediate experience depends upon the Law of Sufficient Reason, which is the expression in logic of the choice of the best on the part of God. Since God conceivably could have chosen another world for realization, rather than this best of all possible worlds, these truths can never equal in certainty the truths of reason, which depend not on God's will, but on the Principle of Contradiction, which not even God himself can make to be false.—*F.L.W.*

Vicious circle: A vicious circle in proof (*circulus in probando*) occurs if p_1 is used to prove p_2, p_2 to prove $p_3, \ldots, p_{n-1}$ to prove p_n, and finally p_n to prove p_1 — $p_1, p_2, \ldots, p_n$ being then taken as all proved. This is a form of the fallacy of *petitio principii* (*q.v.*).

A vicious circle in definition (*circulus in definiendo*) occurs if A_1 is used in defining A_2, A_2 in defining $A_3, \ldots, A_{n-1}$ in defining A_n, and finally A_n in defining A_1. (The simplest case is that in which $n = 1$, A_1 being defined in terms of itself.) There is, of course, a fallacy if $A_1, A_2, \ldots, A_n$ are then used as defined, absolutely. Apparent exceptions, such as definition by *recursion* (*q.v.*), require special justification, e.g., by finding an equivalent form of definition which is not circular.

The term *vicious circle fallacy* is used by Whitehead and Russell (1910) for arguments violating their *ramified theory of types* (*q.v.*). Similarly, the name *circulus vitiosus* is applied by Hermann Weyl (1918) to an argument involving *impredicative definition* (*q.v.*).—*A.C.*

Vidyā: (Skr.) Knowledge; especially knowledge of the real, noumenal.—*K.F.L.*

Vienna Circle: See *Scientific Empiricism I*.

Vijñāna: (Skr.) Consciousness; the faculty of apprehension or individualization of experience, and as such perhaps equivalent to *ahaṁkāra*.—*K.F.L.*

Vijñāna-vāda: (Skr.) Theory (*vāda*) of consciousness, specifically that consciousness is of the essence of reality; also the Buddhist school of subjective idealism otherwise known as Yogācāra (*q.v.*).—*K.F.L.*

Virtue: (Gr. *arete*) In Aristotle's philosophy that state of a thing which constitutes its peculiar excellence and enables it to perform its function well; particularly, in man, the activity of reason and of rationally ordered habits.

(Lat. *virtus*) In Roman philosophy, virtue became associated with virility and strength of character. In the Italian renaissance, e.g. Machiavelli, (Ital. *virtu*), the word means shrewd prudence.—*G.R.M.*

Viṣṇu: (Skr.) Deity of the Hindu trinity (see *Trimurti*). In philosophy, the principle of conservation, maintenance, or stability, the principle worshipped in Vishnuism (q.v.).—K.F.L.

Vishnuism: (Viṣṇuism) One of the major philosophico-religious groups into which Hinduism has articulated itself. It glorifies Vishnu as the supreme being who creates and maintains the world periodically by means of his *bhuti* and *kriyā śaktis* (q.v.) or powers of becoming and producing, corresponding to the *causae materialis et efficiens*. The place of man's soul in this development is explained variously, depending on the relation it maintains to the world-ground conceived in Vishnuite fashion.—K.F.L.

Viśiṣṭādvaita: (Skr.) "Qualified non-duality," the Vedāntic (q.v.) doctrine of qualified monism advocated by Rāmānuja (q.v.) which holds the Absolute to the personal, world and individuals to be real and distinct (*viśiṣṭa*), and salvation attainable only by grace of God earned through *bhakti* (q.v.).—K.F.L.

Vitalism: (Lat. *vita,* life) The doctrine that phenomena of life possess a character sui generis by virtue of which they differ radically from physico-chemical phenomena. The vitalist ascribes the activities of living organisms to the operation of a "vital force" such as Driesch's "entelechy" or Bergson's élan vital. (See H. Driesch, *Der Vitalismus als Geschichte und als Lehre* (1905); *The Science and Philosophy of Organism,* 2 Vols. (1908); *The Problem of Individuality* (1914); H. Bergson, *Creative Evolution*). Opposed to Vitalism is biological mechanism (see *Mechanism*) which asserts that living phenomena can be explained exclusively in physico-chemical terms. (See J. Loeb, *The Organism as a Whole from a Physico-Chemical View-Point,* 1919; *The Dynamics of Living Matter,* 1910. See also C. D. Broad, *The Mind and Its Place in Nature,* ch. II.)—L.W.

Vivarta: (Skr. turning, whirling) The Cyclonic process of manifestation by which the One becomes the (illusory) Many, an essentially Vedāntic (q.v.) concept of cosmogonic as well as psychologico-philosophical implications.—K.F.L.

Volket, Johannes: (1848-1930) Was influenced by the traditions of German idealism since Kant. His most important work consisted in the analysis of knowledge which, he contended, had a double source; for it requires, first of all, empirical data, insofar as there can be no real knowledge of the external world apart from consciousness, and also logical thinking, insofar as it elaborates the crude material of perception. Consequently, knowledge may be described as the product of rational operations on the material of pure experience. Thus he arrived at the conclusion that reality is "trans-subjective;" that is to say, it consists neither of mere objects nor of mere data of consciousness, but is rather a synthesis of both elements of existence.—R.B.W.

Main works: *Erfahrung u. Denken,* 1886; *System d. Aesthetik,* 1905-14; *Phänomenologie u. Metaphysik d. Zeit,* 1925; *Problem d. Individualität,* 1928.

Voltaire, Francois Marie Arouet de: (1694-1778) French dramatist and historian. He was one of the leading Encyclopaedists. He preached a natural religion of the deist variety. Though characterized as an atheist because of his fervent antagonism to the bigotry he found in the organized religions, he nevertheless believed in a righteous god. He was opposed to all intolerance and fought passionately to right the evils he discerned in religion and in society in general. In ethics, he based his views on the universal character of morals in which he firmly believed. His famous *Candide* is illustrative of his keen satire in its blasting of the Leibnizean best of all possible worlds.—L.E.D.

Main works: *Lettres philosophiques,* 1734; *Eléménts de la philos. de Newton,* 1738; *Essai sur les moeurs et l'esprit des nations* (*Philosophie de Christoire*), 1756; *Traité de tolérance,* 1763; *Dict. philosophique,* 1764.

Voluminousness: (Lat. *volumen,* volume) The vague, relatively undifferentiated spatiality characterizing sensations of every sense. See W. James, *The Principles* of Psychology, Vol. II, p. 134 ff. See *Extensity.*—L.W.

Voluntarism: (Lat. *voluntas,* will) In ontology, the theory that the will is the ultimate constituent of reality. Doctrine that the human will, or some force analogous to it, is the primary stuff of the universe; that blind, purposive impulse is the real in nature. (a) In psychology, theory that the will is the most elemental psychic factor, that striving, impulse, desire, and even action, with their concomitant emotions, are alone dependable. (b) In ethics, the doctrine that the human will is central to all moral questions, and superior to all other moral criteria, such as the conscience, or reasoning power. The subjective theory that the choice made by the will determines the good. Stands for indeterminism and freedom. (c) In theology, the will as the source of all religion, that blessedness is a state of activity. Augustine (353-430) held that God is absolute will, a will independent of the Logos, and that the good will of man is free. For Avicebron (1020-1070), will is indefinable and stands above nature and soul, matter and form, as the primary category. Despite the metaphysical opposition of Duns Scotus (1265-1308) the realist, and William of Occam (1280-1347) the nominalist, both considered the will superior to the intellect. Hume (1711-1776) maintained that the will is the determining factor in human conduct, and Kant (1724-1804) believed the will to be the source of all moral judgment, and the good to be based on the human will. Schopenhauer (1788-1860) posited the objectified will as the world-substance, force, or value. James (1842-1910) followed up Wundt's notion of the will as the purpose of the good with the notion that it is the essence of faith, also manifest in the will to believe. See *Will, Conation.* Opposed to *Rationalism, Materialism, Intellectualism.*—J.K.F.

Vortices: (Lat. *vortex*) Whirling figures used in Cartesian physics to explain the differentiation on geometrical principles of pure extension into various kinds of bodies. See: *Cartesianism.*—V.J.B.

Vyāpakatva: (Skr.) "All-reaching-ness," omnipresence.—K.F.L.

Vyāvahārika: (Skr.) Relating to practical or empirical matters.—K.F.L.

W

Wai tan: External alchemy, as a means of nourishing life, attaining Tao, and immortality, including transmutation of mercury into gold (also called chin tan), medicine, charms, magic, attempts at disappearance and change of bodily form. (Taoist religion).—*W.T.C.*

Wai wang: Often used as referring to the man who through his virtues and abilities gains the necessary qualifications of a ruler. (Mencius).—*H.H.*

Wang Chung. (Wang Chung-jên, c. 27—100 A.D.) Although strongly Taoistic in his naturalism, was independent in thinking. His violent and rational attack on all erroneous beliefs resulted in a strong movement of criticism. He was a scholar and official of high repute. (*Lun Hêng,* partial Eng. tr. by A. Forke, *Mettcilungen des Seminars für Orientalische Sprächen,* Vols. IX-XI.)—*W.T.C.*

Wang tao: The ideal institutions described by Mencius constitute the 'Kingly Way,' one that is a kingly or virtuous government.—*H.H.*

Wang Yang-ming: (Wang Shou-jên, Wang Poan, 1473-1529) Was a count, a cabinet member, and a general credited with many successful campaigns against invaders and rebels. Drawing his inspiration from the teachings of Lu Hsiangshan, he developed Neo-Confucianism (li hsüeh) on the basis of the doctrine of the Mind (hsin hsüeh). His complete works, *Wang Yang-ming Ch'üan-chi* (partial Eng. tr. by F. G. Henke: *The Philosophy of Wang Yang Ming*) consist of 38 *chüans* in several volumes.—*W.T.C.*

Watson, John Broadus: (1878-1958) American psychologist and leading exponent of Behaviorism (see *Behaviorism*), studied and served as Instructor at the University of Chicago, and was appointed Professor of Experimental Psychology at Johns Hopkins University 1908 where he served until 1920. Since then he engaged in the advertising business in New York City. The program for a behavioristic psychology employed the objective methods of the biological sciences and excluded the introspective method of earlier psychology; it is formulated by Watson in *"Psychology as the Behaviorist Views It,"* Psychological Review XX (1913), and *Behavior: An Introduction to Comparative Psychology,* 1914.—*L.W.*

Wave mechanics: See *Quantum mechanics.*

Weber, Max: (1864-1920) Weber started his career as a jurist in Berlin and later taught political economy at Freiburg, Heidelberg and Munich. He was a founder of the Deutsche Gesellschaft für Soziologie and editor of *Archiv für Sozialwissenschaft und Sozialpolitik.* Much of his scholarly work was devoted to the sociology of religion. He participated in the Peace Conference at Versailles, and argued against ratification of the treaty; but later he became a member of the committee on the constitution for the German Republic. The provision in that constitution for the popular election of the president was inserted largely because of Weber's pressure. Main works: *Gesammelte Aufsätze z. Religionssoziologie* (1920); *z. Soziologie u. Sozialpolitik* (1922); *z. Wissenschaftelehre* (1924).—*M.B.M.*

Weber-Fechner Law: Basic law of psychophysics which expresses in quantitative terms the relation between the intensity of a stimulus and the intensity of the resultant sensation. E. H. Weber applying the method of "just noticeable difference" in experiments involving weight discrimination found that the ability to discriminate two stimuli depends not on the absolute difference between the two stimuli but on their relative intensities and suggested the hypothesis that for each sense there is a constant expressing the relative intensities of stimuli producing a just noticeable difference of sensation. Fechner, also employing the method of just perceptible difference, arrived at the formula that the sensation varies with the logarithm of the stimulus:

$$S = C \log R$$

where S represents the intensity of the sensation, R that of the stimulus and C a constant which varies for the different senses and from individual to individual and even for the same individual at different times.—*L.W.*

Wei: The product of culture, social order, and training; ability acquired through training and accomplishment through effort; human activity as a result of the cogitation of the mind, as opposed to what is inborn. (Hsün

Tzŭ, c. 335—288 B.C.).—*W.T.C.*

Wei wo: "For the self," in the sense of "preserving life and keeping the essence of our being intact and not to injure our material existence with things," erroneously interpreted by Mencius as egotism, selfishness, "everyone for himself." (Yang Chu, c. 440—360 B.C.).—*W.T.C.*

Well-ordered: See *Ordinal number*.

Weltanschauung: (Ger.) The compound term means world-view, perspective of life, conception of things.

Wen: (a) Culture: evidences of the Confucian Moral Law (tao), such as propriety, music, social institutions, governmental systems, education, etc.; the tradition of the Chou dynasty which Confucius attempted to preserve.

(b) Appearance: polish; superficiality.

(c) Letters: literature, one of the four things Confucius taught (ssŭ chiao).—*W.T.C.*

Wertfrei: (Ger. *value-free*) Seeing the central strength of the scientific attitude in its valuational neutrality, Max Weber (1864-1920) insisted that the deliberate abstention from taking sides for the value or against the disvalue of a thing when under scientific scrutiny was essential to progress in the social sciences.—*H.H.*

Wertheimer, Max: (1880-1943) One of the originators—along with Koffka and Köhler—of *Gestalt* psychology. The three began their association at Frankfort about 1912 and later Wertheimer and Köhler worked together at the University of Berlin. Wertheimer was led to the basic conception of *Gestalt* in the course of his investigations of apparent movement which seemed to indicate that the perception of movement is an integral experience and not the interpretative combination of static sensations. *"Experimental studien über das Sehen von Bewegungen," Zeitschrift für Psychologie*, 1912, Vol. 61, pp. 161-265.—*L.W.*

Wesen: (Ger. being, essence, nature) Designates essential being without which a thing has no reality. It has been conceived variously in the history of philosophy, as Ousia or constant being by Aristotle; as *essentia*, real or nominal, or *species*, by the Schoolmen; as principle of all that which belongs to the possibility of a thing, by Kant; generally as that which is unconditionally necessary in the concept of a thing or is not dependent on external, causal, temporal or special circumstances. Its contrast is that which is *unwesentlich* (defined by Schuppe as that which has relation to or for something else), accidental, contingent.—*K.F.L.*

Wesensschau: (Ger. intuition of essence) In Scheler: The immediate grasp of essences.—*P.A.S.*

Wesenswissen, i.e., Wesensschau (in Max Scheler): The knowledge of essences conditioned by the elimination of acts which posit reality and by the inclusion of pure devotion to the qualities of objects as such (this type of knowledge is opposed to scientific knowledge, which is "outer knowledge," not *Wesenswissen*).—*P.A.S.*

Whitehead, Alfred North: British philosopher. (1861-1947). Fellow of Trinity College, Cambridge, 1911-14. Lecturer in Applied Mathematics and Mechanics at University College, London, 1914-24. Professor of Applied Mathematics at the Imperial College of Science and Technology, London. From 1924 until retirement in 1938, Professor of Philosophy at Harvard University. Among his most important philosophical works are the *Principia Mathematica,* 3 vols. (1910-13) (with Bertrand Russell); *An Enquiry concerning the Principles of Natural Knowledge* (1919); *The Concept of Nature* (1920); *Science and the Modern World* (1926); *Religion in the Making* (1926); *Symbolism* (1928); *Process and Reality* (1929); and *Adventures of Ideas* (1933). The principle of relativity in physics is the key to the understanding of metaphysics. Whitehead opposes the current philosophy of static substance having qualities which he holds to be based on the simply located material bodies of Newtonian physics and the "pure sensations" of Hume. This 17th century philosophy depends upon a "bifurcation of nature" into two unequal systems of reality on the Cartesian model of mind and matter. The high abstractions of science must not be mistaken for concrete realities. Instead, Whitehead argues that there is only one reality; what appears, whatever is given in perception, is real. There is nothing existing beyond what is present in the experience of subjects, understanding by subject any actual entity. There are neither static concepts nor substances in the world; only a network of events. All such events are actual extensions or spatio-temporal unities. The philosophy of organism, as Whitehead terms his work, is based upon the patterned process of events. All things or events are sensitive to the existence of all others; the relations between them consisting in a kind of feeling. Every actual entity is then a "prehensive occasion," that is, it consists of all those active relations with other things into which it enters. An actual entity is further determined by "negative prehension," the exclusion of all that which it is not. Thus every feeling is a positive prehension; every abstraction a negative one. Every actual entity is lost as an individual when it perishes, but is preserved through its relations with other entities in the framework of the world. Also, whatever has happened must remain an absolute fact. In this sense, past events have achieved "objective immortality." Except for this, the actual entities are involved in flux, into which there is the ingression of eternal objects from the realm of possibilities. The eternal objects are universals whose selection is necessary to the actual entities. Thus the actual world is a certain selection of eternal objects. God is the principle of concretion which determines the selection. "Creativity" is the primal cause whereby possibilities are selected in the advance of actuality toward novelty. This movement is termed the consequent nature of God. The pure possibility of the eternal objects themselves is termed his primordial nature.—*J.K.F.*

Whole: The term "whole" has been used frequently in attempts to describe or to explain certain features of biological, psychological, or sociological (but sometimes also of physical and chemical) phenomena which were said to be inaccessible to a "merely mechanistic" or "summative" analysis. In fact, most applications of the concept of whole explicitly resort to a principle which asserts that a whole is *more* than the sum of its parts.

From the viewpoint of empiricist methodology, that whole-part principle, and in most cases also the use of the term "whole" is open to various objections: In particular, the meanings of the terms "whole," "part," "sum," and "more" are far from clear and change from case to case, and accordingly, so does the meaning and the validity of the part-whole principle: In many cases, a whole is simply meant to be an object of study which has parts (in some one of the many senses of the word), and the part-whole principle is taken to assert either (1) that for a complete knowledge of such an object or system, not only those parts, but also their mutual relationships have to be known, or (2) that such an object has properties which can be found in none of its parts. In either of these interpretations, the part-whole principle is trivially true in every case, but just for this reason it cannot furnish an explanation of any empirical phenomenon such as the specific behavior of a developing embryo, taken as a "biological whole," or of visual gestalten, etc.

For that explanatory function, empirical laws are needed, and occasionally the part-whole principle is tacitly identified with some specific law (or group of laws) governing the phenomenon under consideration. Whatever explanation is achieved in such a case, is obviously due, not to the vague part-whole principle but rather to the specific empirical law which is tacitly supplanted for it; and any empirial law which might be chosen here, applies to a certain specific type of phenomena only and cannot pass for a comprehensive principle governing all kinds of wholes.

According to another interpretation of the notion of whole and of the part-whole principle, a whole is an object whose parts are mutually interdependent in the sense that a change affecting one of its parts will bring about changes in all of the other parts; and because of this interdependence the whole is said to be "more" than the sum of its parts. The part-whole principle then obviously is true simply by definition, and again, lacks explanatory value. Besides, if the above interdependence criterion for wholes is taken literally, then any object turns out to be a whole. What the concept of whole is actually meant to refer to, are specific types of interdependence as found in living organisms, etc.; but then, again, an adequate description and explanation of those phenomena can be attained only by a study of their special regularities, not by a sweeping use of the vague concept of whole and of the unclear part-whole principle. (For the points referred to in the preceding remarks, see also *Emergent Evolution, Gestalt, Holism, Mechanism, Vitalism.*)

Recently, the Polish logician St. Lesniewski has developed a formal theory of the part-whole relationship within the framework of a so-called calculus of individuals; one of the theorems of this theory states that every object is identical with the sum of its parts. This is, of course, a consequence of the way in which the axioms of that calculus were chosen, but that particular construction of the theory was carried out with an eye to applications in logical and epistemological analysis, and the calculus of individuals has already begun to show its value in these fields. See Leonard and Goodman, *The Calculus of Individuals and Its Uses,* The Journal of Symbolic Logic, 5 (1940), pp. 45-55.—*C.G.H.*

Wieman, Henry Nelson: (1884-1975) American philosopher of religion, the chief contemporary representative of religious naturalism. Among his works are *The Source of Human Good* (*c.* 1946) and *Intellectual Foundation of Faith* (1961). He rejects supernaturalism on the one hand and atheism on the other, searching for a middle way.—*S.E.N.*

Will: a) In the widest sense, will is synonymous with conation. See *Conation.*

b) In the restricted sense, will designates the sequence of mental acts eventuating in decision or choice between conflicting conative tendencies. An act of will of the highest type is analyzable into:

(1) The envisaging of alternative courses of action, each of which expresses conative tendencies of the subject.

(2) Deliberation, consisting in the examination and comparison of the alternative courses of action with special reference to the dominant ideals of the self.

(3) Decision or choice consisting in giving assent to one of the alternatives and the rejection of the rest.—*L.W.*

Will, Frederick L.: (1909-   )American philosopher and teacher. Since 1938 Will has been teaching at the University of Illinois at Urbana-Champaign, where he is currently Professor (Emeritus) of Philosophy.

Will has been largely influenced by Logical Positivism (*q.v.*), classical American philosophers such as Peirce (*q.v.*), James (*q.v.*), Dewey (*q.v.*), and Royce (*q.v.*), and Hegelianism (*q.v.*), though the wide scope and highly original nature of his thought precludes his classification in any particular philosophical school. He has done extensive work on probability and induction, though his latest work, *Induction and Justification: An Investigation of Cartesian Procedure in the Philosophy of Knowledge,* represents a significant break with his earlier thinking. In the book he argues against the individualist view of knowledge and justification of knowledge contained in what can be broadly understood as the "Cartesian" tradition in philosophy, which conceives of knowledge as a complex, layered structure, at whose base reside certain incorruptible intuitions or immediate "givens" to individual minds, exemplified by Descartes' conception of "clear and distinct ideas." In its place Will proposes a more social view of knowledge and the workings of reason, laying emphasis on the collective nature of human inquiry and, following Peirce, on the impossibility of completely unmediated "first cognitions" or intuitions.

"Will the Future Be Like the Past?;" "Consequences and Confirmation" (1966); "Thoughts and Things" (1969); "Truth and Correspondence" (1977); "The Concern About Truth" (1979).—*T.P.S.*

Will (Scholastic): Will is one of the two rational faculties of the human soul. Only man, as a rational animal, possesses will. Animals are prompted to action by the sensory appetites and in this obey the law of their nature, whereas human will is called free insofar as it determines itself towards the line of action it chooses. Though the objects of will are presented by the intellect, this faculty does not determine will which may still act against the intellect's judgment. The proper object of rational will is good in its universal aspect. Goodness is one of the original ("transcendental") aspects of being; envisioned under this aspect, it becomes a possible end of will. As such, it is apprehended by reason, arousing a simple volitive movement. Follow the approval of "synderesis" (v. there), striving, deliberation, consent, final approval by reason, choice of means and execution. Thus, there is a complicated interplay of intellectual and volitive performances which finally end with action. Action being necessarily about particulars and these being material, will, an "immaterial" faculty cannot get directly in touch with reality and needs, as does on its part intellect, an intermediary; the sensory appetites are the ultimate executors, while the *vis cogitativa* or practical reason supplies the link on the side of intellectual performance. True choice exists only in rational beings; animals appearing to deliberate are, in truth, only passively subjected to the interference of images and appetites, and their actions are automatically determined by the relative strength of these factors. While man's will is essentially free, it is restricted in the exercise of its freedom by imagination, emotion, habit. Whatever an end will aims at, it is always a good, be it one of a low degree.—*R.A.*

Will, free: See *Free Will.*

Will, the Free Elective: (in Kant's ethics) Kant's "free elective will" *(freie Willkür)* is a will undetermined by feeling at the time of willing, even though it is destined to be sanctioned and confirmed by a subsequent accrual of feeling. Such a will, Kant says, is freedom.—*P.A.S.*

Will to Believe: A phrase made famous by William James (1842-1910) in an essay by that title (1896). In general, the phrase characterizes much of James's philosophic ideas: a defence of the right and even the necessity to believe where evidence is not complete, the adventurous spirit by which men must live, the heroic character of all creative thinking, the open-mind to possibilities, the repudiation of the stubborn spirit and the will-not-to-know, the primacy of the will in successful living, the reasonableness of the whole man acting upon presented data, the active pragmatic disposition in general. This will to believe does not imply indiscriminative faith; it implies a genuine option, one which presents an issue that is lively, momentous and forced. Acts of indecision may be negative decisions.—*V.F.*

William of Champeaux: (1070-1121) He was among the leading realists holding that the genus and species

were completely present in each individual, making differences merely incidental. He was one of the teachers of Abelard.—*L.E.D.*

Windelband, Wilhelm: Windelband (1848-1915) was preëminently an outstanding historian of philosophy. He has nowhere given a systematic presentation of his own views, but has expressed them only in unconnected essays and discourses. But in these he made some suggestions of great import on account of which he has been termed the founder and head of the "South-Western German School." He felt that he belonged to the tradition of German Idealism without definitely styling himself a Neo-Kantian, Neo-Fichtean or Neo-Hegelian. His fundamental position is that whereas it is for science to determine facts, it is for philosophy to determine values. Facts may be gathered from experience, but values, *i.e.,* what "ought" to be thought, felt and done, cannot and hence must in some sense be *a priori.* Of particular significance was his effort—later worked out by H. Rickert—to point out a fundamental distinction between natural and historical science: the former aims at establishing general laws and considers particular facts only insofar as they are like others. In contrast to this "nomothetic" type of science, history is "idiographic," *i.e.,* it is interested in the particular as such, but, of course, not equally in all particulars, but in such only as have some significance from the point of view of value.—*H.G.*

Main works: *Geschichte u. Naturwissenschaft,* 1894; *Präludien,* 1924 (9th ed.); *History of Modern Philosophy* (Eng. tr.).

Wisdom, A. John T. D.: (1904-) A British analytic philosopher at Cambridge, he strongly believed that philosophical problems should be attacked through rational means as well as through a close examination of the deeper philosophical motives which led the protagonists to react in the way that they did. He was the author of articles and essays dealing with both philosophy and psychoanalysis including *Problems of Mind and Matter,* (1934), *Other Minds* (1952), *Philosophy and Psychoanalysis* (1953) and *Paradox and Discovery* (1965).—*L.L.*

Wissenschaftslehre: (Ger. doctrine of science) Since Fichte who understood by it critical philosophy in general and his idealistic system based on consciousness of the absolute ego apart from any definite content of knowledge in particular, a term characterizing philosophy as a scientific system of knowledge embracing the principles and methodology of all sciences under exclusion of their factual content or specific conclusions.—*K.F.L.*

Wittgenstein, Ludwig: (1889-1951) Lecturer in philosophy at University of Cambridge, 1929-1939; professor and head of department since 1939. Author of *Tractatus Logico-Philosophicus,* 1921 and *Philosophical Investigations,* 1953.

Apart from technical innovations in logical theory (notably in the discussion of tautology and probability), Wittgenstein's main contribution to contemporary philosophy has been his demonstration of the importance of a study of language. The *Tractatus* is concerned chiefly to determine the conditions which any symbolism, qua representation of fact, must necessarily satisfy. Such a "language" must consist of elements combined in such ways as to mirror in one-one correspondence the elements and structure of the "world." A crucial distinction is made between "saying" (*aussagen*) and "showing" (*zeigen*); a statement is able to assert a certain state of affairs by virtue of having the same structure as that which it represents. The common structure, however, cannot itself be asserted, can only be shown *in* the symbols. Much philosophy is held to consist of trying to say what can only be shown, a misguided proceeding provoked by failure to understand "the logic of our language." Certain mystical conclusions follow.

Wittgenstein's doctrines were a major influence in the evolution of Logical Positivism (*q.v.*) though his later work is out of sympathy with that movement. Later lectures (in the form of unpublished mimeographed notes) embody a more relativistic approach to language, and are largely devoted to the inculcation of a therapeutic method directed against the perennial temptation to ask senseless questions in philosophy.

References: Russell, Introduction to English edition of the Tractatus. J. Weinberg, *Examination of Logical Positivism*, Ch. 1. M. Black, "Some problems connected with language," *Proc. Aris. Soc.*, 39, 43.—*M.B.*

Wolff, Christian: (1679-1754) A most outstanding philosopher of the German Enlightenment, and exponent of an all pervasive rationalism, who was professor of mathematics at Halle. He was a dry and superficial systematic popularizer of dogmatic philosophy whose laws have for him a purely logical and rational foundation.—*H.H.*

Main works: In German a series of works *Vernünftige Gedänke* (Rational Thoughts) on logic, psychologie, ethics, etc. followed by a similar series *Empirical psychology*, etc.

Woodbridge, Frederick James Eugene: (1867-1940) Was Professor of Philosophy of Columbia University and one of the Editors of the Journal of Philosophy. He was an important member of the realist school. For him consciousness was a relation of meaning, a connection of objects, and structure was a notion of greater philosophic value than substance. His best known works are: *Philosophy of Hobbes, The Realm of Mind* and *Nature and Mind.*—*L.E.D.*

World-event: An event conceived in four dimensions, including its duration. See *Space-Time.*—*R.B.W.*

World Ground: The source, cause, essence, or sustaining power within or behind the World. See *Absolute.*—*W.L.*

World-line: A line conceived in four dimensions; a line cutting across space-time. See *Space-Time.*—*R.B.W.*

World-point: A four-dimensional point; a durationless geometrical point. See *Space-Time.*—*R.B.W.*

World soul: 1. An intelligent, animating, in-dwelling principle of the cosmos, conceived as its organizing or

integrating cause, or as the source of its motion; thus posited on the analogy of the human soul and body. Such a doctrine, common among primitive peoples, was taught by Plato, Stoicism, Neo-Platonism, Renaissance Platonism, Bruno, etc.

2. This view has affinities with, and has occasionally developed into, the notion of a World Mind or Absolute Mind as posited in Vedantic and Buddhist idealism, patristic and scholastic Christian theism, objective idealism, and absolute idealism. See *Idealism, The Absolute.*—*W.L.*

Wrong action: Any action that is not right. See: *Right action.*—*C.A.B.*

Wu: 'Eternal Non-Being' is that which is opposed to being of material objects; refers to the essence of *Tao*, the first principle. (Lao *Tzŭ*).—*H.H.*

Wu: Creatures; things; matter; the material principle; the external world; the non-self; objects of the senses and desires; affairs.—*W.T.C.*

Wu ch'ang: (a) The Five Constant Virtues of ancient Confucianism: righteousness on the part of the mother, brotherliness on the part of the elder brother, respect on the part of the young brother, and filial piety on the part of the son. Also called wu chiao and wu tien.

(b) The Five Constant Virtues of Confucianism from the Han dynasty (206 B.C.-220 A.D.) on: benevolence (jên), righteousness (i), propriety (li), wisdom (chih), and good faith (hsin). Also called wu hsing and wu tê.

(c) The Five Human Relationships of Confucianism (wu lun).—*W.T.C.*

Wu chi: The Non-Ultimate. See: *T'ai Chi.*—*W.T.C.*

Wu chiao: The Five Teachings. See: *wu ch'ang.*

Wu hsing: (a) The Five Agents, Elements, or Powers of Water, Fire, Wood, Metal and Earth, the interaction of which gives rise to the multiplicity of things, and which have their correspondence in the five senses, tastes, colors, tones, the five virtues, the five atmospheric conditions, the five ancient emperors, etc. Also called wu tê. (The Yin Yang School in the third and fourth centuries B.C. and the Han dynasty, especially Pan Ku, 32-92 A.D., and Tung Chung-shu, 177-104 B.C.).

(b) The Five Agents which are the five vital forces (ch'i) engendered by the transformation of yang, the active cosmic principle, and its union with yin, the passive cosmic principle, each with its specific nature. When the being of the Great Ultimate (T'ai Chi) and the essence of yin and yang come into mysterious union, determinate being ensues, with the heavenly principle, yang, constituting the male element and the earthly principle, yin, constituting the female element, giving rise to the myriad things. (Chou Lien-hsi, 1017-1073).

(c) The Five Constant Virtues. See: *wu ch'ang.*—*W.T.C.*

Wu hua: The transformation of things, that is, the conception that entities should be, and could be, so transformed, spiritually speaking, that absolute identity may exist between them, especially between the self and the non-self, and between man and things. (Chuang Tzŭ, between 399 and 295 B.C.).—*W.T.C.*

Wu lun: The five human relationships, "those between

the father and the son, the ruler and subordinates, husband and wife, the elder and the younger, and friends." Also called the Five Constants (wu ch'ang). "Between father and son, there should be affection; between sovereign and ministers, there should be righteousness; between husband and wife, attention to their separate functions; between old and young, a proper order; and between friends, good faith (hsin)." (Mencius).—*W.T.C.*

Wundt, Wilhelm Max: (1832-1920) German physiologist, psychologist and philosopher, who, after studying medicine at Heidelberg and Berlin and lecturing at Heidelberg, became Professor of Philosophy at Leipzig in 1875 where he founded the first psychological laboratory in 1879. Wundt's psychological method, as exemplified in his *Principles of Physiological Psychology,* 1873-4, combines exact physical and physiological measurement of stimulus and response along with an introspective analysis of the "internal experience" which supervenes between stimulus and response; he affirmed an exact parallelism or one-to-one correspondence between the physiological and the psychological series. Wundt's psychology on its introspective side, classified sensations with respect to modality, intensity, duration, extension, etc.; and feelings as: (a) pleasant or unpleasant, (b) tense or relaxed, (c) excited or depressed. He advanced but later abandoned on introspective grounds the feeling of innervation (discharge of nervous energy in initiating muscular movement). Among psychologists influenced by Wundt are Cattell, Stanley Hall and Titchener.—*L.W.*

Other works: *Logik,* 1880-3; *Ethik,* 1886; *Völkerpsychologie,* 10 vols. (3d ed., 1910-20).

Wu shih: The Five Origins of Order in the medieval Confucian interpretation of history, namely, the beginning of Heaven is rectified by the depth of the Prime; the government of the empire is rectified by the beginning of Heaven; the position of the princes is rectified by the government of the empire; and the order of the state is rectified by the position of the princes. (Tung Chung-shu, 177-104 B.C.).—*W.T.C.*

Wu te: (a) The Five Powers, or the characteristics of the Five Agents or Elements (wu hsing) of the Yin Yang school.

(b) The Five Constant Virtues. See: *wu ch'ang.* —*W.T.C.*

Wu tien: The Five Constant Virtues. See: *wu ch'ang.*

Wu wei: Following nature; non-artificiality; non-assertion; inaction; inactivity or passivity. It means that artificiality must not replace spontaneity, that the state of nature must not be interfered with by human efforts, superficial morality and wisdom. "Tao undertakes no activity (wu wei), and yet there is nothing left undone. If kings and princes would adhere to it, all creatures would transform spontaneously." (Lao Tzŭ).

"The true man of old did not know what it was to love life or to have death. He did not rejoice in birth nor resist death. Spontaneously he went; spontaneously he came; that was all. He did not forget whence he came; nor did he seek whence he would end. He accepted things gladly, and returned them to nature without reminiscence. This is called not to hurt Tao with the human heart, nor to assist heaven with man." (Chuang Tzŭ, between 399-295 B.C.).

"The meaning of 'wu wei' is that there is no going in advance of nature. The meaning of 'wu pu wei' (there is nothing undone) is that, in following Tao, everything is done. The meaning of 'wu chih' (no governing) is that there is no interference with naturalness. And the phrase 'wu pu chih' (there is nothing that is not governed) is that the end is attained in accordance with the mutual fitness of things." (Huai-nan Tzŭ, 122 B.C.).—*W.T.C.*

Wu wu: To regard things as things, that is, to regard things with objectivity and no attachment or selfishness, on the one hand, and, with the conviction that the self and the non-self form an organic unity on the other.—*W.T.C.*

X

Xenophanes of Colophon (c. 570—480 B.C.): A contemporary of Pythagoras who may have been a student of Anaximander. Usually associated with the Milesian school, his studies carried him into an examination of the phenomena of nature. He held that all living creatures had an origin, that plants and animals had natural origins.—*E.H.*

To Xenophanes is due the saying: "The gods of the Ethiopians are dark-skinned and snub-nosed; the gods of the Thracians are fair and blue-eyed; if oxen could paint, their gods would be oxen."

Xirau Palau, Joaquin: Born in Figueras, Spain, Xirau specialized in philosophy, literature and law, obtaining his Ph.D. from the Central University of Madrid in 1918. Studied and worked under Ortega y Gasset, Serra Hunter, Cossío, and Morente. Main Works: *Las Condiciones de la Verdad Eterna en Leibniz*, 1921; *Rousseau y las Ideas Politicas Modernas*, 1923; *El Sentido de la Verdad*, 1927; *Descartes y el Idealismo Subjetivista Moderno*, 1927; *Amor y Mundo*, 1940; *Introduccion a la Fenomenología*, 1941.

According to Xirau the very essence of philosophic thought (Influence of Husserl and Heidegger) opposes the conception of philosophy as mere play of ideas or speculation of concepts. Philosophy is, above all, called upon to develop man in the sense of actualizing his inborn potentialities and bringing the fact and concept of personality to full fruition. Philosophy thus becomes pedagogical, and as such it will always have a great destiny to realize.—*J.A.F.*

Y

Ya evam veda: (Skr.) "He who knows this," a common Upanishadic (*q.v.*) refrain suggesting compensation of some nature for one conversant with philosophic truth.—*K.F.L.*

Yajna: (Skr.) Sacrifice, a Vedic (*q.v.*) institution which became philosophically interpreted as the self-sacrifice of the Absolute One which, by an act of self-negation (*nisedha-vyāpāra*) became the Many.—*K.F.L.*

Yājnavalkya: One of the foremost teachers in the classic age of Upanishads (*q.v.*).—*K.F.L.*

Yama: (Skr.) Restraint, particularly moral restraint as the first condition for attaining the object of Yoga (*q.v.*), including *ahimsā* (*q.v.*) and *brahmacarya* (*q.v.*), relinquishing theft and desire for gratuities.—*K.F.L.*

Yang: (a) The active, male cosmic principle or force. See: *yin yang*.

(b) The school of Yang Chu (c. 440—360 B.C.) and his followers, whose main doctrines are neither hedonism as *Lieh Tzŭ* seems to represent him, nor egoism as Mencius interpreted him, but rather the Taoist doctrines of following nature, of "preserving life and keeping the essence of our being intact and not injuring our material existence with things," of "letting life run its course freely," and of "ignoring not only riches and fame but also life and death."—*W.T.C.*

Yang ch'i: (a) Nourishing one's vital force, the basis of the human body, by the practice of benevolence, righteousness, and uprightness, and the obedience of the moral law (tao) so that the vital force may be most great and most strong "to the extent of filling up all between Heaven and Earth." See: *hao jan chih ch'i*. (Confucianism).

(b) Nourishing life through breath control. (Taoism).—*W.T.C.*

Yang Chu: (c. 440-360 B.C.) Was a great Taoist whose teachings, together with those of Mo Tzŭ, "filled the empire" and strongly rivaled Confucianism at the time of Mencius (371-289 B.C.). His main doctrines of following nature and preserving life and the essence of being have been distorted as hedonism and egoism in the work bearing his name (Ch. VII of *Lieh Tzŭ*, c. 300 A.D.; Eng. tr. by A. Forke: *Yang Chu's Garden of Pleasure*).—*W.T.C.*

Yang-hsing: 'Nurturing the bodily frame,' by which some early Taoists implied an attitude towards life rather than a system of hygiene.—*H.H.*

Yang sheng: "Nurturing life," conserving one's vital powers, by which later Taoists understood sex life, breath control, the physical exercises and diet.—*H.H.*

Yeh ch'i: The "air of the night," i.e., the strength or force obtained through the rest and recuperation during the night, suggestive of the moral invigoration from the calmness and repose of the mind which is necessary for the realization of one's good nature. (Mencius, 371-289 B.C.).—*W.T.C.*

Yi: Change. See: *i*.

Yin yang: (a) Passive and active principles, respectively, of the universe, or the female, negative force and the male, positive force, always contrasting but complimentary. Yang and yin are expressed in heaven and earth, man and woman, father and son, shine and rain, hardness and softness, good and evil, white and black, upper and lower, great and small, odd number and even number, joy and sorrow, reward and punishment, agreement and opposition, life and death, advance and retreat, love and hate, and all conceivable objects, qualities, situations, and relationships.

(b) The Two Modes (i — — and — in trigram, or kua, symbols) of the Great Ultimate (T'ai Chi), from the interplay of which all things are engendered.

(c) A system constituted by the Five Agents or Elements (wu hsing) of Water, Fire, Wood, Metal, and Earth, which in turn constitute the Great Ultimate. (Chou Lien-hsi, 1017-1073).

(d) The two forces of ch'i, or the vital force which is the material principle of the universe. (Neo-Confucianism).

(e) Name of a school (400-200 B.C.) headed by Tsou Yen, which advocated that all events are manifestations of the passive or female force and the active or male force of the universe, and which was closely associated with popular geomancy, astrology, etc.—*W.T.C.*

Yo: Music, or the social and cosmic principle of harmony. See: *li* (propriety).—*W.T.C.*

Yoga: (Skr. "yoking") Restraining of the mind (see *Manas*), or, in Patañjali's (*q.v.*) phrase: *citta vṛtti nirodha,* disciplining the activity of consciousness. The object of this universally recommended practice in India is the gaining of peace of mind and a deeper insight into the nature of reality. On psycho-physical assumptions, several aids are outlined in all works on Yoga, including moral preparation, breath control, posture, and general toning up of the system. *Karma* or *kriyā* Yoga is the attainment of Yoga ends primarily by doing, *bhakti* Yoga by devotion, *jñāna* Yoga by mental or spiritual means. The Yogasutras (*q.v.*) teach eight paths: Moral restraint (see *yama*), self-culture (see *niyama*), posture (see *āsana*), breath-control (see *prāṇāyama*), control of the senses (see *pratyāhāra*), concentration (see *dhāraṇa*), meditation or complete surrender to the object of meditation (see *samādhi*). See *Hathayoga.*—*K.F.L.*

Yogācāra: A Mahāyāna (*q.v.*) Buddhist school which puts emphasis on Yoga (*q.v.*) as well as *ācāra,* ethical conduct. Believing in subjective idealism, it is also designated as Vijñāna-vāda (*q.v.*). Since we know the world never apart from the form it has in consciousness, the latter is an essential to it. All things exist in consciousness; they cannot be proven to exist otherwise.—*K.F.L.*

Yogasūtras: Famous work by Patañjali (*q.v.*) on which is founded Yoga, one of the great systems of Indian philosophy (*q.v.*). It is essentially a mental discipline in eight stages (see Yoga) for the attainment of spiritual freedom without neglecting physical and moral preparation. In philosophic outlook, the *sutras* (*q.v.*) and most commentaries on them are allied to the Sāṅkhya (*q.v.*), yet not without having theistic leanings.—*K.F.L.*

Yogin, Yoginī: (Skr.) The man, the woman, practicing Yoga (*q.v.*).—*K.F.L.*

Yoni: (Skr. womb) Source, origin, matrix, first cause. See *garbha.*—*K.F.L.*

Yu: Being, existence, the mother of all things, which comes from Non-Being (wu). Both Being and Non-Being are aspects of Tao.—*W.T.C.*

Yu: Space, or "what extends to different places" and "covers the four directions." (Neo-Mohism).—*W.T.C.*

Yu: Desire, which the Taoists regard as detrimental to a good life and the understanding of Tao, but which the Confucians accept as natural and reasonable if under control. "The nature of man is tranquil, but when it is affected by the external world, it begins to have desires. . . When the likes and dislikes are not properly controlled and our conscious minds are distracted by the material world, we love our true selves and the principle of reason in Nature is destroyed. . . The people are therefore controlled through the rituals and music instituted by the ancient kings." As Tai Tung-yüan (1723-1777) puts it, "Man and creatures all have desires, and desires are the functionings of their nature. . . If functionings and operations do not err, they are in harmony with the characteristics of Heaven and Earth. . . Goodness is nothing but the transformation of Heaven and Earth and the functionings and capabilities of nature. . . We should not be without desires, but we should minimize them."—*W.T.C.*

Yu: "Eternal being" refers to the function of the metaphysical principle *Tao.* It is no mere zero or nothingness, having as first principle brought all things into being. (Lao Tzŭ, Taoists).—*H.H.*

Yuan: (a) The Beginning. For the One-Prime, see: *i yüan.*

(b) The beginning of number, one.

(c) The beginning of the material principle or the vital force (ch'i).

(d) The originating power of the Heavenly Element (chien) in the system of the Eight Elements (pa kua); "being attentive to the fundamentals—the first and the chief quality of goodness," one of the four virtues (ssŭ tê).

(e) The great virtue of Heaven and Earth which expresses itself in production and reproduction.—*W.T.C.*

Yuan: The method of analogy in argumentation. See: *pien.*—*W.T.C.*

Yuan ch'i: The primal fluid or the Prime-Force, the product of the cosmos. Its pure and light portion collected to form Heaven and its impure and heavy portion, Earth. (Huai-nan Tzŭ, d. 122 B.C.).—*W.T.C.*

Yung: Courage, one of the universally recognized moral qualities of man ((ta tê), especially of the superior man.—*W.T.C.*

Yung: (a) Harmony.

(b) What is common, ordinary, universal. To the Confucians this is "the eternal law of the universe." See: *chung yung.* To Chuang Tzŭ (between 399 and 295 B.C.) "the common and the ordinary are the natural function of all things, which expresses the common nature of the whole. Following the common nature of the whole, they are at ease. Being at ease, they are near perfection. This is letting nature take its course, without being conscious of the fact. This is Tao."—*W.T.C.*

Z

Zaddik, Joseph Ibn: Judge at Cordova (1080-1149). Philosophic work written in Arabic is the *Microcosm* (Heb. *Olam Katon*). See *Jewish Philosophy*.

Zarathustra: A historic personality whose life became enshrouded in legend. He lived not later than the 6th century B.C. in ancient Persia (Iran or Bactria) and is credited with establishing a dualism called after him Zoroastrianism (*q.v.*). In *Also sprach Zarathustra,* Nietzsche makes him, though dissociated from his doctrines, the bearer of his message.—*K.F.L.*

Zen: The Japanese Zen has its origin in the early *Ch'an* schools of Chinese Buddhism, and has had influence in the West in its Japanese interpretation. Basis of Zen teachings is philosophical introspection by which Mind, in Tao-istic manner, can see the Eternal Law and become One with the Eternal Mind. When the Buddha Mind has been touched, Enlightenment is attained.

Zendavesta: (from Middle Persian *Zend u Avistā,* "commentary and text") The Commentary, still used today as sacred scripture among the Parsis (see *Zoroastrianism*), on the basic text which was composed by the followers of Zarathustra (*q.v.*), but had become unintelligible due to its archaic nature.—*K.F.L.*

Zeno of Elea: (about 490-430 B.C.) Disciple of Parmenides; defended the doctrine of his master that only changeless "Being" is real by indirect proofs exposing the logical absurdities involved in the opposite view, namely that plurality and change are real. Zeno's famous arguments against the possibility of motion were intended as proofs that motion was full of contradictions and that it could not therefore serve as a principle for the explanation of all phenomena, as the atomists, Heraclitus, Empedocles and others had taught.—*M.F.*

Zeno the Stoic: (c. 340-265 B.C.) A native of Cyprus and the founder of the Stoic School in Athens. His philosophy was built on the principle that reality is a rational order in which nature is controlled by laws of Reason, interpreted in the vein of pantheism. Men's lives are guided by Providence against which it is futile to resist and to which wise men willingly submit.—*R.B.W.*

Zermelo, Ernst (Friedrich Ferdinand): (1871-1953) German mathematician. Professor of mathematics at Zurich, 1910-1916, and at Freiburg, 1926-. His important contributions to the foundations of mathematics are the Zermelo axiomatic set theory (see *logic, formal,* § 9), and the explicit enunciation of the axiom of *choice* (*q.v.*) and proof of its equivalence to the proposition that every class can be well-ordered.—*A.C.*

Zetetic: (Gr. *zeteo,* to seek) A procedure by inquiry. A search (in mathematics) after unknown quantities. A seeker.—*V.F.*

Ziehen, Theodor: (1862-1950) A German thinker whose main interest lay in the field of physiological psychology.—*R.B.W.*

Zoroastrianism: (from Zoroaster) A life-affirming Indo-Iranian religion, also known as Mazdaism, Bah Dīn, Parsiism, and Fire-worship, established by Zarathustra (*q.v.*), weakened by the conquests of Alexander the Great, resuscitated, then practically extinguished by the advance of Mohammedanism, but still living on in the Gabar communities of Persia and the Parsis of Bombay. It is ethical and dualistic in that the struggle between good and evil is projected into cosmology and symbolized by a warfare between light and darkness which is conceived on the one hand naturalistically and manifesting itself in a deification of the shining heavily bodies, veneration of fire, fear of defilement, and purificatory rites, and, on the other, mythologically as the vying for supremacy between Ormazd and Ahriman (*q.v.*) and their hosts of angels and demons. Man must choose between light and darkness, truth and falsehood, moral right and wrong, and thus gain either eternal bliss or agony.—*K.F.L.*

Zwingliism: The theological thought of Ulrich Zwingli (1484-1531), early Protestant Reformer of Zurich, Switzerland. His theology was theocentric: God's activity is all-pervading and widely revealed. He was a student of the Greek N.T. and of humanistic subjects, a friend of Erasmus. (See *Reformation*). He followed Augustine's doctrine of man's original sin and sinfulness with some modifications. He anticipated Calvin's doctrine of election (see *Calvinism*) as an act of the Divine good and rational will; and he held the feudalistic theory of the atonement of substitution framed by Anselm. The sacraments were not mystical conveyors of divine grace to him; they were rather outward signs of an inward spiritual grace. In the famous Marburg Colloquy, he broke with Luther and his followers on the interpretation of the Lord's Supper.—*V.F.*